Lecture Notes in Computer Science 5873

Rachid Guerraoui   Franck Petit (Eds.)

Stabilization, Safety, and Security of Distributed Systems

11th International Symposium, SSS 2009
Lyon, France, November 3-6, 2009
Proceedings

Springer

Volume Editors

Rachid Guerraoui
Ecole Polytechnique Fédérale de Lausanne
CH 1015 Lausanne, Switzerland
E-mail: rachid.guerraoui@epfl.ch

Franck Petit
LIP
ENS Lyon
46 allée d'Italie
69364 Lyon cedex 07, France
E-mail: franck.petit@ens-lyon.fr

Library of Congress Control Number: 2009936486

CR Subject Classification (1998): C.2.4, C.3, F.1, F.2.2, K.6

LNCS Sublibrary: SL 1 – Theoretical Computer Science and General Issues

ISSN 0302-9743
ISBN-10 3-642-05117-0 Springer Berlin Heidelberg New York
ISBN-13 978-3-642-05117-3 Springer Berlin Heidelberg New York

springer.com

Printed in Germany

Typesetting: Camera-ready by author, data conversion by Scientific Publishing Services, Chennai, India
Printed on acid-free paper SPIN: 12779949 06/3180 5 4 3 2 1 0

Preface

The papers in this volume were presented at the 11th International Symposium on Stabilization, Safety, and Security of Distributed Systems (SSS), held November 3–6, 2009 in Lyon, France.

SSS is an international forum for researchers and practitioners in the design and development of fault-tolerant distributed systems with self-* attributes, such as self-stabilization, self-configuration, self-organization, self-management, self-healing, self-optimization, self-adaptiveness, self-protection, etc. SSS started as the Workshop on Self-Stabilizing Systems (WSS), the first two of which were held in Austin in 1989 and in Las Vegas in 1995. Starting in 1995, the workshop began to be held biennially; it was held in Santa Barbara (1997), Austin (1999), and Lisbon (2001). As interest grew and the community expanded, in 2003, the title of the forum was changed to the Symposium on Self-Stabilizing Systems (SSS). SSS was organized in San Francisco in 2003 and in Barcelona in 2005. As SSS broadened its scope and attracted researchers from other communities, a couple of changes were made in 2006. It became an annual event, and the name of the conference was changed to the International Symposium on Stabilization, Safety, and Security of Distributed Systems (SSS). The last three SSS conferences were held in Dallas (2006), Paris (2007), and Detroit (2008).

This year the Program Committee was organized into several tracks reflecting most topics related to self-* systems. The tracks were: Alternative Systems and Models, Autonomic Computational Science, Cloud Computing, Embedded Systems, Fault-Tolerance in Distributed Systems / Dependability, Formal Methods in Distributed Systems, Grid Computing, Mobility and Dynamic Networks, Multicore Computing, Peer-to-Peer Systems, Self-Organizing Systems, Sensor Networks, Stabilization, and System Safety and Security. We received 126 submissions from 34 countries. Each submission was reviewed by four to six Program Committee members with the help of external reviewers. A rebuttal phase was added for the authors to respond to the reviews before the final deliberation. Out of the 126 submitted papers, 49 papers were selected for presentation. The symposium also included 14 brief announcements. Selected papers from the symposium will be published in a special issue of the *ACM Transactions on Autonomous and Adaptive Systems* (TAAS).

This year, we were very fortunate to have three distinguished invited speakers: Anne-Marie Kermarrec, David Peleg, and Roger Wattenhofer. They also graciously provided a summary of their talks in advance to be included in this volume.

Among the 49 selected papers, we considered three papers for special awards. The best paper award was given to François Bonnet and Michel Raynal for their paper entitled "Looking for the Weakest Failure Detector for k-Set Agreement in Message-Passing Systems: Is Π_k the End of the Road?". The best student paper was shared by Danny Dolev, Ezra N. Hoch, and Yoram Moses for "An Optimal Self-Stabilizing Firing Squad" and Gérard Wagener, Radu State, Alexandre Dulaunoy, and Thomas Engel for "Self-Adaptive High Interaction Honeypots Driven by Game Theory."

On behalf of the Program Committee, we would like to thank all the authors who submitted their work to SSS. We thank all the Vice-Program Chairs, all the members of the Program Committee, and the external reviewers for their tremendous effort and valuable reviews. We also thank the members of the Steering Committee for their invaluable advice. The process of paper submission, selection, and compilation in the proceedings was greatly simplified due to the strong and friendly interface of the *EasyChair* system (`http://www.easychair.org`). We owe a lot to the EasyChair creators and maintainers for their commitment to the scientific community. We gratefully acknowledge the Organizing Committee members for their time and invaluable effort that greatly contributed to the success of this symposium.

November 2009

Rachid Guerraoui
Franck Petit

Conference Organization

General Chair

Ajoy K. Datta — UNLV, Las Vegas, USA

Program Chairs

Rachid Guerraoui — EPFL, Lausanne, Switzerland
Franck Petit — INRIA/LIP, ENS Lyon, France

Program Vice-Chairs

Tarek Abdelzaher
Anish Arora
Raouf Boutaba
Giovanna Di Marzo Serugendo
Pascal Felber
Christof Fetzer
Eric Fleury
Thomas Fuhrmann
Mohamed G. Gouda
Indranil Gupta
Jason Hallstrom
Salima Hassas
Ted Herman
Martin Hutle
Sandeep Kulkarni
Sayan Mitra
Manish Parashar
Franck Petit
Thierry Priol
Omer F. Rana
Josef Widder

Local Arrangements Chair

Eddy Caron

Webmaster

Benjamin Depardon

Publication Chairs

Stéphane Devismes
Cédric Tedeschi

Publicity Chairs

Doina Bein
Borzoo Bonakdarpour
Jiannong Cao
Stéphane Devismes
Yoshiaki Katayama
Ji-Cherng Lin

Program Committee

Alternative Systems and Models

Murat Demirbas
Hoai Ha Phuong
Ted Herman (*Chair*)
Mehmet Karaata
Xenofon Koutsoukos
Håkan Sundell
Paulo Tabuada
Suresh Venkatasubramanian
Lin Zhong

Autonomic Computational Science

Rosa Badia
Jose Fortes
Geoffrey Fox
Shantenu Jha
Nagarajan Kandasamy
Zhiling Lan
Manish Parashar (*Chair*)
Thierry Priol
Omer F. Rana (*Chair*)
Jordi Torres
David Walker
Dongyan Xu

Cloud Computing

Marcos Aguilera
Mahesh Balakrishnan
Gregory Chockler
Brian Cooper
John Dunagan
Indranil Gupta (*Chair*)
Anthony Joseph
Flavio Junqueira
Petr Kuznetsov
Arvind Krishnamurthy
Gopal Pandurangan
Hakim Weatherspoon
Praveen Yalagandula

Embedded Systems

Tarek Abdelzaher (*Chair*)
Karl-Erik Arzen
Hakan Aydin
Ted Baker
Riccardo Bettati
Albert Cheng
Chris Gill
Vana Kalogeraki
Insup Lee
Xue Liu
Lucia Lo Bello
Chenyang Lu
Ying Lu
Frank Mueller
Binoy Ravindran
Bruno Sinopoli
Oleg Sokolsky
Eduardo Tovar
Dakai Zhu

Fault-Tolerance in Distributed Systems / Dependability

James Anderson
Xavier Défago
Felix Freiling
Martin Hutle (*Chair*)
Ricardo Jimenez
Zbigniew Kalbarczyk
Miroslaw Malek
Achour Mostefaoui
Dave Powell
Luís E.T. Rodrigues
Nicola Santoro
Neeraj Suri
Tatsuhiro Tsuchiya
Paulo Veríssimo
Jennifer Welch
Josef Widder (*Chair*)

Formal Methods in Distributed Systems

Gul Agha
Borzoo Bonakdarpour
Ali Ebnenasir
Vijay Garg
Seth Gilbert
Sandeep Kulkarni (*Chair*)
Oded Maler
Jose Meseguer
Sayan Mitra (*Chair*)
Aditya Nori
Natarajan Shankar
Scott Smolka

Grid Computing

Artur Andrzejak
Alvaro Arenas
Jean-Pierre Banâtre
Rajkumar Buyya
Franck Cappello
Eddy Caron
José C. Cunha
Marco Danelutto
Frédéric Desprez
Thomas Fahringer
Geoffrey Fox
Paraskevi Fragopoulou
Sergei Gorlatch
Hai Jin
Dieter Kranzlmueller
Craig Lee
Norbert Meyer
Zsolt Nemeth Sztaki
Manish Parashar
Ronald H. Perrott
Thierry Priol (*Chair*)
Domenico Talia
Dora Varvarigou
Zhiwei Xu
Ramin Yahyapour
Wolfgang Ziegler

Mobility and Dynamic Networks

Stefano Basagni
Marin Bertier
Jiannong Cao
Pierluigi Crescenzi
Marcelo Dias de Amorim
Andras Farago
Eric Fleury (*Chair*)
Paola Flocchini
Pierre Fraigniaud
Seth Gilbert
Jean Loup Guillaume
Shay Kutten
Thomas Moscibroda
David Peleg

Christian Poellabauer
Violet R. Syrotiuk
Sébastien Tixeuil
Koichi Wada
Masafumi Yamashita

Multicore Computing

Andrea Acquaviva
Ali-Reza Adl-Tabatabai
Cedric Bastoul
Pascal Felber (*Chair*)
Christof Fetzer (*Chair*)
Tim Harris
Maurice Herlihy
Michael Hohmuth
Gilles Muller
Nir Shavit
Per Stenstrom
Osman Unsal

Peer-to-Peer Systems

James Aspnes
Olivier Beaumont
Giuseppe Ciaccio
Paolo Costa
Fabrice Le Fessant
Davide Frey
Thomas Fuhrmann (*Chair*)
JoAnne Holliday
Riko Jacob
Márk Jelasity
Kendy Kutzner
Massouli Laurent
Giancarlo Ruffo
Christian Scheideler
Christian Schindelhauer
Pierre Sens
Georgios Smaragdakis
Burkhard Stiller
Kurt Tutschku
Nalini Venkatasubramanian
Spyros Voulgaris
Klaus Wehrle

Self-organizing Systems

Matthias Baumgarten
Jake Beal
Yuriy Brun
Vincent Chevrier
Rogerio De Lemos
Giovanna Di Marzo Serugendo (*Chair*)
Simon Dobson
Bruce Edmonds
Carlos Gershenson
Marie-Pierre Gleizes
Michael Grottke
David Hales
Salima Hassas (*Chair*)
Christian Igel
Mark Jelasity
Anthony Karageorgos
Marco Mamei
Gero Muehl
Wolfgang Renz
Martijn Schut
Mikhail Smirnov
Aad Van Morsell
Rolf Wuertz

Sensor Networks

Anish Arora (*Chair*)
Habib M. Ammari
Jan Beutel
David Du
Jason Hallstrom (*Chair*)
Bhaskar Krishnamachari
Santosh Kumar
Chenyang Lu
Nigamanth Sridhar
Andreas Terzis
Yu-Chee Tseng
Hongwei Zhang

Stabilization

James Aspnes
Joffroy Beauquier
Doina Bein
Christian Boulinier
Alain Cournier
Sylvie Delaët
Stéphane Devismes
Shlomi Dolev
Bertrand Ducourthial
Hugues Fauconnier
Paola Flocchini
Felix Freiling
Sukumar Ghosh
Hirotsugu Kakugawa
Mehmet H. Karaata
Yoshiaki Katayama
Lawrence L. Larmore
Toshimitsu Masuzawa
Fabien Mathieu
Mikhail Nesterenko
Boaz Patt-Shamir
Franck Petit (*Chair*)
Maria Gradinariu Potop-Butucaru
Cédric Tedeschi
Sébastien Tixeuil
Vincent Villain
Masafumi Yamashita

System Safety and Security

Raouf Boutaba (*Chair*)
Jorge Cobb
Mourad Debbabi
Mohamed G. Gouda (*Chair*)
Stefanos Gritzalis
Urs Hengartner
Jiankun Hu
Chin-Tser Huang
Eunjin (E.J.) Jung
Ninghui Li
Alex X. Liu
Dan Massey
Neeraj Mittal
Refik Molva
Peter Muller
Radu State
Gene Tsudik
Carlos Becker Westphall

Steering Committee

Sukumar Ghosh
Anish Arora
Ajoy K. Datta
Shlomi Dolev
Mohamed G. Gouda
Ted Herman
Toshimitsu Masuzawa
Vincent Villain

Additional Reviewers

Hrishikesh B. Acharya
Luca Maria Aiello
Ismet Aktas
Mishari Almishari
Habib M. Ammari
Zakia Asad
Thomas Aynaud
Rosa M. Badia
Zinaida Benenson
Andrew Berns
Josep Berral
Jan Beutel
Hamad Binsalleh
Francois Bonnet
Amine Boukhetouta
Zohir Bouzid
Olga Brukman
Janna Burman
Jan Calta
Jian Chang
Xin Che
Hyun-Chul Chung
Kendra Cooper
Scott Coull
Brian DeVries
Carole Delporte
Benjamin Depardon
Yoann Dieudonné
Andreas Dittrich
Jing Dong
Swan Dubois
Yong Fu
Matthias Függer
Daniel Graff
Vincent Gramoli
Gregory Hackmann
Sammy Haddad
Rachid Hadid
Daniel Hagimont
Kai Han
Claus Hertling
Yu Hua
Shing-Tsaan Huang
Taisuke Izumi
Tomoko Izumi
Georgios Kambourakis
Sayaka Kamei
Giorgos Karopoulos
Vincent Keller
Matthew Kellett
Kyungbaek Kim
Sebastian Kniesburges
Ioannis Krontiris
Petr Kuznetsov
Hyunyoung Lee
Julien Legriel
Joao Leitao
Yawei Li
Yan Li
Peter Likarish
Jó Agila Bitsch Link
Xiaohui Liu
Miroslaw Malek
Nicolas Markey
Marco Milanesio
Neeraj Mittal
Noman Mohammed
Nicolas Nisse
Stephen Olivier
Lucia Draque Penso
Olivier Peres
Marie-Laure Potet
Giuseppe Prencipe
Michel Raynal
Ryan Riley
Yvan Rivierre
Paolo Romano
Gautam Roy
Srikanth Sastry
Gregor Schiele
Elad Michael Schiller
Stefan Schmid
Florian Schmidt
Klaus Schneider
Michael Segal
Massoud Seifi
Zubair Shafiq
John Solis
Anil Somayaji
Claudio Soriente
Srdjan Stipic
Andreas Tielmann
Peter Tröger
Kasturi Varadarajan
Kapil Vaswani
Saira Viqar
Ramesh Viswanathan
Sally Wahba
Christopher Weyer
Qiao Xiang
Alex Yakovlev
Yukiko Yamauchi
Ziming Zheng
Liu Xuan

Table of Contents

Invited Talks

Regular Papers

Brief Announcements

Challenges in Personalizing and Decentralizing the Web: An Overview of GOSSPLE*

Anne-Marie Kermarrec

INRIA, Rennes Bretagne-Atlantique, France
Anne-Marie.Kermarrec@inria.fr

Abstract. Social networks and collaborative tagging systems have taken off at an unexpected scale and speed (Facebook, YouTube, Flickr, Last.fm, Delicious, etc). Web content is now generated by you, me, our friends and millions of others. This represents a revolution in usage and a great opportunity to leverage collaborative knowledge to enhance the user's Internet experience. The GOSSPLE project aims at precisely achieving this: automatically capturing affinities between users that are potentially unknown yet share similar interests, or exhibiting similar behaviors on the Web. This fully personalizes the search process, increasing the ability of a user to find relevant content. This personalization calls for decentralization. (1) Centralized servers might dissuade users from generating new content for they expose their privacy and represent a single point of attack. (2) The amount of information to store grows exponentially with the size of the system and centralized systems cannot sustain storing a growing amount of data at a user granularity. We believe that the salvation can only come from a fully decentralized user centric approach where every participant is entrusted to harvest the Web with information relevant to her own activity. This poses a number of scientific challenges: How to discover similar users, how to define the relevant metrics for such personalization, how to preserve privacy when needed, how to deal with free-riders and misheavior and how to manage efficiently a growing amount of data.

1 Introduction

While the Internet has fully moved into homes, creating tremendous opportunities to exploit the huge amount of resources at the edge of the network, the Web has changed dramatically over the past years. There has been an exponential growth of user generated content (Flickr, Youtube, Delicious, ...) and a spectacular development of social networks (Twitter, FaceBook, etc). This represents a fantastic potential in leveraging such kinds of information about the users: their circles of friends, their interests, their activities, the content they generate. This also reveals striking evidence that navigating the Internet goes beyond traditional search engines. New and powerful tools that could empower individuals in ways that the Internet search will never be able do are required.

The objective of GOSSPLE is to provide an innovative and fully decentralized approach to navigating the digital information universe by placing *users affinities and preferences* at the heart of the search process. Where traditional search engines fail to provide information unless it is properly indexed, GOSSPLE will seek the information where it ultimately is: *at the user*.

* This work is supported by the ERC Starting Grant GOSSPLE number 204742.

R. Guerraoui and F. Petit (Eds.): SSS 2009, LNCS 5873, pp. 1–16, 2009.

GOSSPLE aims at capturing the interactions and affinities on the fly and fully leveraging the huge resource potential available on edge nodes, to efficiently search, dynamically index and asynchronously disseminate and recommend information to interested users based on their preferences. Building on the peer to peer communication paradigm and harnessing the power of gossip-based algorithms, GOSSPLE aims at personalizing Web navigation, by means of a fully decentralized solution, for the sake of scalability and privacy.

A number of technical challenges underlie GOSSPLE and its objective of combining personalization and decentralization:

- **Personalization:** GOSSPLE should address appropriate metrics to compute distances between users and identify and capture the affinities between users.
- **Scalability:** GOSSPLE should provide scalable mechanisms to deal with a huge and growing amount of information.
- **Privacy:** while entrusting users to hold and maintain their personal data give them full control on them, further mechanisms are required in GOSSPLE to leverage personal information and detect affinities between user without exposing personal information about the requests of a user or the content she generates.
- **Support for misbehavior:** while fully decentralized approaches buy scalability, they remove any form of central authority, leaving holes for misbehavior: GOSSPLE should tackle the whole range of misbehavior from attempts to free-ride the system, to attempts to try to exploit it (through spamming for example) and even hurt it with Byzantine behaviors.

The rest of the paper provides the context and motivation (Section 2), the technical challenges (Section 3), the scientific background (Section 4) before concluding and providing the current status of the GOSSPLE project.

2 Time for a Navigation Shift in the Internet

The past decade has witnessed a dramatic scale shift in the area of distributed computing. Meanwhile, the Internet has entered our homes together with various kinds of digital assets. This has resulted into a radical change in the way people are communicating, companies are organized and data is managed all over the world. Social networking in the forms of social networks (Facebook, Twitter) or folksonomies (Delicious, Flickr) has taken off at an unexpected scale. The Internet we are now looking at is composed of millions of computing devices and as many users, generating contents at a high speed, Terabytes of dynamic data, scattered all over the world, shared, disseminated and searched for.

2.1 Personalized Navigation within the Internet

Although computer science in general and more specifically distributed computing has gradually taken into account this digital revolution, we now have reached the point where incremental changes are no longer sustainable. Traditional search engines are performing extremely well but do hardly encompass alternative and very dynamic sources of information such as user-generated contents, blogs, peer-to-peer file-sharing systems instant messaging as well as content distribution frameworks. This is mainly due to their lack of adaptivity to dynamics and their not taking into account correlations between contents and users preferences. They are also limited by their reliance upon centralized indexing: they periodically scan the whole web, build an index in their data centre, then distribute it back out to smaller centres that respond to queries. Typically, corporate pages are visited frequently while individual information may be visited rarely: *the individual is at a disadvantage*. This reveals striking evidence that complementary and novel fully decentralized alternatives to traditional search engines are now required to capture the dynamic, collaborative and heterogeneous nature of the digital universe as well as to to leverage individual preferences and social affinities.

2.2 Illustration: Looking for a Baby-Sitter

To illustrate the inadequacy of state of the art solutions, let us consider the following concrete example. Following a long stay in the UK, a French family is looking for an English speaking student who would be willing to trade baby-sitting hours against accommodation, say in the city of Rennes to allow kids to keep up with English. Given the high number of students in Rennes, there is no doubt that such an offer would be of interest for many English speaking students.

Yet, satisfying this simple, slightly unusual, request is challenging and in fact almost impossible. The most natural way for the family to find a match is to launch a Google request "Baby-sitter anglophone Rennes"[1]. The first hits on Google lead to baby-sitting services, student announces, including different geographical areas and has nothing to do with English speaking. All subsequent reformulated requests, in French or English, lead to equally unsatisfactory results. Yet, would this family be able to reach all English speaking students in Rennes, there will definitely be some candidates.

The data is clearly out there but it is difficult to achieve the match between the offer and the supply. If the offer effectively exists in some proper indexed form, even though a search engine forces to continuously probe the system, it will probably achieve the match eventually. Alternative sites such as Craigslist, a centralized network of online communities featuring free classified advertisements, extremely popular in the US, could also be used in this case, provided that the user follows the imposed structure. However, if the offer does not exist in the proper indexed form, current technology simply does not fit. This is mostly due to the fact that *baby-sitter* is mainly associated with *daycare* or local baby sitting companies. None of the family Facebook buddies can help either as known of them has ever looked for an English-speaking baby-sitter. The best solution would be for the family to post a request on some mailing list or appropriate forum gathering the potential candidate baby-sitters and wait for the responses.

Now, consider Alice living in Strasbourg, who has looked for a similar deal for her kids. Alice is lucky enough to discover through a (real-life) friend that primary school teaching assistants are a very good match for they have the same working hours as kids and tend to enjoy living with a family. If Alice associates *baby-sitter* with *teaching assistant* in the system and if the French family above is able to leverage this information,

[1] "English speaking baby-sitter Rennes".

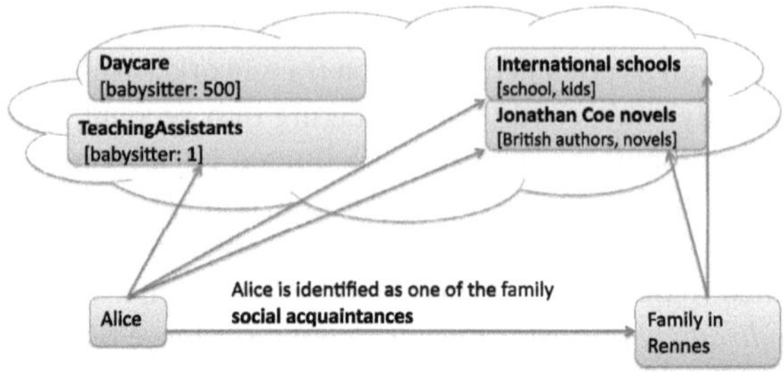

Fig. 1. Babysitter example: while the association between babysitter and daycare dominates, Alice associates babysitter to teaching assistant. The goal of GOSSPLE is to establish a connection between Alice and the French family in Rennes so that it could benefit from Alice's association.

the request can be successful. The goal of GOSSPLE is to establish such a connection, called an implicit social link, between Alice and that French family in Rennes. Note they do not need to know each other. Yet their past history of French people leaving in an English speaking country, their interest in English novels and International school for example, could be conveyed in their online behavior and automatically captured by a system. This is illustrated on Figure 1.

2.3 Where GOSSPLE Comes into Place

In fact, the collaborative and social nature of the Internet is leveraged in many social systems [28] such as delicious, Twitter, Facebook, Twine or Orkut to cite a few. Such systems connect users sharing interests, professional or social, and enable them to share data, blogs, etc. Their functioning is however hurt by the dynamic nature of users behavior. Some users get connected, loose interest and remain connected without participating. Also, the user feedback is hardly leveraged and while the blog feature is widely used, search is mostly absent. Similarly, the semantic Web improves automation through machine understandable descriptions [11]. Yet, such tools mostly rely on static structures. Above all, all those systems remain centralized. This an issue for two main reasons: scalability and privacy. An efficient personalization mechanism requires to store a large amount of data per user and maintain it, potentially limiting the scalability of the system and hurting the desire of users to preserve their personal information. In addition, centralized systems are more vulnerable to denial of service attacks such as the one observed in August 2009 on Twitter, Facebook and LiveJournal.

To cope with dynamics and the huge amount of information that need to be managed on a per user basis, entrusting each user with discovering and managing the data relevant to her is the solution to both scalability and privacy preservation.

GOSSPLE stems from the observation that social connections can be leveraged by a system to collaboratively help Web search and recommendation. Yet such social connections need not to be explicitly established as in social networks ala Facebook. Instead the system should capture such social connections and discover relevant users. As opposed to globally harvest and organize the Web, the basic idea behind GOSSPLE is that each user is in charge of harvesting the network in her own personalized way.

Coming back to our example, even if the answer to the request actually does not exist as such (say no foreign student has figured out that some families would offer such a deal), GOSSPLE would actually enable to dynamically *attract it*. There are several ways this could be achieved by GOSSPLE, by expanding the query in a relevant manner or by having the request navigate in the network to the right places. With GOSSPLE, the family would gradually get connected to relevant matching users typically representing adequate communities (say English speaking people in Rennes). Then the object would dynamically turn into an ad, in a sense *creating the need* and subsequently the matches. In turn, potential response objects would travel back to the family acquaintances in the form of notifications or ads, and subsequently create the need for other related families (those who wouldn't have thought of the deal but actually like the idea). At the heart of this procedure lies dynamic overlays based on *users affinities and preferences*. This goes far beyond discovering indexed data. All along, the connection procedures, both sides, will be continuously fed by the feedback from the users to refine the quality of the connections, as well as by recommendations on possibly matching objects from other users with similar preferences on similar requests. The interacting model is inherently collaborative, asynchronous and iterative.

Obviously, this example is not meant to restrict the usage of GOSSPLE to this application. However, we believe that the simple scenario illustrates the dynamic and collaborative navigation idea. These, implemented in a fully-decentralized manner, can be applied to a large spectrum of applications (content sharing, dissemination, instant messaging, RSS feeds, or virtual communities).

3 The GOSSPLE Challenges

The existing technology of distributed and personalized search is in its infancy. We are reaching the limits of what we could call the "Google style" of problem solving: periodically cull all the pages on the web into their data centre, index them, and then answer queries for pages for some period of time. So far, the information space has mostly been composed of Web pages, indexation ruled by search engines and navigation ensured mostly manually by the users, largely favouring the "mass". Effectively, the page rank algorithms of Google-like systems favour popular pages. Although GOSSPLE does not come as a replacement of such engines but rather as a complementary tool, it provides a fresh look at the information space management and favour communities at a disadvantage. More specifically it offers a new way to navigate the digital space.

The GOSSPLE's challenge is to provide the following features in a fully decentralized way.

1. Full-fledged personalization
2. Scalable management of the information space
3. Privacy-aware implementation
4. Resilience to misbehavior

3.1 A Network of Affinities

We are seeking search solutions leveraging the live nature of the data and the collaborative nature of its users. GOSSPLE exploits the social dimension of the Internet to get "related" users indirectly connected and refine each other's filtering procedures through implicit preferences. The network will be organized around such preferences and affinities between users. This will provide a radically different approach to managing digital assets, navigating within the Internet and bringing new dimensions for collaborative applications. Such a network of affinities is at the heart of GOSSPLE and represents the first challenge of Gossple. Providing each user with a personalized view of the network requires solving several issues:

- **Sampling the network:** the second challenge is to be able to discover such users. This is particularly challenging in a fully decentralized system where no entity has a global knowledge of the system and is able to make a match between similar users. A related issue is to connect all GOSSPLE users in a connected mesh: although a user should be connected to similar users, she should be able to navigate the whole network if needed.
- **Affinity metrics:** the first challenge is to be able to identify the fact that two users share similar interests. This requires to compute a distance between users and can depend on the content they generate, their past activity, the feedback they provide, the application they are running, etc.
- **Coping with dynamics:** the third challenge is to be able to maintain a personalized network up-to-date and to take into account the changes and the dynamics of the system with respect to the users, the data, the changes in the interests or the activity of the users.

GOSSPLE will heavily rely on peer to peer overlay networks to achieve personalization of the network. Basically, GOSSPLE will manage a large set of GOSSPLE peers (users, items, etc). More specifically, we envision a basic layer where all potential nodes are, at least temporarily, connected and maintained despite dynamics in content and connectivity patterns, providing gateways and efficient routing to higher level overlays (See Figure 2). At the basic abstraction layer, a GOSSPLE peer represents a machine connected to the Internet. The same physical computer may host several logical GOSSPLE peers: the request of the family, a user in a virtual community, a file, etc. A major GOSSPLE challenge is to build, on top of its basic layer, many overlay networks that will dynamically evolve, based on users affinities and common preferences.

GOSSPLE will leverage the sampling features of gossip-based protocols to provide users with the ability to sample the network and identify similar users.

Figure 2 conveys an example of a federation of overlays as we foresee it in GOSSPLE. The bottom layer ensures connectivity, on top of which the federation of overlays is maintained. Each GOSSPLE peer associated with a user may be part of one or several sub-overlay networks, whose nature may vary depending on the functionalities required by the application they are running. This amounts to having a physical peer running many instances of different P2P overlay networks. Yet, a fair amount of information may be shared between these instances. We will investigate the mutualization of the state associated with each overlay in order to limit the overhead for a similar, or even better, performance. More specifically, we will identify for each overlay the application-dependent connections, which will have to be maintained independently of other sub-networks such as the "closest" peers according to the "affinity" metric.

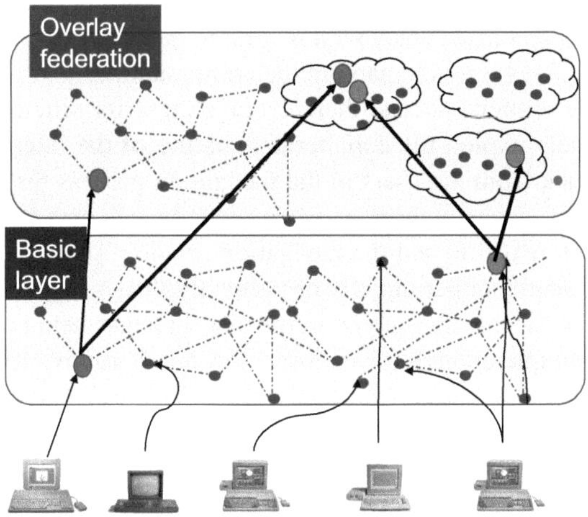

Fig. 2. Gossple Overlay Federation

Identifying the relevant users requires appropriate metrics to compute a distance between users. The refinement of connections between peers is crucial: each GOSSPLE peer will keep in its *personalized view* of the system for a given overlay a set of acquainted peers. In most cases, this choice is done on a peer basis, that is depending on its own characteristics. The correlation between all the peers present in the view could also be exploited to cover as much as possible all the range of interests of a user. All these aspects should be investigated in the project.

3.2 Scalable Data Management

A scalable personalization of the network, operating a navigation shift on the Internet, calls for a fully decentralized system and requires the following features:

- **Efficient management of personal information:** this refers to the amount and the type of personal data that should be stored per user and exchanged between users in order to evaluate the proximity of interests between users and achieve personalization.
- **Efficient search, recommendation and navigation algorithms:** this refers to the algorithms to search content, process queries, implement efficient notification mechanisms, routing features, etc.

Identifying the relevant discovery space, the granularity of the search protocol and data representation are crucial to the design of an efficient digital navigation. The navigation criteria should be simple and flexible enough to preserve the efficiency and simplicity of an underlying gossip-based discovery protocol. A related issue is the trade-off between expressiveness and exhaustivity. Expressiveness refers to the accuracy of a request formulation (exact search, keyword-based search, range queries), or the *quality* of a request. This is highly dependent on the number of dimensions of the search space, the type of query, the correlation between various attributes of the request. The degree of exhaustivity refers to the accuracy with respect to *quantity*.

A key aspect of GOSSPLE is to capture the commonalities and preferences of users from their matching refinements and then leverage these for efficient navigation. This is crucial to genuinely exploit the collaborative nature of the Internet. GOSSPLE will integrate the feedback from the users in the navigation process through recommendation mechanisms. The acquaintances between related users may take the form of recommendations, as in real life, and the navigation protocol should take those as direct inputs to refine the search either directly or indirectly through specific overlays. These aspects have been so far mostly ignored in the distributed system community and specific mechanisms, simple enough for the user, and not disruptive for the system, need to be investigated.

There are many connections with the information retrieval community. However, most approaches are centralized, complex and require a large amount of knowledge of the whole system. GOSSPLE borrows from this community to represent and track similarities between data and/or users.

3.3 Preserving Privacy

Apart from the fact that centralized systems may be subject to DOS attacks, one of the main motivations to provide a fully decentralized system is to fulfil the need for privacy of users and fight their fear (or the real risk) of the *Big Brother Syndrome*. In the realm of recent developments of social networks, the associated companies have consistently shown their eagerness to exploit personal information: in 2009, Facebook tried to change its terms of use so that any content ever published on Facebook was doomed to a perpetual licence to Facebook. Likewise in 2007, Facebook proposed a feature called beacon to expose Web navigation history of users [2]. Similarly, many personal information are stored by Google [3].

A fully decentralized system avoids such issues as no single entity keeps the control of personal data. Instead, the users are in charge of managing such data themselves. In order to get the most of users communities, personal information must be disclosed to some extent. Yet, the association between a user and her personal information is not always required. The challenge here, with respect to privacy, is to ensure that personal information can be fully leveraged while masking the association between user profile and identity whenever this is required.

GOSSPLE leverages this fact by masking the association between a user and her information whenever this is possible. GOSSPLE will also include a lightweight mechanism to track potential intruders, including colluding ones.

3.4 Fighting Misbehavior

Fully decentralized systems are particularly vulnerable to misbehavior, the very fact that there is no central control authority allow users to misbehave with impunity, ranging

[2] Note that those proposals did not get through due to users reaction.

[3] To further illustrate this, the launching of Google Latitude on the iPhone, a location-based social network, in July 2009, raised many concerns with respect to privacy. Indeed, many people are extremely reluctant to disclose people whereabouts.

from free-riding behaviors, to malicious ones. Fighting such misbehavior is of the utmost importance for a wide adoption of a system.

Several angles can be investigated:

- Measuring the degree of collaboration in order to characterize the benefit of a user with respect to her contribution
- Detecting misbehavior
- Punishing misbehaving nodes thus creating an incentive to non-malicious behaviors

Load balancing, referring to the fact that the load is evenly shared between participating entities has been at the heart of the design of P2P systems to ensure scalability regardless of the capacities of peers. *Fairness* has not. In this context fairness is related to the ratio between the benefit a peer gets from the system from its contribution. We mean by a fair system one in which peers contribute to the system proportionally to the benefit they get. This is crucial for a collaborative system to provide incentives to contribute. The fact that fairness has been ignored so far is mostly due to the low-level nature of distributed systems, where the perception by a user is not prevalent. This is no longer the case because users and machines are closely related, now more than ever. A user does not want a software to store data for others or use her bandwidth without being rewarded to a certain extent for this. Should users perceive that they contribute to the system more than what they get out of it, they could decide to get disconnected. Thus, an unfair distribution of the workload can lead to increasing artificially the system dynamics and impact the reliability and scalability of a decentralized system. This is particularly important in GOSSPLE where inputs from the users and their affinities are prevalent.

Ensuring fairness implies characterizing the load, being able to measure it, and devising adaptive mechanisms to account for it. Fairness also intrinsically limits the impact of selfish (free-riders) users. Yet, some users may exhibit some arbitrary behavior, voluntarily or not. Clearly, GOSSPLE might suffer from the same potential attacks as a traditional P2P system [4]. In addition, the misbehavior might also target the data that are exchanged in the system in order to personalize the system. Indeed, GOSSPLE introduces some specificities in this area related to the targeted applications such as false recommendations, wrong feedback or stale objects.

4 Background: Peer to Peer, Gossip and the Small World Nature of the Internet

Decentralization is a core characteristic of GOSSPLE. In this section, we provide the networking background on which GOSSPLE will heavily rely.

Traditional structured and unstructured overlays exhibit almost orthogonal properties and are complementary with respect to locating data in a large-scale system. Structured overlays associate keys with nodes and provide an exact match interface. This approach is highly efficient when the exact identifier of an item is known but not as straightforward when it comes to performing a *range query* or a *keyword-based search*. In addition, the maintenance cost of a structured overlay may be high in dynamic environments where the peers leave and join the system frequently. On the other hand, unstructured networks handle range queries and keyword searches more easily and are highly adaptive to dynamic environments. In particular, the inherent randomness of gossip-based protocols makes their corresponding unstructured networks ideal for scalable information dissemination. However, they tend to generate a large number of messages for each search request as they do not recall any history. Besides, they do not always guarantee an exhaustive search.

We aim at taking the best of all worlds, by combining structured and unstructured overlays within GOSSPLE. More specifically, we will make use of a gossip-based protocol for basic navigation, combined with structured networks derived from the affinities of users.

Self-* emerging structures. Current search engines are mostly centralized [4]. Not only do we aim at revolutionizing navigation, but we also believe that it is no longer conceivable to rely on a few companies to index the digital world [5]. The total absence of centralization is the key to both scalability and privacy preservation. A fully decentralized system, as envisioned in GOSSPLE is sustainable if and only if it is able to be self-organizing, self-healing, self-parametrizing and self-managing. To this end, GOSSPLE will harness the power of gossip-based algorithms, strongly rely on the scalable peer to peer communication paradigm and overlay networks.

Connectivity: Peer to peer communication paradigm. In peer to peer (P2P) systems, each node may be both a client and a server and takes individual decisions based on an extremely restricted knowledge of the network. Yet expected global system properties emerge. This makes P2P computing robust, self-organizing and scalable. Following this model, nodes organize in a logical (overlay) network, structured or not, on top of a physical network (typically the Internet). Many such overlays have been proposed in the past five years [37, 32]. Yet, real deployments remain limited and their potential goes far beyond file sharing, voice over IP or content distribution. In GOSSPLE, we step away from general-purpose overlay networks and consider dynamic application-tailored collaborative overlays.

Navigability: Small-world networks. Small world networks have been introduced as an analytical way of modelling the *six degrees of separation* [26] stating that two random individuals are separated by short chains of acquaintances that can be discovered. When applied to computing networks, the small world phenomenon [23] is defined as the combination of a high degree of clustering, small diameter in the connection graph and navigability properties. Such a model matches pretty well the real interactions between humans and more specifically between users over the Internet. A small-world network can be defined as a system where each node in a mesh knows its *closest*[6] neighbors and has additional shortcuts in the graph. The asymptotic routing performance depends on the way shortcuts are chosen (random [44] or following a specific distribution (*d*-harmonic) [23]). Kleinberg [23] determined the magnitude order of this routing complexity results in such networks. This work has been of the up-most importance in the community, leading to a full range of works.

[4] Obviously central servers in this context refer to huge data centres.

[5] One can imagine the impact of Google falling apart.

[6] The proximity metric may be application-dependent.

Dynamicity: Gossip-based networking. Gossip-based protocols implement the P2P communication paradigm in an unstructured manner. Inspired by the spreading of rumours or epidemics, these protocols are very powerful for disseminating information and quickly discovering acquaintances between users. Their implementation typically relies on a periodic peer-wise exchange of information. It turns out that depending on the peer chosen locally for the interaction and the information exchanged, gossip-based protocols can be used to build and maintain arbitrary structures. As such, gossip-based protocols are attractive for developing large-scale distributed systems and do have a substantial power. They combine convergent behavior, ability to let emergent structures appear, simplicity of programming and deployment. They also impose a bounded load on participants, are independent of the underlying topology and are robust to network disruptions and continuous changes. Gossip-based protocols will constitute a basic building block for the design and implementation of GOSSPLE.

In short, a generic version of a gossip-based protocol, consists in having each peer run periodically a protocol that can be fully characterized by the three following parameters [21]: *(i) Peer selection* refers to the peer selected for the gossip exchange. Each peer has an extremely limited knowledge of the system (list of other peers) and selects a peer from this *view* of the system; *(ii) Data exchanged* refers to the nature of the data exchanged during the gossip interaction. This is highly application-dependent; *(iii) Data processing* refers to the computation operated on the data after the exchange. Again, data processing is highly application dependent. This simple algorithm and its associated set of parameters are surprisingly powerful and can be applied in a wide variety of settings. More specifically, when the data exchanged is related to peer themselves, this provides a generic tool to build and maintain large-scale overlay networks, structured, unstructured, random, or clustered [15, 19]. They also cope extremely well with network dynamics. For example, more than 70% of the nodes are required to be down for a network to become partitioned [21]. When the data exchanged is related to information to be disseminated, this provides a scalable and reliable dissemination system [15].

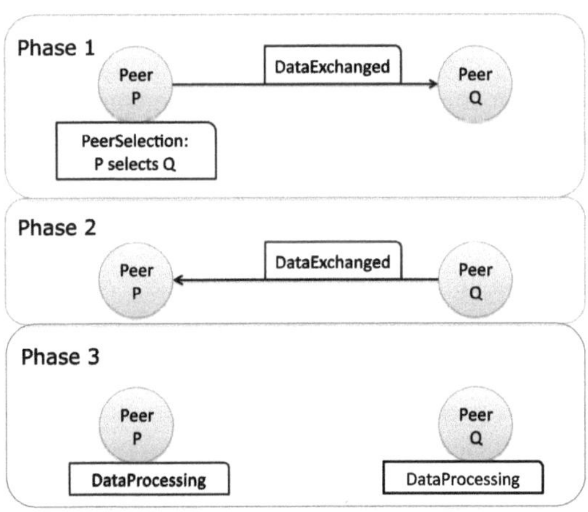

Fig. 3. Phases of a gossip initiated by Peer P: P picks Q among its neighbors (its view)

Distributed computations can also be implemented by simply tuning adequately the data exchanged and data processing parameters [20, 25]. Gossip-based protocols have also been used to create clustered overlays optimized with respect to application-specific metrics [42, 41]. To illustrate this further, epidemic protocols may be used to construct P2P overlay networks achieving graph properties very close to those of random graphs [21]. The protocol is illustrated on Figure 3.

These protocols scale extremely well and are closely matched to the style of social networking problems GOSSPLE targets. In GOSSPLE, we will go one step further to explore their huge potential over the Internet and in particular consider them with respect to arbitrary metrics.

5 Personalizing the Web: Related Projects

The related work in networks has been presented above. In this section, we provide a brief overview of the work that has been conducted to personalize the Web. Since the Web has been acknowledged as a read-write platform with growing user-generated content, a lot of research has tried to leverage this in many areas [34, 24, 40]. Yet, to the best or our knowledge no existing work combines personalization, decentralization, privacy and resilience to misbehavior.

Personalized search. The social semantics between users exhibits a huge potential to leveraging social connections should they be explicit through social networks connections or implicit trough similar tagging behavior. One example of system leveraging explicit social connections is Peerspective [27] where the search results of a user's skype buddies are used for the user subsequent search operations. Yet, as pointed out in [9], the utility of the information gathered from such networks turns out however to be very limited. We believe that there is much more to leverage in unknown social acquaintances or user activities such as user's query histories [36], browsing histories [38], and tagging behaviors [31].

In the context of top-k processing, the notion of user affinity has been often discussed [33, 3], yet, most personalized approaches are centralized such as [33] or [2]. In the context of query expansion, collecting and exploiting information about the past activity of a user has been considered in [12, 22]. The work presented in [8] is a first step to personalization through social relation: the scoring model is personalized, the associated query expansion mechanism is not.

Finally, there have been several user-centric approaches in the area of search, and recommendation [30, 47, 45, 17, 9, 29, 46, 39, 7, 18, 49], as well as query expansion [48]. None is decentralized though.

Decentralized approaches. The closest work with respect to distributed systems are semantic overlays, relying on the peer-to-peer communication paradigm. These systems [14, 35, 6, 16] cluster peers hosting similar data or interested in similar topics [43] in order to improve the efficiency of query resolution in peer-to-peer data sharing systems. Their focus is nevertheless mainly on exploiting similarities to locate objects in a distributed data repository. None of these approaches attempt to discover social connections between peers.

Metrics. There has been a lot of work, mostly in the area of information retrieval on personalization metrics to measure the distance between tags or items in collaborative systems, and folksonomies in particular. These include *co-occurrence count* [30], *cosine similarity* to compute distance between users [47, 49] or tags [13, 46], *edit-distance* [45] and *relative centrality*. Yet, there are still many application-dependent metrics that should be considered.

Finally, recommendation systems ([1] for example) have been proposed and analyzed from a theoretical standpoint, there are yet to be put in practice in a decentralized setting.

6 Conclusion and Work in Progress

The combination of the penetration of Internet into homes, huge computing power at the edge of the network, an exponential growth of user-generated content, a striking need for personalizing Web navigation with respect to search, notification, recommendation, and a call for decentralization to remove the fear of the *Big brother* syndrome and the potential vulnerabilities to attacks of centralized systems, paves the way for a new generation of systems. GOSSPLE should hopefully be one of them. The main originality of GOSSPLE is to make every user responsible for harvesting the Web in a personalized way through the use of efficient gossip-based protocol. Apart from the GOSSPLE challenge that we mentioned above, the challenge of digging out the right tools and scientific backgrounds from as many areas as distributed computing, information retrieval and database is a challenge in itself.

Personalization has been in the air for a while. This has been even more striking as users generate contents. Yet, we are not there yet and combining personalization, security and scalability remains an open track that GOSSPLE tries to fill.

Many challenges need to be tackled in GOSSPLE There are currently three main tracks currently under investigation.

Personalized networks. At the core of Gossple lies the notion of personalized network. GOSSPLE achieves this through gossiping: based on a random peer sampling protocol providing each user with a random subset of other users, GOSSPLE implements a biased sampling protocol that speeds up convergence. Each user periodically contacts a close user, they exchanged their knowledge on the other users and retain the best ones according to a given metric to form the personalized network. Such a protocol enables the quick discovery of related (with respect to a given metric) users in a very large system in a fully distributed manner and with every user storing a small amount of information about the system.

Query expansion in GOSSPLE. In this work, we provide a personalized query expansion mechanism. In the context of a collaborative tagging system ala delicious, Gossple builds, for each user, a personal network of acquaintances through a gossip protocol as explained above. This network is composed of a set of other users that together cover all the interests of the user. This is achieved without revealing the associations between users and their profiles. The information gathered from the personal network is used to create a personalized view of the correlations between tags. This data structure called the TagMap represents a user-centric personalized view of the relations between tags and is used to expand queries in a meaningful manner. Experimental results conducted on traces crawled from CiteULike, a collaborative tagging system for bibliographic references, and Delicious, show that by storing and exchanging little information between users, the user experience is improved through the query expansion mechanism both with respect to the quality of the results and the number of results obtained. More details can be found in [10].

Top-k processing in GOSSPLE. We are considering decentralized and personalized top-k processing, the protocol is called P3K [5]. It has been shown in [2] that personalizing top-k processing could significantly improve the quality of the results. This was achieved firstly in a centralized way and secondly considering that a social network was known explicitly in advance. We go beyond this approach in P3K. We discover a personal network of acquaintances computing a distance between users based on the similarities observed in their tagging behaviors. In this protocol, we show that using only the information gathered from similar users in a decentralized way, we are able to achieve similar results to those of a centralized approach. We are currently studying a gossip-based alternative to process personalized top-k queries, improving the scalability of the system.

Acknowledgments

I would like to warmly thank all the members of the GOSSPLE team: Xiao Bai, Marin Bertier, Antoine Boutet, Davide Frey, Kevin Huguenin, Vincent Leroy, Afshin Moin, Guang Tan, Christopher Thraves, as well as Rachid Guerraoui who is actively collaborating with us on the project. I also would like to thank Jacques-Henri Jourdan, Fabrice le Fessant and Vivien Quéma for their help.

References

[1] Alon, N., Awerbuch, B., Azar, Y., Patt-Shamir, B.: Tell me who i am: An interactive recommendation system. In: ACM Symposium on Parallelism in Algorithms and Architectures (2006)
[2] Amer-Yahia, S., Benedikt, M., Lakshmanan, L., Stoyanovich, J.: Efficient network aware search in collaborative tagging sites. In: International conference on Very Large Data Bases (VLDB), vol. 1, pp. 710–721. VLDB Endowment (2008)
[3] Amer-Yahia, S., Marlow, C., Yu, C., Stoyanovich, J.: Leveraging tagging to model user interests in del.icio.us. In: AAAI SIP: Social Information (2008)
[4] Awerbuch, B., Scheideler, C.: Towards scalable and robust overlay networks. In: International Workshop on Peer-to-Peer Systems (2007)
[5] Bai, X., Bertier, M., Guerraoui, R., Kermarrec, A.-M.: Toward personalized peer-to-peer top-k processing. In: International workshop on Social Network Systems (2009)
[6] Banaei-Kashani, F., Shahabi, C.: Swam: a family of access methods for similarity-search in peer-to-peer data networks. In: ACM Conference on Information and Knowledge Management (2004)
[7] Bao, S., Xue, G., Wu, X., Yu, Y., Fei, B., Su, Z.: Optimizing web search using social annotations. In: International conference on World Wide Web (WWW), pp. 501–510. ACM, New York (2007)

[8] Bender, M., Crecelius, T., Kacimi, M., Michel, S., Neumann, T., Xavier Parreira, J., Schenkel, R., Weikum, G.: Exploiting social relations for query expansion and result ranking. In: International Conference on Data Engineering Conference (ICDE) Workshops (2008)
[9] Bender, M., Crecelius, T., Kacimi, M., Michel, S., Xavier Parreira, J., Weikum, G.: Peer-to-peer information search: Semantic, social, or spiritual? Bulletin of Computer Society Technical Committee on Data Engineering (2007)
[10] Bertier, M., Guerraoui, R., Kermarrec, A.-M., Leroy, V.: Toward personalized query expansion. In: International workshop on Social Network Systems, SNS (2009)
[11] Sheth Cardoso, A.: J. Semantic Web Services: Theory, Tools and Applications. Springer, Heidelberg (2007)
[12] Carman, M., Baillie, M., Crestani, F.: Tag data and personalized information retrieval. In: ACM Workshop on Search in Social Media, SSM (2008)
[13] Cattuto, C., Benz, D., Hotho, A., Stumme, G.: Semantic analysis of tag similarity measures in collaborative tagging systems. In: Workshop on Ontology Learning and Population (2008)
[14] Crespo, A., Molina, H.H.G.: Semantic overlay networks for p2p systems (2002)
[15] Eugster, P., Handurukande, S., Guerraoui, R., Kermarrec, A.-M., Kouznetsov, P.: Lightweight probabilistic broadcast. ACM Transaction on Computer Systems 21(4) (November 2003)
[16] Eyal, A., Gal, A.: Self organizing semantic topologies in p2p data integration systems. In: International Conference on Data Engineering Conference, ICDE (2009)
[17] Fogaras, D., Rácz, B., Csalogány, K., Sarlós, T.: Towards scaling fully personalized pagerank: Algorithms, lower bounds, and experiments. Journal of Internet Mathematics 2(3), 333–358 (2005)
[18] Hotho, A., Jäschke, R., Schmitz, C., Stumme, G.: Information retrieval in folksonomies: Search and ranking. In: Sure, Y., Domingue, J. (eds.) ESWC 2006. LNCS, vol. 4011, pp. 411–426. Springer, Heidelberg (2006)
[19] Jelasity, M., Babaoglu, O.: T-Man: Gossip-based overlay toplogy management. In: Brueckner, S.A., Di Marzo Serugendo, G., Hales, D., Zambonelli, F. (eds.) ESOA 2005. LNCS (LNAI), vol. 3910, pp. 1–15. Springer, Heidelberg (2006)
[20] Jelasity, M., Montresor, A.: Epidemic-style proactive aggregation in large overlay networks. In: International Conference on Distributed Computing Systems, ICDCS 2004 (2004)
[21] Jelasity, M., Voulgaris, S., Guerraoui, R., Kermarrec, A.-M., van Steen, M.: Gossip-based peer sampling. ACM Transactions on Computer Systems (August 2007)
[22] Jie, H., Zhang, Y.: Personalized faceted query expansion. In: SIGIR (2006)
[23] Kleinberg, J.: The small-world phenomenon: An algorithmic perspective. In: ACM Symposium on Theory of Computing (2000)
[24] Lawrence, S.: Context in web search. IEEE Data Engineering Bulletin 23, 25–32 (2000)
[25] Le Merrer, E., Kermarrec, A.-M., Massoulié, L.: Peer-to-peer size estimation in large and dynamic networks: a comparative study. In: IEEE International Symposium on High Performance Distributed Computing, HPDC 15 (2006)
[26] Milgram, S.: The small-world problem. Psychology Today, 60–67 (1967)
[27] Mislove, A., Gummadi, K., Druschel, P.: Exploiting social networks for internet search. In: HotNets. ACM, New York (2006)
[28] Monroe, D.: Just for you. Communications of the ACM 52(8) (2009)
[29] Morrison, J.: Tagging and searching: Search retrieval effectiveness of folksonomies on the world wide web. Journal of Information Processing and Management (2008) (Corrected Proof) (in press)
[30] Niwa, S., Doi, T., Honiden, S.: Web page recommender system based on folksonomy mining for itng 2006 submissions. In: International Conference on Information Technology: New Generations, INTG (2006)

[31] Noll, M., Meinel, C.: Web search personalization via social bookmarking and tagging. In: Aberer, K., Choi, K.-S., Noy, N., Allemang, D., Lee, K.-I., Nixon, L.J.B., Golbeck, J., Mika, P., Maynard, D., Mizoguchi, R., Schreiber, G., Cudré-Mauroux, P. (eds.) ASWC 2007 and ISWC 2007. LNCS, vol. 4825, pp. 367–380. Springer, Heidelberg (2007)

[32] Rowstron, A., Druschel, P.: Pastry: Scalable, decentralized object location, and routing for large-scale peer-to-peer systems. In: Guerraoui, R. (ed.) Middleware 2001. LNCS, vol. 2218, p. 329. Springer, Heidelberg (2001)

[33] Schenkel, R., Crecelius, T., Kacimi, M., Michel, S., Neumann, T., Xavier Parreira, J., Weikum, G.: Efficient top-k querying over social tagging networks. In: SIGIR (2008)

[34] Schenkel, R., Crecelius, T., Kacimi, M., Neumann, T., xavier Parreira, J., Spaniol, M., Weikum, G.: Social wisdom for search and recommandation. Bulletin of the IEEE Computer Society Technical Committee on Data Engineering 31(12), 40–49 (2008)

[35] Sedmidubsky, J., Barton, S., Dohnal, V., Zezula, P.: Adaptive approximate similarity searching through metric social networks. In: International Conference on Data Engineering Conference, ICDE (2008)

[36] Speretta, M., Gauch, S.: Personalized search based on user search histories. In: IEEE/WIC/ACM International Conference on Web Intelligence (2005)

[37] Stoica, I., Morris, R., Karger, D., Kaashoek, F., Balakrishnan, H.: Chord: A scalable peer-to-peer lookup service for internet applications. In: ACM SIGCOMM Conference, San Diego, California (2001)

[38] Sugiyama, K., Hatano, K., Yoshikawa, M.: Adaptive web search based on user profile constructed without any effort from users. In: International conference on World Wide Web (2004)

[39] Teevan, J., Dumais, S.T., Horvitz, E.: Personalizing search via automated analysis of interests and activities. In: SIGIR (2007)

[40] Teevan, J., Dumais, S.T., Horvitz, E.: Characterizing the value of personalizing search. In: SIGIR, pp. 757–758. ACM, New York (2007)

[41] Voulgaris, S., Rivière, E., Kermarrec, A.-M., van Steen, M.: Sub-2-sub: Self-organizing content-based publish and subscribe for dynamic and large scale collaborative networks. In: International Workshop on Peer-to-Peer Systems (2006)

[42] Voulgaris, S., van Steen, M.: Epidemic-style management of semantic overlays for content-based searching. In: Cunha, J.C., Medeiros, P.D. (eds.) Euro-Par 2005. LNCS, vol. 3648, pp. 1143–1152. Springer, Heidelberg (2005)

[43] Wang, Q., Li, R., Chen, L., Lian, J., Tamer Özsu, M.: Speed up semantic search in p2p networks. In: ACM Conference on Information and Knowledge Management (2008)

[44] Watts, D.J., Stogatz, S.H.: Collective dynamics of small-world networks. Nature 393, 440–442 (1998)

[45] Wong, B., Slivkins, A., Sirer, E.G.: Approximate matching for peer-to-peer overlays with cubit. Technical report, Cornell University, Computing and Information Science Technical Report (2008)

[46] Xu, S., Bao, S., Fei, B., Su, Z., Yu, Y.: Exploring folksonomy for personalized search. In: SIGIR, New York, NY, USA (2008)

[47] Yildirim, H., Krishnamoorthy, M.S.: A random walk method for alleviating the sparsity problem in collaborative filtering. In: ACM Conference on recommander systems, RecSys (2008)

[48] Zanardi, V., Capra, L.: Social ranking: uncovering relevant content using tag-based recommender systems. In: ACM Conference on recommander systems, RecSys (2008)

[49] Zhao, S., Du, N., Nauerz, A., Zhang, X., Yuan, Q., Fu, R.: Improved recommendation based on collaborative tagging behaviors. In: International conference on intelligent user interfaces (2008)

Local Algorithms: Self-stabilization on Speed

Christoph Lenzen[1], Jukka Suomela[2], and Roger Wattenhofer[1]

[1] Computer Engineering and Networks Laboratory TIK
ETH Zurich, 8092 Zurich, Switzerland
lenzen@tik.ee.ethz.ch, wattenhofer@tik.ee.ethz.ch
http://www.dcg.ethz.ch

[2] Helsinki Institute for Information Technology HIIT
P.O. Box 68, FI-00014 University of Helsinki, Finland
jukka.suomela@cs.helsinki.fi
http://www.hiit.fi

1 Introduction

Fault tolerance is one of the main concepts in distributed computing. It has been tackled from different angles, e.g. by building replicated systems that can survive crash failures of individual components, or even systems that can tolerate a minority of arbitrarily malicious ("Byzantine") participants.

Self-stabilization, a fault tolerance concept coined by the late Edsger W. Dijkstra in 1973 [1,2], is of a different stamp. A self-stabilizing system must survive arbitrary failures, beyond Byzantine failures, including for instance a total wipe out of volatile memory at all nodes. In other words, the system must self-heal and converge to a correct state even if starting in an arbitrary state, provided that no further faults happen.

Local algorithms, on the other hand, have no apparent relation to fault tolerance. Instead, the basic question studied is whether one can build efficient network algorithms, where any node only knows about its immediate neighborhood. What problems can be solved in such a framework, and how efficiently? Local algorithms have first been studied about 10 years after Dijkstra proposed the notion of self-stabilization [3,4,5,6]; recently they experience an Indian summer because of new application domains, such as overlay or sensor networks [7].

It seems that the world of self-stabilization (which is asynchronous, long-lived, and full of malicious failures) has nothing in common with the world of local algorithms (which is synchronous, one-shot, and free of failures). However, as shown in the late 1980s, this perception is incorrect [8,9]; indeed one can prove quite easily that the two areas are essentially equivalent. Intuitively, this is because (i) asynchronous systems can be made synchronous by using synchronizers [10], (ii) self-stabilization concentrates on the case after the last failure, when the system tries to become correct again, and (iii) one-shot algorithms can just be executed in an infinite loop.

R. Guerraoui and F. Petit (Eds.): SSS 2009, LNCS 5873, pp. 17–34, 2009.

One can show that upper and lower bounds in either area more or less transfer directly to the other area.[1] Unfortunately, it seems that this equivalence has been somewhat forgotten in the last decades. For instance, hardly ever does a paper from one area cite work from the other area. We take the opportunity of this invited paper to summarize the basics, to discuss the latest developments, and to point to possible open problems. We believe that the two areas can learn a great deal from each other!

2 Deterministic Algorithms

The connection between local algorithms and self-stabilizing algorithms is particularly straightforward in the case of deterministic algorithms: any deterministic local algorithm is also a deterministic self-stabilizing algorithm. Furthermore, any deterministic, synchronous local algorithm whose running time is T synchronous communication rounds provides a self-stabilizing algorithm that stabilizes in time T. In this section, we review the conversion in detail, first through an example and then in the general case.

2.1 An Example: Graph Coloring

Throughout this work we consider distributed systems that consist of computational devices and communication links between them. The distributed system is represented as a graph $\mathcal{G} = (V, E)$ with $n = |V|$ nodes: each node $v \in V$ is a device, and two nodes can communicate directly if they share an edge $\{u, v\} \in E$.

Although the connection between local algorithms and self-stabilizing algorithms is more general, in this text we focus on distributed algorithms that solve graph problems. We use the problem of finding a graph coloring as a running example. In this case we want to assign a color $c(v)$ to each node $v \in V$ such that no two adjacent nodes share the same color, i.e., the nodes of each color form an independent set. In general it is NP-hard to determine the minimum number of colors required to color a graph, so we settle for $(\Delta + 1)$-colorings, where Δ is the maximum node degree. Each node v must produce a *local output* from the set $\{0, 1, \ldots, \Delta\}$ such that for any pair of adjacent nodes the local outputs are different.

2.2 A Deterministic Local Algorithm for Graph Coloring

Perhaps the simplest model of distributed computing is a synchronous distributed algorithm. In a synchronous algorithm, all nodes in the network perform steps in parallel: during each *synchronous communication round*, all nodes

[1] So was local algorithms just old wine in new skins? Not really, because the two areas had quite a different focus. Whereas self-stabilization mostly dealt with correctness, local algorithms were all about complexity and efficiency. Today, this difference is disappearing, as also self-stabilization is more and more about efficiency.

in parallel (i) perform local computation, (ii) send out messages to their neighbors, (iii) wait for the messages to propagate along the edges, and (iv) read the incoming messages. Finally the nodes determine their output and terminate. A synchronous *local algorithm* is simply a distributed algorithm that completes in T synchronous communication rounds. Typically T is a constant [6,11] or a slowly-growing function of n [3,4,5].

In T communication rounds, information is propagated for only T hops in the communication graph; hence the output of a node v can only depend on the structure of the graph $\mathcal{G}$ in the radius-T neighborhood of v. This is the very idea suggested by the term "local algorithm": nodes make decisions based on *local* information, yet the decisions must be globally consistent.

We start with a variant of a very fast and elegant algorithm, the well-known Cole–Vishkin algorithm [4], which 3-colors an n-cycle in $O(\log^* n)$ rounds. The function $\log^* n$ is defined as the number of times the logarithm has to be applied to n until the result is a constant. This function grows exceptionally slowly and is bounded by a small number for any reasonable size of n. In the Cole–Vishkin algorithm, the local input of a node is a unique identifier with $O(\log n)$ bits, and the local output of a node will be a color from the set $\{0, 1, 2\}$:

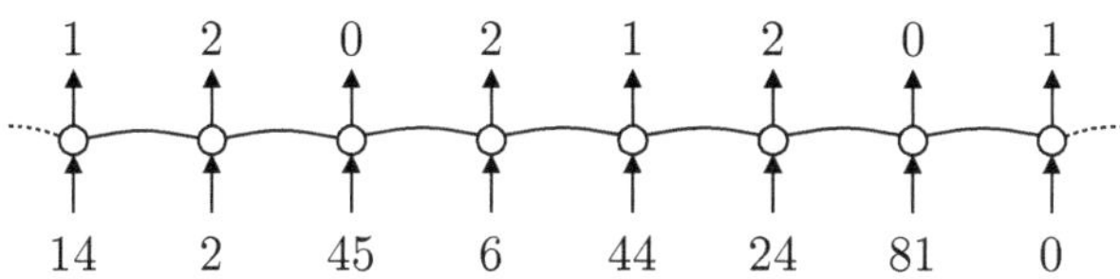

To keep things simple, we assume that the nodes know an upper bound on n, and the cycle has a consistent orientation such that each node has one successor and one predecessor:

The algorithm works as follows. Initially, the color of a node is equal to its unique identifier; the idea is to repeatedly decrease the number of colors required. In each round, each node v sends its current color to its successor w. The node w compares bitwise its own color to the received one to determine the least significant bit where they differ. It binary encodes the position and appends the differing bit, resulting in its new color in the form of a bit string. The new color of w cannot be identical to the new color of its predecessor v: either the indices of the bits v and w determined are not the same, meaning that the colors have a different prefix, or the computed indices referred to bits with different values, i.e., the new colors differ in their terminal bits.

The following example shows two iterations of the algorithm on a part $t \to u \to v \to w$ of a cycle:

$$\begin{aligned}
t&: 1010110000 \to \;\ldots\; \to \ldots \\
u&: 0010110000 \to 10010 \to \ldots \\
v&: 1010010000 \to 01010 \to 111 \\
w&: 0110010000 \to 10001 \to 001.
\end{aligned}$$

The initial colors, i.e., the nodes' unique identifiers, have $O(\log n)$ bits. After one step, the colors consist of $O(\log \log n)$ bits, namely a binary encoded position in a string of length $O(\log n)$ plus one bit. Applying this observation also to subsequent rounds, we see that after $O(\log^* n)$ rounds, the number of bits—and thus colors—has become constant. At this point, a simple constant-time algorithm can be used to reduce the number of colors to $\Delta + 1 = 3$: in each round, we remove the largest color.

In summary, we have an algorithm for 3-coloring an n-cycle in $O(\log^* n)$ rounds; furthermore, this running time is asymptotically optimal [5]. The approach can be generalized to bounded-degree graphs and rooted trees [12,13]. Recently, the technique was utilized to find colorings in bounded-independence graphs in $O(\log^* n)$ rounds [14]; we will discuss recent work in more detail in Sect. 4.1.

2.3 A Self-stabilizing Algorithm for Graph Coloring

The local algorithm presented in the previous section is not fault-tolerant in any way. We assumed that all nodes are activated simultaneously in a specific initial state, and the network does not change during the execution of the algorithm. The algorithm eventually stops, after which it does not react in any way to changes in the network. Furthermore, we assumed that all nodes perform computations in a synchronous manner, as if a global clock pulse was available.

Nevertheless, it is possible to convert this local algorithm into an efficient asynchronous *self-stabilizing* algorithm. A self-stabilizing algorithm, by definition, provides an extreme form of fault tolerance [2,15,16]: an adversary can choose an arbitrary initial configuration, and a self-stabilizing algorithm is still guaranteed to converge into a correct output.

For the sake of concreteness, we use the shared-memory model here: we assume that each communication link $\{u, v\} \in E$ consists of a pair of communication registers, one which is written by u and read by v, and one for passing information in the opposite direction. Typically support of atomic reads and writes is assumed.

In this model, a *configuration* of the system consists of the local outputs of the nodes, the contents of the local variables of the nodes, and the contents of the communication registers. In a *legitimate configuration* the system behaves as intended—in our example, a legitimate configuration simply refers to any configuration in which the local outputs of the nodes form a valid coloring. We refer to Dolev's book [16, §2] for more details on these definitions and on the model of self-stabilizing algorithms in general.

We now convert the variant of the Cole–Vishkin algorithm presented in Sect. 2.2 into an asynchronous self-stabilizing algorithm. Asynchronicity means here that there are no guarantees on how fast computations are done and information is exchanged. Rather, the algorithm must be resilient to a worst-case situation where a non-deterministic distributed daemon may schedule any computational step at any node next. The algorithm must reach a legitimate state regardless of the decisions of the daemon. The time complexity of an asynchronous self-stabilizing algorithm is defined as the number of *asynchronous cycles* required to converge from an arbitrary state to a legitimate configuration; an asynchronous cycle is an execution during which each node at least once reads its input and incoming messages, and infers and writes its new output and outgoing messages.

The algorithm from Sect. 2.2 can be adapted to this model as follows. Let $T = O(\log^* n)$ be the running time of the Cole–Vishkin algorithm. For each edge in the cycle, we divide the associated communication register (in the described algorithm communication is unidirectional, hence a single register suffices) into T parts, each of which represents one round of the local algorithm. Let v be a node in the oriented cycle, with predecessor u and successor w. Now the state of the communication register on the edge $\{u, v\}$ corresponds to *all* messages that u sends to v during the execution of the Cole–Vishkin algorithm; similarly, the register on the edge $\{v, w\}$ corresponds to the messages sent by v to w.

The node v continuously reads its input (its unique identifier) and the values in the communication register on the edge $\{u, v\}$. The node v *simulates* its own actions during a complete execution of the Cole–Vishkin algorithm, *assuming* that these incoming messages are correct, and writes its own outgoing messages to the communication register on the edge $\{v, w\}$. The node also continuously re-writes its local output based on this simulation.

Naturally, in the beginning the output might be nonsense, as the initial memory state is arbitrary. After one asynchronous cycle, however, the nodes will have (re)written their identifiers into the parts of the registers responsible for the messages in round one of the Cole–Vishkin algorithm. In the next cycle, their neighbors will read them, compute the new colors, and write them into the parts for round two, and so on. After $T + 1$ asynchronous cycles, the initial state of the system has been erased and replaced by the values the local algorithm would compute in a single run, independently of the schedule the daemon chooses. Hence the same arguments as in the previous section prove that the output must be correct at all nodes. Moreover, no further state transitions occur, as the outcome of all steps of the computation depends only on the local inputs (unique identifiers) of the nodes.

We conclude that the algorithm stabilizes within $T + 1$ asynchronous cycles, where T is the running time of the local algorithm. Hence in the conversion from local to self-stabilizing algorithms, we can guarantee much more than mere *eventual* convergence into a legitimate configuration: we can show that the convergence is *fast*.

Note that the algorithm is also efficient in terms of the number of bits sent and the required memory. In total

$$\sum_{i=1}^{T} O(\log^{(i)} n) = O(\log n)$$

bits need to be exchanged along each edge, where $\log^{(i)} n$ denotes the i times iterated logarithm. Apart from the presented special case where edges are oriented, this bit complexity is asymptotically optimal [17], a result also holding for randomized algorithms which are presented in Sect. 3. No additional memory beyond the communication registers is needed.

2.4 General Case

The example of Sect. 2.3 was fairly simple: in the original local algorithm, each node sends messages to only one neighbor. However, the general case is not much more complicated: there are two communication registers on each edge, and all registers are divided in T parts, one part for each communication round.

Figure 1 shows the basic idea behind the conversion: given any deterministic distributed algorithm $\mathcal{A}$ with running time T, we can construct an equivalent *circuit* that produces the same output as $\mathcal{A}$. The figure shows the conversion in the case where the communication graph $\mathcal{G}$ is a cycle, but the same idea can be applied to arbitrary graphs.

Each node v in Fig. 1a is replaced by $T+1$ virtual nodes $v_0, v_1, \ldots, v_T$ in Fig. 1b. The node v_0 represents the initial state of the node v in the algorithm $\mathcal{A}$, and the node v_i for $i = 1, 2, \ldots, T$ represents the state of the node v in the algorithm $\mathcal{A}$ after the synchronous communication round i. A directed edge from v_{i-1} to u_i represents the message sent by v to u during the synchronous communication round i. Clearly the output of the circuit is equal to the output of the original algorithm $\mathcal{A}$.

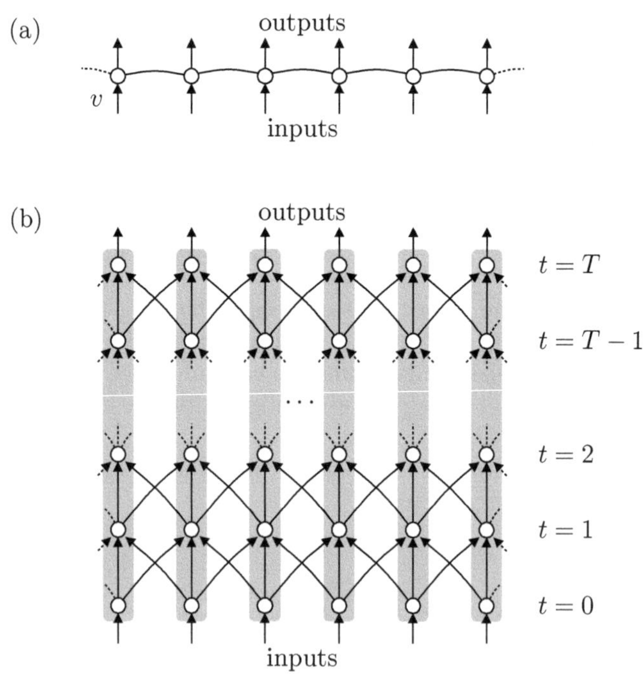

Fig. 1. (a) A distributed system that executes a local deterministic algorithm $\mathcal{A}$ with running time T. (b) A circuit that computes the same output.

So far we seem to have gained little: we have just an alternative representation of the original local algorithm $\mathcal{A}$. However, the key observation is that it is easy to *simulate* the computations of the circuit of Fig. 1b by a self-stabilizing algorithm. Furthermore, the simulation can be realized in virtually any model of distributed computing (assuming, of course, that the model allows us to implement any kind of reliable computation at all).

In essence, we simply replace each diagonal edge from v_{i-1} to u_i by a point-to-point communication channel from the node v to u. The node v continuously

1. re-reads its local input and all incoming messages,
2. simulates the behavior of $\mathcal{A}$ for each time step, assuming that the incoming messages are correct, and
3. re-writes its local output and all outgoing messages.

After $i + 1$ asynchronous cycles, the outgoing signals of the virtual nodes v_i are correct, and after $T + 1$ asynchronous cycles, the output of each node is correct, regardless of the initial configuration.

In the example of Sect. 2.3 we implemented point-to-point communication from u to v by using a communication register that was written by u and read by v. Equally well we could use the message-passing model and a self-stabilizing implementation of unit capacity data links; see, e.g., Awerbuch et al. [18].

Naturally, if T is large, say, $T = \Theta(n)$, then the conversion of Fig. 1 is of little use. However, in the case of local algorithms, typically $T \ll n$ and in some cases even $T = O(1)$. Hence this simple and easy-to-implement conversion yields an efficient self-stabilizing algorithm for most deterministic local algorithms. In particular, constant-time distributed algorithms are also self-stabilizing algorithms that stabilize in constant time. Furthermore, the memory requirement and message size is increased only by a factor of T: for example, if the original local algorithm transmits m-bit messages on each edge, the self-stabilizing algorithm sends (Tm)-bit messages.

2.5 The Simple Conversion in Literature

The observation that deterministic distributed algorithms can be easily converted into self-stabilizing algorithms is by no means new. The conversion of Fig. 1 is, in essence, equal to the "simulator" introduced by Awerbuch and Sipser [8] more than 20 years ago. Awerbuch and Sipser explicitly referred to the problem of simulating local algorithms, even though the field of local algorithms barely existed back then. While Awerbuch and Sipser did not focus on self-stabilizing algorithms, all key ingredients were already present. Their algorithm was triggered by a topology change in the network; equally well we can trigger the algorithm by periodically re-reading the inputs, and we obtain a self-stabilizing algorithm.

Awerbuch and Varghese [9] make the connection between synchronous distributed algorithms and self-stabilizing algorithms explicit. They use the term "rollback compiler" to refer to a simple conversion similar to that of Fig. 1. In their terminology, the states of the virtual nodes $v_0, v_1, \ldots, v_T$ together with the incoming messages constitute a *log* that contains the full execution history of the node v; hence the node can *verify* that the execution of the algorithm $\mathcal{A}$ is correct from its own perspective. If the execution is correct from the perspective of all nodes, then also the outputs are correct and the algorithm has stabilized. By keeping track of the execution history, we have made the output of the distributed algorithm locally checkable.

The simple conversion can also be interpreted as an application of local checking and correction that is introduced in Awerbuch et al. [18]. We can *locally check* the state of each directed edge in Fig. 1b. If a link (u_{i-1}, v_i) is in an inconsistent state, we can *locally correct* the state of v_i. By construction, each dependency chain in this system has length at most T, and hence the system will stabilize in time $T + 1$.

However, even though the simple conversion itself is well-known [16, §5.1], it seems that fairly little attention has been paid to it in the literature. The main focus has been on non-local problems such as spanning trees and leader election. Even in Awerbuch and Varghese's [9] work the main contribution is related to the conversion of non-local distributed algorithms whose running time T is larger than the diameter of the network.

A notable exception is Mayer et al. [19]. In this work—which is a follow-up of the seminal paper by Naor and Stockmeyer [6] that initiated the study of strictly local (constant-time) distributed algorithms—Mayer et al. specifically draw attention to the connection between local algorithms and fault-tolerance in dynamic systems. However, the field of local algorithms was still in its infancy in 1995, and positive examples of local algorithms were scarce.

We believe it is time to revisit the issue now, as we have numerous recent examples of local algorithms. In Sect. 4, we survey highlights from the field of local algorithms—both positive and negative results—and explain what implications they have from the perspective of self-stabilizing algorithms. However, we will first have a look at the much more complicated issue of randomized local algorithms.

3 Randomized Algorithms

So far we have restricted our attention to *deterministic* local algorithms. There is a considerable number of local algorithms that are *randomized*, i.e., each node has access to (uniformly) random bits. These can be useful to break symmetry or locally take decisions that probably perform well on a global scale, creating algorithms which are likely to be faster than their deterministic counterparts, to achieve better approximation guarantees, or to yield correct solutions despite short running times.

3.1 Basic Symmetry Breaking

Sometimes deterministic algorithms are even incapable of solving a particular task. Coloring an anonymous cycle, i.e., a cycle without a means to distinguish between nodes, is impossible without randomization. Due to total symmetry, when executing a deterministic algorithm, all nodes must take the same actions and eventually attain the same color.[2] On the other hand, running the Cole–Vishkin algorithm from Sect. 2 with $O(\log n)$ random bits as "identifier" at each node will result in a correct output *with high probability* (w.h.p.), i.e., for any choice of a constant $c > 0$ we can bound the probability of failure by $1/n^c$. Using random bit strings of length $(c + 2)\log n$, any pair of nodes will have distinct bit strings with probability $1/n^{c+2}$. Summing over all pairs of nodes, the probability of two nodes having the same string can be bounded by $n(n-1)/(2n^{c+2}) < 1/n^c$. Thus, with probability at least $1 - 1/n^c$, we can interpret the random bits as correct input of the deterministic Cole–Vishkin algorithm relying on unique identifiers.

When this technique is to be employed in the self-stabilizing world, we cannot guarantee globally unique identifiers any more unless accepting a stabilization time of $\Omega(D)$, since there is no way to distinguish a corrupted memory state from a correct one if not comparing the identifiers. However, for many algorithms, in particular routines such as Cole–Vishkin dealing with breaking of *local* symmetry, a locally unique labeling, i.e., *any* coloring, will do. Assuming (an approximation of) n is known, we merely need to continuously compare the "random identifiers" of neighbors, and generate a new random bit string if a conflict is observed. This very simple algorithm self-stabilizes w.h.p. within one or two cycles, depending on the precise model, and can be a building block for more sophisticated algorithms.

3.2 Pseudo-Randomization

The general transformation from Sect. 2.4 fails for randomized algorithms. On the one hand, if nodes make their random choices in advance and proceed deterministically, an adversary may tamper with the state of the memory holding the random bits, and the algorithm will be slow, yield bad approximations, or even completely fail. On the other hand, if nodes take random choices in each step of the algorithm "on the fly", the execution of the algorithm itself is not deterministic. In this case, we cannot represent the state of a node in a given (synchronous) round as function of the states of the nodes in the previous round, and thus also not represent the respective computations by a Boolean circuit. Rather, to guarantee uncorrupted random choices, nodes would have to continuously renew their random bits, preventing convergence to a fixed output.

From a practical point of view, this problem can be tackled easily: Instead of generating actual random numbers, we use fixed unique random seeds, i.e., node identifiers, as part of the input. These bits are read-only and can be seen as part of the protocol itself, i.e., they are not subject to the arbitrariness of initial states. Using a pseudo-random function with the node identifier in conjunction with the round number as input, nodes can generate pseudo-random

[2] Asynchrony might break symmetry, but in the worst case it will certainly not. Here the worst case ironically is the system being perceived as synchronous.

bits for use by a randomized algorithm. Since these bits are computed deterministically at running time, the conversion from Sect. 2.4 can be applied again to infer asynchronous and self-stabilizing algorithms from synchronous randomized counterparts.

Assuming that no correlation between the random seeds and the problem-specific input exists, and provided that a well-behaving pseudo-random function is used, the performance of the algorithm will be indistinguishable from a "true" randomized algorithm's: We simply ensured a supply of random bits in advance by storing a previous random choice in non-volatile memory to avoid corruption. Hence, in practice also randomized local algorithms lead to efficient self-stabilizing solutions in a straightforward manner.

3.3 Theoretical Questions

From a theoretical point of view, the use of pseudo-randomization is noneffective. Regardless of the computations made, previously stored values do not replace randomly generated numbers. At best, if the stored bits have been generated uniformly at random and the other input is independent of these choices, each stored bit can be used once as a random bit. At worst, a sufficiently powerful adversary might learn about nodes' pseudo-random choices by experimentation or having access to the complete state of nodes, and afterwards modify the input in a way such that the pseudo-random choices are badly suited to the created problem instance. After all, pseudo-randomness does not change the deterministic behavior of the algorithm, and therefore any lower bound applicable to deterministic algorithms must hold.

In fact, to the best of our knowledge, little is known about which randomized local algorithms can be made self-stabilizing efficiently. We presented a trivial, yet important example at the beginning of the section which tolerates asynchronicity. Synchronous randomized algorithms may require synchronous systems to self-stabilize quickly, as the random choices of a given round need to be correlated. This however might limit their usability in an asynchronous environment, since a self-stabilizing synchronizer requires time in the order of the diameter of the network to stabilize [20], a bound that—at least when ignoring other complexity measures—is trivial to local algorithms, since nodes may learn about the whole topology and all local inputs in that time.

4 Results on Local Algorithms

In this section, we present selected results from the field of local algorithms, with the main focus on recent discoveries. Most of the results are deterministic algorithms or lower-bound results, each of which has a direct self-stabilizing counterpart. We have also included examples of randomized local algorithms—some of these can be made self-stabilizing by using the symmetry breaking technique discussed in Sect. 3, while developing self-stabilizing versions of others provides challenges for future research. We begin with the theme that we have used as a running example in Sections 2 and 3, graph coloring.

4.1 Colorings, Independent Sets, and Matchings

In the study of traditional centralized algorithms, graph coloring is often seen from the perspective of *optimization*: the goal is to minimize the number of colors. This perspective leads to many famous results in graph theory and computer science; finding an optimal coloring is a classical NP-hard problem, and numerous (in)approximability results, practical heuristics, and exponential-time exact algorithms are known.

However, in distributed computing, graph coloring is usually regarded as a fundamental *symmetry-breaking* primitive. From this point of view, minimizing the number of colors is not necessary—a coloring with $\Delta + 1$ colors is sufficient for symmetry-breaking purposes. While such a coloring is trivial to find in a centralized setting by using a greedy algorithm, the problem of finding such colorings efficiently in a distributed setting has been a central question from the very first days of the field to the present day. These efforts have resulted in fast algorithms and tight impossibility results, both of which transfer directly to a self-stabilizing setting.

Before reviewing the key results, it is worth mentioning that there is another symmetry-breaking problem that is essentially equal to graph coloring: the problem of finding a *maximal independent set*. Given a k-coloring, it is easy to find a maximal independent set in time k. Conversely, if we have an algorithm for finding a maximal independent set, we can use it to find a $(\Delta + 1)$-coloring [5]. Another related symmetry-breaking problem is finding a *maximal matching*. In particular, in the case of directed cycles a maximal matching is equivalent to a maximal independent set: the outgoing edges of independent nodes form a matching and vice versa.

From this background it comes as no surprise that all these problems have essentially the same time complexity in bounded-degree graphs, already familiar from Sect. 2: if $\Delta = O(1)$, then it is possible to find a $(\Delta+1)$-coloring, a maximal independent set, and a maximal matching in $O(\log^* n)$ rounds, and not faster.

Deterministic Algorithms. Naturally, all deterministic algorithms that break the symmetry require some kind of initial symmetry-breaking information [21]. The algorithms that we discuss here assume that each node has a unique identifier. The unique identifiers do not make the problems trivial, though. Linial's results [5] show that even in the case of directed cycles with unique identifiers, there is no constant-time algorithm for finding a graph coloring, maximal independent set, or maximal matching. Any such algorithm requires $\Omega(\log^* n)$ communication rounds.

We already presented the Cole–Vishkin algorithm [4] for coloring a cycle in Sect. 2; the running time of this algorithm matches Linial's lower bound. Since the publication of Cole and Vishkin's seminal work in 1986, numerous algorithms have been presented for the problem of coloring an arbitrary graph with $\Delta + 1$ colors; typically, such algorithms have time complexity of the form $O(f(\Delta) + \log^* n)$. Examples of these include an algorithm by Goldberg et al. [22] with a running time of $O(\Delta^2 + \log^* n)$ rounds, and by Kuhn et al. [23] with running time $O(\Delta \log \Delta + \log^* n)$. The recent algorithms by Barenboim and Elkin [24] and Kuhn [25] finally push the running time down to $O(\Delta + \log^* n)$. These results also provide a deterministic algorithm for finding a maximal independent set in $O(\Delta + \log^* n)$ rounds. Schneider et al. [14] study *bounded-independence graphs*, i.e., graphs in which any constant-radius subgraph contains at most $O(1)$ independent nodes. In this family, a maximal independent set, a maximal matching, or a $(\Delta + 1)$-coloring can be found in $O(\log^* n)$ rounds.

There are also efficient distributed algorithms that directly solve the problem of finding a maximal matching. Some of the algorithms have running times of the familiar form $O(f(\Delta)+\log^* n)$: Panconesi and Rizzi [26] find a maximal matching in $O(\Delta + \log^* n)$ rounds. However, there are also algorithms that perform well even if $\Delta = \Theta(n)$. For example, Hańćkowiak et al. [27] find a maximal matching in $O(\log^4 n)$ rounds.

In summary, at least for bounded-degree graphs (or more general bounded-independence graphs), these three symmetry-breaking problems admit very efficient and asymptotically optimal deterministic solutions.

Randomized Algorithms. In the case of deterministic algorithms, we assumed that we have unique identifiers in the network. However, a much weaker assumption is usually sufficient: it is enough to have a graph coloring (possibly with an unnecessarily large number of colors). Many deterministic graph coloring algorithms, including the original Cole–Vishkin algorithm, simply perform *color reductions* steps: in each iteration, a k-coloring is replaced with an $O(\log k)$-coloring.

Therefore we can apply a randomized graph coloring algorithm, such as the one mentioned in Sect. 3.1, to obtain an initial k-coloring, and then use deterministic local algorithms to find a $(\Delta+1)$-coloring, a maximal independent set, or a maximal matching. Such a composition results in a randomized self-stabilizing algorithm that can be used in anonymous networks without unique identifiers.

There are also randomized local algorithms that find a maximal independent set directly, without resorting to a randomized graph coloring algorithm. The most famous example is Luby's [3] randomized algorithm from 1986 that finds a maximal independent set in $O(\log n)$ rounds w.h.p.; similar results were also presented by Alon et al. [28] and Israeli et al. [29] around the same time. Recently, Métivier et al. [30] presented a new variant featuring a simpler analysis. While we are not aware of a self-stabilizing version of Luby's algorithm, there has been progress in this direction. Already in 1988, Awerbuch and Sipser [8] studied Luby's algorithm in dynamic, asynchronous networks, and more recently the algorithm has been studied in a fault-tolerant setting by Kutten and Peleg [31].

4.2 Linear Programs

Now we change the perspective from symmetry-breaking problems to optimization problems. Many resource-allocation questions in computer networking can be naturally formulated as *distributed linear programs* (LPs): each (physical or virtual) node in the network represents a variable or a constraint, with an edge between a variable and each constraint that depends on it. Papadimitriou and

Yannakakis [32] raised the question of solving such linear programs in a local manner so that the value of each variable is chosen using only information that is available in its local neighborhood in the network.

Clearly such algorithms cannot produce an optimal solution—in some cases even finding a feasible solution requires essentially global information on the problem instance. However, there are important families of linear programs that admit *local approximation algorithms*, i.e., algorithms that find a solution that is guaranteed to be feasible and near-optimal.

The most widely-studied families are *packing and covering LPs*. In a packing LP, the objective is to maximize $\boldsymbol{c}^\top \boldsymbol{x}$ subject to $A\boldsymbol{x} \leq \boldsymbol{1}$ and $\boldsymbol{x} \geq \boldsymbol{0}$ for a non-negative matrix A; a covering LP is the dual of a packing LP. Distributed approximation algorithms for packing and covering LPs have been presented by Bartal et al. [33] and by Kuhn et al. [34,35].

For example, in the case of $\{0, 1\}$ coefficients, Kuhn et al. [35] find a $(1+\epsilon)$-approximation in $O(\epsilon^{-4} \log^2 \Delta)$ rounds; here the degree bound Δ is the maximum number of non-zero elements in any row or column of the matrix A. If Δ is a constant, the algorithm is strictly local in the sense that the approximation ratio and the running time are independent of the number of nodes. Moreover, it is a *local approximation scheme*: an arbitrarily good approximation ratio can be achieved. The algorithm is deterministic, an therefore it can be easily converted into a self-stabilizing algorithm.

It is also known that the dependency on Δ in the running time is unavoidable. Kuhn et al. [35,36] present lower bound constructions that, in essence, show that finding a constant-factor approximation of a packing or covering LP requires $\Omega(\log \Delta / \log \log \Delta)$ rounds, even in various special cases such as the LP relaxations of minimum vertex cover and maximum matching. The same construction also gives a lower bound of $\Omega(\sqrt{\log n / \log \log n})$ rounds as a function of n. Such lower bounds have applications far beyond linear programming, as they also give lower bounds for the original combinatorial problems. Incidentally, the lower bounds by Kuhn et al. hold even in the case of randomized algorithms with probabilistic approximation guarantees.

The family of *max-min LPs* combines packing and covering constraints. In a max-min LP, the objective is to maximize ω subject to $A\boldsymbol{x} \leq \boldsymbol{1}$, $C\boldsymbol{x} \geq \omega\boldsymbol{1}$, and $\boldsymbol{x} \geq \boldsymbol{0}$ for non-negative matrices A and C. While arbitrarily good approximation factors can be achieved for packing and covering LPs in bounded-degree graphs with a strictly local algorithm, this is no longer the case for max-min LPs—indeed, a tight pair of positive [37] and negative [38] results is known for the approximation factor achievable with a strictly local algorithm. Nevertheless, for certain families of graphs better approximation algorithms are known [39].

4.3 Randomized LP Rounding

In addition to being the workhorse of operations research, linear programming has found numerous applications in the field of combinatorial optimization [40]. Many of the best polynomial-time approximation algorithms build on the theory of linear programming [41]. The case is the same in the field of local algorithms.

Putting together the LP approximation schemes discussed in Sect. 4.2 and the technique of *randomized rounding* [34,35,42], it is possible to find good approximations for many classical combinatorial problems. For example, in the case of the minimum dominating set problem, we can study the *LP relaxation* of the problem. This is a covering LP, and using the LP approximation schemes, we can find a near-optimal solution, i.e., a near-optimal fractional dominating set.[3] Now the challenge is to construct an integral dominating set whose size is not much worse than the size of the fractional dominating set; this can be solved by using a two-step randomized algorithm which provides an $O(\log \Delta)$-approximation in expectation. In addition to covering problems such as dominating set, this approach can be applied to solve packing problems: the expected approximation factor is $O(\Delta)$ for maximum independent sets and $O(1)$ for maximum matchings. The running time is essentially equal to the running time of the LP approximation scheme.

One of the main drawbacks of this approach is that the use of randomness seems to be unavoidable, and it is not obvious how to design a self-stabilizing algorithm with the same performance guarantees. However, there are various other techniques that can be used to design local approximation algorithms; we review these in the following section.

4.4 Other Combinatorial Approximation Algorithms

The classical problem of finding a minimum-size vertex cover serves as a good example of alternatives to randomized LP rounding. There are at least three other approaches. First, it turns out that vertex cover can be approximated well by using a deterministic LP-based algorithm. The LP approximation schemes by Kuhn et al. [35] together with a simple deterministic rounding technique [43] yield a $(2+\epsilon)$-approximation in $O(\epsilon^{-4} \log \Delta)$ rounds. This algorithm as a whole can be made self-stabilizing directly by using the approach from Sect. 2.

Second, we can use maximal matchings. The endpoints of a maximal matching form a 2-approximation of vertex cover. Hence from the results mentioned in Sect. 4.1, we immediately have deterministic 2-approximation algorithms for vertex cover with running times $O(\log^4 n)$ [27] and $O(\Delta + \log^* n)$ [26].

Third, there is a recent deterministic algorithm that finds a 2-approximation of a minimum vertex cover in $O(\Delta^2)$ rounds [44] without resorting to maximal matchings. The algorithm does not require unique identifiers, making it particularly easy to convert into a self-stabilizing algorithm even in anonymous networks.

Finally, there are also strong lower-bound results. For example, in the case of a constant Δ, the above-mentioned algorithm finds a 2-approximation of a minimum vertex cover in constant time. This approximation factor is tight: lower bound results [45,46] show that a $(2-\epsilon)$-approximation is not possible in constant time for any constant $\Delta \geq 2$. Furthermore, the lower bound result by

[3] A fractional dominating set assigns to each node a weight from $[0, 1]$ such that the sum of a node's own and neighbors' weights is at least 1.

Kuhn et al. [36] proves that a constant Δ is necessary if we want constant running time and constant approximation factor.

In summary, the problem of approximating vertex covers by distributed algorithms is nowadays well understood: there is a whole range of deterministic algorithms from which to choose, and there are also strong lower-bound results. All these results have straightforward corollaries in a self-stabilization setting.

Also the minimum dominating set problem that we used as an example in Sect. 4.3 admits deterministic approximation algorithms—at least for special cases and variants of the problem. Recent results include two constant-time distributed algorithms that find a constant-factor approximation of a minimum dominating set in a planar graph [45,47]. There is also a deterministic $O(\log^* n)$-time algorithm that finds a constant-factor approximation of a minimum connected dominating set in bounded-independence graphs [14].

The classical optimization problem of finding a maximum-size independent set can be used to illustrate the trade-off between randomization and running time. As the maximum independent set problem is hard to approximate even in a centralized setting, we focus on the special case of planar graphs. Czygrinow et al. [45] present both deterministic and randomized local approximation schemes: the deterministic algorithm finds a good approximation in $O(\log^* n)$ rounds, while the randomized algorithm finds a good approximation in $O(1)$ rounds w.h.p. Together with the recent lower bound results [45,46], this work shows that randomized local algorithms are asymptotically faster than deterministic local algorithms in some optimization problems, giving additional motivation for studying the conversion of local randomized algorithms into self-stabilizing randomized algorithms.

We refer to Elkin's [48] survey for more information on distributed approximation algorithms. There is also a recent survey [11] that focuses specifically on constant-time distributed algorithms.

5 Conclusion

We misused this invited paper to remind the local algorithms and self-stabilization communities that they share a long history. After recapitulating the elementary observation that *any* deterministic local algorithm has a self-stabilizing analogon, we highlighted recent results on efficient local algorithms. We are convinced the relation goes in both directions—we believe that a similar article could be written from a vantage point of self-stabilization.

Several issues are still open. In our view randomization is not fully understood in this context. We thus encourage experts from both fields to explore to what extent randomization techniques can be transferred between the two areas. Also, we merely touched the surface of bit complexity, the quality of an algorithm in terms of the number of exchanged bits. In the last decades considerable progress has been made both in minimizing the bit complexity of local algorithms as well as in establishing lower bounds. We conjecture that both communities can profit from ascertaining each others' results. And finally, there are several areas related to both local algorithms and self-stabilization, e.g. dynamic networks or self-assembly [49].

Acknowledgements. This work was supported in part by the Academy of Finland, Grant 116547, by Helsinki Graduate School in Computer Science and Engineering (Hecse), and by the Foundation of Nokia Corporation.

References

1. Dijkstra, E.W.: Self-stabilization in spite of distributed control. Manuscript EWD391 (October 1973)
2. Dijkstra, E.W.: Self-stabilizing systems in spite of distributed control. Communications of the ACM 17(11), 643–644 (1974)
3. Luby, M.: A simple parallel algorithm for the maximal independent set problem. SIAM Journal on Computing 15(4), 1036–1053 (1986)
4. Cole, R., Vishkin, U.: Deterministic coin tossing with applications to optimal parallel list ranking. Information and Control 70(1), 32–53 (1986)
5. Linial, N.: Locality in distributed graph algorithms. SIAM Journal on Computing 21(1), 193–201 (1992)
6. Naor, M., Stockmeyer, L.: What can be computed locally? SIAM Journal on Computing 24(6), 1259–1277 (1995)
7. Suomela, J.: Optimisation Problems in Wireless Sensor Networks: Local Algorithms and Local Graphs. PhD thesis, University of Helsinki, Department of Computer Science, Helsinki, Finland (May 2009)
8. Awerbuch, B., Sipser, M.: Dynamic networks are as fast as static networks. In: Proc. 29th Symposium on Foundations of Computer Science (FOCS), pp. 206–219. IEEE, Los Alamitos (1988)
9. Awerbuch, B., Varghese, G.: Distributed program checking: a paradigm for building self-stabilizing distributed protocols. In: Proc. 32nd Symposium on Foundations of Computer Science (FOCS), pp. 258–267. IEEE, Los Alamitos (1991)
10. Awerbuch, B.: Complexity of network synchronization. Journal of the ACM 32(4), 804–823 (1985)
11. Suomela, J.: Survey of local algorithms (manuscript, 2009)
12. Goldberg, A.V., Plotkin, S.A.: Parallel $(\Delta+1)$-coloring of constant-degree graphs. Information Processing Letters 25(4), 241–245 (1987)
13. Peleg, D.: Distributed Computing – A Locality-Sensitive Approach. SIAM, Philadelphia (2000)
14. Schneider, J., Wattenhofer, R.: A log-star distributed maximal independent set algorithm for growth-bounded graphs. In: Proc. 27th Symposium on Principles of Distributed Computing (PODC), pp. 35–44. ACM Press, New York (2008)
15. Schneider, M.: Self-stabilization. ACM Computing Surveys 25(1), 45–67 (1993)
16. Dolev, S.: Self-Stabilization. The MIT Press, Cambridge (2000)
17. Kothapalli, K., Scheideler, C., Onus, M., Schindelhauer, C.: Distributed coloring in $\tilde{O}(\sqrt{\log n})$ bit rounds. In: Proc. 20th International Parallel and Distributed Processing Symposium (IPDPS). IEEE, Los Alamitos (2006)
18. Awerbuch, B., Patt-Shamir, B., Varghese, G.: Self-stabilization by local checking and correction. In: Proc. 32nd Symposium on Foundations of Computer Science (FOCS), pp. 268–277. IEEE, Los Alamitos (1991)

19. Mayer, A., Naor, M., Stockmeryer, L.: Local computations on static and dynamic graphs. In: Proc. 3rd Israel Symposium on the Theory of Computing and Systems (ISTCS), pp. 268–278. IEEE, Los Alamitos (1995)
20. Awerbuch, B., Kutten, S., Mansour, Y., Patt-Shamir, B., Varghese, G.: Time optimal self-stabilizing synchronization. In: Proc. 25th Symposium on Theory of Computing (STOC), pp. 652–661. ACM Press, New York (1993)
21. Angluin, D.: Local and global properties in networks of processors. In: Proc. 12th Symposium on Theory of Computing (STOC), pp. 82–93. ACM Press, New York (1980)
22. Goldberg, A.V., Plotkin, S.A., Shannon, G.E.: Parallel symmetry-breaking in sparse graphs. SIAM Journal on Discrete Mathematics 1(4), 434–446 (1988)
23. Kuhn, F., Wattenhofer, R.: On the complexity of distributed graph coloring. In: Proc. 25th Symposium on Principles of Distributed Computing (PODC), pp. 7–15. ACM Press, New York (2006)
24. Barenboim, L., Elkin, M.: Distributed $(\Delta + 1)$-coloring in linear (in Δ) time. In: Proc. 41st Symposium on Theory of Computing (STOC), pp. 111–120. ACM Press, New York (2009)
25. Kuhn, F.: Weak graph colorings: Distributed algorithms and applications. In: Proc. 21st Symposium on Parallelism in Algorithms and Architectures (SPAA). ACM Press, New York (to appear, 2009)
26. Panconesi, A., Rizzi, R.: Some simple distributed algorithms for sparse networks. Distributed Computing 14(2), 97–100 (2001)
27. Hańćkowiak, M., Karoński, M., Panconesi, A.: On the distributed complexity of computing maximal matchings. SIAM Journal on Discrete Mathematics 15(1), 41–57 (2001)
28. Alon, N., Babai, L., Itai, A.: A fast and simple randomized parallel algorithm for the maximal independent set problem. Journal of Algorithms 7(4), 567–583 (1986)
29. Israeli, A., Itai, A.: A fast and simple randomized parallel algorithm for maximal matching. Information Processing Letters 22(2), 77–80 (1986)
30. Métivier, Y., Robson, J.M., Nasser, S.D., Zemmari, A.: An optimal bit complexity randomised distributed MIS algorithm. In: SIROCCO 2009. LNCS, vol. 5869. Springer, Heidelberg (to appear, 2009)
31. Kutten, S., Peleg, D.: Tight fault locality. SIAM Journal on Computing 30(1), 247–268 (2000)
32. Papadimitriou, C.H., Yannakakis, M.: Linear programming without the matrix. In: Proc. 25th Symposium on Theory of Computing (STOC), pp. 121–129. ACM Press, New York (1993)
33. Bartal, Y., Byers, J.W., Raz, D.: Global optimization using local information with applications to flow control. In: Proc. 38th Symposium on Foundations of Computer Science (FOCS), pp. 303–312. IEEE Computer Society Press, Los Alamitos (1997)
34. Kuhn, F., Wattenhofer, R.: Constant-time distributed dominating set approximation. Distributed Computing 17(4), 303–310 (2005)
35. Kuhn, F., Moscibroda, T., Wattenhofer, R.: The price of being near-sighted. In: Proc. 17th Symposium on Discrete Algorithms (SODA), pp. 980–989. ACM Press, New York (2006)
36. Kuhn, F., Moscibroda, T., Wattenhofer, R.: What cannot be computed locally! In: Proc. 23rd Symposium on Principles of Distributed Computing (PODC), pp. 300–309. ACM Press, New York (2004)
37. Floréen, P., Kaasinen, J., Kaski, P., Suomela, J.: An optimal local approximation algorithm for max-min linear programs. In: Proc. 21st Symposium on Parallelism in Algorithms and Architectures (SPAA). ACM Press, New York (to appear, 2009)

38. Floréen, P., Hassinen, M., Kaski, P., Suomela, J.: Tight local approximation results for max-min linear programs. In: Fekete, S.P. (ed.) ALGOSENSORS 2008. LNCS, vol. 5389, pp. 2–17. Springer, Heidelberg (2008)
39. Floréen, P., Kaski, P., Musto, T., Suomela, J.: Approximating max-min linear programs with local algorithms. In: Proc. 22nd International Parallel and Distributed Processing Symposium (IPDPS). IEEE, Los Alamitos (2008)
40. Papadimitriou, C.H., Steiglitz, K.: Combinatorial Optimization: Algorithms and Complexity. Dover Publications, Inc., Mineola (1998)
41. Vazirani, V.V.: Approximation Algorithms. Springer, Heidelberg (2001)
42. Kuhn, F., Moscibroda, T., Wattenhofer, R.: Fault-tolerant clustering in ad hoc and sensor networks. In: Proc. 26th International Conference on Distributed Computing Systems (ICDCS). IEEE Computer Society Press, Los Alamitos (2006)
43. Hochbaum, D.S.: Approximation algorithms for the set covering and vertex cover problems. SIAM Journal on Computing 11(3), 555–556 (1982)
44. Åstrand, M., Floréen, P., Polishchuk, V., Rybicki, J., Suomela, J., Uitto, J.: A local 2-approximation algorithm for the vertex cover problem. In: Proc. 23rd Symposium on Distributed Computing (DISC). Springer, Heidelberg (to appear, 2009)
45. Czygrinow, A., Hańćkowiak, M., Wawrzyniak, W.: Fast distributed approximations in planar graphs. In: Taubenfeld, G. (ed.) DISC 2008. LNCS, vol. 5218, pp. 78–92. Springer, Heidelberg (2008)
46. Lenzen, C., Wattenhofer, R.: Leveraging Linial's locality limit. In: Taubenfeld, G. (ed.) DISC 2008. LNCS, vol. 5218, pp. 394–407. Springer, Heidelberg (2008)
47. Lenzen, C., Oswald, Y.A., Wattenhofer, R.: What can be approximated locally? In: Proc. 20th Symposium on Parallelism in Algorithms and Architectures (SPAA), pp. 46–54. ACM Press, New York (2008)
48. Elkin, M.: Distributed approximation: a survey. ACM SIGACT News 35(4), 40–57 (2004)
49. Sterling, A.: Self-assembling systems are distributed systems. Manuscript, arXiv:0907.1072 [cs.DC] (July 2009)

As Good as It Gets: Competitive Fault Tolerance in Network Structures

David Peleg*

Department of Computer Science and Applied Mathematics,
The Weizmann Institute of Science, Rehovot, 76100 Israel
david.peleg@weizmann.ac.il

Abstract. Consider a logical structure $\mathcal{S}$, constructed over a given network G, which is intended to efficiently support various services on G. This logical structure is supposed to possess certain desirable properties, measured with respect to G and represented by some requirement predicate $\mathcal{P}(\mathcal{S}, G)$. Now consider a failure event F affecting some of the network's vertices and edges. Making $\mathcal{S}$ fault-tolerant means reinforcing it so that subsequent to the failure event, its surviving part $\mathcal{S}'$ continues to satisfy $\mathcal{P}$. One may insist on imposing the requirements with respect to the *original network* G, i.e., demanding that the surviving structure $\mathcal{S}'$ satisfies the predicate $\mathcal{P}(\mathcal{S}', G)$. The idea behind *competitive fault tolerance* is that it may sometimes be more realistic and more productive to evaluate the performance of the surviving $\mathcal{S}'$ after the failure event not with respect to G (which at the moment is no longer in existence anyway), but rather with respect to the *surviving network* $G' = G \setminus F$, which in a sense is the best one can hope for. Hence, we say that the structure $\mathcal{S}$ enjoys *competitive fault-tolerance* if subsequent to a failure event F, its surviving part $\mathcal{S}'$ satisfies the requirement predicate $\mathcal{P}(\mathcal{S}', G')$. The paper motivates the notion of competitive fault tolerance, compares it with the more demanding alternative approach, and illustrates it on a number of representative examples.

1 Introduction

Logical Network Structures

A central theme in the theory of networks concerns the construction of *logical information structures* on top of the network, that possess some desirable properties and can be used for improving the performance of relevant applications. Common examples include a variety of spanning trees such as shortest-path trees, minimum-weight spanning trees, Steiner trees, optimum communication trees [24,31], and shallow-light trees [4,26], distance-sensitive skeletal structures such as spanners (cf. [30,35,36]), preservers [11], emulators [19,40] and tree covers

* Supported by a grant from the Israel Ministry of Science.

R. Guerraoui and F. Petit (Eds.): SSS 2009, LNCS 5873, pp. 35–46, 2009.

[7,15,30], clustered representations such as partitions [8], covers [3], decompositions [6,5] and hierarchical organizations of different types (cf. [30]), informative labeling schemes for a variety of graph functions [1,2,22,25,33,34], data structures supporting different types of topology-related queries such as distance oracles [9,37,39] and connectivity oracles [20], routing schemes (cf. [3,30,32,38]), and more.

In all of these cases, given a network G, one is interested in constructing a logical information structure $\mathcal{S}(G)$ enjoying some useful properties. The set of desired properties can be represented abstractly as a *requirement predicate* $\mathcal{P}(\mathcal{S}, G)$. Typically, the optimization problem corresponding to such a structure involves also some *cost measure* $\texttt{cost}(\mathcal{S})$ associated with constructing or maintaining the structure $\mathcal{S}$, and the goal is to select a cheap (preferably, the cheapest) structure $\mathcal{S}$ satisfying $\mathcal{P}(\mathcal{S}, G)$.

As a running example illustrating the notions and terminology under discussion, let us consider the basic requirement of *connectivity*. Let our structure $\mathcal{S}$ be simply a subgraph of G, and let the requirement predicate $\mathcal{P}_{conn}$ specify that the structure $\mathcal{S}$ must ensure, for every two vertices u, w in G, that if u and w are connected in G, then they are connected in $\mathcal{S}$ as well. A structure satisfying this predicate is hereafter referred to as a *connectivity structure*. For concreteness, let the cost measure $\texttt{cost}(\mathcal{S})$ correspond to the number of edges included in the subgraph $\mathcal{S}$.

Clearly, if G is composed of ℓ connected components $G_1, \ldots, G_\ell$, then one can obtain a connectivity structure $\mathcal{S} = \mathcal{S}(G)$ by selecting a forest composed of any collection of ℓ trees $T_1, \ldots, T_\ell$ such that T_i spans the connected component G_i for every $1 \leq i \leq \ell$. Such a structure will achieve the task optimally, with a minimum cost of $n - \ell$ edges.

Fault Tolerance

This paper addresses the question of making logical information structures in networks *fault-tolerant*. The underlying assumption is that the vertices and edges of the network may occasionally fail or malfunction. Consider some failure event, represented by a subset F of vertices or edges (or both) that have failed. As a result of such a failure event, the network G is partially destroyed, and we are left with the surviving part of the network, $G' = G \setminus F$. It is clear, however, that such a failure event affects not only the network G, but also any logical structure $\mathcal{S} = \mathcal{S}(G)$ constructed for it, as presumably this structure too makes use of some of the vertices and edges of G, so the failure event F partially destroys $\mathcal{S}$ as well, leaving us with the structure $\mathcal{S}' = \mathcal{S} \setminus F$. In our connectivity example, for instance, if the set of failed edges F contains a edge of the forest $\mathcal{S} = \mathcal{S}(G)$, then after the failure, one of the trees T_i' of the surviving partial structure $\mathcal{S}' = \mathcal{S} \setminus F$ may be disconnected and can no longer be used as a spanning tree for the corresponding connected component G_i of G. In our formal terminology, the requirement predicate $\mathcal{P}(\mathcal{S}', G)$ might no longer hold.

The natural question that arises is, therefore, whether $\mathcal{S}(G)$ can somehow be *reinforced* and made fault tolerant, i.e., ensure the property that the requirement predicate $\mathcal{P}$ still holds subsequent to a failure event. A relaxed, but equally natural, variant of the question calls for a construction of a structure $\mathcal{S}(G)$ that can guarantee the desired properties in some weakened form, namely, ensure that some relaxed requirement predicate $\mathcal{P}'$ holds subsequent to a failure event.

Rigid vs. Competitive Fault Tolerance

The notion of "fault tolerance" in logical information structures, as formulated so far, still contains a hidden ambiguity. One possible (and common) interpretation to the above description calls for constructing the structure $\mathcal{S}(G)$ in such a way that subsequent to a failure event F, the requirement predicate $\mathcal{P}(\mathcal{S}', G)$ continues to hold (on the *original* network G). Hereafter, we refer to this demanding interpretation as the *"rigid"* (or *"static"*) approach to fault tolerance. Our focus in this paper is on highlighting an alternative, more flexible approach, referred to as *competitive fault tolerance*. Following this approach, we lower our expectations, and settle for a structure $\mathcal{S}$ that ensures that subsequent to a failure event F, the surviving structure $\mathcal{S}'$ satisfies only $\mathcal{P}(\mathcal{S}', G')$, namely, it satisfies the requirement predicate $\mathcal{P}$ with respect to the *surviving network* G', and not with respect to the original network G (which at the moment is no longer in existence anyway).

While competitive fault-tolerance appears to be a weaker notion than rigid fault-tolerance, it is important to realize that rigid fault-tolerance is sometimes impossible to attain, or is attainable only under some restrictive conditions on the instance at hand, or only in some weakened form (namely, with a weaker requirement predicate $\mathcal{P}'$). In contrast, competitive fault tolerance can often be attained without having to resort to imposing constraints on the instance or weakening the requirement predicates. In that sense, ensuring competitive fault tolerance for a logical structure essentially means ensuring that the situation is "as good as it gets" under the existing circumstances.

To illustrate the distinction between the two notions of fault-tolerance, let us return to our connectivity example and consider the fault-tolerant variant of the problem. Suppose that we are required to construct a connectivity structure $\mathcal{S}$ capable of withstanding a single edge failure ($|F| = 1$). Note that the rigid version of the problem does not always admit a solution. For example, suppose the original network G itself is a single connected tree. Then necessarily $\mathcal{S} = G$, and the elimination of any edge $e = (u, v)$ of G will cause the surviving subgraph $\mathcal{S}' = \mathcal{S} \setminus F$ to violate the requirement predicate $\mathcal{P}_{conn}(\mathcal{S}', G)$ (as u and v, for instance, are connected in G but not in $\mathcal{S}$).

Hence the only way to achieve rigid fault-tolerance for connectivity structures is to impose some conditions on the network G under consideration. For instance, we may impose a biconnectivity requirement on the connected components of the original G, namely, require each connected component G_i of G to be 2-edge-connected. This will ensure the existence of a feasible rigid fault-tolerant spanning subgraph $\mathcal{S}$ that satisfies the requirement predicate $\mathcal{P}_{conn}$ with respect to G. In particular, taking $\mathcal{S} = G$ as our connectivity structure will satisfy the problem requirements. In fact, a reasonably low cost can be guaranteed as well.

In particular, for a network G with ℓ connected components $G_1, \ldots, G_\ell$, each of which is 2-edge-connected, at most $2n - 2\ell$ edges will suffice for a rigid 1-fault-tolerant connectivity structure $\mathcal{S}$. To see this, consider the following construction for a connectivity structure. Start with an arbitrary collection of ℓ trees $T_1, \ldots, T_\ell$ spanning $G_1, \ldots, G_\ell$ (respectively). For each edge $e \in E(T_i)$, whose elimination from T_i disconnects it into T_{i1}^e and T_{i2}^e, let $backup(e) = \{e'\}$ for some edge $e' \in E(G_i) \setminus E(T_i)$ connecting T_{i1}^e and T_{i2}^e. (Such an edge must exist since G_i is 2-edge-connected.) It is easy to verify that taking $\mathcal{S}$ to be

$$\mathcal{S} = \bigcup_{i=1}^{\ell} \left(E(T_i) \cup \bigcup_{e \in E(T_i)} backup(e) \right)$$

ensures that $\mathcal{S}' = \mathcal{S} \setminus \{e\}$ satisfies $\mathcal{P}_{conn}(\mathcal{S}', G)$, for any $e \in E(G)$.

The rigid approach to fault-tolerance is of course highly significant from both the theoretical and practical standpoints, and in fact it is the approach of choice during the design stage of the underlying physical network G. At that stage, one must ensure both the reliability and survivability of G itself and the resilience of logical information structures to be embedded on top of it. The rigid approach to fault tolerance allows us to analyze the basic a-priori conditions that the network G must meet in order to support logical information structures satisfying the desired requirements in the presence of failures, and thus enables us (given sufficient time in advance) to reinforce the physical network G itself so as to strengthen its accompanying logical structures as necessary. In the example of connectivity, this can be achieved by adding edges to G so as to ensure 2-edge connectivity on every component G_i that requires rigid fault-tolerant (1-edge) connectivity.

It is equally clear, however, that the rigid approach to fault-tolerance might be inappropriate in situations where the underlying physical network has already been fixed, and can no longer be modified, yet it is necessary to assess the fault-resilience of new logical information structures embedded on it. In such situations, it may be more realistic and more productive to turn to competitive fault-tolerance.

Returning to our connectivity example, one realizes that ensuring competitive fault tolerance does not require imposing any conditions on the network, and a suitable competitive fault tolerant connectivity structure can be constructed for every G. To demonstrate this claim for the simple case of a single edge failure ($|F| = 1$), for instance, observe that taking $\mathcal{S} = G$ solves the problem, as $\mathcal{P}_{conn}(\mathcal{S}', G')$ always holds. This is because no matter which edge $e = (u, w)$ fails in F, it is guaranteed that $\mathcal{S}' = G'$, and therefore, if the failure of e disconnects u from w in $\mathcal{S}$, then u and w must be disconnected in G' as well.

In fact, a competitive fault tolerant connectivity structure of cost as low as that of the rigid fault-tolerant solution outlined above is also feasible, as one can apply the same construction method, with the following small change. For each edge $e \in E(T_i)$, whose elimination from T_i disconnects it into T_{i1}^e and T_{i2}^e, if a backup edge is unavailable for e, we take $backup(e) = \emptyset$. That is, we define the backup edges as

$$backup(e) = \begin{cases} \{e'\}, & \exists e' \in E(G_i) \setminus E(T_i) \text{ connecting } T^e_{i1} \text{ and } T^e_{i2}, \\ \emptyset, & \text{otherwise.} \end{cases}$$

To verify that the resulting structure $\mathcal{S}$ guarantees $\mathcal{P}_{conn}(\mathcal{S}', G')$, consider an edge $e = (u, w)$ that has failed, and suppose that in G', the vertices u and w are connected. Then necessarily u and w belong to the same connected component of G, say, G_i. If e is not in T_i, then u and w are still connected in $\mathcal{S}$ via T_i. If e is in T_i, then its elimination disconnects T_i into T^e_{i1} and T^e_{i2}, with u in one of the parts and w in the other. But in this case, $\mathcal{S}$ must contain also an edge $e' \in backup(e)$ (since if no such edge existed in G_i, then T^e_{i1} and T^e_{i2} would be disconnected in G'_i as well, and so would u and w, contradicting our assumption). Hence u and w are still connected in $\mathcal{S}$.

The remainder of this paper presents several additional examples illustrating the concept of competitive fault-tolerance in the context of different logical information structures in networks, contrasting it against the alternative notion of rigid fault-tolerance, and reviewing some recent results in the area.

2 Examples of Competitive Fault Tolerance

We now present a number of additional examples for logical information structures in networks and discuss the possibility of turning them into rigid or competitive fault-tolerant structures.

MST Structures

Consider a connected network G with edge weights $\omega : E \mapsto \mathbb{R}^+$. For any subgraph H of G, let $\omega(H) = \sum_{e \in H} \omega(e)$. Suppose that our goal is to maintain a logical structure, referred to as an *MST structure*, ensuring the availability of a spanning tree of minimum weight. Letting $MST(G)$ be an arbitrary minimum weight spanning tree of G, our logical structure $\mathcal{S}$ is again a subgraph of G, and the requirement predicate we wish it to satisfy, denoted $\mathcal{P}_{mst}(\mathcal{S}, G)$, specifies that $\mathcal{S}$ contains a spanning tree T of weight $\omega(T) = \omega(MST(G))$. A natural cost measure for MST structures may be $\texttt{cost}(\mathcal{S}) = \omega(\mathcal{S})$.

In the non-fault-tolerant setting, simply taking $\mathcal{S} = MST(G)$ yields a feasible MST structure satisfying $\mathcal{P}_{mst}$. However, this structure clearly fails to solve the problem in a failure-prone setting. (As discussed earlier, such a solution will fail to guarantee even connectivity, let alone low weight).

Moreover, it is clear that a rigid fault tolerant MST structure (i.e., one satisfying $\mathcal{P}_{mst}(\mathcal{S}', G)$) does not always exist, even in the presence of a single edge fault, and even by taking $\mathcal{S} = G$, for arguments similar to those mentioned in our discussion of the connectivity example. (As an exercise, the reader is invited to contemplate a-priori conditions on G that may ensure the existence of a rigid fault tolerant MST structure.)

Turning to competitive fault tolerance, the problem becomes more managable. In particular, it is clear that there always exists an MST structure $\mathcal{S}$ for G satisfying $\mathcal{P}_{mst}(\mathcal{S}', G')$. However, the problem of computing a minimum cost MST structure is NP-hard [14], so it may be necessary to resort to approximate solutions. In fact, one may consider several different types of approximation problems. One type concerns the construction of a competitive fault tolerant MST structure of near-minimum cost. A second, more relaxed, type of problem concerns the construction of what one may call a competitive fault tolerant *Approx-MST structure*, namely, a structure $\mathcal{S}$ with the property that for any set F of failed edges, the surviving structure $\mathcal{S} \setminus F$ contains a tree T' spanning G' whose weight $\omega(T')$ is close to $\omega(MST(G'))$. The most relaxed version of the problem is the one involving both notions of approximation, namely, seeking to construct a competitive fault tolerant Approx-MST structure of near-minimum cost. The latter type of structures may be easier to construct than the former two.

Flow Structures

Consider a network G with edge capacities $\gamma(e)$, and with a specified source vertex $\hat{s}$ and destination vertex $\hat{d}$. Suppose that a certain client of the network services desires to guarantee its long term ability to push as much flow as possible from $\hat{s}$ to $\hat{d}$, and for that purpose it intends to lease a certain (nonnegative) amount of capacity $\tilde{\gamma}(e)$ on each edge e, where $0 \leq \tilde{\gamma}(e) \leq \gamma(e)$. Let $\texttt{flow}(\hat{s}, \hat{d}, G)$ denote the maximum flow that can be pushed from $\hat{s}$ to $\hat{d}$ in G. The logical structure $\mathcal{S}$ maintaining the leased capacities, referred to as a *flow structure*, is a copy of G, with leased capacity values $\tilde{\gamma}(e)$ for each edge e, that are sufficient to support the desired flow from $\hat{s}$ to $\hat{d}$. This guarantee is formally captured by the requirement predicate $\mathcal{P}_{flow}(\mathcal{S}, G)$. Supposing further that the price of leasing a unit of capacity on the edge e is $\texttt{price}(e)$, the overall cost of a flow structure $\mathcal{S}$ is $\texttt{cost}(\mathcal{S}) = \sum_{e \in E(G)} \texttt{price}(e) \cdot \tilde{\gamma}(e)$. Our goal is thus to construct a minimun cost flow structure $\mathcal{S}$ (ensuring the maximum level of flow possible).

Considering the problem in a failure-free setting, it is clear that in order to determine the values of leased capacity $\tilde{\gamma}(e)$ necessary for every edge e in a minimum cost flow structure $\mathcal{S}$, all that needs to be done is solve the corresponding min-cost max-flow problem.

Turning to the failure-prone setting, let us first consider rigid fault tolerance. Here, once again, it is not possible to guarantee a solution for the problem (namely, a flow of $\texttt{flow}(\hat{s}, \hat{d}, G)$ units) under all circumstances, as is realized, say, by considering a network G consisting of a single edge $(\hat{s}, \hat{d})$ of capacity 1. A weaker type of rigid guarantee $\mathcal{P}'_{flow}$ may be obtained as follows. Given the flow structure $\mathcal{S} = \{\tilde{\gamma}(e) \mid e \in E(G)\}$, let e_{max} be the edge of maximum $\tilde{\gamma}$. Then $\mathcal{S}$ can be thought of as an approximate flow structure, ensuring a flow of at least $\texttt{flow}(\hat{s}, \hat{d}, G) - \tilde{\gamma}(e_{max})$ units. However, this guarantee is dissatisfactory, as in some cases it may be sub-optimal. For instance, look at the network G depicted in Figure 1. Suppose that in this network all edges have unit capacities ($\gamma(e) = 1$), and the flow structure $\mathcal{S}$ consists of leasing in full the capacities of the edges of the upper path (namely, e_1, e_2, e_3, e_4). In the presence of faults, this flow structure is worthless if the edge e_2 gets disconnected, in the sense that in the surviving structure $\mathcal{S}'$, no flow can be pushed at all, despite the existence of a surviving $\hat{s} - \hat{d}$ path of capacity 1.

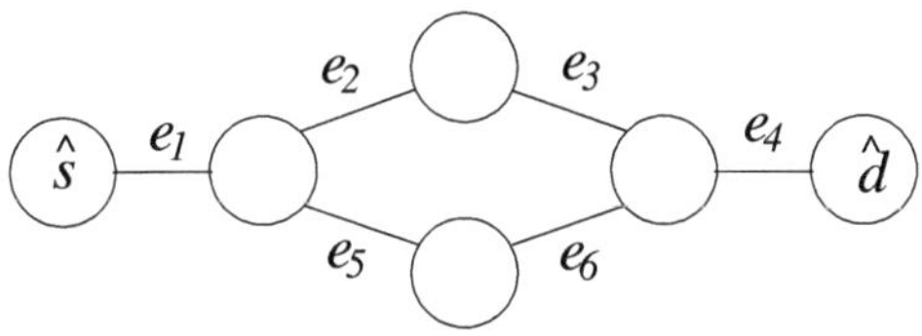

Fig. 1. An example flow network

A (non-min-cost) competitive fault-tolerant flow structure for this simple example (as for any other example) would be to take $\mathcal{S} = (G, \gamma)$, namely, to lease all the available capacity on all the edges. In this case, for every disconnected edge, if the surviving network G' allows a maximum flow of $\mathtt{flow}(\hat{s}, \hat{d}, G')$ from $\hat{s}$ to $\hat{d}$, then the surviving flow structure $\mathcal{S}'$ will enable the same amount of flow, i.e., the requirement predicate $\mathcal{P}_{flow}(\mathcal{S}', G')$ will still hold.

An algorithm for the construction of minimum cost competitive fault tolerant flow structures is presented in [14].

k-Spanners

As our next example, let us consider the structure of k-spanners (cf. [30,35,36]). A graph spanner $\mathcal{S}$ can be thought of as a skeleton structure that generalizes the concept of spanning trees and allows us to faithfully represent the underlying network using few edges, in the sense that for any two vertices of the network, the distance in the spanner is stretched by only a small factor. More formally, consider a weighted graph G and let $k \geq 1$ be an integer. Let $\mathtt{dist}(u, v, G)$ denote the (weighted) distance between u and v in G. For a subgraph $\mathcal{S}$, the requirement predicate $\mathcal{P}_{k-span}(\mathcal{S}, G)$ specifies that $\mathtt{dist}(u, v, \mathcal{S}) \leq k \cdot \mathtt{dist}(u, v, G)$ for every $u, v \in V$. A subgraph $\mathcal{S}$ satisfying this predicate is a k-spanner of G.

Turning to *fault tolerant* k-spanners, the rigid approach leads to the following definition: a subgraph $\mathcal{S}$ is an f-edge fault-tolerant k-spanner of G if $\mathtt{dist}(u, v, \mathcal{S} \setminus F) \leq k \cdot \mathtt{dist}(u, v, G)$ for any set $F \subseteq E$ of size at most f and any pair of vertices $u, v \in V$. (A similar definition applies to f-vertex fault-tolerant k-spanners.)

By the same connectivity argument as before, we note that this requirement may be unattainable for some graphs. For instance, if G is not f-edge-connected, then so is $\mathcal{S}$, in which case the elimination of the edges of F from $\mathcal{S}$ might disconnect it, preventing it from satisfying the requirement. In fact, even if the set of failures F leaves G connected by some fortunate turn of events, it may still happen that no selection of $\mathcal{S}$ could possibly work. Consider for example an n-vertex ring G and $f = 1$; clearly, even if all the edges are selected to the spanner, setting $\mathcal{S} = G$, the elimination of a single edge $F = \{e = (u, w)\}$ from G will leave $\mathcal{S}' = G \setminus \{e\}$ connected but increase the distance between the endpoints u and w from $\mathtt{dist}(u, w, G) = 1$ to $\mathtt{dist}(u, w, \mathcal{S}') = n - 1$.

Rigid fault-tolerance can thus be ensured only in some special cases. One particular such case is when G is a complete Euclidean graph (with $\mathtt{dist}(u, v, G)$

defined as $|uv|$, the Euclidean distance between u and v). In this case, it is possible to construct a rather sparse fault-tolerant spanner for G. Indeed, the notion of (rigid) fault tolerant spanners was introduced in the geometric setting in [27], which presented an efficient algorithm that given a set V of n points in d-dimensional Euclidean space, constructs an f-vertex fault tolerant geometric $(1+\epsilon)$-spanner for V, namely, a sparse graph $\mathcal{S}$ satisfying that $\mathtt{dist}(u, v, \mathcal{S} \setminus F) \leq (1+\epsilon)|uv|$ for any set $F \subseteq V$ of size f, and for any pair of points $u, v \in V \setminus F$. A fault tolerant geometric spanner of improved size was later presented in [28], and finally a fault tolerant geometric spanner with optimal maximum degree and total weight was presented in [17].

In contrast, the competitive approach yields the following definition. We say that a subgraph $\mathcal{S}$ is a *competitive f-edge fault-tolerant k-spanner* of G if $\mathtt{dist}(u, v, \mathcal{S} \setminus F) \leq k \cdot \mathtt{dist}(u, v, G \setminus F)$ for any set $F \subseteq E$ of size at most f, and any pair of vertices $u, v \in V$. (A similar definition applies to competitive f-vertex fault-tolerant k-spanners.) As in the previous examples, we note that under this definition, the task of constructing a competitive f-edge fault-tolerant k-spanner for a given graph G is never infeasible, as in particular, taking $\mathcal{S} = G$ yields a competitive f-edge fault-tolerant 1-spanner of G for any f.

The question of whether it is possible to construct a sparse fault tolerant spanner for an arbitrary undirected weighted graph, raised in [17], was answered in the affirmative in [13] employing competitive fault tolerance and presenting algorithms for constructing a competitive f-vertex fault tolerant $(2k-1)$-spanner of size $O(f^2 k^{f+1} \cdot n^{1+1/k} \log^{1-1/k} n)$ and a competitive f-edge fault tolerant $2k-1$ spanner of size $O(f \cdot n^{1+1/k})$ for a graph of size n. This should be contrasted with the best stretch-size tradeoff currently known for non-fault-tolerant spanners [38], namely, $2k-1$ stretch with $\tilde{O}(n^{1+1/k})$ edges.

Fault-Tolerant Distance Oracles

A *distance oracle* [9,37,39] is a succinct data structure capable of supporting efficient responses to distance queries on a weighted graph G. A distance query (s, t) requires finding, for a given pair of vertices s and t in V, the distance (namely, the length of the shortest path) between u and v in G. A distance oracle $\mathcal{S}$ satisfies the requirement predicate $\mathcal{P}_{DO}(\mathcal{S}, G)$ if its query protocol correctly answers distance queries on G.

In a *competitive fault tolerant distance oracle*, the query may include also a set F of failed edges or vertices (or both). To satisfy the requirement predicate $\mathcal{P}_{DO}(\mathcal{S}', G')$, the distance oracle $\mathcal{S}$ must return, in response to a query (s, t, F), the distance between s and t in $G' = G \setminus F$. Such a structure is sometimes called an *F-sensitivity distance oracle.*

It has been shown in [18] that given a directed weighted graph G of size n, it is possible to construct in time $\tilde{O}(mn^2)$ a 1-sensitivity fault tolerant distance oracle of size $O(n^2 \log n)$ capable of answering distance queries in $O(1)$ time in the presence of a single failed edge or vertex. The preprocessing time was recently improved to $\tilde{O}(mn)$, with unchanged size and query time [10]. A 2-sensitivity fault tolerant distance oracle of size $O(n^2 \log^3 n)$, capable of answering 2-sensitivity queries in $O(\log n)$ time, was presented in [20].

Label-based fault-tolerant distance oracles for graphs of bounded clique-width are presented in [16]. The structure is composed of a label $L(v)$ assigned to each vertex v, and handles queries of the form $(L(s), L(t), F)$ for a set of failures F. For an n-vertex graph of tree-width or clique-width k, the constructed labels are of size $O(k^2 \log^2 n)$.

A relaxed variant of distance oracles, in which distance queries are answered by *approximate* distance estimates instead of *exact* ones, was introduced in [39], where it was shown how to construct, for a given weighted undirected n-vertex graph G, an approximate distance oracle of size $O(n^{1+1/k})$ capable of answering distance queries in $O(k)$ time, where the *stretch* (multiplicative approximation factor) of the returned distances is at most $2k-1$.

In the competitive fault tolerant setting, an f-sensitivity approximate distance oracle $\mathcal{S}$ is presented in [12]. For an integer parameter $k \geq 1$, the size of $\mathcal{S}$ is $O(kn^{1+\frac{8(f+1)}{k+2(f+1)}} \log(nW))$, where W is the weight of the heaviest edge in G, the stretch of the returned distance is $2k-1$, and the query time is $O(|F| \cdot \log^2 n \cdot \log\log n \cdot \log\log d)$, where d is the distance between s and t in $G \setminus F$.

Fault Tolerant Routing Schemes

The concept of competitive fault tolerance is suitable also in the context of handling message routing in communication networks. A *competitive fault-tolerant routing protocol* is a distributed algorithm that, for any set of failed edges F, enables any source vertex $\hat{s}$ to route a message to any destination vertex $\hat{d}$ along a shortest or near-shortest path in the surviving network $G \setminus F$ in an efficient manner (and without knowing F in advance).

In addition to route efficiency, it is often desirable to optimize also the amount of memory stored in the routing tables of the vertices, possibly at the cost of lower route efficiency, giving rise to the problem of designing compact routing schemes (cf. [3,30,32,38]).

Label-based fault-tolerant routing schemes for graphs of bounded clique-width are presented in [16]. To route from s to t, the source needs to specify the labels $L(s)$ and $L(t)$ and the set of failures F, and the scheme efficiently calculates the shortest path between s and t that avoids F. For an n-vertex graph of tree-width or clique-width k, the constructed labels are of size $O(k^2 \log^2 n)$.

Competitive fault-tolerant compact routing schemes are considered in [12], for up to two edge failures. Given a message M destined to t at a source vertex s, in the presence of a failed edge set F of size $|F| \leq 2$ (unknown to s), the scheme presented therein routes M from s to t in a distributed manner, over a path of length at most $O(k)$ times the length of the optimal path (avoiding F). The total amount of information stored in vertices of G on average is bounded by $O(kn^{1+1/k})$. This should be compared with the best memory-stretch tradeoff currently known for non-fault-tolerant compact routing [38], namely, $2k-1$ stretch with $\tilde{O}(n^{1+1/k})$ memory per vertex.

3 Discussion

In this paper we addressed the question of making logical information structures in networks *fault-tolerant*. We formalized and motivated the notion of competitive fault tolerance, compared it with the more demanding alternative approach of rigid fault tolerance, and illustrated the distinction between the two approaches on a number of representative examples.

Let us remark that the notion of competitive fault tolerant structures is somewhat similar to, but distinct from, the notion of maintaining a *dynamic* structure (namely, maintaining a structure in a dynamically changing environment). There, the structure in question can be *modified* repeatedly, in response to changes in the topology, and the algorithmic / complexity questions revolve around the (worst case or amortized) update costs, and the three-way tradeoffs between those costs, the memory costs of the structure and the query times. The problem of maintaining connectivity in a dynamic network, for instance, has received considerable attention under various models of dynamic changes, cf. [21,23,29].

Many interesting research directions related to competitive fault tolerance are left for future study. In adition to the obvious technical questions related to points left unsettled throughout the above discussion, several natural extensions of the model present themselves.

One such extension concerns probabilistic failure models. In some settings, it may be natural to assume that different failure events have different probabilities of occurring, and moreover, the failure probability of edges and vertices can be estimated based on their past history. This may facilitate constructions of lower cost (rigid or competitive) fault-tolerant structures.

When the distribution of failures is not known in advance, it may be useful to formulate and study an online version of the problem, in which decisions must be made in each step without knowledge of the future, and the incurred cost (which depends on the online decisions) should be compared against the cost of the best (offline) solution.

Finally, it may be interesting to consider non-uniform fault-tolerance requirements, capable of modeling situations where some sub-components of the structures under consideration are more vital than others, and hence their protection is more crucial. This could be reflected via the definition of suitable cost models for fault-tolerance violations, and may model various quality-of-service aspects.

Acknowledgements. I am grateful to Shiri Chechik, Mike Langberg and Liam Roditty for many stimulating and fruitful discussions.

References

1. Abiteboul, S., Kaplan, H., Milo, T.: Compact labeling schemes for ancestor queries. In: Proc. 12th ACM-SIAM Symp. on Discrete Algorithms, pp. 547–556 (2001)
2. Alstrup, S., Bille, P., Rauhe, T.: Labeling schemes for small distances in trees. In: Proc. 14th ACM-SIAM Symp. on Discrete Algorithms (2003)

3. Awerbuch, B., Bar-Noy, A., Linial, N., Peleg, D.: Compact distributed data structures for adaptive network routing. In: Proc. 21st ACM Symp. on Theory of Computing, pp. 230–240 (1989)
4. Awerbuch, B., Baratz, A., Peleg, D.: Efficient broadcast and light-weight spanners. Unpublished manuscript (1991)
5. Awerbuch, B., Berger, B., Cowen, L., Peleg, D.: Fast network decomposition. In: Proc. 11th ACM Symp. on Principles of Distributed Computing, pp. 169–177 (1992)
6. Awerbuch, B., Goldberg, A., Luby, M., Plotkin, S.: Network decomposition and locality in distributed computation. In: Proc. 30th IEEE Symp. on Foundations of Computer Science, pp. 364–369 (1989)
7. Awerbuch, B., Kutten, S., Peleg, D.: On buffer-economical store-and-forward deadlock prevention. In: Proc. INFOCOM, pp. 410–414 (1991)
8. Awerbuch, B., Peleg, D.: Sparse partitions. In: 31st IEEE Symp. on Foundations of Computer Science, pp. 503–513 (1990)
9. Baswana, S., Sen, S.: Approximate distance oracles for unweighted graphs in expected $O(n^2)$ time. ACM Trans. Algorithms 2(4), 557–577 (2006)
10. Bernstein, A., Karger, D.: A nearly optimal oracle for avoiding failed vertices and edges. In: Proc. 41st ACM Symp. on Theory of Computing, pp. 101–110 (2009)
11. Bollobás, B., Coppersmith, D., Elkin, M.: Sparse distance preservers and additive spanners. SIAM J. on Discr. Math. 19(4), 1029–1055 (2006)
12. Chechik, S., Langberg, M., Peleg, D., Roditty, L.: f-sensitivity distance oracles and routing schemes (June 2009) (manuscript)
13. Chechik, S., Langberg, M., Peleg, D., Roditty, L.: Fault-tolerant spanners for general graphs. In: Proc. 41st ACM Symp. on Theory of computing, pp. 435–444 (2009)
14. Chechik, S., Peleg, D.: Fault resilient network structures (2009) (in preparation)
15. Cohen, E.: Fast algorithms for constructing t-spanners and paths with stretch t. In: Proc. 34th IEEE Symp. on Foundations of Computer Science, pp. 648–658 (1993)
16. Courcelle, B., Twigg, A.: Compact forbidden-set routing. In: Proc. 24th Symp. on Theoretical Aspects of Computer Science, pp. 37–48 (2007)
17. Czumaj, A., Zhao, H.: Fault-tolerant geometric spanners. Discrete & Computational Geometry 32 (2003)
18. Demetrescu, C., Thorup, M., Chowdhury, R., Ramachandran, V.: Oracles for distances avoiding a failed node or link. SIAM J. Computing 37, 1299–1318 (2008)
19. Dor, D., Halperin, S., Zwick, U.: All-pairs almost shortest paths. SIAM J. Computing 29(5), 1740–1759 (2000)
20. Duan, R., Pettie, S.: Dual-failure distance and connectivity oracles. In: Proc. 20th ACM-SIAM Symp. on Discrete Algorithms (2009)
21. Eppstein, D., Galil, Z., Italiano, G.F., Nissenzweig, N.: Sparsification – A technique for speeding up dynamic graph algorithms. J. ACM 44 (1997)
22. Gavoille, C., Peleg, D.: Compact and localized distributed data structures. Distributed Computing 16, 111–120 (2003); PODC Jubilee Special Issue
23. Holm, J., Lichtenberg, K., Thorup, M.: Poly-logarithmic deterministic fully-dynamic algorithms for connectivity, minimum spanning tree, 2-edge, and biconnectivity. J. ACM 48(4), 723–760 (2001)
24. Hu, T.C.: Optimum communication spanning trees. SIAM J. Computing 3, 188–195 (1974)
25. Kannan, S., Naor, M., Rudich, S.: Implicit representation of graphs. In: Proc. 20th ACM Symp. on Theory of Computing, May 1988, pp. 334–343 (1988)

26. Khuller, S., Raghavachari, B., Young, N.: Balancing minimum spanning and shortest paths trees. In: Proc. 4th ACM-SIAM Symp. on Discrete Algorithms, Austin, Texas (1993)
27. Levcopoulos, C., Narasimhan, G., Smid, M.: Efficient algorithms for constructing fault-tolerant geometric spanners. In: Proc. 30th ACM Symp. on Theory of computing, pp. 186–195 (1998)
28. Lukovszki, T.: New results on fault tolerant geometric spanners. In: Dehne, F., Gupta, A., Sack, J.-R., Tamassia, R. (eds.) WADS 1999. LNCS, vol. 1663, pp. 193–204. Springer, Heidelberg (1999)
29. Pătraşcu, M., Thorup, M.: Planning for fast connectivity updates. In: Proc. 48th IEEE Symp. on Foundations of Computer Science, pp. 263–271 (2007)
30. Peleg, D.: Distributed Computing: A Locality-Sensitive Approach. SIAM, Philadelphia (2000)
31. Peleg, D., Reshef, E.: Deterministic polylog approximation for minimum communication spanning trees. In: Proc. 25th Int. Colloq. on Automata, Languages & Prog., pp. 670–681 (1998)
32. Peleg, D., Upfal, E.: A tradeoff between size and efficiency for routing tables. J. ACM 36, 510–530 (1989)
33. Peleg, D.: Proximity-preserving labeling schemes and their applications. In: Widmayer, P., Neyer, G., Eidenbenz, S. (eds.) WG 1999. LNCS, vol. 1665, pp. 30–41. Springer, Heidelberg (1999)
34. Peleg, D.: Informative labeling schemes for graphs. In: Nielsen, M., Rovan, B. (eds.) MFCS 2000. LNCS, vol. 1893, pp. 579–588. Springer, Heidelberg (2000)
35. Peleg, D., Schäffer, A.A.: Graph spanners. J. of Graph Theory 13, 99–116 (1989)
36. Peleg, D., Ullman, J.D.: An optimal synchronizer for the hypercube. SIAM J. Computing 18(2), 740–747 (1989)
37. Roditty, L., Thorup, M., Zwick, U.: Deterministic constructions of approximate distance oracles and spanners. In: Proc. 32nd Int. Colloq. on Automata, Languages & Prog., pp. 261–272 (2005)
38. Thorup, M., Zwick, U.: Compact routing schemes. In: Proc. 14th ACM Symp. on Parallel Algorithms and Architecture, Hersonissos, Crete, pp. 1–10 (2001)
39. Thorup, M., Zwick, U.: Approximate distance oracles. J. ACM 52, 1–24 (2005)
40. Thorup, M., Zwick, U.: Spanners and emulators with sublinear distance errors. In: 17th Symp. on Discrete Algorithms (SODA), pp. 802–809. ACM-SIAM, New York (2006)

Multicore Constraint-Based Automated Stabilization

Fuad Abujarad and Sandeep S. Kulkarni

Department of Computer Science and Engineering
Michigan State University
East Lansing, MI 48824, USA
{abujarad,sandeep}@cse.msu.edu
http://www.cse.msu.edu/~{abujarad,sandeep}

Abstract. Given the non-determinism and race conditions in distributed programs, the ability to provide assurance about them is crucial. Our work focuses on incremental synthesis where we modify a distributed programs to add self-stabilization. We concentrate on reducing the time complexity of such synthesis using parallelism. We apply these techniques in the context of constraint satisfaction. In particular, incremental synthesis of self-stabilizing programs requires adding recovery actions to satisfy the constraint that are true in the legitimate states. We consider two approaches to speedup the synthesis algorithm: first, the use of the multiple constraints that have to be satisfied during synthesis; second, the use of the distributed nature of the programs being synthesized. We show that our approaches provide significant reductions in the synthesis time.

Keywords: Stabilization, Program Synthesis, Multicore Algorithms, Program Transformation, Distributed Programs.

1 Introduction

Self-stabilization, the ability to recover from an arbitrary state to a legitimate state, is an important feature of distributed programs. It ensures that programs can recover to their legitimate states even if they are perturbed by unexpected and unknown transient faults. It is also well-known that designing self-stabilizing programs is especially challenging. Hence, techniques that permit one to *add* self-stabilization to existing programs is highly desirable.

Techniques for adding stabilization to distributed programs can be classified in two categories. The first category includes approaches based on *distributed reset* [6], where the program utilizes approaches such as *distributed snapshot* [9] and reset the system to a legitimate state if the current state is found to be illegitimate. Approaches from this category suffer from several drawbacks. In particular, it requires the designer to know the set of all legitimate states. The cost of detecting the global state can be high. Additionally this approach is heavy-handed since it requires a reset of the entire system even if the fault may be localized. And, in some cases, e.g., [16], the generated program may utilize

R. Guerraoui and F. Petit (Eds.): SSS 2009, LNCS 5873, pp. 47–61, 2009.

variables with unbounded domain even though the original program used only variables with bounded domain.

The second category includes approaches based on *constraint satisfaction*, where we identify constraints that should be satisfied in the legitimate states. Typically, the constraints are local (e.g., involving one node or a node and its neighbors) therefore, detecting their violation is easy. Since the constraints are local, the recovery actions to fix them are also local. Moreover, with this approach, if we begin with a program where the domain of variables is bounded, then the same property is preserved in the generated program.

However, this approach suffers from one important drawback: local actions taken to fix one constraint may violate other constraints. Consequently, these constraints need to be ordered. Furthermore, we need to ensure that satisfying one constraint does not violate constraints *earlier* in the order. Since verifying that recovery actions for satisfying one constraint do not affect other constraints is a demanding task; automated techniques that ensure correctness by construction are highly desirable. Such techniques ensure that the synthesized program is correct by construction. However, algorithms for designing programs that are correct by construction suffer from high complexity and, hence, techniques to expedite them need to be developed.

With these motivations, this paper focuses on the use of multicore computing for parallel synthesis of distributed self-stabilizing programs. We consider two approaches for parallelization: (1) use of multiple constraints that have to be satisfied during synthesis, and (2) use of the distributed nature of the programs being synthesized. The contributions of the paper are as follows:

- We present a multicore algorithm to synthesize distributed self-stabilizing programs by partitioning the satisfaction of the constraints among available threads.
- We briefly describe an algorithm that utilizes the distributed nature of programs being synthesized by parallelizing them.
- We illustrate our algorithm in the context of two case studies.
- As a part of this work, we modify the MDD (Multi-valued Decision Diagrams) library [20] to make it reentrant and to use it in the parallel synthesis.

Organization of the paper. The rest of the paper is organized as follows. In Section 2, we define distributed programs and specifications. We describe the algorithms for the automated addition of self-stabilization in Section 3. We present our multicore algorithms in Section 4 and experimental results in Section 5. Finally, we discuss related work in Section 6 and conclude in Section 7.

2 Programs and Specifications

In this section we define the notion of distributed programs, faults, and the problem statement for adding self-stabilization. Those definitions are based on the ones given by Arora and Gouda [5]. We also identify how the notion of fairness can be modeled for automated addition of self-stabilization.

For the following definitions of *enabled* and *fairness* let S_s be a set of states. A transition over S_s is of the form (s_0,s_1), where $s_0,s_1 \in S_s$. Let α, $\alpha_1, \alpha_2, \alpha_3, ...\alpha_m$ be sets of transitions over S_s. In other words, α, $\alpha_1, \alpha_2, \alpha_3, ...\alpha_m$ are subsets of $S_s \times S_s$.

Enabled. Intuitively, α is enabled in s_0 if α contains some transitions that begins in s_0. Formally, α is *enabled* in a state s_0 iff there exists a state s_1, such that $(s_0,s_1) \in \alpha$.

Fairness. Intuitively, if a sequence is fair with respect to $(\alpha_1, \alpha_2, \alpha_3, ...\alpha_m)$ and α_i is continuously enabled in that sequence then that sequence includes a transition in α_i. Formally, an infinite sequence $\langle s_0, s_1, s_3, ...\rangle$ is fair with respect to $(\alpha_1, \alpha_2, \alpha_3, ...\alpha_m)$ iff for each i, k the following condition is satisfied:

$$(\alpha_i \text{ is } \textit{enabled} \text{ in each state } s_k, s_{k+1}, ...) \quad \Rightarrow (\exists l : l \geq k : (s_l, s_{l+1}) \in \alpha_i \ ).$$

Note that this definition is equivalent to *weak fairness* from [3,1,10].

Program. A program p is specified in terms of its state space, S_p and the transitions sets $(\alpha_1, \alpha_2, \alpha_3, ...\alpha_m)$, where for each i, $\alpha_i \in S_p \times S_p$. The transitions of p, δ_p, are equal to $\alpha_1 \cup \alpha_2 \cup \alpha_3 \cup ... \cup \alpha_m$. We use the notation $\langle S_p, (\alpha_1, \alpha_2, \alpha_3, ...\alpha_m)\rangle$ to denote such programs. Whenever it is clear from the context, we use p and its transitions δ_p interchangeably. A sequence of states, $\sigma = \langle s_0, s_1, ...\rangle$ is a computation of p iff (1) $(\forall j : 0 < j < length(\sigma) : (s_{j-1}, s_j) \in \delta_p)$, that is, in each *step* of this sequence, a transition of p is executed, (2) if the sequence is finite and terminates in s_j then $\forall s' :: (s_j, s') \notin p$, i.e., a computation is finite only if it reaches a state from where the program does not have any outgoing transition, and (3) if the sequence is infinite then it is fair with respect to $(\alpha_1, \alpha_2, \alpha_3, ...\alpha_m)$.

A state predicate C of program p is a subset, say S_C, of S_p. In our MDD [20] based implementation, we represent it using an equivalent function f_C with domain S_p and range {true, false} where $f_C(s) = true$ iff $s \in S_C$. Let $C1$ and $C2$ be two state predicates represented with sets S_{C1} and S_{C2}, respectively. Let f_{C1} and f_{C2} be corresponding functions. Observe that the function corresponding to $S_{C1} \cap S_{C2}$ is $f_{C1 \wedge C2}$ where $f_{C1 \wedge C2}(s) = f_{C1}(s) \wedge f_{C2}(s)$. In other words, the intersection of two state predicates corresponds to the conjunction of corresponding functions. Likewise, disjunction corresponds to union, and so on. Hence, throughout the rest of the paper, we use these boolean operators for constructing different state predicates, as this directly corresponds to our MDD based implementation. Likewise, in our implementation, to represent a set of transitions over state space S_p, we use a function with domain $S_p \times S_p$ and range {true, false}. Thus, a conjunction of such formula is equivalent to the intersection of corresponding sets of transitions and so on.

Invariant. Legitimate states of a program, say p, are characterized by a set of constraints $C_1, C_2 ... C_m$, where each C_i is a subset of the state space S_p. Thus, predicate $I = C_1 \wedge C_2 ... \wedge C_m$, denoted as *invariant* of p, identifies all legitimate states of p. In other words, if a computation of p begins in a state that is in I then (1) I is true at all states in that computation and (2) the computation is *correct*. Note that the notion of this *correctness* has to deal with the *fault-intolerant* program that is assumed to be correct. We assume that each transition of p preserves each constraint in the invariant, i.e. for each i, if (s_0, s_1) is transition of p and $s_0 \in C_i$ then $s_1 \in C_i$.

Faults. Let f be the class of faults to which tolerance is to be added. Faults for program p are specified as a subset of $S_p \times S_p$. Note that this allows modeling of different types of faults, such as transients, Byzantine, crash faults, etc.

The goal of an algorithm that adds self-stabilization is to begin with a fault-intolerant program p, its invariant I, and faults f, and to derive the self-stabilizing program, say p', such that in the presence of faults, p' eventually converges to I. Furthermore, computations of p' that begin in I must be the same as that of p.

Based on this discussion, we define the problem of adding self-stabilization fault-tolerance as follows:

Problem statement 1. Given p, I, and f, identify p' such that:

- Transitions within the invariant remain unchanged:
  - $s_0 \in I \Rightarrow (\forall s_1 :: (s_0, s_1) \in p \Longleftrightarrow (s_0, s_1) \in p')$
- All program transitions eventually converge to the invariant
  - $s_0 \in S_p \wedge \langle s_0, s_1, ...\rangle$ is a computation of $p' \Rightarrow \quad (\exists j : j \geq 0 : s_j \in I)$

Note that since each constraint is preserved by the original program p, closure property of the self-stabilizing program p' is satisfied from the first constraint of the problem statement. Hence, it is not explicitly specified above.

3 Synthesis Algorithm of the Self-stabilization

In this section, we describe the approach for adding self-stabilization to fault-intolerant programs based on [6, 2]. The goal of self-stabilization is to ensure that starting from any state in the program state space, the program eventually reaches one of the legitimate states in I where, $I = C_1 \wedge C_2 ... \wedge C_m$. Faults perturb the program to a state in $(\neg\, I)$. Hence, in the presence of f, one or more of the constraints from $C_1, C_2 ... C_m$ are violated. The goal of this algorithm is to automatically synthesize the recovery actions such that when faults stop occurring, the constructed recovery actions in conjunction with the original program actions will, eventually, converge the program to a state where I holds.

Since we focus on the design of distributed programs, for brevity, we specify the state space of a program in terms of its variables. Thus, the state space of the program is obtained by assigning each variable each possible value from its domain. Furthermore, we specify the transitions of the program in terms of a set of processes, where every process can read and write a subset of the program variables. Transitions of a process are obtained by considering how that process updates the program variables. And, finally, the transitions of the program are the union of the transitions of its processes.

Read restrictions of distributed programs. A process in a distributed program has a partial view of the program variables. Therefore, when a new program transition is added/removed, we need to add/remove a *group* of transitions based on the variables that cannot be read by that process. For instance, let j be a process, let R_j be the set of variables that j can read, and let $v_a(s_0)$ denote the value of variable v_a in the state s_0. Then if $t = (s_0, s_1)$ is a transition that j can execute then the group of transitions associated with t must also include transitions of the form (s_2, s_3) where s_0 and s_2 (respectively s_1 and s_3) are undistinguishable for j, i.e., they differ only in terms of the variables that j cannot read. The synthesis algorithm uses the function *Group* to include these additional transitions. The *group* it self is given by the following formula:

$$
\begin{aligned}
group_j(t) = \bigvee_{(s_2,s_3)} \quad & \\
(\bigwedge_{v \notin R_j}(v(s_0) = v(s_1) \;\; \wedge \;\; v(s_2) = v(s_3)) \wedge & \\
\bigwedge_{v \in R_j}(v(s_0) = v(s_2) \;\; \wedge \;\; v(s_1) = v(s_3))) &
\end{aligned}
$$

3.1 Constraint Satisfier

The algorithm for adding stabilization is as shown in Algorithm 1. The input for the algorithm is the constraint array C and program p.

In this algorithm, the constraints from the constraint array are satisfied one after another. The algorithm starts by computing the invariant as the intersection of all constraints in the constraint array (Lines 3). To satisfy constraint $C[i]$, the algorithm constructs the transitions that start from $(\neg C[i])$ and reach a state where $C[i]$ is true (Line 6)[1]. Since the algorithm is adding new transitions, it needs to include their *group*. Moreover, no transition should start from a state in the invariant and target a state outside the invariant. It also needs to remove the group of transitions that violates I (Line 7).

The algorithm needs to ensure that none of the transitions used to satisfy the constraint, say $C[i]$, violates the pre-satisfied constraints $C[0]$ to $C[i-1]$. Hence, it lets V include the transitions that originate from a state where $C[i-1]$ is *true* and end in a state where $C[i-1]$ is $false$ as well as similar transitions for the constraints $C[0]$ to $C[i-2]$ (Line 10). The transitions in V are used to ensure that recovery transitions do not violate other pre-satisfied constraints. The algorithm ensures that none of the transitions in *temp* interfere with earlier constraints. Therefore, it removes the transitions in V from *temp* if any is found (Line 8). At this point the algorithm collects all recovery transitions in *rec* (Line 9). Steps $4-11$ are repeated until all the recovery actions that satisfy all the constraints in the array C are found. Finally, it returns the recovery actions of the program p.

---

[1] $(X \wedge \langle Y \rangle')$ refers to the transitions that start in a state in X and reach Y.

Algorithm 1. ConstraintSatisfier

Input: constraint array C, and program transitions p.
Output: recovery transitions rec.

1: $temp,\ V := false, false$;

2: $m\ :=\ SizeOf(C) - 1$;

//Compute, I, the intersection of all constraints

3: $I\ := \bigwedge_{i=0}^{m} C[i]$;

4: **for** $i := 0$ **to** m **do**

5: //$temp$ are the transitions that start in a state in $\neg C(i)$ and reach $C(i)$

6: $temp\ :=\ Group((\neg\ C[i]) \wedge \langle C[i]\rangle')$;

//ensure that no recovery transitions violate I

7: $temp\ :=\ temp\ \wedge\ \neg\ Group(temp * (I \wedge \langle \neg I\rangle'))$;

8: $temp := temp\ \wedge\ \neg\ V$;

// Combine current recovery transitions with the new recovery transition.

9: $rec := rec\ \vee\ temp$;

//Compute, V, the set of the transitions that violating the constraints

10: $V\ := V\ \vee\ Group(C[i] \wedge \langle \neg C[i]\rangle')$

11: **end for**

// return the recovery transition.

12: **return** rec;

Algorithm 1 has the following property (The proof is similar to Theorem 1 in [6]):
Given are :

- Fault-intolerant program p, constraints $C_1, C_2 ... C_m$, and faults f.
- Let $I = C_1 \wedge C_2 ... \wedge C_m$.
- Let $rec =\ ConstraintSatisfier(C,\ p)$.
  If $\forall s_0 : s_0 \in S_p - I : (\exists s_1 : s_1 \in S_p : (s_0, s_1) \in rec)$
  Then $\langle S_p, (rec, \delta_p)\rangle$ solves the constraints in Problem statement 1.

4 Using Parallelism in Synthesis

In Section 3, we described the sequential approach for synthesizing self-stabilizing distributed programs from fault-intolerant versions. In this section, we present our approaches for expediting the synthesis with multicore computing.

There are two main factors that contribute to the execution time for the algorithm *ConstraintSatisfier* (c.f. Algorithm 1). The first factor is the number of constraints to be satisfied. One can notice that the main loop of the algorithm *ConstraintSatisfier* (Lines 4-11) is controlled by the number of constraints to be satisfied (i.e. *SizeOf(C)*). Therefore, one approach to speedup this algorithm is to distribute the job of this loop among the available cores/processors. The second factor are the operations performed by the statements within this loop, namely the *group* computation in Lines 6, 7, and 10. The group computation is required based on the nature of the distributed programs and the read/write restrictions imposed on the program variables. A sequential *group* algorithm goes through several computations for each process that causes *group* computation to take a substantial amount of time. One way to speedup the *group* computation is to split it among available cores/processors. With this motivation, in Sections 4.1, and 4.2, we present two multicore algorithms to target the bottlenecks described above.

Parallelizing the MDD library. Since we are using MDD-based symbolic synthesis, the constraints are characterized by Boolean formulae involving the variables in the program being synthesized. The MDD package [20] is not designed to be reentrant and assumes that at most one MDD package is active at any given time. Hence, multiple threads cannot operate on the same MDD package simultaneously. Also, different threads cannot access different MDD packages simultaneously. We considered two approaches to solve this problem: (1) utilize a reentrant version of the MDD package, or (2) utilize multiple independent MDD packages and handle consistency issues explicitly. We followed the second approach. We modified the MDD package so that multiple instances could be used simultaneously. We also added a *Transfer* function to transfer an MDD object from one MDD package to a different MDD package. Hence, during the parallel algorithms, a *master* thread spawns several *worker* threads, each running on a different processor core in parallel with an instance of its own MDD package. The instance of the MDD package assigned to each worker thread is initialized using MDDs (i.e. program transitions MDD) transferred from the MDD package of the master thread.

4.1 Partitioning the Constraints Satisfaction

The amount of time required by the automated synthesis of self-stabilizing programs depends on the number of constraints to be satisfied by the synthesis algorithm. Furthermore, in some cases, this number can be multiples of the number of the processes in the fault-intolerant program. To remedy this restriction, we present a multicore algorithm that partitions the satisfaction of such constraints among available threads.

Algorithm sketch. Intuitively, our algorithm works as follows. During constraint satisfaction, a *master* thread spawns several *worker* threads each running on a different processor core in parallel with an instance of its own MDD package. The instance of the MDD package assigned to each worker thread is initialized using MDDs for an array of constraints, program transitions, an array of constraints violating transitions, and invariant predicate. The master thread partitions the constraints and provides each worker thread with one such partition. Subsequently, worker threads start resolving their assigned set of constraints in parallel by adding the required *recovery* actions. Upon completion, the master thread *merges* the results returned by each worker thread.

Parallel Constraints Satisfaction. Our algorithm for satisfying the constraints in parallel is as shown in Algorithm 2. This algorithm begins with the

Algorithm 2. ParallelConstraintsSatisfaction [Master Thread]

Input: constraint array C, program transitions p, and number of threads n.
Output: recovery transitions $recAll$.

1: $gAll := false$;
2: $I := \bigwedge_{i=0}^{m} C[i]$;
   // $C[i] \wedge \langle \neg C[i] \rangle'$ *refers to transitions that start in* $\neg C[i]$ *and ends in* $C[i]$
3: **for** $i := 1$ **to** $n-1$ **do**
4: SpawnThread $\rightsquigarrow$ ComputeViolate(i);
5: **end for**
6: **for** $i := 1$ **to** $SizeOf(C) - 1$ **do**
7: $V[i] := V[i-1] \vee V[i]$;
8: **end for**
9: **for** $i := 0$ **to** $n-1$ **do**
10: $C_p[i] = Split(i, C)$;
11: $V_p[i] = Split(i, V)$;
12: **end for**
13: **for** $i := 1$ **to** $n-1$ **do**
14: $rec[i]$:= SpawnThread $\rightsquigarrow$ PConstraintSatisfier($C_p[i]$, p, $V_p[i]$, I);
15: **end for**
16: ThreadJoin($0..n-1$);
17: $recAll := \bigvee_{i=0}^{n-1} rec[i]$; // *Merging the results from all threads*
18: **return** $recAll$;

array of constraints to be satisfied C, fault-intolerant program p, and the number of worker threads to be spawned n. The goal of the algorithm is to discover the set of recovery transitions $recAll$ such that all the constraints in C are satisfied in a way that enables the fault-tolerant program to recover to its legitimate states. Initially, the algorithm starts by computing the invariant as the intersection of all constraints in the constraint array (Lines 2). Now, the algorithm constructs the array V such that $V[i]$ includes the transitions that start from a state where $C[i]$ is true and end in a state where $C[i]$ is false as well as the similar transitions for the constraints $C[j]$, where $0 \leq j \leq i-1$ (Lines 3-8). Observe that in the sequential algorithm (c.f. Algorithm 1), V is being updated while the constraints being satisfied. However, in this algorithm, V is computed before the constraints satisfaction starts. The reason for the early computation of V is that if each thread wants to find $V[i]$, where $i < 0 \leq sizeOf(C)$, it needs to consider the constraints from 0 to $i-1$, which unnecessarily repeats part of the computation. A more efficient way to do this is when the master thread uses the worker threads such that each thread computes its share of V elements. Once all threads are done, the master thread updates the array V such that $V[i] = V[i-1] \vee V[i]$. In other words, $V[i]$ contains all transitions that violate the constraint $C[0]$ to $C[i]$.

After constructing the array V, the algorithm proceeds to evenly distribute C and V among the worker threads (Lines 9-12), such that $C_p[i]$ includes the array of constraints assigned to thread i, and $V_p[i]$ includes the array of corresponding constraints violating transitions. Note that the availability of the array V_p enables each worker thread to work independently without interfering with the other threads. Now, the master thread spawns the worker threads such that each thread has its own set of constraints with their corresponding constraint violating transitions and a copy of I, and p. To compute the respective recovery transitions, each worker thread (Lines 13-15) calls the algorithm *PConstraintSatisfier*, which is similar to the Algorithm 1 except that in addition to C_p and p it also takes V_p and I as an input rather than computing them. Once all worker threads complete their jobs (Line 16), the master thread collects all the recovery transitions returned by worker threads in *recAll* (Lines 17-19) and returns the overall recovery transitions.

4.2 Using the Distributed Nature of the Program Being Synthesized

Based on the nature of distributed programs and their need to account for the read/write restrictions on the program variables, the synthesis algorithm is required to compute the *group* associated with any set of transitions added/removed from the program transitions. In this section, we present a multicore algorithm to perform the *group* computation using two or more cores/processes.

Algorithm sketch. Given transition set *tr* the goal of this algorithm is to compute the *Group* of transitions associated with the set *tr*. The sequential algorithm will go through many computations for each process, one after another. However, in the parallel algorithm, we split the *Group* computation over the available number of threads. In particular, rather than having one thread find the *Group* for all the processes, we let each thread compute the *Group* for a subset of the processes. Since the tasks assigned to each thread require a very small amount of the processor time, there is considerable overhead associated with the threads creation/destruction every time the *Group* is computed. Therefore, we let the master thread create the worker threads at the initialization stage of the synthesis algorithm. The worker threads stay idle until the master thread needs to compute the *Group* for a set of transitions. The Master thread activates/deactivates the worker threads through a set of mutexes. When all worker threads are done, the main thread collects the results of all worker threads in one *Group*.

5 Case Studies

In Subsections 5.1-5.2, we describe and analyze two case studies, namely the Self-Stabilizing Mutual Exclusion [19], and the stabilization of Data Dissemination Problem in Sensor Networks [17]. Of these, the first case study is of the classic problems from distributed computing and illustrate the feasibility of algorithms that add self-stabilization. In the second case study we demonstrate the applicability of our approach on a real world problem in the field of sensor networks. In both case studies, we find that parallelism significantly reduces the total synthesis time.

To concisely describe the transitions of the program we use guarded command notation: $\langle guard \rangle \rightarrow \langle statement \rangle$, where guard is a Boolean expression over program variables and the statement describes how program variables are updated and it always terminates. A guarded command of the form $g \rightarrow st$ corresponds to transitions of the form $\{(s_0, s_1) |\ g$ evaluates to true in s_0 and s_1 is obtained by executing st from $s_0\}$.

Throughout this section, all experiments are run on a Sun Fire V40z with 4 dual-core Opteron processors and 16 GB RAM. The MDD representation of the Boolean formulae has been done using a modified version of the MDD/BDD Glu 2.1 package [20] developed at the University of Colorado [20].

5.1 Case Study 1: Self-stabilizing Mutual Exclusion Program

Mutual exclusion is one of the fundamental problems in distributed/concurrent programs. One of the classical solutions to this problem is the token-based solution due to Raymond [19]. In this solution, the processes form a directed rooted tree, a *holder tree*, in which there is a unique token held at the tree root. If a process wants to access the critical section, it must first acquire the token. Our goal in this case study is to add stabilization to the fault-intolerant program in [7]. When faults occur and perturb the holder tree, the new program will self-stabilize and reconstruct a correct holder tree within a finite number of steps under weak fairness assumption.

Fault-Intolerant Program. In Raymond's algorithm, the processes are organized in a logical tree, denoted as a parent. The holder tree is superimposed on top of the parent tree such that the root of the holder tree is the process that has the token. The holder variable forms a directed path from any process in the tree to the process currently holding the token. In this program, a process can send the token to one of its neighbors. In particular, if j and k are adjacent (in the parent tree), then the action by which k sends the token to j is as follows:

$$NM1 :: (h.k = k \ \wedge \ j \in Adj.k) \ \wedge \ (h.j = k\ ) \ \longrightarrow \ h.k, h.j := j, j;$$

Constraints. Recall from Section 2 that we define the invariant to be a set of constraints on the program state space. In this case study, this set is the conjunction of the constraints $S1$, $S2$, and $S3$, described next. Moreover, each of these constraints is specified for each process separately. Therefore, if n is the number of processes then we have $3n$ constraints to satisfy.Constraint $S1$ requires that j's holder can either be j's parent, j itself, or one of j's children. $S2$ requires that the holder tree conforms to the parent tree. Finally, S3 requires that there are no cycles in the holder relation. Thus, predicates $S1$, $S2$, and $S3$ are as follows:

$$(S1) \quad \forall j : (h.j = P.j) \vee (h.j = j) \vee (\exists k : (P.k = j) \wedge (h.j = k))$$
$$(S2) \quad \forall j : (P.j \neq j) \Rightarrow (h.j = P.j) \vee (h.(P.j) = j)$$
$$(S3) \quad \forall j : (P.j \neq j) \Rightarrow \neg((h.j = P.j) \wedge (h.(P.j) = j))$$

Faults. Since we focus on self-stabilizing fault-tolerance, we consider faults that perturb the holder relation of all processes to an arbitrary value. Thus the fault action is as follows:

$$(F1) \quad true \longrightarrow \{h.j = \text{any arbitrary value from its domain}\};$$

Fault-Tolerant Program. To add stabilizing fault-tolerance to the above program, we used the synthesis algorithm as follows. The fault intolerant program for each process is specified by actions $NM1$; the faults are specified by the fault action $F1$; and the constraints are from $S1$, $S2$, and $S3$. We specified these constraints in the following order: first, we specified constraints $S1$ for the root, then its children, then its grandchildren and so on. Subsequently, we specified constraint $S2$ likewise. Finally, we specified constraint $S3$ in the reverse order. The recovery actions computed by the synthesis algorithm are as follows:

$$\begin{aligned}
&(R1)\ \neg((h.j = P.j) \vee (h.j = j) \vee (\exists k : (P.k = j) \wedge (h.j = k))) \\
&\qquad\qquad \longrightarrow h.j := j \mid h.j := P.j \mid h.j := \{\text{child of } j\}; \\
&(R2)\ \neg((P.j \neq j) \Rightarrow (h.j = P.j) \vee (h.(P.j) = j)) \\
&\qquad\qquad \longrightarrow h.j := P.j \mid h.(P.j) := j; \\
&(R3)\ \neg((P.j \neq j) \Rightarrow \neg((h.j = P.j) \wedge (h.(P.j) = j))) \\
&\qquad\qquad \longrightarrow h.j := j \mid h.(P.j) := P.j \mid h.(P.j) := P.(P.j);
\end{aligned}$$

Analysis of experimental results. Figure 1 shows the results of using parallelism during constraints satisfaction in synthesizing the self-stabilizing Mutual Exclusion program.The table illustrate the results for various numbers of processes organized in linear topology using different numbers of processors/cores. It shows the time needed, in seconds, to satisfy the constraints, and the total synthesis time. It also shows the amount of memory in megabytes. As we can see from this figure, using parallelism has substantially reduced the time needed for the synthesis. As a concrete example, observe that the time required to synthesize a stable mutual exclusion program with 50 processes dropped from 623 seconds, using the sequential algorithm, to 378 seconds when two cores were used, and to 274 seconds when four cores were used.

No. of Processes	reachable states	*Sequential* Cnst t(s)	Syn t(s)	Mem (MB)	*2 threads* Cnst t(s)	Syn t(s)	Mem (MB)	*4 threads* Cnst t(s)	Syn t(s)	Mem (MB)	*8 threads* Cnst t(s)	Syn t(s)	Mem (MB)
20	10^{26}	8	8	6	6	6	23	3	3	33	4	4	42
30	10^{44}	47	48	13	35	36	42	23	24	66	21	22	91
40	10^{64}	188	191	14	154	157	41	88	90	71	79	80	120
50	10^{84}	619	623	15	416	378	46	243	246	77	228	233	132
60	10^{106}	1242	1252	16	945	954	51	579	588	82	492	502	136
70	10^{129}	2683	2725	17	2033	2071	74	1398	1439	114	1174	1215	188

Fig. 1. Self-Stabilizing Mutual Exclusion using *Constraints* partitioning. **Cnst t(s)** : Total time spent in constraints satisfaction in seconds. **Syn t(s)**: Total synthesis time in seconds. **Mem (MB)**: Memory usage in MB.

No. of Processes	reachable states	*Sequential* Grp t(s)	Syn t(s)	Mem (MB)	*2 threads* Grp t(s)	Syn t(s)	Mem (MB)	*4 threads* Grp t(s)	Syn t(s)	Mem (MB)	*8 threads* Grp t(s)	Syn t(s)	Mem (MB)
20	10^{26}	8	8	6	5	5	16	3	4	25	3	4	42
30	10^{44}	47	48	13	36	38	32	21	24	50	20	25	83
40	10^{64}	185	191	14	124	133	40	84	93	68	74	89	121
50	10^{84}	611	623	15	361	378	44	247	274	74	233	276	133
60	10^{106}	1228	1252	16	773	808	45	586	640	71	570	658	124
70	10^{129}	2628	2725	17	1830	1961	47	1358	1516	77	1039	1280	136

Fig. 2. Self-Stabilizing Mutual Exclusion using *Group* threading. **Grp t(s)** : Total time spent in *Group* computation in seconds. **Syn t(s)**: Total synthesis time in seconds. **Mem (MB)**: Memory usage in MB.

Figure 2 shows the results of exploiting the distributed nature of the program being synthesized (i.e. *Group* parallelism) in synthesizing the self-stabilizing Mutual Exclusion program. It shows the time needed, in seconds, to compute the *group*, and the total synthesis time. It also shows the amount of memory in megabytes needed by our algorithm.

5.2 Case Study 2: Data Dissemination in Sensor Networks

In this problem, a base station initiates a computation in which a block of data is to be sent to all sensors in the network. The data message is split into fixed size packets. Each packet is given a sequence number. The base station starts transmitting the packets to its neighbor(s) in specified time slots, in the order of the packet sequence number. Subsequently, when the neighbor(s) receive a message, they, in turn, retransmit it to their neighbors and so on. The computation ends when all sensors in the network receive all the messages.

Our goal in this case study is to synthesize a fault-tolerant version of the data dissemination program that can tolerate a finite number of lost packets (This program satisfies the constraints only from states reached in the presence of faults, although not necessarily from all states). The synthesized program is the same as Infuse [17] that is designed manually. With regard to the limited space, we will only include the experimental results showing the benefit of parallelism details of the fault-intolerant algorithm shown in [2].

Figure 3 shows the results of synthesizing the data dissemination protocol with various numbers of processes by partitioning the constraints among available threads. Note that, in the case of the data dissemination problem, there were only 5 constraints to satisfy. Hence, when the synthesis is launched with 8 threads, we are only utilizing 5 of them. As can be seen from Figure 3 if the number of constraints is not large enough then the speedup gained from portioning the constraints is limited.

Figure 4 shows the results of synthesizing the data dissemination protocol with various numbers of processes by exploiting the distributed nature of this program.

No. of Processes	reachable states	*Sequential* Cnst t(s)	Syn t(s)	Mem (MB)	*2 threads* Cnst t(s)	Syn t(s)	Mem (MB)	*4 threads* Cnst t(s)	Syn t(s)	Mem (MB)	*8 threads* Cnst t(s)	Syn t(s)	Mem (MB)
50	10^{47}	8	9	11	6	6	28	5	6	44	7	8	62
100	10^{95}	67	70	13	48	53	40	60	64	65	66	70	110
150	10^{143}	321	330	15	187	197	41	188	197	68	248	259	114
200	10^{190}	977	984	16	471	497	47	536	564	73	545	573	116

Fig. 3. Data Dissemination program using *Constraints* partitioning

No. of Processes	reachable states	*Sequential* Grp t(s)	Syn t(s)	Mem (MB)	*2 threads* Grp t(s)	Syn t(s)	Mem (MB)	*4 threads* Grp t(s)	Syn t(s)	Mem (MB)	*8 threads* Grp t(s)	Syn t(s)	Mem (MB)
50	10^{47}	8	9	11	5	7	26	3	5	43	2	5	67
100	10^{95}	63	70	13	38	51	39	23	42	66	17	47	119
150	10^{143}	321	330	15	187	197	41	188	197	68	248	259	114
200	10^{190}	948	984	16	369	457	46	203	324	73	174	358	127

Fig. 4. Data Dissemination program using *Group* threading

Memory Usage. Notice that the amount of memory needed during synthesis is proportional to the number of threads being used. It is approximately the amount of memory used by the sequential algorithm multiplied by the number of cores being used. Clearly, this is expected since for every thread used, we create a new MDD package.We argue that using extra memory to gain a speedup is acceptable, since in the automated synthesis, time complexity is a far more serious barrier than space complexity.

6 Related Work

Automated program synthesis is studied from different perspectives. One approach (e.g., [4]) focuses on synthesizing fault-tolerant programs from their specification in a temporal logic (e.g., CTL, LTL, etc.). Our approach for adding self-stabilization is based on satisfying constraints that should be true in legitimate states. An orthogonal approach is to utilize primitives such as distributed reset [16] where one detects whether the system is in a consistent state and resets it to a legitimate state, if needed. Examples of these approaches include [16,22]. Our approach can be utilized to design the distributed reset protocol itself.

Parallelization of symbolic reachability analysis has been studied in the model checking community from different perspectives. In [11,12,13], the authors propose solutions and analyze different approaches to parallelization of the *saturation*-based generation of state space in model checking. In particular, in [12], the authors show that in order to gain speedup in saturation-based parallel symbolic verification, one has to pay a penalty for memory usage of up to 10 times that of the sequential algorithm. Other efforts range from simple approaches that essentially implement BDDs as two-tiered hash tables [18, 21], to sophisticated approaches relying on *slicing* BDDs [15] and techniques for *workstealing* [14]. However, the resulting implementations show only limited speedup.

7 Conclusion

In this paper, we focused on automated addition of fault-tolerance to hierarchical programs. In particular, we considered programs where legitimate states are specified in terms of constraints that are true in legitimate states. The goal of adding self-stabilizing fault-tolerance was to ensure that if these constraints are violated by faults then eventually the program would reach a state from where all the constraints are satisfied and, hence, subsequent behavior would be correct.

We focused on improving the synthesis of fault-tolerant programs from their fault-intolerant version. We showed that the use of multicore technology to parallelize the synthesis algorithm reduces the synthesis time substantially. We parallelized constraint satisfaction by: (1) partitioning the constraints and (2) utilizing the nature of distributed programs. We showed that parallelism provides a substantial benefit in reducing the time needed in synthesis.

We illustrated our approach with two case studies: self-stabilizing mutual exclusion, and a data dissemination problem for sensor networks. The complexity analysis demonstrated that automated synthesis in these case studies was feasible and achieved in a reasonable time speedup in all case studies.

Based on the results in this paper, there is potential for further reduction in synthesis time if the level of parallelism is increased (e.g., if there are more processors). Although the level of parallelism is fine-grained, we showed that the overhead of parallel computation is small. Hence, another future work is to evaluate the limits of parallel computation in improving performance of the synthesis algorithm and include this in the tools (e.g., SYCRAFT [8]) for synthesizing fault-tolerance.

References

1. Abadi, M., Lamport, L.: Conjoining specifications. ACM Transactions on Programming Languages and Systems (TOPLAS) 17(3), 507–535 (1995)
2. Abujarad, F., Kulkarni, S.S.: Multicore constraint-based automated stabilization. In: Guerraoui, R., Petit, F. (eds.) SSS 2009. LNCS, vol. 5873, pp. 47–61. Springer, Heidelberg (2009)
3. Aminof, B., Ball, T., Kupferman, O.: Reasoning about systems with transition fairness. In: Baader, F., Voronkov, A. (eds.) LPAR 2004. LNCS (LNAI), vol. 3452, pp. 194–208. Springer, Heidelberg (2005)
4. Arora, A., Attie, P.C., Emerson, E.A.: Synthesis of fault-tolerant concurrent programs. In: Principles of Distributed Computing (PODC), pp. 173–182 (1998)
5. Arora, A., Gouda, M.G.: Closure and convergence: A foundation of fault-tolerant computing. IEEE Transactions on Software Engineering 19(11), 1015–1027 (1993)
6. Arora, A., Gouda, M.G., Varghese, G.: Constraint satisfaction as a basis for designing nonmasking fault-tolerant systems. Journal of High Speed Networks 5(3), 293–306 (1996)

7. Arora, A., Kulkarni, S.S.: Designing masking fault-tolerance via nonmasking fault-tolerance. In: Proceedings of the Fourteenth Symposium on Reliable Distributed Systems, Bad Neuenahr, vol. 14, pp. 174–185 (1995)
8. Bonakdarpour, B., Kulkarni, S.S.: Sycraft: A tool for automated synthesis of fault-tolerant distributed programs. In: International Conference on Concurrency Theory (2008)
9. Chandy, K.M., Misra, J.: Parallel program design: a foundation. Addison-Wesley Longman Publishing Co., Inc., Boston (1988)
10. Emerson, E.A., Lei, C.L.: Temporal model checking under generalized fairness constraints. In: Proc. 18th Hawaii International Conference on System Sciences, pp. 277–288 (1985)
11. Ezekiel, J., Lüttgen, G.: Measuring and evaluating parallel state-space exploration algorithms. In: International Workshop on Parallel and Distributed Methods in Verification, PDMC (2007)
12. Ezekiel, J., Lüttgen, G., Ciardo, G.: Parallelising symbolic state-space generators. In: Damm, W., Hermanns, H. (eds.) CAV 2007. LNCS, vol. 4590, pp. 268–280. Springer, Heidelberg (2007)
13. Ezekiel, J., Lüttgen, G., Siminiceanu, R.I.: Can Saturation be parallelised? on the parallelisation of a symbolic state-space generator. In: Brim, L., Haverkort, B.R., Leucker, M., van de Pol, J. (eds.) FMICS 2006 and PDMC 2006. LNCS, vol. 4346, pp. 331–346. Springer, Heidelberg (2007)
14. Grumberg, O., Heyman, T., Ifergan, N., Schuster, A.: Achieving speedups in distributed symbolic reachability analysis through asynchronous computation. In: Borrione, D., Paul, W. (eds.) CHARME 2005. LNCS, vol. 3725, pp. 129–145. Springer, Heidelberg (2005)
15. Grumberg, O., Heyman, T., Schuster, A.: A work-efficient distributed algorithm for reachability analysis. Formal Methods in System Design (FMSD) 29(2), 157–175 (2006)
16. Katz, S., Perry, K.: Self-stabilizing extensions for message passing systems. Distributed Computing 7, 17–26 (1993)
17. Kulkarni, S.S., Arumugam, M.: Infuse: A TDMA based data dissemination protocol for sensor networks. International Journal of Distributed Sensor Networks 2(1), 55–78 (2006)
18. Milvang-Jensen, K., Hu, A.J.: BDDNOW: A parallel BDD package. In: Gopalakrishnan, G.C., Windley, P. (eds.) FMCAD 1998. LNCS, vol. 1522, pp. 501–507. Springer, Heidelberg (1998)
19. Raymond, K.: A tree based algorithm for mutual exclusion. ACM Transactions on Computer Systems 7, 61–77 (1989)
20. Somenzi, F.: CUDD: Colorado University Decision Diagram Package, `http://vlsi.colorado.edu/~fabio/CUDD/cuddIntro.html`
21. Stornetta, T., Brewer, F.: Implementation of an efficient parallel BDD package. In: Design automation (DAC), pp. 641–644 (1996)
22. Theel, O., Gartner, F.C.: An exercise in proving convergence through transfer functions. In: Proc. 4th Workshop on Self-stabilizing Systems, Austin, Texas, pp. 41–47 (1999)

A Theory of Network Tracing

Hrishikesh B. Acharya[1] and Mohamed G. Gouda[1,2]

[1] The University of Texas at Austin, USA
[2] The National Science Foundation, USA
{acharya,gouda}@cs.utexas.edu

Abstract. Traceroute is a widely used program for computing the topology of any network in the Internet. Using Traceroute, one starts from a node and chooses any other node in the network. Traceroute obtains the sequence of nodes that occur between these two nodes, as specified by the routing tables in these nodes. Each use of Traceroute in a network produces a trace of nodes that constitute a simple path in this network. In every trace that is produced by Traceroute, each node occurs either by its unique identifier, or by the anonymous identifier"∗". In this paper, we introduce the first theory aimed at answering the following important question. Is there an algorithm to compute the topology of a network N from a trace set T that is produced by using Traceroute in network N, assuming that each edge in N occurs in at least one trace in T, and that each node in N occurs by its unique identifier in at least one trace in T? We prove that the answer to this question is "No" if N is an even ring or a general network. However, it is "Yes" if N is a tree or an odd ring. The answer is also "No" if N is mostly-regular, but "Yes" if N is a mostly-regular even ring.

1 Introduction

Traceroute is arguably the most popular mechanism for computing the topology of a network in the Internet [1] and [2]. Executing Traceroute between any two nodes, say nodes x and y, in a network produces a sequence of node identifiers that corresponds to a simple path between x and y in the network. This sequence of node identifiers is usually referred to as a *trace* between x and y.

Traceroute can be used to compute the topology of a network N in the Internet as follows [1] :

1. Identify the "terminal" nodes in network N (preferably at the perimeter of N for good coverage).
2. Execute Traceroute between every pair of terminal nodes of N, identified in Step 1, to produce traces of nodes that occur between each pair (as per the routing tables in the nodes of N).
3. Put the traces produced in Step 2 together in order to compute the topology of network N.

It turns out that this procedure for using Traceroute to compute the topology of network N has a problem. As observed in [3], [4], and [5], some of the nodes in the

R. Guerraoui and F. Petit (Eds.): SSS 2009, LNCS 5873, pp. 62–74, 2009.

traces produced in Step 2 occur by anonymous identifiers, rather than by their unique identifiers. This causes Step 3 to compute many candidate topologies, rather than one unique topology, for network N.

To solve this problem, Yao et al. [3] have suggested that Step 3 compute only the topology with the smallest number of anonymous nodes, subject to some constraints (trace preservation and distance preservation). This suggestion has two problems of its own. First, the choice, that the topology of network N be the one with the smallest number of anonymous nodes, is an arbitrary one. Second, it turns out that the problem of computing the network topology with the smallest number of anonymous nodes, from a given set of traces, is NP-complete. In order to solve this second problem, Jin et al. [4] and Gunes et al.[5] propose several heuristics (with complexity polynomial in the number of unique identifiers) that can be used to compute a network topology with a "small" number of anonymous nodes. Clearly, these heuristics cannot always compute a network topology with the smallest possible number of anonymous nodes.

In this paper, we take a different approach to the problem of computing one unique topology for network N from a given trace set T that is generated by executing Traceroute over N. Our approach is based on the assumption that the given trace set T satisfies a number of "conditions". The assumption, that the given trace set T satisfies these conditions, is made with the hope that the computed topology for network N is unique. These conditions can be summarized as follows: (Formal statements of these conditions are given in section 2).

- *Unique node identifiers:* Each node in network N has exactly one unique identifier, and if this node occurs in a trace in T, then it occurs in this trace either by this unique identifier, or by an anonymous identifier.
- *Complete coverage:* Each edge in network N occurs in at least one trace in the trace set T. Also, each node in N occurs by its unique identifier in at least one trace in T.
- *Stable and symmetric routing:* The routing tables in the nodes of network N indicate exactly one route between any two nodes in N.

These conditions may appear to be too strong to hold in practice. However, it is straightforward to show that if the given trace set T does not satisfy any one of these conditions, then more than one candidate topology for network N can be computed from T.

For example, assume that the given trace set T does not satisfy the first condition: a node occurs by identifier a in one trace in T, and occurs by a second identifier b in another trace in T. In this case, one can infer at least two candidate topologies for network N : in one topology, a and b indicate one node in N, and in the other, they indicate two distinct nodes in N.

Our main result in this paper is negative. This means that, even when the given trace set T satisfies the above (admittedly strong) conditions, it is not always possible to compute a unique topology for network N from T. Thus, adopting the above conditions has the effect of strengthening our primary (negative) results.

2 Network Tracing

A network N is a connected, undirected graph where nodes have unique identifiers. Every node in a network is designated either *terminal* or *non-terminal.* Also, every node is either *regular* or *irregular.*

A *trace* t is *generable from* a network N iff t is a sequence of node identifiers that represents a simple path between two terminal nodes in N. A regular node occurs in t by its unique identifier. An irregular node occurs in t either by its unique identifier, or by the anonymous identifier $*_i$, where i is a unique integer in t. The first and last nodes of t occur by their unique identifiers in t.

We adopt the following notation in our graphical representations.

1. A terminal node is represented by a box.
2. A non-terminal node is represented by a circle.
3. A regular node x is labeled by its unique identifier "x".
4. An irregular node x is labeled "x/*".

Note that a trace t that is generable from a network N is a sequence of nodes that corresponds to a simple path in N. Thus, there are two ways to write the sequence of nodes in t. For example, t can be written as $(e, *_1, *_2, *_3, a)$, or it can be written as $(a, *_3, *_2, *_1, e)$. We regard the differences between these two ways of writing t as immaterial. Later on, when we mention that a trace is of the form $(x, \ldots, y)$, we mean that this trace could also be of the form $(y, \ldots, x)$.

For trace t, we adopt the notation $|t|$ to indicate the number of edges in t. For example, $|(e, *_1, *_2, *_3, a)| = 4$.

A *trace set* T is *generable from* a network N iff T satisfies the following five conditions :

1. T is a set of traces, each of which is generable from N.
2. For every pair of terminal nodes x, y in N, T has at least one trace $(x, \ldots, y)$.
3. Every edge in N occurs in at least one trace in T.
4. The unique identifier of every node in N occurs in at least one trace in T.
5. T is *consistent*: for every two distinct nodes x and y, if x and y occur in two or more traces in T, then the exact same set of nodes occur between x and y in every trace in T where both x and y occur.

Two comments concerning Condition 5 in this definition are in order. First, if a trace set T has two traces of the form $(x, *_2, z)$ and (u, x, y, z), then from Condition 5, we can conclude that node $*_2$ is in fact node y.

Second, if a trace set T has a trace of the form $(x, *_2, z)$, then from Condition 5, T cannot have a trace of the form $(u, x, *_5, y, z)$. This is because the number of nodes between x and z in the first trace is 1, and their number in the second trace is 2, in violation of Condition 5.

The *network tracing problem* is to design an algorithm that takes as input a trace set T that is generable from a network, and produces a network N such that T is generable from N and not from any other network.

3 Impossibility of Network Tracing

Obviously, the network tracing problem is solvable for *regular* networks, those where every node is regular. However, it turns out that the problem is *not* solvable for general networks. In fact, if a network is permitted to have just one irregular node, then the network tracing problem is unsolvable, as shown by the following theorem.

Theorem 1. *There is no algorithm that takes as an input a trace set T that is generable from a network with one irregular node, and produces as output a network N with one irregular node such that:*

- *T is generable from N, and*
- *T is not generable from any other network with at least one irregular node.*

Proof. (By contradiction) Assume that such an algorithm exists. The following trace set T_1 is generable from network N_1 in Figure 1.

$$T_1 = \{(a, b), (a, *_1, d), (a, f), \\ (b, c, d), (b, f), \\ (d, e, f)\}$$

If T_1 is given as an input to the assumed algorithm, the algorithm produces network N_1 as output. This implies that T_1 is not generable from any other network, which contradicts the fact that T_1 is also generable from network N_2 in Figure 1. □

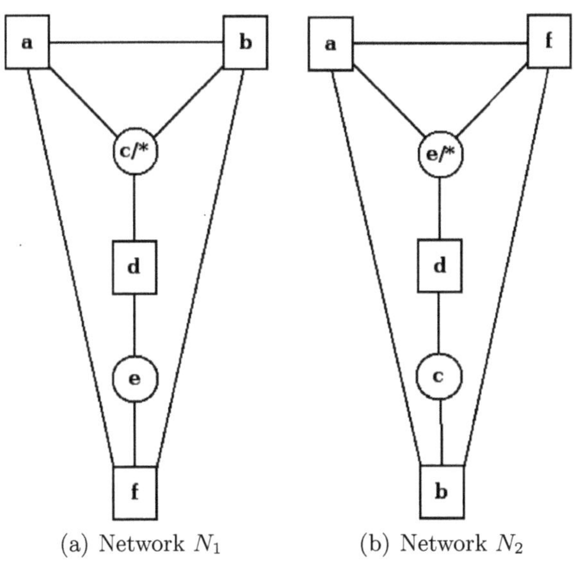

Fig. 1. Theorem 1

Theorem 1 provides a strong negative result for the network tracing problem. Nevertheless, we identify, in the next three sections, classes of networks for which the network tracing problem is solvable:

1. Tree networks in Section 4.
2. Odd rings in Section 5.
3. Mostly regular even rings in Section 6.

4 Tracing of Tree Networks

A network N is called a *tree* iff N is acyclic. In this section, we show that the network tracing problem is solvable for tree networks.

Theorem 2. *There is an algorithm that takes as an input a trace set T that is generable from a tree network, and produces as output a tree network N such that:*

- *T is generable from N, and*
- *T is not generable from any other tree network.*

Proof. (By construction) We prove Theorem 2 by providing the algorithm mentioned. The algorithm consists of the following eight steps:

1. Initially, tree N is empty.
2. Apply procedure *Leaf*, discussed below, to compute, from T, the unique identifier of each leaf node in N.
3. Apply procedure *Parent*, discussed below, to compute from T, the unique identifier of the parent of each leaf node in N.
4. For every node y that is the parent of a leaf node x, add to tree N an (undirected) edge between nodes x and y.
5. For every node y that is the parent of a leaf node x, replace in T each trace of the form $(x, *_i, \ldots)$ by a trace of the form $(x, y, \ldots)$.
6. Shorten the traces in T by replacing in T each trace of the form $(x, y, \ldots)$, where x is a leaf node, by the trace $(y, \ldots)$ and by discarding from T each trace that has only one node or is empty.
7. Repeat the algorithm, starting from Step 2, on the trace set T, that results from Step 6, provided that the resulting set T is non-empty.
8. The algorithm outputs N and terminates when the resulting T from Step 6 is empty.

Next, we specify the two procedures *Leaf* and *Parent* that are used in Steps 2 and 3, respectively, of the above algorithm. The correctness of procedure *Leaf* follows from the observation that each leaf node in N occurs as a terminal node in some trace in T, but the converse is not necessarily true. Procedure *Leaf* is specified as follows:

procedure *Leaf*
for each terminal node y in any trace in T
if T has three traces
$t = (x, \ldots, y), t' = (y, \ldots, z), t'' = (x, \ldots, z)$,
such that $|t| + |t'| = |t''|$
then y is a non-leaf node in N
else y is a leaf node in N
end

The correctness of procedure *Parent* follows from the observation that the parent of each leaf node in N occurs by its unique identifier in some trace in T. Procedure *Parent* is specified as follows:

procedure *Parent*
for each leaf node x in N,
if T has a trace of the form $(x, y \ldots)$,
or T has two traces of the form $(x, *_i, z)$ and $(z, y, \ldots)$
where z is a leaf node in N
then the unique identifier of the parent of node x is y
end

□

5 Tracing of Ring Networks

In this section, we discuss the solvability of the network tracing problem for ring networks. Surprisingly, we show that the problem is solvable for odd rings (i.e. cycles with an odd number of nodes), but not solvable for even rings (i.e. cycles with an even number of nodes).

Theorem 3. *There is an algorithm that takes as an input a trace set T that is generable from an odd ring network, and produces as output an odd ring network N such that:*

- *T is generable from N, and*
- *T is not generable from any other odd ring network.*

Proof. (By construction) We prove Theorem 3 by describing the algorithm that is mentioned in the theorem. The algorithm consists of the following five steps:

1. Construct an unlabeled ring N with n nodes, where n is the number of unique identifiers that occur in the traces in T. The algorithm terminates when each node in N is labeled by a distinct unique identifier from those that occur in the traces in T.

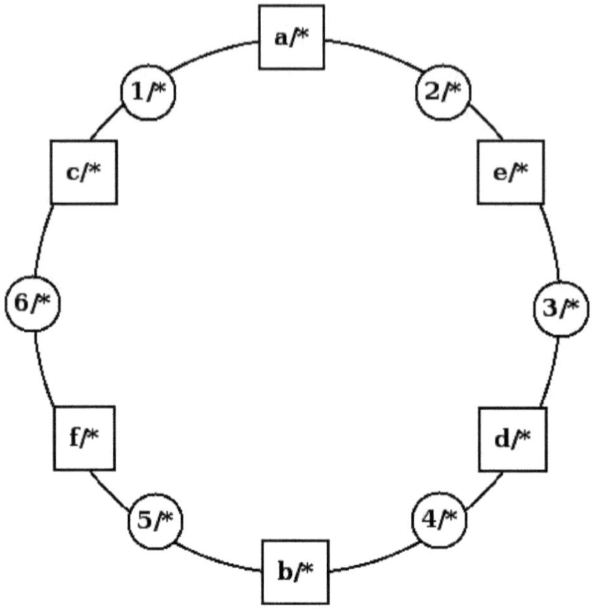

(a) Network N_3

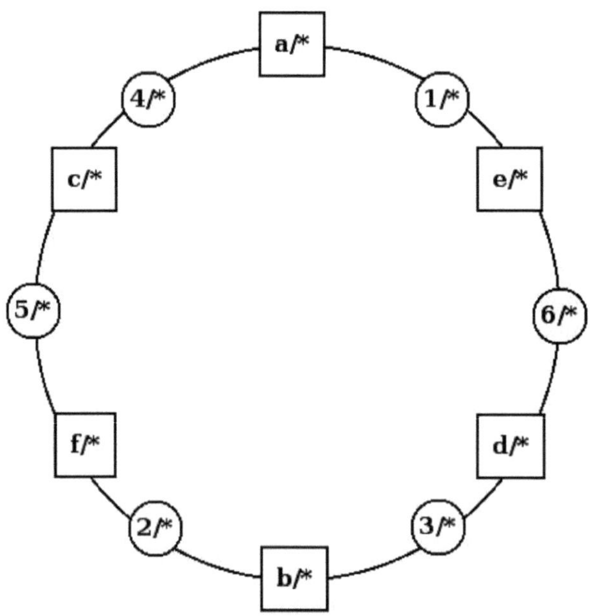

(b) Network N_4

Fig. 2. Theorem 5

2. Choose any trace $t = (a, \ldots, b)$ in T. Label any node in N with the unique identifier "a", and label the node in N, that is reachable by traversing $|t|$ edges clockwise starting from node a, with the unique identifier "b".
3. For every pair of traces $t' = (a, \ldots, c)$ and $t'' = (b, \ldots, c)$ in T,
   if $|t| = |t'| + |t''|$ or $|t'| = |t| + |t''|$
   then label the node in N, that is reachable by traversing $|t'|$ edges clockwise starting from node a, with the unique identifier "c".
   else label the node in N, that is reachable by traversing $|t'|$ edges counter-clockwise starting from node a, with the unique identifier "c".
4. Note that by the end of Step 3, every unique identifier of a terminal node in a trace in T is used to label one node in ring N.
5. Consider any trace $t' = (x, \ldots, y)$ in T, and note that $|t'|$ cannot be equal to $n/2$ since $|t'|$ is a positive integer, and n is odd. Consequently, one can determine whether any trace $t = (x, \ldots, y)$ goes, either clockwise or counter-clockwise, from node x to node y. Thus, if trace t has a unique identifier z that has not yet been used to label any node in N, then one can identify the node in N that should be labeled with z. □

Theorem 4. *There is no algorithm that takes as an input a trace set T that is generable from an even ring network, and produces as output an even ring network N such that:*

- *T is generable from N, and*
- *T is not generable from any other even ring network.*

Proof. (By contradiction) The proof proceeds as for Theorem 1, using the observation that the following trace set T_2 is generable from two even ring networks, N_3 and N_4, in Figure 2.

$$\begin{aligned} T_2 = \{&(a, 1, *_1, 6, *_2, *_3, b), (a, *_4, c), (a, *_5, *_6, *_7, d), (a, *_8, e), (a, *_9, *_{10}, *_{11}, f),\\ &(b, *_{12}, *_{13}, *_{14}, c), (b, *_{15}, d), (b, *_{16}, *_{17}, *_{18}, e), (b, *_{19}, f),\\ &(c, *_{20}, *_{21}, 2, *_{22}, 3, d), (c, *_{23}, *_{24}, *_{25}, e), (c, *_{26}, f),\\ &(d, *_{27}, e), (d, *_{28}, *_{29}, *_{30}, f),\\ &(e, *_{31}, *_{32}, 4, *_{33}, 5, f)\} \end{aligned}$$ □

6 Tracing of Mostly-Regular Networks

A network, where each node has at most one irregular neighbor, is called *mostly-regular*. The following theorem shows that the network tracing problem is solvable for mostly-regular even rings.

Theorem 5. *There is an algorithm that takes as an input a trace set T that is generable from a mostly-regular even ring network, and produces as output a mostly-regular even ring network N such that:*

- *T is generable from N, and*
- *T is not generable from any other mostly-regular even ring network.*

Proof. (By construction). The algorithm is given in our technical report [6]. □

Encouraged by Theorem 5, one may have hoped that the network tracing problem is solvable for the whole class of mostly-regular networks. Unfortunately, as shown by the next theorem, this turns out not to be the case.

Theorem 6. *There is no algorithm that takes as an input a trace set T that is generable from any mostly-regular network, and produces as output a mostly-regular network N such that:*

- *T is generable from N, and*
- *T is not generable from any other mostly-regular network.*

Proof. (By contradiction) Suppose such an algorithm exists. As any network with exactly one irregular node is clearly mostly-regular, this algorithm takes any trace set generable from a network N with one irregular node, and returns N (and only N). This contradicts Theorem 1. □

7 The Weak Network Tracing Problem

The reason that the network tracing problem is not solvable in most cases, one may argue, is that the given trace set T is required to be generable from one, and only one, network N. One may hope, then, that if this strict requirement is somewhat relaxed, then the resulting weak version of the network tracing problem becomes solvable in many cases. The *weak network tracing problem* can be stated as follows:

"Design an algorithm that takes as input a trace set T, that is generable from a network, and produces a small set $\{N_1, .., N_k\}$ of networks such that T is generable from each network in this set and not from any network outside this set."

The requirement that the produced set $\{N_1, .., N_k\}$ be small means, mathematically, that the cardinality k of this set be a constant rather than a function of the number of unique node identifiers in the given trace set T.

There are both practical and theoretical reasons for this requirement. From a practical point of view, the smaller the produced set, the better. From a theoretical point of view, allowing the cardinality of the produced set to be a function of n, the number of unique identifiers, makes the weak network tracing problem trivially solvable (by exhaustive enumeration, setting each $*_i$ to each unique identifier).

Unfortunately, the following theorem shows that the weak network tracing problem is not solvable in general.

Theorem 7. *There is no algorithm that takes as an input a trace set T that is generable from a network, and computes a set of networks $\{N_1 \ldots N_k\}$ such that:*

- *T is generable from every network in the set $\{N_1 \ldots N_k\}$,*
- *T is not generable from any other network, and*
- *k is a constant whose value is not a function of the number of node identifiers in T.*

Proof. We prove this theorem by exhibiting an infinite sequence of trace sets TS_6, $TS_8, TS_{10} \ldots$ such that each trace set TS_n satisfies the following three conditions:

- TS_n has 1 anonymous node identifier.
- TS_n has n unique node identifiers.
- TS_n is generable from any one of $\frac{n-2}{2}$ distinct networks.

Consider the first trace set in the sequence.

$$
\begin{aligned}
TS_6 = \{&(a, x_1, b), (a, *_1, m_1), (a, x_2, m_2),\\
&(b, *_2, m_1), (b, x_2, m_2),\\
&(m_1, m_2)\}
\end{aligned}
$$

This trace set is generable from the two networks N_5 and N_6 in Figure 3.

We now add two nodes, x_3 and m_3, to the trace set TS_6 to form the trace set TS_8 and increase the number of possible networks (from which the trace set TS_8 is generable) by 1. Node x_3 connects m_3 to both a and b, so we add the traces (a, x_3, m_3) and (b, x_3, m_3). Also, m_3 is directly connected to every m_i, so we add (m_1, m_3) and (m_2, m_3). The resulting trace set TS_8 is as follows:

$$
\begin{aligned}
TS_8 = \{&(a, x_1, b), (a, *_1, m_1), (a, x_2, m_2), (a, x_3, m_3),\\
&(b, *_2, m_1), (b, x_2, m_2), (b, x_3, m_3),\\
&(m_1, m_2), (m_1, m_3), (m_2, m_3)\}
\end{aligned}
$$

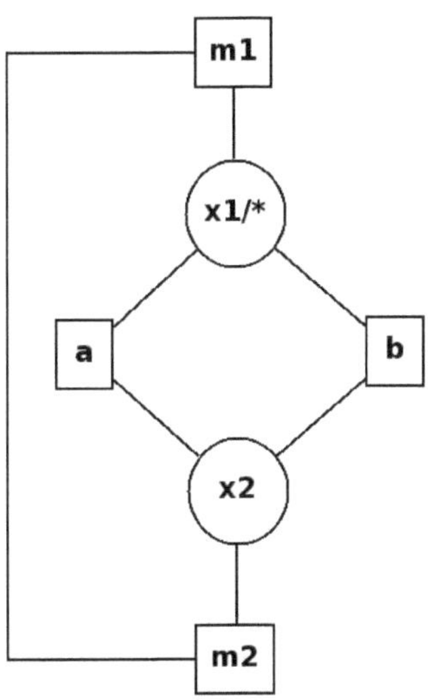

(a) Network N_5

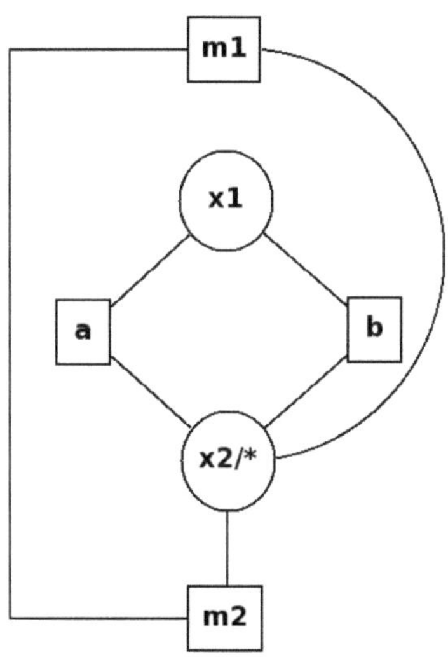

(b) Network N_6

Fig. 3. Two networks

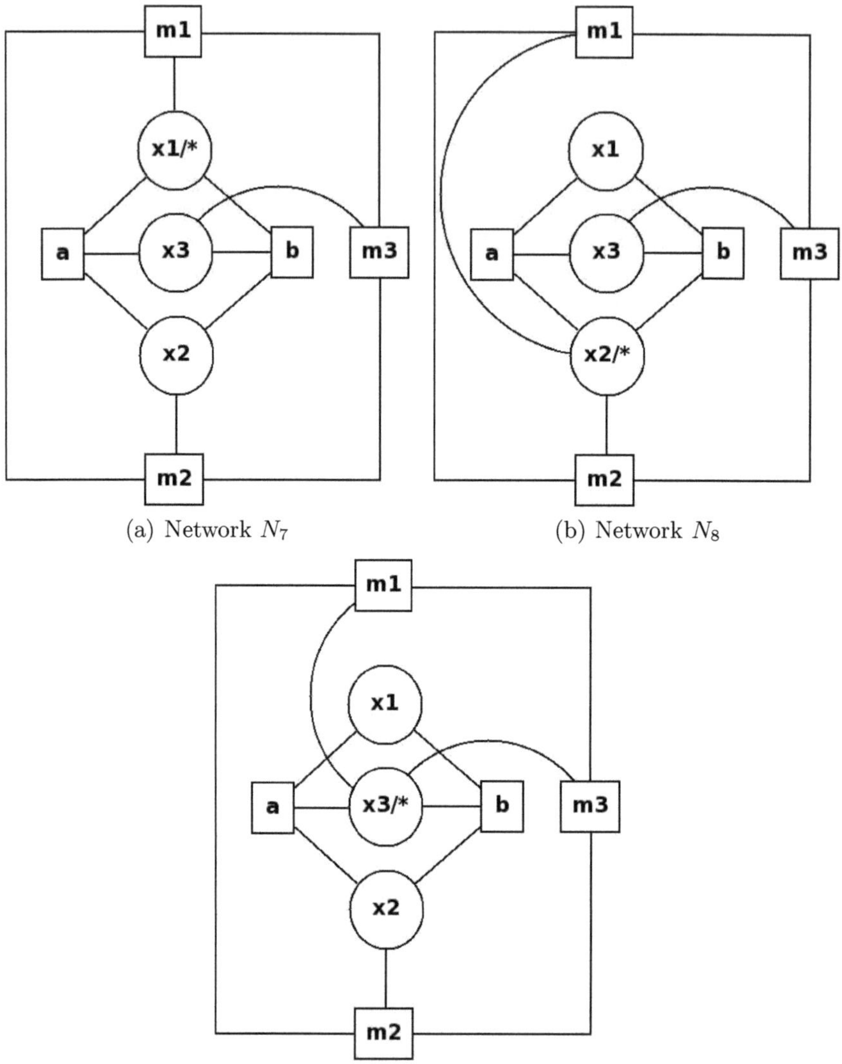

(a) Network N_7 (b) Network N_8

(c) Network N_9

Fig. 4. Three networks

The trace set TS_8 is generable from any of the three networks N_7, N_8 and N_9 in Figure 4.

By repeating this procedure $k-2$ times, we produce a trace set that is generable from every member of a set of k distinct networks. As each step adds two new nodes, each of these networks has $2k+2$ nodes. The number of unique identifiers being n, we have $k = \frac{n-2}{2}$. □

8 Discussion and Related Work

There have been three attacks on the anonymity problem. Casting it as an optimization problem, Yao et al. [3] try building the smallest possible topology by combining anonymous nodes. They consider two constraints, trace preservation and distance preservation. Proving that optimum topology inference under these conditions is NP-complete, they propose a $O(n^5)$ heuristic that merges anonymous nodes, keeping the constraints invariant. Distance preservation requires that merging nodes never reduces the length of the shortest path between any two nodes in the computed network; this assumes not only consistency, but also shortest-path routing. Their study also assumes that anonymous nodes are strictly anonymous, and their unique identifiers are never revealed.

Jin et al. propose two heuristics to address the problem in [4]. The first is $O(n^3)$, uses link delays or node connectivity as attributes, and performs ISOMAP-based dimensionality reduction. It ignores the difficulty of estimating one-hop delays from RTTs in path traces [7]. The second, a simple $O(n^2)$ neighbor matching heuristic, has high rates of both false positives and false negatives. In [5], Gunes et al. apply five heuristics in succession and get performance strictly better than $O(n^3)$.

This paper addresses the problem and provides a theoretical basis for stating which instances of trace set can be used to compute exactly one network, and which cannot. We give a metric for reduction - the irregularity number - and bounds on algorithms such as in the above papers. We also give polynomial-time exact algorithms for several network cases of interest.

9 Concluding Remarks

We have made three contributions in this paper. First, we formally state the network tracing problem. We then develop the theory by identifying some important network classes for which this problem is solvable, and some for which it is not. This includes some very surprising results.

We then extend this research using a weaker version of the network tracing problem, and show that it is not only not possible in general to take a trace set T and compute a single network N, such that T is generable from N and only N, it is also not possible to generate a small (with constant cardinality) set of networks such that T is generable only from members of this set.

In future work, we intend to investigate whether it is possible to relax our assumptions (consistent routing, unique identifiers, and complete coverage) while maintaining the effectiveness and elegance of the theory.

References

1. Cheswick, B., Burch, H., Branigan, S.: Mapping and visualizing the internet. In: ATEC 2000: Proceedings of the annual conference on USENIX Annual Technical Conference, Berkeley, CA, USA, pp. 1–12. USENIX Association (2000)

2. Viger, F., Augustin, B., Cuvellier, X., Magnien, C., Latapy, M., Friedman, T., Teixeira, R.: Detection, understanding, and prevention of traceroute measurement artifacts. Computer Networks 52, 998–1018 (2008)
3. Yao, B., Viswanathan, R., Chang, F., Waddington, D.: Topology inference in the presence of anonymous routers. In: Twenty-Second Annual Joint Conference of the IEEE Computer and Communications Societies, INFOCOM 2003, vol. 1, pp. 353–363. IEEE, Los Alamitos (2003)
4. Jin, X., Yiu, W.P.K., Chan, S.H.G., Wang, Y.: Network topology inference based on end-to-end measurements. IEEE Journal on Selected Areas in Communications 24, 2182–2195 (2006)
5. Gunes, M., Sarac, K.: Resolving anonymous routers in internet topology measurement studies. In: INFOCOM 2008. The 27th Conference on Computer Communications, pp. 1076–1084. IEEE, Los Alamitos (2008)
6. Acharya, H.B., Gouda, M.G.: Tr-09-02: The theory of network tracing. Technical report, University of Texas, Austin (2009), `http://www.cs.utexas.edu/research/publications/ncstrl/ncstrl2html.cgi`
7. Feldman, D., Shavitt, Y.: Automatic large scale generation of internet pop level maps. In: IEEE Global Telecommunications Conference (GLOBECOM), pp. 1–6 (2008)

Developing Autonomic and Secure Virtual Organisations with Chemical Programming

Alvaro E. Arenas[1], Jean-Pierre Banâtre[2], and Thierry Priol[2]

[1] STFC Rutherford Appleton Laboratory, UK
[2] INRIA Rennes - Bretagne Atlantique, France
alvaro.arenas@stfc.ac.uk, Jean-Pierre.Banatre@inria.fr,
Thierry.Priol@inria.fr

Abstract. This paper studies the development of autonomic and secure Virtual Organisations (VOs) when following the chemical-programming paradigm. We have selected the Higher-Order Chemical Language (HOCL) as the representative of the chemical paradigm, due mainly to its generality, its implicit autonomic property, and its potential application to emerging computing paragidms such as Grid computing and service computing. We have advocated the use of aspect-oriented techniques, where autonomicity and security can be seen as cross-cutting concerns impacting the whole system. We show how HOCL can be used to model VOs, exemplified by a VO system for the generation of digital products. We develop patterns for HOCL, including patterns for traditional security properties such as authorisation and secure logs, as well as autonomic properties such as self-protection and self-healing. The patterns are applied to HOCL programs following an aspect-oriented approach, where aspects are modelled as transformation functions that add to a program a cross-cutting concern.

1 Introduction

The concept of Virtual Organisation (VO) is given attention by researchers within a wide range of fields, from social anthropology and organisational theory to computer science. Its importance resides in providing an abstraction to represent organisational collaborations, a topic of fresh interest given the current exploitation of Internet to create virtual enterprises [5], or the sharing of resources across different organisations as envisaged by Grid computing [7].

This paper studies the development of VOs when using a chemical programming paradigm. Chemical programming is a computational paradigm inspired by the chemical metaphor, where computation is seen as reactions between molecules in a chemical solution. Examples of chemical-programming frameworks include P-Systems [13], the Higher-Order Chemical Language (HOCL) [1] and Fraglets [14], among others. Potentiality of the paradigm has been shown by its application to solve problems as diverse as page ranking of biochemical databases [12], coordination of services [3], or protocol resilience [15].

A VO can be seen as a temporary or permanent coalition of geographically dispersed organisations that pool resources, capabilities and information in order

R. Guerraoui and F. Petit (Eds.): SSS 2009, LNCS 5873, pp. 75–89, 2009.

to achieve common goals. Autonomicity is an important property in VOs, since coalition members should act autonomously in order to achieve the VO goals. The chemical programming paradigm is very relevant to the programming of autonomic systems as it captures the intuition of a collection of cooperative components which evolve freely according to some predefined constraints (reaction rules). Security is also an important concern in VOs, since such a coalition may include unknown organisations that are untrusted by other VO partners.

We introduce here a method for modelling autonomic and secure VOs in HOCL using aspect-oriented techniques. We have selected HOCL as the language representative of the chemical paradigm, due mainly to its generality, its implicit autonomic property — HOCL is based on the Gamma calculus [1], which is also the foundation of other chemical frameworks such as Fraglets — and its potential application to emerging computing paradigms such as service computing [3]. We define first a set of patterns for HOCL programs, representing security and autonomic properties. Each property is modelled then as an aspect, defined using the patterns, which is weaved following a code pre-processing technique.

The structure of the paper is the following. Section 2 introduces HOCL. Section 3 discusses the autonomic properties of HOCL and describes its application to VOs, exemplified by a system for the generation of digital products. Section 4 presents security patterns for chemical programs. Section 5 describes the use of aspect-oriented techniques in HOCL. Next, section 6 shows how to apply the security patterns by using aspect-oriented programming. Section 7 relates our work with others. Finally, section 8 concludes the paper and highlights future work.

2 The Higher-Order Chemical Language

In this section we introduce the main features of HOCL, referring the reader to [2] for a more complete presentation. A chemical program can be seen as a (symbolic) chemical solution where data is represented by floating molecules and computation by chemical reactions between them. When some molecules match and fulfill a reaction condition, they are replaced by the body of the reaction. That process goes on until an inert solution is reached: the solution is said to be inert when no reaction can occur anymore.

In HOCL, a chemical solution is represented by a multiset and reaction rules specify multiset rewritings. Every entity is a molecule, including reaction rules. A program is a molecule, that is to say, a multiset of atoms $(A_1, \ldots, A_n)$ which can be constants (integers, booleans, etc.), sub-solutions $(\langle M \rangle)$ or reaction rules. Compound molecules (M_1, M_2) are built using the associative and commutative operator ",", which formalises the Brownian motion and can always be used to reorganise molecules. The execution of a chemical program consists in triggering reactions until the solution becomes inert. A reaction involves a reaction rule **replace-one** P **by** M **if** C and a molecule N that satisfies the pattern P and the reaction condition C. The reaction consumes the rule and the molecule N, and produces M. Formally:

$$(\textbf{replace-one } P \textbf{ by } M \textbf{ if } C),\ N \longrightarrow \phi M \quad \text{if } P \text{ } match \text{ } N = \phi \text{ and } \phi C$$

where ϕ is the substitution obtained by matching N with P. It maps every variable defined in P to a sub-molecule from N. For example, the rule in

$$\langle 0,\ 10,\ 8,\ \textbf{replace-one } x \textbf{ by } 9 \textbf{ if } x > 9\rangle$$

can react with 10. They are replaced by 9. The solution becomes the inert solution $\langle 0,\ 9,\ 8\rangle$.

A molecule inside a solution cannot react with a molecule outside the solution (i.e. the construct $\langle . \rangle$ can be seen as a membrane). A HOCL program is a solution which can contain reaction rules that manipulate other molecules (reaction rules, sub-solutions, etc.) of the solution.

In the remaining of the paper, we use some syntactic sugar such as declarations **let** $x = M_1$ **in** M_2 which is equivalent to M_2 where all the free occurrences of x are replaced by M_1. The reaction rules **replace-one** P **by** M **if** C are one-shot: they are consumed when they react. Their variant denoted by **replace** P **by** M **if** C are n-shot, i.e. they do not disappear when they react.

There are usually many possible reactions making the execution of chemical programs highly parallel and non-deterministic. Since reactions involve only a few molecules and react independently of the context, many distinct reactions can occur at the same time. For example, consider the program of Figure 1 that computes the prime numbers lower than 10 using a chemical version of the Eratosthenes' sieve.

let *sieve* = **replace** x, y **by** x **if** x `div` y **in**
$\langle sieve,\ 2, 3, 4, 5, 6, 7, 8, 9, 10\rangle$

Fig. 1. Chemical prime numbers program

The rule *sieve* reacts with two integers x and y such that x divides y, and returns x (i.e. removes y). Initially several reactions are possible, for example $sieve, 2, 8$ (replaced by $sieve, 2$) or $sieve, 3, 9$ (replaced by $sieve, 3$) or $sieve, 2, 10$, etc. The solution becomes inert when the rule *sieve* cannot react with any couple of integers in the solution, that is to say, when the solution contains only prime numbers. The result of the computation in our example is $\langle sieve,\ 2, 3, 5, 7\rangle$.

An important feature of HOCL is the notion of *multiplets*. A multiplet is a finite multiset of identical elements. In this paper, we limit ourselves to multiplets of basic values (integers, booleans, strings). In HOCL multiplets are defined and matched using an exponential notation: if v is a basic value then v^k $(k > 0)$ denotes a multiplet of k elements v. Likewise, for variable x having a basic type, notation x^k denotes a multiplet of k elements. We could also have variables in the exponentiation of constants or patterns, indicating that the size of a multiplet becomes dynamic.

3 Virtual Organisations in HOCL

3.1 Autonomicity in HOCL

Autonomic computing provides a vision in which systems manage themselves according to some predefined goals. The essence of autonomic computing is self-organisation. Like biological systems, autonomic systems maintain and adjust their operation in the face of changing components, workloads, demands and external conditions, such as hardware or software failures, either innocent or malicious. The autonomic system might continually monitor its own use and check for component upgrades. HOCL is very appropriate as a programming model to express programs with autonomic behaviours. The reason is twofold. First, HOCL is intrinsically dynamic: rules are executed until an inert state is reached. When the multiset is modified, then reactions rules are executed to achieve again the inertness. Secondly, the high-order promoted by HOCL allows some policies to be replaced at runtime by new ones. Policies can be expressed by a set of rules that are stored in the multiset and thus can be replaced thanks to the execution of some other rules (high-order). An autonomic system is implemented using control loops that monitor the system and executes a set of operations to keep its parameters within a desired scope. A control loop has four basic steps: *monitor*, *analyse*, *plan* and *execute*. All these steps can be mapped onto chemical objects. *Monitor* and *execute* can be represented by external input/output operations into the multiset by generating molecules whereas *analyse* and *plan* are a set of chemical rules that express the autonomic behavior. A simple autonomic mail system [2] has been developed as an example of programming self-organisation with HOCL.

3.2 Programming Autonomic Virtual Organisations in HOCL

We model here a VO with the goal of generating products resulting from the collaboration of several dispersed organisations, which possesses the following characteristics:

1. The VO aims at producing some complex, sophisticated 'digital' product (e.g. a software system, or some multimedia product).
2. The VO consists of a defined number of members (organisations), each one contributing to the generation of products.
3. The product generation is considered a *knowledge-intensive* and *content-intensive* activity. VO members depend on and need access to several sources of knowledge as well as digital content assets, which they assemble/use to create the product.
4. The production process is structured along some workflow (e.g. a software production process, or a Web/content publishing process), and foresees several phases. Policies may be applied to control access to the assets, which may vary according to the phase or state in the project workflow.

For our scenario, we are assuming a very simple workflow depicted in Figure 2. The workflow consists of four phases. In the *Edit* phase, work is distributed

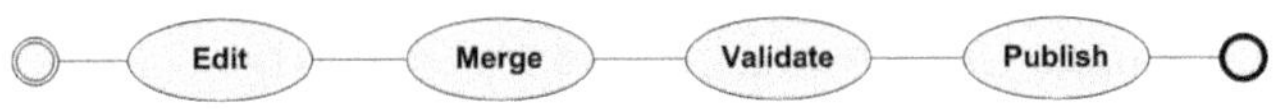

Fig. 2. Workflow process for the VO supporting the generation of a product

among all VO members contributing to the generation of a product. In the *Merge* phase, parts of the product created by each VO member are combined in order to create a global product. Once the global product is created, it is passed to the VO members in the *Validate* phase, so they can "validate" the product. Finally, the process finalises if the product is approved by a determined number of members by sending the product to *Publish*.

For the case of our VO for product generation, the whole VO is modelled as a solution, which contains sub-solutions $S_i{:}\langle\cdots\rangle$ that represent the VO members. The product under construction is modelled as a molecule that could be tagged by another molecule representing the product status (`EDITING`, `EDITED`, `GENERATE`, `VALIDATING`, `VALIDATED`, `ACCEPTING` and `PUBLISHED`). Workflow operations (*edit*, *merge*, *publish*, etc.) are represented as reactions. Table 1 summarises the chemical modelling of the main elements of our VO.

Table 1. Chemical representation of the main elements of a virtual organisation for the collaborative generation of products

VO Concept	Chemical Representation
VO	Solution
VO Member	Sub-solution
Workflow Operation	Reaction
Product	Molecule
Product Status	Molecule

Figure 3 shows the HOCL program for generating a product. It consists of a solution containing all VO members —represented as subsolutions S_i for $i = 1, \cdots, k$, and molecule *GlobalProduct*, the product to be published.

The reaction rule *edit* distributes the global product to all VO members. Here we are assuming the existence of k VO members, where k is a predefined integer constant. Reaction *merge* generates a local product, and marks the contribution of the corresponding member to the product generation by adding constant `GENERATE` to the global solution. It also includes operation $Merge$, which combines both the local and global products. The edition of a product finalises when VO members have contributed, which is represented by having $NumMerges(k)$ copies of molecule `GENERATE`. Function $NumMerges(k)$ is a domain-specific function indicating the number of copies needed to generate a product; if it is the identity function, i.e. equal to k, all participant solutions must contribute to the product generation. Note that we are exploiting here the existence of multiplets in HOCL: molecule $\mathtt{GENERATE}^{NumMerges(k)}$ acts as a synchronisation barrier indicating when reaction *valid* can occur. Reaction

$$
\begin{array}{ll}
\textbf{let } \mathit{publish} = & \textbf{replace } \mathit{GlobalProduct}, \texttt{ACCEPTING}^x, \texttt{GENERATE}^y \\
& \quad \textbf{by } \texttt{PUBLISHED:}\mathit{GlobalProduct} \\
& \quad \textbf{if } x \geq \mathit{MinApproval}(k) \wedge y = \mathit{NumMerges}(k) \\
\textbf{in} & \\
\textbf{let } \mathit{accept} = & \textbf{replace } S{:}\langle \texttt{VALIDATING:}\mathit{Product}\rangle \\
& \quad \textbf{by } S{:}\langle \texttt{VALIDATED}\rangle, \texttt{ACCEPTING} \\
& \quad \textbf{if } \mathit{AgreeProduct}(\mathit{Product}) \\
\textbf{in} & \\
\textbf{let } \mathit{valid} = & \textbf{replace } S{:}\langle \texttt{EDITED}\rangle, \mathit{GlobalProduct}, \texttt{GENERATE}^y \\
& \quad \textbf{by } S{:}\langle \texttt{VALIDATING:}\mathit{GlobalProduct}\rangle, \mathit{GlobalProduct}, \texttt{GENERATE}^y \\
& \quad \textbf{if } y = \mathit{NumMerges}(k) \\
\textbf{in} & \\
\textbf{let } \mathit{merge} = & \textbf{replace } S{:}\langle \texttt{EDITING:}\mathit{Product}\rangle, \mathit{GlobalProduct} \\
& \quad \textbf{by } S{:}\langle \texttt{EDITED}\rangle, \mathit{Merge}(\mathit{Product}, \mathit{GlobalProduct}), \texttt{GENERATE} \\
& \quad \textbf{if } \mathit{FinishProduct}(\mathit{Product}) \\
\textbf{in} & \\
\textbf{let } \mathit{edit} = & \textbf{replace } S{:}\langle\rangle, \mathit{GlobalProduct} \\
& \quad \textbf{by } S{:}\langle \texttt{EDITING:}\mathit{GlobalProduct}\rangle, \mathit{GlobalProduct} \\
\textbf{in} & \\
\multicolumn{2}{l}{\langle S_1{:}\langle\rangle, \cdots, S_k{:}\langle\rangle, \ \mathit{GlobalProduct}, \ \mathit{edit}, \ \mathit{merge}, \ \mathit{valid}, \ \mathit{accept}, \ \mathit{publish}\rangle}
\end{array}
$$

Fig. 3. HOCL Program for collaborative generation of a digital product

valid distributes the final *GlobalProduct* among the members in order to get their approval. Reaction *accept* allows a VO member to vote for the approval of the product, which results in adding molecule `ACCEPTING` in the global solution. The whole process finalises as soon as $MinApproval(k)$ VO members approve the final product by executing reaction *publish*, which sends the final product to publishing. Function $MinApproval(k)$ is an abstraction of the protocol used to decide when to publish a product; for instance, if it is equal to $ceil(k/2)$, we would be using a majority vote protocol.

4 Patterns for Chemical Programming

A composition pattern is a design model that specifies the design of a cross-cutting requirement independently of any design it may potentially cross-cut, and how that design may be re-used wherever it may be required [6]. In this section we define composition patterns for HOCL programs. These patterns serve as templates that guide the definition of aspects by instantiating them with domain-specific information. We define patterns for important security properties, namely *Authorisation* and *Security Logs*; as well as patterns for autonomic properties such as *Self-Protection* and *Self-Healing*.

Authorisation Pattern. Authorisation is concerned with the verification that an entity can perform a particular action. In the context of chemical programs, authorisation refers to the verification that a reaction could occur in a solution.

$$\begin{array}{l} authoZ(S,R) \mathrel{\widehat{=}} \textbf{let } R = \textbf{replace } P \textbf{ by } M \\ \qquad\qquad\qquad\qquad\qquad\quad \textbf{if } C \wedge Authorised(S,R) \\ \qquad\qquad\qquad \textbf{in } S{:}\langle \omega, R \rangle \end{array}$$

Fig. 4. HOCL Pattern for Authorisation

The authorisation pattern, described in Figure 4, indicates that whenever a solution S reacts using reaction R, the authorisation condition $Authorised(S, R)$ holds.

The authorisation condition is considered as a generic condition that should be instantiated with domain-specific information. In this paper, we are interested in defining authorisation for three particular cases of attributed-based authorisation: role-based access control, authorisation based on trust values, and authorisation based on environmental conditions such as date, time, etc.

In the case of role-based access control, we associate solutions to roles and indicate which reactions can be executed by roles. Let *SolutionRole* be a predicate associating a solution with a role, and *RoleReaction* a predicate associating a role with a reaction. In this case the *Authorisation* condition takes the form $SolutionRole(S, Rol) \wedge RoleReaction(Rol, R)$.

In the case of authorisation based on trust values, we assume there is a function $TrustValue(S)$ returning the trust value associated to a solution S. The *Authorisation* condition is simply a predicate comparing the trust value of a solution with a particular value.

In the case of authorisation based on environmental conditions, we assume there are predicates such as *Date* and *Time* which could restrict when a reaction occurs.

Security Log Pattern. In the case of security-critical operations, it might be required to maintain a security log of such operations. In chemical programming, this corresponds to storing in a log a reaction as well as the changes it has produced. Let R = **replace** P **by** M **if** C be a reaction. The security log pattern, described in Figure 5, indicates that whenever reaction R happens, it is stored in solution *Log* a molecule with information about the solutions and molecules participating in R. The *Log* solution can be seen as a trusted third party in charge of storing and maintaining the security log.

$$\begin{array}{l} logging(R) \mathrel{\widehat{=}} \textbf{let } R = \textbf{replace } P,\ Log{:}\langle \omega \rangle \textbf{ by } M,\ Log{:}\langle \omega, R{:}P{:}M \rangle \textbf{ if } C \\ \qquad\qquad\quad\ \textbf{in } S{:}\langle \omega, R \rangle \end{array}$$

Fig. 5. HOCL Pattern for Security Logging

Self-Protection Pattern. Self-protection refers to the ability of anticipating problems, and taking steps to avoid or mitigate them. It can be decomposed in two phases: a detection phase and a reaction phase [9]. The detection phase

$$selfprot(S, R) \mathrel{\hat{=}} \textbf{let } R = \textbf{replace } P, Q \textbf{ by } Protect(Q) \textbf{ if } Filter(P) \textbf{ in } S{:}\langle\omega, R\rangle$$

Fig. 6. HOCL Pattern for Self-Protection

consists mainly in filtering data (pattern matching). The reaction phase consists in preventing offensive data from spreading and sometimes also in counter-attacking. This mechanism can easily be expressed with the condition-reaction scheme of the chemical programming. Figure 6 shows the self-protection pattern. Function *Filter* rule out undesirable data; on the other hand, function *Protect* represents the application of a protection mechanism to the rest of the data.

Self-Healing Pattern. Another important autonomic property is self-healing, which refers to the automatic discovery and correction of faults in a system. We define a pattern for the case in which a partner in a VO — represented as a solution— fails by replacing it by a *back-up partner*. The back-up partner offers his own resources while the original partner cannot contribute to the VO objective. Functions $Failure(S)$ and $Recover(S)$ are associated to the system functionality capable of detecting whether a system has failed or recovered from a previous problem.

$$fail(S) \mathrel{\hat{=}} \textbf{replace } S{:}\,\langle\omega\rangle \textbf{ by } S_{backup}{:}\,\langle\omega\rangle \textbf{ if } Failure(S)$$
$$repair(S) \mathrel{\hat{=}} \textbf{replace } S_{backup}{:}\,\langle\omega\rangle \textbf{ by } S{:}\,\langle\omega\rangle \textbf{ if } Recover(S)$$

Fig. 7. HOCL Pattern for Self-Healing

5 Aspects for Chemical Programming

Aspect-oriented programming (AOP) is a paradigm that explicitly promotes separation of concerns. In the context of security, aspects mean that the main program should not need to encode security information; instead, it should be moved into a separate, independent piece of code [16].

AOP is based on the idea that computer systems are better programmed by separately specifying the various concerns of a system and some description of their relationships, and then relying on mechanisms in the underlying AOP environment to weave or compose them together into a coherent program. The goal of AOP is to make designs and code more modular, meaning the concerns are localised rather than scattered and have well-defined interfaces with the rest of the system. This provides the usual benefits of modularity, including making it possible to reason about different concerns in relative isolation, making them (un)pluggable, amenable to separate development, and so forth.

This section introduces the main concepts of aspects and relates them with chemical programming.

5.1 Basic Concepts on AOP

Cross-cutting concerns are concerns whose implementation cuts across a number of program components. This results in problems when changes to the concern have to be made —the code to be changed is not localised but is in different places across the system. Cross-cutting concerns can range from high level notions like security and quality of service to low-level notions such as caching and buffering. They can be functional, like features or business rules, or nonfunctional, such as synchronization and transaction management. The following are the main terminology used in AOP:

- *Join point*: Point of execution in the application at which cross-cutting concern needs to be applied. In the case of chemical programming, join points could be associated with reactions where the concerns need to be applied.
- *Advice*: This is the additional code that one wants to apply to an existing model. In the case of chemical programming, advice are applied to joint points (reactions) by adding/replacing some of the components of the reaction.
- *Aspect*: An aspect is an abstraction which implements a concern; it is the combination of a join point and an advice.
- *Weaving*: The incorporation of advice code at the specific joint points. There are three approaches to aspect weaving: source code pre-processing, link-time weaving, and execution-time weaving.

There is an additional concept called the *Kind of an Aspect* indicating if an advice is applied before, after, or around a join point. Since there is not a notion of sequentiality (execution order) in a chemical program, we do not exploit this feature. All aspects for chemical programming can be seen as around aspects.

5.2 Defining Aspects for Chemical Programming

In this work we have followed a code pre-processing technique to weave aspects in a chemical program. To do so, we represent aspects as a collection of transformation functions Ψ_{C_i}, each one modelling a different cross-cutting concern C_i. Each function Ψ_{C_i} is applied to a reaction and returns a modified version of the reaction that has been transformed according to the aspect.

Let *Reaction* denote the set of reaction rules and Σ denote the state of a chemical program. State here refers to the solution and molecules participating in a program. The signature of a transformation function Ψ_C is defined as follows: $\Psi_C: Reaction \times \Sigma \rightarrow Reaction$

As a way of illustration, let us define transformation Ψ_{RBAC} that applies the role-based authorisation concern to a reaction, indicating that a solution could react using a particular reaction if it is playing a role in the system. Function Ψ_{RBAC} takes as input a reaction, a solution name, and a role name, producing a new version of the reaction where the condition has been strengthened with the predicates *SolutionRole* and *RoleReaction*, as presented in the authorisation pattern defined in sub-section 4. Upper part of Figure 8 shows the definition of

$$\Psi_{RBAC}\colon \mathit{Reaction} \times \mathit{SolutionName} \times \mathit{RoleName} \rightarrow \mathit{Reaction}$$

$$\begin{array}{l} \forall R\colon \mathit{Reaction},\, S\colon \mathit{SolutionName},\, \mathit{Rol}\colon \mathit{RolName} \\ R = \textbf{replace}\ P\ \textbf{by}\ M\ \textbf{if}\ C \quad \rightarrow \\ \quad \Psi_{RBAC}(R, S, \mathit{Rol}) = R = \textbf{replace}\ P\ \textbf{by}\ M \\ \qquad\qquad \textbf{if}\ C \wedge \mathit{SolutionRole}(S, \mathit{Rol}) \wedge \mathit{RoleReaction}(\mathit{Rol}, R) \end{array}$$

$$\begin{array}{l} \Psi_{RBAC}(\mathit{merge}, S, \mathit{Editor}) \quad = \\ \quad \mathit{merge} = \textbf{replace}\ S\colon \langle \texttt{EDITING:}\mathit{Product}\rangle\ ,\ \mathit{GlobalProduct} \\ \qquad\qquad \textbf{by}\ S\colon \langle \texttt{EDITED}\rangle\ ,\ \mathit{Merge}(\mathit{Product}, \mathit{GlobalProduct}),\ \texttt{GENERATE} \\ \qquad\qquad \textbf{if}\ \mathit{FinishProduct}(\mathit{Product}) \wedge \\ \qquad\qquad\quad \mathit{SolutionRole}(S, \mathit{Editor}) \ \wedge\ \mathit{RoleReaction}(\mathit{Editor}, \mathit{merge}) \end{array}$$

Fig. 8. Weaving an aspect: applying the RBAC aspect to reaction *merge*

the transformation function Ψ_{RBAC}. Let us assume that the *merge* reaction in the VO system presented in Figure 3 can react when the solution containing it is playing the *Editor* role. Lower part of Figure 8 shows the result of applying the transformation function Ψ_{RBAC} to *merge*.

6 Applying Patterns and AOP to 'Chemical' VOs

In general, our approach for applying AOP techniques to chemical programs comprises the following steps. First, requirements for the system under construction are defined. Second, the requirements are modelled as aspect functions, following the patterns introduced in section 4. Third, we define the join points where the aspects functions should be applied. Finally, aspects are weaved producing a new chemical program. The rest of this section describes the application of such approach to the VO for product generation introduced in section 3.2.

Requirements for Product Generation. The system for product generation has the following security requirements:

1. Organisations participating in the VO could play the roles *Editor* or *Validator*.
2. VO members playing the role *Editor* can execute only operations related to the edit and merge phases of the workflow.
3. VO members playing the role *Validator* can execute only operations related to the validate phases of the workflow.
4. Acceptance of a product is considered a security-critical operation requiring to be registered in a security log.
5. Acceptance is allowed only for those VO members with a trust value higher than 0.5.
6. The system must check automatically that any product to be merged is free of virus.
7. The VO member assigned to location 1, i.e. the member identified as S_1, is considered critical one and must be replaced by a back up member in case of failure.

Ψ_{RBAC}: *Reaction* × *SolutionName* × *RoleName* → *Reaction*

∀*R*: *Reaction*, *S*: *SolutionName*, *Rol*: *RolName*
$R =$ **replace** P **by** M **if** C →
$\Psi_{RBAC}(R, S, Rol) = R =$ **replace** P **by** M
if $C \wedge SolutionRole(S, Rol) \wedge RoleReaction(Rol, R)$

Ψ_{TRUST}: *Reaction* × *SolutionName* × $\Re$ → *Reaction*

∀*R*: *Reaction*, *S*: *SolutionName*, *t*: $\Re$
$R =$ **replace** P **by** M **if** C →
$\Psi_{TRUST}(R, S, t) = R =$ **replace** P **by** M
if $C \wedge TrustValue(S) > t$

Ψ_{LOG}: *Reaction* → *Reaction*

∀*R*: *Reaction*
$R =$ **replace** $S{:}P$ **by** M **if** C →
$\Psi_{LOG}(R) = R =$ **replace** $S{:}P,\ Log{:}\langle\omega\rangle$
by $M,\ Log{:}\langle\omega,\ S{:}R\rangle$
if C

Fig. 9. Aspect functions for securing the VO for product generation

Requirements 1 to 5 are classical security requirements; requirement 6 is a self-protection one; and requirement 7 is a self-healing requirement.

Aspect Transformation Functions. Figure 9 shows the aspect functions defined for our VO to deal with the security requirements presented above, and Figure 10 illustrates the aspect functions defined for self-protection and self-healing requirements.

In Figure 9, function Ψ_{RBAC} models role-based authorisation, following the authorisation pattern introduced in sub-section 4. We are assuming the underlying execution system includes functions *SolutionRole*, associating a solution with a role, and *RoleReaction*, associating a role with the reaction that can perform. Likewise, function Ψ_{TRUST} models authorisation based on trust values, following also the pattern from sub-section 4. Here, it is assumed the existence of function *TrustValue*, returning the trust value of a solution. Finally, function Ψ_{LOG} models the secure log concern.

In Figure 10, function $\Psi_{NOVIRUS}$ models self-protection according to the pattern presented in subsection 4. Here, we are assuming there is a system function called $NoVirus$ in charge of checking there is not virus in a digital product. On the other hand, functions Ψ_{FAIL} and $\Psi_{RECOVER}$ model self-healing according to the pattern presented previously.

Defining Join Points. Table 2 illustrates the joint points for our VO according to the requirements defined previously.

$\Psi_{NOVIRUS}$: *Reaction* → *Reaction*

$\forall R$: *Reaction*

$R =$ **replace** S: ⟨EDITING:P⟩ , ω **by** S: ⟨EDITED⟩ , M **if** C →
$\Psi_{NOVIRUS}(R) = R =$ **replace** S: ⟨EDITING:P⟩ , ω
by S: ⟨EDITED⟩ , M
if $C \wedge NoVirus(P)$

Ψ_{FAIL}: *SolutionName* × *SolutionName* → *Reaction*
$\Psi_{RECOVER}$: *SolutionName* × *SolutionName* → *Reaction*

$\forall S, S_{backup}$: *SolutionName*
$\Psi_{FAIL}(S, S_{backup}) = fail =$ **replace** S: ⟨ω⟩ **by** S_{backup}: ⟨ω⟩ **if** $Failure(S)$
$\Psi_{RECOVER}(S, S_{backup}) = recover =$ **replace** S_{backup}: ⟨ω⟩ **by** S: ⟨ω⟩ **if** $Recover(S)$

Fig. 10. Aspect functions for self-protection and self-healing in the VO for product generation

Table 2. Join points to apply aspect functions to the product generation VO

Requirement	Aspect	Requirement	Aspect
1, 2	$\Psi_{RBAC}(edit,\ S,\ Editor)$	5	$\Psi_{TRUST}(accept,\ S,\ 0.5)$
1, 2	$\Psi_{RBAC}(merge,\ S,\ Editor)$	6	$\Psi_{NOVIRUS}(merge)$
1, 3	$\Psi_{RBAC}(valid,\ S,\ Validator)$	7	$\Psi_{FAIL}(S_1, S_{1_{backup}})$
1, 3	$\Psi_{RBAC}(accept,\ S,\ Validator)$	7	$\Psi_{RECOVER}(S_1, S_{1_{backup}})$
4	$\Psi_{LOG}(accept)$		

At this stage, we can see the modularity obtained by applying AOP techniques. Any change in the security requirements implies only changes in the definition of aspect functions and join points, without altering the business logic of the program. For instance, if the requirement that the *accept* reaction should be performed only by solutions with their trust above a particular value is removed, then the only changes required are to remove Ψ_{TRUST} function and to eliminate the corresponding rule in Table 2.

Aspect Weaving. Finally, the aspects are weaved producing a new program. The chemical program resulting after weaving the aspects defined in Table 2 is presented in Figure 11. For instance, comparing reaction *merge* with the original version presented in Figure 3, we can notice that the condition of the rule has been strengthened restricting the execution only to solutions playing the role *Editor* and when the product to be generated is free of any virus.

7 Related Work

The work presented here has been inspired by Viega, Bloch and Chandra's work on applying aspect-oriented programming to security [16]. They have developed an

$$
\begin{array}{ll}
\textbf{let } \mathit{publish} = & \textbf{replace } \mathit{GlobalProduct}, \mathtt{ACCEPTING}^x, \mathtt{GENERATE}^y \\
& \quad \textbf{by } \mathtt{PUBLISHED}{:}\mathit{GlobalProduct} \\
& \quad \textbf{if } x \geq \mathit{MinApproval}(k) \ \wedge \ y = \mathit{NumMerges}(k) \\
\textbf{in} & \\
\textbf{let } \mathit{accept} = & \textbf{replace } S{:}\langle \mathtt{VALIDATING}{:}\mathit{Product}\rangle, \ \mathit{Log}{:}\langle\omega\rangle \\
& \quad \textbf{by } S{:}\langle \mathtt{VALIDATED}\rangle, \mathtt{ACCEPTING}, \ \mathit{Log}{:}\langle\omega, \ S{:}\mathit{accept}\rangle \\
& \quad \textbf{if } \mathit{AgreeProduct}(\mathit{Product}) \ \wedge \\
& \qquad \mathit{SolutionRole}(S, \mathit{Validator}) \ \wedge \ \mathit{RoleReaction}(\mathit{Editor}, \mathit{accept}) \ \wedge \\
& \qquad \mathit{TrustValue}(S) > 0.5 \\
\textbf{in} & \\
\textbf{let } \mathit{valid} = & \textbf{replace } S{:}\langle \mathtt{EDITED}\rangle, \mathit{GlobalProduct}, \mathtt{GENERATE}^y \\
& \quad \textbf{by } S{:}\langle \mathtt{VALIDATING}{:}\mathit{GlobalProduct}\rangle, \mathit{GlobalProduct}, \mathtt{GENERATE}^y \\
& \quad \textbf{if } y = \mathit{NumMerges}(k) \ \wedge \\
& \qquad \mathit{SolutionRole}(S, \mathit{Validator}) \ \wedge \ \mathit{RoleReaction}(\mathit{Validator}, \mathit{valid}) \\
\textbf{in} & \\
\textbf{let } \mathit{merge} = & \textbf{replace } S{:}\langle \mathtt{EDITING}{:}\mathit{Product}\rangle, \mathit{GlobalProduct} \\
& \quad \textbf{by } S{:}\langle \mathtt{EDITED}\rangle, \mathit{Merge}(\mathit{Product}, \mathit{GlobalProduct}), \mathtt{GENERATE} \\
& \quad \textbf{if } \mathit{FinishProduct}(\mathit{Product}) \ \wedge \\
& \qquad \mathit{NoVirus}(\mathit{Product}) \ \wedge \\
& \qquad \mathit{SolutionRole}(S, \mathit{Editor}) \ \wedge \ \mathit{RoleReaction}(\mathit{Editor}, \mathit{merge}) \\
\textbf{in} & \\
\textbf{let } \mathit{edit} = & \textbf{replace } S{:}\langle\rangle, \mathit{GlobalProduct} \\
& \quad \textbf{by } S{:}\langle \mathtt{EDITING}{:}\mathit{GlobalProduct}\rangle, \mathit{GlobalProduct} \\
& \quad \textbf{if } \mathit{SolutionRole}(S, \mathit{Editor}) \ \wedge \ \mathit{RoleReaction}(\mathit{Editor}, \mathit{edit}) \\
\textbf{in} & \\
\textbf{let } \mathit{fail} = & \textbf{replace } S_1{:}\langle\omega\rangle \\
& \quad \textbf{by } S_{1_{backup}}{:}\langle\omega\rangle \\
& \quad \textbf{if } \mathit{Failure}(S_1) \\
\textbf{in} & \\
\textbf{let } \mathit{recover} = & \textbf{replace } S_{1_{backup}}{:}\langle\omega\rangle \\
& \quad \textbf{by } S_1{:}\langle\omega\rangle \\
& \quad \textbf{if } \mathit{Recover}(S_1) \\
\textbf{in} & \\
\multicolumn{2}{l}{\langle S_1{:}\langle\rangle, \cdots, S_k{:}\langle\rangle, \ \mathit{GlobalProduct}, \ \mathit{fail}, \ \mathit{recover}, \ \mathit{edit}, \ \mathit{merge}, \ \mathit{valid}, \ \mathit{accept}, \ \mathit{publish}\rangle}
\end{array}
$$

Fig. 11. HOCL program for the VO system for product generation after weaving aspects

aspect-oriented extension to the C programming language following also a transformational approach, where aspects are defined independently of the main application, and are then weaved into a single program at compilation time. Their emphasis is on security, developing aspects to replace insecure function calls by secure ones. Our approach follows a transformational approach as proposed by Viega, with the difference that the aspect definition is guided by the existence of security patterns. Previous work on the application of aspect-oriented techniques to chemical programming include [10,11]. In [10], Mentré *et al* present the design of shared-virtual-memory protocols using the Gamma formalism; then, aspect-oriented techniques are used to translate this design into a concrete implementation, modelling cross-cutting concerns such as control and data representation.

Comparing with our work, they also used a transformational approach, weaving at compilation time a Gamma program to produce an automaton; however, they do not represent cross-cutting concerns as patterns. The work by Mousavi *et al* [11] centred on extending Gamma with aspect-oriented concepts, including aspects for timing and distribution. For each aspect, they present new syntactic constructors and give them a structured operational semantics. The weaving process map the different aspects into a common formal semantics domain based on timed process algebra with relative intervals and delayable actions. Our work has the advantage that there is not need of changing the underlying semantic model (all our aspects are in HOCL) and exploiting the existence of composition patterns.

8 Conclusion and Future Work

This paper has described an approach to program autonomic and secure Virtual Organisations (VOs) when using the Higher-Order Chemical Language (HOCL). Our approach is based on composition patterns and aspect-oriented techniques. We represent aspects as a collection of transformation functions, each one modelling a different cross-cutting concern. The functions are applied (weaved) to a HOCL program in order to generate a new program that include the concerns.

Our working example has been a VO for the production of digital product, and the cross-cutting concerns have been security properties such as attribute-based authorisation and security logs, as well as autonomic properties such as self-protection and self-healing. The approach comprises the following steps. First, security requirements for the system under construction are defined. Second, the requirements are modelled as transformational aspect functions following a library of compositional patterns. Third, it is defined the join points where the aspects functions should be applied. Finally, aspects are weaved producing a new chemical program.

There are several avenues to follow as future work. Firstly, we are currently studying the weaving of several aspects on the same reaction, analysing conditions that guarantee properties such as commutativity and associativity of aspects. Secondly, we plan to investigate patterns for weaving aspects at run-time, exploiting the high-order potentiality of HOCL. Thirdly, we are interested in evaluating the effectiveness of our approach to improve modularisation of cross-cutting concerns in HOCL; an initial step is to adapt quantitative methods to evaluate AOP [8]. Finally, there are several similarities between chemical programming and other evolutionary approaches such as genetic programming [4]; we plan to investigate how our approach to secure and autonomic cooperations can be applied when using genetic programming.

Acknowledgments

This work has been partially funded by the EU CoreGRID (IST FP6 No 004265) and GridTrust (IST FP6 No 033817) projects. We would like to thank Yann Radenac and Benjamin Aziz for comments to early drafts of this paper.

References

1. Banâtre, J.-P., Fradet, P., Le Métayer, D.: Gamma and the Chemical Reaction Model: Fifteen Years After. In: Calude, C.S., Pun, G., Rozenberg, G., Salomaa, A. (eds.) Multiset Processing. LNCS, vol. 2235, pp. 17–44. Springer, Heidelberg (2001)
2. Banâtre, J.-P., Fradet, P., Radenac, Y.: Chemical Specification of Autonomic Systems. In: Proceedings of the 13th International Conference on Intelligent and Adaptive Systems and Software Engineering (IASSE 2004) (July 2004)
3. Banâtre, J.-P., Priol, T., Radenac, Y.: Service Orchestration Using the Chemical Metaphor. In: Brinkschulte, U., Givargis, T., Russo, S. (eds.) SEUS 2008. LNCS, vol. 5287, pp. 79–89. Springer, Heidelberg (2008)
4. Banzhaf, W., Koza, J.R., Ryan, C., Spector, L., Jacob, C.: Genetic Programming. IEEE Intelligent Systems and their Applications 15(3), 74–84 (2000)
5. Camarihna-Matos, L.M., Afsarmanesh, H. (eds.): Collaborative Networked Organisations — A Research Agenda for Emerging Business Models. Kluwer, Dordrecht (2004)
6. Clarke, S., Walker, R.J.: Composition Patterns: An Approach to Designing Reusable Aspects. In: International Conference on Software Engineering (2001)
7. Foster, I., Kesselman, C., Tuecke, S.: The Anatomy of the Grid: Enabling Scalable Virtual Organizations. Int. Journal of Supercomputer Applications 15(3) (2001)
8. Garcia, A., Sant Anna, C., Figueiredo, E., Kulesza, U., Lucena, C., von Staa, A.: Modularizing Design Patterns with Aspects: A Quantitative Study. In: Rashid, A., Aksit, M. (eds.) Transactions on Aspect-Oriented Software Development I. LNCS, vol. 3880, pp. 36–74. Springer, Heidelberg (2006)
9. Kephart, J.O., Chess, D.M.: The Vision of Autonomic Computing. Computer 36(1), 41–50 (2003)
10. Mentré, D., Le Métayer, D., Priol, T.: Formalization and Verification of Coherence Protocols with the Gamma Framework. In: Symposium on Software Engineering for Parallel and Distributed Systems (PDSE 2000), pp. 105–113 (2000)
11. Mousavi, M.R., Reniers, M.A., Basten, T., Chaudron, M.R.V.: Separation of Concerns in the Formal Design of Real-Time Shared Data-Space Systems. In: ACSD, pp. 71–81. IEEE Computer Society, Los Alamitos (2003)
12. Muskulus, M.: Application of Page Ranking in P Systems. In: 9th Workshop on Membrane Computing. IEEE Computer Society, Los Alamitos (2008)
13. Păun, G.: Membrane Computing. An Introduction. Springer, Berlin (2002)
14. Tschudin, C.: Fraglets - a Metabolistic Execution Model for Communication Protocols. In: 2nd Annual Symposium on Autonomous Intelligent Networks and Systems (AINS). IEEE Computer Society Press, Los Alamitos (2003)
15. Tschudin, C., Yamamoto, L.: A Metabolic Approach to Protocol Resilience. In: Smirnov, M. (ed.) WAC 2004. LNCS, vol. 3457, pp. 191–206. Springer, Heidelberg (2005)
16. Viega, J., Bloch, J.T., Chandra, P.: Applying Aspect-Oriented Programming to Security. Cutter IT Journal 14(2), 31–39 (2001)

Making Population Protocols Self-stabilizing

Joffroy Beauquier[1,*], Janna Burman[2,**], and Shay Kutten[2,***]

[1] University Paris Sud, LRI, UMR 8623, Orsay, F-91405
jb@lri.fr

[2] Dept. of Industrial Engineering & Management, Technion, Haifa 32000, Israel
{bjanna,kutten}@technion.ac.il

Abstract. Developing *self-stabilizing* solutions is considered to be more challenging and complicated than developing classical solutions, where a proper initialization of the variables can be assumed. This remark holds for a large variety of models. Hence, to ease the task of the developers, some automatic techniques have been proposed to design self-stabilizing algorithms. In this paper, we propose an *automatic transformer* for algorithms in *population protocols model*. This model introduced recently for networks with a large number of resource-limited mobile agents. For our purposes, we use a variant of this model. Mainly, we assume agents having characteristics (e.g., moving speed, communication radius) affecting their intercommunication "speed" and considered through the notion of *cover time*. The automatic transformer takes as an input an algorithm solving a static problem and outputs a self-stabilizing algorithm for the same problem. We prove that our transformer is correct and we analyze its stabilization complexity.

Keywords: population protocols, cover time, self-stabilization, transformer.

1 Introduction

Mobile sensor networks have been developed recently in applications ranging from environment monitoring to emergency search-and-rescue operations. For instance, ZebraNet [17] is a habitat monitoring application where sensors are attached to zebras and collect biometric information (e.g., heart rate and body temperature) and information about their behavior and migration patterns (via GPS). All zebras in the population meet each other and ZebraNet's agents (zebras' attached sensors) send data to peer agents. Each agent stores its own sensor data as well as data of other sensors that were in range in the past. They upload data to a base station whenever it is near by. Another example, where mobile

* The work of this author was partially supported by grants from Grand Large project, INRIA Saclay.

** *Contact author.* The work of this author was partially supported by grants from Israel Science Foundation.

*** The work of this author was partially supported by grants from Israel Science Foundation.

R. Guerraoui and F. Petit (Eds.): SSS 2009, LNCS 5873, pp. 90–104, 2009.

sensors move in a more predictable manner, is EMMA project [18] - a pollution monitoring network of sensors attached to different kinds of public transport vehicles. In EMMA, agents may share information whenever two vehicles meet and later, forward it to a central server at a major bus or train stop.

As mobile sensors networks have their own specificity, attempts have been made for developing specific models. Angluin et al. [2] have proposed the population protocols model to describe networks of tiny mobile agents, where the size of the population is large and possibly unknown. Each agent is represented as a finite state machine. Agents are anonymous and move in an asynchronous way. More precisely, the assumptions about the motion of the agents are that it is "passive (not under the control of the sensors), sufficiently rapid and unpredictable for stable routing strategies to be infeasible, and that each pair of sensors will repeatedly be close enough to communicate..." [2]. It has been emphasized that, due to the very nature of potential applications, the available memory in each sensor has to be small. It has been less often stressed that such sensors are exposed to failures. In this paper, we address the latter problem too.

It was shown in [4] that the set of applications that can be solved in the original population protocols model of [2] is rather limited. Hence, various extensions were suggested to the model of [2] (e.g., [15,9,12,3]). In [12], an oracle for eventual leader detection is assumed, and even with the help of oracle, it is shown that constructing uniform self-stabilizing leader election in (communication) rings is impossible when a local fairness is used (somewhat weaker fairness than in [2]). In the present paper, we consider a variant of population protocols that enables us to construct a general automatic transformer that transforms a non-self-stabilizing population protocol into its self-stabilizing version.

The model we use here has been introduced in [7]. In this model, a complete communication graph is considered and each agent v is allocated with a *cover time*, $\mathbf{cv}_v$. The cover time is an abstraction of agent's intercommunication/mobility characteristics such as physical speed, movement pattern, frequencies to visit different places, communication range or reliability of a sensor. For instance, in ZebraNet, it can be expected that grown up (or healthy) zebras move faster than calf (or ill animals) and thus, have a smaller cover time. See Sec. 2.2 for details on the cover time. In addition to the cover times, we assume a distinguishable agent, the *base station* (BS), which is resource-unlimited in contrast with the other agents. Note that this is a natural assumption, because an agent as BS is present in many sensor network applications, and even in the original population protocols model [2], BS is assumed to start all the agents simultaneously by a transmission of a global signal. In addition, a distinguishable agent is used in other extensions of population protocols (e.g., [9,3]).

Self-stabilization deals with transient failures and is related to the self-* techniques. The transient failures can corrupt the states of the agents, but not the code of the algorithm they execute. Note that dynamic events, in which the set of agents changes, can be modeled as transient failures. After an arbitrary number of transient failures a self-stabilizing system recovers, by itself and without any external intervention and in a bounded time, to a correct behavior. In the model, it is assumed that all the transient failures happen at the beginning of the execution (the next ones could occur only in a sufficiently long time). That is equivalent to consider that the system is started in any possible configuration. In the sequel, we will use the term *classical* for an algorithm assuming initialization, in contrast to a self-stabilizing algorithm.

Self-stabilizing population protocols were studied in [5] and [12]. There, variants of population protocols (such as assuming complete or ring communication graphs, local fairness, or assuming an oracle for eventual leader detection [12]) are considered and some self-stabilizing protocols for problems like leader election and token circulation are given. The main difference with these works is that we are not concerned in specific self-stabilizing solutions, but in a general transformer that converts any algorithm that works in a failure-free environment into a self-stabilizing one.

Developing self-stabilizing solutions (and proving them) is considered to be more challenging and complicated than developing classical ones. Thus, it is desirable to lighten the task of designers by providing automatic transformers, that receive an input algorithm (that is correct when initialized properly) and output its self-stabilizing version. Numerous self-stabilizing transformers has been designed and studied (cf., for instance, [1,6,10,13,14]) but, to the best of our knowledge, up to now, no one concerns population protocols. Note that the transformer presented in [11] deals with crash faults as well as transient faults, but it assumes a bound on the number of these faults, contrary to the common assumption made in self-stabilization.

An extended version of this paper appears on the web [8]. It mainly extends the paper by giving examples of problems and their solutions subject to the transformation.

2 The Model

2.1 Transition System

A *system*, $\mathcal{S}$, is given as a set, A, of agents , where $|A| = \mathbf{n}$ and $\mathbf{n}$ is unknown to agents. As in [9], among the agents, there is a distinguishable one, the *base station* (BS), which is (usually) non-mobile[1] and can be resource-unlimited in contrast with the other agents. All the other agents are finite-state, anonymous and referred in the paper as *mobile*.

Population protocols can be modeled as transition systems. An agent is modeled as a set of *states* and a set of *transitions* between states. The state of an agent is the sequence of the values of its variables. The transitions are of the form $(s_i, s_j) \rightarrow (s'_i, s'_j)$, where s_i and s'_i are two states of agent P_i, and s_j and s'_j two states of another agent P_j. A transition can be interpreted as follows: when P_i meets agent P_j , denoted by *event* (P_i, P_j), they communicate and exchange values, and as a result, P_i and P_j set their states to s'_i and s'_j respectively. A *configuration* is a vector of states of all the agents. We extend the transitions

[1] If BS is mobile, it will not change the analysis in this paper.

between states to configurations as follows. First, without loss of generality and as in [2], we assume that no two events happen "simultaneously". Then, there is a transition between two configurations C and C', iff there is a transition $(s_i, s_j) \to (s'_i, s'_j)$ for two agents P_i and P_j. The states of all the other ($\neq P_i, P_j$) agents are identical, in C and C'.

An *execution* e of $\mathcal{S}$ is a sequence of couples (configuration, transition): $(C_0, t_0)(C_1, t_1)(C_2, t_2)\ldots$ such that C_{i+1} is obtained from C_i by the transition t_i. An execution is said to be *finite*, by convention, iff from some point any applicable transition doesn't change the configuration. This configuration is said to be *terminal.* When a terminal configuration is reached, we say that the *termination* has occurred. Each execution corresponds to a unique sequence of events. If an execution e is finite, its *length*, denoted by $|e|$ is the minimum number of events until the termination.

Intuitively, it is convenient to view executions as if a *scheduler* (an adversary) "chooses" which two agents participate in the next event. Formally, a scheduler $\mathcal{D}$ is a predicate on the sequences of events. A *schedule* of $\mathcal{D}$ is a sequence of events that satisfies predicate $\mathcal{D}$. A scheduler $\mathcal{D}$ is said to be *fair*, iff for every agent x, in any infinite schedule of $\mathcal{D}$, x is chosen by $\mathcal{D}$ infinitely many times. This *fairness* is somewhat weaker (and more common in the literature) than the one used in the model of [2]. Refer to, e.g., [5,12] for discussion on fairness.

As in [19], a *specification* $\mathcal{P}$ of a problem is a predicate on the executions. We say that an algorithm $\mathcal{A}$ solves the specification $\mathcal{P}$, iff any execution of $\mathcal{A}$ satisfies the predicate $\mathcal{P}$. The specifications we consider here not only ask for termination, but also for a *property of the terminal configuration* of an execution. This property is given as a predicate on a subset of variables which are called *output variables.* We call *legal* a terminal configuration satisfying the property of terminal configuration. In a legal configuration, output variables are said to be *correct.* We call this type of specification a *static problem.*

Self-Stabilization. We adopt the definitions related to self-stabilization of [19], in particular for the notions of *convergence* and *correctness.* Classical algorithms assume that every execution is started from an initial configuration. That is not the case for self-stabilizing algorithms, whose executions can be started from any possible configuration. It is well known that self-stabilizing algorithms cannot be explicitly terminating. Given a static problem $\mathcal{P}$, we say that algorithm $\mathcal{A}$ *stabilizes* for $\mathcal{P}$ if there exists a subset $\mathcal{L}$ of the set of configurations, called *legitimate configurations*, such that: *i*) (convergence:) every execution from any possible initial configuration reaches a configuration in $\mathcal{L}$. *ii*) (correctness:) every execution from a configuration in $\mathcal{L}$ only reaches configurations satisfying the property of terminal configuration of $\mathcal{P}$. In other words, an algorithm $\mathcal{A}$ stabilizes for $\mathcal{P}$, iff it converges towards the subset of legitimate configurations and, once converged, never reaches configurations in which the property of terminal configuration of $\mathcal{P}$ is not satisfied. When it happens, we say that the *stabilization* has occurred.

Definition 1 (Local and Global Counting)
Let l be any non-negative integer and x an agent in A.

- *Then,* l locally counted events at x*, denoted by* $[l]^x$*, are* l *consecutive events in which agent* x *participates.*
- *And,* l globally counted events *or just* l (global) events *represent a segment of length* l *in an execution, in which different agents are involved.*

Note that during $[l]^x$*, at least* l *globally counted events occur.*

Definition 2 (Event Complexity). *The* worst case event complexity *(or just* event complexity*) of a system* $\mathcal{S}$ *(or of an algorithm* $\mathcal{A}$*) is the maximum length (counted by the number of global events) of an execution until termination, in case of a system* $\mathcal{S}$ *with initialization, or until stabilization, in case of a self-stabilizing system* $\mathcal{S}$*. In the latter case, we also call it* stabilization complexity.

2.2 Cover Time Property

The cover time, defined below, is an abstraction of agent's mobility characteristics detailed in the introduction. Informally, it indicates the "time" for a mobile agent to communicate successfully with all the other agents. As the systems we consider are asynchronous, implying no real time, the "time" reference here is the total number of communications (events) during some interval.

Given $\mathbf{n}$ agents, a vector $\mathtt{CV} = (\mathbf{cv}_1, \mathbf{cv}_2, \ldots, \mathbf{cv}_\mathbf{n})$ of positive integers (the *cover times*) and a scheduler $\mathcal{D}$, $\mathcal{D}$ (and any of its schedules) is said to satisfy the *cover time property*, if in any $\mathbf{cv}_i$ ($i \in \{1 \ldots \mathbf{n}\}$) consecutive events of each schedule of $\mathcal{D}$, an agent i meets every other agent at least once (participates in at least one event with every other agent). Any *execution* of a system under such a scheduler we consider is one that *satisfies the cover time property.*

For two agents x and y, if $\mathbf{cv}_x < \mathbf{cv}_y$, then x is called *faster* than y, and y *slower* than x. The minimum cover time value is denoted by $\mathbf{cv}_\mathbf{min}$ and the maximum one by $\mathbf{cv}_\mathbf{max}$. A *fastest/slowest* agent z has $\mathbf{cv}_z = \mathbf{cv}_\mathbf{min}/\mathbf{cv}_z = \mathbf{cv}_\mathbf{max}$.

Remark 1. A scheduler satisfying the cover time property is fair. The fairness defined in Sec. 2.1 ensures that each agent communicates with other agents infinitely many times. With cover times, we are able to express the frequency of the meetings of an agent. This can be considered a natural extension of this fairness. Still, notice that the cover time property provides a kind of a strong fairness in the sense that every agent is able to communicate frequently with every other.

Agents are Not Assumed to Know Cover Times. Instead, we do assume that when two agents meet, they are able to detect which of them is faster (unless none of them is). One way to quantify that, is to assume that each agent x is given with a *category* number $\mathbf{cat}_x$ (a positive integer). For instance, different kinds of public transport vehicles (moving according to different itineraries) in the EMMA project [18] can correspond to different categories. In ZebraNet [17], a measured temperature (or pulse) far from the normal can imply an ill animal (that is less mobile) - a category. We assume that for each two agents x and y,

$\mathbf{cat}_x < \mathbf{cat}_y \Longleftrightarrow \mathbf{cv}_x < \mathbf{cv}_y$.[2] The number of different categories, $\mathbf{m}$, is generally much smaller than the size of the population $\mathbf{n}$ ($\mathbf{m} \ll \mathbf{n}$) and agents do not know the value of $\mathbf{m}$. Note that categories are not identifiers, because there can be an arbitrary number of agents in the same category and because agents in the same category are indistinguishable.

For BS, we need the following stronger requirement. We assume that BS, but not a mobile agent, is able either to estimate a tight upper bound or to know an exact $\mathbf{cv}$ of an agent *it meets*. Recall that BS is resource-unlimited, which helps it in this task. E.g., BS may maintain a table telling it what is the maximal cover time of each category. For the sake of simplicity, in the presentation of the code in BS (and its analysis), for each agent j that meets BS, we will use $\mathbf{cv}_j$ assuming that this is the cover time that BS has estimated based on $\mathbf{cat}_j$.

2.3 Start of Computation

For a non-self-stabilizing algorithm, there are two options to start the computation : *simultaneously* (or synchronously) and *non-simultaneously* (or asynchronously). In the non-simultaneous case, at least one agent has to start the computation spontaneously. Then, each time an already started agent i meets a not yet started agent j, agent j starts too. The simultaneous start, is a particular case of the non-simultaneous one, in which the agents have to respond simultaneously to some global signal, e.g., from BS, to initiate the computation.

The simultaneous start can be difficult to realize in practice. It implies that BS has a communication power strong enough to broadcast, instantaneously, an information to each mobile agent, at whatever distance it could be. We assume a general and a more natural non-simultaneous start.

3 The Transformer

In this part, we consider classical (assuming initialization) algorithms solving static problems and satisfying the condition below. We present a transformer (compiler) that takes as an input such algorithm $\mathcal{A}$, which solves a static problem $\mathcal{P}$. The transformer outputs the self-stabilizing version of $\mathcal{A}$ solving the self-stabilizing version of $\mathcal{P}$.

Conditions on the input algorithm.
The required conditions are as follows. First, the classical input algorithm $\mathcal{A}$ solves a static problem $\mathcal{P}$ such that $\mathcal{A}$ assumes a non-simultaneous start (see Sec. 2). Second, $\mathcal{A}$ legally terminates with the same vector of correct output values (finds the same solution) starting from a predetermined initial configuration and regardless of the schedule "chosen" by the scheduler. Note that, in fact, the transformer requires somewhat weaker condition than the first one. It is sufficient that $\mathcal{A}$ solves $\mathcal{P}$ assuming only a subset of all the possible non-simultaneous starts, the subset where BS is the first agent that starts the computation.

[2] In some cases, a weaker relation between cover times and categories may be enough.

We assume that an upper bound on the worst case event complexity of the input algorithm $\mathcal{A}$ is known and is correct assuming a non-simultaneous start. In addition, the bound is given as a function of the cover times of the agents $\{\mathbf{cv_1}, \mathbf{cv_2}, \ldots, \mathbf{cv_n}\}$. Hence, we can express the bound as a function of $\mathbf{cv_{min}}$ and $\mathbf{cv_{max}}$, because any cover time value is at most $\mathbf{cv_{max}}$. We denote this upper bound expressed in that way by $\overline{\mathtt{WCC}_{\mathcal{A}}}$.

Main idea of the transformer. Basically, the transformer algorithm is a composition of three modules, *TServerMin* algorithm (Sec. 3.1), *TClient* algorithm (Sec. 3.2) and *TServerMax* (described later in this section). The composition is made in the following way. First, *TServerMin* and *TClient* are combined in a *fair composition* [16,19] to get "a first step" transformer. This transformer is used to construct the *TServerMax* module. Then, all three *self-stabilizing* modules are combined together to get "the final" transformer. *Independently* from each other, both *TServerMax* and *TServerMin* are combined with *TClient*, each one using a fair composition. *TServerMax* and *TServerMin* perform independently and provide inputs to *TClient*.

TClient uses a repetition of three non-overlapping rounds synchronized at BS. In the first round, all the agents are initialized according to the input classical algorithm $\mathcal{A}$. In the second round, agents are informed that the previous round is accomplished. This is to ensure (in the *asynchronous* model we use) that no initialization transition is done during the next, third, round. In the third round, assuming that a proper initialization of $\mathcal{A}$ is done, a "simulation" of an execution of $\mathcal{A}$ is performed (with a non-simultaneous start, where the first agent that starts is BS). Each round is initialized by BS and then is propagated (together with executing the appropriate transitions) to the other agents. To know when to switch to the next round, BS locally counts an appropriate number of events. Below, we show that in order to fully perform the first two rounds, BS has to count at least $2\mathbf{cv_{min}}$ events for each of those rounds; and to fully perform the third round - at least $\max(2\cdot\mathbf{cv_{min}}, \overline{\mathtt{WCC}_{\mathcal{A}}})$ events. To be able to count, BS has to evaluate (at least, to estimate the maximum values of) $\mathbf{cv_{min}}$ and $\mathbf{cv_{max}}$ (and then, also $\overline{\mathtt{WCC}_{\mathcal{A}}}$). Algorithm *TServerMin* in Sec. 3.1 provides an estimated value of $\mathbf{cv_{min}}$ as an input to *TClient* (via variable `mincv`). Algorithm *TServerMax* below provides an estimated value of $\mathbf{cv_{max}}$ as an input to *TClient* (via variable `maxcv`). An evaluated $\overline{\mathtt{WCC}_{\mathcal{A}}}$ in *TClient* (see Fig. 2) is denoted by $\mathtt{WCC}_{\mathcal{A}}$.

Self-stabilizing computation of $\mathbf{cv_{max}}$ - algorithm *TServerMax*. To design this algorithm we use the transformer presented here itself. First, we use the proposed below classical algorithm *NSSmaxcv* that computes an estimated $\mathbf{cv_{max}}$ in BS (from a non-simultaneous start at BS) in $3\cdot\mathbf{cv_{min}}$ events and hence, $\overline{\mathtt{WCC}_{NSSmaxcv}} = 3\cdot\mathbf{cv_{min}}$. Then, by the correctness of the transformer (Sec. 3.2, Lem. 4) when $\overline{\mathtt{WCC}_{\mathcal{A}}}$ is a function of $\mathbf{cv_{min}}$ only, the transformation of *NSSmaxcv* outputs a required self-stabilizing algorithm *TServerMax*.

In *NSSmaxcv*, every agent x (including BS) has a variable $\mathtt{maxcat}_x$ which is initialized to $\mathbf{cat}_x$. When a started agent x meets agent y (first, y becomes started, if not started already, and then), x assigns $\mathtt{maxcat}_x := \max(\mathtt{maxcat}_x, \mathtt{maxcat}_y)$. In $\mathbf{cv_{min}}$ events, all fastest agents meet some started agent and start the computation. Then, in additional $\mathbf{cv}_{\mathbf{min}}$ events, every fastest agent x meets a slowest agent and x assigns its $\mathtt{maxcat}_x$ to a maximum category number. And finally, in additional $\mathbf{cv}_{\mathbf{min}}$ events (after $3 \cdot \mathbf{cv}_{\mathbf{min}}$ in overall), some fastest agent meets BS, $\mathtt{maxcat}_{BS}$ is assigned to a maximum category number and BS saves the correct estimation of $\mathbf{cv}_{\mathbf{max}}$ (according to the value of $\mathtt{maxcat}_{BS}$) in maxcv.

3.1 Algorithm *TServerMin* (Fig. 1)

The purpose of this algorithm running at BS is to compute $\mathbf{cv}_{\mathbf{min}}$ in a self-stabilizing manner. The output of *TServerMin* is saved in mincv and used as an input to the *TClient* algorithm.

TServerMin executes in rounds, using an event counter (variable $\mathtt{counter}^{\mathrm{srv}}$) to start a new round when counter becomes 0 or smaller (line 1). The output mincv is updated once in a round (line 2). A *round* is a segment of an execution of *TServerMin* which ends at line 2; and a *complete round* is a round that had *also* been started at line 3. *Incomplete* rounds arise from a bad (faulty) initialization.

By Lem. 1 below, each round lasts at most $[\mathbf{cv}_{\mathbf{min}} + 1]^{BS}$ events. The output mincv is updated to the *correct* value after each *complete* round (in line 2). Hence, the convergence and correctness are ensured after $[2 \cdot \mathbf{cv}_{\mathbf{min}} + 1]^{BS}$.

Memory in a mobile agent $j \neq$ BS:
$\mathbf{cat}_j$: positive integer (* category number of j *)
Memory in BS:
$\mathtt{counter}^{\mathrm{srv}}$: integer (* counter of the events of a round *)
$\mathtt{mincv}, \mathtt{mincv}'$: positive integer (* mincv is an output variable *)
$\mathbf{cv}_j$: positive integer (* cover time value of j **estimated** by BS based on $\mathbf{cat}_j$*)

When an agent j communicates with BS:
1 **if** $\mathtt{counter}^{\mathrm{srv}} \leq 0$ **then**
2 $\quad \mathtt{mincv} := \mathtt{mincv}'$ (* end of a round - output update *)
3 $\quad \mathtt{mincv}' := \mathbf{cv}_j$; $\mathtt{counter}^{\mathrm{srv}} := \mathbf{cv}_j$ (* start of a round - initialization *)
4 **else**
5 $\quad \mathtt{counter}^{\mathrm{srv}} := \min(\mathtt{counter}^{\mathrm{srv}}, \mathtt{mincv}') - \max(1, \mathtt{mincv}' - \mathbf{cv}_j + 1)$
6 $\quad \mathtt{mincv}' := \min(\mathbf{cv}_j, \mathtt{mincv}')$

Fig. 1. *TServerMin*

Lemma 1. *Each TServerMin round lasts at most* $[\mathbf{cv}_{\mathbf{min}}+1]^{BS}$. *In addition, at the end of a complete round, the output of TServerMin is correct, i.e.,* $\mathtt{mincv} = \mathbf{cv}_{\mathbf{min}}$.

Proof: If at the first local event of the round at BS, the condition in line 1 is true, the round (an incomplete one) is ended and the lemma holds trivially. Otherwise, there are two cases: (1) at the beginning of a round (just after the faults or at the beginning of a *complete* round, in line 3), $\mathtt{mincv}' \geq \mathbf{cv}_{\mathbf{min}}$ and $\mathtt{counter}^{\mathrm{srv}} \geq \mathbf{cv}_{\mathbf{min}}$; or (2) the initial value of $\mathtt{mincv}' < \mathbf{cv}_{\mathbf{min}}$ or/and the initial value of $\mathtt{counter}^{\mathrm{srv}} < \mathbf{cv}_{\mathbf{min}}$ (cannot be the case of a complete round; see line 3).

First, note that in both cases ((1) and (2)), $\mathtt{mincv}'$ is assigned to $\mathbf{cv}_j$ (line 3) or $\min(\mathbf{cv}_j, \mathtt{mincv}')$ (line 6), at least once in the round (at least at the first local event at BS in the round). After that, during the round, we have $\texttt{mincv}' \leq \mathbf{cv_{max}}$.

We treat case (1) first. Let e_x be an event (BS, j) and also the $[x]^{BS}th$ event of a round such that this is the first time in the round when BS meets some *fastest* agent (j, in this case). In this event, $\texttt{mincv}' \geq \mathbf{cv}_j$ ($= \mathbf{cv_{min}}$). In e_x, in line 5, a counter is updated such that $\texttt{counter}^{\texttt{srv}} \leq (\mathbf{cv_{max}} - (x-1) - (\mathbf{cv_{max}} - \mathbf{cv_{min}} + 1)) = \mathbf{cv_{min}} - x$. In the next line, 6, $\texttt{mincv}'$ becomes $\mathbf{cv_{min}}$. In at most additional $\mathbf{cv_{min}} - x + 1$ local events, the condition in line 1 becomes true and $\texttt{mincv}$ becomes $\texttt{mincv}'$ which is equal to $\mathbf{cv_{min}}$ ($\texttt{mincv}'$ has stayed unchanged since e_x). Thus, in total, in case (1), in at most $\mathbf{cv_{min}} + 1$ local events, the round ends (and the new one starts) and at line 2, $\texttt{mincv}$ is assigned to $\mathbf{cv_{min}}$ as required.

In case (2), it is easy to see by the code (line 5) that the round ends in less than $\mathbf{cv_{min}} + 1$ local events (see details in [8]). ∎

3.2 Algorithm *TClient* (Fig. 2)

TClient executes at BS and at the mobile agents. It uses as an input a classical algorithm $\mathcal{A}$, the output (`mincv`) of *TServerMin* and the output (`maxcv`) of *TServerMax*. As *TServerMin* and *TServerMax* are self-stabilizing, they will eventually furnish the correct output values in `mincv` and `maxcv`. Below, we prove that *TClient* is itself self-stabilizing given that `mincv` and `maxcv` are correct.

The main operation of *TClient* is aimed to properly initialize and execute $\mathcal{A}$ repeatedly. At the end of each such repetition, *TClient* acquires a correct output of $\mathcal{A}$, if no faults occur during the current repetition. Otherwise, a correct output will be acquired at the end of the next repetition. To achieve such operation, *TClient* executes three different rounds (0-`round`, 1-`round` and 2-`round`) in a cyclic manner. Each new round is started by BS and then, propagated from agent to agent via round indicators (`round`) of agents.

Definition 3 (Complete and Incomplete i-`round`). *Each* i-`round` *is a segment of an execution of TClient during which the* `round` *indicator at BS equals i. A* complete 0-`round` *is a 0-*`round` *which starts in line 16 (Fig. 2) and ends in line 9. A* complete 1-`round` *is a 1-*`round` *which starts in line 9 and ends in line 12. A* complete 2-`round` *is a 2-*`round` *which starts in line 12 and ends in 16.*

An incomplete i-`round` *is an i-*`round` *which is not a complete one. Incomplete rounds arise from a bad (faulty) initialization.*

Each of the three rounds has a task to perform. BS counts local events to learn when the task terminates and then, switches to the next round. 0-`round` is used to "reset" (initialize) the states of all the agents to start the upcoming execution of $\mathcal{A}$ with properly initialized variables. In this round, just before each agent performs the initialization action, it saves the output values from the previous execution of $\mathcal{A}$ (see details below). 1-`round` is used to inform that the previous "reset" round is fully accomplished and to ensure that no "reset" action is performed during the next round, 2-`round`, in which an execution of $\mathcal{A}$ takes place. When 2-round ends, during the next 0-round, all the output variables of $\mathcal{A}$ are saved in the corresponding variables of *TClient*, which are designed as generic type variables $\texttt{output}_i$ for every agent i (see Fig. 2). These variables are the output variables of *TClient* and of the output (transformed) self-stabilizing algorithm. Note lines 4, 17 and 21 in the code of *TClient* where these variables are updated and saved. This is necessary, because the variables of $\mathcal{A}$ (and possibly its output variables) are re-initialized just after, during the 0-round, while the output variables of *TClient* are not modified until the very end of the *next* 2-round. As $\mathcal{A}$ is assumed to terminate with the same vector of correct output values from a predetermined initial configuration, these output values are identically re-computed in each "complete" (repetition of the) execution of $\mathcal{A}$, while the population does not change. This provides a stabilization of the output algorithm.

Lemma 2. *Assume that the value of* mincv *is correct (equals* $\mathbf{cv_{min}}$*). Then, each* complete *0-*round *lasts* $[2 \cdot \mathbf{cv_{min}}]^{BS}$ *events. In addition, at the end of the round (line 9), the* round *indicators of all the agents are set to 0 and all the agents are initialized according to the non-self-stabilizing algorithm* $\mathcal{A}$*. The* fastest *bit of every fastest agent is set to 1, and to 0 for others (these bits stay unchanged thereafter).*

Proof: The lemma considers a complete 0-round (see Def. 3), hence it has started in line 16. In this line, $\texttt{counter}^{\texttt{cnt}}$ is set to $2 \cdot \texttt{mincv}$. Hence and by line 2, the 0-round lasts $[2 \cdot \mathbf{cv_{min}}]^{BS}$ (during which at least $2 \cdot \mathbf{cv_{min}}$ global events occur in the system). After the round has started at line 16, in $\mathbf{cv_{min}}$ events, every fastest agent f meets BS and sets $\texttt{round}_f := 0$ (line 18) and $\texttt{fastest}_f := 1$ (line 6). From this point, no line of the code can change $\texttt{fastest}_f$ of any f (see lines 6, 7 and 19). Hence, line 24 cannot be executed for any fastest agent. Line 26 cannot be executed for f with $\texttt{round}_f := 0$. Hence, $\texttt{round}_f$ value cannot change during the remaining events of the corresponding 0-round. Hence, since $\texttt{round}_f = 0$ and $\texttt{fastest}_f = 1$ at this round, lines 14 and 26 (the transitions of $\mathcal{A}$) cannot be executed for any fastest f until the end of the round. Note that f is initialized in line 5, at the same meeting with BS, when it assigns $\texttt{round}_f = 0$ and $\texttt{fastest}_f = 1$. Hence, after the first $\mathbf{cv_{min}}$ events of the round, every fastest agent and BS initialize $\mathcal{A}$ internal variables in line 5 and these variables stay unchanged at least until the end of the round.

Starting with the first event of the round, in $\mathbf{cv_{min}}$ events, every fastest agent meets every other non-fastest agent s and its $\texttt{fastest}_s$ bit is set to 0 (in line 19). After the first $\mathbf{cv_{min}}$ events of a complete 0-round, all the fastest bits stay unchanged (lines 6-7 and 19). After additional $\mathbf{cv_{min}}$ events, in $2 \cdot \mathbf{cv_{min}}$ events in total, every non-fastest agent meets a fastest one, sets its round indicator to 0 and initializes its $\mathcal{A}$ variables, in line 22. From this point and until the end of the round, lines 14, 26 (the only lines that can change the variables of $\mathcal{A}$) cannot be executed. Line 24 cannot be executed either and thus, the round indicators of all the agents stay unchanged until the end of the round. ∎

```
Memory in a mobile agent j ≠ BS:
  round_j ∈ {0,1,2}                                   (* the round indicator of j *)
  fastest_j ∈ {0,1}                                   (* a bit to mark a fastest agent *)
  output_j        (* set of output variables of the new self-stabilizing algorithm *)
  cat_j : positive integer                            (* category number of j *)

Memory in BS:
  counter^cnt : integer                      (* counter of the local events at BS *)
  round ∈ {0,1,2}                            (* the round indicator of BS *)
  mincv : positive integer       (* output of TServerMin; used here as an input *)
  maxcv : positive integer       (* output of TServerMax; used here as an input *)
  WCC_A : positive integer              (* evaluated WCC_A‾ (by mincv and maxcv) *)
  output_BS       (* set of output variables of the new self-stabilizing algorithm *)
  cv_j : positive integer    (* cover time value of j estimated by BS based on cat_j *)

When agent j communicates with BS:
  WCC_A := ⟨WCC_A‾ evaluated by mincv and maxcv⟩
  counter^cnt := min(counter^cnt, max(2·mincv, WCC_A)) − 1
  if round = 0 then
      if round_j = 2 ⟨update output_j by the corresponding output variables of A⟩
      ⟨initialize variables of A at j and BS⟩
     if (cv_j = mincv) then fastest_j := 1       (* j is one of the fastest agents *)
      else fastest_j := 0
      if counter^cnt ≤ 0 then
        counter^cnt := 2·mincv;  round := 1                   (* start of 1-round *)
   else if round = 1 then
      if counter^cnt ≤ 0 then
        counter^cnt := max(2·mincv, WCC_A);  round := 2        (* start of 2-round *)
  else (* round = 2 *)
      ⟨perform a transition of A for event (BS, j)⟩
      if counter^cnt ≤ 0 then
        counter^cnt := 2·mincv;  round := 0                   (* start of 0-round *)
      ⟨update output_BS and output_j by the corresponding output variables of A⟩
   round_j := round

When agent j communicates with an agent i ≠ BS:
  if cat_j > cat_i then fastest_j := 0                  (* j is a non-fastest agent *)
  if (round_i = 0 ∧ fastest_i ∧ ¬fastest_j) then
      if round_j = 2 then ⟨update output_j by the corresponding output of A⟩
      round_j := 0; ⟨initialize variables of A at j⟩
  else if (round_i = 1 ∧ fastest_i ∧ ¬fastest_j) then
      round_j := 1
  else if (round_i = 2 ∧ round_j ≠ 0) then
      round_j := 2; ⟨perform a transition of A for event (i, j)⟩
```

Fig. 2. *TClient*

Lemma 3. *Assume that the value of* `mincv` *is correct. Let e be a TClient execution sequence composed of 2 sequential* complete *i*-`round`s *such that e ≡ [0-*`round` *1-*`round`*]. Then, at the end of e (line 12), the* `round` *indicator of every agent equals 1 and all the agents are initialized according to the non-self-stabilizing algorithm $\mathcal{A}$. In addition, a corresponding 1-*`round` *lasts* $[2 \cdot \mathbf{cv_{min}}]^{BS}$ *events.*

Proof: By Lem. 2, at the end of a complete 0-`round`, all the round indicators are equal to 0 and the `fastest` bits of all the fastest agents are equal to 1 and 0 for others. In addition, at BS, the counter $\mathtt{counter}^{cnt}$ is set to $2 \cdot \mathbf{cv_{min}}$ and the `round` indicator to 1 (start of a 1-`round`). Then, during the next $[2 \cdot \mathbf{cv_{min}}]^{BS}$ events, the `round` indicator at BS is 1 (line 2, 9, 10-12) and hence, line 14 cannot be executed during the round. During the first $\mathbf{cv_{min}}$ events in 1-`round`, every fastest agent f meets BS and sets its $\mathtt{round}_f$ indicator to 1 (line 18). Now, we prove by induction on the events that line 26 cannot be executed (either), during the corresponding 1-`round`. First of all, note that during 1-`round` round indicator can be set to 2 in line 26 only and only if one of the agents in the event have the round indicator set to 2. By Lem. 2, at the beginning of the corresponding 1-`round`, no round indicator in agents equals 2 and hence, the basis of induction is correct. By the induction hypothesis, during the first k events (of the 1-`round`) line 26 cannot be executed. Hence, by the end of the kth event no round indicator in agents equals 2 too. Thus, the induction is also correct for event $k+1$.

Thus, during all the 1-`round`, round indicators can be set to 1 or to 0 by a fastest agent (lines 22, 24) and to 1 by BS (line 1). After the first $\mathbf{cv_{min}}$ events in the 1-`round`, round indicators can be set to 1 only (by the fastest agents, line 24). Hence, in $2 \cdot \mathbf{cv_{min}}$ events, all the round indicators are set to 1 and stay unchanged until the end of the corresponding 1-`round`. In addition, by Lem. 2 and since we showed that lines 14 and 26 cannot be executed during the corresponding 1-`round`, all the agents are initialized according to the non-self-stabilizing algorithm $\mathcal{A}$ at the end of the round. ∎

Lemma 4. *Assume that the output variables of TServerMin (variable* `mincv`*) and of TServerMax (variable* `maxcv`*) are correct. Let e be a TClient execution sequence composed of 3 sequential* complete *i*-`round`s *such that e ≡ [0-*`round` *1-*`round` *2-*`round`*]. Then, at the end of e (line 16), the* `round` *indicator of all the agents equals 2 and the output variables of $\mathcal{A}$ are correct. In addition, the corresponding 2-*`round` *lasts* $[\max(2 \cdot \mathbf{cv_{min}}, \overline{\mathtt{WCC}_{\mathcal{A}}})]^{BS}$ *events.*

If $\overline{\mathtt{WCC}_{\mathcal{A}}}$ is a function of $\mathbf{cv_{min}}$ only, the statements in the lemma hold even if `maxcv` *is incorrect.*

Proof: By Lem. 3, at the end of 1-`round` in e, the round indicators of all the agents are equal to 1 and each agent is in an initial state according to $\mathcal{A}$. Hence, during the next complete 2-`round` in e, lines 5 or 22 ($\mathcal{A}$ initialization) cannot be executed (this ensures that no initialization actions are executed).

BS is the first agent that starts a complete 2-`round` by setting its round indicator to 2 in line 12. Then, any agent communicating with BS during this 2-`round`, sets its round indicator to 2, and both agents perform a transition of $\mathcal{A}$ (line 14). Then, each time an agent i with a round indicator equal to 2 meets another agent j with round 1, agent j sets its round indicator to 2, and both agents perform a transition of $\mathcal{A}$ (line 26). When any two agents, both with round indicators equal to 2, meet, they perform a transition of $\mathcal{A}$ too (line 26).

Such a behavior simulates an execution of $\mathcal{A}$ with a non-simultaneous start at BS. In addition, due to the correctness of `mincv` and `maxcv`, $\mathtt{WCC}_{\mathcal{A}}$ is correctly evaluated at line 1. Hence, the 2-`round` in e lasts at least $[\max(2 \cdot \mathbf{cv}_{\mathbf{min}}, \overline{\mathtt{WCC}_{\mathcal{A}}})]^{BS}$ events (line 12), which are at least $\overline{\mathtt{WCC}_{\mathcal{A}}}$ global events. Hence, at the end of the 2-`round` in e, the output variables of $\mathcal{A}$ are correct.

By the above, the corresponding 2-`round` lasts at least $2 \cdot \mathbf{cv}_{\mathbf{min}}$ events and thus (see the following explanation), the round indicators in all agents are set to 2 by the end of the round. During the first $\mathbf{cv}_{\mathbf{min}}$ events in this 2-`round`, every fastest agent meets BS and sets its round indicator to 2. After this setting and till the end of the round, this indicator stays unchanged, because the conditions in lines 20 and 23 are false (for any meeting (i, j)). Then, in additional $\mathbf{cv}_{\mathbf{min}}$, a fastest agent meets all the others and they sets their indicators to 2 in line 26. These indicators stay unchanged too, until the end of e, by the same reason.

Note that if $\overline{\mathtt{WCC}_{\mathcal{A}}}$ is a function of $\mathbf{cv}_{\mathbf{min}}$ only, the proof is correct even if `maxcv` is incorrect. ∎

Lemma 5. *Assume that the output variables of TServerMin (variable* `mincv`*) and of TServerMax (variable* `maxcv`*) are correct. Let e be a TClient execution sequence composed of 4 sequential* complete i-`rounds` *such that* $e \equiv$ *[0-*`round` *1-*`round` *2-*`round` *0-*`round`*]. Then, at the end of e (line 9), the output variables of TClient (*`output`*) are correct (satisfy the property of terminal configuration of* $\mathcal{P}$ *that* $\mathcal{A}$ *solves) and stay correct thereafter.*

If $\overline{\mathtt{WCC}_{\mathcal{A}}}$ *is a function of* $\mathbf{cv}_{\mathbf{min}}$ *only, the statements in the lemma hold even if* `maxcv` *is incorrect.*

Proof: In the first event of the last 0-`round` in e, in line 17, BS and agent j update the output variables of *TClient* to the *correct* ones of $\mathcal{A}$ (by Lem. 4).

By Lem. 4, at the end of the 2-`round` in e, all the round indicators are set to 2. Hence, in the next 0-`round`, any (other than j) fastest agent (by Lem. 2, the `fastest` bits are correct in this round) meets BS in $\mathbf{cv}_{\mathbf{min}}$ events and updates the output variables of *TClient* (to the *correct* ones) in line 4 (j does it in line 17, at the first event of the round). Then, in additional $\mathbf{cv}_{\mathbf{min}}$ events, all the other agents update these variables in line 21 (if they did not make it already in this round, in this line, or in line 4).

Note that line 26 cannot be executed during the last 0-`round` in e for an agent that has already set its round indicator to 0. Thus, the round indicators stay unchanged during this 0-`round` after they have been set to 0. Hence, during this round, the update of the output variables of *TClient* by those of $\mathcal{A}$ (in lines 4, 17 and 21) is done *exactly once for every agent.* From this moment, it is easy to see that the output variables of *TClient* stays untouched until the *end* of the next 2-`round` that starts *after* e. Then, during the next additional 0-`round`, these variables are updated again (and exactly once for each agent) to the correct values by the same points as above. Hence, the lemma holds. ∎

The complexity of the transformation.

Lemma 6. *Assume that the output variables of TServerMin (variable* `mincv`*) and of TServerMax (variable* `maxcv`*) are correct. Then, each i-*`round` *lasts at most* $[\max(2 \cdot \mathbf{cv_{min}}, \overline{\mathtt{WCC}_{\mathcal{A}}})]^{BS}$.

If $\overline{\mathtt{WCC}_{\mathcal{A}}}$ *is a function of* $\mathbf{cv_{min}}$ *only, the statement in the lemma holds even if* `maxcv` *is incorrect.*

The correctness of the lemma is directly implied by Def. 3 and line 2 (Fig. 2).

Theorem 1. *Let the input of the presented transformer be a classical algorithm* $\mathcal{A}$ *that solves a static problem* $\mathcal{P}$ *from a non-simultaneous start and terminates with the same vector of correct output values from a predetermined initial configuration. In addition, the upper bound on the worst case complexity of* $\mathcal{A}$ *is given as a function of* $\mathbf{cv_{min}}$ *and* $\mathbf{cv_{max}}$ *and denoted by* $\overline{\mathtt{WCC}_{\mathcal{A}}}$*. Then, the output of the transformer is an algorithm that stabilizes for* $\mathcal{P}$ *in* $O(\frac{\mathbf{cv_{max}}}{\mathbf{n}-1} \cdot \max(2 \cdot \mathbf{cv_{min}}, \overline{\mathtt{WCC}_{\mathcal{A}}}))$ global *events.*

An additional memory requirement for the transformation (on top of the memory requirement for $\mathcal{A}$*) is* $O(1)$ *for every mobile agent.*

Proof: First, assume that the output variables of *TServerMin* and *TServerMax* are correct. Then, consider an execution sequence e composed of 4 sequential *complete* i-`rounds` such that $e \equiv$ [0-`round` 1-`round` 2-`round` 0-`round`]. Let us define the legitimate configurations for the output algorithm as the configurations reached after a sequence e. Then, by Lem. 5, *TClient* stabilizes.

Now, we drop the assumption on the outputs of *TServerMin* and *TServerMax*. The analysis of *TServerMin* and *TServerMax* in this section, shows that these algorithms indeed stabilize to the correct outputs in $O([\mathbf{cv_{min}}]^{BS})$ events. In addition, it is clear that *TServerMin* and *TServerMax* make no use of any of the *TClient* variables, so that the variable condition for the fair composition is satisfied.

By Lem. 6, any suffix of e is of length at most $4 \cdot [\max(2 \cdot \mathbf{cv_{min}}, \overline{\mathtt{WCC}_{\mathcal{A}}})]^{BS}$. Hence, after the stabilization of both *TServerMin* and *TServerMax* and in less than additional $2|e|$ events (at most $|e|$ events for the suffix of e and additional $|e|$ events for the complete e, with no faults), in overall $O([\max(2 \cdot \mathbf{cv_{min}}, \overline{\mathtt{WCC}_{\mathcal{A}}})]^{BS})$ events, the convergence and correctness of the transformer are ensured.

Now, let us express the complexity by the number of *global* events instead of the local ones at BS. By the cover time property (see Sec. 2.2), in any $\mathbf{cv}_{BS}$ consecutive global events, BS participates in at least one event with every other agent out of $\mathbf{n} - 1$ and hence, locally counts at least $\mathbf{n} - 1$ events. Thus, in $O(\frac{\mathbf{cv_{max}}}{\mathbf{n}-1} \cdot \max(2 \cdot \mathbf{cv_{min}}, \overline{\mathtt{WCC}_{\mathcal{A}}}))$ global events, the convergence and correctness of the transformer (or the output algorithm) are ensured. ∎

References

1. Afek, Y., Kutten, S., Yung, M.: The local detection paradigm and its application to self-stabilization. Theor. Comput. Sci. 186(1-2), 199–229 (1997)
2. Angluin, D., Aspnes, J., Diamadi, Z., Fischer, M.J., Peralta, R.: Computation in networks of passively mobile finite-state sensors. In: PODC, pp. 290–299 (2004)

3. Angluin, D., Aspnes, J., Eisenstat, D.: Fast computation by population protocols with a leader. DC 21(3), 183–199 (2008)
4. Angluin, D., Aspnes, J., Eisenstat, D., Ruppert, E.: The computational power of population protocols. Distributed Computing 20(4), 279–304 (2007)
5. Angluin, D., Aspnes, J., Fischer, M.J., Jiang, H.: Self-stabilizing population protocols. TAAS 3(4) (2008)
6. Awerbuch, B., Patt-Shamir, B., Varghese, G., Dolev, S.: Self-stabilization by local checking and global reset (extended abstract). In: Tel, G., Vitányi, P.M.B. (eds.) WDAG 1994. LNCS, vol. 857. Springer, Heidelberg (1994)
7. Beauquier, J., Burman, J., Clement, J., Kutten, S.: Brief announcement: Non-self-stabilizing and self-stabilizing gathering in networks of mobile agents - the notion of speed. In: PODC (2009)
8. Beauquier, J., Burman, J., Kutten, S.: Making population protocols self-stabilizing, extended version (2009), `http://tx.technion.ac.il/~bjanna/transformerBBK_all.pdf`
9. Beauquier, J., Clement, J., Messika, S., Rosaz, L., Rozoy, B.: Self-stabilizing counting in mobile sensor networks with a base station. In: Pelc, A. (ed.) DISC 2007. LNCS, vol. 4731, pp. 63–76. Springer, Heidelberg (2007)
10. Beauquier, J., Datta, A.K., Gradinariu, M., Magniette, F.: Self-stabilizing local mutual exclusion and daemon refinement. Chicago J. Theor. Comput. Sci. (2002)
11. Delporte-Gallet, C., Fauconnier, H., Guerraoui, R., Ruppert, E.: When birds die: Making population protocols fault-tolerant. In: Gibbons, P.B., Abdelzaher, T., Aspnes, J., Rao, R. (eds.) DCOSS 2006. LNCS, vol. 4026, pp. 51–66. Springer, Heidelberg (2006)
12. Fischer, M., Jiang, H.: Self-stabilizing leader election in networks of finite-state anonymous agents. In: Shvartsman, M.M.A.A. (ed.) OPODIS 2006. LNCS, vol. 4305, pp. 395–409. Springer, Heidelberg (2006)
13. Ghosh, S., Gupta, A., Herman, T., Pemmaraju, S.V.: Fault-containing self-stabilizing algorithms. In: PODC, pp. 45–54 (1996)
14. Gouda, M.G., Haddix, F.F.: The alternator. DC 20(1), 21–28 (2007)
15. Guerraoui, R., Ruppert, E.: Even small birds are unique: Population protocols with identifiers. Technical Report CSE-2007-04. York University (September 10, 2007)
16. Herman, T.: Adaptivity through Distributed Convergence (Ph.D. Thesis). University of Texas at Austin (1991)
17. Juang, P., Oki, H., Wang, Y., Martonosi, M., Peh, L., Rubenstein, D.: Energy-efficient computing for wildlife tracking: design tradeoffs and early experiences with zebranet. In: ASPLOS, pp. 96–107 (2002)
18. Lahde, S., Doering, M., Pöttner, W., Lammert, G., Wolf, L.C.: A practical analysis of communication characteristics for mobile and distributed pollution measurements on the road. Wireless Communications and Mobile Computing 7(10), 1209–1218 (2007)
19. Tel, G.: Introduction to Distributed Algorithms, 2nd edn. Cambridge University Press, Cambridge (2000)

Analysis of Wireless Sensor Network Protocols in Dynamic Scenarios*

Cinzia Bernardeschi[1], Paolo Masci[1,2], and Holger Pfeifer[3]

[1] Department of Information Engineering, University of Pisa, Italy
cinzia.bernardeschi@ing.unipi.it
[2] Institute of Information Science and Technologies, CNR, Pisa, Italy
masci@isti.cnr.it
[3] Institute of Artificial Intelligence, Ulm University, Germany
holger.pfeifer@uni-ulm.de

Abstract. We describe an approach to the analysis of protocols for wireless sensor networks in scenarios with mobile nodes and dynamic link quality. The approach is based on the theorem proving system PVS and can be used for formal specification, automated simulation and verification of the behaviour of the protocol. In order to demonstrate the applicability of the approach, we analyse the reverse path forwarding algorithm, which is the basic technique used for diffusion protocols for wireless sensor networks.

1 Introduction and Motivation

Wireless devices have a limited transmission range and multi-hop communication protocols must be adopted when the network has a physical extension which exceeds the transmission range of nodes. Wireless Sensor Networks (WSNs) represent an example of wireless networks that are gaining more and more attention from the research community. In particular, WSNs are distributed systems consisting of a large number of spatially distributed, autonomous and cooperating nodes. The nodes of the network, referred to as *sensor nodes*, are battery-operated devices which provide limited computation capabilities, low-rate and low-range wireless communication, and are equipped with a number of sensors and actuators to monitor physical or environmental conditions [1].

Protocols for wireless networks are difficult to test on real devices, and simulation is currently the main technique used to investigate protocol behaviour. Software-based simulators are widely used to provide controlled environments in which experiments are to yield reproducible results. Protocols are commonly analysed with ad hoc simulators built on top of readily available network simulators, such as *Omnet++* [2], or distributed system simulators, such as *ptolemy* [3]. Currently, there is no established standard simulation framework.

Formal modelling is of outstanding importance for reasoning about the behaviour of systems, and formal analysis methods are widely accepted as a method

* This work was partially supported by the European Commission through the Network of Excellence ReSIST (IST-026764).

R. Guerraoui and F. Petit (Eds.): SSS 2009, LNCS 5873, pp. 105–119, 2009.

to provide additional confidence in the correctness of a system. For wireless sensor networks, there is increasing interest in using formal methods to verify key properties of popular routing algorithms [4], to evaluate protocol performance [5], and to validate simulation results [6].

In order to analyse protocols for wireless sensor networks, in this work we build on a framework [7] based on the *Prototype Verification System (PVS)*. PVS is a formal tool that combines an expressive specification language with an interactive theorem prover and it has been successfully employed for formal reasoning in several application domains (see [8] for an overview). The framework [7] allows an easy specification of the characteristics of wireless networks, such as limited communication range and lossy transmissions. In this work we introduce in the framework mechanisms to automate the analysis of dynamic scenarios with mobile nodes and quality changes of communication links. With our approach, a high-level clear description of the protocol can be developed. The formal specification can be animated and conveniently used to debug the specification and to obtain quantitative evaluations. Moreover, the approach opens the possibility of formally proving the correctness of the specification with respect to properties of interest.

In order to demonstrate the applicability of the approach, we show its application to the reverse path forwarding (RPF) algorithm, which is the basic technique used for diffusion protocols for WSNs. We employ a mechanism provided by the framework to automatically translate the formal specification into executable code, and simulate the algorithm in dynamic scenarios with mobile nodes and degraded / faulty wireless links. Moreover, by using the theorem prover of PVS, we prove that our specification satisfies desired properties of interest when the routing table is static, i.e., when the routing table is guaranteed to remain unchanged during protocol execution.

2 Basic Concepts of the Formal Framework

The framework presented in [7] combines formal verification and simulation to build an integrated approach that can be employed to improve the confidence in the behaviour of a system. The framework relies on the *Prototype Verification System (PVS)* [8].

2.1 PVS

The Prototype Verification System (PVS) is a specification and verification system which combines an expressive specification language with a powerful automated theorem prover. The PVS specification language builds on classical typed higher-order logic with the usual base types, `bool`, `nat`, `integer`, `real`, among others, and the function type constructor `[A -> B]`. Predicates are simply functions with range type `bool`. The type system of PVS also includes record types, dependent types, and abstract data types. The most powerful concept are *predicate subtypes*, which can be used to check for violations, such as division by zero, or to express complex consistency requirements.

PVS specifications are packaged as *theories* that can be parametric in types and constants. Theorems and lemmas contained in PVS theories can be formally proved using the theorem prover of PVS. A built-in prelude and loadable libraries provide standard specifications and proved facts for a large number of theories. A theory can use definitions and theorems of another theory by importing it.

PVS also provides a *ground evaluator* [9] that can be used to animate functional specifications i.e., to translate the formal specifications into executable code. Indeed, although the specification language of PVS is based on higher-order logic and features a rich type system, a large subset of it is executable. The ground evaluator translates the executable constructs of PVS into efficient *Lisp* code. Furthermore, in order to still be able to simulate theories that also involve declarative specifications, the ground evaluator can be augmented by so-called *semantic attachments*, through which the user can supply pieces of Lisp code and attach them to the declarative parts. Using this mechanism, the *PVSio* package [10] extends the ground evaluator with a predefined library of imperative programming language features such as side effects and input/output operations, and also provides a high-level interface for writing user-defined semantic attachments.

2.2 Modelling and Analysing Network Protocols

The formal specifications of a network protocol consists of a collection of PVS theories. A PVS theory may represent a service installed on a node (e.g., packet logger, clock), a structural property of the network (e.g., network graph), a communication functionality (e.g., packet forwarding). For each PVS theory, a number of different versions can be provided in order to specify and analyse algorithms under several perspectives and at desired level of detail. The most abstract theory provides the declaration of types for a minimum set of mandatory attributes and the declaration of functions. More detailed theories can be derived from the abstract definition by specifying the behaviour of functions and by extending types.

In the following, we recall the basic aspects of the framework. For a more complete description of the theories, we refer to [7].

Nodes and Network Structure. Nodes in the network are identified by a unique identifier `node_id`. The base station has a special identifier `base_station`. The network is represented with a directed graph, and the external library [11] is used to benefit from various concepts and proved facts. To simplify graph specification, an auxiliary topology function is defined, which identifies, for each node, the set of neighbouring nodes.Once the topology is given, the network graph can be instantiated with an utility function that transforms a topology into a directed graph.

Communication Primitives. Nodes can exchange packets. Communication primitives take into account the structure of the network and enable packet reception only for nodes in the communication range of the sender: if node x sends out a broadcast packet, it is received only by the neighbours of x. Ideal and lossy communication are modelled through special addresses. Basically, lossy addresses are functions that return a subset of nodes with respect to their ideal counterpart. A number of different single-hop primitives were modelled to ease the specification of communication protocols: *Inject*, which can be used to send out packets generated by nodes; *Forward*, which is suitable to relay packets previously received by nodes; *Drop*, which is used to discard received packets. Additionally, nodes are also allowed to perform the *Idle* transition, i.e., a transition in which nodes do not perform any operation on incoming or outgoing packets. The implemented primitives are suitable for unicast, multicast and broadcast communication.

Protocols. A protocol is specified as a cyclic procedure executed on a generic node. The specification of the protocol may use services installed on the node, and the protocol itself can be used to define new services. Examples of services are *packet logger*, which stores statistics about sent and received packets, *receive buffer*, which models the buffer that holds received packets waiting to be processed, and *node scheduler*, which abstracts the clock of nodes and the medium-access control mechanism with the sequence of nodes that execute the algorithm. The *state* of a node is defined by the services installed on the node. The *network state* maintains the state of all nodes in the network.

3 Modelling Dynamic Scenarios

In this section we present extensions of the framework which support the specification of dynamic scenarios. Specifically, we show mechanisms suitable to express mobility patterns of nodes, possibility of link quality changes, and to automate the generation of routing tables.

Node Mobility. Node mobility can be expressed with functions that change network connectivity with the following three steps: *i)* select a target direction among those allowed by topology, *ii)* determine the new set of neighbours of the mobile node, *iii)* return a new topology according to the actual parameters. The `node_mobility_th` theory shows the definition of such a function in PVS. Three auxiliary functions are used to implement the corresponding steps.

```
node_mobility_th: THEORY
 BEGIN
 IMPORTING network_graph_th

   %-- select a target direction
   select_target(s: finite_set[node_id]): node_id

   %-- generate the new set of neighbours for the mobile node
   new_neighbours(tp: topology, mobile_node, target_node: node_id): finite_set[node_id] =
       {n: node_id | (n /= mobile_node) AND (tp(target_node)(n) OR n = target_node)}

   %-- change topology tp according to the new neighbourhood of the mobile node
   change_topology(tp: topology)(mobile_node: node_id, nbs: finite_set[node_id]): topology =
       LET tp = remove_node(mobile_node, tp)
        IN add_node(mobile_node, nbs, tp)
```

```
  %-- node mobility function
  node_mobility(m: node_id, tp: topology): topology =
      LET target  = select_target(tp(m)), new_nbs = new_neighbours(tp, m, target)
       IN change_topology(tp)(m, new_nbs)

  %-- ... more definitions omitted
END node_mobility_th
```

The target direction of the mobile node can be selected through a set of rules. Rules depend on the mobility model, and they can be either deterministic or random. For instance, suppose that a node moves according to a random walk, i.e., the mobile node takes a decision about the direction option for the next step according to a random distribution. Random walk is a well-known searching technique for resource discovery in decentralised networks. In the framework, such a mobility pattern can be specified by means of a function `random_walk`, which moves the mobile node n times:

```
random_walk_th: THEORY
  BEGIN
  IMPORTING node_mobility_th

  random_walk(n: nat)(ng: network_graph): RECURSIVE network_graph =
    IF n = 0 THEN ng
    ELSE LET tp = node_mobility(mobile_node, new_topology(ng)), ng = new_network_graph(tp)
          IN random_walk(n-1)(ng) ENDIF
      MEASURE n
 END random_walk_th
```

Theory `random_walk_th` can be used to study protocols in dynamic scenarios. In the following we show an example where a mobile base station moves according to a random walk pattern and periodically injects a new packet; sensor nodes execute the flooding protocol to diffuse packets.

```
mobile_scenario_th: THEORY
  BEGIN %--... imports and some declarations omitted

  mobile_scenario(n: nat)(net: network_state, ng: network_graph)
         (sched_grp: finite_set[node_id]): RECURSIVE network_state =
    IF n = 0 THEN net
    ELSE LET ng = random_walk(S)(mobile_node, ng), %-- move the base station of S steps
             scheduled_id = flooding_app_scheduler(sched_grp),
             net = IF scheduled_id = base_station
                   THEN inject(scheduled_id)(net, ng) %-- the base injects a new packet
                   ELSE flooding(scheduled_id)(net, ng) %-- nodes execute flooding
                   ENDIF
          IN mobile_scenario(n-1)(net, ng)(remove(scheduled_id, sched_grp))
    ENDIF
      MEASURE n

 END mobile_scenario_th
```

Note that the specification above is executable and can be animated to perform simulation. Examples of random walks traced by the mobile node during simulation on a grid with 64 places with 8 columns and rows are shown in Figure 1. In our simulations, the mobile node is initially placed on the top-left corner of the grid. Different initial positions can, of course, be chosen. Grids with larger number of places and different structure can be used as well. For the sake of simplicity, the figure reports only the trace drawn by the mobile node without any direction indication.

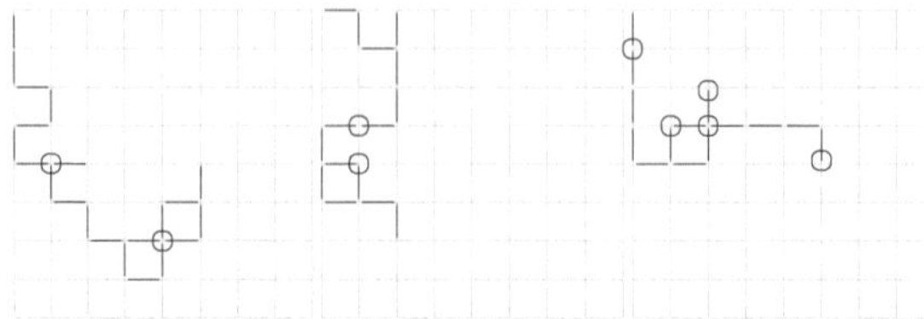

Fig. 1. Examples of random walks that can be generated during simulations. Circles represent places where the mobile node stopped for at least one step.

Automated Generation of Routing Tables. Routing tables are, by definition, tables that store, for each node, a path suitable to reach other nodes. Hence, we specified the routing table with a function which returns, for any node, a vector of paths: given a network graph G and a routing table rt, the vector of paths starting from i is $rt(i)$, and the path from i to j is $rt(i)(j)$. In this definition, we benefit from the definition of paths provided in [11]: a path from i to j is a `prewalk` of nodes (i.e., a sequence of nodes) that must be traversed on the network graph to reach j starting from i.

```
routing_table_th: THEORY
BEGIN
IMPORTING network_graph_th, digraphs[node_id]

   routing_table: TYPE = [i: node_id -> [j: node_id -> prewalk[node_id]]]
   routing_table?(rt: routing_table, g: network_graph): bool =
                                     FORALL (i, j: node_id): route?(g, rt(i)(j), i, j)

   valid_route?(g: network_graph, p: prewalk[node_id], i, j: node_id): bool =
       ((i /= j) AND (l(p) > 1) AND path_from?(g, p, i, j))

   valid_routing_table?(rt: routing_table, g: network_graph): bool =
       routing_table?(rt,g) AND FORALL (i, j: node_id): valid_route?(g, rt(i)(j), i, j)

   %-- ... more definitions omitted
 END routing_table_th
```

In order to automate the generation of routing tables, we extended the framework with a new theory `rtgen_th` which defines a service that, given a network graph, generates a routing table. Basically, `rtgen_th` models a technique that is frequently used in WSNs to generate routing tables. The technique is based on a protocol which performs the following actions. A node forwards a received packet only if the packet is received for the first time, otherwise the packet is dropped; packets carry a hop-count field in their payload that is incremented every time the packet is forwarded. To build a routing table with the above algorithm, the base station sends out a *beacon* packet with hop-count equal to 0; as the packet gets forwarded in the network, nodes learn about their own distance from the base station, and nodes are also able to estimate the distance of their neighbours by inspecting the sender address and hop-count fields of the received packets.

In the framework, the service can be specified as follows:

```
rtgen_th: THEORY
 BEGIN
IMPORTING routing_table_th    %-- ... more imports omitted

  rtgen(x:node_id)(net:network_state, g:network_graph)
       (bs:node_id, rt:routing_table): network_state =
    IF empty?(net_receive_buffer(net)(x)) THEN idle(x)(net, g, rt)
    ELSE LET received_pk = getpacket(net_receive_buffer(net)(x)),
             hopcount = getpayload(received_pk)(COUNTER_FIELD)
          IN IF forwarded_packets(x, net_log(net)) = 0
             THEN forward(received_pk WITH [destination_addr := lossy_bcast_addr,
                                                    payload := new_payload(hopcount+1)])
                         (x)(net,g,rt)
             ELSE drop(received_pk)(x)(net, g, rt)
             ENDIF
    ENDIF

  rtgen_service(net: network_state, g: network_graph, rt: routing_table):
         RECURSIVE network_state =
      LET grp = next_rpf_group(net_receive_buffer(net), net_log(net))
       IN IF zero?(grp) THEN net
          ELSE LET scheduled_id = random(grp),
                   net_prime = rtgen_rec(scheduled_id)(net, g)(0, rt)
                IN rtgen_service(net_prime, g, rt)
        ENDIF
       MEASURE size(next_rpf_group(net_receive_buffer(net), net_log(net)))

   %-- ... more definitions omitted
 END rtgen_th
```

Routing tables can be generated either with ideal or lossy transmissions. In the case of ideal transmissions, routing tables always define a spanning tree with minimum hop distance from the base station. With lossy transmissions, on the other hand, the generated routing tables define a spanning tree with a random structure. For lossy transmissions, we can instantiate the probability P_{rx} for which node $x \in$ `lossy_bcast_addr`. When lossy transmissions are used, a `check` predicate controls if the generated routing table is valid. In the case that the routing table is not valid – this may happen with lossy transmissions when some nodes are not reached by the beacon packet sent by the base station to build the routing table – the procedure was instrumented to automatically try to generate a new routing table.

4 Case Study: The Reverse Path Forwarding Algorithm

In this section we will apply the proposed approach to the reverse path forwarding (RPF) algorithm, which is the basic technique used for diffusion protocols for WSNs. RPF is a broadcast routing method which exploits the information contained in the routing table to deliver packets generated by a base station to all other nodes in a multi-hop network. With RPF, packets are propagated with the following policy: a node n accepts a packet received from node p only if n believes that p is the best next hop on the path to the base station, as specified in the routing table. It is well known that, under the assumption of a static routing table, the reverse path forwarding algorithm delivers exactly one copy of the broadcast packet to all nodes. If, however, the routing table is dynamic, as is usually the case in real-world deployments, then such guarantees cannot be made for RPF [12].

In our framework, the algorithm is specified as follows: a broadcast packet received by node x is accepted for forwarding if the sender address of the packet is the best next hop of x towards the base station. The best next hop can be derived from the routing table. The specification of the algorithm is:

```
rpf_th: THEORY
  BEGIN IMPORTING routing_table_th    %-- ... more imports omitted

 rpf(x: node_id)(g:network_graph, base_station:node_id, rt:routing_table)
    (net: network_state): network_state =
   IF empty?(net_receive_buffer(net)(x)) THEN idle(x)(net, g, rt)
   ELSE LET received_pk = getpacket(net_receive_buffer(net)(x)),
            source_addr = source_addr(received_pk),
            sender_addr = sender_addr(received_pk),
            next_hop = next_hop(x, base_station)(g, rt)
         IN IF sender_addr = next_hop
            THEN forward(received_pk)(x)(net,g,rt)
            ELSE drop(received_pk)(x)(net, g, rt)
            ENDIF
   ENDIF

   %-- ... more definitions omitted
 END rpf_th
```

The main property of the RPF algorithm is the following:

Property P. *If the routing table is correct and static, then exactly one copy of the broadcast packet sent by the base station will be delivered to all nodes in the network.*

5 Simulation

To simulate RPF, we need to specify an application scenario that takes into account how the system evolves. As RPF itself does not generate routing tables, we use the PVS function `rtgen` shown in Section 3 for that purpose.

In our simulations, we generated routing tables by using `lossy_bcast_addr` with $P_{rx} = 0.94$, which can be a reasonable value for low power wireless devices [13]. A semantic attachment of the PVSio library is used to generate pseudo-random numbers. Moreover, a theory for generating random sets of nodes has been implemented. In our simulations, a uniform distribution is used, but other distributions can be adopted as well, either providing an executable specification or changing the semantic attachment. On a desktop computer with a 2 GHz processor, a valid routing table can be generated in seconds for networks of 100 nodes placed on a grid. For a network of 1000 node placed on a grid, the average time is of few minutes.

In our setting, the base station periodically injects packets in the network, and other nodes apply the RPF algorithm. Each packet injected by the base station is uniquely identified: this way we can derive useful statistics by inspecting the log of nodes. In our simulations, a random node is scheduled at each simulator step. The scheduler is specified so that fairness of execution between nodes is guaranteed, i.e., all nodes are able to execute the algorithm and make progress at the same speed. Nodes operate in burst mode, i.e., when a node is scheduled, all packets in the receive buffer are processed according to the RPF algorithm.

We aim at evaluating the delivery ratio and the overhead due to duplicates in some representative scenarios of dynamic environment. The delivery ratio of a node x is the number of packets delivered to node x over the number of packets sent to node x. If the delivery ratio is one, then all packets were delivered to the intended destination. The overhead due to duplicates is the amount of traffic due to packet replicas. Such overhead can be caused by the RPF algorithm when the routing table is not static [12].

In the following paragraphs, we show simulation results obtained for networks of 64 nodes placed on a grid with 8 columns. Networks with larger number of nodes and different structures can be simulated as well.

Link Quality

Link quality is a measure of the probability of successful communication over a link. In wireless networks, nodes can estimate the quality of the links with their neighbours, e.g., through the received signal strength intensity (RSSI), which is automatically computed by the wireless radio chip whenever a packet gets received [14]. In wireless environments, link quality may dramatically change because of many factors, ranging from hardware/software nodes failure to environmental factors (e.g., humidity, obstacles). In multi-hop wireless networks, link failures may lead to network partitioning because of the limited communication range of the radio equipment. Hence, whenever a link between two neighbouring nodes fails, such nodes must choose a new next hop in order to recover the routing table.

We evaluate the RPF algorithm in a scenario where the routing table always contains paths with the best local link quality. The base station periodically injects a new packet in the network, and all nodes apply the RPF algorithm to diffuse the packet. We assume that the quality of different links is not correlated, and that link quality may change with a uniform probability P_c. The specification of the application scenario used to simulate the network for n steps is shown in the following.

```
rpf_sim_th: THEORY
  BEGIN
   %-- ...imports omitted

link_quality_app(Pc:real)(n:nat)(net:network_state, ng:network_graph, rt:routing_table)
                (base_station:node_id, sched_grp:finite_set[node_id]):
        RECURSIVE network_state =
  IF n = 0 THEN net
  ELSE LET (rt, nf) = change_routing_table(Pc)(n)(base_station, ng, rt),
           sched_id = random_scheduler(sched_grp),
           net_prime = IF sched_id = base_station
                       THEN inject_service(sched_id,n)(net,ng)(rt)
                       ELSE rpf_service(sched_id)(net,ng)(base_station,rt)
                       ENDIF
        IN link_quality_app(Pc)(n - 1)(net_prime, ng, rt)
                           (base_station, update_sched(sched_id, sched_grp))
  ENDIF MEASURE n
   %-- ... more definitions omitted
  END rpf_sim_th
```

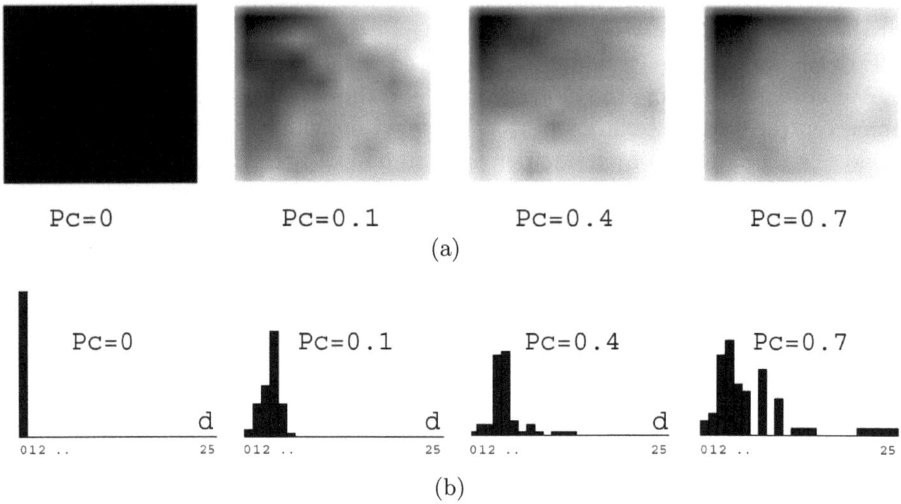

Fig. 2. Examples of simulation results with different link quality change probability Pc. (a) Delivery ratio at the end of different simulation runs. (b) Distribution of duplicates.

Function `change_routing_table` reflects the possible changes in the routing table due to changes in the quality of the links, and uses `rt_gen` to generate new routing tables.

The results of four simulations runs in which RPF has been evaluated with different probabilities Pc are shown in Figure 2. For each simulation run, routing tables were chosen randomly, and link quality changed if the value of a random variable was higher than a given threshold. Figure 2(a) shows a snapshot of the grid network at the end of simulation runs. The images relate the physical position of nodes with colours that highlight the number of packets successfully delivered (darker colours for higher delivery ratios). The base station is placed in the top-left corner of the grid. As expected, the delivery ratio is 1, i.e., all packets are delivered, when the link quality does not change (Pc=0). In the case of dynamic scenarios (Pc≠0), on the other hand, some nodes are not able to receive the packet sent out by the base station. Moreover, we can notice that the delivery ratio is relatively high for nodes that are closer to the source node (i.e., the base station), while it decreases rapidly for distant nodes. Figure 2(b) reports the distribution of duplicates among nodes. The x-axis of the histogram reports the number *d* of duplicates, the y-axis reports the number of nodes that received *d* duplicates. It can be noticed how the number of duplicates rapidly grows with the dynamics of the network.

These kinds of analyses can be applied to communication protocols to derive useful information about possibly unexpected behaviours. For instance, if energy consumption is a main concern for the application, results may point out that developers should combine their algorithm with a mechanism that efficiently suppresses duplicates.

Node Mobility

We also evaluated the RPF algorithm with changing routing table due to a mobile base station. In our scenario, the base station moves according to a random walk pattern, i.e., the base station takes a decision about the direction option for the next step according to a random distribution. Random walks are well-known searching techniques for resource discovery in decentralised networks. Every time the base station moves, a new routing table is generated and a new packet is sent out. The application used to simulate n steps of the network is similar to that of link quality changes. The main difference, with respect to the specification used for link quality changes, is the function used to generate the new routing table. In this case, first, the topology of the network is updated to reflect the mobility of the base station; second, a new routing table is generated:

```
rpf_sim_th: THEORY
  BEGIN %-- ...imports omitted

node_mobility_app(n:nat)(net:network_state, ng:network_graph, rt:routing_table)
                 (base_station: node_id, sched_grp: finite_set[node_id]):
        RECURSIVE network_state =
  IF n = 0 THEN net
  ELSE LET (ng, rt)  = move_base_station(n)(base_station, ng, rt),
          sched_id  = random_scheduler(sched_grp),
          net_prime = IF sched_id = base_station
                      THEN inject_service(sched_id,n)(net,ng)(rt)
                      ELSE rpf_service(sched_id)(net,ng)(base_station,rt)
                      ENDIF
       IN node_mobility_app(n - 1)(net_prime, ng, rt)
                           (base_station, update_sched(sched_id, sched_grp))
  ENDIF
MEASURE n
   %-- ... more definitions omitted
  END rpf_sim_th
```

Figure 3 shows some results of simulations where the base station was initially placed on the top-left corner of the grid. The random walks traced by the mobile base station during three simulation runs are shown in Figure 3(a). For the sake of simplicity, the figure reports only the trace drawn by the mobile node without any direction indication. Figure 3(b) shows the delivery ratio obtained for a simulation run (the walk performed by the mobile node is shown in overlay). It can be noticed that the delivery ratio is higher for nodes closer to the path

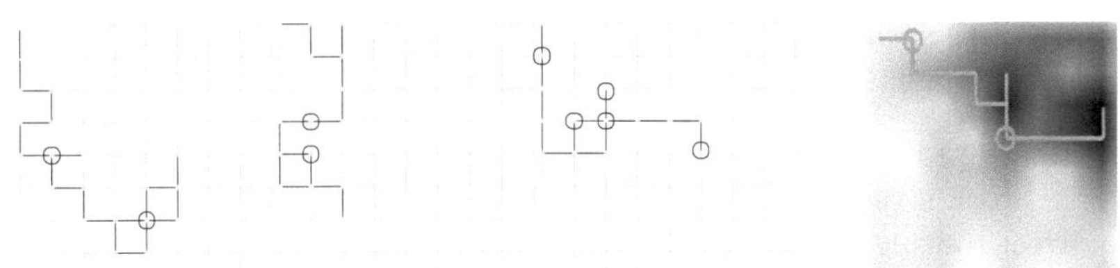

(a) (b)

Fig. 3. Example of simulations results with a mobile base station. (a) Random walks; circles represent places where the mobile node stopped. (b) Delivery Ratio; the random walk is shown in overlay.

traversed by the base station. The average delivery ratio is between 0.23 and 0.59, with an average value of 0.34; with more details, the average delivery ratio of nodes that were immediate neighbours of the mobile node is 0.4, while for other nodes it is only 0.29 in average. Such results are coherent with respect to the results presented in [15], where RPF was evaluated for a mobile base station following a random waypoint mobility pattern.

6 Formal Verification

In this section, we outline the proof that the specification of RPF satisfies property **P** when the routing table is static. The execution of the RPF algorithm is specified as a sequence of network states which starts from an initial state and repeatedly applies a state transition function. For RPF, the initial state models the injection of a packet in the network by the base station. The state transition function models the execution of the algorithm of a generic node x, which is applied recursively to all received packets using an auxiliary `rpf_service` function:

```
rpf_proof_th: THEORY
  BEGIN %-- ... imports omitted

   rpf_service(t: nat)(x: node_id)
             (ns:network_state, g:network_graph, rt:routing_table) : network_state =
     LET scheduled_node = scheduler(t),
         n = size(net_receive_buffer(ns)(scheduled_node))
      IN execute(rpf(scheduled_node)(g,base_station, rt))(n)(ns)

   rpf_transition(ns0, ns1: network_state, t: nat)
                (g: network_graph, rt: routing_table): bool =
     ns1 = rpf_service(scheduled_node)(ns0, g)(base_station, rt)

   rpf_trace(seq: sequence[network_state])(g: network_graph, rt: routing_table): bool =
     seq(0) = initial_rpf_state(base_station) AND
      FORALL(t:nat): rpf_transition(seq(t),seq(t+1),t)(base_station,g,rt)

   %-- ... more definitions omitted
  END rpf_proof_th
```

The formal proof of property **P** is by an induction on the execution traces of RPF, i.e., on sequences that start with the initial state and apply the RPF transition function to generate subsequent states states. Furthermore, the proof makes use of the following properties and constraints, which can be expressed as additional lemmas, or sub-type conditions:

- the routing table is correct and does not change
- the network is not partitioned
- a correct routing table rt exists, which defines a spanning tree rooted at the base station
- all nodes are guaranteed to be scheduled at least once every N steps of the execution trace, where N is the number of nodes in the network
- all nodes operate in burst mode: when a node is allowed to transmit, it sends out all packets waiting to be transmitted

To accomplish the overall proof, the following lemmas proved useful:

Lemma 1. *For all execution traces and network states, for every node x, the number of packets with sender address equal to the next hop of x in the receive log of node x, is equal to the number of packets in the forward log of the next hop of x (by definition, the next hop of the base station is the base station itself).* ◇

Lemma 2. *For all execution traces and network states, for every node x, the number of packets with sender address equal to the next hop of x in the forward log of node x is less than or equal to the number of packets in the receive log of node x.* ◇

Lemma 3. *For all execution traces and all network states, for every node x, if the number of packets with sender address equal to the next hop of x in the receive log of x is ≥ 1 at time t, then the number of packets in the forward log of node x is ≥ 1 at time $(t+N)$, where N is the number of nodes in the network.* ◇

The delivery of the broadcast packet is assessed through the receive log of nodes. To this end, the proof of property **P** is split into two parts: first we prove that the number of received packets is at most one; second, we prove that the number of received packets is at least one. The proofs have been developed and mechanically checked with the theorem prover of PVS.

Theorem 1. *For every node x, the number of received packets with sender equal to next hop of x is at most one.*

Proof outline. *The proof is given by induction on the number k of hops between the node and the base station on the spanning tree defined by the routing table.*

Base: $k = 1$. *The proof follows from the assumption that the base station injects only one packet.*

Induction: $k = n + 1$. *The path p between the base station and node x is split into a path p' between the base station and next hop of x and an edge between next hop of x and x. The length of p' is n. Hence, the inductive hypothesis holds for the next hop of x, which receives at most one packet. By using Lemma 2, we obtain that x receives at most one packet from the next hop* ◇

Theorem 2. *For every node x, the number of packets with sender equal to next hop of x is at least one.*

Proof Outline. *The proof is given by induction on the number k of hops between the node and the base station on the spanning tree defined by the routing table and by using the assumption on fairness for transmissions.*

Base: $k = 1$. *By construction of the initial state, the base station has injected a packet at time $t = 0$. Hence the receive log of neighbours of the base station contains the packet sent by the base station at time $t = 0$.*

Induction: $k = n + 1$. *The path p between the base station and node x is split into a path p' between the base station and next hop of x and an edge between* *next hop of x and x. The length of p' is n. Hence, the inductive hypothesis holds for the next hop of x, which receives at least one packet at a time t. By using Lemma 3, we obtain that next hop of x forwarded at least one packet at time $t + N$. By Lemma 1, there is at least one packet with sender address equal to next hop of x in the receive log of x.* ◇

7 Related Work and Conclusions

The need for formal modelling and analysis of algorithms for wireless networks has been pointed out in many papers. In [4], basic properties of the Reverse Path Forwarding algorithm have been analysed with FDR and Alloy Analyser. Scalability is the main problem of such an approach: only very simple and small network configurations were analysed, and specific hypotheses were assumed in a hand-proof of the correctness the algorithm . In [5], Lamport's Temporal Logic of Actions is used to model and simulate diffusion protocols for discovering routing trees for gathering and disseminating data. The analysis focuses on performance variation of push and pull phases of the diffusion protocol for routing trees with different shapes, however without the objective of algorithm design evaluation. In [16], Real-Time Maude has been applied to the OGDC density control algorithm and networks of several hundred nodes were analysed. The approach allows modelling the algorithm at high levels of detail, using broadcast and unicast communication primitives; results are claimed to be often more accurate compared to other network simulators.

In this paper we show an approach based on the PVS system to analyse protocols for WSNs in dynamic scenarios with mobile nodes and link quality changes. As case study, we developed a formal specification for RPF. Through simulation, we evaluated the algorithm and we have obtained results that are coherent with those reported in other papers. Furthermore, we used the theorem prover of PVS to verify core correctness properties of RPF when the routing table is guaranteed to remain unchanged.

The approach allows an easy specification of the characteristics of wireless networks, such as limited communication range, lossy transmissions, node mobility. The advantages of our approach are that it allows to develop a formal specification of the protocol at different levels of abstraction, opening the possibility to make complex systems tractable, and that the same formal specification can be automatically translated into executable code suitable for simulations and as basis for formal reasoning in a theorem proving system.

References

1. Akyldiz, I., Su, W., Sankarasubramaniam, Y., Cayirci, E.: Wireless Sensor Networks: a Survey. Computer Networks 38, 393–422 (2002)
2. Varga, A.: The Omnet++ Discrete Event Simulation System. In: Proceedings of the European Simulation Multiconference (ESM 2001) (June 2001)

3. Buck, J., Ha, S., Lee, E.A., Messerschmitt, D.G.: Ptolemy: a Framework for Simulating and Prototyping Heterogeneous Systems. In: Readings in hardware/software co-design, pp. 527–543. Kluwer Academic Publishers, Dordrecht (2002)
4. Bolton, C., Lowe, G.: Analyses of the Reverse Path Forwarding Routing Algorithm. In: Proc. Intl. Conf. on Dependable Systems and Networks, pp. 485–494. IEEE Computer Society, Los Alamitos (2004)
5. Nair, S., Cardell-Oliver, R.: Formal Specification and Analysis of Performance Variation in Sensor Network Diffusion Protocols. In: Proc. Symp. on Modeling, Analysis and Simulation of Wireless and Mobile Systems, pp. 170–173. ACM, New York (2004)
6. Bhargavan, K., Gunter, C., Lee, I., Sokolsky, O., Kim, M., Obradovic, D., Viswanathan, M.: Verisim: Formal Analysis of Network Simulations. IEEE Trans. Software Engineering 28(2), 129–145 (2002)
7. Bernardeschi, C., Masci, P., Pfeifer, H.: Early Prototyping of Wireless Sensor Network Algorithms in PVS. In: Harrison, M.D., Sujan, M.-A. (eds.) SAFECOMP 2008. LNCS, vol. 5219, pp. 346–359. Springer, Heidelberg (2008)
8. Owre, S., Rushby, J., Shankar, N., Henke, F.v.: Formal Verification for Fault-Tolerant Architectures: Prolegomena to the Design of PVS. IEEE Trans. on Software Engineering 21(2), 107–125 (1995)
9. Crow, J., Owre, S., Rushby, J., Shankar, N., Stringer-Calvert, D.: Evaluating, testing, and animating PVS specifications. Technical Report, Computer Science Laboratory, SRI International, Menlo Park, CA (2001)
10. Muñoz, C.: Rapid prototyping in PVS. Technical Report NIA Report No. 2003-03, NASA/CR-2003-212418, National Institute of Aerospace, Hampton, VA (2003)
11. Butler, R., Sjogren, J.: A pvs graph theory library. Nasa Technical Memorandum 1998-206923, NASA Langley Research Center, Hampton, Virginia (1998)
12. Dalal, Y., Metcalfe, R.: Reverse Path Forwarding of Broadcast Packets. Communications of ACM 21(12), 1040–1048 (1978)
13. Woo, A., Tong, T., Culler, D.: Taming the Underlying Challenges of Reliable Multihop Routing in Sensor Networks. In: SenSys 2003, pp. 14–27. ACM Press, New York (2003)
14. Texas Instruments: Chipcon CC2420 Datasheet (2007), `http://focus.ti.com/lit/ds/symlink/cc2420.pdf`
15. Clausen, T., Larsen, N., Olesen, T., Viennot, L.: Investigating Data Broadcast Performance in Mobile ad hoc Networks. In: The 5th International Symposium on Wireless Personal Multimedia Communications, WPMC (2002)
16. Ölveczky, P., Thorvaldsen, S.: Formal Modeling and Analysis of the OGDC Wireless Sensor Network Algorithm in Real-Time Maude. In: Bonsangue, M.M., Johnsen, E.B. (eds.) FMOODS 2007. LNCS, vol. 4468, pp. 122–140. Springer, Heidelberg (2007)

Consensus When All Processes May Be Byzantine for Some Time

Martin Biely[1,2,⋆] and Martin Hutle[3]

[1] Ecole polytechnique, 91128 Palaiseau Cédex, France
[2] TU Wien, Embedded Computing Systems Group (182/2) 1040 Wien, Austria
biely@ecs.tuwien.ac.at
[3] Ecole Polytechnique Fédérale de Lausanne (EPFL) 1015 Lausanne, Switzerland
martin.hutle@epfl.ch

Abstract. Among all classes of faults, Byzantine faults form the most general modeling of value faults. Traditionally, in the Byzantine fault model, faults are statically attributed to a set of up to t processes. This, however, implies that in this model a process at which a value fault occurs is forever "stigmatized" as being Byzantine, an assumption that might not be acceptable for long-lived systems, where processes need to be reintegrated after a fault.

We thus consider a model where Byzantine processes can recover in a predefined recovery state, and show that consensus can be solved in such a model.

1 Introduction

Consensus is the fundamental problem of achieving agreement among distributed processes in the presence of faults. When considering process faults, the most general assumption is that processes may behave arbitrarily. This class of faults was termed Byzantine [1]. It is a quite old and well-known result that in order to tolerate up to t faulty processes, at least $n = 3t + 1$ processes are necessary. The usual assumption on failures puts a severe restriction on the distribution of faults in a system. Consider the case of $n = 4$ and $t = 1$: Once a single fault occurs at one process, say p, from this time on, further faults are allowed to occur *only* at p, without violating the fault assumptions.

The reason for this is that traditionally, faults are considered to be *permanent*: a process that is faulty once, is considered to be faulty forever. In [2] it was shown that in the case of benign faults this is an unnecessary restriction, and that consensus can be solved even if all processes are unstable as long as they are up long enough. In the case of arbitrary value faults, however, a transient fault can leave a process with a corrupted state, and thus the assumption of permanent faults seems to be justified for these kind of faults. However, its very unlikely that Byzantine faults live forever: often processes with a corrupted

⋆ Martin Biely is partially supported by the Austrian BM:vit FIT-IT project *TRAFT* (proj. no. 812205).

R. Guerraoui and F. Petit (Eds.): SSS 2009, LNCS 5873, pp. 120–132, 2009.

state crash [3], can be detected to be erroneous [4,5], or are subject to proactive recovery [6].

This leads us to investigate systems where processes recover from being Byzantine. Such a fault assumption is especially favorable for long-lived systems and systems with high costs for hardware. There, the reintegration of components that were subject to a soft error (that is a transient fault caused by a single event upset) is essential. Such radiation induced soft errors were usually only considered a problem in aerospace applications (where they are more or less ubiquitous due to cosmic radiation, e.g., [7,8]). More recent research shows that soft error rates are bound to increase also on ground level due to the decreasing feature sizes and operating voltages (e.g., [9,10,11]).

When considering recovery in the case of benign faults, one distinguishes between systems with or without stable storage [2]. In case of value faults, stable storage is of no help, as a process can corrupt it arbitrarily when it is faulty. We are thus limited to systems without stable storage. As failures can not only corrupt the stable storage but also the state of the process, losing a process's state and putting the process in a well-defined recovery state is not a restriction but a wanted feature in this case. This, however, adds a difficulty to the problem of solving consensus: if too many processes lose their state, the information about previous decision values or initial values might get lost, and may thus lead to violation of agreement and/or validity. Are we thus back to an assumption where only some processes might ever be faulty?

The key to answer this question in the negative is that not all processes are faulty *at the same time*. When looking at long-lived systems, it is also not very likely that the system is constructed such that error probabilities are high enough for that. As we show in this paper, if we generalize t to be a threshold on the number of faults during some period of time, we actually can solve consensus even in the case where *all* processes are temporarily faulty in an execution. After recovery, the previously faulty processes must be reintegrated, that is they need to learn about the current state of the computation, among other things about the initial values or even previous decisions. For this, we can only rely on the information distributed in the system (as it is the case for benign recovery without stable storage) to let a recovering process learn about these values. This is only possible if we assume a recovering process receives sufficiently many messages before another process can fail instead of it. In perpetually synchronous systems with perpetually good communication this is easily achieved by making the fault turnover interval large enough.

Our model, however, is a relaxation of the famous model of [12] where the system is allowed to alternate between good and bad periods [2], where in good periods the synchrony assumptions hold for correct processes and messages between them, whereas in bad periods there is no such assumption. We consider only good periods that are larger than some minimum length, which will suffice to allow a recovering process to learn a new state. The threshold t is defined such that it is the maximum number of faulty processes in any bad period together with its adjacent good periods. This "overlapping" definition guarantees that no new processes can fail before recovered processes have learned about the past. Finally, in order to decide we require a good period in which all processes have recovered. In Section 4 we discuss how to relax this condition.

1.1 Related Work

With respect to consensus protocols in partial synchronous systems with Byzantine faults, beside the seminal work of Dwork et al. [12], the protocols BFT [6] and Fast Byzantine Paxos [13] have received a lot of attention. There have been several approaches to make BFT more practical, e.g., [14,15,16,17]. Fast Byzantine Paxos shares some algorithmic similarities with $\mathcal{A}_{T,E}$ [18] and thus also with our algorithm. Even weaker synchrony assumptions (but higher link reliability assumptions) are considered in [19]. None of these papers considers a consensus algorithm with recovery in the Byzantine case.

The replication protocol of BFT [6] has a variant that supports proactive recovery. However, in their case, recovery may occur only between several consensus instances. For a single instance of consensus, BFT has a fixed set of faulty processes. Their approach heavily relies on cryptography, so that a process after recovery enters the system with a new identity, makes use of stable storage and tries to verify whether this stored state is still valid. It also uses extra recovery messages to integrate a new replica into the system.

This is in contrast to our work, where we do not need any of these means. Our solution allows recoveries *during* a consensus instance and does not specify the reason for recoveries. As it is the case for recovery in the benign case, whether recovery during a consensus instance is a relevant case in practice depends highly on the application. For our work, it is mainly important to show that it is *possible*.

Recovery from arbitrary faults was previously considered in the context of clock synchronization [20,21,22]. A stronger model, where the system is synchronous and Byzantine processes eventually crash (but do not recover) is considered in [3] to solve consensus.

Although our work may seem to be related to self-stabilization [23], this is not the case, as we do not allow all processes to be in an arbitrary state. Indeed the consensus problem is trivially impossible to solve in such systems. Examples of agreement problems solvable in the context of self-stabilization include clock synchronization [24] and iterated consensus [25].

1.2 Algorithm Idea

Our algorithm maintains a round structure where, for each process that is correct, a round model is simulated, *i.e.*, at the beginning of each round a process sends messages to all other processes and at the end of the round, every process has received (some of) these messages. Moreover, this round model is communication closed, which means that messages are only delivered in the round they are sent.

In general rounds are not synchronized during a bad period, and thus there is no guarantee to receive all messages, but the algorithm ensures that a group of correct processes keep their rounds synchronized and no correct process is in a higher round than any member of this group. As soon as a good period starts (and this period is sufficiently long), our algorithm ensures that all correct processes resynchronize with this group of processes and that all processes that recovered update their state so that they are properly integrated in the protocol. This ensures that after some bounded time in a good period, every correct process receives a message from every correct process in every round. Furthermore, by filtering the stored messages our algorithm ensures an "isolation" property, so that no message from a faulty process will be used in a higher round where this process is not "counted as faulty" anymore. That is, there was a good period between the times these rounds were entered (cf. the definition of t above). We will discuss the message filtering and other concepts central to our solution in more detail in Section 3.

The consensus part of our solution is based on the $\mathcal{A}_{T,E}$ algorithm of [18], shown here as Algorithm 1. This algorithm was developed in a high-level round model where no process faults occur but transmission value faults are allowed to be transient and dynamic. More specifically, every process may receive up to α faulty messages per round, where the faulty links may be different in different rounds. It solves consensus with appropriate choices of the parameters T and E, that is, if $n \geq E$ and $n \geq T > 2(n+2\alpha-E)$.[1] In our context with process faults we have $\alpha = t$, and this bound is ensured by the isolation property mentioned above. In order to allow recovering processes to learn new values, we need to fix $T = n - t$, otherwise the faulty processes could prevent a process that just recovered from learning a suitable estimate value denoted x_p, by just not sending any message. From this it follows that $n > 5t$ and, in the minimum case $n = 5t + 1$, that $E = n$.

The core intuition of the consensus protocol is the following: once a correct process decides a value v, it has received $E = n$ messages proposing this value. Thus, at least $T = n - t$ correct processes had v as their estimate x_p in the current round. Therefore, in this and all subsequent rounds, a correct process can only update its x_p to v (line 8).

Similar to the approach of [2] our solution can be interpreted as an implementation of this abstraction in a lower level system model. However, since the system assumptions are quite different (there are no state corruptions and thus no need for reintegration in the round model of [18]), from a formal point of view a sharp separation between the algorithm and the implementation by using only a predicate as interface is not possible (which contrasts [2]). Consequently, our resulting algorithm is given as a monolithic one.

We like to emphasize that the requirement $n > 5t$ stems from the fact that our algorithm is a *fast* one [13], *i.e.*, in good runs it permits a decision in one round. The recovery part of the algorithm has no extra demand in resilience. We have chosen this algorithm instead of an algorithm with $n > 3t$ because of its simplicity.

[1] Contrary to [18], we exchanged the use of $>$ and $\geq$ in Algorithm 1 and these formulas, which leads to the same results, but simplifies presentation.

Algorithm 1. The $\mathcal{A}_{T,E}$ algorithm of [18], parametrized by the thresholds T and E (see text)

Variable Initialization:
  $x_p \in V$, initially v_p /* v_p is the initial value of p */

Round r **:**
  Sending function S_p^r:
    send $\langle x_p \rangle$ to all processes;

  Transition function T_p^r:
    if received at least T messages **then**
      $x_p :=$ the smallest most often received value in this round
    if at least E values received are equal to v **then**
      DECIDE(v)

This paper is organized as follows. In Section 2 we formally specify our model of Byzantine faults with recovery and state the definition of the consensus variant we solve. In Section 3 we present our algorithm. Proofs of correctness are omitted here due to space constraints but can be found in the associated technical report [26]. In Section 4 we discuss possible extensions of our approach. We conclude the paper in Section 5.

2 Model and Problem Definition

We consider a network of n distributed processes Π which communicate by message-passing. For analysis we assume the existence of global real time which takes values $\tau \in \mathbb{R}$. Processes only have access to an estimate of this global time, given by their unsynchronized local clocks $clock_p(\tau)$. For simplicity, we assume that clocks are always correct. However, it can be seen easily that this is only necessary in good periods, in bad periods only monotonicity is necessary.[2]

Processes make progress by performing steps. In a send step, a single message to another process is sent. (That is, sending a message to oneself does not require a send step.) In a receive step a set S of messages can be received (cf. [12]).

Processes can fail by exhibiting a behavior that is not in compliance with their protocol. For any point in time τ we denote with the right-continuous function $\mathcal{F}(\tau) \subseteq \Pi$ the set of processes faulty at τ. For convenience we denote by $\mathcal{C}(\tau) = \Pi \setminus \mathcal{F}(\tau)$ the set of correct processes at time τ.

We generalize the notion of faulty and correct in a natural way for an interval $I = [\tau_1, \tau_2) \subset \mathbb{R}$, *i.e.*, $\mathcal{F}(I) = \bigcup_{\tau \in I} \mathcal{F}(\tau)$ and $\mathcal{C}(I) = \Pi \setminus \mathcal{F}(I) = \bigcap_{\tau \in I} \mathcal{C}(\tau)$. For an arbitrary contiguous time interval I, we say a process p is I-correct if it is not faulty at any time within that interval, *i.e.*, $p \in \mathcal{C}(I)$; else it is I-faulty, *i.e.*, $p \in \mathcal{F}(I)$.

[2] Further, also for simplicity, we ignore clock drift. While the algorithm (and proofs) can be adapted to include clock drift, it clutters up the presentation and makes their understanding cumbersome.

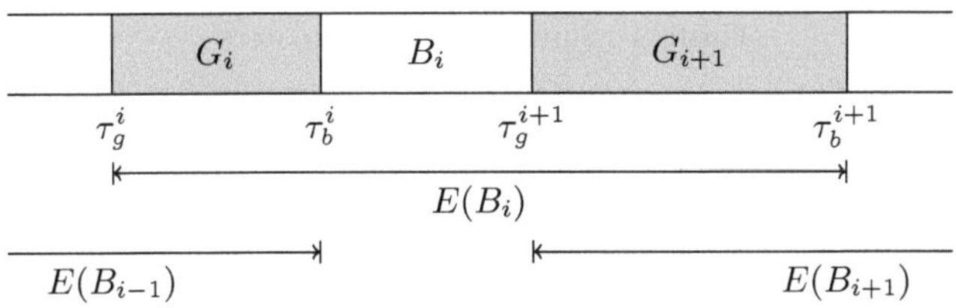

Fig. 1. Good, bad, and enclosing periods: definitions

In general, $\mathcal{F}(\tau)$ can be arbitrary, but we assume that processes can recover from being faulty only by entering a special recovery state. Thus — when we denote by *state*(p, τ) the state of process p at time τ — we get:

$$\forall p \in \Pi, \forall [\tau', \tau) \subset \mathbb{R} : p \in \mathcal{F}([\tau', \tau)) \ \wedge \ p \in \mathcal{C}(\tau) \\ \implies \mathit{state}(p, \tau) = \mathit{recoverystate}_p.$$

For every contiguous interval $I \subset \mathbb{R}$ we say that the processes speed bound Φ holds in I, if and only if every process p that is I-correct makes finitely many but at least one step in any contiguous subinterval of length Φ.[3]

For every contiguous interval $I = [\tau_1, \tau_2) \subset \mathbb{R}$ we say that the communication bound Δ holds in I, if and only if for any message sent from I-correct process p to I-correct process q at time τ_s, the following holds:

(i) If $\tau_s \in I$, q makes a receive step at time $\tau_r \geq \tau_s + \Delta$, and $\tau_r \in I$, then this message is received in this receive step or any receive step q made since τ_s.
(ii) If $\tau_s < \tau_1$, q makes a receive step at time $\tau_r \geq \tau_1 + \Delta$, and $\tau_r \in I$, then this message is received in this receive step or any receive step q made since τ_s or it is never received.

Note that these definitions allow the actual reception by the algorithm to occur later than $\tau_s + \Delta$, which is necessary under certain conditions, for instance when the receiving process performed only send steps since τ_s.

We call an interval I a *good period*, if the process speed bound Φ and the communication bound Δ hold in I. Our system alternates between good and bad periods, and we consider only maximal good periods of length $|I| \geq W$, where the parameter W is to be determined later. We denote τ_g^i the beginning of the ith good period with $|I| \geq W$, and τ_b^i its end; $G_i = [\tau_g^i, \tau_b^i)$. Thus, $B_i = [\tau_b^i, \tau_g^{i+1})$ denotes a bad period (cf. to Figure 1). From the above definitions, it follows that the system is in a bad period from $-\infty$ to at least τ_0, where we assume the computation to start by the first process making a step. This bad period is denoted B_0. For simplicity, we assume w.l.o.g. $\tau_0 = 0$. Note that 0 may not be

[3] There is a subtle difference to the model of [12]. We use continuous time and not discrete time so that our definition of Φ does not put an upper bound on the speed of Byzantine processes (as it is the case in [12]). We think that this weaker modeling fits better the intuition of an arbitrary fault.

Table 1. Summary of Parameters

Parameter	Lower Bound	Typical value	Upper bound
Retransmission delay (η)	$n\Phi$		ϑ
ROUND message timeout (ϑ)	$(3n-1)\Phi + 2\Delta$	$2\Delta + 3n\Phi$	
Max. message age (ζ)	$\vartheta + n\Phi + \Delta$	$3\Delta + 4n\Phi$	$W - \Delta - 2n\Phi$
Min. length of good period (W)	$3\vartheta + (7n-4)\Phi + 3\Delta$	$9\Delta + 16n\Phi$	
Min. length of deciding period (D)	$W + \vartheta + (3n-1)\Phi + \Delta$	$13\Delta + 18n\Phi$	

the start of a good period. Moreover, our definitions imply that a message from a bad period is received at most Δ after the start of a good period, or is lost.

We define $f(I) = |\mathcal{F}(I)|$. If B_i (with $i > 0$) is a bad period, let $E(B_i)$ denote the *enclosing* period, *i.e.*, the bad period with its two adjacent good periods; and $E(B_0)$ is defined as the union of B_0 and G_1. In the remainder of the paper we assume that the resilience bound t holds, that is for any bad period B_i, $f(E(B_i)) \leq t$. Moreover, recall that for decision we assume a good period of length $D \geq W$ where all processes are correct.

In contrast to systems with perpetual faults, our definition of consensus allows processes to decide several times, but we guarantee that all decisions of correct processes are the same. Each process p has an initial value v_p taken from the set of all possible initial values V, and decides according to the following rules:

Agreement: When two processes p and q decide v_p and v_q at times τ_p and τ_q and $p \in \mathcal{C}(\tau_p) \ \wedge \ q \in \mathcal{C}(\tau_q)$, then $v_p = v_q$.

Validity: If all initial values are v and if p decides v_p at time τ_p and $p \in \mathcal{C}(\tau_p)$ then $v_p = v$.

Termination: Every process eventually decides.

3 Algorithm

Our protocol (Algorithm 2) requires $n > 5t$, and uses the timeout parameters ϑ, η, and ζ. Determining the range of values for these parameters is done in the technical report version of this paper [26]; the results can be found in Table 1.

The algorithm operates in rounds, where in each round r basically the following takes place: (i) the ROUND message for round r is sent, and (ii) a timeout is started; (iii) during the timeout, messages are received and processed; (iv) at the end of a round a FIN message is used to synchronize with other processes, before (v) the round ends and the consensus code for this round is executed. The concepts of the algorithm are described in more detail below.

Variables and Initialization. For a process p, the estimate of the consensus decision is stored in x_p, the decision value in $decision_p$. When the process normally starts its execution in line 1 of our algorithm it sets x_p to its initial value. The algorithm starts in round 1, with r_p denoting p's current round number.

The information from a received message is stored in three variables: For each round r', estimates from other processes are stored in $Rcv_p[r']$, where only the value for the current round and the following one are kept. This variable is used

Algorithm 2. Consensus in the Byzantine/recovery model, code for p

$x_p \leftarrow v_p$ /* initial value */
$r_p \leftarrow 1$
$decision_p \leftarrow \perp$
$\forall r', q : Rcv_p[r'][q] \leftarrow \perp$
$\forall r' : R_p[r'] \leftarrow \emptyset, F_p[r'] \leftarrow \emptyset$

while true **do**
  send $\langle \text{ROUND}, r_p, x_p \rangle$ to all
  $timeout \leftarrow clock_p + \vartheta$
  $r_{next} \leftarrow r_p$
  while $clock_p \leq timeout$ **and** $r_p = r_{next}$ **do**
    receive-and-process()
    $r_{next} \leftarrow \max \left\{ r' : \left| \bigcup_{r'' \geq r'} Proc(R_p[r''] \cup F_p[r'']) \right| \geq t+1 \right\}$
  $timeout \leftarrow -\infty$
  while $r_p = r_{next}$ **do**
    if $clock_p \geq timeout$ **then**
      send $\langle \text{FIN}, r_p, x_p \rangle$ to all
      $timeout \leftarrow clock_p + \eta$
    receive-and-process()
    if $|Proc(F_p[r])| \geq n - t$ **then**
      $r_{next} \leftarrow r_p + 1$
    $r_{next} \leftarrow \max \left(\{r_{next}\} \cup \left\{ r' : \left| \bigcup_{r'' \geq r'} Proc(R_p[r''] \cup F_p[r'']) \right| \geq t+1 \right\} \right)$
  while $r_p < r_{next}$ **do**
    if $|\{q \in \Pi : Rcv_p[r_p][q] \neq \perp\}| \geq n - t$ **then**
      $x_p \leftarrow \min \{v' : \#(v') = \max_{v''} \{\#(v'')\}\}$
    if $\exists v \in V : \forall q \in \Pi, Rcv_p[r_p][q] = v$ **then**
      $decision_p \leftarrow v$
    $r_p \leftarrow r_p + 1$

function receive-and-process() **:**
  $S \leftarrow$ receive step
  for each $\langle q, \langle \text{ROUND}, r', - \rangle \rangle \in S$ **do**
    $R_p[r'] \leftarrow R_p[r'] \cup \{\langle q, clock_p \rangle\}$
  for each $\langle q, \langle \text{FIN}, r', - \rangle \rangle \in S$ **do**
    $F_p[r'] \leftarrow F_p[r'] \cup \{\langle q, clock_p \rangle\}$
  for each r' **do**
    for each $\langle q, c \rangle \in R_p[r']$ where $c < clock_p - \zeta$ **do**
      remove $\langle q, c \rangle$ from $R_p[r']$
    for each $\langle q, c \rangle \in F_p[r']$ where $c < clock_p - \zeta$ **do**
      remove $\langle q, c \rangle$ from $F[r']$
  for each $\langle q, \langle \text{ROUND}, r', x' \rangle \rangle \in S$ and each $\langle q, \langle \text{FIN}, r', x' \rangle \rangle \in S$ **do**
    if $r' \in \{r_p, r_p + 1\}$ **then**
      $Rcv_p[r'][q] \leftarrow x'$

on recovery do
  $x_p \leftarrow \perp$
  $r_p \leftarrow 0$
  goto 3

in the consensus core of the algorithm, while the variables R_p and F_p are used in the round synchronization part. These contain the information if and when a ROUND resp. FIN message has been received by p. In this context we use the following abbreviations in the algorithm:

$$Proc(S) := \{p \in \Pi \ : \ \exists c : \ \langle p, c\rangle \in S\}$$
$$\#(v) := |\{q \in \Pi \ : \ Rcv_p[r_p][q] = v\}|$$

where $\langle p, c\rangle$ denotes a pair of a process id and a time. Thus $Proc(S)$ denotes the set of processes which have an entry (with some time) in S. The abbreviation $\#(v)$ just counts the number of times v was received in the current round.

Consensus core. The consensus core, based on Algorithm 1, corresponds to the shaded lines in Algorithm 2. The sending part S_p^r of a round (line 5 of Algorithm 1) corresponds to sending ROUND messages to all other processes at the beginning of a round (line 7). At the end of each round the lines 23–26 are executed, which correspond to the transition function of $\mathcal{A}_{T,E}$ (cf. lines 7 to 10 in Algorithm 1). Here, we use the values stored in $Rcv_p[r_p]$ to determine the messages received in the current round.

Progress in good periods. The aforementioned ROUND message is also used for round synchronization; as such it indicates that the sending process has started a new round (line 7). Subsequently the process sets a timeout of length ϑ and starts collecting messages. Once the timeout expires, it is ready to proceed to the next round, since it can be sure that in a good period all correct processes received a message from all correct processes by that time. The process indicates this fact to the other processes by sending a FIN message. In good periods this message serves only one purpose: it keeps a group of correct processes in a bad period "together", *i.e.*, their round numbers differ by at most 1. Once a process received $n - t$ FIN messages, it ends the round and advances to the next round (line 20). However, since good periods do not always start at the beginning of a round, FIN messages are retransmitted every η time (lines 15–17). Therefore, they also serve as retransmissions of the ROUND messages. This allows the progression through the rounds to continue (shortly) after the beginning of a good period even if all messages are lost in a bad period.

Resynchronization. Not all correct processes will follow the group with the highest round numbers in a bad period. In order to resynchronize, the algorithm has a "catch-up" rule that allows such processes to resynchronize with this group. Once a process receives at least $t+1$ messages with a round number r'' that is higher or equal to some higher round number $r' > r$, the algorithm immediately advances to round r' (lines 12 and 21). Because there are at most t faulty processes in an enclosing period $E(B)$, faulty processes can not cause a premature end of a round for a correct process.

Note that recovering processes (which, due to line 44, start at round 0) also catch up through this resynchronization mechanism.

Message filtering. In order to deal with the additional challenges of the recovery model, we need to do the following two adaptions (cf. function receive-and-process() in Algorithm 2): Firstly, we record quorums for each round together with a time-stamp and remove entries that are older than ζ time. With the right choice of ζ, due to the "overlapping" definition of t it can be ensured that no message from a faulty process sent in a bad period survives a good period. Thus a changing set of faulty processes cannot harm the round structure.

Secondly, we record messages only for the current and the next round. Since (as we show in the next section) for two different bad periods, correct processes have distinct round numbers, this prevents bad processes to place erroneous estimates into Rcv for rounds where they might be correct.

Both adaptations are thus designed to limit the impact of a Byzantine process of a bad period on later periods, when it is no longer faulty.

Recovery. In case of recovery, a process starts in line 42, where it starts executing in round 0 (which is not used elsewhere in the protocol) and with no estimate ($\perp$ will be ignored in lines 23–24). From that time on, it participates in the protocol like a process that never left round 0, until it is able to resynchronize with the rest of the system. This is guaranteed to happen in the next good period, where the recovering process is guaranteed to receive more than $n - t$ messages for a round, and thus also sets its estimate to a value consistent with Agreement and Validity.

Choice of timeouts. The key point of proving the correctness of this algorithm is now to find suitable choices of the algorithm parameters ϑ, η, and ζ, as well for the system parameter W, and the length of a fault-free good period for termination D, so that indeed the algorithm solves consensus. For space reasons, the derivation of the bounds on these figures as well as the proof of correctness are done in the technical report version of this paper [26]. Table 1 summarizes our results, where the "Typical values" listed in the table match the lower bound but are rounded to the next higher multiple of $n\Phi$.

Lemma 1 (Agreement). *If $n > 5t$, if two processes p and q decide v_p and v_q at times τ_p and τ_q and $p \in \mathcal{C}(\tau_p) \wedge q \in \mathcal{C}(\tau_q)$, then $v_p = v_q$.*

Lemma 2 (Validity). *If $n > 5t$ and all initial values are v and if p decides v_p at time τ_p and $p \in \mathcal{C}(\tau_p)$ then $v_p = v$.*

Lemma 3 (Termination). *If there is a good period G_i which has a subinterval I of length $W + \vartheta + (3n - 1)\Phi + \Delta$ in which all processes are correct then, every process decides.*

When all processes are correct, have the same value, and consensus is started synchronously at all processes and in a good period (an *initial good period*), termination is much faster.

Corollary 1 (Fast decision). *If there is an initial good period of duration $\vartheta + 3n\Phi + \Delta$ in which all processes boot simultaneously there are no faulty processes, and all processes initially agree on some value v, then processes decide within one round.*

4 Extensions

In this section we briefly discuss some extensions that can be applied to our algorithm to increase its efficiency.

Multiple instances. First we illustrate how our algorithm can be modified to work for several instances of consensus. The straightforward approach would be of course to use an extra instance of Algorithm 2 for each instance. This is, however, not necessary. In fact, the same round structure can be shared by all instances. This stems from the fact that an execution does not have to start in round 1: since the algorithm allows any number of rounds where "nothing" happens, any new instance of consensus just starts in the current round of the algorithm. The only variables that need thus to be duplicated for each instance are the decision value and the array *Rcv*. For the latter, another optimization is possible. Obviously only the value of the current round and the following round are needed by the algorithm. Thus the size of this variable reduces to $2n$ entries per instance.

Additional permanent crashes. Another fairly straightforward improvement of the current algorithm is to allow permanent crash faulty processes as well, which also allows decisions when some processes are still down. This can be achieved by setting E (recall Algorithm 1) to a value smaller than n. It is easy to see that if we want to tolerate t_c crashes in addition to t Byzantine/recovery faults, we need to set the first threshold $T = n - t - t_c$ and the second one to $E = n - t_c$. The resulting resilience bound $n > 5t + 3t_c$ can then be deduced from the formulas in Section 1.2.

Fast decision. Our algorithm is already fast in the classical sense, *i.e.*, if all processes are correct, have the same value and consensus is started at the same time at all processes, it terminates within one round. However, as Algorithm 2 is written, this round might still last $\vartheta + 3\Phi + \Delta$. A simple modification makes the algorithm really fast without invalidating any of our results: in the first round, if a process receives n ROUND messages containing the same v, it can immediately decide on that value. This can be achieved by executing the transition function part (lines 23 to 26) for the first round as soon as one has received a message from every other process. So a decision within the duration of an *actual* transmission delay, which might be much smaller than Δ, is possible. This behaviour is called weakly one-step in [27], where it is also shown that $n = 5t + 1$ is the lower bound for such algorithms, thus our solution is optimal in this respect. For strongly one-step algorithms, *i.e.*, those that can decide within one δ even when up to t processes behave Byzantine from the start but all correct processes share the same initial value, a lower bound of $n = 7t + 1$ is shown. We conjecture that our algorithm could also be made strongly one-step quite easily. In order to do so we would have to change the algorithm such that it decides when it receives $n - 2t$ messages with the same value ([27] shows that this is a necessary condition for every strongly fast algorithm). When setting $E = n - 2t$ the conditions on

n, T, and E (cf. Section 1.2) lead to the requirement that $n > 9t$, causing our algorithm to be suboptimal in this respect.

5 Conclusion

Our paper shows that it is possible to solve consensus in a system where processes may recover from arbitrary faults. The algorithm is *fast*, *i.e.*, in good runs it decides in the first round. The requirement $n > 5t$ is thus also optimal [13,27]. Nevertheless, when looking at the duration of our rounds in the non-fast case there might be room for improvement. Addressing this could be a promising future work, since we believe that our weak fault model is of high practical interest.

References

1. Pease, M., Shostak, R., Lamport, L.: Reaching agreement in the presence of faults. Journal of the ACM 27, 228–234 (1980)
2. Hutle, M., Schiper, A.: Communication predicates: A high-level abstraction for coping with transient and dynamic faults. In: Dependable Systems and Networks (DSN 2007), pp. 92–101. IEEE, Los Alamitos (2007)
3. Widder, J., Gridling, G., Weiss, B., Blanquart, J.P.: Synchronous consensus with mortal Byzantines. In: Dependable Systems and Networks, DSN 2007 (2007)
4. Alvisi, L., Malkhi, D., Pierce, E., Reiter, M.K.: Fault detection for Byzantine quorum systems. IEEE Trans. Parallel Distributed Systems 12, 996–1007 (2001)
5. Haeberlen, A., Kouznetsov, P., Druschel, P.: The case for Byzantine fault detection. In: HOTDEP 2006: Proceedings of the 2nd conference on Hot Topics in System Dependability, Berkeley, CA, USA, p. 5. USENIX Association (2006)
6. Castro, M., Liskov, B.: Practical Byzantine fault tolerance and proactive recovery. ACM Trans. Computer Systems 20, 398–461 (2002)
7. Dyer, C., Rodgers, D.: Effects on spacecraft & aircraft electronics. In: Proceedings ESA Workshop on Space Weather, ESA WPP-155, Nordwijk, The Netherlands, ESA, pp. 17–27 (1998)
8. Taber, A., Normand, E.: Single event upset in avionics. IEEE Trans. Nuclear Science 40, 120–126 (1993)
9. Baumann, R.C.: Radiation-induced soft errors in advanced semiconductor technologies. IEEE Trans. Device and Materials Reliability 5, 305–316 (2005)
10. Gordon, M., Goldhagen, P., Rodbell, K., Zabel, T., Tang, H., Clem, J., Bailey, P.: Measurement of the flux and energy spectrum of cosmic-ray induced neutrons on the ground. IEEE Trans. on Nuclear Science 51, 3427–3434 (2004)
11. Shivakumar, P., Kistler, M., Keckler, S.W., Burger, D., Alvisi, L.: Modeling the effect of technology trends on the soft error rate of combinational logic. In: Dependable Systems and Networks (DSN 2002), pp. 389–398. IEEE, Los Alamitos (2002)
12. Dwork, C., Lynch, N., Stockmeyer, L.: Consensus in the presence of partial synchrony. Journal of the ACM 35, 288–323 (1988)
13. Martin, J.P., Alvisi, L.: Fast Byzantine consensus. In: Dependable Systems and Networks (DSN 2005), pp. 402–411. IEEE, Los Alamitos (2005)

14. Abd-El-Malek, M., Ganger, G.R., Goodson, G.R., Reiter, M.K., Wylie, J.J.: Fault-scalable Byzantine fault-tolerant services. SIGOPS Operating Systems Review 39, 59–74 (2005)
15. Cowling, J., Myers, D., Liskov, B., Rodrigues, R., Shrira, L.: HQ replication: a hybrid quorum protocol for Byzantine fault tolerance. In: OSDI 2006: Proceedings of the seventh Symposium on Operating Systems Design and Implementation, Berkeley, CA, USA, pp. 177–190. USENIX Association (2006)
16. Kotla, R., Alvisi, L., Dahlin, M., Clement, A., Wong, E.L.: Zyzzyva: speculative Byzantine fault tolerance. In: Proceedings of the twenty first ACM Symposium on Operating Systems Principles, SOSP 2007, pp. 45–58 (2007)
17. Rodrigues, R., Castro, M., Liskov, B.: Base: using abstraction to improve fault tolerance. In: Proceedings of the eighteenth ACM symposium on Operating Systems Principles, pp. 15–28. ACM, New York (2001)
18. Biely, M., Charron-Bost, B., Gaillard, A., Hutle, M., Schiper, A., Widder, J.: Tolerating corrupted communication. In: Proceedings of the 26th Annual ACM Symposium on Principles of Distributed Computing (PODC 2007). ACM Press, New York (2007)
19. Aguilera, M.K., Delporte-Gallet, C., Fauconnier, H., Toueg, S.: Consensus with Byzantine failures and little system synchrony. In: Dependable Systems and Networks (DSN 2006), pp. 147–155 (2006)
20. Anceaume, E., Delporte-Gallet, C., Fauconnier, H., Hurfin, M., Le Lann, G.: Designing modular services in the scattered Byzantine failure model. In: 3rd International Symposium on Parallel and Distributed Computing (ISPDC 2004), pp. 262–269. IEEE Computer Society, Los Alamitos (2004)
21. Anceaume, E., Delporte-Gallet, C., Fauconnier, H., Hurfin, M., Widder, J.: Clock synchronization in the Byzantine-recovery failure model. In: Tovar, E., Tsigas, P., Fouchal, H. (eds.) OPODIS 2007. LNCS, vol. 4878, pp. 90–104. Springer, Heidelberg (2007)
22. Barak, B., Halevi, S., Herzberg, A., Naor, D.: Clock synchronization with faults and recoveries (extended abstract). In: Proceeding of the 18th Annual ACM Symposium on Principles of Distributed Computing (PODC 2000), Portland, Oregon, United States, pp. 133–142. ACM Press, New York (2000)
23. Dolev, S.: Self-Stabilization. MIT Press, Cambridge (2000)
24. Dolev, S., Welch, J.L.: Self-stabilizing clock synchronization in the presence of Byzantine faults. Journal of the ACM 51, 780–799 (2004)
25. Dolev, S., Kat, R.I., Schiller, E.M.: When consensus meets self-stabilization. In: Shvartsman, M.M.A.A. (ed.) OPODIS 2006. LNCS, vol. 4305, pp. 45–63. Springer, Heidelberg (2006)
26. Biely, M., Hutle, M.: Consensus when all processes may be Byzantine for some time. Research Report 47/2009, Technische Universität Wien, Institut für Technische Informatik, Treitlstr. 1-3/182-1, 1040 Vienna, Austria (2009)
27. Song, Y.J., van Renesse, R.: Bosco: One-Step Byzantine Asynchronous Consensus. In: Taubenfeld, G. (ed.) DISC 2008. LNCS, vol. 5218, pp. 438–450. Springer, Heidelberg (2008)

A Superstabilizing $\log(n)$-Approximation Algorithm for Dynamic Steiner Trees

Lélia Blin[2], Maria Gradinariu Potop-Butucaru[1], and Stephane Rovedakis[2]

[1] Univ. Pierre & Marie Curie - Paris 6,
LIP6-CNRS UMR 7606, France
maria.gradinariu@lip6.fr
[2] Université d'Evry, IBISC, CNRS, France
LIP6-CNRS UMR 7606, France
{lelia.blin,stephane.rovedakis}@ibisc.univ-evry.fr

Abstract. This paper proposes a fully dynamic self-stabilizing algorithm for the Steiner tree problem. The Steiner tree problem aims at constructing a Minimum Spanning Tree (MST) over a subset of nodes called Steiner members, or Steiner group usually denoted S. Steiner trees are good candidates to efficiently implement communication primitives such as publish/subscribe or multicast, essential building blocks in the design of middleware architectures for the new emergent networks (e.g. P2P, sensor or adhoc networks). Our algorithm returns a $\log |S|$-approximation of the optimal Steiner tree. It improves over existing solutions in several ways. First, it is fully dynamic, in other words it withstands the dynamism when both the group members and ordinary nodes can join or leave the network. Next, our algorithm is self-stabilizing, that is, it copes with nodes memory corruption. Last but not least, our algorithm is *superstabilizing*. That is, while converging to a correct configuration (i.e., a Steiner tree) after a modification of the network, it keeps offering the Steiner tree service during the stabilization time to all members that have not been affected by this modification.

1 Introduction

The design of efficient distributed applications in the newly distributed emergent networks such as MANETs, P2P or sensor networks raises various challenges ranging from models to fundamental services. These networks face frequent churn (nodes and links creation or destruction) and various privacy and security attacks that cannot be easily encapsulated in the existing distributed models. Therefore, new models and new algorithms have to be designed.

Communication services are the building blocks for any distributed system and they have received a particular attention in the lately years. Their efficiency greatly depends on the performance of the underlying routing overlay. These overlays should be optimized to reduce the network overload. Moreover, in order to avoid security and privacy attacks the number of network nodes that are used only for the overlay connectivity have to be minimized. Additionally, the overlays have to offer some quality of services while nodes or links fail.

R. Guerraoui and F. Petit (Eds.): SSS 2009, LNCS 5873, pp. 133–148, 2009.

The work in designing optimized communication overlays for the new emergent networks has been conducted in both structured (DHT-based) and unstructured networks. Communication primitives using DHT-based schemes such as Pastry, CAN or Chord [1] build upon a global naming scheme based on hashing nodes identifiers. These schemes are optimized to efficiently route in the virtual name space. However, they have weak energy performances in MANETs or sensor networks where the maintenance of long links reduces the network perennial. Therefore, alternative strategies [2], mostly based on gossip techniques, have been recently considered. These schemes, highly efficient when nodes have no information on the content and the topology of the system, offer only probabilistic guarantees on the message delivery.

In this paper we are interested in the study of overlays targeted to efficiently connect a group of nodes that are not necessarily located in the same geographical area (e.g. sensors that should communicate their sensed data to servers located outside the deployment area, P2P nodes that share the same interest and are located in different countries, robots that should participate to the same task but need to remotely coordinate). Steiner trees are good candidates to implement the above mentioned requirements since the problem have been designed for efficiently connect a subset of the network nodes, referred as Steiner members.

The Steiner tree problem. The Steiner tree problem can be informally expressed as follows: given a weighted graph in which a subset S of nodes is identified, find a minimum-weight tree spanning S. The Steiner tree problem is one of the most important combinatorial optimization problems and finding a Steiner tree is NP-hard.

A survey on different heuristics for constructing Steiner trees with different approximation ratios can be found in [3]. In our work we are interested in dynamic variants of Steiner trees first addressed in [4] in a centralized online setting. They propose a $\log |S|$-approximation algorithm for this problem that copes only with Steiner member arrivals. At first step, a member becomes the root of the tree then at each step a new member is connected to the existing Steiner tree by a shortest path. This algorithm can be implemented in a decentralized environment (see [5]).

Our work considers the fully dynamic version of the problem where both Steiner members and ordinary nodes or communication links can join or leave the system. Additionally, our work aims at providing a superstabilizing approximation of a Steiner tree. The property of self-stabilization [6,7] enables a distributed algorithm to recover from a transient fault regardless of its initial state. The superstabilization [8] is an extension of the self-stabilization property for dynamic settings. The idea is to provide some minimal guarantees while the system repairs after a topology change.

To our knowledge there are only two self-stabilizing approximations of Steiner trees [9,10]. Both works assume the shared memory model and an unfair centralized scheduler. In [9] the authors propose a self-stabilizing algorithm based on a pruned minimum spanning tree. The computed solution has an approximation ratio of $|V| - |S| + 1$, where V is the set of nodes in the network. In [10], the authors proposed a four-layered algorithm which is built upon the techniques proposed in [11] to obtain a 2 approximation.

The above cited algorithms work only for static networks. In [10] the members can become ordinary nodes and ordinary nodes can become members, but the network does not change.

Our results. We describe the first distributed super-stabilizing algorithm for the Steiner tree problem. This algorithm has the following novel properties with respect to the previous constructions:

- it is specially designed to cope with the system dynamism. In other words, our solution tolerates nodes (or links) join and leave the system, while using $O(\delta \log n)$ memory bits with δ the maximal degree of the network (or $O(\log n)$ in the classical message passing model)[1].
- it's design includes self-stabilizing policies. Starting from an arbitrary state (nodes local memory corruption, counter program corruption, or erroneous messages in the network buffers), our algorithm is guaranteed to converge to a tree spanning the Steiner members. Additionally, it is *superstabilizing*. That is, while a topology change occurs, i.e., during the restabilization period, the algorithm offers the guarantee that only the subtree connected through the crashed node/edge is reconstructed.

Table 1. Distributed (deterministic) algorithms for the Steiner tree problem

	Dynamicity	Superstabilizing	Self-Stabilizing	Approximation ratio
[12]	No	No	No	2
[9]	No	No	Yes	$\|V\| + \|S\| - 1$
[10]	No	No	Yes	2
This paper	Yes	Yes	Yes	$\log \|S\|$

Table 1 summarizes our contribution compared to previous works. The approximation ratio of our algorithm is logarithmic, which is not as good as the 2-approximation of the algorithm proposed by Kamei and Kakugawa in [10]. However, this latter algorithm is not superstabilizing. Designing a superstabilizing 2-approximation algorithm for the Steiner tree problem is a challenge. Indeed, all known 2-approximation distributed algorithms (self-stabilizing or not) for the Steiner tree problem use a minimum spanning tree (MST) computation, and the design of a superstabilizing algorithm for MST is a challenge in itself.

2 Model and Notations

We consider an undirected weighted connected network $G = (V, E, w)$ where V is the set of nodes, E is the set of edges and $w : E \to \mathbb{R}^+$ is a positive cost

[1] To solve the problem, one can use a self-stabilizing reset algorithm with a centralized algorithm computing a Steiner tree on each node but this requires at least $O(n \log n)$ memory bits because the map of the network have to be stored on each node.

function. Nodes represent processors and edges represent bidirectional communication links. Each node in the network has an unique identifier. $S \subseteq V$ defines the set of members we have to connect. For any pair of nodes $u, v \in V$, we note $d(u, v)$ the distance of the shortest path $P(u, v)$ between u and v in G (i.e. $d(u, v) = \sum_{e \in P(u,v)} w(e)$). For a node $v \in V$, we denote the set of its neighbors $\mathcal{N}(v) = \{u, (u, v) \in E\}$. A Steiner tree, T in G is a connected acyclic sub-graph of G such that $T = (V_T, E_T)$, $S \subseteq V_T \subseteq V$ and $E_T \subset E$. We denote by $W(T)$ the cost of a tree T, i.e. $W(T) = \sum_{e \in T} w(e)$. We consider an asynchronous communication message passing model with FIFO channels (on each link messages are delivered in the same order as they have been sent).

A *local state* of a node is the value of the local variables of the node and the state of its program counter. We consider a fined-grained communication atomicity model [13,7]. That is, each node maintains a local copy of the variables of its neighbors. These variables are refreshed via special messages (denoted in the sequel `InfoMsg`) exchanged periodically by neighboring nodes. A *configuration* of the system is the cross product of the local states of all nodes in the system plus the content of the communication links. The transition from a configuration to the next one is produced by the execution of an atomic step at a node. An *atomic step* at node p is an internal computation based on the current value of p's local variables and a single communication operation (send/receive) at p. An *computation* of the system is an infinite sequence of configurations, $e = (c_0, c_1, \ldots c_i, \ldots)$, where each configuration c_{i+1} follows from c_i by the execution of a single atomic step.

Given $\mathcal{L}_{\mathcal{A}}$ a non-empty *legitimacy predicate*[2] an algorithm $\mathcal{A}$ is *self-stabilizing* iff the following two conditions hold: (i) Every computation of $\mathcal{A}$ starting from a configuration satisfying $\mathcal{L}_{\mathcal{A}}$ preserves $\mathcal{L}_{\mathcal{A}}$ (*closure*). (ii) Every computation of $\mathcal{A}$ starting from an arbitrary configuration contains a configuration that satisfies $\mathcal{L}_{\mathcal{A}}$ (*convergence*). A *legitimate configuration* for the Steiner Tree is a configuration that provides an instance of a tree T spanning S. Additionally, we expect a competitiveness of $\log(z)$, i.e., $\frac{W(T)}{W(T^*)} \leq \log(z)$, with $|S| = z$ and T^* an optimal Steiner tree.

In the following we propose a self-stabilizing Steiner tree algorithm. We expect our algorithm to be also *superstabilizing* [8]. That is, given a class of topology changes Λ and a passage predicate, an algorithm is superstabilizing with respect to Λ iff it is self-stabilizing, and for every computation[3] e beginning at a legitimate state and containing a single topology change event of type Λ, the passage predicate holds for every configuration in e.

In the following we propose a self-stabilizing Steiner tree algorithm and extend it to a superstabilizing Steiner tree algorithm that copes with the Steiner members and tree edges removal. During the tree restabilization the algorithm verifies a passage predicate detailed below. Then, we discuss the extension of the algorithm to fully dynamic settings (the add/removal of members, nodes or links

[2] A legitimacy predicate is defined over the configurations of a system and is an indicator of its correct behavior.

[3] [8] use the notion of trajectory which is the computation of a system enriched with dynamic actions.

join/leave). This second extension offers no guarantees during the restabilization period.

3 Stabilizing Steiner Tree Algorithm S3T

This section describes a stabilizing algorithm for the Steiner tree problem, called S3T. It implements the technique proposed by Imase and Waxman [4][4], in a stabilizing manner. In our implementation we assume a rooted network where the root is a special node chosen in the Steiner group. This node will be also the root of the constructed Steiner tree. The choice of the root is beyond the scope of the current paper. In the following we assume the system augmented with a leader oracle that returns to every node in the system its status: leader or follower. The single node that receives "leader" while invoking the leader oracle is the root and is allowed to execute the root code detailed below. Several implementations for leader oracles fault-tolerant, stabilizing or dynamic can be found for example in [14,15,16].

The idea of our Steiner Tree algorithm is as follows. All nodes in the network (Steiner or not) compute their distances to the existing Steiner tree. Steiner members send asynchronously their connexion requests to the existing Steiner tree via a shortest path and join the tree. Each connection may disturb the coherency of the data maintained by the nodes in the system. Therefore, all nodes in the system have to recompute their distances to the new Steiner tree.

Note that in a stabilizing setting the initial configuration may be arbitrary hence nodes have to perpetually verify the coherency of their variables with those maintained by their neighbors.

3.1 Variables and Predicates

For any node $v \in V(G)$, $N(v)$ is the neighbors set of v in the network G (our algorithm is built upon an underlying self-stabilizing protocol that regularly updates the neighbor set of every node). We denote by $\mathrm{ID}_v \in \mathbb{N}$ the unique network identifier of v. Every node v maintains seven variables for constructing and maintaining a Steiner tree. Three of them are integers, and the others are booleans.

- $\mathtt{p}_v$: ID of the parent of node v in the current tree;
- ℓ_v: (Level) number of nodes on the path between the root and v in spanning tree;
- $\mathtt{d}_v$: the shortest distance to a node already connected to the current tree;
- $\mathtt{member}_v$: *true* if $v \in S \subseteq V$, *false* otherwise (this is not a variable written by the algorithm but only read);
- $\mathtt{need}_v$: *true* if $v \in S \subseteq V$ or v has a descendant which is a member, *false* otherwise;
- $\mathtt{connect}_v$: *true* if v is in the current tree, *false* otherwise;
- $\mathtt{connect\_pt}_v$: *true* if v is a member or v has more than one children in the current tree, *false* otherwise.

[4] Each Steiner member is connected to the existing Steiner tree via a shortest path.

$$
\begin{array}{l}
\mathtt{CRoot}(v) \equiv \mathtt{d}_v = 0 \wedge \mathtt{p}_v = \mathrm{ID}_v \wedge \mathtt{need}_v \wedge \mathtt{connect}_v \wedge \mathtt{connect\_pt}_v \wedge \ell_v = 0 \\
\mathtt{CParent}(v) \equiv (\exists u \in N(v), \mathtt{p}_v = \mathrm{ID}_u) \wedge (\ell_v = \ell_{\mathtt{p}_v} + 1) \wedge (\nexists u \in N(v), \mathtt{p}_u = \mathrm{ID}_v \wedge \\
\qquad \ell_u \neq \ell_v + 1) \\
\mathtt{Asked\_Connect}(v) \equiv (\exists u \in N(v), \mathtt{p}_u = \mathrm{ID}_v \wedge \mathtt{need}_u) \\
\mathtt{Better\_Path}(v) \equiv (\neg \mathtt{connect}_v \wedge \mathtt{d}_v \neq \mathtt{d\_NotConnect}(v)) \vee (\mathtt{connect}_v \wedge \\
\qquad \mathtt{d}_v \neq \mathtt{d\_Connect}(v)) \\
\mathtt{Connect\_Pt\_Stab}(v) \equiv (\mathtt{member}_v \wedge \mathtt{connect\_pt}_v) \vee (\neg \mathtt{member}_v \wedge \\
\qquad \mathtt{connect\_pt}_v = (|\{u : u \in N(v) \wedge \mathtt{p}_u = \mathrm{ID}_v \wedge \mathtt{connect}_u\}| > 1)) \\
\mathtt{Connect\_Stab}(v) \equiv [\mathtt{member}_v \vee (\neg \mathtt{member}_v \wedge \mathtt{Asked\_Connect}(v))] \wedge \mathtt{need}_v \wedge \mathtt{connect}_{\mathtt{p}_v} \\
\mathtt{d\_NotConnect}(v) \equiv \min(\min\{w(u,v) : u \in N(v) \wedge \mathtt{connect}_u\}, \mathtt{d}_u + w(u,v) : \\
\qquad u \in N(v) \wedge \neg \mathtt{connect}_u\}) \\
\mathtt{d\_Connect}(v) \equiv \min(\min\{w(u,v) : u \in N(v) \wedge \mathtt{connect}_u \wedge \mathtt{connect\_pt}_u\}, \\
\qquad \min\{\mathtt{d}_u + w(u,v) : u \in N(v) \wedge [\neg \mathtt{connect}_u \vee (\mathtt{connect}_u \wedge \neg \mathtt{connect\_pt}_u))\} \\
\mathtt{p\_Connect}(v) \equiv \arg(\mathtt{d\_Connect}(v)) \\
\mathtt{p\_NotConnect}(v) \equiv \arg(\mathtt{d\_NotConnect}(v))
\end{array}
$$

Fig. 1. Predicates used by the algorithm

3.2 Description of the Algorithm

Every node $v \in V$ sends periodically its local variables to each of its neighbors using `InfoMsg` messages. Upon the reception of this message a neighbor updates the local copy of its neighbor variables. The description of a `InfoMsg` message is as follows: $\mathtt{InfoMsg}_v[u] = \langle \mathtt{InfoMsg}, \mathtt{p}_v, \ell_v, \mathtt{d}_v, \mathtt{need}_v, \mathtt{connect}_v, \mathtt{connect\_pt}_v \rangle$.

Our algorithm is a four phase computation: (1) first nodes update their distance to the existing Steiner tree, then (2) nodes request connection (if they are members or they received a connection demand), then (3) they establish the connection, and finally (4) they update the state of the current Steiner tree. These phases have to be performed in the given order. That is, a node cannot initiate a request for connection for example if it has not yet updated its distance.

Note that if a node detects a distance modification in its neighborhood, it can change its connection to the current tree. Therefore, a node must update its distance to the current tree before executing any other action.

Every node in the network, maintains a parent link. The parent of a node is one of its neighbors having the shortest distance to the current tree. Note that erroneous initial configurations may create cycles in the parent link. To break these cycles, we use the notion of tree level, defined by the variable ℓ: the root has the level zero and each node has the level equal to its parent level plus one.

When a member tries to connect to the tree, it sets its variable `need` to *true*. When a node in the current tree receives a demand for connection, an acknowledgment is sent back along the requesting path enabling every node along this path to set a variable `connect` to *true*. Nodes with `connect` set *true* are called "connected nodes". Whenever a node detects an incoherency in its neighborhood it disconnects from the current tree (see rules $\mathcal{DR}_1$ and $\mathcal{CR}_2$).

Algorithm: Upon the reception of a InfoMsg nodes correct their local state via the rules explained below then broadcast their new local state in their local neighborhood.

Root: In a coherent state the root has a distance and a level equal to zero, variables need and connect are *true* since the root is always connected (it always belongs to the Steiner tree). Variable connect_pt is *true* because the root is a member so a connection point. Whenever the state of the root is incoherent the Rule $\mathcal{RR}$ below is enabled.

$\mathcal{RR}$: (Root reinitialization)

If $\texttt{Is\_Root}(v) \wedge \neg\texttt{CRoot}(v)$ **then**

$\texttt{d}_v := 0$; $\texttt{p}_v := \text{ID}_v$; $\texttt{need}_v := true$; $\texttt{connect}_v := true$;

$\texttt{connect\_pt}_v := true$; $\ell_v := 0$;

Distance update: Rule $\mathcal{DR}_1$ enables to a unconnected node to compute its shortest path distance to the Steiner tree as follows: Take the minimum between the edge weights with connected neighbors and the distances with unconnected neighbors. If a unconnected node detects it has a better shortest path (see Predicate Better_Path) then it updates its distance (using Predicates d_NotConnect and d_Connect) and changes its other variables accordingly.

The same rule is used to reinitiate the state of a node if it observes that its parent is no more in its neighborhood.

Similarly, Rule $\mathcal{DR}_2$ enables a connected node to compute its shortest path distance. In order to execute this rule a connected node must have a stabilized connection. The distance is computed as for a unconnected node but a connected node compares this distance with its local distance towards its connection point and takes the minimum.

$\mathcal{DR}_1$: (Distance stabilization for unconnected nodes)

If $\neg$ $\texttt{Is\_Root}(v) \wedge [(\neg\texttt{connect}_v \wedge \texttt{Better\_Path}(v)) \vee (\neg\texttt{CParent}(v) \wedge \texttt{d}_{\texttt{p}_v} \neq \infty)]$ **then**

$\texttt{d}_v := \texttt{d\_NotConnect}(v)$; $\texttt{p}_v := \texttt{p\_NotConnect}(v)$;

$\texttt{connect}_v := false$; $\texttt{connect\_pt}_v := false$; $\ell_v := \ell_{\texttt{p}_v} + 1$;

$\mathcal{DR}_2$: (Distance stabilization for connected nodes)

If $\neg$ $\texttt{Is\_Root}(v) \wedge \texttt{connect}_v \wedge \texttt{Connect\_Stab}(v) \wedge \texttt{Better\_Path}(v) \wedge \texttt{CParent}(v) \wedge$ $\texttt{Connect\_Pt\_Stab}(v)$ **then**

$\texttt{d}_v := \texttt{d\_Connect}(v)$; $\texttt{p}_v := \texttt{p\_Connect}(v)$;

$\ell_v := \ell_{\texttt{p}_v} + 1$;

Request to join the tree: Variable need is used by a unconnected node to ask to its parent a connection to the current Steiner tree. Since a member must be connected to the Steiner tree, each member sets this variable to *true* using Rule $\mathcal{NR}_1$. A not member and unconnected node which detects that a child wants to be connected (see Predicate Asked_Connect) changes its variable need to *true*. This connection request is forwarded in the spanning tree until a unconnected node neighbor of a connected node is reached. A unconnected node sets its variable need to *false* using Rule $\mathcal{NR}_2$ if it is not a member and it has no child requesting a connection.

$\mathcal{NR}_1$: **(Nodes which need to be connected)**

If $\neg$ $\texttt{Is\_Root}(v) \wedge \neg \texttt{need}_v \wedge \neg \texttt{connect}_v \wedge \neg \texttt{Better\_Path}(v) \wedge \texttt{CParent}(v) \wedge [\texttt{member}_v \vee (\neg \texttt{member}_v \wedge \texttt{Asked\_Connect}(v))]$
then $\texttt{need}_v := \mathit{true}$;

$\mathcal{NR}_2$: **(Nodes which need not to be connected)**

If $\neg$ $\texttt{Is\_Root}(v) \wedge \neg \texttt{connect}_v \wedge \texttt{need}_v \wedge \neg \texttt{member}_v \wedge \neg \texttt{Asked\_Connect}(v) \wedge \neg \texttt{Better\_Path}(v) \wedge \texttt{CParent}(v)$ **then** $\texttt{need}_v := \mathit{false}$;

Member connection: When a unconnected node neighbor of a connected node (i.e. which belongs to the Steiner tree) detects a connection request from a child (i.e. Predicate `Asked_Connect` is *true*), an acknowledgment is sent backward using variable `connect` along the request path. Therefore every unconnected node on this path uses Rule $\mathcal{CR}_1$ and sets `connect` to *true* until the member that asked the connection is connected. Only a node that has (1) no better path, (2) its variable `need` $=$ *true* and (3) a connected parent can use Rule $\mathcal{CR}_1$. A connected node becomes unconnected if its connection path is no more stabilized (i.e. Predicate `Connect_Stab` is false). Therefore, it sets `connect` to *false* using Rule $\mathcal{CR}_2$. The parent distance is used for the disconnection of a subtree whenever a fault occurs in the network. If a fault occurs (parent distance is infinity), a connected node in the subtree below a faulty node or edge in the spanning tree must be disconnected using Rule $\mathcal{CR}_3$. So the node sets `connect` to false and `d` to infinity and waits until all its subtree is disconnected (i.e. it has no connected child).

$\mathcal{CR}_1$: **(Nodes which must be connected)**

If $\neg$ $\texttt{Is\_Root}(v) \wedge \neg \texttt{connect}_v \wedge \texttt{Connect\_Stab}(v) \wedge \neg \texttt{Better\_Path}(v) \wedge \texttt{CParent}(v)$
then $\texttt{connect}_v := \mathit{true}$;

$\mathcal{CR}_2$: **(Nodes which must not be connected)**

If $\neg$ $\texttt{Is\_Root}(v) \wedge \texttt{connect}_v \wedge \neg \texttt{Connect\_Stab}(v) \wedge \texttt{CParent}(v) \wedge \texttt{d}_{\texttt{p}_v} \neq \infty$ **then** $\texttt{connect}_v := \mathit{false}$;

$\mathcal{CR}_3$: **(Consequence of a deletion)**

If $\neg$ $\texttt{Is\_Root}(v) \wedge \texttt{connect}_v \wedge \neg \texttt{Connect\_Stab}(v) \wedge \texttt{d}_{\texttt{p}_v} = \infty$
then $\texttt{connect}_v := \mathit{false}$; $\texttt{d}_v := \infty$; $\texttt{connect\_pt}_v := \mathit{false}$;
send $\texttt{InfoMsg}_v$ to all $u \in N(v)$ and wait until $(\nexists u \in N(v), \texttt{p}_u = \mathrm{ID}_v \wedge \texttt{connect}_u)$

Update the Steiner tree: Since we use shortest paths to connect members to the existing Steiner tree, we must maintain distances from members to connection points. A connection point is a connected member or a connected node with more than one connected children, i.e. the root of the branch connecting a member. Every connected node updates its distance if it has a better path. So thanks to connection points and distance computation, we maintain a shortest path between a member and the Steiner tree in order to respect the construction in [4]. Rule $\mathcal{TR}$ is used by a connected node to change its variable `connect_pt` and to become or not a connection point. This rule is executed only if the connected node has a stabilized connection path (i.e. Predicate `Connect_Stab` is *true*).

$\mathcal{TR}$: **(Connected path stabilization)**

If $\neg$ Is_Root(v)$\wedge$connect$_v$$\wedge$Connect_Stab($v$)$\wedge$CParent($v$)$\wedge$$\neg$Connect_Pt_Stab($v$)
then If member$_v$ **then** connect_pt$_v$:= *true*;
Else connect_pt$_v$:= $|\{u : u \in N(v) \wedge$ p$_u$ = ID$_v \wedge$ connect$_u\}| > 1$;

4 Correctness Proof in Static Settings

Definition 1 (Legitimate state of DST). *A configuration of algorithm is legitimate iff each process $v \in V$ satisfies the following conditions:*

1. *a Steiner tree T spanning the set of members S is constructed;*
2. *a shortest path connects each member $v \in S$ to the existing tree.*

Lemma 1. *Eventually a unique rooted spanning tree is constructed in the network.*

Proof. Function Is_Root(v) is a perfect oracle which returns true if v is the root of the tree and false otherwise. So we assume that there is a time after which only one root exists in the network. Moreover, Rule $\mathcal{RR}$ is only used by the root to correct its corrupted variables.

Since there is only one root in the network, to have a spanning tree we must show that each node has one parent and there is no cycle. First note that each node v could have at each time a single parent in its neighborhood (see Predicate CParent(v)) stored in variable p$_v$ (only the root has its parent equal to itself). Each node maintains its level stored in variable $\mathfrak{l}_v$ which is updated by Rules $\mathcal{RR}$ (maintains a zero distance for the root), $\mathcal{DR}_1$ and $\mathcal{DR}_2$ (selects as parent a neighbor of minimum distance to the Steiner tree for unconnected or connected nodes respectively). The level of each node must be equal to the level of its parent plus one, except for the root which has a zero level (see Rule $\mathcal{RR}$). Suppose there is a cycle in the constructed structure. This implies there is at least one node x with a smaller level than its parent y in the cycle, i.e., for x we have $\mathfrak{l}_x \neq \mathfrak{l}_y + 1$ and for y we have p$_x$ $= ID_y \wedge \mathfrak{l}_x \neq \mathfrak{l}_y + 1$. So Predicate CParent is false for x and y, thus x and y can execute Rule $\mathcal{DR}_1$ to reset their variables to break the cycle by choosing as parent the neighbor with minimum distance according to Function d_NotConnect. Therefore, there is a time after which no cycle exists in the constructed structure. Since there is only one root in the network (i.e., $\mathfrak{l}_v = 0$ and p$_v$ $= ID_v$), the constructed structure describes a single spanning tree. □

Lemma 2. *Eventually each unconnected node knows its distance to the current Steiner tree.*

Proof. A node v is connected iff need$_v$ $= true$ and connect$_v$ $= true$. There is at least one connected node because the root is always connected (see Rule $\mathcal{RR}$), otherwise there is a time when the root corrects its variables using Rule $\mathcal{RR}$. According to Lemma 1, a tree spanning the network is constructed. Let x be a unconnected node, d_x the distance of the shortest path from x to the nearest connected node and y its neighbor on this shortest path. Suppose d$_x$ $> d_x$, thus it exists a time after which a neighbor offers a better path (i.e., a neighbor with a distance lower than $\mathtt{d}_x$, see Predicate $\mathtt{Better\_Path}(x)$) and x can execute Rule $\mathcal{DR}_1$ because Predicate $\mathtt{Better\_Path}(x)$ is true. So x corrects $\mathtt{d}_x$ as the minimum distance in its neighborhood (see Function $\mathtt{d\_NotConnect}(x)$). Thus, there is a time after which $\mathtt{d}_x = d_x$. Moreover, when x executes Rule $\mathcal{DR}_1$ the variable $\mathtt{p}_x$ is modified respectively to variable $\mathtt{d}_x$ (see Function $\mathtt{p\_NotConnect}(x)$). So $\mathtt{p}_x$ stores the neighbor of x which offers to x the shortest path to the nearest connected node. Therefore, there is a time after which $\mathtt{d}_x = d_x$ and $\mathtt{p}_x = y$. □

Lemma 3. *Eventually each Steiner member is linked to root by a path of connected nodes.*

Proof. A node v is connected iff $\mathtt{need}_v = true$ and $\mathtt{connect}_v = true$. There is at least one connected node because the root must always be connected (see Rule $\mathcal{RR}$), otherwise there is a time when the root corrects its variables using Rule $\mathcal{RR}$. According to Lemma 1, there is only one rooted spanning tree. Thus, there exists a path between each member and the root and Predicate $\mathtt{CParent}(v)$ returns true for every node v in the tree.

To prove the lemma, we first show that for each node v on the path connecting a member to the root we have $\mathtt{need}_v = true$. Each node v (except the root) can change the value of its variable $\mathtt{need}_v$ to true or false with Rule $\mathcal{NR}_1$ or $\mathcal{NR}_2$ respectively, only when v has no neighbor with a lower distance than its parent (i.e., v has no better path so $\mathcal{DR}_1$ and $\mathcal{DR}_2$ are not executable). Otherwise $\mathtt{Better\_Path}(v)$ returns true and Rules $\mathcal{DR}_1$ or $\mathcal{DR}_2$ are uppermost used to correct $\mathtt{d}_v$ and $\mathtt{p}_v$. So we suppose that $\mathtt{Better\_Path}(v)$ returns false. Note that for any node v (except the root), if we have $\mathtt{need}_v = false$ then we can suppose that $\mathtt{connect}_v = false$ (otherwise v can execute Rule $\mathcal{CR}_2$ because Predicate $\mathtt{Connect\_Stab}(v)$ is false).

There are two cases: member or not member nodes. Consider the member node v. If $\mathtt{need}_v \neq true$ then v can execute Rule $\mathcal{NR}_1$ to set $\mathtt{need}_v$ to true (because $\mathtt{connect}_v = false$, $\mathtt{Better\_Path}(v) = false$ and $\mathtt{CParent}(v) = true$). Otherwise, consider a (not member) node v on the path connecting a member to the root of the tree (this path exists according to Lemma 1). If $\mathtt{need}_v \neq true$ then we have Predicate $\mathtt{Asked\_Connect}(v) = true$ because there is a time when v has at least a child u s.t. $\mathtt{need}_u = true$. Moreover, we have $\mathtt{connect}_v = false$, $\mathtt{Better\_Path}(v) = false$ and $\mathtt{CParent}(v) = true$. Thus v can change the value of its variable $\mathtt{need}_v$ to true by executing Rule $\mathcal{NR}_1$. Therefore one can show by induction using the same scheme that for each node v on the path between a member and the root we have $\mathtt{need}_v = true$.

It remains to show that for each node v on the path connecting a member to the root we have $\mathtt{connect}_v = true$. Each node v (except the root) with $\mathtt{connect}_v = false$ can correct its variable $\mathtt{connect}_v$ using Rule $\mathcal{CR}_1$ or $\mathcal{CR}_2$ only when Rule $\mathcal{NR}_1$ is not executable (i.e., we have $\mathtt{need}_v = true$). Otherwise, Predicate $\mathtt{Connect\_Stab}(v) = false$ and Rule $\mathcal{CR}_1$ or $\mathcal{CR}_2$ can not be executed. Since the root is always connected (i.e., $\mathtt{connect}_{root} = true$), each child v of the root with $\mathtt{need}_v = true$ and $\mathtt{connect}_v = false$ can execute Rule $\mathcal{CR}_1$ to change $\mathtt{connect}_v$ to true because we have Predicate $\mathtt{Connect\_Stab}(v) = true$,

$\texttt{Better\_Path}(v) = false$ and $\texttt{CParent}(v) = true$. Thus, using the same argument one can show by induction that for any node v on the path between a member and the root we have $\texttt{connect}_v = true$. □

Lemma 4. *Eventually* $\texttt{Connect\_Pt\_Stab}(v)$ *is true for every connected node* v *on the path between each member and the root in the network.*

Proof. Predicate $\texttt{Connect\_Pt\_Stab}(v)$ notices if the variable $\texttt{connect\_pt}_v$ is locally stabilized. According to Lemma 3, there is a time after which we have paths of connected nodes between members and the root. Note that in this case Predicates $\texttt{Connect\_Stab}(v)$ and $\texttt{CParent}(v)$ are true for every node v on a path connecting a member to the root (including the members).

Suppose that $\texttt{Connect\_Pt\_Stab}(v)$ for a connected node v is false. If v is a member then this implies that $\texttt{connect\_pt}_v = false$ (see predicate $\texttt{Connect\_Pt\_Stab}(v)$), so v can execute Rule $\mathcal{TR}$ to change the value of $\texttt{connect\_pt}_v$ to true and we have $\texttt{Connect\_Stab}(v) = true$. Otherwise, let v be the parent of a member u on the path of connected nodes connecting u to the root. This implies that $\texttt{connect\_pt}_v \neq |\{u : u \in N(v) \wedge \texttt{p}_u = \text{ID}_v \wedge \texttt{connect}_u\}| > 1$ (see predicate $\texttt{Connect\_Pt\_Stab}(v)$), so v can execute Rule $\mathcal{TR}$ to update $\texttt{connect\_pt}_v$ and we have $\texttt{Connect\_Stab}(v) = true$. Thus one can show by induction on the height of the tree that it exists a time where $\texttt{Connect\_Pt\_Stab}(v)$ is true for every connected node v on the path between each member and the root. □

Lemma 5. *Eventually each member is connected by a shortest path to the current Steiner tree.*

Proof. Let T_{i-1} be the Steiner tree constructed by the algorithm before the connection of the member v_i. To prove the lemma, we must show that for any member v_i we have a shortest path P_i from v_i to T_{i-1} when $\texttt{Connect\_Pt\_Stab}(v_i) = true$ and $\texttt{Better\_Path}(v_i) = false$ (i.e., Rule $\mathcal{DR}_2$ can not be executed by a member because there is no better path to connect the member). Initially, according to Rule $\mathcal{RR}$ the root v_0 is always connected and we have $\texttt{Connect\_Pt\_Stab}(v_0) = true$ and $\texttt{Better\_Path}(v_0) = false$ (because $\texttt{d}_{v_0} = 0$). We show by induction on the number of members that the property is satisfied for each member. At iteration 1, let v_1 be a unconnected member. According to Lemma 2, the path P_1 from v_1 to v_0 in the spanning tree is a shortest path (otherwise Predicate $\texttt{Better\_Path}(v_1) = true$ and v_1 can execute Rule $\mathcal{DR}_2$ to compute its shortest path to v_0) so there is a time s.t. P_1 is a path of connected nodes (see Lemma 3) and $\texttt{Connect\_Pt\_Stab}(v_1) = true$ (see Lemma 4). Since P_1 is a shortest path between v_1 and v_0, we have $\texttt{Better\_Path}(v_1) = false$, thus the property is satisfied for v_1. We suppose that the tree T_i satisfies the desired property for every member $v_j, j \leq i$. At iteration $i+1$, when member v_{i+1} is unconnected, according to Lemma 2 the path P_{i+1} from v_{i+1} to T_i is a shortest path, so there is a time s.t. P_{i+1} is a path of connected nodes (see Lemma 3) and $\texttt{Connect\_Pt\_Stab}(v_{i+1}) = true$ (see Lemma 4). Since P_{i+1} is a shortest path between v_{i+1} and T_i, we have $\texttt{Better\_Path}(v_{i+1}) = false$ and the property is satisfied for v_{i+1}.

Note that a member v_{i+1} can create a new connection point u (i.e., $\texttt{connect\_pt}_u = true$) on the path P_j connecting a member $v_j, j \leq i$. In this case, the property is still satisfied for v_j because the path between u and v_j is part of P_j so it is a shortest path since a subpath of a shortest path is a shortest path. Moreover, when we have $\texttt{connect\_pt}_u = true$ for u then all nodes on the path between u and v_j update their distance with Rule $\mathcal{DR}_2$ (see Predicate Better_Path). □

Lemma 6. *Eventually a Steiner tree is constructed.*

Proof. Let T be the spanning tree constructed by the algorithm (see Lemma 1). Since T is a spanning tree, the Steiner group S is also spanned by T. Let $ST \subseteq T$ be the subtree of T such that every node v of ST is connected (i.e., we have $\texttt{need}_v = true$ and $\texttt{connect}_v = true$) and there is a path of connected nodes between each member $s \in S$ and the root (these paths eventually exist according to Lemma 3). Moreover, for every node v in ST we have $\texttt{Better\_Path}(v) = false$ and $\texttt{CParent}(v) = true$ because we consider that all member nodes are connected to the Steiner tree with a shortest path. To prove the lemma we must show that every leaf of ST is a member.

We consider every leaf node v in ST. Note that since v is a leaf, this implies that v has no connected child in ST and thus Predicate $\texttt{Asked\_Connect}(v)$ is false. Suppose that v is not a member. Predicate $\texttt{Connect\_Stab}(v)$ is false because v is not a member and Predicate $\texttt{Asked\_Connect}(v)$ is false. Thus, v can execute Rule $\mathcal{CR}_2$ to set $\texttt{connect}_v$ to false. Then, the guard of Rule $\mathcal{NR}_2$ is satisfied and v can change the value of $\texttt{need}_v$ to false. Therefore v is unconnected and is no more a leaf of ST. By using the same scheme we can show by induction on the height of ST that every node on a path of connected nodes which contains no member nodes can not belong to ST after a finite bounded of time.

Now suppose that v is a member. The guard of Rule $\mathcal{CR}_2$ is not satisfied because Predicate $\texttt{Connect\_Stab}(v) = true$ and thus $\texttt{connect}_v$ remains true. Since $\texttt{connect}_v = true$, the guard of Rule $\mathcal{NR}_2$ is not satisfied and $\texttt{need}_v$ remains true too. Therefore, v is maintained by the algorithm as a leaf of ST. □

Lemma 7 (Convergence). *Starting from an illegitimate configuration eventually the algorithm reaches in a finite time a legitimate configuration.*

Proof. Let C be an illegitimate configuration, i.e. $C \notin \mathcal{L}$. According to Lemmas 1, 5 and 6, in a finite time a legitimate state is reached for any process $v \in V$. Thus in a finite time a legitimate configuration is reached in the network. □

Lemma 8 (Closure). *The set of legitimate configurations is closed.*

Proof. According to the model, InfoMsg messages are exchanged periodically with the neighborhood by all nodes in the network, so InfoMsg messages maintain up to date copies of neighbor states. Thus, starting in a legitimate configuration the algorithm maintains a legitimate configuration. □

5 Correctness Proof in Dynamic Settings

In this section, we consider dynamic networks and we prove that topology changes can be correctly handled by using the extended algorithm given in Figure 2 with the rules previously presented. Moreover, we show that a passage predicate is satisfied during the restabilizing execution of our algorithm with extensions.

In the following, we define the topology change events, noted ε, we consider:

- an add (resp. a removal) of a member v to (resp. from) S (v remains in the network) noted $\mathtt{add}_v$ (resp. $\mathtt{del}_v$);
- an add (resp. a removal) of an edge (u, v) in the network noted $\mathtt{recov}_{uv}$ (resp. $\mathtt{crash}_{uv}$);
- an add (resp. a removal) of a neighbor node u of v in the network noted $\mathtt{recov}_u$ (resp. $\mathtt{crash}_u$).

The algorithm given in Figure 2 completes the self-stabilizing algorithm described in precedent sections and allows to a node v to take into account topology change events. In the sequel, we suppose that after every topology change event the network remains connected. We prove in the next that the algorithm of Figure 2 has a superstabilizing property for a particular class of topology change events. We provide below definitions of the topology change events class Λ and passage predicate for the protocol given in Figure 2.

Do forever: send $\mathtt{InfoMsg}_v$ to all $u \in N(v)$
Upon receipt of $\mathtt{InfoMsg}_u$ from u:
  use all the rules to correct the local state of v
  send $\mathtt{InfoMsg}_v$ to all $u \in N(v)$
Interrupt Section:
  If ε is a $\mathtt{del}_v$ event or ((ε is a $\mathtt{crash}_{uv}$ or $\mathtt{crash}_u$ event) and $\mathtt{p}_v = ID_u$)
  then $\mathtt{connect}_v := false$; $\mathtt{d}_v := \infty$; $\mathtt{connect\_pt}_v := false$;
    send $\mathtt{InfoMsg}_v$ to all $u \in N(v)$
    wait until ($\nexists u \in N(v), \mathtt{p}_u = ID_v \wedge \mathtt{connect}_u$);

Fig. 2. Algorithm for message exchanges and treatment of topology change events

Definition 2 (Class Λ of topology change events). $\mathtt{del}_v, \mathtt{crash}_{uv}$ *and* $\mathtt{crash}_v$ *compose the class Λ of topology change events.*

Definition 3 (Passage predicate). *The parent of a node v can be modified if v is in the subtree connected by the removed member, edge or node, and the parent is not changed for any other node in the tree.*

Lemma 9. *Starting from a legitimate configuration, if a member x leaves the set of members S or node x or edge (y, x) is removed from the network then each connected node v in the subtree of x is disconnected from the tree and a legitimate configuration is reached by the system.*

Proof. According to the description of the complete algorithm, when a member x leaves the set of members S then x changes first its variables as following: $\texttt{connect}_x = false$ and $\texttt{d}_x = \infty$, then x sends its state to its neighborhood and finally x waits until it has no connected child. In the same way, if a node x (resp. edge (y, x) (assume $\texttt{p}_x = ID_y$)) is removed from the network then each child v of x (resp. x) changes first its variables as following: $\texttt{connect}_v = false$ and $\texttt{d}_v = \infty$ (resp. $\texttt{connect}_x = false$ and $\texttt{d}_x = \infty$), then v (resp. x) sends its state to its neighborhood and finally v (resp. x) waits until it has no connected child. When a connected child u of v (resp. of x) receives message $\texttt{InfoMsg}_v$ from v (resp. $\texttt{InfoMsg}_x$ from x), since Predicate $\texttt{Connect\_Stab}(u)$ is false (because $\texttt{connect}_{parent_u} = false$) and $\texttt{d}_{parent_u} = \infty$ the node u can execute Rule $\mathcal{CR}_3$. As a consequence, the variables of u are changed like v's or x's variables, u sends its state to its neighborhood and waits until it has no connected child. According to Lemma 11, no node in the subtree of x can execute Rule $\mathcal{CR}_3$ and can perpetually wait it has no connected child. As a consequence, after a finite time every connected node v in the subtree of x is no more connected.Since each node in the subtree of x is unconnected, there is at least one of those nodes v such that Predicate $\texttt{Better\_Path}(v)$ is true (because we assume the network is always connected). Thus, v can execute Rule $\mathcal{DR}_1$. According to Lemmas 1 and 2, there is a time after which each node in the subtree of x knows its correct shortest path distance to a connected node. Moreover, by Lemmas 3 and 5 each unconnected member will be connected by a shortest path to a connected node in the existing Steiner tree. Therefore, in a finite number of steps the system reaches a legitimate configuration $C' \in \mathcal{L}$. □

Lemma 10. *The proposed protocol is superstabilizing for the class Λ of topology change events, and the passage predicate (Definition 3) continues to be satisfied while a legitimate configuration is reached.*

Proof. Consider a configuration $\Delta \vdash \mathcal{L}$. Suppose ε is a removal of edge (u, v) from the network. If (u, v) is not a tree edge then the distances of u and v are not modified neither u nor v changes its parent and thus no parent variable is modified. Otherwise, let $\texttt{p}_v = u$, u's distance and u's parent are not modified, it is true for any other node not contained in the subtree of v since the distances are not modified (i.e., Predicate $\texttt{Better\_Path}$ is not satisfied). However, u is no more a neighbor of v so according to the handling of an edge removal by the algorithm v's variables are reseted. So v sends its state to its neighborhood and waits until it has no connected child. According to Lemma 9, all its children will become unconnected and eventually will change their parent by executing Rule $\mathcal{DR}_1$ because there is a better path (i.e., Predicate $\texttt{Better\_Path}$ is satisfied). Therefore, only a node in the subtree connected by the edge (u, v) may change its parent.

Suppose ε is a removal of node (resp. member) u from the network (resp. from the Steiner group S). Any node not contained in the subtree of u do not change its parent relation because the distances are not modified (i.e., Predicate $\texttt{Better\_Path}$ is not satisfied). Consider each edge (u, v) between u and its child v, we can apply the same argument described above for an edge removal. So only any node contained in the subtree connected by u may change its parent. □

A fault which occurs in the network is detected using a infinity distance value. To handle a fault, we introduce Rule $\mathcal{CR}_3$ to bootstrap connected nodes in the subtree below a faulty node/edge. We show in Lemma 11 that even Rule $\mathcal{CR}_3$ is executed when no fault occurs in the network then no node perpetually waits (no deadlock) because of Rule $\mathcal{CR}_3$.

Lemma 11. *Starting from an arbitrary configuration, Rule $\mathcal{CR}_3$ introduces no deadlock in the network.*

Proof. Consider a configuration which simulates the presence of a fault in the network (but there is not really a fault) and allows the execution of Rule $\mathcal{CR}_3$ by a node v (i.e., v is a connected node and has a unconnected parent u with $\mathtt{d}_{\mathtt{p}_v} = \infty$). According to Rule $\mathcal{CR}_3$, v becomes a unconnected node and sets its distance to infinity (i.e., $\mathtt{connect}_v = false$ and $\mathtt{d}_v = \infty$), then it sends its state to its neighbors and waits until it has no connected child. There are two cases: (1) v has no connected child or (2) v has at least one connected child. In case (1), v is a leaf of the connected subtree and does not wait. Otherwise, in case (2) since there is no deadlock for the leaves of the connected subtree (see case (1)) the subtree of connected nodes rooted in v has a finite height. Thus, we can show by induction that in a finite time every node in the subtree of v executes Rule $\mathcal{CR}_3$. So, in a finite time v has no more connected child and wakes up. □

6 Conclusion

We propose a self-stabilizing algorithm for the Dynamic Steiner tree problem, based on the heuristic proposed in [4], and achieves starting from any configuration a competitiveness of $log(z)$ in $O(zD)$ rounds[5], with z the number of members and D the diameter of the network. Additionally, we show that our algorithm works for dynamic networks in which a fault may occur on a node or edge. Moreover, we prove that if a subclass of faults (i.e., a member, a node or an edge removal) occurs in a legitimate configuration our algorithm is superstabilizing and is able to satisfy a "passage predicate" defined on the tree structure. For future works, it will be interesting to design a self-stabilizing algorithm in dynamic networks, which achieves a constant competitiveness of 2 (e.g., by using the algorithm in [10] extended for dynamic networks or another heuristic).

References

1. Castro, M., Druschel, P., Hu, Y., Rowstron, A.: Topology-aware routing in structured peer-to-peer overlay networks. In: Future Directions in Distributed Computing, pp. 103–107 (2003)
2. Kermarrec, A.M., van Steen, M.: Gossiping in distributed systems. Operating Systems Review 41(5), 2–7 (2007)

[5] Due to lack of space the complexities and competitiveness proof are discussed in [17].

3. Winter, P.: Steiner problem in networks: a survey. Networks 17(2), 129–167 (1987)
4. Imase, M., Waxman, B.: Dynamic steiner tree problem. SIAM J. Discrete Math. 4(3), 369–384 (1991)
5. Gatani, L., Re, G.L., Gaglio, S.: A dynamic distributed algorithm for multicast path setup. In: Cunha, J.C., Medeiros, P.D. (eds.) Euro-Par 2005. LNCS, vol. 3648, pp. 595–605. Springer, Heidelberg (2005)
6. Dijkstra, E.: Self-stabilizing systems in spite of distributed control. Commun. ACM 17(11), 643–644 (1974)
7. Dolev, S.: Self-Stabilization. MIT Press, Cambridge (2000)
8. Dolev, S., Herman, T.: Superstabilizing protocols for dynamic distributed systems. Chicago J. Theor. Comput. Sci. 1997 (1997)
9. Kamei, S., Kakugawa, H.: A self-stabilizing algorithm for the steiner tree problem. In: SRDS, p. 396 (2002)
10. Kamei, S., Kakugawa, H.: A self-stabilizing algorithm for the steiner tree problem. IEICE Transactions on Information and System E87-D(2), 299–307 (2002)
11. Wu, Y.F., Widmayer, P., Wong, C.: A faster approximation algorithm for the steiner problem in graphs. Acta Inf. 23(2), 223–229 (1986)
12. Chen, G.H., Houle, M., Kuo, M.T.: The steiner problem in distributed computing systems. Informtion Sciences 74(1-2), 73–96 (1993)
13. Burman, J., Kutten, S.: Time optimal asynchronous self-stabilizing spanning tree. In: Pelc, A. (ed.) DISC 2007. LNCS, vol. 4731, pp. 92–107. Springer, Heidelberg (2007)
14. Delporte-Gallet, C., Devismes, S., Fauconnier, H.: Robust stabilizing leader election. In: Masuzawa, T., Tixeuil, S. (eds.) SSS 2007. LNCS, vol. 4838, pp. 219–233. Springer, Heidelberg (2007)
15. Piergiovanni, S., Baldoni, R.: Brief announcement: Eventual leader election in the infinite arrival message-passing system model. In: Taubenfeld, G. (ed.) DISC 2008. LNCS, vol. 5218, pp. 518–519. Springer, Heidelberg (2008)
16. Welch, J., Walter, J.: An asynchronous leader election algorithm for dynamic networks. In: Proc. of Inter. Par. and Distrib. Proc. Symp., IPDPS (2009)
17. Blin, L., Potop-Butucaru, M., Rovedakis, S.: A superstabilizing log(n)-approximation algorithm for dynamic steiner trees. Technical Report hal-00363003, HAL (2009)

Looking for the Weakest Failure Detector for k-Set Agreement in Message-Passing Systems: Is Π_k the End of the Road?

François Bonnet and Michel Raynal

IRISA, Université de Rennes 1, 35042 Rennes, France
{francois.bonnet,raynal}@irisa.fr

Abstract. In the k-set agreement problem, each process (in a set of n processes) proposes a value and has to decide a proposed value in such a way that at most k different values are decided. While this problem can easily be solved in asynchronous systems prone to t process crashes when $k > t$, it cannot be solved when $k \leq t$. Since several years, the failure detector-based approach has been investigated to circumvent this impossibility. While the weakest failure detector class to solve the k-set agreement problem in read/write shared-memory systems has recently been discovered (PODC 2009), the situation is different in message-passing systems where the weakest failure detector classes are known only for the extreme cases $k = 1$ (consensus) and $k = n-1$ (set agreement). This paper introduces a candidate for the general case. It presents a new failure detector class, denoted Π_k, and shows $\Pi_1 = \Sigma \times \Omega$ (the weakest class for $k = 1$), and $\Pi_{n-1} = \mathcal{L}$ (the weakest class for $k = n-1$). Then, the paper investigates the structure of Π_k and shows it is the combination of two failures detector classes denoted Σ_k and Ω_k (that generalize the previous "quorums" and "eventual leaders" failure detectors classes). Finally, the paper proves that Σ_k is a necessary requirement (as far as information on failure is concerned) to solve the k-set agreement problem in message-passing systems. The paper presents also a Π_{n-1}-based algorithm that solves the $(n-1)$-set agreement problem. This algorithm provides us with a new algorithmic insight on the way the $(n-1)$-set agreeement problem can be solved in asynchronous message-passing systems (insight from the point of view of the non-partitioning constraint defined by Σ_{n-1}).

1 Introduction

The k-set agreement problem. This problem is a coordination problem (also called *decision* task). It involves n processes and is defined as follows [6]. Each process proposes a value and every non-faulty process has to decide a value (termination), in such a way that any decided value is a proposed value (validity) and no more than k different values are decided (agreement). The problem parameter k defines the coordination degree; $k = 1$ corresponds to its most constrained instance (consensus problem) while $k = n - 1$ corresponds to its weakest non-trivial instance (set agreement problem).

Considering the process crash failure model, let t be the maximal number of processes that may crash in a run ($0 \leq t < n$). When $t < k$, the k-set agreement can

R. Guerraoui and F. Petit (Eds.): SSS 2009, LNCS 5873, pp. 149–164, 2009.

always be solved, be the system synchronous or asynchronous. When $t \geq k$, the situation is different. While the problem can always be solved in synchronous systems, [7] (see [26] for a survey), it has no solution in asynchronous systems [3,18,28].

The failure detector-based approach. A failure detector is a distributed oracle that provides each alive process with hints on process failures [4]. Failure detectors have been investigated to solve k-set agreement problem since 2000 [22][1]. Lower bounds to solve the k-set agreement in asynchronous message-passing systems enriched with limited accuracy failure detectors have been conjectured in [22] and proved in [17]. The question of the weakest failure detector class for the k-set agreement problem ($k > 1$) has been stated first in [25].

The case $k = 1$ and the case $k = n - 1$. When $k = 1$, as already indicated k-set agreement boils down to consensus, and it is known that the failure detector class Ω is the weakest to solve consensus in asynchronous message-passing systems where $t < n/2$ [5]. Ω ensures that there is an unknown but finite time after which all the processes have the same non-faulty leader (before that time, there is an anarchy period during which each process can have an arbitrarily changing leader). This lower bound result is generalized in [11] where it is shown that $\Sigma \times \Omega$ is the weakest failure detector class to solve consensus when $t < n$. This means that Σ is the minimal additional power (as far as information on failures is concerned) required to overcome the barrier $t < n/2$ and attain $t \leq n - 1$. Actually the power provided by Σ is the minimal one required to implement a shared register in a message-passing system [10,11]. Σ provides each process with a quorum (set of process identities) such that the values of any two quorums (each taken at any time) intersect, and there is a finite time after which any quorum includes only correct processes [10]. Fundamentally, Σ prevents partitioning. A failure detector of the class $\Sigma \times \Omega$ outputs a pair of values, one for Σ and one for Ω.

The weakest failure detector classes for the $(n - 1)$-set agreement have been established in 2008, but they are not the same in the shared memory model and the message-passing model. More precisely, the weakest class for solving the $(n - 1)$-set agreement problem in the asynchronous read/write shared memory model is Anti-Ω (denoted here $\overline{\Omega}_{n-1}$) [29]. Such a failure detector provides each process with a set of $(n-1)$ "leaders" that can change with time but these sets are such that, after some unknown but finite time, they all contain the same non-faulty process[2].

Differently, the weakest class for solving $(n - 1)$-set agreement in the asynchronous message-passing model, is the *Loneliness* failure detector class (denoted $\mathcal{L}$) [12]. Such a failure detector provides each process p with a boolean (that p can only read) such that the boolean of at least one process remains always false and, if all but one process crash, the boolean of that process becomes and remains true forever.

The general case for read/write shared memory. The failure detector class $\overline{\Omega}_k$ has first been presented at the PODC'07 rump session [27] where it has been conjectured to be the weakest failure detector class for solving the k-set agreement problem in read/write

[1] Similarly to consensus, the randomized approach also has been investigated to solve the k-set agreement problem [23].

[2] Anti-Ω is defined in a different but equivalent way in [29].

shared memory systems. This conjecture has been very recently (PODC 2009) proved by three independent groups [13,14,15] (a slightly weaker result is proved in [14] using k-resilient environment). A failure detector of the class $\overline{\Omega}_k$ provides each process with a (possibly always changing) set of k processes such that after some unknown but finite time all the sets that are output have in common the same non-faulty process.

The optimality of $\overline{\Omega}_k$ to solve k-set agreement in shared memory systems seems to be related to the fact that this problem is equivalent to the k-simultaneous consensus problem [1], in which each process executes k independent consensus instances (to which it proposes the same input value), and is required to terminate in one of them. As shown in [29], this problem has been instrumental in determining the weakest failure detector for wait-free solving the $(n-1)$-set agreement problem in asynchronous shared memory systems.

Content of the paper. This paper proposes and investigates a new failure detector class for solving the k-set agreement problem in asynchronous message-passing systems. Its main contributions are the following.

- A new family of failure detector classes, denoted $\{\Pi_k\}_{1 \leq k < n}$, is introduced. Its first interest lies in the fact that (1) $\Pi_1 \simeq \Sigma \times \Omega$ (i.e., it allows expressing the weakest failure detector class for consensus with a one-dimensional output, namely a set of process identities), and (2) $\Pi_{n-1} = \mathcal{L}$, from which it results that Π_k is optimal for the extreme values of k when one wants to solve the k-set agreement problem in message-passing systems. Expressing the power of both $\Sigma \times \Omega$ and $\mathcal{L}$ with a single formalism was not a priori evident.
- It is shown that the class Π_k is actually equivalent to the class $\Sigma_k \times \Omega_k$ where Σ_k is an appropriate generalization of Σ.[3] We have $\Sigma_1 \equiv \Sigma$, and very interestingly $\Pi_{n-1} \simeq \Sigma_{n-1} \simeq \mathcal{L}$ which sheds a new light on the weakest failure detector class for the $(n-1)$-set agreement problem.
- It is proved that for any k, Σ_k is a necessary requirement (as far as information on failures is concerned) to solve the k-set agreement problem in message-passing systems. It is worth noticing that the proof of this necessity requirement does rely neither on an heavy machinery, nor on a reduction to a previous impossibility result. It is purely constructive and particularly simple.

The paper additionally presents a message-passing $(n-1)$-set agreement algorithm directly based on Π_{n-1} (i.e., Σ_{n-1}). As already indicated, this provides us with a new algorithmic insight on the way the $(n-1)$-set agreement can be optimally solved.

Last but not least, an output of this paper is the following intriguing question. As already indicated, the k-set agreement problem and the k-simultaneous consensus problem are equivalent in read/write shared memory systems [1], which means that k-set agreement can be solved by executing k independent consensus instances. From a "minimal information on failures" point of view, each such instance relies on the shared memory (i.e., on Σ) to ensure agreement, and on an instance of Ω to ensure termination. For the k-set agreement we only need that one instance does terminate. This is

[3] Interestingly, a failure detector class weaker than $\Sigma \times \Omega_k$ is proposed in [8] to solve k-set agreement in message-passing systems. It is easy to show that $\Sigma \times \Omega_{n-1}$ is stronger than $\mathcal{L}$.

what is captured by $\overline{\Omega}_k$ (that eventually provides the processes with sets of k leaders that can arbitrarily change but contain forever the same correct process).

So, the question is: Which is the relation between the k-set agreement problem and the k-simultaneous consensus problem in message-passing systems? Understanding this link and its nature would give us a better understanding of the fundamental difference between shared memory communication and message-passing communication. The intertwining between sharing and agreeing seems to be subtle [9].

Roadmap. This paper is made up of 7 sections. Section 2 describes the computation model and Section 3 defines the failure detector class Π_k. Then, Section 4 shows that the classes $\{\Pi_k\}$ and $\Sigma_k \times \Omega_k$ are equivalent, and Section 5 shows that Π_{n-1} and $\mathcal{L}$ are equivalent. Section 6 presents a Π_{n-1}-based $(n-1)$-set agreement algorithm. Section 7 proves that Σ_k is a necessary requirement for failure detector-based k-set agreement in message-passing systems. Due to page limitation, the missing proofs can be found in [2].

2 System Model and k-Set Agreement

2.1 System Model

Process model. The system consists of a set of $n > 2$ asynchronous processes denoted $P = \{p_1, \ldots, p_n\}$. Each process executes a sequence of atomic steps (internal action, sending of a message, or reception of a message). A process executes its code until it possibly crashes. After it has crashed a process executes no more step. A process that crashes during a run is *faulty* in that run, otherwise it is *correct*. Given a run, C denotes the set of processes that are correct in that run. Up to $(n-1)$ processes can crash in a run. This is called the *wait-free environment*.

Communication model. The processes communicate by sending and receiving messages through channels. Every pair of processes is connected by a bidirectional channel. The channels are failure-free (there is no creation, alteration, duplication or loss of messages) and asynchronous (albeit the time taken by a message to travel from its sender to its destination process is finite, there is no bound on transfer delays). The notation "broadcast MSG_TYPE(m)" is used to send a message m (the type of which is MSG_TYPE) to all the processes. It is a (non-atomic) shortcut for "**for each** $j \in \{1, \ldots, n\}$ **do** send MSG_TYPE(m) to p_j **end for**".

Notation. The previous asynchronous message-passing model is denoted $\mathcal{AS}_n[\emptyset]$. When enriched with any failure detector of a given class X, it will be denoted $\mathcal{AS}_n[X]$.

2.2 The k-Set Agreement Problem

As already indicated, the k-set agreement problem has been introduced by S. Chaudhuri [6]. It generalizes the consensus problem (that corresponds to $k = 1$). It is defined as follows. Each process proposes a value and has to decide a value in such a way that the following properties are satisfied:

- Termination. Every correct process decides a value.
- Validity. A decided value is a proposed value.
- Agreement. At most k different values are decided.

3 Failure Detector Classes Definition

If xx_i is the local variable that contains the output of the failure detector at process p_i, xx_i^τ denotes its value at time τ.

3.1 The Eventual Leaders Families (The Omega Families)

Each process p_i is endowed with a local variable $leaders_i$ that satisfies the following properties.

The eventual leaders family Ω_k ($1 \leq k \leq n-1$). This family has been introduced by Neiger [24]. The local variables $leaders_i$ satisfy the following properties.

- Validity. $\forall i : \forall \tau : leaders_i^\tau$ is a set of k process identities.
- Eventual leadership. $\exists \tau : \exists LD = \{\ell_1, \ldots, \ell_k\} : (LD \cap \mathcal{C} \neq \emptyset) \wedge (\forall \tau' \geq \tau : \forall i : leaders_i^{\tau'} = LD)$.

Let us notice that τ is finite but unknown. Before τ, there is an anarchy period during which the local sets $leaders_i$ can contain unrelated values. After τ, these sets are equal to the same set LD that contains at least one correct process.

$\Omega = \Omega_1$ is the weakest failure detector class to solve consensus [5] in message-passing systems with a majority of correct processes, and in shared memory systems [16,19]. An Ω_k-based algorithm that solves the k-set agreement in message-passing systems where $t < n/2$ is described in [21]. This algorithm can easily be modified to replace the $t < n/2$ assumption by a failure detector of the class Σ_1 (see below).

The eventual leaders family $\overline{\Omega}_k$ ($1 \leq k \leq n-1$). The class $\overline{\Omega}_{n-1}$ (called anti-Omega) has been introduced in [29] where it has been shown to be weakest failure detector class to solve $(n-1)$-set agreement in shared memory systems. It has been generalized in [27] (as cited in [29]). The local variables $leaders_i$ satisfy the following properties.

- Validity. $\forall i : \forall \tau : leaders_i^\tau$ is a set of k process identities.
- Weak Eventual leadership. $\exists \tau : \exists \ell \in \mathcal{C} : \forall \tau' \geq \tau : \forall i : \ell \in leaders_i^{\tau'}$.

$\overline{\Omega}_1$ is the same as Ω_1. For $k > 1$, $\overline{\Omega}_k$ is weaker than Ω_k: it requires only that after some (finite but unknown) time the sets $leaders_i$ contain the same correct process. Very recently, it has been shown that $\overline{\Omega}_k$ is the weakest failure detector class to solve k-set agreement in shared memory systems [13,14,15]. As noticed in the Introduction, this family of failure detectors is related to the k simultaneous consensus problem [1].

3.2 The Quorum Family Σ_k ($1 \leq k \leq n-1$)

Each process p_i is endowed with a local variable qr_i that satisfies the following properties.

- Intersection. Let $id_1, \ldots, id_{k+1}$ denote a multiset of $k+1$ process identities, and $\tau_1, \ldots, \tau_{k+1}$ be any multiset of $k+1$ arbitrary time instants. $\forall id_1, \ldots, id_{k+1} : \forall \tau_1, \ldots, \tau_{k+1} : \exists i, j : 1 \leq i \neq j \leq k+1 : (qr_{id_i}^{\tau_i} \cap qr_{id_j}^{\tau_j} \neq \emptyset)$.
- Liveness. $\exists \tau : \forall \tau' \geq \tau : \forall i \in \mathcal{C} : qr_i^{\tau'} \subseteq \mathcal{C}$.

After a process p_i has crashed (if it ever does), we have (by definition) $qr_i = \{1, \ldots, n\}$ forever.

Σ_k is a generalization of the quorum failure detector class Σ introduced in [11] (that does correspond to Σ_1), where it is shown to be the weakest failure detector class to implement an atomic register in a message-passing system whatever the number of process failures ("wait-free" environment). It is interesting to notice that the intersection property of Σ_k is the same as the one used to define k-coteries [20].

3.3 The Agreement Quorum Family Π_k $(1 \leq k \leq n-1)$

Each process p_i is endowed with a local variable qr_i that satisfies the Intersection and Liveness properties of the quorum family Σ_k plus the following property:

- Eventual leadership. $\exists \tau : \exists LD = \{\ell_1, \ldots, \ell_k\} : \forall \tau' \geq \tau : \forall i : qr_i^{\tau'} \cap LD \neq \emptyset$.

After a process p_i has crashed (if it ever does), we have (by definition) $qr_i = \{1, \ldots, n\}$ forever. Moreover, let us observe that the Eventual leadership property of Π_k is weaker than the Eventual leadership property of Ω_k or $\overline{\Omega}_k$: it is not required that, after τ, qr_i must always contain the same correct process.

It follows from the Intersection property that a quorum can never be empty. Moreover, it follows from the Liveness property that the set $LD = \{\ell_1, \ldots, \ell_k\}$ defined in the Eventual leadership property is such that $LD \cap C \neq \emptyset$ (which means that this set contains at least one correct process). Let us also observe that the intersection requirement in the Eventual leadership property is similar to but weaker than the intersection property used in the definition of a k-arbiter [20].

3.4 Relations between Failure Detector Classes

Definition 1. *The failure detector class A is* stronger *than the failure detector class B (denoted $A \succeq B$ or $B \preceq A$) if it is possible to build a failure detector of the class B in $\mathcal{AS}_n[A]$.*

It follows from their definitions that (1) for any k: $\Omega_k \succeq \overline{\Omega}_k$, and (2) FD standing for any of Σ, Ω, $\overline{\Omega}$, and Π: $FD_1 \succeq \cdots FD_k \succeq FD_{k+1} \cdots \succeq FD_{n-1}$.

Definition 2. *Class A is* strictly stronger *than B ($A \succ B$) if $A \succeq B$ and $\neg(B \succeq A)$.*

Definition 3. *The classes A and B are* equivalent *($A \simeq B$) if $A \succeq B$ and $B \succeq A$.*

4 Π_k vs $\Sigma_k \times \Omega_k$ $(1 \leq k \leq n-1)$

4.1 From $\Sigma_k \times \Omega_k$ to Π_k

An algorithm that builds a failure detector of the class Π_k from a failure detector of the class $\Sigma_k \times \Omega_k$ is described in Figure 1.

Theorem 1. *The algorithm described in Figure 1 is a wait-free construction of a failure detector of the class Π_k in $\mathcal{AS}_n[\Sigma_k \times \Omega_k]$.* (Proof in [2].)

Init: $queue_i \leftarrow < 1, \ldots, n >$.
Task $T1$: **repeat periodically** broadcast ALIVE(i) **end repeat**.
Task $T2$: **when** ALIVE (j) **received**: suppress j from $queue_i$; enqueue j at head of $queue_i$.
when p_i reads qr_i: **let** ℓ **be** the first id of $queue_i$ that belongs to the output of Ω_k;
return (output of $\Sigma_k \cup \{\ell\}$).

Fig. 1. From $\Sigma_k \times \Omega_k$ to Π_k (code for p_i)

4.2 From Π_k to Σ_k and Ω_k

It is trivial to build Σ_k in $\mathcal{AS}_n[\Pi_k]$: the output of Σ_k is the output of Π_k. The rest of this section focuses on the construction of Ω_k in $\mathcal{AS}_n[\Pi_k]$.

Description of the Algorithm. Each process p_i manages a local variable $quorum\_set_i$ that contains a set of quorums. (Its initial value is the current value of qr_i, the local output supplied by Π_k). The principle of the algorithm is to maintain invariant the following property where $\ell_1, \ldots, \ell_k$ are different process identities:

$$(\exists\{\ell_1, \ldots, \ell_k\} : \forall qr \in quorum\_set_i : qr \cap \{\ell_1, \ldots, \ell_k\} \neq \emptyset)$$

and "extract" Ω_k from it. As we are about to see, this property guarantees that, if the process p_i was alone, it could consider $\{\ell_1, \ldots, \ell_k\}$ as its local output of Ω_k. So, in addition of maintaining the previous property invariant, the processes additionally use a reset mechanism and a gossip mechanism in order to ensure that all the local outputs $(\{\ell_1, \ldots, \ell_k\})$ eventually satisfy the leadership property of Ω_k.

The algorithm is described in Figure 2 in which each **when** statement is assumed to be executed atomically. Each process p_i executes a sequence of phases, locally identified by ph_nb_i. The behavior of p_i is as follows.

- Initially, p_i broadcasts NEW$(quorum_set_i, ph_nb_i)$ to inform the other processes of its value qr_i locally supplied by Π_k. It does the same broadcast each time the value of $quorum\_set_i$ changes (line 15 whose execution is entailed by the invocation of pres_inv&gossip() at lines 02 or 07).
- When p_i receives a NEW$(qset, ph_nb)$ message, its behavior depends on ph_nb.
  - If $ph\_nb > ph\_nb_i$, p_i jumps to the phase ph_nb, adopts the quorum set $qset$ it receives (line 03), and broadcasts its new state (line 04).
  - If $ph\_nb < ph\_nb_i$, p_i discards the message.
  - If $ph\_nb = ph\_nb_i$, p_i and the message are at same phase. In that case, p_i adds $qset$ to its quorum set $quorum\_set_i$. Moreover, if this addition has changed its value, p_i gossips it (line 07).
- The procedure pres_inv&gossip() is invoked in a **when** statement when $quorum\_set_i$ has been modified (line 02 or line 07). It has a reset role and a gossip role.
  - Reset. The first is to preserve the invariant property stated before. To that end, p_i resets $quorum\_set_i$ if the property was about to be violated (lines 13-14). In that case, p_i starts a new phase.
  - Gossip. Then, in all cases, p_i broadcasts the new value of $quorum\_set_i$.

– Finally, the algorithm defines as follows the value returned as the current local output of Ω_k (lines 09-12). The process p_i first considers all the increasing sequences of k process identities the intersection of which with each quorum currently in $quorum\_set_i$ are not empty (lines 09-10). Let us notice that each of these sequences satisfies the invariant property. Then, p_i deterministically selects and returns one of them (e.g., the first in lexicographical order, lines 11-12).

Init: $ph\_nb_i \leftarrow 0$; $quorum\_set_i \leftarrow \{qr_i\}$; broadcast NEW$(quorum_set_i, ph_nb_i)$.

when the value of qr_i changes:
(01) $quorum\_set_i \leftarrow quorum\_set_i \cup \{qr_i\}$;
(02) **if** ($quorum\_set_i$ has changed) **then** pres_inv&gossip() **end if**.

when NEW$(qset, ph_nb)$ **is received**:
(03) **case** $ph\_nb > ph\_nb_i$ **then** $ph\_nb_i \leftarrow ph\_nb$; $quorum\_set_i \leftarrow qset$;
(04) broadcast NEW$(quorum_set_i, ph_nb_i)$
(05) $ph\_nb < ph\_nb_i$ **then** discard the message
(06) $ph\_nb = ph\_nb_i$ **then** $quorum\_set_i \leftarrow quorum\_set_i \cup qset$;
(07) **if** ($quorum\_set_i$ modified) **then** pres_inv&gossip() **end if**
(08) **end case**.

when p_i reads $leaders_i$:
(09) **let** k_seqs the set of length k increasing sequences of process ids
(10) $\ell_1 < \cdots < \ell_k$ such that $\forall qr \in quorum\_set_i$: $qr \cap \{\ell_1, \ldots, \ell_k\} \neq \emptyset$;
(11) **let** $\ell_1, \ldots, \ell_k$ **be** the first sequence of k_seqs (according to lexicographical order);
(12) return$(\{\ell_1, \ldots, \ell_k\})$. % local output of Ω_k %

procedure pres_inv&gossip():
(13) **if** ($\nexists \{\ell_1, \ldots, \ell_k\} : \forall qr \in quorum\_set_i : qr \cap \{\ell_1, \ldots, \ell_k\} \neq \emptyset$)
(14) **then** $ph\_nb_i \leftarrow ph\_nb_i + 1$; $quorum\_set_i \leftarrow \{qr_i\}$ **end if**;
(15) broadcast NEW$(quorum_set_i, ph_nb_i)$.

Fig. 2. From Π_k to Ω_k (code for p_i)

Proof of the Algorithm. As Ω_k is defined by an *eventual* property, let us consider the time instant definition with respect to a run of the algorithm described in Figure 2.

Lemma 1. *Let X be the value of the the greatest local variable ph_nb_i at time τ. X is finite and no ph_nb_i variable becomes greater than $X + 1$.* (Proof in [2]).

Lemma 2. *There is a finite time after which no message is exchanged.* (Proof in [2].)

Lemma 3. *The set k_seqs defined at line 09 is never empty, and each of its elements is a non-empty set.* (Proof in [2].)

Lemma 4. $\exists LD = \{\ell_1, \ldots, \ell_k\} : LD \cap C \neq \emptyset : \exists \tau' \geq \tau$: $\forall \tau'' \geq \tau'$: $\forall i \in C$: $leaders_i^{\tau''} = LD$.

Proof. Let M be the greatest phase number ever attained by a correct process. Due to Lemma 1 this phase number does exist. Moreover, due to the lines 15 and 03, all the correct processes enter the phase M.

During the phase M, each correct process p_i exchanges its quorum set $quorum\_set_i$ each time this set is modified (lines 02 and 07). It follows from the network reliability and the fact that, during a phase, $quorum\_set_i$ can take a bounded number of distinct valucs, that there is a finite time after which all the correct processes have the same set of quorums in their local variables $quorum\_set_i$ (line 03). Let QS be this set of quorums.

Let τ' be a time after which all the processes p_i are such that $quorum\_set_i = QS$. The first part of the lemma follows from the fact that, after τ', the processes compute deterministically the same set LD of k leaders from the (never changing) same input QS (lines 09-12).

The fact that LD contains a correct process follows from the the liveness property of Π_k (there is a finite time after which each qr_i contains only correct processes), from which we conclude that the quorum set QS contains only quorums made up of correct processes. Due to its very definition, it follows that LD contains at least one correct process. $\Box_{Lemma\ 4}$

Theorem 2. *The algorithm described in Figure 2 is a wait-free quiescent construction of a failure detector of the class* Ω_k *in* $\mathcal{AS}_n[\Pi_k]$.

Proof. The fact that the algorithm constructs a failure detector of the class Ω_k follows from Lemma 3 (validity), and Lemma 4 (eventual leadership). The fact that the algorithm is quiescent follows from Lemma 2. Finally, it is trivially wait-free as there is no wait statement. $\Box_{Theorem\ 2}$

Theorem 3. $\Pi_k \simeq \Sigma_k \times \Omega_k$.

Proof. Theorem 1 has proved that $\Sigma_k \times \Omega_k \geq \Pi_k$. Theorem 2 has proved that $\Pi_k \geq \Omega_k$. Finally, (as already noticed), taking the output of Π_k as the output of Σ_k proves that $\Pi_k \geq \Sigma_k$. $\Box_{Theorem\ 3}$

5 Π_{n-1} vs. $\mathcal{L}$

5.1 The Failure Detector Class $\mathcal{L}$

The failure detector class $\mathcal{L}$ (for loneliness) has been introduced in [12] where it is shown to be the weakest failure detector class that solves the $(n-1)$-set agreement problem in message-passing systems. ([12] also shows that $\overline{\Omega}_{n-1} \succ \mathcal{L} \succ \Sigma$.) The class $\mathcal{L}$ is defined as follows. Each process p_i is provided with a boolean variable $alone_i$ that it can only read. These variables are such that:

- Stability. There is at least one process whose boolean remains always *false*.
- Loneliness. If only one process is correct, eventually its boolean outputs *true* forever.

By definition, after a process p_i has crashed (if it ever crashes) its boolean $alone_i$ is set to *false* and keeps that value forever.

Let us notice that nothing prevents the value of a boolean $alone_i$ to change infinitely often (as long as the corresponding process p_i is neither the one whose boolean remains always false, nor the only correct process in the the case where all the other process crash).

5.2 From Π_{n-1} to $\mathcal{L}$

The algorithm that constructs a failure detector of the class $\mathcal{L}$ from any failure detector of the class Π_{n-1} is described in Figure 3. It is pretty simple: the boolean of a process p_i becomes true (and remains true forever) only if the quorum of that process contains only its own identity. (A similar construction is described in [12] to show that Σ is stronger than $\mathcal{L}$.)

> **Init**: $alone_i \leftarrow false$.
> **when** $qr_i = \{i\}$: $alone_i \leftarrow true$.

Fig. 3. From Σ_{n-1} to $\mathcal{L}$ (code for p_i)

Theorem 4. *The algorithm described in Figure 3 builds a failure detector of the class $\mathcal{L}$ in $\mathcal{AS}_n[\Sigma_{n-1}]$.* (Proof in [2].)

As $\Pi_{n-1} = \Sigma_{n-1} \times \Omega_{n-1}$, the previous algorithm builds a failure detector of the class $\mathcal{L}$ in $\mathcal{AS}_n[\Pi_{n-1}]$.

5.3 From $\mathcal{L}$ to Π_{n-1}

The algorithm that constructs a failure detector of the class Π_{n-1} from any failure detector of the class $\mathcal{L}$ is described in Figure 4. Each process p_i periodically sends ALIVE(i) messages, processes the messages it receives, and set qr_i to $\{i\}$ when $alone_i$ becomes true (then, qr_i is no longer modified).

> **Init**: $qr_i \leftarrow \{i,j\}$ where $j \neq i$.
> **Task** $T1$: **repeat periodically** broadcast ALIVE(i) **end repeat**.
> **Task** $T2$: **when** $alone_i$ **becomes** $true$: $qr_i \leftarrow \{i\}$.
> **when** ALIVE(j) **is received**: **if** $\big((i \neq j) \wedge (|qr_i| \neq 1)\big)$ **then** $qr_i \leftarrow \{i,j\}$ **end if**.

Fig. 4. From $\mathcal{L}$ to Π_{n-1} (code for p_i)

Theorem 5. *The algorithm described in Figure 4 is a wait-free construction of a failure detector of the class Π_{n-1} in $\mathcal{AS}_n[\mathcal{L}]$.*

Proof. The proof considers each property of Π_{n-1} separately.

Proof of the Intersection property. As $k = n-1$, we have to prove that $\forall\{\tau_1,\ldots,\tau_n\} : \exists i,j : 1 \leq i \neq j \leq n : (qr_i^{\tau_i} \cap qr_j^{\tau_j} \neq \emptyset)$. Due to the Stability property of $\mathcal{L}$, there is at least one process (say p_i) such that $alone_i$ never becomes $true$. So, until p_i crashes (if it ever crashes), we have $|qr_i| = 2$. Consequently, there is always a process p_j such that $qr_i = \{i,j\}$, from which it follows that there is always a process p_j (not necessarily always the same) such that at any time $qr_i \cap qr_j \neq \emptyset$, which proves the property until p_i crashes. After p_i has crashed (if it does), the Intersection property is trivially satisfied.

Proof of the Liveness property. Let p_i be a correct process. We consider two cases.

- The boolean $alone_i$ takes (at least once) the value $true$. In that case, we will have $qr_i = \{i\}$. Then, qr_i remains forever equal to $\{i\}$, and the Liveness property is satisfied.
- The boolean $alone_i$ never takes the value $true$, and consequently we will never have $qr_i = \{i\}$. In that case, there are other correct processes (at least one). As, after some finite time, there are only correct processes, p_i will receive infinitely often messages ALIVE(j) from each of these correct processes p_j (and it will receive messages only from them). It follows that, after some time, qr_i contains only ids of correct processes.

Proof of the Eventual leadership property. We have to prove that $\exists \tau : \exists LD = \{\ell_1, \ldots, \ell_{n-1}\} : \forall \tau' \geq \tau : \forall i : qr_i^{\tau'} \cap LD \neq \emptyset$. Let us recall that any boolean (but one) can flip infinitely often between *false* and *true*. Let τ be the time after which no more boolean moves from *false* to *true* for the first time. Let $Z = \{i | \exists \tau : alone_i^{\tau} = true\}$. It follows from the definition of $\mathcal{L}$ that $0 \leq |Z| \leq n-1$. We consider two cases.

- $|Z| = n-1$. Let $Z = \{\ell_1, \ldots, \ell_{n-1}\}$ and take $LD = Z$. We show that, in that case, after τ, we always have $\forall i : LD \cap qr_i \neq \emptyset$. This is trivial for any process p_{ℓ_x}, $1 \leq x \leq n-1$, as we always have $\ell_x \in qr_{\ell_x}$. Let us now consider the process p_{ℓ_n} such that $alone_{\ell_n}$ remains always equal to *false* (due to definition of $\mathcal{L}$, p_{ℓ_n} does exist). Due to the algorithm of Figure 4, the process p_{ℓ_n} is such that we always have $|qr_{\ell_n}| = 2$. Consequently, the predicate $qr_{\ell_n} \cap LD \neq \emptyset$ is always satisfied, which completes the proof of the case.
- $|Z| < n-1$. Let $|Z| = z$. Let us recall that each process p_i in Z is such that after some finite time we always have $qr_i = \{i\}$. In that case, let us add $(n-1) - z$ processes to Z in order to obtain a set LD of $(n-1)$ processes. Due to the definition of Z and the algorithm of Figure 4, it follows that the process (say p_{ℓ_n}) that is not in LD is such that $|qr_{\ell_n}| = 2$. Consequently (as in the previous item) the predicate $qr_{\ell_n} \cap LD \neq \emptyset$ is always satisfied. Hence, the set LD satisfies the Eventual leadership property, which completes the proof of the theorem.

$\Box_{Theorem\ 5}$

5.4 Σ_{n-1}, $\mathcal{L}$ and Ω_{n-1}

Theorem 6. $\Sigma_{n-1} \simeq \mathcal{L} \simeq \Pi_{n-1} \simeq \Sigma_{n-1} \times \Omega_{n-1}$. (Proof in [2].)

This theorem generalizes a result of [10] where it is shown that $\Sigma_1 \simeq \Sigma_1 \times \Omega_1$ in systems made up of $n = 2$ processes. The following corollaries are an immediate consequence of the previous theorem and the definition of Σ_k. The second one generalizes a result of [12] that (expressed with our notations) states $\Sigma_1 \succ \mathcal{L} \succ \overline{\Omega}_{n-1}$.

Corollary 1. *Σ_{n-1} is stronger than Ω_{n-1}.*

Corollary 2. $\Sigma_1 \succ \Sigma_2 \succ \ldots \succ \Sigma_{n-2} \succ \Sigma_{n-1} \simeq \mathcal{L}$.

6 A Σ_{n-1}-Based $(n-1)$-Set Agreement Algorithm

An $\mathcal{L}$-based $(n-1)$-set agreement algorithm is presented in [12]. Hence, the stacking of this algorithm on top of the algorithm described in Figure 4 (that builds Π_{n-1}, i.e., Σ_{n-1}, in $\mathcal{AS}_n[\mathcal{L}]$), supplies a Σ_{n-1}-based $(n-1)$-set agreement algorithm. This Section describes a $(n-1)$-set agreement algorithm that is directly built on top of Σ_{n-1} and consequently saves the construction of $\mathcal{L}$ when one is provided with a failure detector of the class Π_{n-1}.

The algorithm. The code of the algorithm for a process p_i is described in Figure 5. The local variable est_i contains p_i's current estimate of the decision value, while $qsize_i$ contains a quorum size, namely, the size of smallest quorum that allowed computing the current value of est_i.

The processes proceed in n asynchronous rounds. At the end of the last round, p_i returns (decides) the current value of est_i (line 09). During a round r, a process p_i first broadcasts it current state (the pair $(qsize_i, est_i)$) and waits for the current states of the processes in its current quorum qr_i (lines 03-04). Then, considering these states $(qsize, est)$ plus its local state, p_i selects the smallest one according to their lexicographical ordering[4] (line 06). Finally, p_i updates $qsize_i$ and est_i (line 07). The local estimate est_i is updated to the estimate value est_x of the processes p_x of $q = qr_i \cup \{i\}$ such that $qsize_x$ is the smallest; $qsize_i$ is set to $\min(qsize_x, |q|)$ to take into account the size of the quorum that allowed computing est_i (line 07). The proof of correctness (with respect to the set-agreement problem) of this algorithm appears in [2].

Function set_agreement$_{n-1}$ (v_i):
(01) $est_i \leftarrow v_i$; $qsize_i \leftarrow n$;
(02) **for** r_i **from** 1 to n **do**
(03) broadcast PROPOSE$(r_i, qsize_i, est_i)$;
(04) **wait until** (PROPOSE$(r_i, -, -)$ **received from all the processes in** qr_i);
(05) **let** q **be** $\{i\}\cup$ the quorum qr_i that allowed the **wait** statement to terminate;
(06) **let** $(qsize, est)$ **be** the smallest pair (lex. order) rec. from the processes $\in q$;
(07) $qsize_i \leftarrow \min(qsize, |q|)$; $est_i \leftarrow est$
(08) **end for**;
(09) return(est_i).

Fig. 5. Σ_{n-1}-based $(n-1)$-set algorithm (code for p_i)

7 Necessity of Σ_k to Solve k-Set Agreement

This section shows that Σ_k is necessary to solve the k-set agreement problem as soon as we are looking for a failure detector-based solution. To that end, given any algorithm A that solves the k-set agreement problem with the help of a failure detector $\mathcal{D}$, we provide an algorithm that emulates the output of Σ_k. This means that it is possible to build a failure detector of the class Σ_k from any failure detector $\mathcal{D}$ that can solve the

[4] Recall that $(q1, est1) < (q2, est2) \stackrel{\text{def}}{=} ((q1 < q2) \vee (q1 = q2 \wedge est1 < est2))$.

k-set agreement problem (according to the usual terminology, Σ_k can be *extracted from* the $\mathcal{D}$-based algorithm A). The output of Σ_k at p_i is kept in qr_i.

Interestingly enough, and in addition of being more general, the proposed construction (Figure 6) provides us with a proof of the necessity of Σ_1 to solve the consensus problem that is simpler than the one described in [10].

Underlying principle. As in [12], the proposed extraction algorithm does not rely on the asynchronous impossibility of a problem. Its design principle is the following. Each process p_i participates in several runs of A. Let $R_{\{i\}}$ denote a run of A in which only the process p_i participates, $R_{\{i,j\}}$ $(i \neq j)$ a run of A in which only the processes p_i and p_j participate, etc., and $R_{\{1,2,\ldots,n\}}$ a run of A in which all the processes participate. This means that in a run denoted R_Q only the processes of Q take steps, and each process of Q either decides, blocks forever or crashes[5]. So, the extraction algorithm uses $2^n - 1$ runs of A. Let us observe that, due to asynchrony and the fact that any number of processes can crash ("wait-free" environment), any prefix of any of these runs can occur in a given execution.

The algorithm. The algorithm executed by each process p_i is described in Figure 6. It is made up of four tasks. Each process manages two local variables: a set of sets denoted S_i and a queue denoted $queue_i$. The aim of S_i is to contain all the sets Q such that p_i decides in the run R_Q (Task $T1$), while $queue_i$ is managed as the queue with the same name in Figure 1 (tasks $T2$ and $T3$). The important point here is that the correct processes eventually appear before the faulty processes in $queue_i$.

The idea is to select a set of S_i as the current output of Σ_k. As we will see in the proof, any $(k+1)$ sets of S_i are such that two of them do intersect which will supply the intersection property. The main issue is to ensure the liveness property of Σ_k (namely, eventually the set qr_i associated with p_i contains only correct processes), while preserving the intersection property. This is done as follows with the help of $queue_i$. The current output of Σ_k is the set (quorum) of S_i that appears as being the "first" in $queue_i$. The formal definition of "first set of S_i wrt $queue_i$" is stated in the task $T3$. To make it easy to understand let us consider the following example. Let $S_i = \{\{3,4,9\},\{2,3,8\},\{4,7\}\}$, and $queue_i =< 4,8,3,2,7,5,9,\cdots >$. The set $F = \{2,3,8\}$ is the first set of S_i with respect to $queue_i$ because each of the other sets $\{3,4,9\}$ and $\{4,7\}$ includes an element (9 and 7, respectively) that appears in $queue_i$ after the elements of F. (In case several sets are "first", any of them can be selected).

Remark. Initially S_i contains the set $\{1,\ldots,n\}$. As only sets of processes can be added to S_i (task $T1$), S_i is never empty. Moreover, it is not necessary to launch a run in which all the processes participate. This is because, as the $\mathcal{D}$-based k-set agreement algorithm A is correct, it follows that all the correct processes decide in that run $R_{\{1,\ldots,n\}}$. This case is directly taken into account in the initialization of S_i (thereby saving the run $R_{\{1,\ldots,n\}}$).

[5] As the processes that are not in Q do not participate, the messages sent by the processes of Q to these processes are never received. Alternatively, as in [12], we could say that the processes of Q "omit" sending messages to the processes that are not in Q.

Init: $S_i \leftarrow \{\{1\ldots,n\}\}$; $queue_i \leftarrow < 1,\ldots,n >$;
for each $Q \in (2^{\Pi} \setminus \{\emptyset,\{1,\ldots,n\}\})$ **such that** $(i \in Q)$ **do**
let A_Q denote the $\mathcal{D}$-based instance of A in which participate only the processes of Q;
p_i proposes i to the instance A_Q **end for**.

Task $T1$: **when** p_i decides in the instance of A in which participate only the processes of Q:
$S_i \leftarrow S_i \cup \{Q\}$.

Task $T2$: **repeat periodically** broadcast ALIVE(i) **end_repeat**.

Task $T3$: **when** ALIVE (j) **received**: suppress j from $queue_i$; enqueue j at head of $queue_i$.

Task $T4$: **when** p_i reads qr_i:
let $m = \min_{Q\in S_i}(\max_{x\in Q}(rank[x]))$ where $rank[x]$ denotes the rank of x in $queue_i$;
return (a set Q such that $\max_{x\in Q}(rank[x]) = m$).

Fig. 6. Extracting Σ_k from a k-set agreement failure detector-based algorithm A

Theorem 7. *Given any algorithm A that solves the k-set agreement problem with the help of a failure detector $\mathcal{D}$, the algorithm described in Figure 6 is a wait-free construction of a failure detector of the class Σ_k.*

Proof. The Intersection property of Σ_k is proved by contradiction. Let us first notice that a set qr_i returned to a process p_i is a set Q of S_i. Let us assume that there are $k+1$ subsets of processes $Q_1,\ldots,Q_{k+1}$ such that (1) $\forall x : 1 \le x \le k{+}1 : Q_x \in \bigcup_{1\le i\le n} S_i$, and (2) $\forall x,y : 1 \le x \ne y \le k+1 : Q_x \cap Q_y = \emptyset$ (pairwise independence). The item (1) means that Q_x can be returned as the value of qr_i by a process p_i.

Let $Q = Q_1 \cup \ldots \cup Q_{k+1}$. Let R be the run of A in which (1) only the processes of Q participate, and (2) for each x, $1 \le x \le k+1$, the processes of Q_x behave exactly as in R_{Q_x} (as defined in the **Init** part of Figure 6). Due to the second item, in R, the processes in Q_x, $1 \le x \le k+1$, that decide do decide as in R_{Q_x}. It follows that, even if the processes in each Q_x would decide the same value, up to $k+1$ different values could be decided. This contradicts the fact that A solves the k-set agreement in the run R, from which we conclude that $\exists x,y : 1 \le x \ne y \le k+1 : Q_x \cap Q_y \ne \emptyset$ which proves the Intersection property of Σ_k.

As far as the Liveness property, let us consider the run of A in which the set of participating processes is exactly $\mathcal{C}$ (the set of correct processes). Due to the termination property of A, every correct process does terminate in that instance. Consequently, in the extraction algorithm, the variable S_i of each correct process p_i eventually contains the set $\mathcal{C}$.

Moreover, after some finite time, each correct process p_i receives ALIVE(j) messages only from correct processes. This means that, for each correct process p_i, all the correct processes eventually precede the faulty processes in $queue_i$. Due to the definition of "first set of S_i wrt $queue_i$" stated in the task $T4$, and the fact that $\mathcal{C} \in S_i$, it follows that the quorum Q selected by the task $T4$ is such that $Q \subseteq \mathcal{C}$, which proves the liveness property of Σ_k. $\Box_{Theorem\ 7}$

Remark. The previous theorem provides us with a register-free proof of the necessity of Σ to solve consensus in the asynchronous message-passing model.

References

1. Afek, Y., Gafni, E., Rajsbaum, S., Raynal, M., Travers, C.: Simultaneous consensus tasks: A tighter characterization of set-consensus. In: Chaudhuri, S., Das, S.R., Paul, H.S., Tirthapura, S. (eds.) ICDCN 2006. LNCS, vol. 4308, pp. 331–341. Springer, Heidelberg (2006)
2. Bonnet, F., Raynal, M.: Looking for the Weakest Failure Detector for k-Set Agreement in Message-passing Systems: Is Π_k the End of the Road? Tech. Report #1929, 19 pages, IRISA, Université de Rennes 1 (France) (May 2009)
3. Borowsky, E., Gafni, E.: Generalized FLP Impossibility Results for t-Resilient Asynchronous Computations. In: Proc. 25th ACM Symposium on Theory of Computation (STOC 1993), San Diego, CA, pp. 91–100 (1993)
4. Chandra, T., Toueg, S.: Unreliable Failure Detectors for Reliable Distributed Systems. Journal of the ACM 43(2), 225–267 (1996)
5. Chandra, T., Hadzilacos, V., Toueg, S.: The Weakest Failure Detector for Solving Consensus. Journal of the ACM 43(4), 685–722 (1996)
6. Chaudhuri, S.: More Choices Allow More Faults: Set Consensus Problems in Totally Asynchronous Systems. Information and Computation 105, 132–158 (1993)
7. Chaudhuri, S., Herlihy, M., Lynch, N., Tuttle, M.: Tight Bounds for k-Set Agreement. Journal of the ACM 47(5), 912–943 (2000)
8. Chen, W., Zhang, J., Chen, Y., Liu, X.: Weakening failure detectors for k-set agreement via the partition approach. In: Pelc, A. (ed.) DISC 2007. LNCS, vol. 4731, pp. 123–138. Springer, Heidelberg (2007)
9. Delporte-Gallet, C., Fauconnier, H., Guerraoui, R.: Sharing is harder than agreeing. In: 27th ACM Symp. on Princ. of Distributed Computing (PODC 2008), pp. 85–94. ACM Press, New York (2008)
10. Delporte-Gallet, C., Fauconnier, H., Guerraoui, R.: Shared Memory vs Message Passing. Technical Report2003-77, EPFL Lausanne (2003)
11. Delporte-Gallet, C., Fauconnier, H., Guerraoui, R., Hadzilacos, V., Kouznetsov, P., Toueg, S.: The weakest failure detectors to solve certain fundamental problems in distributed computing. In: Proc. 23th ACM Symposium on Principles of Distributed Computing (PODC 2004), pp. 338–346. ACM Press, New York (2004)
12. Delporte-Gallet, C., Fauconnier, H., Guerraoui, R., Tielmann, A.: The Weakest Failure Detector for Message Passing Set-Agreement. In: Taubenfeld, G. (ed.) DISC 2008. LNCS, vol. 5218, pp. 109–120. Springer, Heidelberg (2008)
13. Delporte-Gallet, C., Fauconnier, H., Guerraoui, R., Tielmann, A.: The disagreement power of an adversary. In: Proc. 28th ACM Symposium on Principles of Distributed Computing (PODC 2009). ACM Press, New York (2009)
14. Fernandez Anta, A., Rajsbaum, S., Travers, C.: Weakest failure detectors with an edge-laying simulation. In: Proc. 28th ACM Symposium on Principles of Distributed Computing (PODC 2009). ACM Press, New York (2009)
15. Gafni, E., Kuznetzov, P.: The weakest failure detector for solving k-set agreeemnt. In: Proc. 28th ACM Symp. on Principles of Distributed Computing (PODC 2009). ACM Press, New York (2009)
16. Guerraoui, R., Kouznetsov, P.: Failure detectors as types boosters. Distributed Computing 20, 343–358 (2008)
17. Herlihy, M.P., Penso, L.D.: Tight Bounds for k-Set Agreement with Limited Scope Accuracy Failure Detectors. Distributed Computing 18(2), 157–166 (2005)

18. Herlihy, M.P., Shavit, N.: The Topological Structure of Asynchronous Computability. Journal of the ACM 46(6), 858–923 (1999)
19. Lo, W.-K., Hadzilacos, V.: Using failure detectors to solve consensus in asynchronous shared-memory systems. In: Tel, G., Vitányi, P.M.B. (eds.) WDAG 1994. LNCS, vol. 857, pp. 280–295. Springer, Heidelberg (1994)
20. Manabe, Y., Baldoni, R., Raynal, M., Aoyagia, S.: K-arbiter: a safe and general scheme for h-out of-k mutual exclusion. Theoretical Computer Science 193(1-2), 97–112 (1998)
21. Mostéfaoui, A., Rajsbaum, S., Raynal, M., Travers, C.: On the Computability Power and the Robustness of Set Agreement-oriented Failure Detector Classes. Distributed Computing 21(3), 201–222 (2008)
22. Mostéfaoui, A., Raynal, M.: k-Set Agreement with Limited Accuracy Failure Detectors. In: 19th ACM Symp. on Principles of Distributed Computing (PODC 2000), pp. 143–152 (2000)
23. Mostéfaoui, A., Raynal, M.: Randomized Set Agreement. In: Proc. 13th ACM Symposium on Parallel Algorithms and Architectures (SPAA 2001), pp. 291–297. ACM Press, New York (2001)
24. Neiger, G.: Failure Detectors and the Wait-free Hierarchy. In: 14th ACM Symposium on Principles of Distributed Computing (PODC 1995), pp. 100–109. ACM Press, New York (1995)
25. Raynal, M., Travers, C.: In search of the holy grail: looking for the weakest failure detector for wait-free set agreement. In: Shvartsman, M.M.A.A. (ed.) OPODIS 2006. LNCS, vol. 4305, pp. 3–19. Springer, Heidelberg (2006)
26. Raynal, M., Travers, C.: Synchronous Set Agreement: a concise guided tour (including a new algorithm and a list of open problems). In: Proc. 12th IEEE Pacific Rim Int'l Symposium on Dependable Computing (PRDC 2006), pp. 267–274. IEEE Computer Press, Los Alamitos (2006)
27. Raynal, M.: K-anti-Omega. In: Rump Session at 26th ACM Symposium on Principles of Distributed Computing, PODC 2007 (2007)
28. Saks, M., Zaharoglou, F.: Wait-Free k-Set Agreement is Impossible: The Topology of Public Knowledge. SIAM Journal on Computing 29(5), 1449–1483 (2000)
29. Zielinski, P.: Anti-Omega: the weakest failure detector for set agreement. In: Proc. 27th ACM Symp. on Principles of Distributed Computing (PODC 2008), pp. 55–64. ACM Press, New York (2008)

Optimal Byzantine Resilient Convergence in Asynchronous Robots Networks

Zohir Bouzid, Maria Gradinariu Potop-Butucaru, and Sébastien Tixeuil

Université Pierre et Marie Curie - Paris 6, LIP6-CNRS 7606, France

Abstract. This paper addresses the byzantine resilience lower bound for the convergence in semi-synchronous robot networks. We prove that $3f+1$ robots are needed for convergence to tolerate up to f Byzantine robots. Our work generalizes the previously established lower bound proved for the class of cautious algorithms only. Additionally we propose the first deterministic algorithm that matches this lower bound and performs in the asynchronous CORDA model. Our algorithm works under bounded scheduling assumptions for oblivious robots moving in a uni-dimensional space.

1 Introduction

Convergence is a fundamental agreement primitive in robot networks and is used in the implementation of a broad class of services (*e.g.* the construction of common coordinate systems or specific geometrical patterns). Given a set of oblivious robots with arbitrary initial locations and no agreement on a global coordinate system, *convergence* requires that all robots asymptotically approach the same, but unknown beforehand, location. Convergence is hard to achieve in asynchronous systems, when robots obtain information only *via* visual sensors, since they are unable to distinguish between a moving or a stationary robot. The problem becomes even harder when some robots are Byzantine (*i.e.* those robots can exhibit arbitrary behavior). In that case correct robots are required to converge independently of the behavior of the faulty ones.

Robots operate in *cycles* that comprise *Look*, *Compute*, and *Move* phases. The Look phase consists in taking a snapshot of the other robots positions using its visibility sensors. In the Compute phase a robot computes a target destination based on the previous observation. The Move phase simply consists in moving toward the computed destination using motion actuators. The robots that we consider have weak capacities: they are *anonymous* (they execute the same protocol and have no mean to distinguish themselves from the others), *oblivious* (they have no memory that is persistent between two cycles), and have no compass whatsoever (they are unable to agree on a common direction or orientation).

In order to capture the essence of distributed coordination in robot networks, two main computational models are proposed in the literature: the ATOM [1] and CORDA [2] models. The main difference between the two models comes

R. Guerraoui and F. Petit (Eds.): SSS 2009, LNCS 5873, pp. 165–179, 2009.

from the granularity of the execution of the *Look-Compute-Move* cycle. In the ATOM model, the whole cycle is atomic while in the CORDA model, the cycle is executed in a continuous manner. That is, in the ATOM model, robots executing concurrently always remain in the same phase while in CORDA it is possible that e.g. a robot executes its Look phase while another robot performs its Move phase, or that a robot executes its Compute phase while its view (obtained during the Look phase) is already outdated.

Related works. Since the pioneering work of Suzuki and Yamashita [1], gathering[1] and convergence have been addressed in *fault-free* systems for a broad class of settings. Prencipe [2] studied the problem of gathering in both ATOM and CORDA models, and showed that the problem is intractable without additional assumptions such as being able to detect the multiplicity of a location (*i.e.*, knowing if there is more than one robot in a given location). Flocchini *et al.* [3] proposed a gathering solution for oblivious robots with limited visibility in the CORDA model, where robots share the knowledge of a common direction given by a compass. The subsequent work by Souissi *et al.* [4] consider a system in which compasses are not necessarily consistent initially. In [5] the authors address convergence with limited visibility in fault-free environments. Convergence with inaccurate sensors and movements is addressed in [6]. Recently, in [7] the authors study the same problem under a uniform sensing error model. Ando *et al.* [5] propose a gathering algorithm for the ATOM model with limited visibility.

The case of *fault-prone* robot networks was recently tackled by several academic studies. The faults that have been investigated fall in two categories: *crash* faults (*i.e.* a faulty robots stops executing its cycle forever) and *Byzantine* faults (*i.e.* a faulty robot may exhibit arbitrary behavior and movement). Of course, the Byzantine fault model encompasses the crash fault model, and is thus harder to address. *Deterministic* fault-tolerant gathering is addressed in[8] where the authors study a gathering protocol that tolerates one crash, and an algorithm for the ATOM model with fully synchronous scheduling that tolerates up to f byzantine faults, when the number of robots is (strictly) greater than $3f$. In [9] the authors study the feasibility of *probabilistic* gathering in crash-prone and Byzantine-prone environments. *Deterministic* fault-tolerant convergence was first addressed in [10,11], where algorithms based on convergence to the center of gravity of the system are presented. Those algorithms work in CORDA model and tolerate up to f $(n > f)$ crash faults, where n is the number of robots in the system. Most related to this paper is [12], where the authors studied convergence in byzantine-prone environments when robots move in a uni-dimensional space. In more details, [12] showed that convergence is impossible if robots are not endowed with strong multiplicity detectors which are able to detect the exact number of robots that may simultaneously share the same location. The same paper defines the class of *cautious* algorithms which guarantee that correct robots always move inside the range of positions held by correct robots, and proved that any cautious convergence algorithm that can

[1] Gathering requires robots to actually *reach* a single point within finite time regardless of their initial positions.

tolerate f Byzantine robots requires the presence of at least $2f+1$ robots in fully-synchronous ATOM networks and $3f+1$ robots in semi-synchronous ATOM networks. The lower bound for the ATOM model naturally extends to the CORDA model, yet the protocol proposed in [12] for the asynchronous CORDA model requires at least $4f+1$ robots.

Table 1. Crash and byzantine resilience bounds for deterministic gathering and convergence

Reference	**Model**	**Faults**	**Bounds**
[6]	ATOM	inaccurante sensors movements and calc.	-
[8]	ATOM Fully-Sync ATOM	crash **Byzantine**	$f = 1$ $n > 3f$
[10]	ATOM	crash	$n > f$
[11]	**CORDA**	crash	$n > f$
[12]	Fully-Sync ATOM ATOM **CORDA**	**Byzantine** **Byzantine** **Byzantine**	$n > 2f$ $n > 3f$ $n > 4f$
This paper	**CORDA**	**Byzantine**	$n > 3f$

Table 1 summarizes the results related to crash and byzantine resilience of gathering and convergence deterministic protocols that are known in robot netwoks. The bold values denote the least specialized (and more difficult) hypothesises.

Our contributions. In this paper we generalize the byzantine resilience lower bound result for convergence in semi-synchronous robot networks. The previously established lower bound proven in [12] restricted to the class of cautious algorithms[2]. Additionally, we propose an optimal (with respect to the number of Byzantine robots) Byzantine resilient solution for convergence when robots execute their actions in the CORDA model. That is, our solution tolerates f byzantine robots in $3f+1$-sized networks, which matches our lower bound.

Outline. The remaining of the paper is organized as follows: Section 2 presents our model and robot network assumptions. Section 3 presents the formal specification of the convergence problem and recalls the necessary and sufficient conditions to achieve convergence in Byzantine prone systems. In Section 4 we derive the lower bound on the number of faulty robots. Section 5 describes our protocol and its complexity, while concluding remarks are presented in Section 6.

2 Model

Most of the notions presented in this section are borrowed from[1,13,8]. We consider a network that consists of a finite set of n robots arbitrarily deployed

[2] In this class correct robots always move inside the range of positions held by correct robots.

in a uni-dimensional space. The robots are devices with sensing, computing and moving capabilities. They can observe (sense) the positions of other robots in the space and based on these observations, they perform some local computations that can drive them to other locations.

In the context of this paper, the robots are *anonymous*, in the sense that they can not be distinguished using their appearance, and they do not have any kind of identifiers that can be used during the computation. In addition, there is no direct mean of communication between them. Hence, the only way for robots to acquire information is by observing their positions. Robots have *unlimited visibility*, *i.e.* they are able to sense the entire set of robots. Robots are also equipped with a strong multiplicity sensor referred to as *multiples detector* and denoted hereafter by $\mathcal{M}$. This sensor provides robots with the ability to detect the exact number of robots that may simultaneously occupy the same location[3]. We assume that the robots cannot remember any previous observation nor computation performed in any previous step. Such robots are said to be *oblivious* (or *memoryless*).

Each robot runs a *program* that consists in executing *Look-Compute-Move cycles* infinitely many times. That is, the robot first observes its environment (Look phase). An observation returns a snapshot of the positions of all robots within the visibility range. In our case, this observation returns a snapshot (also called *local configuration* hereafter) of the positions of *all* robots denoted with $P^i(t) = \{P^i_1(t), ..., P^i_n(t)\}$. The positions of correct robots are referred as $U^i(t) = \{U^i_1(t), ..., U^i_m(t)\}$ where m denotes the number of correct robots. Note that $U^i(t) \subseteq P^i(t)$. The observed positions are *relative* to the observing robot, that is, they use the coordinate system of the observing robot. Based on its observation, a robot then decides — according to its program — to move or stay idle (Compute phase). When a robot decides a move, it moves to its destination during the Move phase.

The network of n robots executes a *protocol* which is a collection of n *programs*, one operating on each robot. Given a global coordinate system and a global unit of distance a *global configuration* of the network, denoted with $P(t) = \{P_1(t), ..., P_n(t)\}$, is a snapshot at time t of the positions of the n robots relative to the global coordinate system. In order to ease the presentation, in the following we will not explicitly indicate when the configurations are local or global. This will be deduced from the context. An *execution* $e = (c_0, \ldots, c_t, \ldots)$ of the protocol is an infinite sequence of configurations, where c_0 is the initial configuration[4] of the system, and every transition $c_i \rightarrow c_{i+1}$ is associated to the execution of a subset of the previously defined actions.

A *scheduler* is a predicate on computations, that is, a scheduler defines a set of *admissible* computations, such that every computation in this set satisfies the scheduler predicate. A *scheduler* can be seen as an entity that is external to the

[3] In [12], it is proved that $\mathcal{M}$ is necessary to deterministically solve the convergence problem in a uni-dimensional space even in the presence of a single Byzantine robot.

[4] Unless stated otherwise, we make no specific assumption regarding the respective positions of robots in initial configurations.

system and selects robots for execution. As more power is given to the scheduler for robot scheduling, more different executions are possible and more difficult it becomes to design robot algorithms. In the remaining of the paper, we consider that the scheduler is *k-bounded* if, between any two activations of a particular robot, any other robot can be activated at most k times[5].

We now review the main differences between the ATOM [1] and CORDA [13] models. In the ATOM model, whenever a robot is activated by the scheduler, it performs a *full* computation cycle. Thus, the execution of the system can be viewed as an infinite sequence of rounds. In a round one or more robots are activated by the scheduler and perform a computation cycle. The *fully-synchronous ATOM* model refers to the fact that the scheduler activates all robots in each round, while the *semi-synchronous ATOM* model enables the scheduler to activate only a subset of the robots. In the CORDA model, robots may be interrupted by the scheduler after performing only a portion of a computation cycle. In particular, actions (look, compute, move) of different robots may be interleaved. For example, a robot a may perform a look phase, then a robot b performs a look-compute-move complete action, then a computes and moves based on its previous observation (that does not correspond to the current configuration anymore). As a result, the set of executions that are possible in the CORDA model are a strict superset of those that are possible in the ATOM model. So, an impossibility result that holds in the ATOM model also holds in the CORDA model, while an algorithm that performs in the CORDA model is also correct in the ATOM model. Note that the converse is not necessarily true.

The faults we address in this paper are *Byzantine* faults. A byzantine (or malicious) robot may behave in arbitrary and unforeseeable way. In each cycle, the scheduler determines the course of action of faulty robots and the distance to which each non-faulty robot will move in this cycle. However, a correct robot i is guaranteed to move a distance of at least δ_i towards its destination before it can be stopped by the scheduler. In this model, a Byzantine robot can not be ubiquitous, which is realistic for mobile robots. However, the adversary (*i.e.* scheduler) can, by scheduling activations and controlling the actions of Byzantine robots, deceive correct robots and "display" several different locations for a single Byzantine robot.

Our convergence algorithm performs operations on multisets. A multiset or a bag S is a generalization of a set where an element can have more than one occurence. The number of occurences of an element a is referred as its *multiplicity* and is denoted by $mul(a)$. The total number of elements of a multiset, including their repeated occurences, is referred as the *cardinality* and is denoted by $|S|$. $\min(S)$(resp. $\max(S)$) is the smallest (resp. largest) element of S. If S is nonempty, $range(S)$ denotes the set $[\min(S), \max(S)]$ and $diam(S)$ (diameter of S) denotes $\max(S) - \min(S)$.

[5] Note that we prove the impossibility result with $n = 3f$ robots using a 2-bounded scheduler.

3 The Byzantine Convergence Problem

Given an initial configuration of n autonomous mobile robots (m of which are correct such that $m \geq n-f$), the *point convergence problem* requires that all correct robots asymptotically approach the exact same, but unknown beforehand, location. In other words, for every initial configuration there exists a point c such that for every $\epsilon > 0$, there exists a time t_ϵ from which all correct robots are within distance of at most ϵ of c (and thus within distance of at most 2ϵ of each other).

Definition 1 (Byzantine Convergence). *A system of oblivious robots satisfies the Byzantine convergence specification if and only if for every initial configuration, $\exists c$, a position in the space, such that $\forall \epsilon > 0, \exists t_\epsilon$ such that $\forall t > t_\epsilon$, $\forall i \leq m$, $distance(U_i(t), c) < \epsilon$, where $U_i(t)$ is the position of some* correct *robot i at time t, and where $distance(a, b)$ denotes the Euclidian distance between two positions.*

Definition 1 requires the convergence property only from the *correct* robots. Note that it is impossible to obtain the convergence for all robots since Byzantine robots may exhibit arbitrary behavior and never join the position of correct robots.

In the following we recall the necessary conditions to achieve convergence in systems prone to Byzantine failures. We first focus on the definition of *shrinking* algorithms (algorithms that eventually decrease the range between any two correct robots). In [12] is proved that this condition is necessary but not sufficient for convergence even in fault-free environments. We then recall the definition of *cautious* algorithms (algorithms that ensure that the position of correct robots always remains inside the range of the correct robots). This condition combined with the previous one is sufficient to reach convergence in fault-free systems [12].

By definition, convergence aims at asymptotically decreasing the range of possible positions for the correct robots. The shrinking property captures this property. An algorithm is shrinking if there exists a constant factor $\alpha \in (0, 1)$ such that starting in any configuration the range of correct robots eventually decreases by a multiplicative α factor. Note that to deal with the asynchrony of the model, the diameter calculation takes into account both the positions and destinations of correct robots.

Definition 2 (Shrinking Algorithm). *An algorithm is* shrinking *if and only if $\exists \alpha \in (0, 1)$ such that $\forall t, \exists t' > t$, such that $diam(U(t') \cup D(t')) < \alpha * diam(U(t) \cup D(t))$, where $U(t)$ and $D(t)$ are respectively the the multisets of positions and destinations of correct robots.*

A natural way to solve convergence is to never let the algorithm increase the diameter of correct robot positions. In this case the algorithm is called *cautious*. This notion was first introduced in [14]. A cautious algorithm is particularly appealing in the context of Byzantine failures since it always instructs a correct robot to move inside the range of the positions held by the correct robots regardless of the locations of Byzantine ones. The following definition introduced first in [12] customizes the definition of cautious algorithm proposed in [14] to robot networks.

Definition 3 (Cautious Algorithm). *Let $D_i(t)$ be the last destination calculated by the robot i before time t and let $U^i(t)$ the positions of the correct robots as seen by robot i before time t.* [6] *An algorithm is* cautious *if it meets the following conditions:*

- ***cautiousness:*** $\forall t,\ D_i(t) \in range(U^i(t))$ *for each robot i.*
- ***non-triviality:*** $\forall t$, *if* $diameter(U(t)) \neq 0$ *then* $\exists t' > t$ *and a robot i such that* $D_i(t') \neq U_i(t')$ *(at least one correct robot changes its position whenever convergence is not achieved).*

The following theorem will be further used in order to prove the correctness of our convergence algorithm.

Theorem 1. *[12] Any algorithm that is both cautious and shrinking solves the convergence problem in fault-free robot networks.*

4 Lower Bound on the Number of Faulty Robots

In this section we study the lower bound on the number of robots for Byzantine convergence when the activation of robots is handled by a semi-synchronous ATOM scheduler. In [12] we already proved for the class of cautious algorithms that the presence of at least $3f+1$ robots is required to tolerate up to f Byzantine robots. In this section, we generalize this lower bound for any convergence algorithm (whether it is cautious or not). The result is proved for the weaker ATOM model, and thus extends to CORDA model.

The intuition behind the lower bound is that if there are less than $3f+1$ robots in the network, the adversary (i.e. scheduler) is able for some initial configurations to make the robots indefinitely alternate between two non terminal configurations while ensuring fairness. Very important to the proof is the notion of equivalence between configurations. Informally speaking, two configurations of robots are equivalent if: (1) the number of robots is the same in both configurations and (2) each configuration can be obtained from the other by translation, symmetry or rotation. That is, the number of locations points, their multiplicity and their relative distances are maintained. To capture this notion formally, we introduce the following definition:

Definition 4. *Two configurations P and P' of n mobile robots are equivalent if there exists some real factor α such that either (1) $\forall\ 0 < i \leq n,\ (P_i - P_{i-1}) = \alpha * (P'_i - P'_{i-1})$ or (2) $\forall\ 0 < i \leq n,\ (P_i - P_{i-1}) = \alpha * (P'_{n+1-i} - P'_{n-i})$.*

The following lemma is fundamental to our proof. Its states that if a majority of at least $n-f$ robots are colocated in the same position, then any convergence algorithm will instruct them to stay in this position. Formally, we have:

[6] If the last calculation was executed at time $t' \leq t$ then $D_i(t) = D_i(t')$.

Lemma 1. *Let S be a set of at least $n - f$ robots that are colocated in the same position p at time t; then all destinations of robots in S that are computed by any convergence algorithm at time $t' \geq t$ are equal to p.*

Proof. We consider any initial configuration C_1 such that at least $n - f$ robots are located in the same position p. Let $SetP$ denote the set of these robots.

The proof of our lemma proceeds by contradiction. We assume there exists a convergence algorithm A that instructs the robots of $SetP$ to move to some position $q \neq p$ when they are activated by the scheduler. Assume without loss of generality that $q < p$, that is p is to the right of q. This order is only given for ease of presentation and is unknown to robots that can not use it in their algorithms.

We now inductively create an execution in which the correct robots that run algorithm A form a moving multiplicity point, that is they stay always together but they move indefinitely to the right by a distance equal to $distance(p, q)$ at each movement. Hence, convergence is prevented.

Let C_2 be an equivalent configuration to C_1 (take $\alpha = 1$ and keep the same positive direction), but where all the correct robots are at p. This is possible since in C_1, $|SetP| \geq n - f$. We again denote by $SetP$ the set of robots located at p. Note that $SetP$ may contain also some Byzantine robots. Since C_1 and C_2 are equivalent, they are completely indistinguishable to individual robots which must behave similarly in both cases (as they run the same deterministic algorithm A). This results from the absence of a common coordinate system between robots. Thus the origin, the positive direction of the axis and the unit of distance may be different from one robot to another and their algorithms can not exploit global coordinates or exact metric distances between robots.

Hence, when the correct robots of $SetP$ are activated in C_2, their computed destination by A is equal to q. Assume that the scheduler activates all the robots of $SetP$ simultaneously and does not stop them before they reach their destination q. At the same time, each Byzantine robot i is moved by the scheduler to the right by a distance equal to $distance(p, q)$. Denote by C_3 the resulting configuration. Clearly, C_3 is equivalent to C_2. Therefore, by repeating the same actions indefinitely, the adversary is able to make the correct robots move at each cycle by a distance equal to $distance(p, q)$. Thus, convergence is prevented which contradicts the assumption of A being a correct convergence algorithm. This proves our lemma. □

Now we are ready to present the main result of this section. The following theorem provides the lower bound for Byzantine convergence in semi-synchronous ATOM model.

Theorem 2. *Byzantine-resilient convergence is impossible for $n \leq 3f$ in the semi-synchronous ATOM model and a 2-bounded scheduler.*

Proof. Our proof is based on a particular initial setting in which we prove that no convergence algorithm is possible if a third or more of the robots are Byzantine. So consider a network of n robots, f of which are Byzantine with $n \leq 3f$. We

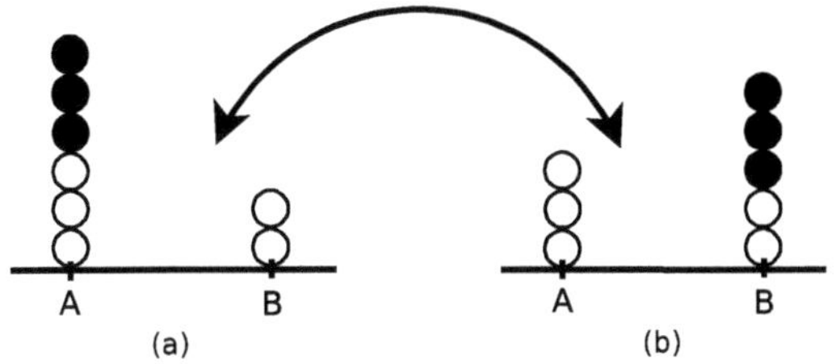

Fig. 1. Impossibility of convergence in ATOM with $n \leq 3f$, black robots are Byzantine. (a) Configuration C_1. (b) Configuration C_2.

only consider networks with at least two correct robots since the convergence of a single correct robot is trivial. Thus $f + 2 < n \leq 3f$.

Now assume that the correct robots are spread over two distinct points A and B in a uni-dimensional space. Let C_1 be an initial configuration in which $\lceil \frac{n-f}{2} \rceil$ correct robots are located at A and the remaining $\lfloor \frac{n-f}{2} \rfloor$ correct robots are at B. Note that both A and B contain at least one correct robot each. All the Byzantine robots robots in C_1 are located at A (refer to Figure 1(a)).Therefore, the total number of robots at A (whether correct or not) is $\lceil \frac{n-f}{2} \rceil + f$ which is at least equal to $n - f$ since $n \leq 3f$.

Thus, according to lemma 1, when the correct robots at A are activated they remain in their location (A) and do not move. Next, the adversary moves the Byzantine robots to B which leads to the configuration C_2 (see figure 1(b)). Again, the total number of robots at B in C_2 is at least equal to $n - f$. Therefore, the correct robots at B do not move upon their activation.

So by repeatedly alternating between the two configurations C_1 and C_2, the adversary ensures that every robot is activated infinitely often in the execution yet prevents convergence at the same time since robots at A and B remain always at their initial positions and never converge. □

5 Deterministic Asynchronous Convergence

In this section we propose a deterministic convergence algorithm and prove its correctness in the CORDA model under a k-bounded scheduler. This algorithm matches the lower bound on the number of robots proved in the last section and works correctly for $n > 3f$. The idea of Algorithm 1 is as follows: each robot computes the center of the positions of the robots seen in its last Look phase ignoring the f largest positions if they are larger than his own position and the f smallest positions if they are smaller than his own position.

Algorithm 1 uses two functions, $trim_f^i()$ and $center()$. The choice of the function $trim_f^i()$ makes the difference between this algorithm and that of [12]. Indeed, in [12] the trimming function removes the f largest and the f smallest values from the multiset given in parameter. That is, the returned multiset does not depend on the position of the calling robot. In Algorithm 1, $trim_f^i()$ removes

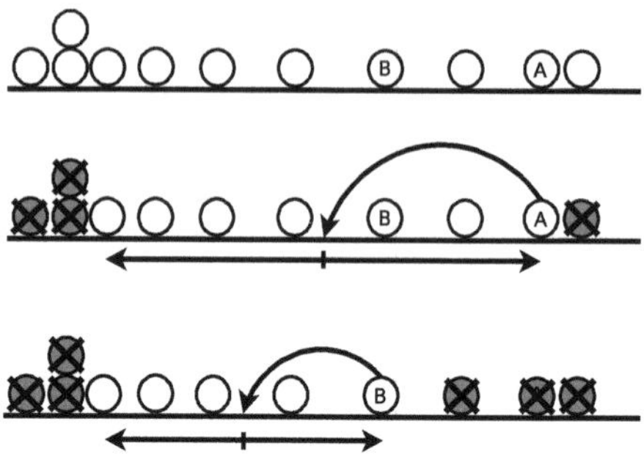

Fig. 2. Illustration of functions $trim^i_f$ and *center* for robots A and B in a system of $n = 11$ robots ($f = 3$)

among the f largest positions *only* those that are greater than the position of the calling robot i. Similarly, it removes among the f smallest positions only those that are smaller than the position of the calling robot.

Formally, let $minindex_i$ be the index of the minimum position between $P_i(t)$ and $P_{f+1}(t)$ (if $P_i(t) < P_{f+1}(t)$ then $minindex_i$ is equal to i, otherwise it is equal to $f+1$). Similarily, let $maxindex_i$ be the index of the maximum position between $P_i(t)$ and $P_{n-f}(t)$ (if $P_i(t) > P_{n-f}(t)$ then $maxindex_i$ is equal to i, otherwise it is equal to $n-f$). $trim^i_f(P(t))$ is the multiset consisting of positions $\{P_{minindex_i}(t), P_{minindex_i+1}(t), ..., P_{maxindex_i}(t)\}$. $center()$ returns the center point of the input range. The two functions are illustrated in Figure 2) .

Algorithm 1. Byzantine Tolerant Convergence

Functions:
- $trim^i_f(P(t))$: removes up to f largest positions that are larger than $P_i(t)$ and up to f smallest positions that are smaller than $P_i(t)$ from the multiset $P(t)$ given in parameter.
- *center*: returns the center point of the input range.

Actions:
move towards $center(trim^i_f(P(t)))$

In the following we prove the correctness of Algorithm 1 in the CORDA model under a k-bounded scheduler. In order to show that Algorithm 1 converges, we prove first that it is cautious then we prove that it satisfies the specification of a shrinking algorithm. Convergence then follows from Theorem 1.

5.1 Algorithm 1 Is Cautious

In this section we prove that Algorithm 1 is a cautious algorithm (see Definition 3) for $n > 3f$. The following lemma states that the range of the trimmed multiset $trim^i_f(P(t))$ is contained in the range of correct positions.

Lemma 2. *Let i be a correct robot executing Algorithm 1, it holds that*

$$range(trim_f^i(P(t))) \subseteq range(U(t))$$

A direct consequence of the above property is that correct robots always compute a destination within the range of positions held by correct robots, whatever the behavior of Byzantine ones. Thus, the diameter of positions held by correct robots never increases. Consequently, the algorithm is cautious. The formal proof is proposed in the following lemma.

Lemma 3. *Algorithm 1 is cautious for $n > 3f$.*

Proof. According to Lemma 2, $range(trim_f^i(P(t))) \subseteq range(U(t))$ for each correct robot i, thus $center(trim_f^i(P(t))) \in range(U(t))$. It follows that all destinations computed by correct robots are located inside $range(U(t))$ which proves the lemma.

5.2 Algorithm 1 Is Shrinking

In this section we prove that Algorithm 1 is a shrinking algorithm (see Definition 2). The following lemma states that a robot can not compute a destination that is far from its current position by more than half the diameter of correct positions. More specifically, a robot located on one end of the network can not move to the other end in a single movement.

Interestingly, the property of lemma 4 is guaranteed even though robots are not able to figure out the range of correct positions nor to compute the corresponding diameter. The bound on the movements of robots is achieved by taking into account the position of the calling robot when computing the trimming function. It is important to note that if all robots compute their destinations using the same trimming function irrespective of the position of the calling robot, convergence requires the presence of more than $4f$ robots to tolerate the presence of up to f Byzantine robots [12].

Lemma 4. *$\forall t, \forall i$, correct robot, if i computes its destination point at time t, then at t, $distance(U_i^i(t), D_i(t)) \leq diameter(U^i(t))/2$*

The following lemmas describe some important properties on the destination points computed by correct robots which will be used in proving the shrinkingness of Algorithm 1. These properties are verified whatever the positions of Byzantine robots are, and thus they capture the limits of the influence of Byzantine robots on the actions undertaken by correct robots.

The next lemma shows that the correct positions $\{U_{f+1}(t), ..., U_{m-f}(t)\}$ are always included in the trimmed range (the output range of the function $trim_f^i$) regardless of the positions of Byzantine robots.

Lemma 5. *It holds that $range(trim_f(U(t))) \subseteq range(trim_f(P(t)))$.*

Let $D(t)$ be the set of destinations computed with Algorithm 1 in systems with $n > 3f$, and let $UD(t)$ be the union of $U(t)$ and $D(t)$. If a robot i executed its last Look phase at time $t' \leq t$, then $UD^i(t) = UD(t')$. The following lemma proves that the destination computed by each correct robot i is always within the range $[(min(UD^i(t)) + U^i_{m-f}(t))/2, (U^i_{f+1}(t) + max(UD^i(t)))/2]$ independently of the positions of Byzantine robots.

Lemma 6. *The following properties hold:*
$\forall i$, each destination point calculated by a correct robot i at time t is (1) smaller than $(U^i_{f+1}(t) + max(UD^i(t)))/2$ and (2) greater than $(min(UD^i(t)) + U^i_{m-f}(t))/2$.

Lemma 7. *Let $S(t)$ be a multiset of $f+1$ arbitrary elements of $U(t)$. The following properties hold: (1) $\forall t$, $U_{f+1}(t) \leq \max(S(t))$ and (2) $\forall t$, $U_{m-f}(t) \geq \min(S(t))$*

The next lemma generalizes and extends the properties of Lemmas 5 and 6 (proven for a fixed time instant) to a time interval. It describes bounds on the destination points computed by correct robots during a time interval $[t_1, t_2]$. It states that if there is a subset of $f+1$ robots whose positions are less than S_{max} during $[t_1, t_2]$, then all destinations computed during $[t_1, t_2]$ by all correct robots in the network are necessarily smaller than $(S_{max} + Max(UD(t_1)))/2$.

Lemma 8. *Let a time $t_2 > t_1$ and let $S(t)$ be a multiset of $f+1$ arbitrary elements in $U(t)$. If $\forall p \in S(t)$ and $\forall t \in [t_1, t_2]$ $p \leq S_{max}$ then all calculated destination points at time interval $[t_1, t_2]$ are smaller than $(S_{max} + Max(UD(t_1)))/2$.*

The next Lemma states that if some calculated destination point is in the neighborhood of one end of the network, then a majority of $m - f$ correct robots are necessarily located in the neighborhood of this end.

Lemma 9. *If some correct robot i executes its Look phase at time t and then compute (in the Compute phase which immediatly follows) a destination D_i such that $D_i < min(UD(t)) + b$ (with b any distance smaller than $diameter(UD(t))/2$), then at t, there are at least $m - f$ correct robots whose positions are (strictly) smaller than $min(UD(t)) + 2b$.*

We are now ready to give the proof of shrinkingness of our algorithm in the CORDA model. The general idea of the proof is to show that the destination points computed by correct robots are located either around the middle of the range of correct positions or/and in the neighborhood of only one end of this range.

If all computed destinations are located around the middle of the range of correct robots then the diameter of this range decreases and the algorithm is shrinking. Otherwise, if some computed destinations are located in the neighborhood of one end of the range, it is shown that there is a time at which no correct robot will be in the neighborhood of the other end of the range, which leads again to a decrease in the range of correct positions and shows that the algorithm is shrinking.

Lemma 10. *Algorithm 1 is shrinking in the CORDA model with $n > 3f$ under a k-bounded scheduler.*

Proof. Let $U(t_0) = \{U_1(t_0), ..., U_m(t_0)\}$ be the configuration of correct robots at initial time t_0 and $D(t_0) = \{D_1(t_0), ..., D_m(t_0)\}$ the multiset of their calculated destination points at the same time t_0 and $UD(t_0)$ is the union of $U(t_0)$ and $D(t_0)$. Let t_1 be the first time at which all correct robots have been activated and executed their Look and Compute phase at least once since t_0 ($U(t_1)$ and $D(t_1)$ are the corresponding multisets of positions and destinations). Assume that robots are ordered from left to right and define d_0 and d_1 as their diameters at t_0 and t_1 respectively. Since the model is asynchronous, the diameter calculation takes into account both the positions and the destinations of robots. So $d_0 = diameter(UD(t_0))$ and $d_1 = diameter(UD(t_1))$. Let b be any distance that is smaller than $d_0/4$, for example take $b = d_0/10$.

We consider the actions of correct robots after t_1 and we separate the analysis into two cases:

- *Case A*: All calculated destinations by all correct robots after t_1 are inside $[min(UD(t_0))+b, max(UD(t_0))-b]$. So when all correct robots are activated at least once, their diameter decreases by at least $\min\{2\delta, 2b = d_0/5\}$. Thus by setting $\alpha_1 = \max\{1 - 2\delta/d_0, 4/5\}$, the algorithm is shrinking.
- *Case B*: Let $t_2 > t_1$ be the first time when a robot, say i, execute a Look phase such that the Compute phase that follows compute a destination point, say D_i, that is outside $[min(UD(t_0))+b, max(UD(t_0))-b]$. This implies that either $(D_i < min(UD(t_0)) + b)$ or $(D_i > max(UD(t_0)) - b)$. Since the two cases are symmetric, we consider only the former which implies according to Lemma 9 that the range $[min(UD(t_0)), min(UD(t_0)) + 2b]$ must contain at least $m - f$ correct positions.

  If some robots among these $m - f$ robots are executing a Move phase, their destination points have necessarily been calculated after t_0 (since at t_1 each robot has been activated at least once). And we have by lemma 4 that the distance between each robot and its destination can not exceed half the diameter, so we conclude that at t_2 the destination points of these $m - f$ robots are all inside $[min(UD(t_0)), min(UD(t_0)) + b + d_0/2]$.

  Let $S(t_2)$ be a submultiset of $UD(t_2)$ containing the positions and destinations of $f + 1$ arbitrary robots among these $m - f$ whose positions and destinations are inside $[min(UD(t_0)), min(UD(t_0)) + b + d_0/2]$. So $\max(S(t_2)) \leq min(UD(t_0))+b+d_0/2$. And since we choosed $b < d_0/4$, we have $\max(S(t_2)) < max(UD(t_0)) - 3d_0/4$. Let $t_3 \geq t_2$ be the first time each correct robot in the system has been activated at least once since t_2. We prove in the following that at t_3, $\max(S(t_3)) < max(UD(t_0)) - 3d_0/2^{k(f+1)+2}$.

  To this end we show that the activation of a single robot of $S(t)$ can not reduce the distance between the upper bound of $max(S)$ and $max(UD(t_0))$ by more than half its precedent value, and since the scheduler is k-bounded, we can guarantee that this distance at t_3 is at least equal to $3d_0/2^{k(f+1)+2}$.

  According to Lemma 6, if some robot i calculates its destination D_i at time $t \in [t_2, t_3]$, $D_i \leq (U_{f+1}(t) + max(UD(t)))/2$. But $U_{f+1}(t) \leq max(S(t))$

by Lemma 7 and $max(UD(t)) \leq max(UD(t_0))$ due to cautiousness. This gives us $D_i \leq (max(S(t) + max(UD(t_0)))/2$. Therefore, an activation of a single robot in $S(t)$ to execute its Compute phase can reduce the distance between $Max(UD(t_0))$ and $max(S(t))$ by at most half its precedant value.

So at t_3, after a maximum of k activations of each robot in $S(t)$, we have $max(S(t_3)) \leq Max(UD(t_0)) - 3d_0/2^{k(f+1)+2}$, and by Lemma 8, all calculated destinations by all correct robots between t_2 and t_3 are less than or equal to $Max(UD(t_0)) - 3d_0/2^{k(f+1)+3}$.

Since robots are guaranteed to move toward their destinations by at least a distance δ before they can be stopped by the scheduler, after t_3, no robot will be located beyond $Max(UD(t_0)) - min\{\delta, 3d_0/2^{k(f+1)+3}\}$. Hence by setting $\alpha = \max\{\alpha_1, 1 - \delta/d_0, 1 - 3/2^{k(f+1)+3}\}$ the lemma follows. □

The convergence proof of Algorithm 1 directly follows from Lemma 10 and Lemma 3. Algorithm 1 solves the Byzantine convergence problem in the CORDA model for $n > 3f$ under a k-bounded scheduler.

6 Conclusions and Discussions

In this paper we consider networks of oblivious robots with arbitrary initial locations and no agreement on a global coordinate system. Robots obtain system related information only *via* visual sensors and some of them are Byzantine (*i.e.* they can exhibit arbitrary behavior). In this weak scenario, we studied the *convergence* problem that requires that all robots asymptotically approach the exact same, but unknown beforehand, location. We proved that the Byzantine resilience lower bound for convergence in semi-synchronous networks is $3f + 1$ where f is the number of Byzantine robots. Additionally, we proposed a Byzantine resilient solution that matches this lower bound when robots execute their actions asynchronously as defined in the CORDA model.

Two immediate open problems are raised by our work. Our algorithm is proved correct under bounded scheduling assumption. We conjecture that this hypothesis is necessary for achieving convergence in the class of cautious algorithms. The second open problem is the study of asynchronous byzantine-resilient convergence in a multi-dimensional space is still open.

References

1. Suzuki, I., Yamashita, M.: Distributed anonymous mobile robots: Formation of geometric patterns. SIAM Journal of Computing 28(4), 1347–1363 (1999)
2. Prencipe, G.: On the feasibility of gathering by autonomous mobile robots. In: Pelc, A., Raynal, M. (eds.) SIROCCO 2005. LNCS, vol. 3499, pp. 246–261. Springer, Heidelberg (2005)
3. Flocchini, P., Prencipe, G., Santoro, N., Widmayer, P.: Gathering of asynchronous mobile robots with limited visibility. Theoretical Computer Science 337, 147–168 (2005)

4. Souissi, S., Défago, X., Yamashita, M.: Eventually consistent compasses for robust gathering of asynchronous mobile robots with limited visibility. Research Report IS-RR-2005-010, JAIST, Ishikawa, Japan (July 2005)
5. Ando, H., Oasa, Y., Suzuki, I., Yamashita, M.: Distributed memoryless point convergence algorithm for mobile robots with limited visibility. IEEE Transactions on Robotics and Automation 15(5), 818–828 (1999)
6. Cohen, R., Peleg, D.: Convergence of autonomous mobile robots with inaccurate sensors and movements. In: Durand, B., Thomas, W. (eds.) STACS 2006. LNCS, vol. 3884, pp. 549–560. Springer, Heidelberg (2006)
7. Yamamoto, K., Izumi, T., Katayama, Y., Inuzuka, N., Wada, K.: Convergence of mobile robots with uniformly-inaccurate sensors. In: Sirocco (2009)
8. Agmon, N., Peleg, D.: Fault-tolerant gathering algorithms for autonomous mobile robots. In: Proceedings of the fifteenth annual ACM-SIAM symposium on Discrete algorithms, vol. 11(14), pp. 1070–1078 (2004)
9. Defago, X., Gradinariu, M., Messika, S., Parvedy, P.: Fault-tolerant and self-stabilizing mobile robots gathering. In: Dolev, S. (ed.) DISC 2006. LNCS, vol. 4167, pp. 46–60. Springer, Heidelberg (2006)
10. Cohen, R., Peleg, D.: Robot convergence via center-of-gravity algorithms. In: Kralovic, R., Sýkora, O. (eds.) SIROCCO 2004. LNCS, vol. 3104, pp. 79–88. Springer, Heidelberg (2004)
11. Cohen, R., Peleg, D.: Convergence properties of the gravitational algorithm in asynchronous robot systems. SIAM Journal on Computing 34(6), 1516–1528 (2005)
12. Bouzid, Z., Potop-Butucaru, M.G., Tixeuil, S.: Byzantine-resilient convergence in oblivious robot networks. In: Garg, V., Wattenhofer, R., Kothapalli, K. (eds.) ICDCN 2009. LNCS, vol. 5408, pp. 275–280. Springer, Heidelberg (2009)
13. Prencipe, G.: CORDA: Distributed coordination of a set of autonomous mobile robots. In: Proc. 4th European Research Seminar on Advances in Distributed Systems (ERSADS 2001), Bertinoro, Italy, May 2001, pp. 185–190 (2001)
14. Dolev, D., Lynch, N., Pinter, S., Stark, E., Weihl, W.: Reaching approximate agreement in the presence of faults. Journal of the ACM (JACM) 33(3), 499–516 (1986)

FoG: Fighting the Achilles' Heel of Gossip Protocols with Fountain Codes

Mary-Luc Champel[1], Anne-Marie Kermarrec[2], and Nicolas Le Scouarnec[1]

[1] Thomson R&D, Cesson-Sevigné, France
[2] INRIA Rennes Bretagne-Atlantique, Rennes, France

Abstract. Gossip protocols are well known to provide reliable and robust dissemination protocols in highly dynamic systems. Yet, they suffer from high redundancy in the last phase of the dissemination. In this paper, we combine fountain codes (rateless erasure-correcting codes) together with gossip protocols for a robust and fast content dissemination in large-scale dynamic systems. The use of fountain enables to eliminate the unnecessary redundancy of gossip protocols. We propose the design of FoG, which fully exploits the first exponential growth phase (where the data is disseminated exponentially fast) of gossip protocols while avoiding the need for the shrinking phase by using fountain codes. FoG voluntarily increases the number of disseminations but limits those disseminations to the exponential growth phase. In addition, FoG creates a split-graph overlay that splits the peers between encoders and forwarders. Forwarder peers become encoders as soon as they have received the whole content. In order to benefit even further and quicker from encoders, FoG biases the dissemination towards the most advanced peers to make them complete earlier.

We assess FoG through simulation. We show that FoG outperforms by 50% a simple push protocol with respect to overhead and improves by 30% the termination time.

1 Introduction

Gossip protocols are now recognized as a solid and robust approach for disseminating content in large scale-systems. They provide an efficient alternative to tree-based approaches, typically fragile in highly dynamic environments. In gossip protocols, peers periodically push contents to f (called the fanout in the sequel) peers picked uniformly and randomly among all peers. A message is first disseminated from a source. When receiving the message for the first time, a peer forwards it to f other random peers until the message reaches only peers that have already received it. In gossip, two phases can be distinguished in the dissemination: *(i) an exponential growth phase* during which the message spreads exponentially fast since initially the probability to reach a peer that has not yet been reached is very high; and *(ii) a shrinking phase* where the rate of dissemination diminishes, as eventually the probability to reach already informed peers increases drastically [1]. This phase typically generates a large number of

R. Guerraoui and F. Petit (Eds.): SSS 2009, LNCS 5873, pp. 180–194, 2009.

duplicates. Yet it is necessary to achieve a reliable dissemination. This shrinking phase is generally recognized as the Achilles' heel of gossip protocols: this is a fatal pitfall but also the price to pay for achieving reliability in highly dynamic systems. Moreover, the cost associated with the shrinking phase becomes an increasingly serious issue, overhead wise, as the size of the content to disseminate increases. This typically explains the recent success of video streaming protocols which relies on a push gossip protocol for locating the content with small messages while the content is subsequently pulled ([2,3]).

In this paper, we propose to combine the use of gossip protocols with fountain codes to benefit fully from the exponential growth phase of gossip protocols while avoiding suffering from the shrinking phase. Fountain codes typically encode the full content so that encoded chunks embed redundancy [4,5]. However, the use of fountain codes precisely removes the notion of useless redundancy. Typically, a fountain code generates infinity of encoded chunks from an original content of k chunks. Any $k(1+\epsilon)$ chunks, with $\epsilon \approx 0.04$ for long enough codes ($k > 1000$), are enough to decode the full content. Even though network codes [6] are usually considered as more powerful than fountain codes, we choose to rely on fountain codes which have a lower complexity[1]. Their lower complexity makes them more practical to deploy in environments where the amount of data to be encoded is important and the computation resources are scarce.

We propose the design and evaluation of FoG a dissemination gossip protocol relying on fountain codes. FoG fully leverages the potential of gossip protocols through the following principles.

- First, FoG removes the need for the shrinking phase by simply increasing the number of exponential phases. This is due to a clever use of content encoded through fountain codes. Typically k gossips are turned into $z > k$ shorter gossips[2] where only the exponential growth is considered. The basic intuition behind this is that peers that have been missed during the exponential phase for one dissemination recover by being reached over the subsequent ones. Eventually, all peers receive the z chunks required to decode the full content. This increases the marginal utility of any chunk's dissemination.
- Second, FoG implements a biased dissemination to favor the most advanced peers so that completed peers (peers that have received the full content) become sources since they have the ability to produce new innovative chunks by re-encoding the content as soon as possible. This exploits the fact that peers can receive the z distinct chunks from any source. All encoded chunks are equally useful, and two encoders produce distinct and independent encoded chunks thanks to the infinite size of the set of encoded chunks. To this end, FoG gradually builds a split-graph overlay by sampling the system over all non-completed peers. This means that the f gossip targets on each

[1] Network codes involves a Gaussian elimination $O(k^3)$ for decoding while practical fountain codes such as LT Codes [7] exploit belief propagation decoding $O(k \ln k)$.

[2] z is automatically determined by the protocol which disseminates as long as some peers have not completed.

peer are chosen randomly among the peers that have not yet received the full content.

We evaluate FoG through extensive simulations by comparing it against standard push gossip protocols. We are mainly interested in the termination of peers when they can decode and use the content. We compare the progression of the decoding for all peers. We conclude that peers using FoG complete 30% earlier than peers using a standard gossip do.

We describe the design rationale in Section 2. The details of FoG are provided in Section 3. Experimental results are reported in Section 4. We review related works in Section 5 before concluding in Section 6.

2 FoG in a Nutshell

In this section, we first present the system model and then explain the design of FoG.

2.1 System Model

We consider a system of n peers in which peers cooperate to disseminate a file. Each peer is supposed to cooperate as specified: byzantine and selfish behaviors are outside of the scope of this paper. A peer that has a full copy of the file is called *complete*, *incomplete* otherwise. In the figures of this paper, the complete peers are black and the incomplete ones are white.

The n peers are connected by an unstructured overlay network. The overlay network is maintained by a gossip-based peer sampling protocol [8]. Such protocols tend to build overlay network the topology of which is close to a d-regular random graph where d is the out-degree of peers. To this end, each peer maintains a view of size d, constantly updated by the gossip peer sampling protocol. In FoG, the complete peers have no incoming edges and never appear in samples provided by the peer sampling service. This means although complete peers remains connected by maintaining a view, they are absent of any views and they are never picked during the dissemination.

The dissemination protocol runs over the network of n peers following a push protocol. Initially, the source is assumed to be the only complete peer. A dissemination is considered finished, when all the n peers have a copy of the file. The file is divided in k small chunks. Those chunks are disseminated independently. The source sends chunks periodically to one of its neighbors. When a peer receives a new chunk, it forwards it to f *(fanout)* neighbors. This scheme ensures a complete dissemination with high probability as long as $f = O(\log n)$. To limit flooding, we introduce a *TTL (time to live)* that significantly reduces the number of peers that receive the chunk thus reducing multiple receptions and removing the shrinking phase. However, removing the shrinking phase results in significantly more peers not receiving the chunk.

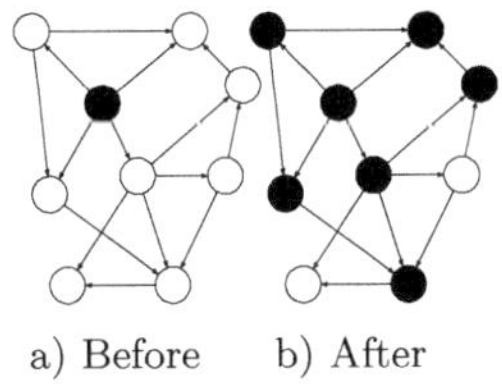

Fig. 1. Shrinking phase

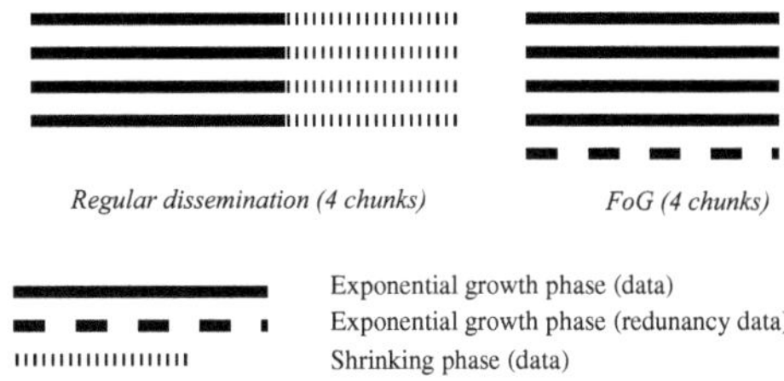

Fig. 2. FoG keeps only growth phases

2.2 Design Rationale

As mentioned earlier, gossip dissemination is implicitly characterized by a first phase, called exponential growth, where the data is spread exponentially fast, followed by a second phase, called the shrinking phase, where a lot of redundancy is introduced (i.e. peers which have already received the message receive it again) but is required to reach the remaining peers. This is due to the random selection of the peers to gossip to. As illustrated on Figure 1, without adding mechanism to ensure full dissemination, some peers are not able to receive the data. The idea behind FoG is to exploit fully the strength of gossip dissemination, namely the exponential growth phase, without suffering from its weakness, the shrinking phase. FoG achieves this by increasing the number of disseminations, but limiting them to the exponential growth phase. Obviously, a gossip dissemination stopping after the exponential growth phase misses many peers. We therefore use fountain codes so that the number of sources is infinite and the number of disseminations can be infinite. The termination of the dissemination is naturally detected overall as the complete peers are gradually removed from the views.

FoG replaces the shrinking phases by additional exponential growth phases. To illustrate, consider a content of k chunks to disseminate to a set of peers. Chunks are disseminated in parallel by independent exponential-growth phases. At the end of each exponential-growth phase, $\frac{n}{2}$ peers have received the disseminated chunk. Note that this is achieved by associating an empirically determined finite TTL to each chunk, enough to reach $\frac{n}{2}$ peers. At each dissemination, $\frac{n}{2}$ peers miss the data disseminated. To ensure that all peers complete regardless, additional disseminations of encoded data are performed. We "factor out" the shrinking phases of all disseminations in a few disseminations of redundant content, as shown on Figure 2.

To keep the shrinking phase, $TTL = \infty$ so that we would reach all n peers at the end of each dissemination and no peer would miss the data with high probability.

The dissemination protocol disseminates data to peers that are provided by a peer sampling protocol ([8]) that builds an overlay network. FoG structures the overlay network as a split-graph (Figure 3) that is a composition of a random graph connecting incomplete peers and a bipartite-graph connecting complete

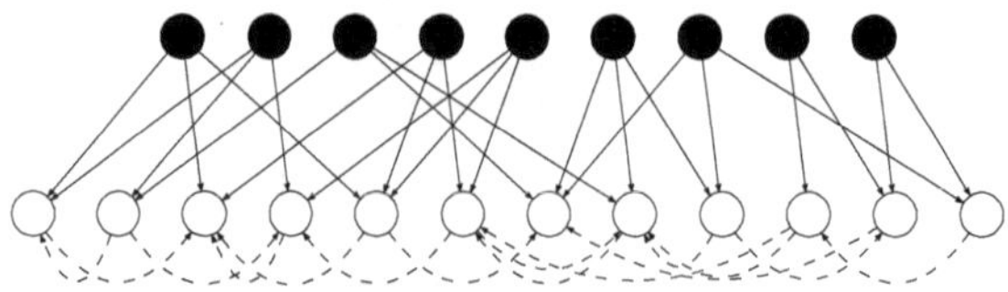

Fig. 3. A split-graph overlay

peers to incomplete peers. This structure matches the dissemination progress. This enables complete peers to act as additional sources and speed up the dissemination: they encode the content and inject new encoded chunks in the clique (the random graph connecting incomplete peers). Incomplete peers cooperate to disseminate the encoded chunks to each other so that no bandwidth is lost.

In order to ensure termination, FoG keeps disseminating as long as some peers miss some chunks they require in order to be able to decode and recover the original data. Complete peers remove all their incoming links. This is achieved simply by filtering out complete peers during merges and not propagating their information between incomplete peers. They leave the clique of the split-graph and do not receive redundant data once they have finished. The overlay maintenance protocol also automatically detects termination. A complete peer, acting as a source, stops sending data when its view becomes empty: it means that it does not know any incomplete peer. Therefore, the protocol eventually terminates.

The proposed protocol needs all chunk disseminations to be independent and equally useful so that any combination of $k(1+\epsilon)$ chunks received during exponential growth phases can be decoded to recover the original data. This is achieved in FoG through the use of fountain codes.

Fountain codes are erasure-correcting codes that allow building an infinite set of encoded chunks from k source chunks. As soon as $k(1+\epsilon)$ encoded chunks are received, it is possible to recover the original k chunks. Erasure-correcting codes are usually characterized by a rate r which actually defines the number $l = k/r$ of distinct encoded block that are generated. Generally, any k distinct chunks out of l are enough to decode and recover the original data. Virtually, fountain codes are erasure-correcting codes with a rate $r = 0$.

Fountain codes [9,4,5], as any erasure-correcting codes [10], require the complete original data so as to generate new encoded chunks. Therefore, only peers that hold the complete data can encode and produce new encoded chunks. Fountain codes differ from network codes [6]. Network codes allow a peer that only hold some encoded (and possible some decoded) data to recombine all this data to produce new encoded chunks. For this reason, network codes are usually considered as more powerful than fountain codes. Yet, the lack of structure of network codes makes them decodable only using Gaussian elimination, which is complex and requires heavy computation. On the contrary, some fountain codes [7,11] are decodable using more efficient algorithms like Belief-Propagation decoding which are less complex. Therefore, even if network codes are more powerful, using fountain codes may be more interesting and more practical when

(a) The incomplete peer receives the chunk of data a twice

(b) Incomplete peers cannot cooperate as they both receive a.

Fig. 4. Difficulties in cooperation

decoding complexity matters as this is for instance the case when such codes are used for video distribution among embedded devices with limited computational resources since the amount of distributed content is important.

In FoG, fountain codes allow many distinct sources to start distinct disseminations without coordination. All the disseminations distribute different encoded chunks and never conflict. Without fountains codes, we would suffer redundancy between disseminations as shown on Figure 4.

Fountain codes allow sources to start new disseminations as long as some peers have not completed. All this disseminations are independent and useful regardless of the chunks the remaining peers miss.

Eventually, as only peers that hold the whole data can produce new encoded blocks using fountain codes, the peers that hold the whole data are much more useful than the other peers are. Therefore, we bias the dissemination to deliberately favor some peers that will be useful to other peers as soon as possible. As incomplete peers are not able to encode and generate new innovative chunks, the dissemination favors complete peers. This point differs from many p2p protocols where peers tend to progress at the same speed and finish all together.

3 FoG in Details

The FoG dissemination protocol relies on random (uniform) samples of incomplete peers provided by a gossip-based peer sampling service. The peer sampling service is based on a *gossip-based peer sampling service* [8] that builds a d-regular random graph. We modified the protocol to systematically exclude complete peers from samples. Both the dissemination protocol and the peer sampling service are biased for a more efficient dissemination and are presented below.

3.1 FoG Peer Sampling: Split-Graph Overlay

FoG relies on a peer sampling service that creates a split-graph overlay network upon which the dissemination is implemented (Figure 3). Each peer maintains a *view*, which is a sample of the system provided by a peer sampling protocol. A view is a compound of information about at most s peers. Each peer entry in the view contains its IP, its completion level and its age. The peer sampling service

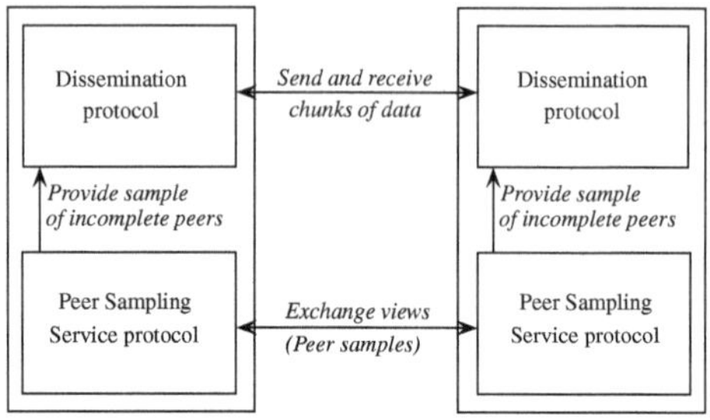

Fig. 5. Organisation of protocols

in FoG ensures that each peer p has a view v_p that corresponds to a uniform random sample of the incomplete peers in the system. The peer sampling service provides this sample of peers to the dissemination protocol as shown in Figure 5.

In the split-graph overlay, the incomplete peers are connected through a random graph while the complete peers are connected to some incomplete peers but not reciprocally. This is achieved by ensuring that the view of each peer, be it complete or incomplete, contains only references to incomplete peers. The structure of the overlay emerges naturally as complete peers have only outgoing edges and as only incomplete peers have incoming edges. Therefore, complete peers are forcibly kept outside of the clique.

More specifically, the peer sampling protocol runs two threads on each peer p_{myself} as in [8]. An active thread periodically chooses a random peer p_{random} and p_{myself} sends its view to p_{random}. A passive thread receives views and handles them. When p_{random} receives the view v, it replies by sending its own view to p_{myself}. Finally, both peers merge the view they have received with the view they had before and get a new view of size s. p_{random} merges v_{random} with v. First, any duplicates are removed. Any references to complete peers are removed to ensure a *split-graph* structure. The view is then truncated to match the view size following the protocol of [8] [3]

Incomplete peers and complete peers differ in the view they send during the exchange. As complete peers have no incoming edges, they receive less up-to-date information. An incomplete peer applies the protocol as defined in [8]. However, complete peers apply a slightly different protocol when exchanging view. Instead of sending their own view, they send only information about themselves. The goal is to avoid overwriting an incomplete peer's up-to-date information with out-dated information coming from a complete peer.

Interestingly enough, the FoG split-graph could be also implemented using T-Man [12][4], which builds any structure by gossiping, using an infinite distance

[3] The H oldest entries are removed to ensure *self-healing*. S entries that were just sent to the other peer are removed to ensure *low information losses*. Finally, if needed, some random entries are removed to get back to a view of size s.

[4] The T-Man gossip protocol converges to any structure defined by an ordering relation between peers. Upon gossip, peers merge the two sets of neighbors and keep the closest neighbors.

between any peer to a complete peer and distance 1 between any peer to an incomplete peer. We would simply need to add a few features to T-Man to ensure that a peer is able to decide not to keep information about some peer as it is too "far". Moreover, we also need the information about completion to be available in views.

3.2 FoG Dissemination Protocol

We first present the basic dissemination protocol followed by the biased dissemination protocol towards the most advanced peers.

Dissemination and Foutain codes. FoG aims at disseminating a whole file to all peers in the system. The dissemination is complete when all peers have completed. FoG relies on fountain codes (rateless erasure-correcting codes) to get rid of the unnecessary redundancy of gossip dissemination protocols as explained in the design rationale. To this end, a TTL is attached to every chunk. As in a standard dissemination protocol, each peer contributes to the dissemination process. The peers that hold the full content can encode and send these encoded chunks of data to some random peers. The other peers buffer at most the B most recent received chunks and try to forward those chunks to f *(fanout)* other randomly chosen peers from their views. Each peer forwards a given chunk once; if a chunk is received twice, it is simply dropped. In order to avoid the shrinking phase of gossip, the chunks are forwarded over at most TTL *(time to live)* hops, enough to implement the exponential growth phase.

Due to the random nature of the algorithm, a peer may miss some chunks. However, as the view of peers permanently evolves, the probability that a peer misses m consecutive chunks decreases exponentially. We leverage this property in FoG by assuming the peers that were not reached by a given chunk, have a high probability to be reached by the following disseminations.

In FoG, the roles of peers differ depending on their being complete or not. As soon as a peer is complete, it can become a new source. Complete peers run a permanent task that produces new encoded chunks using fountain codes and start disseminating. Note that incomplete peers also collaborate to the dissemination by forwarding chunks but they cannot encode the content as they miss some chunks, as the whole file is needed to encode using fountain codes.

Biasing the dissemination. The more complete peers, the more new independent chunks are injected in the system. To benefit even further of complete peers as additional sources, FoG favors the most advanced peers with respect to the completion so that they can help the system as soon as possible.

This is achieved simply by adding a bias in the dissemination. Basically we aim at allowing the progression of peers to be different amongst peers. Typically, some peers should progress much faster and help the rest of the system once they have completed. The bias is implemented as follows: when a complete peer chooses to serve some incomplete peer, it serves the one that has the highest completion first. Incomplete peers also have a bias in the dissemination to ensure that there are always incomplete peers with a high completion.

The dissemination is biased by biasing the probability to choose a given peer to gossip depending on its level of completion. All peers keep a reference to the last peer *last* to which they have sent data and keep a view v of other peers. To send data, a peer *self* chooses another peer *dest*. *self* builds a set of candidates $C = \{c || c \in v \cup \{last\} \wedge c.completion < self.completion\}$. Then, it chooses *dest* to be a peer $c \in C$ with a probability proportional to the completion level of c.

More formally, the choice is performed as explained bellow. Let j be the peer running the algorithm, l_j be the completion of peer j, v_j be the view of j and $last_j$ be the last peer to which j sent data. Let $c_{i,j}$ be the completion of peer i from the point of view of j. m_j is the highest completion $c_{i,j}$ with $i \in v_j \cup \{last_j\}$ such that $m_j < l_j$. For each peer, we compute $d_{i,j} = m_j - c_{i,j}$ if $m_j - c_{i,j} > 0$ or $d_{i,j} = 1$ else.

Complete peer j chooses to send data to peer i of its view with a probability $p_i = \frac{(1-(d_i))^e}{\sum_{k \in v_j \cup \{last_j\}} (1-(d_k))^e}$ that depends on the completeness of the peer so that the higher the completeness, the higher the probability. The parameter e expresses the level of aggressivity of the bias.

Incomplete peers sort the peers in increasing order of the value $d_{i,j}$ and choose the first peer to which chosen chunk of data has not been sent. Therefore, they send chunks to peers that are the most complete but that are not more complete than they are. This avoids the creation of cycles in the dissemination process.

The peers and the active links of the overlay look like a multi-layered graph where peers move from bottom to top slowly. There is a little subset at the top that progresses quickly and a large pool of peers at the bottom. It should exhibit a long tail distribution for the completion of peers: the majority of peers have a low completion while a few peers have a high completion.

4 Evaluation

We performed extensive simulations of FoG and some reference protocols. The protocol has been simulated in an event-based simulation using PeerSim [13]. The time information displayed on the graph is arbitrary as it matches the event management.

We simulated a 25,000 peer network, peers maintain a view of size 21. During the selection process, the healing parameter H was set to 8 while the swapping parameter S was set to 12. These values are chosen to quickly remove peers that have completed or have left the network as explained in [8]. We disseminate a file of 1000 chunks. The upload bandwidth was constrained as follows: each peer can send a chunk every unit of time. It also exchanges a gossip message to update the overlay every 10 units of time.

The source and encoder peers continuously encode, using a fountain encoder, and send chunks of data. The incomplete peers buffer at most 48 chunks of data. The fanout (f), the number of peers a received chunk is forwarded to, is set to 6 while the number of hops a chunk is forwarded (TTL) over is set 6. Forwarder peers forward data until their buffers become empty. The selectiveness parameter e is set to 20 for the biased dissemination protocol.

We are mainly interested in the termination of the dissemination. A file can only be used once all the chunks are available. Therefore, we plot the average value of completion (chunks received over chunks needed) for all peers. When the completion is 1.0, all peers have a full copy of the file and the dissemination is complete.

We compare our protocol with and without the biased dissemination against the two first of these following variants of traditional push-based dissemination protocols along termination time and overhead in term of useless messages. The two protocols are traditional protocols over which we have simply added fountain codes.

- **Peers stay in the overlay after completion.** Those peers receive more chunks of data even if they do not need to receive them. Keeping the peers in the overlay helps to maintain connectivity. However, they can be on the paths between the source and peers that still need data. In this case, the dissemination slows down when almost all peers have completed, as complete peers do not forward data.
- **Peers leave the overlay gracefully.** The peers leave the overlay by excluding themselves when exchanging views. As they continue to maintain the overlay, the overlay should not be split. Thanks to the self-healing property, the peers are removed progressively. However, they do not contribute to the system once they have completed. In this case, the download does not slow down as the diameter of the network decreases and peers that do not have completed are close to the source.

By comparing our protocol to these, we can assess that adding foutain codes is not enough to get good performances: one need to modify the protocol to leverage the coding ability.

The graph on Figure 6(a) presents the completion results. FoG with or without overhead is faster than the reference protocols. As shown on Figure 6(a), biased FoG achieves 95% completion at time 2667 while unbiased FoG achieves same completion at time 3333. The two traditional protocols are slower as they achieve

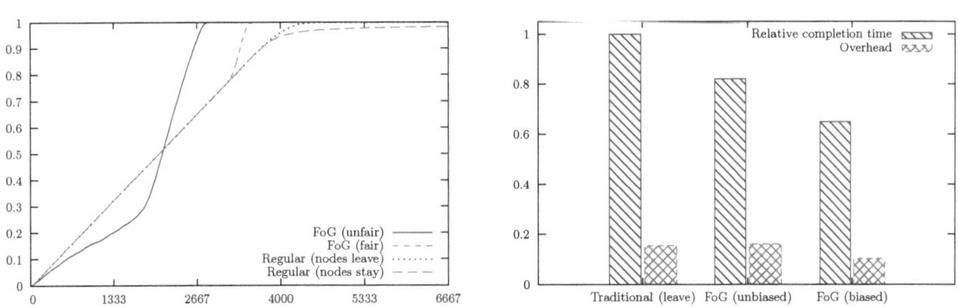

(a) Average completion

(b) Completion time and overhead

Fig. 6. FoG outperforms traditional dissemination protocols the same completion at time 4000 if peers leave when they complete and at time 4400 if peers stay in the overlay once they have completed. Finally, biased FoG achieves full completion at time 2800, unbiased FoG achieves full completion at 3733 and the traditional protocol where peers leave the overlay once complete achieves full completion at time 4667. We observe a slight slowdown if peers depart gracefully while the progress becomes slow if peers do not leave as it can be seen at time 4000. Biased FoG completes almost twice earlier than a traditional dissemination protocol (the one where peers leave once they have complete) and it even offers a slightly lower overhead as shown on Figure 6(b).

Based on these results, we can conclude that FoG completes faster than the two variants of traditional push protocols. We observe that an unbiased FoG is not faster than competitors are as the number of complete peers acting as encoders increases only in the end, at time, when some peers complete. This confirms the relevance of introducing a bias to the dissemination.

4.1 Impact of the Biased Dissemination

We observe on Figure 6(a) that the dissemination in unbiased FoG speeds up at time 3333 when the download process is almost over. This is mostly due to peers completing and acting as additional sources late in the process. Introducing a bias towards the most advanced peers enables to exploit earlier complete peers. At time 2000, biased FoG becomes faster than unbiased FoG. Consequently, the delay for all peers to get the whole content is reduced from 3733 to 2800.

We have studied the density of completion at different times for the two, unbiased and biased, protocols. The probability density function at time t, $d_t(x)$, is defined such that the probability that, at time t, a peer has a completion rate $c \in [a, b]$ is $p_t = \int_a^b d_t(x)dx$. The density functions at different times are plotted for each protocol on Figure 7. As an example, at time $t = 960$, in the unbiased version, all peers have a completion of approximately 60%. On the other side, at the same time, the biased version shows that some of the peers have a completion of 40% while half of them have already completed and a few of them are between

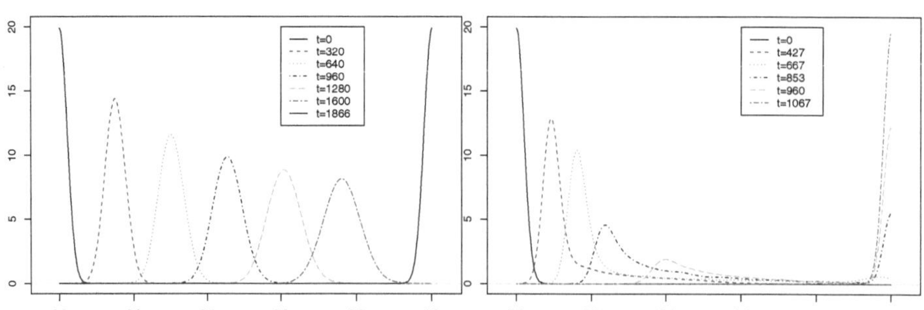

(a) Unbiased dissemination (b) Biased dissemination

Fig. 7. Density of probability that a peer has a completion c attime t. The first curve is the bell-shaped curve on the leftside. The last one is on the right side.

40% and 100%. The unbiased version of the protocol exhibits a density that is Gaussian while the biased version has a density function that resembles a power law. When the dissemination is unbiased, all peers complete at the same speed. Therefore, no peer is able to encode data and help other peers. When a bias is introduced in the dissemination, a few peers behave differently from the majority and complete early resulting in the biased version outperforming the unbiased one.

4.2 Impact of Coding

In the previous experiments, we disseminate data encoded with fountain codes. During the definition of our protocol, we asserted that using fountain codes (rateless erasure-correcting codes) was needed. We check this assertion by comparing our protocol with a rateless encoder (fountain encoder), with a fixed-rate ($\frac{1}{4}$) encoder or without encoder. We also study the impact of using codes with a traditional dissemination protocol where peers simply leave the overlay when they complete.

When disseminating with rate $\frac{1}{4}$ encoding, sources send encoded data cyclically in order. When disseminating non-coded data, original data is sent cyclically by sources. If a new source is created, the starting point in the stream is chosen randomly.

The results are shown on Figure 8. The graph shows that encoding improves the dissemination in all settings. Clearly, the protocols that use some form of coding (either rateless codes or fixed-rate codes) outperform the protocols that do not use codes. Completion becomes slow at time 933 when we use non-coded data: this time matches the time at which the source will loop over and start disseminating again chunks that have already been disseminated.

The better performance of the protocols using codes can easily be explained. Peers complete faster as cooperation is easier and as redundancy in the chunks they receive is lower. Therefore, our assumption that we need coding holds. Moreover, fountain and fixed rate codes both result in curves having similar shapes. This shows that even though we provide an infinite amount of redundancy through the use of fountain codes, a finite amount ($4k$) is enough for our

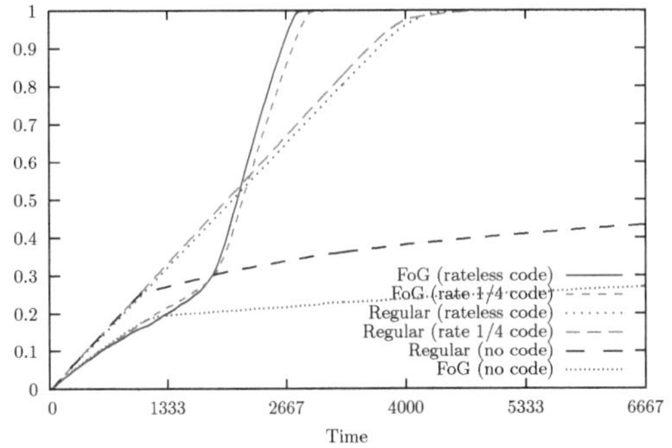

Fig. 8. Encoding enhances the performance of dissemination algorithms

protocol to work: the additional redundancy only brings very little enhancement. However, low complexity fixed-rate codes use the same decoder as fountain codes and have the same decoding complexity. Therefore, there is no reason to drop the more elegant design of using fountain codes for using fixed-rate erasure-correcting codes.

5 Related Works

Dissemination protocols can either be streaming protocols where peers exchange data within a window of interesting data or be file swarming protocols where all peers cooperate to get a full copy of a file. The streaming case is widely used in live streaming of video or audio streams. In such protocols, losses of some chunks of data, even if not desirable, are possible. File swarming protocols are more useful to get a full copy of a file where no losses are allowed. FoG is used to download a full copy of a file as file swarming protocols through push protocols. Encoding content adds the constraint that the content need to be entirely downloaded and decoded before it can be used. However, the content we disseminate need to be entirely downloaded before being used. Therefore, encoding data does not constrain more the use that can be done of our protocol.

There has been many works in peer-to-peer based dissemination, we focus on systems using coding to enhance the performance. Various coding techniques have been used for enhancing dissemination process. *Avalanche* [14,15] uses network coding [6] in order to reduce redundancy in exchanged chunks. Simulations of *Avalanche* result in the conclusion that it can make throughput 2 or 3 times better than transmitting unencoded chunks over *Bittorrent*-like networks [16]. However, as random linear network codes decoding involves complex computation ($O(k^3)$ Gaussian elimination) , some people [2] compared network coding in *Avalanche* to systems that do not use coding and had less optimistic conclusion. They claim that network coding is too complex and does not enhance the performance enough to justify its use [17,18]. Locher and al. [19] propose to add source coding to *Bittorrent* instead of relying on costly network coding. As source coding increases diversity, it enhances the performance of Bittorrent and helps the tit for tat mechanism. Their work is based on random linear codes that have high decoding complexity, but their work can directly be extended to any other code with lower complexity ($O(k \cdot \ln k)$ Belief-propagation decoding) such as LT codes [7]. In our paper, we decided to avoid network coding and use lower complexity ($O(k \cdot \ln k)$) source codes such as LT.

A protocol[20,21,22] is said to push data if it sends data to a peer without being requested to do so. A protocol pulls data if it sends data to a peer after being requested. Push protocols have lower control overhead as they do not involve a query prior to pushing data. Moreover, push protocols have lower delay, because, as soon as a peer has some data, it can immediately push it to other peers. Pull protocols have higher delay as peer regularly poll for their neighbors to get new data and new data is only sent once the other peer asked it. Pull protocols have lower overhead as they allow the receiver to choose the data it gets, it avoids getting the same chunk twice. Our choice was to implement a push dissemination protocol in order to reduce the amount of control messages needed. The article by Karp and al. [1] studies push protocol and their behavior. They study the performance of push-only and pull-only scheme before proposing a push&pull scheme that tries to take the best of two.

6 Conclusion

In this paper, we presented FoG, a protocol that aims at keeping the strength of gossip protocols, exponential-growth phases, while removing the need for their weakness, shrinking phases. To this end, we ensure completion through more dissemination of content encoded using fountain codes instead of relying on the shrinking phase of gossip based dissemination that produces a high level of redundancy.

In this context, we build an overlay (a split-graph) that matches dissemination progress. The overlay is structured so that only incomplete peers have incoming edges. Therefore, peers do not receive more data once they have completed. Moreover, peers that complete can act as new sources.

In order to leverage further completed peers as additional sources, we bias the dissemination towards the most advanced peers. This enables peers to complete earlier and exploit further fountain codes.

Experiments show that FoG outperforms by 50% for the overhead and by 30% for the termination time traditional push protocols.

The bias introduced in FoG is needed for its performance. The fact that peers that are favored get the file earlier may be seen as a natural incentive to contribute. However, FoG leverages such peers that must then serve other peers. Selfish peers could in turn leverage this to stop collaborating, making FoG sensitive to their presence. Preserving FoG's performance in the context of selfish peers is an interesting line of research for future work.

References

1. Karp, R., Schindelhauer, C., Shenker, S., Vöcking, B.: Randomized rumor spreading. In: FOCS (2000)
2. Li, H.C., Clement, A., Wong, E.L., Napper, J., Roy, I., Alvisi, L., Dahlin, M.: Bar gossip. In: OSDI (2006)
3. Zhang, X., Liu, J., Li, B., Yum, T.S.P.: Coolstreaming/donet: A data-driven overlay network for efficient live media streaming. In: INFOCOMM (2005)
4. Byers, J.W., Luby, M., Mitzenmacher, M.: A digital fountain approach to asynchronous reliable multicast. IEEE JSAC, Special Issue on Network Support for Multicast Communication 20(8), 1528–1540 (2002)
5. Mitzenmacher, M.: Digital fountains: A survey and look forward. In: ITW (2004)
6. Ahlswede, R., Cai, N., Li, S.Y.R., Yeung, R.W.: Network information flow. IEEE Transactions On Information Theory 46(4), 1204–1216 (2000)
7. Luby, M.: LT Codes. In: FOCS (2002)

8. Jelasity, M., Voulgaris, S., Guerraoui, R., Kermarrec, A.M., van Steen, M.: Gossip-based peer sampling. ACM Transactions on Computer Systems 25 (2007)
9. Byers, J., Considine, J., Mitzenmacher, M., Rost, S.: Informed content delivery across adaptive overlay networks. IEEE/ACM Transactions on Networking 12, 767–780 (2004)
10. MacKay, D.J.: Information Theory, Inference, and Learning Algorithms. Cambridge University Press, Cambridge (2002)
11. Shokrollahi, A.: Raptor codes. IEEE/ACM Transactions on Networking 14, 2551–2567 (2006)
12. Jelasity, M., Babaoglu, O.: T-man: Gossip-based overlay topology management. In: Brueckner, S.A., Di Marzo Serugendo, G., Hales, D., Zambonelli, F. (eds.) ESOA 2005. LNCS (LNAI), vol. 3910, pp. 1–15. Springer, Heidelberg (2006)
13. Jelasity, M., Montresor, A., Jesi, G.P., Voulgaris, S.: The peersim simulator, `http://peersim.sourceforge.net/`
14. Gkantsidis, C., Rodriguez, P.R.: Network coding for large scale content distribution. In: INFOCOMM (2005)
15. Gkantsidis, C., Miller, J., Rodriguez, P.: Anatomy of a p2p content distribution system with network coding. In: IPTPS (2006)
16. Cohen, B.: Incentives build robustness in bittorrent. In: P2PEcon (June 2003)
17. Wang, M., Li, B.: How practical is network coding? In: IWQoS (2006)
18. Ma, G., Xu, Y., Lin, M., Xuan, Y.: A content distribution system based on sparse network coding. In: NetCod (2007)
19. Locher, T., Schmid, S., Wattenhofer, R.: Rescuing tit-for-tat with source coding. In: P2P (2007)
20. Picconi, F., Massoulié, L.: Is there a future for mesh-based live-video streaming? In: P2P (2008)
21. Massoulié, L., Twigg, A., Gkantsidis, C., Rodriguez, P.: Randomized decentralised broadcasting algorithms. In: INFOCOMM (2007)
22. Bonald, T., Massoulié, L., Mathieu, F., Perino, D., Twigg, A.: Epidemic live streaming: Optimal performance trade-offs. In: SIGMETRICS (2008)

How to Improve Snap-Stabilizing Point-to-Point Communication Space Complexity?*

Alain Cournier[1], Swan Dubois[2], and Vincent Villain[1]

[1] MIS Laboratory, Université de Picardie Jules Verne
[2] LIP6 - UMR 7606 Université Pierre et Marie Curie - Paris 6/INRIA Rocquencourt

Abstract. A *snap-stabilizing* protocol, starting from any configuration, always behaves according to its specification. In this paper, we are interested in message forwarding problem in a message-switched network. In this problem, we must manage resources of the system to deliver messages to any processor of the network. In this purpose, we use information given by a routing algorithm. By the context of stabilization (in particular, the system starts in any configuration), this information can be corrupted. In [1], authors show that there exists snap-stabilizing algorithms for this problem (in the *state model*). That implies that we can ask the system to begin forwarding messages without losses even if routing informations are initially corrupted.

In this paper, we propose another snap-stabilizing algorithm for this problem which improves the space complexity of the one of [1].

1 Introduction

The quality of a distributed system depends on its *fault-tolerance*. Many fault-tolerant schemes have been proposed. For instance, *self-stabilization* [2] allows to design a system tolerating arbitrary transient faults. A self-stabilizing system, regardless of the initial state of the system, is guaranteed to converge into the intended behavior in a finite time. Another paradigm is *snap-stabilization* ([3]). A snap-stabilizing protocol guarantees that, starting from any configuration, it always behaves according to its specification. Hence, a snap-stabilizing protocol is a self-stabilizing protocol which stabilizes in 0 time unit.

In a distributed system, it is commonly assumed that each processor can exchange messages only with its *neighbors* (*i.e.* processors with which it shares a communication link) but processors may need to exchange messages with *any* processor of the network. To perform this goal, processors have to solve two problems: the determination of the path which messages have to follow in the network to reach their destinations (it is the *routing problem*) and the management of network resources in order to forward messages (it is the *message forwarding problem*). These two problems received a great attention in literature. The routing problem is studied for example in [4,5,6] and self-stabilizing

* This work has been supported in part by the ANR project SPADES (08-ANR-SEGI-025).

R. Guerraoui and F. Petit (Eds.): SSS 2009, LNCS 5873, pp. 195–208, 2009.

approaches can be found in [7,8,9]. The forwarding problem has also been well studied, see [10,11,12,13,14,15]. As far we know, only [1] deals with this problem using a stabilizing approach.

Informally, the goal of forwarding is to design a protocol which allows all processors of the network to send messages to any destination of the network (knowing that a routing algorithm computes the path that messages have to follow to reach their destinations). Problems come of the following fact: messages traveling through a message-switched network ([16]) must be stored in each processor of their path before being forwarded to the next processor on this path. This temporary storage of messages is performed with reserved memory spaces called buffers. Obviously, each processor of the network reserves only a finite number of buffers to the message forwarding. So, it is a problem of bounded resources management which exposes the network to deadlocks and livelocks if no control is performed. In this paper, we focus about a message forwarding protocol which deals withthe problem using a stabilizing approach. The goal is to allow the system to forward messages regardless of the state of the routing tables. Obviously, we need that these routing tables repair themselves within a finite time. So, we assume the existence of a self-stabilizing protocol to compute routing tables.

In the following, a valid message is a message which has been sent out by a processor. As a consequence, an invalid message is present in the initial configuration. We can now specify the problem. We propose a specification of the problem where duplications (*i.e.* the same message reaches many time its destination while it has been sent out only once) are forbidden:

Specification 1 ($\mathcal{SP}$). *Specification of the message forwarding problem.*
- Any message can be sent out in a finite time.
- Any valid message is delivered to its destination once and only once in a finite time.

In [1], authors show that it is possible to transform a forwarding algorithm of [11] into a snap-stabilizing one without any significant over cost (with respect to time of forwarding and amount of memory per processor). But this algorithm needs $\Theta(n)$ buffers per processor (where n is the number of processors of the networks). The scope of this paper is the improvement of this space complexity. We achieve this goal by providing a snap-stabilizing forwarding algorithm which requires $\Theta(D)$ buffers per processor (where D is the diameter of the network). Even if this improvement can be seen as quite useful from a theoretical point of view (since n and D are close values in the worst case), we believe that it could be very interesting from a practical point of view. Indeed, practical networks have in general a diameter which is very smaller than the number of nodes (for example, [17] shows that the diameter of Internet is near to 6 in 2000 although it had near to 14,000 nodes).

The remaining of this paper is organized as follows: we present first our model (section 2), then we give and prove our solution in the state model (section 3). Finally, we conclude in section 4.

2 Preliminaries

We consider a network as an undirected connected graph $G = (V, E)$ where V is a set of processors and E is the set of bidirectional asynchronous communication links. In the network, a communication link (p, q) exists if and only if p and q are neighbors. We assume that the labels of neighbors of p are stored in the set N_p. We also use the following notations: respectively, n is the number of processors, Δ the maximal degree, and D the diameter of the network. If p and q are two processors of the network, we denote by $dist(p, q)$ the length of the shortest path between p and q. In the following, we assume that the network is identified, *i.e.* each processor has an identity which is unique on the network. Moreover, we assume that all processors know the set I of all identities of the network.

State model. We consider the classical local shared memory model of computation (see [16]) in which communications between neighbors are modeled by direct reading of variables instead of exchange of messages. In this model, the program of every processor consists in a set of shared variables (henceforth, referred to as variables) and a finite set of actions. A processor can write to its own variables only, and read its own variables and those of its neighbors. Each action is constituted as follows: $<$ label $>::<$ guard $>\longrightarrow<$ statement $>$. The guard of an action in the program of p is a boolean expression involving variables of p and its neighbors. The statement of an action of p updates one or more variables of p. An action can be executed only if its guard is satisfied. The state of a processor is defined by the value of its variables. The state of a system is the product of the states of all processors. We refer to the state of a processor and the system as a (local) state and (global) configuration, respectively. We note $\mathcal{C}$ the set of all configurations of the system. Let $\gamma \in \mathcal{C}$ and A an action of p ($p \in V$). A is said enabled at p in γ if and only if the guard of A is satisfied by p in γ. Processor p is said to be enabled in γ if and only if at least one action is enabled at p in γ. Let a distributed protocol $\mathcal{P}$ be a collection of binary transition relations denoted by $\rightarrow$, on $\mathcal{C}$. An execution of a protocol $\mathcal{P}$ is a maximal sequence of configurations $\Gamma = (\gamma_0, \gamma_1, ..., \gamma_i, \gamma_{i+1}, ...)$ such that, $\forall i \geq 0, \gamma_i \rightarrow \gamma_{i+1}$ (called a step) if γ_{i+1} exists, else γ_i is a terminal configuration. *Maximality* means that the sequence is either finite (and no action of $\mathcal{P}$ is enabled in the terminal configuration) or infinite. All executions considered here are assumed to be maximal. $\mathcal{E}$ is the set of all executions of $\mathcal{P}$. As we already said, each execution is decomposed into steps. Each step is shared into three sequential phases atomically executed: (i) every processor evaluates its guards, (ii) a daemon chooses some enabled processors, (iii) each chosen processor executes its enabled action. When the three phases are done, the next step begins. A daemon can be defined in terms of fairness and distribution. There exists several kinds of fairness assumption. Here, we use only the weakly fairness assumption, meaning that we assume that every continuously enabled processor is eventually chosen by the daemon. Concerning the distribution, we assume that the daemon is distributed meaning that, at each step, if one or more processors are enabled, then the daemon chooses at least one of these processors to execute an action. We consider that any processor p is neutralized in the step $\gamma_i \rightarrow \gamma_{i+1}$ if p was enabled in γ_i and not enabled in γ_{i+1}, but did not execute any action in $\gamma_i \rightarrow \gamma_{i+1}$. To compute the time complexity, we use the definition of round [18]. This definition captures the execution rate of the slowest processor in any execution. The first round of $\Gamma \in \mathcal{E}$, noted Γ', is the minimal prefix of Γ containing the execution of one action or the neutralization of every enabled processor from the initial configuration. Let Γ'' be the suffix of Γ such that $\Gamma = \Gamma'\Gamma''$. The second round of Γ is the first round of Γ'', and so on.

Message-switched network. Today, most of computer networks use a variant of the *message-switching* method (also called *store-and-forward* method). It's why we have chosen to work with this switching model. In this section, we quickly present this method (see [16] for a detailed presentation). The model assumes that each buffer can store a whole message and that each message needs only one buffer to be stored. The switching method is modeled by four types of moves:

1- ***Generation:***when a processor sends a new message, it "creates" a new message in one of its empty buffers. We assume that the network may allow this move as soon as at least one buffer of the processor is empty.
2- ***Forwarding:***a message m is forwarded (copied) from a processor p to an empty buffer in the next processor q on its route (determined by the routing algorithm). We assume that the network may allow this move as soon as at least one buffer buffer of the processor is empty.
3- ***Consumption:***A message m occupying a buffer in its destination is erased and delivered to this processor. We assume that the network may always allow this move.
4- ***Erasing:***a message m is erased from a buffer. We assume that the network may allow this move as soon as the message has been forwarded at least one time or delivered to its destination.

Stabilization. We recall here some formal definitions.

Definition 1 (Self-Stabilization [2]).
Let $\mathcal{T}$ be a task, and $\mathcal{S}_\mathcal{T}$ a specification of $\mathcal{T}$. A protocol $\mathcal{P}$ is self-stabilizing for $\mathcal{S}_\mathcal{T}$ if and only if $\forall \Gamma \in \mathcal{E}$, there exists a finite prefix $\Gamma' = (\gamma_0, \gamma_1, ..., \gamma_l)$ of Γ such that all executions starting from γ_l satisfies $\mathcal{S}_\mathcal{T}$.

Definition 2 (Snap-Stabilization [3]).
Let $\mathcal{T}$ be a task, and $\mathcal{S}_\mathcal{T}$ a specification of $\mathcal{T}$. A protocol $\mathcal{P}$ is snap-stabilizing for $\mathcal{S}_\mathcal{T}$ if and only if $\forall \Gamma \in \mathcal{E}$, Γ satisfies $\mathcal{S}_\mathcal{T}$.

This definition has the two following consequences. We can see that a snap-stabilizing protocol for $\mathcal{S}_\mathcal{T}$ is a self-stabilizing protocol for $\mathcal{S}_\mathcal{T}$ with a stabilization time of 0 time unit. A common method used to prove that a protocol is snap-stabilizing is to distinguish an action as a "starting action" (*i.e.* an action which initiates a computation) and to prove the following property for every execution of the protocol: if a processor requests it, the computation is initiated by a starting action in a finite time and every computation initiated by a starting action satisfies the specification of the task. We use these two remarks to prove snap-stabilization of our protocol in the following.

3 Proposed Protocol

3.1 Description

To simplify the presentation, we assume that the routing algorithm induces only minimal paths in number of edges. We have seen that, by default, the network always allows message moves between buffers. But, if we do no control on these moves, the network can reach unacceptable situations such as deadlocks, livelocks or message losses. If such situations appear, specifications of message forwarding are not respected. Now, we quickly present solutions brought by the literature in the case where routing tables are correct in the initial configuration. In order to avoid deadlocks, we must define an algorithm which permits or forbids various moves in the network (functions of the current occupation of buffers) in order to prevent the network to reach a deadlock. Such algorithms are called deadlock-free controllers (see [16] for a much detailed description). Livelocks can be avoided by fairness assumptions on the controller for the generation and the forwarding of messages. Message losses are avoided by the using of identifier on messages (for example, the concatenation of the identity of source and a two-value flag). [11] introduced a generic method to design deadlock-free controllers. The key idea is to restrict moves of messages along edges of an oriented graph BG (called buffer graph) defined on the network buffers. Authors show that cycles on BG can lead to deadlocks and that, if BG is acyclic, they can define a deadlock-free controller on this buffer graph. The main idea in [1] is to adapt a graph buffer of [11] in order to obtain a snap-stabilizing forwarding protocol.

In this paper, we are interested in another buffer graph introduced in [11]. Each processor have $D+1$ buffers ranked from 1 to $D+1$. New messages are always generated in the buffer of rank 1 of the sender processor. When a message occupying a buffer of rank i is forwarded to a neighbor q, it is always copied in the buffer of rank $i+1$ of q. It is easy to see that this graph is acyclic since messages always "come upstairs" the buffer rank (the reader can find an example of such a graph in Figure 1). We need $D+1$ buffers per processor since, in the worst case, there are D forwarding of a message between its generation and its consumption.

Our idea is to adapt this scheme in order to tolerate transient faults. To perform this goal, we assume the existence of a self-stabilizing silent algorithm $\mathcal{A}$ to compute routing tables (see e.g. [7,8,9]) which runs simultaneously to our message forwarding protocol provided in Algorithm 1 ($\mathcal{SSMFP}$ means $\mathcal{S}$nap-$\mathcal{S}$tabilizing $\mathcal{M}$essage $\mathcal{F}$orwarding $\mathcal{P}$rotocol). Moreover, we assume that $\mathcal{A}$ has priority over $\mathcal{SSMFP}$ (*i.e.* a processor which has enabled actions for both algorithms always chooses the action of $\mathcal{A}$). This guarantees us that routing tables are correct and stable within a finite time. We assume that $\mathcal{SSMFP}$ can have access to the routing table via a function, called $nextHop_p(d)$. This function returns the identity of the neighbor of p to which p must forward messages of destination d. Our idea is as follows: we allow the erasing of a message only if we are ensured that the message has been delivered to its destination. In this goal, we use a scheme with acknowledgment which guarantees the reception of the message. More precisely, we associate to each copy of the message a type which have 3 values: E (Emission), A (Acknowledgment) and F (Fail). Forwarding of a valid message m (of destination d) follows the above scheme:

1- Generation of m with type E in a buffer of rank 1 by $(\boldsymbol{R_1})$.
2- Forwarding[1] of m with type E without any erasing by $(\boldsymbol{R_8})$ or $(\boldsymbol{R_{12}})$).
3- If m reaches d:
3.1- It is delivered and the copy of m takes type A by $(\boldsymbol{R_4})$ or $(\boldsymbol{R_{10}})$.
3.2- Type A is spread to the sink following the incoming path by $(\boldsymbol{R_7})$.
3.3- Buffers are allowed to free themselves once the type A is propagated to the previous buffer on the path by $(\boldsymbol{R_9})$, $(\boldsymbol{R_{11}})$, or $(\boldsymbol{R_{14}})$.
3.4- The sink erases its copy by $(\boldsymbol{R_3})$ or $(\boldsymbol{R_5})$, thus m is erased.
4- If m reaches a buffer of rank $D+1$ without crossing d:
4.1- The copy of m takes type F by $(\boldsymbol{R_{13}})$.
4.2- Type F is spread to the sink following the incoming path by $(\boldsymbol{R_7})$.
4.3- Buffers are allowed to free themselves once the type F is propagated to the previous buffer on the path by $(\boldsymbol{R_9})$, $(\boldsymbol{R_{11}})$, or $(\boldsymbol{R_{14}})$).
4.4- Then, the sink of m gives the type E to its copy, that begin a new cycle: m is sending once again by $(\boldsymbol{R_2})$ or $(\boldsymbol{R_6})$.

Obviously, it is necessary to take in account invalid messages: we have chosen to let them follow the forwarding scheme and to erase them if they reach step 4.4 (by rules from $(\boldsymbol{R_{15}})$ to $(\boldsymbol{R_{18}})$). The key idea of the snap-stabilization of our algorithm is the following: since a valid message is never erased, it is sent again after the stabilization of routing tables (if it never reaches its destination before) and then it is normally forwarded. To avoid livelocks, we use a fair scheme of selection of processors allowed to forward a message for each buffer. We can manage this fairness by a queue of requesting processors. Finally, we use a specific flag to prevent message losses. It is composed of the identity of the next processor on the path of the message, the identity of the last processor crossed over by the message, the identity of the destination of the message and the type of the message (E, A or F).

We must manage a communication between our algorithm and processors in order to know when a processor has a message to send. We have chosen to create a boolean shared variable $request_p$ (for any processor p). Processor p can set it at $true$ when it is at $false$ and when p has a message to send. Otherwise, p must wait that our algorithm sets the shared variable to $false$ (when a message is sent out).

3.2 Proof of the Snap-Stabilization

In this section, we give ideas[2] to prove that $\mathcal{SSMFP}$ is a snap-stabilizing message forwarding protocol for specification $\mathcal{SP}$. We introduce a second specification $\mathcal{SP}'$ of the problem. This specification is identical to $\mathcal{SP}$ but it allows message duplications. Our proof has the following map. First, we prove that

[1] With copy in buffers of increasing rank.

[2] Due to the lack of place, formal proofs are omitted. A full version of this work is available in [19].

Algorithm 1. $\mathcal{SSMFP}$: protocol for processor p

Data:
- n, D : natural integers equal resp. to the number of processors and to the diameter of the network.
- $I = \{0, ..., n-1\}$: set of processor identities of the network.
- N_p : set of neighbors of p.

Message:
- (m, r, q, d, c) with m useful information of the message, $r \in N_p$ identity of the next processor to cross for the message (when it reaches the node), $q \in N_p$ identity of the last processor cross over by the message, $d \in I$ identity of the destination of the message, $c \in \{E, A, F\}$ color of the message.

Variables:
- $\forall i \in \{1, ..., D+1\}$, $buf_p(i)$: buffer which can contain a message or be empty (denoted by ε)

Input/Output:
- $request_p$: boolean. The higher layer can set it to "true" when its value is "false" and when there is a waiting message. We consider that this waiting is blocking.
- $nextMes_p$: gives the message waiting in the higher layer.
- $nextDest_p$: gives the destination of $nextMes_p$ if it exists, $null$ otherwise.

Procedures:
- $nextHop_p(d)$: neighbor of p computed by the routing for destination d (if $d = p$, we choose arbitrarily $r \in N_p$).
- $\forall i \in \{2, ..., D+1\}, choice_p(i)$: fairly chooses one of the processors which can send a message in $buf_p(i)$, *i.e.* $choice_p(d)$ satisfies predicate $((choice_p(i) \in N_p) \wedge (buf_{choice_p(i)}(i-1) = (m, p, q, d, E)) \wedge (choice_p(i) \neq d))$. We can manage this fairness with a queue of length $\Delta + 1$ of processors which satisfies the predicate.
- $deliver_p(m)$: delivers the message m to the higher layer of p.

Rules:

/* Rules for the buffer of rank 1 */

/* Generation of messages */

$(\boldsymbol{R_1})$ :: $request_p \wedge (buf_p(1) = \varepsilon) \wedge (nextDest_p = d) \wedge (nextMes_p = m) \wedge (buf_{nextHop_p(d)}(2) \neq (m, r', p, d, c)) \longrightarrow buf_p(1) := (m, nextHop_p(d), r, d, E)$ with $r \in N_p$; $request_p := false$

/* Processing of acknowledgment */

$(\boldsymbol{R_2})$ :: $(buf_p(1) = (m, r, q, d, F)) \wedge (d \neq p) \wedge (buf_r(2) \neq (m, r', p, d, F)) \longrightarrow buf_p(1) := (m, nextHop_p(d), q, d, E)$

$(\boldsymbol{R_3})$ :: $(buf_p(1) = (m, r, q, d, A)) \wedge (d \neq p) \wedge (buf_r(2) \neq (m, r', p, d, A)) \longrightarrow buf_p(1) := \varepsilon$

/* Management of messages which reach their destinations */

$(\boldsymbol{R_4})$ :: $buf_p(1) = (m, r, q, p, E) \longrightarrow deliver_p(m)$; $buf_p(1) := (m, r, q, p, A)$

$(\boldsymbol{R_5})$ :: $buf_p(1) = (m, r, q, p, A) \longrightarrow buf_p(1) := \varepsilon$

$(\boldsymbol{R_6})$ :: $buf_p(1) = (m, r, q, p, F) \longrightarrow buf_p(1) := (m, r, q, p, E)$

/* Rule for buffers of rank 1 to D : propagation of acknowledgment */

$(\boldsymbol{R_7})$ :: $\exists i \in \{1, ..., D\}, ((buf_p(i) = (m, r, q, d, E)) \wedge (p \neq d) \wedge (buf_r(i+1) = (m, r', p, d, c)) \wedge (c \in \{F, A\})) \longrightarrow buf_p(i) := (m, r, q, d, c)$

End of Algorithm 1:

/* Rules for buffers of rank 2 to D */

/* Forwarding of messages */

$(\boldsymbol{R_8})$ :: $\exists i \in \{2,...,D\}, ((buf_p(i) = \varepsilon) \wedge (choice_p(i) = s) \wedge (buf_s(i-1) = (m,p,q,d,E)) \wedge (buf_{nextHop_p(d)}(i+1) \neq (m,r,p,d,c))) \longrightarrow buf_p(i) := (m, nextHop_p(d), s, d, E)$ /* Erasing of messages which acknowledgment has been forwarded */

$(\boldsymbol{R_9})$ :: $\exists i \in \{2,...,D\}, ((buf_p(i) = (m,r,q,d,c)) \wedge (c \in \{F,A\}) \wedge (d \neq p) \wedge (buf_q(i-1) = (m,p,q',d,c)) \wedge (buf_r(i+1) \neq (m,r',p,d,c)) \longrightarrow buf_p(i) := \varepsilon$

/* Rules for buffers of rank 2 to $D+1$ */

/* Consumption of a message and generation of the acknowledgment A */

$(\boldsymbol{R_{10}})$ :: $\exists i \in \{2,...,D+1\}, buf_p(i) = (m,r,q,p,E) \longrightarrow deliver_p(m);\ buf_p(i) := (m,r,q,p,A)$

/* Erasing of messages for p which acknowledgment has been forwarded */

$(\boldsymbol{R_{11}})$ :: $\exists i \in \{2,...,D+1\}, ((buf_p(i) = (m,r,q,p,c)) \wedge (c \in \{F,A\}) \wedge (buf_q(i-1) = (m,p,q',p,c))) \longrightarrow buf_p(i) := \varepsilon$

/* Rules for the buffer of rank $D+1$ */

/* Forwarding of messages */

$(\boldsymbol{R_{12}})$ :: $(buf_p(D+1) = \varepsilon) \wedge (choice_p(D+1) = s) \wedge (buf_s(D) = (m,p,q,d,E)) \longrightarrow buf_p(D+1) := (m, nextHop_p(d), s, d, E)$

/* Generation of the acknowledgment F */

$(\boldsymbol{R_{13}})$ :: $(buf_p(D+1) = (m,r,q,d,E)) \wedge (d \neq p) \longrightarrow buf_p(D+1) := (m,r,q,d,F)$

/* Erasing of messages of which the acknowledgment has been forwarded */

$(\boldsymbol{R_{14}})$ :: $(buf_p(D+1) = (m,r,q,d,c)) \wedge (c \in \{F,A\}) \wedge (d \neq p) \wedge (buf_q(D) = (m,p,q',d,c)) \longrightarrow buf_p(D+1) := \varepsilon$

/* Correction rules: erasing of tail of abnormal caterpillars of type F, A */

$(\boldsymbol{R_{15}})$ :: $\exists i \in \{2,...,D\}, ((buf_p(i) = (m,r,q,d,c)) \wedge (c \in \{F,A\}) \wedge (buf_r(i+1) \neq (m,r',p,d,c)) \wedge (buf_q(i-1) \neq (m,p,q',d,c'))) \longrightarrow buf_p(i) := \varepsilon$

$(\boldsymbol{R_{16}})$ :: $\exists i \in \{2,...,D\}, ((buf_p(i) = (m,r,q,d,c)) \wedge (c \in \{F,A\}) \wedge (buf_r(i+1) \neq (m,r',p,d,c)) \wedge (buf_q(i-1) = (m,p,q',d,c')) \wedge (c' \in \{F,A\} \backslash \{c\} \vee q = d)) \longrightarrow buf_p(i) := \varepsilon$

$(\boldsymbol{R_{17}})$ :: $(buf_p(D+1) = (m,r,q,d,c)) \wedge (c \in \{F,A\}) \wedge (buf_q(D) \neq (m,p,q',d,c')) \longrightarrow buf_p(D+1) := \varepsilon$

$(\boldsymbol{R_{18}})$ :: $(buf_p(D+1) = (m,r,q,d,c)) \wedge (c \in \{F,A\}) \wedge (buf_q(D) = (m,p,q',d,c')) \wedge (c' \in \{F,A\} \backslash \{c\} \vee q = d) \longrightarrow buf_p(D+1) := \varepsilon$

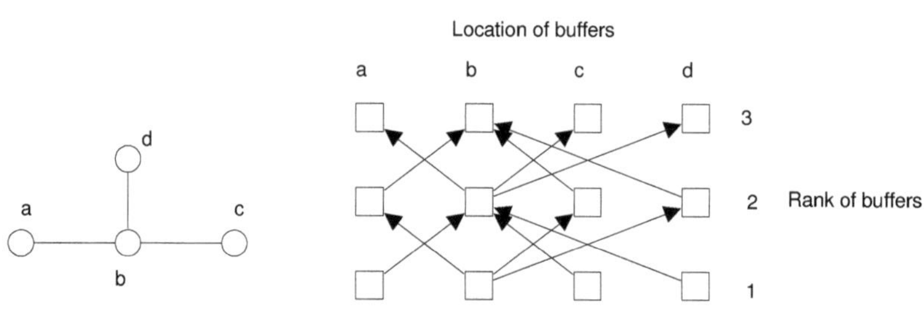

Fig. 1. Example of our buffer graph (on the right) for the network on the left

$\mathcal{SSMFP}$ is a snap-stabilizing message forwarding protocol for specification $\mathcal{SP}'$ if routing tables are correct in the initial configuration (Proposition 1). Then, we can show that $\mathcal{SSMFP}$ is a self-stabilizing message forwarding protocol for specification $\mathcal{SP}'$ even if routing tables are corrupted in the initial configuration (Proposition 2). Finally, we obtain that $\mathcal{SSMFP}$ is a snap-stabilizing message forwarding protocol for specification $\mathcal{SP}$ even if routing tables are corrupted in the initial configuration (Proposition 3). In this proof, we consider that the notion of message is different from the notion of useful information. This implies that two messages with the same useful information sent by the same processor are considered as two different messages. We must prove that the algorithm does not lose one of them thanks to the use of the flag. Let γ be a configuration of the network. A message m is existing in γ if at least one buffer contains m in γ.

Definition 3 (Caterpillar of a message m). *Let m be a message of destination d existing in a configuration γ. We define a caterpillar associated to m (noted C_m) as the longest sequence of buffers $C_m = buf_{p_1}(i)...buf_{p_t}(i+t-1)$ (with $t \geq 1$) which satisfies:*

- $\forall j \in \{1, ..., t-1\}$, $p_j \neq d$ *and* $p_{j+1} \neq p_j$.
- $\forall j \in \{1, ..., t\}$, $buf_{p_j}(i+j-1) = (m, r_j, q_j, d, c_j)$.
- $\forall j \in \{1, ..., t-1\}$, $r_j = p_{j+1}$.
- $\forall j \in \{2, ..., t\}$, $q_j = p_{j-1}$.
- $\exists k \in \{1, ..., t+1\}$, $\begin{cases} \forall j \in \{1, ..., k-1\},\ c_j = E \text{ and} \\ (\forall j \in \{k, ..., t\},\ c_j = A) \vee (\forall j \in \{k, ..., t\},\ c_j = F) \end{cases}$

We call respectively $buf_{p_1}(i)$, $buf_{p_t}(i+t-1)$ and $lg_{C_m} = t$ the tail, the head and the length of C_m.

Definition 4 (Characterization of caterpillar of a message m). *Let m be a message of destination d in a configuration γ and $C_m = buf_{p_1}(i)...buf_{p_t}(i+t-1)$ $(t \geq 1)$ a caterpillar associated to m. Then,*

- *C_m is a normal caterpillar if $i = 1$. It is abnormal if $i \geq 2$.*
- *C_m is a caterpillar of type E if $\forall j \in \{1, ..., t\}$, $c_j = E$ (i.e. $k = t+1$).*
- *C_m is a caterpillar of type A if $\exists j \in \{1, ..., t\}$, $c_j = A$ (i.e. $k < t+1$).*
- *C_m is a caterpillar of type F if $\exists j \in \{1, ..., t\}$, $c_j = F$ (i.e. $k < t+1$).*

The reader can find in Figure 2 an example for some type of caterpillar. It is obvious that, for each caterpillar C_m, either C_m is normal or abnormal. In the same way, C_m is only of type E, A or F.

When we study the behavior of these caterpillars from some configurations, we obtain the following properties:

Lemma 1. *Let γ be a configuration and m be a message existing in γ. Under a weakly fair daemon, every abnormal caterpillar of type F (resp. A) associated to m disappears in a finite time or becomes a normal caterpillar of type F (resp. A).*

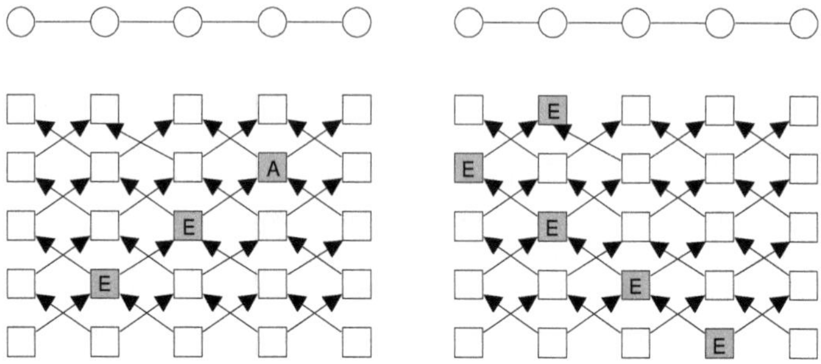

Fig. 2. Examples of caterpillar: abnormal of type A (left) and normal of type E (right)

Lemma 2. *Let γ be a configuration and m be a message existing in γ. Under a weakly fair daemon, every normal caterpillar of type A associated to m disappears in a finite time.*

Lemma 3. *Let γ be a configuration and m be a message existing in γ. Under a weakly fair daemon, every normal caterpillar of type F associated to m becomes a normal caterpillar of type E of length 1 in a finite time.*

Lemma 4. *Let γ be a configuration and m be a message existing in γ. Under a weakly fair daemon, every caterpillar of type E associated to m becomes a caterpillar of type A or F in a finite time.*

Assume that there exists a normal caterpillar of type E in a configuration γ in which routing tables are correct, then we can observe that, under a weakly fair daemon:
- by lemma 4, C_m becomes a caterpillar of type A or F in a finite time.
- in the latter case, lemma 3 allows us to say that C_m becomes a caterpillar of type E in a finite time. Then, C_m becomes of type A in a finite time by lemma 4 and the fact that routing tables are correct. So, we have the lemma:

Lemma 5. *Let γ be a configuration in which routing tables are correct and m be a message existing in γ. Under a weakly fair daemon, every normal caterpillar of type E associated to m becomes a caterpillar of type A in a finite time.*

Assume that a processor p has a message m to forward in a configuration in which routing tables are correct. Lemmas 3, 5 and 2 allow us to say that the buffer of rank 1 of p is empty in a finite time. Then, it is easy to see that the rule $(\boldsymbol{R_1})$ is enabled in a finite time and remains forever. So, the weakly fair daemon allows us to state:

Lemma 6. *If routing tables are correct, every processor can generate a message (*i.e.* execute $(\boldsymbol{R_1})$) in a finite time under a weakly fair daemon.*

Assume that a processor generate a message in a configuration in which routing tables are correct. This implies the creation of a normal caterpillar of type E.

By the lemma 5, this caterpillar become of type A in a finite time. That means that the message has been delivered to its destination by rule $(\boldsymbol{R_1})$ or $(\boldsymbol{R_4})$. Then, we have:

Lemma 7. *If a message m is generated by $\mathcal{SSMFP}$ in a configuration in which routing tables are correct, $\mathcal{SSMFP}$ delivers m to its destination in a finite time under a weakly fair daemon.*

Assume that routing tables are correct in the initial configuration. To prove that our algorithm is a snap-stabilizing message forwarding protocol for specification $\mathcal{SP}'$, we must prove that $(\boldsymbol{R_1})$ (the starting action) is executed within a finite time if a computation is requested. Lemma 6 proves this. After a starting action, the protocol is executed in accordance to $\mathcal{SP}'$. If we consider that $(\boldsymbol{R_1})$ have been executed at least one time, we can prove that: the first property of $\mathcal{SP}'$ is always verified (by Lemma 6 and the fact that the waiting for the sending of new messages is blocking) and the second property of $\mathcal{SP}'$ is always verified (by Lemma 7). By the remark which follows the definition 2, this implies the following result:

Proposition 1. *$\mathcal{SSMFP}$ is a snap-stabilizing message forwarding protocol for $\mathcal{SP}'$ if routing tables are correct in the initial configuration.*

We recall that a self-stabilizing silent algorithm $\mathcal{A}$ for computing routing tables is running simultaneously to $\mathcal{SSMFP}$. Moreover, we assume that $\mathcal{A}$ has priority over $\mathcal{SSMFP}$ (*i.e.* a processor which have enabled actions for both algorithms always chooses the action of $\mathcal{A}$). This guarantees us that routing tables are correct and stable within a finite time regardless of their initial states. As we are guaranteed that $\mathcal{SSMFP}$ is a snap-stabilizing message forwarding protocol for specification $\mathcal{SP}'$ from a such configuration by Proposition 1, we can conclude:

Proposition 2. *$\mathcal{SSMFP}$ is a self-stabilizing message forwarding protocol for $\mathcal{SP}'$ even if routing tables are corrupted in the initial configuration when $\mathcal{A}$ runs simultaneously.*

Assume that a processor p generate a message m. This implies the creation of a normal caterpillar of type E. While m is not deliver to its destination, we know by lemma 4 and 3 that C_m is continuously transforming in type F (not A since m is not deliver) then in type E. This implies that there exists a copy of m in the buffer of rank 1 of p until m is deliver to its destination, that proves:

Lemma 8. *Under a weakly fair daemon, $\mathcal{SSMFP}$ does not delete a valid message without deliver it to its destination even if $\mathcal{A}$ runs simultaneously.*

It is obvious that the emission of a message by rule $(\boldsymbol{R_1})$ only creates one caterpillar of type E. Then, we can observe that all rules are designed to obtain the following property: if a caterpillar has one head in a configuration, it has also one head in the following configuration whatever rules have been applied. Indeed, it is important to remark that the next processor on the path of a message is computed when the message is copied into a buffer not when it is forwarded to a neighbor (this why routing table moves have no effects on caterpillars). Then, we have:

Lemma 9. *Under a weakly fair daemon, $\mathcal{SSMFP}$ never duplicates a valid message even if $\mathcal{A}$ runs simultaneously.*

Proposition 2 and Lemma 8 allows us to conclude that $\mathcal{SSMFP}$ is a snap-stabilizing message forwarding protocol for specification $\mathcal{SP}'$ even if routing tables are corrupted in the initial configuration on condition that $\mathcal{A}$ run simultaneously. Using this remark and Lemma 9, we have:

Proposition 3. *$\mathcal{SSMFP}$ is a snap-stabilizing message forwarding protocol for $\mathcal{SP}$ even if routing tables are corrupted in the initial configuration when $\mathcal{A}$ run simultaneously.*

3.3 Time Complexities

In this section, we give time complexities results[3]. Since $\mathcal{SSMFP}$ needs a weakly fair daemon, there is no points to study complexities in terms of steps. It's why all results of this section are given in terms of rounds. Let $R_{\mathcal{A}}$ be the stabilization time of $\mathcal{A}$ in terms of rounds.

Proposition 4. *In the worst case, $\Theta(nD)$ invalid messages are delivered to a processor.*

Proposition 5. *In the worst case, an accepted message needs $O(max\{R_{\mathcal{A}}, nD\Delta^D\})$ rounds to be delivered to its destination.*

Proposition 6. *The delay (waiting time before the first emission) and the waiting time (between two consecutive emissions) of $\mathcal{SSMFP}$ is $O(max\ \{R_{\mathcal{A}}, nD\Delta^D\})$ rounds in the worst case.*

The complexity obtained in Proposition 5 is due to the fact that the system delivers a huge quantity of messages during the forwarding of the considered message. It's why we are now interested in the amortized complexity (in rounds) of our algorithm. For an execution Γ, this measure is equal to the number of rounds of Γ divided by the number of delivered messages during Γ (see [20] for a formal definition).

Proposition 7. *The amortized complexity (to forward a message) of $\mathcal{SSMFP}$ is $O(max\{R_{\mathcal{A}}, D\})$ rounds if there is no invalid messages.*

4 Conclusion

In this paper, we provide an algorithm to solve the message forwarding problem in a snap-stabilizing way (when a self-stabilizing algorithm for computing routing tables runs simultaneously) for a specification which forbids message losses and duplication. This property implies the following fact: our protocol can forward

[3] Due to the lack of space, proofs are omitted but available in [19].

any emitted message to its destination regardless of the state of routing tables in the initial configuration. Such an algorithm allows the processors of the network to send messages to other without waiting for the routing table computation. As in [1], we show that it is possible to adapt a fault-free protocol into a snap-stabilizing one without memory over cost. This new algorithm improve the one proposed in [1] since it needs $\Theta(D)$ buffers per processor versus $\Theta(n)$ for the former. But the following problem is still open: what is the minimal number of buffers to allow snap-stabilization on the message forwarding problem ?

References

1. Cournier, A., Dubois, S., Villain, V.: A snap-stabilizing point-to-point communication protocol in message-switched networks. In: IPDPS (to appear, technical report available [19]) (2009)
2. Dijkstra, E.W.: Self-stabilizing systems in spite of distributed control. Commun. ACM 17(11), 643–644 (1974)
3. Bui, A., Datta, A.K., Petit, F., Villain, V.: Snap-stabilization and pif in tree networks. Distributed Computing 20(1), 3–19 (2007)
4. Chandy, K.M., Misra, J.: Distributed computation on graphs: Shortest path algorithms. Commun. ACM 25(11), 833–837 (1982)
5. van Leeuwen, J., Tan, R.B.: Compact routing methods: A survey. In: SIROCCO, pp. 99–110 (1994)
6. Merlin, P., Segall, A.: A failsafe distributed routing protocol. IEEE Trans. Communications 27(9), 1280–1287 (1979)
7. Huang, S.T., Chen, N.S.: A self-stabilizing algorithm for constructing breadth-first trees. Inf. Process. Lett. 41(2), 109–117 (1992)
8. Kosowski, A., Kuszner, L.: A self-stabilizing algorithm for finding a spanning tree in a polynomial number of moves. In: Wyrzykowski, R., Dongarra, J., Meyer, N., Waśniewski, J. (eds.) PPAM 2005. LNCS, vol. 3911, pp. 75–82. Springer, Heidelberg (2006)
9. Johnen, C., Tixeuil, S.: Route preserving stabilization. In: Huang, S.-T., Herman, T. (eds.) SSS 2003. LNCS, vol. 2704, pp. 184–198. Springer, Heidelberg (2003)
10. Duato, J.: A necessary and sufficient condition for deadlock-free routing in cut-through and store-and-forward networks. IEEE Trans. Parallel Distrib. Syst. 7(8), 841–854 (1996)
11. Merlin, P.M., Schweitzer, P.J.: Deadlock avoidance in store-and-forward networks. In: Jerusalem Conference on Information Technology, pp. 577–581 (1978)
12. Schwiebert, L., Jayasimha, D.N.: A universal proof technique for deadlock-free routing in interconnection networks. In: SPAA, pp. 175–184 (1995)
13. Toueg, S.: Deadlock- and livelock-free packet switching networks. In: STOC, pp. 94–99 (1980)
14. Toueg, S., Steiglitz, K.: Some complexity results in the design of deadlock-free packet switching networks. SIAM J. Comput. 10(4), 702–712 (1981)
15. Toueg, S., Ullman, J.D.: Deadlock-free packet switching networks. SIAM J. Comput. 10(3), 594–611 (1981)
16. Tel, G.: Introduction to Distributed Algorithms, 2nd edn. Cambridge University Press, Cambridge (2000)
17. Faloutsos, M., Faloutsos, P., Faloutsos, C.: On power-law relationships of the internet topology. In: SIGCOMM, pp. 251–262 (1999)

18. Dolev, S., Israeli, A., Moran, S.: Uniform dynamic self-stabilizing leader election. IEEE Trans. Parallel Distrib. Syst. 8(4), 424–440 (1997)
19. Cournier, A., Dubois, S., Villain, V.: Two snap-stabilizing point-to-point communication protocols in message-switched networks. Technical Report arXiv:0905.2540, INRIA (2009)
20. Cormen, T., Leierson, C., Rivest, R., Stein, C.: Introduction à l'algorithmique, 2nd edn. Eyrolles (2002)

Fault-Containment in Weakly-Stabilizing Systems

Anurag Dasgupta, Sukumar Ghosh, and Xin Xiao

The University of Iowa
{adasgupt,ghosh,xinxiao}@cs.uiowa.edu

Abstract. This paper presents an exercise in fault-containment on a weakly-stabilizing system. The exercise uses the weakly stabilizing leader election algorithm in [3], and shows how the effect of single faults can be contained both in space and in time. Our algorithm confines the effect of any single fault to the constant-distance neighborhood of the faulty process, and the contamination number is restricted to 4 with high probability for an array of processes. We also show that the expected recovery time from a single fault is independent of the array size, i.e., the solution is fault-containing in time too.

1 Introduction

A distributed system is *weakly stabilizing* [11][3], if from any starting configuration, there exists at least one computation that leads the system to a *legitimate configuration*, and the legitimate configuration is closed under the given system actions. Arbitrary configurations may be caused by transient failures that can corrupt the system state. Due to the weakening of the stabilization property, it is not possible to bound the stabilization time under a deterministic scheduler, and randomized scheduling becomes necessary to guarantee eventual recovery. Furthermore, in well-designed systems, the possibility of a massive failure is quite low, and single failures are much more likely to occur. The problem of containing the effect of minor failures is becoming increasingly important due to the dramatic growth of network sizes. In many stabilizing systems, a single transient failure can potentially contaminate a large portion of the system. To increase the efficiency of fault-tolerance, it is important to guarantee a much faster recovery from all single failures, while also guaranteeing eventual recovery from more major failures. This motivates the current work.

The tight containment of the effect of single failures depends on the context: *containment in time* implies that all observable variables of the system recover to their legitimate values in $O(1)$ time, whereas *containment in space* means that the processes at $O(1)$ distance from the faulty process make observable changes. For optimal performance, both of these properties should hold.

From the point of system design, the mean time between failures (commonly termed as MTBF), is an important issue. While a fault-containing system recovers from a single failure, a minimum time is required before the system becomes

R. Guerraoui and F. Petit (Eds.): SSS 2009, LNCS 5873, pp. 209–223, 2009.

ready to recover from the next single failure with the same efficiency. This is an important metric, and is called the *fault-gap* [14]. If the next failure hits the system sooner than this time duration, then the guarantee of constant time recovery falls apart. Thus fault-gap determines the availability of the fault-free system, and a low fault-gap is desirable as it reflects better availability. The growth of the network size increases the probability of the occurrence of failures. So scale-free fault-gap is an important design goal.

1.1 Our Contributions

In this paper, we present a probabilistic solution to the fault-containment problem for leader election on an array. The solution can be extended for a tree network. Our solution uses a randomized scheduler, and is both weakly self-stabilizing and fault-containing. We consider single-fault scenarios and our algorithm confines the effect of any single fault to the constant-distance neighborhood of the faulty process with high probability (w.h.p.[1]) We show that the contamination number is at most 4 w.h.p., thus the algorithm is spatially fault-containing. The expected recovery time from a single fault is independent of the array size, i.e., the solution is fault-containing in time too. Furthermore, the system is fault-containing from multiple failures provided that the failures occur at more than distance-8 apart from each other on the array. When the distance between two faulty processes is 8 or less, fault-containment property is no longer guaranteed, but stabilization property of the system still holds.

Most current solutions to fault-containment are designed for the traditional (strongly) stabilizing systems, and the important class of weakly stabilizing systems have been largely ignored, with the exception of [2][3]. Our work fills this gap. Many solutions to fault-containment that we know of, achieve a fault-gap of $O(n)$ or worse. This seriously undermines the availability of the fault-free system. Our solution guarantees that the fault-gap is independent of the size of the array, which significantly increases the *availability* of the fault-free system.

1.2 Related Work

In [2], the authors provided a probabilistic fault-containment algorithm for the persistent-bit protocol. The solution is both weakly fault-containing and self-stabilizing and uses a randomized scheduler. *Weak fault-containment* means that from all single failures, the expected recovery time (as well as the fault-gap) is dependent only on the degree of the nodes, and independent of the network size. Furthermore, observable changes are confined to only the immediate neighbors of the faulty processes w.h.p. In [3], the authors investigated the relative power of weak, self, and probabilistic stabilization and provided a deterministic weak-stabilizing leader election algorithm on a tree network using a strongly fair scheduler. Our fault-containing algorithm for an array is an extension of this

[1] An event e happens with high probability (w.h.p) if $\lim_{m \to \infty} \Pr(e) = 1$, where m is a user defined parameter. This is slightly different from the traditional definition of w.h.p. [17] in randomized algorithms, but used in the same spirit.

– by introducing additional rules, we incorporate the fault-containment feature without compromising the weak stabilization property.

For specific problems, self-stabilizing protocols that exhibit certain fault-containment properties have been studied in the past [13] [15] [10]. Kutten and Peleg [4] introduced a protocol for fault-mending that corrects the systems from minor failures, but provides no guarantee for stabilization. Ghosh et al [14][5] demonstrated how containment can be combined with stabilization, and analyzed the cost of it. Dolev and Herman introduced *superstabilizing* protocols [9], which, in addition to being stabilizing, guarantee that during convergence from configurations that arise from legitimate states by small-scale topology changes, certain passage predicates are satisfied.

Herman's self-stabilizing protocol [12] for mutual exclusion on a ring contains the effect of any spurious token that may have been generated by a single-process fault. Kutten and Patt-Shamir [1] proposed an asynchronous stabilizing algorithm for the persistent-bit problem – their solution leads to recovery in $O(k)$ time from any k-faulty configuration. A similar protocol for mutual exclusion appears in [6]. Beauquier et al investigated the 1-strong property [7] that guarantees strong spatial confinement, and time-adaptive recovery.

1.3 Organization of the Paper

This paper has six sections. Section 2 describes the model of computation. Section 3 presents the main algorithm for fault-containment. Section 4 describes the recovery steps from different single-fault configurations. Section 5 presents the results of containment in time and space and their proofs. Section 6 contains some concluding remarks.

2 The Model of Computation

Let $G = (V, E)$ denote an array of a distributed system, where $V = \{0, 1, \cdots, n-1\}$ represents the set of processes, and each edge $(i, j) \in E$ represents a link between processes i and j. We use the notation $N(i)$ to represent the neighbors of process i:thus $(i, j) \in E \Leftrightarrow j \in N(i)$ and $i \in N(j)$. Each process i contains two variables: the *parent* variable (primary variable or the observable variable) denoted by $P(i)$, and a secondary variable $x(i)$. By definition, $P(i) \in \{N(i) \cup \perp\}$, where $\perp$ denotes *null*. Process j is called the parent of process i if $P(i) = j$. The purpose of the secondary variable is to contain the effect of single faults. $x(i)$'s domain is the set of non-negative integers. If a process i is the parent of all the processes in its neighborhood $N(i)$, then i is called the leader, denoted by L. In a legal configuration, there can only be a single leader in the system. Processes communicate with their immediate neighbors (also called the distance-1 neighbors) using the shared memory model. Each process i executes a program that consists of one or more guarded actions $g \rightarrow A$, where g is a predicate involving the variables of i and those of its immediate neighbors, and A is an action that updates one or more variables of i. A central daemon serializes all guarded actions. The global state consists of the local states of all the processes. A *computation*is a finite or infinite sequence of global states that satisfies two properties: (a) if s and s' are two consecutive states in the sequence, then there exists a process i such that i has an enabled guard in s and execution of the corresponding action results in the state s', and (b) if the sequence is finite, then in the last state of the sequence, no process has an enabled guard. We assume a randomized scheduler, where the central daemon *randomly chooses* an action with an enabled guard with uniform probability. We focus on a class of systems for which the actions are *reversible*, i.e. if there exists an action that changes the local state of a process from s to s', then there exists another action that changes the state from s' to s.

A stabilizing system converges to a legal configuration LC that is traditionally defined in terms of the observable or *primary* variables. However, in most cases, fault-containment requires the use of auxiliary or *secondary variables* too. We define the local state of each process i as an ordered pair $\langle p_i, s_i \rangle$, where p_i denotes the primary variables, and s_i denotes the secondary variables. Correspondingly, we write the global state as an ordered pair $\langle p, s \rangle$, where p is the collection of all primary variables and s is the collection of all secondary variables. For any global state $\langle p, s \rangle$, $\langle p, s \rangle \in LC \Rightarrow p \in LC_p$ and $s \in LC_s$.

Definition 1 (Fault-Containment in Time). *The* containment time *is the time needed to establish LC_p from any single-fault configuration. Ideally it should be $O(1)$.*

Definition 2 (Stabilization Time). *The* stabilization time *is the maximum time needed to establish LC from an arbitrary initial configuration.*

Definition 3 (Fault-Containment in Space). *Containment in space means that the primary variables of the processes at $O(1)$ distance from the faulty process make observable changes.*

Definition 4 (Contamination Number). *The* contamination number *is the maximum number of processes that change the primary part of their local states during recovery from any single-fault configuration.*

Definition 5 (Fault Gap). *The* fault gap *is the worst case time, starting from any single-fault state, to reach a state in LC.*

3 Probabilistic Algorithm for Fault-Containment

Our starting point is the weakly-stabilizing leader election algorithm on a tree network presented in [3]. For implementing it on an array, we make minor modifications for the stabilization rules. An array is a special case of a tree where each node except the end nodes has a degree of 2. Therefore we replace the notations of Δ from [3], and just consider the two neighbors (or the only neighbor if it is an end node) of a particular process. For the fault-containment part though, we need to add new rules. The basic idea is the same as presented in [2]. To make the protocol fault-containing, we add to each process i a secondary variable $x(i)$ whose domain is the set of non-negative integers. In a way, $x(i)$ will reflect the priority of process i in executing an action to update $P(i)$. Process i will update $P(i)$ and increase its $x(i)$ value with respect to its neighbors when the following conditions hold:

1. The randomized scheduler chooses i,
2. $\{(\exists j \in N(i) : P(i) = j)\}$,
3. $\{(\exists k \in N(i) : P(k) = l \neq i)\}$,
4. $\{x(i) \geq x(k)\}$.

After updating $P(i)$, process i will increase its $x(i)$ value accordingly: $\{x(i) \leftarrow \max_{q \in N(i)} x(q) + m\}$, $m \in \mathbb{Z}^+$.

If the first three conditions hold, but not the fourth one, process i increases its $x(i)$ value by 1, but leaves $P(i)$ unchanged. The same thing happens when the first two conditions hold, but not the fourth, and the third condition is modified to $\exists k \in N(i) : P(k) = \bot$.

Observe that once a process i updates $x(i)$, it becomes difficult for its neighbors to change their P-values, since their x-values will lag behind that of i. The larger is the value of m, the greater is the difficulty. A neighbor j of i will be able to update $P(j)$ if it is chosen by the random scheduler m times, without choosing i even once (except case R5 of Algorithm 1, where the update happens immediately when recovery is in sight within a single future move). On the other hand, after making a move, it becomes easier for i to update $P(i)$ again in the near future. With a large value of m, the probability of j being able to change its parent pointer compared to i is very low. This explains the mechanism of containment. The complete algorithm is described below for a process i:

Algorithm 1. *containment: Program for process i*

- Variable: $P(i) \in N(i) \cup \{\bot\}$.
- Macro: $C(i) = \{q \in N(i) | P(q) = i\}$
- Predicates: $Leader(i) \equiv (P(i) = \bot) \wedge (\forall j \in N(i) : P(j) = i)$
- Actions:

R1 $(P(i) \neq \bot) \wedge (|C(i)| = |N(i)|) \longrightarrow P(i) \leftarrow \bot$

R2 $(P(i) = \bot) \wedge (|C(i)| < |N(i)|) \longrightarrow P(i) \leftarrow (N(i) \setminus C(i))$

R3 a) $(\exists j \in N(i) : P(i) = j) \wedge (\exists k \in N(i) : P(k) = l \neq i) \wedge (x(i) \geq x(k)) \longrightarrow (P(i) \leftarrow k) \wedge \left(x(i) \leftarrow \max_{q \in N(i)} x(q) + m\right), m \in \mathbb{N}$

b) $(\exists j \in N(i) : P(i) = j) \wedge (P(j) \neq \bot) \wedge (\exists k \in N(i) : P(k) = l \neq i) \wedge (x(i) < x(k)) \longrightarrow x(i) \leftarrow x(i) + 1$

R4 a) $(\exists j \in N(i) : P(i) = j) \wedge (\exists k \in N(i) : P(k) = \bot) \wedge (x(i) \geq x(k)) \longrightarrow P(i) \leftarrow k$

b) $(\exists j \in N(i) : P(i) = j) \wedge (\exists k \in N(i) : P(k) = \bot) \wedge (x(i) < x(k)) \longrightarrow x(i) \leftarrow x(i) + 1$

R5 $(\exists j \in N(i) : P(i) = j) \wedge (P(j) = \bot) \wedge (\exists k \in N(i) : P(k) = l \neq i) \longrightarrow P(i) \leftarrow k$

1. R1 describes the situation when a process i has a parent, but all its neighbors consider i as their parent. So i sets its parent pointer to null and start considering itself as the leader.
2. R2 describes the situation when a process i has no parent and one of its neighbors q does not satisfy the condition $P(q) = i$. Note that for a single-fault scenario it cannot happen that both of i's neighbors do not satisfy the same condition. This means i is not unanimously selected as the leader by its neighbors. As a consequence, i stops considering itself as a leader by setting its parent pointer to q, i.e., $P(i) = q$.
3. R3 a) describes the situation when parent of i is j, and i has a neighbor k whose parent is a node l. Node l is at distance-2 from i. Now if $x(i) \geq x(k)$, then i sets k as its new parent and increases its $x(i)$ value with respect to its neighbors.
4. R3 b) describes the the situation when parent of i is j, j has a parent, and i has a neighbor k whose parent is a node l. Node l is at distance-2 from i. Now if $x(i) < x(k)$, then i does not alter its parent pointer but it just increments its x value by 1.
5. R4 a) describes the situation when parent of i is j, and i has a neighbor k whose parent pointer is set to null. Now if $x(i) \geq x(k)$, then i sets k as its new parent.
6. R4 b) describes the situation when parent of i is j, and i has a neighbor k whose parent is set to null. Now if $x(i) < x(k)$, then i does not alter its parent pointer but it just increments its x value by 1.
7. R5 is necessary for recovery. The intuition is if a node finds out that its change of parent will help the system to recover in a single future move, then it makes the move. When parent of i is j, and j has no parent, and there is a neighbor k of i such that k whose parent is a node l. Node l is at distance-2 from i. Now regardless of the value of $x(i)$ i sets k as its new parent.

4 Recovery

In this section, we describe the different cases of single-fault configuration and the recovery steps. It is to be noted that we have to consider cases up to distance-4 from the leader, as beyond distance-4, all cases of recovery are similar to each other for single-fault configuration. For convenience, we consider an array of length n and denote process i on the array as v_i where $i = 0, \cdots, n-1$. In each figure; the grey node denotes the original leader in the system, the node with a square is the node hit by the single fault, and the nodes with a $\star$ above are the nodes whose guards are true after the single fault hits the system. If there is an arrow from i to j, that indicates $P(i) = j$.

4.1 Fault at the Leader

In Fig. 1, v_4 is the leader where the fault hits, and v_3 becomes the parent of v_4. In this case, the system recovers trivially in a single step. If the scheduler

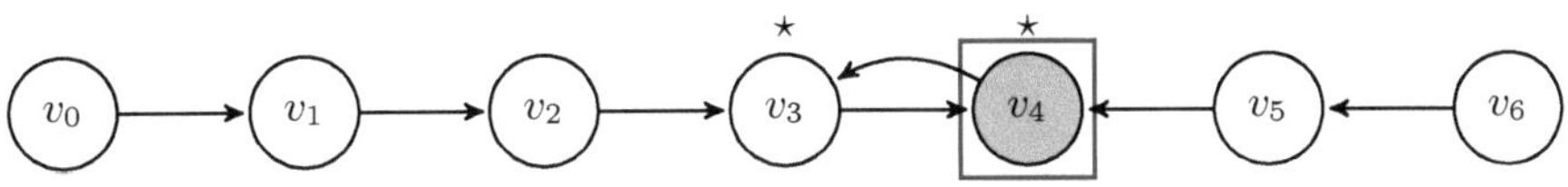

Fig. 1. Fault at leader v_4. Due to the fault v_3 becomes v_4's parent.

chooses either of v_3 or v_4, R1 can be applied at v_3 or v_4. Note that, if v_4 makes the move, the system goes back to the initial legal configuration, whereas if v_3 makes the move, v_3 becomes the new leader of the system after recovery.

4.2 Fault at Distance-1 Neighbor from the Leader

a) The parent pointer of distance-1 neighbor from the leader becomes null. The fault hits v_3 (Fig 2). If v_3's parent pointer becomes null, again the recovery happens trivially in a single step. If the scheduler chooses either of v_3 or v_4, R2 can be applied at v_3 or v_4 and a legal configuration can be reached in a single step. Note that, if v_3 makes the move, the system goes back to the initial legal configuration, whereas if v_4 makes the move, v_3 becomes the new leader.
b) A new node becomes the parent of the distance-1 faulty node. In Fig 3, if $P(v_3) = v_2$, then v_2, v_3, and v_4's guards are true. If v_3 is selected first, and if $x(v_3) \geq x(v_4)$, the system trivially recovers in a single step (by R4a at v_3). Otherwise, v_3 would not make a parent change. If the scheduler chooses v_4, then the recovery happens in two steps. First, v_4 applies R2 and after that either v_2 or v_3 makes a move (R1). Note that if v_3 makes the move, the leader shifts one place compared to the original legal configuration, whereas if v_2 makes the move, the leader shifts two places.

If v_2 makes the first move, R1 can be applied at v_2. After that if the scheduler chooses v_4, recovery is immediate as R2 can be applied at v_4. But if the scheduler chooses v_3 repeatedly and $x(v_3) \geq x(v_4)$ and $x(v_3) \geq x(v_2)$, oscillations can occur in the system for some period of time due to the fact that R4a is applicable at v_3. v_2 and v_4 alternately becomes v_3's parent. But whenever v_2 or v_4 is chosen

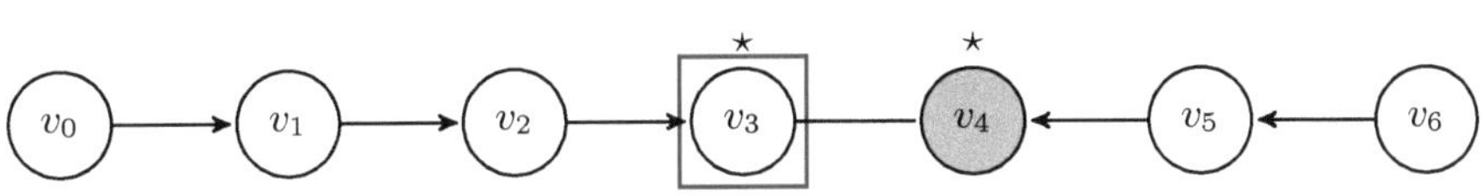

Fig. 2. Fault at distance-1 neighbor from the leader. v_3's parent pointer becomes null due to the fault.

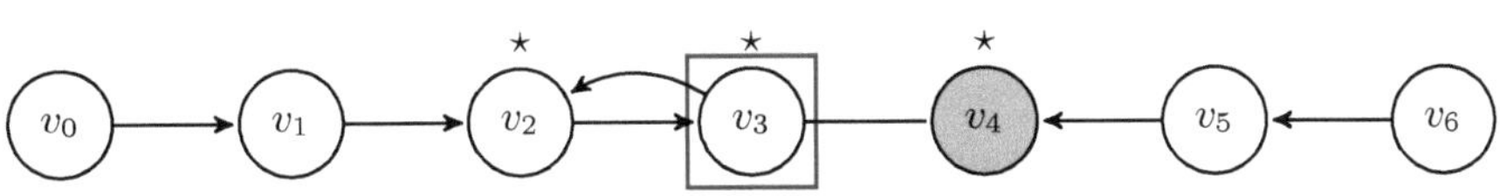

Fig. 3. Fault at distance-1 neighbor from the leader. Due to the fault v_2 becomes v_3's new parent.

by the scheduler next, the system recovers (R2). In the case, $x(v_3) < x(v_2)$ or $x(v_3) < x(v_4)$, recovery is complete when the scheduler next chooses v_2 or v_4 respectively.

4.3 Fault at Distance-2 from the Leader

a) The parent pointer of distance-2 neighbor from the leader becomes null. Consider Fig 4. The fault hits the system at v_2. If the scheduler chooses v_2, the system trivially recovers in a single step (R2). If v_3 is chosen by the scheduler, the system has a potential for oscillations, i.e., v_4 or v_2 alternately may become v_3's parent, depending on the x values of v_2, v_3, v_4. The system recovers by applying R2 at v_2 or v_4 respectively when either of them is chosen next by the scheduler.
b) A new node becomes the parent of the distance-2 faulty node. Consider Fig 5. If v_1 becomes the new parent of v_2, then either v_1, v_2 or v_3 can make a move. If v_2 is selected first, the situation is like the one described in 4.2b), except that R3 a) can be applied now at v_2 as v_3 has a parent if $x(v_2) \geq x(v_3)$. If v_3 is selected first, v_3 can select v_2 as its new parent if $x(v_3) \geq x(v_2)$. The recovery is complete following v_2, v_1's (or v_1, v_2's) moves (R1) followed by v_4's move (R2) or vice versa. If both v_3 and v_2 are unable to change their parents due to smaller x values, then recovery is complete by v_1's move first (R1), followed by v_3's move (now R5 can be applied at v_3) and v_4's move (R2).

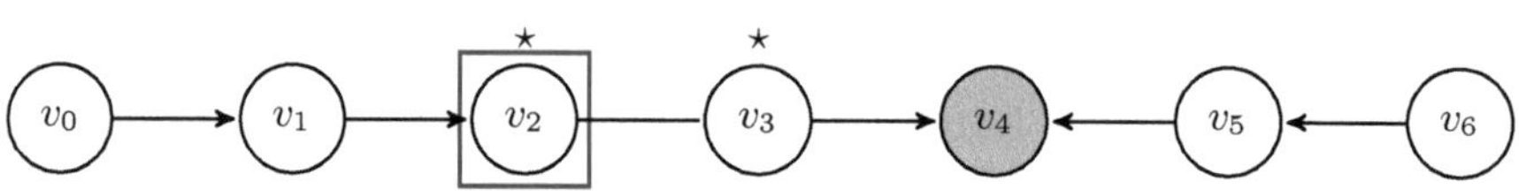

Fig. 4. Fault at distance-2 from the leader. v_2's parent pointer becomes null due to the fault.

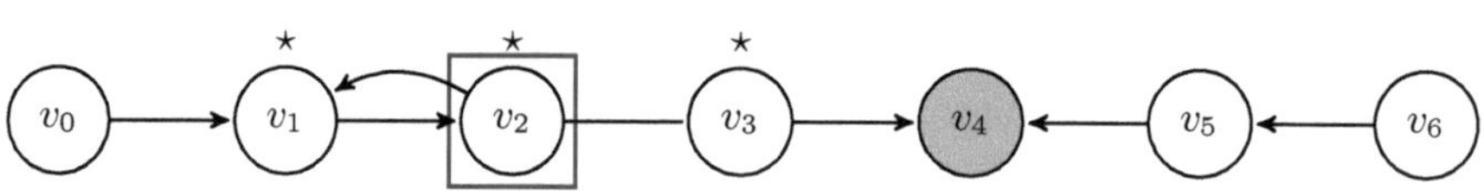

Fig. 5. Fault at distance-2 from the leader. v_1 becomes the new parent of the v_2 due to the fault.

4.4 Fault at Distance-3 Neighbor from the Leader

a) The parent pointer of distance-3 neighbor from the leader becomes null. Consider Fig 6. If the scheduler chooses v_1, recovery trivially happens in a single step (R2). If v_2 is chosen first, then it can alternately choose v_1 or v_3 as its parent for a while, if its x value is greater than that of both v_1 and v_3. Recovery completes when v_1 is selected (R2). Note that, because of higher x value of v_2, v_3 is unlikely to change its parent. If it does, then recovery happens by applying R5 at v_3 followed by R2 at v_4.

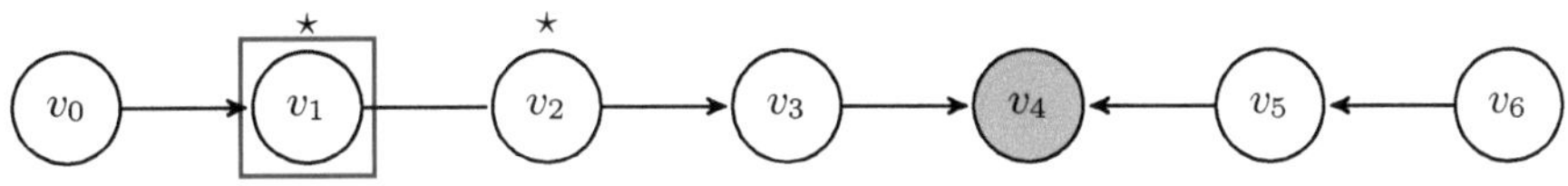

Fig. 6. Fault at distance-3 from the leader. v_1's parent pointer becomes null due to the fault.

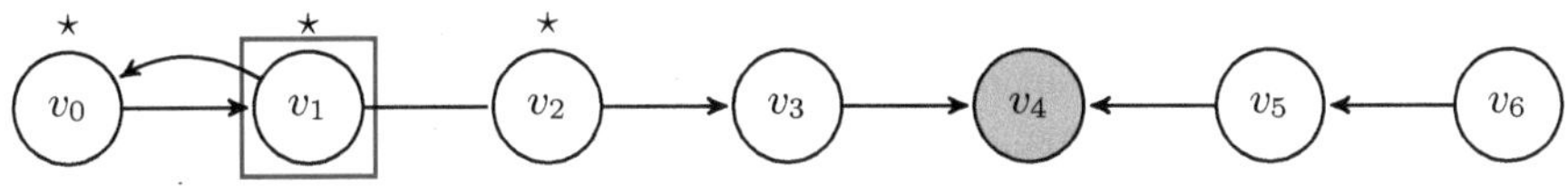

Fig. 7. Fault at distance-3 from the leader. v_0 becomes the new parent of v_1.

b) A new node becomes the parent of the distance-3 faulty node. Consider Fig 7. If v_0 becomes the new parent of v_1, then v_0, v_1, and v_2's guards are true. If v_1 is selected first, then the situation is the same as described above in 4.3b). If v_0 is chosen by the scheduler first, R1 can be applied at v_0. The system recovers when v_1 chooses v_2 as its parent afterwards (using R3a if applicable) and v_0 makes a move next (R2 can be applied at v_0 possibly after some oscillations of v_1). If v_2 is selected to make a move and if $x(v_2) \geq x(v_1)$, then v_2 chooses v_1 as its parent and increases its x value (R3a). Now v_3 is still able to change its parent to v_2 regardless of the value of x at v_2 (R5) provided v_0 had made a prior move. Recovery is completed by v_4's move (R2). Otherwise, if v_0 had not made a move prior to v_3, the higher x value of v_2 will prevent v_3 to change its parent. Then the recovery is completed by v_1's move (R5) followed by v_0's move (R2). Note that even if v_0 is not an end node, this still applies.

4.5 Fault at Distance-4 Neighbor or beyond from the Leader

a) The parent pointer of distance-4 neighbor from the leader becomes null. Consider Fig 8. If v_1 is selected by the scheduler, recovery occurs immediately by R2 or after some oscillations at v_2. Otherwise, if $x(v_2) \geq x(v_1)$, then v_1 becomes v_2's new parent (R4a). Similarly v_2 may become v_3's new parent, but this time v_3 sets its x value higher (R3a). Recovery is completed by v_4's move (R5) followed by v_5's move (R2). Note that for fault occurring at distance-4 and beyond from the leader, R5 will no more applicable at the distance-1 neighbor from the leader (v_4 in this case). Therefore, we do not consider hereafter the cases beyond fault at distance-4 beyond the leader.

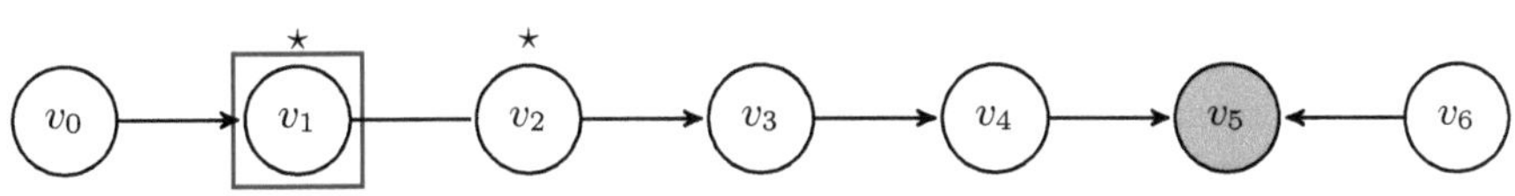

Fig. 8. Fault at distance-4 from the leader. v_1's parent pointer becomes null.

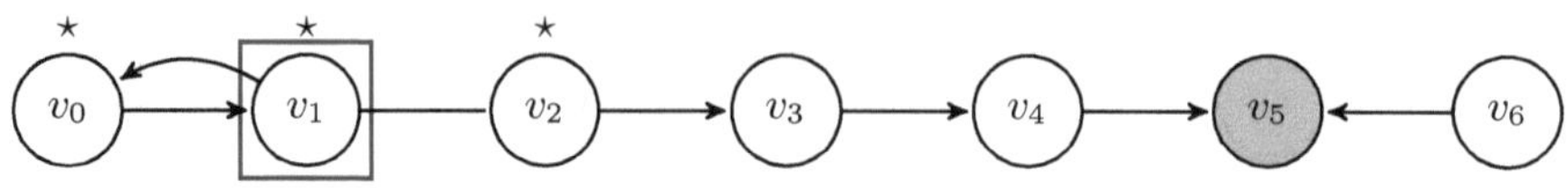

Fig. 9. Fault at distance-4 from the leader. v_0 becomes the new parent of v_1.

b) A new node becomes the parent of the distance-4 faulty node. Consider Fig 9. If v_0 becomes the new parent of v_1, then v_0, v_1, and v_2's guards are true. If v_1 is selected to make a move first, then the situation is the same as described above in 4.4b). If v_0 is chosen by the scheduler first, R1 can be applied at v_0. The system recovers when v_1 chooses v_2 as its parent afterwards (R3a if applicable) and v_0 makes a move next (R2 can be applied at v_0 possibly after some oscillations of v_1). If v_2 is selected to make a move and if $x(v_2) \geq x(v_1)$, then v_2 chooses v_1 as its parent and increases its x value (R3a). Now v_3 cannot apply R5 anymore and it is unlikely that the fault will propagate beyond v_2. The recovery proceeds through the following steps - v_0 makes a move (R1), after some oscillations at v_2, v_1 chooses v_2 as its parent (R5), and finally v_0 selects v_1 as its parent (R2). Note that even if v_0 is not an end node, this still applies.

Note that all cases of single-fault configuration beyond distance-4 from the leader will not involve any different recovery steps that are already not covered in the previous scenarios. This is because even if we shift the original place of the fault further away from the leader, its neighborhood that is going to be affected by subsequent recovery steps will remain unchanged. In the recovery mechanism, R3b) and R4b) are not shown as we only highlighted the moves where the change of parent pointers occurs leading to the recovery of the system.

5 Results

5.1 Fault-Containment in Space

Theorem 1. *With high probability, the effect of a single failure is restricted within distance-4 of the faulty process on an array, and the contamination number is at most 4, i.e., algorithm* containment *is spatially fault-containing.*

To prove the result of spatial containment, we need to find out how far the observable variables change from the faulty node w.h.p. We consider all the subcases of the recovery mechanism.

1. Fault at leader: The fault propagates to at most distance-1.
2. Fault at distance-1 neighbor from the leader:
   (a) Parent pointer of the distance-1 neighbor becomes null: The fault propagates to at most distance-1.
   (b) A new node becomes the parent of the distance-1 faulty node: In the recovery steps, we showed that in Fig 3, at most v_2 or v_4's parent might change. Thus, the fault propagates to at most distance-1.

3. Fault at distance-2 neighbor from the leader:
   (a) The parent pointer of the distance-2 neighbor becomes null: Consider Fig 4. If v_2 is selected the system recovers immediately. Another possible recovery is through the sequence of moves of v_3 followed by v_4. In the latter case the contamination happens up to distance-2 of the original faulty node.
   (b) A new node becomes the parent of the distance-2 faulty node: Consider Fig 5. The worst case scenario happens when v_3 makes a move and after that v_4 completes the recovery. Contamination happens up to distance-2 of the original faulty node in this case.
4. Fault at distance-3 neighbor from the leader:
   (a) The parent pointer of the distance-3 neighbor becomes null: Consider Fig 6. The worst case scenario happens when v_4 has to change its parent. The fault propagates to at most distance-3.
   (b) A new node becomes the parent of the distance-3 faulty node: Consider Fig 7. The worst case scenario happens when v_4 has to change its parent. The fault propagates to at most distance-3.
5. Fault at distance-4 from the leader:
   (a) The parent pointer of the distance-4 neighbor becomes null: This is the scenario where the highest spatial contamination occurs. Consider Fig 8. In the worst case, a distance-4 node from the faulty node might have to change its parent pointer. In Fig 8, v_5 is this node.
   (b) A new node becomes the parent of the distance-4 faulty node: Consider Fig 9. The fault propagates up to distance-1 w.h.p. The probability of the fault contaminating beyond distance-1 is $(1 - 1/2^m) \times 1/2^m$ and $\lim_{m\to\infty}(1 - 1/2^m) \times 1/2^m = 0$.

Note that for fault occurring at distance-4 and beyond from the leader, R5 will no more be applicable to the distance-1 neighbor from the leader. Hence algorithm *containment* is spatially fault-containing and the highest contamination number is 4 w.h.p. □

Corollary 1. *The algorithm* containment *is fault-containing from multiple failures provided that the failures occur at more than distance-8 apart from each other.*

5.2 Fault-Containment in Time

Theorem 2. *The expected number of steps needed to contain a single fault is independent of n, i.e., the number of nodes in the array. Hence algorithm* containment *is fault-containing in time.*

Proof. To prove that algorithm *containment* is fault-containing in time, we again consider each individual subcase of fault. We show that each subcase can be bounded and each of them is independent of n, i.e., the size of the array. For each individual case, we calculate the expected number of moves required for recovery. Essentially that means we are considering the probabilities of the system recovering in a single move, in two moves, in three moves etc. We denote the number of moves (which is a random variable) as X, and $\Pr(X = x)$ denotes the probability that the system recovers using x moves.

1. Fault at leader: Consider Fig. 1. This is a trivial case. In this scenario, both v_4 and v_3 have their guards true. Each of them has an equal probability to execute, given a chance. The system recovers in a single move if either of them executes. So the expected number of moves required for recovery is $1 \times 1/2 + 1 \times 1/2 = 1$.
2. Fault at distance-1 from the leader:
   (a) The parent pointer of the faulty node becomes null: Consider Fig. 2. This is again a trivial case. The system recovers in a single move if either v_4 or v_3 executes. The expected number of moves for recovery is the same as before, i.e., $1 \times 1/2 + 1 \times 1/2 = 1$.
   (b) A new node becomes parent of the faulty node: The system can recover following different sequences:
      - v_4, v_2 or v_4, v_3.
      - $v_3, \cdots, v_3$ ($x(4) - x(3)$ times)
      - $v_3, \cdots, v_3$ ($x(4) - x(3) - 1$ times) followed by v_4, v_2 or v_4, v_3
      - v_2, v_4
      - $v_2, v_3, \cdots, v_3$ followed by v_2 or v_4.

      The length of recovery sequences of the first four situations is finite and independent of n, and only the last sequence may be arbitrarily long. We show that its expectation is finite. After v_2 makes a move applying R2, both of v_3's neighbor consider themselves as the leader. Hence depending on the parent of v_3, each time there are at most two enabled nodes: v_2 and v_3 or v_3 and v_4. Therefore, the probability that the scheduler chooses v_3 is $1/2$ before recovery completes. Hence, the probability of v_3 being selected consecutively n times is $1/2^n$. Therefore, if v_2 is selected by the scheduler first, the expected length of the recovery sequence is $2 + \sum_{n=1}^{\infty} n/2^n = 4$.
3. Fault at distance-2 from the leader
   (a) The parent pointer of the faulty node becomes null: Regardless of the values of $x(2)$, $x(3)$ and $x(4)$, no matter which node the scheduler chooses, there is always $1/2$ probability that the system recovers after the selected node makes a move. Hence, the expected recovery time is $\sum_{n=1}^{\infty} n/2^n = 2$.
   (b) A new node becomes parent of the faulty node: In our proof so far, we assumed the value of x to be different. Proceeding in the same manner, the rest of the expectation calculation can be done. However, for subsequent cases, the computation will be more complex. The constant factors in the result will still hold, since the time complexity calculation for each subcase will involve products of several terms like $(1 - 1/2^m)$ and $1/2^m$. For the sake of simplicity, we assume the value of x to be identical for the rest of the proof.

Following the above assumption, the expected number of moves for recovery will be:

$$\mathbb{E}(X) = 1\times\frac{1}{3} + 3\left(\frac{1}{3}\times\frac{1}{2}\times\frac{1}{2} + \frac{1}{3}\times\frac{1}{2}\times\frac{1}{2} + \frac{1}{3}\times\frac{1}{4}\times\frac{1}{2} + \frac{1}{3}\times\frac{1}{4}\times\frac{1}{2}\right)$$
$$+\frac{2}{3}\sum_{n=2}^{\infty}\frac{2n+1}{2^{2n}}$$
$$=\frac{151}{108}$$

In the same manner, the expected number of moves for recovery will be $\frac{131}{54}$ and $\frac{115}{36}$ for fault at distance-3 from the leader, and the expected number of moves for recovery will be $\frac{10}{9}$ and $\frac{29}{27}$ for fault at distance-4 from the leader. □

5.3 Computing the Availability

An interesting aspect of the proposed algorithm is that there is no overhead for stabilizing the secondary variables. $LC_s = true$ as long as $x(i) \in \mathbb{Z}^+$. So, LC holds as soon as LC_p holds. This leads to the following theorem:

Theorem 3. *For single failures, the fault gap equals the containment time.*

5.4 Convergence

We use martingale convergence theorem to prove the convergence of algorithm *containment*. We first give the definition of martingales, and then we provide the statement of martingale convergence theorem with a corollary derived by the martingale convergence theorem [16]. Finally we show that the corollary can be applied in our problem.

Definition 6. *Let $\mathcal{F}_n$ be an increasing sequence of σ-fields, and let $X_n \in \mathcal{F}_n$ for all n. X is said to be a martingale with respect to $\mathcal{F}_n$ if the following conditions hold:*

1. $\mathbb{E}(|X_n|) < \infty$,
2. *X_n is adapted to $\mathcal{F}_n$,*
3. *$\mathbb{E}(X_{n+1}|\mathcal{F}_n) = X_n$ for all n*

If $=$ in the last condition is replaced by $\leq$ or $\geq$, then X_n is said to be a supermartingale or submartingale, respectively.

Theorem 4 (The martingale convergence theorem). *If X_n is a submartingale with $\sup\mathbb{E}(X_n^+) < \infty$ then as $n \to \infty$, X_n converges almost surely (i.e. the probability that X_n converges is 1) to a limit X with $\mathbb{E}(|X|) < \infty$.*

Corollary 2. *If $X_n \geq 0$ is a supermartingale then as $n \to \infty$, $X_n \to X$ almost surely and $\mathbb{E}(X) \leq \mathbb{E}(X_0)$.*

Theorem 5. *Algorithm* containment *is weakly-stabilizing.*

Proof. We denote the number of nodes whose guards are true at step i by X_i. Let $\mathcal{F}_i = \sigma < X_0, X_1, \cdots, X_i >$, we first prove that the sequence of X_i is a supmartingale with respect to $\mathcal{F}_i$: (a) $\mathbb{E}(X_i) < \infty$ is trivially true as there are n nodes in the system, so $\mathbb{E}(X_i) \leq n$. (b) $X_i \in \mathcal{F}_i$ by the definition of $\mathcal{F}_i$; (c) We show that $\mathbb{E}(X_{i+1}|X_i) \leq X_i$ by enumerating all possible values of X_i. X_i can only be 0, 2 or 3. Note that X_i's value cannot be 1. There is no single-fault configuration for which only one node's guard can be true in the system.

1. When $X_i = 0$, $X_{i+1} = 0$ as the system has reached the non-faulty configuration.
2. When $X_i = 2$, $\mathbb{E}(X_{i+1}|X_i) = 1/2 \times 0 + 1/2 \times 2 = 1 \leq 2$.
3. When $X_i = 3$, $\mathbb{E}(X_{i+1}|X_i) = 1/3 \times 0 + 1/3 \times 2 + 1/3 \times 4 = 2 \leq 3$.

As the number of nodes whose guards are true are nonnegative, we apply corollary 2 and thus $X_n \to X$, *i.e.*, the number of nodes whose guards are true converge. □

6 Conclusion

The unbounded variable $x(i)$ can be bounded using the method described in [2]. Our proposed algorithm for array can easily be extended to tree networks. An array is a special case of a tree network. In case of a general tree topology, one will have to consider all the neighbors of a process i when executing the rules of the algorithm, instead of considering at most two neighbors for an array. The analysis will involve Δ, the maximum degree of a node,, and instead of expected recovery in constant number of moves, the results will yield an expression in terms of Δ. Note that this result will satisfy the definition of weak fault-containment [2].

References

1. Kutten, S., Patt-Shamir, B.: Stabilizing time-adaptive protocols. Theor. Comput. Sci. 220, 93–111 (1999)
2. Dasgupta, A., Ghosh, S., Xiao, X.: Probabilistic fault-containment. In: Masuzawa, T., Tixeuil, S. (eds.) SSS 2007. LNCS, vol. 4838, pp. 189–203. Springer, Heidelberg (2007)
3. Devismes, S., Tixeuil, S., Yamashita, M.: Weak vs. Self vs. Probabilistic Stabilization. In: 28th IEEE International Conference on Distributed Computing Systems (ICDCS 2008), Beijing, China, June 17-20 (2008)
4. Kutten, S., Peleg, D.: Fault-local distributed mending. In: Proceedings of the 14th Annual ACM Symposium on Principles of Distributed Computing, pp. 20–27 (1995)
5. Ghosh, S., Gupta, A., Herman, T., Pemmaraju, S.V.: Fault- containing self-stabilizing distributed algorithms. In: Proceedings of the 15th Annual ACM Symposium on Principles of Distributed Computing, pp. 45–54 (1996)

6. Beauquier, J., Genolini, C., Kutten, S.: Optimal reactive k-stabilization the case of mutual exclusion. In: Proceedings of the 18th Annual ACM Symposium on Principles of Distributed Computing, pp. 209–218 (1999)
7. Beauquier, J., Delaet, S., Haddad, S.: A 1-Strong Self-Stabilizing Transformer. In: Proceedings of the Eighth Symposium on Self-Stabilizing Systems (2006)
8. Coolidge, J.L.: The Gambler's Ruin. The Annals of Mathematics 10(4), 181–192 (1909)
9. Dolev, S., Herman, T.: Superstabilizing protocols for dynamic distributed systems. In: Proceedings of the Second Workshop on Self-Stabilizing Systems, pp. 3.1-3.15 (1995)
10. Ghosh, S., Gupta, A., Pemmaraju, S.V.: Fault-containing network protocols. In: Proceedings of 12th Annual ACM Symposium on Applied Computing (1997)
11. Gouda, M.G.: The Theory of Weak Stabilization. In: Datta, A.K., Herman, T. (eds.) WSS 2001. LNCS, vol. 2194, pp. 114–123. Springer, Heidelberg (2001)
12. Herman, T.: Superstabilizing mutual exclusion. In: Proceedings of 1st International Conference on Parallel and Distributed Processing: Techniques and Applications (1995)
13. Ghosh, S., Gupta, A.: An exercise in fault-containment: Self- stabilizing leader election. Informat. Process. Lett. 5(59), 281–288 (1996)
14. Ghosh, S., Gupta, A., Herman, T., Pemmaraju, S.V.: Fault-containing self-stabilizing distributed protocols. Distributed Computing (2007)
15. Ghosh, S., Gupta, A., Pemmaraju, S.V.: A fault-containing self-stabilizing algorithm for spanning trees. J. Comput. Informat. 2, 322–338 (1996)
16. Durrett, R.: Probability: theory and examples. Duxbury Press, Belmont (1996)
17. Mitzenmacher, M., Upfal, E.: Probability and Computing: Randomized Algorithms and Probabilistic Analysis. Cambridge University Press, Cambridge (2005)

Stability of Distributed Algorithms in the Face of Incessant Faults

Robert E. Lee DeVille and Sayan Mitra

University of Illinois at Urbana Champaign
{rdeville,mitras}@illinois.edu

Abstract. For large distributed systems built from inexpensive components, one expects to see incessant failures. This paper proposes two models for such faults and analyzes two well-known self-stabilizing algorithms under these fault models. For a small number of processes, the properties of interest are verified automatically using probabilistic model-checking tools. For a large number of processes, these properties are characterized using asymptotic bounds from a direct Markov chain analysis and approximated by numerical simulations.

1 Introduction

Self-stabilization guarantees automatic fault-tolerance: after a fault, the system may deviate from its desirable behavior for a finite amount of time, but it eventually reaches a desirable (or *legal*) state automatically. This property is particularly attractive in large distributed systems where manual failure management is impractical. Self-stabilizing algorithms for mutual exclusion, leader election, spanning tree construction and other distributed computation tasks have been extensively studied (see for example [1,2,3]). These algorithms guarantee that *once failures cease* a legal state is reached in a finite number of steps. Often the number of steps (and therefore the amount of time) required for recovery from even a single failure grows at least linearly with the size of the system, and it is assumed that no further failures occur during this period. For these algorithms to be valid, the failure probability times the number of components must be significantly less than one.

Distributed systems built from off-the shelf components and deployed in harsh environments [4,5,6] will experience frequent component failures. As a result, these systems may not experience failure-free periods which are long enough to recover completely to a legal state. In this paper, we initiate a systematic investigation of distributed algorithms in the face of such *incessant failures*. Random transmission and link failures have been studied recently in [7,8]. Also, fault-tolerance with respect to a locally bounded number of faults (as opposed to globally bounded) has been studied in [9]. To the best of our knowledge, however, our work is the first attempt at investigating distributed systems under random failures with bounded failure rate.

In the face of incessant faults, the system will not stabilize, i.e. enter a legal state and remain there. However, not all illegal states are equivalent; some are

R. Guerraoui and F. Petit (Eds.): SSS 2009, LNCS 5873, pp. 224–237, 2009.

worse than others. For a given distributed system with state space X, define $Q : X \to \mathbb{R}$, which determines "how far" each state is from legal: legal states are those for which $Q = 0$, and high Q states are ones which are particularly bad. We show below how to use a Markov chain to model a distributed system under incessant faults. The Markov chain (under weak assumptions) will have a unique invariant measure π which leads to natural global measures of performance (e.g. the mean of Q, $Prob(Q > k)$ for some k, etc.). If one knows π, then one can compute all of these, but in general, it is difficult to compute π explicitly.

Two observations emerge from the results in this paper. First, the measure π depends significantly on the types of allowed faults, i.e. changing the fault model leads to a significantly different "typical state" during the evolution of a system. Secondly, since a post-fault state depends on the pre-fault state, which itself depends on the output of the algorithm after a random number of steps, etc., *one can no longer assume that the stabilization process and the faults are decoupled.* That is, when the faults occur on a timescale comparable to (or shorter than) the stabilization time, the system and the faults interact in complicated ways. This leads to some surprising and non-intuitive phenomena and requires a novel approach to the analysis of such systems.

In this paper, we take a first step towards development of this general theory. Specifically, we do the following:

We define two incessant fault models, the *update (U)* fault and the *sleep-update (S/U)* fault. Roughly, an update fault only occurs when a process attempts to update its state; a sleep-update fault can occur at any time. Each type of fault transforms a given stochastic automaton model of a fault-free distributed algorithm into a new stochastic automaton with additional probabilistic transitions. In particular, for synchronous distributed algorithms, the resulting fault-transformed system is a Markov chain. Next, we analyze Dijkstra's self-stabilizing token ring algorithm (TR) [10] and a randomized graph coloring algorithm (GC) from [11] under incessant faults. First, for a small number ($N \approx 7$) of participating processes, we verify quantitative properties of these algorithms using probabilistic model checkers [12,13]. This analysis is automatic and provides exact values for quantitative properties, however, owing to the state space explosion it does not scale well with N. Second, we use techniques from probability theory to analyze the underlying Markov processes of TR. The insight gained from the Markov chain analysis allows us to understand how TR tends to fail under the U and S/U fault models, and this naturally leads to a modified version, namely TR2, which, as we show, performs significantly better under incessant faults. Finally, we perform simulations of both algorithms for large N to give an idea how several performance metrics depend on parameters.

The results of this paper suggest performing an analogous analysis of many well-known self-stabilizing algorithms for routing, maximal independent set, leader election [3], etc. We expect that the specific phenomena observed here will be representative of a wide range of models, and analysis along these lines will be very useful in developing new algorithms which are robust to incessant faults. Moreover, the scaling problems we encounter with standard model checkers suggests the exploration of parallelizable statistical tools such as [14,15], and further emphasizes the need for new tools and techniques.

2 Background and Fault Models

There are several formalisms for compositionally specifying randomized distributed algorithms (see, for example [16,17,18,19] and the references therein). We describe fault-prone algorithms as *stochastic automata*, which are simplified versions of the Probabilistic I/O Automata of [20].

We denote the set of probability distributions over a set S by $\mathcal{P}(S)$. In describing the states of processors in a distributed system, we find it convenient to use a variable structure. Let X be a set of variables. Each variable $x \in X$, is associated with a *type*, denoted by *type(x)*, which is the set of values that x may take. A *valuation* of the variables in X is a function that associates each $x \in X$ with a value in $type(x)$. A particular valuation for a set of variables X is written as $\mathbf{x}$, and the value of an individual variable x is denoted by $\mathbf{x}.x$. The set of all valuations of X is denoted by $Val(X)$. For a valuation $\mathbf{x} \in Val(X)$, the restriction of $\mathbf{x}$ to $Y \subseteq X$ is denoted by $\mathbf{x} \lceil Y$. For a probability distribution $\mu \in \mathcal{P}(Val(X))$ the marginal distribution of μ on $Y \subseteq X$ is denoted by $\mu \lceil Y$.

2.1 Stochastic Automata

Definition 1. *A* Stochastic Automaton (SA) $\mathcal{A}$ *is a 4-tuple* $(X, U, \bar{\mu}, \rightarrow)$, *where (1)* X *is a set of* state variables, $Val(X)$ *is called the set of* states, *(2)* U *is a set of* input variables, *(3)* $\bar{\mu} \subseteq \mathcal{P}(Val(X))$ *is an* initial distribution *on states, and (4)* $\rightarrow \subseteq Val(U) \times Val(X) \times \mathcal{P}(Val(X))$ *is a set of* probabilistic transitions, *satisfying:* **(D)** *for each* $\mathbf{u} \in Val(U), \mathbf{x} \in Val(X)$, *there exists* $\mu \in \mathcal{P}(Val(X))$ *such that* $(\mathbf{u}, \mathbf{x}, \mu) \in \rightarrow$.

The input variables provide a mechanism for modeling inter-automata communication. For example, the state variable of one automaton may act as inputs to others. In a synchronous distributed system, this variable-based communication can be implemented by message passing. In this paper, we assume existence of unique initial distribution of SA for the sake of convenience; the metrics we analyze in Sections 3 and 4 are in fact independent of the initial distributions.

Notation. If $(\mathbf{u}, \mathbf{x}, \mu) \in \rightarrow$, we write $(\mathbf{u}, \mathbf{x}) \rightarrow \mu$. For a SA $\mathcal{A}$ we denote its components by $U_{\mathcal{A}}, X_{\mathcal{A}}, \bar{\mu}_{\mathcal{A}}$ and $\rightarrow_{\mathcal{A}}$, respectively, and for a SA $\mathcal{A}_1$ its components are denoted by $U_1, X_1, \bar{\mu}_1$ and $\rightarrow_1$.

Informally, each execution or run of $\mathcal{A}$ is a (possibly infinite) sequence $(\mathbf{u}_0, \mathbf{x}_0)$, $(\mathbf{u}_1, \mathbf{x}_1)$, ... Each pair in the sequence corresponds to a probabilistic transition or a step. Throughout this paper, we use the "time" and "number of steps" synonymously. As in [20], we can define the probability measures over sets of executions of $\mathcal{A}$ by resolving the nondeterminism with a scheduler, however, for this paper we work with a restricted class of SAs which simplifies the formal framework.

$\mathcal{A}$ is said to be *finite* if $Val(X_{\mathcal{A}})$ is finite, *closed* if $U_{\mathcal{A}} = \emptyset$, *pure* if for every $\mathbf{u} \in Val(U), \mathbf{x} \in Val(X)$ there exists a *unique* μ satisfying condition **(D)**, and *deterministic* if for every $(\mathbf{u}, \mathbf{x}) \rightarrow_{\mathcal{A}} \mu$, μ is a Dirac delta distribution. A particular probabilistic transition $\mathbf{u}, \mathbf{x} \rightarrow \mu$ is said to be *active* if $\mu \neq \delta_{\mathbf{x}}$, otherwise it is *passive*. (Throughout this paper $\delta_{\mathbf{x}}$ is the Dirac measure at $\mathbf{x}$.) A state $\mathbf{x} \in Val(X)$ is said to be *stable* if for all $\mathbf{u} \in Val(U)$ there are no active transitions from $(\mathbf{u}, \mathbf{x})$. Clearly, a closed, pure SA $\mathcal{A}$ is equivalent to a discrete time Markov chain (DTMC) with state space $Val(X_{\mathcal{A}})$. Suppose $P_{\mathcal{A}}$ is the transition matrix of this equivalent Markov chain.

Example 1. The pseudocode in Figure 1 specify ordinary (*Left*) and special (*Right*) processes participating in Dijkstra's token ring [10]. The natural numbers N and K are parameters. TR_i, $0 < i < N$, is a deterministic, finite-state SA with the following components: (1) set of state variables $X_i = \{x_i\}$, where x_i is a variable of type $\{0, \ldots, K-1\}$, (2) set of input variables $U_i = \{x_{i-1}\}$, where x_{i-1} is a variable of type $\{0, \ldots, K-1\}$, (3) $\bar{\mu}$ is the uniform distribution over $Val(X_i)$, (4) for each $\mathbf{u} \in Val(U_i), \mathbf{x} \in Val(X_i), (\mathbf{u}, \mathbf{x}) \rightarrow \mu$ iff (i) $\mathbf{u}.x_{i-1} = \mathbf{x}.x_i$ and $\mu = \delta_{\mathbf{x}}$, or (ii) $\mathbf{u}.x_{i-1} \neq \mathbf{x}.x_i$ and $\mu = \delta_{\mathbf{x}'}$, where $\mathbf{x}'$ is the valuation that assigns $\mathbf{u}.x_{i-1}$ to x_i.

```
automaton TR(N,K:ℕ,const i ≠ 0)
variables
  state x_i: {0,...,K − 1} := uni[{0,...,K − 1}]
  input x_{i−1}: {0,...,K − 1}

transitions
  pre x_i ≠ x_{i−1}
  eff x_i := x_{i−1}
```

```
automaton TR(N,K:ℕ,const i = 0)
variables
  state x_0: {0,...,K − 1}
        := uni[{0,...,K − 1}]
  input x_{N−1}: {0,...,K − 1}

transitions
  pre x_0 = x_{N−1}
  eff x_0 := x_0 + 1 mod K
```

Fig. 1. SA models for token ring. *Left:* processes $i = 1 \ldots N-1$, *Right* process $i = 0$.

The parallel composition operation on SA is used for building models of distributed systems where several processes execute concurrently and communicate through shared input variables. Roughly, the composed SA is obtained by taking the union of the variables of the component automata and merging the transitions.

Definition 2. *Two SA are* compatible *if they have disjoint set of state variables. Given a pair of compatible SA $\mathcal{A}_1$ and $\mathcal{A}_2$ their* composition, *denoted by $\mathcal{A}_1 \| \mathcal{A}_2$, is defined as the structure $(U, X, \bar{\mu}, \rightarrow)$, where (1) $X = X_1 \cup X_2$, (2) $U = (U_1 \cup U_2) \setminus X$, (3) $\bar{\mu} = \bar{\mu}_1 \times \bar{\mu}_2$, and (4) $\rightarrow$ is defined as follows: for each $\mathbf{u} \in Val(U), \mathbf{x} \in Val(X), \mu \in \mathcal{P}(Val(X))$, $(\mathbf{u}, \mathbf{x}) \rightarrow \mu$ iff for each $i \in \{1, 2\}$ $((\mathbf{u}, \mathbf{x}) \lceil U_i, (\mathbf{u}, \mathbf{x}) \lceil X_i) \rightarrow_i \mu_i \lceil X_i$.*

It is easy to check that (finite, pure, deterministic) SA are closed under composition. The composition operation is inductively extended to multiple SA in the obvious way. A particular probabilistic transition $\mathbf{u}, \mathbf{x} \rightarrow \mu$ of the composed stochastic automaton $\mathcal{A} = \mathcal{A}_1 \| \mathcal{A}_2$ is said to be *active with respect to* $\mathcal{A}_1$ if $\mu \lceil X_1 \neq \delta_{\mathbf{x} \lceil X_1}$.

Example 2. The overall token-ring system $\mathsf{TR}(N, K)$ is specified as composition of $\mathsf{TR}(N, K, 0) \| \mathsf{TR}(N, K, 1) \| \ldots \mathsf{TR}(N, K, N-1)$. We define the following functions which will be useful later:

$$token(\mathbf{x}, i) = (i = 0 \ \wedge \ \mathbf{x}.x_0 = \mathbf{x}.x_{N-1}) \vee (i \neq 0 \ \wedge \ \mathbf{x}.x_i \neq \mathbf{x}.x_{i-1})$$
$$hastoken(\mathbf{x}) = \{i \mid token(\mathbf{x}, i)\}, \quad legal(\mathbf{x}) = (|hastokens(\mathbf{x})| = 1).$$

Here $\mathbf{x}$ is a valuation of all the variables of TR and $i \in \{0, \ldots, N-1\}$.

2.2 Incessant Fault Models

We introduce two models for random incessant faults. These faults introduce additional probabilistic transitions in a SA $\mathcal{A}$ which capture the effect of the faults on state variables of $\mathcal{A}$. Update faults capture (possibly transient) faults in the memory, disk drives, network interface cards, while sleep-update faults capture the effects of stochastic disturbances such as transient hardware faults, power surges, cosmic rays, and corruption of messages. First, we define how incessant faults transform the SA models for individual processes. In the *update(U)* fault model, whenever a SA $\mathcal{A}$ performs a computation and sets new values to its state variables, with some probability a fault occurs and the variable is set to an arbitrary value.

Definition 3. *Given a SA $\mathcal{A}$, the* U-faulty *version of $\mathcal{A}$ with rate $\epsilon \in (0,1]$ is a SA $\mathcal{B} = (X_{\mathcal{B}}, U_{\mathcal{B}}, \bar{\mu}_{\mathcal{B}}, \rightarrow_{\mathcal{B}})$, where $U_{\mathcal{B}} = U_{\mathcal{A}}$, $X_{\mathcal{B}} = X_{\mathcal{A}}$, $\bar{\mu}_{\mathcal{B}} = \bar{\mu}_{\mathcal{A}}$, and $\rightarrow_{\mathcal{B}}$ is defined as follows: for every $(\mathbf{u}, \mathbf{x}) \rightarrow_{\mathcal{A}} \mu$ where $\mu \neq \delta_{\mathbf{x}}$, $(\mathbf{u}, \mathbf{x}) \rightarrow_{\mathcal{B}} \mu'$, where for every $\mathbf{x}' \in Val(X)$, $\mu'(\mathbf{x}')$ is defined as $(1-\epsilon)\mu(\mathbf{x}') + \frac{\epsilon}{|Val(X)|}$.*

It is clear from the above that if $\mathcal{A}$ is pure (also closed) then so is $\mathcal{B}$. Also, once $\mathcal{B}$ reaches a stable state, update faults do not occur. The above is the definition of U-faults for a single process; the faulty model for a complete distributed system is obtained by composing the transformed SA for the individual processes.

Sleep-update faults may affect the state of the system even after a stable state is reached: at every step, each state variable may be reset to an arbitrary value with some small probability.

Definition 4. *Given a SA $\mathcal{A}$, the* S/U-faulty *version of $\mathcal{A}$ with rate $\epsilon \in (0,1]$ is a SA $\mathcal{B} = (X_{\mathcal{B}}, U_{\mathcal{B}}, \bar{\mu}_{\mathcal{B}}, \rightarrow_{\mathcal{B}})$, where $U_{\mathcal{B}} = U_{\mathcal{A}}$, $X_{\mathcal{B}} = X_{\mathcal{A}}$, $\bar{\mu}_{\mathcal{B}} = \bar{\mu}_{\mathcal{A}}$, and $\rightarrow_{\mathcal{B}}$ is defined as follows: for every $(\mathbf{u}, \mathbf{x}) \rightarrow_{\mathcal{A}} \mu$, $(\mathbf{u}, \mathbf{x}) \rightarrow_{\mathcal{B}} \mu'$ where for every $\mathbf{x}' \in Val(X)$, $\mu'(\mathbf{x}') = (1-\epsilon)\mu(\mathbf{x}') + \frac{\epsilon}{|Val(X)|}$.*

Example 3. The pseudocode in Figure 2 specifies the version of TR_i under S/U-faults. The parameter ϵ serves as the rate for incessant faults. STR_i, $i \neq 0$, is a SA with set of state variables, input variables, and initial distribution identical to that of TR_i of Figure 1. The specification of the version with U-faults, denoted by UTR_i, is identical to STR_i, except that the second set of probabilistic transitions is absent. The code for the transitions specify the probabilistic transitions.

```
automaton STR(N,K:ℕ,const i ≠ 0, ε : (0,1))     transitions
variables                                          pre x_i = x_{i-1}
  state x_i: {0,...,K-1}                           eff x_i := x_{i-1} with prob (1-ε) +
         := uni[{0,...,K-1}]                              k : {0,...,K-1} with prob ε/K;
  input x_{i-1}: {0,...,K-1}
                                                   pre x_i = x_{i-1}
                                                   eff x_i := x_i with prob (1-ε) +
                                                          k : {0,...,K-1} with prob ε/K;
```

Fig. 2. TR with incessant sleep-update (S/U) faults

3 Token Ring

In this section, we analyze S/U-faulty and U-faulty version of Dijkstra's token ring algorithm $\mathsf{TR}(N, K)$ (see Figure 2). First, we use probabilistic model-checking to exactly verify quantitative properties of the faulty systems. These techniques are automatic and they provide exact answers to a rich class of quantitative questions; however, they do not scale to systems with large number of processes. Our second approach analyzes the Markov chain corresponding to these systems directly; this allows us to determine bounds on the probabilities of various events. This analysis enables us to prove properties of the faulty system with arbitrarily large number of processes assuming that the fault rates are not too large; specifically, we assume that faults are rare enough so that it is unlikely to see more than one fault during any single transition, but common enough that many faults may occur during a self-stabilization process.

Analysis for small N. Probabilistic model checking tools (including PRISM [12] and MRMC [13]) can be used for verifying quantitative properties of Stochastic Automata, Markov Chains, and Markov Decision Processes. Given (a) a description of the model and (b) a property, a model checker returns true or false depending on whether the property is satisfied in all states of the system or not. For probabilistic model checking, properties may include boolean predicates as well as quantitative statements about the probability of certain states and executions (paths). These properties are described using probabilistic extensions of temporal logics such as Probabilistic Computational Tree Logic (PCTL) [12], Continuous Stochastic Logic (CSL) [21], and QuaTEx [14].

For the token ring system under U-faults and S/U-faults we are interested in the following quantitative properties:

Steady State(SS). For each $k \in \{1, \dots, N\}$, define $SS(k)$ as the probability of the system being in any state $\mathbf{x}$ with $|hastokens(\mathbf{x})| = k$, where this probability is taken with respect to the invariant measure of the Markov chain.

Expected Stabilization Time (EST). For a state $\mathbf{y}$, define $L(\mathbf{y})$ to be the expected number of steps required to reach a state $\mathbf{x}$ satisfying $legal(\mathbf{x})$. The EST of an algorithm under a certain error model is then defined as $max_{\mathbf{y}} L(\mathbf{y})$. (N.B.: Under S/U-faults the legal states are no longer absorbing, so this quantity is more pertinent for U-faults.)

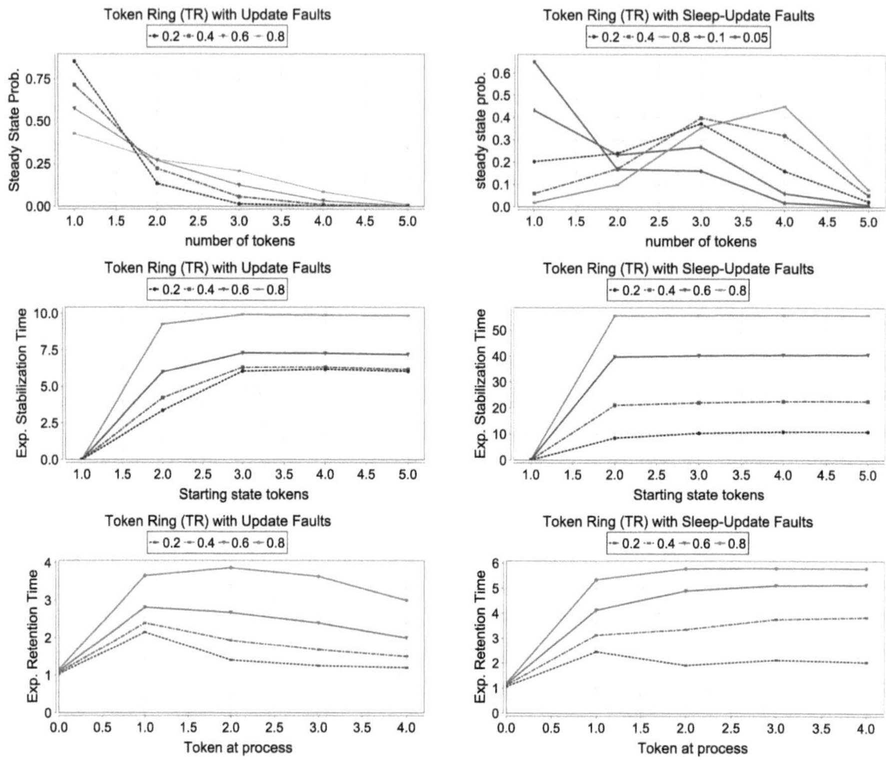

Fig. 3. *Top:* Steady state probabilities (SS) for TR under U-faults (*Left*) and S/U-faults (*Right*). *Bottom:* EST for TR under U-faults (*Left*) and S/U-faults (*Right*).

Expected Retention Time (ERT). Define $R(i)$ as the expected time to reach a state $\mathbf{y}$ with $\neg token(\mathbf{y}, i)$, given that we start at a state $\mathbf{x}$ with $token(\mathbf{x}, i)$, and define the ERT as $\max_i R(i)$.

The EST metric is useful in applications where just reaching a stable state allows a higher level application to make progress. For example, in a wireless system where graph coloring (see Section 4) is used for channel frequency assignments, reaching a stable coloring means that a node can send a packet successfully (at least for one round). We computed SS, EST, and ERT for $N = 4 \ldots 7$[1] with different fault rates $\epsilon = 0.2, 0.4, 0.6$ and 0.8. Typical results are shown in Figure 3. In the case of U-faults (UTR), as $\epsilon \to 0$ the probability of observing $k > 1$ tokens drops off and the probability of observing a single token approaches 1. In the case of S/U-faults (STR), the probability of observing $k > 1$ tokens also drops to 0 but at a slower rate. These observations comport with general results on limits of regularly-perturbed Markov chains [22].

[1] Modelchecking larger systems proved to be impractical with PRISM.

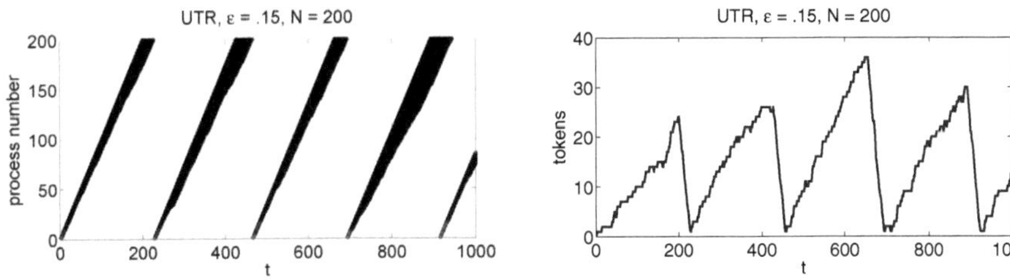

Fig. 4. Simulation of UTR for $N = 200, K = 201, \epsilon = 0.15$. *Left:* a raster plot of the locations of the tokens versus time. *Right:* Total number of tokens versus time; the number of tokens in each cycle grow to about $\epsilon N = 30$; this process is roughly periodic with period N.

For computing the expected stabilization times (EST) we assign a reward of 1 unit to every transition of the system and then we check for the following property in PRISM: $\mathbf{R}_{=?}[\mathbf{F}\ legal\ \{|hastokens| = k\}]$. Here $\mathbf{F}$ is the eventual operator and $\mathbf{R}$ is the expected reward operator in temporal logic. Both the EST and ERT increase with fault rates, and this increment is much more pronounced in STR.

Analysis for large N. For large N, we consider the Markov chain corresponding to UTR(N, K, ϵ) and analyze it directly; our observable Q will be the number of tokens.

We denote $t \in \mathbb{N}$ as the round number, T_t as the (random) number of tokens at round t, and L_t as the (random) subset of $\{0, \ldots, N-1\}$ giving the locations of the tokens at round t. Whenever a process changes value, it goes to the correct value with probability $1 - \epsilon(K-1)/K$ (there is a ϵ/K probability of a fault accidentally giving the right answer) and to any given incorrect state with probability $\delta := \epsilon/K$).

First consider the case of a single token in the system: $T_t = 1, L_t = \{n\}, n \neq 0$. Then $x_i = a$ for $i = 0, \ldots, n-1$ and $x_i = b$ for $i = n, \ldots, N-1$ for some $a \neq b$. The only process which will change is the nth, and without a fault the new value would be a; however, with faults we have $P(x_n \mapsto a) = 1 - \epsilon + \delta, P(x_n \mapsto b) = \delta, P(x_n \mapsto c) = (K-2)\delta$, where $c \neq a, c \neq b$. Changing to b is an error, but does not change the number of tokens, so the probability of having two tokens after the update is $(K-2)\delta$. Thus, if $T_t = 1 \wedge L_t = \{n\}, n \neq 0$, then $P(T_{t+1} = 1) = 1 - (K-2)\delta, P(T_{t+1} = 2) = (K-2)\delta$. On the other hand, if $L_t = \{0\}$, then the state of the system is $x_i = a$ for all i. The correct transition would be for $x_0 \mapsto a+1$, but even if there is an incorrect transition $x_0 \mapsto b \neq a+1$, the process still has one correct token.

Now consider the case of multiple tokens. We first assume that there are multiple tokens in a row, but away from the 0 process: $T_t = q, L_t = \{n, n+1, \ldots, n+q-1\}, 0 \notin L_t$. We show the result of one update, where we assume correct execution, and we denote by stars those states for which an error is possible:

process:	$n-1$	n	$n+1$	$n+2$	...	$n+q-2$	$n+q-1$	$n+q$
before:	x_{n-1}	x_n	x_{n+1}	x_{n+2}	...	x_{n+q-2}	x_{n+q-1}	x_{n+q-1}
after:	x_{n-1}	x^*_{n-1}	x^*_n	x^*_{n+1}	...	x^*_{n+q-3}	x^*_{n+q-2}	x_{n+q-1}

Consider the $(n+1)$st process; it should have a token under correct execution. But even if there is an update fault, unless the new value is one of the two values x_{n-1}, x_{n+1}, then it will still have a token. If the fault occurs at the $(n+1)$st process, then the probability of decreasing the number of tokens is either 2δ or δ (it is the latter if $x_{n-1} = x_{n+1}$). This holds true for all of the processes $n+1, \ldots, n+q-1$. The process cannot decrease the number of tokens if the update fault occurs at process n. Thus the probability of decreasing the number of tokens by one is, to leading order, bounded above by $(2q-1)\delta$. If the new value of process n is anything other than x_{n-1} or x_n, then this increases the number of tokens, so the probability of an increase in tokens is $(K-2)\delta$. Therefore, whenever $T_t = q, L_t = \{n, n+1, \ldots, n+q-1\}$, we have $P(T_{t+1} = q+1) = \delta(K-2)+O(\delta^2)$, and $P(T_{t+1} = q-1) \leq \delta(2q-1) + O(\delta^2)$.

Finally, consider the case where there are multiple tokens, but the set of tokens is not contiguous. Each contiguous block of tokens will act as if there are no other tokens in the system, since the entire algorithm is local. Thus, if we have l blocks of lengths q_l, with $\sum q_l = q$, then the probability of decreasing the number of tokens is then bounded above by $\delta \sum_l (2q_l-1)+O(\delta^2) \leq \epsilon(2q-1)/(K-1)+O(\epsilon^2)$, while the probability of increasing the number of tokens is $\delta \sum_l (K-2)+O(\delta^2) = \epsilon l(K-2)/(K-1)+O(\epsilon^2)$. In short, more blocks means more likelihood of gaining a token, since tokens are created on the boundaries of blocks of tokens.

Consider a run of tokens next to the 0 process, i.e. $L_t = \{N-q, \ldots, N-1\}$. If none of the values $x_{N-q}, \ldots, x_{N-1}$ are equal to x_0, then each of these values updates to its predecessor, but the 0 process would stay fixed (notice the 0 process is sleeping throughout). This ends with exactly one token at 0 after q updates. If, however, one of these tokens is equal to x_0, this creates an erroneous token; as these q updates progress, we create an erroneous token each time there is a coincidence between states $N-1$ and 0. Since the incorrect states are chosen randomly, we expect about q/K of these coincidences.

We are now prepared to describe the typical "life cycle" of UTR. Start with a single token at process 0. The earliest a token can cycle around and reach 0 again is after N computational steps, so we want to compute the number of tokens we would expect to have after N steps, or T_N. Using the bounds on tokens increasing or decreasing, define $\widetilde{T}_t$ as the stochastic process with $\widetilde{T}_0 = 1$ and

$$\begin{aligned} P(\widetilde{T}_{t+1} = \widetilde{T}_t + 1) &= \epsilon(K-2)/(K-1), \\ P(\widetilde{T}_{t+1} = \widetilde{T}_t - 1) &= \epsilon(2q-1)/(K-1), \end{aligned} \tag{1}$$

and $\widetilde{T}_{t+1} = \widetilde{T}_t$ otherwise. By Chernoff's Theorem [23, Theorem 9.3], we have that $\mathcal{P}(\widetilde{T}_t < T_t) \sim e^{\rho t}$ for some $\rho < 0$. Rescaling and passing to the limit [24,

Theorem 5.3] that, with probability exponentially close (in N) to one,

$$\widetilde{T}_N = \frac{N}{2}(1 - e^{-2\epsilon}) + o(N) \approx \epsilon N.$$

Thus if the system starts with a single token at the 0 process, the process will eventually generate a run of tokens of length $q \approx \epsilon N$, but this run will be effectively cleared up when it reaches process 0 — in fact, the mean number of tokens which survive after this run of tokens is absorbed by zero is about $q/K \approx \epsilon N/K < \epsilon$.

The simulations shown in Figure 4 corroborate the above analysis. These results are obtained by encoding a virtual token ring in Matlab. In every time-step, we first compute the correct transition. We then determine which processes could have a fault in this step (for the U model, the processes which updated; for the S/U model, all processes). For each processes which could have a fault, we chose an random number in [0,1]; if it was less than ϵ, then that process has an error, i.e. it is set to a randomly chosen value in $\{0, ..., K-1\}$.

Modified Token Ring algorithm TR2. The TR algorithm does not perform well in the presence of incessant faults, even if they are only U-faults. One insight gained in the probabilistic arguments above is that, in the U-fault model, multiple tokens tend to come in runs. A simple way to correct this is to change

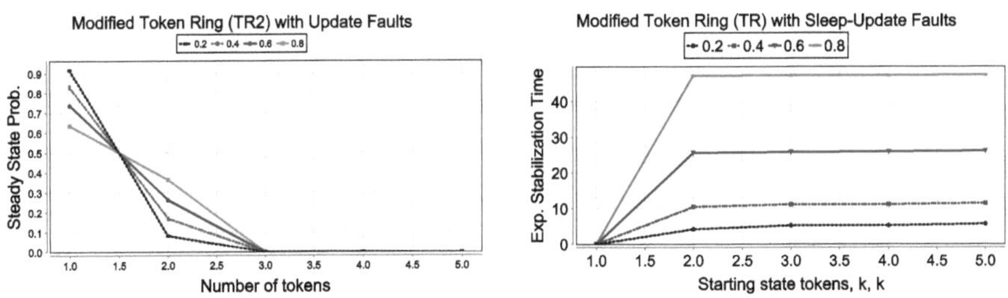

Fig. 5. *Left:* Steady state distribution of TR2 under update faults. *Right:* EST of TR2 under sleep-update faults for $N = 5$.

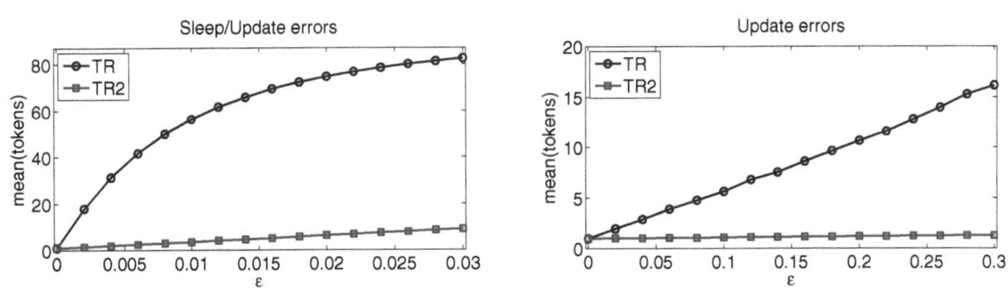

Fig. 6. Mean number of tokens in the steady state of TR and TR2 in both error models with $N = 100$. The mean is taken over 10^5 updates after the system is started in a correct state.

automaton TR2(N,K:$\mathbb{N}$,**const** $i > 1$)
variables
  state x_i: $\{0,\ldots,K-1\}$:= **uni**[$\{0,\ldots,K-1\}$]
  input x_{i-1}, x_{i-2}: $\{0,\ldots,K\}$
transitions
  pre $x_i \neq x_{i-1} \wedge x_{i-1} = x_{i-2}$
  eff $x_i := x_{i-1}$

Fig. 7. Modified token ring algorithm

the algorithm so that no process attempts to enter a state in which both it, and its predecessor, have a token. One such method is a "two lookbacks" version of TR, where each process looks at the inputs from two predecessors; we call this algorithm TR2. Basically, the algorithm looks to the two previous processors, and updates to its predecessor only if the previous two agree, otherwise it sleeps (see Figure 7). In Figure 5 we display the performance of TR2 with 5 processes using PRISM, and in Figure 6 for 100 processes using simulations. TR2 works significantly better than TR for both error models and in all parameter regimes.

4 Graph Coloring

We analyze S/U-faulty and U-faulty versions of the randomized graph coloring algorithm from [11]. The pseudocode in Figure 8 describes the self-stabilizing graph coloring algorithm. Fix an undirected graph G with N vertices. For each vertex $i \in \{0,\ldots,N-1\}$ in the graph, the set of neighbors (adjacent vertices) of i is denoted by NB_i, $K = \max_i |NB_i|$ is the maximum degree of G, and define the *palette* P of colors as the set $\{0,\ldots,K\}$. GC_i, $0 \leq i \leq N-1$, is a SA with the following components: (1) A set of state variables $X_i = \{x_i\}$, where x_i is of type P, and the value of x_i is the color of vertex i. (2) A set of input variables $U_i = \{x_j | j \in NB_i\}$, where each x_j is a variable of type P. NC_i is a derived variable; its value is the set of colors (values) of the neighbors of i. (3) An initial distribution $\bar{\mu}$ that is uniform over $Val(X_i)$, and (4) a set of probabilistic transitions we now define. We say that there is a collision at vertex i if the color of i is in NC_i. If there is a collision at i, process i picks a color in $P \setminus NC_i$ uniformly at random. Define

$$conflict(\mathbf{x}, i) = \exists\ j \in NB_i, \mathbf{x}.x_j = \mathbf{x}.x_i$$
$$hasconflict(\mathbf{x}) = \{i | conflict(\mathbf{x}, i)\}, \quad legal(\mathbf{x}) = (|hasconflict(\mathbf{x})| = 0).$$

For the graph coloring algorithm under U-faults and S/U-faults we are interested in the following quantitative properties:

Steady State(SS) : $SS(k)$ is the probability of the system being in a state $\mathbf{x}$ satisfying $|hasconflicts(\mathbf{x})| = k$, for some $k \in \{0,\ldots,N\}$.

Expected Stabilization Time (EST) : Starting from an arbitrary state with k conflicts, the maximum expected time to reach a legal state.

automaton GC(N:ℕ, P:set[ℕ], **const** $i \neq 0$)
variables
  state x_i: P := **uni**[P]
  input x_j: P **where** $j \in NB_i$

derived
  NC_i: Set[P] := $\{x_j | j \in NB_i\}$

transitions
  pre $x_i \in NC_i$
  eff x_i := **uni**[$P \setminus NC_i$]

Fig. 8. Self-stabilizing graph coloring algorithm *autoGC*

Analysis for Small N. Just as was done for the token ring system, our analysis for UGC and SGC for a small number of processes employs the PRISM and MRMC model checkers. We compute SS and EST for randomly generated graphs with $N = 4 \ldots 7$ with different error rates $\epsilon = 0.2, 0.4, 0.6$ and 0.8. Typical results are shown in Figures 9. For U-faults (UGC), the states with no conflicts have a steady-state probability of 1. This is because under U-faults, once a legal configuration is reached, the system undergoes no further transitions, i.e. the legal states are absorbing states of UGC. In the case of S/U-faults (SGC), the steady-state probability of observing $k > 0$ conflicts is positive but it drops to 0 as the error rate goes to 0. For example, we observe that with an error rate of $\epsilon = 0.2$, there is a 5% probability of observing 4 conflicts in the long run. This type of quantitative results will be useful for analyzing performance of higher-level applications that use graph coloring as a service, e.g., assignment of channels in a multi-channel wireless network. Both for UGC and SGC, the expected time to stabilize (EST) to a legal state decreases as the error rate decreases. As expected the value of the EST for SGC is higher than that of UGC.

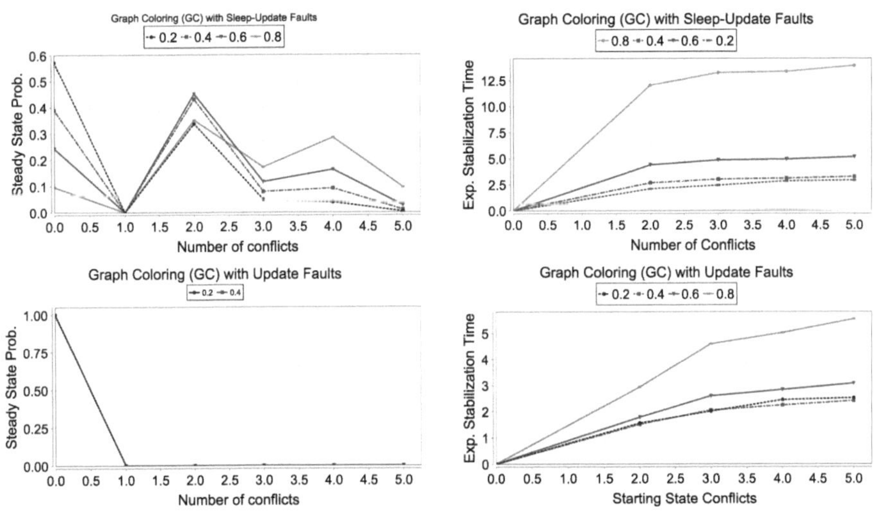

Fig. 9. GC(5, 4) under sleep-update (*Top*) faults SGC and update faults (*Bottom*) UGC. *Left:* Steady state distribution. *Right:* Expected Stabilization Times (EST).

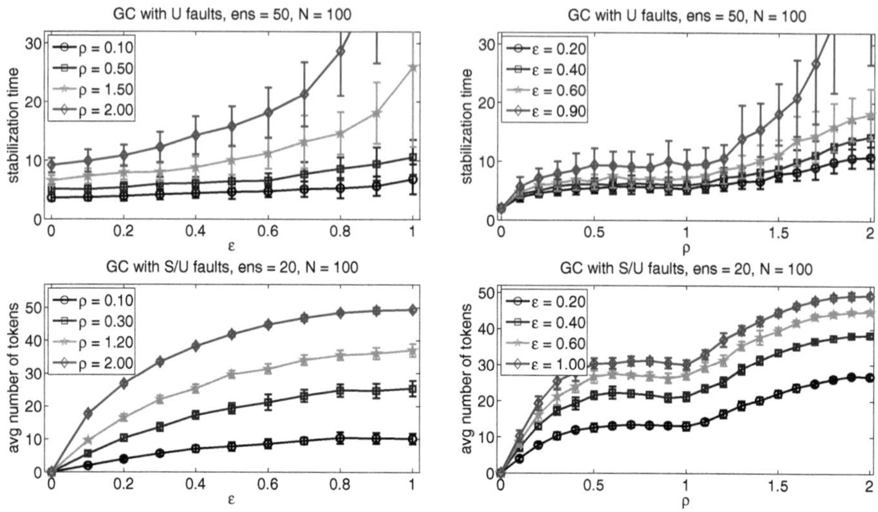

Fig. 10. Numerical simulation for UGC (*Top*) showing the time to reach a legal state and and SGC (*Bottom*) showing the mean number of collisions. In each case, we plot the same data versus both ϵ and ρ.

Analysis for Large N. We present numerical simulations for UGC and SGC in Figure 10. The obtain the undirected random graphs we choose N vertices uniformly at random in the unit disk, fix a *communication radius* $\rho \in [0, 2]$, and add edges between vertices that are within distance ρ of one another. Each data point corresponds to choosing an ensemble of *ens* graphs with a given ρ, each of which is simulated with fault rate ϵ; the point plotted is the ensemble mean and the error bars are the ensemble standard deviation. For UGC we plot the EST; for SGC, we instead plot the average number of collisions over a long run. In either case, a higher number is a signature of the poor performance. Of course, both of these metrics worsen when ϵ is increased, but there is a plateau (perhaps even a nonmonotonicity) for $\rho \in (1/2, 1)$. Surprisingly, in this range increasing the communication radius does not adversely affect performance.

References

1. Dolev, S.: Self-stabilization. MIT Press, Cambridge (2000)
2. Schneider, M.: Self-stabilization. ACM Comput. Surv. 25, 45–67 (1993)
3. Herman, T.: A comprehensive bibliography on self-stabilization. A Working Paper in the Chicago Journal of Theoretical Computer Science (2002), `http://www.cs.uiowa.edu/ftp/selfstab/bibliography/`
4. Steiner, C.: Bot in the delivery:KIVA systems. Forbes Magazine (2009), `http://www.forbes.com/forbes/2009/0316/040_bot_time_saves_nine.html`
5. of Energy, U. (Smart Grid), `http://www.oe.energy.gov/smartgrid.htm`

6. Akyildiz, L.F., Su, W., Sankarasubramaniam, Y., Cayirci, E.: A survey on sensor networks. IEEE Communications Magazine 40, 102–114 (2002)
7. Pelc, A., Peleg, D.: Feasibility and complexity of broadcasting with random transmission failures. Theoretical Computer Science 370, 279–292 (2007)
8. Kar, S., Moura, J.: Distributed average consensus in sensor networks with random link failures. In: Acoustics, Speech and Signal Processing, vol. 2, pp. II–1013–II–1016. IEEE, Los Alamitos (2007)
9. Nesterenko, M., Arora, A.: Local tolerance to unbounded byzantine faults. In: IEEE SRDS, pp. 22–31 (2002)
10. Dijkstra, E.W.: Self-stabilizing systems in spite of distributed control. Commun. ACM 17, 643–644 (1974)
11. Ghosh, S., Karaata, M.H.: A self-stabilizing algorithm for coloring planar graphs. Distrib. Comput. 7, 55–59 (1993)
12. Hinton, A., Kwiatkowska, M., Norman, G., Parker, D.: PRISM: A tool for automatic verification of probabilistic systems. In: Hermanns, H., Palsberg, J. (eds.) TACAS 2006. LNCS, vol. 3920, pp. 441–444. Springer, Heidelberg (2006)
13. Katoen, J.P., Kemna, T., Zapreev, I., Jansen, D.N.: Bisimulation minimisation mostly speeds up probabilistic model checking. In: Grumberg, O., Huth, M. (eds.) TACAS 2007. LNCS, vol. 4424, pp. 87–101. Springer, Heidelberg (2007)
14. Agha, G., Meseguer, J., Sen, K.: PMaude: Rewrite-based specification language for probabilistic object systems. In: 3rd Workshop on Quantitative Aspects of Programming Languages, QALP 2005 (2005)
15. Younes, H.: Ymer: A statistical model checker. In: Etessami, K., Rajamani, S.K. (eds.) CAV 2005. LNCS, vol. 3576, pp. 429–433. Springer, Heidelberg (2005)
16. Hermanns, H.: Interactive Markov Chains: The Quest for Quantified Quality. Springer, Heidelberg (2002)
17. Segala, R.: A compositional trace-based semantics for probabilistic automata. In: Lee, I., Smolka, S.A. (eds.) CONCUR 1995. LNCS, vol. 962, pp. 234–248. Springer, Heidelberg (1995)
18. Wu, S.H., Smolka, S., Stark, E.: Composition and behaviors of probabilistic I/O automata. Theoretical Computer Science 176, 1–38 (1997)
19. de Alfaro, L.: Formal Verification of Probabilistic Systems. PhD thesis, Stanford University, CA, Technical Report STAN-CS-TR-98-1601 (1997)
20. Canetti, R., Cheung, L., Kaynar, D., Liskov, M., Lynch, N., Pereira, O., Segala, R.: Task-structured Probabilistic I/O Automata. In: Proc. of the 8th Intl. Workshop on Discrete Event Systems – WODES 2006. IEEE catalog number 06EX1259 (2006)
21. Aziz, A., Sanwal, K., Singhal, V., Brayton, R.: Model-checking continuous-time markov chains. ACM Trans. Comput. Logic 1, 162–170 (2000)
22. Young, P.: The evolution of conventions. Econometrica 61, 57–84 (1993)
23. Billingsley, P.: Probability and Measure. John Wiley & Sons, New York (1995)
24. Shwartz, A., Weiss, A.: Large deviations for performance analysis. Chapman & Hall, London (1995)

Dependability Engineering of Silent Self-stabilizing Systems*

Abhishek Dhama[1], Oliver Theel[1], Pepijn Crouzen[2], Holger Hermanns[2], Ralf Wimmer[3], and Bernd Becker[3]

[1] System Software and Distributed Systems, University of Oldenburg, Germany
{abhishek.dhama,theel}@informatik.uni-oldenburg.de
[2] Dependable Systems and Software, Saarland University, Germany
{crouzen,hermanns}@cs.uni-saarland.de
[3] Chair of Computer Architecture, Albert-Ludwigs-University Freiburg, Germany
{wimmer,becker}@informatik.uni-freiburg.de

Abstract. Self-stabilization is an elegant way of realizing non-masking fault-tolerant systems. Sustained research over last decades has produced multiple self-stabilizing algorithms for many problems in distributed computing. In this paper, we present a framework to evaluate multiple self-stabilizing solutions under a fault model that allows intermittent transient faults. To that end, metrics to quantify the dependability of self-stabilizing systems are defined. It is also shown how to derive models that are suitable for probabilistic model checking in order to determine those dependability metrics. A heuristics-based method is presented to analyze counterexamples returned by a probabilistic model checker in case the system under investigation does not exhibit the desired degree of dependability. Based on the analysis, the self-stabilizing algorithm is subsequently refined.

1 Introduction

Self-stabilization has proven to be a valuable design concept for dependable systems. It allows the effective realization of non-masking fault-tolerant solutions to a problem in a particularly hostile environment: an environment subject to arbitrarily many transient faults potentially corrupting the self-stabilizing system's run-time state of registers and variables. Consequently, designing a self-stabilizing system is not an easy task, since many scenarios due to faults must correctly be handled beyond the fact that the system has to solve a given problem when being undisturbed by faults. The formal verification of a self-stabilizing solution to a given problem is therefore often quite complicated. It consists of a 1) convergence proof showing that the system eventually returns to a set of system states (called *safe* or *legal states*) where it solves the given problem and 2) a closure proof showing that once within the set of legal states, it does not leave this set voluntarily in the absence of faults occurring. Whereas the closure proof

* This work was supported by the German Research Foundation (DFG) under grant SFB/TR 14/2 "AVACS," www.avacs.org

R. Guerraoui and F. Petit (Eds.): SSS 2009, LNCS 5873, pp. 238–253, 2009.

is often not too complicated, the convergence proof may become extremely challenging. It requires some finiteness argument showing the return of the system to the legal state set in a finite number of computational steps in the absence of newly manifested faults.

As discussed, finding a self-stabilizing solution to a given problem as well as proving its self-stabilization property are generally not easy and present areas of agile research. But what, if multiple self-stabilizing solutions to a problem are already known? Which solution should be preferred and therefore be chosen? Clearly, many criteria do exists and their relevance depends on the concrete application scenario.

In this paper, we focus on dependability properties of those systems. For example: "Does the given self-stabilizing system exhibit a system availability of at least p?" with system availability being only an example of a dependability metrics. Other metrics are, e.g., reliability, mean time to failure, and mean time to repair. Based on the evaluation of relevant dependability metrics, a decision should be taken of which solution out of the set of present solutions should be chosen and put to work for ones purposes. By building on [1], we present useful dependability metrics for differentiating among self-stabilizing solutions and show how to evaluate them. For this purpose, we propose the modeling of a self-stabilizing algorithm together with the assumed fault model in terms of a discrete-time Markov decision process or a discrete-time Markov chain. Whereas the former modeling allows – with the help of a probabilistic model checker – to reason about the behavior of the system under any fair scheduler, the latter modeling is suitable if concrete information about the scheduler used in the system setting is available. The self-stabilizing solution exhibiting the best dependability metrics value can then easily be identified and used.

Furthermore, we show a possible way out of the situation where all available self-stabilizing solutions to a given problem have turned out to fail in the sense described above: if the dependability property under investigation cannot be verified for a particular system, then an automatically generated counterexample (being a set of traces for which, as a whole, the property does not hold) is prompted. By analyzing the counterexample, the self-stabilizing algorithm is then refined and again model-checked. This refinement loop is repeated until the dependability property is finally established or a maximal number of refinement loops has been executed.

In the scope of the paper, wrt. abstraction scheme and system refinement, we restrict ourselves to *silent* self-stabilizing algorithms and a dependability metrics being a notion of limiting (system) availability called *unconditional limiting availability* in a system environment where faults "continuously keep on occurring." Silent self-stabilizing algorithms do not switch among legal states in the absence of faults. Unconditional limiting availability is a generalization of limiting availability in the sense that any initial state of the system is allowed. Finally, with the more general fault model, we believe that we can analyze self-stabilizing systems in a more realistic setting: contrarily to other approaches, we do not analyze the system only after the last fault has already occurred but always allow faults to hamper with the system state.

The paper is structured as follows: in Section 2, we give an overview of related work. Then, in Section 3, we introduce useful dependability metrics for self-stabilizing systems. Additionally, we state the model used for dependability metrics evaluation based on discrete-time Markov decision processes or discrete-time Markov chains. Section 4 describes the refinement loop and thus, dependability engineering based on probabilistic model-checking, counterexample generation, counterexample analysis, and silent self-stabilizing system refinement along with an abstraction scheme to overcome scalability problems. Section 5, finally, concludes the paper and sketches our future research.

2 Related Work

The body of literature is replete with efforts towards the engineering of fault-tolerant systems to increase dependability. In [2], a formal method to design a – in a certain sense – multitolerant system is presented. The method employs *detectors* and *correctors* to add fault tolerance with respect to a set of fault classes. A detector checks whether a state predicate is satisfied during execution. A corrector ensures that – in the event of a state predicate violation – the program will again satisfy the predicate. It is further shown in [3] that the detector-corrector approach can be used to obtain masking fault-tolerant from non-masking fault-tolerant systems. But, despite its elegance, the fault model used in their applications admits only transient faults.

Ghosh *et al.* described in [4] an approach to engineer a self-stabilizing system in order to limit the effect of a fault. A transformer is provided to modify a non-reactive self-stabilizing system such that the system stabilizes in constant time if a single process is faulty. However, there is a trade-off involved in using the transformer as discussed in [5]. The addition of such a transformer to limit the recovery time from a single faulty process might lead to an increase in stabilization time.

A compositional method, called "cross-over composition," is described in [6] to ensure that an algorithm self-stabilizing under a specific scheduler converges under an arbitrary scheduler. This is achieved by composing the target "weaker" algorithm with a so-called "strong algorithm" such that actions of the target algorithm are synchronized with the strong algorithm. The resultant algorithm is self-stabilizing under any scheduler under which the strong algorithm is proven to be self-stabilizing. However, the properties of the strong algorithm determine the class of schedulers admissible by the composed algorithm.

Recent advances in counterexample generation for stochastic model checking has generated considerable interest in using the information given by the counterexamples for debugging or optimizing systems. An interactive visualization tool to support the debugging process is presented in [7]. The tool renders violating traces graphically along with state information and probability mass. It also allows the user to selectively focus on a particular segment of the violating traces. However, it does not provide any heuristics or support to modify the system in order to achieve the desired dependability property. Thus, the user must modify systems by hand without any tool support. In addition to these shortcomings, only models based on Markov chains are handled by the tool. In particular, models containing non-determinism cannot be visualized.

We will next describe the method to evaluate dependability metrics of self-stabilizing systems with an emphasis on silent self-stabilizing systems.

3 Dependability Evaluation of Self-stabilizing Systems

We now present a procedure with tool support for evaluating dependability metrics of self-stabilizing systems. A self-stabilizing BFS spanning tree algorithm given in [8] is used as a working example throughout the sections to illustrate each phase of our proposed procedure. Note that the method nevertheless is applicable to any other self-stabilizing algorithm as well.

3.1 Dependability Metrics

The definition and enumeration of metrics to quantify the dependability of a self-stabilizing system is the linchpin of any approach for dependability evaluation. This becomes particularly critical in the case of self-stabilizing systems as the assumptions made about the frequency of faults may not hold true in a given implementation scenario. That is, faults may be intermittent and the temporal separation between them, at times, may not be large enough to allow the system to converge. In this context *reliability*, *instantaneous availability*, and *limiting availability* have been defined for self-stabilizing systems in [1]. An important part of these definitions is the notion of a system doing “something useful.” A self-stabilizing system is said to do something useful if it satisfies the safety predicate (which in turn specifies the set of legal states) with respect to which it has been shown to be self-stabilizing.

We now define the mean time to repair (MTTR) and the mean time to failure (MTTF) along with new metrics called *unconditional instantaneous availability* and *generic instantaneous availability* for self-stabilizing systems. These metrics are *measures* (in a measure theoretic sense) provided the system under study can be considered as a stochastic process. It is natural to consider discrete-state stochastic processes, where the set of states is divided into a set of operational states (“up states”) and of disfunctional states (“down states”).

The basic definition of instantaneous availability at time t quantifies the probability of being in an “up state” at time t [9]. Some variations are possible with respect to the assumption of the system being initially available, an assumption that is not natural in the context of self-stabilizing systems, since these are designed to stabilize from any initial state. Towards that end, we define *generic instantaneous availability* and *unconditional instantaneous availability* and apply them in the context of self-stabilizing systems. Our natural focus is on systems evolving in discrete time, thus where the system moves from states to states in steps. Time is thus counted in steps, and s_i refers to the state occupied at time i.

Generic instantaneous availability at step k $A_{\mathcal{G}}(k)$ is defined as probability $Pr(s_k \models \mathcal{P}_{\text{up}} \mid s_0 \models \mathcal{P}_{\text{init}})$, where $\mathcal{P}_{\text{up}}$ is a predicate that specifies the states where the system is operational, doing something useful, $\mathcal{P}_{\text{init}}$ specifies the initial states.

Unconditional instantaneous availability at step k $A_{\mathcal{U}}(k)$ is defined as the probability $Pr(s_k \models \mathcal{P}_{\text{up}} \mid s_0 \models \text{true})$.

Unconditional instantaneous availability is the probability that the system is in "up state" irrespective of the initial state. Generic instantaneous availability is the probability that the system is in "up state" provided it was started in some specific set of states. As k approaches ∞ – provided the limit exists – instantaneous, unconditional, and generic instantaneous availability are all equal to limiting availability.

The above definitions can be readily used in the context of silent self-stabilizing systems by assigning $\mathcal{P}_{\text{up}} = \mathcal{P}_{\mathcal{S}}$, where $\mathcal{P}_{\mathcal{S}}$ is the safety predicate of the system. Hence, unconditional instantaneous availability of a silent self-stabilizing system is the probability that the system satisfies its safety predicate at an instant k irrespective of its starting state. Generic instantaneous availability of a silent self-stabilizing system is the probability of satisfying the safety predicate provided it started in any initial state characterized by predicate $\mathcal{P}_{\text{init}}$.

Mean time to repair (MTTR) of a self-stabilizing system is the average time (measured in the number of computation steps) taken by a self-stabilizing system to reach a state which satisfies the safety predicate $\mathcal{P}_{\mathcal{S}}$. The average is taken over all the executions which start in states not satisfying the safety predicate $\mathcal{P}_{\mathcal{S}}$. As mentioned earlier, a system has "recovered" from a burst of transient faults when it reaches a safe state. It is also interesting to note that the MTTR mirrors the average case behavior under a given implementation scenario unlike bounds on convergence time that are furnished as part of convergence proofs of self-stabilizing algorithms.

Mean time to failure (MTTF) of a self-stabilizing system is the average time (again measured in the number of computation steps) before a system reaches an unsafe state provided it started in a safe state. This definition may appear trivial for a self-stabilizing system as the notion of MTTF is void given the closure property of self-stabilizing systems. However, under relaxed fault assumptions, the closure is not guaranteed because transient faults may "throw" the system out of the safe states once it has stabilized. Thus, MTTF may well be finite.

There is an interplay between MTTF and MTTR of a self-stabilizing system since its limiting availability also agrees with MTTF/(MTTR + MTTF) [9]. That is, a particular value of MTTF is an environment property over which a system designer has often no control, but the value of MTTR, in the absence of on-going faults, is an intrinsic property of a given implementation of a self-stabilizing algorithm alongwith the scheduler used (synonymously referred to as self-stabilizing *system*). One can modify the self-stabilizing system leading to a possible decrease in average convergence time. The above expression gives a compositional way to fine tune the limiting availability by modifying the MTTR value of a self-stabilizing system despite a possible inability to influence the value of MTTF.

3.2 Model for Dependability Evaluation

The modeling of a self-stabilizing system for performance evaluation is the first step of the toolchain. We assume that the self-stabilizing system consists of a number of concurrent components which run in parallel. These components cooperate to bring the system to a stable condition from any starting state. Furthermore, we assume that at any time a fault may occur which brings the system to an arbitrary state.

Guarded command language. We can describe a self-stabilizing system using a *guarded command language* (GCL) which is essentially the language used by the probabilistic model checker PRISM [10].

The model of a component consists of a finite set of variables describing the state of the component, initial valuations for the variables and a finite set of guarded commands describing the behavior (state change) of the component. Each guarded command has the form

```
[label] guard -> prob1 : update1 + ... + probn : updaten
```

Intuitively, if the guard (a Boolean expression over the set of variables) is satisfied, then the command can be executed. One branch of the command is selected probabilistically and the variables are updated accordingly. Deterministic behaviour may be modeled by specifying only a single branch. The commands in the model may be labeled. Figure 1 gives a sketch of a self-stabilizing BFS algorithm of [8] with three components representing a process each. Fault inducing actions are embedded in every component. There are a number of important properties inherent in the model in Figure 1. First, at every step, it is open whether a fault step or a computational step occurs. If a computational step occurs, it is also unclear which component executes a command. Finally, in the case of a fault step, it is unclear which fault occurs, i.e. what the resulting state of the system will be. The model in Figure 1 is thus *non-deterministic* since it does not specify how these choices must be resolved.

Schedulers. To resolve the non-determinism in the model, and thus to arrive at a uniquely defined stochastic process, one usually employs *schedulers*. In essence, a scheduler is an abstract entity resolving the non-determinism among the possible choice options at each time step. A set of schedulers is called a *scheduler class*. For a given scheduler class, one them aims at deriving worst-case and best-case results for the metric considered, obtained by ranging over all stochastic processes induced by the individual schedules in the class. This computation is performed by the probabilistic model checking machinery.

Schedulers can be characterized in many ways, based on the power they have: A scheduler may make decisions based on only the present state (*memoryless* scheduler) or instead based on the entire past history of states visited (*history-dependent* scheduler). A scheduler may be *randomized* or simply be *deterministic*. A randomized scheduler may use probabilities to decide between choice options, while deterministic ones may not. For instance, we can consider the class of randomized schedulers that, when a fault step occurs, chooses the particular fault randomly with a uniform distribution. When adding this assumption to the GCL specification of the fault model, the resulting system model becomes partially probabilistic as shown in Figure 2 for the root module. It is still non-deterministic with respect to the question whether a fault step occurs, or which component performs a step. Here, we encoded the probabilistic effect of the schedulers considered inside the GCL specification, while the remaining non-determinism is left to the background machinery. It would also be possible to specify a choice according to a probability distribution that is obtained using information collected from the history of states visited (*history-dependent* scheduler), or according to a distribution gathered from statistics about faults occuring in real systems.

```
module root
  variable x02,x01 : int ...;
  [stepRoot] true -> 1: x01' = 0 & x02'=0
  [faultRoot1] true -> 1: x01' = 0 & x02'=1
       ...
  [faultRootn] true -> 1: x01' = 2 & x02'=2 ;
 endmodule

module proc1
  variable x10,x12,dis1 : int ...;
  [stepProc1] true -> 1: (dis1'=
       min( min(dis1,x01,x21)+1,N))
      & (x10' = ...) & (x12'=...) ;
  [faultProc11] true -> 1: (dis1'=0)
      &(x10'=0)&(x12'=1)
                          ...
  [faultProc1n] true -> 1:(dis1'=2)
      &(x10'=2)&(x12'=2);
endmodule

module proc2
  ...
endmodule
```

Fig. 1. Non-deterministic self-stabilizing BFS algorithm with faults

Markov decision processes. The formal semantics of a GCL model is a *Markov decision process* (MDP). A MDP is a tuple $\mathscr{D} = \{\mathtt{S}, \mathtt{A}, P\}$ where $\mathtt{S}$ is the set of states, $\mathtt{A}$ is the set of possible actions, and $P \subseteq \mathtt{S} \times \mathtt{A} \times \mathit{Dist}(\mathtt{S})$ is the transition relation that gives for a state and an action the resulting probability distribution that determines the next state. In the literature, MDPs are often considered equipped with a reward structure, which is not needed in the scope of this paper.

Intuitively, we can derive a MDP from a GCL model in the following way. The set of states of the MDP is the set of all possible valuations of the variables in the GCL model. The set of actions is the set of labels encountered in the GCL model. For each state we find a set of commands for which the guard is satisfied. Each such command then gives us an entry in the transition relation where the action is given by the label associated with the command and the resulting distribution for the next state is determined by the distribution over the updates in the GCL description. In Figure 3 (left), we see an example of a MDP state with its outgoing transitions for our example model from Figure 1 (where the choice of fault is determined probabilistically as in Figure 2). We see that in every state either a fault may occur, after which the resulting state is chosen probabilistically or a computational step may occur. The choice between faults or different computational steps is still non-deterministic.

```
module root
  variable x02,x01 : int ...;
  [stepRoot] true -> 1: x01' = 0 & x02'=0
  [faultRoot] true -> 1/n: x01' = 0 & x02'=1 +
                       ...
                       1/n: x01' = 2 & x02'=2;
 endmodule
```

Fig. 2. Root module with a randomized scheduler for n distinct faults

Markov chain. When we consider a specific scheduler that resolves all non-deterministic choices either deterministically or probabilistically, we find a model whose semantics is a particular kind of MDP, namely that has for each state s exactly one transition (s, a, μ) in the transition relation P. If we further disregard the actions of the transitions, we arrive at a model which can be interpreted as a *Markov chain.* We define a Markov chain as a tuple $\mathscr{D} = \{\mathtt{S}, P\}$ where $\mathtt{S}$ is the set of states and $P \subseteq \mathtt{S} \rightarrow \mathit{Dist}(\mathtt{S})$ is the transition relation that gives for a state the probability distribution that determines the next state. A Markov chain is a stochastic process which is amenable to analysis.

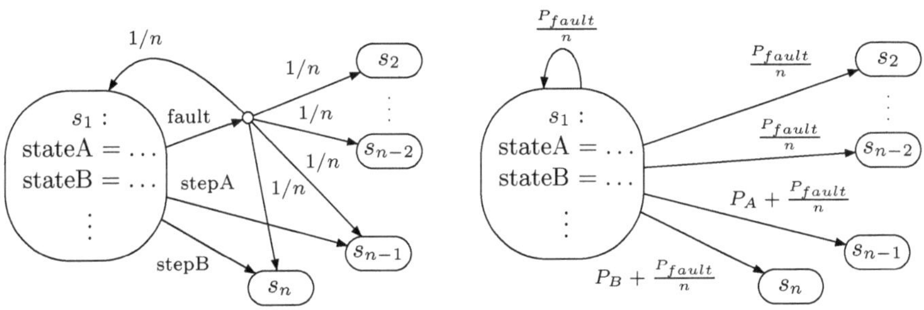

Fig. 3. Segment of a self-stabilizing system modeled as an MDP (left) or a Markov Chain (right)

For our example, we can find a Markov chain model if we assume a scheduler that chooses probabilistically whether a fault occurs, which component takes a step in case of normal computation and which fault occurs in case of a fault step. Figure 4 shows the probabilistic model for the root module and Figure 3 (right) shows part of the resulting model, where P_A, P_B and P_{fault} denote the probabilities that, respectively, component A takes a step, component B takes a step, or a fault occurs.

```
module root
  variable x02,x01 : int ...;
  [stepRoot] true -> STEP_PROB: x01' = 0 & x02'=0+
                  (1-STEP_PROB)/n: x01' = 0 & x02'=1+
                  ...
                  (1-STEP_PROB)/n: x01' = 2 & x02'=2;
 endmodule
```

Fig. 4. Root module modeled to have a fully randomized scheduler

Choosing a scheduler class. Scheduler classes form a hierarchy, induced by set inclusion. For MDPs, the most general class is the class of history-dependent randomized schedulers. Deterministic schedulers can be considered as specific randomized schedulers that schedule with probability 1 only, and memoryless schedulers can be considered as history-dependent schedulers that ignore the history apart from the present state.

In the example discussed above (Figure 2 and Figure 4), we have sketched how a scheduler class can be shrinked by adding assumptions about a particular probabilistic behaviour. We distinguish two different strategies of doing so: *Restricted resolution* refers to scheduler classes where some non-determinstic options are pruned away. In *partially probabilistic resolution* some of the choices are left non-deterministic, while others are randomized (as in Figure 3, left). A *fully randomized* scheduler class contains a single scheduler only, resolves all non-determinism probabilistically. Recall that deterministic schedulers are specific randomized schedulers. Figure 5 provides an overview of the different resolution strategies.

Choosing a class of schedulers to perform analysis on is not trivial. If we choose too large a class, probability estimations can become so broad as to be unusable (e.g. the model checker may conclude that a particular probability measure lies somewhere between 0 and 1). Choosing a smaller class of schedulers results in tighter bounds for our probability measures. However, choosing a small scheduler class requires very precise information about the occurrence of faults and the scheduling of processes. Furthermore, such analysis would only inform us about one very particular case. A more general result is usually desired, that takes into account different fault models or scheduling schemes.

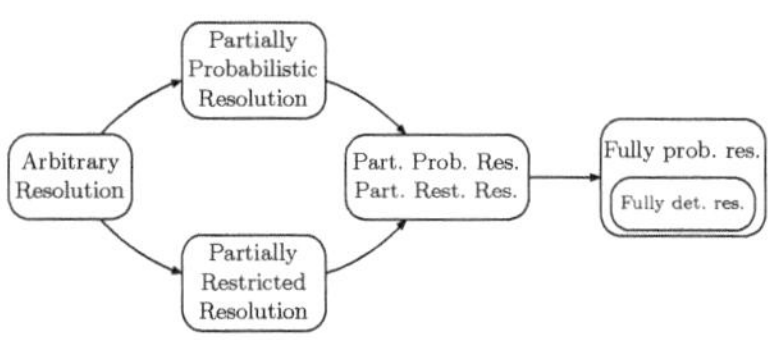

Fig. 5. Overview of different resolution strategies

More advanced scheduler classes are also possible. For the scheduling of n processes, we allow only those schedules where each process performs a computational step at least every k steps. This is akin to assuming that the fastest process is at most twice as fast as the slowest one. While such assumptions are interesting to investigate, they also make analysis more difficult. To implement such a *k-bounded* scheduler, it is required to track the last computational step of every process. Though, the size of the state space does not scale well for large n and k.

Model checking. A model checker, such as PRISM [10] may be employed to answer reachability questions for a given MDP model. The general form of such a property is $P_{<p}\left[A \cup^{\leq k} B\right]$ which checks whether the probability that a state with property B is reached within k steps via a path consisting of states in which A holds only, is smaller than p. In this way instantaneous availability properties can be checked. If the property does not hold, a *counterexample* is generated.

We next explain the methods to re-engineer a self-stabilizing system based on a counterexample provided by a probabilistic model checker.

4 Dependability Engineering for Self-stabilizing Systems

In order to meet the quality of service requirements, the counterexample returned by the model checker can be used to optimize the system. An important distinction between counterexample generation of qualitative model checking versus quantitative model checking is the fact that quantitative model checking returns a *set of paths* as counterexample. This distinction needs to be taken into account while devising a method for exploiting the counterexample. We explain a heuristics-based method to modify a system given such a set of paths. The self-stabilizing BFS spanning tree algorithm implemented on a three-process graph under a fully randomized scheduler is used as an illustrative example. We used the stochastic bounded model checker `sbmc` [11] alongwith PRISM to generate counterexamples. Please note that this particular method applies beneficently only to scenarios where faults follow a uniform probability distribution over the system states.

4.1 Counterexample Structure

An understanding of the structure of the elements of the set of paths returned as counterexample is important to devise a method to modify the system. In the scope of this section, we are interested in achieving a specific unconditional instantaneous availability $A_{\mathcal{U}}(k)$ which is basically the step-bounded reachability probability of a legal state. However, the tool used to generate the counterexample can only generate counterexamples for queries that contain an upper bound on the probability of reaching a set of certain states. Therefore, a reformulated query is presented to the model checker. Instead of asking queries of the form "Is the probability of reaching a legal state within k steps greater than p?," i.e. $P_{>p}\left[\text{true} \cup^{\leq k} \text{legal}\right]$ the following query is given to the model checker: $P_{\leq(1-p)}\left[\neg\text{legal}\, \mathcal{W}^{\leq k}\, \text{false}\right]$. The reformulated query ascertains whether the probability of *reaching non-legal* states with in k steps is *less than* $1-p$. The probability p used in the queries is equal to the desired value of $A_{\mathcal{U}}(k)$, namely unconditional instantaneous availability at step k.

In case the probability of reaching non-legal states is larger than the desired threshold value, the probabilistic model checker returns a set of paths of length k. This set consists of k-length paths such that all the states in the path are non-legal states. The probability of these paths is larger than the threshold specified in the query. This set of paths constitutes a counterexample because the paths as a whole violate the property being model-checked.

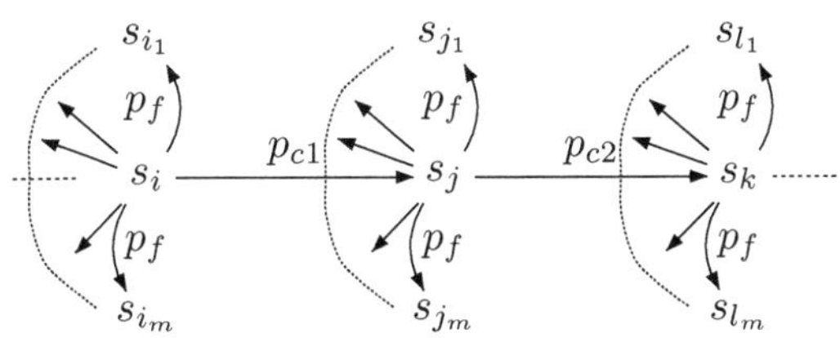

In order to devise a system optimization method we "dissect" a generic path – annotated with transition probabilities – of length 2 (shown below) for a system with a uniform fault probability distribution.

p_{c1} and p_{c2} are probabilities of state transitions due to a computation step whereas p_f is the probability of a fault step. Note that due to the uniform fault probability distribution there is a pair of fault transitions between each pair of system states. If the above path is seen in contrast with a fault-free computation of length 2, one can identify the reason for the loss of probability mass. Consider a path that reaches state s_k from state s_i in two steps.

$$\cdots\cdots\; s_i \xrightarrow{1} s_j \xrightarrow{1} s_k \;\cdots\cdots$$

Such a path can be extracted from a MDP-based model by choosing a specific scheduler. It results in a fully deterministic model because of the absence of fault steps, thereby leaving the model devoid of any stochastic behavior. The probability associated with each of the two transitions is 1 and therefore the probability of the path is 1 as well [12]. However, the addition of fault steps to the model reduces probabilities associated with computation steps and thus, reduces the probability of the path. In the light of this discussion, we next outline a method to modify the system in order to achieve a desired value of $A_{\mathcal{U}}(k)$.

4.2 Counterexample-Guided System Re-engineering

We consider the set of paths of length k returned by the probabilistic model checker. In Step 1, we remove the extraneous paths from the counterexample. In Step 2, we add and remove certain transitions to increase $A_{\mathcal{U}}(k)$.

Step 1. As explained above, a counterexample consists of all those paths of length k whose probability in total is greater than the threshold value. This set also consists of those k-length paths where some of the transitions are fault steps. The number of possible paths grows combinatorially as k increases because the uniform fault model adds transitions between every pair of states. For example, as there are (fault) transitions between each pair of states, the probabilistic model checker can potentially return all the transitions of the Markov chain for $k = 1$. Hence, the problem becomes intractable even for small values of k. Therefore, such paths are removed from the set of paths. The resultant set of paths consists of only those k-length paths where all the transitions are due to computation steps. The self-stabilizing BFS spanning tree algorithm was model checked to verify whether the probability of reaching the legal state within three steps is higher than 0.65. The example system did not satisfy the property and thus, the conjunction of PRISM and `sbmc` returned a set of paths as counterexample. This set contains 190928 paths in total out of which a large number of paths consist of fault steps only. An instance of such a path is shown below.

$$\langle 2,2,1,2,2,1,1,2\rangle \rightarrow \langle 2,2,1,2,2,0,0,0\rangle \rightarrow \langle 2,2,0,0,0,0,0,0\rangle \rightarrow \langle 2,2,0,0,0,0,0,1\rangle$$

A state in the path is represented as a vector $s_i = \langle x_{01}, x_{02}, x_{12}, x_{10}, \mathrm{dis}_1, x_{20}, x_{21}, \mathrm{dis}_2\rangle$ where x_{ij} is the communication register owned by process proc_i and dis_i is the local variable of proc_i. The removal of such extraneous paths lead to a set of 27 paths.

Step 2. The probability of a path without a loop is the product of the individual transition probabilities. Due to the presence of fault steps and associated transition probabilities, one cannot increase the probability measure of the path without decreasing the path length. Consider a path

$$s_i \xrightarrow{p_i} s_j \xrightarrow{p_j} s_k \xrightarrow{p_k} s_l$$

and the modified path obtained by 1) adding a direct transition between states s_i and s_l and 2) disabling the transition between states s_i and s_j.

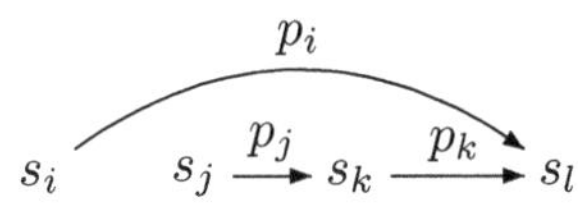

The addition of a direct transition to state s_l and thereby the reduction of the path length leads to an increase in probability of reaching state s_l from state s_i. The method thus strives to increase the value of $A_{\mathcal{U}}(k)$ by reducing the length of the paths. As we have no control over the occurrence of fault steps, such transitions can neither be removed nor the probabilities associated with these transitions be altered. Thus, in essence, we increase the number of paths with length less than k and decrease k-length paths to the legal state.

The paths in the counterexample are arranged in decreasing order of probability. The following procedure is applied to all the paths starting with the most probable path. We begin with the first state s_0 of a path. In order to ensure that a transition is feasible between s_i and s_j, we determine the variables whose valuations need to be changed to reach state s_j from state s_i. A transition is deemed feasible for addition to a system if the variable valuations can be changed in a single computation step under a specific sequential randomized scheduler. If a transition from state s_0 to the legal state s_l is deemed feasible, then a guarded command to effect that state transition is added to the system. In case such a direct transition is not feasible, then transitions are added to modify the local states of the processes to decrease the convergence time. This method can be iterated over the initial states of the paths returned till the desired threshold is achieved or all the returned paths are used up.

Addition of such transitions, however, requires some knowledge of the algorithm under consideration. For instance, a state transition to s_l that leads to a maximal decrease in convergence time might require change of variables belonging to more than one process. Such a transition is not feasible if an algorithm is implemented with a sequential scheduler. Infeasibility of a direct state transition to s_l may also result from the lack of "global knowledge." Let $s_i \longrightarrow s_l$ be the transition that leads to a maximal decrease in convergence time and let proc_x be the process whose local state must be changed to effect the aforementioned state transition. Process proc_x, therefore, needs a guarded command that changes its *local state* if system is in a *specific global state*. However, process proc_x cannot determine local states of *all* processes in a system unless the communication topology of system is a completely connected graph. Transition $s_i \longrightarrow s_l$, in this, is infeasible for communication topologies which are not completely connected. This is, however, an extremal case because usually processes – instead of global knowledge – require knowledge of their extended "neighborhood."

We applied the above procedure on the example system by analyzing the resultant set of paths after removing paths with fault steps. The state $s_b = \langle 2,2,1,2,2,1,1,2\rangle$ was the most probable *illegal* state. The paths having this state as the initial state were inspected more closely; a direct transition to the legal state $\langle 0,0,1,1,1,1,1,1\rangle$ was not feasible because it required changes in variable valuations in all three processes in a *single* step. However, a transition could be added to correct the local state of the non-root processes so that if the system is in state s_b, then the (activated) process corrects its local state. The communication topology of the example system allows each process to access the local states of all the process. Thus, guarded commands of the form

```
[stepstateB] state=stateB -> state'= correctstate
```

were added to the processes proc_1 and proc_2. The modification of the system led to an increase in probability (of reaching the legal state from state s_b) from 0.072 to 0.216.

The method described above can be used to modify the system for a given scheduler under a fault model with ongoing faults. However, the very fact that the scheduler is fixed limits the alternatives to modify the system. For instance, many transitions which could have potentially increased $A_{\mathcal{U}}(k)$ were rendered infeasible for the example system. This, in turn, can lead to an insufficient increase in $A_{\mathcal{U}}(k)$ or a rather large number of iterations to achieve the threshold value of $A_{\mathcal{U}}(k)$. The problem can be circumvented if one has leeway to fine-tune the randomized scheduler or modify the communication topology.

4.3 Randomized Scheduler Optimization

The probabilities with which individual processes are activated in each step by a scheduler affects the convergence time and thus the unconditional instantaneous availability of the system. However, a counterexample can be exploited to identify the processes whose activation probabilities need to be modified. For instance, consider a path returned by the conjunction of PRISM and `sbmc`:

$$\langle 2,2,1,2,2,1,1,2\rangle \rightarrow \langle 0,0,1,2,2,1,1,2\rangle \rightarrow \langle 0,0,1,1,1,1,1,2\rangle \rightarrow \langle 0,0,1,1,1,1,1,2\rangle$$

In the second last state of the path, activation of the root process does not bring any state change and thus leads only to an increase in convergence time. Hence, if the probability of activating a non-root process in the scope of the example algorithm is increased, then the probability associated with such sub-optimal paths can be decreased. We varied the probability of activating the root process in the example system to see the effect on $A_{\mathcal{U}}(k)$. As Figure 6 shows, unconditional instantaneous availability increases as the probability of activating the root is decreased. This is because one write operation of the root process alone corrects its local state; further activations are time-consuming only. But once the root process has performed a computation step, any activation of a non-root process corrects its local state. The paths in the counterexample can be analyzed in order to identify those processes whose activations lead to void transitions. The respective process activation probabilities of the scheduler can then be fine-tuned to increase $A_{\mathcal{U}}(k)$.

4.4 Abstraction Schemes for Silent Self-stabilization

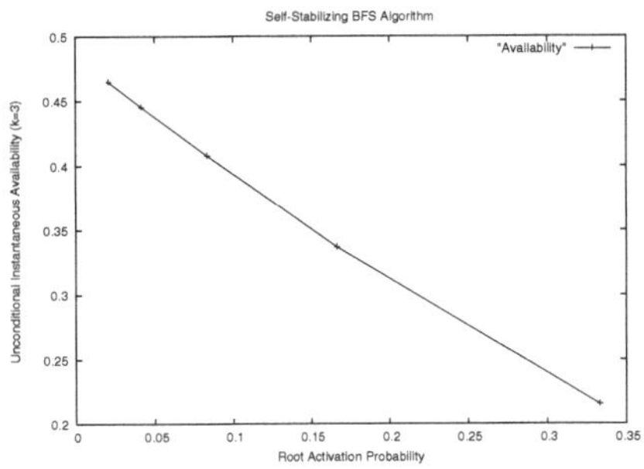

Fig. 6. Variation of unconditional instantaneous availability

Probabilistic model checking of self-stabilizing systems suffers from the state space explosion problem even for a small number of processes. This is due to the fact that the set of initial states of a self-stabilizing system is equal to the entire state space. As we intend to quantify the dependability of a self-stabilizing algorithm in an implementation scenario, we may be confronted with systems having a large number of processes. This necessitates a method to reduce the size of the model before giving it to the model checker. Often, data abstraction is used to reduce the size of large systems while preserving the property under investigation [13]. We next evaluate existing abstraction schemes and identify a suitable abstraction scheme for silent self-stabilizing systems.

Data abstraction constructs an abstract system by defining a finite set of abstract variables and a set of expressions which maps variables of the concrete system to the domain of the abstract variables. A form of data abstraction is predicate abstraction where a set of Boolean predicates is used to partition the concrete system state space [14]. Doing so results in an abstract system whose states are tuples of boolean variables. However, predicate abstraction can only be used to verify safety properties as it does not preserve liveness properties [15]. Since convergence is a liveness property, predicate abstraction cannot be used to derive smaller models of self-stabilizing systems.[1]

Ranking abstraction overcomes the deficiency of predicate abstraction by adding a *non-constraining progress monitor* to a system [15]. A progress monitor keeps track of the execution of the system with the help of a ranking function. The resulting augmented system can then be abstracted using predicate abstraction.

An important step in abstracting a system using a ranking abstraction is the identification of a so called *ranking function core*. This need not be a single ranking function – parts of it suffice to begin the verification of a liveness property. The fact that we are trying to evaluate a silent self-stabilizing system makes the search of a ranking function core easier. The proof of the convergence property of a self-stabilizing system is drawn using either a ranking function [17],

[1] However, for the properties considered here, which are step-bounded properties, this reasoning does not apply. In fact, we experimented with the predicate-abstraction-based probabilistic model checker PASS [16] that also supports automatic refinement. This was not successful because PASS seemingly was unable to handle the many distinct guards appearing in the initial state abstraction.

for instance a Lyapunov function [18], or some other form of well-foundedness argument [19]. Thus, one already has an explicit ranking function (core) and, if that is not the case, then the ranking function core can be "culled" from the proof of a silent self-stabilizing system. Further, we can derive an abstracted self-stabilizing system with the help of usual predicate abstraction techniques once the system has been augmented with a ranking function.

5 Conclusion and Future Work

We defined a set of metrics, namely unconditional instantaneous availability, generic instantaneous availability, MTTF, and MTTR, to quantify the dependability of self-stabilizing algorithms. These metrics can also be used to compare different self-stabilizing solutions to a problem. We also showed how to model a self-stabilizing system as a MDP or as a MC to derive these metrics. Further, heuristic-based methods were presented to exploit counterexamples of probabilistic model checking and to re-engineer silent self-stabilizing systems.

There are still open challenges with respect to dependability engineering of self-stabilizing systems. An abstraction scheme suitable for non-silent self-stabilizing algorithms is required to make their dependability analysis scalable. As discussed, there are multiple ways to refine a system which in turn leads to the challenge of finding the most viable alternative. We would also like to increase the tool support for dependability engineering of self-stabilizing systems. We believe that the identification of optimal schedulers and the determination of feasible transitions are the most promising candidates for solving the problem.

References

1. Dhama, A., Theel, O., Warns, T.: Reliability and Availability Analysis of Self-Stabilizing Systems. In: Datta, A.K., Gradinariu, M. (eds.) SSS 2006. LNCS, vol. 4280, pp. 244–261. Springer, Heidelberg (2006)
2. Arora, A., Kulkarni, S.S.: Component Based Design of Multitolerant Systems. IEEE Trans. Software Eng. 24, 63–78 (1998)
3. Arora, A., Kulkarni, S.S.: Designing Masking Fault-Tolerance via Nonmasking Fault-Tolerance. IEEE Trans. Software Eng. 24, 435–450 (1998)
4. Ghosh, S., Gupta, A., Herman, T., Pemmaraju, S.V.: Fault-Containing Self-Stabilizing Algorithms. In: PODC, pp. 45–54 (1996)
5. Ghosh, S., Pemmaraju, S.V.: Tradeoffs in fault-containing self-stabilization. In: WSS, pp. 157–169 (1997)
6. Beauquier, J., Gradinariu, M., Johnen, C.: Randomized Self-Stabilizing and Space Optimal Leader Election under Arbitrary Scheduler on Rings. Distributed Computing 20, 75–93 (2007)
7. Aljazzar, H., Leue, S.: Debugging of Dependability Models Using Interactive Visualization of Counterexamples. In: QEST, pp. 189–198. IEEE Computer Society, Los Alamitos (2008)
8. Dolev, S., Israeli, A., Moran, S.: Self-Stabilization of Dynamic Systems Assuming Only Read/Write Atomicity. Distributed Computing 7, 3–16 (1993)

9. Trivedi, K.S.: Probability and Statistics with Reliability, Queuing, and Computer Science Applications. John Wiley and Sons, Chichester (2001)
10. Hinton, A., Kwiatkowska, M.Z., Norman, G., Parker, D.: PRISM: A Tool for Automatic Verification of Probabilistic Systems. In: Hermanns, H., Palsberg, J. (eds.) TACAS 2006. LNCS, vol. 3920, pp. 441–444. Springer, Heidelberg (2006)
11. Wimmer, R., Braitling, B., Becker, B.: Counterexample Generation for Discrete-Time Markov Chains Using Bounded Model Checking. In: Jones, N.D., Müller-Olm, M. (eds.) VMCAI 2009. LNCS, vol. 5403, pp. 366–380. Springer, Heidelberg (2009)
12. Baier, C., Katoen, J.P.: Principles of Model Checking. MIT Press, Cambridge (2008)
13. Cousot, P., Cousot, R.: Abstract Interpretation: A Unified Lattice Model for Static Analysis of Programs by Construction or Approximation of Fixpoints. In: POPL, pp. 238–252 (1977)
14. Graf, S., Saïdi, H.: Construction of Abstract State Graphs with PVS. In: Grumberg, O. (ed.) CAV 1997. LNCS, vol. 1254, pp. 72–83. Springer, Heidelberg (1997)
15. Balaban, I., Pnueli, A., Zuck, L.: Modular Ranking Abstraction. Int. J. Found. Comput. Sci. 18, 5–44 (2007)
16. Hermanns, H., Wachter, B., Zhang, L.: Probabilistic CEGAR. In: Gupta, A., Malik, S. (eds.) CAV 2008. LNCS, vol. 5123, pp. 162–175. Springer, Heidelberg (2008)
17. Kessels, J.L.W.: An Exercise in Proving Self-Stabilization with a Variant Function. Inf. Process. Lett. 29, 39–42 (1988)
18. Oehlerking, J., Dhama, A., Theel, O.: Towards Automatic Convergence Verification of Self-Stabilizing Algorithms. In: Tixeuil, S., Herman, T. (eds.) SSS 2005. LNCS, vol. 3764, pp. 198–213. Springer, Heidelberg (2005)
19. Gouda, M.G., Multari, N.J.: Stabilizing Communication Protocols. IEEE Trans. Computers 40, 448–458 (1991)

Robustness and Dependability of Self-Organizing Systems - A Safety Engineering Perspective

Giovanna Di Marzo Serugendo

Birkbeck College, University of London
dimarzo@dcs.bbk.ac.uk

Abstract. This paper analyses the robustness of self-organizing (engineered) systems to perturbations (faults or environmental changes). It considers that a self-organizing system is embedded into an environment, the main active building blocks are agents, one or more self-organizing mechanisms regulate the interaction among agents, and agents manipulate artifacts, i.e. passive entities maintained by the environment. Perturbations then need to be identified at the level of these four design elements. This paper discusses the boundaries of normal and abnormal behaviour in self-organizing systems and provides guidelines for designers to determine which perturbation in which part of the system leads to a failure.

1 Introduction

Self-organizing artificial (engineered) systems are appealing because they provide a "natural" robustness to changes and failures, while being composed of relatively simple entities. This claim, although backed by observation through simulations or experiments, has not been thoroughfully investigaged. For instance, questions such as: To what changes in their environment/faults are these systems naturally robust to, and what changes/faults are they not able to overcome (naturally)? What does "naturally" mean in this context? The boundary between the normal behaviour and the abnormal one is usually blurred since the self-* part of these systems contains (built-in or intrinsic) recovery capabilities. So, what is the normal operational mode of such systems, what is their abnormal one? This is also pointed out by Alderson et al. [1], in the context of complex systems: "Robustness is the invariance of [a property] of [a system] to [a set of perturbations]". The main point here is that a given system preserves a specific property for a specific set of perturbations, but may be fragile for *another property* or *other perturbations*.

The aim of this paper is twofold. First, it intends to clarify the notions of "normal", "dependable" and "resilient" behaviour in self-organizing systems. Second, it guides the designer of self-organizing systems in identifying the limits of the "natural" robustness, i.e. in identifying the *properties* and set of *perturbations* that render the system fragile. This is similar to the Failure Mode and Effects Analysis (FMEA)[1] technique followed by safety engineers when they analyse the

[1] http://en.wikipedia.org/wiki/Failure_mode_and_effects_analysis

R. Guerraoui and F. Petit (Eds.): SSS 2009, LNCS 5873, pp. 254–268, 2009.

design of a system to find what faults can occur. Starting from a block diagram of the system, the safety engineer considers what happens when each block fails and subsequently proposes changes to the system to make it safer. In the context of self-organizing systems, the designer determines which changes/faults in which part of the system lead to a failure. To this end, the paper lists the *design elements* of a self-organizing system, *properties* of self-organizing systems, *types of faults* for self-organizing systems and considers *means to reach dependability* in self-organizing systems. To illustrate our discussion, we consider a simple self-organizing systems and discuss its dependability to different changes and faults. This paper does not intend to be complete, additional investigations, experiments and measurements are necessary. The main goal of this paper is to lay the foundations for additional thorough investigation into these systems' behaviour.

2 Dependability and Resilience

This section provides a short summary of Avizienis et al. [2] and Laprie [3] papers. We extract (almost verbatim) here the essential elements of these papers that suit the purpose of our discussion and render our paper self-contained as we will refer to these notions in the next sections.

Robustness and Dependability. A computing system is *robust* if it retains its ability to deliver a service in conditions which are beyond its normal domain of operation [4]. *Dependability* is the ability to deliver a service that can justifiably be trusted.

Dependability Attributes. Dependability is measured against the following criteria: *Availability* - readiness for correct service; *Reliability* - continuity of correct service; *Safety* - absence of catastrophic consequences on the user(s) and the environment; *Integrity* - absence of improper system alterations; *Maintainability* - ability to undergo modifications and repairs.

Threats to dependability. A *failure* is an event that occurs when the delivered service deviates from correct service (service does not comply with functional specification). It is a transition from correct service to incorrect service. A service failure means that one or more of external service states deviates from the correct service state. The deviation is called an error. An *error* is a part of the total state of the service that may lead the system to its subsequent service failure. A *fault* is the cause of an error.

Means to attain dependability. *Fault Prevention* encompasses the improvement of development processes in order to reduce the number of faults introduced in the produced systems. *Fault Tolerance* aims at failure avoidance and is carried out through error detection and system recovery. *Fault Removal* occurs during system development or during system use. *Fault Forecasting* consists in evaluating the system's behaviour with respect to fault occurrence.

Resilience. In a recent paper, Laprie [3] provides an insight into the notion of resilience and its relationship with dependability. The considered systems are ubiquitous systems and the main point is to maintain dependability in spite of continuous changes. *Resilience* is then defined as the persistence of dependability when facing changes.

Self-organizing systems permanently face changes; this definition of resilience thus applies directly to self-organizing systems.

3 Self-Organizing Systems

Self-organizing applications are applications generally made of *multiple autonomous entities* with a knowledge limited to their *local environment* and that *locally interact* (directly or indirectly) to produce a result. Autonomous entities usually work in a *decentralised manner*, the global behaviour (function) generally "emerges" from the local interactions of the different entities. The entire "global" function is encoded in none of the individual entities. The result is generally obtained when the system reaches, converges to, a stable state. Typical examples of natural self-organizing system include swarms (ant, flocks of birds, wasps, etc.), immune system, human social behaviour (markets, trust, gossip). Artificial (engineered) systems include unmanned vehicles, swarms of robots, P2P systems, immune computer or trust-based access control.

3.1 Design Elements

Our discussion starts with the following consideration driven by design concerns [5,6]. The elements of a self-organizing (SO) system are: the *environment* in which it evolves (operating system, physical world, or network), the autonomous individual active entities - the *agents* - that constitute the system itself (software agent, robots, peer nodes), the *self-organizing mechanism* defining the rules (all) the agents apply (continuously) when evolving in the environment and letting them (re-)organise in case of changes or failures, and the *artifacts*, which are the passive entities maintained by the environment, created, modified and/or sensed by the agents (e.g. digital pheromone spread in the environment or information exchanged among agents).

SO System = Environment + Agents + SO Mechanism (rules) + Artifacts

Agents evolve into an environment, which they use to interact and carry on their behaviour. The boundary between an agent and its environment must be identified, but may vary from system to system. Depending on the system, it may be more convenient to consider an agent as a piece of software and everything else as its environment (in particular the underlying operating system or the node the agent is residing in). In other cases, it is more convenient to consider the agent as the combination of the piece of software *and* the node it is executing in. This is the case, when the agent is an autonomous (maybe mobile) robot, or when the agent is a node itself. Artificial systems usually take inspiration from nature - the SO mechanism being an ad hoc translation of the natural SO mechanism.

Sections 5 provides an example of SO Systems (stigmergy) identifying the environment, the agents, the SO mechanism, the artifacts together with examples of respective failures. Babaoglu et al. [7] describe this mechanism as well as others under the form of patterns and analyse in details these mechanisms and their corresponding implemented algorithms. Additional patterns for self-organisatin can be found in [8].

3.2 Types of Faults in SO Systems

In order to identify faults arising in a SO system, it is then convenient to consider faults (individually or as a combination) arising from each of these elements, i.e. faults from the environment, from the agents, from the SO mechanism itself, or from the artifacts, as shown in Figure 1.

Environmental Faults include all network related faults and communication faults arising among the agents; operational faults of the computing entities (nodes) present in the environment; any storage related fault (database, memory problem) affecting agent programs or artifacts; as well as any faults from the physical world in which the agents evolve (hole in the ground, unexpected obstacle). Environmental faults are a type of Interaction faults, more precisely they are System Boundaries faults (External faults), those that "originate outside the system boundary and propagate errors into the system by interaction or interference".

Agents Faults cover development faults affecting agent code and behaviour; when the node, in which the agent program resides, is considered part of the agent, then node faults are also Agents faults. We distinguish those faults from the ones directly affecting sensing and acting capabilities of the agents (vision camera fault or robot arm fault). Finally, an agent can be maliciously faulty. Agents faults may be Physical faults (hardware or software fault) and/or Development faults introduce during the system development. Agents interact with

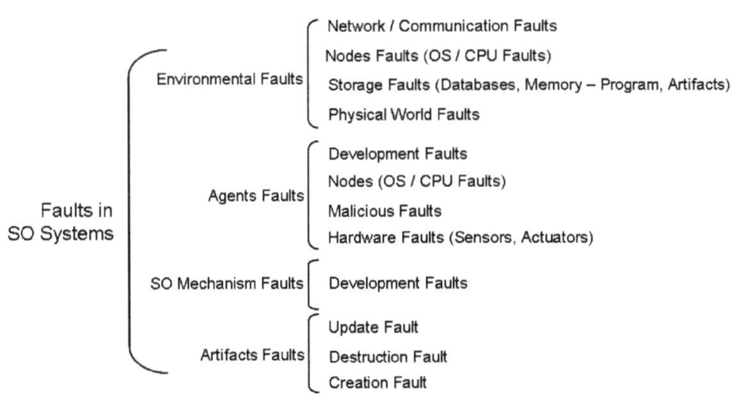

Fig. 1. Characterisation of Types of Faults in SO Systems

each other directly or indirectly through the environment. Agents faults may then also contribute to Interaction faults. Both Environmental and Agents faults may be the result of some malicious intent.

SO Mechanism Faults are Development faults, essentially due to errors in the design and implementation of the SO mechanism rules.

Artifacts Faults are all those faults affecting the integrity of the artifacts. Artifacts faults are likely to be caused by the Environment, the Agents or the SO Mechanism, since Artifacts themselves are essentially passive. We consider a fault to be an Artifact fault when it affects an artifact - through uncorrect modification, destruction, production or management of the artifact. For instance, an artificial pheromone whose evaporation rate is different than the expected one or that suddenly dissapears is an Artifact fault, in this case mostly caused by the Environment.

Environment and Agent faults may be either permanent or transient, while SO Mechanisms faults are permanent.

3.3 SO Systems Properties

We identify here the properties of self-organizing systems (Figure 2) that have to be questioned for the types of faults identified above.

Invariants. An invariant is any property that must be satisfied by the system at all time, i.e. it must be true at any state of the system.

SO Systems Robustness Attributes. *Convergence.* An important property of SO systems is whether the system actually converges towards the intended goal (correct value). *Speed of convergence.* How quickly does the system reaches its goal? *Stability.* Once the goal is reached, does the system maintain it? *Scalability.* How is the system affected by the number of agents and artifacts?

Dependability Attributes. These are the dependability attributes listed in Section 2: *Availability, Reliability, Safety, Integrity, Maintainability.*

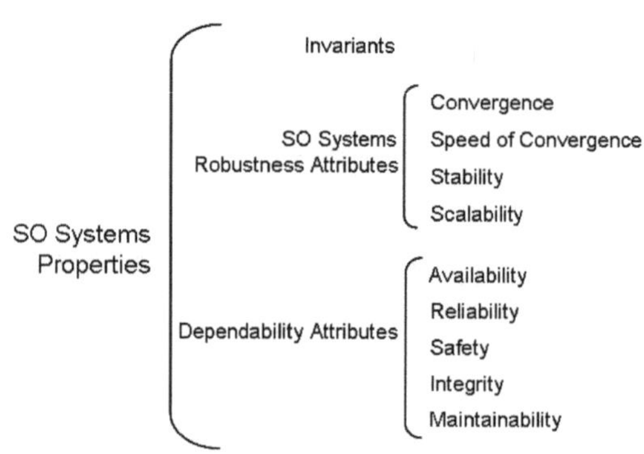

Fig. 2. SO Systems Properties

4 Normal vs. Self-Organizing vs. Resilient

4.1 Dependability at Run-Time - Traditional Systems

Figure 3 (a) sketches the normal vs abnormal states in "traditional" systems (where no SO mechanism is involved). As discussed in Section 2, the means to reach dependability at run-time are: fault tolerance, fault removal and fault forecasting. In each case, this consists in *identifying the error state* and undertaking appropriate steps so that the system *goes back to a normal state*. The *Normal* operational mode of these systems occurs when the system is not in an error state. An identified error state triggers appropriate techniques (exception handlers, patches, etc.) to bring the system back to normal. *Dependability* thus extends to include all those error states. When the system cannot be brought back to normal, then the error state leads to a *Failure*, where the fault causing the error cannot be recovered.

4.2 Resilience at Run-Time - Self-Organizing Systems

The main difference between "traditional" systems and SO systems resides in the fact that an SO system recovers from an error *without error detection*, i.e. without specifically identifying an erroneous state and applying a specific recovery action.

Figure 3 (b) shows the different states of a SO system. *Normal* represents the ideal mode of operation of the system. The one when none of the faults discussed in Section 3.2 occur. *Self-** includes all the changes that the system overcomes without changing its mode of operations. These changes occur from the faults identified above. The SO system does not identify these changes as errors, it just carries on with its normal behaviour (that is why we do not call them errors). This is the area where the SO mechanism is enough to overcome the perturbation. In fact the *Normal* states could extend to the *Self-** ones. A SO mechanism has its limits, i.e. there are cases where carrying on as usual doesn't solve the problem (e.g. system does not converge or is unstable). *Resilience* thus refers to all the states where the SO system actually identifies an error and

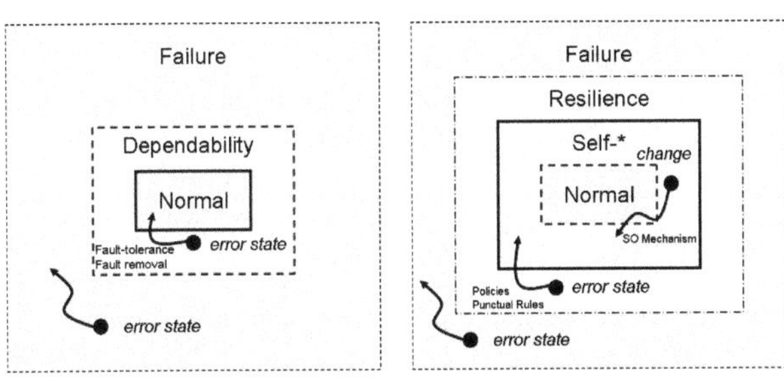

(a) Traditional Systems (b) SO Systems

Fig. 3. Systems' States

specifically and *punctually* applies a recovery action. The system goes back to the *Self-** area again, where the usual SO mechanism rules apply. Finally, *Failure* refers to all the cases where the error cannot be recovered.

4.3 Analysis of Robustness and Dependability

In order to analyse robustness and dependability of SO systems, we need to determine which *perturbations* (change or fault) lead to which *property* being violated.

Properties. We consider the following properties:

```
Properties = Invariants - Robustness Attributes - Dependability Attributes
```

Invariants are all the invariant properties that the SO system has to preserve during its execution. *Robustness attributes* are convergence, speed of convergence, stability, and scalability (discussed in Section 3.3). *Dependability attributes* are availability, reliability, safety, integrity, maintainability (discussed in Section 2).

Perturbations. As we have seen above, the design elements of a SO system are the *Environment*, *Agents*, *SO mechanism* and *Artifacts*. The perturbations are any faults / changes / threats the system is likely to undergo originating from these elements (discussed in Section 3.2).

```
Perturbation = Changes or Faults in:
                    Environment - Agents - SO Mechanism - Artifacts
```

Analysis. Similarly to the FMEA technique, the designer needs to *question each element of the design* (environment, agents, SO mechanism and artifact), establish for each of them any *potential fault or change* that can actually occur, and *determine its impact on the properties* listed above.

```
Analysis = for all Design Elements
                for all Changes and Types of Faults
                    if change / fault can happen
                      is any Invariant modified?
                      is any Robustness Attribute affected?
                      is any Dependability Attribute affected?
```

An example of such a questioning could be:

> "Is it possible that in the considered system the environment behaves maliciously, if yes then:
>
> – how is this affecting any invariant property (e.g. the value of a sum that has to be computed),
> – how is this affecting any robustness property (e.g. will the system still converge and at which speed), and

– what is the impact on any dependability attribute (e.g. is the service provided by the system always available or will there be disruptions)?"

Different faults, originating from different elements of the design, may have similar effects. For instance, a fault compromising the integrity of an artifact may be due to a fault in the environment (responsible to maintain the artifact), or to a malicious agent or to the artifact itself. In order to correct the fault, it becomes important to determine the origin of the fault by identifiyng the appropriate design element responsible for the fault.

Once a change or fault and its effect is identifed, a mean to attain dependability has to be identified through design change or additional resilience mechanism (see below).

4.4 Means to Attain Dependability in SO Systems

Let us discuss here the four means to attain dependability, as identified by Avizienis et al. and reported in Section 2, for the specific case of self-organizing systems (Figure 4).

Fault prevention. The design of self-* algorithms can be verified, to some extent, with mathematical analysis, but *simulations* are the most preferred tool at the moment.

Fault tolerance. For "traditional" software, fault tolerance consists in detecting an error and subsequently recovering from that error (with a bunch of diverse techniques). As said above, this is where SO systems differ from "traditional" software. We distinguish two levels.

First, the intrinsic fault-tolerance: the *SO mechanism* is robust enough to recover from errors *without* explicitly detecting an error and subsequently recovering from it. The SO system then "naturally" recovers from states which are not part of the ideal mode of operation. If a source of food suddenly disappears in an ant-based system, the SO system just carries on exploring the environment for food until the system finds another source. The disappearance of the food

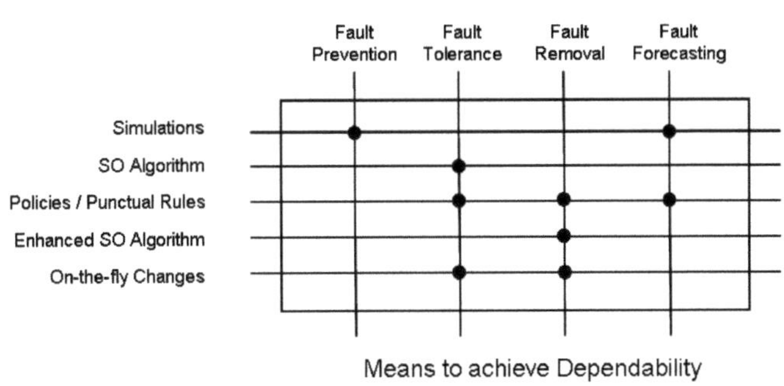

Fig. 4. Means To Attain Dependability in SO Systems

does not trigger any specific error, the system continues to run as in the normal case and just recovers (*Self-** in Figure 3).

Seond, similarly to fault tolerance in traditional software, the *Resilience* case expresses the limits of the SO mechanism to recover from errors. This is similar to "traditional" software: errors are detected (locally or globally) and appropriate measures apply in order to tackle the error. *Policies or punctual rules* then apply in order to recover from the error. These rules are different from the rules of the SO mechanism that are applied permanently by the entities of the system.

Fault removal. This encompasses: *enhanced SO mechanisms* with policies becoming part of the rules, or modified rules (so that what was before an error is now part of the normal operational behaviour); *on-the-fly changes*, such as switching among different SO mechanisms (rules) or adapting the rules, depending on the environmental conditions, or replacing outdated SO mechanism or policies with new ones on the fly during system execution.

As an example of enhanced SO mechanisms, we can mention the case of optimisation problems. The original Particle Swarm Optimisation algorithm detects one static optimum only, but is not able to cope with multiple or dynamic optimums. QSO is an algorithm that overcomes this problem, but still there is the problem of the swarm getting stuck in one optimum [9]. Multi-swarm is a solution to this that allows to find all optimums [10].

Fault Forecasting. This is similar to the *Resilience* case, through monitoring, exceeded thresholds are identified and policies punctually recover before the system reaches an error state.

5 Stigmergy - Ant-Based System

This example is a simulation of an ant colony foraging (see Figure 5 (a)).

SO System Elements. The *environment* is the physical world where ants evolve, where their nest is positioned, and where food is available. Ants deposit pheromone in the environment for marking paths food. The nest diffuses also a scent which helps the ants go back home with pieces of food. The *agents* are the ants. The *SO mechanism* works as follows:

- Ants are either looking for food, or going back to the nest once they have found food.
- When looking for food, ants leave the nest and walk randomly until they sense a pheromone scent in their locality. They then move in the direction where the pheromone scent is stronger.
- When they have found food, ants go back to the nest following the nest's scent. They follow the nest's scent in the direction where it is stronger.
- When they go back to the nest with food, they drop a pheromone scent at each step. This pheromone scent adds up to any other pheromone scent already present at the same place.

Finally, the *artifacts* are: the nest (in the center), the three food sources (upper-left corner, bottom-left corner and middle-right), pheromone scent (marking the path from food to nest) and nest's scent. The pheromone has an evaporation rate (how long it lasts) and a diffusion rate (how far it can be sensed). The pheromone is updated regularly by the environment (diffused and evaporated).

As we see from this description, the environment plays an important role when the SO system employs a SO mechanism using indirect communication such as stigmergy. Agents rely strongly on the environment and an Environmental faults can lead to a failure. In this example, the environment must host the pheromone and update it properly.

This system has no particular invariant, we list here the robustness attributes.

SO Systems Robustness Attributes. They are as follows:

- Convergence takes two dimensions here.
  Exploration: ants explore their environment properly - entirely and regularly - so as to spot any source of food.
  Exploitation: ants eventually bring back all the food to the nest.
- Speed of convergence:
  Exploration: how quickly ants can spot a new source of food once the current one is exhausted; *Exploitation*: how efficiently they can get the whole source back to the nest.
- Stability: ants focus on exploiting a source of food.
- Scalability: convergence and speed of convergence are not affected by the number of ants

We started from the original simulation of [11], which is part of the NetLogo package. We altered it so as to insert different types of faults. We report here on some experiments we made in order to illustrate our discussion. A thorough investigation of the algorithm would require more experiments and precise measurements.

Real world applications taking advantage of stigmergy include static and dynamic optimisation problems as well as coordination of unmanned vehicles [12].

5.1 Environmental Faults

Ants disappear (or die). The system continues finding food, it converges but at a slower pace. If the number of agents is very low, then the pheromone path is not maintained and exploitation is less efficient, stability is compromised, but all food is eventually retrieved (Figure 5 (b)). This is similar to an agent crash and can also be seen as an Agent Fault.

Obstacle (Physical World). An obstacle (hole or rock) is now part of the environment mid-way between the upper-left source of food and the nest. The nest's scent on the obstacle is very low. Agents lay down the pheromone around the obstacle, thus adapting the path to find the food (Figure 5 (c)). None of the properties seems to be affected by this fault.

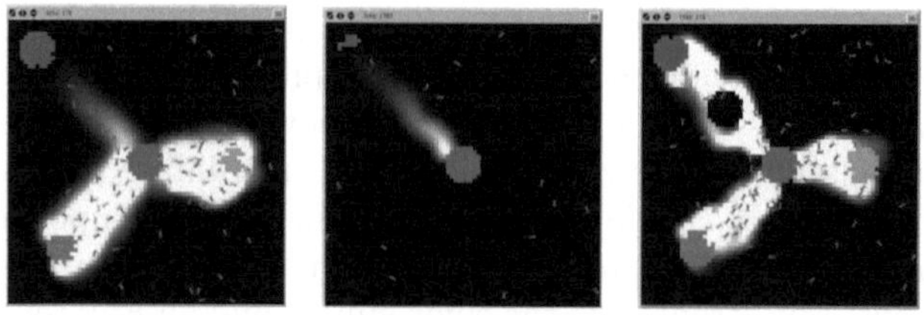

(a) Normal (b) Ants Die (c) Obstacle

Fig. 5. Normal Behaviour and Environmental Faults

5.2 Agents Faults

Malicious agents. A subset of agents (25%) are not looking for food, but deposit pheromone at the wrong place (25% or 100% of the time) Depending on the quantity of wrongly added pheromone, paths to the food are more or less compromised (speed of convergence is slower and lack of focus on a source of food compromises stability). The system eventually converges and exploits all food. (Figure 6 (a) and (b)).

No Pheromone. Agents look for food, bring it to the nest, but do not deposit pheromone at all. Agents just look for food at random. All food is eventually retrieved but slowly. This is similar to the evaporation rate of the pheromone that is too quick.

5.3 SO Mechanism Faults

Pheromone Scent. Agents take a wrong direction when detecting the pheromone scent. As a result, agents avoid the paths leading to the food. Paths tend to

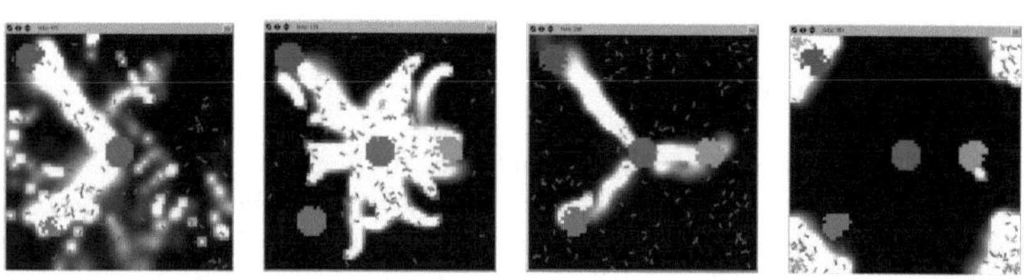

(a) Malicious Agents (b) Malicious Agents (c) Wrong direction - Pheromone (d) Wrong direction - Nest

Fig. 6. Agents and SO Mechanism Faults

disappear. There is no systematic exploitation. Food is eventually brought back to nest, but the system converges slowly (Figure 6 (c)).

Nest's Scent. Agents take a wrong direction when detecting the nest's scent. Agents avoid the nest, do not find it, cannot deposit food and remain stuck at the opposite of the nest. The system does not converge at all (Figure 6 (d)).

5.4 Artifacts Faults

Evaporation rate of pheromone. Rate of 0% (or too slow): the pheromone scent does not evaporate (or not quickly enough), it stays where it has been laid down. The environment gets filled with pheromone, the ants continue following the paths even when food is exhausted. The system converges (it eventually retrieves all the food), but exploitation is not efficient (Figure 7 (a)). A small evaporation rate (above 6%) is enough for maintaining the paths without filling the environment with unnecessary scent. Rate of 100% (or too quick). Pheromone evaporates before ants can build a path and maintain it. Similarly to above, the system converges but is not efficient (speed is slow and stability is compromised).

Diffusion rate of pheromone. Rate of 0% (or too thin): the paths are thin and do not build up fully. A small rate (10%) is enough to construct solid paths (Figure 7 (b)). Rate of 100% (or too large): paths are large, ants do not go straight to food.

Nest's scent. The environment disperses the nest scent. In the simulation we first put random values instead of increasing values leading to the nest. Ants do not find the nest quickly anymore. Pheromone scent starts filling the whole environment. Efficient exploitation is compromised, but ants eventually exhaust all the food. Second, the nest's scent is randomised in a restricted portion of the environment, between the upper-left corner source of food and the nest, that portion of the environment is filled with pheromone (Figure 7 (c)). Efficient exploitation is compromised, but ants eventually exhaust all the food.

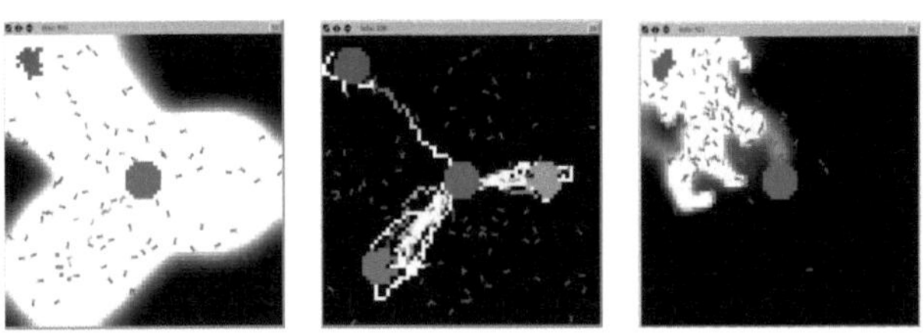

(a) Evaporation Rate - Slow

(b) Diffusion Rate - Thin

(c) Nest Scent

Fig. 7. Artifacts Faults

Food disappearance. This is a case of a change in the environment instead of a fault. After a short while the pheromone leading to the disappeared source of food vanishes, the ants just continue looking for food as usual, find and exploit other sources of food.

5.5 Analysis of Resilience

This example has no invariants, we discuss here robustness attributes; dependability attributes are discusssed in the next section. There are basically 3 categories of perturbations that affect robustness attributes: those that affect speed of convergence and stability (ants are moving randomly or not focusing on a source of food, thus taking longer to exhaust it); those that do not particularly affect the system (paths are maintained); and those that compromise convergence. Globally, we can say that when the system converges with a convenient speed of convergence and stability behaviour, it behaves normally (*Normal* box of Figure 3(b)). When the system eventually converges (despite slow speed of convergence and/or instability), the SO mechanism succeeded in overcoming the perturbation (*Self-** box of Figure 3(b)). If the system does not converge, an invariant is not preserved, the speed of convergence is too slow to be acceptable or if the instability becomes an issue, then we reach the limits of the "natural" robustness. Extra resilience is needed to support the SO mechanism. For instance, in the case of the ants, they may detect that they do not follow a path but go at random, and may decide to lay down another type of pheromone. This could overcome malicious ants trying to confuse them with pheromone deposited at the wrong place. Regarding scalability, a low number of ants affects speed of convergence and stability, while a large number helps building paths to find food. A large number of sources of food scattered all over the environment may also affect speed of convergence and stability.

6 Discussion

From the examples we have investigated so far, we can draw the following preliminary conclusions regarding the robustness and dependability attributes.

Invariants and Robustness. Convergence and invariants are key elements to determine the dependability limits of an SO system. A system that converges and maintains its invariants despite perturbations "naturally" overcomes those perturbations. An SO system needs additional resilience techniques when convergence cannot be reached, invariants are not satisfied, or speed of convergence and stability are not acceptable.

Availability. SO systems are always ready to work, but the service they provide may not be correct at first. It may take a certain time before the system converges.

Reliability. SO systems usually imply latency. Therefore, reliability is not necessarily ensured: a service is (necessarily) discontinued while the SO system re-organises/adapts to the new conditions. It may not stop, but will not be correct.

Safety. SO systems usually overcome a large range of changes/faults. However, the adaptation may imply latency. During this period, safety may not be guaranteed. In addition, in some cases the SO system is at a loss of overcoming the problem and may get stuck in a bad situation.

Integrity. Artifacts are at a high risk of integrity concerns/issues. They are not necessarily equipped with specific protection and are vulnerable because agents need the environment to exchange them, to modify or maintain them. Agents themselves are also at risk of integrity: they depend on the environment for their execution, their data or their physical movements.

Maintainability. We have seen that SO systems naturally adapt to changing software / hardware on-the-fly. In the case of SO system, we can contemplate changes at each level: changes in the environment, the agents, the SO mechanism and the artifacts in order to determine the maintainability level of the system.

7 Conclusion

This paper discusses the notions of robustness and dependability in the context of self-organizing systems. It proposes to analyse robustness and dependability by identifying perturbations (changes or faults) arising from each design element and studying their impact on invariants, robustness and dependability properties. Many research issues related to dependability of SO systems need to be investigated. Among others testing and formal verification of SO systems, or fault removal on the fly, which has not received much attention yet (e.g. switching SO mechanism, adapting the rules, applying specific policies to SO systems).

Acknowledgements

The author thanks John Fitzgerald for fruitful discussions on dependability and resilience as well as the anonymous reviewers for their feedback and comments on the paper.

References

1. Alderson, D.L., Doyle, J.C.: Can complexity science support the engineering of critical network infrastructures? In: IEEE International Conference on Systems, Man and Cybernetics, SCM 2007 (2007)
2. Avizienis, A., Laprie, J.C., Randell, B., Landwehr, C.: Basic concepts and taxonomy of dependable and secure computing. IEEE Transactions on Dependable and Secure Computing 1(1), 11–33 (2004)
3. Laprie, J.C.: From dependability to resilience. In: IEEE/IFIP International Conference on Dependable Systems and Networks (DSN 2008 - Fast Abstracts) (2008)

4. Anderson, T. (ed.): Resilient Computing Systems. Collins (1985)
5. Ricci, A., Viroli, M., Omicini, A.: Programming MAS with artifacts. In: Bordini, R.H., Dastani, M.M., Dix, J., El Fallah Seghrouchni, A. (eds.) PROMAS 2005. LNCS (LNAI), vol. 3862, pp. 206–221. Springer, Heidelberg (2006)
6. Picard, G., Gleizes, M.P.: The ADELFE Methodology-Designing Adaptive Cooperative Multi-Agent Systems. In: Bergenti, F., Gleizes, M.P., Zambonelli, F. (eds.) Methodologies and Software Engineering for Agent Systems, pp. 157–175. Springer, Heidelberg (2004)
7. Babaoglu, O., Canright, G., Deutsch, A., Di Caro, G., Ducatelle, F., Gambardella, L., Ganguly, N., Jelasity, M., Montemanni, R., Montresor, A., Urnes, T.: Design patterns from biology for distributed computing. ACM Transactions on Autonomous and Adaptive Systems 1(1), 26–66 (2006)
8. De Wolf, T., Holvoet, T.: Design patterns for decentralised coordination in self-organising emergent systems. In: Brueckner, S.A., Hassas, S., Jelasity, M., Yamins, D. (eds.) ESOA 2006. LNCS (LNAI), vol. 4335, pp. 28–49. Springer, Heidelberg (2007)
9. Poli, R., Kennedy, J., Blackwell, T.: Particle swarm optimization - an overview. Swarm Intelligence 1, 33–57 (2007)
10. Blackwell, T., Branke, J.: Multiswarms, exclusion, and anti-convergence in dynamic environments. IEEE Transactions on Evolutionary Computation 10(4), 459–472 (2006)
11. Wilensky, U.: NetLogo Ants model. Center for Connected Learning and Computer-Based Modeling. Northwestern University, Evanston (1997), `http://ccl.northwestern.edu/netlogo/models/Ants`
12. Sauter, J.A., Matthews, R., Parunak, H.V.D., Brueckner, S.A.: Performance of digital pheromones for swarming vehicle control. In: 4th International Joint Conference on Autonomous Agents and Multiagent Systems (AAMAS 2005), The Netherlands, pp. 903–910. ACM, New York (2005)

Efficient Robust Storage Using Secret Tokens*

Dan Dobre, Matthias Majuntke, Marco Serafini, and Neeraj Suri

TU Darmstadt, Hochschulstr. 10, 64289 Darmstadt, Germany
{dan,majuntke,marco,suri}@cs.tu-darmstadt.de

Abstract. We present algorithms that reduce the time complexity and improve the scalability of robust storage for unauthenticated data. Robust storage ensures progress under every condition (wait-freedom) and never returns an outdated value (regularity) nor a forged value (Byzantine fault tolerance). The algorithms use *secret tokens*, which are values randomly selected by the clients and attached to the data written into the storage. Tokens are secret because they cannot be predicted by the attacker before they are used, and thus revealed, by the clients. Our algorithms do not rely on unproven cryptographic assumptions as algorithms based on self-verifying data. They are optimally-resilient, and ensure that reads complete in two communication rounds if readers do not write into the storage, or in one communication round otherwise.

1 Introduction

We study the problem of efficiently implementing a robust storage for unauthenticated data from Byzantine storage components. Robust storage is an abstraction which supports read and write operations that are always live (wait-freedom) and read operations that never return an outdated or a spurious value (regularity). A robust algorithm uses passive storage components called *base objects* (or *objects*) that may suffer Nonresponsive-arbitrary faults [1]. Robust storage implementations for unauthenticated data are attractive because they do not incur the overhead of cryptography and they are invulnerable to cryptographic attacks. Existing unauthenticated algorithms with optimal resilience and optimal time-complexity [2, 3, 4, 5, 6] have a much higher (worst-case) read latency compared to algorithms storing self-verifying data, using digital signatures [7, 8, 9]. This is critical because many practical workloads are dominated by read operations. Therefore, the natural question arises if it is also possible to achieve minimal read latency without fundamentally strengthening the assumptions of the system model.

In this paper we propose two robust storage implementations for unauthenticated data with optimal resilience and optimal time complexity. The first algorithm supports unbounded readers and features constant read complexity. The second algorithm features fast reads, i.e., every read operation terminates after one round of communication with the base objects. Our algorithms circumvent the lower bounds established in [2, 4] by using *secret tokens*. A secret token (briefly token) is a value randomly selected by

* Research funded in part by EC INSPIRE, Microsoft Research and DFG GRK 1362 (TUD GKmM).

R. Guerraoui and F. Petit (Eds.): SSS 2009, LNCS 5873, pp. 269–283, 2009.

the client and attached to the messages sent to the base objects. The secrecy property of a token selected by a correct client is that the adversary can not generate its value before the client actually uses the token.

Secret tokens are useful because they prevent faulty base objects from simulating client operations (read or write) that have not yet been invoked but will actually occur at some later point. However, tokens are weaker than signatures, because they cannot prevent a faulty base object from successfully forging a value that is never written. Consider for instance the lower bound of reading from a safe storage with optimal resilience [4]. It states that with t faulty objects, a read that does not modify the base objects takes at least $t+1$ communication rounds before it can read a value. In each read round, a different malicious object simulates a concurrency with the same write, thereby triggering a new read round. With secret tokens, the second read round definitely reveals which value can be returned and the read terminates.

The assumption that tokens are secret can be violated with some probability. However, this probability can be arbitrarily reduced, for example, by uniformly and independently generating random tokens of k bits and by increasing the value of k. Note that in practice, assumptions in general hold only with a certain probability, e.g., the assumption that no more than t base objects fail.

Our first algorithm does not require readers to modify the base objects. As a consequence, it supports an unbounded number of possibly malicious readers. Every read completes after two communication rounds, which we show to be a tight bound. Thus, the algorithm improves on the read complexity of $t + 1$ rounds established for unauthenticated storage with optimal resilience when readers do not write [4]. Our second algorithm guarantees that every read is *fast*, i.e. it terminates after a one communication round by allowing readers to modify the base objects. The general lower bound of two rounds for reading from a robust storage with optimal resilience [2] is circumvented using tokens which are written by readers into the storage.

An alternative approach to the use of secret tokens to reduce the time-complexity is the use of cryptography, namely digital signatures [7, 8, 9]. Digital signatures generally require the generation of a secret (e.g. private) key, which entails the generation of a random bit string. Secret tokens have the following advantages over signatures: (1) no certification and key pre-distribution/sharing is needed, eliminating the need for a PKI and/or a trusted dealer; (2) no unproven assumptions such as the hardness of factorization or of discrete logarithm computation are needed; (3) the assumption of a computationally bounded adversary is not needed; (4) sampling of secret tokens can be done offline or asynchronously, without imposing an overhead in the critical execution path of the algorithm as done if signatures are used. Our algorithms are also designed to gracefully degrade their properties if the secrecy of the tokens is violated, whereas existing authenticated protocols do not discuss the system behaviors if signatures can be forged by the adversary.

1.1 Previous and Related Work

The different types of read/write storage *safe*, *regular* and *atomic* (in increasing strength) have been introduced by Lamport [10]. The study of reliable distributed storage using faulty storage components was initiated in [11] for the crash model and was extended to the Byzantine model in [7]. Since then, several Byzantine resilient distributed storage algorithms have been developed. However, only a few of them exhibit the features of robustness and optimal resilience. For instance, some implementations do not ensure wait-freedom [12] but weaker termination guarantees, such as obstruction-freedom [13] introduced in [14], or finite-writes [4]. Other works implement only weaker safe storage semantics [1,7,4,2]. Safe storage may return arbitrary values under concurrency.

Distributed storage has also been studied in a model where active base objects are able to push messages to subscribed clients and that are able to communicate with each other [15, 16, 17]. In our work we consider passive base objects which are only able to respond to client requests and do not communicate. Different works assume a stronger model where data is authenticated (called self-verifying data) [7, 8, 9], typically using digital signatures. As discussed, such solutions entail a certification and a key pre-distribution phase, they are often based on unproven assumptions, they are not secure against computationally unbounded adversaries and they entail a noticeable computation overhead.

Lower bounds have shown that protocols using the optimal number of $3t+1$ base objects [15] require at least *two rounds* to implement both read and write operations [2,4]. If readers are not allowed to modify the state of the base objects, the read latency is linear in the number of the base objects [4]. Our algorithms have a write complexity of two rounds, which is optimal. The read lower bounds mentioned above are circumvented using secret tokens.

The authors of [3,5] study the best case complexity of robust atomic storage. However, reads are not bounded wait-free, requiring an unbounded number of rounds in the worst case. Recent works have studied amnesic distributed storage [5, 18, 19, 6]. Amnesic storage algorithms do not store the entire history of written values in the base objects [19].

1.2 Summary of Contributions

We now briefly summarize our contributions.

(1) We show that secret tokens can be used to reduce the read complexity of unauthenticated storage with optimal resilience from $O(n)$ rounds [4], where n is the number of base objects, to just two communication rounds. The resulting algorithm supports a possibly unbounded number of malicious readers. Our implementation is gracefully degrading. Even if the secrecy of tokens is violated, the algorithm preserves the safety properties of regular storage.

(2) We show that if readers do not write, then the cost of two communication rounds of the read operation is a lower bound for every unauthenticated storage algorithm with optimal resilience. The lower bound of [4] does not hold in a model that allows the use of secret tokens. Therefore, the time complexity of our first algorithm is optimal.

(3) Under the assumption that readers can modify the base objects, we exhibit an implementation in which every read completes after one communication round. The read lower bound of two communication rounds [2] is circumvented also in this case by using secret tokens. This algorithm is also gracefully degrading. It preserves wait-freedom and never returns a forged value. It may however return an outdated value if the secrecy of tokens is violated.

2 System Model and Definitions

We consider an asynchronous distributed system consisting of a collection of clients, interacting with a finite collection of n storage elements (called base objects). Clients are divided into a singleton writer process and a (possibly infinite) set of reader processes. When needed, the number of readers is denoted by r. Up to $t \leq \lfloor n/3 \rfloor$ base objects can be nonresponsive-arbitrary [1]. Any number of reader processes can suffer Byzantine failures and the writer may fail by crashing. Clients communicate with the base objects by message-passing using point-to-point reliable communication channels. Base objects do not communicate with each other and do not push messages to clients.

We assume the existence of a function GetToken used by clients that takes no arguments and outputs a value in $\{0,1\}^*$ and has the following property:
Secrecy: The adversary cannot generate the ith output of function GetToken before the ith invocation of GetToken.

This assumption can be implemented by sampling a value (called token) randomly, uniformly and independently from $\{0,1\}^k$. With 2^k different tokens and large k (in practice a few bytes suffice), the probability of creating a token before learning it is negligibly small.

A storage abstraction is a data structure with an initial value v_0 and two operations: WRITE(v), which stores $v \neq v_0$ in the storage and READ, which returns the value from the storage. We say that an operation *op* is *complete* in a run if the run contains a response step for *op*. For any two operations *op* and *op'*, when the response step of *op* precedes the invocation step of *op'*, we say *op precedes op'*. If neither *op* nor *op'* precedes the other then they are *concurrent*.

A regular storage returns the value of the last complete WRITE preceding READ, or of some concurrent WRITE. A safe storage behaves like a regular one only if no WRITE overlaps the READ. Else, it may return arbitrary values.

The time-complexity (or latency) of a distributed storage algorithm is defined as the number of communication round-trips from the clients to the base objects and back.

3 An Implementation Supporting Unbounded Readers

Our first algorithm uses $n \geq 3t+1$ base objects to implement a multi-reader single-writer (MRSW) regular storage and features optimal time complexity for both operations (see Section 3.4). In the following we give a detailed description of the algorithm.

3.1 Overview

Both READ and WRITE operations take at most two rounds. In each round, the client sends a message to all objects. Each round terminates at the latest after receiving matching replies from $n-t$ correct objects. A value is written in two consecutive phases, called *pre-write* and *write* phase. In the first READ round, the reader samples a set of candidates such that the value returned after the second round is among them. In the second round, the reader collects from the objects copies of the values in the candidate set, until it finds a value to return.

The base objects maintain the array $history[0\ldots]$ used by the base objects to keep track of the values written. The entry $history[ts].pw$ stores a timestamp-value pair $tsval$ of the form $\langle ts, v\rangle$ and $history[ts].w$ the pair $\langle tsval, token\rangle$. The initial token value is the empty token denoted ϵ. Variable ts stores the timestamp of the last written value. The variables of an object are collectively called *fields*.

In the pre-write phase, of WRITE(v), the writer: (1) increases its timestamp ts, (2) assigns the timestamp-value pair $\langle ts, v\rangle$ to its variable pw and (3) writes pw to $n - t$ objects' $history[ts].pw$ field (short pw field). In the write phase, the writer (1) saves the previously written value w in the variable w_p, (2) invokes GetToken and assigns its output to variable $w.token$, (3) assigns pw to $w.tsval$ and (4) writes both w and w_p to $n - t$ objects' $history[ts].w$ and $history[ts - 1].w$ fields respectively (short w fields). The algorithms of the writer and the base objects appear in Figures 1 and 2 respectively.

In the following we detail the READ implementation since it is more involved and constitutes the main focus of this paper.

```
Initialization:
    ts ← 0; w ← ⟨⟨0, v0⟩, ϵ⟩

WRITE(v)
    /* Pre-write Phase */
    inc(ts)
    pw ← ⟨ts, v⟩
    send pw⟨ts, pw⟩ to all objects
    wait for reception of pw_ack⟨ts⟩ from n − t objects
    /* Write Phase */
    wp ← w
    w.token ← GetToken()
    w.tsval ← pw
    send wr⟨ts, w, wp⟩ to all objects
    wait for reception of wr_ack⟨ts⟩ from n − t objects
    return ack
```

Fig. 1. Algorithm of the writer

3.2 READ Implementation

The full algorithm of the readers can be found in Figure 3. As mentioned earlier, READ performs in two rounds. In the first round, the reader collects from $n-t$ base objects the latest and the second latest values written w and w_p and adds them to the set of return candidates C. For this purpose the reader sends a message *rd1* to all objects (line 18) and awaits $n - t$ matching responses of type *rd1_ack* (line 20).

In the second round, the reader gathers copies of the candidate values in C from the history of pw and the w fields of the base objects until it finds a candidate it can safely return. For this purpose, in the second round (1) the reader adds the timestamps of the candidates in C to a set TS (line 21) and (2) sends a message *rd2* to all objects (line 22). Upon reception of a *rd2* message, each correct object constructs two sets PW and W, and for each timestamp $ts \in TS$ it adds to PW and W the corresponding value from the $history[ts].pw$ and $history[ts].w$ fields, if present. Finally, it sends a *rd2_ack* message containing PW and W back to the reader. When the reader receives a matching *rd2_ack* message from base object i for the first time, it records PW and W in its variables $PW[i]$ and $W[i]$, and removes all candidates from C which are incomplete (lines 23–25). If a value c is incomplete then it is missing from $n - t$ objects' history of w fields. In this case, the WRITE of c does not precede READ and thus c can be disregarded without violating regularity. The reader keeps waiting for additional *rd2_ack* messages until there is a candidate $c \in C$ such that no candidate in C has a higher timestamp (i.e., predicate highCand(c) holds) and c is stored at $t+1$ base objects in the pw or w field (i.e., predicate safe(c) holds).

Our implementation guarantees that the condition in line 26 is eventually satisfied in every READ. In the following we give a rough intuition of why this is true (the detailed proof can be found in Section 3.3).

Observe that $C \neq \emptyset$ because the second-last written value reported by a correct object is never incomplete. Assume by contradiction that READ never completes, i.e. there is a candidate $c \in C$ such that c is never eliminated from C and c is never safe. Consider the following two cases. Case (1): c is reported in the first READ round *after* the pre-write phase of $c.tsval$ has completed. In this case, $c.tsval$ is pre-written to $t+1$ correct objects before any of them is accessed by the second READ round. Hence $t+1$ correct objects eventually report $c.tsval$ from their pw history and c becomes safe. Case (2): c is reported during the first READ round *before* the pre-write phase of $c.tsval$ has completed. Clearly, c is reported by a malicious object. By the Secrecy assumption, the token used by the adversary is different from the token which is indeed written together with $c.tsval$. Hence, no correct object reports c and c is eliminated from C. Therefore, each value either becomes safe or is removed from the set of candidates.

It is important to note that the algorithm implements a regular storage even if the Secrecy assumption does not hold. Specifically, the proof of regularity below does not rely on the inability of the adversary to guess the token.

3.3 Correctness

Lemma 1 (Regularity). *The* READ *operation either returns the latest value written before* READ *is invoked or one that is written concurrently with* READ.

Proof. Note that if READ returns a value $c.tsval.val$, then safe(c) holds. This implies that $t+1$ objects respond with $c.tsval$ and some of these is correct. Hence, either $c.tsval$ has been written or is $\langle 0, v_0 \rangle$. We now show that READ does not return values older that the latest WRITE preceding READ.

If no WRITE completes before READ then we are done. Else, let R be a READ invocation and W $=$ WRITE(v) be the last WRITE that completes before R is invoked. Let ts be the timestamp associated with v. We need to show that if $c.tsval.val$ is returned, then $c.tsval.ts \geq ts$.

We assume by contradiction that $c.tsval.ts < ts$. Since W precedes R, the write phase of $\langle ts, v \rangle$ completes at $t+1$ correct objects before any of them is accessed by R.

```
Initialization:
    ts ← 0; history[0].pw ← ⟨0, v0⟩; history[0].w ← ⟨pw, ϵ⟩
upon reception of pw⟨ts′, pw⟩ from writer
    history[ts′].pw ← pw
    send pw_ack⟨ts′⟩ to writer
upon reception of wr⟨ts′, w, w_p⟩ from writer
    if ts′ > ts then ts ← ts′
    history[ts′].w ← w; history[ts′ − 1].w ← w_p
    send wr_ack⟨ts′⟩ to writer
upon reception of rd1⟨tsr⟩ from reader j
    send rd1_ack⟨tsr, history[ts].w, history[ts − 1].w⟩ to reader j
upon reception of rd2⟨tsr, TS⟩ from reader j
    PW ← {history[ts′].pw : ts′ ∈ TS}
    W ← {history[ts′].w : ts′ ∈ TS}
    send rd2_ack⟨tsr, PW, W⟩ to reader j
```

Fig. 2. Algorithm of the base objects

```
Predicates:
    safe(c) ≜ |{i ∈ Q : c.tsval ∈ PW[i] ∨ c ∈ W[i]}| ≥ t + 1
    incomplete(c) ≜ |{i ∈ Q : c ∉ W[i]}| ≥ n − t
    highCand(c) ≜ c ∈ C : (∀c′ ∈ C : c.tsval.ts ≥ c′.tsval.ts)

READ()
    C ← TS ← Q ← ∅
    PW[i] ← W[i] ← ∅, 1 ≤ i ≤ n
    /* Round 1 */
    inc(tsr)
    send rd1⟨tsr⟩ to all objects
    repeat
        if received rd1_ack⟨tsr, w, w_p⟩ then C ← C ∪ {w, w_p}
    until received rd1_ack⟨tsr, ∗⟩ from n − t objects
    TS ← {c.tsval.ts : c ∈ C}
    /* Round 2 */
    send rd2⟨tsr, TS⟩ to all objects
    repeat
        if received rd2_ack⟨tsr, PW, W⟩ from object i then
            Q ← Q ∪ {i}; PW[i] ← PW; W[i] ← W
            C ← C \ {c ∈ C : incomplete(c)}
    until (received rd2_ack⟨tsr, ∗⟩ from n − t objects) ∧
        (∃c ∈ C : safe(c) ∧ highCand(c))
    return c.tsval.val
```

Fig. 3. Algorithm of the readers

Therefore, these $t + 1$ objects report to the first round of R values with timestamp ts or higher. Since READ waits for $n - t$ responses, it receives a response from one of these $t + 1$ correct objects. Let i denote this object and let c' be the value with the lowest timestamp of the two values reported by i such that $c'.tsval.ts \geq ts$. We show that c' is not incomplete. Assume the contrary.

By definition of incomplete, c' is missing from the history of $n-t$ objects. There are two cases to consider. If c' is reported in w, then by the choice of c', it holds that $c'.tsval = \langle ts, v \rangle$. Otherwise, c' is reported in w_p, which implies that WRITE($c'.tsval.val$) precedes the second round of R. In both cases c' has been stored in the history of w fields of $t+1$ correct objects before the second read round starts. Hence, c' is missing from the history of w fields of at most $n-t-1$ objects, a contradiction. Consequently, c' is not incomplete and is never removed from the set C of candidates. As $c'.tsval.ts \geq ts > c.tsval.ts$, c is not highCand, contradicting the assumption that R returns $c.tsval.val$. □

Lemma 2 (Wait-freedom). READ *and* WRITE *operations are wait-free.*

Proof. As the WRITE operation waits for at most $n - t$ objects to respond and by assumption there are $n - t$ correct objects, it never blocks. We now show that the READ operation does not block.

We assume by contradiction that READ blocks in line 23. We consider the time after which all correct objects (at least $n-t$) have responded. We first show that $C \neq \emptyset$. Let c be the second-last value written to a correct object and reported in w_p (line 19). Observe that WRITE($c.tsval.val$) is complete before the second round of R starts. Therefore c is missing from the history of at most $n - t - 1$ objects and thus, c is never eliminated from C.

We now show that for all $c \in C$, safe(c) holds. Assume by contradiction that there exists $c \in C$ and c is not safe. We distinguish the following two cases:

Case (1): c is reported in the first round by some correct object. This implies that $c.tsval$ is pre-written to $t + 1$ correct objects before any of them is read in the second round. Therefore, these $t + 1$ correct objects respond with $c.tsval$ in PW and c is safe. Case (2): only malicious objects respond with c in the first read round. If no correct object reports c in the second read round, then c is incomplete and hence $c \notin C$. Else, if some correct object reports $c' = c$, then $c'.token = c.token$. By the Secrecy property, the malicious base objects report c only after the WRITE of c' has invoked GetToken. As the pre-write phase precedes the invocation of GetToken, $c.tsval$ is pre-written to $t+1$ correct objects before the second READ round starts and therefore c is safe. □

Theorem 1. *The Algorithm appearing in figures 1, 2 and 3 wait-free implements a MRSW regular storage.*

Proof. Follows directly from Lemma 1 and Lemma 2. □

Efficiency After having proved the correctness, we now discuss the efficiency of the algorithm. As the algorithm stores the history of written values in the base objects, the storage requirements depend on the number of write operations. Note that, if readers do not write, storing less values is an open problem [19]. The messages used are of constant size except the second read round messages which are $O(n)$. Observe that neither the storage requirements of the base objects nor the communication complexity (i.e. message size) depends on the number of readers in the system. Thus, the algorithm is scalable, supporting a possibly unbounded number of malicious clients. As announced, the time-complexity of both READs and WRITEs is of two rounds in the worst case.

In the following we show that the round-complexity of the algorithm is tight.

3.4 Optimality: Fast Reads Must Write

In this section we give a rough intuition of why the presented algorithm has optimal time-complexity. Due to space limitations, we make only a statement of the result. A detailed proof can be found in our technical report [20].

Theorem 2. There is no fast READ implementation of a single-reader single-writer (*SRSW*) safe storage from $4t$ base objects if the reader does not modify the base objects' state.

This result, together with the lower bound of two rounds for the WRITE [4], imply that our first algorithm exhibits optimal time-complexity.

Our proof derives from three indistinguishable runs. In the first run, READ is concurrent with WRITE, all correct base objects have responded and the faulty objects have crashed. In the second run, WRITE precedes READ but the faulty objects are malicious and hide the written value from the reader, simulating the concurrency of the first run. In the third run, no value is written and the malicious base objects forge the value of the writer. The reader finds itself in a situation in which it cannot distinguish between the second and the third run. If the reader returns a value, then it returns the same value in both runs, which violates safety either in the second or the third run. Else if the reader waits for more base objects, then it would block in the first run, which violates liveness.

4 An Implementation of Fast READs

The second algorithm we present in this paper also uses $n \geq 3t + 1$ base objects and implements a MRSW regular storage. The main difference to the previous algorithm is that every READ operation completes after one communication round.

4.1 Overview

In each round the client (reader or writer) sends a message to all objects and waits until it has received matching replies from at most $n - t$ correct objects. Like in the previous algorithm, a value is written in two phases, a pre-write and a subsequent write phase. Unlike in the previous algorithm, in the pre-write phase, in addition to writing data, the writer also reads control data from the base objects. Readers write control data and read data written by the writer.

The base objects maintain in addition to the history of written values an array $tsrtoken[1...r]$ which is updated by the readers. The entry $tsrtoken[j]$ stores a timestamp-token pair of the form $\langle tsr, token \rangle$, where tsr is the most recent timestamp of reader j and $token$ the corresponding token value.

In the pre-write phase, of WRITE(v), the writer: (1) increases its timestamp ts, (2) stores the last pre-written value in pw_p (3) assigns the timestamp-value pair $\langle ts, v\rangle$ to its variable pw, (4) writes pw and w to $n-t$ objects' $history[ts].pw$ and $history[ts-1].w$ fields respectively, (5) reads the objects' $tsrtoken[*]$ fields written by the readers and (6) for each reader j adds $tsrtoken[j]$ to the set $Tsrtokens[j]$. In the write phase, the writer (1) assigns $\langle pw, Tsrtokens\rangle$ to variable w and (2) writes both w and pw_p to $n-t$ objects' $history[ts].w$ and $history[ts-1].pw$ fields respectively. The algorithm of the writer appears in Figure 4.

In the following we detail the READ implementation and the interaction with the base objects, which is slightly more involved.

Initialization:
    $Inittsrtokens[j] \leftarrow \emptyset, 1 \leq j \leq r$
    $ts \leftarrow 0$; $pw \leftarrow \langle 0, v_0\rangle$; $w \leftarrow \langle pw, Inittsrtokens\rangle$

WRITE(v)
    /* *Pre-Write Phase* */
    $Tsrtokens \leftarrow Inittsrtokens$
    inc(ts)
    $pw_p \leftarrow pw$
    $pw \leftarrow \langle ts, v\rangle$
    send *pw*$\langle ts, pw, w\rangle$ to all objects
    repeat
        if received *pw_ack*$\langle ts, tsrtoken\rangle$ from object i **then**
            Tsrtokens$[j] \leftarrow Tsrtokens[j] \cup \{tsrtoken[j]\}, 1 \leq j \leq r$
    until received *pw_ack*$\langle ts, *\rangle$ from $n-t$ objects
    /* *Write Phase* */
    $w \leftarrow \langle pw, Tsrtokens\rangle$
    send *wr*$\langle ts, pw_p, w\rangle$ to all objects
    wait for reception of *wr_ack*$\langle ts\rangle$ from $n-t$ objects
    return *ack*

Fig. 4. Algorithm of the writer

4.2 READ Implementation

The full algorithm of the base objects is given in Figure 5 and that of the readers in Figure 6. As mentioned earlier, READ completes in one communication round. The reader (1) increments its timestamp tsr, (2) selects a secret token $token$ and (3) sends a message *rd* containing tsr and $token$ to all objects. Upon reception of *rd* from reader j, each correct object (1) stores $\langle tsr, token\rangle$ in $tsrtoken[j]$, (2) computes a timestamp ts_{max} such that any higher timestamped value stored has been written concurrently with READ and (3) sends a message *rd_ack* containing three values with timestamps $ts_{max}-1$, ts_{max} and $ts_{max}+1$ (if available) back to the reader. When the reader receives a *rd_ack* message from object i for the first time, it stores the value with timestamp ts_{max} in $w[i]$ and adds $w[i]$ to the set of candidates C. The other two values are added to $PW[i]$. In addition it removes all incomplete candidates from C. A candidate is incomplete when $n-t$ objects have reported candidates with lower timestamps. Observe that the choice of ts_{max} as candidate is crucial: (a) values with higher timestamps can be safely disregarded without violating regularity and (b) the value corresponding to ts_{max} is stored in $t+1$ correct objects' pw field before any of them is read. The latter property is critical because otherwise, a candidate might never become safe. The termination condition is the existence of a candidate which is both highCand and safe. Our implementation guarantees that this condition is eventually satisfied in every READ. We now give an intuition of why this is true.

Recall that, for every candidate c it holds that c is pre-written to $t+1$ correct objects before any of them is read. We now explain why. The negation thereof implies that at least $t+1$ correct objects store the timestamp-token pair of READ *before* c is pre-written to them. At least one of them reports the token in the pre-write phase, such that c and all higher timestamped values are stored together with the token in the write phase. Consequently, all correct objects (at least $n-t$) report to READ only values with lower timestamps and c is eliminated from C. It is not difficult to see that if the correct base objects report the entire pw history, then every candidate would eventually become safe. Our approach simulates this behaviour, but the correct objects send at most three values, with consecutive timestamps centered around ts_{max}. The reasoning behind it is the following: if some candidate is lower than the first, then it is not highCand. Else, if it is higher than the third, then it is removed from C.

4.3 Correctness

Lemma 3 (Regularity). *The* READ *operation either returns the latest value written before* READ *is invoked or one that is written concurrently with* READ.

Proof. Observe that if READ returns a value $c.val$, then safe(c) holds. This implies that $t+1$ objects respond with c and some of these is correct. Hence, either c has been written or is $\langle 0, v_0\rangle$. We now show that READ does not return values older than the latest WRITE preceding READ.

If no WRITE completes before READ then we are done. Else, let R be a READ invocation of reader j and W $=$ WRITE(v) be the last WRITE that completes before R is invoked. Let ts be the timestamp associated with v. We need to show that if $c.val$ is returned, then $c.ts \geq ts$.

We assume by contradiction that $c.ts < ts$. Let $\langle tsr, token\rangle$ be the timestamp-token pair of R. Since W precedes R, GetToken is invoked by R after W is complete. If some malicious object reports $\langle tsr, token'\rangle$ to W, then the Secrecy assumption implies that $token \neq token'$. Therefore, W does not include $\langle tsr, token\rangle$ in the set $Tsrtokens[j]$ corresponding to $\langle ts, v\rangle$. Furthermore, the write phase of $\langle ts, v\rangle$ completes at $t+1$ correct base objects before any of them is accessed by R. As $\langle tsr, token\rangle \notin Tsrtokens[j]$, these $t+1$ correct objects report values with timestamp ts or higher from their w field.

Let c' be the value with the lowest timestamp received from the w field of any of the $t+1$ objects. As R waits for at least $n-t$ objects to respond, such a value exists. We show that c' is not incomplete. Assume the contrary. By definition of incomplete, $n-t$ objects must report values with timestamps lower than $c'.ts$ from their w field. At

Initialization:

$\quad$ *Inittsrtokens*$[j] \leftarrow \emptyset$; $tsrtoken[j] \leftarrow \langle 0, \epsilon \rangle, 1 \leq j \leq r$

$\quad$ $history[0].pw \leftarrow \langle 0, v_0 \rangle$; $history[0].w \leftarrow \langle \langle 0, v_0 \rangle, Inittsrtokens \rangle$

upon reception of $pw\langle ts, pw, w \rangle$ from writer

$\quad$ $history[ts].pw \leftarrow pw$; $history[ts-1].w \leftarrow w$

$\quad$ send $pw\_ack\langle ts, tsrtoken \rangle$ to writer

upon reception of $wr\langle ts, pw_p, w \rangle$ from writer

$\quad$ $history[ts-1].pw \leftarrow pw_p$; $history[ts].w \leftarrow w$

$\quad$ send $wr\_ack\langle ts' \rangle$ to writer

upon reception of $rd\langle tsr, token \rangle$ from reader j

$\quad$ **if** $tsr > tsrtoken[j].tsr$ **then** $tsrtoken[j] \leftarrow \langle tsr, token \rangle$

$\quad$ $ts_{max} \leftarrow \max\{ts : tsrtoken[j] \notin history[ts].w.Tsrtokens[j]\}$

$\quad$ $w \leftarrow history[ts_{max}].w.tsval$

$\quad$ $PW \leftarrow \{history[ts_{max}-1].pw, history[ts_{max}+1].pw\}$

$\quad$ send $rd\_ack\langle tsr, PW, w \rangle$ to reader j

Fig. 5. Algorithm of the base objects

Predicates:

$\quad$ safe$(c) \triangleq |\{i \in Q : c \in PW[i] \cup \{w[i]\}\}| \geq t+1$

$\quad$ incomplete$(c) \triangleq |\{i \in Q : w[i].ts < c.ts\}| \geq n-t$

$\quad$ highCand$(c) \triangleq \forall c' \in C : c.ts \geq c'.ts$

READ()

$\quad$ $C \leftarrow Q \leftarrow \emptyset$

$\quad$ $PW[i] \leftarrow \emptyset$; $w[i] \leftarrow \perp, 1 \leq i \leq n$

$\quad$ $inc(tsr)$

$\quad$ $token \leftarrow$ GetToken()

$\quad$ send $rd\langle tsr, token \rangle$ to all objects

$\quad$ **repeat**

$\quad\quad$ **if** received $rd\_ack\langle tsr, PW, w \rangle$ from object i **then**

$\quad\quad\quad$ $Q \leftarrow Q \cup \{i\}$; $PW[i] \leftarrow PW$; $w[i] \leftarrow w$; $C \leftarrow C \cup \{w\}$

$\quad\quad\quad$ $C \leftarrow C \setminus \{c \in C :$ incomplete$(c)\}$

$\quad$ **until** (received $rd\_ack\langle tsr, * \rangle$ from $n-t$ objects) $\wedge$

$\quad\quad$ $(\exists c \in C :$ safe$(c) \wedge$ highCand$(c))$

$\quad$ **return** $c.val$

Fig. 6. Algorithm of the readers

least one of these is a correct object i among the $t+1$ updated by W. By the choice of c', $w[i].ts \geq c'.ts$. Therefore, c' is not incomplete and is never removed from the set C of candidates. As $c'.ts \geq ts > c.ts$, c is not highCand, contradicting the assumption that c is returned by R. □

Lemma 4 (Wait-freedom). READ *and* WRITE *operations are wait-free.*

Proof. As the WRITE operation waits for at most $n-t$ objects to respond and by assumption there are $n-t$ correct objects, it never blocks. We now show that the READ operation does not block.

We assume by contradiction that READ blocks in line 23. We consider the time after which all correct objects (at least $n-t$) have responded. We first show that $C \neq \emptyset$. Let c be the $t+1$st highest value reported in the w field of a correct object. Clearly, c is not incomplete and thus it is not removed from C.

Let $c \in C$ be the highest value reported in the w field of a correct object. We show that (1) highCand(c) holds and (2) safe(c) holds.

Step (1): If c is not highCand, then there exists $c' \in C$ and $c'.ts > c.ts$. By the choice of c, there are $n-t$ correct objects i that report values $w[i]$ such that $w[i].ts < c'.ts$. This implies that $c' \notin C$, a contradiction.

Step (2): Observe that $t+1$ correct objects have stored c in their pw field before any of them replies to READ. Else, no correct object would reply with c in the w field (line 11). Let i be any of these correct objects. We assume by contradiction that $c \notin PW[i] \cup \{w[i]\}$. Let ts_{max} be the timestamp computed by object i in line 11. If $c.ts - 1 \leq ts_{max} \leq c.ts+1$, then c is reported either from $PW[i]$ or $w[i]$ and we are done. Observe that, since c is pre-written to i together with the last written value (with timestamp $c.ts-1$), it holds that $ts_{max} \geq c.ts-1$. Therefore, the only remaining case is $ts_{max} > c.ts+1$. This implies that c' exists such that $ts_{max} > c'.ts > c.ts$. Since the value with timestamp ts_{max} is pre-written to $t+1$ correct objects before they are read, c' is written to $t+1$ correct objects before they are read. Hence, c' or a higher timestamped value is not incomplete, contradicting the assumption that c is highCand. □

Theorem 3. *The Algorithm appearing in figures 4, 5 and 6 wait-free implements a MRSW regular storage.*

Proof. Follows directly from Lemma 3 and Lemma 4. □

Efficiency. We now discuss the efficiency of the algorithm. Like in the previous algorithm, the storage requirements depend on the number of write operations. In addition, the base objects store up to $n \cdot r$ timestamp-token pairs together with each value written to them. Messages exchanged between the reader and the base objects are of constant size. The WRITE messages *pw_ack* (respectively *wr*) contain r (respectively $n \cdot r$) timestamp-token pairs. The time-complexity of the READ is one communication round in the worst case, which is clearly optimal. Every WRITE completes after two rounds which is also optimal [4].

5 Conclusion

The algorithms presented effectively circumvent lower bounds established for unauthenticated storage by using secret tokens. The first algorithm supports unbounded readers and features constant read complexity. The second algorithm features fast reads, i.e., every read terminates after one round of communication with the base objects. Even if the secrecy assumption of the token is violated both algorithms are gracefully degrading. The first algorithm fully preserves regularity and the second algorithm never blocks and never returns a forged value. However, the probability of property violation is negligibly small if the token space is large enough. The algorithms are secure against a computationally unbounded adversary because tokens are purely random and therefore they cannot be computed.

Both algorithms require base objects to store all the values they receive from the writers. If readers do not write, storing less values is an open problem [19]. Concerning the second algorithm, a sophisticated arbitration mechanism as shown in [6] is needed to overcome this problem, which goes beyond the scope of the paper. Although some very practical storage systems [21] rely on the same assumption this might raise issues of storage exhaustion and needs careful garbage collection.

References

1. Jayanti, P., Chandra, T.D., Toueg, S.: Fault-tolerant wait-free shared objects. J. ACM 45(3), 451–500 (1998)
2. Guerraoui, R., Vukolić, M.: How fast can a very robust read be? In: PODC 2006: Proceedings of the twenty-fifth annual ACM symposium on Principles of distributed computing, pp. 248–257. ACM, New York (2006)
3. Guerraoui, R., Levy, R.R., Vukolić, M.: Lucky read/write access to robust atomic storage. In: DSN 2006: Proceedings of the International Conference on Dependable Systems and Networks (DSN 2006), pp. 125–136 (2006)
4. Abraham, I., Chockler, G., Keidar, I., Malkhi, D.: Byzantine disk paxos: optimal resilience with byzantine shared memory. Distributed Computing 18(5), 387–408 (2006)
5. Guerraoui, R., Vukolić, M.: Refined quorum systems. In: PODC 2007: Proceedings of the twenty-sixth annual ACM symposium on Principles of distributed computing, pp. 119–128 (2007)
6. Dobre, D., Majuntke, M., Suri, N.: On the time-complexity of robust and amnesic storage. In: Baker, T.P., Bui, A., Tixeuil, S. (eds.) OPODIS 2008. LNCS, vol. 5401, pp. 197–216. Springer, Heidelberg (2008)
7. Malkhi, D., Reiter, M.: Byzantine quorum systems. Distrib. Comput. 11(4), 203–213 (1998)
8. Cachin, C., Tessaro, S.: Optimal resilience for erasure-coded byzantine distributed storage. In: DSN 2006: Proceedings of the International Conference on Dependable Systems and Networks (DSN 2006), Washington, DC, USA, pp. 115–124. IEEE Computer Society, Los Alamitos (2006)
9. Liskov, B., Rodrigues, R.: Tolerating byzantine faulty clients in a quorum system. In: ICDCS 2006: Proceedings of the 26th IEEE International Conference on Distributed Computing Systems, Washington, DC, USA, p. 34. IEEE Computer Society, Los Alamitos (2006)
10. Lamport, L.: On interprocess communication. part II: Algorithms. Distributed Computing 1(2), 86–101 (1986)

11. Attiya, H., Bar-Noy, A., Dolev, D.: Sharing memory robustly in message-passing systems. J. ACM 42(1), 124–142 (1995)
12. Herlihy, M.: Wait-free synchronization. ACM Trans. Program. Lang. Syst. 13(1), 124–149 (1991)
13. Hendricks, J., Ganger, G.R., Reiter, M.K.: Low-overhead byzantine fault-tolerant storage. In: SOSP 2007: Proceedings of twenty-first ACM SIGOPS symposium on Operating systems principles, pp. 73–86. ACM, New York (2007)
14. Herlihy, M., Luchangco, V., Moir, M.: Obstruction-free synchronization: Double-ended queues as an example. In: ICDCS 2003: Proceedings of the 23rd International Conference on Distributed Computing Systems, Washington, DC, USA, p. 522. IEEE Computer Society, Los Alamitos (2003)
15. Martin, J.P., Alvisi, L., Dahlin, M.: Minimal Byzantine Storage. In: Malkhi, D. (ed.) DISC 2002. LNCS, vol. 2508, pp. 311–325. Springer, Heidelberg (2002)
16. Bazzi, R.A., Ding, Y.: Non-skipping timestamps for byzantine data storage systems. In: Guerraoui, R. (ed.) DISC 2004. LNCS, vol. 3274, pp. 405–419. Springer, Heidelberg (2004)
17. Aiyer, A., Alvisi, L., Bazzi, R.A.: Bounded wait-free implementation of optimally resilient byzantine storage without (Unproven) cryptographic assumptions. In: Pelc, A. (ed.) DISC 2007. LNCS, vol. 4731, pp. 7–19. Springer, Heidelberg (2007)
18. Abraham, I., Chockler, G., Keidar, I., Malkhi, D.: Wait-free regular storage from byzantine components. Inf. Process. Lett. 101(2) (2007)
19. Chockler, G., Guerraoui, R., Keidar, I.: Amnesic Distributed Storage. In: Pelc, A. (ed.) DISC 2007. LNCS, vol. 4731, pp. 139–151. Springer, Heidelberg (2007)
20. Dobre, D., Majuntke, M., Serafini, M., Suri, N.: Efficient robust storage using secret tokens. Technical report, Technische Universität Darmstadt, http://www.deeds.informatik.tu-darmstadt.de/dan/dms2TR.pdf
21. Goodson, G.R., Wylie, J.J., Ganger, G.R., Reiter, M.K.: Efficient byzantine-tolerant erasure-coded storage. In: DSN 2004: Proceedings of the 2004 International Conference on Dependable Systems and Networks (DSN 2004), Washington, DC, USA, p. 135. IEEE Computer Society, Los Alamitos (2004)

An Optimal Self-stabilizing Firing Squad

Danny Dolev[1,*], Ezra N. Hoch[1], and Yoram Moses[2]

[1] The Hebrew University of Jerusalem
Jerusalem, Israel
[2] Technion—Israel Institute of Technology
Haifa, Israel

Abstract. Consider a fully connected network where up to t processes may crash, and all processes start in an arbitrary memory state. The self-stabilizing firing squad problem consists of eventually guaranteeing simultaneous response to an external input. This is modeled by requiring that the non-crashed processes "fire" simultaneously if some correct process received an external "GO" input, and that they only fire as a response to some process receiving such an input. This paper presents FIRE-SQUAD, the first self-stabilizing firing squad algorithm.

The FIRE-SQUAD algorithm is optimal in two respects: (a) Once the algorithm is in a safe state, it fires in response to a GO input as fast as any other algorithm does, and (b) Starting from an arbitrary state, it converges to a safe state as fast as any other algorithm does.

1 Introduction

The firing squad problem was first introduced in [2,3]. Informally, it is assumed that at any given round a process may receive an external "GO" input, which is considered a request for the correct processes to simultaneously "fire." Roughly, a good solution is a protocol satisfying three properties: (a) if some process fires in round r then all the non-crashed processes fire simultaneously in round r; (b) if a correct process receives a GO input in round r' then it will fire at some later round $r > r'$; and (c) a process fires in round r only if some process received a GO input in some round $r' < r$. (The formal definition disallows a solution in which a single input induces a constant firing.)

Requiring the processes to fire simultaneously captures an important aspect of distributed systems: There are cases in which it is important that activities begin in the same round, *e.g.*, when one distributed algorithm ends and another one begins, and the two may interfere with each other if executed concurrently. Similarly, many synchronous algorithms are designed assuming that all sites start participating in the same round of communication. Finally, simultaneity may be motivated by the fact that a distributed system interacts with the outside world, and these interactions should often be simultaneously consistent. A

* This research was supported in part by Israeli Science Foundation (ISF) Grant number 0397373.

R. Guerraoui and F. Petit (Eds.): SSS 2009, LNCS 5873, pp. 284–296, 2009.

non-simultaneous announcement to financial (stock) markets may enable unfair arbitrage trading, for example.

Coordinating simultaneous actions is not subsumed by the consensus task. Indeed, even when no transient failures are considered possible (so there is a global clock and no self-stabilization is required), solving the firing squad problem or simultaneously deciding in a consensus task can be considerably harder than plain consensus [4,8]. This implies, in particular, that clock synchronization [7,11,6,12,18] does not suffice for solving the firing squad problem in a self-stabilizing manner; as it can be seen as providing round-numbers to a self-stabilizing environment, which still leaves the firing squad problem as a non-trivial problem.

The firing squad problem is a primary example of a problem requiring simultaneously coordinated actions by the non-faulty processes. Simultaneous coordination has been shown to be closely related to the notion of common knowledge [10,9], and this connection has been used to characterize the earliest time required to reach simultaneous consensus, firing squad, and related problems in a variety of failure models [8,15,1,17,13,16]. One of the consequences of this literature is the fact that the time at which a simultaneous action that is based on initial values or external inputs can be performed depends in a crucial way on the pattern in which failures occur.

A general form of simultaneous agreement called *continuous consensus* was defined in [13]. In this problem, each of the processes maintains a list of events of interest that have taken place in the run, and it is guaranteed that the lists at all non-faulty processes are identical at all times. They present an optimal (non-stabilizing) implementation of such a service, which is a protocol called ConCon. If we define as the events to be monitored by ConCon to be of the form (go, p, k), corresponding to a go message arriving at process p at the end of round k, then a firing squad protocol can be obtained from ConCon simply by having the non-faulty processes fire exactly when a (go, p, k) event first appears in their identical copies of the "common" list. We shall refer to this solution to the firing squad problem based on ConCon by CCfs.

Traditionally, the firing squad problem assumes that processes do not recover, *i.e.*, failed processes stay failed forever. Moreover, even though it is easy to extend the firing squad problem so that it can be repeatedly executed (*i.e.*, allow for multiple firings over time, given that multiple go inputs are received), it assumes that nothing in the system goes amiss—except possibly for the crash failures being accounted for. Adding support for handling transient faults increases the robustness of a firing squad algorithm in this aspect. Indeed, a self stabilizing solution will, in particular, be able to cope with process recovery: Following process recoveries, the system will eventually converge to a valid state and continue operating correctly.

Transient faults alter a process's memory state in an arbitrary way. A self-stabilizing algorithm [5] is assumed to start in an arbitrary state and be guaranteed to eventually reach a state from which it operates according to its intended specification. Starting the operation at an arbitrary state enables the adversary to "plant" false information, such as the receipt of GO messages in the past, which can cause the algorithm to unjustifiably fire, either immediately, or within a few rounds. One of the challenges in designing an efficient self-stabilizing firing squad algorithm is in bounding the damage that can be caused by such false information in the initial state.

Perhaps the first candidate solution would be to initiate an instance of CCFS in every round, with $t+1$ instances executing concurrently at any given time, where t is an upper bound on the number of possible crashed processes. Firing would then take place if it is dictated by any of the instances. Since the component instances of such a solution are not themselves stabilizing, all we can show is that such a solution is guaranteed to stabilize after $t+1$ rounds, regardless of the failure pattern. We shall present a solution that does not consist of such a concurrent composition. Moreover, it performs subtle consistency checks to restrict the impact of false information that appears in the initial state. As a result, in some cases we obtain stabilization in as little as two rounds.

The above discussion points out the stabilization time as an important aspect of a self-stabilizing firing squad algorithm. Another central performance parameter is its swiftness: Once the algorithm has stabilized, how fast does it fire given that some process receives a GO input? In addition to solving the self-stabilizing firing squad problem, the algorithm presented in this paper is also optimal in terms of both its stabilization time, and its swiftness.

The main contributions of this paper are:

- A self-stabilizing variant of the firing squad problem is defined, and an algorithm solving it in the case of crash failures is given.
- The proposed algorithm, called FIRE-SQUAD, is shown to be optimal both in terms of the time it requires to stabilize and in terms of the time it takes, after stabilization, to fire in response to a GO input.
- Finally, the optimality is demonstrated in a fairly strong sense: For every possible failure pattern, both stabilization time and swiftness are the fastest possible, in any correct algorithm. In extreme cases this enables stabilization in two rounds and firing in one round.

The rest of the paper is organized as follows. Section 2 describes the model and defines the problem at hand. Section 3 provides lower bounds for the optimality properties. Section 4 describes the proposed solution, FIRE-SQUAD, and proves its correctness and optimality. Finally, Section 5 concludes with a discussion.

2 Model and Problem Definition

The system consists of a set $\mathcal{P} = \{1, \ldots, n\}$ of processes. Communication is done via message passing, and the network is synchronous and fully connected. The system starts out at time[1] $k = 0$, and a communication round r starts at time $k = r - 1$ and ends at time $k = r$. At time k each process computes its state according to its state at time $k - 1$, the internal messages it received by time

[1] All references to "time" in this paper refer to non-negative integer times.

k (sent by other processes at time $k-1$) and external inputs (if any) that it received at time k. In addition, at any time $k \geq 0$ a process can produce an external output (such as "firing").

Let $\mathcal{I}_p^k \in \{0,1\}$ represent the external input of process p at time k. We say that p received an external GO input at time k if $\mathcal{I}_p^k = 1$; Otherwise, (if $\mathcal{I}_p^k = 0$), we say that p *did not* receive a GO input. Let $\mathcal{I}_p = \{\mathcal{I}_p^k\}_{k=0}^{\infty}$, let $\mathcal{I}^k = \{\mathcal{I}_p^k\}_{p=1}^{n}$ and let $\mathcal{I} = \{\mathcal{I}_p\}_{p=1}^{n}$. $\mathcal{I}$ is "the input pattern", and $\mathcal{I}^k$ is the (joint) input at time k. In a similar manner define $\mathcal{O}_p^k \in \{0,1\}, \mathcal{O}_p, \mathcal{O}^k$ and $\mathcal{O}$ as the output pattern. If $\mathcal{O}_p^k = 1$ we say that p fires at time k, and if $\mathcal{O}_p^k = 0$ we say p does not fire at time k. It will be convenient to say that a fire action occurs at time k if $\mathcal{O}_p^k = 1$ for some process p, and similarly that a GO input is received at time k if $\mathcal{I}_p^k = 1$ for some p.

Denote by t an *a priori* bound on the number of faulty processes in the system. For ease of exposition, we assume that $t < n-1$, so that there are at least two processes that need to coordinate their actions. We assume the *crash* failure model, in which a faulty process p does not send any messages after its failing round; it behaves correctly before its failing round, and sends an arbitrary subset of its intended messages during its failing round.

A failure pattern describes for each time k which processes have failed by time k, and for each process that fails in round k (*i.e.*, did not fail by time $k-1$), which of its outgoing communication channels are blocked (and hence do not deliver its messages) in round k. Notice that a process may fail in round k even if all of its messages are delivered. We denote a failure pattern by $\mathcal{F}$, and by $\mathcal{F}^k$ the set of processes that fail in $\mathcal{F}$ by time k. Observe that $\mathcal{F}^k \subseteq \mathcal{F}^{k+1}$; in the crash failure model failed processes do not recover. Similarly, we use $\mathsf{G}^k = \mathcal{P} \setminus \mathcal{F}^k$ to denote the set of processes that are non-faulty at time k. Finally, G will denote the set of processes that remain non-faulty throughout $\mathcal{F}$, *i.e.*, $\mathsf{G} = \bigcap_{k=0}^{\infty} \mathsf{G}^k$. Notice that the set G is always defined in terms of a failure pattern $\mathcal{F}$, which is typically clear from the context.

In addition to crashes, there are also transient faults. Formally, we denote by $\mathcal{S}_p^k$ the state of a process p at time k. We denote by $\mathcal{S}^k = (\mathcal{S}_1^k, \ldots, \mathcal{S}_p^k, \ldots, \mathcal{S}_n^k)$ the state of the entire system at time k. Transient faults are captured by the assumption that the system may start from any (arbitrary) state, and there is some round r such that for all rounds $r' \geq r$ the intended algorithm operates as written. In other words, for any possible state S, if $\mathcal{S}^0 = S$ then eventually (starting from some round r) the algorithm operates correctly.

For the following analysis, each algorithm $\mathcal{A}$ is assumed to have an initial state $\mathcal{S}_{init}^{\mathcal{A}}$. For self-stabilizing algorithms, we fix an arbitrary state as $\mathcal{S}_{init}^{\mathcal{A}}$ (as the algorithm should converge starting from any initial state). The *a priori* bound of t on the number of failures is assumed to be hard-wired into the algorithm, and is not affected by transient faults. Such an algorithm is assumed to be executed only in the context of failure patterns in which at most t processes crash. For such failure patterns $\mathcal{F}$, the algorithm $\mathcal{A}$ produces an output pattern $\mathcal{O}$ starting from state $\mathcal{S}$ given an input $\mathcal{I}$; we denote this output pattern by $\mathcal{O} = \mathcal{A}(\mathcal{S}, \mathcal{I}, \mathcal{F})$.

Informally, the Firing Squad problem requires that: (1) all processes fire together (*"simultaneity"*); (2) if a GO input is received then a fire action occurs (*"liveness"*); and (3) the number of fire actions is not larger than the number of received GO inputs (*"safety"*). Formally,

Definition 1. *Let $\mathcal{O} = \mathcal{A}(\mathcal{S}, \mathcal{I}, \mathcal{F})$ and let* G *denote the set of processes that remain non-faulty throughout $\mathcal{F}$. We say that $\mathcal{O}$ satisfies the* $\mathtt{FS}(k)$ *properties (capturing correct firing-squad behavior from time k on) w.r.t. $\mathcal{I}$, $\mathcal{F}$, and $\mathcal{O}$, if the following conditions hold for all $k' \geq k$:*

1. *(simultaneity) If $\mathcal{O}_p^{k'} = 1$ for some $p \in \mathcal{P}$ then $\mathcal{O}_q^{k'} = 1$ for all $q \in \mathsf{G}$;*
2. *(liveness) If $\mathcal{I}_p^{k'} = 1$ for some $p \in \mathsf{G}$, then there is $k'' > k'$ s.t. $\mathcal{O}_p^{k''} = 1$;*
3. *(safety) The number of times k'' satisfying $k \leq k'' \leq k'$ at which a fire action occurs at k'' is not larger than the number of times h in the range $0 \leq h < k'$ at which* GO *inputs are received.*

We can use the $\mathtt{FS}(k)$ properties to define when an algorithm solves the firing squad problem in a self stabilizing manner. We first use it to define the stabilization time of an algorithm as follows:

Definition 2 (Stabilization time). *The* stabilization time *of $\mathcal{A}$ on $\mathcal{S}$, $\mathcal{I}$ and $\mathcal{F}$, denoted by $\mathtt{stab}(\mathcal{A}, \mathcal{S}, \mathcal{I}, \mathcal{F})$, is the minimal $k \geq 0$ such that $\mathtt{FS}(k)$ holds with respect to $\mathcal{I}$, $\mathcal{F}$, and $\mathcal{O} = \mathcal{A}(\mathcal{S}, \mathcal{I}, \mathcal{F})$. (If $\mathtt{FS}(k)$ holds for no finite k, then $\mathtt{stab}(\mathcal{A}, \mathcal{S}, \mathcal{I}, \mathcal{F}) = \infty$.)*

Notice that the *"safety"* property in $\mathtt{FS}(k)$ relates outputs starting from time k to inputs starting from time 0. Here's why: Since we consider time 0 to be the point at which transient errors end, if the system starts in a state in which "it appears as if" GO inputs were received before time 0, the good processes may fire after time 0 without a GO message actually having been received. Once all firings induced by such "phantom" GO inputs have occurred, we can legitimately require firing events to happen only in response to genuine GO message receipts. We thus think of the stabilization time, at which in particular the safety property of $\mathtt{FS}(k)$ holds, as one after which no firing will occur in response to phantom GO messages. Rather, every firing will be justifiable as a response to some GO message received at or after time 0.

Definition 3 (SSFS Algorithm). *An algorithm $\mathcal{A}$ solves the Self stabilizing Firing Squad problem ($\mathcal{A}$ is an SSFS algorithm, for short) if there exists a $k < \infty$ such that $\mathtt{stab}(\mathcal{A}, \mathcal{S}, \mathcal{I}, \mathcal{F}) \leq k$ for every system state $\mathcal{S}$, input pattern $\mathcal{I}$ and failure pattern $\mathcal{F}$.*

Observe that in a setting with no transient faults, an algorithm $\mathcal{A}$ solves the (non-self-stabilizing) Firing Squad problem if it satisfies $\mathtt{FS}(0)$ with respect to $\mathcal{I}$, $\mathcal{F}$, and $\mathcal{O}$, for every $\mathcal{I}$, $\mathcal{F}$ and $\mathcal{O} = \mathcal{A}(\mathcal{S}_{init}^{\mathcal{A}}, \mathcal{I}, \mathcal{F})$.

Notice that Definition 3 implies that any SSFS algorithm $\mathcal{A}$ has at least one memory state from which the firing squad properties are guaranteed to hold. Denote one of these memory states by $\mathcal{S}_{stab}^{\mathcal{A}}$, or simply $\mathcal{S}_{stab}$ when $\mathcal{A}$ is clear from the context.

2.1 Optimality Measures

In this work we are interested in finding an optimal SSFS algorithm. We start by defining stabilization time optimality, which measures how quickly algorithm $\mathcal{A}$ stabilizes.

Definition 4. *An SSFS algorithm $\mathcal{A}$ is said to* optimally stabilize *if the following holds for every SSFS algorithm $\mathcal{B}$ and every failure pattern $\mathcal{F}$:*

$$\max_{\mathcal{S},\mathcal{I}}\{\mathtt{stab}(\mathcal{A},\mathcal{S},\mathcal{I},\mathcal{F})\} \le \max_{\mathcal{S},\mathcal{I}}\{\mathtt{stab}(\mathcal{B},\mathcal{S},\mathcal{I},\mathcal{F})\} .$$

Definition 4 defines optimality of an algorithm $\mathcal{A}$ with respect to its stabilization time, *i.e.*, how quickly $\mathcal{A}$ starts to operate according to all of the FS requirements. The intuition behind defining optimality in terms of worst-case $\mathcal{S}$ and $\mathcal{I}$ is to avoid algorithms that are "specific" to an initial memory state or input pattern. Thus, by requiring optimality in the worst-case we ensure that the algorithm cannot be hand-tailored to a specific setting, but rather needs to solve the SSFS problem in a "generic" manner.

We now turn to the issue of comparing the responsiveness of distinct firing squad algorithms. Specifically, we are concerned with how quickly an algorithm fires after a GO message is received (once the algorithm has stabilized). For simplicity, we consider receipts of GO by non-faulty processes, since the problem specification forces a firing following such a receipt. Another subtle issue is that if GO messages are received in different rounds between which there is no firing, then it may be difficult to figure out which GO message the next firing is responding to. Again for simplicity, we will be interested in what will be called *sequential* input patterns, in which a GO is not received before all previous GO's have been followed by firings. More formally, we define:

Definition 5 (Sequential inputs). *Let $\mathcal{A}$ be an SSFS algorithm. We say that the input $\mathcal{I}$ is sequential with respect to ($\mathcal{A}$, $\mathcal{S}$, $\mathcal{F}$) if (i) no* GO *inputs are received according to $\mathcal{I}$ at times $k < \mathtt{stab}(\mathcal{A},\mathcal{S},\mathcal{I},\mathcal{F})$, (ii)* GO *inputs are received in $\mathcal{I}$ only by processes from G, and (iii) if $k_1 < k_2$ and* GO *inputs are received at both k_1 and k_2, then there is an intermediate time $k_1 < k' \le k_2$ at which a fire action occurs.*

The following definition formally captures the number of firing events that occur between the stabilization time and a given time k.

Definition 6. *Let $\mathcal{A}$ be an SSFS algorithm and let $\mathcal{O} = \mathcal{A}(\mathcal{S},\mathcal{I},\mathcal{F})$. We define $\#[(\mathcal{A},\mathcal{S},\mathcal{I},\mathcal{F}),k]$ to be the number of rounds k' in the range $\mathtt{stab}(\mathcal{A},\mathcal{S},\mathcal{I},\mathcal{F}) \le k' \le k$ such that $\mathcal{O}_p^{k'} = 1$ holds for some process p (*i.e., *a firing occurs at time k').*

By definition, if $k < \mathtt{stab}(\mathcal{A},\mathcal{S},\mathcal{I},\mathcal{F})$ then $\#[(\mathcal{A},\mathcal{S},\mathcal{I},\mathcal{F}),k] = 0$. With the last two definitions, we are now able to formally compare the responsiveness of different SSFS algorithms:

Definition 7 (Swiftness). *Let $\mathcal{A}$ and $\mathcal{B}$ be SSFS algorithms. We say that $\mathcal{A}$ is* at least as swift as *$\mathcal{B}$ if $\mathcal{A}$ fires at least as quickly as $\mathcal{B}$ on all sequential inputs. Formally, we require that for every failure pattern $\mathcal{F}$, input $\mathcal{I}$, and states $\mathcal{S}_{\mathcal{A}}$ of $\mathcal{A}$ and $\mathcal{S}_{\mathcal{B}}$ of $\mathcal{B}$, the following holds. If $\mathcal{I}$ is sequential both with respect to ($\mathcal{A}$, $\mathcal{S}_{\mathcal{A}}$, $\mathcal{F}$) and with respect to ($\mathcal{B}$, $\mathcal{S}_{\mathcal{B}}$, $\mathcal{F}$), then $\#[(\mathcal{A}, \mathcal{S}_{\mathcal{A}}, \mathcal{I}, \mathcal{F}), k] \geq \#[(\mathcal{B}, \mathcal{S}_{\mathcal{B}}, \mathcal{I}, \mathcal{F}), k]$ holds for every time k. An SSFS algorithm $\mathcal{A}$ is optimally swift if it is at least as swift as $\mathcal{B}$ for every SSFS algorithm $\mathcal{B}$.*

We are now in a position to state the main result of the paper: The FIRE-SQUAD algorithm of Figure 1 is an SSFS algorithm, is optimally stabilizing and is optimally swift (Theorem 3).

3 Lower Bounds

In this section we provide lower bounds for the stabilization time and for the swiftness of any SSFS algorithm $\mathcal{A}$. The lower bounds build upon previous results in the field of simultaneous agreement.

Recall that if $\mathcal{A}$ is a non-self-stabilizing Firing Squad algorithm, then $\mathtt{stab}(\mathcal{A}, \mathcal{S}^{\mathcal{A}}_{init}, \mathcal{I}, \mathcal{F}) = 0$ for all $\mathcal{I}$ and $\mathcal{F}$. Therefore, in the non-self-stabilizing case, it only makes sense to compare algorithms in terms of their "swiftness." In a non-self-stabilizing setting, the firing squad protocol CCFS (based on CONCON [13]) is optimally swift. We will use it as a benchmark and yardstick for expressing and analyzing the performance of self-stabilizing firing squad protocols. To compare the performance of different algorithms, we make use of the following definitions.

Definition 8. *We denote by $\delta(\mathcal{F}, k)$ the number of processes known at time k to be faulty by the processes in G^k in a run of* CCFS *with failure pattern $\mathcal{F}$.*

Intuitively, $\delta(F, k)$ stands for the number of failures that are *discovered* by time k in a run with pattern $\mathcal{F}$. We remark that $\delta(\mathcal{F}, k)$ is well-defined, because the same number of faulty processes are discovered (at the same times) in all runs of CCFS that have failure pattern $\mathcal{F}$. Moreover, since CCFS detects failures as a full-information protocol does, no algorithm $\mathcal{A}$ can discover more failed processes than CCFS does (see [8]). Thus, $\delta(\mathcal{F}, k)$ is an upper bound on the number of failed process discovered by time k by any algorithm $\mathcal{A}$.

CCFS makes essential use of a notion of *horizon*, which is roughly the time by which past events are guaranteed to become common knowledge. This motivates the following definitions.

Definition 9 (Horizons). *Given a failure pattern $\mathcal{F}$, the* horizon distance *at time k, denoted by $\mathtt{disH}(\mathcal{F}, k)$, is $t + 1 - \delta(\mathcal{F}, k)$. The* absolute horizon *at time k, denoted $\mathtt{absH}(\mathcal{F}, k)$, is $k + \mathtt{disH}(\mathcal{F}, k)$.*

While the absolute horizon is an upper bound on when events become common knowledge, the publication time is a lower bound on this time. It is defined as follows:

Definition 10 (Publication Time). *Given a failure pattern $\mathcal{F}$, the* publication time *for (time) k, denoted by $\pi(\mathcal{F},k)$, is* $\min_{k' \geq k}\{\texttt{absH}(\mathcal{F},k')\}$.

When $\mathcal{F}$ is clear from the context, it will be omitted from $\delta(k)$, $\texttt{disH}(k)$, $\texttt{absH}(k)$ and $\pi(h)$.

As shown in [13], for a given failure pattern $\mathcal{F}$, a GO input received at time k is "common knowledge" not before time $\pi(\mathcal{F},k)$. Thus, for a specific algorithm $\mathcal{A}$, the publication time for 0 bounds (from below) the time k at which the first firing action can occur in $\mathcal{O} = \mathcal{A}(\mathcal{S}_{stab}, \mathcal{I}, \mathcal{F})$.

The publication time $\pi(\mathcal{F},k)$ is a generalization of notions developed in [8] for Simultaneous (single-shot, non-stabilizing) Consensus. In that paper, a notion of the *waste* of $\mathcal{F}$ is defined, and information about initial values—which can be viewed in our setting as being about external inputs at time 0—becomes common knowledge at time $t+1-$ *waste*. In our terminology, this occurs precisely at the publication time $\pi(\mathcal{F},0)$ for events of time 0.

The intuition behind the first lower bound is that if CCFS receives a GO input at time 0, then it fires at time $\pi(0)$ (Lemma 1). Since CCFS is optimal, an SSFS algorithm $\mathcal{A}$ cannot fire faster. Therefore, if we consider $\mathcal{A}$ starting in a memory state where $\mathcal{A}$ "thinks" it received a GO input 1 round ago, $\mathcal{A}$ will fire not before time $\pi(0)-1$.

Lemma 1. *Let $\mathcal{F}$ be any failure pattern and let $\mathcal{I}$ be an input pattern for which $\mathcal{I}_q^k = 0$ for every process q and time $k \geq 0$, except for one process $p \in \mathsf{G}$ for which $\mathcal{I}_p^0 = 1$. The first fire action of $\mathcal{O} = \text{CCFS}(\mathcal{S}_{init}^{\text{CCFS}}, \mathcal{I}, \mathcal{F})$ occurs at time $\pi(\mathcal{F},0)$.*

Following is the first lower bound result, stating that the worst case stabilization time of every SSFS algorithm $\mathcal{A}$ is at least $\pi(0)$.

Theorem 1. $\max_{\mathcal{S},\mathcal{I}}\{\texttt{stab}(\mathcal{A},\mathcal{S},\mathcal{I},\mathcal{F})\} \geq \pi(\mathcal{F},0)$ *holds for every SSFS algorithm $\mathcal{A}$ and every failure pattern $\mathcal{F}$.*

Our second lower bound result, informally stating that any SSFS algorithm cannot fire faster than CCFS, is captured by the following theorem. (Notice that the claim is made with respect to sequential input patterns.)

Theorem 2. *Let $\mathcal{A}$ be an SSFS algorithm, $\mathcal{I}$ a sequential input, $\mathcal{F}$ a failure pattern and $\mathcal{O} = \mathcal{A}(\mathcal{S}_{stab}, \mathcal{I}, \mathcal{F})$. For every $k \geq 0$ for which a GO input is received in $\mathcal{I}^k$ there is no fire action in $\mathcal{O}$ during times k' satisfying $k < k' < \pi(\mathcal{F},k)$.*

4 Solving SSFS

The algorithm FIRE-SQUAD in Figure 1 is an SSFS algorithm that is both optimally stabilizing and is optimally swift. For swiftness, the algorithm is based on the approach used in the CCFS algorithm, in which the horizon is computed by monitoring the number of failures that occur, and a firing action takes place when the receipt of a GO becomes common knowledge. The horizon computation at a process p makes use of reports that p receives from other processes regarding failures that they have observed. Following a transient fault, the state of a process may contain arbitrary (including false) information about failures. In the crash failure model, a process q will learn about (truly) crashed processes in the first round. Consequently, p will compute a correct horizon one round later, once it receives reports from all such processes. Roughly speaking, this can be used as a basis for a (nontrivial) solution that stabilizes within two rounds of the optimal time.

In order to improve on the above and obtain an optimal algorithm, FIRE-SQUAD employs a couple of subtle consistency checks. The first one involves checking the information obtained from other processes regarding failures they observed before the current round started. In the crash failure model, every failure observed by q by time $k-1$ must be directly observable by p no later than time k. So if the set of failures reported to p contains failures that p has not directly observed, then it must be time $k \leq 1$, and p will use the set of failures that it has directly observed in computing the horizon, instead of the set of reported failures. A subtle proof shows that, in this case, the computed horizon works correctly if $k = 1$, which is crucial for the algorithm's stabilization optimality. The second consistency check is based on the fact that in normal operation the horizon distance is (weakly) monotone decreasing. The local state contains information about previous horizon computations, and our second consistency check forces it to satisfy weak monotonicity.

We now turn to describe the details of FIRE-SQUAD. The following discussion and lemmas are stated w.r.t. the algorithm and its components. For a variable *var*, we denote by var_p^k the value of *var* at process p after the computation step at time k.

Each process p has a vector $Requests_p[i]$, which represents p's information about a GO input received by some process i time units ago; and this request was not fulfilled yet. More precisely, if $Requests_p^k[i] = 1$, then some process received a GO input at time $k - i$, and no firing action occurred between time $k - i + 1$ and time k. The vector *Requests* contains values for the previous $t+1$ time units and the current time; a total of $t + 2$ entries.

In addition, each process has a set *Failed*, which consists of the processes it has seen to be failed in the current round. That is, at time k, process p's $Failed_p^k$ set contains all processes that process p did not received messages from during round k (*i.e.*, messages sent at time $k - 1$). *Failed'* is the union of all *Failed* sets (as received from other processes) of the previous round. That is, at time k, ${Failed'}_p^k$ is the union of $Failed_q^{k-1}$ as computed at time $k - 1$ by every process q that p received messages from during round k.

Finally, each process keeps track of a vector *Views*. If $Views_p^k[i] = z$ it means that at time $k+i$, data from time $k-z$ is common knowledge. The vector *Views* contains $t + 1$ entries, for the current round and the coming t rounds.

For ease of exposition every process p is assumed to send messages to itself. Moreover, a process executing the algorithm is unaware of the current round

Algorithm FIRE-SQUAD (t)

do forever: /* *executed on process p at time k* */
/* *process p is unaware of the value of k* */
  receive all available ($Requests_q$, $Failed_q$, $Views_q$) messages from process $q \in \mathcal{P}$;

  /* *update variables according to messages of round k and external input* */
  set $Requests[0] := \mathcal{I}_p^k$;
  for $1 \leq i \leq t+1$: **set** $Requests[i] := \max_q\{Requests_q[i-1]\}$;
  set $Failed' := \bigcup_q Failed_q$;
  set $Failed$:= all processes that p did not hear from this round;
  for $1 \leq i \leq t$: **set** $Views[i-1] := \min_q\{Views_q[i]\} + 1$;

  /* *calculate horizon at time k − 1* */
  set $Horizon := t + 1 - \min\{|Failed'|, |Failed|\}$; /* *consistency check I* */
  set $Views[Horizon\text{-}1] := 1$;
  for $0 \leq i \leq t$: **set** $Views[i] := \max\{Views[i], Horizon - i\}$; /* *check II* */

  /* *should we fire?* */
  if for some $i' \geq Views[0]$ it holds that $Requests[i'] = 1$ then
    for $i' \leq i'' \leq t+1$: **set** $Requests[i''] := 0$;
    do "Fire";
  fi;

  /* *send round k + 1 messages to all processes* */
  send ($Requests$, $Failed$, $Views$) to all;
od.

Clean up:
$Requests$ contains only $\{0, 1\}$ values. $Views$ contains only values $\in \{0, \ldots, t+1\}$.

Fig. 1. FIRE-SQUAD: A self-stabilizing firing squad algorithm

number. We refer to such rounds using numbers k etc. for ease of exposition in describing and analyzing the algorithm.

4.1 Correctness Proof

A central notion in the analysis of simultaneous actions under crash failures is that of a *clean round* [8]. In the non-stabilizing setting, a round r is clean according to failure pattern $\mathcal{F}$ if no process considered non-faulty by all processes at time $r-1$ is known to be faulty by one or more (non-crashed) processes at time r. In a setting that allows transient faults, we use a slightly different definition for the exact same notion. Consider a process p that fails in round k. We say that p fails *silently* in round k if it is not blocked according to $\mathcal{F}$ from sending messages in round k to any of the processes $q \in \mathsf{G}^k$. Thus, no process surviving round k can detect p's failure in this round.

Definition 11 (Clean Round). *Round r in failure pattern $\mathcal{F}$ is a* clean round *if (i) no process fails silently in round $r-1$, and (ii) all processes (if any) that fail in round r fail silently.*

This definition of a round r being clean in $\mathcal{F}$ coincides with the standard definition of clean rounds previously used in non-stabilizing systems [8]. In protocols such as FIRE-SQUAD, with the property that every process sends the same message to all other processes in every round, all (non-crashed) processes receive the same set of messages in a clean round.

Due to lack of space we present an overview of the proof. The full proof will appear in the full version of the paper. Following is the main result of the paper:

Theorem 3. FIRE-SQUAD *solves the SSFS problem, it optimally stabilizes and is optimally swift.*

Proof Overview. First, notice that once a clean round has occurred, all processes receive the same set of messages, and different processes agree on the value of *Requests* (except for *Requests*[0]). Moreover, in the following round all processes agree on the value of *Requests* perhaps except for the value of *Requests*[0] and *Requests*[1]. In a similar manner, k rounds after a clean round the values of $Requests[k+1], Requests[k+2], \ldots$ are the same at all processes.

Second, consider the value of $Views^k[0]$. By Line 6, $Views^k[0]$ equals the value of $Views^{k-1}[1]+1$. In a similar manner, if $Views^k[i]$ is updated by Line 8 then $Views^{k+i}[0] = Views^k[i]+i$. If k was the last clean round prior to round $k+i$, then $Views[0] = i+1$ holds at time $k+i$. Together with the claim from the previous paragraph, we have that once there was a clean round, if different processes agree on the value of $Views[0]$, then they all agree on the values of $Requests[Views[0]], Requests[Views[0]+1], \cdots$. Thus, if processes agree on the value of $Views[0]$ then they are guaranteed to act simultaneously, either firing together or, together, refraining from firing. Therefore, we turn our attention to analyzing the behavior of $Views[0]$ at the different processes.

Intuitively, the reason the above discussion does not show that all processes agree on the value of $Views[0]$, is the following: Even though all processes update the value of *Views* in a similar manner (Line 6) each process p updates its own $Views_p$ according to the failures that p has seen in the current round. To show that all processes have the same value of $Views[0]$ (for all rounds following a clean round) we show two things: (1) if $Views^k[0]$ is updated in round k, then $Horizon = 1$, *i.e.*, $|Failed'| = t$. This will be observed by all processes, and so they will all set $Views^k[0] = 1$; (2) if $Views^k[0]$ was not updated in round k, then let $k-i$ be the latest round in which the value of $Views^{k-i}[Horizon^{k-i}-1]$ was updated. The proof shows that there must be a clean round between round $k-i$ and round k, thus ensuring that all processes will agree on the value in $Views[0]$ by round k.

Up till now, we have given an overview of the proof that FIRE-SQUAD solves the SSFS problem. To show that it optimally stabilizes and is optimally swift a precise analysis of the convergence of SSFS is required, along with a proof that SSFS will fire no later than any other algorithm (on sequential inputs). To illustrate the tools used in those proofs, we define the following:

Definition 12. *Let*
- $\texttt{minHG}(\mathcal{F}, k) = \min_{p \in \mathsf{G}} Horizon_p^k$, *and*
- $\texttt{bestH}(\mathcal{F}, k) = \min_{k' \geq k}\{k' + \texttt{minHG}(\mathcal{F}, k'+1)\}$.

We write $\texttt{bestH}(k)$ *when* $\mathcal{F}$ *is clear from the context.*

The main point behind this definition is that bestH is the equivalent of π with respect to FIRE-SQUAD (recall that π is computed according to CCFS). In the non-self-stabilizing model π is shown to be a lower bound on when a GO input becomes "common knowledge". Thus, the following two lemmas conclude that FIRE-SQUAD is optimally swift.

Lemma 2. $\texttt{bestH}(k) \leq \pi(k)$, *for every* $k \geq 0$.

Lemma 3. *Let input* $\mathcal{I}$ *be sequential with respect to* (FIRE-SQUAD, $\mathcal{S}, \mathcal{F}$). *If* $\mathcal{I}_p^k = 1$ *for process* p *at time* k *then* $\mathcal{O}_p^{k'} = 1$ *for* $k < k' \leq \texttt{bestH}(k)$.

Finally, we wish to point out a main difference between the proofs of the lower and upper bounds in the self-stabilizing model as opposed to the classical model (with respect to the firing squad problem): in the first round of FIRE-SQUAD the value of *Failed'* (the set of processes that have failed in the previous round) might be contaminated. That is, a process may start in a state where it thinks that some other processes are failed, even though they are correct. Thus, a major property that is used in the classical proofs cannot be used freely in the self-stabilizing model's proofs: the monotonicity of crash failures. In the classical model, the perceived set of crashed processes can only increase, while in the self-stabilizing model it may decrease following the first round.

This explains the purpose of Line 7, which is to perform a consistency check, comparing the reported $Failed_q$ values (from the previous round) to failures that are directly observed by p in the current round (stored in $Failed_p$). This comparison together with a delicate treatment in the proofs, ensures the optimality of FIRE-SQUAD. That is, to prove that FIRE-SQUAD is optimal up to an additive constant of 1 round is much easier than to prove that FIRE-SQUAD is optimal. We prove the latter, stronger, property.

5 Conclusions and Open Problems

This paper presents FIRE-SQUAD, the first self-stabilizing firing squad algorithm. FIRE-SQUAD is optimal in two important respects: It optimally stabilizes, and is optimally swift. There are many directions in which this work can be extended. These include:

- FIRE-SQUAD assumes the crash fault model. What can be said about the omission fault model? And what about the *Byzantine* fault model? Each such extension seems to be a nontrivial step.

- FIRE-SQUAD works when we assume that failures are permanent. Being an ongoing and everlasting service, firing squad is expected to operate for long periods, in which processes may recover. A more reasonable assumption in this case is that there is a bound (of t) on the number of failures over every interval of m rounds, for some m. (Non-stabilizing) Continuous consensus has recently been studied in this model [14], and it would be interesting to see if the same can be done for self-stabilizing firing squad.

References

1. Bazzi, R., Neiger, G.: The possibility and the complexity of achieving fault-tolerant coordination. In: PODC 1992, pp. 203–214. ACM, New York (1992)
2. Burns, J.E., Lynch, N.A.: The byzantine firing squad problem. Advances in Computing Research: Parallel and Distributed Computing 4, 147–161 (1987)
3. Coan, B.A., Dolev, D., Dwork, C., Stockmeyer, L.J.: The distributed firing squad problem. SIAM J. Comput. 18(5), 990–1012 (1989)
4. Dolev, D., Reischuk, R., Strong, R.H.: Early stopping in byzantine agreement. J. ACM 37(4), 720–741 (1990)
5. Dolev, S.: Self-Stabilization. MIT Press, Cambridge (2000)
6. Dolev, S., Welch, J.L.: Self-stabilizing clock synchronization in the presence of byzantine faults. Journal of the ACM 51(5), 780–799 (2004)
7. Dolev, S.: Possible and impossible self-stabilizing digital clock synchronization in general graphs. Real-Time Systems 12(1), 95–107 (1997)
8. Dwork, C., Moses, Y.: Knowledge and common knowledge in a Byzantine environment: crash failures. Information and Computation 88(2), 156–186 (1990)
9. Fagin, R., Halpern, J.Y., Moses, Y., Vardi, M.Y.: Reasoning about Knowledge. MIT Press, Cambridge (1995)
10. Halpern, J.Y., Moses, Y.: Knowledge and common knowledge in a distributed environment. Journal of the ACM 37(3), 549–587 (1990); A preliminary version appeared in PODC 1984
11. Hoch, E.N., Dolev, D., Daliot, A.: Self-stabilizing byzantine digital clock synchronization. In: Datta, A.K., Gradinariu, M. (eds.) SSS 2006. LNCS, vol. 4280, pp. 350–362. Springer, Heidelberg (2006)
12. Lamport, L., Melliar-Smith, P.M.: Synchronizing clocks in the presence of faults. Journal of the ACM 32(1), 52–78 (1985)
13. Mizrahi, T., Moses, Y.: Continuous consensus via common knowledge. Distributed Computing 20(5), 305–321 (2008)
14. Mizrahi, T., Moses, Y.: Continuous consensus with failures and recoveries. In: Taubenfeld, G. (ed.) DISC 2008. LNCS, vol. 5218, pp. 408–422. Springer, Heidelberg (2008)
15. Moses, Y., Tuttle, M.R.: Programming simultaneous actions using common knowledge. Algorithmica 3, 121–169 (1988)
16. Moses, Y., Raynal, M.: Revisiting simultaneous consensus with crash failures. J. Parallel Distrib. Comput. 69(4), 400–409 (2009)
17. Neiger, G., Tuttle, M.R.: Common knowledge and consistent simultaneous coordination. Distrib. Comput. 6(3), 181–192 (1993)
18. Patt-Shamir, B.: A Theory of Clock Synchronization. Doctoral thesis, MIT (October 1994)

Anonymous Transactions in Computer Networks*
(Extended Abstract)

Shlomi Dolev[1] and Marina Kopeetsky[2]

[1] Department of Computer Science, Ben-Gurion University of the Negev, Beer-Sheva, 84105, Israel
dolev@cs.bgu.ac.il

[2] Department of Software Engineering, Sami-Shamoon College of Engineering, Beer-Sheva, 84100, Israel
marinako@sce.ac.il

Abstract. We present schemes for providing anonymous transactions while privacy and anonymity are preserved, providing user anonymous authentication in distributed networks such as the Internet. We first present a practical scheme for anonymous transactions while the transaction resolution is assisted by a Trusted Authority. This practical scheme is extended to a theoretical scheme where a Trusted Authority is not involved in the transaction resolution. Given an authority that generates for each player hard to produce evidence *EVID* (e. g., problem instance with or without a solution) to each player, the identity of a user U is defined by the ability to prove possession of said evidence. We use Zero-Knowledge proof techniques to repeatedly identify U by providing a proof that U has evidence *EVID*, without revealing *EVID*, therefore avoiding identity theft.

In both schemes the authority provides each user with a unique random string. A player U may produce unique user name and password for each other player S using a one way function over the random string and the IP address of S. The player does not have to maintain any information in order to reproduce the user name and password used for accessing a player S. Moreover, the player U may execute transactions with a group of players S^U in two phases; in the first phase the player interacts with each server without revealing information concerning its identity and without possibly identifying linkability among the servers in S^U. In the second phase the player allows linkability and therefore transaction commitment with all servers in S^U, while preserving anonymity (for future transactions).

1 Introduction

Due to the rapid development of the Service Oriented Architecture (SOA) and web services in supporting different multiphase business processes, the issue of

* Partially supported by Deutsche Telekom, Rita Altura Trust Chair in Computer Sciences, Lynne and William Frankel Center for Computer Sciences.

R. Guerraoui and F. Petit (Eds.): SSS 2009, LNCS 5873, pp. 297–310, 2009.

providing services which preserve user anonymity, is very important nowadays. SOA is defined as a group of services that communicate with each other. The process of communication involves a number of services coordinating a common activity. The purpose of this paper is to design the new protocols for providing the multiphase transactions between users and a set of servers while maintaining the user anonymity.

We provide anonymous authentication in distributed networks. We define and present protocols for executing anonymous transactions between a user and a set of servers. Both the user privacy and anonymity are preserved during the transaction. Protocols for providing anonymous communications via insecure communication channels were proposed in, e. g. [7], [8], [12] and [3]. Our scope is beyond the actual anonymous communications assuming one of the above protocols is used to provide such a service.

Several protocols devoted to the performance of anonymous transactions have been recently proposed. For example protocols for providing anonymous credentials were proposed and analyzed in [17], [4] and [2]. The authors proposed pseudonym systems which allow users to interact with multiple organizations anonymously, using unlinkable pseudonyms. In [4] an accumulator scheme is proposed. Dynamic accumulators enable efficient revocation of credentials in the anonymous credential systems. A special P-signature scheme which enables a practical design of a non-interactive anonymous credential system is proposed in [2]. The scope of the above works is user centric, where the servers do not communicate directly. In such a user centric design the communication and computation over the user is high.

A system for anonymous personalized web browsing was proposed in [11]. A new cryptographic function, namely the Janus function that satisfies a number of properties, including anonymity, consistency, secrecy, uniqueness of an alias, and protection from creation of dossiers provides user anonymity in a computationally secure aspect. This function translates the user name (for example, e-mail address) to a unique user alias. The computation of the Janus function and the translation of the real user name to the corresponding alias is performed by the centralized Janus proxy server which is usually placed in the firewall which connects a particular Intranet to the Internet.

Our contribution. The contribution of our paper is in the design of new schemes for providing user with anonymous transactions. A transaction is defined as a two stage operation. During the first stage a player (user) U anonymously authenticates himself/herself by means of a unique pseudonym to several other players (servers) S^U. In the second stage U can prove to each sever S from S^U that the same entity interacted with all the servers and therefore has done all the preparations to execute a (composite) transaction. Each user has a one way function F. The user U may produce a unique user name and password for each other player (user or server) S using both a random seed and the IP address of S. The user U does not have to maintain any information in order to reproduce the user name and password used for accessing a server S. Moreover, the user U may execute transactions with a group of players (servers or users) S^U and prove without revealing information concerning the identity of U that U is the one that accessed each player in S^U. The pseudonym generated by a user for accessing any server in a group of servers, is unique for each user-server pair. The pseudonym uniqueness is provided by the server's IP address which is one of the parameters of the seed that generates pseudo random sequence by a given one way function.

We present two protocols for anonymous transactions. The first Anonymous Transactions Protocol ATP_1 is based on the approval of the Trusted Authority (*TA*) for the transaction resolution. The *TA* may limit the number of possible transactions carried out by the same user. The transactions are performed in two modes: unlinkable and linkable transactions. The different user's transactions can be unlinkable in the sense that different players from a set of network users do not know that the same anonymous identity requested a service from them. The transactions linkability may also be satisfied as the users get tools to verify whether they have received service from the same anonymous identity. The transactions mode is chosen by the player who accesses the *TA* in order to carry out the transactions.

The advanced theoretical protocol ATP_2 uses the *TA* in the initialization stage only, while the anonymous transactions are carried out by a player (user) without involving the *TA*. In the advanced scheme the *TA* generates a hard to produce evidence $EVID$ for each user U e.g., a problem instance with or without a solution. The user's pseudonym in this scheme is based on the server's IP address, a hard to produce evidence $EVID$, and a one way function granted to the user by the *TA* during the system initialization. The pseudonym includes the anonymous user name (login), and the password. The pseudonym is created as a pseudo random sequence. This pseudo random sequence is generated by the one way function and a seed calculated by $XOR-ing$ the server's IP address and an evidence $EVID$. In order to perform the transaction resolution and prove to the group of players S^U that a user U processed all accesses needed to complete the transaction, the user performs an interactive Zero Knowledge Proof to prove that he/she knows $EVID$ which is computationally hard to produce by a polynomial time adversary. The advanced ATP_2 protocol uses Zero-Knowledge proof techniques to repeatedly identify the user U without exposing the $EVID$ and its solution, therefore avoiding an identity theft. Hence, the *TA* in ATP_2 is involved only once during the system initialization.

Compared with the Janus system, our protocol has several advantages.

Anonymity between users, Trusted Authority, and servers in the network. Anonymity is provided between all players: a user which performs a transaction; a group of servers participating in the transaction; and a Trusted Authority.

Performing the transactions without involving a Trusted Authority. The ATP_2 protocol involves the *TA* only once during the system initialization. The future ATP_2 protocol's functionality is implemented by the user which locally computes the pseudonym and resolves the transaction by himself/herself.

Low computational cost combined with a very high security level. Our first protocol continuously uses the pseudo random sequences generation by the cryptographic one way functions and XOR calculation as a source for preserving the security level of the anonymous user's pseudonym. Therefore, low computational power is required in comparison with the standard cryptographic techniques. The Zero-Knowledge proof performed by the user in the transaction resolution stage computationally prevents an adversary from impersonating himself/herself on behalf of the legal user. In contrast to the Janus system our protocol does not rely on a Secure Socket Layer (SSL) [19] or any other security protocol that assumes the involvement of the Trusted Authority.

Permanent validity of the secret granted to the users by the *TA*. The secret number granted by the TA to the user in the ATP_1 protocol and the corresponding hardly producible $EVID$ in ATP_2 are valid forever, and only user encryptions of the secret value are updated during different transactions.

Linkability and unlinkability of the transactions. The encryption scheme for the pseudonym generation may be chosen adaptively on user demand. The user may choose the unlinkable mode while neither network players (users and servers) can identify that they communicated with the same anonymous identity during different transactions. The user may also perform transactions in a linkable mode while the other players acquire tools to ascertain that the same player executed with them different transactions, whereas the user's identity remains anonymous.

Compared with the recent papers on anonymous credentials, such as [17], [4] and [2] our anonymous transactions protocols ATP_1 and ATP_2 have the following benefits.

Complete anonymity to Trusted Authority. A user in our scheme gets the permission for providing the transactions in the completely anonymous manner, without using Public Key Infrastructure.

Proof of linkability. A user in ATP_1 protocol must not prove the linkability, whereas the servers verify the linkability on their own, unlike the anonymous credential schemes.

Pseudonym storage. User in our scheme does not have to remember and store his/her pseudonym to each server in the system. The pseudonym is efficiently generated by a user each time when he/she intends to access a server.

Scale to number of servers. A user in ATP_1 and ATP_2 protocols proves the transaction correctness simultaneously to a group of servers, while in the anonymous credential systems a user cannot prove the possession of the credentials simultaneously to a group of organizations.

Simplicity. ATP_1 is not based on the ZKPs as credential schemes in [17], [4] and [2].

Performing transaction by a single operation. In our model a user performs a transaction by a single operation. Hence, the transaction resolution in our model is atomic. In the anonymous credential system a user is highly involved with each organization separately for validation of his/her credential transfer (performing the transaction).

Involving of Trusted Authority. In the ATP_2 protocol the Trusted Authority is involved in the initialization stage only, while in the anonymous credential systems the TA carries out the transaction resolution.

Paper organization. The formal system description appears in Section 2. The basic protocol for anonymous transactions ATP_1 is introduced in Section 3. The advanced protocol, impractical in current technology, ATP_2 protocol which provides transaction resolution anonymously without involving the Trusted Authority, is presented in Section 4. Conclusions appear in Section 5. Proofs are omitted from this extended abstract and can be found in [9].

2 Security Model for Anonymous Transactions

We consider the set of network players (users and servers), and a Trusted Authority *TA* which comprise the anonymous network. The set of network players includes two sub-sets that may intersect: the set of users $U = \{U_1, \ldots, U_n\}$ and the set of servers $S = \{S_1, \ldots, S_l\}$. A user $U_i \in U$ initiates and carries out an anonymous transaction with the servers from the corresponding server set S^{U_i}. The transaction is defined as a two stage operation:

(a) The first stage is the authentication stage. During this stage a user U_i anonymously authenticates himself/herself and interacts with each server S_j from the server set S^{U_i}.
(b) The second stage is the transaction resolution. In this stage U_i proves to each server from the S^{U_i} set that he/she is the identity that provided authentication and visited all the servers from S^{U_i} during the previous stage. Note that this stage is optional and depends on U_i's choice.

According to [7], we use two cryptographic primitives: *encryption* and *authentication*. *Encryption* guarantees the secrecy of messages, while *authentication* ensures that if a sender sends a message to a receiver and an adversary alters this message, then with overwhelming probability the receiver can detect this fact (see [7] for details and [14] for formal definitions). Denote the kth transaction carried out by the user U_i with the servers from the corresponding server set S^{U_i} as T_i^k. Each T_i^k starts with the authentication message t_{ij} sent by U_i to each $S_j \in S^{U_i}$, and ends when each $S_j \in S^{U_i}$ confirms the transaction resolution by sending the message $r_i{=}Confirm_i^k$, or rejects it by sending the message $r_i{=}Reject_i^k$. The message t_{ij} consists of the anonymous user name and password pair (u_{ij}, p_{ij}) which is, in essence unique for a given user U_i and a server S_j. The transaction resolution is initiated by the user U_i and is performed by sending the message $Resolve_i^k$ to each $S_j \in S^{U_i}$.

The security parameter in our model is ϵ which is equal to the length of the seed c_{ij} that generates the pseudo random sequence for the anonymous user name and password. The larger ϵ is compared to the pseudo random sequence length, the higher the computational security level of the proposed scheme is.

Given the features of the proposed model, we describe the basic anonymous transactions protocol ATP_1, and the advanced ATP_2 protocol. The transaction resolution in ATP_1 is executed by the TA when each server S_j passes the $Resolve_i^k$ message received from U_i to the TA, while the TA confirms the transaction correctness by sending the message $r_i = Confirm_i^k$, or rejects the transaction by sending the $r_i = Reject_i^k$ to all servers from the S^{U_i} set.

The transaction resolution provided by ATP_2 is performed by the user U_i while U_i proves that he/she knows the hardly producible evidence $EVID$ to each server from the corresponding server set S^{U_i} in the interactive ZKP. We assume a polynomial time restricted semi-honest adversary A [20]. A can impersonate as the legal user and, therefore can get access to the server resources. A can also try to prove to the group of servers that he/she is a legal user that initiated the transaction. Nevertheless, A must follow the protocol fairly.

We define the requirements for the ATP_1 and ATP_2 protocols.

(R_1)-anonymity: If a user U_i performs a transaction, neither the network players, including the TA nor the servers get information about U_i's real identity.

(R_2)-Anonymous authentication to TA: The user U_i authenticates himself/herself to the TA and gets the credit for the execution of a certain number of transactions via an anonymous secure channel.

(R_3)-Pseudonym uniqueness: the pseudonym which is composed of the user's user name and password is unique for any user-server pair that participated in the transaction.

(R_4)-Pseudonym consistency: The user pseudonym is consistent for each server in the sense that the server can recognize the pseudonym in the course of the repeated user visits in the same transaction.

(R_5)-Atomicity: The transaction resolution is executed simultaneously for all servers in the corresponding servers' set.

(R_6)-Optionality of the transaction mode (linkability and unlinkability of a transaction): A user can choose for himself/herself one of two transaction modes: linkable and unlinkable. In the linkable mode the servers from the corresponding servers set can verify that the same user executed with them a certain number of transactions, whereas in the unlinkable mode the servers have no tools to identify the same anonymous identity.

The model presented and the corresponding requirements are defined as a function of the security parameter ϵ that assures the computationally secure level of the anonymous transactions.

The anonymous transactions protocol ATP_1 and the advanced ATP_2 protocol are introduced in the next sections.

3 The Anonymous Transactions Protocol ATP_1

3.1 ATP_1 Description

The ATP_1 protocol is described in Figures 1 and 2. In order to carry out a certain transaction with a group of servers S^{U_i} a user $U_i \in U$ performs the following operations:

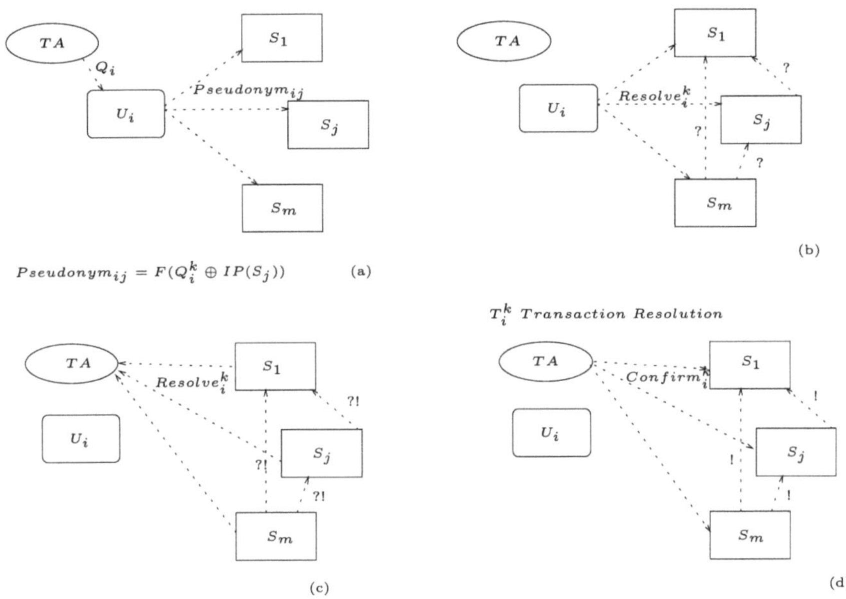

Fig. 1. ATP_1: Stages in Executing a Transaction

(a) Initialization stage: The Trusted Authority *TA* grants the user U_i a secret random number Q_i. It is assumed that there is common knowledge of a one-way function F. t possible transactions are permitted by the *TA* to U_i (Figure 1, (a), Figure 2, lines 1-4). Note that anonymous communication is provided between the *TA* and the user because the *TA* gets no information about the user's identity.

(b) In order to start the kth transaction T_i^k U_i locally computes $Pseudonym_{ij}$ that consists of the anonymous user name u_{ij} and password p_{ij}.

$Pseudonym_{ij} = (u_{ij} \| p_{ij}) = F((Q_i^k) \oplus IP(S_j))$ (Figure 1, (a), Figure 2, lines 5-13). Here $IP(S_j)$ is the corresponding IP address of the server S_j, and Q_i^k, $k = 1, .., t$ is the kth sub-string of the Q_i string. It should be noted that if the Q_i string is short, Q_i may be used as a seed for generating a pseudo random sequence $c_F(Q_i)$ by the F function for any k^{th} transaction instead of the Q_i^k sub-string. In this case $c_F(Q_i)$ should be divided on t sequential sub-strings $c_F^1(Q_i), \ldots, c_F^t(Q_i)$. Each $c_F^k(Q_i)$ will generate the user name and password pair for any k^{th} user's transaction.

Assuming that F is a proper collision-resistant one way function [20], the generated $Pseudonym_{ij}$ is unique for all interactions between U_i and any $S_j \in S^{U_i}$. Note, that the user's U_i $Pseudonym_{ij}$ is different for any server S_j from S^{U_i}, and therefore the servers do not know whether U_i is the same identity that visited any server from the corresponding server set. The question marks in Figure 1 (b) relate to this case.

	ATP_1. Protocol for User U_i		ATP_1. Protocol for Server S_j
1:	Initialization:	1:	
2:	Get (Q_i, t)	2:	
3:	from TA	3:	
4:	int $k = 1$	4:	
5:	Start k^{th} transaction T_i^k	5:	
6:	User's U_i authentication	6:	
7:	to any $S_j \in S^{U_i}$	7:	
8:	for $j = 1..m$	8:	
9:	$F_{ij} = F(Q_i^k \oplus IP(S_j))$	9:	
10:	$F_{ij} = (u_{ij} \Vert p_{ij})$	10:	
11:	$Pseudonym_{ij} = (u_{ij} \Vert p_{ij})$	11:	
12:	Send $t_{ij} = Pseudonym_{ij}$ to S_j	12:	Upon reception of t_{ij}
13:	End user's U_i authentication	13:	Confirm U_i^{th} authentication
14:	k^{th} Transaction Resolution	14:	k^{th} Transaction Resolution
15:	$Resolve_i^k = Q_i^k \oplus IP(S_j)$	15:	Upon reception of $Resolve_i^k$
16:	Send $Resolve_i^k$ to all S_j from S^{U_i}	16:	
17:	If r_i=$Confirm_i^k$	17:	If $TA(Resolve_i^k)$=$Confirm_i^k$
18:	return	18:	Send $r_i = Confirm_i^k$ to U_i
19:	*Transaction Resolution*	19:	
20:	else	20:	If $TA(Resolve_i^k) = Reject_i^k$
21:	return	21:	Send $r_i = Reject_i^k$ to U_i
22:	*Transaction Failure*	22:	
23:	if $k \prec t$ $k := k + 1$	23:	if $k \prec t$ $k := k + 1$
24:	else Last Transaction	24:	else Last Transaction

Fig. 2. Anonymous Transactions Protocol ATP_1

(c) In order to convince each server from the S^{U_i} set that U_i is the same identity that visited any server from the server set, U_i opens the part Q_i^k of the secret Q_i, or the sub-string $c_F^k(Q_i)$ of the pseudo random sequence $c_F(Q_i)$, respectively used in k^{th} transaction by sending the message $Resolve_i^k = (Q_i^k) \oplus IP(S_j)$ (or $Resolve_i^k = c_F^k(Q_i) \oplus IP(S_j)$, respectively) to all servers. This stage is provided by the user for himself/herself (Figure 1 (b), Figure 2, lines 14-16). The question marks in Figure 1 (b), denote that the servers do not know yet that they interacted with the same anonymous user.

(d) Transaction resolution is performed simultaneously when each S_j sends the Q_i^k (or $c_F^k(Q_i)$) to *TA* revealed from the $Resolve_i^k$ message which was previously received from U_i. *TA* verifies whether Q_i^k (or $c_F^k(Q_i)$) is the correct Q_i^{th} sub-string, or correct sub-string generated by F from the secret number Q_i. If so, then the *TA* sends $Confirm_i^k$ message to each S_j from S^{U_i} and resolves the kth transaction T_i^k. Otherwise, the *TA* sends $Reject_i^k$ message to each S_j, and rejects T_i^k (Figure 1 (c), (d), Figure 2, lines 17-22). The question marks that appear together with the exclamation marks, in Figure 1 (c), denote that the servers may verify that they interacted with the same anonymous user. The exclamation marks in Figure 1 (d) denote that the transaction resolution has been carried out simultaneously and each server has been convinced that the same anonymous user carried out the transaction.

3.2 Linkable and Unlinkable Transactions

Linkable mode. Let us assume that a certain user U_i wishes that his/her different transactions T_i^k and T_i^l, $k \prec l$ with the same group of servers S^{U_i} will be linkable in the sense that after executing the T_i^k transaction any S_j from S^{U_i} can be convinced that the T_i^k and T_i^l transactions have been performed by the same anonymous user. We propose to use the authentication scheme suggested by Lamport [15]. In this case k^{th} encryption of the secret Q_i used in T_i^k transaction equals to $F^{t-k}(Q_i)$,and the corresponding user name and password pair is $(u_{ij}, p_{ij}) = F(F^{t-k}(Q_i) \oplus IP(S_j))$. It should be noted that the one way function F generates the pseudo random sequence $F(Q_i)$ from the seed Q_i. t denotes the maximum number of the transactions permitted to the user U_i by the *TA*. $F^{t-k}(Q_i)$ denotes $t-k$ sequential applications of the one way function F on the secret seed Q_i. The value revealed by the user U_i in the $Resolve_i^k$ message is, consequently the internal seed $F^{t-k}(Q_i) \oplus IP(S_j)$ used to compute (u_{ij}, p_{ij}). Assume that the user U_i has provided T_i^k, $T_i^{k+1}, \ldots$, T_i^l sequential transactions with the servers from the S^{U_i} set. U_i remains linkable after any transaction that follows the T_i^k transaction because each $S_j \in S^{U_i}$ can verify by repeatedly applying $l-k$ times the one way function F on Q_i that Q_i^{th} encryptions $F^{t-k}(Q_i)$ and $F^{t-l}(Q_i)$ used in the kth and l^{th} transactions, respectively satisfy the following equality $F^{t-k}(Q_i) = F^{l-k}(F^{t-l}(Q_i))$.

Unlinkable mode. We propose the following encryption scheme in order to ensure the user's U_i unlinkability during his/her transactions with the group of servers from the S^{U_i} set. In this case the *TA* grants U_i the pair (Q_i, W_i) of secret seeds. The U_i^{th} user's user name and password in the T_i^k transaction are calculated in the following manner $(u_{ij}, p_{ij}) = F(F^{t-k}(Q_i) \oplus F^k(W_i))$. In doing so, the pseudo random sequence $F^k(W_i)$, generated by the secret seed W_i by the k sequential compositions of the one way function F, provides the one way "lock" $F^{t-k}(Q_i)$ of the encrypted secret Q_i.

Note that the use of the different seeds Q_i^1, $Q_i^2, \ldots$, Q_i^t in the different transactions divided from the secret string Q_i, also provide the transactions unlinkability. The reason is that the different independent seeds, e. g. Q_i^k and Q_i^l result in the different independent pseudo random sequences $F(Q_i^k)$ and $F(Q_i^l)$, respectively.

The security parameter ϵ equals the length of the seed Q_i or W_i which are used as the arguments of the F function for generating the pseudo random sequence. Note that the larger ϵ is, the higher the encryption level provided in the transactions is.

The following Theorem proves that ATP_1 satisfies the model requirements and provides the anonymous transactions in the computationally secure manner.

Theorem 1. ATP_1 satisfies the following requirements:
(R_1)-anonymity;
(R_2)-Anonymous authentication to TA;
(R_3)-Pseudonym uniqueness;
(R_4)-Pseudonym consistency;
(R_5)-Atomicity;
(R_6)-Optionality of the transaction mode (linkability and unlinkability of a transaction).
ATP_1 is computationally secure regarding the security parameter ϵ that determines the computational security level.

The proof of Theorem 1 is presented in [9].

4 The Anonymous Transactions Protocol ATP_2

4.1 ATP_2 Description

The advanced anonymous transactions protocol ATP_2 enables the user to carry out and resolve the anonymous transactions by himself/herself. Hence, the TA is involved in the system only once during the initialization stage. The idea is to provide a user with an evidence which is hard to produce, say a very long prime number [6]. Only a powerful entity may have enough resources to obtain such evidences. ATP_2 is described in Figures 3 and 4. The user's U_i transaction with the servers from the corresponding set S^{U_i} is executed in the following way.

(a) Initialization Stage: As in the the ATP_1 case, a particular commonly known proper one way function F generates the pseudo random sequence for the anonymous user's pseudonym. An evidence $EVID$ which is hard to produce, is also granted to U_i. After the initialization stage the TA leaves the system forever (Figure 3 (a) and Figure 4, lines 1-3).

(b) In order to initiate the T_i^k transaction, U_i visits the servers from the S^{U_i} set and authenticates himself/herself to each $S_j \in S^{U_i}$ by means of the anonymous $Pseudonym_{ij} = (u_{ij}, p_{ij})$. Here u_{ij} and p_{ij} are the anonymous user name and password, as in the ATP_1 case. Now the anonymous U_i^{th} identity is computed as $Pseudonym_{ij} = (u_{ij}, p_{ij}) = F(Com_i^k(EVID) \oplus IP(S_j))$. The question marks in Figure 3 (b) mean that the servers do not know whether they are interacting with the same anonymous user. As in the ATP_1 case, $IP(S_j)$ is the S_j^{th} IP address, and F is the one way function provided to the user by the TA during the initialization stage. The parameter $Com_i^k(EVID)$ is the kth commitment to the instance $EVID$ [13]. Compared to the ATP_1 protocol, the computationally hard evidence $EVID$ is granted to U_i by the TA instead of a secret random number. As in the ATP_1 case the message sent by U_i to each S_j is $t_{ij} = (u_{ij}, p_{ij})$ (Figure 3 (a) and Figure 4, lines 4-13).

(c) In order to resolve the T_i^k transaction, U_i opens and sends each $S_j \in S^{U_i}$ in the $Resolve_i^k$ message the $Com_i^k(EVID)$ string (Figure 3 (b) and Figure 4, lines 15-17). The question marks in Figure 3 (b) denote that the servers do not know yet that they interacted with the same anonymous user.

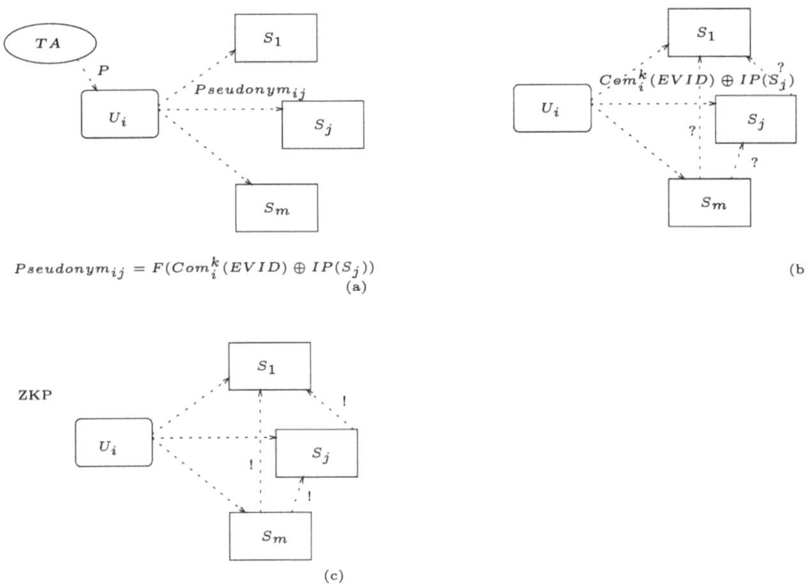

Fig. 3. ATP_2: Stages in Executing a Transaction

The T_i^k transaction is resolved by the user when U_i provides the computationally secure Interactive ZKP [13] that U_i is the same anonymous identity that knows *EVID* (Figure 3 (*c*) and Figure 4, lines 15-24). The exclamation marks in Figure 3 (*c*) relate to the transaction resolution.

The following Theorem proves that ATP_2 protocol satisfies the following requirements and provides the anonymous transactions in the computationally secure manner without involving the *TA*.

Theorem 2. ATP_2 satisfies the following requirements:
(R_1)-anonymity;
(R_2)-Anonymous authentication to *TA*;
(R_3)-Pseudonym uniqueness;
(R_4)-Pseudonym consistency;
(R_5)-Atomicity.
The ATP_2 protocol's computational security level is determined by the security parameters of the ZKP performed by the user to the servers from the corresponding servers' set.

The proof of Theorem 2 is presented in [9].

4.2 Possible ZKPs of Primality

In order to provide a user's permanent identity, the *TA* must generate a hard to produce evidence *EVID* and its solution, so it is computationally unfeasible to produce *EVID* and, hence to guess *EVID* in an adversarial manner. We suggest

ATP_2. Protocol for User U_i	ATP_2. Protocol for Server S_j
Initialization:	
Get $EVID$	
from TA	
int $k = 1$	
Start k^{th} transaction T_i^k	
User's U_i authentication	
to any $S_j \in S^{U_i}$	
for $j = 1..m$	
$F_{ij} = F(Com_i^k(EVID) \oplus IP(S_j))$	
$F_{ij} = (u_{ij} \| p_{ij})$	
$Pseudonym_{ij} = (u_{ij} \| p_{ij})$	
Send $t_{ij} = Pseudonym_{ij}$ to S_j	
End user's U_i authentication	Upon reception of t_{ij}
	Confirm U_i^{th} authentication
k^{th} Transaction Resolution	k^{th} Transaction Resolution
$Resolve_i^k = Com_i^k(EVID)$	Upon reception of $Resolve_i^k$
Send $Resolve_i^k$ to all S_j from S^{U_i}	Provide ZKP U_i knows $EVID$
Provide ZKP that U_i knows $EVID$	If ZKP correct
If $r_i = Confirm_i^k$	Send $r_i = Confirm_i^k$ to U_i
return	else
$Transaction\ Resolution$	Send $r_i = Reject_i^k$ to U_i
else	
return	
$Transaction\ Failure$	
$k := k + 1$	$k := k + 1$
if $k \prec t$ $k := k + 1$	if $k \prec t$ $k := k + 1$
else Last Transaction	else Last Transaction

Fig. 4. Anonymous Transactions Protocol ATP_2

making use of the difficulty of the prime numbers generation and the primality proof. As a matter of fact, the generation of large prime numbers is an extremely hard problem ([6]), and therefore only an extremely powerful authority such as a government is able to produce large primes. The proposed hard evidence *EVID* is a very large prime number P.

Assume that the purpose of the user U_i is to convince the servers from the S^{U_i} set that U_i anonymously interacted with each $S_j \in S^{U_i}$ and provided a kth transaction T_i^k in a legitimate manner. The user U_i acts as follows: he/she computes a commitment to P for T_i^k transaction and proves in the $T_i^{k\ th}$ second phase that P is a very large prime. We suggest the use of the ZKP proofs of primality proposed in [5] or [16]. The ZKP protocols presented in these papers are based on the randomized primality tests which provide a very high confidence level of the committed number being prime. The main advantage of these schemes is that the target number is not revealed, and only its commitment participates in the ZKP. Based on these results, the prime evidence P granted to the user by the *TA* is valid forever for any number of possible transactions. Hence, only commitment to P is updated for a new transaction. In ([5]) the first efficient statistical ZKP protocol for proof that a committed number is pseudo prime is presented. A prover (in our context a user) performs the correct computation of a modular addition, modular multiplication, or a modular exponentiation, where all values including the modulus are committed but not publicly available ([5]). The authors implement the randomized Lehmann primality test in Zero Knowledge (see [1]). The computational security power is based on the hardness of the discrete logarithm problem in finite groups ([20]).

The authors of [16] propose a more efficient ZKP of primality. The primality certificate is investigated based on the proof that a given number has only one prime factor and that it is square free. The algebraic settings are: Let $G = \langle g \rangle$ be a finite group of large known order Q and let h be a second group generator while the discrete logarithm $log_g h$ is unknown to the prover-user and the verifier-server. A commitment scheme in [5] and [16] is as follows: in order to commit to any element x participated in the ZKP the prover-user chooses a random number r_x and sends the commitment to x $c_x = g^x h^{r_x}$ to the verifier-sender. Given $c_x = g^x h^{r_x}$ it is computationally infeasible for the verifier or any other adversary to obtain any information about x, while it is infeasible to find different pairs $(x, r_x$ and $x', r_{x'}$ such that $c_x = g^x h^{r_x} = g^{x'} h^{r_{x'}}$ unless the prover can compute $log_h g$ (see [5], [16]). The ZKP of primality in [16] is provided in two phases: firstly, the prover proves that a committed in $c_P = g^P h^{r_P}$ number P has only one prime factor; and next that P is square free. The ZKP is based on the quadratic residues and the LaGrange theorem [1]. For example, in order to perform the secret modular computation $\forall\ a \in Q\ a^P = a(mod\ P)$, the basic secret modular multiplication, exponentiation, and quadratic residue computations are provided. The Lehmann primality test in [5] is also based on these building blocks. The ZKP proves that P is in a given range, and its upper bound may be as large as desired as presented in [16], which suits our model.

The application of ATP_2 requires the users and the servers to deal with computations that are very long and, therefore requires them to be powerful machines as well.

5 Conclusions and Extensions

We define a framework for providing anonymous transactions in computer networks. Two schemes are proposed and analyzed. The first scheme is based on an approval of each transaction by a third party, namely Trusted Authority for the transaction resolution. This scheme is flexible in the sense that the *TA* may limit the maximal number of the transactions permitted to a user by the *TA*; the transactions can be performed in both the linkable and unlinkable mode. The transactions mode is chosen by the user for himself/herself. The advanced scheme uses the *TA* in the initialization stage only, while the anonymous transactions are provided by the user without involving the *TA*. Nevertheless, this scheme is mainly of theoretical interest. The reason is that it is based on computationally expensive Zero Knowledge Proof techniques. Hence, this scheme is implementable only by very powerful computers.

References

1. Bach, E., Shallit, J.: Algorithmic Number Theory. Efficient Algorithms, vol. 1. MIT Press, Cambridge (1996)
2. Belenkiy, M., Chase, M., Kohlweiss, M., Lysyanskaya, A.: Non-Interactive Anonymous Credentials. IACR Cryptology ePrint Archive, Report 2007/384
3. Camenisch, J., Lysyanskaya, A.: A Formal Treatment of Onion Routing. In: Shoup, V. (ed.) CRYPTO 2005. LNCS, vol. 3621, pp. 169–187. Springer, Heidelberg (2005)
4. Camenisch, J., Lysyanskaya, A.: Dynamic Accumulators and Application to Efficient Revocation of Anonymous Credentials. In: Yung, M. (ed.) CRYPTO 2002. LNCS, vol. 2442, p. 61. Springer, Heidelberg (2002)
5. Camenisch, J., Michels, M.: Proving in Zero Knowledge that a Number is the Product of Two Safe Primes. Basic Research in Computer Science (BRICS) Report Series (1998)
6. Cooperative Computing Awards, `http://w2.eff/org/awards/coop.php`
7. Beimel, A., Dolev, S.: Buses for Anonymous Message Delivery. Journal of Cryptology 16, 25–39 (2003)
8. Dolev, S., Ostrovsky, R.: Xor-Trees for Efficient Anonymous Multicast and Reception. ACM Transactions on Information and System Security 3(2), 63–84 (2000)
9. Dolev, S., Kopeetsky, M.: Anonymous Transactions in Computer Networks. Department of Computer Science, Ben Gurion University of the Negev, Technical Report, Number 09-04 (2009)
10. Feige, U., Fiat, A., Shamir, A.: Zero-Knowledge Proofs of Identity. Journal of Cryptology 1(2) (1988)
11. Gabber, E., Gibbons, P., Matias, Y., Mayer, A.: How to Make Personalized Web Browsing Simple, Secure, and Anonymous. In: Luby, M., Rolim, J.D.P., Serna, M. (eds.) FC 1997. LNCS, vol. 1318. Springer, Heidelberg (1997)
12. Golle, P., Jakobsson, M., Juels, A., Syverson, P.: Universal Re-encryption for Mixnets. In: The Cryptographer's Track at RSA conference, San Francisco, CA, USA, pp. 163–178 (2004)
13. Goldreich, O.: Foundations of Cryptography, vol. 1. Cambridge University Press, Cambridge (2003)
14. Goldreich, O.: Foundations of Cryptography, vol. 2. Cambridge University Press, Cambridge (2003)
15. Lamport, L.: Password Authentication with Insecure Communication. Communications of the ACM 24(11) (1981)
16. Lee, T.V., Nguyen, K.Q., Varadharajan, V.: How to Prove that a Committed Number is Prime. In: Lam, K.-Y., Okamoto, E., Xing, C. (eds.) ASIACRYPT 1999. LNCS, vol. 1716, pp. 208–218. Springer, Heidelberg (1999)
17. Lysyanskaya, A., Rivest, R.L., Sahai, A., Wolf, S.: Pseudonym Systems. In: Heys, H.M., Adams, C.M. (eds.) SAC 1999. LNCS, vol. 1758, pp. 184–199. Springer, Heidelberg (2000)
18. Naor, M., Ostrovsky, R., Venkatesan, R., Yung, M.: Perfect Zero-Knowledge Arguments for NP Using any One-Way Permutation. In: Brickell, E.F. (ed.) CRYPTO 1992. LNCS, vol. 740, pp. 196–214. Springer, Heidelberg (1993)
19. Stallings, W.: Network Security Essentials: Applications and Standards. Prentice Hall, Englewood Cliffs (2007)
20. Stingson, D.R.: Cryptography. Theory and Practice, 3rd edn. Chapman and Hall/CRC, Boca Raton (2006)

Nash Equilibria in Stabilizing Systems

Mohamed G. Gouda[1,2] and Hrishikesh B. Acharya[2]

[1] The National Science Foundation, USA
[2] The University of Texas at Austin, USA
{gouda,acharya}@cs.utexas.edu

Abstract. The objective of this paper is three-fold. First, we specify what it means for a fixed point of a stabilizing distributed system to be a Nash equilibrium. Second, we present methods that can be used to verify whether or not a given fixed point of a given stabilizing distributed system is a Nash equilibrium. Third, we argue that in a stabilizing distributed system, whose fixed points are all Nash equilibria, no process has an incentive to perturb its local state, after the system reaches one fixed point, in order to force the system to reach another fixed point where the perturbing process achieves a better gain. If the fixed points of a stabilizing distributed system are all Nash equilibria, then we refer to the system as perturbation-proof. Otherwise, we refer to the system as perturbation-prone. We identify four natural classes of perturbation-(proof/prone) systems. We present system examples for three of these classes of systems, and show that the fourth class is empty.

1 Introduction

The main objective of this paper is to argue that Nash equilibria, which were introduced as termination criteria of games [1], can be used to discourage malicious perturbations in stabilizing distributed systems. But let us start, from the beginning, by describing how a Nash equilibrium can be used as a termination criterion for a well-known game called the two-prisoner dilemma [2].

Consider a "game" that involves two prisoners: prisoner 0 and prisoner 1. This game ends when each prisoner settles on one strategy, out of the two possible strategies of "stay silent" or "betray other prisoner", that maximizes the value of its gain function.

Each prisoner i has a variable $x.i$ whose value, 0 or 1, is assigned as follows:

$$x.i = \begin{cases} 0 & \text{if prisoner } i \text{ selects the "stay silent" strategy} \\ 1 & \text{if prisoner } i \text{ selects the "betray other prisoner" strategy} \end{cases}$$

The gain function $g.i$ of prisoner i is defined, based on the values of the two variables $x.0$ and $x.1$, as follows:

$$\begin{aligned} g.i = & \ 1 \text{ if } x.i = 0 \wedge x.(i+1 \bmod 2) = 0 \\ & -1 \text{ if } x.i = 1 \wedge x.(i+1 \bmod 2) = 1 \\ & \ 2 \text{ if } x.i = 1 \wedge x.(i+1 \bmod 2) = 0 \\ & -2 \text{ if } x.i = 0 \wedge x.(i+1 \bmod 2) = 1 \end{aligned}$$

R. Guerraoui and F. Petit (Eds.): SSS 2009, LNCS 5873, pp. 311–324, 2009.

Thus, the value of the gain function of prisoner i is increased (either from 1 to 2, or from -2 to -1) when the value of variable $x.i$ is changed from 0 to 1 while the value of the other variable $x.(i+1 \bmod 2)$ remains unchanged. In other words, the action of prisoner i to select a strategy, out of the two possible strategies, is as follows:

$$x.i = 0 \rightarrow x.i := 1$$

Note that this action of prisoner i can be executed only when its execution is guaranteed to increase the value of the gain function of prisoner i.

This game of selecting strategies by the two prisoners can start at any global state, for example one where $x.0 = 0 \wedge x.1 = 0$, and then the enabled actions of the two prisoners can be executed, one at a time, until the game reaches the fixed point where $x.0 = 1 \wedge x.1 = 1$ and the game terminates (since neither action can be executed at this fixed point). The fixed point of this game, of selecting strategies, is a Nash equilibrium.

Thus, a Nash equilibrium of a game is a global state of the game where no player can execute an action to change its local state and increase the value of its own gain function.

The subject matter of this paper is to discuss the role of Nash equilibria in stabilizing distributed systems, rather than in games. On the surface, games and stabilizing distributed systems seem similar. On one hand, a game involves several players, and each player is specified by some local variables, some actions, and a gain function. On the other hand, a stabilizing distributed system involves several processes, and each process is specified by some local variables, some actions, and a gain function.

But as one looks deeper, significant differences between games and stabilizing distributed systems become clear:

1. The actions of each player in a game are intended only to increase the value of the gain function of that player, whereas the actions of each process in a system are intended to perform other functions (e.g. construct a spanning tree, elect a leader, or reach consensus) and may not always increase the value of the gain function of that process.
2. Each fixed point of a game is a Nash equilibrium, whereas some fixed points of a system may not be Nash equilibria. Assume for example that a system has a fixed point s such that if a process i perturbs its local state at s, then the system reaches another fixed point s' where the value of the gain function of i at s' is higher than its value at s. In this case, the fixed point s can not be considered a Nash equilibrium for this system.
3. The role of Nash equilibria in a game is to signal game termination. By contrast, the role of Nash equilibria in a stabilizing distributed system is to discourage the system processes from maliciously perturbing their local states to force the system into fixed points with higher values of their gain functions.

The notion that each process in a stabilizing distributed system may have a distinct gain function (that the process seeks to maximize during the system execution) has appeared in the pioneering work of [3] and [4]. There are, however, substantial differences between the problems addressed in the current paper and those addressed in [3] and [4].

1. In [3] and [4], the gain function of each process in a stabilizing distributed system is defined at each state (whether stable or not) of the system. By contrast, in the current paper, the gain function of each process in the system is defined only at the (stable) fixed points of the system.
2. In [3] and [4], the actions of each process in the system are intended to increase the value of the gain function of that process. In the current paper, the actions of each process are only intended to force the system into a fixed point.
3. In [3] and [4], once the system reaches a fixed point, no process can perturb its local state. In the current paper, once the system reaches a fixed point, any process can perturb its local state in order to push the system towards another fixed point, provided that the gain function of the process has a higher value at this new fixed point.

2 Stabilizing Systems and Nash Equilibria

A *distributed system* consists of n processes that communicate through their shared memory, as described below. Each *process* i in a distributed system, where i is in the range $0 \ldots (n-1)$, has a number of local variables and a number of actions. Each *action* of process i is of the following form:

$$< \mathit{guard} > \rightarrow < \mathit{statement} >$$

where $< \mathit{guard} >$ is a boolean expression over the local variables of process i and the local variables of the neighboring processes of process i, and $< \mathit{statement} >$ is an assignment statement that reads the local variables of process i and the local variables of the neighboring processes of process i and writes the local variables of process i.

A *local state* of process i in a distributed system is defined by a value for each local variable in process i. A *global state* of a distributed system is defined by a local state of every process in the distributed system.

A *transition* of a distributed system is a pair (s, s') where the following two conditions hold:

1. Both s and s' are global states of the distributed system.
2. There is an action c in some process in the distributed system such that the guard of c is true when the system is in state s and executing the statement of the action c when the system is in state s yields the system in state s'.

A global state s of a distributed system is called a *fixed point* of the system iff the guard of each action in each process in the system is false when the system is in state s.

A *computation* of a distributed system is a sequence $(s.0, s.1, \ldots)$ where the following three conditions hold:

1. Each of the sequence elements $s.0, s.1, \ldots$ is a global state of the distributed system.
2. Each pair of consecutive states $(s.j, s.(j+1))$ in the sequence is a transition of the distributed system.
3. Either the sequence is infinite, or it is finite and its last global state is a fixed point of the system.

A global state s' is said to be *reachable from* a global state s iff the distributed system has a computation, where s is the initial state and s' is a state in the computation.

A distributed system is called *stabilizing* iff every computation of the system is finite.(Thus, each computation of a stabilizing distributed system is guaranteed to end at a fixed point of the system.)

Consider a stabilizing distributed system that has n processes. A *gain function* $g.i$ for process i in this system is a function that assigns, to the local state of process i and to the local states of the neighboring processes (of process i) when the system is in a fixed point s, an integer value called the value of the gain function $g.i$ at the fixed point s.

Note that the value of a gain function is defined only when the system is at a fixed point.

Henceforth we adopt the notation $\{g.i\}$ to indicate a set of gain functions that contains exactly one gain function $g.i$ for each process i in the system.

Consider a stabilizing distributed system. Let s be a fixed point of this system, and $\{g.i\}$ be a set of gain functions for this system. The fixed point s is called a *Nash equilibrium* w.r.t. $\{g.i\}$ iff for every process i in the system and for every global state s', that results from perturbing (i.e. changing in any way) the local state of process i starting from state s, the following condition holds:

The value of the gain function $g.i$ at some fixed point s'', reachable from s', is no more than the value of $g.i$ at the fixed point s.

Equivalently, the fixed point s is not a Nash equilibrium w.r.t. $\{g.i\}$ iff there exists a process i in the system, and there exists a global state s', that results from perturbing the local state of process i starting from state s, such that the following condition holds:

The value of the gain function $g.i$ at every fixed point s'', reachable from s', is more than the value of $g.i$ at the fixed point s.

The significance of a fixed point of a stabilizing distributed system being a Nash equilibrium w.r.t. $\{g.i\}$ can be explained as follows. Recall that each computation of the system is guaranteed to end at a fixed point since the system is stabilizing. Now assume that the system computation ends at a fixed point s. If s is a Nash equilibrium w.r.t. $\{g.i\}$, then no process i in the system has an incentive to perturb its local state - any such perturbation may lead the system to a fixed point where the value of $g.i$ is no more than its value at s. On the other hand, if s is not a Nash equilibrium w.r.t. $\{g.i\}$, then at least one process i in the system has an incentive to perturb its local state in some way, because this perturbation is guaranteed to lead the system to a fixed point where the value of $g.i$ is more than its value at s.

In summary, whereas a Nash equilibrium in a game is an indication that no move by a game player is gainful to this player, a Nash equilibrium in a stabilizing distributed system is an indication that no perturbation of the local state of a system process is gainful to this process.

3 Verification of Nash Equilibria

In this section, we present some theorems that state sufficient conditions under which a fixed point of a stabilizing distributed system is, or is not, a Nash equilibrium. These sufficient conditions are convenient to use in verifying that a fixed point is, or is not, a Nash equilibrium, as illustrated by the system examples in the following sections.

The first theorem states a sufficient condition for a given fixed point, of a given stabilizing distributed system, to be a Nash equilibrium w.r.t. a given set of gain functions.

Theorem 1. *Consider a stabilizing distributed system that has n processes. Let s be a fixed point of this system, and $\{g.i\}$ be a set of gain functions for this system. The fixed point s is a Nash equilibrium w.r.t. $\{g.i\}$ if, for each i in the range $0 \dots (n-1)$, at least one of the following two conditions holds:*

(a) The gain function $g.i$ has its maximum value at s.
(b) For each global state s' that results from perturbing the local state of process i at s,
  - *either s' is a fixed point where the value of $g.i$ at s' is no more than its value at s,*
  - *or process i has an action whose execution starting at s' returns the system to state s.*

Proof. We show that, if either (a) or (b) holds, then no perturbation of the local state of process i can guarantee that the value of the gain function $g.i$ (of process i) will increase. Thus, there is no incentive for any process to perturb its local state at s, and s is a Nash equilibrium w.r.t. $\{g.i\}$.

If (a) holds, then the value of the gain function $g.i$ at any fixed point s', other than s, cannot be greater than its value at the fixed point s. Thus, when s is the state of the system, no perturbation of the local state of process i will increase the value of $g.i$.

If (b) holds,then any perturbation of the local state of process i at s will either lead back to s, or lead to another fixed point s', where the value of $g.i$ is no more than its value at s. In either case, the perturbation of the local state of process i will not increase the value of $g.i$. □

The next theorem states a sufficient condition for a given fixed point, of a given stabilizing distributed system, to not be a Nash equilibrium w.r.t. a given set of gain functions.

Theorem 2. *Consider a stabilizing distributed system that has n processes. Let s be a fixed point of this system, and $\{g.i\}$ be a set of gain functions for this system. The fixed point s is not a Nash equilibrium w.r.t. $\{g.i\}$ if there exists an i in the range $0 \dots (n-1)$ such that the following condition holds:*

The system has a second fixed point s' where s and s' differ only in the local state of process i and the value of $g.i$ at s is less than its value at s'.

Proof. Let s and s' be two fixed points of a stabilizing distributed system whose set of gain functions is $\{g.i\}$. Assume that s and s' differ only in the local state of process i. Also assume that the value of the gain function $g.i$ (of process i) at state s is less than its value at state s'. Therefore, if process i perturbs its local state, starting from state s and forcing the system into state s', then the value of its gain function $g.i$ is guaranteed to increase. Thus, the fixed point s is not a Nash equilibrium. □

The next theorem states a sufficient condition for a given fixed point, of a given stabilizing distributed system, to be a Nash equilibrium w.r.t. every set of gain functions.

Theorem 3. *Consider a stabilizing distributed system that has n processes. Let s be a fixed point of this system. The fixed point s is a Nash equilibrium w.r.t. every set of gain functions of this system if the following condition holds for every i in the range $0 \dots (n-1)$:*

For each global state s' that results from perturbing the local state of process i at s, process i has an action whose execution starting at s' returns the system to the fixed point s.

Proof. Let s be a fixed point of a stabilizing distributed system. Assume that for each process i in the system, and for each global state s' that results from perturbing the local state of process i at s, process i has an action whose execution, starting at s', returns the system to s. Therefore, no process i can be guaranteed to increase the value of its gain function by perturbing its local state at s. As no process has an incentive to perturb its local state at s, s is a Nash equilibrium w.r.t. any set of gain functions. □

The next theorem states sufficient conditions under which one can construct a set of gain functions to make every fixed point, of a stabilizing distributed system, a Nash equilibrium, or to make one fixed point, of a stabilizing distributed system, not a Nash equilibrium.

Theorem 4. *Consider any stabilizing distributed system that has n processes.*

(a) There is a set of gain functions $\{g.i\}$ for this system such that every fixed point of the system is a Nash equilibrium w.r.t. $\{g.i\}$.

(b) If the system has two fixed points that differ only in the local state of one process, then there is a set of gain functions $\{g.i\}$ for this system such that one of the two fixed points is not a Nash equilibrium w.r.t. $\{g.i\}$.

Proof. For Part(a), define each gain function $g.i$ to have the (same) value 0 at every fixed point of the stabilizing distributed system. From Theorem 1 Part(a), every fixed point of the system is a Nash equilibrium w.r.t. this set of defined gain functions $\{g.i\}$.

For Part(b), let s and s' be two fixed points of the system that differ only in the local state of one process, say process i. Now define the gain function $g.i$ of process i to have the value 0 at state s and 1 at state s'. Thus, if process i perturbs its local state at s, forcing the system to state s', then the value of $g.i$ will increase from 0 to 1 . Therefore, state s is not a Nash equilibrium w.r.t. $\{g.i\}$. □

Based on the above definition of a fixed point being or not being a Nash equilibrium, we identify, in the next four sections, four classes of perturbation proof/prone systems. We give nontrivial examples of systems in the first three classes and then show that the fourth class of systems is empty.

4 Relatively Perturbation-Proof Systems

A stabilizing distributed system is called *relatively perturbation-proof* iff there is a set of gain functions $\{g.i\}$ for this system such that every fixed point of the system is a Nash equilibrium w.r.t. $\{g.i\}$.

In this section, we present an example of a relatively perturbation-proof system. Our objective of this exercise is two-fold. First, we want to show how to use Theorem 1 (above) in verifying that a stabilizing distributed system is relatively perturbation-proof. Second, we want to demonstrate that the class of relatively perturbation-proof systems admits interesting systems.

Consider a maximal matching bidirectional ring that consists of n processes.

Each process i in this ring has two neighbors: process $i-1$ and process $i+1$. Note that, henceforth, we use $i-1$ and $i+1$ to denote $(i-1 \mod n)$ and $(i+1 \mod n)$, respectively. Each process i in this ring has only one local variable named $m.i$ whose value is taken from the set $\{i-1, i, i+1\}$. When the value of $m.i$ is $i-1$ or $i+1$, we say that process i is *matched* to process $i-1$ or process $i+1$, respectively. When the value of $m.i$ is i, we say that process i is not matched. Process i in this ring is specified as follows:

process $i : 0 \ldots (n-1)$
variable $m.i : \{i-1, i, i+1\}$
begin

$$m.i = i-1 \wedge m.(i-1) = i-2 \rightarrow m.i := i$$
$$[]\ m.i = i+1 \wedge m.(i+1) = i+2 \rightarrow m.i := i$$
$$[]\ m.i = i \wedge m.(i-1) \neq i-2 \rightarrow m.i := i-1$$
$$[]\ m.i = i \wedge m.(i+1) \neq i+2 \rightarrow m.i := i+1$$

end

To show that this ring is stabilizing, we first specify a ranking function R that assigns to each global state s of the ring a nonnegative integer. We then establish that for each action execution, that causes the global state of the ring to change from s to s', $R(s) > R(s')$. A ranking function R for this ring can be specified as follows:

$$R = R.0 + R.1 + \ldots + R.(n-1)$$

where each $R.i$ is specified as follows:

$$\begin{aligned} R.i = {} & 3 \text{ if } (m.i = i-1 \wedge m.(i-1) = i-2) \vee \\ & \qquad (m.i = i+1 \wedge m.(i+1) = i+2) \\ & 2 \text{ if } (m.i = i) \\ & 1 \text{ if } (m.i = i-1 \wedge m.(i-1) = i-1) \vee \\ & \qquad (m.i = i+1 \wedge m.(i+1) = i+1) \\ & 0 \text{ if } (m.i = i-1 \wedge m.(i-1) = i) \vee \\ & \qquad (m.i = i+1 \wedge m.(i+1) = i) \end{aligned}$$

To show that the following predicate P holds at each fixed point of this ring:

$$\begin{aligned} P = & (\forall \text{i, where i is in the range } 0 \ldots n-1, \\ & (m.i = i-1 \rightarrow m.(i-1) = i) \wedge \\ & (m.i = i+1 \rightarrow m.(i+1) = i) \wedge \\ & (m.i = i \rightarrow m.(i-1) = i-2 \wedge m.(i+1) = i+2)) \end{aligned}$$

it is sufficient to argue that the guard of each action in the ring is false when predicate P holds.

Specify the gain function $g.i$ for each process i in this ring as follows:

$$\begin{aligned} g.i = & 0 \text{ if } m.i = i \\ & 1 \text{ otherwise} \end{aligned}$$

We use Theorem 1 to show that each fixed point of this ring is a Nash equilibrium w.r.t. this set of gain functions $\{g.i\}$. Consider a fixed point s of this ring where predicate P holds. At s, each $m.i$ has one of the three values $i-1$, $i+1$, or i. If $m.i$ has the value $i-1$ or $i+1$ at s, then $g.i$ has its maximum value 1 at s, and process i has no incentive to perturb the value of $m.i$ when the ring is at s. It remains now to consider the case where $m.i$ has the value i at s which implies, from predicate P, that $(m.(i-1) = i-2 \wedge m.(i+1) = i+2)$ at s. If process i perturbs the value of its $m.i$ from i to $i-1$, then the first action in process i can be executed causing the ring to return to s and the value of $g.i$ to remain unchanged. Thus, process i has no incentive to perturb the value of $m.i$ from i to $i-1$.

Similarly, we can argue that process i has no incentive to perturb the value of $m.i$ from i to $i+1$. Therefore, s is a Nash equilibrium w.r.t. $\{g.i\}$.

Because each fixed point of this ring is a Nash equilibrium w.r.t. the set of gain functions $\{g.i\}$ specified above, this ring is relatively perturbation-proof.

5 Relatively Perturbation-Prone Systems

A stabilizing distributed system is called *relatively perturbation-prone* iff there is a set of gain functions $\{g.i\}$ for this system such that some fixed point of the system is not a Nash equilibrium w.r.t. $\{g.i\}$.

In this section, we present an example of a relatively perturbation-prone system and use Theorem 2 (above) to verify that the system is indeed relatively perturbation-prone.

Consider a ring that has n processes. Each process i has one local variable named $c.i$ that can be regarded as the color of process i. The value of $c.i$ is taken from the set $\{0, 1, 2\}$. At each fixed point of this ring, every two neighboring processes have distinct colors. Process i in this ring is specified as follows:

process $i : 0 \ldots (n-1)$
variable $c.i : 0, 1, 2$
begin
$i > 0 \wedge c.(i-1) = c.i \rightarrow c.i := (c.i + 1 \bmod 3)$
$[\!]\ i = n-1 \wedge c.(i+1) = c.i \rightarrow c.i := (c.i + 1 \bmod 3)$
end

It is straightforward to show that this ring is stabilizing and that the following predicate P holds at each fixed point of the ring:

$$P = (\text{ For every } i, \text{ where } i \text{ is in the range } 0 \ldots n-1, c.i \neq c.(i+1))$$

Specify the gain function $g.i$ for each process i in this ring as follows:

$$\begin{aligned} g.i = & 0 \text{ if } c.i = 0 \\ & 1 \text{ if } c.i \neq 0 \text{ and } c.(i-1) \neq 0 \text{ or } c.(i+1) \neq 0 \\ & 2 \text{ if } c.i \neq 0 \text{ and } c.(i-1) = 0 \text{ and } c.(i+1) = 0 \end{aligned}$$

We use Theorem 2 to show that some fixed point of this ring is not a Nash equilibrium w.r.t. this set of gain functions. Consider the following fixed point s of the ring (assuming that n is even):

$$c.0 = 1 \wedge c.1 = 0 \wedge c.2 = 1 \wedge c.3 = 0 \wedge \ldots \wedge c.(n-1) = 0$$

To show that s is not a Nash equilibrium w.r.t. $\{g.i\}$, it is sufficient, by Theorem 2, to exhibit another fixed point s' where s and s' differ only in the value of exactly one $c.i$, say $c.1$, and show that the value of $g.1$ at s is less than its value at s'. Now consider the following fixed point s' of the ring:

$$c.0 = 1 \wedge c.1 = 2 \wedge c.2 = 1 \wedge c.3 = 0 \wedge \ldots \wedge c.(n-1) = 0$$

The two fixed points s and s' differ only in the value of $c.1$ and the value of $g.1$ at s is 0, less than its value 1 at s'. This proves that s is not a Nash equilibrium w.r.t. $\{g.i\}$. (Note that, as the value of the gain function $g.1$ increases from 0 to 1, the values of each of the two gain functions $g.0$ and $g.2$ is decreased from 2 to 1.)

Because some fixed point of this ring is not a Nash equilibrium w.r.t. the set of gain functions $\{g.i\}$ specified above, the ring is relatively perturbation-prone.

6 Absolutely Perturbation-Proof Systems

A stabilizing distributed system is called *absolutely perturbation-proof* iff for every set of gain functions $\{g.i\}$ for this system, every fixed point of the system is a Nash equilibrium w.r.t. $\{g.i\}$.(Note that a system is absolutely perturbation-proof iff it is not relatively perturbation-prone).

Consider the case where the designers of a stabilizing distributed system wish to make this system perturbation-proof. In this case, if the designers can determine the natural set of gain functions for this system, then they should design the system to be relatively perturbation-proof w.r.t. this set of gain functions. On the other hand, if the designers cannot determine the one natural set of gain functions for this system, then they should design the system to be absolutely perturbation-proof.

In this section, we give an example of an absolutely perturbation-proof system and use Theorem 3 (above) to show that this system is indeed absolutely perturbation-proof.

Consider a ring that has n processes. Each process i has one local variable named $c.i$ that can be regarded as the color of process i. In specifying the actions of each process in this ring we adopt the notation $A \equiv B$ to indicate that the two sets A and B are equal, and adopt the notation $A \subseteq B$ to indicate that set A is a subset of set B. Process i in this ring is specified as follows:

process $i : 0 \ldots (n-1)$
variable $c.i : \{0, 1, 2\}$
begin

$c.i \neq 0 \wedge \{c.(i-1), c.(i+1)\} \equiv \{1, 2\} \rightarrow c.i := 0$
$[\!]\ c.i \neq 1 \wedge \{c.(i-1), c.(i+1)\} \equiv \{0, 2\} \rightarrow c.i := 1$
$[\!]\ c.i \neq 1 \wedge \{c.(i-1), c.(i+1)\} \equiv \{2\} \rightarrow c.i := 1$
$[\!]\ c.i \neq 2 \wedge \{c.(i-1), c.(i+1)\} \subseteq \{0, 1\} \rightarrow c.i := 2$

end

A ranking function R for this ring can be specified as follows:

$$\begin{aligned} R = {} & 3\times\#(\{i | c.i = c.(i-1) \vee c.i = c.(i+1)\}) \\ & +\#(\{i | c.i = 0\}) \\ & +\#(\{i | c.i = 1 \wedge c.(i-1) = 0 \wedge c.(i+1) = 0\}) \end{aligned}$$

It is straightforward to show that each action execution in this ring causes the value of this ranking function R to decrease by at least 1. (For example, if the first action in process 0 is executed starting at a global state where $c.(n-1) = 1$ and $c.0 = 1$ and $c.1 = 2$, then this execution changes the value of $c.0$ to 0 and causes the value of R to be reduced by at least 4.) The existence of such a ranking function for this system guarantees that the system will eventually reach a global state where no action can be executed, i.e. a fixed point.

The following predicate P holds at each fixed point of this ring:

$$
\begin{aligned}
P = (\forall i, & i \text{ is in the range } 0 \ldots (n-1),\\
& (c.i = 0 \wedge \{c.(i-1), c.(i+1)\} \equiv \{1,2\}) \vee \\
& (c.i = 1 \wedge \{c.(i-1), c.(i+1)\} \equiv \{0,2\}) \vee \\
& (c.i = 1 \wedge \{c.(i-1), c.(i+1)\} \equiv \{2\}) \vee \\
& (c.i = 2 \wedge \{c.(i-1), c.(i+1)\} \subseteq \{0,1\}))
\end{aligned}
$$

Note that when predicate P holds, the value of each $c.i$ is different from the values of $c.(i-1)$ and $c.(i+1)$.

We use Theorem 3 to show that each fixed point of this ring is a Nash equilibrium w.r.t. any set of gain functions. Consider a fixed point s of this ring where P holds. At s, each $c.i$ has any one of the values 0, 1, or 2. If the value of $c.i$ is 0 at s, and if this value is perturbed to 1 or 2 yielding the ring in a global state s', then the first action of process i can be executed at s' to return the ring to the fixed point s. Also if the value of $c.i$ is 1 at s, and if this value is perturbed to 0 or 2 yielding the ring in a global state s', then either the second or third action of process i can be executed at s' to return the ring to s. Similarly, if the value of $c.i$ is 2 at s, and if this value is perturbed to 0 or 1 yielding the ring in a global state s', then the fourth action of process i can be executed at s' to return the ring to s. Thus, by Theorem 3, the fixed point s is a Nash equilibrium w.r.t. any set of gain functions.

Because each fixed point of this ring is a Nash equilibrium w.r.t. any set of gain functions, we conclude that this ring is absolutely perturbation-proof.

This system example illustrates a method, implied by Theorem 3, for designing absolutely perturbation-proof systems. This method can be summarized as follows. To ensure that a stabilizing distributed system is absolutely perturbation-proof, consider each global state s of this system, where s differs from a fixed point s' of the system only in the local state of process i, then ensure that process i has an action whose execution starting at s yields the system in s'.

The next theorem identifies an interesting subclass of absolutely perturbation-proof system.

Theorem 5. *Any stabilizing distributed system, that has exactly one fixed point, is absolutely perturbation-proof.*

Proof. Consider a stabilizing distributed system that has only one fixed point s. If any process i perturbs its local state at s, the system (being stabilizing) is guaranteed to stabilize and thus return to state s. Therefore, the value of the gain function of process i remains unchanged. Thus, no process has an incentive to perturb its local state at s, so s is a Nash equilibrium w.r.t. any set of gain functions. The system is absolutely perturbation-proof. □

7 Absolutely Perturbation-Prone Systems

A stabilizing distributed system is called *absolutely perturbation-prone* iff for every set of gain functions $\{g.i\}$ for this system, there is a fixed point of the system that is not a Nash equilibrium w.r.t. $\{g.i\}$.

The next theorem, which follows directly from Theorem 4(a), states, in effect, that the class of absolutely perturbation-prone systems is empty.

Theorem 6. *No stabilizing distributed system is absolutely perturbation-prone. (In other words, every stabilizing distributed system is relatively perturbation-proof.)*

Proof. By Theorem 4(a), for every stabilizing distributed system there exists at least one set of gain functions $\{g.i\}$ such that every fixed point of the system is a Nash equilibrium w.r.t. $\{g.i\}$. This implies that every stabilizing distributed system is relatively perturbation-proof, and the theorem holds. □

Based on Theorem 6, we have the taxonomy of stabilizing distributed systems shown in Figure 1.

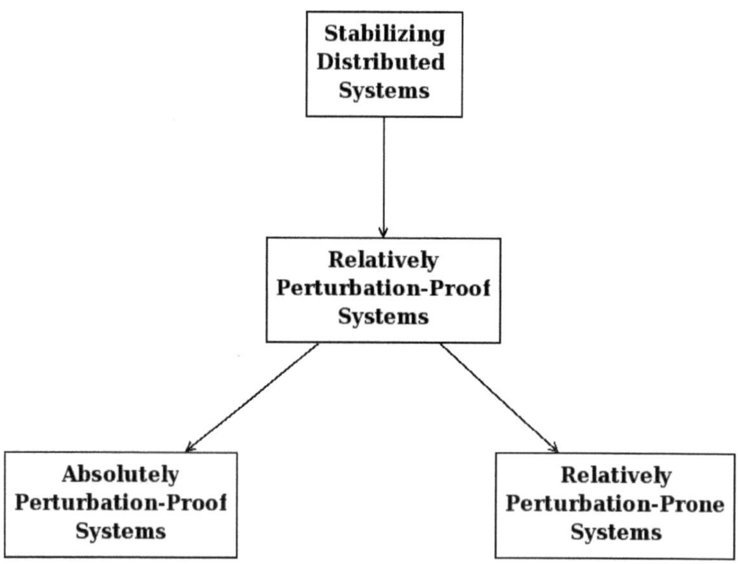

Fig. 1. A taxonomy

8 Concluding Remarks

A stabilizing distributed system is a system that is guaranteed to return to a fixed point every time a "fault" yields the system in an arbitrary state that is not a fixed point. Thus, the property of stabilization makes systems recover from the effects of a large class of faults [5].

Unfortunately, stabilization does not protect a system from state perturbations caused by system processes that prefer one fixed point over another in accordance with some gain functions for these processes. To ensure that no process in a system has an incentive to intentionally perturb the system state, the system should be designed such that any perturbation caused by any process i in the system is not guaranteed to increase the value of the gain function of process i. This can be accomplished by ensuring that each fixed point of the system is a Nash equilibrium with respect to the given set of gain functions, one for each process in the system. We refer to a system, where each fixed point is a Nash equilibrium, as a perturbation-proof system.

In this paper, we identify two classes of perturbation-proof systems: relatively perturbation-proof systems and absolutely perturbation-proof systems. In a relatively perturbation-proof system, each fixed point is a Nash equilibrium w.r.t. a given set of gain functions (one for each process in the system). In an absolutely perturbation-proof system, each fixed point is a Nash equilibrium w.r.t. each possible set of gain functions (one for each process in the system).

Clearly, the concept of a relatively perturbation-proof system is useful when the set of gain functions for the system processes can be uniquely and completely identified. On the other hand, the concept of an absolutely perturbation-proof system is useful when there are multiple candidates for the set of gain functions.

The fact that one can design an absolutely perturbation-proof system, as indicated by Theorem 3, is the main contribution of this paper. Theorem 3 suggests that an absolutely perturbation-proof system can be designed as follows:

1. Consider each global state gs that is not a fixed point of the system and where changing the local state of one process i from ls to ls' changes the global state of the system from gs to a fixed point gs'.
2. Ensure that process i has an action that can be executed when the global state of the system is gs and when the local state of process i is ls, and ensure that the execution of this action causes the local state of process i to become ls'.

It has been suggested recently that the definition of a Nash equilibrium can be extended to make it more relevant to Computer Science. (See for instance [6], [7], and [8].) It is interesting to explore how these extensions of Nash equilibrium can impact our theory of Perturbation-Freedom outlined in this paper.

References

1. Nash, J.F.: Equilibrium points in n-person games. Proceedings of the National Academy of Sciences of the United States of America 36, 48–49 (1950)
2. Flood, M.M.: Some experimental games. Management Science 5, 5–26 (1958)
3. Bhattacharya, A., Ghosh, S.: Self-optimizing peer-to-peer networks with selfish processes. In: Proceedings of the First International Conference on Self-Adaptive and Self-Organizing Systems, pp. 340–343 (2007)

4. Cohen, J., Dasgupta, A., Ghosh, S., Tixeuil, S.: An exercise in selfish stabilization. ACM Trans. Auton. Adapt. Syst. 3, 1–12 (2008)
5. Arora, A., Gouda, M.: Closure and convergence: A foundation for fault-tolerant computing. IEEE Transactions on Computers 19, 1015–1027 (1993)
6. Abraham, I., Dolev, D., Gonen, R., Halpern, J.: Distributed computing meets game theory: robust mechanisms for rational secret sharing and multiparty computation. In: Proceedings of the twenty-fifth annual ACM symposium on Principles of distributed computing, pp. 53–62. ACM, New York (2006)
7. Abraham, I., Dolev, D., Halpern, J.: Lower bounds on implementing robust and resilient mediators. In: Canetti, R. (ed.) TCC 2008. LNCS, vol. 4948, pp. 302–319. Springer, Heidelberg (2008)
8. Halpern, J.Y.: Beyond nash equilibrium: Solution concepts for the 21st century. In: van Breugel, F., Chechik, M. (eds.) CONCUR 2008. LNCS, vol. 5201, p. 1. Springer, Heidelberg (2008)
9. Dijkstra, E.W.: Self-stabilizing systems in spite of distributed control. Commun. ACM 17, 643–644 (1974)
10. Dolev, S.: Self-stabilization. MIT Press, Cambridge (2000)
11. Gouda, M.G.: The triumph and tribulation of system stabilization. In: Helary, J.-M., Raynal, M. (eds.) WDAG 1995. LNCS, vol. 972, pp. 1–18. Springer, Heidelberg (1995)
12. Goddard, W., Hedetniemi, S.T., Jacobs, D.P., Srimani, P.K.: Self-stabilizing protocols for maximal matching and maximal independent sets for ad hoc networks. In: Proceedings of the 17th International Symposium on Parallel and Distributed Processing, Washington, DC, USA, p. 162.2. IEEE Computer Society, Los Alamitos (2003)
13. Huang, S.T., Hung, S.S., Tzeng, C.H.: Self-stabilizing coloration in anonymous planar networks. Information Processing Letters 95, 307–312 (2005)

ACCADA: A Framework for Continuous Context-Aware Deployment and Adaptation

Ning Gui, Vincenzo De Florio, Hong Sun, and Chris Blondia

PATS group, University of Antwerp, Belgium
and IBBT, Ghent-Ledeberg, Belgium
{ning.gui,vincenzo.deflorio,chris.blondia}@ua.ac.be

Abstract. Software systems are increasingly expected to dynamically self-adapt to the changing environments. One of the principle adaptation mechanisms is dynamic recomposition of application components. This paper addresses the key issues that arise when external context knowledge is used to steer the run-time (re)composition process. In order to integrate such knowledge into this process, A Continuous Context-Aware Deployment and Adaptation (ACCADA) framework is proposed. To support run-time component composition, the essential runtime abstractions of the underlying component model are studied. By using a layered modeling approach, our framework gradually incorporates design-time as well as run-time knowledge into the component composition process. Service orientation is employed to facilitate the changes of adaptation policy. Results show that our framework has significant advantages over traditional approaches in light of flexibility, resource usage and lines of code. Although our experience was done based on the OSGi middleware, we believe our findings to be general to other architecture-based management systems.

Keywords: Adaptive middleware, context-specific knowledge, run-time composition, service oriented architecture.

1 Introduction

Software systems today increasingly operate in changing environments and with diverse user needs, resulting in the continued increasing complexity for managing and adapting these systems. As a consequence, software systems are increasingly expected to dynamically self-adapt to accommodate resource variability, changing user needs, and system faults. However, mechanisms that support self-adaptation currently are hardwired within each application. These approaches are often highly application-specific, static in nature, and tightly bound to the code. Being static, such mechanisms can hardly cope with dynamic context changes. Furthermore, the localized treatments of application adaptation could not effectively deal with those complex environments in which many multi-influencing applications coexist.

In order to deal with the adaptation problem outside single application scope, architecture-based adaptation frameworks are proposed in [1] [2] to handle the cross system adaptation. Rather than scatter the adaptation logics in different applications and

R. Guerraoui and F. Petit (Eds.): SSS 2009, LNCS 5873, pp. 325–340, 2009.

represent them as low-level binary code, architecture-based adaptation uses external models and mechanisms in a closed-loop control fashion to achieve various goals by monitoring and adapting system behavior across application domains. A well-accepted design principle in architecture-based management consists in using a component-based technology to develop management system and application structure [3-6] .

However, in traditional approaches, design-time knowledge for application structure is largely lost during the off-line application construction process. Without this knowledge, it is nearly impossible for external engines to effectively change a application' structure with the assurance that the new configuration would perform as intended. On the other hand, Integration of external context knowledge[1] to application becomes very difficult as that knowledge can only be available well after an application was built.

During our research on run-time adaptation, we observed that in order to achieve effective architecture-based adaptation framework, three important prerequisites must be fulfilled. First, when building application, those practices of rigid location and binding between component instances should be replaced with run-time, context-specific composition. Second, selected design-time information must be exposed and those constraints must be made explicitly verifiable during run-time. Third, since different contexts have radically different properties of interest and require dynamic modification strategies, it is critical that the architectural control model and modification strategies could be easily tailored to various system contexts.

Our framework tackles these problems from different perspectives. A run-time application construction methodology is proposed to provide a continuum between the design and run-time process. An architecture-based management framework structure is designed to facilitate the integration of context-specific adaptation knowledge. In order to support run-time component composition, a declarative component model with uniform management interface and meta-data based reflection is proposed. By adopting a service oriented architecture-based implementation, our framework provides efficient mechanisms for adapting to specific context requirements. The effectiveness of our architecture is demonstrated both from qualitative and a quantitative point of view. Simulation results show the soundness of our implementation in term of line of code, memory and adaptation capabilities.

The rest of the paper is organized as follows. Section 2 exposes our design methodology and a context-specific management framework and those challenges in realizing this framework. Section 3 presents the structure of our management framework as well as the component model and construction process. The ideas exposed in this paper have been validated by a set of comparison from different aspects in Section 4. Related work is discussed in Section 5, and we conclude in Section 6.

2 Architecture-Based Adaptation

Architecture-based adaptation is proposed to deal with cross system adaptation. In principle, such external control mechanisms provide a more effective engineering solution with respect to internal mechanisms for self-adaptation because they abstract

[1] By context, we refer to [7] and define it as "any information that characterizes a situation related to the interaction between humans, applications and the surrounding environment."

the concerns of problem detection and resolution into separable system modules[2]. However, systematic support for multi-context knowledge integration is largely missing. An important contribution of this paper is the designing and developing architectural principles and design patterns to integrate different context-specific knowledge into architecture-based adaption framework. We design the context-specific application methodology to better support run-time component composition,

2.1 Context-Specific Application Construction Methodology

In order to more effectively deal with run-time component composition, we propose a new methodology to explicitly incorporate context-specific knowledge into the software composition & adaptation process. The new architecture design & composition flow, depicted in Fig. **1.**, represents a procedure which tries to incorporate the functional design information with context concerns in compositing run-time software architecture. Depending on the employed design languages and corresponding tools, the compliance with the functional interface is enforced during the design process. However, unlike traditional approach, in which a component's functional knowledge is lost during this compiling process, in this case the design time information is explicitly exposed and maintained.

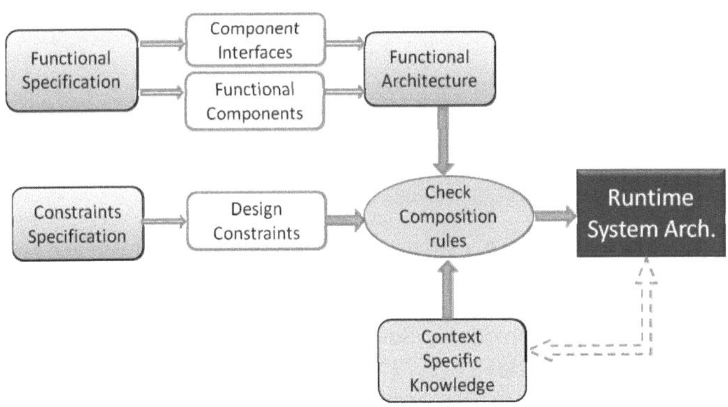

Fig. 1. Context-specific Application Construction Flow

As an application is constructed during run-time, in order to achieve correct and pointed adaptation, a set of constraints must be maintained. In this process, three main aspects constraints should be evaluated. 1) The functional dependence constraints must be satisfied 2) a component's non-functional constraints must be guaranteed: this information includes, for instance, requirements for CPU speed, screen size or that some property value be within a certain range. 3) context-specific knowledge, which specifies the domain related information and adaptation strategy should also hold valid after adaptation process.

As the dashed arrow points out, a managed application is continuously restructured and evolved according to context switches. The combined knowledge enables automatically run-time verification for constraints from various aspects which allows the system to change the software structure according to its hosting environment and without violating constraints from these three aspects.

2.2 Motivation Example

To better illustrate all the complexities in introducing the context knowledge into the application composition process, we make use of an example scenario that will be revisited several times throughout the course of this paper.

Today we are surrounded by an ever increasing number of networked equipment which can be harnessed to do something for you for temporal or long-term base. The open-system approach implies that a set of new applications will be installed into the host devices without thoroughly system analysis.

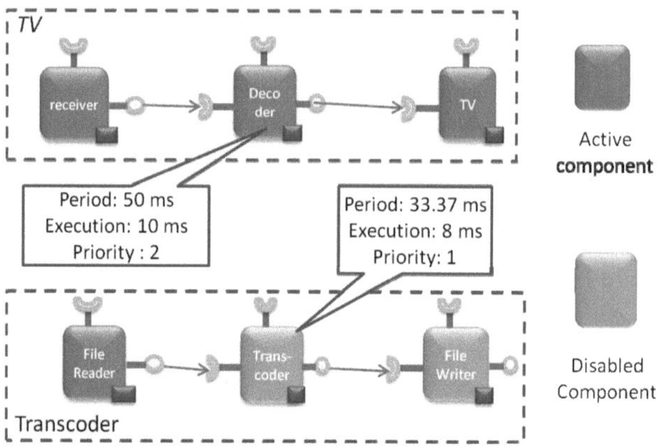

Fig. 2. QoE adaptation Demonstration

As an example, let us consider a Set-top device with Open platform support. The basic application of such device is TV processing. In brief, this application will received streaming video data from remote server, decode this data and output it to the TV port. As an open system, Set-top can also install certain applications to enhance its usability. For example, a user can install a new application which transcode recorded High Definition TV stream to IPhone format for later display on his/her mobile devices. Figure 2 shows the simplified component graph for those two applications, which will be further studied in later sections. As a typical multi-task system, if a user starts those two applications, a Set-top will try to execute the two applications simultaneously no matter whether the Set-top device has enough resources. If that is not the case, this may eventually lead to possibly transient timing problems of TV decoding task including missing frame, data overflows etc. These kinds of time breaches can result in poor video quality and bad user experience.

Context-specific knowledge, however, can help the architecture automatically determine which actions should be taken according to the current context. One possible strategy can choose to disable the computationally intensive transcoding component and reserve enough system resources for TV application. This is because a user normally prefers to give highest priority to those applications that matter their experience most. Figure 2 shows the snapshot of component states after such adaptation.

3 Architectural Framework

We adopt a standard view of software architecture that is typically used today at design time to characterize an application to be built. Specifically, an application is represented as a graph of interacting computational elements. Nodes in the graph, called *components*, represent the system's principal computational elements (software or hardware) and data stores. The connections represent the pathways for interaction between the components. Additionally, the component may be annotated with various properties, such as expected throughputs, latencies, and protocols of interaction.

In our framework, applications are run-time composed from a set of managed component instances. Context-specific adaptation is achieved by dynamic (re)composing application components according to context knowledge.

3.1 Architecture-Based Management Framework

Figure 3 shows our ACCADA architecture for adaptation. As can be clearly seen from that picture, our approach makes use of an extended control loop, consisting of five basic modules – *Event Monitor, Adaptation Actuator, Structural Modeler, Context-Specific Modeler* and *Context Selector*. ACCADA uses an abstract architectural model to monitor a running system's run-time properties, evaluate the model for (functional as well as context-specific) violation, and – if a problem occurs – performs global and component-level adaptations on the running system.

The Event Monitor module observes and measures various system states. It sends notifications to trigger a new round of the adaptation process. The possible source of adaptation may include, for example, a new component being installed or the CPU or memory utilization reaching a status that may have significant effect on the existing system configuration. It could also be a simple Timer that triggers periodically at certain time intervals. The Adaptation Actuator carries out the actual system modification. The actual action set is tightly related to the component implementation. From our developing experience, in order to achieve effective architecture-based adaptation, the basic set of actions should include component lifecycle control, attribute configuration, and component reference manipulation.

The above two modules provide an interface to manage the installed component instances and form the ACCADA Management Layer (discussed in Section 3.4). The other three modules constitute what we call the Modeling Layer which builds the system architectural model according to the changing contexts(Section 3.3).

Building a software system architecture model is not a trivial endeavor – it includes handling design-time knowledge such as interfaces or constraints as well as run-time aspects on environment changes. By using the Divide and Conquer principle, we assign the management of these two aspects to two different modules to more effectively deal with two different requirements – software architecture management and context-specific knowledge integration.

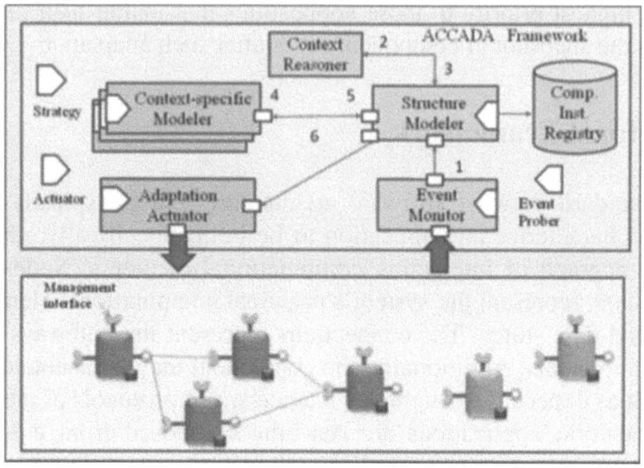

Fig. 3. ACCADA framework

One module, the *Structural Modeler*, manages functional dependences between installed components – checking whether the required and provided interfaces are compatible – and maintains application's software architecture. This module is comparably stable as it is only determined by the component implementation model and will not change with context. So, it is designed as the core module in our system. In addition to those functional dependence managements, the traces of all the adaptation steps performed is also monitored and exposed for later analysis. The other set of modules are the *Context-specific Modeler*. In order to cope with dynamically changing environments, rather than going for the traditional approach of "one adaptor for all possible contexts", our framework supports more than one *Context-specific Modelers* specifically designed for different contexts in the system. By reasoning upon various system metrics, *Context Selector* is designed to determine the most appropriate *Modeler* to date.

Service-oriented Approach. In order to achieve more reusability and flexibility, our framework is designed according to the Service Oriented model. Each module is designed and implemented as a service provider. Modules implement and register their interfaces into the system service registry. Thanks to such loosely coupled structure, a candidate service provider can be easily interchanged during system run-time. In doing so, many existing and/or future more sophisticated context adaptation policies can be plugged into our framework.

3.2 Requirements for Component Model

In ACCADA, a component represents a single unit of functionality and deployment. In order to achieve architecture-based run-time composition, a component model with following attributes is needed:

Uniform management interface. As components are individually installed and configured by the system service, it is very important that a component could be managed through a uniform management interface. With this interface, components are reified in a uniform way for configuration, state monitoring and management. This approach enables system management services such as *Event Monitor* and the *Adaptation Actuator* to be designed in a generic way and used across multiple application domains. The management interface supports lifecycle control and get/set component properties. It can be accessed via two different approaches – either accessing directly or mediated through an architectural layer which, apart from performing the requested actions, also coherently updates the status of the global software architecture. In order to maintain a coherent and accurate global configuration, it is vital that this uniform management interface can only be accessed through architecture- exposed methods. Our previous work provides the detailed design of such interface.

Component description and introspection. In order to support different types of components, a component model should be able to describe the component's distinguished stable characteristics. These Features include a component's provided and required interfaces, component's properties as well as other constraints, for example, the type of CPU that is required. Interface-based introspective and reflective component models are proposed in Fractal [8] and OpenCom [9, 10], in which a general interface is designed for such knowledge discovery.

Instead of following these approaches, a concise management interface is used to control and capture the components' run-time state, while meta-data is applied to expose component-specific knowledge. Compared to the interface-based introspection, it provides designers with a more light-weighted and explicit solution. Compared to Interface-based approach, meta-data approach enables components to be identified prior to their initialization; furthermore, this reduces the burden of component developers to implement those introspection interfaces, as meta-data already provides much design-time structural information. Those meta-data can be naturally abstracted from application design, validated in the verification process, and then reused during the run-time composition process. In this approach, a component design knowledge actually winds through its whole lifecycle. The ACCADA framework can dynamically discover and retrieve a component's structural characteristics as soon as they are installed into the system.

In our previous work in the Declarative Real-time component model (DRCom), a simple declarative language is designed. Please refer [11]for details.

3.3 Modeling Layer

As already mentioned, modeling the whole system architecture and making pointed adaptation decisions is a very complex process. That is especially true in our framework, as not only functional dependences but also the context knowledge are considered in the composition process. These two aspects have been kept separated and assigned to what we call *Structural Modeler* and *Context-specific Modeler*, described in what follows.

3.3.1 Structural Modeler

As the application is constructed, configured and reconstructed during system run-time, how to derive the functional and structural dependency among components becomes one of the key problems in run-time component composition.The Structural Modeler consists of several processes, the most important of which are:

Dependence Compatibility Check. This component first checks all the installed components dependence relationship. A component can only be initialized when all its required interfaces (Receptacles) have corresponding provided interfaces.. This also guarantees component initialization orders. According to different component model, different policies may be employed, such as the interface based matching – used in the model of Declarative Service and Fractal model – or data communication matching as it is the case in DRCom model.

Such function is quite important for run-time composition as it provides a general matching service which is indispensable in maintaining application architecture during system configuration changes.

Maintenance of Application architecture (Reference update). As component will be installed and uninstalled during run-time, the issue of reference update during component exchange must be addressed. When one component is exchanged for another it is necessary to update the references that point to the old component such that they refer to the new one. Doing so is necessary to ensure that the program continues to execute correctly. For example, when a component is disabled, the modeler will firstly check whether another component with the same functional attributes exists. If such a candidate is successfully found, the modeler will repair the references between components to change the old references with the new one, and then destroy the invalid connections. Otherwise, all components which depend on this disabled component will also be disabled. All these adaptations are performed during run-time without disabling the whole application. By having the system managing the run-time reference update, an application's architecture integrity can be preserved even in the face of configuration changes.

Many run-time composition approaches, such as Servicebinder [12] and Perimorph [13], provide similar layer to manage the references between components. However, without context information integration, this functional layer itself could not solve conflicts when several functional configurations are available. Such kind of ambiguity can only be handled with context knowledge.

3.3.2 Context-specific Modeler

As the *Structural Modeler* deals with the functional related constraints in building and maintaining the software architecture, the *Context-specific Modeler* deals with constraints related to the knowledge of context. All components that satisfy functional requirements will be further evaluated by context knowledge. As a result, the modeler will build a context-specific architecture model using its knowledge and adaptation strategy. This model will be checked periodically and/or on request. If a constraints violation occurs, it determines the course of action and delegates such actions to the adaptations execution module.

In ACCADA, several context modelers with different context adaptation knowledge can be installed simultaneously. They implement the same context modeler service interface with different attributes describing their target concerns. Such concerns could be e.g. prolonging mission life in case of low batteries, or maximizing user experience when watching movies on a given mobile device. Service orientation enables the architecture to support different or future unpremeditated adaptation strategies. Another benefit from this approach is that one modeler instance just needs to deal with a fraction of all possible adaptation concerns. Compared to "one size fits all" approach, our solution makes the modeler very concise, easy to implement and consuming fewer resources. By switching Context-specific Modeler, the system architecture model as well as the adaptation behavior can be easily altered, which could be beneficial in matching different environmental conditions. Here, which Context-specific Modeler is to be used is determined by the Context Selector .

3.3.3 Context Selector

As several Context-specific Reasoners may co-exist in a specific time, only one of them will be selected according to current system context. It will return an active context modeler "best matching" the current environment. According to different system requirements, the reasoning logic may be as simple as using CPU status as decision logics, or as complex as using a semantic reasoning engine or some other artificial intelligence approach. By separating three kinds of responsibilities -knowing when a modeler is useful, selecting among different modelers, and using a modeler, new modelers can be integrated into software system in a way that is transparent to users. One simple interface is designed to return the best matched reference:

```
public interface ContextSelector
           { public ContextAdaptor findCurrentFitAdaptor();  }
```

3.4 Management Layer

This layer provides an abstract interface to manage the interactions between modeling layer and component instances. It consists of two main elements: Event Monitor and Adaptation Actuator. Event Monitor tracks installed components' state changes as well as probes the measured attributes across different system components. The value of a managed component's attribute can be retrieved via the getProperty(…) methods. Adaptation Actuator implements the atomic adaptation actions that the system can take. This can include actions that manage a component's lifecycle state – start, stop, pause, stop – as well as properties manipulations via setProperty(…), for example, changing the computation task's priority, period… The uniform management interface simplifies the design of the actuator as the actions can be taken in a general way and can be easily reused to different component models

3.5 General Adaptation Process

The above five key modules residing in the modeling and management layers are orchestrated so as to form an external control loop across different application domain. When a significant change has been detected, the modeling layer is notified to check whether existing constraints are being violated. Algorithm 1 describes the general adaptation process.

Algorithm 1. General adaptation process

Requires: An architecture-based management system with context-specific adaptation logic

Ensure: Keep constraints satisfied in the face of changes, both functional as non-functional, through Context-specific knowledge

1. A system change triggers adaptation process
2. Structural Modeler gets the set of satisfied components in terms of functional dependence
3. Context Selector returns Context-specific modeler's reference
4. The selected Context-specific Modeler builds an adaptation plan
5. Structure modeler merges two adaptation plan
6. The Adaptation Actuator executes the adaptation plan

4 Implementation and Simulation

In this section, we will discuss our implementation to achieve a context-specific architecture-based adaptation. This framework has been validated both from a qualitative and a quantitative point of view including such concerns as implementation complexity, adaptation flexibility, memory usage, etc.

4.1 System Implementation

Equinox, a popular, free, open source OSGi Platform developed by the Eclipse organization, is used as our basic development platform. In current state, our implementation focused on providing a light-weight implementation for local applications managements. However, it can be generally extended to distributed environment via using R-OSGi (Remote OSGi) support. We use slightly revised DRCom model[11, 14]. It was originally designed for the construction of dynamically configurable & reflective real-time systems.

Table 1. Lines of code for Architecture-based adaptation

	Functions	Line of code	Binary size (byte)
Monitoring	Reflections of code	142	2353
	Monitoring	354	7407
Parsing	Model class	1329	2353
	Parser class	1450	36000
Structural Modeler	Functional constraints	200	15230
	Reference management	249	5382
Adaptation executor	Dispose management	459	11782
	Instance management	369	8795
	Meta-function Invoking	280	6714
Context-specific adaptation	Plug-in constraint adaptor	108	3798
Context Reasoner	Simple context match	90	2620
Auxiliary code		500+	

As discussed in Section 3.1, this system is implemented via five key modules. The lines of code of each implemented modules is shown at Table 1. Our framework also provides such mechanisms as deployment support and version control by simply reusing OSGi system service, which leads to a lean and quite concise implementation.

One of the basic services in our system is the Meta-data Parsing. This module parses the meta-data and stores it in the form of meta-data objects. A simple component meta-data language is defined to describe component characteristics. This component model designs an extensible XML format that supports future more complex description languages: Due to page limits, here we will not go into details. Clearly the complexity of Context Selector and Context-specific Modeler is highly implementation specific, thus the lines of code listed here are just the simple adaptation algorithm for our TV scenario described in section 4.

4.2 Adaptation to different context

In the traditional approach towards application-based adaptation, in order to achieve adaptation matching different context requirements, developers normally need to reprogram the whole adaptation architecture. There are, to name but a few, modules for detection, modules for component management, adaptation logic as well as the execution modules.

Table 2. Application-based vs. Architecture-based Adaptation

	Application adaptation	ACCADA Framework
Adaptation logic	Prefixed	Change in runtime
Context knowledge Integration	Static/Internal	Flexible/Architecture
Implementation Complexity	High	Low
Multi-context support	NA or static	Yes and flexible
Context-specific Adaptor implementation	Complex	Concise
Separation of design concerns	Mixed	Yes
Level of Adaptation	Inside specific Application	Across several applications

However, during context changes, only the adaptation strategy should be altered to express the context-specific knowledge. Without the burden to support software maintenance, a context-specific adaptor can be implemented very concisely. For instance, the adaptation module to guarantee the QoE of the TV application can be implemented in less than 120 lines of codes. On the other hand, an ad-hoc approach need re-implement new version of a basic component management run-time (in our case, about 2000 lines). Thus, programmers can focus on adaptation logic rather than having to take care of those low level details. Table 2 shows the comparison between application specific adaptation approaches and our framework.

Certain component frameworks provide tools to help programmers to automatically generate auxiliary codes. Examples include Juliac [2]- a Fractal [8] toolchain backend, which generates Java source code corresponding to the application architecture

[2] Available at http://fractal.ow2.org/

specified by the designer. In the following section, we compare our approach with Juliac-based approach in adaptation complexity.

4.3 Adaptation Complexity

In the Juliac approach, ADL language is used to generate the glue code and the codes for introspection. The simplest "hello world" example uses two components – Client and Server. The Client will try to invoke the service exposed interface to print the "hello world" string. Table 3 shows that, for such simple application with only two functional components, the business code is about 100 lines, including import and interface definitions. With Juliac, about 3500 lines of Java codes will be generated. In comparison, in ACCADA, no process for off-line auxiliary code generation is needed. An application mainly contains its business code, simple and easy to manage.

Table 3. Line of codes

	Application size	Lines of code(business)	Lines of code (generated)
Juliac	95.7 KB	100	3500
ACCADA	4.7 KB	140	0

Resource consumption. we executed this application with different number of instances. With the Juliac approach, the memory consumption will increase considerably (about 470 KB for each application) when the number of applications grows, while in our framework it will increase of about 42Kbyte for each installed application. For each installed component, about 13Kbyte memory are needed to store the parsed meta-data information and reference relations. This overhead is comparably small with respect to the more than 430Kbyte memory required by the Fractal model. This discrepancy comes from the different models employed. Each Juliac application has to carry a full set of system run-time, with the increasing number of application; the overhead from the basic system service can be intolerably high. In contrast, ACCADA framework is designed to support a set of managed components and is decoupled from application business logics. No matter how many applications are deployed, only one set of basic services is needed.

In this test, we used equinox, a general purpose OSGi platform. Other implementation, such as Concierge OSGi [15], achieves memory consumption less than 200Kbytes memories. In other words, by simply changing OSGi implementation, the resource consumption can be further reduced.

4.4 Architecture Performance

To evaluate the performance of the Automatic Configuration Service, we instrumented a test to measure the time for fetching, parsing, reference management, and configuring. We focused on the time for installing a single component as we vary the number of managed components by the framework. Here, each component has one in port, one out port, and one attribute. The size of each component is the same – 20.6

KB. We use a Dell D630 laptop with 2.2 GHz dual core T7500 CPU, 2GB RAM and 80 GB 7200RPM HDD. The JVM we adopted is JAVA 1.6.0.2 SDK on Linux.

Here, we use a different Context Modeler with the one described in section 4. It checks following constraints (1). The arrival component will only be enabled when (1) holds true. In order to best test framework's performance, all these component execution tasks remains disabled during the experiment. Here, in the newly installed component, the component initialization time is not counted as it may varied according to different implementations.

$$\sum \frac{\text{Execution time}}{\text{Period}} < 1 \text{ for all enabled components} \quad (1)$$

Installing a new component normally consists of five main steps: component loading, meta-data processing, structural modeling, context modeling, and actuation. Figure 4 shows the absolute times spent in each steps. Each value is the arithmetic mean of 250 runs of the experiment. In order to better illustrate the trend of different steps, we use two Y direction axes in expressing data. Values in stacked column use the main Y axis (left) and those values in marked lines use the secondary Y axis (right) . The time scale used in both axes is micro-seconds (μs).

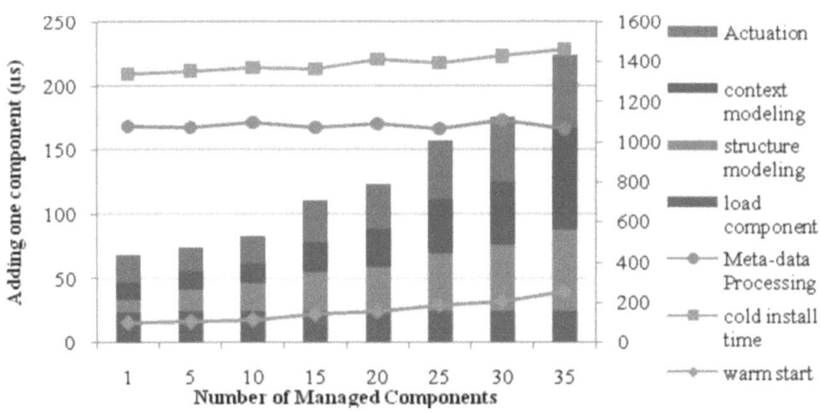

Fig. 4. Framework Performance on adding one component

With the number of managed components grows, component installation time grows very slowly. It mainly due to the fact that two key elements –component loading time, meta-data processing time which count more than 80% total time, keep comparably stable when component number *n* grows. In contrast, the other three key elements, the structural modeling, context modeling and actuation will increase lineally with n as it has computing complexity O (n). Context modeling process which checks whether the new component can satisfy the resource requirements also have complexity of O (n) (stateless implementation, no optimization). Here, the actuation process also includes time for post-processing the modeling results from two modeling processes so it changes with the system scales. As most of the installation time results from the large meta-data processing task, we optimized the installation process by parsing a component's meta-data prior to its usage (without initiating the component). We call this a “warm-start”. This approach can effectively reduce a component response time – from 1000 μs to about 200μs.

Simulation results show that our framework scales well when the number of managed components grows. However, the Context modeling time confines to the simple algorithm described here. Other more complex reasoning policies may not perform well when the number of managed components grows. This is highly policy dependent and is out of the scope of this paper. The Context Selector also has similar characteristics.

5 Related Work

There is a substantial body of literature on reconfigurable middleware systems. Compared to on our earlier work on the DRCom component mode, our framework exhibits a richer and more coherent set of features to support context-specific knowledge and provides a systematic approach to integrate such knowledge.

SmartFrog [4] is a framework for the management of configuration-driven systems. The framework provides mechanisms for describing these component collections and for deploying and managing their life cycle. However, there also lack of support of how to support the context-specific adaptation and the description of component is static and could not support non-functional properties and constraints.

Sylvain etc. identifies novel requirements on reflective component models for architecture-based management systems [5].The construct layer is designed for the meta-data checkpoint and replication. A faulty component can be repaired by restore its state and all the meta-data information outside of the component instance. However, their approach does not have clear definition and separation between system services. The hard-wired architecture makes it very hard to reuse their framework across different contexts.

Garlan etc. propose a general architecture-based self-adaptation framework [2]. The Rainbow framework uses software architectures and a reusable infrastructure to support self-adaptation of software systems. The use of external adaptation mechanisms allows the explicit specification of adaptation strategies for multiple system concerns and domains. However, their approach lacks of component composition support which is also important in building applications.

In order to deal with component dynamicity, Cervantes and Hall [12] propose a service-oriented component based framework for constructing adaptive component-based applications. The key part of the framework is the Service Binder which automatically controls the relationship between components. Our approach mimics theirs in dealing with component's dynamicity. However, our approach can provide more flexible adaptation compared to its static resolving policy.

Kasten etc. propose the Perimorph framework to achieve run-time composition and state management for adaptive system [13] It enables an application designer to quantify and codify collateral changes in terms of factor sets. However, due to lack of a clear defined component model, it hard to extern their approach to cross applications adaptation. Their approach also doesn't consider how to integrate the context adaptation knowledge.

In order to handle the complex dependence between components, Kon etc. propose an integrated architecture for managing dependencies in distributed component based systems [3]. The architecture supports automatic configuration and dynamic resource management in distributed heterogeneous environments. However, how to support the context changes is not specified in their approach.

6 Conclusion and Future Work

In this paper we have described our approach to continuous context-aware deployment and adaptation. We have shown in particular how to integrate context-specific knowledge in run-time component composition. By designing the uniform management interface, the architecture provides a unified programming model over a wide range of components. The design time knowledge is maintained as meta-data and reused during run-time component composition. Service-oriented model is used in implementing architecture basic modules thus achieving more flexible system architecture. This framework is easy to be configured to fit with different contexts. Although our experience was done based on the OSGi middleware, we believe our findings to be general to architecture-based management systems using reflective component models.

References

1. Oreizy, P., et al.: An architecture-based approach to self-adaptive software. IEEE Intelligent Systems & Their Applications 14(3), 54–62 (1999)
2. Garlan, D., et al.: Rainbow: Architecture-based self-adaptation with reusable infrastructure. Computer 37(10), 46–54 (2004)
3. Kon, F., et al.: Design, implementation, and performance of an automatic configuration service for distributed component systems. Software-Practice & Experience 35(7) (2005)
4. Anderson, P., Goldsack, P., Paterson, J.: SmartFrog meets LCFG: Autonomous reconfiguration with central policy control. In: Usenix Association Proceedings of the Seventeenth Large Installation Systems Administration Conference (2003)
5. Sylvain, S., Fabienne, B., Noel De, P.: Using components for architecture-based management: the self-repair case. In: Proceedings of the 30th international conference on Software engineering. ACM, Leipzig (2008)
6. Costa, P., et al.: The RUNES middleware for networked embedded systems and its application in a disaster management scenario. In: Fifth Annual IEEE International Conference on Pervasive Computing and Communications (2007)
7. Dey, A.K., Abowd, G.D., Salber, D.: A conceptual framework and a toolkit for supporting the rapid prototyping of context-aware applications. Human-Computer Interaction 16(2-4), 193–212 (2001)
8. Seinturier, L., Pessemier, N., Duchien, L., Coupaye, T.: A component model engineered with components and aspects. In: Gorton, I., Heineman, G.T., Crnković, I., Schmidt, H.W., Stafford, J.A., Szyperski, C., Wallnau, K. (eds.) CBSE 2006. LNCS, vol. 4063, pp. 139–153. Springer, Heidelberg (2006)
9. Coulson, G., et al.: A generic component model for building systems software. ACM Transactions on Computer Systems 26(1) (2008)

10. Clarke, M., Blair, G.S., Coulson, G., Parlavantzas, N.: An Efficient Component Model for the Construction of Adaptive Middleware. In: Guerraoui, R. (ed.) Middleware 2001. LNCS, vol. 2218, p. 160. Springer, Heidelberg (2001)
11. Gui, N., et al.: A framework for adaptive real-time applications: the declarative real-time OSGi component model. In: The 7th Workshop on Adaptive and Reflective Middleware (ARM), Leuven,Belgium (2008)
12. Hall, R.S., Cervantes, H.: Challenges in building service-oriented applications for OSGi. IEEE Communications Magazine 42(5), 144–149 (2004)
13. Kasten, E.P., McKinley, P.K.: Perimorph: Run-time composition and state management for adaptive systems. In: 24th International Conference on Distributed Computing Systems Workshops, Proceedings (2004)
14. Gui, N., et al.: A Hybrid real-time component model for reconfigurable embedded systems. In: ACM symposium on Applied computing, Fortaleza, Ceara, Brazil (2008)
15. Rellermeyer, J.S.: Concierge: A Service Platform for Resource-Constrained Devices. Operating Systems Review 41(3), 245 (2007)

A Self-stabilizing Approximation Algorithm for Vertex Cover in Anonymous Networks

Volker Turau and Bernd Hauck

Hamburg University of Technology
Institute of Telematics
Schwarzenbergstrasse 95
D-21073 Hamburg
{turau,hauck}@tuhh.de

Abstract. This paper presents a deterministic self-stabilizing algorithm that computes a 3-approximation vertex cover in anonymous networks. It reaches a legal state after $O(n+m)$ moves or $2n+1$ rounds respectively and recovers from a single fault within a constant containment time. The contamination number is $2\Delta+1$. An enhanced version of this algorithm achieves a 2-approximation on trees.

Keywords: self-stabilizing algorithms, vertex cover, distributed algorithms, anonymous networks.

1 Introduction

Distributed algorithms substantially depend on the properties of the underlying network. The most common model assumes all nodes to have unique identifiers. These can be used to prevent neighbored nodes to perform a particular operation concurrently, that is, to ensure local mutual exclusion. For instance, only the node with locally highest id is allowed to execute. Non-uniform networks can use another mechanism to break the symmetry, they have a node that takes on a special role. These two network models are equivalent [3]. In uniform networks without unique identifiers it is possible to use randomness to break symmetry. Availing oneself of randomization results in a probabilistic algorithm, though. A network is called *anonymous* if it is uniform and there are no further symmetry breaking mechanisms such as unique identifiers or randomization. In some anonymous networks nodes are allowed to order adjacent edges. This is a very weak assumption called *port numbering* [1].

A lot of research has been done in the field of algorithms in anonymous networks. Angluin made the most remarkable publication in that area [1]. She proved several impossibility results subject to the different anonymity properties of the network. In particular she showed that it is impossible to break symmetry via a port numbering in general graphs.

Particular problems in graph theory cannot be solved at all with a distributed algorithm on an anonymous network, for instance, it is impossible to find a valid vertex coloring, a minimal vertex cover, a minimal dominating set, or a maximal matching on such a network with a distributed algorithm [1,10]. Recently Suomela presented a

R. Guerraoui and F. Petit (Eds.): SSS 2009, LNCS 5873, pp. 341–353, 2009.

valuable survey of local algorithms [10], that includes results for distributed algorithms on anonymous networks, e.g. limitations for approximation ratios.

The concept of self-stabilization is a general approach to make a system tolerate arbitrary transient faults by design. A distributed system is called *self-stabilizing* if it reaches a consistent state in a finite number of steps by itself without external intervention and remains in a consistent state, starting from any possible global configuration. Detailed information and a more formal definition of self-stabilization can be found e.g. in [3].

In this paper we present the first self-stabilizing algorithm that calculates a 3-approximation vertex cover on anonymous networks using the shared-variable model. An enhanced version of this algorithm achieves a 2-approximation on trees. The basic idea is as follows: Any maximal matching on the graph implies a 2-approximation vertex cover by selecting all nodes adjacent to a matching edge. Unfortunately it is impossible to establish a maximal matching via a distributed algorithm in an anonymous network [10]. Hańćkowiak et al. developed an algorithm that calculates a maximal matching on a bicolored graph [6] without unique identifiers, but Rosenkrantz, Shukla and Ravi proved that a self-stabilizing algorithm that provides a 2-coloring of an anonymous network cannot exist [9]. For this reason, our algorithm makes use of the *Kronecker double cover* of the underlying graph, which is a bicolored graph. A maximal matching in the Kronecker double cover leads to a vertex cover in the original graph.

The vertex cover problem has been studied by several authors recently. Kiniwa presented a self-stabilizing algorithm that calculates a $(2 - 1/\Delta)$-approximation vertex cover [7]. This algorithm needs unique identifiers, though. A number of not-self-stabilizing algorithms compute a vertex cover with a good approximation ratio: Polishchuk and Suomela developed a local algorithm that finds a 3-approximation vertex cover in anonymous networks [8]. Vishwanathan showed that finding a vertex cover of size $2 - \varepsilon$ for graphs with vector chromatic number at most $2 - \delta$ (for small δ) with a non-distributed algorithm is as hard as for general graphs [11]. Grandoni et al. published a distributed algorithm that approximates a *minimum weight* vertex cover via maximal matchings [5].

2 Algorithm

A self-stabilizing algorithm consists of a set of rules, with each rule having a precondition and a statement. The execution of a statement is referred to as a *move*. A rule is *enabled* if its corresponding precondition is *true*. A node is called *enabled* if at least one of its rules is enabled.

Self-stabilizing algorithms operate in *steps*. At the beginning of every step, all nodes check the preconditions of their rules. Then a scheduler selects a subset of the enabled nodes to make a move. Since a central scheduler (only a single node makes its move in every step) trivially breaks the symmetry of the network, only the distributed scheduler (any nonempty subset of the enabled nodes can make their moves simultaneously), and the synchronous scheduler (all enabled nodes make their moves simultaneously) are considered in this paper. Note that the distributed scheduler subsumes the other types of schedulers and is the most general concept. With the distributed scheduler the complexity of an algorithm can also be measured in *rounds*. A round is a minimal sequence of steps during which any node that was enabled at the beginning of the round has either made a move or become disabled.

Let $G = (V, E)$ be an undirected graph, $|V| = n$ and $|E| = m$. A vertex cover of G is a subset C of G such that each $e \in E$ is incident to at least one node of C. Trivially, V itself forms a vertex cover of G. A vertex cover is called *optimal* if there is no other vertex cover that contains less nodes. The algorithm uses a *matching* to determine a vertex cover. A matching is a subset M of independent edges of G. M is a *maximal matching* if there is no matching M' with $M \subset M'$.

To calculate a vertex cover on a graph G the algorithm simulates the *Kronecker double cover* $K(G) = G \times K_2$. Figure 1 illustrates how this double cover is established: Every node is equipped with a black and a white pointer (Figure 1b) which can point to its neighbors' pointers each. A black pointer can only point towards a neighbor's white pointer and vice versa (Figure 1c). This creates a 2-colored graph (Figure 1d).

In this way we can use the concept developed by Hańćkowiak et al. [6]: It is possible to calculate a maximal matching on $K(G)$. Then, the established matching is transformed to a set of paths and rings in G. This results in a 3-approximation vertex cover. The matching on $K(G)$ is established by making the vertices try to match their black pointers with the white pointer of one of their neighbors. The white pointers will choose one of the "offering" black pointers. All nodes that are matched with at least one of their pointers establish the vertex cover of G. The same approach is used by Polishchuk and Suomela to develop a local algorithm that finds a 3-approximation vertex cover in anonymous networks [8]. Their algorithm is not self-stabilizing, though.

To formally define the rules the following notation is defined for each node v: The black (resp. white) pointer is denoted by $v.black$ (resp. $v.white$). There are two predicates that evaluate to $true$, if and only if the node that v is pointing to on its part points back to v:

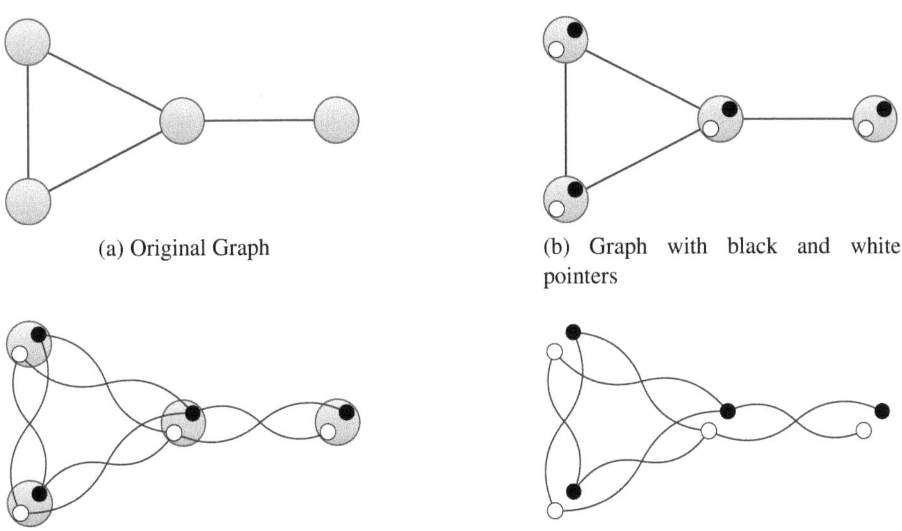

(a) Original Graph

(b) Graph with black and white pointers

(c) Pointers are connected

(d) Kronecker Double Cover

Fig. 1. Simulating the Kronecker Double Cover

- $blackMatched(v) \equiv (v.black \neq null) \wedge ((v.black).white = v)$
- $whiteMatched(v) \equiv (v.white \neq null) \wedge ((v.white).black = v)$

Furthermore, two functions are defined for each node v. They return a neighbor a node can point to with its particular pointer. A black pointer can only head for a white pointer that is set to *null* itself, whereas a white pointer can only be directed to black pointers that are currently pointing back to it. The select operator $select(S)$ refers to an arbitrary function that selects one element of the specified set S in a deterministic manner. If nodes have a port numbering it can be implemented as the minimum function. For the algorithm it is irrelevant, *which* node is chosen. Note that the select operation is extended, such that $select(\emptyset) = null$.

- $selectWhite(v) = select\{x \in N(v) \mid x.white = null\}$
- $selectBlack(v) = select\{x \in N(v) \mid x.black = v\}$

The term *white node* (resp. *black node*) refers to the white (resp. black) pointer of a given node. Algorithm 1 shows the set of rules for every node v. These rules establish a maximal matching on $K(G)$ which implies a vertex cover.

Algorithm 1. Vertex Cover

R_1: $(\neg whiteMatched) \wedge ((white \neq null) \vee (white \neq selectBlack))$
    $\longrightarrow$ **if** $(white \neq null)$
        then $white := null$
    else if $(white \neq selectBlack)$
        then $white := selectBlack$

R_2: $(\neg blackMatched) \wedge ((black = null) \vee (black.white \neq null)) \wedge (black \neq selectWhite)$
    $\longrightarrow black := selectWhite$

An execution of rule R_1 (resp. rule R_2) will also be referred to as *white move* (resp. *black move*). Note that rule R_1 has a higher priority than R_2, i.e. if a node is enabled to make a white move, it will not make a black move. Let VC be the set of nodes that are matched via their black or white pointer by Algorithm 1.

Lemma 1. *If all nodes are disabled with respect to Algorithm 1 then the following conditions hold:*
a) All pointers are either matched or they point to null.
b) The set VC forms a vertex cover.

Proof. Obviously, if a node's white (resp. black) pointer is neither matched nor it points to *null*, rule R_1 (resp. R_2) is enabled for this node. This verifies statement a). Since all nodes are disabled with respect to Algorithm 1, for every edge (u,v) at least one of its nodes is matched via at least one of its pointers. Otherwise, because rule R_1 is not enabled, u and v both had their white pointers set to *null* and hence, rule R_2 would be enabled for both nodes. This proves statement b). □

3 Approximation Ratio

Lemma 2. *In an anonymous network a non-probabilistic self-stabilizing algorithm that calculates a k-approximation vertex cover with $k < 2$ for arbitrary graphs cannot exist under a synchronous scheduler (and therefore under a distributed scheduler).*

Proof. Consider a ring consisting of n nodes, where n is an even number. If all nodes start in the same state, this property will hold all the time. Thus, all of them will be selected for the vertex cover. An optimal vertex cover only contains every second node. □

Theorem 1. *Algorithm 1 calculates a 3-approximation vertex cover.*

Proof. Let $G = (V, E)$ be a graph. The graph G' is derived from $G|_{VC}$ by removing all edges whose adjacent nodes do not have set at least one pointer to the other one. Every node only has two pointers and therefore its degree is at most 2, hence G' consists of components that form a path or a ring.

In both, a path and a ring, at least every second node has to be part of a vertex cover. Hence, even selecting all nodes of a ring or of a path with an even number of nodes leads to a 2-approximation. On a path p with an odd number of nodes at least $(|p| - 1)/2$ nodes have to be part of a vertex cover, thus any vertex cover of p will exceed the number of nodes of an optimal vertex cover by a factor of 3 at most. The worst case is a path consisting of three nodes, where Algorithm 1 might select all nodes instead of only the one in the middle. □

The approximation ratio depends on the underlying graph. In any regular graph with n nodes, the smallest vertex cover contains at least $\lceil n/2 \rceil$ nodes, hence even selecting all nodes results in a 2-approximation.

Algorithm 1 can be improved to achieve an approximation ratio of 2 on certain topologies. Section 5 shows that combining this algorithm with some vertex exclusion rules leads to a 2-approximation for a vertex cover in trees. This modification also improves the results on arbitrary graphs in practice. However, the worst case on arbitrary graphs is still a 3-approximation.

3.1 Move Complexity

Lemma 3. *While executing Algorithm 1 a node directs its black pointer towards a given neighbor at most once.*

Proof. According to Algorithm 1, for u being enabled to point to v, v must have its white pointer set to *null*. After that the black pointer of u (and of all other nodes that point towards v) is disabled until v moves its white pointer. After that v's white pointer is matched with one of the nodes that where pointing at it and will not make a move again. Besides, from that time on, a node cannot point towards v with its black pointer since v does not point to *null*. □

Some notation is introduced for the upcoming proof. We assume that Algorithm 1 has stabilized and are going to analyze the sequence of steps that led to that state.

- Steps in which at least one node matches with one of its neighbors by directing its white pointer towards it are called *Matching-steps*.
- The total number of Matching-steps is denoted by s.
- V_i contains the nodes that match via their white pointer in the i-th Matching-step.
- X_i contains the nodes that are matched in the i-th Matching-step by the white move of a node contained in V_i.

Lemma 4. *Algorithm 1 stabilizes after at most $O(n+m)$ moves under the distributed scheduler.*

Proof. There are at most 2 white moves per node. It can first point to *null* if it does not already and then it accepts an offer from a black node. This black pointer cannot move its pointer, unless the white pointer is directed to another node, thus, there will be no further white moves. Hence, there are at most $2n$ white moves in total.

After the nodes in V_i made their white matching move, the nodes in X_i cannot make any further black move. Now we show that before the nodes of V_i made this move, the maximum number of black moves made by $x_i \in X_i$ is limited to $\min(2i, 2d(x_i))$.

If node x_i sets its black pointer towards a node v, this node has its white pointer set to *null*. To make x_i move its black pointer again, v has to direct its white pointer to another node, that also points at it via its black pointer. Obviously, if that happens i times, there are i steps in which nodes were matched via their white pointer *before* a node of V_i can match with x_i, in contradiction to the assumption. Assuming that x_i points to *null* every time before directing its pointer to a new node this results in at most $2i$ black moves. On the other hand, node x_i can point to any node only once via its black pointer. Thus, its black moves are also limited to $2d(x_i)$. Hence, the total number of black moves is

$$2\sum_{i=1}^{s}\sum_{x_i\in X_i}\min(i, d(x_i)).$$

Note that in the worst case $V_i = \{v_i\}$ for all $i \in \{1,\ldots,s\}$ and thus, $s = n$, which results in a total of

$$2\sum_{i=1}^{n}\min(i, d(v_i)) \in O(n+m)$$

black moves. In particular, this situation is given if Algorithm 1 runs under a central scheduler. □

3.2 Round Complexity

Lemma 5. *Algorithm 1 stabilizes after at most $2n+1$ rounds under the distributed scheduler.*

Proof. The basic idea is to show that at least every second round a white pointer is matched with a neighbor's black pointer after the first round. If a node has its white pointer set to *null* and at least one of its neighbors point to it via a black pointer (otherwise it does not get enabled to make a white move), then before the end of the next round it will match with one of these neighbors. Note that due to the priority of R_1

over R_2 after the first round all white pointers are either matched or they point to *null*. Therefore any node will make at most one further white move and this move will match the white pointer (cf. proof of Lemma 4).

Consider a round without white moves. Rule R_1 is not enabled, hence, all white pointers are either matched or they point to *null* without having a neighbor that points towards them. If Algorithm 1 has not stabilized yet, there is at least one enabled black node. If there is no node having its white pointer set to *null*, all enabled black nodes will set their pointer to *null* and the system is in a legal state after this round. So, let x be a black node having at least one neighbor that has its white pointer set to *null*. Node x will move its black pointer to one of these nodes, which therefore becomes enabled to perform a white move. Hence, in every round that does not contain a white move, at least one white node gets enabled.

There might be one final round in which some unmatched black pointers have to be set to *null*. However, this cannot happen, if *all* white pointers are matched. Thus, after at most $2n+1$ rounds Algorithm 1 has stabilized. □

The following example proves that the bound of Lemma 4 is sharp. Let $G = \{v_1, v_2, \ldots, v_n\}$ be the complete Graph K_n. Initially, all nodes have set their white pointer to v_{n-1} and their black ones to v_n. We assume a distributed scheduler and divide the execution of Algorithm 1 in *phases*. The first phase consists of five steps:

a) All nodes except v_n set their white pointer to *null*.
b) Node v_1 sets its black pointer to v_2 and all other nodes except v_n set their black pointer to v_1.
c) Node v_n sets its white pointer to *null*.
d) Node v_n sets its black pointer to v_1.
e) Node v_2 matches its white pointer with v_1's black pointer.

These steps are followed by $n-1$ phases that consist of the following moves each:

a) All nodes that are not yet matched via their black pointer direct it towards the smallest node that is not yet matched via its white pointer.
b) This node chooses the smallest of them and matches its white pointer with it.

This results in $2n$ white moves and $\sum_{i=1}^{n/2}((n-1)-2(i-1))$ black moves and hence, $O(n+m)$ moves in total.

4 Fault Containment

We assume the system to be in a stable state with respect to Algorithm 1. This section analyzes the impact of the transient error of a single node, e.g. due to a memory fault. The *containment time* is defined as the worst case number of rounds (resp. moves) until the system has returned to a legitimate state. The *contamination number* denotes the worst case number of nodes that execute a rule within that time [4].

Lemma 6. *If the system is in a stable state with respect to Algorithm 1 and a single node changes its state erroneously, the system re-stabilizes with a containment time of* 9 *rounds (resp.* $4\Delta+4$ *moves) under the distributed scheduler and the contamination number is* $2\Delta+1$.

Proof. Let v be the node that changed its state erroneously. All pointers that are matched to any node but v do not get activated by the changing of v. The effect of an erroneously changed black or white pointer is analyzed separately. They do not influence each other since a black pointer only interacts with its neighbors' white pointers and vice versa.

Case a) v changed its black pointer.

If v was not matched before all its neighbors' white pointers are matched already. Thus, no other node becomes enabled, v will reset its pointer to *null* and thus, the system is in the same stable state as before. So assume v to have switched its black pointer erroneously from node x to node u. Node x can set its white pointer to *null* which could cause all its neighbors that are not already matched via their black pointer to point to it. The node will choose one of them and point back to it, the others will reset their black pointer to *null*. Two cases have to be considered for node u:

- $u = null$
  Node v can point to any of its neighbors that is not already matched via its white pointer. If this node is not x it will point back at v. If v pointed to x once more, this node might choose another node to match with which would make v reset its pointer to *null*. This leads to at most $2|N(x)\backslash\{v\}| - 1 + 2 + 1 + 1 = 2|N(x)| + 1$ moves until stabilization in the worst case and only $|N(x)| + 2$ nodes are affected, namely v, x and all its other neighbors and one other neighbor of v.
- $u \neq null$ If u is matched via its white pointer already it will not become enabled. In that case v can point back to x or to *null*. Assume u not to be matched via its white pointer. Since u points to *null* node v cannot take its pointer away. Node u will point back at v so these two nodes will be matched. This scenario leads to at most $2|N(x)\backslash\{v\}| - 1 + 2 + 1 = 2|N(x)|$ moves (resp. 4 rounds) until stabilization in the worst case and only $|N(x)| + 2$ nodes are affected, namely v, x and all its other neighbors and one other neighbor of v.

Case b) v changed its white pointer.

If v was not matched before all its neighbors' black pointers are matched already. Thus, no other node becomes enabled, v will reset its pointer to *null* and thus, the system is in the same stable state as before. So assume v to have switched its white pointer erroneously from node x to node u. If $u \neq null$, v is enabled to point to *null* after x has made a move. A node can only direct its black pointer towards one of its neighbors if this neighbor points to *null* with its white pointer. Hence, if v does not point to *null*, only v itself and x are enabled.

Node x can point to all neighbors that have their white pointer set to *null*. Let x point to a node $y \neq v$. If $y \neq null$ it will point back at x so they will be matched. Otherwise x will be treated as any other neighbor of v. When v points to *null*, all its neighbors that are not matched via their black pointer already, could point towards v. Node v will choose one of them to point back, the other nodes will reset their pointers to *null*. This leads to at most $2|N(v)| + 3$ moves (resp. 5 rounds) until stabilization in the worst case and only $|N(v)| + 2$ nodes are affected at worst, namely v, all its neighbors, and one further neighbor of x.

Note that in combining cases a) and b) the node v does not necessarily point to the same node with each pointer. Hence the nodes that might become enabled due to the erroneous move of v are in the worst case v, the two nodes it was pointing to before and all their neighbors as well as two further neighbors of v. This results in a contamination number of $2\Delta+1$. Adding the number of moves in the cases a) and b) yields a total number of at most $4|N(x)|+4 \leq 4\Delta+4$ moves until the system has re-stabilized. In the worst case a node executes only one rule per round, hence the containment time in rounds is $4+5=9$. □

5 Improving the Approximation Ratio

As shown in Lemma 2, a self-stabilizing algorithm that calculates a vertex cover with an approximation ratio better than 2 is impossible for anonymous networks. It is possible to improve Algorithm 1 in a way that it achieves a 2-approximation vertex cover on trees. On general graphs, however, the approximation ratio remains 3.

In the original algorithm all nodes that have at least one pointer matched are in VC, the others are not. The idea of the improved algorithm is to check, whether a node that is matched with exactly one pointer has only neighbors that have both their pointers matched. If this is the case, it can leave the vertex cover since all its neighbors are in VC and cannot leave it theirselves. If two neighboring nodes both have the same pointer matched, or they are both matched with both pointers it is impossible to let exactly one of them leave the vertex cover due to the impossibility of symmetry breaking. To formally define the additional rules the following predicates are specified for each node v:

- $isLooseBlack(v) \equiv$
  $blackMatched(v) \wedge v.white = null \wedge \forall x \in N(v):\ x.white \neq null$
- $isLooseWhite(v) \equiv$
  $whiteMatched(v) \wedge v.black = null \wedge \forall x \in N(v):\ x.black \neq null$

Algorithm 2 consists of the rules of Algorithm 1 and additional three rules that change the value of a boolean variable vc indicating whether a node is part of the vertex cover or not.

Algorithm 2. Vertex Cover, improved

R_1 and R_2 as in Algorithm 1

R_3: $((isLooseBlack \vee isLooseWhite) \wedge vc = true)$
$\longrightarrow vc := false$

R_4: $(white = null \wedge black = null \wedge vc = true)$
$\longrightarrow vc := false$

R_5: $((white \neq null \wedge \neg isLooseWhite) \vee (black \neq null \wedge \neg isLooseBlack)) \wedge (vc = false)$
$\longrightarrow vc := true$

Note that rules R_1 and R_2 have a higher priority than the other rules. The moves (rules, respectively) of type R_3, R_4 and R_5 will also be referred to as *vc-moves* (*vc-rules*, respectively). The first two rules are extended so that they also set the *vc*-variable according to the *vc*-rules. Thus, a node is not enabled to perform a *vc*-move after an execution of R_1 or R_2 before a neighbor also executes one of the first two rules. Obviously, every node can execute rule R_4 at most once, namely as its first move. The priority setting as well as the update of the vc-variable in the first two rules helps to reduce the number of moves in practice. It does not improve the worst case, though.

Lemma 7. *While executing Algorithm 2 on a distributed scheduler there are at most $O(\Delta(n+m))$ vc-moves.*

Proof. Let $S = S_1, S_2, S_3 ...$ be an execution of Algorithm 2. A vc-move of a node v in step S_i with $i > 1$ is called *belated*, if neither v nor any of its neighbors performed a move of type R_1 or R_2 in step S_{i-1}. Since a node does not read a neighbor's vc variable in Algorithm 2, all belated moves can be executed in the corresponding preceding step and this results in a valid execution with the same total number of moves. Let execution $\widetilde{S} = \widetilde{S}_1, \widetilde{S}_2, \widetilde{S}_3 ...$ be derived from S by shifting all belated moves into the corresponding preceding step (several times, if necessary) until there is no belated move left. Apart from the very first step all vc-moves of $\widetilde{S}$ are now preceded by a neighbor's move of type R_1 or R_2. Let $x_i = \left|\{w \in \widetilde{S}_{i-1} \mid w \text{ executes rule } R_1 \text{ or } R_2\}\right|$, for $i > 1$. Hence, in step $\widetilde{S}_i$ there are at most Δx_{i-1} vc-moves. In the worst case there are n vc-moves in the first step. From Lemma 4 we know that $\sum x_i \in O(n+m)$. This results in a total number of at most $O(\Delta(n+m))$ vc-moves. □

The following lemma shows that Algorithm 2 still computes a vertex cover. Let $G = (V,E)$ be a graph and $V_A = \{v \in V \mid v.vc = true\}$.

Lemma 8. *If no node of G is enabled with respect to Algorithm 2 then V_A is a vertex cover of G.*

Proof. It suffices to prove that all neighbors of a node v with $v.vc = false$ have their vc variable set to $true$. Assume, there was a node $x \in N(v)$ with $x.vc = false$. According to the assumption, the rules R_1 and R_2 are not enabled for both nodes. If one of the two nodes is matched via both its pointers then it is enabled to execute rule R_5, hence both nodes have at least one pointer set to $null$. If one of the two nodes has both pointers set to $null$ then one of them is enabled to execute rule R_2, so assume both nodes to have exactly one pointer set to $null$. If these pointers have the same color then rule R_5 is enabled for both nodes, otherwise the node that has its black pointer set to $null$ is enabled to point to the other one via rule R_2. □

Lemma 9. *Let $T = (V,E)$ be a tree with $|V| > 2$ and I the set of inner nodes, i.e. $I = \{v \in V \mid d(v) > 1\}$. Let M be a maximum cardinality matching of T. Then I is a vertex cover of T and $|I| \leq 2|M|$.*

Proof. Obviously I is a vertex cover of T, any leaf has a neighbor in I. The rest is shown by induction on the number of nodes. Obviously, the statement holds for $|V| = 3$. Let $|V| > 3$, and x be a leaf of T. The neighbor of x is denoted by y. We distinguish two cases:

a) $d(y) > 2$
Let $T' = T \backslash \{x\}$. The set of inner nodes does not change by removing x from the

graph, i.e. $I' := I$. By induction $|I'| \leq 2|M'|$, where M' is a maximum cardinality matching of T'. Furthermore, $|M| \geq |M'|$, since the matching cannot become larger by removing a node. Putting all this together results in $|I| = |I'| \leq 2|M'| \leq 2|M|$.

b) $d(y) = 2$
Let $T' = T \backslash \{x, y\}$. Node $y \notin I'$ and maybe its other neighbor is a leaf in T', hence $|I'| \leq |I| + 2$. By induction $|I'| \leq 2|M'|$, where M' is a maximum cardinality matching of T'. $M' \cup \{(x,y)\}$ is a maximum cardinality matching of T, thus, $|M'| + 1 = |M|$. Putting all this together results in $|I| = |I'| + 2 \leq 2|M'| + 2 \leq 2|M|$.
□

Theorem 2. *Algorithm 2 calculates a 2-approximation vertex cover in case the graph is a tree.*

Proof. Let $T = (V, E)$ be a tree. Lemma 8 yields that V_A is a vertex cover. Let M_1 be the set of nodes that are matched to one neighbor via both pointers each, i.e. $M_1 = \{v \in V \mid v.black = v.white \neq null\}$.

We define the forest $T' = T \backslash M_1$ and show that all leaves of T' have their *vc* variable set to $false$. Let x be a leaf of T' and assume $x.vc = true$. Then, obviously, x must matched with a node y via at least one of its pointers. If its other pointer does not point to *null*, then it must have a second neighbor in T' and therefore it is not a leaf. Note that a vertex of T' cannot be matched with the same neighbor via both its pointers. If y has its second pointer set to *null* one of the two nodes is enabled to execute rule R_2, hence y is also matched with another node. All other neighbors of x in T belong to M_1 anyway, thus rule R_3 must be enabled for x. Thus, all leaves of T' must have their *vc* variable set to $false$.

Let I' be the set of nodes of T' without the leaves and let M_2 be a maximum cardinality matching of T'. From Lemma 9 we derive that $I' \leq 2|M_2|$. The set $M_1 \cup M_2$ is a maximum cardinality matching of T. Hence, from König's theorem [2] we deduce:
$|V_A| \leq 2|M_1| + |I'| \leq 2|M_1| + 2|M_2| = 2|M_1 \cup M_2| \leq 2|VC_{opt}|$ □

The behavior in case of a transient error of a single node is similar to the behavior of Algorithm 1. Only the nodes mentioned in Lemma 6 can change their pointers. However, the neighbors of a node that changed a pointer might execute two *vc*-moves each. A node does not read a neighbor's *vc*-variable, hence the contamination radius is increased by only one hop.

It is an open question whether Theorem 2 can be extended to other classes of graphs. The following example shows that the approximation ratio of Algorithm 2 in general is 3, even on a bipartite graph.

Example 1. Let G_k with $k = 5$ be the graph depicted in Figure 2a. There is a node l on the left, a node r on the right and a node t on the top. Furthermore there are k simple line graphs consisting of three nodes r_i, m_i and r_i each, with connections from r_i to r and l_i to l respectively.

The optimal vertex cover consists of l, r and the nodes $m_1, \ldots, m_k$, and accordingly $k+2$ nodes in total. However, in the worst case Algorithm 2 selects all nodes of G: Figure 2b shows all nodes m_i (and t respectively) to have both their pointers matched. Let each m_i have its white pointer matched with l_i (l, respectively) and their black

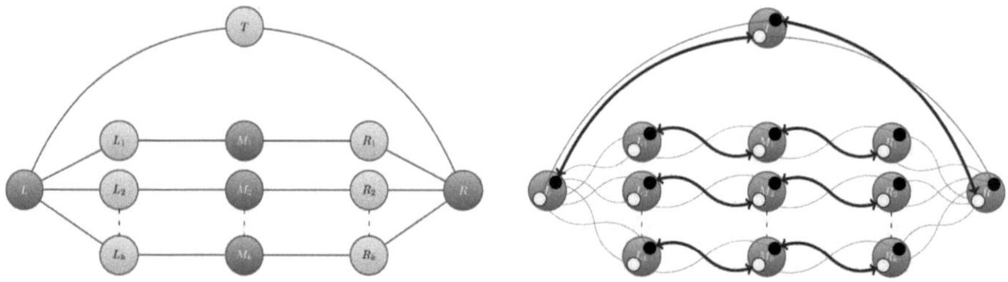

(a) Optimal vertex cover on graph G (b) Worst case solution of Algorithm 2

Fig. 2. Comparison of optimal solution and worst case solution

pointer matched with r_i (r, respectively). Now any node that has an unmatched pointer has a neighbor with an unmatched pointer of the same color. Thus, it is not enabled to set its *vc* variable to $false$. Hence, all nodes are selected. G consists of $3k+3$ nodes and thus the approximation ratio is $(3k+3)/(k+2) = 3 - 3/(k+2)$.

6 Conclusion

This paper presented the first self-stabilizing algorithm for a 3-approximation vertex cover in anonymous networks. It stabilizes after $O(n+m)$ moves and the contamination number is $2\Delta+1$. An improved version of the algorithm yields a 2-approximation in case the graph is a tree. We conclude this paper with a conjecture.

Conjecture. *Algorithm 2 requires* $O(n+m)$ *vc-moves using a distributed scheduler.*

Acknowledgments

This research was partially funded by the German Research Foundation (DFG), contract number TU 221/3-1.

References

1. Angluin, D.: Local and global properties in networks of processors (extended abstract). In: STOC 1980: Proceedings of the twelfth annual ACM symposium on Theory of computing, pp. 82–93. ACM, New York (1980)
2. Diestel, R.: Graph Theory, 3rd edn. Graduate Texts in Mathematics, vol. 173. Springer, Heidelberg (2005)
3. Dolev, S.: Self-stabilization. MIT Press, Cambridge (2000)
4. Ghosh, S., Gupta, A., Herman, T., Pemmaraju, S.V.: Fault-containing self-stabilizing distributed protocols. Distributed Computing 20(1), 53–73 (2007)
5. Grandoni, F., Könemann, J., Panconesi, A.: Distributed weighted vertex cover via maximal matchings. ACM Trans. Algorithms 5(1), 1–12 (2008)

6. Hańćkowiak, M., Karoński, M., Panconesi, A.: On the distributed complexity of computing maximal matchings. In: SODA 1998: Proceedings of the ninth annual ACM-SIAM symposium on Discrete algorithms, Philadelphia, PA, USA, pp. 219–225. Society for Industrial and Applied Mathematics (1998)
7. Kiniwa, J.: Approximation of self-stabilizing vertex cover less than 2. In: Herman, T., Tixeuil, S. (eds.) SSS 2005. LNCS, vol. 3764, pp. 171–182. Springer, Heidelberg (2005)
8. Polishchuk, V., Suomela, J.: A simple local 3-approximation algorithm for vertex cover. Inf. Process. Lett. 109(12), 642–645 (2009)
9. Shukla, S.K., Rosenkrantz, D.J., Ravi, S.S.: Observations on self-stabilizing graph algorithms for anonymous networks. In: Proceedings of the Second Workshop on Self-Stabilizing Systems, pp. 7–1 (1995)
10. Suomela, J.: Survey of local algorithms (unpublished manuscript, 2009)
11. Vishwanathan, S.: On hard instances of approximate vertex cover. ACM Trans. Algorithms 5(1), 1–6 (2008)

Separation of Circulating Tokens*

Kajari Ghosh Dastidar and Ted Herman

Department of Computer Science, University of Iowa

Abstract. Self-stabilizing distributed control is often modeled by token abstractions. For a cyber-physical system, tokens may represent physical objects whose movement is controlled. The problem studied in this paper is to ensure that a synchronous system with m circulating tokens has at least d distance between tokens. This problem is first considered in a ring where d is given whilst m and the ring size n are unknown. The protocol solving this problem can be uniform, with all processes running the same program, or it can be non-uniform, with some processes acting only as token relays. The protocol for this first problem is simple, and can be expressed with Petri net formalism. A second problem is to maximize d when m is given, and n is unknown. For the second problem, the paper presents a non-uniform protocol with a single corrective process.

1 Introduction

Distributed computing deals with the interaction of concurrent entities. Asynchronous models permit irregular rates of computation whereas pure synchronous models can impose uniform steps across the system. For either mode of concurrency the application goals may benefit from controlled reduction of some activity. Mutual exclusion aims to reduce the activity to one process at any time; some scheduling tasks require that certain related processes not be active at the same time. System activation of a controlled functionality is typically abstracted as a process *having a token*, which constitutes permission to engage in some controlled action. Many mechanisms for regulating token creation, destruction, and transfer have been published. This paper explores a mechanism based on timing information in a synchronous model. In a nutshell, each process has one or more timers used to control how long a token rests or moves to another process. An emergent property of a protocol using this mechanism should be that tokens move at each step, tokens visit all processes, and no two tokens come closer than some given distance (or, alternatively, that tokens remain as far apart as possible). The challenge, as with all self-stabilizing algorithms, is that tokens can initially be located arbitrarily and the variables encoding timers or other variables may have unpredictable initial values.

One motivating application is physical process control, as formalized by Petri nets. The tokens of a Petri net can represent physical objects. As an example, one can imagine a closed network where some objects are conveyed from place to

* Research supported by NSF Grant 0519907.

R. Guerraoui and F. Petit (Eds.): SSS 2009, LNCS 5873, pp. 354–368, 2009.

place, with some physical processing (loading, unloading, modifications to parts) done at each place. For the health of the machinery it may be useful to keep the objects at some distance apart, so that facilities at the different places have time to recharge resources between object visits. Figure 1 partially illustrates such a situation, with an unhealthy initial state (three objects are together at one place). The circuit of the moving objects is a ring for this example. The formalism of Petri nets allows us to add additional places, tokens and transitions so that a self-stabilizing network can be constructed: eventually, the objects of interest will be kept apart by some desired distance. Section 4 presents a self-stabilizing algorithm for this network.

The figure shows a large ring and two smaller rings, where each smaller ring is connected by a joint transition (which can only fire when a token is present on each of its inputs) to the larger ring. On the right side a portion of the larger (clockwise) token ring is represented, with three tokens shown resting together at the same place. Two other smaller, counterclockwise rings are partially shown on the left side, each with one token. The joint transition will prevent the three resting tokens from firing until the token on the smaller ring completes its traversal. Thus the smaller rings, each having exactly one token in any state, behave as delay mechanisms. The algorithm given in Section 4 uses conventional process notation instead of a Petri net, and the smaller rings are replaced by counters in a program.

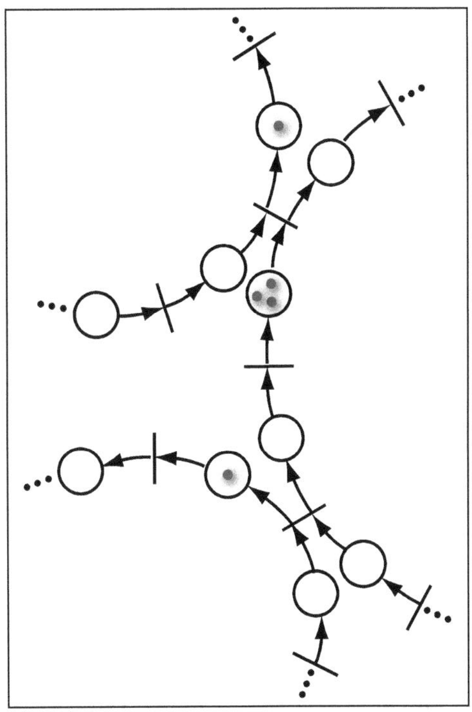

Fig. 1. Petri Net Embodiment

Another motivating application comes from wireless sensor networks, where power management is important. A strategy for limiting power consumption is to limit the number of sensors that are on at any time, presumably selecting enough sensors to be on for adequate coverage of a field of interest, yet rotating which nodes deploy sensors over time, to extend lifetime and to improve robustness with regard to variation in sensor calibration. One solution to this problem would be to use clock synchronization, with a periodic schedule for sensing activity based on a global time. Alternatively, token circulation could be considered to activate sensors. Unlike a schedule purely based on synchronized clocks, a token-based solution provides some assurance and feedback in cases where nodes are faulty (*e.g.,* when a token cannot be passed from one node to another due to a failure, such failure may be recognized and an alarm could be triggered). The abstraction of tokens put into messages may also allow aggregated sensor data or commands to be carried with a token, further enabling application behavior. Keeping tokens apart may relate to coverage goals for the sensor network: if tokens circulate in parallel and satisfy some distance constraint between them, then the sensors that are on at any time may provide adequate spatial diversity over the field of interest. An optimal solution to satisfy a coverage constraint is beyond the scope of this paper. Our investigation is confined to the problem of self-stabilizing circulation of tokens with some desired separation between them.

Related Work. Perhaps the earliest source on self-stabilization is [1], which briefly presents an algorithm to distribute N points equally on a circle. The algorithm given in Section 5 distributes m tokens equally around a ring, however the objective is a behavior (circulating tokens) rather than a final state. Papers on coordinated robot behavior, for example [2,8,3], are similar to [1] in that a geometric, physical domain is modeled. Most such papers consider a final robot configuration as the objective of distributed control and give the robots powerful vision and mobility primitives. Like the example of robot coordination, our work can have a physical control motivation, but we have a behavior as the objective. For results in this paper, the computation model is discrete and fully synchronous, where processes communicate only with neighbors in a ring. As for the sensor network motivation sketched above, duty-cycle scheduling while satisfying coverage has been implemented [4] (numerous network protocol and system issues are involved in this task [5]). These sensor network duty-cycle scheduling efforts are not self-stabilizing to our knowledge.

Within the literature of self-stabilization, a related problem is model transformation. If an algorithm P is correct for serial execution, but not for a parallel execution, then one can implement a type of scheduler that only allows a process p of P to take a step provided that no neighbor q is activated concurrently [6]; this type of scheduling is known to correctly emulate a serial order of execution. The problem we consider, separating tokens by some desired distance d, can be specialized to $d = 2$ and be comparable to such a model transformation. For larger values of d, the nearest related work is the general stabilizing philosopher problem [7], which considers conflict graphs between non-neighboring philosophers. By equating philosopher activity (dining) to holding a token, [7] yields a solution to the problem of ensuring tokens are at some desired distance, and also allowing tokens to move as needed. The synchronous token behavior in this paper differs from the philosopher problem because token circulation is not demand-based, and therefore solutions to the problem are obtained through timing.

Literature on self-stabilizing mutual exclusion includes token abstractions [10], generalizations of mutual exclusion to k-exclusion or k-out-of-ℓ exclusion [11], multitoken protocols for a ring [13], and group mutual exclusion [12]. Most of the literature does not constrain tokens to be separated by some desired distance d (unlike the philosopher problem cited above), which differentiates our work from previous multitoken protocols. However, in applying the methods of this paper to some applications, it can be useful to employ self-stabilizing token or multitoken protocols at a lower layer: Section 4.2 expands on this idea of using self-stabilizing token protocols as a basis for our work.

2 Desired Behavior

Desired properties of a token circulation protocol are labeled as D1–D5, as follows. D1: at any time, m tokens are present in the system; D2: the minimum distance between any two tokens is at least d; D3: a token moves in each step from one process to a neighboring process; D4: every process has a token equally often; *i.e.*, in an execution of k steps, for any process p_i, there is a token at p_i for $k \cdot m/n$ steps; D5: following a transient failure that corrupts state variables of any number of processes, the system automatically recovers to behavior satisfying D1–D4.

In many topologies, not all of D1–D5 are achievable. As an instance, for D3 to hold, the center node of a star topology or a simple linear chain is necessarily visited by tokens more often than other nodes, conflicting with D4. The constructions of this paper are able to satisfy D1–D5 for a ring topology. Though it is straightforward to map a virtual ring on a complete walk over an arbitrary network, property D2 may not hold: nodes at distance d in a virtual ring could be at much smaller distance in the base network.

3 Notation and Model

Consider a ring of n processes executing synchronously, in lock-step. Each process perpetually executes steps of a program, which are called *local steps*. In one *global step*, every process executes a local step. Programs are structured as infinite loops, where the body of a loop contains statements that correspond to local steps. We assume that all processes execute the loop steps in a coordinated manner: for processes running the same program, all of them execute the first statement step in unison. Similarly, if two processes run distinct programs, we suppose they begin the body of the loop together, which may entail padding the loop of one program to be the same number of steps as the other program. This assumption about coordination of steps is for convenience of presentation, since it is possible to engineer all programs to have a loop body with a single, more powerful statement. The execution of all statements in the loop, from first to last, is called a *round*.

The notion of distance between locations in the ring can be measured in either clockwise or counterclockwise direction. In program descriptions and proof arguments, it is convenient to refer to the clockwise (counterclockwise) neighbor of a process using subscript notation: process p_i's clockwise neighbor is p_{i+1} and its counterclockwise neighbor is p_{i-1}. The distance from p_i to itself is zero, the clockwise distance from p_i to p_{i+1} is one, and the counterclockwise distance from p_i to p_{i+1} is $n-1$; the counterclockwise distance from p_i to p_{i-1} is one, and general definitions of distance between p_i and p_j for arbitrary ring locations can be defined inductively. The counterclockwise neighbor of p_i is called the *predecessor* of p_i, and the clockwise neighbor is called the *successor*.

The local state of a process p_i is specified by giving values for its variables. The global state of the system is an assignment of local states for all processes. A protocol, specified by giving programs for each p_i, should satisfy the desiderata of Section 2. A protocol is *self-stabilizing* if, eventually, D1–D5 hold throughout the suffix of any execution. For simplicity, in the presentation of our protocols, we make some unusual model choices: in one case, p_i assigns to a variable of p_{i-1}; and we assume that m tokens are present in any initial state of any execution. After presenting programs in Section 4, we discuss in Subsection 4.2 these choices in reference to the two illustrative applications, Petri nets and sensor networks.

4 Protocol with Known Separation

This section presents a protocol to achieve and maintain a separation of at least $C+1$ links between tokens in the unidirectional ring. An implementation of the protocol uses four instantiation parameters, n, m, C, and the choice of which of two programs are used for nodes in the ring. Only the separation parameter C is used in the protocol, as the domain of a counter, whereas the ring size n and the number of tokens m are unknown for the programs. The separation by $C+1$ links cannot be realized for arbitrary $n > 1$ and $m > 1$; we require that

$$m(C+1) \quad \leq \quad n \tag{1}$$

The protocol consists of two programs delay and relay. At least one process in the system executes the delay and any processes not running delay run the relay program. Processes running either program have two variables, q and r; a process running delay has an additional variable c. To specify the variable of a particular process, we subscript variables, for instance, q_i is the q variable of process p_i. The domains of q and r are nonnegative integers; the domain of c is the range of integers in $[0, C]$.

The q and r variables model the abstraction of tokens in a ring. At any global state σ, process p_i said to have t tokens if $r_i + q_i = t$. We say that k tokens are *resting* at p_i if $r_i = k$, and ℓ tokens are *queued* (for moving forward) if $q_i = \ell$. The objective of the protocol is to circulate m tokens around the ring so that the distance from one token to the next (clockwise) token exceeds parameter C, and in each round every token moves from its current location to the successor. In some cases, it is handy to refer to the value of a variable at a particular state in an execution. The term r_i^σ denotes the value of r_i at a state σ. In most cases, the state is implicitly the present (current) state with respect to a description or a predicate definition.

Define the *minimum clockwise distance* between p_i and a token to be the smallest clockwise distance from p_i to p_j such that p_j has $t > 0$ tokens. Observe that if p_i has a token, then the minimum clockwise distance to a token is zero. Similarly, let the minimum counterclockwise distance from p_i to a token be defined. Let $Rdist_i$ denote the minimum clockwise distance to a token for p_i and let $Ldist_i$ denote the minimum counterclockwise distance to a token for p_i.

4.1 Programs

The delay and relay programs are shown in Figure 2. Both programs begin with steps to move any queued tokens from the predecessor's queue to rest at p_i. The relay program enqueues one token, if there are any resting tokens, in line 3 of the program. The delay program may or may not enqueue a token, depending on values of the counter c_i and the number of resting tokens r_i. In terms of a Petri net, the relay program corresponds to simple, deterministic, unit delay with at most one token firing in any step on the output transition. The delay program expresses a joint transition, with two inputs and two outputs: the variable c_i becomes a ring of $C+1$ places and line 4 of delay represents the joint transition.

In application, it is possible that all n processes run the delay program, and no process runs relay. This would be a *uniform* protocol to achieve D1–D5. An advantage of including relay processes can be to limit the cost of construction for physical embodiments of the logic. Using multiple relay processes can model more general cases of token delay: a consecutive sequence of k relay processes is equivalent to a process that always delays an arriving token by k rounds.

4.2 Application to Models

The relay/delay programs given can be translated to other models. For lack of space in these proceedings, discussion of translation to standard models, including the possibility of asynchronous execution, has been moved to [16].

Petri Net. It is usual for self-stabilization that transient faults, which inject variable corruption, are responsible for creating new initial states, and the event of a transient fault is not explicitly modeled. However for an application where tokens represent physical objects, which is plausible for Petri nets, a transient

```
   delay ::
        do forever
1          r_i ← r_i + q_{i-1} ;
2          q_{i-1} ← 0 ;

3          if  c_i > 0  then
                 c_i ← c_i − 1
4          else if c_i = 0 ∧ r_i > 0 then
                 c_i ← C ;
                 r_i ← r_i − 1 ;
                 q_i ← q_i + 1
```

```
   relay ::
        do forever
1          r_i ← r_i + q_{i-1} ;
2          q_{i-1} ← 0 ;

3          if  r_i > 0  then
                 r_i ← r_i − 1 ;
                 q_i ← q_i + 1
```

Fig. 2. delay and relay programs

fault neither destroys nor creates objects. Thus we think it reasonable to suppose that $m > 1$ tokens satisfying (1) are present in any initial state.

Observe that line 2 of either delay or relay has p_i assign to q_{i-1} (whereas the usual convention in the literature of self-stabilization is that a process may only assign to its own variables). The assignment $q_{i-1} \leftarrow 0$ models the transfer of a token from a transition to its target place in a Petri net. For the firing of a Petri net transition, p_i increments q_i in line 4 of delay or line 3 or relay. Figure 1 illustrates both relay and delay programs. The portions of the two rings on the left side of the figure are modeled by the c variables in relay nodes; these are "minor" rings with $C + 1$ nodes, whereas the "major" ring has n nodes. The situation of a token on a minor ring being ready for a transition shared by the major ring is modeled by $c_i = 0$. Observe that when a token on the major ring is present at the same transition where a minor ring token exists, then transition firing is enabled at line 4, because $r_i > 0$ and $c_i = 0$. We assume that tokens of major and minor rings are of different nature; a transient fault cannot move a token from minor to major or from major to minor ring. A transient fault can move tokens arbitrarily on their respective rings.

Wireless Sensor Network. Wireless networks use messages rather than shared variables for communication, and self-stabilizing clock synchronization [17] can be used to implement a synchronous step of all delay/relay cycles. Two important technical details from the programs to consider are the reading and assignment to q_{i-1} by p_i and the possibility that any token representation is corrupt in the initial state, so we cannot assume m tokens are present in the initial state. The assignment to q_{i-1} can be eliminated in favor of having each p_i obtain token information in a message from p_{i-1} at the start of each round. As for initially corrupt token representation, the simplest solution is to leverage a standard self-stabilizing, unidirectional token or multitoken protocol. For instance, if m independent copies of a self-stabilizing, token-based mutual exclusion are emulated in the adaptation of delay/relay, then each of these copies will converge to having one token in each emulated ring. In such an emulation, it is important that each process emulate the m copies fairly, to ensure that they each converge to having a single token [16].

4.3 Verification

A legitimate state for the protocol is a global state predicate, defining constraints on values for variables. To define this predicate, let *tokdist* denote the minimum, taken over all i such that $r_i + q_i > 0$, of $Rdist_i$. The predicate delay_i is *true* for process p_i running delay and *false* for the relay processes.

Definition 1. *A global state σ is legitimate iff*

$$\sum_i q_i = m \quad \wedge \quad \sum_i r_i = 0 \quad \wedge \quad (\forall i :: \ q_i \leq 1) \tag{2}$$

$$\wedge \quad tokdist > C \tag{3}$$

$$\begin{array}{lll} \wedge & (\forall i: \textsf{delay}_i \ \wedge\ c_i > 0 \ \wedge\ q_i = 0: \ Rdist_i = C - c_i) & (4) \\ \wedge & (\forall i: \textsf{delay}_i \ \wedge\ q_i = 0: \ Ldist_i > c_i) & (5) \\ \wedge & (\forall i: \textsf{delay}_i \ \wedge\ q_i = 1: \ c_i = C) & (6) \end{array}$$

In an initial state, variables may have arbitrary values in their domains, subject to constraint (1).

Lemma 1 (Closure). *Starting from a legitimate state σ, the execution of a round results in a legitimate state σ'.*

Proof. The conservation of tokens expressed by (2) is simple to verify from the statements of delay and relay programs, so we concentrate on showing that (3)–(6) are invariant properties. Assume that σ is a legitimate state. We consider two cases for a process p_i running delay, either there is no token at p_i and $q_i = 0$, or $q_i = 1$ at σ.

▶ $q_i = 1$: observe that $c_i = C$ by (6). For σ' we have $r_i = 0$ because from (3) there is no token at p_{i-1} and we have $q_i = 0 \ \wedge\ c_i = C - 1$ by lines 1-2 of either delay or relay at p_{i+1}, and line 3 of delay at p_i. This validates (2) with respect to the token passed, and (3) holds because every token moves to the successor starting from a legitimate state. Property (4) holds at σ' with respect to p_i because $Rdist_i = 1 = C - c_i$. Finally, (5) is validated for p_i because, if (5) holds for σ when $c_i = C$, then a token moving one process closer to p_i validates (5) by $c_i = C - 1$ at σ'.

▶ $q_i = 0$: there are two subcases, either $c_i = 0$ or $c_i > 0$. In the former case, if no token arrives to p_i in the transition from σ to σ', properties (2)-(6) directly hold with respect to p_i in σ'. If a token arrives to p_i, then $q_i = 1 \ \wedge\ c_i = C$ result by line 4 of delay, and we use properties (3)-(6) of p_{i-1} at σ to infer that the same properties hold of p_i at σ'. If $c_i > 0$ at σ, then by (3)-(5) and legitimacy of all processes within distance $C + 1$ in either direction from p_i, tokens move to the successor process while c_i decrements, which establishes (3)-(5) for p_i at σ'. ❒

To prove convergence, we start with some elementary claims and define some useful terms. Suppose rounds are numbered in an execution, round t starts from state σ, and that $q^{\sigma}_{i-1} = v$. For such a situation, we say that v tokens *arrive* at p_i in round t.

Lemma 2. *In any execution, $\sum_i r_i + q_i \ = \ m$ holds invariantly.*

Proof. As explained in Section 3, $m > 1$ tokens are present in the initial state, represented by r_i and q_i variables. Statements of delay or of relay conserve the number of tokens in the system, because we assume that all processes execute lines 1 and 2 synchronously in any round. Line 4 of delay or line 3 of relay similarly conserve the number of tokens in a process. ❒

Lemma 3. *Within one round of any execution,*

$$(\,\forall i :: \quad q_i \leq 1\,) \tag{7}$$

holds and continues to hold invariantly for all subsequent rounds.

Proof. In every round, line 2 of delay or relay assigns $q_{i-1} \leftarrow 0$, and may assign $q_i \leftarrow 1$. ❐

For the remainder of this section, we consider only executions that start with a state satisfying (7). For such executions, a corollary of Lemma 3 is: at most one token arrives to any process in any round.

Lemma 4. *If $m > 0$, then for every execution of the protocol and $0 \leq k < C \wedge 0 \leq i < n$, the variable $c_i = k$ at infinitely many states.*

Proof. The proof is by contradiction. First, we show that at least some token moves infinitely often. Since $m > 0$, there is a token at some process p_i because $r_i > 0$ or $q_i > 0$; the case $q_i > 0$ implies immediate token movement in the next round, so we look at the other case, $r_i > 0 \wedge q_i = 0$. In one round, p_i either assigns $q_i \leftarrow 1$ program, and thus a token moves in the next round, or p_i assigns $c_i \leftarrow c_i - 1$ because $c_i > 0$. Therefore, after at most C rounds, a state where $c_i = 0 \wedge r_i > 0$ is reached, and the next round enqueues a token for movement. The preceding argument shows that *some* token movement occurs infinitely often in any execution. There are m tokens throughout the execution by (2), hence at least one token can be considered to move infinitely many times. Note that the token abstraction is represented by r and q variables only: we cannot be sure that one token does not overtake another token. However, it will be our convention to model token queuing as first-in, first-out order. Thereby we find that if one token moves infinitely many times clockwise around the ring, all tokens do so as well. Returning to the claim, suppose that some c_i variable eventually never has some value $k \in [0, C-1]$. But p_i experiences infinitely many tokens arriving and assigns $q_i \leftarrow 1$ infinitely often, so lines 3 and 4 of delay execute infinitely often at p_i, which is a contradiction. ❐

Lemma 5. *For any process p_i running the* delay *program, eventually p_i assigns $q_i \leftarrow 1$ at most once in any $C + 1$ consecutive rounds.*

Proof. Lemma 4 shows that p_i eventually assigns $c_i \leftarrow C$. In delay, only line 4 assigns $q_i \leftarrow 1$, and the same step assigns $c_i \leftarrow C$. Thus, if we number rounds t, $t + 1$, and so on, the values of c_i and q_i variables *at the end* of each round is shown by:

round	t	$t+1$	$t+2$	$\cdots$	$t+(C-1)$	$t+C$	$t+(C+1)$
c_i	C	$C-1$	$C-2$	$\cdots$	1	0	C
q_i	1	0	0	$\cdots$	0	0	1

The table makes the worst-case assumption that $r_i > 0$ at round $t + (C + 1)$, to illustrate that through at least C consecutive rounds, q_i remains zero. ❐

Lemma 6. *Let σ be a state that occurs after sufficiently many rounds so that every token has arrived at least once at some process running the* delay *program. In the (suffix) execution following σ, if a token arrives at p_i in round t, then no token arrives at p_i during rounds $t + 1$ through $t + C$.*

Proof. After σ, a token departs from any given delay process p_i only at line 4 of delay, which has precondition $c_i = 0$ and postcondition $c_i = C$. Thus, each delay process releases a token once every $C+1$ rounds (or less often, if $r_i = 0$ holds). A relay process p_j could potentially release tokens once per round, if r_j remains positive, however we have supposed that each token has entered some delay process before σ. A simple inductive argument shows that $r_j = 0$ holds throughout the execution following σ. Therefore, each process experiences token arrival at most once every $C+1$ rounds. ❒

Below we consider only executions that start with a state σ satisfying (6). For such executions, a corollary of Lemma 6 is: the token arrival rate to any process is at most $1/(C+1)$.

Lemma 7. *Let σ be a state in any execution identified by Lemma 6. Then, throughout the remainder of the execution,*

$$(\forall i :: \quad r_i \leq 1 + r_i^\sigma) \tag{8}$$

Proof. If some r_i increases in a round, then because of Lemma 6, no additional token arrives to p_i for $C+1$ rounds; this is an adequate number of rounds to ensure that p_i will release a token, thus putting r_i back to its original value. ❒

Lemma 7 allows us to introduce the notion of a *resting bound* for any process p_i. With respect an execution E with an initial state σ as defined in Lemma 6, for each p_i executing the delay program there is a bound $1 + r_i^\sigma$ on the number of tokens that may rest together at p_i during the remainder of E. After any round in E producing a state β, let us consider three possibilities for any particular delay process p_i's number of resting tokens:

$$r_i^\beta = (1 + r_i^\sigma) \quad \vee \quad r_i^\beta = r_i^\sigma \quad \vee \quad r_i^\beta < r_i^\sigma$$

Notice that for the first two disjuncts, the resting bound of r_i is unchanged. However, for the third disjunct, where p_i released a token in the round and has fewer than r_i^σ resting tokens, the argument of Lemma 7 can be applied to state β, lowering the resting bound for p_i to $1 + r_i^\beta$. More generally, there might be other processes that lower their resting bounds during the round obtaining β. Thus, the resting bound developed by Lemma 7 for each process may improve during an execution. At any particular point in E, the best bound for r_i is $1+r_i^\delta$, where δ is determined by the most recent round that lowered r_i's resting bound; if there is no such preceding round, then let $\delta = \sigma$. Below, we find special cases with more accurate bounds.

Resting bounds are the basis for a variant function on protocol execution. Let F be a tuple formed by listing the resting bounds for all delay processes. Since no process increases its resting bound in any round, it follows that valuations of F can only decrease during execution. If all components of tuple F are zero, then it is possible to show that the protocol has reached a legitimate state. We say that F is positive if any of its components is nonzero. In order to prove convergence, two more claims are needed. First, a special case is required for a resting bound of zero (since Lemma 7's form is inappropriate); second, it must be shown that F eventually does decrease if it is positive.

Lemma 8. *Let E be an execution originating from a state σ identified by Lemma 6, and suppose α is a state in E where p_i running* delay *satisfies $r_i^\alpha = 0 \wedge c_i^\alpha = 0$. Then, for the execution following α, the resting bound of r_i is zero.*

Proof. The proof is by induction over the execution following α, based on the sequence of rounds associated with token arrival at p_i. When a token arrives at p_i after state α, the predicate $r_i = 0 \ \wedge \ c_i = 0$ holds. The delay program establishes $q_i = 1 \ \wedge \ r_i = 0 \ \wedge \ c_i = C$ when processing the arriving token. Lemma 6 ensures that no additional token will arrive to p_i during the following C rounds, so that $c_i = 0$ holds when the next token arrival occurs for p_i. ❒

Lemma 9. *Let E be an execution originating from a state σ identified by Lemma 6. F cannot be positive and constant throughout E.*

Proof. Proof by contradiction. Suppose, for each delay p_i, that the resting bound never decreases. We analyze scenarios for this supposition and derive necessary conditions, which are used to show a contradiction. Lemma 4 implies that p_i receives a token infinitely often in E and releases a token infinitely many times. If each token reception coincides with releasing a token, which entails $c_i = 0$, then $r_i > 0$ would remain constant throughout E. For such a continuing scenario, p_i must receive at token once every $C+1$ rounds. The other possible scenario is that of r_i incrementing to the resting bound, then decrementing, and repeating this pattern. For this scenario, c_i decrements to zero, then resets to C, continuously during E. Because we have supposed that r_i never decrements twice before incrementing again (otherwise F would decrease), tokens need to arrive sufficiently often to p_i. Suppose $c_i = k > 0$ when a token arrives. Then another token must arrive after exactly $C+1$ rounds so that $c_i = k$ upon token arrival. If instead, a token arrives after $C+1+d$ rounds, then $c_i = k - d$ would hold upon token arrival, $d \leq k$. More generally, the spacing in token arrivals over E could be $C+1+t_1$, then $C+1+t_2$, and so on up to a delay gap of $C+1+t_\ell$ rounds, so long as $\sum_{j=1}^{\ell} t_j \leq k$. Each time there is a delay gap of $C+1+t_j$ rounds with $t_j > 0$, the counter c_i decreases in this scenario. A decrease resulting in $c_i = 0$ would then force all future delays to be $C+1$, so that tokens arrive exactly as they are released, preventing a reduction of r_i.

Having exposed the scenarios for F remaining constant over execution E, thus at least one $r_i > 0$ throughout E, we observe that from $m(C+1) \leq n$ there exists a segment of the ring, with more than $C+1$ processes, containing no token, at every state in E. The existence of such a segment implies that some delay p_i will receive a token after a delay of more than $C+1$ rounds (a more detailed argument could take into account processes identified by Lemma 8, which merely pass along tokens when they arrive). Thus, infinitely often, a delay between token arrivals is at least $C+2$ rounds. It follows that eventually, c_i decreases to zero for some p_i before a token arrives, at which point it will decrease r_i, contradicting the assumption that F remains constant. ❒

Lemma 10 (Convergence). *Every execution of the protocol eventually contains a legitimate state.*

Proof. The proof is by induction on Lemma 9, so long as F is positive. Therefore, the resting bound for every delay process is zero eventually. To establish that the resulting state is legitimate, it is enough to verify the behavior of a delay process p_i during the $C+1$ rounds preceding token arrival to see that (3)-(5) hold with respect to p_i. ❐

We sketch an argument bounding the worst-case convergence time using elements from the proof of convergence. The variant function F is applied to an execution suffix satisfying (7), and Lemma 6; such a suffix occurs within $O(n)$ rounds of any execution: the worst case occurs when one delay process p_i holds all m tokens, which it releases after at most $m \cdot C$ rounds, and the last of these tokens takes $O(n)$ rounds to again arrive at a delay process; since $m \cdot C \leq n$ by (1), we have $O(n)$ rounds overall to obtain the suffix for Lemma 6. To bound the worst case for F reducing in an execution, we observe that there are at most n components to F, each with an initial maximum value of m. Suppose each component decreases sequentially, therefore requiring $n \cdot m \cdot f$ time, where f is the worst-case number of rounds to reduce one component of F. We bound f by the proof argument of Lemma 9. A ring segment of length at least $C+2$ and devoid of tokens implies some decrease of a resting bound in the proof argument. This decrease may take $O(C)$ time to occur, as a c variable reduces while a process awaits a token; however a token may take $O(n)$ rounds to reach the waiting process. A conservative bound is therefore $O(m \cdot n^2) = O(n^3)$ rounds.

As an aside, we note that the algorithms are deterministic, execution is fully synchronous (there is no nondeterministic adversary), and the program model fits the Petri net formalism; therefore a formulation using the max-plus algebra [9] can express system execution, and there exist tools to compute eigenvalues for a matrix representing the system. We did not investigate such an approach, since the choice of which processes run delay would be an extra complication.

In [16] we report on simulations of the protocol for various values of n, m, C, and different choices for the number of delay processes. The simulations suggest that a bound $O(n^3)$ may be loose for the average case; simulation result suggest that expected convergence time could be linear in n. Another point of the simulation is to investigate the influence of having multiple delay processes on convergence time; simulations suggest that having at least a few delay processes is beneficial.

Theorem 1. *The delay/relay protocol, with at least one delay process, and with $n > 1$, $m > 1$, $d = C+1$, and $m \cdot d \leq n$, self-stabilizes to desiderata* D1-D5.

Proof. Lemma 2 attends to D1. The definition of legitimate state validates D2. A property of a legitimate state is that $c_i = 0$ whenever a token arrives to p_i, hence the behavior of delay is like relay: a token moves in each round, as required by D3. The ring topology and the unidirectional movement of tokens satisfies D4. Finally, lemmas 10 and 1 provide the technical basis for the theorem, showing D5. ❐

5 Protocol with Unknown Ring Size

A parameter C, upon which the target separation between tokens is based, is given to the protocol of Section 4. Here we consider another design alternative, where the separation between tokens should be maximized, but the ring size is unknown. The technique is straightforward: building upon the delay program, additional variables are added to count the number of rounds needed to circulate a token, that is, the new program calculates n. Two extra assumptions are used for the new protocol: the value of m is known and the number of processes running the delay program is exactly one. We discuss this limitation in Section 6.

Figure 3 presents the revised delay program, which introduces $timing_i$, t_i, $ignore_i$, and $ClockBase_i$. The program uses $ClockBase_i$ in place of parameter C, which is periodically recalculated.

Lemma 11. *With the delay program of Figure 3 at one process and relay at all other processes, the system is self-stabilizing for* $C = \lfloor n/m \rfloor - 1$, *if* $m \leq \lfloor n/2 \rfloor$.

Proof. Due to space restrictions in these proceedings, the proof has been moved to [16]. We sketch some key points of the proof here. Let p_k be the sole delay process. For convergence it is enough to show that $ClockBase_k$ obtains the maximum feasible value for m tokens, that is, $ClockBase_k = \lfloor n/m \rfloor - 1$ holds throughout a suffix execution. Lemmas 1 and 10 then apply to verify self-stabilization. The proof hinges on two cases, (*1*) either $(\forall i : \ i \neq k : \ r_i = 0)$

```
delay ::
    do forever
        t_i ← t_i + 1 ;
        if q_{i-1} > 0 ∧ timing_i then
            ignore_i ← ignore_i − 1 ;
            if ignore_i < 1 then
                timing_i ← false ;
                ClockBase_i ← ⌊t_i/m⌋ − 1

        r_i ← r_i + q_{i-1} ;
        q_{i-1} ← 0 ;

        if  c_i > 0  then
            c_i ← c_i − 1
        else if c_i = 0 ∧ r_i > 0 then
            c_i ← ClockBase_i ;
            r_i ← r_i − 1 ;
            q_i ← q_i + 1 ;
            if ¬timing_i then
                timing_i ← true ;
                t_i ← 0 ;
                ignore_i ← m − r_i − 1
```

Fig. 3. delay program revised to calculate ring size

or (*2*) some tokens rest at relay processes. In case (*1*), because p_k releases at most one token per round, and because all relay processes pass along any tokens they receive in each round, it follows that (*1*) holds invariantly. Provided $m > 0$, process p_k infinitely often receives and releases a token in any execution, so lines 5-6 and lines 16-18 of Figure 3 are executed repeatedly. Line 18 calculates one fewer than the number of tokens that do not rest at p_k at the instant a token is released from p_k to p_{k+1}. Provided (*1*) holds, it will be n subsequent rounds before this token circulates the ring and returns to p_k. Lines 1-6 compute the elapsed time between this release of the token and its return, so that $t_k = n$ when line 6 calculates the value of $ClockBase_k$, and this drives convergence in the remainder of the execution. Case (*2*) can be shown to eventually disappear, because $ClockBase_k > 1$ is calculated in each execution of line 6; resting tokens for relay processes therefore do not persist. ❐

6 Conclusion

This paper provides fault tolerant constructions for a timing behavior in which m loci of control are separated. The program mechanisms are simple: tokens carry no data and processes use few variables. The first construction can be uniform, distinguished (with one unique corrective process), or hybrid. The second construction requires one distinguished process.

An interesting question is whether there can be a hybrid or uniform protocol when the ring size and separation constant are unknown. For the style of algorithm in Section 5 we conjecture the answer is negative. If one delay process p_i has an accurate estimate for maximum separation $d = c_i + 1$ and does not delay any arriving token, another process p_j may have either a larger, inaccurate estimate, or may perceive that tokens are unaligned with its counter and therefore delay some arriving tokens. Such delay would lead to p_i detecting an apparently larger ring size, since the measured traversal time around the ring would include p_j's delays. Hence p_i would raise its estimate for the separation value. Note that the problem may admit other types of algorithms: for example, if tokens are allowed to carry data, this would enable processes to communicate. Whether such increased communication power is useful is an open question. Another direction would be to use randomized timing, so that different delay processes do not interfere.

The program of Section 4 conforms to the standard Petri net model of behavior control if we replace counters by auxiliary token rings, as shown in Figure 1. This restriction enables tokens to model a physical system. However, programs that use tokens to carry data and thus communicate with explicit data rather than mere timing of tokens would need more functionality from a physical embodiment than Section 4's programs use in their timing-only mechanism. We have preferred for the present to investigate algorithms that use only the timing of tokens to overcome an unpredictable initial state.

References

1. Dijkstra, E.W.: EWD386 The solution to a cyclic relaxation problem. In: Selected Writings on Computing: A Personal Perspective, pp. 34–35. Springer, Heidelberg (1982)
2. Asahiro, Y., Fujita, S., Suzuki, I., Yamashita, M.: A self-stabilizing marching algorithm for a group of oblivious robots. In: Baker, T.P., Bui, A., Tixeuil, S. (eds.) OPODIS 2008. LNCS, vol. 5401, pp. 125–144. Springer, Heidelberg (2008)
3. Cieliebak, M., Flocchini, P., Prencipe, G., Santoro, N.: Solving the robots gathering problem. In: Baeten, J.C.M., Lenstra, J.K., Parrow, J., Woeginger, G.J. (eds.) ICALP 2003. LNCS, vol. 2719, pp. 1181–1196. Springer, Heidelberg (2003)
4. He, T., Krishnamurthy, S., Luo, L., Yan, T., Gu, L., Stoleru, R., Zhou, G., Cao, Q., Vicaire, P., Stankovic, J.A., Abdelzaher, T.F., Hui, J., Krogh, B.: VigilNet: an integrated sensor network system for energy-efficient surveillance. ACM Transactions on Sensor Networks 2(1), 1–38 (2006)
5. Wang, L., Xiao, Y.: A Survey of energy-efficient scheduling mechanisms in sensor networks. Mobile Networks and Applications 11(5), 723–740 (2006)
6. Gouda, M.G., Faddix, F.: The alternator. In: WSS 1999, pp. 48–53 (1999)
7. Danturi, P., Nesterenko, M., Tixeuil, S.: Self-stabilizing philosophers with generic conflicts. In: Datta, A.K., Gradinariu, M. (eds.) SSS 2006. LNCS, vol. 4280, pp. 214–230. Springer, Heidelberg (2006)
8. Flocchini, P., Prencipe, G., Santoro, N.: Self-deployment of mobile sensors on a ring. Theoretical Computer Science 402(1), 67–80 (2008)
9. Baccelli, F., Cohen, G., Olsder, G.J., Quadrat, J.P.: Synchronization and Linearity: An Algebra for Discrete Event Systems. Wiley, Chichester (1992)
10. Dolev, S.: Self-Stabilization. MIT Press, Cambridge (2000)
11. Datta, A.K., Hadid, R., Villain, V.: A new self-stabilizing k-out-of-ℓ exclusion algorithm on rings. In: Huang, S.-T., Herman, T. (eds.) SSS 2003. LNCS, vol. 2704, pp. 113–128. Springer, Heidelberg (2003)
12. Cantarell, S., Petit, F.: Self-stabilizing group mutual exclusion for asynchronous rings. In: OPODIS 2000, pp. 71–90 (2000)
13. Flatebo, M., Datta, A.K., Schoone, A.A.: Self-stabilizing multi-token rings. Distributed Computing 8(3), 133–142 (1995)
14. Arora, A., Gouda, M.G.: Distributed reset. IEEE Trans. Comput. 43(9), 1026–1038 (1994)
15. Afek, Y., Brown, G.M.: Self-stabilization of the alternating-bit protocol. Distributed Computing 7, 27–34 (1993)
16. Ghosh Dastidar, K., Herman, T.: Separation of circulating tokens (2009), `http://arxiv.org/abs/0908.1797`
17. Herman, T., Zhang, C.: Stabilizing clock synchronization for wireless sensor networks. In: Datta, A.K., Gradinariu, M. (eds.) SSS 2006. LNCS, vol. 4280, pp. 335–349. Springer, Heidelberg (2006)

Visiting Gafni's Reduction Land: From the BG Simulation to the Extended BG Simulation

Damien Imbs and Michel Raynal

IRISA, Université de Rennes 1, 35042 Rennes, France

Abstract. The *Borowsky-Gafni* (BG) *simulation* algorithm is a powerful tool that allows a set of $t+1$ asynchronous sequential processes to wait-free simulate (i.e., despite the crash of up to t of them) a large number n of processes under the assumption that at most t of these processes fail (i.e., the simulated algorithm is assumed to be t-resilient). The BG simulation has been used to prove solvability and unsolvability results for crash-prone asynchronous shared memory systems.

In its initial form, the BG simulation applies only to colorless decision tasks, i.e., tasks in which nothing prevents processes to decide the same value (e.g., consensus or k-set agreement tasks). Said in another way, it does not apply to decision problems such as renaming where no two processes are allowed to decide the same new name. Very recently (STOC 2009), Eli Gafni has presented an *extended BG simulation* algorithm (GeBG) that generalizes the basic BG algorithm by extending it to "colored" decision tasks such as renaming. His algorithm is based on a sequence of sub-protocols where a sub-protocol is either the base agreement protocol that is at the core of BG simulation, or a commit-adopt protocol.

This paper presents the core of an extended BG simulation algorithm that is particularly simple. This algorithm is based on two underlying objects: the base agreement object used in the BG simulation (as does GeBG), and (differently from GeBG) a new simple object that we call *arbiter*. More precisely, (1) while each of the n simulated processes is simulated by each simulator, (2) each of the first $t+1$ simulated processes is associated with a predetermined simulator that we called its "owner". The arbiter object is used to ensure that the permanent blocking (crash) of any of these $t+1$ simulated processes can only be due to the crash of its owner simulator. After being presented in a modular way, the proposed extended BG simulation algorithm is proved correct.

Keywords: Arbiter, Asynchronous processes, Distributed computability, Fault-Tolerance, Process crash failure, Reduction, t-Resilience, Shared memory system, Wait-free environment.

1 Introduction

What is the Borowsky-Gafni (BG) simulation. Considering an asynchronous system where processes can crash, the (n,k)-set agreement problem is a basic decision task defined as follows [9]. Each of the n processes proposes a value, and every process that does not crash has to decide a value (termination), such that a decided value is a proposed value (validity) and at most k different values are decided (agreement). The consensus problem corresponds to the particular case $k=1$.

R. Guerraoui and F. Petit (Eds.): SSS 2009, LNCS 5873, pp. 369–383, 2009.

A fundamental question related to asynchronous distributed computability is the following. Suppose we have an algorithm that solves the $(15, 4)$-set agreement problem. Can we use this algorithm as a subroutine to solve the $(12, 5)$-set agreement problem, assuming that at most $t < 12$ processes can crash? Intuitively, the answer might be "yes" (as we have less processes and more decided values are allowed). Let us now suppose that we want to use the same $(15, 4)$-set agreement subroutine to solve the $(100, 4)$-set agreement problem. As we have much more proposed values, and the same constraint on the number of decided values, an intuitive answer does not spring in an obvious way. And what is the answer if we want to solve the $(80, 7)$-set agreement problem (much more proposed values but only two more values can be decided), or (assuming $t = 4$) solve the $(5, 4)$-set agreement problem?

Stated in more general terms, the question is: *"Can we use a solution to the (n, k)-set agreement problem as a subroutine to solve the (n', k')-set agreement problem, when at most $t < \min(n, n')$ processes may crash?"* (We say that "the (n', k')-set agreement is reducible to (n, k)-set agreement".) The BG simulation (introduced in [6] and formalized and deeply investigated in [7] where is given a formal definition of "reducibility") answers this fundamental question. It states that the answer is "yes" if $k' \geq k$ and "no" if $k' \leq t < k$. As we can see, the answer "yes" does not depend on the number of processes.

To that end, a BG simulation algorithm is described that allows $n' = t+1$ processes to simulate a large number n of processes that collectively solve a decision task in presence of at most t crashes. Each of the n' simulator processes simulates all the n processes. These n' simulator processes cooperate through underlying objects (the type of which is called here safe_agreement) that allow them to agree on a single output for each of the non-deterministic statements issued by every simulated process.

The important lesson learned from the BG simulation is that, in a failure-prone context, what is important is not the number of processes but the maximal number of possible failures and the actual number of values that are proposed to a decision task. An interesting application of the BG simulation (among several of its applications [7]) is the proof that there is no t-resilient (n, k)-set agreement algorithm for $t \geq k$. This is obtained as follows. As (1) the BG simulation allows reducing the $(k+1, k)$-set agreement problem to the (n, k)-set agreement problem in a system with up to k failures, and (2) the $(k+1, k)$-set agreement problem is known to be impossible in presence of k failures [6,13,17], it follows that there is no k-resilient (n, k)-set agreement algorithm.

The limit of the BG-simulation and the extended BG-simulation. The BG simulation characterizes t-resilient solvability by reducing it to the question of wait-free solvability (i.e., t-resilience in a system of $n = t+1$ processes). Unfortunately, the BG simulation is limited to *colorless* decision tasks, i.e., tasks in which if a process decides a value v, then all the processes can decide that value (the class of colorless tasks is formally defined in [7]). The (n, k)-set decision problem is typically such a task. From an operational point of view, this is due to the fact that, in the BG simulation, each simulator simulates fairly all the processes, and consequently, the crash of a simulator process can manifest itself as the crash of any simulated process (the one it is currently simulating a critical part of code).

The extended BG simulation has been proposed by Eli Gafni to overcome this limitation and consequently fully capture t-resilience [12]. As stated in [12] "With the extended BG simulation we can reduce questions about t-resilience solvability to questions about wait-free solvability. The latter is characterized by the Herlihy-Shavit conditions [13]".

As a result, it applies to both colorless tasks and *colored* decision tasks such as the renaming problem [3]. In that problem, each of the n processes has to decide a new name (from a given new name space) such that no two processes have the same new name. This problem has wait-free solutions when the new name space $[1..M]$ is such that $M \geq 2n - 1$ (see [8] for a deeper insight into the problem).

In his paper [12], Gafni presents several (un)decidability results that can be obtained in a simpler way from the BG simulation. He also uses the extended BG simulation to show that the t-resilient weak symmetry breaking problem is equivalent to t-resilient weak renaming problem.

The core of the BG simulation relies on the following principles: (1) each of the $(t + 1)$ simulators fairly simulates all the processes, and this simulation is such that (2) the crash of a simulator entails the crash of at most one simulated process. The BG simulation is "symmetric" in the sense that each of the n processes is simulated by every simulator, and the $(t + 1)$ simulators are "equal" with respect to each simulated process. One way to be able to simulate colored tasks (without preventing the simulation of colorless tasks), consists in introducing some form of *asymmetry*.

The extended BG simulation [12] realizes the appropriate asymmetry as follows. In addition of simulating an appropriate subset of the n simulated processes, each simulator q is statically associated with exactly one given simulated process p (in our terminology, q is the *owner* of p). This ownership notion is used to ensure that the corresponding simulated process p will not be blocked forever (perceived as crashed) if its owner simulator q does not crash. Hence, if a simulator does not crash, it can always decide the value decided by the simulated process p it "owns". As noticed and demonstrated in [12] "extending the BG simulation by this simple property results in a full characterization of t-resilience in terms of wait-freedom".

Content of the paper. In addition to the introduction of the notion of extended BG simulation, and a full characterization of t-resilience, Gafni presents in [12] an extended BG simulation algorithm (denoted here GeBG). This algorithm is based on a sequence of sub-protocols where each sub-protocol is either the base agreement protocol used in the BG simulation (safe_agreement type objects) or a commit-adopt protocol [11]. This algorithm is presented informally in English.

The present paper presents the core of an extended BG simulation algorithm that is particularly simple. This algorithm is based on two underlying object types: the type safe_agreement (the one used in the BG simulation algorithm and in GeBG), and (differently from GeBG) an object type that we call arbiter. An arbiter object allows exploiting the ownership notion in a simple way to ensure that (1) an object value is always decided when its owner does not crash, and (2) the value of that object is determined either by its owner simulator or by the other simulators.

As far as the whole simulation is concerned, while (as in the BG simulation) each of the n simulated processes is simulated by each simulator, (as in GeBG) each of the first

$t+1$ simulated processes is "associated" with exactly one simulator (its "owner"). As already said, it follows from the appropriate use of the arbiter objects that the permanent blocking (crash) of any of these $t+1$ simulated processes can only be due to the crash of its owner simulator.

The paper is made up of 7 sections. Section 2 presents the model and the definition of decision tasks. Section 3 explains the structure of the simulation. Section 4 defines the base object types used by the simulators to cooperate and realize a correct simulation. Then, the extended BG simulation algorithm is presented in an incremental and modular way. First Section 5 briefly presents the BG simulation algorithm, and then Section 6 enriches it to solve the extended BG simulation. This algorithm is proved in Section 7.

2 Solving Decision Tasks

2.1 Decision Tasks

The problems we are interested in are called *decision tasks*[1]. In every run, each process proposes a value and the proposed values define an input vector I where $I[j]$ is the value proposed by p_j. Let $\mathcal{I}$ denote the set of allowed input vectors. Each process has to decide a value. The decided values define an output vector O, such that $O[j]$ is the value decided by p_j. Let $\mathcal{O}$ be the set of the output vectors.

A decision task is a binary relation Δ from $\mathcal{I}$ into $\mathcal{O}$. A task is *colorless* if, when a value v is decided by a process p_j (i.e., $O[j] = v$), then v can be decided by all the processes). Consensus, and more generally k-set agreement, are colorless tasks. Otherwise the task is *colored*. Renaming is a colored task.

2.2 The Computation Model

Asynchronous processes and fault model. We are interested in distributed algorithms the aim of which is to solve a task in a system made up of n asynchronous sequential processes denoted $p_1, ..., p_n$. A process executes a sequence of atomic steps (as defined by its algorithm). Each process p_j is endowed with a write-once local variable $output_j$ where it deposits the value it decides.

A process can crash in a run. A process executes correctly the steps defined by its algorithm until it crashes (if it ever does). After it has crashed, a process executes no more steps. If it does not crash, a process executes an infinite number of steps.

It is assumed that an arbitrary subset (not known in advance) of up to $t < n$ processes can crash (the crash of one process being independent from the crash of other processes). A process that does not crash in a run is said to be *correct* in that run, otherwise it is faulty. This failure model is called the *t-resilient environment*, and an algorithm designed for such an environment is said to be *t-resilient*. The extreme case $t = n-1$ is called *wait-free environment*, and the corresponding algorithms are called *wait-free algorithms*.

[1] The reader interested in a more formal presentation of decision tasks can consult the literature (e.g., [2,7,12,13]).

Communication model. The n processes cooperate through a shared memory made up of a snapshot object [1] denoted mem. This means that a process p_j can write only the entry $mem[j]$ but can read all the entries by invoking the operation $mem.\mathsf{snapshot}()$. The write and snapshot operations appear as being executed atomically [1]. (These operations can be built on top of a single-writer/multiple-readers atomic registers [1,4]). Initially, $mem[j] = \perp$.

Definition. The previous computation model (asynchronous crash-prone processes that communicate through snapshot objects) is called *snapshot model.*

2.3 Algorithm Solving a Task

An algorithm solves a task in a t-resilient environment if, given any $I \in \mathcal{I}$, each correct process p_j decides (i.e., writes a value v in $output_j$) and there is an output vector O such that $(I, O) \in \Delta$ where O is defined as follows. If p_j decides v, then $\mathcal{O}[j] = v$. If p_j does not decide, $O[j]$ is set to any value v' that preserves the relation $(I, O) \in \Delta$.

A task is solvable in a t-resilient environment if there is an algorithm that solves it in that environment. As an example, consensus is not solvable in the 1-resilient environment [10,15,16]. Differently, renaming with $2n - 1$ names is solvable in the wait-free environment [3,5,13].

3 Simulated Processes vs. Simulator Processes

Aim. Let A be an n-process t-resilient algorithm that solves a decision task in the base snapshot model described previously. The aim is to design a $(t + 1)$-process wait-free algorithm A' that simulates A in the same snapshot model. (The reader is referred to [7] for a formal definition of a simulation.)

Notation. A simulated process is denoted p_j with $1 \leq j \leq n$. Similarly, a simulator process (in short "simulator") is denoted q_i with $1 \leq i \leq t + 1$.

As far as the objects accessed by the simulators are concerned, the following convention is adopted. The objects denoted with upper case letters are the objects shared by the simulators. Differently, an object denoted with lower case letters is local to a simulator (in that case, the associated subscript denotes the corresponding simulator).

What a simulator does. Each simulator q_i is given the code of all the simulated processes $p_1, \ldots, p_n$. It manages n threads, each one associated with a simulated process, and locally executes these threads in a fair way. It also manages a local copy mem_i of the snapshot memory mem shared by the simulated processes.

The code of a simulated process p_j contains writes of $mem[j]$ and invocations of $mem.\mathsf{snapshot}()$. These are the only operations used by the processes $p_1, \ldots, p_n$ to cooperate. So, the core of the simulation is the definition of two algorithms. The first (denoted $\mathsf{sim\_write}_{i,j}()$) has to describe what a simulator q_i has to do in order to correctly simulate a write of $mem[j]$ issued by a process p_j. The second (denoted $\mathsf{sim\_snapshot}_{i,j}()$) has to describe what a simulator q_i has to do in order to correctly simulate an invocation of $mem.\mathsf{snapshot}()$ issued by a process p_j.

4 Base Object Types Used in the Simulation

In addition to snapshot objects, the simulator processes also cooperate through atomic read/write register objects, and specific objects the types of which (safe_agreement and arbiter) are defined in this section. These types can be implemented from multi-reader/multi-writer atomic registers, which in turn can be implemented from snapshot objects. Hence, all the base objects used in the simulation can be implemented in the snapshot computation model described in the previous section.

4.1 The safe_agreement Object Type

The safe_agreement *type.* This object type (defined in [6,7]) is at the core of the BG simulation. It provides each simulator q_i with two operations, denoted $\mathsf{propose}_i(v)$ and $\mathsf{decide}_i()$, that q_i can invoke at most once, and in that order. The operation $\mathsf{propose}_i(v)$ allows q_i to propose a value v while $\mathsf{decide}_i()$ allows it to decide a value. The properties satisfied by an object of the type safe_agreement are the following.

- Termination. If no simulator q_x crashes while executing $\mathsf{propose}_x()$, then any correct simulator q_i that invokes $\mathsf{decide}_i()$, returns from that invocation.
- Agreement. At most one value is decided.
- Validity. A decided value is a proposed value.

An implementation. The implementation of the safe_agreement type described in Figure 1 is from [7]. This construction is based on a snapshot object SM (with one entry per simulator q_i). Each entry $SM[i]$ of the snapshot object has two fields: $SM[i].value$ that contains a value and $SM[i].level$ that stores its level. The level 0 means the corresponding value is meaningless, 1 means it is unstable, while 2 means it is stable.

When a simulator q_i invokes $\mathsf{propose}_i(v)$, it first writes the pair $(v, 1)$ in $SM[i]$ (line 01), and then reads the snapshot object SM (line 02). If there is a stable value in SM, p_i "cancels" the value it proposes, otherwise it makes it stable (line 03).

A simulator q_i invokes $\mathsf{decide}_i()$ after it has invoked $\mathsf{propose}_i()$. Its aim is to return the same stable value to all the simulators that invoke this operation (line 06). To that end, q_i repeatedly computes a snapshot of SM until it sees no unstable value in SM (line 04). Let us observe that, as a simulator q_i invokes $\mathsf{decide}_i()$ after it has invoked $\mathsf{propose}_i(v)$, there is at least one stable value in SM when it executes line 05. Finally, in order that the same stable value be returned to all, q_i returns the stable value proposed by the simulator with the smallest id (line 05).

A formal proof that this algorithm implements the safe_agreement type is given [7]. Another proof is also given [14].

4.2 The arbiter Object Type

Definition. Each object of the type arbiter has a statically predefined owner simulator q_j. Such an object provides the simulators with a single operation denoted $\mathsf{arbitrate}_{i,j}()$ (where i is the id of the invoking simulator and j the id of the owner). A simulator q_i invokes $\mathsf{arbitrate}_{i,j}()$ at most once, and, when it terminates, this invocation returns a value to q_i. The properties of an object of the type arbiter owned by q_j are the following.

```
init: for each x : 1 ≤ x ≤ t+1 do SM[x] ← (⊥,0) end for.

operation propose_i(v):   % 1 ≤ i ≤ t+1 %
SM[i] ← (v,1);
sm_i ← SM.snapshot();
if (∃x : sm_i[x].level = 2) then SM[i] ← (v,0) else SM[i] ← (v,2) end if.

operation decide_i():   % 1 ≤ i ≤ t+1 %
repeat sm_i ← SM.snapshot() until (∀x : sm_i[x].level ≠ 1) end repeat;
let x = min({k | sm_i[k].level = 2); res ← sm_i[x].value;
return(res).
```

Fig. 1. An implementation of the safe_agreement type [7] (code for q_i)

- Termination. If the owner q_j invokes arbitrate$_{j,j}()$ and is correct, or does not invoke arbitrate$_{j,j}()$, or if a simulator q_i returns from its invocation arbitrate$_{i,j}()$, then all the correct simulators return from their arbitrate$_{i,j}()$ invocation.
- Agreement. No two processes return different values.
- Validity. The returned value is 1 (*owner*) or 0 (*not_owner*). Moreover, if the owner does not invoke arbitrate$_{j,j}()$, 1 cannot be returned, and if only the owner invokes arbitrate$_{i,j}()$, 0 cannot be returned.

An implementation. An implementation of an object of the type arbiter is described in Figure 2. It is based on a snapshot object $PART$ (initialized to $[false, \ldots, false]$), and a multi-writer/multi-reader atomic register $WINNER$ (initialized to $\bot$).

When it invokes arbitrate$_{i,j}()$, the simulator q_i announces that it participates (line 01), and issues a snapshot to know the simulators that are currently participating (line 02). If q_i is the owner of the object ($i = j$, line 03), it checks if it is the first participant (predicate $part_i = \{i\}$). If it is, it sets $WINNER$ to 1, otherwise it sets it to 0 (line 04). If q_i is not the owner of the object ($i \neq j$), it checks if the owner is a participating simulator (predicate $j \in part_i$). If it is, q_i waits to know which value has been assigned to $WINNER$. If it is not, it sets $WINNER$ to 0. Finally, q_i terminates by returning the value of $WINNER$.

A proof that this construction implements the arbiter object type is given in [14].

```
operation arbitrate_{i,j}():   % 1 ≤ i,j ≤ t+1 %
(01) PART[i] ← true;
(02) aux_i ← PART.snapshot(); part_i ← {x | aux_i[x]};
(03) if (i = j)   % p_i is the owner of the associated arbiter type object %
(04)    then if (part_i = {i}) then WINNER ← 1 else WINNER ← 0 end if
(05)    else  if (j ∈ part_i) then wait (WINNER ≠ ⊥) else WINNER ← 0 end if
(06) end if;
(07) return(WINNER).
```

Fig. 2. The arbitrate$_{i,j}()$ operation of the arbiter object type (code for q_i)

5 The BG Simulation

This section presents the BG simulation [6,7]: its main principles and the algorithms implementing its base operations $\mathsf{sim\_write}_{i,j}()$ and $\mathsf{sim\_snapshot}_{i,j}()$.

5.1 The Shared Memory $MEM[1..(t+1)]$

The snapshot memory mem shared by the processes $p_1, \ldots, p_n$ is emulated by a snapshot object MEM shared by the simulators (so, MEM has $(t+1)$ entries).

More specifically, $MEM[i]$ is an (unbounded) atomic register that contains an array with one entry per simulated process p_j. Each $MEM[i][j]$ is made up of two fields: a field $MEM[i][j].value$ that contains the last value of $mem[j]$ written by p_j, and a field $MEM[i][j].sn$ that contains the associated sequence number. (This sequence number, introduced by the simulation, is a control data that will be used to produce a consistent simulation of the mem.snapshot() operations issued by the simulated processes).

5.2 The $\mathsf{sim\_write}_{i,j}()$ Operation

The algorithm, denoted $\mathsf{sim\_write}_{i,j}(v)$, executed by q_i to simulate the write by p_j of the value v into $mem[j]$ is described in Figure 3 [7]. Its code is pretty simple. The simulator q_i first increases a local sequence number $w\_sn_i[j]$ that will be associated with the value v written by p_j into $mem[j]$. Then, q_i writes the pair $(v, w\_sn_i[j])$ into $mem_i[j]$ (where mem_i is its local copy of the memory shared by the simulated processes) and finally writes atomically its local copy mem_i into $MEM[i]$.

operation $\mathsf{sim\_write}_{i,j}(v)$:
(01) $w\_sn_i[j] \leftarrow w\_sn_i[j] + 1$;
(02) $mem_i[j] \leftarrow (v, w\_sn_i[j])$;
(03) $MEM[i] \leftarrow mem_i$.

Fig. 3. $\mathsf{sim\_write}_{i,j}(v)$ executed by q_i to simulate $\mathsf{write}(v)$ issued by p_j (from [7])

5.3 The $\mathsf{sim\_snapshot}_{i,j}()$ Operation

This operation is implemented by the algorithm described in Figure 4 [7].

Additional local and shared objects. For each process p_j, a simulator q_i manages a local sequence number generator $snap\_sn_i[j]$ used to associate a sequence number with each mem.snapshot() it simulates on behalf of p_j (line 04).

In addition to the snapshot object $MEM[1..(t+1)]$, the simulators $q_1, \ldots, q_{t+1}$ cooperate through an array $SAFE\_AG[1..n, 0...]$ of safe_agreement type objects.

Underlying principle of the BG simulation [6,7]*: obtaining a consistent value.* In order to agree on the very same output of the $snapsn$-th invocation of mem.snapshot() that is issued by p_j, the simulators $q_1, \ldots, q_{t+1}$ use the object $SAFE\_AG[j, snapsn]$.

Each simulator q_i proposes a value (denoted $input_i$) to that object (line 05) and, due to its agreement property, that object will deliver them the same output at line 06. In order to ensure the consistent progress of the simulation, the input value $input_i$ proposed by the simulator q_i to $SAFE\_AG[j, snapsn]$ is defined as follows.

operation sim_snapshot$_{i,j}$():
(01) $sm_i \leftarrow MEM$.snapshot():
(02) **for each** $y : 1 \leq y \leq n$: **do** $input_i[y] = sm_i[s][y].value$
(03) **where** $\forall x : 1 \leq x \leq t+1 : sm_i[s][y].sn \geq sm_i[x][y].sn$ **end for**;
(04) $snap\_sn_i[j] \leftarrow snap\_sn_i[j] + 1$; **let** $snapsn = snap\_sn_i[j]$;
(05) enter_mutex; $SAFE\_AG[j, snapsn]$.propose$_i(input_i)$; exit_mutex;
(06) $res \leftarrow SAFE\_AG[j, snapsn]$.decide$_i$()
(07) return(res).

Fig. 4. sim_snapshot$_{i,j}$() executed by q_i to simulate mem.snapshot() issued by p_j (from [7])

- First, q_i issues a snapshot of MEM in order to obtain a consistent view of the simulation state. The value of this snapshot is kept in sm_i (line 01).
  Let us observe that $sm_i[x][y]$ is such that (1) $sm_i[x][y].sn$ is the number of writes issued by p_y into $mem[y]$ that have been simulated up to now by q_x, and (2) $sm_i[x][y].value$ is the value of the last write into $mem[y]$ as simulated by q_x on behalf of p_y.
- Then, for each p_y, q_i computes $input_i[y]$. To that end, it extracts from $sm_i[1..t+1][y]$ the value written by the more advanced simulator q_s as far as the simulation of p_y is concerned. This is expressed in lines 02-03.

Once $input_i$ has been computed, q_i proposes it to $SAFE\_AG[j, snapsn]$ (line 05), and then returns the value decided by that object (lines 06-07).

The previous description shows an important feature of the BG simulation. A value $input_i[y] = sm_i[s][y].value$ proposed by simulator q_i can be such that $sm_i[s][y].sn > sm_i[i][y].sn$, i.e., the simulator q_s is more advanced than q_i as far as the simulation of p_y is concerned. This causes no problem, as when q_i will simulate mem.snapshot() operations for p_y (if any) that are between the $(sm_i[i][y].sn)$-th and the $(sm_i[s][y].sn)$-th write operations of p_y, it will obtain a value that has already been computed and is currently kept in the corresponding $SAFE\_AG[y, -]$ object.

Underlying principle of the BG simulation [6,7]*: from wait-freedom to t-resilience.* Each simulator q_i simulates the n processes $p_1, \ldots, p_n$ "in parallel" and in a fair way. But any simulator q_i can crash. The crash of q_i while it is engaged in the simulation of mem.snapshot() on behalf of several processes p_j, $p_{j'}$, etc., can entail their definitive blocking, i.e., their crash. This is because each $SAFE\_AG[j, -]$ object guarantees that its $SAFE\_AG[j, -]$.decide() invocations do terminate only if no simulator crashes while executing $SAFE\_AG[j, -]$.propose() (line 05 of Figure 4).

The simple (and bright) idea of the BG simulation to solve this problem consists in allowing a simulator to be engaged in only one $SAFE\_AG[-, -]$.propose() invocation at a time. Hence, if q_i crashes while executing $SAFE\_AG[j, -]$.propose(), it can entail the crash of p_j only. This is obtained by using an additional mutual exclusion object offering the operations enter_mutex and exit_mutex. (Let us notice that such a mutex object is purely local to each simulator: it solves conflicts among the simulating threads inside each simulator, and has nothing to do with the memory shared by the simulators).

From t-resilience to wait-freedom. As an example let us consider we have a t-resilient algorithm that solves the (n, t) agreement problem. We obtain a wait-free algorithm that solves the $(t+1, t)$ agreement problem as follows. Each simulator q_i $(1 \leq i \leq t+1)$ is initially given a proposed value v_i, and the base objects $SAFE\_AG[1..n, 0]$ are used by the $(t+1)$ simulators as follows to determine the value proposed by p_j. For each j, $1 \leq j \leq n$, the simulator q_i invokes first $SAFE\_AG[j, 0].\mathsf{propose}_i(v_i)$ and then $SAFE\_AG[j, 0].\mathsf{decide}_i()$ that returns it a value that it considers as the value proposed by p_j. It is easy to see that, for any j, all the simulators obtain the same value for p_j. Moreover, this value is one of the $t+1$ values proposed by the simulators. Finally, simulator process q_i can decide any of the values decided by the processes p_j it is simulating. (It is easy to see that the BG simulation is for colorless decision tasks.) A formal proof of this reduction (based on input/output automata) can be found in [7].

From wait-freedom to t-resilience. For colorless decision tasks, t-resilience can easily be reduced to wait-freedom as follows. First, each application process deposits its input value in a shared register. Then, every process of the $t+1$ processes of the wait-free algorithm takes one of those values as its input value and executes its code. Finally, each application process decides any value decided by a process of the wait-free algorithm.

6 The Extended BG Simulation

This section extends the previous algorithms in order to solve the extended BG simulation. Our aim is to obtain an implementation that is "as simple as possible". To that end, we proceed incrementally by "only" enriching the previous base BG simulation. The proposed implementation uses the same snapshot object MEM and the same $\mathsf{sim\_write}_{i,j}()$ operation (Figure 3) as the base BG simulation. It also uses the same $SAFE\_AG[1..n, 0...]$ array made up of safe_agreement type objects.

This section presents the additional shared objects that are used, the underlying principles on which relies the implementation of $mem.\mathsf{snaspshot}()$ issued by a simulator q_i on behalf of a simulated process p_j, and the algorithm (denoted $\mathsf{e\_sim\_snapshot}_{i,j}()$) that implements it.

6.1 The Additional Shared Objects

In addition to MEM and $SAFE\_AG[1..n, 0...]$, the memory shared by the simulators $q_1, \ldots, q_{t+1}$ contains the following objects.

- $ARBITER[1..t+1, 0...]$ is an array of arbiter objects. The objects contained in $ARBITER[j, -]$ are owned by the simulator q_j $(1 \leq j \leq t+1)$.
  The object $ARBITER[j, snapsn]$ is used by a simulator q_i when it simulates its $snapsn$-th invocation $mem.\mathsf{snapshot}()$ on behalf of the simulated process p_j for $1 \leq j \leq t+1$. (As we will see, when $t+1 < j \leq n$, the simulation of $mem.\mathsf{snapshot}()$ on behalf of p_j does not require the help of an arbiter object.)
- $ARB\_VAL[1..t+1, 0...][0..1]$ is an array of pairs of atomic registers. The pair of atomic registers $ARB\_VAL[j, snapsn][0..1]$ is used in conjunction with the arbiter object $ARBITER[j, snapsn]$.

The aim of $ARB\_VAL[j, snapsn][1]$ is to contain the value that has to be returned to the $snapsn$-th invocation mem.snapshot(), on behalf of the simulated process p_j, if the owner q_j is designated as the winner by the associated object $ARBITER[j, snapsn]$. If the owner q_j is not the winner, the value that has to be returned is the one kept in $ARB\_VAL[j, snapsn][0]$.

6.2 The e_sim_snapshot$_{i,j}$() Operation

The enriched algorithm. The algorithm implementing the operation e_sim_snapshot$_{i,j}$() executed by q_i to simulate a mem.snapshot() operation issued by p_j is described in Figure 5. Its first four lines and its last line are exactly the same as in Figure 4. The lines 05-06 are replaced by the new lines N01-N14 that constitutes the "addition" that allows going from the BG to the extended BG simulation.

Underlying principle. Albeit each simulated process p_j ($1 \leq j \leq n$) is simulated by each simulator q_i ($1 \leq i \leq t+1$) as in the BG simulation, each simulated process p_j such that $1 \leq j \leq t+1$ is associated with exactly one simulator that is its "owner": q_i is the owner of p_j if $j = i$ (and also the owner of the corresponding objects $ARBITER[j, -]$). The aim is, for any $snapsn \geq 0$, to associate a single returned value with the $snapsn$-th invocations of e_sim_snapshot$_{i,j}$() issued by the simulators. The idea is to use the ownership notion to "shortcut" the use of $SAFE\_AG[j, snapsn]$ object in appropriate circumstances.

The operation e_sim_snapshot$_{i,j}$() for the simulated processes p_j such that $t+2 \leq j \leq n$, is exactly the same as sim_snapshot$_{i,j}$(). This appears in the lines N02-N03 that are the same as the lines 06-07 of Figure 4 (in that case, there is no ownership notion).

operation e_sim_snapshot$_{i,j}$():
(01) $sm_i \leftarrow MEM$.snapshot():
(02) **for each** $y : 1 \leq y \leq n$: **do** $input_i[y] = sm_i[s, y].value$
(03) **where** $\forall x : 1 \leq x \leq t+1 : sm_i[s, y].sn \geq sm_i[x, y].sn$ **end for**;
(04) $snap\_sn_i[j] \leftarrow snap\_sn_i[j] + 1$; **let** $snapsn = snap\_sn_i[j]$;
(N01) **if** $(j > t+1)$
(N02) **then** enter_mutex; $SAFE\_AG[j, snapsn]$.propose$_i(input_i)$; exit_mutex;
(N03) $res \leftarrow SAFE\_AG[j, snapsn]$.decide$_i$()
(N04) **else if** $(i = j)$
(N05) **then** $ARB\_VAL[j, snapsn][1] \leftarrow input_i$;
(N06) enter_mutex; $win \leftarrow ARBITER[j, snapsn]$.arbitrate$_{i,j}$(); exit_mutex;
(N07) **if** $(win = 1)$ **then** $res \leftarrow input_i$
(N08) **else** $res \leftarrow ARB\_VAL[j, snapsn][0]$ **end if**;
(N09) **else** enter_mutex; $SAFE\_AG[j, snapsn]$.propose$(input_i)$; exit_mutex;
(N10) $ARB\_VAL[j, snapsn][0] \leftarrow SAFE\_AG[j, snapsn]$.decide$_i$();
(N11) $r \leftarrow ARBITER[j, snapsn]$.arbitrate$_{i,j}$();
(N12) $res \leftarrow ARB\_VAL[j, snapsn][r]$
(N13) **end if**
(N14) **end if**;
(07) return(res).

Fig. 5. e_sim_snapshot$_{i,j}$() executed by q_i to simulate mem.snapshot() issued by p_j

The new lines N04-N14 address the case of the simulated processes owned by a simulator, i.e., the processes $p_1, \ldots, p_{t+1}$. The idea is the following: if q_i does not crash, p_i must not crash. In that way, if q_i is correct, p_i will always terminate whatever the behavior of the other simulators. To that end, q_i on one side, and all the other simulators on the other side, compete to define the snapshot value returned by the $snapsn$-th invocations e_sim_snapshot$_{i,j}$() issued by each of them. To attain this goal, the additional objects $ARBITER[j, snapsn]$ and $ARB\_VAL[j, snapsn]$ are used as follows.

All the simulators invoke $ARBITER[j, snapsn]$.arbitrate$_{i,j}$() (at line N06 if q_i is the owner, and line N11 if it is not). According to the specification of the arbiter type, these invocations do not return different values, and do return at least when the owner q_j is correct and invokes that operation (as indicated in the specification, there are other cases where the invocations do terminate). Finally, the value returned indicates if the winner is the owner (1) or not (0).

If the winner is the owner q_j, the value returned by the $snapsn$-th invocations of e_sim_snapshot$_{i,j}$() (one invocation by simulator) is the value $input_j$ computed by the owner. That value is kept in the atomic register $ARB\_VAL[j, snapsn][1]$ (line N05).

If the owner is not the winner, the value returned is the one determined by the other simulators that invoked $SAFE\_AG[j, snapsn]$.propose$_i$($input_i$) (line N09) and $SAFE\_AG[j, snapsn]$.decide$_i$() (line N10). The value they have computed has been deposited in $ARB\_VAL[j, snapsn][0]$ (line N10), and this value is used as the result of the $SAFE\_AG[j, snapsn]$ object.

It is important to notice that the owner q_j does not invoke the propose$_j$() and decide$_j$() operations on the objects it owns. Moreover, the simulator q_j is the only simulator that can write $ARB\_VAL[j, snapsn][1]$, while the other simulators can only write $ARB\_VAL[j, snapsn][0]$.

To summarize, if a simulator q_i crashes, it entails the crash of at most one simulated process. This is ensured thanks to the mutex algorithm. If the simulator q_i crashes, $1 \leq i \leq t+1$, as far the simulated processes are concerned, it can entail either no crash at all (if q_i crashes outside a critical section), or the crash of p_i (if it crashes while executing arbitrate$_{i,j}$() inside the critical section at line N06), or the crash of a process p_j such that $1 \leq j \neq i \leq t+1$ (this can occur only if q_j has crashed and was not winner, and q_i crashes inside the critical section at line N09), or the crash of one of the processes p_{t+2}, ..., p_n (if it crashes at line N02 inside the critical section).

t-Resilience vs wait-freedom. Given a BG simulation algorithm where a simulated process p_j ($1 \leq j \leq t+1 \leq n$) can be blocked forever only if simulator q_j crashes, Gafni shows in [12] that wait-freedom and t-resilience are equivalent for decision tasks (he also shows strong results on equivalence between weak renaming and weak symmetry breaking).

7 Proof of the Extended BG Simulation

Lemma 1. *A simulator can block the progression of only one simulated process at a time.*

Proof. A simulator can block the simulation of a process only during the execution of an e_sim_snapshot() operation, when the simulator uses a safe_agreement (lines N02-N03 or N09-N10) or an arbiter object because it is its owner (line N06). All these invocations are placed in mutual exclusion. Thus a simulator can block the simulation of only a single process at a time. $\square_{Lemma\ 1}$

Lemma 2. *The simulated process p_i is never blocked at the simulator q_i.*

Proof. The e_sim_snapshot() operation, when invoked by simulator q_i for the simulated process p_i (line N04, $i = j$) does not include any wait statement and does not use a safe_agreement object. Due to the properties of the arbiter object type, it cannot be blocked during its invocation of arbitrate(). Thus, the simulated process p_i can never be blocked at simulator q_i. $\square_{Lemma\ 2}$

Lemma 3. *Each simulator receives the decision value of at least $n - t$ simulated processes.*

Proof. Because at most t simulators may crash, and a simulator can block at most a single simulated process at a time (Lemma 1), each simulator can execute the code of at least $n - t$ simulated processes without being blocked forever. Because the simulated algorithm is t-resilient, these $n - t$ processes will then decide a value. $\square_{Lemma\ 3}$

Lemma 4. *All the simulators that return from the simulation of the k-th snapshot issued by the the simulated process p_j do return the same value for that snapshot.*

Proof. If p_j isn't owned by any simulator ($j > t + 1$), because of the properties of the safe_agreement objects, the same value is always returned (lines N02-N03 of Figure 5).

If the owner of p_j chooses the value it has computed for p_j's k-th snapshot, it has written this value in $ARB\_VAL[j, snapsn][1]$ (line N05), and is the winner of the arbiter object (line N06). All other simulators will then read its value (line N12).

If the simulated process p_j has an owner but another process chooses the value it has computed for p_j's k-th snapshot, this process has already agreed on a value with all other non owner processes (safe_agreement object, lines N09-N10) and is the winner of the arbiter object (lines N11-N12). All non-owner processes will then write the same value in $ARB\_VAL[j, snapsn][0]$ (line N10) and the owner will read it (line N08).

Thus, all the simulators that return a value for the k-th snapshot of the simulated process p_j return the same value. $\square_{Lemma\ 4}$

Lemma 5. *At most one decision value can be decided by a simulated process on any simulator.*

Proof. Because every simulator computes the same value for any given snapshot and because the snapshot operations are the only non-deterministic parts of codes of the simulated processes, all simulators that decide a value for a given simulated process decide the same value. $\square_{Lemma\ 5}$

Lemma 6. *The sequences of all writes and snapshots for each simulated process correspond to a correct execution of the simulated algorithm.*

Proof. Every simulator that is not blocked while simulating a process simulates it in the same way (same values written and same snapshots read, Lemma 4).

When simulator q_i executes e_sim_snapshot() for p_j (i.e. the simulation of a snapshot for p_j), it stores in its $input_i$ variable the values written by the simulators that have advanced the most for each simulated process (Figure 3 and lines 01-03 of Figure 5). It can choose its own $input_i$ snapshot value only if no other simulator has already ended the execution of this e_sim_snapshot() (Lemma 4 implies that safe_agreement objects have a "memory" effect). Thus, for each e_sim_snapshot(), q_i returns an $input$ value computed by itself or another simulator. Let us notice that, when this $input$ value has been determined, no simulator had terminated its associated e_sim_snapshot(). (If this was not the case, that simulator would have provided the other simulators with its own $input$ value.) Because processes are simulated deterministically, the $input$ value returned contains the last value written by p_j as seen by q_i. This shows that the simulated process order is respected.

To ensure that the simulation is correct, we then have to show that the writes and snapshots of all processes can be linearized. The linearization point of the writes is placed at line 03 of Figure 3 of the first simulator that executes it. The linearization point of the snapshots is placed at line 01 of Figure 5 of the simulator q_i that imposes its $input_i$ value.

Because the simulator q_i that imposes its $input_i$ value in a e_sim_snapshot() operation reads the most advanced values at the time of its snapshot (lines 02-03 of Figure 5), and because once a simulator finishes the execution of e_sim_snapshot(), the value for this e_sim_snapshot() cannot change (Lemma 4), the linearization correspond to a linearization of a correct execution of the simulated algorithm. $\Box_{Lemma\ 6}$

Theorem 1. *The extended BG simulation algorithms described in Figures 3 and 5 are correct.*

Proof. Lemmas 2, 3, 5 and 6 show that the extended BG simulation algorithms presented here are correct. $\Box_{Theorem\ 1}$

Acknowledgments

The authors want to thank E. Gafni, S. Rajsbaum, and C. Travers for interesting discussions on the BG-simulation, and the referees for their constructive comments.

References

1. Afek, Y., Attiya, H., Dolev, D., Gafni, E., Merritt, M., Shavit, N.: Atomic Snapshots of Shared Memory. Journal of the ACM 40(4), 873–890 (1993)
2. Afek, Y., Gafni, E., Rajsbaum, S., Raynal, M., Travers, C.: Simultaneous consensus tasks: a tighter characterization of set consensus. In: Chaudhuri, S., Das, S.R., Paul, H.S., Tirthapura, S. (eds.) ICDCN 2006. LNCS, vol. 4308, pp. 331–341. Springer, Heidelberg (2006)
3. Attiya, H., Bar-Noy, A., Dolev, D., Peleg, D., Reischuk, R.: Renaming in an Asynchronous Environment. Journal of the ACM 37(3), 524–548 (1990)

4. Attiya, H., Rachman, O.: Atomic Snapshots in O($n \log n$) Operations. SIAM Journal on Computing 27(2), 319–340 (1998)
5. Attiya, H., Welch, J.: Distributed Computing, Fundamentals, Simulation and Advanced Topics, 2nd edn. Wiley Series on Par. and Distributed Computing, 414 pages (2004)
6. Borowsky, E., Gafni, E.: Generalized FLP Impossibility Results for t-Resilient Asynchronous Computations. In: Proc. 25th ACM Symposium on Theory of Computing (STOC 1993), pp. 91–100. ACM Press, New York (1993)
7. Borowsky, E., Gafni, E., Lynch, N., Rajsbaum, S.: The BG distributed simulation algorithm. Distributed Computing 14(3), 127–146 (2001)
8. Castañeda, A., Rajsbaum, S.: New Combinatorial Topology Upper and Lower Bounds for Renaming. In: Proc. 27th ACM Symposium on Principles of Distributed Computing (PODC 2008), Toronto, Canada, pp. 295–304. ACM Press, New York (2008)
9. Chaudhuri, S.: More *Choices* Allow More *Faults:* Set Consensus Problems in Totally Asynchronous Systems. Information and Computation 105, 132–158 (1993)
10. Fischer, M.J., Lynch, N.A., Paterson, M.S.: Impossibility of Distributed Consensus with One Faulty Process. Journal of the ACM 32(2), 374–382 (1985)
11. Gafni, E.: Round-by-round Fault Detectors: Unifying Synchrony and Asynchrony. In: Proc. 17th ACM Symp. on Principles of Distr. Computing (PODC 1998), pp. 143–152. ACM Press, New York (1998)
12. Gafni, E.: The Extended BG Simulation and the Characterization of t-Resiliency. In: Proc. 41st ACM Symposium on Theory of Computing (STOC 2009). ACM Press, New York (2009)
13. Herlihy, M., Shavit, N.: The Topological Structure of Asynchronous Computability. Journal of the ACM 46(6), 858–923 (1999)
14. Imbs, D., Raynal, M.: Visiting Gafni's Reduction Land: from the BG Simulation to the Extended BG Simulation. Tech Report #1931, IRISA, Université de Rennes (F) (2009)
15. Loui, M.C., Abu-Amara, H.H.: Memory Requirements for Agreement Among Unreliable Asynchronous Processes. In: Par. and Distributed Computing. Advances in Comp. Research, vol. 4, pp. 163–183. JAI Press (1987)
16. Lynch, N.A.: Distributed Algorithms, 872 pages. Morgan Kaufmann Pub., San Francisco (1996)
17. Saks, M., Zaharoglou, F.: Wait-Free k-Set Agreement is Impossible: The Topology of Public Knowledge. SIAM Journal on Computing 29(5), 1449–1483 (2000)

Randomized Gathering of Mobile Robots with Local-Multiplicity Detection*

Taisuke Izumi[1], Tomoko Izumi[2], Sayaka Kamei[3], and Fukuhito Ooshita[4]

[1] Graduate School of Engineering, Nagoya Institute of Technology
t-izumi@nitech.ac.jp
[2] College of Information Science and Engineering, Ritsumeikan University
izumi-t@fc.ritsumei.ac.jp
[3] Graduate School of Engineering, Hiroshima University
s-kamei@se.hiroshima-u.ac.jp
[4] Graduate School of Information Science and Technology, Osaka University
f-oosita@ist.osaka-u.ac.jp

Abstract. Let us consider the gathering problem of n anonymous and oblivious mobile robots, which requires that all robots meet in finite time at a non-predefined point. While the gathering problem cannot be solved deterministically without any additional capability to robots, randomized approach easily allows it to be solvable. However, only the randomized solution taking expected round complexity exponential of n is currently known. Motivated by this fact, we investigate the feasibility of polynomial-expected-round randomized gathering in this paper. Our first contribution is to give a negative result about the round complexity of randomized gathering. It is proved that any algorithm without no additional assumption has $\Omega(\exp(n))$ expected-round lower bound. This lower bound yields a question: What additional assumptions are necessary to achieve gathering in polynomial expected rounds? We address this question from the aspect of multiplicity detection. This paper newly introduces two weaker variants of multiplicity detection capability, called *local-strong* and *local-weak* multiplicity, and investigates whether those capabilities permit polynomial-expected-round gathering or not. Our second contribution is to reveal the power of local (strong/weak) multiplicity by showing that local-strong multiplicity detection allows $O(n)$-expected round gathering but local-weak multiplicity detection takes an exponential-time lower bound. These results imply that those two kinds of multiplicity-detection capabilities have inherently large difference about their computational powers.

1 Introduction

1.1 Background and Motivation

Algorithmic studies about cooperations among a large number of autonomous mobile robots are recently emerging in the distributed computing community. In

* This work is supported in part by The Telecommunication Advancement Foundation and Grand-in-Aid for Young Scientists ((B)19700075) of JSPS.

R. Guerraoui and F. Petit (Eds.): SSS 2009, LNCS 5873, pp. 384–398, 2009.

most of those studies, a robot is modeled as a point in a plane, and its capability is quite weak: It is usually assumed that robots are *oblivious* (no memory to record past situations), *anonymous* (no ID to distinguish two robots), and *uniform* (all robots run an identical algorithm). In addition, it is also assumed that each robot has no direct means of communication. The communication between two robots is done in the implicit way that each robot observes the environment, which includes the positions of other robots. From the theoretical aspect, it is an interesting problem to clarify the weakest capability of robot systems to accomplish a given task. The *gathering problem* is one of fundamental coordination tasks in theoretical mobile robotics, which requires that all robots meet in finite time at a point that is not predefined. Because of its simplicity, the gathering problem is actively studied before now. However, it has been proved that the gathering problem is unsolvable in oblivious and anonymous robot systems without no additional assumption. This impossibility result raises the interest to the necessary assumptions for the gathering problem to be solvable. There are a number of studies showing possibility/impossibility results under different assumptions [1, 2, 4, 5, 8, 9, 10, 11, 12, 13, 7, 6, 3, 14].

In this paper, we focus on randomized solutions of the gathering problem in the semi-synchronous model. Since the essential difficulty of the gathering problem derives from the hardness of symmetry breaking among robots, it seems quite easy and trivial to design gathering algorithms by employing randomization. Despite such an intuition, the gathering problem remains hard even if randomization approach is available: It has been already proved that any randomized algorithm cannot solve the gathering problem with no restriction to schedulers [12, 9]. This impossibility can be broken by assuming the bounded regularity to the scheduler (that can be regarded as a certain kind of synchrony assumptions). Actually, there exists a simple randomized gathering algorithm under the bounded regularity [4]. However, the performance of the algorithm is quite poor. Its expected round complexity is exponential of the number of mobile robots. To the best of our knowledge, there has been no randomized gathering algorithm with polynomial expected running time.

1.2 Our Contribution

This paper investigates the feasibility of randomized gathering with polynomial expected rounds. The first question is whether it is possible to reduce such exponential round complexity to the polynomial or not. One of our contribution is to provide the negative answer for this question. We show that without no additional assumption, any algorithm must have $\Omega(\exp(n))$ round complexity under the bounded-regular scheduler. This lower bound yields our second question: What additional assumptions are necessary to achieve polynomial-round gathering? A trivial answer for this question is the assumption that makes the gathering problem deterministically solvable: The agreement of local views among robots [11, 10, 13, 8, 7, 6], a restriction to the initial location [14], and so on. However, in the context of our study, those assumptions should be regarded as too strong ones. Our focus is more weaker assumptions, which are not so powerful as to solve the gathering problem deterministically, but sufficient to permit polynomial-round randomized gathering. In this sense, the objective of our study is the discovery of such "intermediate" assumptions.

We address the second question by introducing two novel types of multiplicity detection capabilities. The multiplicity detection specifies how each robot observes the single location where two or more robots stay. In all of previous works, three types of multiplicity detection are proposed: No multiplicity (each robot cannot distinguish the location with a single robot from that with multiple robots), weak multiplicity (each robot can detect whether the number of robots on a point is only one or more than one), and strong multiplicity (each robot can know the number of robots on a point). In addition to these classification, we further introduce the notion of *locality* for multiplicity detection capability. The local multiplicity detection implies that each robot can detect the multiplicity only for its current location. On the other hand, the global multiplicity allows each robot to detect the multiplicity of any location. Notice that locality is an orthogonal classification to the existing strong/weak classification. Thus, we can obtain five types of multiplicity detection totally: No multiplicity, local-weak multiplicity, local-strong multiplicity, global weak multiplicity, and global strong multiplicity.

Importantly, any kind of multiplicity detection is insufficient to achieve deterministic gathering for arbitrary initial configurations. It can be easily understood by a simple observation. Assume the system consisting of $n = 2n'$ robots. We divide all robots into two groups of n' robots, and consider the initial configuration where all robots in one group are placed on a point P, and the other group are placed on another point P'. Then, if the scheduler always activates all robots in each group simultaneously, each group will behave as a single robot without multiplicity detection (i.e., any multiplicity detection provides no information because two locations are occupied by the same number of robots, and thus they are identically observed). Thus, we can obtain the impossibility of gathering from that in the system without multiplicity detection. Actually, all of previous studies about the gathering problem based on multiplicity detection implicitly assumes that all robots are located on different points initially [2]. In that sense, any kind of multiplicity detection can become a candidate of the assumptions we explore.

This paper clarifies the feasibility of polynomial-round randomized gathering under the assumption of local (strong/weak) multiplicity detection for any initial configuration. The followings are precise descriptions of our results:

- Even if we assume local-weak multiplicity, any randomized gathering algorithm takes $\Omega(\exp(n))$ expected-round lower bound.
- With local-strong multiplicity, we can construct a randomized gathering algorithm which can start from any initial configuration and achieves gathering in $O(n)$ expected rounds.

These two results imply that local-strong multiplicity is sufficient to achieve polynomial-expected-round randomized gathering, and a large gap of computational power lies between local-strong and local-weak multiplicity detection.

Only the known result that considers randomized gathering with multiplicity detection is one by Clement et.al. [3]. It proposes an $O(n)$-expected-round randomized gathering algorithm using global-strong multiplicity detection. Our study can be regarded as an improvement of this result by introducing the notion of local multiplicity detection.

1.3 Organization

In Section 2, we present the model of autonomous mobile robots considered in this paper, and introduce other necessary notations and definitions. Section 3 provides $\Omega(\exp(n))$ expected-round lower bound under the assumption of local-weak multiplicity. We show in Section 4 the possibility result that $O(n)$-expected-round randomized gathering is possible with the support of local-strong multiplicity detection. Finally we conclude this paper in Section 5.

2 Preliminaries

The robot model considered in this paper is the *semi-synchronous model*, which is one of standard models in the context of the algorithmic studies of mobile robots.

2.1 The System Model

The system consists of a set of autonomous mobile robots $\mathcal{R} = \{R_0, R_1, \cdots, R_{n-1}\}$. Robots are *anonymous* and *oblivious*. That is, each robot has no identifier distinguishing itself and others, and cannot explicitly remember the history of its execution. In addition, no device for direct communication is equipped. The cooperation of robots is done in an implicit manner: Each robot has a sensor device to observe the environment (i.e., the positions of other robots). One robot is modeled as a point located on a two-dimensional space. To specify the location of each robot consistently, we introduce the global Cartesian coordinate system. Notice that the global coordinate system is introduced only for ease of explanations, and thus each robot cannot be aware of them. Also, any knowledge about the number of robots n is not available to each robot. Each robot executes the deployed algorithm in *computational cycles* (or briefly *cycles*). At the beginning of a cycle, the robot observes the current environment (i.e., the positions of other robots) and determines the destination point based on the deployed algorithm. Then, the robot moves toward the computed destination. It is guaranteed that each robot necessarily reaches the computed destination at the end of the cycle.

The observation of an environment is represented as the set of points on the *local coordinate system* that the observer has. The local coordinate system of a robot is the Cartesian coordinate system whose origin is the current position of the robot. There is no agreement to the direction and unit length of local coordinate systems among robots.

The point where at least one robot stays is called *robot location* (or briefly *location*). The number of robots staying on a location is called the *multiplicity number* of the location. If a location p has a multiplicity number more than one, we say p is *multiple*. Otherwise, p is said to be *single*. The capability of *multiplicity detection* specifies how each robot observes multiple locations. In this paper, we consider the following two types of multiplicity detection:

- **Local-weak multiplicity**: Each robot can detect whether its current location is multiple or single.
- **Local-strong multiplicity**: Each robot can detect the multiplicity number of its current location.

We assume the semi-synchronism as the timing model. In the semi-synchronous model, an execution is divided into consecutive *rounds*, where at most one cycle can be performed. The set of performing robots for each round is determined by the *scheduler*. At any round $t = 0, 1, 2, \cdots$, the scheduler determines whether each robot is *active* or *inactive*. Active robots perform one cycle in the synchronized manner, and inactive ones wait during the round. In this paper, we assume the *bounded-regular* scheduler, which guarantees that if a robot is activated at round t_1 and t_2 ($t_1 < t_2$), any robot is activated at least once during $[t_1, t_2]$.

Throughout this paper, we use the notations defined as follows: For any two points A and B, $|AB|$ denotes the length of the segment whose endpoints are A and B. A *configuration* is the multiset consisting of all robot locations. We define $C(t)$ as the configuration at t. We also define the point set $P(C)$ of a configuration C to be the set of all locations without multiplicity. For short, we call $P(C(t))$ the point set at t, and it is denoted by $P(t)$.

2.2 Gathering Problem

The *gathering problem* must ensure that all robots eventually meet at a point that is not predefined, starting from any configuration. Formally, we say that an algorithm $\mathcal{A}$ solves the gathering problem if any execution of $\mathcal{A}$ eventually reaches and keeps a configuration with exactly one robot location.

3 $\Omega(\exp(n))$-Round Lower Bound

First, we consider the impossibility of gathering with polynomial expected rounds. More precisely, the primary result shown in this section is the following theorem:

Theorem 1. *In the system of n mobile robots with local-weak multiplicity detection, any gathering algorithm has $\Omega(\exp(n))$ running time in expectation.*

Proof. Let A be a randomized gathering algorithm that works correctly with local-weak multiplicity detection. We show the adversarial bounded-regular schedule of A such that the expected length of the corresponding execution is $\Omega(\exp(n))$. The schedule is constructed by repeating the following strategy:

> Let $P_0, P_1, \cdots, P_k$ be a sequence of robot locations at t ($k \geq 1$), and S_i be the set of robots staying on P_i at t. We assume at least one point has

multiplicity more than three and that point is P_k, i.e., $|S_k| \geq 3$ holds. During each round in $t+r \in [t, t+k-1]$, all robots in S_r are simultaneously activated. At round $t+k$, we consider the following four strategies: (1) Activating only all robots on S_k simultaneously, (2) activating all robots in the system simultaneously, (3-A) activating all robots in the system except for two robots in S_k at $t+k$ and the remaining two robots at $t+k+1$, or (3-B) activating all robots in the system except for two robots in S_k at $t+k$, and then all robots in the system at $t+k+1$. The choice of the scheduler depends on the current configuration and the algorithm (which is explained below).

It is clear that the constructed schedule is bounded-regular. Then, if we prove that the probability p of achieving gathering during $[t, t+k]$ (or $[t, t+k+1]$) is bounded by $O(1/\exp(n))$, it can be concluded that the expected running time of A under our scheduler strategy becomes $\Omega(\exp(n))$. Thus, the remaining part of the proof is to show the upper bound. It is obtained by considering the following cases:

- **Case 1** $|P(t+k)| \geq 3$: The scheduler chooses the strategy (1). Since the number of robot locations decreases at most one at each round, the gathering is never achieved at $t+k+1$ in this case, that is, $p = 0$.
- **Case 2** $|P(t+k)| = 2$: Let $P(t+k) = \{P_l, P_k\}$, and m_l and m_k be the multiplicity numbers of P_l and P_k respectively. Let $x \in \{l, k\}$ be one satisfying $m_x = \max\{m_l, m_k\}$. Notice that $m_x = \Omega(n)$. Among P_l and P_k, we denote the point that is not P_x by P_y. We also define the probability q as one that a robot on P_x at $t+k$ moves to some point other than P_x for its activation. This case is further divided into the following four subcases:
  - **Case2A** $0 < q < 1$: Then, for the strategy (2), the probability that all robots on P_x stay on the same point is bounded by $q^{m_x} + (1-q)^{m_x} = O(1/\exp(n))$. This bounds also can become the upper bound for p.
  - **Case2B** $q = 1$ and $m_x \leq n-2$: Let P' be the midpoint of P_x and P_y. Importantly, in this case, the views observed by robots on P_x and P_y is the same. Thus, for the strategy (2), the movement by the robots on P_y is symmetric about P' to that by the robots on P_x. Then, if all robots are not gathered at $t+k+1$, we clearly obtain $q = 0$ by the strategy (2). Otherwise, the possible scenario achieving gathering by applying the strategy (2) is that all robots gather on P'. If such a scenario occurs, the activations of only the robots on P_k can prevent all robots from gathering at $t+k+1$. That is, we can obtain $q = 0$ by adopting the strategy (1).
  - **Case2C** $q = 1$ and $m_x = n-1$: In this case, we adopt the strategy (3-A) or (3-B). Since all activated robots in S_k leave P_k with probability one, in the strategy (3-A/B), $|P(t+k+1)| > 1$ necessarily holds. If $|P(t+k+1)| \geq 3$ holds, we can reduce this case to Case 1, where the two remaining robots can be regarded as ones on P_k in Case 1, and the choice of the strategy (1) in Case 1 corresponds to adopting the strategy (3-A). Similarly, if $|P(t+k+1)| = 2$ holds, the case can be reduced to

Case2B or 2A, where the choice of the strategy (1) or (2) in those cases corresponds to adopting the strategy (3-A) or (3-B).

- **Case 2D** $q = 0$: We show this case never occurs by leading a contradiction. Consider another system of $2m_x$ robots and its configuration C' such that both P_l and P_k has m_x robots in C' respectively. In this configuration, the view observed by any robot in C' is the same as that by a robots on P_x in $C(t+k)$. Thus, no robot can move for any activation in C', and thus the gathering is impossible. This is a contradiction.

Consequently, the theorem is proved. □

4 $O(n)$-Expected Round Randomized Gathering with Local-Strong Multiplicity

This section shows that gathering is possible with $O(n)$ expected rounds if we assume local-strong multiplicity.

4.1 $O(n)$-Round Line Algorithm

In this subsection, we first show the algorithm ML (Making Line), which is used as a building block of our gathering algorithm. Starting from an arbitrary configuration, algorithm ML guarantees that the system eventually reaches a configuration where all robots are located on a single line within $O(n)$ rounds unless gathering is achieved.

Before presenting the detail of the algorithm, we first introduce several necessary definitions.

Definition 1. *A configuration C is* circular *if there exists a circle such that one location in $P(C)$ is on its center and all other locations are on its boundary.*

Definition 2. *A configuration C is* uniquely-circular *if there exists exactly one circle such that one point in $P(C)$ is on its center and all other locations are on its boundary.*

For any uniquely-circular configuration, we define the *corresponding circle* as one whose boundary and center contain any robot location in $P(C)$. For a round t such that $C(t)$ is uniquely-circular, we denote the corresponding circle of $C(t)$ by $D(t)$. The following propositions are fundamental facts about circular configurations.

Proposition 1. *Almost all circular configurations are uniquely-circular. The only exceptions are that the point set $P(C)$ of circular configuration C consists of (1) a segment, (2) a regular triangle (Figure 1), or (3) a regular diamond (Figure 2).*

Proposition 2. *Let $C(t)$ be a uniquely-circular configuration, and assume that one or more robots on $D(t)$ moves to the center of $D(t)$ at round t. Then, $C(t+1)$ is circular. In addition, if $C(t+1)$ is uniquely-circular, $D(t)$ and $D(t+1)$ have the same center.*

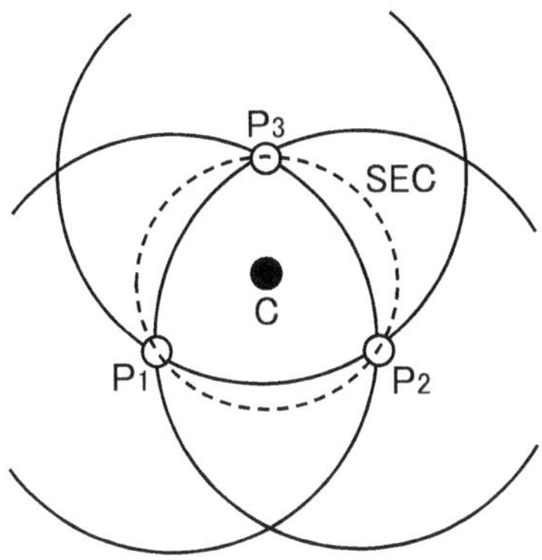

Fig. 1. Regular Triangle: A configuration circular but not uniquely-circular. Three locations P_1, P_2, and P_3 form a regular triangle. This point set has three candidates of corresponding circles (drawn in full line). The dotted circle means the SEC of this configuration.

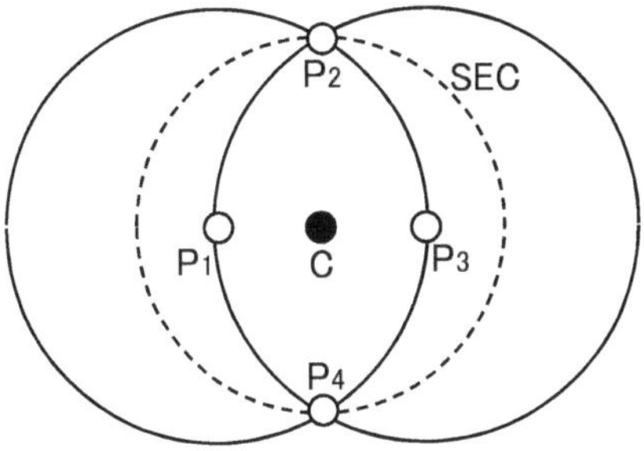

Fig. 2. Regular Diamond: Another configuration circular but not uniquely-circular. Locations P_1, P_2 and P_3 form a regular triangle, and P_1, P_3, and P_4 form its line-symmetric regular triangle. This point set has two candidates of corresponding circles.

The algorithm ML is quite simple. To make the line containing all robots, it tries to make all robots gather on two points: When a robot R_i is activated, it first checks whether the observed configuration is uniquely-circular or not. If it is uniquely-circular and R_i is on the corresponding circle, it moves to the center of the corresponding circle. Otherwise, R_i computes the *smallest enclosing circle* (SEC), which is the minimum-diameter circle containing all locations of robots. In this case, R_i moves to the center of SEC only if it is not on the boundary of SEC.

We concisely explain the correctness of this algorithm. First, we show that two exceptional configurations, regular triangle and regular diamond, are appropriately handled by our algorithm. Let us consider a configuration $C(t)$ where $P(t)$ forms a regular triangle. In this case, by the movement of robots to the center of SEC, the configuration becomes uniquely-circular (SEC becomes the corresponding circle) at $t+1$. After becoming uniquely-circular, any movement by the algorithm preserves the uniquely-circular property unless a line or gathering is achieved, and thus the system eventually reaches a two-location configuration (when only one robot location remains on the boundary of the corresponding circle). The case of regular diamond is also same. Let us consider a regular-diamond configuration $C(t)$. Then, the length of the segment formed by the farthest pair of robot locations in $P(t)$ (P_2 and P_4 in Figure 2) is equivalent to the diameter of the SEC. Thus, the robots on other two locations are not on the boundary of SEC. They move to the center of SEC, and when all of them reach the center, the configuration becomes a line.

The above explanation implies that the point set eventually forms a line if the current configuration is not uniquely-circular but circular. In addition, as long as the uniquely-circular property is kept, the number of robots on the boundary monotonically decreases and thus the configuration eventually becomes a line. These two facts imply that it is sufficient to show the correctness that the configuration eventually becomes circular: If the current configuration is not circular, the robots not on the boundary of SEC move to its center. Then, since robots on the boundary of SEC do not change their positions, SEC is preserved for those movements, and thus the system eventually reaches a circular configuration (If all robots are on the boundary of SEC, the configuration becomes circular when a robot on the boundary moves to the center of SEC).

More strictly, the correctness of the algorithm ML derives from the following lemmas, which can be easily proved from the above arguments.

Lemma 1. *Let t be the round when $C(t)$ is not uniquely-circular but circular. Then, there exists a round $t' \in [t+n]$ such that any location in $P(t')$ is on a common line.*

Lemma 2. *Let t be the round when $C(t)$ is not circular. Then, there exists a round $t' \in [t+n]$ such that $C(t')$ is circular.*

Lemma 3. *Let t be the round when $C(t)$ is uniquely-circular, and k be the number of robots on the boundary of the corresponding circle at t. If $C(t+1)$ is uniquely-circular, at most $k-1$ robots stay on the boundary at $t+1$.*

These lemmas and Proposition 2 imply the following theorem.

Theorem 2. *The algorithm* ML *guarantees that the system reaches a configuration where all robots stay on a common line within $O(n)$ rounds.*

4.2 Gathering from Line Using Local-Strong Multiplicity Detection

In this section, we show a randomized algorithm GfL (Gathering from Line) which guarantees that all robots staying on a line gather into a single point. This algorithm assumes the local-strong multiplicity detection, and takes $O(n)$ expected rounds. Thus, the composition of GfL and ML becomes the randomized gathering algorithm that uses local-strong multiplicity and achieves $O(n)$-expected rounds.

We explain the detailed behavior of algorithm GfL. In algorithm GfL, any movement is performed only on the line where all robots are initially located. Thus, for ease of presentation, we introduce the one-dimensional coordinate system on that line. The behavior of each robot is divided into two cases according to the number of robot locations. We show below the behavior of the algorithm when robot R is activated:

- The number of robot locations is two: Let P_1 and P_2 be the two robot locations, and we assume that R stays on P_2 without loss of generality. In this case, the destination of R is probabilistically determined. With probability $1/(4m)$ (m is the multiplicity number of P_2), R moves toward the opposite direction of P_1 by distance $2|P_1P_2|$. In addition, it also moves to P_1 with probability $1/(4m)$. Otherwise (i.e., with probability $1 - 1/(2m)$), it stays at its current location. See Figure 3(a).
- The number of robot locations is three or more: In this case, any activated robot moves to its nearest endpoint. More precisely, let $P_1, P_2, \cdots, P_k$ be all robot locations ordered by their coordinates in terms of R's local coordinate system, and assume R stays on P_j. In this case, R can move only when $j \neq 1$ and $j \neq k$. Then, R chooses the nearest of P_1 and P_k as its destination. That is, if $|P_1P_j| > |P_jP_k|$ holds, it moves to P_k. Otherwise (including the case of $|P_1P_j| = |P_jP_k|$), it moves to P_1. See Figure 3(b).

For a configuration C with three locations P_1, P_2, and P_3 (ordered by their coordinates), we say C is *isolated* if $|P_1P_2| \neq |P_2P_3|$ holds and the farthest location from P_2 is single. Intuitively, the correctness of algorithm GfL is understood as follows: Clearly, the case of three or more locations can be reduced to a two-location case. For two-location cases, we further consider two subsituations. The first subsituation is one where both of robot locations are multiple.

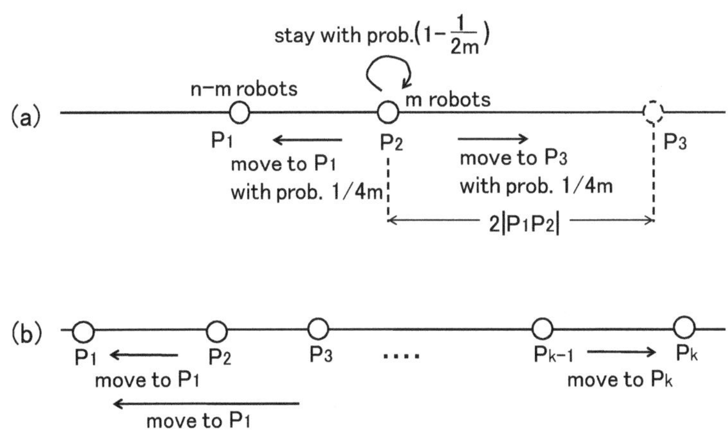

Fig. 3. The behavior of Algorithm GfL

Then, in following executions, exactly one robot R_i leaves those two locations with constant probability. Let P_1 and P_2 be the two robot locations before the movement, and assume R_i moves from P_2 to another point P_3. Then, because of $|P_2P_3| = 2|P_1P_2|$ (by the definition of the algorithm), the configuration after the movement is isolated, and thus any robot on P_2 eventually joins into P_1. Furthermore, since only R_i stays at P_3, the number of robots on P_1 after joining is $n-1$. Consequently, the first situation can be reduced into the second subsituation, where either of two locations is single. In this situation, the robot R_j on the single point joins to the other point with probability $1/4$ at its next activation and gathering is achieved. The only scenario obstructing the gathering is that a robot on the multiple point moves earlier than R_j's activation. However, the probability of occurring such scenario is bounded by a constant, and even if it occurs, the system can recover the second subsituation again within $O(n)$ expected rounds. Therefore, by repeating the second subsituation constant times, gathering is achieved in $O(n)$ expected rounds. In what follows, we give the strict proof of the correctness.

Lemma 4. *If a location P has multiplicity number $n-1$ at t, gathering is achieved by $t+n$ with probability at least* $1/8$.

Proof. Let R_i be the robot that does not stay on P, and t' be the first round after t when R_i is activated. Since we assume the bounded-regular scheduler, each robot is activated at most once during $[t, t']$ (notice that R_i is activated only once during the period). Thus, the probability that no robot on P moves at t' or earlier is lower bounded by

$$\left(1 - \frac{1}{2(n-1)}\right)^{n-1} \geq \left(1 - \frac{1 \cdot (n-1)}{2(n-1)}\right) \geq \frac{1}{2}.$$

Since R_i moves to P with probability $1/4$ for its activation, gathering is achieved at $t'+1$ with a probability more than or equal to $1/8$. In addition, because of bounded regularity of the scheduler, $t'+1 < t+n$ clearly holds. Therefore, the lemma holds. □

Lemma 5. *Assume that two locations P_1 and P_2 have multiplicity number $n-k$ and k $(n/2 \geq k > 1)$ at t_1 respectively. With probability at least* $1/32$, *there exists a round $t' \in [t_1, t_1+n]$ such that $C(t'+1)$ is isolated.*

Proof. Let t_1+t_2 be the earliest round after t_1 such that the times of activations during $[t_1, t_1+t_2]$ becomes more than or equal to n. In what follows, we prove the lemma by showing that the system reaches an isolated configuration at t_1+t_2 or earlier with probability more than or equal to $1/32$. Let X_h $(0 \leq h \leq t_2)$ be the indicator random variable such that $X_h = 1$ if no robot moves during $[t_1, t_1+h]$ and $X_h = 0$ otherwise. We also define Y to be the random variable representing the first round after t when exactly one robot moves (and thus the system becomes isolated). If such round does not exist during $[t_1, t_1+t_2]$, we define $Y = \infty$. We first show the bound for the probability $P[Y = h | X_{h-1} = 1]$

that exactly one robot moves at a round t_1+h under the condition that no robot moves by $t+h-1$. Let $j_1(h)$ and $j_2(h)$ be the number of robots on P_1 and P_2 activated at $t+h$ respectively. Notice that it clearly holds that $0 \le j_1(h) \le n-k$, $0 \le j_2(h) \le k$, and either $j_1(h)$ or $j_2(h)$ is non-zero. The probability is bounded as follows:

$$\begin{aligned}
P[Y=h|X_{h-1}=1] &\ge \binom{j_1(h)}{1}\frac{1}{4(n-k)}\left(1-\frac{1}{2(n-k)}\right)^{j_1(h)-1}\left(1-\frac{1}{2k}\right)^{j_2(h)} \\
&\quad+\binom{j_2(h)}{1}\frac{1}{4k}\left(1-\frac{1}{2(n-k)}\right)^{j_1(h)}\left(1-\frac{1}{2k}\right)^{j_2(h)-1} \\
&\ge \left(\frac{j_1(h)}{4(n-k)}+\frac{j_2(h)}{4k}\right)\left(1-\frac{1}{2(n-k)}\right)^{j_1(h)}\left(1-\frac{1}{2k}\right)^{j_2(h)} \\
&\ge \left(\frac{j_1(h)}{4(n-k)}+\frac{j_2(h)}{4k}\right)\left(1-\frac{j_1(h)}{2(n-k)}\right)\left(1-\frac{j_2(h)}{2k}\right) \\
&\ge \frac{1}{16}\left(\frac{j_1(h)}{(n-k)}+\frac{j_2(h)}{k}\right)
\end{aligned}$$

where we use the inequality $(1-(1/x))^y \ge 1-(y/x)$. Notice that the first line of this inequalities does not hold if $j_1(h)=0$ or $j_2(h)=0$, but even in the case, the second inequality holds and thus we can obtain lower bound $1/16$. We also bound the probability $P[X_{h-1}=1]$:

$$\begin{aligned}
P[X_{h-1}=1] &= \prod_{l=0}^{h-1}\left(1-\frac{1}{2(n-k)}\right)^{j_1(l)}\left(1-\frac{1}{2k}\right)^{j_2(l)} \\
&= \left(1-\frac{1}{2(n-k)}\right)^{\sum_{l=0}^{h-1} j_1(l)}\left(1-\frac{1}{2k}\right)^{\sum_{l=0}^{h-1} j_2(l)} \\
&\ge \left(1-\frac{\sum_{l=0}^{h-1} j_1(l)}{2(n-k)}\right)\left(1-\frac{\sum_{l=0}^{h-1} j_2(l)}{2k}\right)
\end{aligned}$$

From the definition of t_2, activations occur at most $n-1$ times during the period $[t_1, h-1]$ ($\subset [t_1, t_2]$). Furthermore, since we assume the bounded regularity, each robot is activated at most once in that period. This fact implies that $\sum_{l=0}^{h-1} j_1(l) \le (n-k)$ and $\sum_{l=0}^{h-1} j_2(l) \le k$ hold. Thus, we obtain the bound below.

$$\begin{aligned}
P[X_{h-1}=1] &\ge \left(1-\frac{\sum_{l=0}^{h-1} j_1(l)}{2(n-k)}\right)\left(1-\frac{\sum_{l=0}^{h-1} j_2(l)}{2k}\right) \\
&\ge \left(1-\frac{(n-k)}{2(n-k)}\right)\left(1-\frac{k}{2k}\right) \\
&\ge \frac{1}{4}
\end{aligned}$$

For simplicity of the proof, we also define $P[X_{-1} = 1] = 1$. Using the above inequalities, we give a bound for probability $P[Y = h]$:

$$\begin{aligned} P[Y = h] &\geq P[Y = h | X_{h-1} = 1] \cdot P[X_{h-1} = 1] \\ &\geq \frac{1}{64}\left(\frac{j_1(h)}{(n-k)} + \frac{j_2(h)}{k}\right). \end{aligned}$$

The probability p that an isolated configuration appears at t_2 or earlier is lower bounded by $\sum_{h=0}^{t_2} P[Y = h]$. From the definition of t_2, we have $\sum_{l=0}^{t_2} j_1(l) \geq (n-k)$ and $\sum_{l=0}^{t_2} j_2(l) \geq k$. Consequently, we obtain

$$\begin{aligned} p &\geq \sum_{h=0}^{t_2} P[Y = h] \\ &\geq \sum_{h=0}^{t_2} \frac{1}{64}\left(\frac{j_1(h)}{(n-k)} + \frac{j_2(h)}{k}\right) \\ &\geq \frac{1}{64}\left(\frac{\sum_{h=0}^{t_2} j_1(h)}{(n-k)} + \frac{\sum_{h=0}^{t_2} j_2(h)}{k}\right) \\ &\geq \frac{1}{64}\left(\frac{(n-k)}{(n-k)} + \frac{k}{k}\right) \\ &\geq \frac{1}{32}. \end{aligned}$$

The lemma is proved. □

Lemma 6. *If $|P(t)| \geq 3$ holds, there exists a round $t' \in [t, t+n]$ such that $|P(t')| \leq 2$ holds. In addition, if $C(t)$ is isolated, one location in $P(t')$ has multiplicity number $n-1$.*

Proof. Let $P_1, P_2, \cdots, P_k$ be all robot locations at t ordered by their coordinates. Because of the bounded regularity, all robots are activated at least once during the period $[t, t+n]$. Thus, each robot located on $P_2, P_3, \cdots$, or P_{k-1} at t necessarily moves either of P_1 or P_k by $t+n$. Letting $t'-1$ be the first round after t when all robots on $P_2, P_3, \cdots$, or P_{k-1} are activated, $|P(t')| \leq 2$ holds. If $C(t)$ is isolated (then, $k = 3$), all robots on P_2 move to the nearest endpoint (assume it is P_1 without loss of generality). By the definition of isolated configurations, the number of robots staying on P_1 or P_2 is $n-1$. Therefore, at t', P_1 has multiplicity $n-1$ (i.e., the summation of the multiplicity number of P_1 and P_2 at t). The lemma is proved. □

By combining the above three lemmas, we can obtain the following theorem, which directly implies that algorithm GfL achieves gathering in $O(n)$ expected rounds.

Theorem 3. *Starting from any configuration in one-dimensional space,* GfL *achieves gathering within $4n+1$ rounds with probability at least $1/256$.*

5 Concluding Remarks

This paper has investigated the feasibility of polynomial-round randomized gathering with polynomial expected rounds from the aspect of multiplicity detection capability. We first presented the impossibility result that any algorithm must have $\Omega(\exp(n))$ round complexity even under the bounded-regular scheduler and local-weak multiplicity detection capability. Then, we also constructed a randomized gathering algorithm which has the advantages of $O(n)$ expected round complexity, gathering from any initial configuration, and using only local-strong multiplicity detection. These two results imply that a large gap of computational power lies between those two capabilities.

References

1. Agmon, N., Peleg, D.: Fault-tolerant gathering algorithms for autonomous mobile robots. SIAM Journal of Computing 36(1), 56–82 (2006)
2. Cieliebak, M., Flocchini, P., Prencipe, G., Santoro, N.: Solving the robots gathering problem. In: Baeten, J.C.M., Lenstra, J.K., Parrow, J., Woeginger, G.J. (eds.) ICALP 2003. LNCS, vol. 2719, pp. 1181–1196. Springer, Heidelberg (2003)
3. Clement, J., Défago, X., Gradinariu, M., Izumi, T., Messika, S.: The cost of probabilistic agreement in oblivious robot networks (to submitted)
4. Défago, X., Gradinariu, M., Messika, S., Parvédy, P.R.: Fault-tolerant and self-stabilizing mobile robots gathering. In: Dolev, S. (ed.) DISC 2006. LNCS, vol. 4167, pp. 46–60. Springer, Heidelberg (2006)
5. Flocchini, P., Prencipe, G., Santoro, N., Widmayer, P.: Gathering of asynchronous robots with limited visibility. Theoreical Computer Science 337(1-3), 147–168 (2005)
6. Inuzuka, N., Tomida, Y., Izumi, T., Katayama, Y., Wada, K.: Gathering problem of two asynchronous mobile robots with semi-dynamic compasses. In: Shvartsman, A.A., Felber, P. (eds.) SIROCCO 2008. LNCS, vol. 5058, pp. 5–19. Springer, Heidelberg (2008)
7. Izumi, T., Katayama, Y., Inuzuka, N., Wada, K.: Gathering autonomous mobile robots with dynamic compasses: An optimal result. In: Pelc, A. (ed.) DISC 2007. LNCS, vol. 4731, pp. 298–312. Springer, Heidelberg (2007)
8. Katayama, Y., Tomida, Y., Imazu, H., Inuzuka, N., Wada, K.: Dynamic compass models and gathering algorithm for autonomous mobile robots. In: Prencipe, G., Zaks, S. (eds.) SIROCCO 2007. LNCS, vol. 4474, pp. 274–288. Springer, Heidelberg (2007)
9. Prencipe, G.: Impossibility of gathering by a set of autonomous mobile robots. Theoretical Computer Science 384(2-3), 222–231 (2007)
10. Souissi, S., Défago, X., Yamashita, M.: Gathering asynchronous mobile robots with inaccurate compasses. In: Shvartsman, M.M.A.A. (ed.) OPODIS 2006. LNCS, vol. 4305, pp. 333–349. Springer, Heidelberg (2006)
11. Souissi, S., Défago, X., Yamashita, M.: Using eventually consistent compasses to gather memory-less mobile robots with limited visibility. ACM Trans. on Autonomous Adaptive and Adaptive Systems 4(1) (2009)
12. Suzuki, I., Yamashita, M.: Distributed anonymous mobile robots: Formation of geometric patterns. SIAM Journal of Computing 28(4), 1347–1363 (1999)

13. Yamashita, M., Souissi, S., Défago, X.: Gathering two stateless mobile robots using very inaccurate compasses in finite time. In: Proc. of the 1st International Conference on Robot Communication and Coordination (ROBOCOMM), p. 48 (2007)
14. Yamashita, M., Suzuki, I.: Characterizing geometric patterns formable by oblivious anonymous mobile robots (unpublished)

Scalable P2P Overlays of Very Small Constant Degree: An Emerging Security Threat*

Márk Jelasity[1] and Vilmos Bilicki[2]

[1] University of Szeged and Hungarian Academy of Sciences, Hungary
jelasity@inf.u-szeged.hu
[2] University of Szeged, Hungary
bilickiv@inf.u-szeged.hu

Abstract. In recent years peer-to-peer (P2P) technology has been adopted by Internet-based malware as a fault tolerant and scalable communication medium for self-organization and survival. It has been shown that malicious P2P networks would be nearly impossible to uncover if they operated in a *stealth mode*, that is, using only a small constant number of fixed overlay connections per node for communication. While overlay networks of a small constant maximal degree are generally considered to be unscalable, we argue in this paper that it is possible to design them to be scalable, efficient and robust. This is an important finding from a security point of view: we show that stealth mode P2P malware that is very difficult to discover with state-of-the-art methods is a plausible threat. In this paper we discuss algorithms and theoretical results that support the scalability of stealth mode overlays, and we present realistic simulations using an event based implementation of a proof-of-concept system. Besides P2P botnets, our results are also applicable in scenarios where relying on a large number of overlay connections per node is not feasible because of cost or the limited number of communication channels available.

1 Introduction

In recent years peer-to-peer (P2P) technology has been adopted by botnets as a fault tolerant and scalable communication medium for self-organization and survival [1, 2]. Examples include the Storm botnet [1] and the C variant of the Conficker worm [3].

The detection and filtering of P2P networks presents a considerable challenge [4]. In addition, it has been pointed out by Stern [5] that the potential threat posed by Internet-based malware would be even more challenging if worms and bots operated in a "stealth mode", avoiding excessive traffic and other visible behavior. It has also been shown that state of the art techniques for the detection of P2P networks fail if peers communicate with only a small constant number of neighbors during their lifetime [6].

* M. Jelasity was supported by the Bolyai Scholarship of the Hungarian Academy of Sciences.

R. Guerraoui and F. Petit (Eds.): SSS 2009, LNCS 5873, pp. 399–412, 2009.

Fortunately, current infections generate considerable traffic. For example, the Storm worm contacts a huge number of peers, in the range of thousands [2], when joining the network, generating a recognizable communication pattern as well as revealing a large list of botnet members. In general, P2P clients typically contact a large number of neighbors due to maintenance traffic, and regular application traffic such as search. There are only a few notable exceptions, such as Symphony and Viceroy [7,8], which are overlay networks of a constant degree.

It is still an open question whether it is possible to create overlay networks of a very small constant maximal degree that are efficient and scalable. Research activity concerning Symphony or Viceroy has not yet been targeted to the lower end of maximal node degree, potentially as small as 3 or 4. In fact, even negative results are known that indicate the inherent lack of scalability of constant degree networks [9,10]. In this paper we answer this question in the affirmative and show that it is possible to build a Symphony-inspired overlay network of a very small constant degree, and with the application of a number of simple techniques, this overlay network can be made scalable and robust as well. This result calls for more research into the detection of malicious P2P networks that are potentially of a small maximal degree.

Our contribution is threefold. First, we empirically analyze known as well as new techniques from the point of view of improving the search performance in a Symphony-like overlay network. Second, we present theoretical results indicating that if we add $O(\log N)$ (or, in a certain parameter range, $O(\log\log N)$) backup links for all links (where N is the network size), then a constant degree network becomes fault tolerant even in the limit of infinite network size, while its effective degree remains constant (that is, the network can remain in stealth mode) since the backup links are not used for communication unless they become regular links replacing a failed link. This result is counter intuitive because routing in Symphony requires $O(\log^2 N)$ hops on average. Third, we provide event-based simulation results over dynamic and realistic scenarios with a proof-of-principle implementation of a constant degree network, complete with gossip-based protocols for joining and maintenance.

2 Performance of Small Constant Degree Topologies

Our motivation is to understand whether a reasonable routing performance can be achieved in a network that operates in stealth mode; that is, where the maximal node degree is as small as 3 or 4. We will base our discussion on Symphony, a simple constant degree network [7]. We explore several (existing and novel) simple techniques for improving the routing performance of Symphony at the lower extremes of maximal degree. To the best of our knowledge, this problem has not been tackled so far in detail by the research community.

Symphony was proposed by Manku et al. [7] as an application of the work of Kleinberg [11]. Like many other topologies, the Symphony topology is based on an undirected ring that is ordered according to node IDs. Node IDs are drawn uniformly at random from the interval $[0, 1]$ when joining the network. Apart from the two links that belong to the ring, each node draws a constant number of IDs with a probability proportional to $1/d$, where d is the distance from the node's own ID. Subsequently, each node creates undirected long-range links to those peers that have the closest IDs to the IDs drawn. (We note that an implementation needs an approximation of the network size N for normalizing the distribution. A rough, but practically acceptable, approximation exploits the fact that the expected distance of the closest neighbor in the ring is $1/N$.)

Symphony applies a greedy routing algorithm: at each hop the link is chosen that has the numerically closest ID to the target. Due to the undirected ring, the procedure is guaranteed to converge. It can also be proven that routing takes $O(\log^2 N)$ hops on average; the idea of the proof is to show that it takes $O(\log N)$ hops to halve the distance to the target.

In the following we describe techniques for reducing the number of routing hops in small constant degree networks. Subsequently, we systematically analyze these techniques via simulations.

Lookahead. Greedy routing can be augmented by a lookahead procedure where nodes store the addresses of the neighbors of their neighbors locally as well, up to a certain distance. This way, route selection is based on the best 2, 3, etc., hop route planned locally as opposed to a 1 hop route. Routing with a single hop lookahead has been studied in detail [12, 13]. Since small constant degree networks have small local neighborhoods that can easily be stored and updated, we study 2 hop lookahead as well.

Degree balancing. To enforce a strict small upper bound on node degree, nodes that are already of the maximal degree have to reject new incoming long-range links. To make sure that most joining nodes can create long-range links, we need to introduce balancing techniques. In addition to the usual technique of repeated join attempts, we propose degree balancing: when a node of maximal degree receives a join request, it first checks its closest neighbors in the direction of increasing node ID to see whether they have free slots for a link. This need not require extensive communication as neighbor information is available locally (and, for example, the lookahead mechanism described above also requires local neighborhood information).

Stratification. Since each node has only a small constant number of long-range links (1 or 2 in our case), many hops will follow the ring. It is therefore important that neighboring nodes in the ring have different long-range links. We propose a stratified sampling technique that involves dividing the long range links into a logarithmic number of intervals $[e^i/N, e^{i+1}/N]$ $(i = 0, \ldots, [\ln N] - 1)$. All the nodes first choose an interval at random that is not occupied by a long-range link at a neighbor, and then they draw a random ID from that interval with a probability proportional to $1/d$, where d is the distance from the node's own ID.

Short link avoidance. Interestingly, if the average route is long, then it might be beneficial to exclude long-range links that are too short. This way we introduce some extra hops at the end of the route, when routing follows the ring only.

Table 1. The parameter space of the experiments

network size	2^i, $i = 10, 11, \ldots, 20$
maximal degree (k)	3 or 4 (1 or 2 long-range links)
lookahead	0, 1, or 2 hops
stratification	yes or no
join attempts	1, 2, or 4 attempts
degree balancing	1, 5, 10, or 20 neighbors checked
short link avoidance (m)	0, 1, 2, 3, or 4

However, we save hops during the first phases due to the longer long-range links. As we will see later, this technique works well only in very small degree networks where routes are long, but in such cases we can obtain a significant improvement. We implement short link avoidance based on the same intervals defined for stratification above. We introduce a parameter m: the number of shortest intervals that should be excluded when selecting long-range links. For example, for $m = 2$, the first possible interval will be $[e^2/N, e^3/N]$.

We performed experiments using the parameter space in Table 1. For all parameter combinations, we first constructed the network and subsequently we selected 10,000 random node pairs and recorded the hop count of the routing.

A main methodological tool we apply to evaluate the large parameter space is drawing scatter plots to illustrate the *improvement* in the hop count as a function of a varying parameter. In these plots the points correspond to different combinations of the possible values of a subset of parameters. The remaining free parameters are the ones we are interested in; they are used to calculate the coordinates of the points as follows. The hop count for a specified setting for the free parameters is the horizontal coordinate of a point, whereas the vertical coordinate is the ratio of the horizontal coordinate and the hop count that belongs to another (typically baseline) setting of the same parameters.

The improvement brought about by stratification is illustrated in Figure 1 (left). Clearly, for almost all parameter settings, stratification is a better choice (most values fall below 1). The experiments with values higher than 1 were performed on the smallest networks, with no apparent additional common features. The lack of improvement in these cases is most likely due to the larger noise of random sampling in smaller networks. From now on, we restrict our discussion to experiments with stratification.

The improvement brought about by lookahead is shown in Figure 1 (right). We can see that lookahead helps more if the degree of the network is larger. This is plausible since the local neighborhood is exponentially larger in a network of a larger degree. We also notice that lookahead is more useful in larger networks where the routes are longer.

Let us now have a look at the average degree of the networks (Figure 2). The main observation here is that it is important to approximate the maximal degree because in some cases we can observe a performance improvement of almost 30% relative to the baseline approach (that is, when no balancing efforts

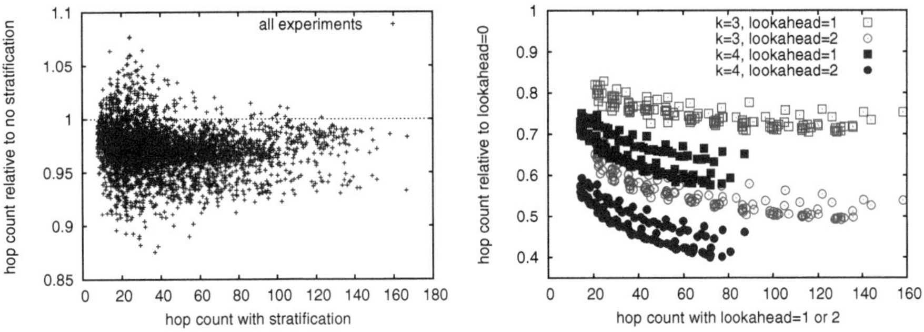

Fig. 1. The improvement in hop count as a result of stratification (left) and lookahead (right)

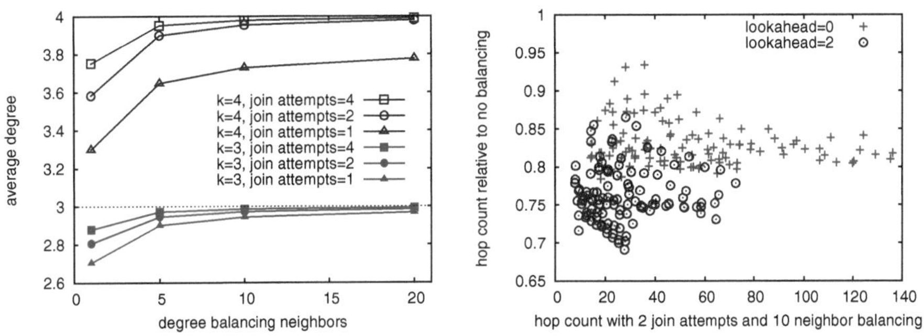

Fig. 2. Average degree for $N = 2^{20}$ (left) and the performance improvement achieved by a good balancing strategy (right). The average degree is practically identical with all the other network sizes too (not shown).

have been made), especially if lookahead has been applied as well. The setting of 2 join attempts with degree balancing over 10 neighbors appears to be a good compromise between cost and performance.

Figure 3 illustrates the effects of short link avoidance. When $m = 2$ (left), performance is improved with each parameter setting, except for $k = 4$ and $lookahead = 2$, where routing is so efficient that even for the largest networks there are too few hops, so short link avoidance does not result in a net gain in hop count. For $m = 3$ (right) the same effect is amplified: for parameter settings with a large hop count the relative improvement is larger, but for short routes the relative cost is larger as well. All in all, the effect of this technique depends on the other parameters, but $m = 2$ appears to be rather robust and results in a slight improvement in most settings. We note that $m = 4$ was not the best setting in any of the experiments, so the maximal reasonable value was $m = 3$ in our parameter space.

Lastly, Figure 4 shows hop count as a function of network size. Theory predicts an $O(\log^2 N)$ hop count complexity; to a good approximation we can observe

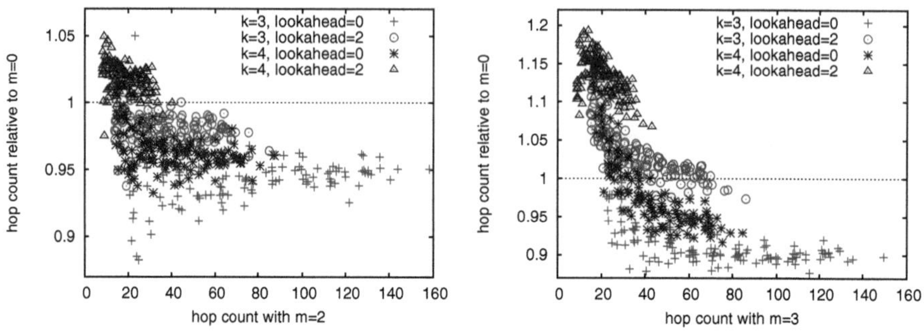

Fig. 3. The improvement in hop count as a result of setting $m \neq 0$

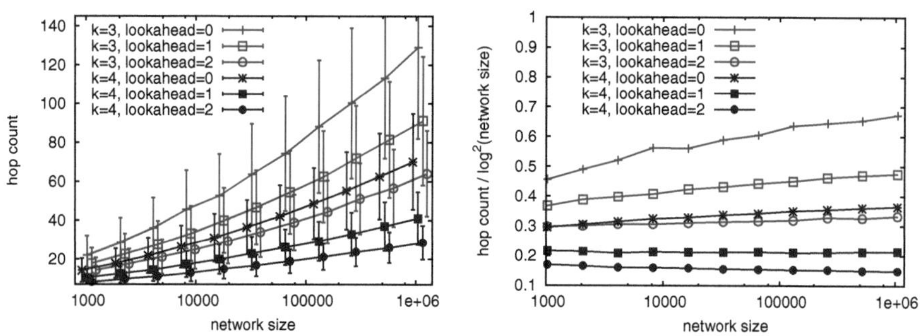

Fig. 4. Scalability of routing. Statistics over 10,000 random node pairs are shown. Stratified sampling was applied, along with 2 join attempts with a degree balancing over 10 neighbors, and we set $m = 2$.

this scaling behavior, especially for $k = 4$. The very large difference between the best and the worst setting is also worth noting. Moving from $k = 3$ to $k = 4$ results in a very significant improvement: 2 long-range links instead of 1 causes the speed of routing to double, as predicted by theory [7].

We may conclude that routing in networks of a very small constant degree is feasible if certain techniques are applied. We found that the most effective technique is lookahead based on locally available information about the neighborhood of the nodes. In addition, degree balancing is very important as well. Further techniques such as short link avoidance and stratification also result in an additional 5-10% improvement, depending on the parameters. With these techniques we can route in around 30 hops in a network of size $N = 2^{20} \approx 1,000,000$ with a maximal node degree of only 4.

3 Scalability of Fault Tolerance

In the above sections we discussed several aspects of scalability. Our focus in this section will be whether the *fault tolerance* of the network diminishes as the network grows. This is crucial from the point of view of P2P networks (in particular, botnets), which have to tolerate a considerable node churn, as well as other types of failures.

We first touch on some important issues regarding the scalability of constant degree topologies, and then we propose the simple technique of using backup links to increase their fault tolerance. We present theoretical results to show that the proposed technique indeed turns constant degree networks scalable in a well defined sense in the presence of node failures.

We consider properties of networks of size N as $N \to \infty$. This means that the results presented here are mainly of theoretical interest, since in practice an upper bound on network size can easily be given, and the algorithm designer can set protocol parameters according to the upper bound even if the algorithm is not scalable in the present sense. Still, our results are somewhat counter intuitive, and as such increase our insight into the behavior of constant degree networks.

The Achilles' heel of constant degree networks is fault tolerance and not performance. Performance is not a problem if the network is reliable. It is well-known that a constant number of neighbors is sufficient to build a connected structure. Not only the trivial constant degree topologies such as the ring or a tree are connected, but also there exist random topologies of constant degree such as the random k-out graphs. In such graphs each node is connected to k random other nodes. It has been shown that for $k \geq 4$ a k-out graph is connected with high probability [14]. It is also well-known that a constant degree is sufficient for an efficient routing algorithm. In the Symphony network routing takes $O(\log^2 N)$ hops while in Viceroy, the optimal $O(\log N)$ hop-count is achieved [8, 7].

Unfortunately, constant degree networks do not tolerate node failure very well. We will examine the case when each node is removed with a fixed constant probability q (that is, the expected number of nodes remaining in the network is $(1-q)N$). For example, the 4-out random graph is no longer connected with high probability in this model. In fact, in order to get a connected random topology in spite of node failures, one needs to maintain $O(\log N)$ neighbors at all nodes [10]. Similarly, it has been shown by Kong et al. [9] that—in this failure model—DHT routing is not scalable in Symphony, while it is scalable on other topologies that are able to find more alternative routes via maintaining $O(\log N)$ links at all the nodes. In the following, we summarize the results of Kong et al. for completeness and extend them to show how to achieve an effectively constant degree, yet scalable, topology.

Kong et al. examined the *success probability* of routing $p(h, q)$, the probability that in a DHT a node h hops away from a starting node will be reached by the routing algorithm under a uniform node failure probability q [9]. Their criterion for scalability is

$$\lim_{N \to \infty} p(h, q) = \lim_{h \to \infty} p(h, q) > 0, \quad 0 < q < 1 - \epsilon, \tag{1}$$

where $\epsilon > 0$, and h is the average routing distance in the topology under study ($h = O(\log^2 N)$ for Symphony). This expresses the requirement that increasing network size should not increase sensitivity to failure without limit. Given this criterion, the proposed methodology consists of finding the exact formula or a lower bound for $p(h, q)$ for a topology of interest, and then calculating the limit to see whether it is positive. To calculate $p(h, q)$, one can create a Markov chain model of the routing process under failure, and determine the probability of reaching the failure state.

Kong et al. proved that Symphony is not scalable. They showed that for each step the probability of failure is a constant (C), so

$$\lim_{h\to\infty} p(h, q) = \lim_{h\to\infty} (1 - C)^h = 0. \tag{2}$$

However, if we assume that there are *backup* links for each link in Symphony, then the situation changes dramatically. We do not go into detail here about how to collect the backup links; Section 4 discusses an actual algorithm. From our point of view here the important fact is that the backup links are such that if a link is not accessible, then the first backup is the best candidate to replace it. If the first backup is down as well, then the second backup is the best replacement, and so on.

Recall that the Symphony topology consists of a ring and a constant number of shortcuts. For the ring, the notion of backup should be clear. A shortcut link is defined by a randomly generated ID: we need to find the numerically closest node in the network to that ID. The first backup in that case is the second closest node in the network, and so on. This notion can be extended to all routing geometries as well.

The backup links do not increase the *effective* degree of an overlay node: a DHT can use the original links if they are available, even if some of the backups were closer to the target. In fact, backup links are *never used* for communication, not even during maintenance or any other function, except when they become regular links after replacing a failed regular link. In addition, as we explain in Section 4, backup links can be collected and updated during regular DHT maintenance without any extra messages.

It seems clear that backup links can turn Symphony scalable. However, the question is how many of them do we need? In the following we show that $O(\log N)$ backup links are sufficient, and under some circumstance even $O(\log\log N)$ links will do.

Lemma 1. *If in a DHT routing network all the links have $f(N)$ backup links then $p(h, q) \geq (1 - q^{f(N)})^h$.*

Proof. The probability of being able to use the best link in the original overlay is $1-q$. Considering the backups this probability becomes $1-q^{f(N)+1} > 1-q^{f(N)}$. Now, if we follow only the optimal link in each step then the probability of success is not smaller than $(1-q^{f(N)})^h$. Clearly, $p(h, q)$ is no less than this value since it accounts for methods for routing around failed links as well.

Lemma 2. $\lim_{N\to\infty}(1 - q^{\log N})^{\log^k N} > 0$ *if* $0 \leq q < 1 - \epsilon$ *and* $k \in \mathbb{R}$.

Proof. For $k <= 0$ the lemma is trivial. For $k > 0$, according to Theorem 1 in [9] we need to prove that

$$\lim_{N\to\infty} q^{\log N} \log^k N < \infty$$

and the lemma follows. The convergence of the above expression can be proven by applying the l'Hospital rule on $(\log^k N)/q^{-\log N}$ a suitable number of times.

Lemma 3. $\lim_{N\to\infty}(1 - q^{\log\log N})^{\log^k N} > 0$ *if* $0 \le q < \min(e^{-k}, 1-\epsilon)$.

Proof. We again need to prove that

$$\lim_{N\to\infty} q^{\log\log N} \log^k N < \infty.$$

Substituting $x = \log N$ we get

$$q^{\log x} x^k = x^{\frac{1}{\log_q e}} x^k = x^{\frac{1}{\log_q e}+k}$$

This means that we need $\frac{1}{\log_q e} + k \le 0$ for convergence. Elementary transformations complete the proof.

Theorem 1. *The Symphony topology is scalable, that is,* $\lim_{h\to\infty} p(h,q) > 0$, *if (i) all the links have* $O(\log N)$ *backup links, or if (ii) all the links have* $O(\log\log N)$ *backup links and* $q \le e^{-2} \approx 0.135$.

Proof. Straightforward application of the previous lemmas for Symphony where $k = 2$, that is, $h = O(\log^2 N)$.

To sum up, we have shown that Symphony-like topologies can be made scalable by adding only $O(\log N)$ backup links for all the links, and under moderate failure rates even $O(\log\log N)$ suffices. This is rather counter-intuitive given that routing still takes $O(\log^2 N)$ steps. It is also promising, because these results suggest that collecting good quality backup links can dramatically improve scalability at a low cost.

4 Experimental Results

In this section we present proof-of-principle experiments with a simple implementation of a small constant degree network in realistic churn scenarios. Our goal is not to present a complete optimized implementation but rather to show that it is indeed possible to achieve acceptable fault tolerance and performance in realistic environments.

We performed the experiments using the PeerSim event-based simulator [15]. In our system model nodes can send messages to each other based on a node address. Nodes have access to a local clock, but these clocks are not synchronized. Messages can be delayed and nodes can leave or join the system at any time. The statistical model of node churn is based on measurement data [16], as we describe later.

Our goal was to design a protocol to construct and maintain a Symphony topology in a fault tolerant way, with backup links (see Section 3). To this end, we applied T-Man, a generic protocol for constructing a wide range of overlay topologies [17]. Here we briefly outline the protocol and the specific details of the present implementation. The reader is kindly requested to consult [17] for more information.

In our experiments each node has a single long-range link; that is, the maximal effective degree is 3. Each node has three local caches: long-range backups, ring backups and random samples. We set a maximal size of 80 for both the long-range and ring backup caches, and 100 for random samples. These values were chosen in an ad hoc way and were not optimized.

The caches contain node descriptors that include the ID and the address of a node. Each node periodically sends the contents of all its caches to all its neighbors. The period of this communication is called the *gossip cycle*, and was set to 1 minute in our experiments.

As described in Section 3, the two backup caches should ideally contain those nodes from the entire network whose IDs are closest to the node's own ID (for the ring neighbors), and the ID of the long-range link, respectively. When receiving a message containing node descriptors, a node updates its own local caches. It also updates the random sample cache, using a stratified sampling approach: the ID space is divided into 100 equal intervals, and each cache entry is selected from one of these intervals. If the random sample cache can be improved using any of the incoming node descriptors, the cache is updated.

In addition, if a node receives a message from a node it should not receive messages from (for example, because the sender has inaccurate knowledge about the topology) the node sends its caches to the sender of the misdirected message as well, so that it can improve its backup caches.

The join procedure starts by generating the node's own ID at random, as well as the ID for the long-range link. The caches need to be initialized as well, using a set of known peers; we applied 50 fixed descriptors for the initialization. Once the caches contain at least one link, the gossip protocol sketched above can start, and all the caches will fill and improve gradually.

When handling a routing request, a node applies greedy routing using the three links: the two ring links and the long-range link. However, before using the currently active ring links or long-range link, the node always checks the best candidate in the backup caches for availability (sending a ping message). Note that we do not check the best candidate for the message to be routed; we check the best candidate for the given link slot (ring or long-range). This way, it is guaranteed that the right links are used based on the current state of the network at any given time.

The scenario we experimented with involves node churn. Applying appropriate models of churn is of crucial importance from a methodological point of view. Researchers have often applied an exponential distribution to model uptime distribution, which corresponds to a failure probability independent of uptime. Measurements of a wide range of P2P networks in [16] suggest that a Weibull distribution of uptime is more realistic, with a shape parameter around $k = 0.5$. In this case the failure rate decreases, that is, the more time a node spends online, the less likely it is to fail. This favors longer sessions, but the Weibull distribution is nevertheless not heavy-tailed.

We applied the Weibull distribution with $k = 0.5$ to model uptime, and scaled the distribution, so that around 30% of the nodes live longer than 30 minutes [16]. The downtime distribution was modeled by a uniform random distribution, with an average downtime of 2 minutes. This average is very short; however, longer downtimes result in a relative increase in the proportion of nodes in the network that have long session lengths. Paradoxically, if the downtime is long, then the network is almost completely stable in the time range we are interested in (around 30 minutes).

As noted in [16], the lengths of the online sessions of a node correlate: there are nodes that tend to be available and nodes that are not. We assigned each node a fixed session length from the distribution above, that remained fixed during the experiment.

We applied a 1 minute gossip cycle. Each experiment lasted for 40 cycles. The network gradually grew to its final size during the first 10 cycles, when we added each node at a random time. During the remaining 30 cycles churn was applied. The network sizes we tested were $N = 2^i$, $i = 10, \ldots, 14$. Parameter m (which controls short link avoidance) was set to $m = 0$ or $m = 3$. Other features such as lookahead, stratification, and degree balancing were not implemented at the time of writing.

Figure 5 illustrates the speed at which the ring topology is being formed despite of the continuous churn. The improvement of the backup links (80 links per node) for the ring links is also illustrated. It can be seen that most nodes collect good quality backups, but some of them seem to have no usable backups at all; these nodes have a very short session time and spend very little time in the network.

One of our main goals was to show that the effective degree—the number of nodes an average node actually communicates with—can be kept low. Figure 6 shows that indeed this can be accomplished. Despite heavy churn, which results in a constant fluctuation of the ring neighbors, the effective degree is small and seems to scale well. Recall that, for example, the Storm worm has been observed to communicate with thousands of neighbors [2].

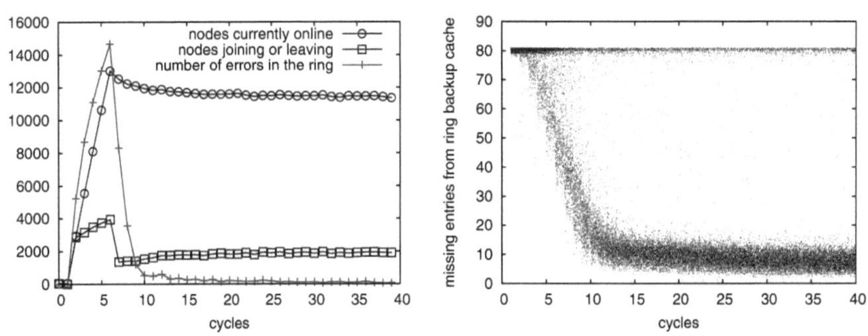

Fig. 5. The evolution of the topology and the backup links for $N = 2^{14}$. In the figure on the right points belong to individual nodes and are randomly shifted so as to visualize the density.

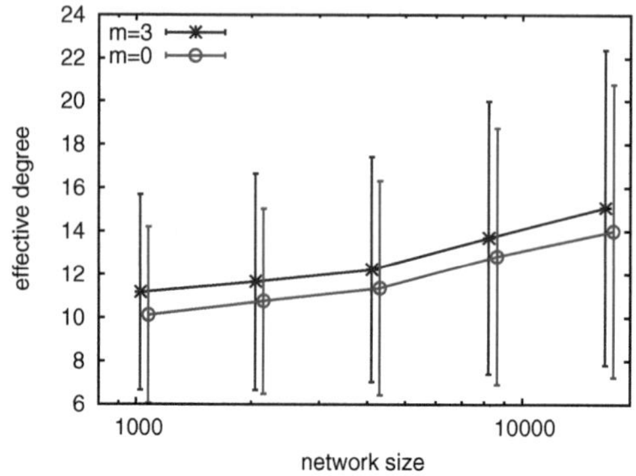

Fig. 6. The observed effective degree by the end of the experiments

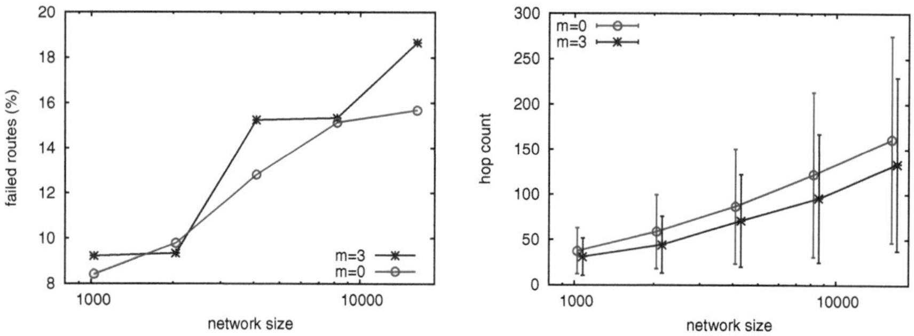

Fig. 7. Routing performance. The figure on the right corresponds to successful routes.

Finally, let us examine the reliability and the efficiency of routing (see Figure 7). Recall that we work with a baseline implementation with no lookahead, stratification, or any other techniques. Only short link avoidance is implemented. When testing routing we pick IDs and not nodes as targets, and consider routing successful if the closest node receives the message at the time of reception. That is, it is possible that the optimal target is different at the start of the routing and at the end of the same routing.

We can see that short link avoidance improves the hop count by a large margin. Overall, we observe almost twice the hop count as in the ideal case shown in Figure 4. However, in our hostile scenario with heavy churn this can be considered acceptable for this baseline approach. We also note that the actual routing performance observed in real botnets can be significantly worse; for example, the success rate of queries has been found to be extremely low in the Storm botnet [2].

5 Conclusions

In this paper we argued for the feasibility of P2P systems that operate in a stealth mode, where nodes communicate only with a very limited number of peers during their lifetime.

Our results have at least two implications. First, they are a strong indication that P2P botnets need to be taken seriously by the P2P community. In our previous work we showed that stealth mode P2P networks are practically invisible for state-of-the art methods for P2P network detection [6]. Current botnets do not exploit P2P technology to its full potential, and by the time they learn how to do that, they will be very difficult to detect and remove.

The second implication is not related to malware. There can be other applications where it is important to utilize very few connections because of a large associated cost. Detailed arguments for a constant degree design can be found in related works as well [8]. For this reason, the research issue that we raised, that is, the investigation of networks of a very small constant degree, is relevant to non-malicious applications as well.

References

1. Holz, T., Steiner, M., Dahl, F., Biersack, E., Freiling, F.: Measurements and mitigation of peer-to-peer-based botnets: a case study on storm worm. In: Proceedings of the 1st USENIX Workshop on Large-Scale Exploits and Emergent Threats (LEET 2008), Berkeley, CA, USA. USENIX Association (2008)
2. Grizzard, J., Sharma, V., Nunnery, C., Kang, B., Dagon, D.: Peer-to-peer botnets: Overview and case study. In: Proceedings of the First USENIX Workshop on Hot Topics in Understanding Botnets, HotBots 2007 (2007)
3. Porras, P., Saïdi, H., Yegneswaran, V.: A foray into Conficker's logic and rendezvous points. In: 2nd USENIX Workshop on Large-Scale Exploits and Emergent Threats (LEET 2009). USENIX (2009)
4. Iliofotou, M., Pappu, P., Faloutsos, M., Mitzenmacher, M., Singh, S., Varghese, G.: Network monitoring using traffic dispersion graphs (TDGs). In: Proceedings of the 7th ACM SIGCOMM conference on Internet measurement (IMC 2007), pp. 315–320. ACM, New York (2007)
5. Stern, H.: Effective malware: The trade-off between size and stealth. In: 2nd USENIX Workshop on Large-Scale Exploits and Emergent Threats (LEET 2009). USENIX (2009) (invited talk)
6. Jelasity, M., Bilicki, V.: Towards automated detection of peer-to-peer botnets: On the limits of local approaches. In: 2nd USENIX Workshop on Large-Scale Exploits and Emergent Threats (LEET 2009). USENIX (2009), `http://www.usenix.org/events/leet09/tech/`
7. Manku, G.S., Bawa, M., Raghavan, P.: Symphony: Distributed hashing in a small world. In: Proceedings of the 4th USENIX Symposium on Internet Technologies and Systems, USITS 2003 (2003)
8. Malkhi, D., Naor, M., Ratajczak, D.: Viceroy: A scalable and dynamic emulation of the butterfly. In: Proceedings of the 21st ACM Symposium on Principles of Distributed Computing (PODC 2002), pp. 183–192. ACM, New York (2002)

9. Kong, J.S., Bridgewater, J.S.A., Roychowdhury, V.P.: A general framework for scalability and performance analysis of DHT routing systems. In: Proceedings of the International Conference on Dependable Systems and Networks (DSN 2006), Washington, DC, USA, pp. 343–354. IEEE Computer Society, Los Alamitos (2006)
10. Kermarrec, A.M., Massoulié, L., Ganesh, A.J.: Probablistic reliable dissemination in large-scale systems. IEEE Transactions on Parallel and Distributed Systems 14(3), 248–258 (2003)
11. Kleinberg, J.: The small-world phenomenon: an algorithmic perspective. In: Proceedings of the 32nd ACM Symposium on Theory of Computing (STOC 2000), pp. 163–170. ACM, New York (2000)
12. Manku, G.S., Naor, M., Wieder, U.: Know thy neighbor's neighbor: the power of lookahead in randomized p2p networks. In: Proceedings of the 36th ACM Symposium on Theory of Computing (STOC 2004), pp. 54–63. ACM, New York (2004)
13. Naor, M., Wieder, U.: Know thy neighbor's neighbor: Better routing for skip-graphs and small worlds. In: Voelker, G.M., Shenker, S. (eds.) IPTPS 2004. LNCS, vol. 3279, pp. 269–277. Springer, Heidelberg (2005)
14. Cooper, C., Frieze, A.: Hamilton cycles in random graphs and directed graphs. Random Structures and Algorithms 16(4), 369–401 (2000)
15. PeerSim, `http://peersim.sourceforge.net/`
16. Stutzbach, D., Rejaie, R.: Understanding churn in peer-to-peer networks. In: Proceedings of the 6th ACM SIGCOMM conference on Internet measurement (IMC 2006), pp. 189–202. ACM, New York (2006)
17. Jelasity, M., Montresor, A., Babaoglu, O.: T-Man: Gossip-based fast overlay topology construction. Computer Networks 53(13), 2321–2339 (2009)

CFlood: A Constrained Flooding Protocol for Real-time Data Delivery in Wireless Sensor Networks*

Bo Jiang[1], Binoy Ravindran[1], and Hyeonjoong Cho[2]

[1] Department of Electrical and Computer Engineering,
Virginia Polytechnic Institute and State University,
Blacksburg, VA 24061, USA
{bjiang,binoy}@vt.edu
[2] Department of Computer and Information Science,
Korea University,
Seoul, Korea 136-701
raycho@korea.ac.kr

Abstract. Real-time performance is critical for many time-sensitive applications of wireless sensor networks. We present a constrained flooding protocol, called CFlood, which enhances the deadline satisfaction ratio per unit energy consumption of time-sensitive packets in sensor networks. CFlood improves real-time performance by flooding, but effectively constrains energy consumption by controlling the scale of flooding, i.e., flooding only when necessary. If unicasting meets the distributed sub-deadline of a hop, CFlood aborts further flooding even after flooding has occurred in the current hop. Our simulation-based experimental studies show that CFlood achieves higher deadline satisfaction ratio per unit energy consumption than previous multipath forwarding protocols, especially in sparsely deployed or unreliable sensor network environments.

1 Introduction

Real-time performance is one of the most important quality of service (QoS) metrics for time-sensitive applications of wireless sensor networks (WSN). For example, a target tracking system [1] may require sensors to collect and report target information to sink nodes before the target leaves the surveillance field. For improving real-time performance, we need to ensure that as many time-sensitive packets as possible, arrive at sink nodes within their deadlines. The delay that a packet may experience during transmission may be caused by many reasons, including those due to network congestion and node/link failures.

Multipath forwarding is a commonly used approach for enhancing various QoS metrics of WSN traffic [2]. With multiple paths, network congestion and node/link failures can be bypassed, and real-time performance can be improved. However, it is possible that network congestion or the connection status is not significant enough throughout the entire path from source to sink to warrant multipath forwarding for each hop.

* This work was supported by research project grants from MKE/MND, South Korea.

R. Guerraoui and F. Petit (Eds.): SSS 2009, LNCS 5873, pp. 413–427, 2009.

Therefore sometimes, the redundant copies of data packets generated by multipath forwarding protocols, which often consume additional energy and bandwidth, are not necessary. Since sensor nodes are battery-powered and therefore energy must be efficiently consumed, energy-efficient forwarding protocols are critical toward enhancing the capability of delivering real-time packets within given end-to-end time constraints, while reducing the energy consumption.

Many previous research efforts [3,4,5,6,7,8] have studied the efficiency of multipath forwarding protocols toward enhancing real-time performance while consuming optimized resources (we discuss related work in Section 5). Majority of these efforts have focused on reducing the number of flooding recipients at each hop so that the additional resource consumption can be minimized and QoS constraints such as real-time can also be satisfied. But even though the number of recipients is reduced, this approach introduces redundancy due to its probability-based recipient selection mechanism. In fact, for those hops in which the connection status is good enough so that unicasting does work, redundant multipath flooding is not necessary. The efficiency of flooding therefore can be further improved by controlling the redundancy.

In this paper, we present a constrained flooding protocol called CFlood that improves the flooding efficiency in sensor networks. The primary objective of CFlood is to enhance the deadline satisfaction ratio per unit energy consumption. We adopt the *deadline satisfaction ratio* (*DSR*) [9] to characterize the real-time performance of a WSN, which is defined as the ratio of the number of real-time packets that arrive at sink nodes meeting their deadlines, to the total number of those transmitted.

CFlood uses flooding to enhance *DSR*, and controls the flooding scale to effectively reduce energy consumption. We design CFlood mainly in four components, including neighborhood table management, real-time guarantee verification, recipient selection and flooding control. CFlood maintains a neighborhood table on each node to save routing information and neighboring relations, and uses periodic HELLO message exchanges to estimate the per-hop delays and update the table entries. We also introduce a deadline partition scheme to distribute the end-to-end deadline to multiple hops. By comparing the estimated per-hop delays and the distributed sub-deadlines, the real-time guarantee verification component justifies whether a neighbor node can meet the deadline for a specific packet. Among the neighbors that can meet the deadline, CFlood selects a primary recipient and several secondary recipients according to the criteria on flooding-controllability, congestion avoidance, and computation simplicity. In addition, CFlood aborts further flooding from secondary recipients if unicasting to the primary recipient can meet the distributed sub-deadline. CFlood is designed as a hop-by-hop routing protocol with no global network information needed. Thus, it is scalable for large-scale sensor networks.

We conducted extensive simulation-based experimental studies to evaluate CFlood's performance. Our results reveal that CFlood achieves a higher deadline satisfaction ratio per unit energy consumption than previous multipath data delivery protocols, such as a multipath routing protocol MCMP [2] and a directional flooding protocol DFP [10], especially in sparse or unreliable network environments.

The paper makes the following contributions:

- We design a constrained flooding protocol that improves the flooding efficiency by enhancing the deadline satisfaction ratio per unit energy consumption. A flooding control mechanism is developed based on the cross-layer design, by adding a plug-in block to the MAC protocol.
- We compare the performance of CFlood against previous efforts through the simulation-based experimental studies. To the best of our knowledge, we are not aware of any other protocols that achieves a higher deadline satisfaction ratio per unit energy consumption than what CFlood yields.

The rest of the paper is organized as follows. In Section 2, we outline our system model. The design details of CFlood are presented in Section 3. Section 4 describes our simulation results. We compare and contrast past and related work against CFlood in Section 5, and conclude the paper in Section 6.

2 System Model

We make the following assumptions:

Network. We assume that homogeneous sensor nodes are randomly and uniformly deployed in a flat architecture. We only consider many-to-one data transmission, i.e., each sensor node sends packets only to a single sink node. Such a many-to-one data transmission is usually called "convergecast" [11].

Nodes. We assume that sensor nodes are static, and their transmission radius (within which nodes can communicate, denoted as R) is fixed.

Communication. We adopt the protocol model in [12], where both transmission and interference depend only on the Euclidean distance between nodes.

MAC protocol. We assume that the underlying MAC protocol supports collision avoidance with the RTS/CTS (Request To Send and Clear To Send) exchange mechanism [13].

For convenience in discussion, we summarize all the notations in Table 1.

Table 1. Notations

R	Transmission radius	$NB(N_i)$	Neighbors of node N_i
r	Sensing radius	$Parent(N_i)$	The parent of node N_i
L_h	Estimated per-hop delay	$Source(N_i)$	The source node from which N_i receives a packet
D_h	Distributed per-hop deadline	$Forward(N_i)$	Flooding recipients of node N_i
PR	Primary recipient	$Hop(N_i)$	The number of hops that N_i is away from the sink
SR	Secondary recipient	ρ	Node density
T_h	The average throughput of a node at hop h	C_h	The number of nodes that are h hops away from the sink node
SL_i	Slack time ratio	DSR	Deadline satisfaction ratio
δ	Real-time capacity per unit energy consumption	e	The average energy for transmitting a single time-sensitive packet

3 CFlood: A Constrained Flooding Protocol

We first describe CFlood's design intuition, and then discuss its functional components in detail.

3.1 Overview

CFlood is a decentralized flooding-based routing protocol. Routes are determined, i.e., recipients are chosen at each hop dynamically during data transmission. CFlood uses flooding to increase the deadline satisfaction ratio. But flooding may not be necessary at each hop. It is desirable to constrain the scale of flooding as much as possible to enhance energy efficiency.

We describe energy efficiency by measuring the average energy e consumed for transmitting a single time-sensitive packet, i.e., the ratio of the total energy consumption to the total number of time-sensitive packets generated. With a flooding protocol, a single packet may be copied multiple times. Thus, the total energy consumption consists of the energy for transmitting and receiving all the copies. We do not emphasize the unit of energy, since it depends on the specific hardware platform. We also define the metric *real-time capacity per unit energy consumption* as $\delta = \frac{DSR}{e}$, which measures what percentage of time-sensitive packets is delivered meeting their deadlines for unit energy consumption. Thus, higher δ is, the more efficient the flooding protocol is. The primary objective of CFlood therefore can be described as improving the real-time capacity per unit energy consumption δ as much as possible.

Our approaches for controlling the flooding scale thereby increasing δ include: 1) reducing the flooding actions as much as possible, and using unicasting instead; and 2) reducing the number of recipients when flooding is necessary.

Our intuition in controlling the flooding scale of CFlood with the first approach is as follows. After a recipient at a given hop finds that the transmission of its next hop can meet the sub-deadline, it is unnecessary for other recipients to continue flooding for the next hop. Thus, this recipient can abort the subsequent flooding of other ones. For this hop, it seems as unicasting is used instead of flooding. This way, the end-to-end time constraint can be satisfied and the energy efficiency can be enhanced.

Even if flooding is necessary, we should reduce the number of recipients. We use several criteria for recipient selection, in which the end-to-end time constraint is the primary one. First, we introduce a deadline partition scheme to distribute the end-to-end deadline to multiple hops. Then, CFlood estimates the per-hop delays between nodes. If the estimated per-hop delay is longer than the distributed sub-deadline, it is highly unlikely that the route through the node can meet the end-to-end time constraint. Otherwise, the node can be chosen as a recipient of the flooding. With this approach, the number of recipients can potentially be reduced with respect to meeting the end-to-end time constraint.

We design CFlood with four functional components, which are shown in a network protocol stack in Figure 1. The components are described as follows:

- *Neighborhood table management.* CFlood maintains a neighborhood table on each node to save the routing information, the neighboring relations, and the estimated

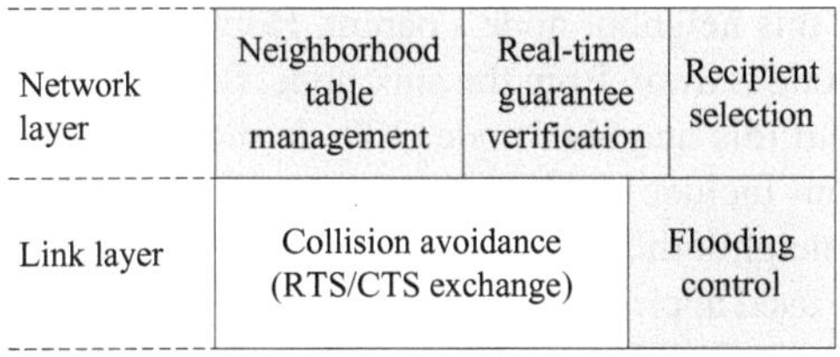

Fig. 1. Functional components of CFlood

per-hop delays. These information fields are shared between neighbors through periodic HELLO message exchanges, and are used for making flooding decisions.

- *Real-time guarantee verification.* Among all the one-hop neighbors, we want to flood only to those nodes that can satisfy the time constraint. This component verifies whether a neighbor can meet the end-to-end time constraint, and therefore could be considered as a flooding recipient. This decision is made by comparing the estimated per-hop delay, denoted as L_h, and the distributed per-hop sub-deadline, denoted as D_h. If $L_h < D_h$, i.e., the transmission at this hop can be completed within the sub-deadline distributed to this hop, then this neighbor could be selected as a prospective recipient.
- *Recipient selection.* First, each node periodically computes a next-hop neighbor (or parent as in [14]), which has the highest probability of meeting the time constraint. This parent node is used as the primary recipient (PR) of flooding. Then, each node also selects several secondary recipients (SRs) based on the time constraint as well as the criteria on flooding-controllability, congestion avoidance and computation simplicity. When unicasting is determined to be sufficient for meeting a packet's time constraint, the PR aborts the SRs' next-hop flooding (this is done through the flooding control mechanism discussed next). Otherwise, the PR and all the SRs continue to flood the packet further.
- *Flooding control.* The working sequence of a MAC protocol, which supports collision avoidance with the RTS/CTS exchange mechanism, can be summarized as RTS-CTS-DATA or RTS-BACKOFF, depending on whether the RTS/CTS exchange succeeds. For controlling the flooding scale, CFlood inserts an ABORT phase after CTS for the PR's flooding, and a WAIT phase before RTS for SRs' flooding. Thus, the working sequence of a PR will be modified as RTS-CTS-ABORT-DATA or RTS-BACKOFF, and that of SRs will be modified as WAIT-ABORT, WAIT-RTS-CTS-DATA or WAIT-RTS-BACKOFF. If a PR finds that the channel is clear after receiving a CTS, it broadcasts an ABORT message so that SRs can abort their subsequent flooding actions.

3.2 Neighborhood Table Management

This component manages the neighborhood table, each entry of which corresponds to a neighbor node. An entry includes the following fields:

(NeighborID, ParentID, HopCount, SendDelay, TTL)

ParentID is the ID of this neighbor node's parent. HopCount is the number of hops by which the neighbor node is away from the sink node. SendDelay is the estimated delay for sending a packet to this neighbor node. TTL is short for Time To Live. The table management operations include adding, updating, expiring, and removing.

The entries in the neighborhood table are updated via HELLO message exchanges, which is a commonly used approach for sharing local knowledge among neighbors [3]. The mechanism has the advantage that it can adapt the network to possible topology changes (e.g., those caused by link failure, node failure). Each HELLO message includes the fields (SenderID, ParentID, HopCount, SendDelay), so that all the receivers may update the entry in their neighborhood tables for the node that sends this HELLO message. For example, at the beginning, when a network is deployed, each node in the network holds an empty neighborhood table. From a HELLO message received from a sink node, all the neighbors of this sink node will know that their HopCount is 1. By iteration, the HopCount will be increased by 1 at each hop from the sink node to all other nodes in the network. (We will discuss the selection of a node's parent and the estimation of SendDelay later in this section.)

3.3 Real-Time Guarantee Verification

As previously discussed, CFlood compares the estimated per-hop delay L_h with the distributed per-hop sub-deadline D_h to determine whether or not a potential recipient can satisfy the time constraint. This component is responsible for estimating L_h, computing D_h, and conducting the comparison.

Per-hop Delay Estimation. The delay experienced at a hop usually consists of the transmission delay, the propagation delay, and the receiving delay. The transmission delay is the time that a packet experiences at the sender's MAC and PHY layers. The propagation delay is the duration when a data signal together with its carrier travels in the air. The receiving delay is the time that a packet experiences at the receiver's PHY and MAC layers. Since the delay includes parts at both the sender and the receiver, the precise measurement will require time synchronization, which is generally energy inefficient [15]. We introduce a feasible mechanism without assuming time synchronization, although our estimation result may not be perfectly precise due to the asymmetry of wireless channels.

The problem of estimating the round-trip delay has been well studied in the past [16]. We simply apply the existing method into the HELLO message exchange mechanism. Suppose the neighbors of a node N are $\{N_i | N_i \in NB(N)\}$. Node N may append a round-trip delay estimation request for a specific neighbor node N_i in a randomly chosen HELLO message (e.g., one out of every twenty continuous HELLO messages). Neighbors other than N_i deal with this HELLO message as usual, while N_i is supposed to reply with a HELLO message immediately. Then a round-trip delay is obtained by node N, the half of which can be used as the estimated per-hop delay and is saved in the SendDelay field of N_i's entry. This does not require time synchronization since the starting and ending time points of the round trip are sampled at the same node.

Per-hop Deadline Computation. Most of the past works on the end-to-end deadline partition [17, 18] have adopted either uniform or exponential models. Uniform distribution allocates the total end-to-end deadline evenly to all the hops from the source to the sink, implicitly assuming that a packet suffers the same delay at each hop. The exponential model computes the per-hop sub-deadline as $D_h = \frac{D}{2^h}$, where h is the number of hops from the sink node and D represents the end-to-end deadline. These schemes are based on analytical models and do not consider the actual throughputs of the network. We now introduce a throughput-based model by establishing a relationship between the per-hop sub-deadline and the number of nodes at each hop in an intuitive manner.

Let ρ denote the node density of the network. Now, the average number of nodes that are h hops away from the sink node, denoted as C_h, can be computed as $\rho(\pi(hR)^2 - \pi[(h-1)R]^2) = \rho\pi R^2(2h-1)$. Intuitively, at a specific hop in a convergecast network, lesser the number of nodes, greater will be the traffic that each node has to transport toward the sink node. Thus, longer will be the delay that a packet will suffer at the hop. Consequently, a longer sub-deadline will be needed for the hop. This relationship can be approximately modeled as $D_h \sim T_h \sim \frac{1}{C_h}$, where T_h is the average throughput of a node at hop h. When the node density ρ is fixed for a given implementation, we have $D_h \sim \frac{1}{2h-1}$. Thus, the end-to-end deadline D over an h-hop transmission can be distributed according to its weight at each hop k as $D_k = \frac{\frac{1}{2k-1}}{\sum_{k=1}^{h} \frac{1}{2k-1}} \cdot D$. Especially the sub-deadline of the first hop from the source is:

$$D_h = \frac{\frac{1}{2h-1}}{\sum_{k=1}^{h} \frac{1}{2k-1}} \cdot D \tag{1}$$

Figure 2 shows the comparison among the uniform model, the exponential model, and the throughput-based model, for an example with a 200 ms end-to-end deadline over 20 hops. We can observe that compared with the uniform model, the throughput-based model is more adaptive for the many-to-one convergecast architecture of WSNs. In addition, unlike the exponential model for which the distributed per-hop deadline decreases quickly to zero, the throughput-based model supports larger-scale networks.

For a single node N, its hop count from the sink node may be different when considering different routes via different neighbor nodes. Therefore the result of (1) needs to be computed for each potential recipient. Suppose HopCount of a neighbor node N_i is h_i. When N_i is used for relaying, the distributed per-hop sub-deadline at this hop is:

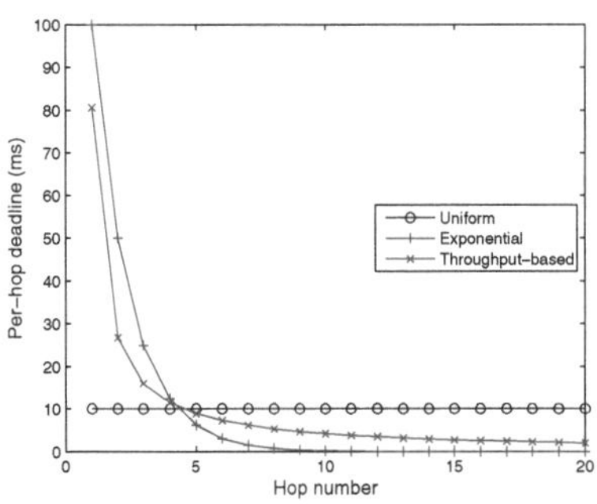

Fig. 2. Deadline Distribution

$$D_{h_i+1} = \frac{\frac{1}{2(h_i+1)-1}}{\sum_{k=1}^{h_i+1} \frac{1}{2k-1}} \cdot D \tag{2}$$

Real-time Guarantee Verification. For a specific neighbor N_i, we establish a function $CanMeetDeadline(N_i)$, in which the per-hop deadline D_{h_i+1} is computed and compared with the per-hop delay L_{h_i+1} (i.e., SendDelay in the neighborhood table). The function $CanMeetDeadline(N_i)$ returns true when $L_{h_i+1} < D_{h_i+1}$ and false otherwise. Only those neighbors that has a true return value will be considered as potential recipients.

3.4 Recipient Selection

The recipient selection component is responsible for selecting the flooding recipients (both a PR and multiple SRs) from the one-hop neighbors. With CFlood, each node computes a parent node as the PR periodically even when no data packets are passing through. The criteria used for SR selection include real-time guarantee, flooding-controllability, congestion avoidance, and simplicity of computation.

Primary Recipient. As one of CFlood's techniques to constrain the flooding scale is to substitute unicasting for flooding as much as possible, a parent needs to be prepared for each node as the next-hop neighbor of unicasting.

For a neighbor N_i, (2) shows the distributed per-hop deadline D_{h_i+1}. We can also estimate the per-hop delay L_{h_i+1} with the round-trip HELLO message exchange. Thus, we define a ratio $SL_i = 1 - \frac{L_{h_i+1}}{D_{h_i+1}}$ to describe the proportion of the slack time, and call it, the *slack time ratio*. The slack time ratio describes how likely N_i can meet a packet's sub-deadline for this hop. Based on our throughput-based deadline partition model, the slack time ratio also describes how likely a route via N_i can meet the end-to-end time constraint. Therefore, we select a neighbor N_i with the maximum SL_i as the parent node, i.e., a neighbor with

$$\max_i(SL_i) \sim \min_i\left\{\frac{L_{h_i+1}}{D_{h_i+1}}\right\} = \frac{1}{D} \cdot \min_i\left\{L_{h_i+1} \cdot \frac{\sum_{k=1}^{h_i+1} \frac{1}{2k-1}}{\frac{1}{2(h_i+1)-1}}\right\}$$

Secondary Recipients. For selecting SRs, we progressively remove those neighbor nodes that cannot satisfy the following criteria:

1. *Real-time guarantee.* An SR should meet the time constraint (i.e., $CanMeetDeadline(N_i)$ returns true).

2. *Flooding-controllability.* The subsequent flooding of an SR should be able to be aborted by the PR.

3. *Congestion avoidance.* An SR should not introduce new congestion, since CFlood's major objective is to quickly bypass network congestion or connection failure. Thus we remove redundant SRs that share the parent with other SRs and have lower probabilities for meeting the time constraint. By strictly prohibiting two recipients from sharing a common parent, the network congestion could be avoided at least for the next hop.

4. *Simplicity of computation.* CFlood is designed to be as simple as possible due to the constrained computing capability of sensor nodes. We use a set of "common sense-based" operations to quickly reduce the problem size before applying the first three ones. These quick reduction operations include: 1) remove all the neighbors whose parent is also a neighbor of the flooding node, and thus also has a chance to receive the packet at this hop, i.e., $Parent(N_i) \in NB(N)$; 2) remove all the neighbors that send packets to the flooding node at the last hop, i.e., $N_i = Source(N)$; and 3) remove all the neighbors that have received packets at the last hop, i.e., $N_i \in Forward(Source(N))$.

Next, we describe the SR selection algorithm at a high-level of abstraction in Algorithm 1. The algorithm complexity is $O(n^2)$ for searching N_i in $Forward(Source(N))$, where n is the average number of one-hop neighbors of a node. The magnitude of n is small. For example, our simulation shows that in a network with node density 0.005 $node/m^2$ (i.e., each node covers an area of 200 m^2), n is only up to 5.

Algorithm 1. Secondary recipient selection

Initialize the SR candidate set as $SR = \{N_i | N_i \in NB(N), Hop(N_i) < Hop(N)\}$;
for all ($N_i \in SR$) **do**
  Examine N_i with the conditions of three quick reduction operations, i.e., remove N_i if ($Parent(N_i) \in NB(N)$) or ($N_i = Source(N)$) or ($N_i \in Forward(Source(N))$);
  Remove N_i if it violates the time constraint, i.e., if ($CanMeetDeadline(N_i)$=**false**);
  Remove N_i if it violates the flooding-controllability criterion, i.e., if it cannot hear from the PR ($N_i \notin NB(PR)$);
  Remove N_i if it violates the congestion avoidance criterion by sharing a parent with the PR, i.e., if ($Parent(N_i) = Parent(PR)$);
end for
if ($SR == \phi$) **then**
  return ϕ
end if
Sort the remaining SRs in a descending order of SL_i;
for all ($N_i \in SR$) **do**
  Remove N_i if it violates the congestion avoidance criterion by sharing a parent with another SR with a higher SL_i, i.e., if ($\exists j < i, Parent(N_i) = Parent(N_j)$);
end for
return SR

3.5 Flooding Control

One of the most important contributions of this paper is the flooding control mechanism, i.e., to abort the subsequent flooding after the current flooding occurs. In detail, the PR and the SRs forward packets in different ways. As the flooding node of the next hop, the PR initiates an RTS/CTS exchange with its PR immediately after receiving a packet. If a CTS is received successfully, the PR broadcasts an ABORT message and then unicasts the data packet. Otherwise, the PR backs off for some period of time and again initiates the RTS/CTS exchange later. Unlike the PR, the SRs set an ABORT timer for each received data packet. If an ABORT message from a PR is received for a buffered data packet, the SRs drop that packet. Otherwise, if the timer runs out first, the SRs know that

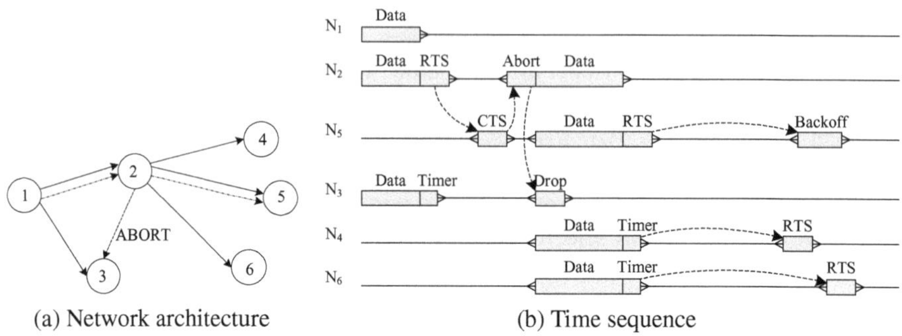

Fig. 3. An example of CFlood's flooding control mechanism

the PR's flooding for the next hop is delayed (i.e., backed off), and therefore they start to flood the packet to the next hop. In this way, when the network condition is good (e.g., the RTS/CTS exchange initiated by the PR succeeds without backoff), the flooding is reduced to unicast (because the SRs drop the packet on receiving the ABORT message).

Overhearing is also an approach for controlling flooding [19], e.g., the SRs abort the subsequent flooding upon overhearing the transmission of the PR. However, overhearing is not a good choice under the time constraint. Not until the SRs overhear the complete packet payload and send it up to the network layer, can they drop the corresponding packet saved in the buffer. Such a transmission through the network stack may introduce extra delays, especially when the data packet is long.

Figure 3 shows an example of CFlood's flooding control mechanism. In the figure, the circle with the number i represents node N_i. In Figure 3a, the dash-dot arrows show the parent relation (e.g., $Parent(N_2) = N_5$), the solid lines show the actual data transmission (e.g., $Forward(N_1) = \{N_2, N_3\}$), and the dotted line represents the ABORT messages. Figure 3b shows the time sequence of the nodes. The dotted curves show the working mechanism of flooding control. When N_2 (as the PR of N_1) finds that the channel is clear on receiving the CTS reply, it broadcasts an ABORT message and then sends out the data packet. Node N_3 (as an SR of N_1) receives the ABORT message from N_2 before the timer runs out. Thus, it aborts the subsequent flooding and drops the packet. On the contrary, N_5 does not receive the CTS reply from its parent node. Thus, it has to backoff for sometime without broadcasting an ABORT message. As N_4 and N_6 do not receive the expected ABORT message before the timer runs out, they have to continue the flooding by initiating the RTS/CTS exchange. The expiration time for the ABORT timers on SRs can be either determined by specific application configurations, or computed as the minimum allowed slack time $\min_i\{D_{h_i+1} - L_{h_i+1}\}$ of that SR node at the next hop.

4 Experimental Evaluation

We evaluated CFlood using the simulation tools Qualnet 4.0 [20] and sQualnet [21], which is an extension to Qualnet for sensor networks. The simulation is based on the CSMA/CA MAC protocol implemented in sQualnet.

4.1 Simulation Environment

We deploy 20 to 150 sensor nodes uniformly in a square area of $200m \times 200m$, and assume Mica motes [22] as the hardware platform. We set $R = 60m$, $r = 30m$, and the data rate as 38.4 kbps. We leverage the statistics provided by sQualnet to estimate the energy consumption.

Each sensor node samples and reports an event (e.g., detection of a target) once per second. We configure the lengths of a data packet, a HELLO message, and an ABORT message as 150 bytes, 50 bytes, and 10 bytes, respectively. Usually 10 bytes (e.g. including the ID of the source node and the ID of this packet) are long enough for an ABORT message to identify a specific data packet.

We compared CFlood against three past competitor algorithms. Mint routing (MR) is a single path delivery protocol [14], which serves as a lower bound on both real-time performance and energy consumption. MCMP [2], a multipath routing protocol, is one of the latest efforts on optimizing data delivery under both real-time and reliability constraints. DFP [10] (short for Directional Flooding Protocol) is a forwarding protocol that optimizes the delivery probability. We measure the performance metrics of interest of CFlood and these protocols under varying degrees of node density, link reliability, and end-to-end time constraint, the default values of which are 0.0015 $node/m^2$, 75%, and $100ms$, respectively.

4.2 Simulation Results

Figure 4 shows the deadline satisfaction ratio of the four protocols under different node densities. Due to the competition of the two factors, the number of recipients and the congestion level, the curves present crests. We observe that CFlood yields the best *DSR*.

Figure 5 shows the average energy consumption per real-time packet under different node densities. We observe that MR, as the lower bound, consumes the least energy, and CFlood consumes the most. But the energy consumption of CFlood is very close to that of DFP.

Figure 6 shows the real-time capacity per unit energy consumption δ under different node densities. We observe that CFlood performs the best, especially when the node density is low. Detailed simulation results show that on average, CFlood is 197%, 346%, and 20% better than MR, MCMP and DFP, respectively.

Figure 7 shows the deadline satisfaction ratio under various per-hop wireless link reliability. Among the four protocols, CFlood yields the best *DSR*, especially when the

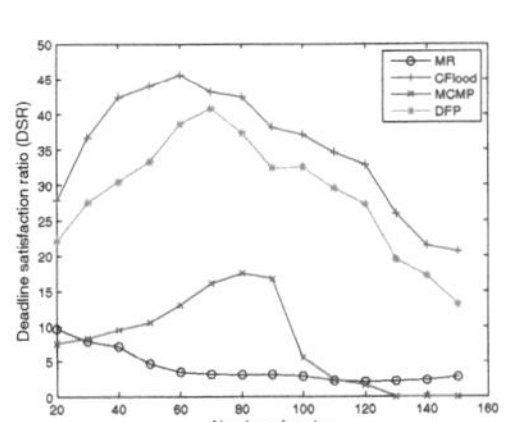

Fig. 4. Deadline satisfaction ratio *DSR* vs. node density

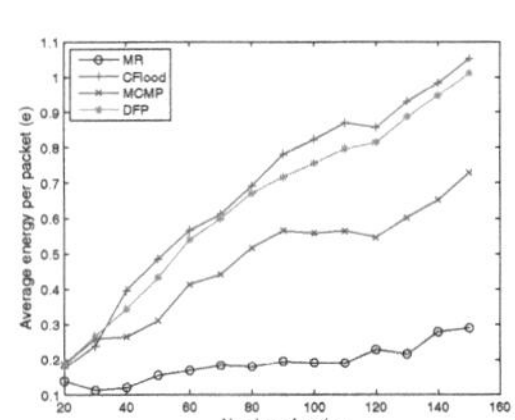

Fig. 5. Average energy consumption *e* vs. node density

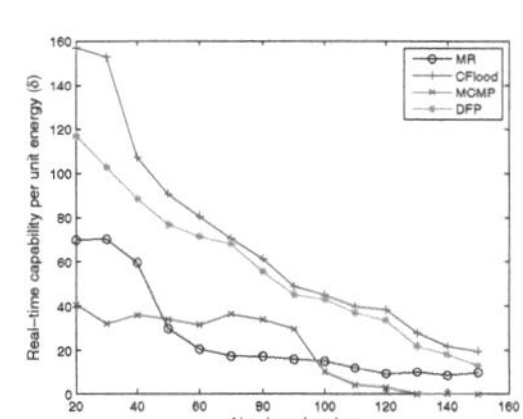

Fig. 6. Real-time capacity δ vs. node density

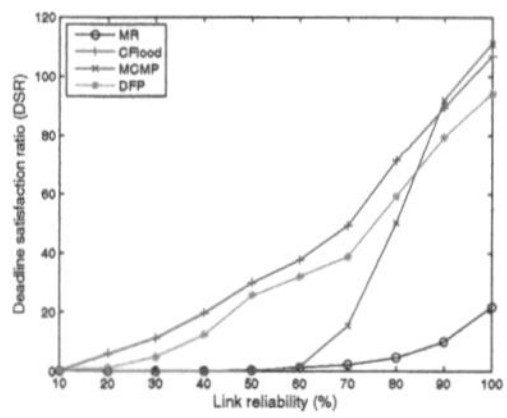

Fig. 7. Deadline satisfaction ratio *DSR* vs. link reliability

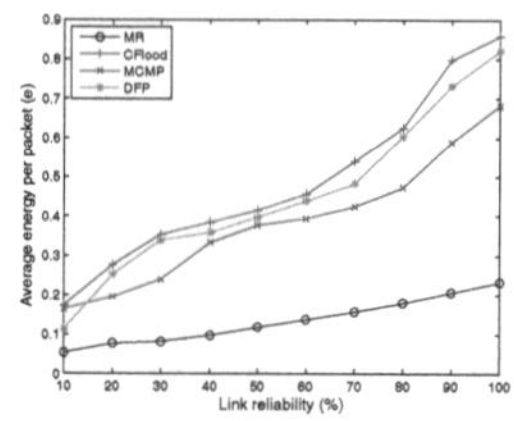

Fig. 8. Average energy consumption *e* vs. link reliability

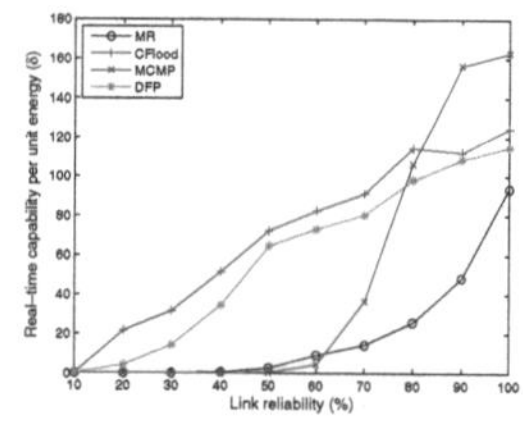

Fig. 9. Real-time capacity δ vs. link reliability

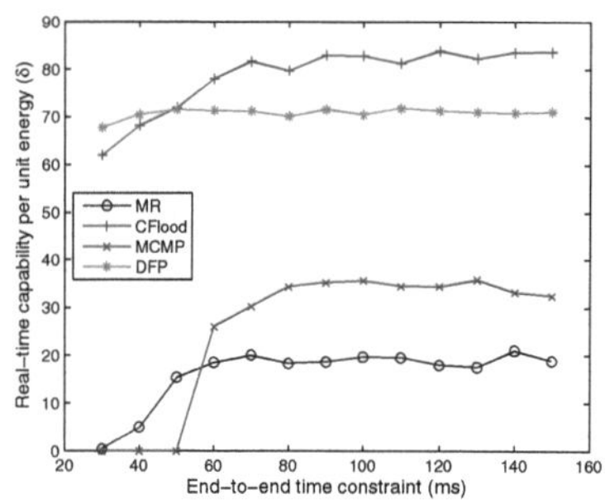

Fig. 10. Real-time capacity δ vs. end-to-end time constraint

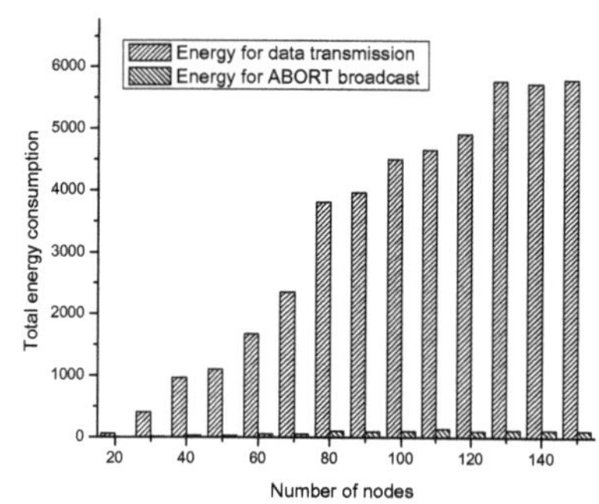

Fig. 11. Energy for data transmission and ABORT broadcast

link reliability is low. As the link reliability increases, the *DSR*s of CFlood, MCMP, and DFP tend to be comparable, and MR remains as the lower bound. We observe that MCMP performs well especially when the network condition is good, while CFlood is more adaptive to unreliable network environments.

Figure 8 shows that CFlood consumes the most energy. However, when we consider the real-time capacity per unit energy consumption δ, CFlood outperforms the other three protocols when the link reliability is lower than 80%, as shown in Figure 9.

Figure 10 shows that the real-time capacity per unit energy consumption δ of CFlood is higher than that of the other three protocols, as long as the end-to-end time constraint is not very tight.

CFlood's flooding control mechanism based on ABORT messages does introduce some overheads. However, the extra energy consumption is negligible. Figure 11 shows the contrast between the energy consumption for data transmission and that for the ABORT message exchange. We observe that the energy consumption for ABORT messages is only about 1% of the energy consumption for data transmission. This implies that CFlood's flooding control mechanism introduces little overhead.

Thus, our simulation results reveal that CFlood achieves better real-time capacity per unit energy consumption than past protocols, especially for sparse node deployment, unreliable wireless links, and loose end-to-end time constraints.

5 Related Work

Existing works on supporting real-time traffic in WSNs have focused on latency and timely delivery from various perspectives. For example, Abdelzaher *et. al.* discussed a WSN's real-time capacity from a macro perspective without making any detailed assumptions [17]. He *et. al.* present detailed delay bounds for each chain of target tracking applications in [1]. Other efforts considered real-time performance as a constraint that must be satisfied [23]. In contrast, we focus on improving the deadline satisfaction ratio per unit energy consumption.

In unreliable network environments, past data delivery protocols use different approaches to guarantee timeliness. Single path forwarding protocols transmit one copy of data along a predetermined single path, and depend on retransmissions to guarantee reliability [24]. In contrast, multipath data delivery protocols transmit a number of copies through multiple routes simultaneously. This will increase the reliability and the probability of delivering real-time data in a timely manner, but often at the expense of additional energy consumption.

Multipath routing protocols can be broadly classified into two categories, static routing and dynamic routing. Static multipath routing protocols setup multiple routes, which are either disjoint [3] or braided [4], before sending out a data packet. The source nodes then either choose one of the routes or combine the resources of all the routes for a single flow. In contrast, dynamic multipath forwarding protocols decide the flooding recipients at each hop so that the data flow is split distributively.

Dynamic routing protocols can be further classified into multicast, broadcast (or flooding), and gossip. Multicast has been extensively studied for WSNs [5], most of which aim at multihop one-to-many communications. Broadcasting and flooding are usually used interchangeably, but there are also works that distinguish them with minor differences [25]. The HHB scheme introduced in [6] is a hop-by-hop broadcast protocol that leverages the broadcasting capability of wireless medium to guarantee the reliable delivery. The HHB protocol broadcasts at each hop with a specific probability to avoid degenerating into a flooding storm. Zhang *et. al.* present a constrained flooding protocol in [7], which exhibits good energy efficiency by constraining retransmissions. Gossip can be considered as a form of probabilistic flooding. In [8], Lu *et. al.* present a gossip algorithm called NBgossip, which forwards the linear combinations of the received messages.

Almost all of the multipath data delivery protocols introduce extra overheads even when unicasting is enough for satisfying QoS constraints such as timeliness. In contrast, CFlood uses flooding but constrains the energy consumption effectively by controlling the scale of flooding.

6 Conclusions

This paper presents a constrained flooding protocol, called CFlood, that enhances the real-time capability per unit energy consumption in WSNs. Besides the fundamental functions of a routing protocol such as neighborhood table management, we present a flooding control mechanism based on ABORT message exchanges, and a recipient selection method to reduce energy consumption. Our experimental evaluation based on Qualnet shows that CFlood outperforms past multipath routing/forwarding protocols, especially for sparsely deployed networks or unreliable wireless links. This result reveals that the cross-layer design of CFlood's flooding control, e.g. substituting unicasting for flooding as much as possible, effectively improves the flooding efficiency.

Directions for future work include: 1) verifying CFlood's performance with real experiments; 2) achieving reliability guarantees; and 3) extending CFlood to sensor networks with multiple sink nodes. With real experiments and corresponding dynamic network conditions, e.g., probabilistic sensing and communication ranges, we would be able to verify CFlood's performance, and make improvements on the design if necessary. For example, we may develop a dynamic configuration method for the frequency of HELLO message exchange, so that the precision of per-hop delay estimation could be optimized under dynamic network conditions.

References

1. He, T., Vicaire, P., Yan, T., Luo, L., Gu, L., Zhou, G., Stoleru, R., Cao, Q., Stankovic, J.A., Abdelzaher, T.: Achieving real-time target tracking using wireless sensor networks. In: RTAS 2006: Proceedings of the 12th IEEE Real-Time and Embedded Technology and Applications Symposium, pp. 37–48 (2006)
2. Huang, X., Fang, Y.: Multiconstrained qos multipath routing in wireless sensor networks. Wirel. Netw. 14(4), 465–478 (2008)
3. Lu, Y.M., Wong, V.W.S.: An energy-efficient multipath routing protocol for wireless sensor networks: Research articles. Int. J. Commun. Syst. 20(7), 747–766 (2007)
4. De, S., Qiao, C., Wu, H.: Meshed multipath routing with selective forwarding: an efficient strategy in wireless sensor networks. Computer Networks 43(4), 481–497 (2003)
5. Silva, J.S., Camilo, T., Pinto, P., Rodrigues, R.R.A., Gaudncio, F., Boavida, F.: Multicast and ip multicast support in wireless sensor networks. Networks, 19–26 (2008)
6. Deb, B., Bhatnagar, S., Nath, B.: Information assurance in sensor networks. In: WSNA 2003: Proceedings of the 2nd ACM international conference on Wireless sensor networks and applications, pp. 160–168 (2003)
7. Zhang, Y., Fromherz, M.: Constrained flooding: A robust and efficient routing framework for wireless sensor networks. In: AINA: Proceedings of the 20th International Conference on Advanced Information Networking and Applications, pp. 387–392 (2006)
8. Lu, F., Chia, L.T., Tay, K.L., Chong, W.H.: Nbgossip: An energy-efficient gossip algorithm for wireless sensor networks. Journal of Computer Science and Technology 23(3), 426–437 (2008)
9. Li, P., Ravindran, B., Wang, J., Konowicz, G.: Choir: A real-time middleware architecture supporting benefit-based proactive resource allocation. In: IEEE International Symposium on Object-Oriented Real-Time Distributed Computing, p. 292 (2003)
10. Ko, Y.B., Choi, J.M., Kim, J.H.: A new directional flooding protocol for wireless sensor networks. In: Kahng, H.-K., Goto, S. (eds.) ICOIN 2004. LNCS, vol. 3090, pp. 93–102. Springer, Heidelberg (2004)
11. Zhang, H., Arora, A., Choi, Y.r., Gouda, M.G.: Reliable bursty convergecast in wireless sensor networks. Comput. Commun. 30(13), 2560–2576 (2007)
12. Gupta, P., Kumar, P.: The capacity of wireless networks. IEEE Transactions on Information Theory 46(2), 388–404 (2000)

13. Part 11: Wireless LAN Medium Access Control (MAC) and Physical Layer (PHY) Specifications. IEEE (approved in 1999, reaffirmed in 2003, revised in 2007)
14. Woo, A., Tong, T., Culler, D.: Taming the underlying challenges of reliable multihop routing in sensor networks. In: SenSys 2003: Proceedings of the 1st international conference on Embedded networked sensor systems, pp. 14–27 (2003)
15. Sivrikaya, F., Yener, B.: Time synchronization in sensor networks: a survey. IEEE Network 18(4), 45–50 (2004)
16. IETF: Rfc 2681 - a round-trip delay metric for ippm, `http://www.ietf.org/rfc/rfc2681.txt?number=2681`
17. Abdelzaher, T.F., Prabh, S., Kiran, R.: On real-time capacity limits of multihop wireless sensor networks. In: RTSS 2004: Proceedings of the 25th IEEE International Real-Time Systems Symposium, pp. 359–370 (2004)
18. Liu, K., Abu-Ghazaleh, N., Kang, K.D.: Jits: just-in-time scheduling for real-time sensor data dissemination. In: Fourth Annual IEEE International Conference on Pervasive Computing and Communications, pp. 5–46 (2006)
19. Basu, P., Redi, J.: Effect of overhearing transmissions on energy efficiency in dense sensor networks. In: Third International Symposium on Information Processing in Sensor Networks (IPSN), pp. 196–204 (2004)
20. Scalable-Networks: Qualnet network simulator, `http://www.scalable-networks.com/`
21. Vasu, B., Varshney, M., Rengaswamy, R., Marina, M., Dixit, A., Aghera, P., Srivastava, M., Bagrodia, R.: Squalnet: a scalable simulation framework for sensor networks. In: SenSys: Proceedings of the 3rd international conference on Embedded networked sensor systems, pp. 322–322. ACM, New York (2005)
22. CrossBow: Mica data sheet, `http://www.xbow.com`
23. Lu, G., Sadagopan, N., Krishnamachari, B., Goel, A.: Delay efficient sleep scheduling in wireless sensor networks. In: INFOCOM 2005. 24th Annual Joint Conference of the IEEE Computer and Communications Societies. Proceedings, vol. 4, pp. 2470–2481. IEEE, Los Alamitos (2005)
24. Willig, A., Karl, H.: Data transport reliability in wireless sensor networks - a survey of issues and solutions. In: Praxis der Informationsverarbeitung und Kommunikation, pp. 86–92 (2005)
25. Pleisch, S., Balakrishnan, M., Birman, K., van Renesse, R.: Mistral: Efficient flooding in mobile ad-hoc networks. In: Proceedings of the 7th ACM International Symposium on Mobile Ad Hoc Networking and Computing (MobiHoc), pp. 1–12. ACM Press, New York (2006)

Cached Sensornet Transformation of Non-silent Self-stabilizing Algorithms with Unreliable Links

Hirotsugu Kakugawa[1,⋆], Yukiko Yamauchi[2], Sayaka Kamei[3,⋆⋆], and Toshimitsu Masuzawa[1,⋆⋆⋆]

[1] Osaka University, Suita, Osaka, Japan
[2] Nara Institute of Science and Technology, Ikoma, Nara, Japan
[3] Hiroshima University, Higashihiroshima, Hiroshima, Japan

Abstract. A wireless sensor network is a set of nodes, each is equipped with sensors and a wireless communication device. Cached Sensornet Transform (CST for short) is a methodology for design and implementation of self-stabilizing algorithms for sensor networks. It transforms a self-stabilizing algorithm in the abstract computational model to a program for sensor networks. In the literature, only CST transformation of silent self-stabilizing algorithms have been investigated, while non-silent ones have not been investigated. Our contribution in this paper is three-fold. We present a counterexample of a non-silent algorithm transformed by CST that does not behave correctly despite the original algorithm is correct. We show a sufficient condition for original algorithms and networks such that a transformed algorithm by CST behaves correctly. We present a token circulation algorithm that behaves correctly by CST, and derive upper bound of its expected convergence time.

1 Introduction

1.1 Background

A wireless sensor network is a set of nodes, each is equipped with wireless communication device and sensors to monitor environment. Software design for wireless sensor networks is a challenging problem because the resource on each node is limited and the wireless communication is unreliable. In addition, a set of sensor nodes in operation dynamically changes because new sensor nodes are deployed in ad-hoc manner and a sensor node stops working when its battery is exhausted. Therefore, self-$*$ is a key concept for system design. Self-stabilization is a theoretical framework for non-masking fault-tolerant distributed systems which is

---

⋆ This work is supported in part by Grant-in-Aid for Scientific Research ((B)20300012 and (B)17300020) of JSPS, Kayamori Foundation of Informational Science Advancement.

⋆⋆ This work is supported in part by Grant-in-Aid for Young Scientists ((B)19700075) of JSPS.

⋆⋆⋆ This work is supported in part by Grant-in-Aid for Scientific Research ((B)19300017) of JSPS, and Global COE (Centers of Excellence) Program of MEXT.

R. Guerraoui and F. Petit (Eds.): SSS 2009, LNCS 5873, pp. 428–442, 2009.

introduced by Dijkstra in 1974 [1]. Specifically, starting from an arbitrary initial configuration (system state), a self-stabilizing system converges to correct system behavior without any human intervention and globally synchronized system reset. This implies that (1) it recovers from any finite number of any kind of transient faults, which are also known as soft errors, e.g., memory and message corruption, and (2) it can adapt to network topology and node set changes.

1.2 Related Works

Although self-stabilization is extremely important in distributed systems, design and verification of a self-stabilizing distributed algorithm is a hard task because such a system must recover from arbitrary transient faults. By this reason, many self-stabilizing distributed algorithms are designed under a computational model what we call the *abstract model* (e.g., coarse-grained atomic action with the state-reading model, which is similar to distributed shared memory) for simplicity of design and verification. However, a big semantic gap lies between such an abstract model and real sensor networks (e.g., fine-grained atomic action with message passing). In this paper, our computational model for sensor networks is called the *sensor network model*. Several model transformation methods that fill in the gap have been proposed so far to execute self-stabilizing distributed algorithms designed in the abstract model on more realistic model such as the sensor network model.

Transformation with exact model equivalence. Transformation in this category guarantees that any execution of a transformed algorithm is exactly the same as an execution under an abstract model. A transformation proposed in [2] is based on optimistic concurrency control from database theory, and update of a local state of a node is considered as a transaction. In [3], a transformation scheme from an abstract (called read/write) model to a sensor network (called write all with collision, WAC) model is presented. Their solution is essentially an execution scheduling protocol for nodes so that no two neighbor nodes execute at the same time like TDMA (time-division multiple access). Because a packet is lost only when neighbor nodes transmit a packet in the WAC model, execution is equivalent to the one in an abstract model.

Transformation with inexact model equivalence. Transformation in this category does not guarantee model equivalence, and a transformed algorithm may produce an execution that never occurs in an abstract model. However, runtime overhead of this transformation category is smaller than that of transformation by exact model equivalence in general. Transformations proposed in [4,5] are based on caching the neighbors' states without any cache maintenance protocols to simulate state-reading model. In each transformation scheme in [4,5], each node maintains a cache of the state of each neighbor node, and each node v_i sends its local state to each neighbor node v_j to update the cache of local state of v_i at v_j. In [4], Huang, Wuu and Tsai propose a transformation for general networks with reliable FIFO communication links. In [5], Herman gives a transformation for wireless sensor networks, named *Cached Sensornet Transform* (CST for short). He assumes that each node has correct cache of each neighbor node in an initial configuration[1] and he also assumes communication is reliable. By these assumptions, correctness of each cache is maintained by sending a new local state when a node updates its local state. In [6], Turau and Weyer show that CST yields a probabilistically self-stabilizing algorithm that converges to a safe configuration[2] with probability 1 from an arbitrary initial configuration. They assume that each node receives a packet from each neighbor with probability $0 < p < 1$, i.e., each communication link is probabilistically unreliable. In [7], Kakugawa and Masuzawa presented upper bounds on the expected convergence time of several self-stabilizing algorithms transformed by CST under the same setting as [6]. Experimental results for CST with real sensor network are found in [6,8] for example.

There are other works on model transformation. The authors of [9] propose a transformation method called conflict manager. It transforms an algorithm in the abstract model in which only one node is executed at each step to an algorithm in the abstract model in which only more than one nodes are executed simultaneously at each step. They propose two types of conflict managers: a deterministic one which guarantees model equivalence and a probabilistic one which guarantees model inequivalence.

1.3 Contribution of This Paper

In this paper, we investigate CST transformation of non-silent self-stabilizing algorithms, e.g., a token circulation algorithm. In [5,6,7], only silent self-stabilizing algorithms, e.g., a maximal independent set algorithm, are investigated, and unfortunately non-silent self-stabilizing algorithms have not been investigated in the literature. Analysis methods in [6,7] for silent self-stabilizing algorithms do not apply to non-silent ones as we will discuss in Section 5. In addition, not all transformed algorithms work correctly in case of non-silent self-stabilizing algorithms, while the transformation works correctly for any silent self-stabilizing algorithm as shown in [6]. Our work is the first one for the transformation of non-silent self-stabilizing algorithms. The contribution of this paper is threefold.

1. Impossibility result. We show a counterexample of a non-silent algorithm transformed by CST that does not behave correctly despite the fact that the original algorithm is correct in the abstract model.
2. Possibility result. One may think that any transformed algorithm does not work in the sensor network model because of packet loss. However, this is not true. We present a sufficient condition for original algorithms and networks such that the transformed algorithm behaves correctly.

---

[1] A configuration is a global state of a distributed system. A formal definition will be presented shortly.

[2] A safe configuration is a configuration in which the specification of an algorithm is satisfied.

3. Convergence time analysis. We present an example algorithm (specifically, token circulation on unidirectional rings) that behaves correctly by the transformation, and derive upper bound of its expected convergence time.

Organization of this paper is as follows. In Section 2, we describe computational models and self-stabilization. In Section 3, CST is reviewed. In Section 4, we present a counterexample algorithm that does not behave correctly by CST. In Section 5, we show a sufficient condition such that a transformed algorithm behaves correctly. In Section 6, we present upper bound of expected convergence time of a token circulation algorithm on unidirectional rings. In Section 7, we give concluding remarks.

2 Preliminary

2.1 The Abstract Model

Let n be the number of nodes, $V = (v_1, v_2, ..., v_n)$ be a set of nodes, and $E \subseteq V \times V$ be a set of directed communication links in a distributed system. Then, the topology of the distributed system is represented as a directed simple graph $G_A = (V, E)$. We assume that G is a connected graph. For each communication link $(v_i, v_j) \in E$, we say that v_j is an *out-neighbor* of v_i, and v_i is an *in-neighbor* of v_j. By N_i, we denote a set of in-neighbors of v_i. By $v_i.x$, we denote a local variable x at node v_i. A set of local variables defines the local state of a node, and let $v_i.q$ be the local state (tuple of all local variables) of node $v_i \in V$. A tuple of local states of nodes $(v_1.q, v_2.q, ..., v_n.q)$ forms a *configuration* (global state) of a distributed system, and let Γ be a set of all configurations.

An algorithm of each node v_i is given as a finite set of guarded commands:

$$*[\ \mathit{Grd}_1 \to \mathit{Act}_1 \ \Box\ \mathit{Grd}_2 \to \mathit{Act}_2 \ \Box\ \cdots \quad \Box\ \mathit{Grd}_L \to \mathit{Act}_L]$$

Each Grd_ℓ ($\ell = 1, 2, ..., L$) is called a *guard* and it is a predicate on v_i's local state and local states of its in-neighbors. For communication model, we assume that each node can read local states of in-neighbors, which is called the *state-reading model.* Although a node can read local states of in-neighbors, it can update its local state only. We say that v_i is *enabled* in configuration γ if and only if at least one guard of v_i is true in γ. If v_i is not enabled, we say that v_i is *disabled.* Each Act_ℓ is called an *action* or *move* which updates the local state of v_i, and the next local state is computed from the current local state of v_i and those of its in-neighbors. We assume that an enabled node becomes disabled by executing an action.

An atomic step of each node v_i consists of the following three internal substeps, which is known as the *composite atomicity* model: read local states of in-neighbors and evaluate guards, execute an action that is associated to a true guard, if any, and update its local state.

For execution model, following two types of schedulers are often assumed in the literature of self-stabilizing distributed algorithms. (1) *The central daemon*:

At each step, only one enabled node is selected arbitrarily, and a selected node executes an action. (2) *The distributed daemon*: At each step, an arbitrary non-empty subset of enabled nodes are selected, and selected nodes execute their actions in parallel. We assume that a self-stabilizing algorithm in the abstract model adopts the central or the distributed daemon in this paper.

2.2 The Sensor Network Model

Communication. Let $V = (v_1, v_2, ..., v_n)$ be a set of nodes. Each node communicates via wireless communication device, and we assume that no two nodes transmit their packets simultaneously. We assume that message delay is zero because two nodes directly communicate via wireless communication. The topology of the distributed system is represented as a directed graph $G_S = (V, E)$. Each communication link $(v_i, v_j) \in E$ is a unidirectional link from v_i to v_j. By N_i we denote a set of in-neighbors of v_i.

Each packet from node v_i is transmitted by a local broadcast to out-neighbors. Each packet from v_i is received by each out-neighbor independently with probability p. Conversely, each out-neighbor drops a packet from v_i independently with probability $1-p$. Note that, when v_i transmits a packet, v_i's some out-neighbor v_j may receive and another out-neighbor v_k may not receive probabilistically.

Scheduler and atomicity. Each node is equipped with a local clock, and all the local clocks proceed with exactly the same rate, however, we do not assume that clock values are synchronized. Each node takes an action on each receive event or timer event.

- Receive event: When a node receives a packet, a message handler of the node is invoked atomically.
- Timer event: When an interval timer by local clock of a node ticks, a timer handler of the node is invoked atomically. We assume that the time intervals are the same at all the nodes.

We imaginary assume a global time of the system, and the global time is divided into a series of rounds. Here, a *round* is the common time interval of interval timers of nodes. Although local clocks of nodes are not synchronized, a timer event occurs at each node exactly once in each round because timer intervals are the same at all the nodes.

As we defined configuration of a system in the abstract model in section 2.1, we can define configuration of a system in the sensor network model. So, a formal definition is omitted.

2.3 Self-stabilization

Self-stabilization property is defined as an ability to converge to a correct system operation in finite time from an arbitrary initial configuration. Let S be a 3-tuple $S = (\Gamma, F, \rightarrow)$, where Γ is a finite set of all configurations, F is a predicate on sequence of configurations, and $\rightarrow$ is a relation on $\Gamma \times \Gamma$. A 3-tuple $S = (\Gamma, F, \rightarrow)$

can be viewed as a transition system defined by given network topology and algorithm. For any configuration γ, let γ' be any configuration that follows γ by a single step of execution. Then, we denote this transition relation by $\gamma \to \gamma'$.

Definition 1. *For any configuration γ_0, a* computation $e(\gamma_0)$ *starting from γ_0 is a maximal (possibly infinite) sequence of configurations $e(\gamma_0) = \gamma_0, \gamma_1, \gamma_2, ...$ such that $\gamma_t \to \gamma_{t+1}$ for each $t \geq 0$. Here, a computation is maximal if (1) it is infinite, or (2) it is finite and no node is enabled in the last configuration.* □

In case an initial configuration γ_0 is clear from context, we denote the computation by e instead of $e(\gamma_0)$.

Definition 2. *A computation $e = \gamma_0, \gamma_1, \gamma_2, ...$ is* legal *with respect to legitimacy predicate F if and only if e satisfies the predicate F.* □

Definition 3. *A configuration γ is* safe *with respect to legitimacy predicate F if and only if any computation that starts from γ is legal with respect to F.* □

Definition 4. *A system $S = (\Gamma, F, \to)$ is (deterministically)* self-stabilizing *if and only if, starting from an arbitrary configuration $\gamma \in \Gamma$, the system reaches a safe configuration with respect to F.* □

Definition 5. *A system $S = (\Gamma, F, \to)$ is* probabilistically self-stabilizing *if and only if, starting from arbitrary configuration $\gamma \in \Gamma$, the system reaches a safe configuration with probability 1.* □

Definition 6. *The* convergence time *of a self-stabilizing algorithm is the number of rounds required so that the system reaches a safe configuration from an initial configuration.* □

Definition 7. *A self-stabilizing system $S = (\Gamma, F, \to)$ is* silent *if and only if once the system reaches a safe configuration, nodes do not change their states. Otherwise, it is* non-silent. □

For example, a token circulation algorithm is non-silent in a legal computation. In this paper, we consider non-silent algorithms.

3 Review of Cached Sensornet Transformation (CST)

3.1 Outline of CST

By CST, a self-stabilizing algorithm assuming the abstract model (Figure 1) is transformed into a program that runs in the sensor network model. Figure 2 shows a structure of a transformed program[3]. Let us describe the outline of

[3] In [5], to deal with message loss, each node maintains a flag for each neighbor in such a way that the flag becomes on when it receives a state-packet from the corresponding neighbor, and all the flags becomes off when a node does not receive a state-packet at expected time from some neighbor; a node takes a step only when all the flags are on. Because the probability that all the flags are on is small if the probability of packet loss is not high enough, we do not use such flags and we discuss a simple CST as shown in Figure 2 in this paper.

```
Local variables of node v_i
  v_i.q  —  the (set of) local variable(s) of original algorithm;
Guarded commands of node v_i
*[  Grd_1  →  Act_1
  □ Grd_2  →  Act_2
      ⋮
  □ Grd_L  →  Act_L
]
```

Fig. 1. An original algorithm in the abstract model

```
Local variables of node v_i
  v_i.q  —  the (set of) local variable(s) of the original algorithm;
  v_i.C[v_k, q]  —  the cache of v_k.q for each neighbor v_k ∈ N_i;
Code of node v_i
  on timer :
    Update;
    transmit ⟨v_i.q⟩;          — broadcast of a state packet
  on message ⟨q'⟩ from v_k ∈ N_i :        — receipt of a state packet
    v_i.C[v_k, q] := q';
  procedure Update
    // For each v_k ∈ N_i, reference to v_k.q is replaced by v_i.C[v_k, q].
    if (Grd_1) then Act_1
    else if (Grd_2) then Act_2
      ⋮
    else if (Grd_L) then Act_L
```

Fig. 2. A transformed program by Cached Sensornet Transformation (CST)

the transformed algorithm by CST shown in Figure 2. Let $v_i.q$ be a (set of) local variable(s) of node v_i in the original algorithm. Then, in the transformed algorithm, each v_i maintains a cache $v_i.C[v_k, q]$ of $v_k.q$ for each in-neighbor $v_k \in N_i$. In the transformed algorithm, each read of $v_k.q$ is replaced by a read of the corresponding cache $v_i.C[v_k, q]$. Periodically, by interval timer event, each node v_i locally broadcasts a packet that contains the value(s) of its local variable(s) $v_i.q$. We call such a message packet *state-packet*. Each out-neighbor receives a state-packet independently with probability p. When node v_i receives a state-packet that contains $v_j.q$ from its in-neighbor v_j, it updates $v_i.C[v_j, q]$ to cache the latest value of $v_j.q$. Every computation in the sensor network model is infinite because timer events infinitely occur at each node.

3.2 Configurations in the Sensor Network Model

We define some terminology for configurations in the sensor network model. Let $S^{\mathrm{A}} = (\Gamma^{\mathrm{A}}, F^{\mathrm{A}}, \rightarrow^{\mathrm{A}})$ be a self-stabilizing system in the abstract model, and let

$S^S = (\Gamma^S, F^S, \to^S)$ be the transformed system in the sensor network model. A set of configurations Γ^S is obtained by augmenting each configuration $\gamma^A \in \Gamma^A$ in such a way that a state of a node v_i in $\gamma^S \in \Gamma^S$ is a tuple of (1) the values of local variables of node v_i in γ^A and (2) the value of local cache $v_i.C[v_k, q]$ for each in-neighbor $v_k \in N_i$ and each local variable q.

Definition 8. *Configuration $\gamma^S \in \Gamma^S$ is an* augmentation *of configuration $\gamma^A \in \Gamma^A$ if and only if local state except the caches of node v_i in γ^S is the same as the one in γ^A for each $v_i \in V$.* □

Definition 9. *For any given infinite computation $e^A = \gamma_0^A, \gamma_1^A, ..., \gamma_i^A, ...$ in the abstract model, a computation*

$$e^S = \gamma_{0,1}^S, \gamma_{0,2}^S, ..., \gamma_{0,k_0}^S, \gamma_{1,1}^S, \gamma_{1,2}^S, ..., \gamma_{1,k_1}^S, ..., \gamma_{i,1}^S, \gamma_{i,2}^S, ..., \gamma_{i,k_i}^S, ...$$

in the sensor network model is an augmentation *of e^A if and only if (1) $\gamma_{i,j}^S$ is an augmentation of γ_i^A for each $i \geq 0$ and $1 \leq j \leq k_i$, (2) $\gamma_{i,j}^S \to^S \gamma_{i,j+1}^S$ for each $i \geq 0$ and $1 \leq j < k_i$, and (3) $\gamma_{i,k_i}^S \to^S \gamma_{i+1,1}^S$ for each $i \geq 0$.* □

Definition 10. *A computation e^S in the sensor network model is* legal *if and only if e^S is an augmentation of some legal computation e^A in the abstract model.*

Definition 11. *For any configuration $\gamma^S \in \Gamma^S$, a configuration γ^S is* cache coherent for node v_i *if and only if $v_j.C[v_i, q] = v_i.q$ for each out-neighbor v_j of v_i and for each local variable q. A configuration γ^S is* cache coherent *if and only if γ^S is cache coherent for each node $v_i \in V$.* □

Definition 12. *A configuration $\gamma^S \in \Gamma^S$ is* cache-coherent augmentation *of a configuration $\gamma^A \in \Gamma^A$ if and only if γ^S is an augmentation of γ^A and γ^S is cache coherent.* □

4 Impossibility Result

In this section, we show a counterexample algorithm whose transformed algorithm by CST does not maintain legal computation. The counterexample algorithm in the abstract model (especially, distributed daemon) is shown in Figure 3, which is a mutual exclusion algorithm for complete networks. This algorithm is based on the idea of [9].

We explain the outline of this algorithm briefly. A node wishing to enter a critical section can make a request only when no node is making a request by raising its request flag (GC2). A node which is making a request can enter critical section if and only if its node identifier is the smallest among requesting nodes (GC3). When a node exits critical section, it downs its request flag (GC4). A safety property of this algorithm is mutual exclusion, i.e., no two nodes enter critical section simultaneously. Formally, a safety predicate is $\forall v_i, v_j (v_i \neq v_j) : \neg(v_i.c \wedge v_j.c)$.

Constant
  N_i: a set of in-neighbor nodes of v_i. ($N_i = V - \{v_i\}$)
Local variables of node v_i
  $v_i.r$: **boolean** — **true** iff v_i is requesting;
  $v_i.c$: **boolean** — **true** iff v_i is in critical section (CS);
Guarded commands of node v_i
*[// GC1 : Fix variable inconsistency
  $\neg v_i.r \wedge v_i.c \rightarrow v_i.c :=$ **false**;
  // GC2 : Make a request if no node is reqesting
□ $\neg v_i.r \wedge \neg v_i.c \wedge (\forall v_j \in N_i : \neg v_j.r) \rightarrow v_i.r =$ **true**;
  // GC3 : Enter CS if its priority is the highest
□ $v_i.r \wedge \neg v_i.c \wedge (\forall v_j \in N_i : \neg v_j.r \vee v_i < v_j) \rightarrow v_i.c =$ **true**;
  // GC4 : Exit CS
□ $v_i.r \wedge v_i.c \rightarrow v_i.c =$ **false**; $v_i.r =$ **false**;
]

Fig. 3. SSMutex : A mutual exclusion algorithm in the abstract model for complete networks

Theorem 1. *The transformed algorithm of SSMutex by CST is not probabilistically self-stabilizing in the sensor network model.*

Proof. We consider the following scenario for two nodes v_i and v_j. Let us assume an initial configuration γ_0 such that (1) γ_0 is a cache-coherent augmentation of a safe configuration of the original algorithm in the abstract model, and (2) no node is requesting ($r =$ false) in γ_0. Then, these two nodes make requests for critical section by raising their request flags ($r =$ true). Suppose that each state-packet that contains the latest value of r is lost. Then, the two nodes enter critical section at the same time by GC3, because each node has no way to know that another node is making a request. This computation is illegal. □

Note that the impossibility does not hold if communication is reliable.

5 Possibility Result

In this section, we show a sufficient condition such that a transformed algorithm is self-stabilizing. Regardless of whether an original self-stabilizing algorithm is silent or non-silent, it is probabilistically guaranteed that a computation of a transformed algorithm by CST reaches a configuration which is a cache-coherent augmentation of a safe configuration of the original algorithm by simple probabilistic argument (See [6] and the proof of Theorem 2). Then, in case that the original algorithm is silent, a configuration simply stays safe forever, as studied in [5,6,7]. In case that the original algorithm is non-silent, however, a configuration may deviate from cache-coherent augmentation of a safe configuration of the original algorithm because of packet loss, and then, behavior of nodes may not obey specification of the original algorithm, as shown in the previous section. Thus, in case of non-silent algorithms, crucial point is the correctness of behavior of nodes after stabilization. The sufficient condition we present in this section guarantees equivalence of executions after stabilization in the abstract model and the sensor network model.

First, we claim that any transformed algorithm does not have any deadlock configuration in the sensor network model.

Lemma 1. *For any algorithm transformed by CST from a non-silent algorithm the probability such that no node is enabled for infinitely long duration is zero.* □

Next, we claim the sufficient condition we mentioned. To make the discussion in the proof simple, we assume that at least one node is enabled in any configuration by Lemma 1.

Theorem 2. *The transformed algorithm by CST is probabilistically self-stabilizing in the sensor network model if an original non-silent self-stabilizing algorithm in the abstract model satisfies the following two conditions. (1) For any two nodes $v_i, v_j \in V$, there is at most one simple path from v_i to v_j. (2) In any safe configuration, the number of enabled nodes is one.*

Proof. We show the following two properties.

1. Probabilistic convergence property: A system in the sensor network model eventually reaches with probability 1 a configuration which is a cache-coherent augmentation of a safe configuration of the abstract model, and
2. Equivalent computation property: For any computation in the sensor network model starting from a configuration which is a cache-coherent augmentation of a safe configuration, there exists an equivalent computation in the abstract model.

First, we show property 1, the probabilistic convergence property. As shown in [6], the probability such that no packet loss does not occur for enough long time is positive, configuration reaches a cache-coherent augmentation of a safe configuration of the original algorithm.

Next, we show property 2, the equivalent computation property. Below, without loss of generality, we suppose that initial configuration γ_0 is a cache-coherent augmentation of a safe configuration. Specifically, we show that the following two properties hold.

- Property 2a. As long as the number of enabled nodes is one, the enabled node has the correct cache values for each in-neighbor.
- Property 2b. The number of enabled nodes is at most one in any configuration that is reachable from γ_0.

These two properties implies that any computation in the sensor network model is equivalent to some computation in the abstract model. Hence correctness of an original algorithm in the abstract model is preserved by CST in the sensor network model.

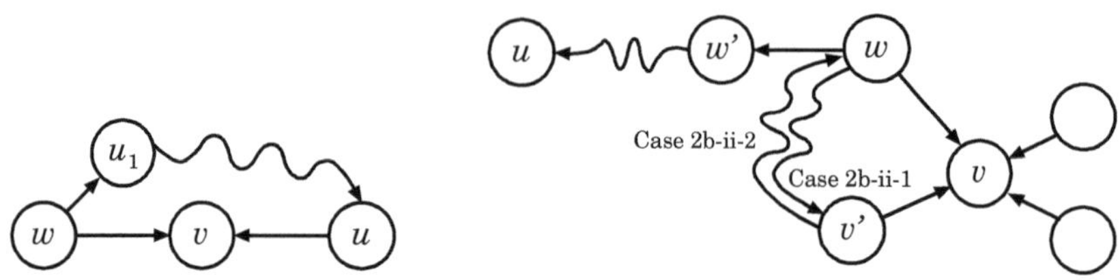

(a) Property 2a (b) Property 2b

Fig. 4. Situations for Property 2a and 2b

We show property 2a. Let γ be any configuration which is reachable from γ_0, and assume that the number of enabled nodes is one from γ_0 to γ. Let v be the enabled node in γ, and let u be the node such that v was enabled by receiving a state-packet of u. Suppose contrary that v does not have the correct cache value for some in-neighbor w of v. Note that $w \neq u$ because v received a state-packet of u and the cache at v for u is correct. (See Figure 4(a).)

Since γ_0 is cache coherent, w makes a move at least once from γ_0 to γ. All the state-packets of w are not received by v from the last move of w because otherwise v has the correct cache value for w.

Because a node is enabled as a result of a move of its in-neighbor, there is a chain of links from w to u, as depicted in Figure 4(a), i.e., (1) after the move of $w(= u_0)$, its out-neighbor, say u_1, is enabled, (2) after the move of u_1, its out-neighbor, say u_2, is enabled, ..., and (3) after the move of u_ℓ ($\ell \geq 0$), its out-neighbor u is enabled.

Because there are two distinct paths (w, v) and $(w, u_1, ..., u_\ell, u, v)$ from w to v, this is a contradiction. Therefore, as long as the number of enabled nodes is one, enabled node has correct cache value for each in-neighbor.

We show property 2b. Suppose contrary that two nodes are enabled in configuration γ_t which follows configuration γ_{t-1} in which only one node is enabled. See Figure 4(b). Let u be the only enabled node in γ_{t-1} and let v be the enabled node in γ_t, i.e., u and v are enabled in γ_t. Let w be a node such that v receives a state-packet of w and v becomes enabled in γ_t. This situation occurs in the following scenario. First, w makes a move, and then, its out-neighbor, say w', becomes enabled as a result. By series of moves by nodes with out-neighbor relation[4], u is enabled in configuration γ_{t-1}. Then, in configuration γ_t, v receives a state-packet of w for the first time after the move of w, and then v is enabled. There are two cases to consider.

- Case 2b-i: None of in-neighbor of v except w makes a move after γ_0. By assumption, w' is enabled after the move of w, and v is also enabled if v receives the state-packet of w because it observes the same local states of its

[4] First, node w is enabled and makes a move. Next, an out-neighbor w' of w is enabled and makes a move. Then, an out-neighbor, say w'', of w' is enabled and makes a move, and so on. Finally, u is enabled.

in-neighbors as in γ_0 except w. This implies that, in the abstract model, both v and w' are enabled after the move of w. Since only one node is enabled in the abstract model, this case does not occur.

– Case 2b-ii: Otherwise, i.e., some in-neighbor v' of v except w makes a move after γ_0.
  - Case 2b-ii-1: w makes a move before the move of v'. In this case, there is a chain of moves by out-neighbor relation $(w, ..., v')$. Thus, there is a path $(w, ..., v', v)$ from w to v. On the other hand, there is a direct path (w, v). So, there are two paths from w to v and hence this case contradicts the assumption.
  - Case 2b-ii-2: v' makes a move before the move of w. In this case, there is a chain of moves by out-neighbor relation $(v', ..., w)$. Thus, there is a path $(v', ..., w, v)$ from v' to v. On the other hand, there is a direct path (v', v). So, there are two paths from v' to v and hence this case also contradicts the assumption.

Therefore, the number of enabled nodes is at most one in any configuration that is reachable from γ_0. □

6 Convergence Time Analysis : A Case Study

In this section, we consider the token circulation problem on unidirectional ring network of size n. We present an algorithm, named SSTokenRing, that is probabilistically self-stabilizing in the sensor network model, and we present a convergence time analysis of the algorithm. Problem specification of the token circulation is that only one token is circulated along the ring, and each node eventually receives the token.

Figure 5 shows the algorithm description of SSTokenRing in the abstract model, which is based on the idea of token circulation algorithms proposed in [10,11]. A set of nodes $v_0, v_1, ..., v_{n-1}$ is arranged in such a way that an out-neighbor of v_i is $v_{i+1 \bmod n}$ for each $i = 0, 1, ..., n-1$. We say that a node has a *token* if it is enabled. By selection of the constant K, there is no configuration in which no node has a token.

Algorithm SSTokenRing in the abstract model is not self-stabilizing under adversarial scheduler (cf. [10]). However, it is interesting that the transformed algorithm is probabilistically self-stabilizing in the sensor network model by probabilistic loss of state-packet as we will show shortly. In the abstract model, if the scheduler is a random one, i.e., a node to be executed is selected uniformly at random from enabled nodes, it is not difficult to see that the algorithm is probabilistically self-stabilizing. In this sense, algorithm SSTokenRing falls into the possible case discussed in Section 5.

6.1 Configuration and Token

First, we explain the behavior of SSTokenRing in the abstract model. One of the safe configurations of the algorithm in the abstract model is as follows.

$$(v_0.x, v_1.x, ..., v_{n-1}.x) = (0, 1, 2, ..., n-2, 0)$$

Constants
v_{i-1}: the predecessor node of v_i in the ring.
$K = n - 1$.
Local variables of node v_i
$v_i.x$: **integer**, $0.., n-2$;
Guarded commands of node v_i
*[// GC1 : Pass the token
$v_i.x \neq v_{i-1}.x + 1 \pmod K \rightarrow v_i.x := v_{i-1}.x + 1 \pmod K$;
]

Fig. 5. SSTokenRing : A token circulation algorithm on unidirectional ring of size n

In this configuration, only v_0 is enabled and it has a token. By λ_0^{A}, we denote this configuration. We define a set of safe configurations in such a way that a configuration γ^{A} is safe if and only if γ^{A} is reachable from λ_0^{A}. After v_0 makes a move, we have a configuration $(1, 1, 2, ..., n-2, 0)$ in which v_1 is enabled.

An example of an unsafe configuration of a network with seven nodes is $(1, 3, 1, 2, 3, 3, 4)$. In this configuration, enabled nodes are v_0, v_1, v_2 and v_5 because each of them does not have a "+1" value of in-neighbor's value, and hence there are four tokens at these nodes. When v_0 makes a move, the two tokens at v_0 and v_1 *collide* and we obtain a configuration $(5, 3, 1, 2, 3, 3, 4)$ in which enabled nodes are v_1, v_2 and v_5, i.e., the token at v_0 is absorbed by the collision. Note that, in the abstract model, it is not difficult to see that the number of tokens never increase.

Next, let us explain safe configurations in the sensor network model. We denote a configuration in the sensor network by

$$((v_0.C[v_{n-1}, x], v_0.x), (v_1.C[v_0, x], v_1.x), ..., (v_{n-1}.C[v_{n-2}, x], v_{n-1}.x)).$$

One of safe configurations is $((0, 0), (0, 1), (1, 2), ..., (n-3, n-2), (n-2, 0))$, in which only v_0 holds a token because it is enabled. By λ_0^{S}, we denote this configuration. We define a set of safe configurations in such a way that a configuration γ^{S} is safe if and only if γ^{S} is reachable from λ_0^{S}. For example, a configuration which is reached by a move by v_0 in the configuration shown above and a state-packet of v_0 is lost, i.e., $((0, 1), (0, 1), (1, 2), ..., (n-3, n-2), (n-2, 0))$, is also safe. In this case, we regard that v_0 still has a token despite it is disabled. In general, we say that v_i *has a token* when (1) v_i is enabled, or (2) v_{i+1} does not have correct cache value of v_i, i.e., $v_i.x \neq v_{i+1}.C[v_i, x]$.

The followings are fundamental properties of the transformed SSTokenRing in the sensor network model.

Lemma 2. *In any configuration, at least one node has a token.* □

Lemma 3. *The total number of tokens is non-increasing.* □

Lemma 4. *In any safe configuration, the total number of tokens is one.* □

6.2 Convergence Time Analysis

We show an upper bound of the expected convergence time of transformed SSTokenRing by CST. Our analysis is based on observation on random walk of tokens and their collisions. Initially, there are several tokens. Then, by random walk of tokens, the number of tokens eventually becomes one by collisions of tokens.

Theorem 3. *The expected convergence time of the transformed SSTokenRing by CST is bounded by* $O(\frac{n^2 \log n}{8p(1-p)})$ *rounds, where* n *is the number of nodes and* p *is the probability that each state-packet is received.*

Proof. First, let us observe random walk of two tokens, say τ_1 and τ_2 on unidirectional ring. We define the distance of the two tokens as $j - i \pmod{n}$, where v_i (resp. v_j) is the node where τ_1 (resp. τ_2) locates. With probability $2p(1-p)$, increase or decrease of the distance occur at each round, and such an event occurs every $1/(2p(1-p))$ expected rounds.

A random walk of these two tokens continues until they collide, i.e., the distance of the two tokens becomes 0 or n. This stochastic process is known as the *gambler's ruin* problem. By the analysis of the gambler's ruin problem, it is known that the expected number of steps that a gambler wins (distance n) or lose (distance 0) is at most $n^2/4$. Hence, $n^2/(8p(1-p))$ is an upper bound of the expected number of rounds for the two tokens collide.

Next, we derive an upper bound of the expected number of rounds until the number of tokens becomes one from arbitrary initial configuration. Suppose that there are ℓ (> 2) tokens $\tau_1, \tau_2, ..., \tau_\ell$ on a ring in this order in an initial configuration. Let us observe collision of two tokens τ_1 and $\tau_{\lceil \ell/2 \rceil}$. If they collide with distance 0, tokens $\tau_2, ..., \tau_{\lceil \ell/2 \rceil - 1}$ disappear, and if they collide with distance n, tokens $\tau_{\lceil \ell/2 \rceil + 1}, ..., \tau_{\ell-1}$ disappear. Thus, by collision of τ_1 and $\tau_{\lceil \ell/2 \rceil}$, at least $\lceil \ell/2 \rceil - 1$ (if n is odd) or $\ell/2$ (if n is even) tokens disappear. Thus, at most $\ell/2+1$ tokens survive by collision of τ_1 and $\tau_{\lceil \ell/2 \rceil}$.

The number of tokens becomes one by repeating such token collisions discussed above at most $O(\log n)$ times because the number of tokens is at most n in any initial configuration. Thus, we have an upper bound $O(n^2 \log n/(8p(1-p)))$. □

7 Conclusion

In this paper, we discussed CST transformation of non-silent self-stabilizing algorithms for sensor networks. Our sufficient condition seems to be too strong, and finding a weaker sufficient condition is a future task. Improvement of the bound of convergence time of the token circulation algorithm is also a future task.

Acknowledgment

The authors would like to thank professor Sébastien Tixeuil for discussion. This work is supported in part by Global COE Program of MEXT, Grant-in-Aid for

Scientific Research ((B)17300020, (B)19300017, (B)20300012) of JSPS, Grant-in-Aid for Young Scientists ((B)19700075) of JSPS, and the Kayamori Foundation of Information Science Advancement.

References

1. Dijkstra, E.: Self-stabilizing systems in spite of distributed control. Communications of the ACM 17(11), 643–644 (1974)
2. Mizuno, M., Kakugawa, H.: A transformation of self-stabilizing programs for distributed computing environments. In: Babaoğlu, Ö., Marzullo, K. (eds.) WDAG 1996. LNCS, vol. 1151, pp. 304–321. Springer, Heidelberg (1996)
3. Kulkarni, S.S., Arumugam, M.: Transformations for write-all-with-collision model. Computer Communications 29(2), 183–199 (2006)
4. Huang, S.T., Wuu, L.C., Tsai, M.S.: Distributed execution model for self-stabilizing systems. In: ICDCS, pp. 432–439 (1994)
5. Herman, T.: Models of self-stabilization and sensor networks. In: Das, S.R., Das, S.K. (eds.) IWDC 2003. LNCS, vol. 2918, pp. 205–214. Springer, Heidelberg (2003)
6. Turau, V., Weyer, C.: Fault tolerance in wireless sensor networks through self-stabilization. International Journal of Communication Networks and Distributed Systems 2(1), 78–98 (2009)
7. Kakugawa, H., Masuzawa, T.: Convergence time analysis of self-stabilizing algorithms in wireless sensor networks with unreliable links. In: Kulkarni, S., Schiper, A. (eds.) SSS 2008. LNCS, vol. 5340, pp. 173–187. Springer, Heidelberg (2008)
8. Yoshida, K., Kakugawa, H., Masuzawa, T.: Observation on lightweight implementation of self-stabilizing node clustering algorithms in sensor networks. In: IASTED SN, Crete, Greece (2008)
9. Gradinariu, M., Tixeuil, S.: Conflict managers for self-stabilization without fairness assumption. In: ICDCS, p. 46 (2007)
10. Burns, J.E., Pachl, J.: Uniform self-stabilizing rings. ACM Transactions on Programming Languages and Systems 11(2), 330–344 (1989)
11. Datta, A.K., Gradinariu, M., Tixeuil, S.: Self-stabilizing mutual exclusion using unfair distributed scheduler. The Computer Journal 47(3), 289–298 (2004)

Analysis of an Intentional Fault Which Is Undetectable by Local Checks under an Unfair Scheduler

Jun Kiniwa[1] and Kensaku Kikuta[2]

[1] Department of Applied Economics, University of Hyogo,
8-2-1 Gakuen nishi-machi, Nishi-ku, Kobe-shi, 651-2197 Japan
Phone: +81-78-794-5844, Fax: +81-78-794-6166
kiniwa@econ.u-hyogo.ac.jp

[2] Department of Strategic Management, University of Hyogo,
Phone: +81-78-794-5829, Fax: +81-78-794-6166
kikuta@biz.u-hyogo.ac.jp

Abstract. We consider a malicious unfair adversary which generates an undetectable fault by local checks, called an intentional fault. Though the possibility of such a fault has ever been suggested, details of its influence and handling are unknown. We assume the intentional fault in a self-stabilizing mutual exclusion protocol, a hybrid of previously proposed ones that complement each other. In the hybrid protocol, we can cope with the fault by using optional strategies, whether or not sending a minor token, which plays a role of preventing the contamination from spreading. We construct a payoff matrix between a group of privileged processes and an adversary, and consider a multistage two-person zero sum game. We interpret the game in two ways: whether it continues or replays the game after an ME(mutual exclusion)-violating repair, in which more than one unexpected privileges are given. For each case, we evaluate the ability of malicious unfair adversary by using a mixed strategy. Our idea is also considered as a general framework for strengthening an algorithm against an intentional fault.

Keywords: self-stabilization, mutual exclusion, safety under convergence, intentional fault model, game theory, multistage two-person zero sum game, unfair scheduler.

1 Introduction

Motivation. Studies on self-stabilization have been extended to vast areas in recent years. One of the areas, which we focus on here, is how to keep a system safe under convergence in self-stabilizing mutual exclusion. The requirement of mutual exclusion is to allow at most one privileged process at any time, called legitimate configurations. Starting from an arbitrary configuration, it is difficult to keep it fully legitimate under convergence. For example, it is known that Dijkstra's 3-state protocol [2] guarantees recovery from arbitrary initial configurations in an n-process ring as illustrated in Fig. 1.

R. Guerraoui and F. Petit (Eds.): SSS 2009, LNCS 5873, pp. 443–457, 2009.

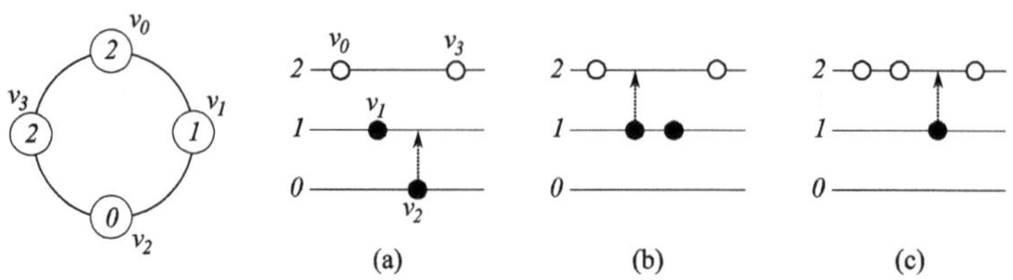

Fig. 1. Dijkstra's 3-State Protocol

Dijkstra's 3-state protocol (addition and subtraction : modulo 3)
process p_0**:** $v_0 + 1 = v_1 \rightarrow v_0 := v_0 - 1$
process p_{n-1}**:** $(v_{n-2} = v_0) \wedge (v_{n-1} \neq v_{n-2} + 1) \rightarrow v_{n-1} := v_{n-2} + 1$
process p_i $(i \neq 0, n-1)$**:** $(v_i + 1 = v_{i-1}) \vee (v_i + 1 = v_{i+1}) \rightarrow v_i := v_i + 1$

In the left hand of the figure, the four processes p_0, p_1, p_2 and p_3 forming a ring, have states $(v_0, v_1, v_2, v_3) = (2, 1, 0, 2)$ and move one by one according to the protocol. An example of state transition is depicted from (a) through (c), where each state is represented by the location of nodes; and privileged processes by black nodes. We call the transition as in Fig. 1 "*ME(mutual exclusion)-violating repair*", where more than one privileges are unexpectedly given to processes under repairing. Hence, the requirement of mutual exclusion is violated temporarily. Such violation occurs because each process acquires a privilege by only the difference of neighboring states in a small domain $\{0, 1, 2\}$.

Kiniwa et al. [14, 15, 17] solved this problem by enlarging the domain from $\{0, 1, 2\}$ to $R = \{0, \ldots, 3L - 1\}$ for a large integer $L \gg n$. Every non-faulty state must take a special value in $I = \{0, L, 2L\}$, called *bases*. Furthermore, a non-faulty process i $(\neq 0, n-1)$ acquires a privilege when it has a state less than a neighboring state by L (**mod** $3L$). Any state other than I, which is easily detected by local checks, is a faulty state. If we consider again the states $(v_0, v_1, v_2, v_3) = (2, 1, 0, 2)$ in the large domain R, only $v_2 \in I$ has a base state and other processes have non-base states, i.e., faulty states. Since the three bases are defined in a large domain, the mutual exclusion is *almost* safe if we assume that faulty states are uniformly distributed over the range. Such an assumption is called a *random fault model.* As far as we know, every conventional argument concerning safety under convergence has used this model [8, 14, 22]. However, there is clearly weakness in the enlarged domain system. Suppose $(v_0, v_1, v_2, v_3) = (2L, L, 0, 2L)$ in R. Then, both p_1 and p_2 have privileges even though every process has a base state. If we assume that an adversary takes aim at the weakness of states, e.g., perturbation limited to I as above, it is called an *intentional fault model.* Yen [22] has ever suggested that

> "In the random failure model, a transient failure can bring the system into any illegitimate state with equal probability",

and that

> "In the malicious failure model, some faulty processors may maliciously try to violate the system legitimacy without being detected by local checks and subsequently cause critical damages".

The term "malicious failure" has been used extensively in the sense of Byzantine failure [21]. So we rename Yen's malicious failure model an intentional fault model. The program of a process can be changed in the Byzantine failure model, whereas the program of a process cannot be changed in the intentional fault model, and only the transient faults are limited to the weakness of the program as if it had malicious intent.

To cope with the intentional fault, we believe that a game theoretic analysis, two-person zero sum game, is useful. Since many processes obtain a privilege as a mutual exclusion system, they are grouped together, called player A. On the other hand, the malicious adversary is called player B. The advantage of player A, corresponding to the disadvantage of player B, is shared by the processes. In our system, the player A has two strategies, whether or not sending a *minor token*, while the player B has five strategies, not causing a fault, causing a *base fault*, a *non-base fault*, a *minor fault* and their mixed faults. The minor token [7, 13], introduced as a coupled use with a *major token*, plays a role of checking every process and repairing the base fault which is undetectable by local checks. In contrast, the non-base fault is detectable by local checks. With the help of game theory, we derive optimal mixed strategies of player A and player B.

Related Work. As Dasgupta et al. [1] pointed out, only little work mixing game theory with self-stabilization has been done. We just know a technique, called a scheduler-luck game, for analyzing the performance of randomized self-stabilization [3]. In the context of distributed non-stabilizing algorithms, however, the behavior of selfish agents has been extensively studied [19], triggered by Koutsoupias and Papadimitriou [18]. They used a term "price of anarchy" to represent a ratio of the largest social welfare achievable to the least social welfare achieved at any Nash equilibrium. A similar framework was preserved in the study of selfish stabilization [1]. Our work, however, owes its technical base to the conventional game theory [9, 20].

The mutual exclusion problem has been one of main topics in self-stabilization since Dijkstra's work [2]. Several new ideas originated from the problem. One of them is an unfair scheduler [10, 11, 12]. Another is the safety under convergence, e.g., superstabilization [7, 13], cryptography [22], fault containment [4, 5, 6] and enlargement of state space [14, 15, 17, 22]. However, as stated above, the safety of each protocol was considered by only the random fault model.

Contributions. Our goal is to develop a game theoretic analysis of the intentional fault model. Our contribution includes

1. the construction of an intentional fault model: We do not assume that the faulty state takes any value over the domain with equal probability. The intentional fault may make the value undetectable by local checks. The study on such an intentional fault model is new.

2. a game theoretic analysis: Grouping a set of privileged processes enables us to consider a multistage two-person zero sum game. The formulation of this game in the self-stabilization is new, and
3. the suggestion of a framework: We propose a framework for strengthening an algorithm against an intentional fault which is undetectable by local checks. The method of strengthening an algorithm is new.

The rest of this paper is organized as follows. Section 2 states our model, introduces underlying protocols, and then presents our protocol. Section 3 provides an analysis of the intentional fault model. First, Section 3.1 considers that a game is continued after every ME-violating repair. Then, Section 3.2 considers that the game is replayed after every ME-violating repair. Finally, Section 4 concludes the paper.

2 Our Method

2.1 Self-stabilizing Model

In this section we describe our method for the mutual exclusion problem on unidirectional rings. A ring consists of n processes $P = \{0, 1, \ldots, n-1\}$ of finite state machines, where process i is connected with its neighboring process $i-1$ **mod** n, called a *predecessor*, and $i+1$ **mod** n, called a *successor*. We also call "the predecessor of the predecessor of i" predecessors, and so forth. Let Σ_i be a finite state space of process i. Each process i has a state $\sigma_i \in \Sigma_i$ consisting of a shared set of states $\sigma_i = (major_i, minor_i, wait_i)$, where $major_i = (vmaj_i, rmaj_i)$ and $minor_i = (vmin_i, rmin_i)$ represent *tokens* for giving a privilege to one process in P. For an integer $H > n$, let $R_H = [0, H) = \{x \mid 0 \leq x < H\}$ be a set of real values, over which a primary variable $vmaj_i$ ranges. Let a function ψ map $vmaj_i \in R_H$ into h digits. That is, $\psi(vmaj_i)$ is represented by h integers which are stored in an array[1]. In the domain R_H, we define H specified integer values $I_H = \{0, 1, \ldots, H-1\}$, called bases, such that every correct $vmaj_i$ must take these values (as a necessary condition). A secondary integer variable $vmin_i$ ranges over I_H (not R_H). The random bit variables $rmaj_i, rmin_i \in \{0, \ldots, L\}$, where $L \gg n$, are used for recognizing a true token with the minimum value.

In addition, σ_i contains an auxiliary boolean variable $wait_i$ for waiting the process with a major token until getting also a minor token. A *configuration* $\mathbf{c}$ is an n-dimensional vector of states $\mathbf{c} = (\sigma_0, \sigma_1, \ldots, \sigma_{n-1})$. The set of all configurations, a global state space, is denoted by $\Omega = \Sigma_0 \times \Sigma_1 \times \cdots \times \Sigma_{n-1}$. Notice that the computation for process $i \pm 1$ uses "**mod** n". For simplicity, we drop the notation of "**mod** n" in the sequel. We assume a *state-reading model* as in [2], that is, process i can directly read (but not write) the states from its predecessor. We assume an unfair *C-daemon* (central daemon) scheduler. Every process has a program of internal computation, **if** G_i **then** A_i or denoted by $G_i \to A_i$, where G_i is called a *guard* and A_i an *action*. If G_i is true, then the

[1] To avoid a computational error in real numbers, we map the value into h digits.

process i is said to be *enabled*. The unfair scheduler does not select every enabled process infinitely often.

We consider a *critical section* in which only a process stays for access to a single resource. We say that a process has a *privilege* if it gains admittance to the critical section. Unlike other papers [2, 13], we distinguish the terms between *enabled* and *privileged* because not all enabled processes can get into the critical section in our protocol. Let $\Lambda \subset \Omega$ be a set of *legitimate* configurations as given in the following definition.

Definition 1. *A configuration* $\mathbf{c}$ *is* legitimate *(*$\mathbf{c} \in \Lambda$*) if*

(1) every process i *has a base* $vmaj_i \in I_H$*,*
(2) there exists at most one $major_i$ *in* $\mathbf{c}$ *such that* $vmaj_i \neq vmaj_{i-1} + 1$*, and*
(3) there exists at most one $minor_i$ *in* $\mathbf{c}$ *such that* $vmin_i \neq vmin_{i-1} + 1$*.* □

In Definition 1, we call the fault which does not satisfy (1) a *non-base fault*, and the fault which does not satisfy (2) but satisfies (1) a *base fault*. We say that process i *has* a major (resp. minor) token if $vmaj_i \neq vmaj_{i-1} + 1$ (resp. $vmin_i \neq vmin_{i-1} + 1$), and that process i *sends* a major (resp. minor) token to $i+1$ if $vmaj_i := vmaj_{i-1} + 1$ (resp. $vmin_i := vmin_{i-1} + 1$) is executed in any configuration. In our protocol, process i has a privilege in two cases. First, if both a major token and a minor token are sent from process $i-1$, it obtains a privilege with some probability. Second, if process i has kept a major token and only a minor token is sent from process $i-1$, it obtains a privilege with probability 1.

2.2 Underlying Protocols

Our protocol is constructed based on three protocols. The first underlying protocol was proposed by Herman [7]. The method guarantees that the system stabilizes from any *1-faulty configuration*, in which the states of at most one process differs from a legitimate configuration, except that the faulty process has a temporary spurious privilege. The feature of his method is that a major token process circulates an additional token, called a minor token, before acquiring a privilege as illustrated in Fig. 2. When the minor token meets a spurious privilege, it corrects the fault. When the minor token meets the process with a major token after a circulation, the process obtains a privilege.

Superstabilizing Protocol [7, 13]

Predicates

$Minor_i \equiv (vmin_i = vmin_{i-1} \wedge i = 0) \vee (vmin_i \neq vmin_{i-1} \wedge i \neq 0)$
$Major_i \equiv (vmaj_i = vmaj_{i-1} \wedge i = 0) \vee (vmaj_i \neq vmaj_{i-1} \wedge i \neq 0)$

Macros

$SendMinor_i \equiv vmin_i := vmin_{i-1}{+}1$ **if**$(i = 0)$, $vmin_i := vmin_{i-1}$ **otherwise**
$SendMajor_i \equiv vmaj_i := vmaj_{i-1}{+}1$ **if**$(i = 0)$, $vmaj_i := vmaj_{i-1}$ **otherwise**
$Privilege_i \equiv$ `perform critical section`; $SendMinor_i$; $SendMajor_i$; $wait_i :=$ `false`

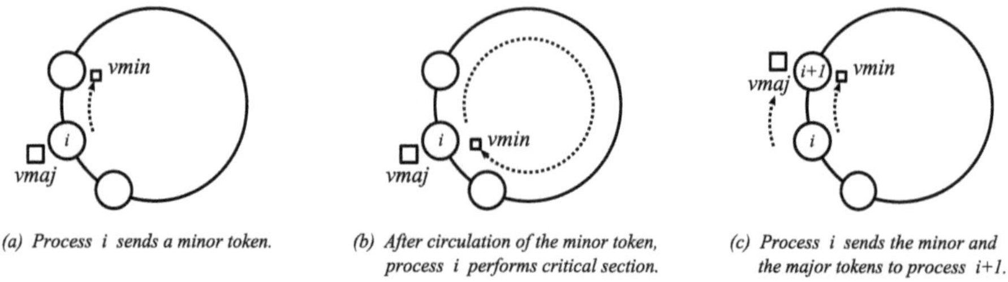

Fig. 2. Superstabilizing Protocol

$Decision_i \equiv Privilege_i$**if**$(wait_i = \texttt{true})$, $wait_i := \texttt{true}$; $SendMinor_i$ **otherwise**

Rules

$Minor_i \wedge \neg Major_i \rightarrow SendMinor_i$
$Minor_i \wedge Major_i \rightarrow Decision_i$

The second underlying protocol, called an enlarged domain protocol[2], was proposed by Kiniwa et al. [15, 17]. Their method guarantees that faulty processes can be detected and rapidly corrected with high probability. The feature is that the enlargement of a state space of Dijkstra's 3-state protocol as stated in Section 1 (see Fig. 3). Since a base fault violates the requirement of mutual exclusion and it is undetectable by local checks, we consider the base fault as an intentional fault.

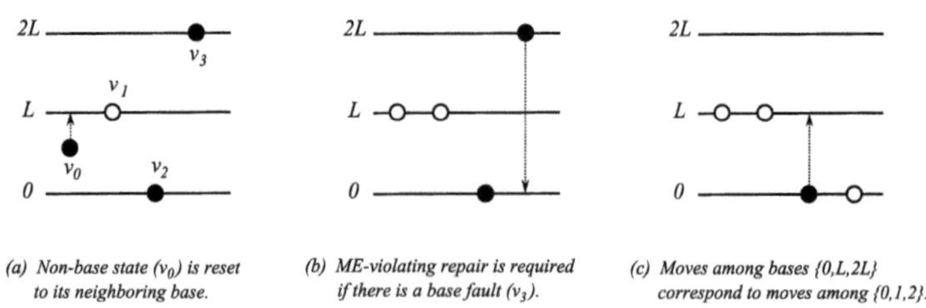

Fig. 3. Enlarged Domain Protocol

Enlarged Domain Protocol [17]

$(v_i \notin I) \wedge (v_{i+1} \in I) \rightarrow v_i := v_{i+1}$; $\quad (v_i \notin I) \wedge (v_{i-1} \in I) \rightarrow v_i := v_{i-1}$
process 0: $(v_0 + L = v_1) \wedge (v_0 \in I) \rightarrow v_0 := v_0 - L$
process $n-1$: $(v_{n-2} = v_0) \wedge (v_{n-1} \neq v_{n-2} + L) \wedge (v_{n-1} \in I) \rightarrow v_{n-1} := v_{n-2} + L$
process i $(\neq 0, n-1)$: $(v_i + L = v_{i-1}) \vee (v_i + L = v_{i+1}) \wedge (v_i \in I) \rightarrow v_i := v_i + L$

[2] For simplicity, deadlock resolution is omitted.

Table 1. Characteristics of Two Underlying Protocols

	advantage	disadvantage
Superstabilizing Protocol	tolerant to a base fault	costly (minor token circulation)
Enlarged Domain Protocol	tolerant to non-base faults, cheap (no minor token)	weak against base faults (ME-violating repair)

The third underlying protocol was proposed by Johnen[10]. The method guarantees that each processor, once stabilized, obtains a token every n computation steps. The feature is that the protocol locks a spurious token forever and it is eventually caught up. Thus, the unfair scheduler has no other choice to move a true token. The method is not effective for the intentional fault, but we use it for tolerating unfair schedulers. Due to the lack of space, we omit the description of the Johnen's protocol.

We briefly summarize the characteristics of the first two underlying protocols in Table 1.

2.3 Description of Our Protocol

Here we present our protocol that combines the previous three protocols[3]. Our method guarantees both advantages in the first two protocols. The feature of our method is that the major token process has the option of whether or not sending a minor token. If the minor token is sent, called a strategy ST, the spreading of base fault contamination can be prevented in any 1-faulty configuration. However, ST is costly because it requires the major token process to wait the circulation of a minor token. If the minor token is not sent, called a strategy NS, the base fault contamination may spread through the system. A non-base fault can be corrected without any aid of minor tokens. Our aim is to know optimal mixed strategies, the probabilities of ST and NS. Notice that $rand\{0 \dots L\}$ picks an integer in $\{0 \dots L\}$ at random, while $rand[0,1)$ picks a real number in $[0,1) = \{x \mid 0 \le x < 1\}$ at random. For simplicity, we omit $ActMajor_i$, $WrongMajor_i$ and $SetRminor_i$ because they are similar to $ActMinor_i$, $WrongMinor_i$ and $SetRmajor_i$, respectively. Though the computation for $vmaj_i$ and $vmin_i$ uses "**mod** H", we drop the notation of "**mod** H" for simplicity.

Our protocol

Predicates

$ActMinor_i \equiv (vmin_i \neq vmin_{i-1}+1) \wedge (vmin_i \neq 0 \vee (rmin_{i-1} \le rmin_i))$

$WrongMinor_i \equiv (vmin_i = vmin_{i-1}+1) \wedge (rmin_i \neq rmin_{i-1}) \wedge (vmin_i \neq 0)$

$Resettable_i \equiv (vmaj_i \notin I_H \wedge vmaj_{i-1} \in I_H) \vee (\neg ActMinor_i \wedge ActMajor_i \wedge wait_i = \texttt{false})$

$Deadlock_i \equiv (ActMinor_i \wedge (wait_i = \texttt{true})) \wedge (vmaj_i, vmaj_{i-1} \notin I_H)$

[3] More precisely, we enlarge the state space of Dijkstra's K-state protocol[2].

Macros

$NewMinor_i \equiv vmin_i := vmin_{i-1}+1;\ rmin_i := rand\{0 \dots L\};\ wait_i := \mathtt{true}$

$SetRmajor_i \equiv rmaj_i := rand\{0 \dots L\}$ **if** $(vmaj_{i-1} = H-1)$,
$rmaj_i := rmaj_{i-1}$ **otherwise**

$PassTokens_i \equiv$ `perform critical section`;
$(vmin_i, vmaj_i) := (vmin_{i-1}+1, vmaj_{i-1}+1);\ wait_i := \mathtt{false}$

$Decision_i \equiv PassTokens_i$ **if** $(wait_i = \mathtt{true}) \vee (rand[0,1) > p)$,
$NewMinor_i$ **else if** $(rand[0,1) \leq p)$

$CorrectBit_i \equiv rmin_i := rmin_{i-1}$ **if** $WrongMinor_i$,
$rmaj_i := rmaj_{i-1}$ **if** $WrongMajor_i$

Rules

$$ActMinor_i \wedge \neg ActMajor_i \rightarrow vmin_i := vmin_{i-1}+1;\ SetRminor_i \quad (1)$$

$$ActMinor_i \wedge ActMajor_i \rightarrow Decision_i;\ SetRmajor_i \quad (2)$$

$$WrongMinor_i \vee WrongMajor_i \rightarrow CorrectBit_i \quad (3)$$

$$Resettable_i \rightarrow vmaj_i := vmaj_{i-1}+1 \quad (4)$$

$$Deadlock_i \rightarrow vmaj_i := rand\{0 \dots H-1\} \quad (5)$$

The predicates $ActMinor_i$ and $ActMajor_i$ describe the unlocked true tokens for the minor token and the major token, respectively. So the rule (1) moves the process with only a minor token, and the rule (2) moves the process with both a minor token and a major token. Both $SetRminor_i$ and $SetRmajor_i$ set the random bit variables in order to send the tokens to the next process. The rule (3) is the correcting rule of the random bits. The rule (4) resets a non-base state. In addition, the rule (5) prevents a deadlock. For lack of space, we omit the correctness proof of our protocol.

3 Game Theoretic Analysis

Our Setting. In this section, we analyze the intentional fault which is undetectable by local checks in our protocol. We summarize our setting as follows.

- We consider a multistage two-person zero sum game played by a set of privileged processes, called player A, and an adversary, called player B. Since a privilege is passed from one process to another, the process playing the role of player A also changes from one to another. We consider a protocol as a multistage game so that we can evaluate the mean costs of players A and B.
- We call the time interval during which a process holds a true privilege a *stage*. The unit stage begins when a process obtains a true privilege and terminates when any fault is removed and the new process obtains a true privilege. The player B can generate faults at most once in each stage. Both the player A and the player B cannot know other player's strategy in advance. A game is represented by the number of remaining stages out of m stages in total.

- A privileged process makes a choice whether or not sending a minor token. The minor token plays a role of preventing contamination from spreading. The reward of detecting a base fault is α and the damage of a base fault is β relative to the cost 1 of not sending a minor token when no fault occurs. On the other hand, the cost of sending a minor token (ST) takes about n times larger than not sending a minor token (NS).
- The goal of player A is to maximize the reward of player A, shared by a set of privileged processes, through the m stages. The mixed strategy of player A consists of sending a minor token (ST) with probability p and not sending a minor token (NS) with probability $1-p$. On the other hand, the mixed strategy of player B consists of causing no faults, base faults, non-base faults, minor faults and their mixed faults with some probabilities.

Since the importance of mutual exclusion can be interpreted in various ways, we consider it from two points of view (Sections 3.1 and 3.2). First, in Section 3.1, we assume that the importance of mutual exclusion is not so crucial, and thus the game is continued after the ME-violating repair. Next, in Section 3.2, we assume that the importance of mutual exclusion is crucial, and thus the game is replayed after the ME-violating repair.

Estimation of Costs. To derive each cost, we have to make some assumptions. First, we assume the following fact according to [11, 12].

Assumption 1. *The scheduler cannot control the random bit in the protocol.* □

Any fault may actually occur at any time. Then, there could be a case where the fault cannot be detected even if a minor token is sent — the fault occurs after the minor token is passed over. For simplicity, we neglect such a case and every fault is always detected when the minor token is sent.

Assumption 2. *Every fault (if any) occurs in the beginning of each stage.* □

The interval time of each step may actually different. Then, it would be very difficult to estimate the cost of each strategy. We consider that the following assumption can be used because we iterate many stages.

Assumption 3. *The interval time of each step is almost equal.* □

We call only a fault with respect to a minor (resp. major) token a *minor fault* (resp. *major fault*). Fig. 4 shows the worst cost of the minor fault. In Fig. 4(a), the unfair adversary sets every different *rmin* value in the ascending order from process $i+1$ to its successors. Then, the adversary moves processes from process i and its predecessors. After all the *rmin* values have been repaired (Fig. 4(b)), that is, the minimum value is propagated, *vmin* values circulate the ring twice (Fig. 4(c)) in order to confirm the true (minimum valued) token. It takes $n(n-1)/2$ steps to repair the *rmin* values and $2n-1$ steps to repair the fault on *vmin*. Let $k = n(n-1)/2 + (2n-1) = (n^2+3n-2)/2$.

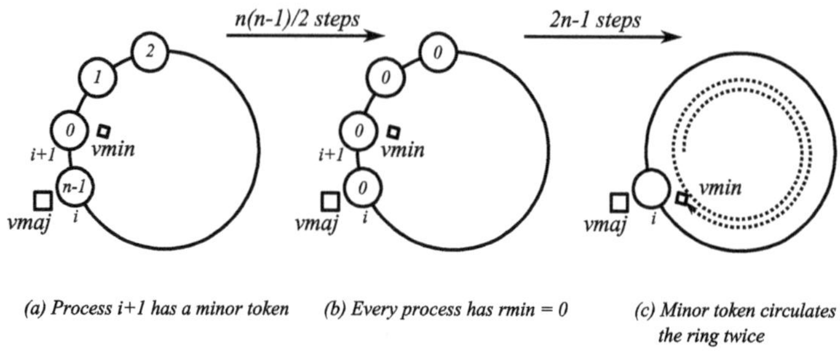

Fig. 4. Cost of Minor Fault (*rmin* values are illustrated in nodes)

Suppose that the player A sends a minor token (ST). There are five cases.

- If there is no fault, the circulation steps n take a cost $-n$ of player A.
- If there are base faults, the reward for detecting the faults is α and the circulation cost is $-n$.
- If there are non-base faults, it takes a reset cost and a circulation cost $-2n$.
- If there are both major faults and minor faults, it gains the reward α for detecting the faults and takes $-k = -(n^2 + 3n - 2)/2$.
- If there are only minor faults, it takes $-k = -(n^2 + 3n - 2)/2$.

Next, suppose that the player A does not send a minor token (NS).

- If there is no fault, we define the reward as 1.
- If there are base faults, we define the cost as $-\beta$.
- If there are non-base faults, it takes a reset cost $-n$.
- If there are minor faults, the cost is fewer than the one for sending a minor token by $2n - 1$.

3.1 Continuing Game after ME-violating Repair

One Stage Game. To begin with, we consider only one stage, i.e., $m = 1$. The payoff matrix is summarized as follows. Each row means player A's strategy and each column means player B's strategy.

	non-fault	base fault	non-base fault	major+minor fault	minor fault
ST	$-n$	$\alpha - n$	$-2n$	$\alpha - k$	$-k$
NS	1	$-\beta$	$-n$	$(2n-1) + \alpha - k$	$(2n-1) - k$

We can exclude the columns of non-fault, non-base fault and major+minor fault because they are dominated by the column of minor fault. Thus, we obtain a simplified payoff matrix as follows.

	base fault	minor fault
ST	$\alpha - n$	$-k$
NS	$-\beta$	$(2n-1) - k$

Let $a = (p, 1-p)$ be the mixed strategy of player A, that is, player A takes the strategy ST with probability p and the strategy NS with probability $1-p$. Then the expected payoffs $E(a, \text{base fault})$ and $E(a, \text{minor fault})$ of player A against the pure strategies {base fault, minor fault} of player B are

$$E(a, \text{base fault}) = p(\alpha - n) + (1-p)(-\beta) = p(\alpha + \beta - n) - \beta, \quad (6)$$
$$E(a, \text{minor fault}) = p(-k) + (1-p)(2n-1-k) = -(2n-1)p + 2n - 1 - k \quad (7)$$

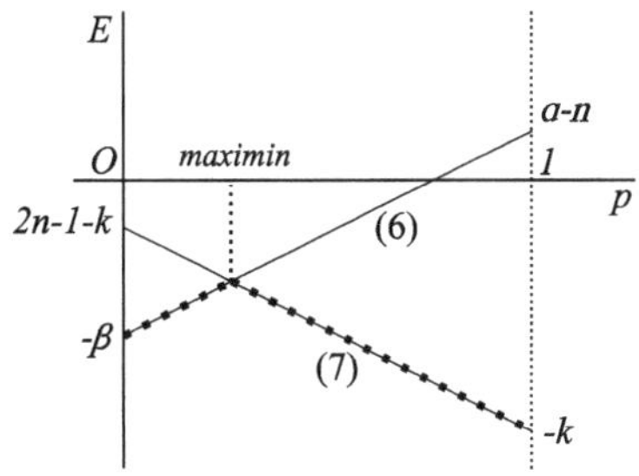

Fig. 5. Maximin Strategy (player B's optimal counterstrategy : dotted line)

Suppose in Fig. 5 that $2n - 1 - k = (n - n^2)/2 > -\beta$, where two lines intersect in $0 \leq p \leq 1$. Since player A is a maximizer, the optimal strategy of player A, derived from the intersection of (6) and (7), is

$$a^* = \left(\frac{\beta + 2n - 1 - k}{\alpha + \beta + n - 1}, \frac{\alpha - n + k}{\alpha + \beta + n - 1} \right).$$

The game value is $u - (\beta + u)(k + u)/(\alpha + \beta + n - 1)$ for $u = 2n - 1 - k$. Since player B does not take the non-fault strategy, let $b = (q, 1-q)$ be the mixed strategy of player B, that is, player B takes the base fault strategy with probability q and the minor fault strategy with probability $1-q$. Then, the expected payoffs of player B against the pure strategies of player A are

$$E(b, \text{ST}) = q(\alpha - n) + (1-q)(-k) \quad \text{and} \quad (8)$$
$$E(b, \text{NS}) = q(-\beta) + (1-q)(2n-1-k). \quad (9)$$

By considering the intersection of (8) and (9), the optimal strategy of player B can be derived as

$$b^* = \left(\frac{2n-1}{\alpha + \beta + n - 1}, \frac{\alpha + \beta - n}{\alpha + \beta + n - 1} \right).$$

The minimax value is $(2n-1)(\alpha + k - n)/(\alpha + \beta + n - 1) - k$.

Next, suppose in Fig. 5 that $2n - 1 - k = (n - n^2)/2 \leq -\beta$, where two lines do not intersect in $0 \leq p \leq 1$. Then, the maximin strategy of player A is $a^* = (0, 1)$ and the minimax strategy of player B is $b^* = (1, 0)$. For simplicity, we assume $(n - n^2)/2 > -\beta$ in the sequel.

Multistage Game. Next, we consider multiple stages of our game. Based on the one stage game, the multistage game $\Gamma(m)$ for $m > 1$ can be expressed as follows.

$$\Gamma(m) = \begin{bmatrix} \alpha - n + \Gamma(m-1) & -k + \Gamma(m-1) \\ -\beta + \Gamma(m-1) & 2n - 1 - k + \Gamma(m-1) \end{bmatrix}$$

Then, the game value v_m for $\Gamma(m)$ can be easily solved as follows. Notice that $v_0 = 0$ holds because there is no reward/cost in playing no game.

$$\begin{aligned} v_m &= val \begin{bmatrix} \alpha - n + v_{m-1} & -k + v_{m-1} \\ -\beta + v_{m-1} & 2n - 1 - k + v_{m-1} \end{bmatrix} \\ &= v_{m-1} + u - \frac{(\beta + u)(k + u)}{\alpha + \beta + n - 1} \\ &= m \left(-\frac{n(n-1)}{2} - \frac{(\beta - n(n-1)/2)\,(2n-1)}{\alpha + \beta + n - 1} \right). \end{aligned}$$

Similar to the argument for $m = 1$, the optimal strategies of players A and B are

$$a^* = \left(\frac{\beta - n(n-1)/2}{\alpha + \beta + n - 1}, \frac{\alpha + (n+2)(n-1)/2}{\alpha + \beta + n - 1} \right) \quad \text{and}$$

$$b^* = \left(\frac{2n-1}{\alpha + \beta + n - 1}, \frac{\alpha + \beta - n}{\alpha + \beta + n - 1} \right),$$

respectively.

3.2 Replaying Game after ME-violating Repair

If ME-violating repair begins, we consider here that the damage of ME-violation can be undone when our game is replayed. Based on the payoff matrix for $m = 1$ in Section 3.1, we start with a multistage game. Since the cases of non-fault, non-base fault and major+minor fault can be excluded, the game $\Gamma(m)$ is

$$\Gamma(m) = \begin{bmatrix} \alpha - n + \Gamma(m-1) & -k + \Gamma(m-1) \\ -\beta + \Gamma(m) & (2n-1) - k + \Gamma(m-1) \end{bmatrix}.$$

Hence, the game value v_m is represented by

$$v_m = val \begin{bmatrix} \alpha - n + v_{m-1} & -k + v_{m-1} \\ -\beta + v_m & (2n-1) - k + v_{m-1} \end{bmatrix},$$

where the game value $v_0 = 0$ because there is no reward/cost in playing no game.

The expected payoffs of player A's mixed strategy $a = (p, 1-p)$ against player B's pure strategies are

$$\begin{aligned} E(a, \text{base fault}) &= p(\alpha - n + v_{m-1}) + (1-p)(-\beta + v_m) \quad \text{and} \\ E(a, \text{minor fault}) &= p(-k + v_{m-1}) + (1-p)\{(2n-1) - k + v_{m-1}\}. \end{aligned}$$

Then, the intersection of them is $p = (\beta+2n-1-k-(v_m-v_{m-1}))/(\alpha+\beta+n-1-(v_m-v_{m-1}))$. Since $v_m - v_{m-1} = (\alpha+\beta-n) - \beta/p$ from $E(a, \text{base fault})$,

$$u_m = (\alpha+\beta-n) - \beta \cdot \frac{(\alpha+\beta+n-1) - u_m}{(\beta+2n-1-k) - u_m}$$

by using $u_m = v_m - v_{m-1}$. Hence $(\alpha-n-u_m)(\beta+2n-1-k-u_m) = \beta(\alpha-n+k)$. By using $x = \alpha-n-u_m$ and $c = \beta-\alpha+3n-1-k$, we have $x^2+cx-\beta(\alpha-n+k) = 0$. Thus, $x = \{-c\pm\sqrt{c^2+4\beta(\alpha-n+k)}\}/2$. Let $x = \gamma, \delta$ $(\gamma < 0 < \delta)$. Suppose $x = \gamma < 0$. Since $v_m - v_{m-1} > \alpha - n$, a contradiction $\beta(1-1/p) > 0$ for $p < 1$ occurs. Thus, $x = \delta > 0$ and $u_m = \alpha - n - \delta$, i.e.,

$$p = \frac{\beta-\alpha+3n-1-k+\delta}{\beta+2n-1+\delta}.$$

Thus we obtain $v_m = v_0 + m(\alpha-n-\delta) = m(\alpha-n-\delta)$. The optimal strategy of player A is

$$a^* = \left(\frac{\beta-\alpha-n(n-3)/2+\delta}{\beta+2n-1+\delta}, \frac{\alpha+(n+2)(n-1)/2}{\beta+2n-1+\delta}\right),$$

where

$$\delta = \frac{1}{2}\{-c+\sqrt{c^2+4\beta(\alpha+(n+2)(n-1)/2)}\} \text{ and } c = \beta-\alpha-n(n-3)/2. \quad (10)$$

On the other hand, the expected payoffs of player B against the pure strategies of player A are

$$E(b, \text{ST}) = q(\alpha-n+v_{m-1}) + (1-q)(-k+v_{m-1}) \quad \text{and} \quad (11)$$
$$E(b, \text{NS}) = q(-\beta+v_m) + (1-q)(2n-1-k+v_{m-1}). \quad (12)$$

By considering the intersection of (11) and (12), the optimal strategy of player B can be derived as

$$b^* = \left(\frac{2n-1}{\beta+2n-1+\delta}, \frac{\beta+\delta}{\beta+2n-1+\delta}\right),$$

where δ satisfies (10).

4 Conclusion

In this paper, we developed not only a game theoretic analysis for an intentional fault, but also a general framework for strengthening an algorithm against the fault. The method is

1. develop two algorithms that complement each other,
2. combine them and specify their strategies to be executed with some probabilities,

3. construct a payoff matrix against an adversary, and
4. determine the maximin value and an optimal strategy.

In our analysis, we assumed a general setting that includes a reward α and a cost β. If we simplify them, e.g., $\alpha = \beta$, we obtain an intuitive result. That is, in the case the game is continued after ME-violating repair, player A's optimal strategy is

$$a^* = \left(\frac{\alpha - n(n-1)/2}{2\alpha + n - 1}, \frac{\alpha + (n+2)(n-1)/2}{2\alpha + n - 1} \right).$$

Thus, if α is sufficiently larger than n^2, the optimal strategy in our protocol is approximately $a^* \simeq (1/2, 1/2)$. Or if α is almost equal to n^2, the optimal strategy is $a^* \simeq (1/4, 3/4)$.

Acknowledgement

This work was partially supported by Grant-in-Aid for Scientific Research ((C)20 510139) of the Ministry of Education, Science, Sports, and Culture of Japan.

References

[1] Dasgupta, A., Ghosh, S., Tixeuil, S.: Selfish stabilization. In: Datta, A.K., Gradinariu, M. (eds.) SSS 2006. LNCS, vol. 4280, pp. 231–243. Springer, Heidelberg (2006)
[2] Dijkstra, E.W.: Self-stabilizing systems in spite of distributed control. Communications of the ACM 17(11), 643–644 (1974)
[3] Dolev, S., Israeli, A., Moran, S.: Analyzing expected time by scheduler-luck games. IEEE Transactions on Software Engineering 21(5), 429–439 (1995)
[4] Ghosh, S., Gupta, A.: An exercise in fault-containment: Self-stabilizing leader election. Information Processing Letters 59, 281–288 (1996)
[5] Ghosh, S., Gupta, A., Herman, T., Pemmaraju, S.V.: Fault-containing self-stabilizing algorithms. In: Proceedings of the 15th Annual ACM Symposium on Principles of Distributed Computing, pp. 45–54 (1996)
[6] Ghosh, S., He, X.: Fault-containing self-stabilization using priority scheduling. Information Processing Letters 73, 145–151 (2000)
[7] Herman, T.: Superstabilizing mutual exclusion. Distributed Computing 13(1), 1–17 (2000)
[8] Herman, T., Pemmaraju, S.: Error-detecting codes and fault-containing self-stabilization. Information Processing Letters 73, 41–46 (2000)
[9] Hohzaki, R.: A compulsory smuggling model of inspection game taking account of fulfillment probabilities of players' aims. Journal of the Operations Research Society of Japan 49(4), 306–318 (2006)
[10] Johnen, C.: Service time optimal self-stabilizing token circulation protocol on anonymous unidirectional rings. In: 21st Symposium on Reliable Distributed Systems, pp. 80–89 (2002)
[11] Kakugawa, H., Yamashita, M.: Uniform and self-stabilizing token rings allowing unfair daemon. IEEE Transactions on Parallel and Distributed Systems 8(2), 154–163 (1997)

[12] Kakugawa, H., Yamashita, M.: Uniform and self-stabilizing fair mutual exclusion on unidirectional rings under unfair distributed daemon. Journal of Parallel and Distributed Computing 62, 885–898 (2002)
[13] Katayama, Y., Ueda, E., Fujiwara, H., Masuzawa, T.: A latency optimal superstabilizing mutual exclusion protocol in unidirectional rings. Journal of Parallel and Distributed Computing 62(5), 865–884 (2002)
[14] Kiniwa, J.: Avoiding faulty privileges in fast stabilizing rings. IEICE Transactions on Fundamentals E85-A(5), 949–956 (2002)
[15] Kiniwa, J.: How to improve safety under convergence using stable storage. IEEE Transactions on Parallel and Distributed Systems 17(4), 389–398 (2006)
[16] Kiniwa, J., Kikuta, K.: Game theoretic analysis of malicious faults which are undetectable by local checks. IEICE Technical Report 108(330), COMP2008-47 (2008)
[17] Kiniwa, J., Yamashita, M.: A randomized 1-latent, time-adaptive and safe self-stabilizing mutual exclusion protocol. Parallel Processing Letters 16(1), 53–61 (2006)
[18] Koutsoupias, E., Papadimitriou, C.H.: Worst-Case Equilibria. In: Meinel, C., Tison, S. (eds.) STACS 1999. LNCS, vol. 1563, pp. 404–413. Springer, Heidelberg (1999)
[19] Nisan, N., Roughgarden, T., Tardos, E., Vazirani, V.V. (eds.): Algorithmic game theory. Cambridge University Press, Cambridge (2007)
[20] Myerson, R.B.: Game theory: analysis of conflict. Harvard University Press (1991)
[21] Nesterenko, M., Tixeuil, S.: Tolerance to unbounded byzantine faults. In: Proceedings of the 21st IEEE Symposium on Reliable Distributed Systems, pp. 22–29 (2002)
[22] Yen, I.-L.: A highly safe self-stabilizing mutual exclusion algorithm. Information Processing Letters 57, 301–305 (1996)

Exploring Polygonal Environments by Simple Robots with Faulty Combinatorial Vision

Anvesh Komuravelli[1,*] and Matúš Mihalák[2]

[1] Department of Comp. Science and Engineering, Indian Institute of Technology Kharagpur, India
anvesh@cse.iitkgp.ernet.in

[2] Institute of Theoretical Computer Science, ETH Zurich, Switzerland
matus.mihalak@inf.ethz.ch

Abstract. We study robustness issues of basic exploration tasks of simple robots inside a polygon P when sensors provide possibly faulty information about the unlabelled environment P. Ideally, the simple robot we consider is able to sense the number and the order of visible vertices, and can move to any such visible vertex. Additionally, the robot senses whether two visible vertices form an edge of P. We call this sensing a *combinatorial vision*. The robot can use pebbles to mark vertices. If there is a visible vertex with a pebble, the robot knows (senses) the index of this vertex in the list of visible vertices in counterclockwise order. It has been shown [1] that such a simple robot, using one pebble, can virtually label the visible vertices with their global indices, and navigate consistently in P. This allows, for example, to compute the map or a triangulation of P. In this paper we revisit some of these computational tasks in a *faulty* environment, in that we model situations where the sensors "see" two visible vertices as one vertex. In such a situation, we show that a simple robot with one pebble cannot even compute the number of vertices of P. We conjecture (and discuss) that this is neither possible with two pebbles. We then present an algorithm that uses three pebbles of two types, and allows the simple robot to count the vertices of P. Using this algorithm as a subroutine, we present algorithms that reconstruct the map of P, as well as the correct visibility at every vertex of P.

1 Introduction

Nowadays one of the main research areas in microrobotics is the study of simple mobile autonomous robots. The recent technological development made it possible to build small mobile robots with simple sensing and computational capabilities at a very low cost, which has launched an interest in the study of distributed robotic systems – computation with *swarms* of robots, not unlike the computational paradigm of wireless sensor networks (where a lot of simple, small and inexpensive devices are spread in the environment, the devices

* The work was done while the author was an internship student at ETH Zurich.

R. Guerraoui and F. Petit (Eds.): SSS 2009, LNCS 5873, pp. 458–471, 2009.

self-deploy in a working wireless network, gather data from the environment and provide simple computational tasks). Simple robots promise to bring mobile computational capabilities into areas where previous approaches (usually of bulky construction) are not feasible or cost-effective. The main advantages are quick and easy deployment, scalability, and cost-effectiveness. This new concept raises new research problems, as the classical schemes designed for centrally operated, or overwhelmingly equipped robots are inapplicable to the lightweight and/or distributed computational models of simple robots.

In this paper we consider one particular model of simple robots, the so called *simple combinatorial robot*. In this model the robot is modeled as a moving point inside a simple polygon P, and the sensing provides only "combinatorial" information about the surroundings. In particular, the robot does not sense any metric information (such as angles, distances, coordinates, or direction). Also, the robot can only move to visible vertices. Study of simple robots with possibly minimum requirements on the sensed information is an attractive topic both in theory and practice, as minimalistic assumptions provide robots that are less susceptible to failures, they are robust against sensing uncertainty and can be very inexpensive to build. In theory, a minimalistic model allows a worst-case computational analysis and provides insights about complexity of various tasks.

The *simple combinatorial robot* was first defined and studied by Suri et al. [1]. The robot operates inside a polygon P. We denote the set of vertices of the polygon P by $V = \{v_0, v_1, \ldots, v_{n-1}\}$, where two vertices v_i and v_{i+1}, $i \geq 0$, form an edge $e_i = v_i, v_{i+1}$ of P.[1] A *visible* vertex of a vertex v is every vertex u of the polygon for which the line uv lies in the polygon P. Similarly, for a robot at vertex v, we say that vertex u is visible to the robot. The robot, initially placed at vertex v_0, can only move to a visible vertex, and while moving, the robot does not sense anything about the environment. When the robot lands at a vertex of P, it senses all visible vertices, but only the presence of vertices – the vertices are unlabelled. The robot senses the vertices in a cyclic order, which is the only way the robot can distinguish the vertices from each other. Thus, a movement operation of the robot is simply of the form "move to the i-th visible vertex". The order of visible vertices is assumed to be counterclockwise (ccw). Additionally, the robot senses whether two visible vertices form a boundary edge of P. Positioned at vertex v, this is modelled by a *combinatorial visibility vector* $\text{cvv}(v) = (c_0, \ldots, c_k)$, which is a binary vector that encodes, given there are $k+1$ visible vertices, whether the i-th and $(i+1)$-th visible vertex, $i = 0, \ldots, k$, form an edge of P ($c_i = 1$) or not ($c_i = 0$). The convention is that the vertex v is visible to itself, and v is the 0-th visible vertex of v. Figure 1 illustrates the concept of cvv's. The robot can use pebbles to mark vertices. If there is a visible vertex with a pebble, the robot also senses the index of this vertex in the list of visible vertices in ccw order. In case the robot uses pebbles of different types, the robot also senses the type of the pebble. Naturally, the goal of computation with pebbles is to use few pebbles and few different types of pebbles.

[1] To avoid notational overhead, we assume all operations on the indices to be modulo the corresponding number (n in this case).

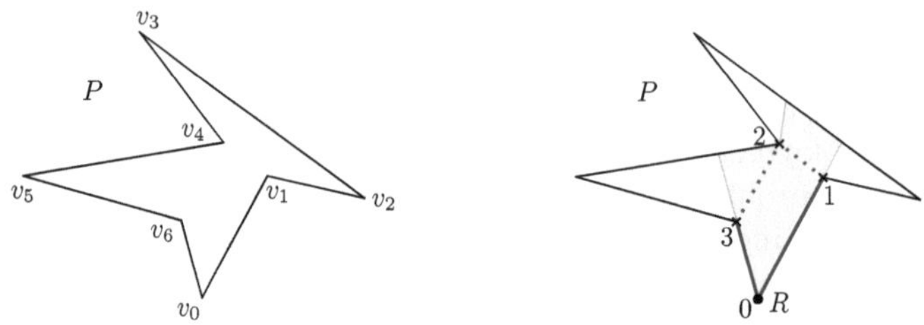

Fig. 1. The left figure depicts a polygon P on vertices $v_0, \ldots, v_6$. On the right figure, a robot R is placed on vertex v_0 of the same polygon. The visible region of the polygon is shaded. The visible vertices (ordered ccw from the robot's position) have only local identifiers 0, 1, 2, and 3 (no global information) stating their position in the ccw order, and the combinatorial visibility vector of v_0 is $\text{cvv}(v_0) = (1, 0, 0, 1)$, as the visible vertices 0, 1 form an edge, vertices 1, 2 form a diagonal, vertices 2, 3 form a diagonal, and vertices 3, 0 form an edge of P.

To understand capabilities of minimalistic robots, one studies what problems are solvable and which not, i.e., one is interested in the possibility only, and does not primarily aim for the best running time of algorithms. Learning and exploring the environment is a prime problem for any robotic system. The results of Suri et al. [1] show that a simple combinatorial robot without a pebble can decide whether the polygon P is convex. On the other hand, without a pebble the robot cannot count the number of vertices, as shows the result of [2]. Allowing the robot to use one pebble, the robot can virtually label the vertices of P and construct a map of P, i.e., the visibility graph $G = (V_{\text{vis}}, E_{\text{vis}})$ of P, a graph with $V_{\text{vis}} = V$ and with an edge between every two vertices that are visible to each other in P. This then allows the robot to consistently navigate inside the polygon, and, for example, compute a triangulation of P. Computing the visibility graph of P is essentially everything the simple combinatorial robot can do with one pebble, as was shown in [2].

In this paper we study the robustness issues of the simple combinatorial robot in scenarios where the sensing does not provide accurate information. In practice, two vertices visible from vertex v can be "seen" as being very close to each other (e.g., they span a very tiny angle with v). If a very "simple" sensory device is used, these two vertices may wrongly be recognized as a single vertex. This creates a faulty sensing for the robot. In this section we model such situations formally and study conditions in which the simple combinatorial robot can reconstruct the visibility graph of a simply-connected polygon P (the visibility graph of P is often called the *map* of the environment). We show in Section 2 that even counting the number of vertices of P is not possible with one pebble. We conjecture that this is still not possible with two pebbles. We then show that using three pebbles of two different types allows the simple combinatorial robot to count the number of vertices of P. In Section 3 we present an algorithm that allows a simple robot with three pebbles of two different types to compute the visibility graph of P, using the algorithm for counting as the main part. We conclude the paper and outline some future work in Section 4.

Modeling Vertex Faults

For a given simply-connected polygon P on vertices V, a *vertex fault* is a set $F \subsetneq V$, $|F| = 2$. We will sometimes refer to a *vertex fault* simply as a *fault.* A vertex that belongs to a vertex fault is called a *faulty vertex.* We denote by $\mathcal{F}$ a collection of vertex faults, i.e., a set $\mathcal{F} = \{F_1, F_2, \ldots, F_m\}$, where every F_i, $i = 1, 2, \ldots, m$, is a vertex fault. We assume that the vertex faults in $\mathcal{F}$ are mutually disjoint, i.e., no vertex belongs to more than one vertex fault.

We define and study the *simple combinatorial robot with vertex faults* (*faulty robot* for short) – a model derived from the simple combinatorial robot that reflects our discussion on unreliable sensing. For a given polygon P and a given set of vertex faults $\mathcal{F}$, a faulty robot sitting at some vertex $v \in V$ senses its surrounding in P via the *faulty combinatorial visibility vector* fcvv(v) which is defined from the cvv in the following way (consult Fig. 2 for illustration). Let cvv(v) be the combinatorial visibility vector of vertex v in polygon P. For any two visible vertices x and y, $x, y \neq v$, that belong to the same vertex fault F and that appear consecutively in the "vision" of vertex v (recall that the visible vertices of v are considered in ccw order), we remove from the cvv the information about the existence of an edge between x and y (i.e., we remove the bit that encodes whether they form an edge or a diagonal in P). Doing so for any such pair of vertices defines the faulty combinatorial visibility vector fcvv of vertex v.

Thus, if vertex v does not see any vertex from a vertex fault, or if vertex v sees at most one vertex from every vertex fault, the cvv and the fcvv are the same. Notice also that according to the definition, the robot at vertex v cannot distinguish between vertices x and y from F only if they lie consecutively next to each other (as observed from vertex v). The reason for this is that from different positions the vertices x and y may cause sensing problems, and from others not.

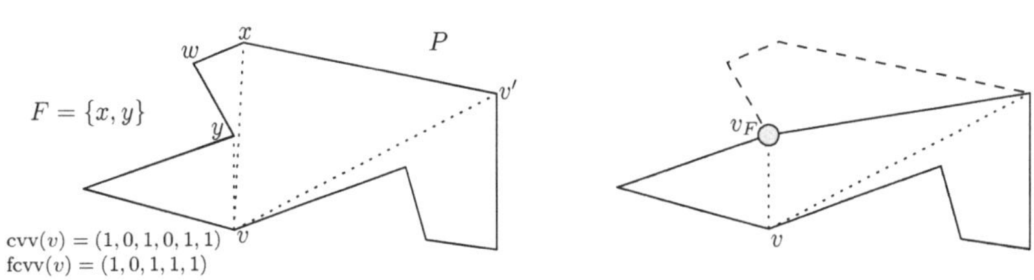

Fig. 2. Illustration of a faulty combinatorial visibility vector. The left figure depicts a polygon P with one vertex fault $F = \{x, y\}$. The vertices x and y appear consecutively in the ccw order as seen from v (the dotted lines are the "vision" lines) and therefore fcvv(v) differs from cvv(v) – the 0 encoding that x and y form a diagonal in P is removed. The right figure depicts an alternative view on fcvv's. The vertex fault $\{x, y\}$ is seen by a robot at v as one virtual vertex v_F, and fcvv(v) is then the cvv of this new (faulty) vision with v_F in it.

Especially, if from some position the vertices x and y do not appear consecutively, i.e., there is at least one vertex w between them, then the robot's sensing can distinguish between x and y. Notice also that if x and y are (mutually) visible in P than a robot at vertex x (or vertex y) always sees y correctly(x). The concept of the fcvv can also be seen as treating the two vertices of a vertex fault as one "virtual" vertex (as observed by a robot), and then defining the fcvv as the cvv with the virtual vertices. In this understanding, the robot thus senses less vertices (than there really are). We will assume that every vertex fault $F = \{u_F, v_F\}$ is visible from a vertex of P, i.e., there is a vertex v in P which sees both u_F and u_F with the correct vision (as otherwise such a vertex fault does not give any faulty vision).

It remains to specify what happens if a robot decides to move to a virtual vertex v_F. In our model we assume that the robot can land non-deterministically at either vertex of F. We study the worst-case behavior of algorithms, and thus assume an *adversary* that decides where the robot lands.

Finally, if a pebble is left at a faulty vertex of a vertex fault F, a robot that sees the virtual vertex v_F also sees the pebble as being placed at the virtual vertex v_F.

To the end of this section we would like to comment on the introduced mathematical model of faulty sensing. Our model is an abstraction, and simplification, and our approach lies rather in theoretical computer science (we are not building real robots), aiming at understanding the basic limitations and strengths of simple robots. We take the worst-case approach. Thus, defining a vertex fault as a set of two vertices, and *requiring* that this two vertices are *always* seen as one virtual vertex, is a simplification, and in a sense a *worst-case* approach – the robot *always* sees wrongly, and can *always* land wrongly (if it moves towards the virtual vertex). A more realistic model, in which a vertex fault $\{x, y\}$ can be sometimes seen correctly, does not change the results presented in this paper – seeing sometimes (but deterministically) correctly makes it only easier for the robot, while in the worst-case (which is our main goal), we may assume the vertex fault is seen wrongly from every vertex.

Related Work

The concept of simple, deterministic robots that sense no metric information (distances, angles, coordinates, etc.) is a relatively new research area. The simple combinatorial robot, the model we consider in this paper, was defined and studied in [1]. The robot was shown be able to compute the visibility graph of P using one pebble. A similar approach to minimalism was studied for example by Yershova et al [3]. They study pursuit-evasion problems with a robot that can only sense the type of the current vertex (reflex or convex angle) and can only move along the boundary edges, but can continue in the same direction after reaching a vertex with reflex angle. In these and similar models (see e.g. [4] or [5] for other examples of similar models) the considered sensing is very simple, yet the reliability of such sensing is crucial for the solutions of the studied problems.

A recent, not directly related, but well studied area of fault-tolerance with mobile robots addresses the computation issues with imprecise compasses. In this model, a set of asynchronous autonomous robots are placed in a plane (i.e., not in a polygon) equipped with a sense of direction (and distance) and capability to move an arbitrary distance in an arbitrary direction. An imprecise compass delivers a direction that can deviate from the actual value, but the error is bounded. In this model, mainly the gathering problem was studied [6,7]. Also for the gathering problem, the issue of not obtaining perfectly accurate sensory input, and not having a perfectly accurate movement was studied in [8] for asynchronous robots.

2 Counting the Number of Vertices

In this section we consider the elementary problem of inferring the number of vertices of a polygon P by a faulty robot. We shall see that this problem, being trivial in the fault-free case using one pebble, becomes non-trivial in the presence of faults even with two pebbles. We will show, however, that a robot with three pebbles of two types can compute the number of vertices of P.

2.1 Counting with 1 Pebble

It is illustrative to consider first the case when there are no vertex faults. In such a case the robot simply leaves a pebble on the current vertex and moves around the boundary, always moving to its first visible vertex (which is its "right" neighbor), counting the number of visited vertices, until the robot comes back to a vertex with the pebble. In case of vertex faults this simple strategy does obviously not work. Consider for example a convex polygon on four vertices v_0, v_1, v_2, v_3 and one vertex fault $F = \{v_1, v_2\}$. Assume that the robot initially sits at vertex v_0. The robot drops the pebble to mark v_0 and moves to its right neighbor, which is a virtual vertex v_F. The adversary makes the robot land on v_2. The robot then continues to v_3 and v_0, visiting only three vertices in total. One could probably easily derive a correct algorithm for this simple case, nonetheless we show that in general, using only one pebble, there is no algorithm for the problem of counting the number of vertices in the presence of vertex faults.

Theorem 1. *Any simple robot with one pebble cannot count the number of vertices of a polygon P with vertex faults.*

Proof. Let $\mathcal{A}$ be an arbitrary (deterministic) algorithm for the simple robot with one pebble. We will show that $\mathcal{A}$ cannot count the number of vertices in every polygon P.

Consider polygons P_1 and P_2 in Fig. 3 with a different number of vertices. The left polygon P_1 is a square and the right polygon P_2 is a convex polygon on six vertices. P_1 has no vertex fault, and P_2 has three vertex faults $F_1 = \{v_0, v_1\}$, $F_2 = \{v_2, v_3\}$ and $F_3 = \{v_4, v_5\}$. Thus, if we consider a robot placed at a vertex of the vertex fault $\{v_0, v_1\}$ for example, it can visually distinguish between the

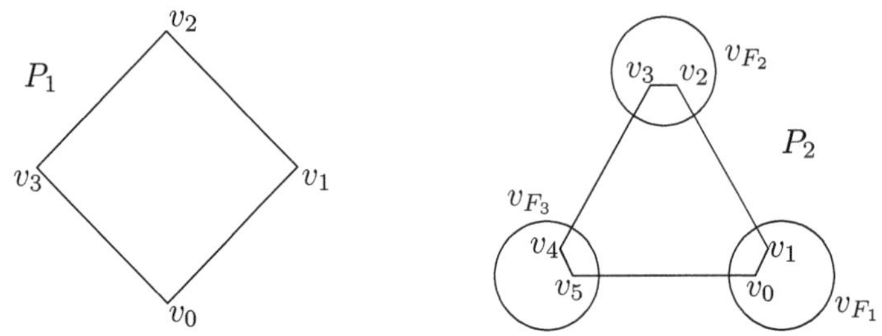

Fig. 3. Polygons used for the proof of Theorem 1

vertices v_0 and v_1, but from either of these vertices the robot sees v_2, v_3 as a single virtual vertex, and v_4, v_5 as another virtual vertex. Let us denote by v_{F_1}, v_{F_2}, and v_{F_3} the virtual vertices that correspond to the vertex faults F_1, F_2, and F_3, respectively.

Observe first that a robot has the same view in both polygons, i.e., $\text{fcvv}(v) = (1, 1, 1, 1)$ for any vertex v in both polygons. Thus, if the robot does not use the pebble, it cannot count the number of vertices because if after ℓ moves and observations in P_1 it determines that polygon has four vertices, then the same movements and observations can be made in the second polygon, and thus the deterministic robot has to claim P_2 has four vertices, which is obviously wrong.

Let us consider the situation when a robot executing $\mathcal{A}$ (in both polygons) drops a pebble. As P_1 and P_2 are symmetric we can, without loss of generality, assume the robot drops the pebble at vertex v_0 when run on any of the two polygons. We now show that any movement of a robot executing $\mathcal{A}$ in P_1 can be mimicked in P_2 as well, by appropriate choices (by the adversary) of a vertex the robot lands at, when moving to a virtual vertex v_{F_i}, $i = 1, 2, 3$, such that the observed fcvv's remain the same, together with the position of the pebble therein. If a robot in P_1 moves to its first visible vertex (i.e., to vertex v_1 in our case), then robot in P_2 attempts to move to v_1 as well, and thus the robot in P_2 lands at v_1 as well. Hence, the position of the pebble in both cases is the same – the pebble is on the vertex which is the robot's left neighbor. Similarly, if the robot in P_1 moves to its last visible vertex (i.e., to vertex v_3), then robot in P_2 attempts to move to vertex v_{F_3} and lands at vertex v_5. If the robot in P_1 moves to the second visible vertex (vertex v_2), then the robot in P_2 lands at vertex v_3. It is easy to check that the position of the pebble is the same in both cases. Now (assuming the pebble is still at vertex v_0) for any position of the robot in P_1 and any movement of the robot to a visible vertex, the adversary can make the robot in P_2 mimic the movement by an appropriate choice of landings in P_2. We do not list all possible movements here, but give one more example only. Assume the robot in P_1 at vertex v_2 moves to vertex v_1 and then to vertex v_3. If the robot in P_2 is at vertex v_3, the algorithm $\mathcal{A}$ moves the robot first to vertex v_2, and then attempts to move the robot to vertex v_{F_3}, and lands at vertex v_5 (by the choice of the adversary).

If the robot picks up the pebble in P_1 so can the robot in P_2, as we have maintained the same vision and the position of the pebble is the same for the robots in both polygons.

Thus, as the adversary can force the algorithm $\mathcal{A}$ to produce the same vision sequence in both polygons, the algorithm cannot compute the number of vertices in both polygons. □

2.2 Counting with 2 Pebbles

A natural question is to study the problem using two pebbles. While we do not know whether two pebbles suffice to compute the number of vertices of any polygon P, we outline the difficulties in designing such an algorithm.

Consider a (big) polygon which consists of "triangular cells" as depicted in Fig. 4. The triangular cell can be seen as a triangle whose tips were cut off. For the construction we cut off just a tiny bit so that the resulting two vertices of a loose end have distance ε (ε as small as needed). Also, the two vertices of every end (corner) of the cell form a vertex fault. We can glue the triangular cells together as depicted in the figure. Starting from a central triangular cell, we can grow the polygon to an arbitrary size by making the newly glued cells smaller and smaller. To make the construction finite, we just sometimes use triangular cells with only one cut off corner (the other two ends are not open and thus nothing can be glued to them). We make the construction such that the two vertices of every vertex fault F appear consecutively in ccw order as seen from any visible vertex, and thus the two vertices will be seen by the robot as a single virtual vertex v_F. For this to achieve, one has to set an appropriate ε and an appropriate angle at which the new cells are glued. For brevity we omit the precise description of the construction. We note that the depiction in Fig. 4 is only schematic. We call the resulting polygon *triangular*. For the moment we assume the polygon is big enough for "anything which follows", while the exact size will naturally become clear at the end of the section.

We first prove a useful lemma that highlights the main technique for the proof of the main result of this subsection.

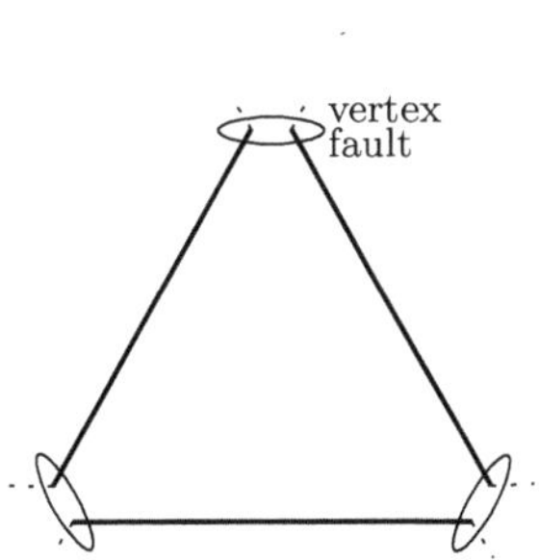

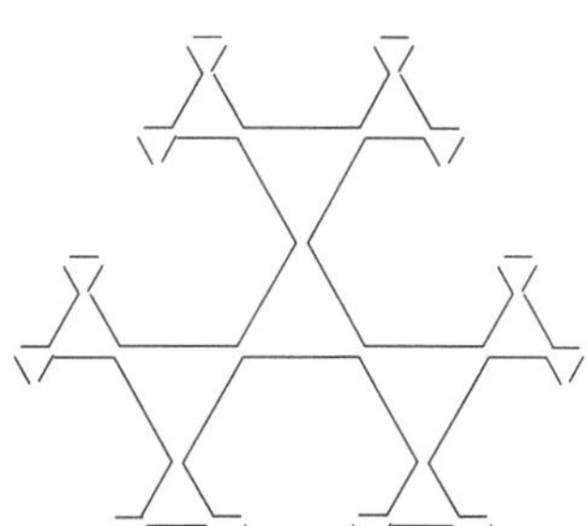

Fig. 4. Left: A "triangular cell" is a triangle with endpoints split into open ends. The two vertices of each open end form a vertex fault. Right: The whole polygon is build from these "triangular cells" by an appropriate rotation and scaling.

Lemma 1. *A simple robot with no pebbles can be made to stay within two neighboring cells in any triangular polygon P. Furthermore, if the initial vertex can be chosen by the adversary, the robot can be made to stay within one cell.*

Proof. The main trick is to choose the proper vertex $v \in F$ where the robot lands when it attempts to move to a virtual vertex v_F. We (the adversary) can choose this vertex arbitrarily (i.e., the robot does not notice the difference) as long as the vision from these two vertices is the same. Observe that if the robot is not at the ending triangular cell, the vision is everywhere the same, fcvv $= (1, 1, 1, 1, 1, 1)$. Our choice of the landing vertex will depend on what the robot wants to do after landing in v_F. For the following discussion, consult Fig. 5. Let s denote the vertex where the robot starts. Let e be the vertex for which $\{s, e\}$ is a vertex fault in P. Vertex s is a "gateway" to two neighboring triangular cells A and B, with vertices as depicted in the figure. We show how to make the robot stay in the cells A and B. Assume for example the robot wants to move to its right neighbor (which is the virtual vertex of the vertex fault $\{a, b\}$). The robot may land at a or b. We have the freedom to choose. Depending on the robot's next move we choose a or b such that after the next move the robot stays in A or B. The important observation is that a robot at a or b has the same sensing (the same fcvv) and thus, as the robot is deterministic, has to do the same movement, regardless of whether it lands at a or b. If the next move is "go to the i-th visible vertex in ccw order", where i is 1 or 2, then we make the robot land at b (as if it landed at a, the next movement would bring the robot out of A and B). Similarly, if the next move is "go to the i-th visible vertex in ccw order", where i is 4 or 5, then we make the robot land at a. Clearly, if the next move is "go to the 3rd visible vertex", the robot stays within the cells A and B regardless of us choosing a or b as the landing vertex. Thus, we only choose a or b according to the robot's first movement that is different from "go to the 3rd visible vertex". After we have chosen the proper vertex a or b for the robot to land, we can similarly argue for all subsequent movements.

From the aforementioned arguments it is now an easy observation that if the adversary can choose the initial vertex (i.e., either s or e) then the robot can be made to stay within one cell (say, cell A in our case). □

Using the ideas of the previous lemma we show the following theorem

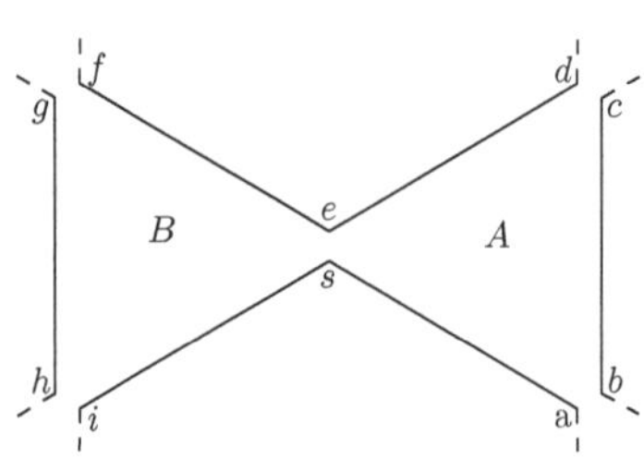

Fig. 5. A robot that does not use a pebble never leaves cells A and B

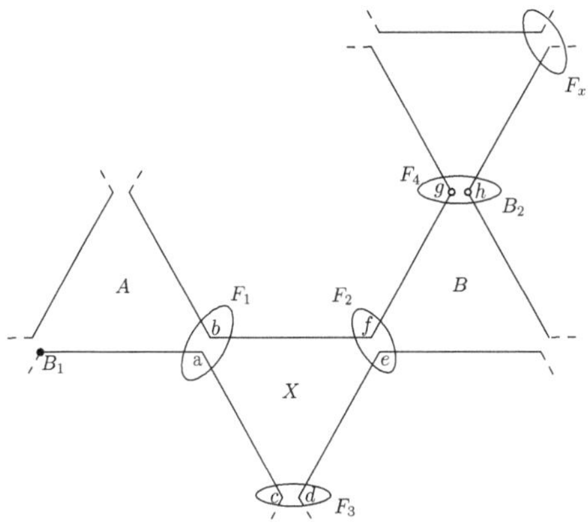

Fig. 6. Pebbles B_1 and B_2 are separated by at least 3 moves

Theorem 2. *If a faulty robot with two pebbles can count the number of vertices of a triangular polygon P, then at any time of the computation the two pebbles are at most two moves (of the robot) apart.*

Proof. Let us consider the situation where the two pebbles B_1 and B_2 are more than two moves apart. Thus, the pebbles are in two cells A and B which do not share a single vertex. Let us consider the moment when the robot places the second pebble B_2 in cell B. We will show that the robot cannot count the number of vertices of P. We will argue that the adversary can choose landings in such a way that the robot will never come back to cell A (where the first pebble B_1 is placed). Thus, effectively, this will lead into a situation of a robot with one pebble only. In this situation, however, the robot cannot lose sight of the second pebble B_2, as otherwise the robot would end up in a situation of Lemma 1, according to which the adversary can make the robot stay in one cell (forever). Clearly, if the robot cannot lose the sight of the second pebble B_2, it cannot visit all vertices of P (as picking up the pebble B_2 results into the situation of Lemma 1, and thus we can make the robot to stay in one cell, never coming back to cell A), and thus it cannot count the number of vertices of P.

Consider the situation in Fig. 6, where B_1 denotes the first pebble, and B_2 denotes the second pebble. B_1 lies in cell A, B_2 lies in cell B, and there is at least one more cell X between the two cells (and B_1 and B_2 do not lie in X). We want to avoid the robot coming to a vertex of vertex fault F_1, the "gateway" to cell A. For this, we first argue about the position of pebble B_2 in cell B. It is placed at a vertex of a vertex fault $F_4 = \{g, h\}$. From the geometry of the setting and from our assumptions it follows that the robot *had* to come to F_4 from a vertex of P that did not see the pebble B_1. Hence, we (the adversary) can choose whether the robot lands at g or h – the visibility will be the same, so the robot decides to place a pebble in either case.

This effectively means that we (the adversary) can decide the location of the pebble B_2 to be g or h. Our decision depends on the next step(s) of the robot.

We may assume that the next step of the robot is a movement (as collecting the right-now dropped pebble is useless and does not help the robot to navigate or compute anything). Let us first consider the case in which we let the robot land at vertex g to place the pebble B_2 there. If the robot never leaves the sight of B_2 then the robot can clearly never come to cell A, and it also cannot count the number of vertices of P. Thus, assume the robot eventually leaves the sight of B_2. Clearly, for one of the choices of landing at g or h, the "leaving" of the robot does not happen at a vertex of F_2 (i.e., if for a particular choice of landing the "leaving" happens at a vertex of F_2, then for the other choice of landing the "leaving" happens at a vertex of F_x – the symmetrically placed vertex fault to F_2; this follows because the robot will do the same sequence of movements in either case). Thus, choosing the proper landing, the robot moves from a vertex of F_x to a cell with no sight of a pebble, and thus it ends up at the situation of Lemma 1, which guarantees the adversary to make the robot stay in one cell (forever). □

Thus, according to the theorem, the two pebbles have to be dropped in adjacent cells, or in the same cell. This hints us that the robot should keep track of the two pebbles such that they are not very far apart. Thus, as the robot moves, it should move the pebbles too. While this may help in visiting vertices, it is not obvious it helps in counting them exactly. This provokes us to make the following conjecture.

Conjecture 1. A simple robot with two pebbles cannot count the number of vertices of a polygon with vertex faults.

2.3 Counting with 3 Pebbles

Now, we present an algorithm for counting the vertices of a polygon with any number of vertex faults using three pebbles of two different types.

Theorem 3. *A simple robot with three pebbles of two different types can count the number of vertices of a polygon P with vertex faults.*

Proof. Our algorithm uses the distinct pebble (pebble of type 2) to mark the start vertex v_0, and two other identical pebbles (pebbles of type 1) to traverse consistently along the boundary of P in ccw order. Starting at vertex v_0, the algorithm's goal is to be able to go to the i-th vertex on the boundary, $i = 1, 2, 3, 4, \ldots$, until the pebble of type 2 is found again, and thus the number of vertices of P is inferred. The pebble of type 2 will not have any other usage in the algorithm.

As we have seen in the previous sections, going to the first vertex is already impossible if no pebble is used (recall, just set $\{v_1, v_2\}$ to be a vertex fault and let the robot land at vertex v_2 instead of landing at v_1). Using two pebbles, traversing the boundary consistently is possible. We will show how to make one *step* of the traversing, i.e., how to move to the next vertex on the boundary. The whole traversing is then just the repetition of these steps.

Assume the robot is at vertex v_0 and it wants to walk to vertex v_1. The robot leaves a pebble (which is always of type 1 from now on) at v_0 and it attempts to move to its first visible vertex (which may be a virtual vertex). Let us denote by v the vertex where the robot landed. Observe now that the robot landed at vertex v_1 if and only if the robot sees the pebble at the *left neighbor* of v – the last visible vertex (possibly virtual) when considered in ccw order. To see this, observe first that if the robot indeed landed at v_1, it sees a pebble at its left neighbor, even if v_0 belongs to a vertex fault F and the left neighbor is seen as a virtual vertex v_F. On the other side, consider the case when the robot did not land at v_1, but at some other vertex v. Thus, $\{v_1, v\}$ has to be a vertex fault of the polygon, and v_0, v_1, and v are mutually visible. We want to show that v does not see a pebble at its left neighbor (even if it is seen as a virtual vertex). This could only be possible if v_0 and the *true* left neighbor w of v formed a virtual vertex for v. However, as v sees vertices v_0, v_1, and w in this order, v_0 and w cannot form a virtual vertex, as v_0 and w do not appear consecutively in the combinatorial vision of v.

The robot can thus easily check whether it landed at the desired vertex. It just looks to its left neighbor and checks whether there is the pebble. If the robot does not land at vertex v_1, but at some vertex v instead, then clearly $\{v_1, v\}$ is a vertex fault in P. Observe that vertex v sees v_0 and v_1. The robot wants to move to v_1. From the view of vertex v, vertex v_1 is the neighboring vertex of v_0 (which is the vertex with the pebble) in ccw order. Thus, the robot attempts to move to this vertex, and, as v and v_1 form a vertex fault, the robot lands correctly at v_1. Let us call this strategy the *remedy procedure.*

Thus, a robot can move to the neighboring vertex on the boundary using one pebble. If the robot had more pebbles, it could just place a new one, move to the neighboring vertex (using the same algorithm), etc. In case of two pebbles only, the robot does the following. It leaves the second pebble at the vertex v_1 (it knows the current vertex is v_1) and moves to the left neighboring vertex, i.e., to v_0. This can be done in a similar way as when the robot walked from v_0 to v_1, just in the reverse, symmetrical order. The robot again checks whether it landed at v_0 (now it is easy, it just checks whether it landed at a vertex with a pebble on it), and performs the (slightly altered) remedy procedure, if needed. This time, if the robot does not land at v_0, the robot sees two pebbles, and thus it has to attempt to walk to the first visible vertex with a pebble (in the order of vertices as seen from the robot's position). A robot at vertex v_0 then collects the pebble and attempts to move to the vertex with the second pebble, the vertex v_1. If the robot lands at v_1, the robot can start the same algorithm again, thus getting from v_1 to v_2, etc. If the robot does not land at v_1, however, then it lands at vertex v which forms with v_1 a vertex fault. From v the robot sees v_1, and it can identify v_1 as the vertex with the pebble. Thus, the robot can attempt to move to v_1 where it also has to land.

We have presented a procedure which allows the robot to move from a vertex to its neighboring vertex on the boundary, and keeps both pebbles with the robot. Thus, repeating this procedure until the robot reaches the pebble of type 2 allows the robot to count the number of vertices of P. □

3 Fault Detection and Map Construction

We have shown that a simple robot with three pebbles of two types can count the number of vertices of a polygon P. Using the traversing procedure we will show that the robot can also reconstruct the correct cvv at every vertex of the polygon, and thus it can reconstruct the visibility graph of P. This is actually a simple task to do while the robot traverses the boundary of P, as the robot at position v_i (before attempting to move to vertex v_{i+1}) can check whether it sees a vertex with the pebble of type 1 (the vertex v_0), and thus it can find out whether v_0 and v_i are visible in P. This proves the following theorem.

Theorem 4. *Simple robot with three pebbles of two different types can reconstruct visibility graph (and all* cvv*'s) of a polygon with vertex faults.*

A related reconstruction-question arises, namely, can a simple robot identify all vertex faults? We present a procedure that allows the robot to identify all vertex faults visible from the vertex v_0. Repeating this procedure for all other vertices v_i, $i = 1, 2, \ldots, n$, then allows to identify all vertex faults. Again, the robot can identify all vertex faults visible from v_0 using three pebbles of two different kinds. First, the robot computes the number of vertices of P using the algorithm of the previous section. After that, the robot at vertex v_0 takes the pebble of type 1 from v_0, and traverses the polygon (using the traversing procedure with the two identical pebbles). The robot checks for every visited vertex v_i, $i = 1, 2, \ldots, n$, whether it is visible from v_0 by leaving the pebble of type 1 at v_i, traversing back to v_0, and checking whether pebble of type 1 is visible from v_0. If vertex v_i is visible from v_0 at the same position (in the ordered list of visible vertices) as the previously visible vertex v', then (and only then) $\{v', v_i\}$ forms a vertex fault visible from v_0.

Theorem 5. *Simple robot with three pebbles of two different types can identify the vertices F of every virtual vertex v_F.*

4 Conclusions and Further Work

We have studied a particular model of faulty sensing of simple combinatorial robots in a polygon P. We have shown that even the otherwise trivial task of computing the number of vertices of P is not possible for a robot with one pebble. We have demonstrated difficulties a robot with two pebbles has to count the number of vertices and conjectured that the robot cannot count. Finally, we have presented algorithms that allows a robot with three pebbles of two different types to count the number of vertices of P, to reconstruct the visibility graph of P, and to identify all vertex faults.

An obvious open problem left is Conjecture 1. Similarly, one might want to get rid of using two types of pebbles. Another interesting question is what happens if we allow the vertex faults to intersect, or we consider more than two vertices in a vertex fault. The presented algorithms do not work for this case (while, obviously, the impossibility results still hold for this case), and this paper leaves this issue unanswered. As a (more distant) future work we would like to study other models of faults for simple combinatorial robots (e.g., movement faults where the robot does not stop at reflex vertices), and possibly a combination of these faults.

References

1. Suri, S., Vicari, E., Widmayer, P.: Simple robots with minimal sensing: From local visibility to global geometry. International Journal of Robotics Research 27(9), 1055–1067 (2008)
2. Brunner, J., Mihalák, M., Suri, S., Vicari, E., Widmayer, P.: Simple robots in polygonal environments: A hierarchy. In: Fekete, S.P. (ed.) ALGOSENSORS 2008. LNCS, vol. 5389, pp. 111–124. Springer, Heidelberg (2008)
3. Yershova, A., Tovar, B., Ghrist, R., LaValle, S.: Bitbots: Simple robots solving complex tasks. In: Proceedings of the Twentieth National Conference on Artificial Intelligence and the Seventeenth Innovative Applications of Artificial Intelligence Conference, pp. 1336–1341 (2005)
4. Tovar, B., Freda, L., LaValle, S.: Using a robot to learn geometric information from permutations of landmarks. Contemporary Mathematics 438, 33–45 (2007)
5. Ganguli, A., Cortés, J., Bullo, F.: Distributed deployment of asynchronous guards in art galleries. In: Proceedings of the American Control Conference, June 2006, pp. 1416–1421 (2006)
6. Souissi, S., Défago, X., Yamashita, M.: Gathering asynchronous mobile robots with inaccurate compasses. In: Shvartsman, M.M.A.A. (ed.) OPODIS 2006. LNCS, vol. 4305, pp. 333–349. Springer, Heidelberg (2006)
7. Katayama, Y., Tomida, Y., Imazu, H., Inuzuka, N., Wada, K.: Dynamic compass models and gathering algorithms for autonomous mobile robots. In: Prencipe, G., Zaks, S. (eds.) SIROCCO 2007. LNCS, vol. 4474, pp. 274–288. Springer, Heidelberg (2007)
8. Cohen, R., Peleg, D.: Convergence of autonomous mobile robots with inaccurate sensors and movements. In: Durand, B., Thomas, W. (eds.) STACS 2006. LNCS, vol. 3884, pp. 549–560. Springer, Heidelberg (2006)

Finding Good Partners in Availability-Aware P2P Networks

Stevens Le Blond[1], Fabrice Le Fessant[2], and Erwan Le Merrer[3,*]

[1] INRIA Sophia Antipolis
stevens.le_blond@inria.fr
[2] INRIA Saclay
fabrice.le_fessant@inria.fr
[3] INRIA Rennes
elemerre@irisa.fr

Abstract. We study the problem of finding peers matching a given availability pattern in a peer-to-peer (P2P) system. Motivated by practical examples, we specify two formal problems of availability matching that arise in real applications: *disconnection matching*, where peers look for partners expected to disconnect at the same time, and *presence matching*, where peers look for partners expected to be online simultaneously in the future. As a scalable and inexpensive solution, we propose to use epidemic protocols for topology management; we provide corresponding metrics for both matching problems. We evaluated this solution by simulating two P2P applications, *task scheduling* and *file storage*, over a new trace of the eDonkey network, the largest available with availability information. We first proved the existence of regularity patterns in the sessions of 14M peers over 27 days. We also showed that, using only 7 days of history, a simple predictor could select predictable peers and successfully predicted their online periods for the next week. Finally, simulations showed that our simple solution provided good partners fast enough to match the needs of both applications, and that consequently, these applications performed as efficiently at a much lower cost. We believe that this work will be useful for many P2P applications for which it has been shown that choosing good partners, based on their availability, drastically improves their performance and stability.

1 Introduction

Churn is one of the most critical characteristics of peer-to-peer (P2P) networks, as the permanent flow of peer connections and disconnections can seriously hamper the efficiency of applications [9]. Fortunately, it has been shown that, for many peers, these events globally obey some availability patterns ([21,22,2]), and so, can be predicted from the uptime history of those peers [18].

To take advantage of these predictions, applications need to be able to dynamically find good partners for peers, according to these availability patterns, even

* Supported by project P2Pim@ges, of the French Media & Networks cluster.

R. Guerraoui and F. Petit (Eds.): SSS 2009, LNCS 5873, pp. 472–484, 2009.

in large-scale unstructured networks. The intrinsic constitution of those networks makes pure random matching techniques to be time-inefficient facing churn. Basic usage of prediction based on node availability exists in the literature, as *e.g.* for file replication [16].

In this paper, we study a generic technique to discover such partners, and apply it for two particular matching problems: *disconnection matching*, where peers look for partners expected to disconnect at the same time, and *presence matching*, where peers look for partners expected to be online simultaneously in the future. These problems are specified in Section 2.

We then propose to use standard epidemic protocols for topology management to solve these problems (see *e.g.* [12,24]); such protocols have proven to be efficient for a large panel of applications, from overlay slicing [13] to IP-TV overlay maintenance [14] for example. However, in order to converge to the desired state or topology (here matched peers), those protocols require good metrics to compute the distance between peers. Such metrics and a well known epidemic protocol, T-Man [12], are described in Section 3.

To evaluate the efficiency of our proposal, we simulated an application for each matching problem: an application of *task scheduling*, where tasks of multiple remote jobs are started by all the peers in the network (disconnection matching), and an application of *P2P file-system*, where peers replicate files on other peers to have them highly available (presence matching). These applications are specified in Section 5.

To run our simulations on a realistic workload, we collected a new trace of peer availability on the eDonkey file-sharing network. With the connections and disconnection of 14M peers over 27 days, this trace is the largest available workload, concerning peers' availability. In Section 4, we show that peers in this trace exhibit availability patterns, and, using a simple 7-day predictor, that it is possible to select predictable peers and successfully predict their behavior over the following week. The new eDonkey trace and this simple predictor are studied in Section 4.

Our simulation results showed that our T-Man based solution is able to provide good partners to all peers, for both applications. Using availability patterns, both applications are able to keep the same performance, while consuming 30% less resources, compared to a random selection of partners. Moreover, T-Man is scalable and inexpensive, making the solution usable for any application and network size. These results are detailed in Section 6.

We believe that many P2P systems and applications can benefit from this work, as a lot of availability-aware applications have been proposed in the literature [3,8,20,5,25]. Close to our work, Godfrey et al. [9] show that strategies based on the longest current uptime are more efficient than uptime-agnostic strategies for replica placement; Mickens et al. [18] introduce sophisticated availability predictors and shows that they can be very successful. However, to the best of our knowledge, this paper is the first to deal with the problem of finding the best partners according to availability patterns in a large-scale network. Moreover, previous results are often computed on synthetic traces or small traces of P2P networks.

2 Problem Specification

This section presents two availability matching problems, disconnection matching and presence matching. Each problem is abstracted from the needs of a practical P2P application that we describe afterward. But first, we start by introducing our system model.

2.1 System and Network Model

We assume a fully-connected asynchronous P2P network of N nodes, with N usually ranging from thousands to millions of nodes. We assume that there is a constant bound n_c on the number of simultaneous connections that a peer can engage in, typically much smaller than N. When peers leave the system, they disconnect silently. However, we assume that disconnections are detected after a time Δ_{disc}, for example 30 seconds with TCP keep-alive.

For each peer x, we assume the existence of an availability prediction $Pr^x(t)$, starting at the current time t and for a period T in the future, such that $Pr^x(t)$ is a set of non-overlapping intervals during which x is expected to be online. Since these predictions are based on previous measures of availability for peer x, we assume that such measures are reliable, even in the presence of malicious peers [19,17].

We note $\bigcup Pr^x(t)$ the set defined by the union of the intervals of $Pr^x(t)$, and $||S||$ the size of a set S.

2.2 The Problem of Disconnection Matching

Intuitively, the problem of *Disconnection Matching* is, for a peer online at a given time, to find a set of other online peers who are expected to disconnect at the same time.

Formally, for a peer x online at time t, an online peer y is a *better match* for Disconnection Matching than an online peer z if $|t^x - t^y| < |t^x - t^z|$, where $[t, t^x[\in Pr^x(t)$, $[t, t^y[\in Pr^y(t)$ and $[t, t^z[\in Pr^z(t)$. The problem of *Disconnection Matching* $DM(n)$ is to discover the n best matches of online peers at anytime.

The problem of disconnection matching typically arises in applications where a peer tries to find partners with whom it wants to collaborate until the end of its session, in particular when starting such a collaboration might be expensive in terms of resources.

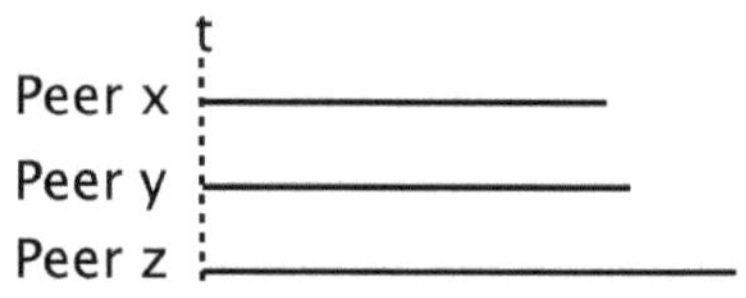

Fig. 1. Disconnection Matching: peer y is a better match than peer z for peer x

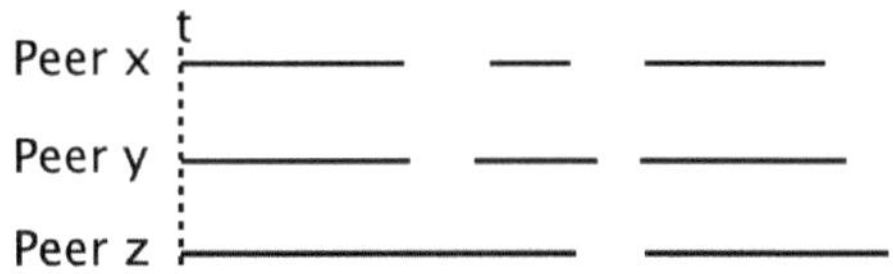

Fig. 2. Presence Matching: peer y is a better match than peer z for peer x

An example of such an application is *task scheduling* in P2P networks. In Zorilla [7] for example, a peer can submit a computation task of n jobs to the system. In such a case, the peer tries to locate n online peers (with expanding ring search) to become partners for the task, and executes the n jobs on these partners. When the computation is over, the peer collects the n results from the n partners. With disconnection matching, such a system becomes much more efficient: by choosing partners who are likely to disconnect at the same time as the peer, the system increases the probability that:

- If the peer does not disconnect too early, its partners will have time to finish executing their jobs before disconnecting and he will be able to collect the results;
- If the peer disconnects before the end of the computation, partners will not waste unnecessary resources as they are also likely to disconnect at the same time.

2.3 The Problem of Presence Matching

Intuitively, the problem of *Presence Matching* is, for a peer online at a given time, to find a set of other online peers who are expected to be connected at the same time in the future.

Formally, for a peer x online at time t, an online peer y is a better match for *Unfair Presence Matching* than an online peer z if:

$$||\bigcup Pr^z(t) \cap \bigcup Pr^x(t)|| < ||\bigcup Pr^y(t) \cap \bigcup Pr^x(t)||$$

This problem is called *unfair*, since peers who are always online appear to be best matches for all other peers in the system, whereas only other always-on peers are best matches for them. Since some fairness is wanted in most P2P systems, offline periods should also be considered. Consequently, y is a better match than z for *Presence Matching* if:

$$\frac{||\bigcup Pr^z(t) \cap \bigcup Pr^x(t)||}{||\bigcup Pr^z(t) \cup \bigcup Pr^x(t)|} < \frac{||\bigcup Pr^y(t) \cap \bigcup Pr^x(t)||}{||\bigcup Pr^y(t) \cup \bigcup Pr^x(t)||}$$

The problem of *Presence Matching* $PM(n)$ is to discover the n best matches of online peers at anytime.

The problem of presence matching arises in applications where a peer wants to find partners that will be available at the same time in other sessions. This is typically the case when huge amount of data have to be transferred, and that partners will have to communicate a lot to use that data.

An example of such an application is storage of files in P2P networks [4]. For example, in Pastiche [6], each peer in the system has to find other peers to store its files. Since files can only be used when the peer is online, the best partners for a peer (at equivalent stability) are the peers who are expected to be online when the peer itself is online.

Moreover, in a P2P backup system[8], peers usually replace the replica that cannot be connected for a given period, to maintain a given level of data redundancy. Using presence matching, such applications can increase the probability of being able to connect to all their partners, thus reducing their maintenance cost.

3 Uptime Matching with Epidemic Protocols

We think that epidemic protocols [12,23,15,24] are good approximate solutions for these matching problems. Here, we present one of these protocols, T-Man[12] and, since such protocols rely heavily on appropriate metrics, we propose a metric for each matching problem.

3.1 Distributed Matching with T-Man

T-Man is a well-known epidemic protocol, usually used to associate each peer in the network with a set of good partners, given a metric (distance function) between peers. Even in large-scale networks, T-Man converges fast, and provides a good approximation of the optimal solution in a few rounds, where each round costs only four messages in average per peer.

In T-Man, each peer maintains two small sets, its *random view* and its *metric view*, which are, respectively, some random neighbors, and the current best candidates for partnership, according to the metric in use. During each round, every peer updates its views: with one random peer in its random view, it merges the two random views, and keeps the most recently seen peers in its random view; with the best peer in its metric view, it merges all the views, and keeps only the best peers, according to the metric, in its metric view.

This double scheme guarantees a permanent shuffle of the random views, while ensuring fast convergence of the metric views towards the optimal solution. Consequently, the choice of a good metric is very important. We propose such metrics for the two availability matching problems in the next part.

3.2 Metrics for Availability Matching

To compute efficiently the distance between peers, the prediction $Pr^x(t)$ is approximated by a bitmap of size m, pred^x, where entry $\mathsf{pred}^x[i]$ is 1 if $[i \times T/m, (i+1) \times T/m[$ is included in an interval of $Pr^x(t)$ for $0 \leq i < m$. Note that these metrics can be used with any epidemic protocol, not only with T-Man.

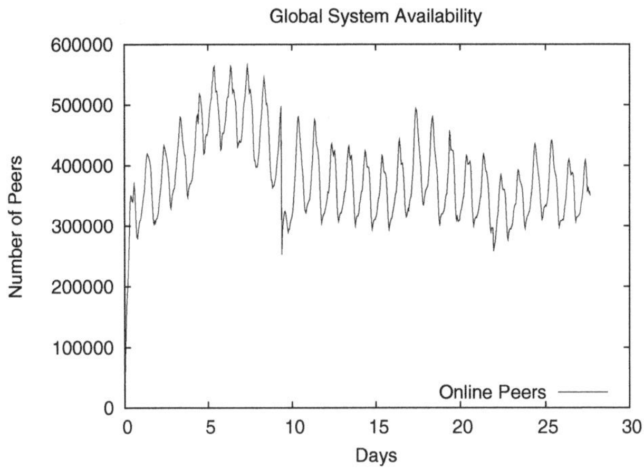

Fig. 3. Diurnal patterns are clearly visible when we plot the number of online peers at any time in our 27-day eDonkey trace. Depending on the time of the day, between 300,000 and 600,000 users are connected to a single eDonkey server.

Disconnection Matching. The metric computes the time between the disconnections of two peers. In case of equality, the PM-distance of 3.2 is used to prefer peers with the same availability periods:

$$\text{DM-distance}(x, y) = |I^x - I^y| + \text{PM-distance}(x, y) \text{ where}$$
$$I^x = min\{0 \leq i < m | \mathsf{pred}^x[i] = 1 \wedge \mathsf{pred}^x[i+1] = 0\}$$

Presence Matching. The metric first computes the ratio of co-availability (time where both peers were simultaneously online) on total availability (time where at least one peer was online). Since the distance should be close to 0 when peers are close, we then reverse the value on [0,1]:

$$\text{PM-distance}(x, y) = 1 - \frac{\sum_{0 \leq i < m} min(\mathsf{pred}^x[i], \mathsf{pred}^y[i])}{\sum_{0 \leq i < m} max(\mathsf{pred}^x[i], \mathsf{pred}^y[i])}$$

Note that, while the PM-distance value is in [0,1], the DM-distance value is in [0,m].

4 Simulation Settings

We evaluated our a solution based on T-Man on two applications, one for each matching problem. In this section, we describe our simulation settings. In particular, we describe the characteristics of the trace we collected for the needs of this study, with more than 300,000 online peers on 27 days. With a few thousand peers online at the same time, most other traces collected on P2P systems [21,10,2] lack massive connection and disconnection trends, for the study of availability patterns on a large scale.

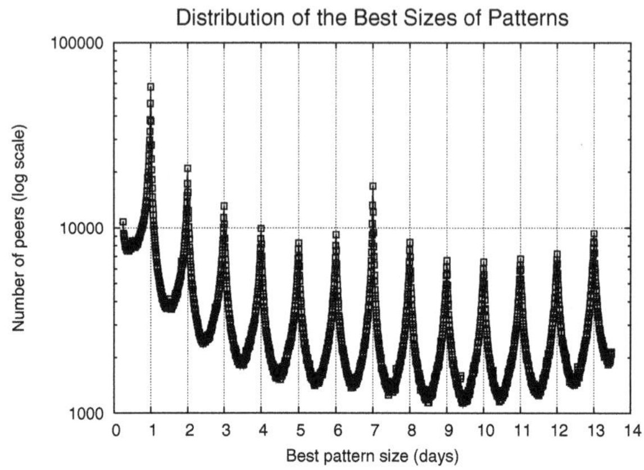

Fig. 4. Peers achieve their best auto-correlation (ressemblance between sessions after a given period) between sessions for a one-day period or a one-week period. Consequently, peers are highly likely to connect at almost the same time the next day or the next week.

4.1 A New eDonkey Trace

In 2007, we collected the connection and disconnection events from the logs of one of the main eDonkey servers in Europe. Edonkey is currently the most used P2P file-sharing network in the world. Our trace, available on our website [1], contains more than 200 millions of connections by more than 14 millions of peers, over a period of 27 days. To analyse this trace, we first filtered useless connections (shorter than 10 minutes) and suspicious ones (too repetitive, simultaneous or with changing identifiers), leading to a *filtered trace* of 12 million peers.

The number of peers online at the same time in the filtered trace is usually more than 300,000, as shown by Fig. 3. Global diurnal patterns of around 100,000 users are also clearly visible: as shown by previous studies [11], most eDonkey users are located in Europe, and so, their daily offline periods are only partially compensated by connections from other continents.

For every peer in the filtered trace, the auto-correlation on its availability periods was computed on 14 days, with a step of one minute. For a given peer, the period for which the auto-correlation is maximum gives its best pattern size. The number of peers with a given best pattern size is plotted on Fig. 4, and shows, as could be expected, that the best pattern size is a day, and much further, a week.

4.2 Filtering and Prediction

Our goal in these simulations was to evaluate the efficiency of our matching protocol, and not the efficiency of availability predictors, as already done in [18]. As a consequence, we implemented a very straightforward predictor, that uses a

7-day window of availability history to compute the *daily pattern* of a peer: for each interval of 10 minutes in a day, its value is the number of days in the week where the peer was available during that full interval:

$$pattern^p[i] = \Sigma_{d \in [0:6]} history^p[d * 24 * 60/10 + i]$$

This predictor has two purposes:

- It should help the application to decide which peers are predictable, and thus, which peers can benefit from an improved quality of service. This gives an incentive for peers to participate regularly to the system;
- it should help the application to predict future connections and disconnections of the selected peers.

To select predictable peers, the predictor computes, for each peer, the maximum and the mean covariance of the peer daily pattern. For these simulations, we computed a set, called *predictable set*, containing peers matching with the following properties:

- The maximum value in *pattern* is at least 5: each peer was available at least five days during the last week exactly at the same time;
- The average covariance in *pattern* is greater than 28: each peer has a sharply-shaped behavior;
- Peer availability is greater than 0.1: peers have to contribute enough to the system;
- Peer availability is smaller than 0.9: peers which are always online would bias positively our simulations.

In our eDonkey trace, this predictable set contains 19,600 such peers. Note that this relatively small amount of peers, *w.r.t.* the total number of peers in our trace, does not mean that eDonkey peers are not predictable: our trace concerns only a part of eDonkey users at measure time (around 10%, those connected to eDonkey Server N.2). Users that leave may join another server (*e.g.* Server N.1, a larger one), which makes them invisible in our trace, even though they are still using eDonkey. For every peer in the set, the predictor predicts that the peer will be online in a given interval if the peer's daily pattern value for that interval is at least 5, and otherwise predicts nothing (we never predict that a peer will be offline). The ratio of successful predictions after a week for the full following week is plotted on Fig. 5. It shows that predictions cannot be only explained by accidental availability, and prove the presence of availability patterns in the trace.

We purposely chose a very simple predictor, as we are interested in showing that patterns of presence are visible and can benefit applications, even with a worst-case approach. Therefore, we expect that better results would be achieved using more sophisticated predictors, such as described in [18], and for an optimal pattern size of one day instead of a week.

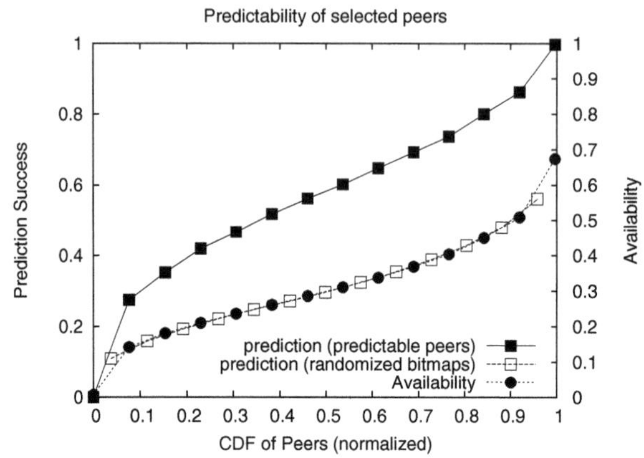

Fig. 5. Whereas availability determines the prediction with random bitmaps, daily patterns improve the prediction with real bitmaps (*e.g.* for 60% of peers (x=0.4), 50% of predictions (y=0.5) are successful, but only 25% with random bitmaps)

4.3 General Simulation Setup

A simulator was developed from scratch to run the simulations on a Linux 3.2 GHz Xeon computer, for the 19,600 peers of the predictable set from Section 4.2. Their behaviors on 14-days were extracted from the eDonkey trace: the first 7 days were used to compute a prediction, and that prediction, without updates, was used to execute the protocol on the following seven days. During one round of the simulator, all online peers in random order evaluate one T-Man round, corresponding to one minute of the trace. As explained later, both applications were delayed by a period of 10 minutes after a peer would come online to allow T-Man to provide a useful metric view. The computation of a complete run did not exceed two hours and 6 GB of memory footprint.

5 Simulated Applications

In this section, we describe the two applications that we used to illustrate the need for an efficient protocol for distributed availability matching. Our goal is not to improve the performance of these applications, as this can be done by an aggressive greedy algorithm, but to save resources using availability information.

5.1 Disconnection Matching: Task Scheduling

To evaluate the efficiency of T-Man and the DM-distance metric, we simulated a distributed task scheduling application. In this application, every peer starts a task after 10 minutes online: a task is composed of 3 jobs of 4 hours on remote partners, and is *completed* if the peer and its partners are still online after 4 hours to collect the results.

The 2 first hours of each job are devoted to the download of the data needed for the computation from a central server. As a consequence, a peer can decide not to start a task to save the bandwidth of the central server. In our simulation, such a decision is taken when the prediction of the peer availability shows that the peer is going to go offline before completion of the task.

5.2 Presence Matching: P2P File-Storage

To evaluate the efficiency of T-Man and the PM-distance metric, we simulated a P2P file storage application. In this application, every peer replicates its data to its partners, ten minutes after coming online for the first time, in the hope that he will be able to use this remote data the next time it will be online.

The size of the data of each peer is supposed to be large, hundred of megabytes of example. As a consequence, it is important for the system to use as little redundancy as possible to achieve high co-availability of data (i.e. availability of the peer and at least one of its data replica). Finding good partners in the network is expected to provide replica which are more likely to be available at the same time as the peer, thus decreasing the need for more replicas.

6 Simulation Results

In this section, we present the results of our simulations of the two applications. We are not interested in the raw performance of these applications, but in the savings that could be achieved by using availability information and partner matching.

6.1 Results for Disconnection Matching

We compared Disconnection Matching with a Random choice of partners (actually, using partners within T-Man random view) for the distributed task scheduling application. The number of completed tasks and the number of aborted tasks are plotted on Fig. 6, for the first day, the 7th day and the whole week.

Prediction of availability decreased by 68% the number of aborted tasks on average over a week, corresponding to 50% of bandwidth savings on the data server, while decreasing the number of completed tasks by only 17%.

These results were largely improved using one-day prediction, since one-week prediction is expected to be less accurate (see auto-correlation in Section 4.1). Indeed, bandwidth savings were about 43% for Disconnection Matching, while completing 20% more tasks. Thus, it is much more interesting from a performance point of view to use one-day prediction every day instead of one-week prediction, although savings are still possible with one-week predictions.

6.2 Results for Presence Matching

We compared Presence Matching with a Random choice of replica locations for the P2P file-system application. The co-availability of the peer and at least one replica is plotted on Fig. 7, for different number of replicas.

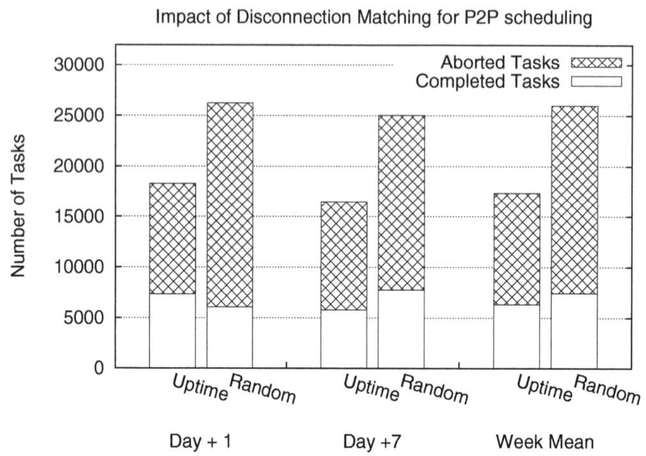

Fig. 6. A task is a set of three remote jobs of 4 hours started by every peer, ten minutes after coming online. A task is successful when the peer and its partners are still online after 4 hours to collect the results. Using availability predictions, a peer can decide not to start a task expected to abort, leading to fewer aborted tasks. Using disconnection matching, it can find good partners and it can still complete almost as many tasks as the much more expensive random strategy.

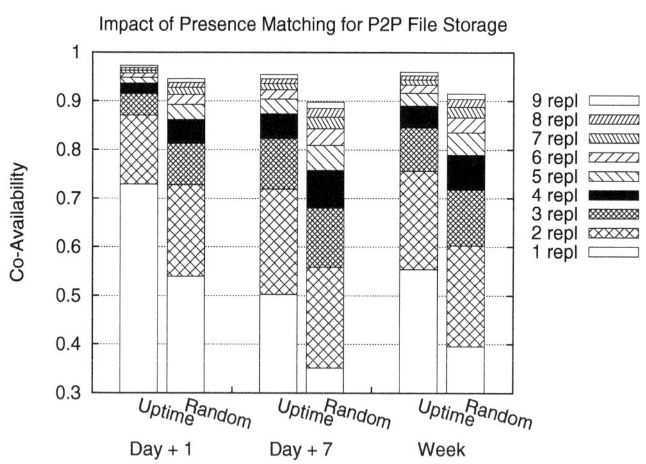

Fig. 7. 10 minutes after coming online for the first time, each peer creates a given number of replica for its data. Co-availability is defined by the simultaneous presence of the peer and at least one replica. Using presence matching, fewer replicas are needed to achieve better results than using a random choice of partners. Even the 7th day, using a 6-day old prediction, the system still performs much more efficiently, almost compensating the general loss in availability.

Using presence matching, fewer replicas were needed to achieve better results than using a random choice of partners. For example, 1 replica with Presence Matching gives a better co-availability than 2 replicas with Random Choice; 5 replicas with Presence Matching give a co-availability of 95% which is only achieved using 9 replicas with Random Choice. As for the other application, week-old predictions performed still better than random choice in the same orders.

7 Discussion and Conclusion

In this paper, we showed that epidemic protocols for topology management can be efficient to find good partners in availability-aware networks. Simulations proved that, using one of these protocols and appropriate metrics, such applications can be less expensive and still perform with an equivalent or better quality of service. We used a worst-case scenario: a simple predictor, and a trace collected from a highly volatile file-sharing network, where only a small subset of peers provide predictable behaviors. Consequently, we expect that a real application would take even more benefit from availability matching protocols.

In particular, until this work, availability-aware applications were limited to using predictions or availability information to better choose among a limited set of neighbors. This work opens the door to new availability-aware applications, where best partners are chosen among all available peers in the network. It is a useful complement to the work done on measuring availability[19,17] and using these measures to predict future availability[18].

References

1. Trace, `http://fabrice.lefessant.net/traces/edonkey2`
2. Bhagwan, R., Savage, S., Voelker, G.: Understanding availability. In: Kaashoek, M.F., Stoica, I. (eds.) IPTPS 2003. LNCS, vol. 2735. Springer, Heidelberg (2003)
3. Bhagwan, R., Tati, K., Cheng, Y.-C., Savage, S., Voelker, G.M.: Total recall: system support for automated availability management. In: NSDI, Symp. on Networked Systems Design and Implementation (2004)
4. Busca, J.-M., Picconi, F., Sens, P.: Pastis: A highly-scalable multi-user peer-to-peer file system. In: Cunha, J.C., Medeiros, P.D. (eds.) Euro-Par 2005. LNCS, vol. 3648, pp. 1173–1182. Springer, Heidelberg (2005)
5. Chun, B.-G., Dabek, F., Haeberlen, A., Sit, E., Weatherspoon, H., Kaashoek, M.F., Kubiatowicz, J., Morris, R.: Efficient replica maintenance for distributed storage systems. In: NSDI, Symp. on Networked Systems Design and Implementation (2006)
6. Cox, L.P., Murray, C.D., Noble, B.D.: Pastiche: Making backup cheap and easy. In: OSDI, Symp. on Operating Systems Design and Implementation (2002)
7. Drost, N., van Nieuwpoort, R.V., Bal, H.E.: Simple locality-aware co-allocation in peer-to-peer supercomputing. In: GP2P, Int'l Work. on Global and Peer-2-Peer Computing (2006)
8. Duminuco, A., Biersack, E.W., En Najjary, T.: Proactive replication in distributed storage systems using machine availability estimation. In: CoNEXT, Int'l Conf. on emerging Networking EXperiments and Technologies (2007)

9. Godfrey, P.B., Shenker, S., Stoica, I.: Minimizing churn in distributed systems. In: SIGCOMM, Conf. on Applications, Technologies, Architectures, and Protocols for Computer Communications (2006)
10. Guha, S., Daswani, N., Jain, R.: An Experimental Study of the Skype Peer-to-Peer VoIP System. In: IPTPS, Int'l Work. on Peer-to-Peer Systems (2006)
11. Handurukande, S.B., Kermarrec, A.-M., Le Fessant, F., Massoulié, L., Patarin, S.: Peer sharing behaviour in the edonkey network, and implications for the design of server-less file sharing systems. In: EuroSys (2006)
12. Jelasity, M., Babaoglu, O.: T-man: Gossip-based overlay topology management. In: Brueckner, S.A., Di Marzo Serugendo, G., Hales, D., Zambonelli, F. (eds.) ESOA 2005. LNCS (LNAI), vol. 3910, pp. 1–15. Springer, Heidelberg (2006)
13. Jelasity, M., Kermarrec, A.-M.: Ordered slicing of very large-scale overlay networks. In: IEEE International Conference on Peer-to-Peer Computing, pp. 117–124 (2006)
14. Kermarrec, A.-M., Le Merrer, E., Liu, Y., Simon, G.: Surfing peer-to-peer iptv: Distributed channel switching. In: Proceedings of Euro-Par (2009)
15. Killijian, M.-O., Courtès, L., Powell, D.: A Survey of Cooperative Backup Mechanisms. Tech. Rep. 06472, LAAS (2006)
16. Kim, K.: Lifetime-aware replication for data durability in p2p storage network. IEICE Transactions 91-B 12, 4020–4023 (2008)
17. Le Fessant, F., Sengul, C., Kermarrec, A.-M.: Pacemaker: Fighting Selfishness in Availability-Aware Large-Scale Networks. Tech. Rep. RR-6594, INRIA (2008)
18. Mickens, J.W., Noble, B.D.: Exploiting availability prediction in distributed systems. In: NSDI, Symp. on Networked Systems Design and Implementation (2006)
19. Morales, R., Gupta, I.: AVMON: Optimal and scalable discovery of consistent availability monitoring overlays for distributed systems. In: ICDCS, Int'l Conf. on Distributed Computing Systems (2007)
20. Sacha, J., Dowling, J., Cunningham, R., Meier, R.: Discovery of stable peers in a self-organising peer-to-peer gradient topology. In: Eliassen, F., Montresor, A. (eds.) DAIS 2006. LNCS, vol. 4025, pp. 70–83. Springer, Heidelberg (2006)
21. Saroiu, S., Gummadi, P.K., Gribble, S.: A measurement study of peer-to-peer file sharing systems. In: MMCN, Multimedia Computing and Networking (2002)
22. Stutzbach, D., Rejaie, R.: Understanding churn in peer-to-peer networks. In: IMC, Internet Measurement Conf. (2006)
23. Voulgaris, S., Gavidia, D., van Steen, M.: CYCLON: Inexpensive membership management for unstructured P2P overlays. J. Network Syst. Manage. 13(2) (2005)
24. Voulgaris, S., van Steen, M., Iwanicki, K.: Proactive gossip-based management of semantic overlay networks: Research articles. Concurr. Comput.: Pract. Exper. 19(17), 2299–2311 (2007)
25. Xin, Q., Schwarz, T., Miller, E.L.: Availability in global peer-to-peer storage systems. In: WDAS, Work. on Distributed Data and Structures (2004)

Churn-Resilient Replication Strategy for Peer-to-Peer Distributed Hash-Tables

Sergey Legtchenko[1], Sébastien Monnet[1], Pierre Sens[1], and Gilles Muller[2]

[1] LIP6/University of Paris VI/CNRS/INRIA
Firstname.Name@lip6.fr
[2] EMN/INRIA
Gilles.Muller@emn.fr

Abstract. DHT-based P2P systems provide a fault-tolerant and scalable mean to store data blocks in a fully distributed way. Unfortunately, recent studies have shown that if connection/disconnection frequency is too high, data blocks may be lost. This is true for most current DHT-based system's implementations. To avoid this problem, it is necessary to build really efficient replication and maintenance mechanisms. In this paper, we study the effect of churn on an existing DHT-based P2P system such as DHash or PAST. We then propose solutions to enhance churn tolerance and evaluate them through discrete event simulations.

1 Introduction

Distributed Hash Tables (DHTs), are distributed storage services that use a structured overlay relying on key-based routing (KBR) protocols [1,2]. DHTs provide the system designer with a powerful abstraction for wide-area persistent storage, hiding the complexity of network routing, replication, and fault-tolerance. Therefore, DHTs are increasingly used for dependable and secure applications like backup systems [3], distributed file systems [4,5] and content distribution systems [6].

A practical limit in the performance and the availability of a DHT relies in the variations of the network structure due to the unanticipated arrival and departure of peers. Such variations, called *churn*, induce at worse the loss of some data and at least performance degradation, due to the reorganization of the set of replicas of the affected data, that consumes bandwith and CPU cycles. In fact, Rodrigues and Blake have shown that using classical DHTs to store large amounts of data is only viable if the peer life-time is in the order of several days [7]. Until now, the problem of churn resilience has been mostly addressed at the P2P routing level to ensure the reachability of peers by maintaining the consistency of the logical neighborhood, e.g., the leafset, of a peer [8,9]. At the storage level, avoiding data migration is still an issue when a reconfiguration of the peers has to be done.

In a DHT, each data block is associated a *root* peer whose identifier is the (numerically) closest to its key. The traditional replication scheme relies on using the subset of the root leafset containing the closest logical peers to store the

R. Guerraoui and F. Petit (Eds.): SSS 2009, LNCS 5873, pp. 485–499, 2009.

copies of a data block [1]. Therefore, if a peer joins or leaves the leafset, the DHT enforces the placement constraint on the closest peers and may migrate many data blocks. In fact, it has been shown that the cost of these migrations can be high in term of bandwidth consumption [3]. A solution to this problem, relies on creating multiple keys for a single data block [10,11]; therefore, only a peer maintaining a key can be affected by a reconfiguration. However, each peer maintaining a data block has to periodically check the state of all the peers possessing a replica. Since copies are randomly spread on the overlay the number of peers to check can be huge.

This paper proposes a variant of the leafset replication strategy that tolerates a high churn rate. Our goal is to avoid data block migrations when the desired number of replicas is still available in the DHT. We relax the "logically closest" placement constraint on block copies and allow a peer to be inserted in the leafset without forcing migration. Then, to reliably locate the block copies, the root peer of a block maintains replicated localization metadata. Metadata management is integrated to the existing leafset management protocol and does not incur additional overhead in practice.

We have implemented both PAST and our replication strategy on top of PeerSim [12]. The main results of our evaluations are:

- We show that our approach achieves higher data availability in presence of churn, than the original PAST replication strategy. For a connection or disconnection occuring every minute our strategy loses two times less blocks than PAST's one.
- We show that our replication strategy induces an average of twice less block transfers than PAST's one.

The rest of this paper is organized as follows. Section 2 first presents an overview of the basic replication schemes and maintenance algorithms commonly used in DHT-based P2P systems, then their limitations are highlighted. Section 3 introduces an enhanced replication scheme for which the DHT's placement constraints are relaxed so as to obtain a better churn resilience. Simulations of this algorithm are presented in Section 4. Section 5 concludes with an overwiew of our results.

2 Background and Motivation

DHT based P2P systems are usually structured in three layers: 1) a routing layer, 2) the DHT itself, 3) the application that uses the DHT. The routing layer is based on keys for identifying peers and is therefore commonly qualified as *Key-Based Routing* (KBR). Such KBR layer hides the complexity of scalable routing, fault tolerance, and self-organizing overlays to the upper layers. In recent years, many research efforts have been made to improve the resilience of the KBR layer to a high churn rate [8]. The main examples of KBR layers are Pastry [13], Chord [2], Tapestry [14] and Kademlia [15]. The DHT layer is responsible for storing data blocks. It implements a distributed storage service that provides persistence and fault tolerance, and can scale up to a large number of peers.

DHTs provide simple get and put abstractions that greatly simplifies the task of building large-scale distributed applications. PAST [1] and DHash [16] are DHTs respectively built on top of Pastry [13] and Chord [2]. Finally, the application layer is a composition of any distributed application that may take advantage of a DHT. Representative examples are the CFS distributed file system [5] and the PeerStore backup system [3].

In the rest of this section we present replication techniques that are used for implementing the DHT layer. Then, we describe related work that consider the impact of churn on the replicated data stored in the DHT.

2.1 Replication in DHTs

In a DHT, each peer and each data block is assigned an identifier (i.e., a key). A data block's key is usually the result of a hash function performed on the block. The peer whose identifier is the closest to the block's key is called the block's *root*. All the identifiers are arranged in a logical structure, such as a ring as used in Chord [2] and Pastry [13] or a d-dimensional torus as implemented in CAN [10] and Tapestry [11].

A peer possesses a restricted local knowledge of the P2P network, i.e., the leafset, which amounts to a list of `L` close neighbors in the ring. For instance, in Pastry the leafset contains the addresses of the `L/2` closest neighbors in the clockwise direction of the ring, and the `L/2` closest neighbors counter-clockwise. Each peer monitors its leafset, removing peers which have disconnected from the overlay and adding new neighbor peers as they join the ring.

In order to tolerate failures, each data block is replicated on `k` peers which compose the *replica-set* of a data block. Two protocols are in charge of the replica management, the initial placement protocol and the maintenance protocol. We now describe existing solutions for implementing these two protocols.

Replica placement protocols. There are two main basic replica placement strategies, leafset-based and multiple key based:

Leafset-based replication. The data block's root is responsible for storing one copy of the block. The block is also replicated on the root's closest neighbors in a subset of the leafset. The neighbors storing a copy of the data block may be either successors of the root in the ring, predecessors or both. Therefore, the different copies of a block are stored *contiguously* in the ring as shown by Figure 1. This strategy has been implemented in PAST [1] and DHash [16]. *Successor replication* is a variant of leafset-based replication where replica peers are only the immediate successors of the root peer instead of being the closest peers [17].

Multiple key replication. This approach relies on computing `k` different storage keys corresponding to different root peers for each data block. Data blocks are then replicated on the `k` root peers. This solution has been implemented by CAN [10] and Tapestry [11]. GFS [18] uses a variant based on random placement to improve data repair performance. *Path* and *symmetric replication* are variants of multiple key based replication [19,17].

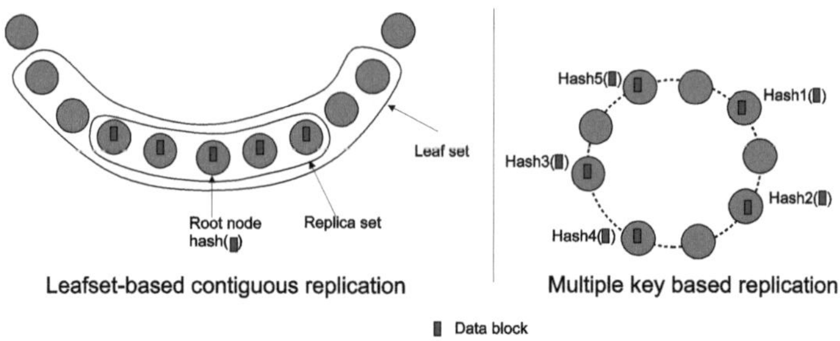

Fig. 1. Leafset-based and multiple key based replication ($k = 5$)

Lian *et al.* propose an hybrid stripe replication scheme where small objects are grouped in blocks and then randomly placed [20]. They show using an analytical framework that their scheme achieves on near-optimal reliability. Finally, several works have focused on the placement strategies based on availability of nodes. Van Renesse [21] proposes a replica placement algorithm on DHT by considering the reliability of nodes and placing copies on nodes until the desired availability was achieved. To this end, he proposes to track the reliability of each node such that each node knows the reliability information about each peer. In FARSITE [22], dynamic placement strategies improve the availability of files. Files are swapped between servers according to the current availability of these latter. With theses approaches, the number of copies can be reduced. However, the cost to track reliability of nodes can be high. Furthermore, such approaches may lead to an high unbalanced distribution whereby highly available nodes contain most of the replicas and can become overloaded.

Maintenance protocols. The maintenance protocols have to maintain `k` copies of each data block without violating the initial placement strategy. This means that the `k` copies of each data block have to be stored on the root peer contiguous neighbors in the case of the leafset-based replication scheme and on the root peers in the multiple key based replication scheme.

The leafset-based maintenance mechanism is based on periodic information exchanges within the leafsets. For instance, in the fully decentralized PAST maintenance protocol [1], each peer sends a bloom filter[1] of the blocks it stores to its leafset. When a leafset peer receives such a request, it uses the bloom filter to determine whether it stores one or more blocks that the requester should also store. It then answers with the list of the keys of such blocks. The requesting peer can then fetch the missing blocks listed in all the answers it receives.

In the case of the multiple key replication strategies, the maintenance has to be done on a "per data block" basis. For each data block stored in the system, it is necessary to periodically check if the different root peers are still alive and are still storing a copy of the data block.

[1] For short, the sent bloom filter is a compact and approximative view of the list of blocks stored by a peer.

2.2 Impact of the Churn on the DHT Performance

A high churn rate induces a lot of changes in the P2P network, and the maintenance protocol must frequently adapt to the new structure by migrating data blocks. While some migrations are mandatory to restore k copies, some others are necessary only for enforcing placement invariants.

A first example arises at the root peer level which may change if a new peer with a closer identifier joins the system. In this situation, the data block will be migrated on the new peer. A second example occurs in leafset-based replication, if a peer possesses an identifier that places it within a replica-set. Therefore, data blocks have to be migrated by the DHT to enforce replicas to maintain the "closest peers from the root" property. It should be noticed that larger the replica-set, higher the probability for a new peer to induce migrations. Kim and Park try to limit this problem by allowing data blocks to interleave in leafsets [23]. However, they have to maintain a global knowledge of the complete leafset: each peer has to know the content of all the peers in its leafset. Unfortunately, the maintenance algorithm is not described in detail and its real cost is unknown.

In the case of the multiple key replication strategy, a new peer may be inserted between two replicas without requiring migrating data blocks, as long as the new peer identifier does not make it one of the data block roots. However, this replication method has the drawback that maintenance has to be done on a per-data block basis; therefore it does not scale up with the number of blocks managed by a peer. For backup and file systems that may store up to thousands of data blocks per peer, this is a severe limitation.

3 Relaxing the DHT's Placement Constraints to Tolerate Churn

The goal of this work to is to design a DHT that tolerates a high rate of churn without degradating of performance. For this, we avoid to copy data blocks when this is not mandatory for restoring a missing replica. We introduce a leafset based replication that relaxes the placement constraints in the leafset. Our solution, named RelaxDHT, is presented thereafter.

3.1 Overview of RelaxDHT

RelaxDHT is built on top of a KBR layer such as Pastry or Chord. Our design decisions are to use replica localization meta-data and separate them from data block storage. We keep the notion of a root peer for each data block. However, the root peer does no longer store a copy of the blocks for which it is the root. It only maintains metadata describing the replica-set and periodically sends messages to the replica-set peers to ensure that they keep storing their copy. Using localization metadata allows a data block replica to be anywhere in the leafset; a new peer may join a leafset without necessarily inducing data blocks migrations.

We choose to restrain the localization of replicas within the root's leafset for two reasons. First, to remain scalable, the number of messages of our protocol does not depend on the number of data blocks managed by a peer, but only on the leafset size. Second, because the routing layer already induces many exchanges within leafsets, the local view of the leafset at the DHT-layer can be used as a failure detector. We now detail the salient aspects of the RelaxDHT algorithm.

Insertion of a new data block. To be stored in the system, a data block is inserted using the `put(k,b)` operation. This operation produces an "insert message" which is sent to the root peer. Then, the root randomly chooses a replica-set of `k` peers around the center of the leafset. This reduces the probability that a chosen peer quickly becomes out of the leafset due to the arrival of new peers. Finally, the root sends to the replica-set peers a "store message" containing:

1. the data block itself,
2. the identity of the peers in the replica-set (i.e., the metadata),
3. the identity of the root.

As a peer may be root for several data blocks and part of the replica-set of other data blocks[2], it stores:

1. a list `rootOfList` of data block identifiers with their associated replica-set peer-list for blocks for which it is the root;
2. a list `replicaOfList` of data blocks for which it is part of the replica-set. Along with data blocks, this list also contains: the identifier of the data block, the associated replica-set peer-list and the identity of the root peer.

A *lease counter* is associated to each stored data block. This counter is set to the value "`Lease`" which is a constant. It is then decremented at each KBR-layer maintenance. The maintenance protocol described below is responsible to periodically reset this counter to "`Lease`".

Maintenance protocol. The goal of this periodic protocol is to ensure that: 1) a root peer exists for each data block. The root is the peer that the closest identifier from the data block's one; 2) each data block is replicated on `k` peers located in the data block root's leafset.

At each period T, a peer `p` executes Algorithm 1, so as to send maintenance messages to the other peers of the leafset. It is important to notice that Algorithm 1 uses the leafset knowledge maintained by the KBR layer which is relatively accurate because the inter-maintenance time of the KBR layer is much smaller than the DHT-layer's one.

The messages constructed by Algorithm 1 contain a set of following two elements:

STORE element for asking a replica node to keep storing a specific data block.

[2] It is possible, but not mandatory, for a peer to be both root and part of the replica-set of a same data block.

Algorithm 1. RelaxDHT maintenance message construction

```
   Result: msgs, the built messages.
1  for data ∈ rootOfList do
2      for replica ∈ data.replicaSet do
3          if NOT isInCenter (replica,leafset) then
4              newPeer =choosePeer (replica,leafset);
5              replace (data.replicaSet, replica,newPeer);
6      for replica ∈ data.replicaSet do
7          add(msgs [replica ],<STORE, data.blockID, data.replicaSet >);
8  for data in replicaOfList do
9      if NOT checkRoot (data.rootPeer,leafset) then
10         newRoot =getRoot (data.blockID,leafset);
11         add (msgs [newRoot ],<NEW ROOT, data.blockID, data.replicaSet >):
12 for p ∈ leafset do
13     if NOT empty (msgs [p ]) then
14         send(msgs [p ],p);
```

NEW ROOT element for notifying a node that it has become the new root of a data block.

These message elements contain both a data block identifier and the associated replica-set peer-list. In order to remain scalable in term of the number of data blocks algorithm 1 sends at most one single message to each leafset member.

Algorithm 1 is composed of three phases: the first one computes STORE elements using the `rootOfList` structure -lines 1 to 7-, the second one computes NEW ROOT elements using the `replicaOfList` structure -from line 8 to 11-, the last one sends messages to the destination peers in the leafset -line 12 to the end-. Message elements computed in the two first phases are added in *msgs[]*. *msgs[q]* is a message containing all the elements to send to node q at the last phase.

Therefore, each peer periodically sends a maximum of `leafset-size` maintenance messages to its neighbors.

In the first phase, for each block for which the peer is the root, it checks if every replica is still in the center of its leafset (line 3) using its local view provided by the KBR layer. If a replica node is outside, the peer replaces it by randomly choosing a new peer in the center of the leafset and it then updates the replica-set of the block (lines 4 and 5). Finally, the peer adds a STORE element in each replica set peers messages (lines 6 and 7). In the second phase, for each block stored by the peer (i.e., the peer is part of the block's replica-set), it checks if the root node did not change. This verification is done by comparing the `replicaOfList` metadata and the current leafset state (line 9). If the root has changed, the peer adds a NEW ROOT message element to announce to the future root peer that it is the root of the data block[3]. Finally, from line 12 to line 14, a loop sends the computed messages to each leafset member.

[3] Note that it is possible (but rare) to temporarily have two different peers acting as a root peer for a same data block but it will not lead to data loss.

Algorithm 2. RelaxDHT maintenance message reception

```
   Data: message, the received message.
1  for elt ∈ message do
2      switch elt.type do
3          case STORE
4              if elt.data ∈ replicaOfList then
5                  newLease(replicaOfList,elt.data);
6                  updateRepSet(replicaOfList,elt.data);
7              else
8                  requestBlock(elt.data);
9          case NEW ROOT
10             rootOfList = rootOfList ∪ elt.data;
```

Maintenance message treatment

For a STORE element (line 3), if the peer already stores a copy of the corresponding data block, it resets the associated lease counter and updates the corresponding replica-set if necessary (lines 4, 5 and 6). If the peer does not store the associated data block (i.e., it is the first STORE message element for this data block received by this peer), it fetches it from one of the peers mentioned in the received replica-set (line 8).

For a NEW ROOT element a peer adds the data block-id and replica-set in the `rootOfList` structure (line 10).

End of a lease treatment. If a data block lease counter reaches 0, it means that no STORE element has been received for a long time. This can be the result of numerous insertions that have pushed the peer outside the center of the leafset of the data block's root. The peer sends a message to the root peer of the data block to ask for the authorization to delete the block. Later, the peer will receive an answer from the root peer. This answer either allows it to remove the data block or asks it to *put* the data block again in the DHT (in the case the data block has been lost).

3.2 Side Effects and Limitations

Our replication strategy for peer-to-peer DHTs, by relaxing placement constraints of data block copies in leafsets, significantly reduces the number of data blocks to be transferred when peers join or leave the system. Thanks to this, we show in the next section that our maintenance mechanism allows us to better tolerate churn, but it implies other effects. The two main ones concern the data block distribution on the peers and the lookup performance. While the changes in data blocks distribution can provide positive effects, the lookup performance can be damaged.

Data blocks distribution. While with usual replication strategies in peer-to-peer DHT's, the data blocks are distributed among peers according to some hash function. Therefore, if the number of data blocks is big enough, data blocks should be uniformly distributed among all the peers. When using RelaxDHT, this remains true if there are no peer connections/disconnections. However, in presence of churn, as our maintenance mechanism does not transfer data blocks if it is not necessary, new peers will store much less data blocks than peers involved for a longer time in the DHT. It is important to notice that this side effect is rather positive: more stable a peer is, more data blocks it will store. Furthermore, it is possible to counter this effect easily by taking into account the quantity of stored data blocks while randomly choosing peers to add in replica-sets.

Lookup performance. We have focused our research efforts on data loss. We show in the next section that for equivalent churn patterns, the quantity of data lost using RelaxDHT is considerably lower than the quantity of data lost using a standard strategy like PAST's one. However, with RelaxDHT, it is possible that temporarily some data block roots are not consistent, inducing a network overhead to find the data. For example, when a peer which is root for at least one data block fails, the data block copies are still in the system but the standard lookup mechanism may not find them: the new peer whose identifier is the closest may not know the data block. This remains true until the failure is detected by one of the peer in the replica-set and repaired using a "new root" message (see algorithms above). It would be possible to flood the leafset or to perform a "limited range walk" when a lookup fails, allowing lookups to find data blocks even in the absence of root. However, note that: 1) some lookups do not need to reach the root peer because the previous hop, arriving in the leafset, reaches one of the replica; 2) a caching mechanism for metadata may limit this problem; and 3) this case is rare.

4 Evaluation

This section provides a comparative evaluation of RelaxDHT and PAST [1]. This evaluation, based on discrete event simulations, shows that RelaxDHT provides a considerably better tolerance to churn: for the same churn levels, the number of data losses is divided by up to two when comparing both systems.

4.1 Experimental Setup

To evaluate RelaxDHT, we have build a discrete event simulator using the PeerSim [12] simulation kernel. We have based our simulator on an already existing PeerSim module simulating the Pastry KBR layer. We have implemented both the PAST strategy and the RelaxDHT strategy on top of this module. It is important to note that all the different layers and all message exchanges are simulated. Our simulator also takes into account network congestion: in our case, network links may often be congested.

For all the simulation results presented in the section, we used a 100-peer network with the following parameters (for both PAST and RelaxDHT):

- a leafset size of 24, which is the Pastry default value;
- an inter-maintenance duration of 10 minutes at the DHT level;

- an inter-maintenance duration of 1 minute at the KBR level;
- 10 000 data blocks of 10 000 KB replicated 3 times;
- network links of 1 Mbits/s for upload and 10 Mbits/s for download with a delay uniformly chosen between 80 and 120 ms.

A 100-peer network may seem a relatively small scale. However, for both replication strategies, PAST and RelaxDHT, the studied behavior is local, contained within a leafset (which size is bounded). It is however necessary to simulate a whole ring in order to take into account side effects induced by the neighbor leafsets. Furthermore, a tradeoff has to be made between system accuracy and system size. In our case, it is important to simulate very precisely all peer communications. We have run several simulations with a larger scale (1000 peers and 100,000 data blocks) and have observed similar phenomenons.

We have injected churn following two different scenarii:

One hour churn. One perturbation phase with churn during one hour. This phase is followed by another phase without connections/disconnections. In this case study, during the churn phase each *perturbation period* we chose randomly either a new peer connection or a peer disconnection. This perturbation can occur anywhere in the ring (uniformly chosen). We have run numerous simulations varying the inter-perturbation delay.

Continuous churn. For this set of simulations, we focus on phase one of the previous case. We study the system while varying the inter-perturbation delay. In this case, "perturbation" can be either a new peer connection or a disconnection.

We also experiment a scenario for which only one peer gets disconnected. We then study the reaction of the system. The first set of experiments allows us to study 1) how many data blocks are lost after a period of perturbation and 2) how long it takes to the system to return to a state where all remaining/non-lost data blocks are replicated `k` times. In real-life systems there will be some period without churn, the system has to take advantage of them to converge to a safer state. The second set of experiments zooms on the perturbation period. It provides the ability to study how the system can resist when it has to repair lost copies in presence of churn. Finally, the last set of simulations is done to measure the reparation of one single failure.

4.2 Losses and Stabilization Time after One Hour Churn

We first study the number of lost data blocks (data block for which the 3 copies are lost) in PAST and in RelaxDHT under the same churn conditions. Figure 2 shows the number of lost data blocks after a period of one hour of churn. The inter-perturbation delay is increasing along the X axis. With RelaxDHT and our maintenance protocol, the number of lost data blocks is much lower than with the PAST's one: it reaches 50% for perturbations interval from lower than 50 *seconds*.

The main reason of the result presented above is that, using PAST replication strategy, the peers have more data blocks to download. This implies that the

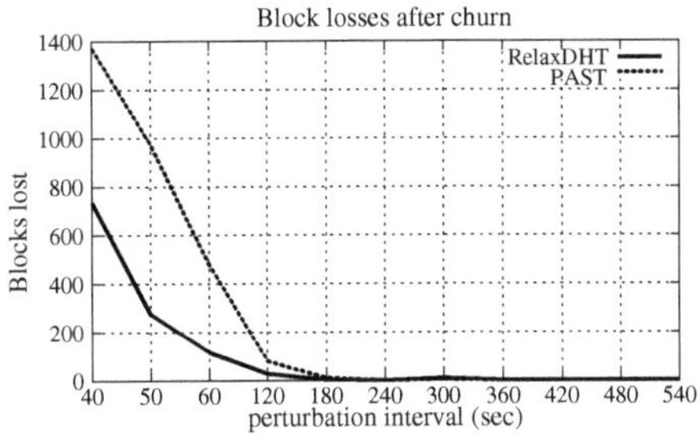

Fig. 2. Number of data block lost (ie. all copies are lost)

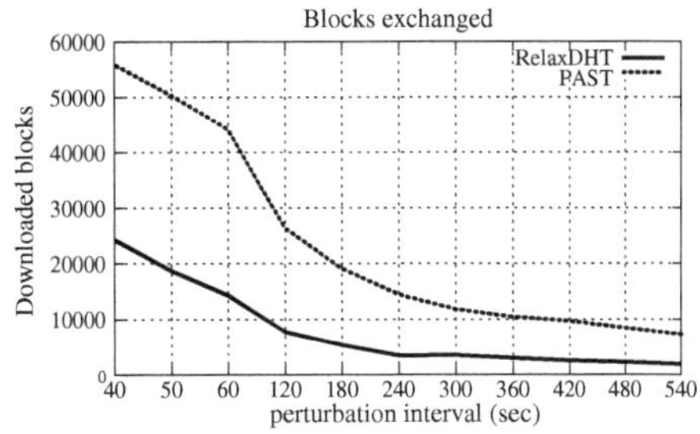

Fig. 3. Number of exchanged data blocks to restore a stable state

mean download time of one data block is longer using PAST replication strategy. Indeed, the maintenance of the replication scheme location constraints generate a continuous network traffic that slows down critical traffic whose goal is to restore lost data block copies.

Figure 3 shows the total number of blocks exchanged for both cases. There again, the X axis represents the inter-perturbation delay. The figure shows that with RelaxDHT the number of exchanged blocks is always near 2 times smaller than in PAST. This is mainly due to the fact that in PAST case, many transfers (near half of them) are only done to preserve the replication scheme constraints. For instance, each time a new peer joins the DHT, it becomes root of some data blocks (because its identifier is closer than the current root-peer's one), or if it is inserted within replica-sets that should remain contiguous.

Using PAST replication strategy, a newly inserted peer may need to download data blocks during many hours, even if no failure/disconnection occurs. During all this time, its neighbors need to send it the required data blocks, using a large part of their upload bandwidth.

In our case, *no* or very *few* data blocks transfers are required when new peers join the system. It becomes mandatory, only if some copies becomes too far from their root-peer in the logical ring[4]. In this case, they have to be transferred closer to the root before their hosting peer leaves the root-peer's leafset. With a replication degree of 3 and a leafset size of 24, many peers can join a leafset before any data block transfer is required.

Finally, we have measured the time the system takes to return in a normal state in which every remaining[5] data block is replicated k times. Figure 4 shows the results obtained while varying the delay between perturbations. We can observe that the recovery time is twice longer in the case where PAST is used compared to RelaxDHT. This result is mainly explained by the number of blocks

[4] The acceptable distance, in number of peers in the logical ring, between a copie and its root-peer is set to 8 in our simulations.

[5] Blocks for which all copies are lost will never retreive a normal state and thus are not taken into account.

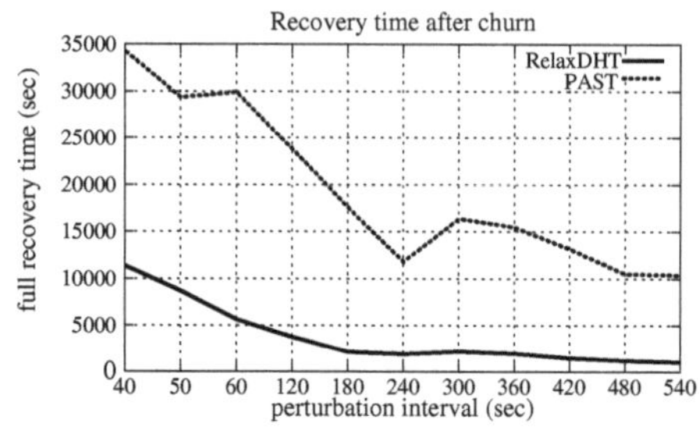

Fig. 4. Recovery time: time for retreiving all the copies of every remaining data block

to transfer which is much more lower in our case: our maintenance protocol transfers only very few blocks for location constraints compared to PAST's one.

This last result shows that the DHT using RelaxDHT repairs damaged data blocks (data blocks for which some copies are lost) faster than PAST. It implies that it will recover very fast, which means it will be able to cope with a new churn phase. The next section describes our simulations with continuous churn.

4.3 Continuous Churn

Before presenting simulation results under continuous churn, it is important to measure the impact of a single peer failure/disconnection.

When a single peer fails, data blocks it stored have to be replicated on a new one. Those blocks are transferred to such a new peer in order to rebuild the initial replication degree k. In our simulations, with the parameters given above, it takes 4609 seconds to PAST to recover the failure: i.e., to create a new replica for each block stored on the faulty peer. While, with RelaxDHT, it takes only 1889 seconds. The number of peers involved in the recovery is much more important indeed. This gain is due to the parallelization of the data blocks-transfers:

- in PAST, the content of contiguous peers is really correlated. With a replication degree of 3, only peers located at one or two hops of the faulty peer in the ring may be used as sources or destinations for data transfers. In fact, only `k+1` peers are involved in the recovery of one faulty peer, where `k` is the replication factor.
- in RelaxDHT, most of the peers contained in the faulty peer leafset (the leafset contains 24 peers in our simulations) may be involved in the transfers.

The above simulation results show that RelaxDHT: 1) induce less data transfers, and 2) remaining data transfers are more parallelized. Thanks to this two points, even if the system remains under continuous churn, RelaxDHT will provide a better churn tolerance.

Such results are illustrated in Figure 5. We can observe that, using the parameters described at the beginning of this section, PAST starts to lose data

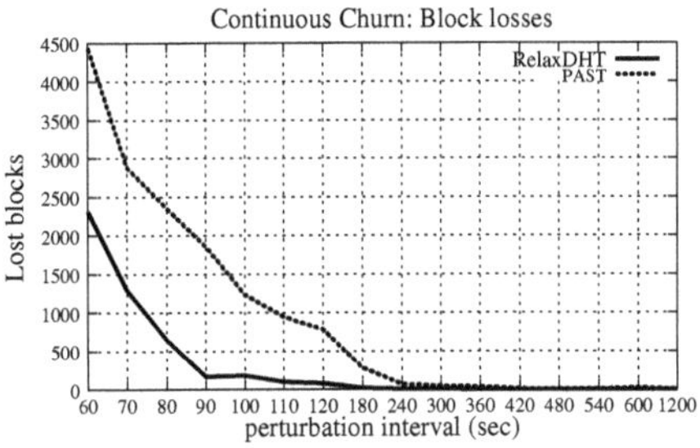

Fig. 5. Number of data blocks losses (all k copies lost) while the system is under continuous churn, varying inter-perturbation delay

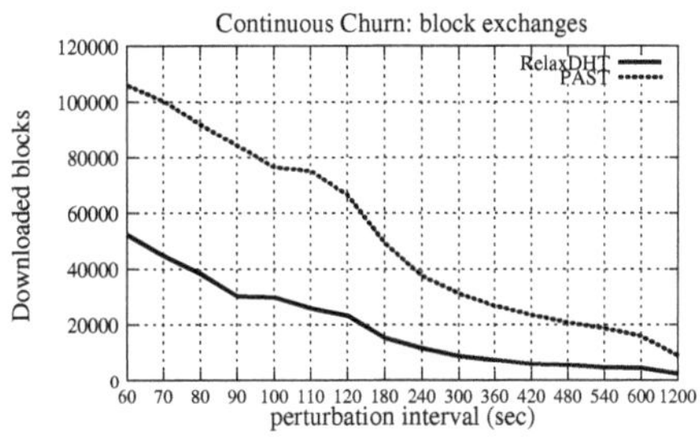

Fig. 6. Number of data blocks transfers required while the system is under continuous churn, varying inter-perturbation delay

blocks when the inter-perturbation delay is around 7 minutes. This delay has to reach less than 4 minutes for data blocks to be lost using RelaxDHT. If the inter-perturbation delay continues to decrease, the number of lost data blocks using RelaxDHT strategy remains near half the number of data blocks lost using PAST strategy.

Finally, Figure 6 confirms that even with a continuous churn pattern, during a 5 hour run, the number of data transfers required by the proposed solution is much smaller (around half) than the number of data transfers induced by PAST's replication strategy.

5 Conclusion

Peer to peer distributed hash tables provide an efficient, scalable and easy-to-use storage system. However, existing solutions do not tolerate a high churn rate or are not really scalable in terms of number of stored data blocks. We have identified the reasons why they do not tolerate high churn rate: they impose strict placement constraints that induces unnecessary data transfers.

In this paper, we propose a new replication strategy, RelaxDHT that relaxes the placement constraints: it relies on metadata (replica-peers/data identifiers) to allow a more flexible location of data block copies within leafsets. Thanks to this design, RelaxDHT entails fewer data transfers than classical leafset-based replication mechanisms. Furthermore, as data block copies are shuffled among a larger peer set, peer contents are less correlated. It results that in case of failure more data sources are available for the recovery, which makes the recovery more efficient and thus the system more churn-resilient. Our simulations, comparing the PAST system to ours, confirm that RelaxDHT 1) induces less data block transfers, 2) recovers lost data block copies faster and 3) loses less data blocks. Furthermore, we have shown that the churn-resilience is obtained without adding a great maintenance overhead.

References

1. Rowstron, A.I.T., Druschel, P.: Storage management and caching in PAST, a large-scale, persistent peer-to-peer storage utility. In: SOSP 2001: Proceedings of the 8th ACM symposium on Operating Systems Principles, December 2001, pp. 188–201 (2001)
2. Stoica, I., Morris, R., Liben-Nowell, D., Karger, D.R., Kaashoek, F.F., Dabek, F., Balakrishnan, H.: Chord: a scalable peer-to-peer lookup protocol for internet applications. IEEE/ACM Trans. Netw. 11(1), 17–32 (2003)
3. Landers, M., Zhang, H., Tan, K.L.: Peerstore: Better performance by relaxing in peer-to-peer backup. In: P2P 2004: Proceedings of the 4th International Conference on Peer-to-Peer Computing, Washington, DC, USA, pp. 72–79. IEEE Computer Society, Los Alamitos (2004)
4. Busca, J.M., Picconi, F., Sens, P.: Pastis: A highly-scalable multi-user peer-to-peer file system. In: Cunha, J.C., Medeiros, P.D. (eds.) Euro-Par 2005. LNCS, vol. 3648, pp. 1173–1182. Springer, Heidelberg (2005)
5. Dabek, F., Kaashoek, F.M., Karger, D., Morris, R., Stoica, I.: Wide-area cooperative storage with CFS. In: SOSP 2001: Proceedings of the 8th ACM symposium on Operating Systems Principles, vol. 35, pp. 202–215. ACM Press, New York (2001)
6. Jernberg, J., Vlassov, V., Ghodsi, A., Haridi, S.: Doh: A content delivery peer-to-peer network. In: Nagel, W.E., Walter, W.V., Lehner, W. (eds.) Euro-Par 2006. LNCS, vol. 4128, pp. 1026–1039. Springer, Heidelberg (2006)
7. Rodrigues, R., Blake, C.: When multi-hop peer-to-peer lookup matters. In: Voelker, G.M., Shenker, S. (eds.) IPTPS 2004. LNCS, vol. 3279, pp. 112–122. Springer, Heidelberg (2005)
8. Rhea, S., Geels, D., Roscoe, T., Kubiatowicz, J.: Handling churn in a DHT. In: Proceedings of the 2004 USENIX Technical Conference, Boston, MA, USA (June 2004)
9. Castro, M., Costa, M., Rowstron, A.: Performance and dependability of structured peer-to-peer overlays. In: DSN 2004: Proceedings of the 2004 International Conference on Dependable Systems and Networks, Washington, DC, USA, p. 9. IEEE Computer Society, Los Alamitos (2004)
10. Ratnasamy, S., Francis, P., Handley, M., Karp, R., Schenker, S.: A scalable content-addressable network. In: SIGCOMM, vol. 31, pp. 161–172. ACM Press, New York (2001)
11. Zhao, B.Y., Huang, L., Stribling, J., Rhea, S.C., Joseph, A.D., Kubiatowicz, J.D.: Tapestry: A global-scale overlay for rapid service deployment. IEEE Journal on Selected Areas in Communications (2003)
12. Jelasity, M., Montresor, A., Jesi, G.P., Voulgaris, S.: The Peersim simulator, `http://peersim.sf.net`
13. Rowstron, A., Druschel, P.: Pastry: Scalable, decentralized object location, and routing for large-scale peer-to-peer systems. In: Guerraoui, R. (ed.) Middleware 2001. LNCS, vol. 2218, pp. 329–350. Springer, Heidelberg (2001)
14. Zhao, B.Y., Huang, L., Stribling, J., Rhea, S.C., Joseph, A.D., Kubiatowicz, J.D.: Tapestry: A resilient global-scale overlay for service deployment. IEEE Journal on Selected Areas in Communications 22, 41–53 (2004)
15. Maymounkov, P., Mazieres, D.: Kademlia: A peer-to-peer information system based on the XOR metric. In: Druschel, P., Kaashoek, M.F., Rowstron, A. (eds.) IPTPS 2002. LNCS, vol. 2429, pp. 53–65. Springer, Heidelberg (2002)

16. Dabek, F., Li, J., Sit, E., Robertson, J., Kaashoek, F.F., Morris, R.: Designing a DHT for low latency and high throughput. In: NSDI 2004: Proceedings of the 1st Symposium on Networked Systems Design and Implementation, San Francisco, CA, USA (March 2004)
17. Ktari, S., Zoubert, M., Hecker, A., Labiod, H.: Performance evaluation of replication strategies in DHTs under churn. In: MUM 2007: Proceedings of the 6th international conference on Mobile and ubiquitous multimedia, pp. 90–97. ACM Press, New York (2007)
18. Ghemawat, S., Gobioff, H., Leung, S.T.: The google file system. In: SOSP 2003: Proceedings of the 9th ACM symposium on Operating systems principles, pp. 29–43. ACM Press, New York (2003)
19. Ghodsi, A., Alima, L.O., Haridi, S.: Symmetric replication for structured peer-to-peer systems. In: Moro, G., Bergamaschi, S., Joseph, S., Morin, J.-H., Ouksel, A.M. (eds.) DBISP2P 2005 and DBISP2P 2006. LNCS, vol. 4125, pp. 74–85. Springer, Heidelberg (2007)
20. Lian, Q., Chen, W., Zhang, Z.: On the impact of replica placement to the reliability of distributed brick storage systems. In: ICDCS 2005: Proceedings of the 25th IEEE International Conference on Distributed Computing Systems, Washington, DC, USA, pp. 187–196. IEEE Computer Society, Los Alamitos (2005)
21. van Renesse, R.: Efficient reliable internet storage. In: WDDDM 2004: Proceedings of the 2nd Workshop on Dependable Distributed Data Management, Glasgow, Scotland (October 2004)
22. Adya, A., Bolosky, W., Castro, M., Chaiken, R., Cermak, G., Douceur, J., Howell, J., Lorch, J., Theimer, M., Wattenhofer, R.: Farsite: Federated, available, and reliable storage for an incompletely trusted environment. In: OSDI 2002: Proceedings of the 5th Symposium on Operating Systems Design and Implementation, Boston, MA, USA (December 2002)
23. Kim, K., Park, D.: Reducing data replication overhead in DHT based peer-to-peer system. In: Gerndt, M., Kranzlmüller, D. (eds.) HPCC 2006. LNCS, vol. 4208, pp. 915–924. Springer, Heidelberg (2006)

Distributed Power Control with Multiple Agents in a Distributed Base Station Scheme Using Macrodiversity

Philippe Leroux and Sébastien Roy

Université Laval, Québec, Canada, G1K-7P4
{lerouxp,sebasroy}@gel.ulaval.ca

Abstract. Power management in wireless networks has been thoroughly studied and applied in many different contexts. However, the problem has not been tackled from a multiple-agent perspective (MA). This paper intends to do so in the context of a wireless network comprised of distributed base stations using macrodiversity. The proposed design is shown to provide efficient use of macrodiversity resources and high energy efficiency when compared with more traditional algorithms. Moreover, the power control mechanism is completely decentralized, while avoiding direct information exchange or excessive signaling, which makes it highly scalable. Its auto-configuration property, stemming from its MA basis, offers high adaptivity when experiencing high or low interference levels. This leads to a naturally balanced resource usage, while also maintaining nearly full efficiency with only a reduced set of discrete power levels, thus making low-cost electronic implementation practical.

1 Introduction

1.1 Power Control

The literature on power control (PC) comprises important contributions, such as the centralized algorithm by Grandhi *et al.* [1] for cellular networks. This algorithm was then modified to offer decentralized properties in [2] and [3]. Yet, these algorithms presented limitations, such as needing a global scaling parameter or converging to infinitesimal power values. Wang [4] offers a compromise solution to obtain a stable fully distributed algorithm. All these algorithms aim to maximize the minimum signal-to-interference ratio (SIR).

Considering macrodiversity, where one mobile is relayed by a set of base stations, power control is furthermore extended to macro PC in a CDMA context by Yanikomeroglu [5]. In such a case, the algorithm does not balance the total received power, as is usually looked for in the CDMA context. Instead, it balances the total SIR, which after proper combination of the diferent signals received at each base station relaying the mobile, is the sum of the individual SIRs. While CDMA is not considered in the present study, the algorithm from [5] remains straightforward to adapt to our context.

R. Guerraoui and F. Petit (Eds.): SSS 2009, LNCS 5873, pp. 500–514, 2009.

Yet, balancing signal to interference ratios has shortcomings in the context of Rice fading where the relative importance of the line of sight can vary greatly for each connection from mobile to the relaying base stations. Hence, the relative signal-to-interference plus noise ratio necessary to achieve a given bit error rate (BER) also varies for all mobiles. In addition, balancing SIR instead of signal to noise plus interference ratio (SINR) can, in certain situations, render some algorithms unstable as will be shown.

1.2 Distributed Base Sations

We focus herein on the distributed base station paradigm, which aims to develop a completely distributed architecture for all aspects of the network. Macrodiversity in [6] is considered in a connection-oriented self-organized system, such that one mobile can be relayed by a set of neighboring distributed base stations (DBS). Yet, these DBS are capacity limited and may not relay all neighboring mobiles. Hence, a combinatorial problem must be solved to allocate connection resources [7]. Moreover, interference cannot be managed with the well-known segregation algorithm since neighboring DBS share channels [8]. Finally, power control is strongly coupled with other aspects of the network since it can greatly influence the potential of macrodiversity and interference management. It also adds another dimension to the resource allocation problem, rendering the solution space analytically intractable without simplifications on either geometry or propagation hypothesis (i.e. considering only Rayleigh fading and not taking into account different K factors for different signal of what would otherwise be Rice fading).

Figure 1 illustrates a simple scenario with two channels. The higher a mobile's power level is (compared to neighboring mobiles), the larger its spatial footprint is, and the more DBS it is able to reach. On the other hand, it also interferes more, preventing other mobiles from linking with a plurality of DBS. Hence, there is a point of equilibrium that each mobile must find, which depends on the surrounding traffic and their own link quality. Moreover, these values change continuously given mobility and changes in shadowing, changes in channel allocation and mobiles joining or leaving the network. Hence, the system is continuously looking for an homeostasis point which balances resources.

In such a context, a Multi-Agent System (MAS) is developed to control mobiles' power level. Such an approach is appropriate given that it relies on the inevitable interdependence of the mobiles' BER related to the propagation factors but, most importantly, to the interference generated by variations of power level and changes in the relay connections. The purpose is therefore to balance BER in an environment with many constraints.

The next section develops in more detail the architectural challenges and explains the key concept in designing MAS, and finally describes the proposed design for power management. Section III proposes a set of simulations to benchmark the proposed design against the mentioned existing algorithms adapted to the DBS context. Finally, Section IV discusses the results.

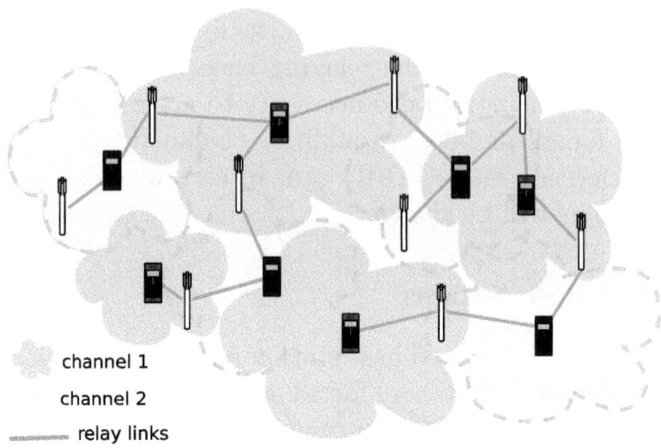

Fig. 1. Illustration of a DBS architecture with 2 channels

2 Multiple Agent Design for DBS Network

2.1 The Distributed Base Station Challenges

In mobile telecommunication networks, the challenges are to provide connectivity to mobiles in spite of the fact that the received signal strength decreases proportionally to a power of up to 4 (in urban environments) of the distance between mobile and base station (BS). Therefore, many BS must be deployed in space. However, mobiles close to one another cannot use the same channels as they will interfere. And, unfortunately, the number of available channels is limited. Cellular mobile networks are an ingenious way of allowing reuse of the resources in space to accommodate a high density of mobiles. Still, these networks require an extensive amount of planning for deployment and exploit expensive base stations, whose siting can be frought with legal and social complications given their radiated power.

The distributed base station architecture aims to answer such network deployment issues, and also offers higher availability of resources to accommodate today's and tomorrow's highly demanding applications in terms of bandwidth. For this, access to a wired network is offered by a plurality of small inexpensive base stations, emitting lower power, and easily installed or hidden inconspicuously in the urban environment. The system is also designed to be completely self-organized to facilitate its installation and configuration. To sustain high throughputs from and to mobiles, macrodiversity is used, such that a set of DBS can relay receive and process different copies of the signal from one mobile to offer a higher aggregate link quality.

Given that a DBS is resource-constrained and may only relay a few mobiles, one problem with such an architecture is to decide which DBS relays which mobiles in a continuously changing environment, with new mobiles connecting and mobiles moving out of the reach of some DBS and into the reach of others. Links must be adjusted dynamically. This has already been answered by a multi agent process in [7] which proved to offer efficient optimization qualities. Also, this system must deal with interference. It can do so by using adequate channel assignment to mobiles, for which a multi agent process has also been proposed in [8]. But resource availability can also be enhanced by using efficient power control, such that some mobiles emit using less power in order to produce less interference for others.

The power control problem is challenging in the DBS network as it is interdependent with the macrodiversity potential. Indeed, a mobile can emit with high power to be reached by many DBS. But because of interference, if all mobiles did this as well, none would gain any benefit. The problem is then to decide which mobile should emit less power to allow others to enjoy better link quality. Many algorithms, either centralized or decentralized, exist in the literature. Yet, all of these are based on maximizing a global criterion. We will see in the following that a multi agent process can offer appropriate and desirable solutions which have not been thought of beforehand. Indeed, instead of striving to maximize a predefined goal based on simplifying assumptions, MAS explore a variety of solutions through empirical experimentation. This brings out novel solutions that would not have been obtained in a classical manner involving reductive hypotheses.

2.2 Multi-agent Design

Swarming agents [9] are interacting entities whose interactions lead to the function we want to generate. Parunak [10] gives heuristics to engineer such a swarming system based on the following three concepts:

1. *Coupling* — processes must continually exchange information;
2. *Auto-catalysis* — whereby interaction is self maintained; and
3. *Function* — the induced organization provides a useful function.

Coupling. To satisfy the coupling requirement, a *distributed environment* is needed where sources of information are not centralized and intelligent behavior can only emerge through constant exchanges. DBS and mobiles do form a distributed environment, with mobiles' requests for connections and QoS being the source of information.

An *active environment* with the use of volatile markers (also referred to as pheromones[1]) aims to generate coupling via at least indirect exchange of information between agents. These markers represent non-intrusive bits of information that an agent imprints on the environment which can be sensed by other agents to obtain information on the present state of the system. Mobiles' requests for connections and QoS, as well as interference and power levels, represent volatile markers since they are sensed by local DBS and mobiles which in turn interact among themselves via multiple relaying.

[1] Where the term denotes the direct inspiration from the information transport medium used by insects as Parunak describes [10].

Agents should be *small in size and scope*, compared to the overall system. Indeed, DBS are small relay stations with a small sphere of influence compared to the classic cellular base stations.

As a final criterion related to coupling, agents should be mapped as *entities, not functions* since an agent does not implement a complete function (e.g., sorting, segmentation).

In the proposed power control system, the agents are mapped to the mobiles and satisfy all of the above criteria. Their actions will continuously adjust mobiles' power levels in an interacting process whose purpose is to obtain a balanced power control functionality.

Auto-catalysis. For agents to maintain their interactions, they must be designed to let the process evolve continuously. Therefore, agents should not be designed based on discrete state transitions, leading to pauses in the process because of unverified conditions. That is why we must favor *flows vs transitions.* One way is for agents to use the volatile markers to inform other agents of their particular state which has to be dealt with, so they can continue their process rather than stop and wait. This is how the mobiles operate in our case, with the mobiles' status being used as markers which can be sensed through the propagation environment itself.

Amplification and limitation is needed. Amplification here implies a positive feedback mechanism such that convergence (to a solution) is favored. In other words, an agent's actions which lead the system in a desirable global direction should influence the surrounding agents to act in the same direction, via the indirect exchange of information by the markers or pheromones (understood here as the mobiles' status).

But limitation implies preventing the whole system from either focusing on one point (exacerbating the convergence of actions to a local minimum) and thus miss a better solution or go past the solution and then diverge from it. Likewise, limitation mechanisms should prevent the system from oscillating.

For a mobile, this means its power level should be amplified or limited depending on the effect its actions have on its QoS, which is necessarily linked to the surrounding mobiles' QoS, e.g. if a mobile increases its power level in order to increase its QoS, but the system cannot support it, all other mobiles will react. In turn, it should force the first mobile to revise its actions. Also, mobiles have a limited power level range and adjustments should therefore also be limited to prevent saturation. Indeed, in such a case, mobiles could saturate to a maximum power level and block the effectiveness of power control.

This striving for amplified/limited adjustments of power level aims to converge to a point of equilibrium: an homeostasis point where the system actually exhibits its expected power control behavior. These actions, to adjust power level, must be sustained (triggered) by an ongoing *flow* to ensure the system continuously explores the solution space and does not get stuck in a dead-end. This flow is analogous to the variations of a stock market title which is influenced by the traders' actions of selling and buying, which in turn influences the traders decisions and actions. The corresponding aspect of our system is created by having mobiles continuously adjust their power level, thus establishing a *flow* of resulting modifications in interference. This flow modifies the mobiles' status (overall QoS) which in turn is sensed by the mobiles so that they take informed decisions at the agent activation.

In the process, the mobiles are transforming the original requests by integrating increasingly global information. Indeed, the agents' actions modify local mobiles' interference. This is sensed by nearby mobiles which, in turn, react to the changes, such that one local action gradually impacts on an increasingly larger neighborhood, thereby coupling local actions to global behavior.

Function. Coupling may be trivial to obtain and auto-catalysis somewhat more involved, but if the process as a whole does not realize a useful function, then it is irrelevant. Hence, we want the flow of adjustments in power levels to actually optimize the QoS of mobiles. *Behavior diversity and alternative behavior* help in realizing the function by forcing agents to break any deterministic pattern through the incorporation of randomness or non linearities. For PC, this means each mobile should adjust its power level differently, in a way that the system never falls in a local minimum where no further improvement is possible. Such non-linearities will make each mobile converge differently to their homeostasis power level point. Hence, the future power level adjustment of a mobile will be dependent on the effect of all mobiles' power level adjustments, which allow power levels to converge to an homeostasis point.

Finally, we need to design a *utility function* which translates the flow sensed (of variations thereof) into rational decisions. That is, it converts a multi-dimensional problem into a one-dimensional quantity upon which decisions for actions are based.

In spite of the fact that many frameworks attempt to provide mathematical support to derive such utility functions (such as Game-Theory [11] or COIN theory [12]), these frameworks mostly consider sophisticated intelligent agents having the ability to learn (eventually using reinforcement learning techniques) which is not the nature of the proposed design. Ultimately, defining simple agent behavior to obtain an intended global behavior still relies on intuition and trial and error such as in Conway's "game of life" [13] or with Wolfram's cellular automata [14]. In fact, no systematic procedure is known which yields the locally-applicable utility function from the desired global behavior.

2.3 Multi-Agent Power Control (MAPC)

Contrary to the algorithms described in the Introduction, the purpose of the agent is not to find a solution that evolves to a common global balance. Rather, it tries to balance resources locally, while generating some interdependence in the power level of neighboring mobiles. That way, and given all mobiles' QoS are interconnected indirectly with macrodiversity relaying and interference, one mobile's power level should evolve to maximize its achievable QoS while not impeding others.

Building upon the DBS architecture developed in [7] (agents for macrodiversity connection management) and [8] (agents for channel allocation in the DBS network), the PC agents sense the mobiles' QoS and modify the mobile's power level. Inevitably, these actions will influence the other two types of agents. However, these interactions are meant to be constructive; an action by one type of agent(power level adjustment) should not impede or exacerbate another agent's action (connection or channel allocation). Hence, limitation of the agents' reactions constitutes an important aspect to maintain stability in the system and to prevent e.g. the PC agents from overreacting while trying to compensate events caused by sudden change of interference due to changes in either channel or connection allocation.

Consider that mobile i has a power level ratio of p_i and an overall link quality defined by

$$Q_i = \frac{\mathrm{Pt}_i}{\mathrm{Pd}_i} = \frac{\log_{10} \mathrm{BER}_i}{\log_{10} \mathrm{BER}_i^R} = \frac{\sum_{k=1}^{M_i} \log_{10}(\mathrm{BER}(i,k))}{\log_{10}(\mathrm{BER}_i^R)}, \tag{1}$$

where Pt_i represents the actual total BER after macrodiversity combining of the signals (i.e a measure of QoS). It is evaluated using the analytical form in [6] (to take into account a Rice fading model). The sum on k iterates through the M_i DBS relaying mobile i. BER_i^R is the requested BER for mobile i. With this normalization, classes of QoS are naturally taken into account in the PC algorithm.

If Q_i is above 1, the mobile is *overserved* (it enjoys a BER better than requested) and should reduce its power level; otherwise it should increase it. Yet, forcing "overserved mobiles" to lower their power level would be restrictive, as local conditions might allow mobiles to enjoy better QoS (due to lower local traffic compared to local resources) without impeding other mobiles overwhelmingly. It would also force mobiles to systematically reduce their power level until they hit the point where SINR is limited by thermal noise, where they become more vulnerable to either sudden deep fading or to the Hidden Terminal Effect (HTE) [15] since very low power levels would prevent nearby DBS from detecting channel use. As well, if mobiles cannot obtain their QoS, they would systematically saturate their transmit power. Therefore, more subtle actions are called for.

The Need variable is introduced to describe what could be the power level of the mobile given its Q_i factor: it is the value to which the mobile's power level should converge to if nothing else changes (which is not the case as other mobiles will adjust their power level). When, for all mobiles, the current Need_i value equals the current power level p_i then the homeostasis point is reached. This variable is evaluated given a shaping function :

$$\mathrm{Need}_i(Q_i) = 2e^{(-SQ_i)} \times (SQ_i + 1) - 1, \tag{2}$$

where the value S is a scaling parameter for Q_i in order to allow mobiles to obtain QoS higher than their requested Pd_i. Therefore, the Need function will not necessarily be smaller than the current power level if $Q_i > 1$. And mobiles can obtain more quality than a global mean value. In the current simulations, QoS is maximized with $S = 0.8$, and it has been observed that this value is adequate across many different conditions of traffic, mobile speeds and available resources.

The exponential in the shaping function (2) generates non-linearities and naturally affects the dynamics of the system. In effect, it affects the mobiles' convergence speed differently given their needs, and this translates into behavior diversity as no mobile will react in a precisely proportional manner. The proposed function is of course not the only possible choice, but it has proved stable and effective. For MAS, effectiveness does not lie in the mathematical exactness of the function, but in the interactions it will generate.

Finally, this Need factor must be converted to a delta (step) value to adjust the power level. Two important functionalities remain to be implemented (1) homeostasis and (2) limitation.

(1) *Homeostasis* is obtained by comparing the Need value to the current power level the mobile has. Hence, the delta value is in the form of $\text{Need}_i - p_i$. The mobile will then try to converge to a Need_i value which depends on local interactions given itself and neighboring mobiles' Q values (given these are indirectly linked via interference). Eventually, a non-linear function helps convergence so that with Need_i and p_i close, the generated delta is kept small to slow down variations and help stabilize the convergence.

$$\Delta_i = \beta \,\text{sign}(\text{Need}_i - p_i)\,(|\text{Need}_i - p_i|)^{1.5}, \tag{3}$$

where the β factor is used to modify the dynamics of the system to help it converge faster, at the expense of stability.

(2) *Limitation:* experience shows that this function is too unstable with high values of β. Still, it can be stabilized with additional scaling parameters, while maintaining fast adaptation in time with large values of $\beta > 5$, which is important for mobility ($\beta = 5$ is used in the presented simulations). Therefore, Δ is scaled with the current power level and also the desired power level (the Need value). That way, if these values are small, Δ is also kept small to prevent strong changes in the system that would otherwise suddenly generate exaggerated interference. Indeed, such changes would lead to complications such as breaking existing links or simply propagating exaggerated reactions throughout the system. Building upon (3), the following function is used:

$$\Delta_i = p_i \times |\text{Need}| \times \beta\text{sign}(\text{Need}_i - p_i)(|\text{Need}_i - p_i|)^{1.5}. \tag{4}$$

Finally, the delta value is constrained to not exceed the power level range:

$$\Delta_i < 0 \Rightarrow \Delta_i' = \max\{\Delta_i, \frac{-p_i}{2}\} \tag{5}$$

$$\Delta_i > 0 \Rightarrow \Delta_i' = \min\{\Delta_i, \frac{1}{2}(1 - p_i)\}. \tag{6}$$

As the mobile's PC agent activates, its power level is adjusted as follows:

$$p_i^{(\nu+1)} = p_i^{(\nu)} + \Delta_i'. \tag{7}$$

3 Simulation Platform

This section begins with a description of two known PC algorithms used for benchmarking purpose. Then, the simulation physical parameters are detailed, as well as a brief description of the emulation platform. Finally, the results are given and detailed.

3.1 Centralized Power Control, CPC

Grandhi's centralized power control (CPC) algorithm [1] is applied in the DBS architecture by considering the M master DBS for the M mobiles on a given channel. g_{ij} denotes the gain of the link (due to the path loss) from mobile i to DBS j, with DBS i being mobile i's master connection. Matrix $\mathbf{A}$ is defined as

$$A_{ij} = g_{ij}/g_{ii} \text{ if } i \neq j, \tag{8}$$

$$A_{ii} = 0. \tag{9}$$

And the SIR at the master DBS is defined as

$$\gamma_i = \frac{p_i}{\sum_{j=1}^{M} A_{ij} p_i j}. \tag{10}$$

The power level for each mobile is then given by the eigenvector associated with the largest positive eigenvalue of $\mathbf{A}$.

Note that this algorithm is not trying to maximize each mobile's SIR. Rather, it finds a set of power levels which maximizes the lowest SIR, thus leading to each mobile's SIR being equal to the minimum (maximized) SIR. Also, the obtained power levels are proportional to the eigenvector and thus need to be scaled to fit inside the mobiles' power level range. This is where the instability of this algorithm lies, since under certain interference conditions, if a mobile is very close to its master DBS, its power level will be very low. Yet, since its SIR is forced to be equal to the other mobiles' SIR, proportionally, the noise at the receiver will have a much stronger impact leading to very poor SINR. Supposing a mobile faces 1W interference power and 0.1W noise power, and emits 10W to obtain a SIR of 10dB, it has a 9.6dB SINR. Now, consider a mobile faced with .1W of interference, it emits 1W to obtain the same 10dB SIR, but has an SINR of 7dB, resulting in an effective penalty of half. In order to minimize this effect, the minimum power level should be high enough so that noise remains as much as possible negligible. Hence, the power levels will be scaled such that the maximum power level evaluated is set to the maximum mobile's range.

On the other hand, a more complex evaluation of such effects would make it possible to lower the maximum power level, keeping it as low as possible, and hence, maximizing the efficiency of the link quality versus the power used per mobile.

3.2 SBMPC

Yanikomeroglu's SIR-balanced macro power control (SBMPC) [5] proposes an interesting algorithm for CDMA distributed antennas using macrodiversity. The algorithm aims to balance, over all mobiles, the sum of the SIR one mobile has (over all antennas). This is a valid approach in the context of Rayleigh fading. However, as mentioned in the introduction, in Rice fading, two similar SIR values can lead to two different BERs given each may not have the same ratio of line of sight component versus reflexions (i.e. different K factor). Therefore, balancing SIR does not balance BER with line of sight components varying depending on mobiles' locations.

As his article suggests, it is straightforward to adapt the algorithm to a general cellular system. For all mobiles on one channel, we consider the matrix $\mathbf{B}$ to describe the connections of mobile i (out of M mobiles) to DBS j (out of L DBS) such that

$$B_{ij} = 1 \text{ if mobile } i \text{ is relayed by DBS } j, \tag{11}$$
$$B_{ii} = 0 \text{ otherwise.} \tag{12}$$

The global SIR for mobile i is then

$$\gamma_{i,SBMPC} = \sum_{j=1}^{L} B_{ij} \frac{g_{ij}p_i}{\left(\sum_{k=1}^{M} g_{kj}p_ik\right) - g_{ij}p_i}. \tag{13}$$

This equation is rearranged to obtain the power level of the $i = \{2, \ldots, M\}$ mobiles given the first in an iterative manner:

$$\mathbf{P}^{(0)} = \{p_i^{(0)}\} = \left\{ \left(\sum_{j=1}^{L} B_{ij}g_{ij} \right)^{-1} \right\}, \forall i, \tag{14}$$

$$\gamma_1^{(\nu)} = \sum_{j=1}^{L} B_{1j} \frac{g_{1j}p_i1^{(\nu)}}{\left(\sum_{k=1}^{M} g_{kj}p_ik^{(\nu)}\right) - g_{1j}p_1^{(\nu)}}. \tag{15}$$

$$p_1^{(\nu+1)} = p_1(\nu), \tag{16}$$

$$p_i^{(\nu+1)} = \frac{\gamma_1^{(\nu)}}{\sum_{j=1}^{L} \frac{B_{ij}g_{ij}}{\left(\sum_{k=1}^{M} g_{kj}p_k^{(\nu)}\right) - g_{ij}p_i^{(\nu)}}}, \; i \in \{2, \ldots, M\}. \tag{17}$$

Similarly to the previous algorithm, the obtained power level vector is scaled to minimize the noise effect.

Given that this is an iterative solution and the purpose is not to evaluate its convergence, the algorithm is run for 20 iterations at each time step of a simulation, which is enough for convergence.

3.3 Simulation Platform

Physical parameters. A square field of 25 square kilometers is considered, in which 1000 mobiles evolve and 100 DBS are scattered randomly. Hence, the traffic and network resource geometries are not uniform, which a priori implies uneven coverage quality. A mobile moves in a random direction at a random speed taken (at the start of a scenario) out of a uniform distribution over $[0, V_{\max}]$. DBS can relay 25 mobiles each, such that the mean number of macrodiversity links per mobile is 2.5. A mobile's maximum transmit power is 1W at 1 meter of its antenna, and the propagation exponent is 4 ($g_ij \sim 1/d^{-4}$). Rayleigh fading is considered, except near a DBS (closer than 100m) where a line of sight component is added with Rice factor $K = 5$ dB. Thermal noise at the receiver is considered for a bandwidth of 30kHz at a temperature of 20°C, yielding $N_0 = -129$ dBW. The number of available channels is denoted Ch.

Agents' emulation. Simulations are run for 1000 seconds and repeated 10 times with different initializations of the geometry (DBS positions and mobile initial positions, directions and speeds). Time is discretized with a time step of 1 second. At each time step, physical parameters are evaluated (mobile's position, propagation, interference, BER, connection outage). Agents activate randomly according to a Poisson distribution with parameter $\lambda = 3$ time steps. At each time step, agents which activate evaluate their local state and take actions accordingly (adjust the power level of the concerned mobile).

Results. At each time step, the set of QoS (total BER level given on a logarithmic scale) for each mobile are sorted, thus providing a snapshot in time of the distribution of the network resources across all mobiles. These sorted distributions are then averaged for all the time steps of the simulation. Given this information, it is then possible to compare how each algorithm distributes resources. The same is done for the power level allocation. Also, to verify the stability over time (considering the dynamic properties) of the algorithm, two factors are interesting to observe to understand how the system handles outage : (1) the mean number $\bar{N_d}$ of mobiles that loose all connections to the network per second, and (2) the mean time $\bar{t_r}$ it takes for the network to reconnect a mobile after it has been disconnected. The latter also provides insight on how well the system is able to provide resources to mobiles with high availability.

4 Results

Figure 2(a) shows the base results, that is, with a static simulation where fading is considered as if mobiles where moving, but mobility is not considered (to observe a nominal capacity without taking into account dynamic adaptation of the algorithms). Noise is also not considered in this case.

The graphic reveals different aspects. First, with no PC, the QoS is clearly not balanced, but more importantly, not all mobiles can be connected as is seen from the right hand side of the graph. With the centralized algorithms, we can clearly see that QoS is balanced, and all mobiles are connected. MAPC on the other hand is able to provide much more QoS to almost all mobiles, while only impeding (compared to SBMPC) very few mobiles.

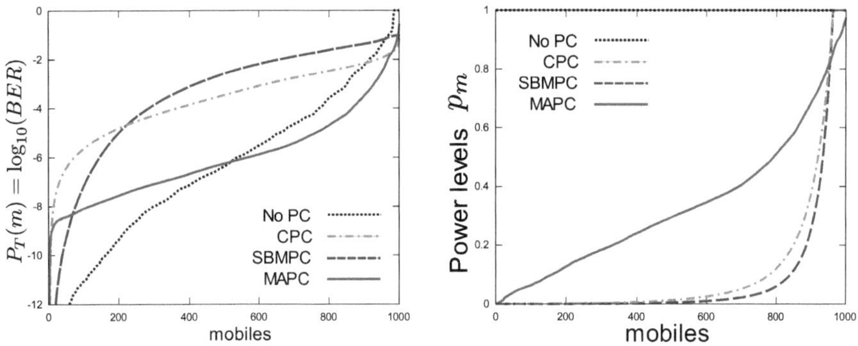

(a) Sorted BER profile averaged in time ($\text{mean}_t(\text{sort}_m(P_T(m)))$)

(b) Sorted power level ratio profile averaged in time ($\text{mean}_t(\text{sort}_i(p_i i))$)

Fig. 2. Ch $= 40$, $N = 0$, $V_{\max} = 0$

In Table 1, it is interesting to note how the CPC handles outage extremely well. It takes only 1 second (1 iteration of the simulation) to reconnect a lost mobile, and the probability that a mobile is disconnected is extremely low. Even SBMPC is not as good, but remains excellent compared to no power control. MAPC is only doing slightly worse, but with a much enhanced QoS provided to all mobiles.

Table 1. Outage behavior without mobility and noise Ch $= 40$

	No PC	CPC	SBMPC	MAPC
$\bar{N_d}$ ($\times 10^{-6}$)	570	8.9	130	190
$\bar{t_r}$ (seconds)	24.2	1	2.0	2.65

Figure 2(b) reveals how both CPC and SBMPC offer similar distributions of the power levels. On the contrary, the MAPC power level allocation is radically different.

Faced with higher interference levels (Ch $= 25$), it can be seen that the centralized algorithms breakdown (Fig. 3(a)). Indeed, in high interference levels, maximizing the minimum SIR leads to very poor SIRs for all mobiles. In turn, this generates many disconnections. Figure 3(a) clearly shows the traditional algorithms are here inefficient and even worse than without PC. However, the MAPC algorithm manages to provide acceptable levels of QoS, while still connecting more mobiles.

The situation deteriorates even more when noise is introduced. Figure 3(b) reveals how noise, as explained previously, renders the traditional algorithms unstable generating lots of disconnections.

Also, facing important mobility (figure not shown due to lack of space), the CPC algorithm loses its strength (of minimizing the outage probability)

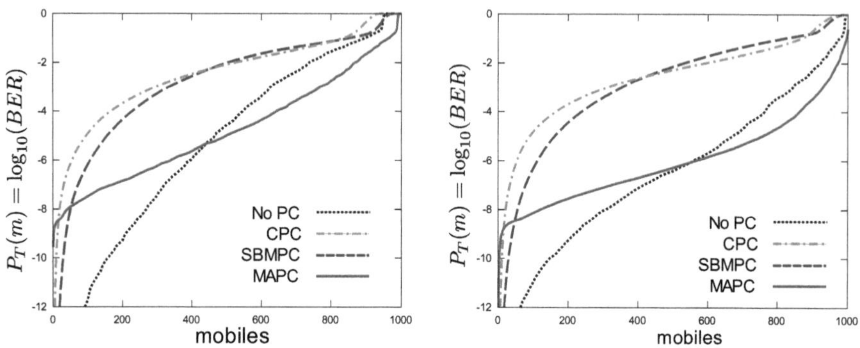

(a) Low channel resources, Ch = 25, $N = 0$, $V_{\max} = 0$

(b) Effect of thermal noise, Ch = 40, $N = -129$dBW, $V_{\max} = 0$

Fig. 3. Sorted BER profile averaged in time ($\text{mean}_t(\text{sort}_m(P_T(m)))$)

as Table 2 reveals. Indeed, with mobility, more interference is present because mobiles do not obtain an optimal reallocation of channels at each iteration. This implies far too many very low power levels with the CPC. This conflicts with the channel agents trying to reorganize the channel allocation as it generates important hidden terminal effects. This also shows that the CPC algorithm loses much of its capacity with even small changes of the efficiency of the channel allocation. In addition, we are not even considering the burden of calculating power levels at each iteration while first centralizing the data bits, which necessarily takes time and would prevent the algorithm from rapidly adapting to the changes in the system. SBMPC is doing much better, yet not as well as MAPC.

Table 2. Outage behavior with mobility ($V_{\max} = 5$ m/s) Ch = 50

	No PC	CPC	SBMPC	MAPC
$\bar{N_d}$ ($\times 10^{-4}$)	9.8	19.1	3.8	1.8
$\bar{t_r}$ (seconds)	5.13	2.4	2.2	1.38

Figure 4(a) shows the behavior of the algorithms with only discrete levels of power. The power level range is uniformly divided into 10 discrete levels. While the MAPC is not as efficient as with a continuous power range, it still remains more efficient at balancing the QoS. The CPC and SBMPC algorithms loose their ability to balance QoS, since in order for them to work properly they need an important dynamic range of power levels especially in the very low powers. However, this necessity is in contradiction with the assumption (on which they rely) that thermal noise is not an important factor. Indeed, mobiles with very low power levels (which in these cases is most of them) will be much affected by the thermal noise parameter, thus resulting in poor SINR. We should note, however, that the CPC and SBMPC algorithms should be much more efficient

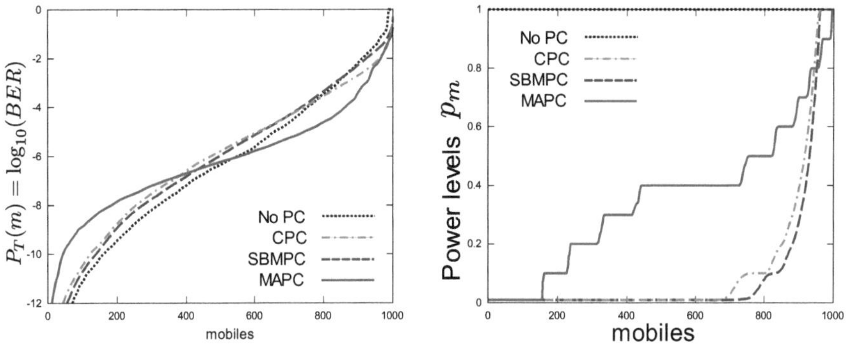

(a) Sorted BER profile averaged in time ($\text{mean}_t(\text{sort}_m(P_T(m)))$)

(b) Sorted power level ratio profile averaged in time($\text{mean}_t(\text{sort}_i(p_i i))$)

Fig. 4. Ch = 40, $N = 0$, $V_{\max} = 0$, discrete power level

than presented herein, if considering a uniform geometry with regularly-spaced DBS and uniform traffic, though this would then be a very academic scenario.

Figure 4(b) shows the allocated power level over all mobiles in the discrete case.

5 Conclusion

This article presents a novel design and approach to power control using multiple agents. Its efficiency is compared with traditional algorithms and proved to be superior in many aspects : robustness, ability to maximize the macrodiversity the DBS architecture offers, as well as adaptability to many situations of high / low traffic/interference or important mobility. The design was developed using Parunak's concepts and adjusted with thorough experiments to understand the interactions involved so that these interactions could be limited or amplified in order to lead to the desired behavior. It is an experimental approach, yet mostly intuitive. Moreover, the design is a proof that striving for a desired solution, such as in the SBMPC or CPC algorithms, which maximizes the minimum SIR, is not necessarily the best way to make the best out of a system. Rather, the MAS concept of first trying to generate coupling and auto-catalysis, and only then trying to push the design in a desired direction (to obtain functionality out of it) leads to un-thought-of solutions which ultimately prove appropriate. Indeed, given the power allocation the MAPC obtains, it might be possible to formulate a mathematical framework to gain further understanding and insight. This is certainly different from the conventional approach in communications which starts from an analytical formulation often made overly simplistic for the sake of tractability.

As it stands, the results obtained with the distributed base station scheme are encouraging and prompt further developments. Indeed, some gains might be obtained if the three agents systems (connections, channel allocation and PC) were more directly coupled to obtain more synergy out of their interactions.

References

1. Grandhi, S., Vijayan, R., Goodman, D., Zander, J.: Centralized power control in cellular radio systems. IEEE Transactions on Vehicular Technology 42(4), 466–468 (1993)
2. Grandhi, S., Vijayan, R., Goodman, D.: Distributed power control in cellular radio systems. IEEE Transactions on Communications 42(234), 226–228 (1994)
3. Lee, T.H., Lin, J.C.: A fully distributed power control algorithm for cellular mobile systems. IEEE Journal on Selected Areas in Communications 14(4), 692–697 (1996)
4. Hongyu, W., Aiging, H., Rong, H., Weikang, G.: Balanced distributed power control, vol. 2, pp. 1415–1419 (2000)
5. Yanikomeroglu, H., Sousa, E.: Sir-balanced macro power control for the reverse link of cdma sectorized distributed antenna system, September 1998, vol. 2, pp. 915–920 (1998)
6. Leroux, P., Roy, S., Chouinard, J.Y.: The Performance of Soft Macrodiversity Based on Maximal-Ratio Combining in Uncorrelated Rician Fading. In: 17th annual IEEE international symposium PIMRC 2006, Helsinki, Finland (September 2006)
7. Leroux, P., Roy, S., Chouinard, J.Y.: An agent system to manage mobile connections in a distributed base station scheme. In: 17th annual IEEE international symposium PIMRC 2006, Helsinki, Finland (September 2006)
8. Leroux, P., Roy, S., Chouinard, J.Y.: A Multi-Agent Protocol to Manage Interference in a Distributed Base Station System. Submited to ATC 2008 (2008)
9. Bonabeau, E., Drigo, M., Theraulaz, G.: Swarm Inteligence: From Natural to Artificial Systems. New York Oxford Univ. Press (1999)
10. Parunak, H.V.D.: Go to the Ant.: Engineering Principles from Natural Agent Systems. Annals of Operations Research (1997)
11. Mackenzie, A., Wicker, S.: Cornell University: Game Theory and the Design of Self Configuring, Adaptive Wireless Networks. IEEE Commun. Mag. (November 2001)
12. Tumer, K., Wolpert, D.: Collectives and the Design of Complex Systems. Springer, NY (2004)
13. Berlekamp, E.R., Conway, J.H., Guy, R.K.: Winning Ways for your Mathematical Plays. Academic Press, New York (1982)
14. Wolfram, S.: A New Kind of Science. Wolfram Media, Champaign (2002)
15. Ware, C., Wysocki, T., Chicharo, J.: Hidden terminal jamming problems in IEEE 802.11 mobile ad hoc networks. In: IEEE International Conference on Communications, ICC 2001, Helsinki, June 2001, pp. 261–265 (2001)

Redundancy Maintenance and Garbage Collection Strategies in Peer-to-Peer Storage Systems

Xin Liu and Anwitaman Datta

School of Computer Engineering, Nanyang Technological University, Singapore
liu_xin@pmail.ntu.edu.sg, anwitaman@ntu.edu.sg

Abstract. Maintaining redundancy in P2P storage systems is essential for reliability guarantees. Numerous P2P storage system maintenance algorithms have been proposed in the last years, each supposedly improving upon the previous approaches. We perform a systematic comparative study of the various strategies taking also into account the influence of different garbage collection mechanisms, an issue not studied so far. Our experiments show that while some strategies generally perform better than some others, there is no universally best strategy, and their relative superiority depends on various other design choices as well as the specific evaluation criterion. Our results can be used by P2P storage systems designers to make prudent design decisions, and our exploration of the various evaluation metrics also provides a more comprehensive framework to compare algorithms for P2P storage systems. While there are numerous network simulators specifically developed even to simulate peer-to-peer networks, there existed no P2P storage simulators - a byproduct of this work is a generic modular P2P storage system simulator which we provide as open-source. Different redundancy, maintenance, placement, garbage-collection policies, churn scenarios can be easily integrated to the simulator to try out new schemes in future, and provides a common framework to compare (future) p2p storage systems designs - something which has not been possible so far.

Keywords: peer-to-peer storage-systems, redundancy maintenance, garbage collection, trace-driven simulations.

1 Introduction

For diverse reasons including fault-tolerance, load-balance or response time or geographic distribution of end users, distributed data stores are of interest. These include traditional systems like distributed databases as well as more recent peer-to-peer systems like *OceanStore* [1] aimed at archival storage, *Freenet* [2] for anonymous file sharing and distributed hash table based cooperative file system [3] among other academic as well as commercial initiatives [4,5,6,7].

There are several somewhat orthogonal design aspects which need to be considered while developing a P2P storage system. Figure 1 summarizes some of

R. Guerraoui and F. Petit (Eds.): SSS 2009, LNCS 5873, pp. 515–530, 2009.

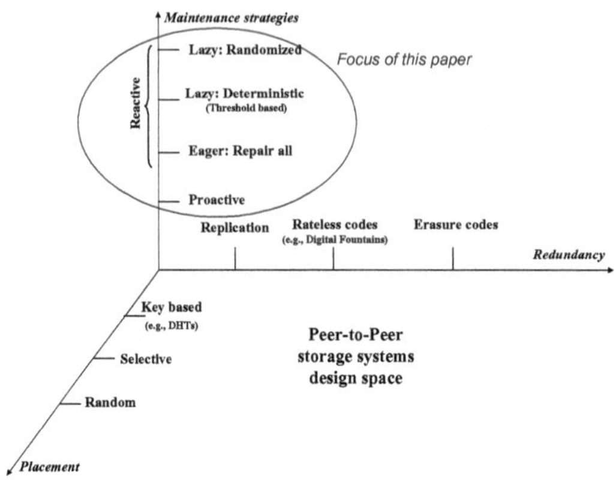

Fig. 1. Important design decisions that need to be considered when designing and deploying a P2P storage system

the most important issues spanning the design space of P2P storage systems. In this paper, we systematically study specifically the influence of one aspect of the design space, namely that of the redundancy maintenance strategies. In the related works section we will elaborate more on existing studies, including studies of the other design choices. The related works also expose the void in current literature in systematic study of the maintenance algorithms - a void we endeavor to partly fill.

Peer-to-peer storage systems need to ensure that once an user (application) stores an object, this object should be available and persist in the network, notwithstanding the unreliability of individual peers and membership dynamics (churn) in the system. This throws open a host of interesting design issues. For resilience, redundancy is essential. Redundancy can be achieved either by replication or using coding techniques. While coding is in principle storage-space efficient for achieving a certain level of resilience, it leads to various kinds of overheads, including computational overhead, and in the context of peer-to-peer systems, communication overhead and even storage overhead to keep track of encoded object fragments, thus making coding mechanisms worthwhile only for relatively larger or rarely accessed objects as in applications like archival storage.

Over time, redundancy is lost unless replenished because of departure of peers. This necessitates some mechanisms to restore redundancy. Trade-off considerations of redundancy maintenance and achieving resilience have led to the design of several maintenance strategies [5,8,9].

The subtle interplay between the dynamics in the system – which tends to deteriorate the system's performance, and the maintenance and garbage collection mechanisms which try to stabilize the system while capping the bandwidth and storage overheads – has been of interest in recent years. Several theoretical work [10,8,11] exist, which however have their own limitations in capturing the whole gamut of design issues, and a complimentary, empirical approach based on simulations and experiments is also called for.

Existing literature on empirical studies however do not systematically compare all these strategies either, and only partial and selective comparison studies exist. The primary objective of this paper is to do a thorough study of all the existing redundancy maintenance mechanisms, also taking into account the influence of garbage collection mechanisms to deal with excessive redundancy, which has significant impact but has not been studied so far. Performance of the different maintenance strategies is evaluated using several metrics and under various circumstances based on system design decisions, workload and environment. Such a comprehensive enumeration is expected to provide P2P storage systems designers guidance in making judicious design choices.

High level summary of our findings are as follows. There is no single strategy which comes across as the best. The randomized lazy maintenance strategy [8] provides a good overall trade-off. It is normal for a complex system influenced by numerous factors that no design choice is good under all circumstances, and it is thus imperative to identify a mechanism which provides good trade-offs and graceful degradation from a multi-objective perspective. This finding, while intuitive, is in contrast to mutually contradicting claims of several previous works because of the selective and limited character of their comparisons.

We demonstrate that different strategies outperform the others depending on the circumstances and also the metrics used to judge them. Also, while encoding based schemes require a minimal number of distinct fragments to recreate the original object, and duplicates of the same fragment do not help in that respect, allowing such duplicates increase the availability of the distinct fragments, and thus indirectly help. In particular, such a strategy turns out to be bandwidth efficient in comparison to other garbage collection decisions allowing no duplicates or using a larger diversity.

2 P2P Storage: Design Space and Related Work

The last years have witnessed numerous prototype P2P storage systems including Pond [12], CFS [3], TotalRecall [5], Glacier [6], Tempo [9] as well as commercial ones like Wuala [4].

Weatherspoon et al [13] carried out an elaborate empirical comparison of several storage systems. Their work focuses on evaluating the system based on specific parameters used to configure the deployed systems but does not discern the effect of specific design choices. Same implementations with other configurations will yield possibly different performance.

Exploring and understanding the effect of the various design choices are crucial. Williams et al [14] studied more diligently the effect of the choice of redundancy, and advocated the use of a hybrid strategy which can leverage on erasure codes to achieve storage space efficiency to guarantee persistence, while using replication to provide performance during regular access. In this paper, we investigate another relatively unexplored axis of the design space to compare the various redundancy maintenance mechanisms, and additionally take into account the effect of different garbage collection strategies. In terms of data placement, often a DHT is used to store the objects [3]. Other placement strategies can also be used, e.g., randomized [5] or other criterions like load or proximity. Using such non-DHT placement strategies increase the complexity of the system's design since it becomes essential to keep track of object fragments.

Several theoretical works complement the experimental studies. Weatherspoon et al [15] conducted an early study to demonstrate that erasure codes are storage efficient compared to replication. Bhagwan et al [5] studied static resilience to determine adequate level of redundancy. Datta et al [8] used Markov models and Di et al [11] used stochastic differential equations to study the combined effect of churn and maintenance operations in a P2P storage system. Our results match well to analytical predictions [8] for the very simple special cases which such analytical studies can model.

2.1 Maintenance (Redundancy Replenishment) Strategies

Individual peers may be unavailable occasionally and (often) unpredictably because users go offline, machines fail, or network gets disconnected. Temporary churn does not directly affect long term persistence, since the peers join back, bringing back in the network whatever is stored in them. Adequate redundancy can mitigate *temporary churn*. However, over a period of time, some participating peers may leave the system permanently, in turn leading to permanent loss of redundancy. *Permanent churn* thus makes the system more vulnerable. Redundancy maintenance schemes need to make the P2P storage system resilient against both regular and relatively predictable temporary and permanent churn as well as unpredictable future correlated failures, while using network and system resources judiciously.

Several redundancy replenishment strategies have been proposed [5,8,9]. Whether the repairs are in response to failures of peers or not they are classified as: (1) *reactive maintenance* and (2) *proactive maintenance.*

For the rest of the paper we will assume that encoding based redundancy is being used in a storage system, such that originally N encoded distinct fragments for an object is stored, of which, retrieving any M (but no less) fragments ensures that the original object can be reconstructed.

Reactive maintenance. The simplest maintenance mechanism is to probe periodically all the peers which are supposed to store encoded fragments of an object, and whenever a probe for some fragments fail, reactively replenish the redundancy by reintegrating new suitable redundant fragments at some live peers. This strategy is referred to as an ***eager maintenance*** strategy. Such an eager reactive maintenance mechanism has been argued and observed [5] that it wastes bandwidth unnecessarily by failing to exploit the fact that often peers come back online along with the stored content. In the design of the TotalRecall storage system, Bhagwan et al [5] advocated a *lazy maintenance strategy* which we call here a deterministic lazy repair strategy, distinguishing it from a randomized strategy proposed subsequently by Datta et al [8] to achieve a more continuous and smoother bandwidth utilization.

In ***deterministic lazy repair*** all peers are probed periodically. When an object has less than parameterized threshold T_{dl} ($M < T_{dl} < N$) encoded fragments available, a repair operation is initiated for that object. Lazy maintenance saves some overheads caused by transient failures. However, this approach may suffer from some undesirable effects: (1) Once the threshold is breached, it tries to replenish all the missing fragments at once, thus causing spikes in bandwidth usage. (2) By waiting for the redundancy to fall below T_{dl}, the system is allowed to degenerate and become more vulnerable to future (correlated) failures. (3) Before maintenance, the available fragments are accessed more frequently, thus causing access overload and imbalance.

The ***randomized lazy repair*** mechanism was proposed to alleviate the shortcomings of the deterministic lazy repair, while trying to preserve its benefits. In this approach, fragments of an object are probed in a random order, until T_{rl} live fragments are detected. A random number $T_{rl} + \mathcal{X}$ of peers are probed to locate such T_{rl} live fragments. The $\mathcal{X}$ (a *random variable*) fragments which are detected to be unavailable are replaced by the system. Adaptivity is inherent in this randomized strategy, because if most of the fragments are online, then $\mathcal{X}$ will be low, and thus there will be fewer replacements, otherwise, more replenishing operations will be carried out.

Proactive maintenance. In a radically different approach, Sit et al [9] argued that if the network is not used at any time point, such bandwidth underutilization is a wastage, and the critical issue is not how much, but how smoothly bandwidth is used. They proposed to continuously generate and integrate new fragments for each object, subject to local bandwidth budget $\mathcal{B}$ at peers, irrespective of the number of fragments of an object in the system.

2.2 Garbage Collection Strategies

The above discussed maintenance operations regenerate lost redundancy. If an offline peer returns, it brings back the fragments stored locally. This may lead to two kinds of excessive redundancy. If the repair operation generates a fragment which is distinct from the fragments that (eventually) come back, then the system may eventually have more than N distinct fragments for an object. Otherwise, the same fragment will have duplicate copies. Both these scenarios lead to excessive redundancy. While extra redundancy can be desirable to an extent, allowing more diversity (a larger number, say up to N_{max} of *distinct* fragments) can make the system more robust against churn, and reduce the need of future maintenance operations. Likewise, even if duplicate copies of encoded fragments do not directly help in increasing availability of an object, they increase the availability of individual fragments, which in turn may help maintaining diversity at a lower future maintenance cost. In all cases the system requires garbage collection to get rid of undesired excessive redundancy. We identify two garbage collection strategies - one to ***limit the diversity of online fragments*** (to N_{max}) and other to ***allow or restrict duplicates of the same fragment***. In our experiments we study the influence of each redundancy replenishment scheme in

Table 1. Simulation parameters

Parameters	Description	Default value
N	The initial number of encoded fragments for each object.	32
M	The required number of fragments to reconstruct the original object.	8
T_{dl}	The threshold number of fragments for *deterministic lazy* repair to trigger the repair operation.	16
T_{rl}	The threshold number of fragments for *randomized lazy* repair to trigger the repair operation.	Table 2
$\mathcal{B}$	The bandwidth budget of each peer (only for *proactive* repair).	Table 2
N_{max}	The maximum redundancy allowed for each object.	32/64
$\mathcal{N}$	The number of nodes in the simulation.	2000
$\mathcal{O}$	The number of objects in the simulation.	4000

conjunction with the garbage collection strategies, which has not been explored in existing literature. Our study demonstrates that it has significant impact on the system's performance.

3 Methodology

We conduct experiments with both real (Skype) and synthetic availability traces[1], and employing the various garbage collection techniques, giving us eight scenarios (see Table 2) to study.

Table 2. Parameters in different scenarios as determined by iteration (explained in Section 3.2) and are measured in terms of object fragments

Scenarios	T_{dl}	T_{rl}	$\mathcal{B}$
Using Skype's peer availability trace [16]			
N_{max} is 32, fragments may have duplicates	16	11	5
N_{max} is 32, fragments don't have duplicates	16	12	8
N_{max} is 64, fragments may have duplicates	16	11	28
N_{max} is 64, fragments don't have duplicates	16	11	12
Using synthetic data (without correlated failures)			
N_{max} is 32, fragments may have duplicates	16	11	3
N_{max} is 32, fragments don't have duplicates	16	12	7
N_{max} is 64, fragments may have duplicates	16	11	7
N_{max} is 64, fragments don't have duplicates	16	11	7

[1] Real (Skype) trace provides a realistic system dynamics scenario, where the rate of churn is always changing; synthetic trace provides insight on the maintenance strategies' resilience against a specific level of churn and the system's dynamic equilibrium, so both real and synthetic traces are necessary in the experiments.

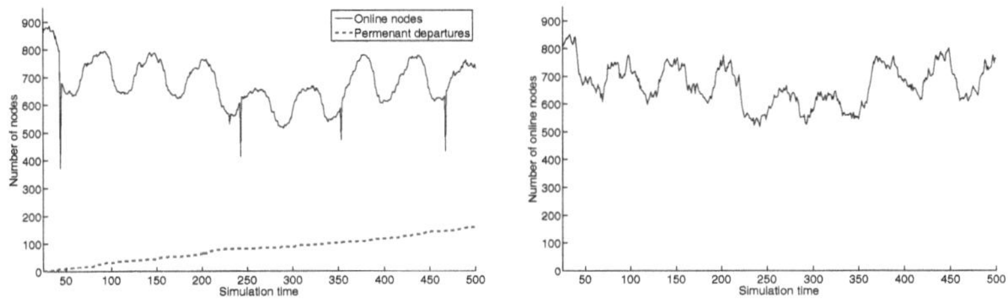

(a) 2000 random Skype peers (b) Synthetic trace (also for 2000 peers)

Fig. 2. Node availability

3.1 Trace Driven Simulation

In our experiments we have used Skype superpeer availability data [16] as well as synthetic data. There is one justification and one excuse for the specific choice of the Skype data set. Availability traces for deployed P2P storage systems are not available. However typical Skype users are very often online on Skype whenever they are online, perhaps because Skype is used as an integral communication tool by many users. Likewise, if a P2P storage system is used as a distributed file system or backup system, the online characteristic can be expected to be similar. Secondly, the main purpose of this paper is to highlight the fact that different maintenance strategies outperform the others in different scenarios, and the current experiments are enough to demonstrate the same. We did experiments with several other availability traces available at the online repository [17] and had similar qualitative results. Apart the diurnal temporal churn, the trace files indicate gradual permanent node departures from the system, besides occasional correlated outages. Figure 2(a) shows Skype node availability [16] after normalization (each time unit stands for 25 minutes).

We also generated synthetic trace for node availability which is shown in Figure 2(b). At each time point, we let online nodes go offline with a probability $p_d(t)$ and offline nodes rejoin the system with a probability $p_r(t)$. To set the values of $p_d(t)$ and $p_r(t)$, we recorded the node availability for a window of 10 time units in the original Skype trace and calculated the average node availability. Based on that, we adapted the departure rate $p_d(t)$ and rejoin rate $p_r(t)$ to make the number of available nodes similar to that in Skype trace in the same period. The synthetic trace helps us study the different maintenance strategies under only transient failures. Since the transient failures dominate in any real system, they also are the principal cause for most of the maintenance overheads, even in the lazier variations. In the experiments with synthetic trace, we try to quantify these overheads.

3.2 Choice of Comparable Parameters

In order to conduct experiments which can be used to compare the different strategies, it is essential to choose parameters for each of the strategies. Maintaining storage redundancy is bandwidth intensive, and thus we consider it to be the cost against which to evaluate the benefits of the various strategies. Ideally we should consider comparable aggregate bandwidth usage while the system is in a steady state as the basis for choosing the parameters to compare the algorithms. In reality, the peer population is never in a steady state but it typically exhibits a diurnal behavior. So we chose the parameter for the deterministic lazy strategy T_{dl} in an ad-hoc manner, and measured the aggregate bandwidth usage over the time window of one such diurnal cycle. We iterated with various values of T_{rl} and $\mathcal{B}$ (We assume $\mathcal{B}$ is unchangeable during the simulation) for the randomized lazy and proactive strategies respectively to determine comparable parameter values where aggregate bandwidth usage over the same time window is similar. Note that over the period of the experiments, the total bandwidth usage of the strategies will vary, because the level of churn changes.

3.3 Evaluation Metrics

We measure several aspects of the system's performance, including the more traditionally studied metrics of *total bandwidth usage*, and *availability of objects*, as well as others like the *probability distribution of the number of fragments of an object* which determines the health of the storage system and thus its vulnerability to further failures (identified in [8]) and *smoothness of bandwidth usage* (identified in [9]).

4 Experiment Environment

We report on eight sets of experiments based on scenarios described above in Section 3 and summarized in Table 2 to compare the four maintenance strategies using a Java based simulator.

4.1 Simulator

Despite numerous simulation based studies of P2P storage systems, and unlike P2P networks (e.g., DHT overlays) for which there exists several simulators, there are no general simulators to study P2P storage systems. So we implemented a modular proprietary simulator for P2P storage systems. The current simulator includes all the maintenance and garbage collection mechanisms mentioned above. We implemented the random placement of fragments as well as others like load-based placement. New strategies for each of the design aspects of P2P storage systems can be integrated as additional modules. A GUI allows the choice of experiment parameters and trace files, facilitating easy usage. The *P2P Storage System Simulator* implementation is available as an open source software at *http://code.google.com/p/p2p3s/*.

4.2 Experiment Settings

While experiments were conducted for various settings, we restrict our report to a smaller set of parameters[2] (default values are summarized in Table 1).

[2] The qualitative trends remained the same across other parameter choices.

Table 3. Summary: Performance of the maintenance strategies considering all metrics

Comparative scenarios	Ranking
N_{max} is 32/fragments may have duplicates/Skype trace	1. Randomized lazy, 2. Proactive, 3. Deterministic lazy, 4. Eager
N_{max} is 32/fragments don't have duplicates/Skype trace	1. Randomized lazy, 2. Proactive, 3. Eager, 4. Deterministic lazy
N_{max} is 64/fragments may have duplicates/Skype trace	1. Randomized lazy, 2. Proactive, 3. Deterministic lazy, 4. Eager
N_{max} is 64/fragments don't have duplicates/Skype trace	1. Randomized lazy, 2. Proactive, 3. Eager, 4. Deterministic lazy
N_{max} is 32/fragments may have duplicates/synthetic trace	1. Randomized lazy, 2. Proactive, 3. Deterministic lazy, 4. Eager
N_{max} is 32/fragments don't have duplicates/synthetic trace	1. Proactive, 2. Randomized lazy, 3. Deterministic lazy, 4. Eager
N_{max} is 64/fragments may have duplicates/synthetic trace	1. Deterministic lazy, 2. Randomized lazy, 3. Eager, 4. Proactive
N_{max} is 64/fragments don't have duplicates/synthetic trace	1. Deterministic lazy, 2. Proactive, 3. Randomized lazy, 4. Eager

We assumed that data objects are stored as erasure encoded fragments, such that any $M = 8$ distinct fragments ensure object reconstruction, and originally $N = 32$ distinct fragments are stored in the network. The encoding scheme used however allowed $N_{max} = 32/64$ unique fragments for each object. The results we discuss below are for $T_{dl} = 16$ and corresponding parameters for other strategies (summarized in Table 2) which were in turn determined by conducting numerous experiments to explore the parameter space. The experiments were run for 500 scaled time units repeated ten times to ascertain that the observed results are consistent. However the results presented are from one instance of such experiments, both because the variance across multiple runs of the experiments was marginal, and also to avoid clutter in the plots. The total peer population used in the experiments comprised of 2000 homogeneous peers and 4000 objects were encoded and placed on online peers using the random placement strategy at the start of the experiments.

5 Results

A different maintenance strategy may be suitable depending on the peer's membership dynamics or other factors like the choice of garbage collection mechanism, as well as depending on which metrics are more important than others for the users. In the discussion below, bandwidth is measured in terms of the number of fragments. The overall performance of the different strategies in different scenarios considering all the evaluation metrics is summarized in Table 3 and explained next.

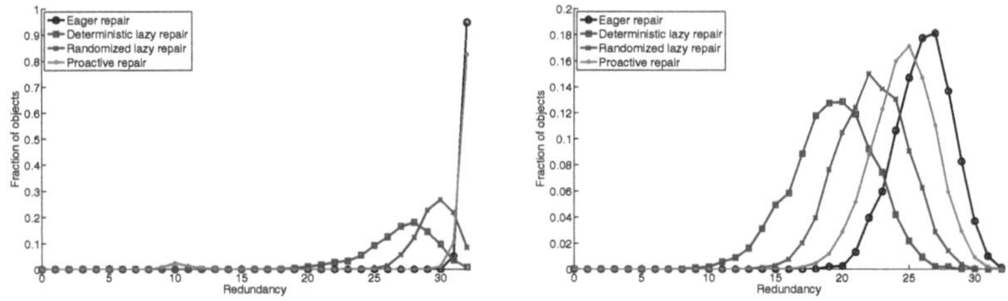

(a) Time 173 (b) Time 243

Fig. 3. Probability distribution of live fragments. N_{max} is 32 and fragments has duplicates. (for Skype trace data).

5.1 Using Skype Trace

To comprehensively understand the behavior of each maintenance and garbage collection strategy, we report on three representative time points from the Skype trace to study - trough at time 173 and peak at time 200 which represent temporary steady states in the peer population with least and most number of online peers (Figure 2(a)) and at time 243 corresponding to correlated departure of many peers. We also studied the system at other time points where the total peer population is transient and the system behavior is somewhere between the system's behavior during the troughs and peaks. These are not reported here due to space constraint and lack of any extra insights.

N_{max} is 32 and fragments may have duplicates. The fact that one fragment may have multiple duplicates makes the system more robust and all objects remain available during the whole period of the experiment. Nevertheless we first consider object availability. Figure 3 shows the probability distribution of distinct live fragments using different strategies at time 173 and time 243. In the long run, the proactive strategy generates a lot of extra redundancy to make it more robust against failures. The general trend from figure 3 is that the eager repair and proactive repair maintain more redundancy than the randomized lazy repair, while the deterministic lazy repair has the least redundancy, making the system vulnerable. However notice that at time 173, ironically for the proactive approach, a small fraction of objects have much smaller number of fragments (a hump around ten fragments), making the system vulnerable. The hump occurs because at each time point each peer can only generate $\mathcal{B} = 5$ fragments at most, so proactive approach can not repair all the objects at once. Thus, unlike in reactive strategies where there are no artificial bandwidth limits, the proactive strategy, by capping bandwidth at each user to smoothen system-wide bandwidth usage which in itself is a desirable property, limits the system's ability to respond and recover fast.

Lower the percentage of fragments with more than one duplicate is, i.e. no wastage for duplicates, the better the performance of the corresponding strategy is in terms of storage space and bandwidth consumption. Referring to figure 4(a)

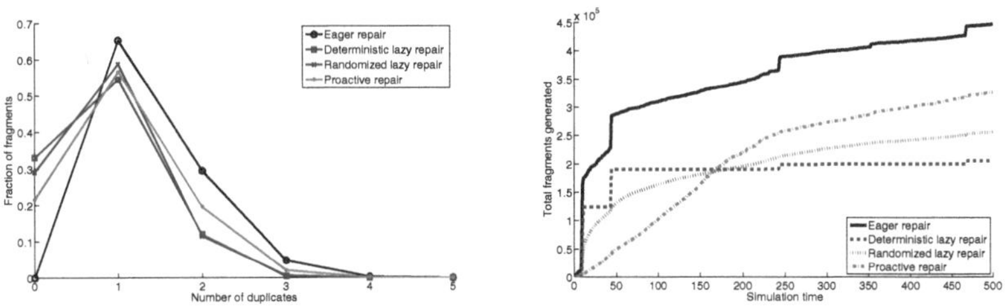

(a) Prob. distribution of duplicates at time 243 (b) Cumulative number of fragments

Fig. 4. N_{max} is 32 and fragments may have duplicates (for Skype trace data)

we see that the lazy repair strategies are the most efficient. Figure 4(b) shows the cumulative number of fragments generated over time. Observe that for eager repair and deterministic lazy repair, there are several spikes in bandwidth usage (manifested as steps since we show the cumulative number of fragments), which may overwhelm the network traffic. In contrast, bandwidth usage of proactive repair is the smoothest. Randomized lazy repair provides a good compromise because its overall bandwidth usage is modest (less than that of proactive or eager approaches) and its bandwidth usage is much smoother than that of other *reactive* strategies. Note that if the system considers only smoothness of the bandwidth usage then proactive repair wins, while in terms of total bandwidth usage, deterministic lazy repair outperformed all others in this scenario, but by making the system vulnerable.

N_{max} is 32 and fragments don't have duplicates. From figure 5(a) we can see that when correlated failures occur, for deterministic lazy repair, 8 objects were lost (the objects that have less than 8 fragments), while the other three strategies all perform better and similar to each other. In terms of aggregate bandwidth usage and the smoothness (figure 5(b)), similar trends can be seen as in the previous scenario, where the randomized lazy repair strategy provides a good trade-off.

N_{max} is 64 and fragments may have duplicates. In this scenario, all the maintenance strategies maintain 100% object availability (Figure 6(a)) at all times. So we conclude that when N_{max} is 64 and multiple duplicates for each live fragment are allowed in the system, all the strategies are robust enough from the viewpoint of object availability, even though, again deterministic lazy repair is the most vulnerable, followed by the eager approach, while proactive strategy is the most robust followed by the randomized lazy approach.

Figure 6(b) shows the cumulative number of fragments generated during the experiment. Eager and deterministic lazy approaches are the most efficient in terms of total bandwidth usage, however the usage itself is spiky (and also recall that they make the system vulnerable), while the proactive strategy consumes

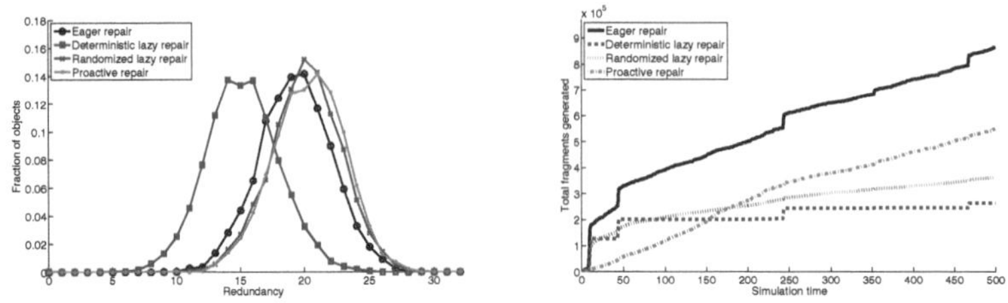

(a) Prob. distribution of live fragments at time 243 (b) Cumulative number of fragments

Fig. 5. N_{max} is 32 and fragments don't have duplicates (for Skype trace data)

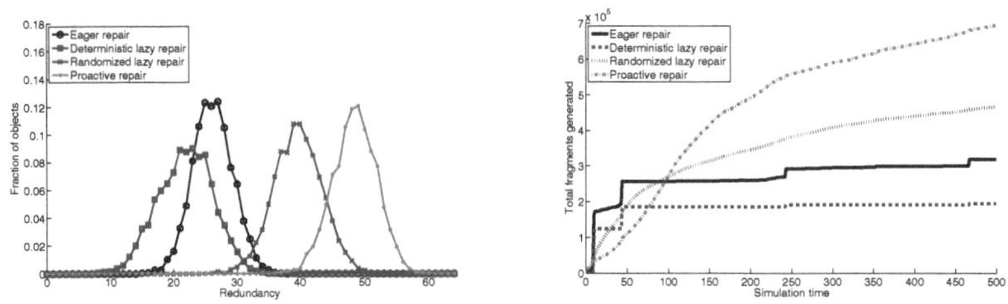

(a) Prob. distribution of live fragments at time 243 (b) Cumulative number of fragments

Fig. 6. N_{max} is 64 and fragments may have duplicates (for Skype trace data)

the most bandwidth, but smoothly. In terms of storage utilization, randomized lazy repair has least duplicates thus is the most efficient.

N_{max} is 64 and fragments don't have duplicates. This scenario is representative of the situation where rateless codes are used, such that no duplicate fragments are created to start with. The proactive strategy in this scenario is also likely to resemble best the way it has been implemented in Tempo [9].

Figure 7(a) shows the comparison of probability distribution of live fragments using different strategies after correlated failures at time 243. In this scenario, deterministic lazy repair can not ensure 100% object availability (1 object was lost). Likewise, the overall conclusions from figure 7 are similar to those observed in the previous scenarios that the randomized lazy strategy provides a good trade-off.

Figures 4(b), 5(b), 6(b) and 7(b) indicate that when N_{max} is 32 and duplicates of fragments are allowed, the bandwidth usage is less in comparison to the scenarios when larger diversity (N_{max} is 64) of distinct fragments are allowed, or when duplicates are not allowed.

5.2 Using Synthetic Data

We also generate synthetic trace (Figure 2(b)) to evaluate the system in presence of only temporary churn, that is when there are no permanent departures and

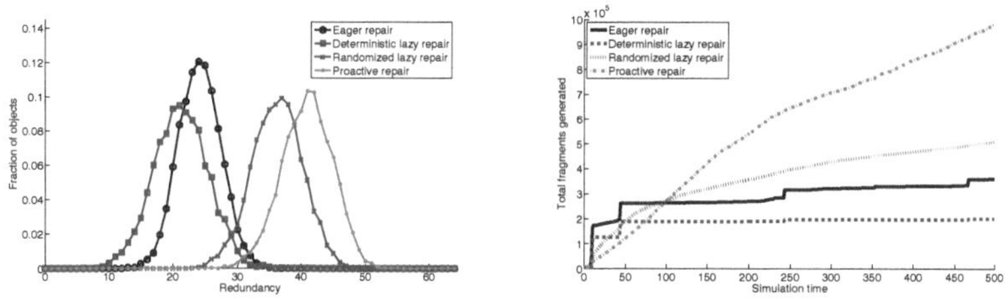

(a) Prob. distribution of fragments at time 243 (b) Cumulative number of fragments

Fig. 7. N_{max} is 64 and fragments don't have duplicates (for Skype trace data)

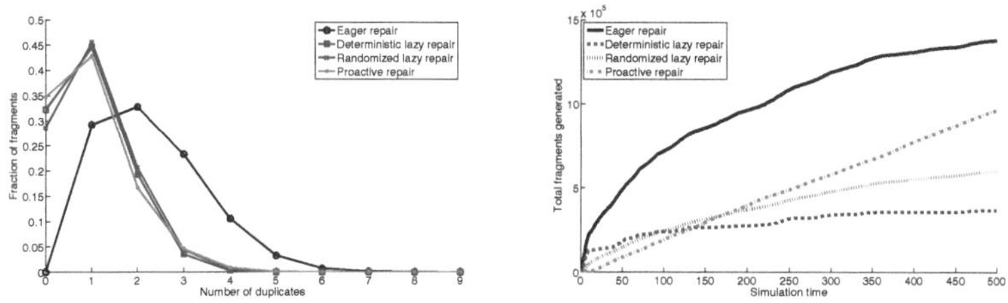

(a) Prob. distribution of duplicates at time 118 (b) Cumulative number of fragments

Fig. 8. N_{max} is 32 and fragments may have duplicates (using synthetic data)

all the objects should stay durable in the long run. We choose a trough (at time 118) and a peak (at time 140) of the curve shown in Figure 2(b).

N_{max} is 32 and fragments may have duplicates. Figures 8(a) and 8(b) show that eager repair wastes much more storage space and bandwidth. All the other mechanisms have similar storage space utilization, however among them the proactive strategy has the smoothest but most bandwidth consumption, while the deterministic lazy repair has the least bandwidth consumption, but its usage is not smooth.

N_{max} is 32 and fragments don't have duplicates. Similar to the previous scenario, eager repair wastes more fragments than the other strategies, which all perform well. The proactive strategy has smoothest and least bandwidth usage and is thus a clear winner for this scenario.

N_{max} is 64 and and fragments may have duplicates. Even though object availability is retained, as opposed to the last scenario, all strategies perform very differently in terms of bandwidth usage (figure 9(b)). Notice that in the previous scenario, even if bandwidth was available, proactive strategy would not have used it simply because N_{max} was low. With a higher N_{max} too much bandwidth is wasted by the proactive strategy. Observe in figures 9(a) that in contrast, the

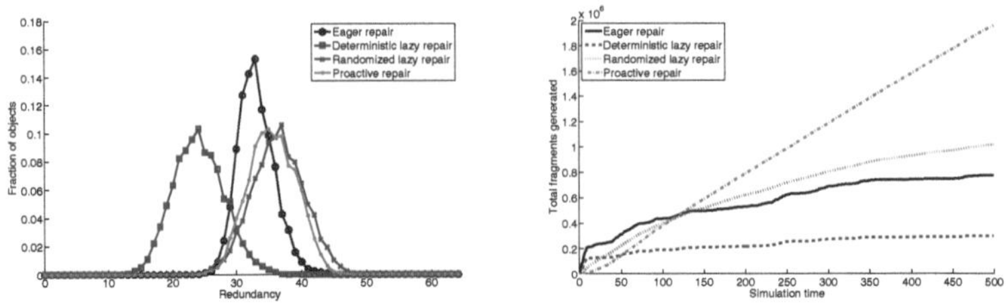

(a) Time 118 (b) Cumulative number of fragments

Fig. 9. N_{max} is 64 and and fragments may have duplicates (using synthetic data)

randomized strategy provides comparable (even better) redundancy at a much lower and relatively smooth bandwidth usage. Even the eager strategy maintains a modest redundancy, and uses even lower amount of bandwidth, but in a spiky manner. The deterministic lazy approach has significantly less bandwidth consumption, though the usage is somewhat spiky and the system is relatively more vulnerable to any further failures, still it has adequate redundancy, making it the best choice in this case.

N_{max} is 64 and and fragments don't have duplicates. In this scenario, deterministic lazy repair strategy requires significantly less bandwidth in comparison to the other strategies, and still maintains modest level of redundancy. Randomized lazy repair and proactive strategies provide better redundancy but at a much higher bandwidth cost, while the eager strategy consumes further more bandwidth for arguable improvement in redundancy.

The synthetic data modeled only temporary churn, and had dramatic effect on the relative standings of the different maintenance strategies. Deterministic lazy repair being the biggest gainer, outperforming other strategies in several scenarios. Also, similar to the experiments using Skype trace, even with artificial data we observe that a moderate diversity of encoded fragments (lower N_{max}) and allowing duplicates of these fragments is the best garbage collection strategy in terms of bandwidth usage.

6 Conclusion

We charted out the various performance metrics typically used in evaluating P2P storage system's performance, and conducted a comprehensive study of existing redundancy maintenance mechanisms, taking into account various aspects including churn and garbage collection mechanism – an issue overlooked in prior works. Our exploration of the various evaluation metrics is novel and also provides a more objective and comprehensive framework to compare P2P storage systems. The only subjective result of the paper is the "overall" ranking, where we consider all the metrics to be of comparable importance. System designers can use our current results as a guide to choose their system design and parameters accordingly. In conclusion, the randomized lazy strategy provides a good overall trade-off under many diverse scenarios based on various performance metrics. In terms of bandwidth usage, allowing fragment duplicates, and using a relatively smaller diversity of distinct fragments (lower N_{max}) turns out to be the most efficient garbage collection strategy. That was so far unexplored and is a good news for P2P storage systems designers because the simplest garbage collection strategy turns out to be the best.

A tangible output of this work is our modular P2P storage system simulator. An interesting extension of the work will be to automatically decide the ranking of the strategies for any arbitrary weightage one may give to the different evaluation metrics. "How do strategies that adapt the design space parameters during the system's lifetime in order to better adapt to changing environment or changing user requirements behave?" is another open ended issue that needs further investigation.

Acknowledgment

This work has been partly supported by the HP Labs Innovation Research Program research grant and A*Star SERC Grant No: 0721340055.

References

1. Kubiatowicz, J., Bindel, D., Chen, Y., Eaton, P., Geels, D., Gummadi, R., Rhea, S., Weatherspoon, H., Weimer, W., Wells, C., Zhao, B.: Oceanstore: An architecture for global-scale persistent storage. In: Proceedings of ACM ASPLOS. ACM, New York (2000)
2. Clarke, I., Miller, S.G., Sandberg, O., Wiley, B.: Protecting free expression online using Freenet. IEEE Internet (2002)
3. Dabek, F., Kaashoek, M.F., Karger, D., Morris, R., Stoica, I.: Wide-area cooperative storage with CFS. In: Proceedings of the 18th ACM Symposium on Operating Systems Principles, SOSP 2001 (2001)
4. AG, C.: (2008), `http://www.wuala.com/`
5. Bhagwan, R., Tati, K., Cheng, Y.C., Savage, S., Voelker, G.M.: Total recall: system support for automated availability management. In: Proceedings of the 1st Symposium on Networked Systems Design and Implementation (2004)
6. Haeberlen, A., Mislove, A., Druschel, P.: Glacier: highly durable, decentralized storage despite massive correlated failures. In: NSDI 2005: Proceedings of the 2nd Symposium on Networked Systems Design & Implementation (2005)
7. Inc., C.: (2007), `http://www.cleversafe.org/dispersed-storage`
8. Datta, A., Aberer, K.: Internet-scale storage systems under churn – a study of the steady-state using markov models. In: Proceedings of the Sixth IEEE International Conference on Peer-to-Peer Computing, Washington, DC, USA (2006)
9. Andreas, E.S., Haeberlen, A., Dabek, F., gon Chun, B., Weatherspoon, H., Morris, R., Kaashoek, M.F., Kubiatowicz, J.: Proactive replication for data durability. In: Proceedings of the 5th Int'l Workshop on Peer-to-Peer Systems, IPTPS (2006)
10. Bhagwan, R., Savage, S., Voelker, G.: Understanding availability. In: Kaashoek, M.F., Stoica, I. (eds.) IPTPS 2003. LNCS, vol. 2735. Springer, Heidelberg (2003)

11. Wu, D., Tian, Y., Ng, K.W., Datta, A.: Stochastic analysis of the interplay between object maintenance and churn. Elsevier Journal of Computer Communications, Special Issue on Foundations of Peer-to-Peer Computing (2008)
12. Rhea, S., Eaton, P., Geels, D., Weatherspoon, H., Zhao, B., Kubiatowicz, J.: Pond: The Oceanstore prototype. In: Proceedings of the USENIX Conference on File and Storage Technologies, FAST (2003)
13. Weatehrspoon, H., Chun, B.G., So, C., Kubiatowicz, J.D.: Long-term data maintenance: A quantitative approach. Technical Report UCB/CSD-05-1404, UC Berkeley (2005)
14. Williams, C., Huibonhoa, P., Holliday, J., Hospodor, A., Schwarz, T.: Redundancy management for p2p storage. In: Proceedings of the Seventh IEEE International Symposium on Cluster Computing and the Grid (2007)
15. Weatherspoon, H., Kubiatowicz, J.: Erasure coding vs. Replication: A quantitative comparison. In: Druschel, P., Kaashoek, M.F., Rowstron, A. (eds.) IPTPS 2001. LNCS, vol. 2429, p. 328. Springer, Heidelberg (2002)
16. Guha, S., Daswani, N., Jain, R.: An Experimental Study of the Skype Peer-to-Peer VoIP System. In: Proceedings of The 5th IPTPS (2006)
17. Godfrey, B.: http://www.cs.berkeley.edu/~pbg/availability/

Model Checking Coalition Nash Equilibria in MAD Distributed Systems

Federico Mari[1], Igor Melatti[1,⋆], Ivano Salvo[1], Enrico Tronci[1], Lorenzo Alvisi[2], Allen Clement[2], and Harry Li[2]

[1] Dep. of Computer Science, University of Rome "La Sapienza"
Via Salaria 113, 00198 Roma, Italy
{mari,melatti,salvo,tronci}@di.uniroma1.it

[2] Dep. of Computer Science, University of Texas at Austin
1 University Station C0500, Austin, Texas, USA
{lorenzo,aclement,harry}@cs.utexas.edu

Abstract. We present two OBDD based model checking algorithms for the verification of Nash equilibria in finite state mechanisms modeling *Multiple Administrative Domains* (MAD) distributed systems with possibly colluding agents (*coalitions*) and with possibly faulty or malicious nodes (Byzantine agents). Given a finite state mechanism, a *proposed protocol* for each agent and the *maximum sizes* f for Byzantine agents and q for agents collusions, our model checkers return PASS if the proposed protocol is an ε-f-q-Nash equilibrium, i.e. no coalition of size up to q may have an interest greater than ε in deviating from the proposed protocol when up to f Byzantine agents are present, FAIL otherwise. We implemented our model checking algorithms within the NuSMV model checker: the first one *explicitly* checks equilibria for each coalition, while the second represents *symbolically* all coalitions. We present experimental results showing their effectiveness for moderate size mechanisms. For example, we can verify coalition Nash equilibria for mechanisms which corresponding normal form games would have more than 5×10^{21} entries. Moreover, we compare the two approaches, and the explicit algorithm turns out to outperform the symbolic one. To the best of our knowledge, no model checking algorithm for verification of Nash equilibria of mechanisms with coalitions has been previously published.

1 Introduction

Cooperative services are increasingly popular distributed systems in which nodes (agents) belong to *Multiple Administrative Domains* (MAD). Thus in a MAD distributed system each node owns its resources and there is no central authority owning all system nodes. Examples of MAD distributed systems include Internet routing [13,23], wireless mesh routing [18], file distribution [8], archival storage [19], cooperative backup [2,9,17].

⋆ Corresponding author: Igor Melatti. Tel.: +39 06 4991 8431 Fax: +39 8541842.

R. Guerraoui and F. Petit (Eds.): SSS 2009, LNCS 5873, pp. 531–546, 2009.

In traditional distributed systems, nodes may deviate from their specifications (*Byzantine nodes*) because of bugs, hardware failures, faulty configurations, or even malicious attacks. In MAD systems, nodes may also deviate because their administrators are *rational*, i.e. selfishly intent on maximizing their own benefits from participating in the system (*selfish nodes*). For example, selfish nodes may change arbitrarily their protocol if that is at their advantage. *Byzantine-Altruistic-Rational* (BAR) protocols provide a realistic model for MAD systems.

Showing that a protocol P for a MAD distributed system satisfies a given specification φ entails two tasks. First, we need to show that P satisfies the given property when all rational nodes follow the protocol *exactly*. Second, we need to show that all rational nodes do, in fact, follow the protocol *exactly*.

As for the first task, well known model checking techniques (e.g. see [6] for a survey) are available to verify that a system satisfies a given property despite the presence of a limited number of Byzantine nodes. It suffices, as usual, to model Byzantine nodes with nondeterministic automata.

As for the second task, this is usually accomplished by proving that no rational agent has an incentive in deviating from the proposed protocol. This is done by proving that the proposed protocol is a *Nash equilibrium* (e.g. see [13,4]).

A symbolic model checking algorithm to automatically verify that a given protocol is a Nash eaquilibrium for a given MAD distributed system has been presented in [20]. However the model checker presented in [20] only addresses the case in which agents do not collude. On the other hand, it is well known from game theory that coalitions of agents may have an advantage in deviating even when no single agent may get any advantage by deviating alone (e.g. see [15]). For example, this is the case for the gossip protocol presented in [16] which is a Nash equilibrium when agents do not collude (no coalitions) and instead is no longer a Nash equilibrium when *large enough* coalitions are allowed.

The above state of affairs motivates the goal of this paper: designing a model checking algorithm to verify if a given protocol is a Nash equilibrium for a MAD distributed system when coalitions up to a given size are allowed.

Our contribution. In Sect. 2 we show how a MAD distributed system with coalitions of players can be modeled as a *Coalition Schema*, that is a suitable synchronous product of *Finite State Machines*. This framework extends *Finite State Mechanisms* presented in [20] which do not account for coalitions.

In Sect. 3 we define the game induced by a Coalition Schema, and in Sect. 4 we give a formal definition of the property we want to verify: ε-f-q-Nash. Intuitively, a mechanism is ε-f-q-Nash if no coalition of size up to q of rational agents has an interest greater than $\varepsilon > 0$ (along the lines of, e.g. [12,14]) in deviating from the *proposed protocol* when there are at most f Byzantine agents (along the lines of [11]). Sufficient conditions to verify ε-f-q-Nash property are given in Theor. 1.

In Sect. 5 we present a verification algorithm that given a coalition schema $\mathcal{Q}$, our desired precision $\delta > 0$ and $(\varepsilon,\ f,\ q)$ as above, returns: PASS if the given mechanism is indeed a $(\varepsilon\ +\ \delta)$-f-q-Nash equilibrium for $\mathcal{Q}$, FAIL otherwise.

From a mathematical point of view, given a coalition schema $\mathcal{Q}$ and a coalition Q, we can build a mechanism $\mathcal{M}_Q$ in which the coalition is just one of the agents. As a consequence, a first approach (that we call *explicit*) to verify that a mechanism is ε-f-q-Nash consists of adapting the symbolic algorithm in [20] to check that $\mathcal{M}_Q$ is a Nash equilibrium for all Q, such that $0 < |Q| \leq q$. If $\mathcal{Q}$ has n players, following this approach entails calling $\mathcal{O}(n^q)$ times a variation of the algorithm in [20] (more specifically, $\sum_{k=1}^{q} \binom{n}{k}$).

To overcome this exponential growth, we propose an alternative approach (that we call *symbolic*) by extending the algorithm in [20] so as to represent symbolically (i.e. using OBDDs [3]) all mechanisms $\mathcal{M}_Q$, where Q is a coalition of size at most q. We implemented our algorithm on top of NuSMV [22] using ADDs (*Arithmetic Decision Diagrams*) [10] to manipulate real valued rewards.

Finally, in Sect. 6 we present experimental results showing effectiveness of our verification algorithm on moderate size mechanisms. For example (Tab. 1 in Sect. 6), within 30 hours using 5GB of RAM we can verify Nash equilibria for mechanisms with 16 agents and coalitions of size up to 2 (i.e. 136 possible coalitions). This corresponds to find Nash equilibria for 136 games each with a normal form of more than 5×10^{21} entries.

Moreover, we compare explicit and symbolic approach performances. To this aim, we note two facts. First, our symbolic approach involves the introduction of auxiliary variables to properly perform the maximin computations required by our algorithm. Second, real valued nodes in ADDs make usual OBDD subtree sharing less effective. As a result, even if the symbolic approach should be asymptotically better, the explicit implementation outperforms the symbolic one in mechanisms we deal with, both in running time and memory usage (Tabs. 1 and 2 in Sect. 6).

Related works. Design of mechanisms for rational agents has been widely studied (e.g. [23,21,5]) as well as the impact of collusions (e.g. [15]). Design methods for BAR protocols have been investigated in [1,16,7,11] .

We differ from such works since our focus here is on automatic verification of Nash equilibria for finite state BAR systems rather than on designing principles for them. The paper closer to ours is [20] where a symbolic algorithm for checking Nash equilibria in mechanisms has been presented. We note however that [20] does not address coalitions.

Summing up, to the best of our knowledge, no model checking algorithm for the automatic verification of Nash equilibria of finite state mechanisms with coalitions has been previously proposed.

2 Coalitions Model

In this section, we present our framework to model protocols. Finite state protocols are modeled via *Finite State Mechanisms*, which suitably extend the usual definition of the synchronous parallel composition of finite state transition systems. The notion of *Coalition Schema* (Sect. 2.2) extends the definition of Mechanism in [20] by specifying the reward function and the discount factor for each possible coalition (i.e. for each subset of players). Indeed, a Coalition Schema represents a class of Mechanisms (Sect. 2.3).

2.1 Basic Notions

We denote with $\mathbb{B}$ the set $\{0,1\}$ of boolean values (0 for *false* and 1 for *true*). We denote with $[n]$ the set $\{1,\ldots,n\}$. The set of subsets of X (with cardinality at most k) will be denoted by $\mathcal{P}(X)$ ($\mathcal{P}_k(X)$).

We denote an n-tuple of objects (of any kind) in boldface, e.g. $\boldsymbol{x}$. Unless otherwise stated we denote with x_i the i-th element of the n-tuple $\boldsymbol{x}$, $\boldsymbol{x_{-i}}$ the $(n-1)$-tuple $\langle x_1,\ldots,x_{i-1},x_{i+1},\ldots,x_n\rangle$, and with $\langle \boldsymbol{x_{-i}}, b\rangle$ the n-tuple $\langle x_1,\ldots,x_{i-1},b,x_{i+1},\ldots,x_n\rangle$. Given a set $Q\subseteq[n]$, we denote the tuple $\langle \boldsymbol{x}_j\rangle_{j\in Q}$ with $\boldsymbol{x}_Q$ and the tuple $\langle \boldsymbol{x}_j\rangle_{j\notin Q}$ with $\boldsymbol{x}_{-Q}$.

2.2 Coalition Schema

Definition 1 (Coalition Schema). *An n players (agents)* coalition schema $\mathcal{Q}$ *is a tuple $\langle \boldsymbol{S},\boldsymbol{I},\boldsymbol{A},\boldsymbol{B},\boldsymbol{T},h,\beta\rangle$ which elements are defined as follows.*

$\boldsymbol{S}=\langle S_1,\ldots,S_n\rangle$ *is an n-tuple of nonempty finite sets (of* local states*). The* state space *of $\mathcal{M}$ is the set (of* global states*)* $S=\prod_{i=1}^n S_i$.

$\boldsymbol{I}=\langle I_1,\ldots,I_n\rangle$ *is an n-tuple of nonempty sets (of* local initial states*) s.t. $I_i\subseteq S_i$. The set of* global initial states *is* $I=\prod_{i=1}^n I_i$.

$\boldsymbol{A}=\langle A_1,\ldots,A_n\rangle$ *is an n-tuple of nonempty finite sets (of* local actions*). The set of* global actions *(i.e. n-tuples of local actions) is $A=\prod_{i=1}^n A_i$. The set of* i-opponents actions *is* $A_{-i}=\prod_{j=1,j\neq i}^n A_j$.

$\boldsymbol{B}=\langle B_1,\ldots,B_n\rangle$ *is an n-tuple of functions s.t., for each $i\in[n]$, $B_i: S\times A_i\times S_i\to\mathbb{B}$. Function B_i models the* transition relation *of agent i, i.e. $B_i(\boldsymbol{s},a,s')$ is true iff agent i can move from (global) state $\boldsymbol{s}$ to (local) state s' via action a. We require B_i to be* serial *(i.e. $\forall \boldsymbol{s}\in S\ \exists a\in A_i\ \exists s'\in S_i$ s.t. $B_i(\boldsymbol{s},a,s')$ holds) and* deterministic *(i.e. $B_i(\boldsymbol{s},a,s')\wedge B_i(\boldsymbol{s},a,s'')$ implies $s'=s''$). We write $B_i(\boldsymbol{s},a)$ for $\exists s'\ B_i(\boldsymbol{s},a,s')$. That is, $B_i(\boldsymbol{s},a)$ holds iff action a is allowed in state $\boldsymbol{s}$ for agent i.*

$\boldsymbol{T}=\langle T_1,\ldots,T_n\rangle$ *is an n-tuple of functions s.t., for each $i\in[n]$, $T_i: S\times A_i\to\mathbb{B}$. We require T_i to satisfy the following properties: 1) $T_i(\boldsymbol{s},a)$ implies $B_i(\boldsymbol{s},a)$; 2) (*nonblocking*) for each state $\boldsymbol{s}\in\boldsymbol{S}$ there exists an action $a\in A_i$ s.t. $T_i(\boldsymbol{s},a)$ holds.*

$h:\mathcal{P}([n])\times\boldsymbol{S}\times\boldsymbol{A}\to\mathbb{R}$ is a function that for each set $Q\subseteq[n]$, for each state $\boldsymbol{s}$ and action $\boldsymbol{a}$, gives the reward $h(Q,\boldsymbol{s},\boldsymbol{a})$ for the coalition *Q.*

$\beta:\mathcal{P}([n])\to\mathbb{R}$ is a function returning for coalition $Q\subseteq[n]$ a value $\beta(Q)\in(0,1)$. We call $\beta(Q)$ the discount factor of coalition Q.

The transition relation B_i models the *underlying* behavior for agent i, that is all possible behaviors of a Byzantine agent or possible choices of a rational one. On the other hand, function T_i models the prescribed behavior (*proposed protocol*) for agent i, i.e. the behavior of *obedient* (or *altruistic*, following [1,16]) agents. For any set Y of Byzantine and rational players such that all players not in Y are altruistic, the dynamic of the system is modeled by the transition relation $BT_{\mathcal{Q}}$ given in the following definition.

Definition 2. *Let $\mathcal{Q} = \langle \boldsymbol{S}, \boldsymbol{I}, \boldsymbol{A}, \boldsymbol{T}, \boldsymbol{B}, h, \beta \rangle$ be an n players coalition schema. We define $BT_{\mathcal{Q}} : \mathcal{P}([n]) \times \boldsymbol{S} \times \boldsymbol{A} \times \boldsymbol{S} \to \mathbb{B}$ as follows: $BT_{\mathcal{Q}}(Y, \boldsymbol{s}, \boldsymbol{a}, \boldsymbol{s}') = \bigwedge_{i=1}^{n} BT_i(Y, \boldsymbol{s}, a_i, s'_i)$, where*

$$BT_i(Y, \boldsymbol{s}, a_i, s'_i) = \begin{cases} B_i(\boldsymbol{s}, a_i, s'_i) & \text{if } i \in Y \\ B_i(\boldsymbol{s}, a_i, s'_i) \wedge T_i(\boldsymbol{s}, a_i) & \text{otherwise.} \end{cases}$$

We write BT for $BT_{\mathcal{Q}}$ when $\mathcal{Q}$ is understood from the context.

2.3 Mechanism

Coalitions are subsets of players that together act as a single rational player. This means that all players in a coalition aim at maximizing the *coalition reward.* This leads to the definition of *mechanism* (with coalitions).

Definition 3 (Mechanism). *A mechanism $\mathcal{M}$ is a pair $\langle \mathcal{Q}, P \rangle$, where $\mathcal{Q}$ is an n players coalition schema, and $P = \{Q_1, \ldots, Q_m\}$ is a partition of $[n]$ (thus each Q_i is a coalition).*

Remark 1. We can recover the definition of mechanism in [20] as a particular case of Def. 3, when all coalitions are singletons, i.e. $P = \{\{1\}, \ldots, \{n\}\}$, $h_i(\boldsymbol{s}, \boldsymbol{a}) = h(\{i\}, \boldsymbol{s}, \boldsymbol{a})$ is the reward of player i and $\beta_i = \beta(\{i\})$ is the discount factor of player i.

Remark 2. Given an n players mechanism $\mathcal{M} = \langle \mathcal{Q}, P \rangle$, where P is $\{Q_1, \ldots, Q_m\}$, there exists an equivalent m players mechanism $\hat{\mathcal{M}}$ with only singleton coalitions. The mechanism $\hat{\mathcal{M}}$ is defined as follows: $\hat{\mathcal{M}} = \langle \hat{\mathcal{Q}}, \hat{P} \rangle$, where $\hat{P} = \{\{1\}, \ldots, \{m\}\}$ and the coalition schema $\hat{\mathcal{Q}} = \langle \hat{\boldsymbol{S}}, \hat{\boldsymbol{I}}, \hat{\boldsymbol{A}}, \hat{\boldsymbol{T}}, \hat{\boldsymbol{B}}, \hat{h}, \hat{\beta} \rangle$ is defined as follows. The set of players of $\hat{\mathcal{Q}}$ is $[m]$. The set of states is $\hat{\boldsymbol{S}} = \langle \hat{S}_1, \ldots, \hat{S}_m \rangle$, where $\hat{S}_i = \prod_{j \in Q_i} S_j$. The set of initial states is $\hat{\boldsymbol{I}} = \langle \hat{I}_1, \ldots, \hat{I}_m \rangle$, where $\hat{I}_i = \prod_{j \in Q_i} I_j$. The set of actions is $\hat{\boldsymbol{A}} = \langle \hat{A}_1, \ldots, \hat{A}_m \rangle$, where $\hat{A}_i = \prod_{j \in Q_i} A_j$. If $\boldsymbol{s} = \langle s_1, \ldots, s_n \rangle \in \boldsymbol{S}$ then $\hat{\boldsymbol{s}} = \langle \boldsymbol{s}_{Q_1}, \ldots, \boldsymbol{s}_{Q_m} \rangle \in \hat{\boldsymbol{S}}$. If $\boldsymbol{a} = \langle a_1, \ldots, a_n \rangle \in \boldsymbol{A}$ then $\hat{\boldsymbol{a}} = \langle \boldsymbol{a}_{Q_1}, \ldots, \boldsymbol{a}_{Q_m} \rangle \in \hat{\boldsymbol{A}}$. The underlying behavior of player i is $\hat{B}_i(\hat{\boldsymbol{s}}, \boldsymbol{a}_{Q_i}, \boldsymbol{s}'_{Q_i}) = \bigwedge_{j \in Q_i} B_j(\boldsymbol{s}, a_j, s_j)$. The proposed protocol for player i of $\hat{\mathcal{Q}}$ is $\hat{T}_i(\hat{\boldsymbol{s}}, \boldsymbol{a}_{Q_i}) = \bigwedge_{j \in Q_i} T_j(\boldsymbol{s}, a_j)$. The discount and reward functions for player i of $\hat{\mathcal{Q}}$ are: $\hat{\beta}(\{i\}) = \beta(Q_i)$ and $\hat{h}(\{i\}, \hat{\boldsymbol{s}}, \hat{\boldsymbol{a}}) = h(Q_i, \boldsymbol{s}, \boldsymbol{a})$.

Since our goal is checking that a given protocol is a Nash equilibrium with respect to *any coalition* of size at most q, we will be working, most of the time, using coalition schemas (Def. 1) rather than mechanisms (Def. 3). Finding a way (Sect. 5) to effectively represent coalition schemas is indeed one of our main contributions.

Without loss of generality, in what follows, we focus on mechanisms $\mathcal{M} = \langle \mathcal{Q}, P \rangle$, with at most one coalition of size greater than 1. That is, partitions P have the form $\{Q, \{j_1\}, \ldots, \{j_{m-1}\}\}$, with $|Q| \geq 1$. By abuse of notation, we denote such kind of partitions with the set of players $Q \subseteq [n]$ forming the non-singleton coalition.

Example 1 (Case Study 1). This case study presents a very simple scenario inspired by peer-to-peer streaming services. Ideally, $n \in \mathbb{N}$ agents have to collaborate to broadcast information in order to maintain a high-quality service. When an agent broadcasts information, it incurs a cost $c \in \mathbb{R}$. All agents have a profit $g \in \mathbb{R}$ if they collaborate and the number of collaborative agents exceeds a threshold pn, where $p \in (0, 1)$ is a real parameter. Otherwise the reward is 0. The set S_i of agent i local states is $\{0, 1\}$. The underlying behavior B_i of each agent $i \in [n]$ is depicted in Fig. 1: each agent in state 0 may choose whether to broadcast information (action *broadcast* which corresponds to the *proposed protocol* T_i) or do nothing (action *sleep*).

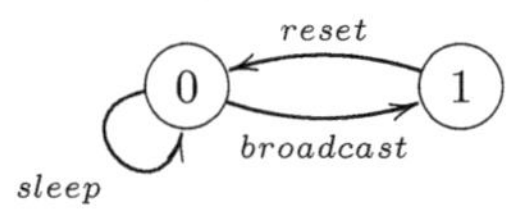

Fig. 1. Underlying behavior B_i for agent i

Following the intuition that members of a coalition may broadcast information only to each other, the reward for a coalition Q is $g|Q|$ if at least pn agents (out of n) and at least $r|Q|$ ($r \in (0, 1)$) agents in the coalition have performed action *broadcast*. This last condition models the fact that a large enough number of agents must collaborate inside the coalition to maintain a high-quality service.

Codifying action *broadcast* with 1 and *sleep* with 0, we give the following formal definition of the reward function h (in state 1, 0 and 1 both codify action *reset*). Defining $f(Q, \boldsymbol{s}, \boldsymbol{a})$ as:

$$f(Q, \boldsymbol{s}, \boldsymbol{a}) = \begin{cases} g|Q| & \text{if } (\sum_{i \in [n]} s_i \geq pn) \wedge (\sum_{i \in Q} s_i \geq r|Q|) \\ 0 & \text{otherwise} \end{cases}$$

the reward function h is $h(Q, \boldsymbol{s}, \boldsymbol{a}) = f(Q, \boldsymbol{s}, \boldsymbol{a}) - c \sum_{i \in Q} \bar{s}_i a_i$.

3 Coalition Schemas as Games

A coalition schema $\mathcal{Q}$ induces a game that has all feasible paths as possible outcomes. The set of feasible paths depends on the $BT_{\mathcal{Q}}$ transition relation given in Def. 2. As a consequence, it depends on a set of players Y that may behave accordingly to the underlying behavior, whereas agents not in Y follow the proposed protocol. The set Y models both Byzantine and rational agents.

In the rest of this section, we assume an n players coalition schema $\mathcal{Q} = \langle \boldsymbol{S}, \boldsymbol{I}, \boldsymbol{A}, \boldsymbol{T}, \boldsymbol{B}, h, \beta \rangle$ and a set of agents $Y \subseteq [n]$ to be given.

Paths. A *path* in ($\mathcal{Q}$, Y) (or simply a *path* when ($\mathcal{Q}$, Y) is understood from the context) is a (finite or infinite) sequence $\pi = \boldsymbol{s}(0)\boldsymbol{a}(0)\boldsymbol{s}(1)\ldots\boldsymbol{s}(t)\boldsymbol{a}(t)\boldsymbol{s}(t+1)\ldots$ where, for each t, $\boldsymbol{s}(t)$ is a global state, $\boldsymbol{a}(t)$ is a global action and $BT(Y, \boldsymbol{s}(t), \boldsymbol{a}(t), \boldsymbol{s}(t+1))$ holds. The *length* $|\pi|$ of a path π is the number of global actions in π. If π is infinite we write $|\pi| = \infty$.

In order to extract the t-th global state and the t-th global action from a given path π, we define $\pi^{(s)}(t) = \boldsymbol{s}(t)$ and $\pi^{(a)}(t) = \boldsymbol{a}(t)$. To extract actions of a set of players Q of size q, we denote with $\pi_Q^{(a)}(t)$ the q-tuple of actions $a_Q(t)$ at stage t of the set of agents Q and with $\pi_{-Q}^{(a)}(t)$ the actions $\boldsymbol{a}_{-Q}(t)$ at stage t of all agents not in Q.

For each set of agents $Q \subseteq [n]$, the *value* of a path π is $v(Q,\pi) = \sum_{t=0}^{|\pi|-1} \beta(Q)^t h\left(Q, \pi^{(s)}(t), \pi^{(a)}(t)\right)$. Note that for any path π and set of agents $Q \subseteq [n]$ the *path value* $v(Q,\pi)$ is well defined also when $|\pi| = \infty$ since the series $\sum_{t=0}^{\infty} \beta(Q)^t h\left(Q, \pi^{(s)}(t), \pi^{(a)}(t)\right)$ converges for all $\beta(Q) \in (0,1)$.

Given a path π and a non-negative integer $k \leq |\pi|$ we denote with $\pi|_k$ the *prefix* of π of length k, i.e. the finite path $\pi|_k = \boldsymbol{s}(0)\boldsymbol{a}(0)\boldsymbol{s}(1)\ldots\boldsymbol{a}(k-1)\boldsymbol{s}(k)$ and with $\pi|^k$ the *tail* of π, i.e. the path $\pi|^k = \boldsymbol{s}(k)\boldsymbol{a}(k)\boldsymbol{s}(k+1)\ldots\boldsymbol{s}(t)\boldsymbol{a}(t)\boldsymbol{s}(t+1)\ldots$.

We denote with $\text{Path}_k(\boldsymbol{s}, Y)$ the set of all feasible paths of length k starting at $\boldsymbol{s}$, when Y is the set of rational/Byzantine agents. Formally, $\text{Path}_k(\boldsymbol{s}, Y) = \{\pi \mid \pi \text{ is a path in } (\mathcal{Q}, Y) \text{ and } |\pi| = k \text{ and } \pi^{(s)}(0) = \boldsymbol{s}\}$. Since we aim to verify that a given protocol is robust with respect to all coalitions of size at most q and all sets of Byzantine agents of size at most f, we introduce the notation $\text{Path}_k(\boldsymbol{s}, f, q)$ to denote the set of all paths of length k feasible with respect to all sets of Byzantine agents of cardinality at most f and all coalitions of size at most q. Formally, $\text{Path}_k(\boldsymbol{s}, f, q) = \bigcup_{|Z| \leq f, 0<|Q|\leq q, Z\cap Q=\varnothing} \text{Path}_k(\boldsymbol{s}, Z \cup Q)$. Unless otherwise stated, in the following we omit the subscript or superscript horizon when it is ∞. For example we write $\text{Path}(\boldsymbol{s}, Y)$ for $\text{Path}_\infty(\boldsymbol{s}, Y)$.

Let $W \subseteq [n]$ be a set of agents. A *path* π in $(\mathcal{Q}, Y)$ is said to be W-*altruistic* if for all $t < |\pi|$, and for all $i \in W$, $T_i(\pi^{(s)}(t), \pi_i^{(a)}(t))$ holds. Note that if $W \cap Y = \varnothing$, all paths in $\text{Path}_k(\boldsymbol{s}, Y)$ are W-altruistic, that is, agents in W behave accordingly to the proposed protocol.

Strategies. As usual in a game theoretical setting, we need to distinguish a player actions (i.e. local actions) from those of its opponents. More in general, we need to distinguish actions of players in a coalition Q from those of players not in Q. This leads to the notion of strategy.

A *strategy* σ for a coalition Q is a (finite or infinite) sequence of actions tuples for the set of players Q. The *length* $|\sigma|$ of σ is the number of actions tuples in σ (thus if $|\sigma| = 0$, the strategy is empty). Let $\sigma = \boldsymbol{a}_0 \ldots \boldsymbol{a}_t \ldots$ be a strategy for coalition Q. We denote with $\sigma(t)$ the t-th action in σ, that is $\boldsymbol{a}_t$. Strategy σ *agrees* with a path π (notation $\pi \simeq^Q \sigma$) if $|\sigma| = |\pi|$ and for all $t < |\sigma|$, $\sigma(t) = \pi_Q^{(a)}(t)$. Given a path π, the strategy (of length $|\pi|$) for a coalition Q associated to π will be denoted by $\sigma(\pi, Q) = \pi_Q^{(a)}(0)\pi_Q^{(a)}(1)\ldots\pi_Q^{(a)}(t)\ldots$.

For any set of agents $Y \subseteq [n]$ the set of Y-*feasible strategies* of length k for a coalition Q in state $\boldsymbol{s}$ is: $\text{Strat}_k(\boldsymbol{s}, Q, Y) = \{\sigma(\pi, Q) \mid \pi \in \text{Path}_k(\boldsymbol{s}, Y)\}$. Our definition of feasible strategy essentially corresponds to the usual one in multi-stage games: global states implicitly represent the sequence of actions in previous periods, i.e. histories. In contrast with the game theoretical model, histories are partitioned into a finite number of equivalence classes, represented as mechanism states.

As for paths, a strategy $\sigma \in \text{Strat}_k(\boldsymbol{s}, Q, Y)$ is said to be Q-*altruistic* if $Q \cap Y = \varnothing$. If $\sigma = a_0 a_1 \ldots a_{k-1} a_k a_{k+1} \ldots$, we use the notations $\sigma|_k = a_0 a_1 \ldots a_{k-1}$ and

$\sigma|^k = a_k a_{k+1}\ldots$ to denote, respectively, the k-prefix and the tail of σ. The set of paths that agree with a set of strategies Σ for a coalition Q is defined as $\text{Path}(\boldsymbol{s}, Q, Y, \Sigma) = \{\pi \in \text{Path}_k(\boldsymbol{s}, Y) \mid \exists \sigma \in \Sigma.\ k = |\sigma| \wedge \pi \simeq^Q \sigma\ \}$. When Σ is the singleton $\{\sigma\}$, we simply write $\text{Path}(\boldsymbol{s}, Q, Y, \sigma)$.

Given a set of Byzantine agents $Z \subseteq [n] \setminus Q$, the *guaranteed outcome* (or the *value*) of a strategy σ in state $\boldsymbol{s}$ for coalition Q is the minimum value of paths that agree with σ. Formally: $v(\boldsymbol{s}, Q, Z, \sigma) = \min\{v(Q, \pi) \mid \pi \in \text{Path}(\boldsymbol{s}, Q, Z \cup Q, \sigma)\}$. The *value* of a state $\boldsymbol{s}$ at horizon k for coalition Q is the guaranteed outcome of the best strategy of length k starting at state $\boldsymbol{s}$. Formally: $v^k(\boldsymbol{s}, Q, Z) = \max\{v(\boldsymbol{s}, Q, Z, \sigma) \mid \sigma \in \text{Strat}_k(\boldsymbol{s}, Q, Z \cup Q)\}$. The *guaranteed outcome of the proposed protocol* in a state $\boldsymbol{s}$ at horizon k for coalition Q is the outcome of the worst Q-altruistic strategy of length k starting at state $\boldsymbol{s}$. Formally, $u^k(\boldsymbol{s}, Q, Z) = \min\{v(\boldsymbol{s}, Q, Z, \sigma) \mid \sigma \in \text{Strat}_k(\boldsymbol{s}, Q, Z)\}$.

The finite horizon value of a state can be effectively computed by using a dynamic programming approach (Prop. 1). This is one of the main ingredients of our verification algorithm (Sect. 5). We omit proofs because of lack of space.

Proposition 1. *Let $\mathcal{Q} = \langle \boldsymbol{S}, \boldsymbol{I}, \boldsymbol{A}, \boldsymbol{T}, \boldsymbol{B}, h, \beta \rangle$ be an n players coalition schema, $\boldsymbol{s} \in S$, and $Q, Z \subseteq [n]$ such that $Z \cap Q = \varnothing$. The state values at horizon k for coalition Q can be computed as follows:*

$$v^0(\boldsymbol{s}, Q, Z) = u^0(\boldsymbol{s}, Q, Z) = 0;$$

$$v^{k+1}(\boldsymbol{s}, Q, Z) = \max_{\boldsymbol{a}_Q \in A_Q} \min_{\boldsymbol{a}_{-Q} \in A_{-Q}} \{\ h(Q, \boldsymbol{s}, \langle \boldsymbol{a}_Q, \boldsymbol{a}_{-Q} \rangle) + \beta(Q)\, v^k(\boldsymbol{s}', Q, Z) \mid BT(Z \cup Q, \boldsymbol{s}, \langle \boldsymbol{a}_Q, \boldsymbol{a}_{-Q} \rangle, \boldsymbol{s}')\};$$

$$u^{k+1}(\boldsymbol{s}, Q, Z) = \min_{\boldsymbol{a}_Q \in A_Q} \min_{\boldsymbol{a}_{-Q} \in A_{-Q}} \{\ h(Q, \boldsymbol{s}, \langle \boldsymbol{a}_Q, \boldsymbol{a}_{-Q} \rangle) + \beta(Q)\, u^k(\boldsymbol{s}', Q, Z) \mid BT(Z, \boldsymbol{s}, \langle \boldsymbol{a}_Q, \boldsymbol{a}_{-Q} \rangle, \boldsymbol{s}')\}$$

Example 2. In the Coalition Schema described in Ex. 1, a rational player may deviate from the proposed protocol if it thinks that the service is compromised because the number of Byzantine agents is larger than $(1-p)n$. In such a case a rational player choose the action *sleep*, which ensures a reward 0, rather than the action *broadcast*, which leads to the negative reward $c \sum_{k \in \mathbb{N}} \beta^{2k}$. A coalition Q may deviate by using the following strategy: some agents broadcast information to other coalition members only, and some agents do not broadcast anything. In such a case, threshold $r|Q|$ of collaborative agents is required to guarantee the service for coalition members. As a consequence, the coalition Q deviates whenever $\lceil r|Q| \rceil < |Q|$. As expected, if all agents are in the coalition, the protocol is not Nash, but the reward of each agent increases (the well known *price of anarchy* phenomenon[15]).

4 Verifying Coalition Nash Equilibria

In this section, we introduce the notion of ε-f-q-Nash coalition schema, in order to verify protocol robustness with respect to coalitions of colluding players. Theor. 1 gives sufficient conditions to check that a coalition schema is ε-f-q-Nash and, together with Prop. 1, it proves the correctness of our verification (Alg. 1 in Sect. 5).

In [20] it is introduced a notion of ε-f-Nash equilibrium for a mechanism. Intuitively, a mechanism $\mathcal{M}$ is ε-f-Nash, if, as long as the number of Byzantine agents is no more than f (e.g. see [11]), no rational agent has an interest greater than ε (e.g. see [12,14]) in deviating from the proposed protocol in $\mathcal{M}$. ε-f-q-Nash extends this notion by requiring that no coalition of rational agents of size at most q has an interest greater than ε in deviating from the proposed protocol.

Definition 4 (ε-f-q-Nash). *Let $\mathcal{Q} = \langle \boldsymbol{S}, \boldsymbol{I}, \boldsymbol{A}, \boldsymbol{T}, \boldsymbol{B}, h, \beta \rangle$ be an n players coalition schema. Let $0 \neq q \in [n]$, $f \leq n - q$, $\varepsilon > 0$ and $Q \subseteq [n]$ be a coalition with $0 < |Q| \leq q$.*

The coalition schema $\mathcal{Q}$ is ε-f-Nash for coalition Q iff $\forall Z \in \mathcal{P}_f([n] \setminus Q)$, $\forall \boldsymbol{s} \in I$, we have:

$$u(\boldsymbol{s}, Q, Z) + \varepsilon \geq v(\boldsymbol{s}, Q, Z).$$

$\mathcal{Q}$ is ε-f-q-Nash if it is ε-f-Nash for all coalitions Q such that $0 < |Q| \leq q$.

In general, Nash equilibria for infinite-horizon games cannot be verified by only looking at finite strategies, since they are not necessarily limits of equilibria of the corresponding finite horizon games (e.g. see [14], or Ex. 1 in [20] for an example in mechanism scenario). However, if we assume that agents cannot distinguish between small variations (ε) in their payoffs, then we can verify Nash equilibria for infinite-horizon games by only looking at *long enough* finite strategies. This has motivated the introduction of ε-Nash equilibria for infinite-horizon games and also motivates Def. 4. Indeed, our definition of ε-0-1-Nash yields the usual definition of ε-Nash equilibria (e.g., see Sect. 4.8 of [14]). We observe that the notion of ε-f-1-Nash is equivalent to the notion of ε-f-Nash in [20]. Thus if a mechanism is ε-f-q-Nash for $q \geq 1$, it is also ε-f-Nash.

ε-f-q-Nash property cannot be verified using finite approximations if for some $Q, Z, \boldsymbol{s}$, $|\, v^k(\boldsymbol{s}, Q, Z) \;-\; u^k(\boldsymbol{s}, Q, Z)\,|$ converges to ε (see Ex. 2 in [20]). However we may get arbitrarily close to this result as stated by the following theorem.

Theorem 1. *Let $\mathcal{Q} = \langle \boldsymbol{S}, \boldsymbol{I}, \boldsymbol{A}, \boldsymbol{T}, \boldsymbol{B}, h, \beta \rangle$ be an n players coalition schema. Let $0 \neq q \in [n]$, $f \leq n - q$, $\varepsilon > 0$ and $\delta > 0$. Furthermore, for each coalition Q, such that $0 < |Q| \leq q$ let:*

1. $M_Q = \max\{|h(Q, \boldsymbol{s}, \boldsymbol{a})| \mid \boldsymbol{s} \in S' \text{ and } \boldsymbol{a} \in A'\}$.
2. $E(Q, k) = 5\, \beta(Q)^k \frac{M_Q}{1-\beta(Q)}$.
3. $\Delta(Q, k) = \max\{v^k(\boldsymbol{s}, Q, Z) \;-\; u^k(\boldsymbol{s}, Q, Z) \mid \boldsymbol{s} \in I, Z \in \mathcal{P}_f([n] \setminus Q)\}$.
4. $\varepsilon_1(Q, k) = \Delta(Q, k) - 2E(Q, k)$.
5. $\varepsilon_2(Q, k) = \Delta(Q, k) + 2E(Q, k)$.

Let k be such that for all coalitions Q such that $0 < |Q| \leq q$, $4E(Q, k) < \delta$ holds. Then we have:

1. *If for all $Q \in \mathcal{P}_q([n])$ $\varepsilon \geq \varepsilon_2(Q, k) > 0$ then $\mathcal{Q}$ is ε-f-q-Nash.*
2. *If there is $Q \in \mathcal{P}_q([n])$ such that $0 < \varepsilon \leq \varepsilon_1(Q, k)$ then $\mathcal{Q}$ is not ε-f-q-Nash. Of course in such a case a fortiori $\mathcal{Q}$ is not 0-f-q-Nash.*

3. *If for all* $Q \in \mathcal{P}_q([n])$, $\varepsilon_1(Q,k) < \varepsilon$ *and there exists* $Q' \in \mathcal{P}_q([n])$ *s.t.* $\varepsilon < \varepsilon_2(Q',k)$ *then* $\mathcal{Q}$ *is* $(\varepsilon+\delta)$-f-q-*Nash.*

Proof. The proof skeleton is essentially the following: first, we show that values of path prefixes converge to the path values, i.e. $v(Q,\pi|_k) \to v(Q,\pi)$. Then, we show that values of strategy prefixes converge to the strategy values, i.e. $v(\boldsymbol{s},Q,Z,\sigma|_k) \to v(\boldsymbol{s},Q,Z,\sigma)$, and finally we show that state values are limits of their finite approximations, i.e. $v^k(\boldsymbol{s},Q,Z) \to v(\boldsymbol{s},Q,Z)$. Bounds in convergence proofs give us the effective test to check if a mechanism is ε-f-q-Nash.

5 Verification Algorithms

Resting on Theor. 1 in this section we present our algorithm (Alg. 1) to verify that a given protocol is ε-f-q-Nash.

Alg. 1 is implemented on top of the NuSMV [22] model checker. Since states ($\boldsymbol{s}$), actions ($\boldsymbol{a}$) and sets of agents (Q,Z) are finite, we can represent them with boolean arrays. We represent boolean functions (such as the transition relations T, B and $BT_{\mathcal{Q}}$) using OBDDs [3] and real valued functions (such as coalition rewards $\lambda \boldsymbol{s}\ Q\ Z.\ u^t(\boldsymbol{s},Q,Z)$ and $\lambda \boldsymbol{s}\ Q\ Z.\ v^t(\boldsymbol{s},Q,Z)$) using ADDs (*Arithmetic Decision Diagrams*) as implemented in the CUDD [10] package.

As usual in OBDD based computations, we represent functions with the expressions defining them. For the sake of clarity, we will present Alg. 1 using a set theoretic notation for sets, predicates and functions over sets, but for example statements in lines 2, 5, 7, and 11 have to be interpreted as ADD manipulations.

The algorithm first computes the number of iterations k needed to reach the precision threshold desired by the user (line 1). Then, for each iteration t from 0 to k, it computes the state value $v^t(\boldsymbol{s},Q,Z)$ and the proposed protocol guaranteed outcome $u^t(\boldsymbol{s},Q,Z)$ using Prop. 1 (lines 2–10). After computing state values, Alg. 1 finds the ADD representing the maximum difference between state values and the guaranteed outcome of the proposed protocol as a function of Q. This is the $\Delta(Q)$ in line 11, representing the best gain that a coalition Q may have in deviating from the proposed protocol. This corresponds to point 3 of Theor. 1. Then in line 12, $\varepsilon_1(Q)$ and $\varepsilon_2(Q)$ are computed as in points 4 and 5 of Theor. 1 respectively. Finally, lines 13–15 determine which statement among 1–3 of Theor. 1 holds.

Verifying that a coalition schema $\mathcal{Q}$ is ε-f-q-Nash requires checking that the hypotheses in statements 1-3 of Theor. 1 hold for all coalitions of size at most q. The number of such coalitions is $\sum_{j=1}^{q}\binom{n}{j}$. We implement two versions of Alg. 1

- in the *explicit* version, the loop in lines 3-10 is performed $\sum_{j=1}^{q}\binom{n}{j}$ times in order to compute state values $u^t(\boldsymbol{s},Q,Z)$ and $v^t(\boldsymbol{s},Q,Z)$ for any possible coalition Q of size at most q. This is almost equivalent to build the single player mechanism $\mathcal{M}_Q$ for each coalition Q and to run (a variation of) the single player verification algorithm presented in [20] with $\mathcal{M}_Q$ as input;
- in the *symbolic* version, all computations are parametric with respect to all mechanisms $\mathcal{M}_Q$: in such a case, line 3 has to be read as a logical predicate rather that an iterative **for** loop.

Algorithm 1. *CheckNash.* Checking if a mechanism is ε-f-q-Nash.

Input: mechanism $\mathcal{Q}$, int f, int q, double ε, δ
Output: (FAIL) or (PASS with a threshold)

1: Let k be such that $\forall Q\ 0 < |Q| \leq q \Rightarrow [4\,E(Q,k) < \delta]$
2: $v^0(\boldsymbol{s}, Q, Z) \leftarrow 0$, $u^0(\boldsymbol{s}, Q, Z) \leftarrow 0$, where $\boldsymbol{s} \in \boldsymbol{S}, Q \in \mathcal{P}_q([n])$ and $Z \in \mathcal{P}_f([n] \setminus Q)$
3: **for all** $Q \in \mathcal{P}_q([n]) \setminus \{\varnothing\}$ **do**
4:     **for** $t = 1$ **to** k **do**
5:         $v^t(\boldsymbol{s}, Q, Z) \leftarrow \max\limits_{a_Q \in A_Q} \min\limits_{\boldsymbol{a}_{-Q} \in A_{-Q}} [h_i(Q, \boldsymbol{s}, \langle a_Q, \boldsymbol{a}_{-Q}\rangle) + \beta(Q) v^{t-1}(\boldsymbol{s}', Q, Z)]$,
6:             where $BT(Q \cup Z, \boldsymbol{s}, \langle a_Q, \boldsymbol{a}_{-Q}\rangle, \boldsymbol{s}'), \boldsymbol{s} \in \boldsymbol{S}, Q \in \mathcal{P}_q([n])$ and $Z \in \mathcal{P}_f([n] \setminus Q)$
7:         $u^t(\boldsymbol{s}, Q, Z) \leftarrow \min\limits_{a_Q \in A_Q} \min\limits_{\boldsymbol{a}_{-Q} \in A_{-Q}} [h_i(Q, \boldsymbol{s}, \langle a_Q, \boldsymbol{a}_{-Q}\rangle) + \beta(Q) u^{t-1}(\boldsymbol{s}', Q, Z)]$,
8:             where $BT(Z, \boldsymbol{s}, \langle a_i, \boldsymbol{a}_{-i}\rangle, \boldsymbol{s}'), \boldsymbol{s} \in \boldsymbol{S}, Q \in \mathcal{P}_q([n])$, and $Z \in \mathcal{P}_f([n] \setminus Q)$
9:     **end for**
10: **end for**
11: $\Delta(Q) \leftarrow \max\{v^k(\boldsymbol{s}, Q, Z) - u^k(\boldsymbol{s}, Q, Z) \mid \boldsymbol{s} \in I, Z \in \mathcal{P}_f([n] \setminus Q)\}$, $Q \in \mathcal{P}_q([n])$
12: $\varepsilon_1(Q) \leftarrow \Delta(Q) - 2E(Q)$, $\varepsilon_2(Q) \leftarrow \Delta(Q) + 2E(Q)$, with $Q \in \mathcal{P}_q([n])$
13: **if** $(\exists Q \in \mathcal{P}_q[n]\ [\varepsilon < \varepsilon_1(Q)])$ **return** (FAIL)
14: **if** $(\forall Q \in \mathcal{P}_q[n]\ [\varepsilon_2(Q) < \varepsilon])$ **return** (PASS with ε)
15:     **else return** (PASS with $(\varepsilon + \delta)$)

Symbolic approach should be asymptotically better. However it requires the introduction of auxiliary state and action variables for maximin computations required by Alg. 1 in lines 5 and 7, which turns out to be much more involved and slower. Moreover, ADDs make usual OBDD memory compression via sharing much less effective. As experimental results show in Sect. 6, in our moderate size mechanisms the explicit implementation outperforms the symbolic one, both in running time and in memory usage.

6 Experimental Results

In order to assess effectiveness of our Nash verifier we present experimental results on its usage on two meaningful and scalable case studies inspired by cooperative services. Case study 1 shown in Ex. 1 is designed to be as simplest as possible, in order to test our verification tool on mechanism with a number of agents as greater as possible. In Sect. 6.1 case study 2 is presented, describing a slightly more complex scenario. Finally, Sect. 6.2 describes experimental settings and assesses tool performances.

6.1 Case Study 2

In this case study we present a slightly more complex and subtle scenario. We are given a set $\mathcal{J} = \{0, \ldots, m-1\}$ of m *jobs* and a set $\mathcal{T} = \{0, \ldots, t-1\}$ of t *tasks*. Function $\eta : \mathcal{J} \rightarrow \mathcal{P}(\mathcal{T})$ defines for each job j the set of tasks $\eta(j)$ needed to complete j, and function $\iota : \mathcal{T} \rightarrow \mathcal{P}(\mathcal{J})$ defines for each task t the set of jobs $\iota(t)$, for which t is needed.

Each agent $i \in [n]$ is supposed to work (*proposed protocol*) on a given sequence of (not necessarily distinct) tasks $\mathcal{T}_i = \langle \tau(i,0), \ldots, \tau(i, \alpha(i)-1) \rangle$ starting from $\tau(i,0)$ and returning to $\tau(i,0)$ after task $\tau(i,\alpha(i)-1)$ has been completed. An agent may *deviate* from the proposed protocol by not executing the task. This behavior models many typical scenarios in cooperative services.

An agent incurs a *cost* w by working towards the completion of its currently assigned task. A job is completed if for each task it needs there exists at least one agent that has completed that task. In such a case, each of such agents receives a *reward*. At the end of each *round* a fixed capital C is equally divided among completed jobs. The reward for a job is in turn equally divided among all agents that executed a task needed to complete the job. Note that even if two (or more) agents have completed the same task all of them get a reward. Finally, we set the reward for a coalition Q to be the sum of its component rewards.

Note that, in this scenario, a coalition may deviate from the proposed protocol in the following way: if two or more players in the coalition are assigned to the same task, it is sufficient that only one of them works. Moreover, if there is a large enough number of Byzantine players, jobs completion is not guaranteed. This may induce a rational player not to work, in order to avoid the cost w.

6.2 Results

In this section we summarize the experimental results we obtain by running the Nash verification algorithm Alg. 1 in both its implementations (i.e. explicit and symbolic) on our case studies.

Results on Case Study 1. We instantiate the class of mechanisms related to our first case study by fixing $p = \frac{3}{4}$, $g = 4$ and $r = \frac{1}{2}$. We then perform our experiments both with the explicit and the symbolic implementation of Alg. 1, by increasing the number of agents n, the coalition maximum size q and the Byzantine agents maximum number b. We set for all coalitions Q, $\beta(Q) = 0.5$.

Results are in Tab. 1. Column meanings in Tab. 1 are as follows. Columns n, q, b show the number of agents, the maximum coalition size, and the maximum number of Byzantine agents. Column **Nash** shows the final verification outcome. In particular, note that the PASS result, in our experiments, always means PASS with ε (case 1 of Theor. 1). Column **CPU expl** (resp., **symb**) shows the computation time in seconds for the explicit (resp. symbolic) implementation. Column **Mem expl** (resp., **symb**) shows the RAM used by the explicit (resp. symbolic) implementation in MBs. Column **BDD expl** (resp., **symb**) shows the number of OBDD/ADD nodes used by the explicit (resp. symbolic) implementation. Finally, column $|\mathcal{P}_q([n])|$ shows the number iterations needed by line 3 of Alg. 1, i.e. $|\mathcal{P}_q([n]) \setminus \{\varnothing\}|$.

Note that "N/A" entries denotes that the corresponding experiment exceeded the available resources, either w.r.t. RAM (needed more than 8 GB) or time (needed more than 3 days). In all experiments we take $\varepsilon = 0.1$ and accuracy $\delta = 0.05$. With such settings the value k in line 1 of Alg. 1 turns out to be at most 15 in all our experiments.

Table 1. Experiments run for the case study of Sect. 1 on a 64-bit Dual Quad Core 3 GHz Intel Xeon Linux PC with 8 GB of RAM

n	q	b	Nash	CPU expl	CPU symb	Mem expl	Mem symb	BDD expl	BDD symb	$\lvert\mathcal{P}_q([n])\rvert$
9	1	3	PASS	2.88e+01	2.82e+03	7.43e+01	1.63e+02	2.59e+05	8.25e+05	9
9	1	4	FAIL	3.03e+01	5.87e+03	7.41e+01	1.63e+02	5.36e+05	7.77e+05	9
9	2	3	PASS	9.26e+01	1.79e+04	7.65e+01	1.64e+02	5.66e+05	1.16e+06	45
9	2	4	FAIL	1.33e+02	3.01e+04	7.54e+01	1.66e+02	2.92e+05	1.67e+06	45
9	3	0	FAIL	1.31e+01	7.73e+02	6.97e+01	1.62e+02	3.91e+05	5.31e+05	129
9	4	0	FAIL	2.25e+01	2.22e+03	7.27e+01	1.63e+02	4.54e+05	3.87e+05	255
9	5	0	FAIL	4.14e+01	6.20e+03	7.61e+01	1.63e+02	5.21e+05	9.30e+05	381
9	6	0	FAIL	7.90e+01	1.03e+04	7.68e+01	1.64e+02	5.95e+05	1.18e+06	465
9	7	0	FAIL	9.01e+01	1.52e+04	7.69e+01	1.63e+02	7.97e+05	1.25e+06	501
9	8	0	FAIL	8.24e+01	1.52e+04	7.69e+01	1.64e+02	7.39e+05	1.45e+06	510
9	9	0	FAIL	8.42e+01	1.58e+04	7.69e+01	1.64e+02	4.55e+05	1.45e+06	511
10	2	3	PASS	2.16e+02	9.21e+04	7.82e+01	5.41e+02	5.79e+05	2.63e+06	55
10	2	4	FAIL	2.70e+02	1.61e+05	8.05e+01	5.45e+02	5.54e+05	3.66e+06	55
11	2	3	PASS	5.97e+02	N/A	8.47e+01	N/A	9.90e+05	2.32e+06	66
16	2	5	FAIL	1.07e+05	N/A	4.48e+03	N/A	7.97e+07	N/A	136
18	2	4	N/A	N/A	N/A	N/A	N/A	N/A	N/A	171

Results on Case Study 2. We instantiate the class of mechanisms related to our second case study as follows. First of all, we take the number n of agents to be greater than or equal to the number t of tasks. Second, we take the number m of jobs to be equal to t. Third, we define $\eta(j)$ (i.e. the set of tasks needed to complete job j) as follows: $\eta(j) = \{j, (j+1) \bmod t\}$. That is, each job requires two tasks and each task participates in two jobs. We take as task sequence for agent i the sequence $\mathcal{T}_i = \langle (i-1) \bmod t, \ldots, t-1, 0, 1, \ldots, ((i-1) \bmod t) - 1\rangle$. In other words, all agents consider tasks with the same order (namely $\langle 0, \ldots, t-1\rangle$). The only difference is that agent i will start its task sequence from task $(i-1) \bmod t$. We set for all coalitions Q, $\beta(Q) = 0.5$. Finally, in order to ease computations we set the cost of working on a task $w = 1440$ and the capital to be divided among completed jobs $C = 4320n$. With the above settings we have the following parameters to be instantiated: n (number of agents), m (number of jobs), q (number of agents in a coalition).

Tab. 2 shows our experimental results on verification of the ε-f-q-Nash property for our case study. Column meanings in Tab. 2 are the same of Tab. 1, with the only addition of column m showing the number of jobs.

In all experiments we take $\varepsilon = 0.1$ and accuracy $\delta = 0.01$. With such settings the value k in line 1 of Alg. 1 turns out to be at most 27 in all our experiments.

Experimental Results Summary. From Tab. 1 and 2 we see that we can effectively handle moderate size mechanisms. Such mechanisms correspond indeed to quite large games. In fact, given a finite horizon k, an n players mechanism can be seen as a game which outcomes are n-tuples $\langle \sigma_1, \ldots, \sigma_n\rangle$ of strategies of

Table 2. Experiments run for the case study of Sect. 6.1 on a 64-bit Dual Quad Core 3 GHz Intel Xeon Linux PC with 8 GB of RAM

n	m	q	b	Nash	CPU expl	CPU symb	Mem expl	Mem symb	BDD expl	BDD symb	$\lvert\mathcal{P}_q([n])\rvert$
4	2	2	0	PASS	1.40e+00	2.74e+00	8.82e+01	8.70e+01	3.99e+05	9.05e+04	10
4	2	4	0	PASS	2.45e+00	4.78e+00	8.82e+01	8.68e+01	8.53e+04	1.14e+05	15
5	2	3	2	FAIL	3.92e+01	2.12e+02	1.14e+02	1.14e+02	2.49e+05	9.27e+05	25
5	2	5	0	PASS	1.36e+01	5.12e+01	1.07e+02	1.14e+02	5.74e+05	6.22e+05	31
6	2	3	3	FAIL	3.33e+02	5.71e+03	1.27e+02	1.87e+02	7.57e+05	1.95e+06	41
6	2	6	0	PASS	8.67e+01	7.61e+02	1.25e+02	1.29e+02	5.68e+05	8.99e+05	63
6	3	1	3	PASS	2.55e+03	4.15e+04	2.57e+02	6.50e+02	2.44e+06	8.19e+06	6
6	3	1	4	FAIL	3.43e+03	5.87e+04	2.71e+02	8.70e+02	2.69e+06	9.77e+06	6
6	3	2	3	PASS	8.96e+03	1.70e+05	2.62e+02	1.70e+03	2.88e+06	1.90e+07	21
6	3	2	4	FAIL	1.04e+04	2.01e+05	2.95e+02	1.75e+03	3.59e+06	4.56e+06	21
6	3	3	0	FAIL	1.23e+03	5.80e+03	1.79e+02	3.64e+02	1.85e+06	4.60e+06	41
6	3	4	0	FAIL	1.88e+03	1.11e+04	1.79e+02	5.11e+02	2.03e+06	6.66e+06	56
6	3	5	0	FAIL	2.20e+03	1.56e+04	1.81e+02	5.27e+02	2.12e+06	6.76e+06	62
6	3	6	0	FAIL	2.28e+03	1.70e+04	1.81e+02	5.34e+02	1.93e+06	9.50e+06	63

length k, where σ_i is the strategy played by agent i. If the underlying behavior of agent i allows two actions for each state, then there are 2^k strategies available for agent i. This would yield a game which normal form has 2^{kn} entries. In the coalition schemas used in Tab. 1, each agent can choose at least among $fib(k)$ (the k-th Fibonacci number) strategies. With n players this yields a normal form game with $fib(k)^n$ entries. If we look at coalitions of size j we have to consider $\binom{n}{j}$ games of size $fib(k)^n$. Since we are considering coalitions of size up to q we are indeed looking at $\sum_{j=1}^{q} \binom{n}{j}$ games of size $fib(k)^n$. For example, with horizon $k = 20$ and $n = 6$ the rows in Tab. 2 with $q = 2$ entail checking Nash equilibria for 21 games each of size $fib(19)^6 = 4181^6 \approx 5 \times 10^{21}$.

For both our case studies, the explicit implementation (in the sense of Sect. 5) outperforms the symbolic one both in RAM and computation time. In particular note that in Tab. 1, for $n = 9, b = 0, q \in [3, 9]$ the number of coalition grows but the symbolic algorithm does not take any advantage of this.

7 Conclusions

We presented two algorithms based on symbolic model checking for verification of Nash equilibria in finite state mechanisms modeling MAD distributed systems with coalitions. The first algorithm, explicitly checks Nash equilibria for any possible coalition within a given size, while the second symbolically represents all coalitions. An experimental comparison shows that the explicit one performs better. Moreover, our experiments show effectiveness of the presented algorithms for moderate size mechanisms. For example, we can handle mechanisms which corresponding normal form games would have more than 5×10^{21} entries.

Future research work include: investigation of more efficient algorithms in order to handle larger size mechanisms, exploiting symmetries in the definition of the mechanism.

References

1. Aiyer, A.S., Alvisi, L., Clement, A., Dahlin, M., Martin, J.-P., Porth, C.: Bar fault tolerance for cooperative services. In: Proc. of SOSP 2005, pp. 45–58. ACM Press, New York (2005)
2. Batten, C., Barr, K., Saraf, A., Trepetin, S.: pStore: A secure peer-to-peer backup system. Technical Memo MIT-LCS-TM-632, Massachusetts Institute of Technology Laboratory for Computer Science (October 2002)
3. Bryant, R.: Graph-based algorithms for boolean function manipulation. IEEE Trans. on Computers C-35(8), 677–691 (1986)
4. Buttyán, L., Hubaux, J.-P.: Security and Cooperation in Wireless Networks - Thwarting Malicious and Selfish Behavior in the Age of Ubiquitous Computing (version 1.5). Cambridge University Press, Cambridge (2007)
5. Chien, S., Sinclair, A.: Convergence to approximate nash equilibria in congestion games. In: Proc. of SODA 2007, pp. 169–178 (2007)
6. Clarke, E.M., Grumberg, O., Peled, D.A.: Model Checking. The MIT Press, Cambridge (1999)
7. Clement, A., Li, H., Napper, J., Martin, J.-P., Alvisi, L., Dahlin, M.: BAR primer. In: Proc. of DSN 2008 (2008)
8. Cohen, B.: Incentives build robustness in bittorrent. In: Kaashoek, M.F., Stoica, I. (eds.) IPTPS 2003. LNCS, vol. 2735. Springer, Heidelberg (2003)
9. Cox, L.P., Noble, B.D.: Samsara: honor among thieves in peer-to-peer storage. In: Proc. of SOSP 2003, pp. 120–132. ACM, New York (2003)
10. CUDD Web Page (2004), `http://vlsi.colorado.edu/~fabio/`
11. Eliaz, K.: Fault tolerant implementation. Review of Economic Studies 69(3), 589–610 (2002)
12. Everett, H.: Recursive games. Contributions to the theory of games. Annals of Mathematical Studies, vol. III, p. 39 (1957)
13. Feigenbaum, J., Sami, R., Shenker, S.: Mechanism design for policy routing. In: Proc. of PODC 2004, pp. 11–20. ACM, New York (2004)
14. Fudenberg, D., Tirole, J.: Game theory. MIT Press, Cambridge (1991)
15. Hayrapetyan, A., Tardos, É., Wexler, T.: The effect of collusion in congestion games. In: Proc. of STOC 2006, pp. 89–98. ACM, New York (2006)
16. Li, H., Clement, A., Wong, E., Napper, J., Roy, I., Alvisi, L., Dahlin, M.: BAR gossip. In: Proc. of OSDI 2006 (2006)
17. Lillibridge, M., Elnikety, S., Birrell, A., Burrows, M., Isard, M.: A cooperative internet backup scheme. In: Proc. of ATEC 2003, p. 3. USENIX Association (2003)
18. Mahajan, R., Rodrig, M., Wetherall, D., Zahorjan, J.: Sustaining cooperation in multi-hop wireless networks. In: Proc. of NSDI 2005, pp. 231–244. USENIX Association (2005)
19. Maniatis, P., Rosenthal, D.S.H., Roussopoulos, M., Baker, M., Giuli, T.J., Muliadi, Y.: Preserving peer replicas by rate-limited sampled voting. In: Proc. SOSP 2003, pp. 44–59. ACM, New York (2003)
20. Mari, F., Melatti, I., Salvo, I., Tronci, E., Alvisi, L., Clement, A., Li, H.: Model checking nash equilibria in mad distributed system. In: Cimatti, A., Jones, R.B. (eds.) Proc. of FMCAD 2008, pp. 85–92. IEEE, Los Alamitos (2008)

21. Nisan, N., Ronen, A.: Algorithmic mechanism design (extended abstract). In: Proc. of STOC 1999, pp. 129–140. ACM, New York (1999)
22. NuSMV Web Page (2006), `http://nusmv.irst.itc.it/`
23. Shneidman, J., Parkes, D.C.: Specification faithfulness in networks with rational nodes. In: Proc. of PODC 2004, pp. 88–97. ACM, New York (2004)

OpenMP Support for NBTI-Induced Aging Tolerance in MPSoCs

Andrea Marongiu[1], Andrea Acquaviva[2], and Luca Benini[1]

[1] DEIS – University of Bologna
Via Risorgimento, 2 – 40136 Bologna, Italy
[2] DAUIN – Politecnico di Torino
Corso Duca Degli Abruzzi, 24 – 10129 Torino, Italy
{a.marongiu,luca.benini}@unibo.it,
{andrea.acquaviva}@polito.it

Abstract. Aging effect in next-generation technologies will play a major role in determining system reliability. In particular, wear-out impact due to Negative Bias Temperature Instability (NBTI) will cause an increase in circuit delays of up to 10% in three years [8]. In these systems, NBTI-induced aging can be slowed-down by inserting periods of recovery where the core is functionally idle and gate input is forced to a specific state. This effect can be exploited to impose a given common target lifetime for all the cores. In this paper we present a technique that allows core-wear-out dependent insertion of recovery periods during loop execution in MPSoCs. Performance loss is compensated based on the knowledge of recovery periods. Loop iterations are re-distributed so that cores with longer recovery are allocated less iterations.

1 Introduction

Embedded multiprocessor systems-on-chips (MPSoCs) fabricated in upcoming nanometer technologies will be increasingly affected by aging mechanisms leading to threshold voltage increase [9] which implies circuit slowdown. As a consequence, guardbands (GB) are inserted to compensate for circuit delay. These guardbands will shrink during core activity until their complete consumption will lead to timing violations. In absence of correction mechanisms, these violations will determine system failure. With respect to single core systems, in multicore platforms an additional reliability issue is that both the initial GB margin and its consumption rate are not uniform across the cores. As a consequence, to prevent the less reliable core to dictate the overall system lifetime, the GB consumption must be equalized as much as possible. At system level, this can be obtained by monitoring the guardband consumption [2,4] and slowing down the aging process of less reliable cores [16].

The strategy to slowdown aging of cores depends on the considered aging effect. The main aging phenomena affecting nanometer devices are Negative Bias Temperature Instability (NBTI) and Hot Carrier Injection (HCI), for which wear-out takes place only during activity periods. In particular, NBTI has gained

R. Guerraoui and F. Petit (Eds.): SSS 2009, LNCS 5873, pp. 547–562, 2009.

much attention from recent research because it is considered a dominant effect [10]. NBTI is due to the dissociation of Si-H bonds along the silicon-oxide interface in presence of a negative bias ($V_{gs} = -V_{dd}$) on PMOS transistors, which causes the generation of traps. These traps lead to the increase in the threshold voltage. Recent studies demonstrate that NBTI will be relevant in forthcoming technologies, leading to up to 10% voltage increase in three year lifetime [8].

The NBTI degradation model is characterized by a recovery effect, caused by the reduction of interface traps when the negative bias is removed. As a result, the threshold voltage decreases. Thus, NBTI-induced aging can be partially compensated by imposing a virtual ground (i.e. a logical "1") to PMOS transistors gates for a certain period of time (the recovery period) where the core is idle from a functional viewpoint. As a result, it is possible to slow-down GB degradation by interleaving core activity with idle periods where the core is placed in a recovery state. The impact of NBTI does not depend on the granularity and distribution of stress/recovery periods but only on their total duration [11]. This allows to efficiently distribute the required idleness with convenient granularity. This can be flexibly tuned to match the characteristics of the workload/programming model chosen to parallelize the target application. The programming model ultimately reflects the features of the underlying hardware platform.

In this paper we consider data-intensive MPSoCs. Aging issues in this kind of platforms can be very critical since they are intensively used during their lifetime, so techniques to hide the effects of aging are desirable. Applications running on these systems focus on a very common data parallel scenario where each core works on a portion of a data structure (e.g. array or matrix) and must synchronize with the others on a barrier. Similar parallelization schemes are typically focused on parallel loops, whose iterations are spread among several concurrent threads. OpenMP is the de-facto standard for such a parallel execution model, and it features a number of MPSoC-suitable implementations [7][12][13][1]. Due to the heterogeneous nature of MPSoCs (i.e. the presence of several non-homogeneous processing units) these implementations are typically OS-less, and the OpenMP runtime environment (RTE) is in full control of all hardware resources. In the OpenMP model, idleness insertion can be managed at the granularity of a single iteration (or chunks of iterations). This choice allows very fine control on the actual duration of idle and active periods, and thus on the entity of stress and recovery phenomena applied to cores.

Idleness insertion impacts workload balancing because of non-uniform GB consumption rates. Starting from a balanced workload distribution, the addition of idleness increases the overall execution time. In barrier-based parallelization schemes, the overall lengthening of the parallel region – hereafter indicated as performance loss – is dictated by the more degraded core (i.e. the one with the longest idle period). This situation is depicted in Figure 1. Residual guard bands are indicated as percentages. Longer idle periods are allocated to processors with smaller GB.

The impact of idleness on loop execution time can be evaluated so that iteration redistribution among the cores can be exploited to minimize it. More

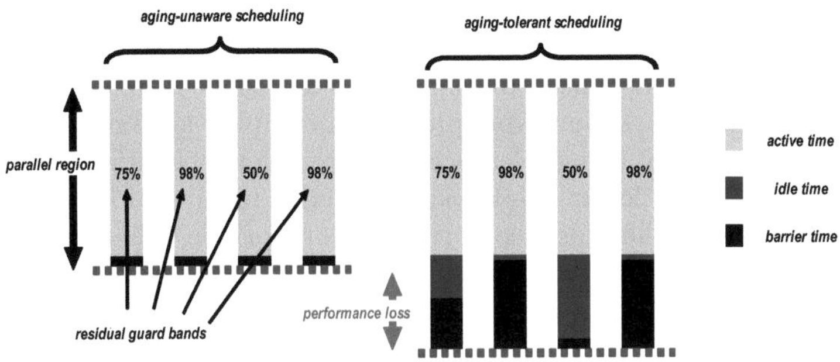

Fig. 1. Performance loss to support aging-tolerant loop parallelization

precisely, performance loss can be compensated by proper re-allocation of workload to cores depending on the idleness distribution. The compiler can allocate less iterations to cores with smaller guard bands (and longer idle periods).

We embedded the workload re-allocation strategy within the GCC (GOMP) compiler. The OpenMP interface has been extended with custom clauses to be coupled with the worksharing directives. These clauses augment the existing static and dynamic parallelization schemes with aging-tolerant scheduling facilities. In a nutshell, the contributions of this paper are the following:

1. The design of a novel compiler level technique for aging tolerance in MPSoCs
2. A work-reallocation policy to minimize the performance impact through compensation of unbalancing introduced by the insertion of idle periods
3. The implementation of the proposed techniques within OpenMP and its validation on a realistic distributed memory MPSoC platform, relying either on static and dynamic scheduling

The paper is organized as follows. In Section 2 we present some background work about aging tolerance techniques, while Section 3 describes the aging model considered in this work. In Section 4 we describe our framework while in Section 5 we show experimental results. Section 6 concludes the paper.

2 Background Work

Aging problems can be tackled at various abstraction levels, ranging from transistor level, architectural and system software level. Software approaches are very attractive because they can exploit workload knowledge to reduce the performance impact of these techniques. A common purpose of various approaches recently proposed is to provide wanted performance and match real-time constraints through statistical scheduling [17] or learning algorithms [18]. In [15] Roberts et al. present a scheduling approach which is aimed at recovering the performance impact due to non-uniform chip degradation. They propose an integer linear programming method to determine an optimal scheduling for streaming applications. Moreover, task migration is also considered as solution to handle the time dependent effect of wear-out. A complete framework, called *Facelift*, performing scheduling and voltage scaling to slow down aging is presented in [16]. It exploits a non linear optimization strategy to find the optimal scheduling.

Comparing to this work, our paper proposes a compiler level strategy, and for this reason we implement aging tolerance at the parallel application level and not at the operating system level. This choice is strongly influenced by the fact that most MPSoCs feature heterogeneous runtime support on different processing tiles. Consequently, typical MPSoC-suitable OpenMP implementations are OS-less. Moreover, our approach reduces the performance hit by playing with loop iteration re-scheduling, which is not possible at the OS-level, where tasks are given. A similar approach is taken by authors of [5]. They propose a variability-aware algorithm that maps computations onto available processors so that each processor runs at its peak frequency rather than simply using chip-wide lowest frequency amongst all cores and highest cache latency. Unlike ours, this technique aims at maximizing performance, but does not cope with wear-out phenomena in any manner. In presence of aging, exercising processors with different degrees of GB consumption at the same rate (i.e. at their peak performance) leads to a situation in which the most degraded core dictates overall system lifetime.

OpenMP implementations for MPSoCs have been presented in [7][12][13]. In [7] the authors deal with implementing parallel tasks in the absence of OS. Authors of [14] face similar problems in using the heterogeneous cores and synchronization support in the Cell BE processor to support OpenMP threads.

Custom extension to the OpenMP API are described in [12][13], but are aimed at enabling parallel execution on DSPs, or to optimize memory allocation exploiting scratchpads [1]. Unlike all those approaches, ours aims at extending the programming model to expose architectural reliability awareness to the compiler. This allows to implement our aging-tolerant policy in the compiler in a manner that is completely invisible to the programmer. This preserves the ease of use of OpenMP, while augmenting it to support aging-related features.

3 Aging Model and Idleness Constraints

Multicore designs in current technologies suffer significant within-die process variation, thus leading to nominally identical processors supporting non-homogeneous maximum frequencies. Furthermore, during processor service life stresses induced on transistors by normal switching activity results in gradually slower critical paths. In order to meet system lifetime constraints, designers add timing guardbands to their designs to absorb any increase in critical path delay. One conservative approach to deal with this source of heterogeneity, which is often employed to simplify the design, is to use a single frequency domain where the slowest core determines the frequency of the whole chip. Moreover, if processors are exercised at a similar rate, the slowest core will consume its own guardband earlier than the others. These effects can strongly impact system lifetime and for this reason an increasing effort is put at the various layers of MPSoC design to detect and compensate them. Designers implemented delay monitors [4,2] spread across the chip that provide degradation information in terms of circuit delay, from which the guardband consumption can be derived. As such, the guardband size provides a upper bound on the allowed ΔV_{th} for each core.

Based on this information, our objective is to equalize GB consumption time among the cores. In principle, we can set a predefined target lifetime, which would be equal for all the cores. In order to achieve a wanted target lifetime, we need to slow down aging rate for less reliable cores (the ones with smaller GB). For NBTI-induced aging, it is possible to slow-down core degradation by imposing idle periods. In this periods, if the core is set into a particular state (recovery state) where the gates of PMOS transistors are tied to a virtual ground (i.e. a logical "1" is applied) the threshold voltage degradation is partially recovered. The increase in V_{th} during the stress phase can be modeled as follows [16]:

$$\Delta V_{th,stress} = A_{NBTI} \cdot t_{ox} \cdot \sqrt{C_{ox}(V_{dd} - V_{th})} \cdot \exp^{(\frac{V_{dd}-V_{th}}{t_{ox}E_0} - \frac{E_a}{kT})} \cdot t_{stress}^{0.25} \tag{1}$$

where t_{stress} is the time under stress, t_{ox} is the oxide thickness and C_{ox} is the gate capacitance per unit area. E_0, E_a and k are constant equal to $0.2V/nm$, $0.13eV$ and $8.6174 \cdot 10^{-5} eV/K$ while A_{NBTI} is a constant dependent on the aging rate. The recovery phase is governed by the following equation:

$$\Delta V_{th} = \Delta V_{th,stress} \cdot (1 - \sqrt{\eta \cdot \frac{t_{rec}}{t_{stress} + t_{rec}}}) \tag{2}$$

where t_{rec} is the time under recovery and η is a constant equal to 0.35. Depending on the guardband value we can compute the maximum ΔV_{th}^i each core i can accommodate before failing. The relationship between ΔV_{th}^i and the guardband value GB^i is given by the following standard switching delay expression:

$$T_s^i = \frac{V_{dd} L_{eff}}{\mu(V_{dd} - V_{th}^i)^\alpha} \tag{3}$$

Now, since $T_s^i = DCP^i + GB^i$ where DCP^i is the initial delay critical path of core i, we can compute the guardband size as a function of the threshold voltage:

$$\Delta V_{th}^i = V_{th}^{init,i} - V_{th}^{stress,i} \tag{4}$$

where $V_{th}^{init,i}$ is the voltage threshold corresponding to the initial critical path delay DCP^i, while $V_{th}^{stress,i}$ is the maximum voltage threshold corresponding to the largest allowed delay (i.e. guardband fully consumed). Thus we can substitute delay expressions into this equation to obtain the maximum allowed voltage increase for each core as a function of its current GB:

$$\Delta V_{th}^{max,i} = f(GB^i) \tag{5}$$

On the other side, Eq. (1) allows to express the voltage increase as a function of the stress and recovery time:

$$\Delta V_{th}^i = f(t_{stress}^i, t_{rec}^i) \tag{6}$$

Combining (1) and (4) and considering a given target lifetime:

$$t_{life} = t^i_{stress} + t^i_{rec} \tag{7}$$

we can compute the amount of recovery time t^i_{rec} needed to consume ΔV^i_{th} in a time t_{life}, the same for all the cores. The recovery time obtained in this way can be used to compute the percentage of idleness I^i to be allocated to maintain the wanted target lifetime:

$$I^i = t^i_{rec}/t_{life}. \tag{8}$$

Cores having larger GBs, whose values can be read from circuit monitors, will be allocated less idleness. Monitors can be implemented either using hardware circuits to measure circuit delays [2] or by monitoring activity (stress) periods and using an analytical model to compute the related circuit delay increase.

The OpenMP extensions we developed leverage this information to perform idleness distribution and iteration allocation at each loop execution to the cores depending on their GB values. We refer to the percentages of idleness needed on different cores to compensate for aging effects as "aging indexes". Aging indexes are computed based on the formulas described above, and can be inspected by the runtime environment to take decisions on workload and idleness distribution. More precisely, we read aging indexes at each loop execution. Based on this feedback, we tune the amount of work on each core by means of a custom partitioning algorithm (see Section 4), and allocate a corresponding recovery period, so that the wanted lifetime is respected.

4 Aging-Aware OpenMP Support Implementation

OpenMP consists of a set of compiler directives, library routines and environment variables that provide a simple means to specify parallel execution within a sequential code. The basic directive, provided for specifying parallel execution within the code is `#pragma omp parallel`. Enclosing a portion of code within the scope of this directive allows the programmer to identify a parallel task, and instructs the compiler to generate code to fork worker threads onto which the parallel task is mapped. The use of this directive is typically coupled with one of the two work-sharing directives, `#pragma omp for` and `#pragma omp sections`. The former enables data parallelism by partitioning the iteration space of a for loop between worker threads, whereas the latter leverages task parallelism. The OpenMP work-sharing model provides means to achieve balanced execution among processors by outlining parallel tasks containing similar amounts of work.

The basic idea of our aging-tolerant policies is that of lengthening the lifetime of degraded cores to match that of the most reliable core, thus meeting expected system service life. This is achieved through explicit insertion of idleness periods, which are interleaved with normal activity. The granularity at which we perform duty cycling (i.e. the duration of active periods) is specified by the use of a particular work-sharing directive. For task parallelism the granularity is that of the task itself, whereas for data parallelism the granularity may be that of a single iteration, or of a chunk of iterations. The compiler inserts time sampling instructions at the beginning and at the end of the work block (with the discussed granularity), then instantiates a call to the custom `omp_sleep` library function passing it the profiled execution time of the work block. The sleep time is a function of the execution time and the aging of the target processor. Information on the aging of each processor is embedded within specific metadata in the custom OpenMP runtime environment (RTE). This "aging index" is as a number between 0 and 1, which expresses the percentage of idleness needed on a core to compensate for its degradation. It can be inspected whenever needed through a call to the custom `omp_get_aging_index` function, which implements the aging model described in Section 3.

The described mechanism efficiently augments OpenMP with an infrastructure for duty cycling. Processors with different aging indexes require different sleep times, thus leading to parallel tasks with non-homogeneous duration and finally implying unbalanced execution. While the balancing issue can be easily addressed by integrating our duty cycling mechanism with the runtime support for dynamic scheduling (see Sec. 4.2), things get more complicated when dealing with static scheduling (see Sec. 4.1). The `schedule(static)` clause is useful when parallelizing loops whose iterations have roughly the same duration, since it affords good balancing with very small scheduling overhead w.r.t. dynamic approaches. Furthermore, smart combination of static scheduling and chunking is the only means provided by the OpenMP API to achieve good data locality. For this reason it is very important to consider static scheduling in our aging-tolerant framework. As described in Section 1 and shown in Figure 1, simply inserting idle periods in presence of static scheduling would lead to very unbalanced overall loop execution time. The barrier implied at the end of the parallel region forces all cores to wait for the less reliable, thus leading to the highest performance degradation.

In the following sections we present custom extensions to the OpenMP API that allow to efficiently address this issue and reduce performance loss.

4.1 Static Scheduling

The simplest algorithm to parallelize a doall loop is that of evenly dividing its iteration space among available worker threads. OpenMP allows to do it with the use of the `schedule(static)` clause combined with the `for` directive: The compiler transforms the loop so that lower and upper bounds are computed locally by each thread, based on the number of concurrent workers and on their IDs. As discussed in the previous section, duty cycling helps in achieving homogeneous guard-band consumption, but introduces imbalance. To achieve load balancing while hiding the effects of aging on system lifetime, we replace the original partitioning algorithm in the compiler with a simple yet effective aging-aware scheduling technique. In what follows the number of iterations (W_i) needed to equalize execution time (T_i) of all the cores is computed.

Let us consider the following parameters:

N	Total loop iterations
M	Number of processors
A_i	Aging index for the i-th core
ΔT	Iteration duration
W_i	Work iterations for i-th core

Overall work time for the i-th core can be expressed like

$$T_{W,i} = \Delta T \cdot W_i \tag{9}$$

Total loop time for processor i is expressed by the formula

$$T_{T,i} = T_{W,i} + T_{S,i} \tag{10}$$

where the sleep time is a function of the active time and the aging index

$$T_{S,i} = (1 - A_i) \cdot T_{W,i} \Rightarrow T_{T,i} = (2 - A_i) \cdot T_{W,i}$$

Loop execution time must be balanced between cores, namely

$$T_{T,i} = T_{T,j} \qquad \forall i, j$$

Sleep times are normalized to that of the less degraded core M, so we consider

$$T_{T,M} = T_{W,M}$$

and express the number of iterations of each slave core as a fraction of the iterations of the master (M) core

$$T_{W,M} = T_{T,i} = (2 - A_i) \cdot T_{W,i} \qquad \forall i \in [1, M)$$

$$W_M \cdot \Delta T = (2 - A_i) \cdot W_i \cdot \Delta T$$

$$W_i = \frac{W_M}{(2 - A_i)} \tag{11}$$

The iterations of the master core can be computed by balancing the iterations

$$\sum_i W_i = N \;\Rightarrow\; W_M + \sum_{i=1}^{M-1} \frac{W_M}{(2 - A_i)} = N$$

which finally leads to

$$W_M = \frac{N}{1 + \sum_{i=1}^{M-1} \frac{1}{(2 - A_i)}} \tag{12}$$

Having W_M we can compute W_i using eq.11.

The aging-aware partitioning algorithm is triggered by the use of the custom `schedule(static_rel)` clause

```
#pragma omp parallel for schedule(static_rel)
  for (i=0; i<N; i++)
    { /* body */ }
```

The compiler has been customized to emit the following parallel code

```
int tid = omp_get_thread_num();
omp_part_iteration_space(N, tid);
int LB = omp_get_lower_bound(tid);
int UB = omp_get_upper_bound(tid);
long start, stop;
  for (i=LB; i<UB; i++)
    {
        start = omp_get_wtick();
        /* body */
        stop = omp_get_wtick();
        omp_sleep(stop-start);
    }
```

Lower and upper bounds for each thread are no longer computed locally, but rather retrieved through calls to the runtime library. Timestamp sampling instructions are inserted to compute the duration of the loop body, which is then passed to the runtime to force the needed amount of idleness.

The `omp_part_iteration_space()` function implements our aging-aware partitioning algorithm. Every thread inspects its aging index, then the master core executes the partitioning algorithm. Slave cores wait on a barrier for lower and upper bounds to be computed for every thread. After this synchronization step, every thread retrieves its chunk of the original iteration space through a call to the custom `omp_get_lower_bound()` and `omp_get_upper_bound()` functions.

The extensions to the OpenMP library (libgomp) are summarized in Tab.1.

4.2 Dynamic Scheduling

Non-uniform duration of different loop iterations can lead to load imbalance issues when using static scheduling schemes. To deal with this problem OpenMP provides a `schedule(dynamic, chunk)` clause. The programmer decides the granularity at which the scheduler is invoked by specifying a chunk size. This parameter represents the number of loop iterations that are folded within a single task. Each thread participating in a dynamically scheduled parallel loop continuously invokes the runtime to obtain the next available work chunk.

When enhancing dynamic scheduling scheme to support duty cycling we no longer need to cope with load balancing issues, since lengthening the execution time of a thread by inserting idle periods has a side effect of having it invoke the scheduler less frequently. More reliable cores will instead increase the number of requests for chunk assignment, thus "stealing" part of the iterations originally assigned to degraded processor. To adapt the framework to support duty cycling one possible solution is that of profiling execution time at chunk granularity. The use of the custom `schedule(dynamic_rel[, chunk])` clause

```
#pragma omp parallel for schedule(dynamic_rel,20)
  for (i=0; i<N; i++)
    { /* body */ }
```

instructs the compiler to generate code that calls custom versions of the library functions for dynamic loop scheduling, namely `GOMP_loop_dynamic_start_rel()` and `GOMP_loop_dynamic_next_rel()`. The scheduling algorithms in these custom functions do not introduce any changes with respect to the original, but

Table 1. API extensions to support aging-tolerant scheduling

`void omp_part_iteration_space (int iterations, int pid)`	Computes lower and upper bound for each thread participating in a parallel loop. Boundaries are computed exploiting our partitioning algorithm and stored in library metadata.
`int omp_get_lower_bound (int pid)`	Returns lower bound for thread pid's iteration space.
`int omp_get_upper_bound (int pid)`	Returns upper bound for thread pid's iteration space.
`GOMP_loop_dynamic_start_rel(...)`	Initializes metadata for aging-aware dynamic scheduling.
`GOMP_loop_dynamic_next_rel(...)`	Dynamically schedules next work chunk in an aging-driven manner.
`int omp_get_wtick (void)`	Returns current timestamp.
`int omp_get_aging_index (int pid)`	Returns current aging index for processor pid.
`int omp_sleep (long cycles)`	Forces wanted idleness on the caller core based on its aging index and on the profiled execution time.

they are enhanced with execution time profiling instructions. The collection of timestamps for execution time profiling at the granularity of a single chunk is performed within these functions. Idleness insertion is forced at every scheduling event, namely every time that a thread queries the runtime for another chunk of iterations to process.

5 Experimental Setup and Results

The MPSoC architectural template that we target in this work is composed by 16 RISC-like processing elements, each featuring private L1 instruction and data caches as well as a scratchpad memory. On-chip shared and private memories are accessed through a shared bus (amba AHB), and synchronization facilities are provided by a hardware semaphore device. We assume all cores to operate at the same frequency. Aging indexes are implemented as special registers that are periodically updated by the aging model, and that can be inspected by the software library.

The proposed aging-tolerant mechanism has been implemented in the GCC 4.3.2 compiler and its support for OpenMP programming (GOMP). The framework relies on a custom implementation for heterogeneous MPSoC platforms [1]. Since accelerators do not run any operating system, the GOMP runtime environment (libgomp) has been re-implemented without pthreads support.

Table 2 lists the benchmarks used to conduct the experiments. We provide four classes of results and plots to highlight:

- **Overhead**: A breakdown of the sources of overhead in our algorithms
- **Idleness**: The precision of our technique in distributing the wanted amount of idleness
- **Balancing**: The load balancing achieved by our partitioning schemes w.r.t. the original application
- **Performance**: The effectiveness of our scheduling policies in minimizing the performance loss due to duty cycling

Table 2. Benchmarks

Benchmark	Source
LU Decomposition (c_lu)	OmpSCR[3]
Loops with dependences (c_loop_dep)	OmpSCR
Jacobi (c_jacobi)	OmpSCR
Computing Π (c_pi)	OmpSCR
Mandelbrot set area (c_mandel)	OmpSCR
Embarassing parallel (ep)	NAS Parallel Benchmarks[6]

For each benchmark we provide results for the following program configurations:

- ***static***: The program is parallelized with the original OpenMP `static` clause. There is no awareness of platform aging at the software level.
- ***static + sleep***: The program is parallelized with the original OpenMP `static` clause, but the framework is aware of system aging, and is augmented with duty cycling. No aging-aware workload distribution policy is enabled, thus leading to worst-case performance loss.
- ***static_rel***: The program is parallelized with the custom `static_rel` clause. Aging-aware loop partitioning takes place.
- ***dynamic***: The program is parallelized with the custom `dynamic_rel` clause to deal with non-uniform duration of loop iterations. Dynamic scheduling of iterations is augmented with duty cycling.

We consider ten different degradation scenarios, namely ten aging index distributions, with worst-case degradation requiring up to 63% idleness. Results are then shown as an average of several program runs. In the following subsections we provide detailed information for each class of results.

5.1 Overhead

Figure 2 shows a breakdown of the considered sources of overhead, namely:

1. *Loop partitioning*: Time taken by the aging-aware partitioning algorithm to compute iteration spaces for every thread
2. *Time sampling*: Overhead due to loop body instrumentation for measuring the duration of iterations
3. *omp_sleep*: Overhead due to computation of idle time (based on profiled active time and aging index) in `omp_sleep` function

For benchmarks ***c_Jacobi***, ***c_Pi***, ***c_mandel*** and ***EP*** the overhead is always very small (under 3%). Parallelizing the main loop in benchmark ***c_LU*** with the `static_rel` clause brings a 9% overhead, which is mainly due to the execution time taken by the partitioning algorithm. This happens because this benchmark features a two-level loop nest, with the innermost nest being parallelized. Since this nest scans the rows of an upper-triangular matrix, decreasing amounts of work are scheduled with repeated invocations to the partitioning algorithm. This overhead notwithstanding, we will show in Section 5.4 that our aging-aware `static_rel` clause achieves the best results in minimizing the performance loss.

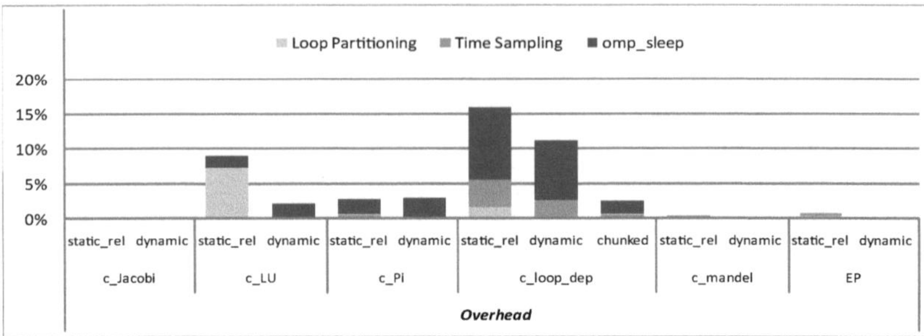

Fig. 2. Sources of overhead

Benchmark ***c_loop_dep*** is a synthetic benchmark in which a backward loop carried dependency is resolved through array replication. Each iteration in this program only contains a single write/read instruction in the array. Thus, in this benchmark all sources of overhead – which are usually negligible in real applications – are visible. When applying static aging-aware partitioning (`static_rel`) the biggest source of overhead ($\approx 10\%$) is the computation of the required sleep time for each core. Second for importance, is the overhead for profiling iteration execution time ($\approx 4\%$). Finally, loop partitioning accounts for an additional 1% overhead. Overall, the overhead introduced by our aging-tolerant facilities amounts to around 15% for static scheduling and 11% for dynamic scheduling. It is important to stress that the overhead is big because of the synthetic nature of the program and the poor computation performed in each iteration. When specifying a chunk size of 10 (i.e. folding ten iterations in a single task) we are able to reduce our techniques' overhead to less than 3% (***chunked*** bar).

5.2 Idleness

Table 3 shows the results of rest time accuracy. Numbers in the table represent the percent error in distributing on each core the target amount of idle time. This error is caused by overhead code which is not managed by our aging-aware balancing policies. Since each parallel region may feature multiple loop nests, as well as code not contained within work-sharing constructs, we compute the actual core idleness as a percentage of the overall parallel region execution time to estimate the error. The results show that the error is always under 4%, thus confirming the effectiveness of the technique in offering idleness distribution precision. Benchmark ***c_LU***

Table 3. Percent error in target idleness distribution

	c_Jacobi	c_LU	c_Pi	c_loop_dep	c_mandel	EP
static + sleep	-0,08	0,02	0,81	-2,84	0,01	-0,30
static_rel	-0,17	-3,98	0,74	-3,26	-0,09	-0,58
dynamic	-0,08	0,24	0,62	-2,32	0,00	-0,29
chunked	-	-	-	-0,65	-	-

has a very small error for ***static + sleep*** and ***dynamic*** configurations. The error is bigger when using static aging-aware scheduling (***static_rel***). This was expected, since as discussed in Section 5.1 the use of this clause carries an overhead that is not considered in duty cycling, thus leading to the error in idleness distribution. Similarly, for benchmark ***c_loop_dep*** sources of overhead present both in static and dynamic parallelization schemes lead to an error in idleness distribution accuracy that is greatly reduced when employing chunked scheduling.

5.3 Load Balancing

As described in Section 4.1, we devised a partitioning algorithm that aims at keeping different threads workload as balanced as possible. In this section we provide results that confirm the effectiveness of the proposed approach.

Standard deviation of parallel execution time over cores has been normalized to the mean to provide a qualitative measure of the load imbalance. Results are shown in Figure 3.a) for different parallelization schemes. The black bars represent the original program parallelized with aging-agnostic OpenMP facilities, and thus is considered as a baseline. Looking at the black bars only, our set of benchmarks can be divided in two categories: ***c_Jacobi***, ***EP***, ***c_Pi*** and ***c_loop_dep*** are regular and balanced. Each of them shows a deviation from average execution time which is contained within 13%.

On the other hand, ***c_LU*** and ***c_mandel*** have a degree of imbalance greater than 30%. ***c_mandel*** is known to have very unbalanced iterations, since decision on whether complex points belong to the Mandelbrot set area are taken within an inner loop which may take very different number of (inner) iterations to reach convergence. Similarly, LU decomposition has decreasing duration of inner loop iterations due to the diminishing number of elements in scanning an upper triangular matrix.

For all benchmarks, the naive ***static + sleep*** approach – which simply introduce idle times without re-allocating workload – un-surprisingly increase imbalance. Our partitioning algorithm (***static_rel***) is expected to never increase imbalance. This is confirmed by the plot. In cases like ***c_LU*** our algorithm reduces imbalance, since it schedules iterations in a smarter way. For example, when there are less iterations than cores, work is allocated to most reliable processors – which require smaller idle times – thus reducing the impact of duty cycling on load imbalance. Dynamic scheduling was originally meant to deal with balancing issues, so – as expected – even when augmented with aging-related features it preserves excellent balancing.

5.4 Performance Loss

As previously discussed, distributing idleness to degraded cores has a cost in terms of performance. Our partitioning algorithm aims at reducing this performance loss. According to the description given in section 4.1, part of the iterations originally assigned to degraded cores are re-distributed to more reliable cores. To estimate the effectiveness of this approach, we compare the parallel execution time of our aging-aware scheduling techniques against the naive ***static***

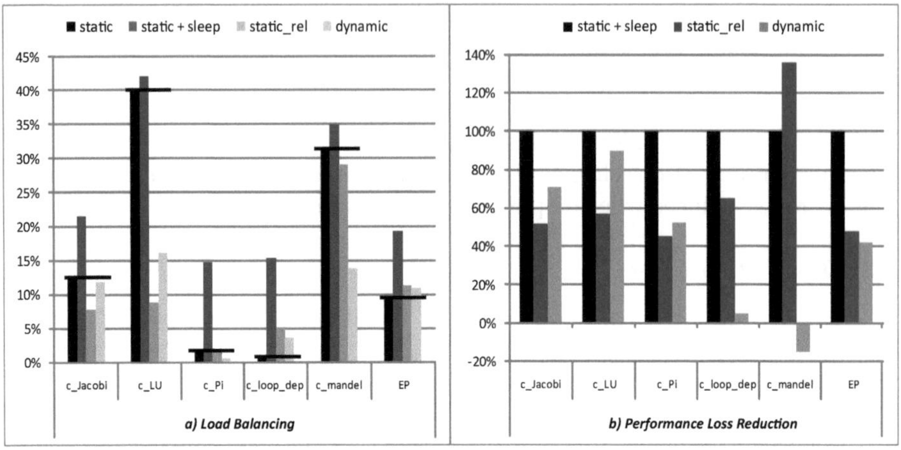

Fig. 3. a)Load balancing b) Performance loss reduction

+ ***sleep*** approach. The results are plot as a series of bars (for different program configurations) in Figure 3.a).

We see that for all benchmarks except ***c_mandel***, our `static_rel` clause affords a significant reduction in performance loss w.r.t. ***static + sleep*** (around 50%). As explained in the previous section, for unbalanced applications such as ***c_mandel*** static scheduling schemes should be avoided. If iterations are known to have different duration, evenly dividing the iteration space among cores results in unbalanced execution time. The same clearly applies to our aging-aware partitioning algorithm, so we did not expect `static_rel` to provide good results. It is important here to stress that this is NOT a problem of our partitioning scheme, but rather an inherent limitation of static parallelization. The knowledgeable programmer would rather employ dynamic scheduling to deal with similar scenarios. For this benchmark in particular, employing a dynamic scheduling policy achieves better performance results than the original static scheduling notwithstanding the idle periods.

6 Summary and Conclusions

In this paper we presented a compiler-supported technique for NBTI-induced aging tolerance in data-intensive MPSoCs. The technique is able to finely insert periods of recovery to various cores within loop executions to compensate non-homogeneous core degradation and minimize the performance impact through loop iteration reallocation among cores. Experimental results performed on a working implementation integrated as an extension of OpenMP parallel compiler on a distributed memory multiprocessor platform demonstrate its accuracy in idleness allocation and performance impact minimization.

References

1. Marongiu, A., Benini, L.: Efficient OpenMP support and extensions for MPSoCs with Explicitly managed memory hierarchy. In: DATE 2009: Proceedings of the 12th International Conference on Design, Automation and Test in Europe, pp. 809–814 (2009)
2. Agarwal, M., Paul, B., Zhang, M., Mitra, S.: Circuit failure prediction and its application to transistor aging. In: Proceedings of the 25th IEEE VLSI Test Symposium table of contents, pp. 277–286 (2007)
3. Dorta, A.J., Rodriguez, C., de Sande, F.: The OpenMP source code repository. In: 13th Euromicro Conference on Parallel, Distributed and Network-Based Processing, PDP 2005, pp. 244–250 (2005)
4. Eireiner, M., Henzler, S., Georgakos, G., Berthold, J., Schmitt-Landsiedel, D.: In-situ delay characterization and local supply voltage adjustment for compensation of local parametric variations. IEEE Journal of Solid-State Circuits 42(7), 1583–1592 (2007)
5. Hong, S., Narayanan, S., Kandemir, M., Ozturk, O.: Process variation aware thread mapping for chip multiprocessors. In: DATE 2009: Proceedings of the 12th International Conference on Design, Automation and Test in Europe, pp. 821–826 (2009)
6. Nas parallel benchmarks, `http://www.nas.nasa.gov/Resources/Software/npb.html`
7. Jeun, W.-C., Ha, S.: Effective OpenMP implementation and translation for multiprocessor system-on-chip without using OS. In: Asia and South Pacific Design Automation Conference, ASP-DAC 2007, pp. 44–49 (2007)
8. Kang, K., Park, S.P., Roy, K., Alam, M.A.: Estimation of statistical variation in temporal NBTI degradation and its impact on lifetime circuit performance. In: ICCAD 2007: Proceedings of the 2007 IEEE/ACM international conference on Computer-aided design, pp. 730–734 (2007)
9. Karl, E., Blaauw, D., Sylvester, D., Mudge, T.: Multi-mechanism reliability modeling and management in dynamic systems. IEEE Transactions on Very Large Scale Integration (VLSI) Systems 16(4), 476–487 (2008)
10. Krishnan, A., Reddy, V., Chakravarthi, S., Rodriguez, J., John, S., Krishnan, S.: NBTI impact on transistor and circuit: models, mechanisms and scaling effects. In: Technical Digest. IEEE International Electron Devices Meeting, IEDM 2003, pp. 14.5.1–14.5.4 (2003)
11. Kumar, S.V., Kim, C.H., Sapatnekar, S.S.: An analytical model for negative bias temperature instability. In: ICCAD 2006: Proceedings of the 2006 IEEE/ACM international conference on Computer-aided design, pp. 493–496 (2006)
12. Liu, F., Chaudhary, V.: Extending OpenMP for heterogeneous chip multiprocessors. In: 2003 International Conference on Parallel Processing, 2003. Proceedings, pp. 161–168 (2003)
13. Liu, F., Chaudhary, V.: A practical OpenMP compiler for system on chips. In: Voss, M.J. (ed.) WOMPAT 2003. LNCS, vol. 2716, pp. 54–68. Springer, Heidelberg (2003)
14. O'Brien, K., O'Brien, K., Sura, Z., Chen, T., Zhang, T.: Supporting OpenMP on cell. In: Chapman, B., Zheng, W., Gao, G.R., Sato, M., Ayguadé, E., Wang, D. (eds.) IWOMP 2007. LNCS, vol. 4935, pp. 65–76. Springer, Heidelberg (2008)
15. Roberts, D., Dreslinski, R.G., Karl, E., Mudge, T., Sylvester, D., Blaauw, D.: When homogeneous becomes heterogeneous. In: Third workshop on Operating Systems for Heterogeneous Multiprocessor Architectures, OSHMA (2007)

16. Tiwari, A., Torrellas, J.: Facelift: Hiding and slowing down aging in multicores. In: 41st Annual IEEE/ACM International Symposium on Microarchitecture (MICRO), pp. 129–140 (2008)
17. Wang, F., Nicopoulos, C., Wu, X., Xie, Y., Vijaykrishnan, N.: Variation-aware task allocation and scheduling for MPSoC. In: ICCAD 2007: Proceedings of the 2007 IEEE/ACM international conference on Computer-aided design, pp. 598–603 (2007)
18. Winter, J., Albonesi, D.: Scheduling algorithms for unpredictably heterogeneous CMP architectures. In: 38th International Conference on Dependable Systems and Networks, pp. 42–51 (2008)

A Self-stabilizing Algorithm for Graph Searching in Trees

Rodica Mihai and Morten Mjelde

Department of Informatics, University of Bergen
{rodica.mihai,mortenm}@ii.uib.no

Abstract. Graph searching games have been extensively studied in the past years. The graph searching problem involves a team of searchers who are attempting to capture a fugitive moving along the edges of the graph. In this paper we consider the graph searching problem in a network environment, namely a tree network. Searchers are software programs and the fugitive is a virus that spreads rapidly. Every node of the network which the virus may have reached, becomes contaminated. The purpose of the game is to clean the network. In real world distributed systems faults can occur and thus it is desirable for an algorithm to be able to facilitate the cleaning of a network in an optimal way, and also to reconfigure on the fly.

In this paper we give the first self-stabilizing algorithm for solving the graph searching problem in trees. Our algorithm stabilizes after $O(n^3)$ time steps under the distributed adversarial daemon. Our algorithm solves the node searching variant of the graph searching problem, but can with small modifications also solve edge and mixed searching.

1 Introduction

We consider a computer network environment, where the nodes are computers or processors and the edges are the connections between them. The computers or processors typically have tasks to perform, and in many instances they collaborate on these tasks. We consider a malicious virus that is moving through the network. Every computer or processor that at some point hosts the virus becomes immediately contaminated, meaning that it may be unable to correctly perform its tasks. Thus clean the network become necessary in order for it to continue its intended function. We assume we have at our disposal a team of software agents that can be used to clean the network and destroy the virus. We make the following assumptions about the virus and the software agents. The virus spreads fast but it cannot contaminate a computer where a software agent is present. The virus is aware of the software agents in the network and it behaves such as to avoid its own detection and removal, while at the same time trying to contaminate as many nodes as possible. A node is cleaned when a software agent is installed on it. A connection between two nodes is cleaned when both end points of the connection have software agents on them.

Our goal is to clean the entire network and neutralize the virus using as few software agents as possible. The constraint on the number of the software agents

R. Guerraoui and F. Petit (Eds.): SSS 2009, LNCS 5873, pp. 563–577, 2009.

is motivated by the cost of installing the software agent on a specific node, as well as the fact that the presence of the software agents may have an adverse effect on the performance of the network. For example, in a wireless network, a large number of software agents may consume too much communication bandwidth. Furthermore, a computer has a limited capacity and a software agent may slow down processes that need to be executed by that specific computer. Thus, the trivial algorithm that at regular intervals install a software agent on each node is not a good choice since it uses as many software agents as nodes in the network.

In the following we denote the malicious virus as a *fugitive*, and the software agents as *searchers*, keeping with the terminology from the graph searching games literature. A node can be in one of the following states: *clean*, meaning it functions normally, *unclean* which represents a possible contamination by the virus, or *searcher* when it contains a searcher/software agent.

Graph searching games were first introduced as a problem from speology [6]. An explorer is lost in a system of caves and the problem is to gather a team of rescuers to find the lost explorer. The challenge is to find the smallest number of rescuers needed to ensure the explorer is found. The explorer might not want to be found and thus will attempt to avoid this. The study of graph searching problem started in 1976 when it was independently introduced by Parsons [21] and Petrov [24], and since then has been studied extensively [2,3,16,18,19,23]. The system of tunnels is represented by a graph. The objective is to search the graph using a sequence of moves of the searchers. The goal is to minimize the number of searchers used at every step of the strategy. In this version of graph searching, called edge searching [17], a search step consists of either placing a searcher on a node, removing a searcher from a node, or sliding a searcher along an edge. An edge is cleaned by sliding a searcher from one of its endpoints to the other endpoint. Kirousis and Papadimitriou [17] introduced a variant of graph searching called node searching. In this version an edge is cleaned if both its endpoints contain searchers.

A third version of the graph searching problem is mixed searching, which combines edge and node searching. In this setting a search step consists, similarly to edge searching, of the following allowed moves: placing a searcher on a node, removing a searcher from a node, or sliding a searcher along an edge. An edge is cleaned if either both its endpoints are occupied by searchers or if a searcher is slid from one of its endpoints towards the other. A searching strategy is *winning* if the number of searchers used is enough to ensure the capture of the fugitive/explorer in the context of the node and mixed searching, and cleaning the graph in the context of edge searching. A cleaned edge e is (re)contaminated at some point if there exists a path P containing e, a contaminated edge and no internal node of P containing a searcher. For example, let u be a node that is incident on a contaminated edge e and is occupied by only one searcher. If this searcher slides from u to v along the edge $uv \neq e$, then the edge uv, which was cleaned by sliding, is immediately recontaminated. A searching strategy is called *monotone* if at any step of this strategy no recontamination occurs. For all three versions of graph searching, recontamination does not allow the graph to be cleaned with fewer searchers [3,18]. That is, on any graph with {edge, mixed, node} search number k there exists a winning monotone {edge, mixed, node} searching program using k searchers.

During the past several years much research has been conducted in the area of graph searching games and decontamination/cleaning of a network. For a bibliography we refer the reader to [13]. Many applications of graph searching games and its variations are in the area of computer networks. In a computer network setting, the graph searching problem serves as a mathematical model for protecting networks against viruses and other unwanted agents, like spyware or eavesdroppers [2,14]. An example is the problem of finding a successful strategy for a group of collaborating software programs that are designed to clean the network from a virus [10]. Distributed versions of the graph searching problem have received considerable attention during the recent years, among the new results are [5,10,11,15,20].

For trees both node and edge searching number can be computed in linear time [22,25]. There are also distributed algorithms to compute the edge searching number of a tree [7]. In the connected graph searching setting at each step the nodes which are cleaned induce a connected subgraph. The connected version of graph searching for trees was proved to be monotone in [1]. An interesting version of a searching game, namely tree decontamination with temporary immunity was introduced in [12]. The algorithm from [12] performs the decontamination of a tree using $2h/(t+2)$ searchers where h is the height of the tree and t the immunity time of a node. Particularly, if $t = 0$, meaning that a node has no immunity then the decontamination of a tree is realized using h searchers.

The main focus in the classical variant of the graph searching games is to find the smallest number of searchers needed to guarantee a winning strategy.

In this paper we focus not only on the node searching strategy that facilitates the cleaning of the network but also on keeping the network clean. Thus we are considering the possibility that errors can occur in the network after it was cleaned.

In general, a network is considered to be dynamic, that is, topology changes may occur regularly. Thus the need for an algorithm that can clean the network in an optimal way but that can also handle possible errors that can appear and cause recontamination.

Self-stabilization is an elegant and powerful approach to manage the possible faults that can appear in the network. We will extend the topic of self-stabilization in Section 2.1.

Our contribution is the first self-stabilizing algorithm for solving the node searching problem in trees. Given a tree T with n nodes and height h, our algorithm stabilizes after $O(n^3)$ time steps under the distributed adversarial daemon and the number of searchers used to clean the tree T is h. Our algorithm can be easily adapted so that it also performs edge and mixed searching of a given tree. We will discuss this in Section 5. Usually, the graph searching strategies studied so far are monotone strategies, meaning that recontamination does not happen. In this paper we consider a searching program which is locally monotone but recontamination can occur. If an error occurs in the network and a previously clean node becomes unclean it can start a recontamination process. The algorithm we introduce is able to handle these kinds of situations

2 Definitions and Motivation

2.1 Self-stabilization

Self-stabilizing algorithms [8,9] are distributed algorithms that permit recovery from transient failures by means of an attractive property: starting from any arbitrary initial state, the system autonomously resumes correct behavior within finite time. Self-stabilization allows failure detection to be bypassed, yet it does not make any assumptions about the nature or the span of those failures, save that they are transient.

In the current paper we use a shared memory model for communication between neighboring nodes. That is, in one atomic step, a node is able to read the state of every neighbor, as well as its own, and then change its own state.

Central to the theory of self-stabilization is the notion of a *daemon*, an abstraction for the scheduling of nodes in the system to execute their local code. A daemon is often viewed as an adversary to the algorithm that tries to prevent stabilization by scheduling the worst possible nodes for execution. The weakest possible requirement is that the daemon is *proper*, i.e. only nodes whose scheduling would change the system state are actually scheduled (these nodes are *privileged*). There are several daemons used to analyse the behavior of self-stabilizing algorithms, and in the current paper we assume a *distributed adversarial daemon.* This daemon may schedule privileged nodes such that the execution of the corresponding moves are simultaneous, however any privileged node may have to wait indefinitely before it is scheduled.

For the adversarial distributed daemon time complexity is measured in time steps, where a time step is one step in the execution during which at least one privileged node executes one move. When no nodes in the graph are privileged, we say that the algorithm is *stable*, or has reached a *stable configuration.* It then follows that in order to prove correctness, an algorithm must be shown to converge toward a stable state regardless of the initial configuration, and that this state is a solution to the problem in question.

2.2 Node Searching Game

We consider the *node searching game*, formally defined as follows. Let $G = (V, E)$ be a graph to be searched. A *searching program* consists of a sequence of discrete steps that involves searchers. Every step is one of the following two types

- Some searchers are placed on some nodes of G (there can be several searchers located in one node);
- Some searchers are removed from G;

At every step of the searching program the edge set of G is partitioned into two sets: *cleaned* edges and *contaminated* edges. Intuitively, the agile and omniscient fugitive with unbounded speed who is invisible for the searchers, is located somewhere on a contaminated territory, and cannot be on cleaned edges. Initially all edges of G are contaminated, i.e., the fugitive can be anywhere. A contaminated edge uv becomes cleaned at some step of the searching program if at this step both its endpoints are occupied by searchers.

2.3 What It Means to Be a Searcher

In this section we will attempt to put the graph searching game problem into a distributed context. As previously mentioned, the aim of self-stabilizing algorithms is to allow a distributed system to recover from transient faults and occurrences without the need for outside intervention. However, many algorithms assume that each individual node is capable of correcting the fault, which may not always be true. Consider for example a computer virus spreading through a wireless network. Then a node that contracts the virus may not be capable of removing it. Indeed, the node may not even detect the virus' presence. Thus it may not be a simple matter of writing a rule that says **if** detect virus **then** remove virus. It may be necessary for unaffected nodes to assist in the removal.

We recall that in our setting, as mentioned in Section 1, a node in the network can be in one of the following states: *clean*, *unclean* or *searcher*.

The *unclean* state defined briefly in the introduction and used throughout the paper may obviously refer to the presence of a virus on the node in question. However, it may also be used by nodes to indicate that a neighbor (or a neighbors neighbor etc.) has become compromised, thereby attracting the attention of the searchers. Indeed, in any practical implementation of our graph searching game algorithm, the choice of becoming unclean may not even reside with the node itself. As was noted above, a node may not be aware that it has been affected by a virus. However, its neighbors can detect this (for example based on messages received from the affected node), in which case they for all intents and purposes label it as unclean.

The searcher may refer to for example software agents that "patrol" the network, perhaps akin a benign virus. Or searchers may be software that resides on all nodes, but is generally turned off in order to preserve battery and/or computational power. The process of actually cleaning the node may for example involve the removal of a virus, or even the complete wipe of the nodes dynamic memory, and then reloading the program from a static memory that can not have been compromised. These are all implementation specific details that we will not address further in this paper. We present them here simply in order to put the problem and algorithm into context.

2.4 Absent Searchers

As we will further elaborate in Section 3, we assume that there is always at least one searcher present in the network. However, this would seem to contradict the claim that our algorithm is self-stabilizing. Consider an initial state where no searcher are present in the graph, and at least one node is contaminated by a virus. In this case, the virus may spread unchecked throughout the entire graph. In this section we will address this issue, and present some possible ways of avoiding it.

One obvious way of solving the above problem is to add a rule that simply sets the root of the tree to be a searcher if this is not the case. This rule then ensures that a searcher will eventually appear in the tree. The disadvantage of this approach is that the root may become a searcher even if other searchers are already present in the tree.

Another possible approach is for every node, at regular intervals, to have a small chance of becoming a searcher (determined by a random dice throw). Thus, even if every searcher disappears due to faults or errors, one can expect new ones to spawn at regular intervals.

Wireless sensor networks are usually expected to report their observations to some base station for example. The same base station may also be employed to inject searchers into the network, should the need arise.

Thus we see that there are several possible ways of resolving a situation where there are no searchers present in the tree. Which of these (or other methods) are employed is an implementation specific detail which we will not further address in this paper.

3 Algorithm

In this section we will describe our algorithm for performing a self-stabilizing graph searching.

Let $T = (V, E)$ be a tree such that V is the set of nodes, E is the set of edges, and $|V| = n$ and $|E| = m$. We define h as the maximum height of the tree and δ as the maximum degree of the nodes in the tree. For every node $v \in V$ the set $N(v)$ is the open neighborhood of v, and $N[v] = N(v) \cup \{v\}$ is the closed neighborhood.

We assume that the tree is rooted at node r. For every node $v \in V$, $p(v)$ is the neighbor that is closest to r (ie. v's parent), and $C(v)$ is the set of v's children. Thus $\{p(v)\} \cup C(v) = N(v)$.

There exists self-stabilizing algorithms that can provide this type of information, such as one given by Blair and Manne in [4]. In this algorithm a node with the lowest maximum distance to every leaf is computed, which is akin to rooting the tree such that the height is minimized.

We assume that exactly one searcher is present in the network before the cleaning process starts. We will call a strategy connected if it is a strategy in which the set of nodes occupied by searchers induce a connected subgraph. We will prove that the cleaning strategy considered here is a connected strategy.

We will refer to the case with more than one initial searcher in the network in Section 4.3.

The classic variant of node searching has the monotonicity property meaning that recontamination does not reduce the number of searchers used. Thus the algorithms that provide a node searching strategy for trees give a strategy

Algorithm 1. A self-stabilizing graph searching algorithm for trees

Rules:

Contamination:

if $s_v = clean \wedge \exists u \in N(v) : s_u = unclean$
then $s_v \leftarrow unclean$
$m_v \leftarrow null$

Descent1:

if $s_v = searcher \wedge \exists c \in C(v) : s_c = unclean \wedge (s_{m_v} = clean \vee m_v \notin C(v))$
then $m_v \leftarrow c$

Descent2:

if $s_v \neq searcher \wedge m_{p(v)} = v \wedge s_{p(v)} = searcher \wedge$
$(\exists c \in C(v) : s_c = unclean \vee s_v = unclean)$
then $s_v \leftarrow searcher$
$m_v \leftarrow null$

Ascent1:

if $s_v = searcher \wedge \nexists c \in C(v) : s_c \in \{searcher, unclean\} \wedge s_{p(v)} \neq searcher \wedge$
$m_v \neq p(v)$
then $m_v \leftarrow p(v)$

Ascent2:

if $s_v = searcher \wedge \nexists c \in C(v) : s_c \in \{searcher, unclean\} \wedge s_{p(v)} = searcher$
then $s_v \leftarrow clean$
$m_v \leftarrow null$

Ascent3:

if $s_v \neq searcher \wedge \exists c \in C(v) : (s_c = searcher \wedge m_c = v)$
then $s_v \leftarrow searcher$
$m_v \leftarrow null$

without recontamination [22,25]. In the graph searching variant that we consider recontamination can happen. If, because of an error in the network, a node in the tree becomes suddenly unclean, recontamination of the network can occur. We will refer to these nodes as contaminators. Our algorithm is designed to handle these kind of situations.

The algorithm uses two local variables for each node. For a node v $s_v \in \{searcher, clean, unclean\}$ is v's current mode and m_v is a pointer used by a searcher v to indicate which neighbor should become a searcher, either in addition to or instead of v.

We give the algorithm as Algorithm 1.

3.1 Informal Description

We now give an informal description of Algorithm 1.

The purpose of the *Contamination* rule is for clean nodes to detect the presence of an unclean neighbor, and thus becoming unclean themselves. While this may seem counterproductive, it allows searchers to avoid areas of the tree that are already clean.

The remaining rules deal with searching the tree. They can be divided up into two groups: The *descent rules* and the *ascent rules*.

The purpose of the descent rules is for a searcher, starting at a node v, to move further down the tree, searching and cleaning each of v's children's subtree, one at a time. Recall that the purpose of the m-variable is to allow a searcher to replicate itself onto a neighboring node. Thus, the *Descent1* rule functions by a searcher v determining if it has an unclean child, in which case it points m_v to such a child if this is not already the case. Following this move, the child will now detect that its parent is a searcher and pointing to it, and become a searcher itself (*Descent2*).

The purpose of the ascent rules is to allow a searcher to climb the tree once a subtree has been cleaned. The *Ascent1* rule becomes privileged for a node v if every child of v is clean, and v's parent is not a searcher. In this case it sets m_v to point to its parent (if this is not the case), indicating that it should become a searcher. If v's parent is a searcher v becomes clean (*Ascent2*), since it no longer needs to function as a searcher. In the first case, when v's parent is not a searcher, then following v's execution of the *Ascent1* rule, its parent become privileged to execute the *Ascent3* rule, after which it becomes a searcher.

4 Proof of Correctness

In this section we show that when Algorithm 1 has reached a stable configuration there are no unclean nodes in the graph, and at most one searcher. We will then bound the complexity of the algorithm for the distributed adversarial daemon, and show that the number of searchers present in the graph at any given time is at most h.

4.1 Correct Stabilization

We now show that if Algorithm 1 reaches a stable configuration there are no unclean nodes, and exactly one searcher, which is at the root of the tree.

Lemma 1. *In a stable configuration there does not exist any pair of neighboring nodes $v, w \in V$ such that $s_v = unclean$ and $s_w = clean$.*

Proof. This follows directly from the *Contamination* rule. □

Lemma 2. *In a stable configuration there does not exist any pair of neighboring nodes $v, w \in V$ such that $s_v = unclean$ and $s_w = searcher$.*

Proof. Assuming that there exists a pair of two neighboring nodes such that one is *unclean* and the other one is *searcher*, we prove that this leads to a contradiction. We show this by induction over the height of the tree. In the following we refer to the set $C'(w)$ as the set of unclean children of w, where w is a node in T. Let i be the distance from the root of the tree to the furthest leaf.

The base case is $i = 1$, ie. for a node w where every child is a leaf. We consider the following two cases. *Case 1*: given a node $v \in C(w)$, then $s_w = unclean$ and $s_v = searcher$. *Case 2*: $s_w = searcher$ and $|C'(w)| > 0$ (ie. there exists at least one child of w that is unclean).

In *Case 1* it follows that since v has no children either v is privileged for an *Ascent1* move (which will cause it to point to w) or w is privileged for an *Ascent2* move (which will cause it to become a searcher).

For *Case 2* either w must be privileged to execute a *Descent1* move and point to $v' \in C'(w)$, or v' must privileged to execute a *Descent2* move, becoming a searcher.

We see that in either of the two cases the configuration is not stable.

Assuming that the induction hypothesis is true for any subtree where the maximum distance from the root to any leaf is less than i, we now show that this implies it is also true for i. We again consider the two cases presented above.

For *Case 1* we know from the induction hypothesis and Lemma 1 that the subtree rooted at v contains no unclean nodes. Thus v must be privileged for an *Ascent1* move or w must be privileged for an *Ascent3* move.

In *Case 2* w must be privileged for a *Descent1* move and point to $v' \in C'(w)$ or v' must be privileged for a *Descent2* move.

In either of the above cases we see that at least one node must be privileged for a move, which contradicts our initial assumption that the configuration is stable. □

From Lemmas 1 and 2 we get the following result.

Lemma 3. *In a stable configuration there does not exists any node $v \in V$ such that $s_v = unclean$.*

Lemma 4. *In a stable configuration there exists exactly one searcher, which is at the root.*

Proof. Recall that in a stable configuration there does not exist any unclean nodes. We note that if there exists a node v such that $s_v = searcher$ and $s_{p(v)} \neq searcher$ then $p(v)$ is privileged for an *Ascent3* move if v is pointing to $p(v)$. If v is not pointing to $p(v)$, it is non-privileged for an *Ascent1* move only if it has at least one child that is a searcher. If $s_v = searcher$ and $s_{p(v)} = searcher$ then v is privileged for an *Ascent2* move if it has no children that are searchers.

Repeating this argument it follows that since a leaf has no child that is a searcher at least one node must be privileged. Furthermore, since the root r of the tree has no parent, r can never become privileged for an *Ascent2* move, and thus it must remain a searcher. □

Based on Lemmas 3 and 4 we get the following.

Theorem 1. *In a stable configuration where $r \in V$ is the root then s_r = searcher and s_v = clean for every node $v \in V \backslash \{r\}$.*

4.2 Convergence for the Distributed Adversarial Daemon

In this section we will show that Algorithm 1 stabilizes in $O(n^3)$ time steps under a distributed adversarial daemon. In the following we refer to *Descent1*, *Descent2*, *Ascent1*, *Ascent2* and *Ascent3* moves as *Cleaning* moves. We here assume that the rooting algorithm by Blair and Manne is stable. That is, there exists exactly one root in the tree, and for every node, the parent is the neighbor that is closest to the root. We will consider the behavior of Algorithm 1 when this is not true in Section 4.4.

From the predicate for each of the *Cleaning* moves, we get the following lemma.

Lemma 5. *A node v can execute a Cleaning move only if there exists at least one node $w \in N[v]$ such that s_w = searcher.*

Next, we show that the set of nodes that are searchers induce a connected tree. We remind the reader that initially there is only one searcher in the network.

Lemma 6. *Let A be the set of nodes a such that s_a = searcher. The nodes in A induce a connected tree.*

Proof. We first note that the only rule that can cause a searcher v to become a non-searcher is the *Ascent2* rule which requires that no children of v are searchers and that $p(v)$ is a searcher. Thus executing this rule will not violate the lemma.

Next we observe that only the *Descent2* and *Ascent3* rules can cause a node to become a searcher, and these require that either v's parent or one of v's children is a searcher, respectively. □

We define T' as the subset of maximum size of T induced by the set of searchers and all unclean nodes for which there exists path of unclean nodes to any searcher. From Lemma 6 we know that T' is a connected tree. Obviously, the nodes in T' can only execute *Cleaning* moves, and we will now show that if no other nodes in the graph can execute a move, T' will stabilize in $O(\delta^h)$ time steps.

Lemma 7. *A connected subset $B \subseteq T$ where the root of B, r_B is a searcher, can execute cleaning moves during at most $O(\delta^{h_B})$ consecutive time steps , where h_B is the height of B.*

Proof. We will show this by induction over the height of B.

For the base case we consider B with height 1, ie. that every child of r_B is a leaf. We assume that r_B is a searcher, and since $|C_r| \neq 0$, r_B may execute a *Descent1* move and point to one of its children. This child can then execute a *Descent2* move and become a searcher. This is followed by an *Ascent2* move, and the child becomes clean. The root r_B may now point to different child, and this process is repeated until all children are clean.

Since r_B has no searcher or unclean children left, it may now execute an *Ascent2* move if $p(r_B)$ is a searcher, and an *Ascent1* move if not. Thus at most $2 \cdot \delta + 2$ moves are executed.

Assuming that the induction hypothesis is true for any subtree with height $i - 1$, we now show that it is true for i. Again we assume that r_B is a searcher. If any children of r_B are searchers, we know by the induction hypothesis that each of their respective subtrees can execute moves during at most $O(\delta^{i-1})$ time steps. If any children are unclean, r_B may execute a *Descent1* move and point to an unclean child. This child will now execute a *Descent2* move and become a searcher. In this case we know that the subtree rooted at this child can execute moves during at most $O(\delta^{i-1})$ time steps. Since r_B has at most δ children, every childs subtree is stable within $O(\delta^i)$ time steps. Since r_B is a searcher, it may now execute an *Ascent2* move if $p(r_B)$ is a searcher, and an *Ascent1* move if not. □

Assuming that r' is the searcher with greatest distance h' from it to any leaf, then it follows that the subtree of T' rooted at r' will stabilize after at most $O(\delta^{h'})$. Following this, since $p(r')$ is not a searcher, r' may execute an *Ascent1* move and point to its parent, which may now execute an *Ascent2* move and become a searcher. Using an induction similar to the proof of Lemma 7 we get the following result.

Lemma 8. *At most $O(\delta^h)$ consecutive cleaning moves can be executed.*

We note that there initially existed a set of unclean nodes, and we refer to these nodes as *contaminators*. We define a *contamination path* $x_0, x_1, ..., x_k$ such that x_0 is a contaminator and every x_j has executed a *Contamination* move due to $s_{x_{j-1}} =$ *unclean*. A *contamination process* is a process started by a contaminator that leads to nodes becoming contaminated by executing the *Contamination* move.

Lemma 9. *Every contaminator w can start a contamination process at most once before it becomes clean.*

Proof. Once a contamination process is started it will spread in a connected way, in the worst case the whole tree is recontaminated. At some point a cleaning process will start at some node u that is a searcher. Consider the unclean subtree rooted at u that contains the contaminator w. We recall that the cleaning strategy is a connected strategy by Lemma 6. The only privileged rules at this point are the *Descent1* and *Descent2* rules. After a finite number of steps w becomes cleaned. Thus w cannot start a contamination process again. □

If a node executing a *Contamination* move has two or more unclean neighbors, we say that it joins only one of its incident contamination paths. This ensures that every node that is a member of a contamination path has exactly one contaminator as its origin (it does however not restrict a single node from being a member of more than one contamination path). Obviously, every node that executes a *Contamination* move is part of a contamination path. We say that a *Contamination* move by a node v is *caused* by a contaminator w if v is a member of a path originating in w. Since such a path can have a length of at most $O(n)$ and by Lemma 9 it follows directly the next lemma.

Lemma 10. *Every contaminator w can cause at most $O(n)$ Contamination moves.*

Note that $O(\delta^h)$ is bounded by $O(n)$. Since there initially existed at most n contaminators in the graph, we get the following theorem.

Theorem 2. *Algorithm 1 will stabilize after at most $O(n^3)$ time steps.*

4.3 Bounding the Number of Searchers

In this section we bound the number of searchers used by Algorithm 1 to clean the graph. We assumed that at the beginning there is only one searcher in the network.

Lemma 11. *The number of searchers used by Algorithm 1 to clean a given tree T is $O(h)$, where h is the height of T.*

Proof. We assume first that the initial searcher present in the tree is situated at the root of the tree. The cleaning process generated by the searcher situated at the root uses at least h searchers. At each node u only one of the subtrees rooted at u is cleaned at any one time. No two subtrees are cleaned at the same time. Thus Algorithm 1 will use at most h searchers.

Let now assume that the initial searcher present in the tree is not situated at the root. Let v be the node of the tree occupied by this searcher. The Algorithm 1 will first perform the cleaning of the subtree rooted at v, since only the Descent moves are privileged at this point. The number of searchers used is h_v, where h_v is the height of the subtree rooted at v. After that the cleaning process is similar to the one described previously for the case when the initial searcher is at the root. Thus Algorithm 1 will use at most h searchers in this case as well. □

If initially there are more than one searcher in the tree, Algorithm 1 will realize the cleaning of the network and it will stabilize after $O(n^3)$ time steps under the distributed adversarial daemon. The number of searchers used may increase in this situation. For each initial extra searcher situated at a node u the number of searchers used to clean the network may increase and become $O(h+h_u))$, where h_u is the height of T_u, the subtree rooted at u and h is the height of T.

4.4 Interaction with the Rooting Algorithm

In the previous sections we have assumed that the rooting algorithm by Blair and Manne is stable. That is, there exists exactly one root in the tree, and for every node, the parent is the neighbor that is closest to the root. In this section we will consider how to deal with situations when this is not true. In the following we denote the algorithm by Blair and Manne as Algorithm 0.

While Algorithm 0 does not use the state of Algorithm 1 in its execution, it is important to ensure that Algorithm 1 will stabilize regardless of the state of Algorithm 0. If this is not the case, Algorithm 1 may execute an infinite number of moves, possibly preventing Algorithm 0 from executing any.

In order to ensure this, we denote a node v as *eligible* if and only if *a)* v is not privileged for an Algorithm 0 move. And *b)*, for every $w \in N(v)$ either $p_v = w$ and $p_w \neq v$, or $p_w = v$ and $p_v \neq w$. That is, v is the parent of every neighbor, save possibly one, which is the parent of v. Note that the set of nodes that are eligible induce a forest (possibly disconnected). Obviously, within each tree in this forest, the parent pointers comply with requirement *b)*, and Algorithm 1 will stabilize within them. Thus, if we only allow eligible nodes to execute Algorithm 1 moves, Algorithm 1 will stabilize regardless of the state of Algorithm 0.

5 Conclusion

We have presented the first self-stabilizing algorithm for solving the graph searching problem in trees. We assumed that before the cleaning process starts there is only one searcher in the network. Recontamination can occur, if for example a node that was previously clean becomes unclean. At each step of the algorithm at most h searchers are used, where h is the height of the tree.

Throughout the paper we focused mainly on the node searching problem, meaning that an edge in the tree is cleaned by placing a searcher on both of its endpoints. Our algorithm can be easily modified to solve the edge and mixed searching problems for trees. The main modification to be done is in the way a new searcher is introduced in the network. In order to solve the edge searching problem a new searcher is introduced first at the parent of a node and afterwards is slid to a specific child. We remind the reader that in the edge searching setting an edge is cleared by sliding a searcher from one of its endpoints towards the other. By introducing the searcher at the parent of a node that needs to become searcher we can easily slide that new introduced searcher through the corresponding edge and clean it. Notice that since the parent node already had one searcher, then by sliding the second searcher, recontamination cannot occur locally. Since mixed searching combines both node searching and edge searching, each of the previously described strategies constitutes a mixed searching strategy. In the mixed searching setting an edge is cleaned either by placing a searcher on each of its endpoints or by sliding a searcher through it.

We believe that these results can be extended to other graph classes and we plan to further explore this possibility.

Acknowledgements

The authors would like to thank Fredrik Manne for useful comments on this paper.

References

1. Barrière, L., Flocchini, P., Fraigniaud, P., Santoro, N.: Capture of an intruder by mobile agents. In: SPAA, pp. 200–209 (2002)
2. Bienstock, D.: Graph searching, path-width, tree-width and related problems (a survey). DIMACS Ser. in Discrete Mathematics and Theoretical Computer Science 5, 33–49 (1991)
3. Bienstock, D., Seymour, P.D.: Monotonicity in graph searching. J. Algorithms 12(2), 239–245 (1991)
4. Blair, J.R.S., Manne, F.: Efficient self-stabilizing algorithms for tree network. In: ICDCS, pp. 20–26. IEEE Computer Society, Los Alamitos (2003)
5. Blin, L., Fraigniaud, P., Nisse, N., Vial, S.: Distributed chasing of network intruders. Theor. Comput. Sci. 399(1-2), 12–37 (2008)
6. Breisch, R.: An intuitive approach to speoleotopology. S.W.Cavers VI 5, 72–78 (1967)
7. Coudert, D., Huc, F., Mazauric, D.: A distributed algorithm for computing and updating the process number of a forest. In: Taubenfeld, G. (ed.) DISC 2008. LNCS, vol. 5218, pp. 500–501. Springer, Heidelberg (2008)
8. Dijkstra, E.W.: Self-stabilizing systems in spite of distributed control. Commun. ACM 17(11), 643–644 (1974)
9. Dolev, S.: Self-stabilization. MIT Press, Cambridge (2000)
10. Flocchini, P., Jun Huang, M., Luccio, F.L.: Contiguous search in the hypercube for capturing an intruder. In: IPDPS. IEEE Computer Society, Los Alamitos (2005)
11. Flocchini, P., Luccio, F.L., Song, L.X.: Size optimal strategies for capturing an intruder in mesh networks. In: d'Auriol, B.J., Arabnia, H.R. (eds.) Communications in Computing, pp. 200–206. CSREA Press (2005)
12. Flocchini, P., Mans, B., Santoro, N.: Tree decontamination with temporary immunity. In: Hong, S.-H., Nagamochi, H., Fukunaga, T. (eds.) ISAAC 2008. LNCS, vol. 5369, pp. 330–341. Springer, Heidelberg (2008)
13. Fomin, F.V., Thilikos, D.M.: An annotated bibliography on guaranteed graph searching. Theor. Comput. Sci. 399(3), 236–245 (2008)
14. Franklin, M.K., Galil, Z., Yung, M.: Eavesdropping games: a graph-theoretic approach to privacy in distributed systems. J. ACM 47(2), 225–243 (2000)
15. Ilcinkas, D., Nisse, N., Soguet, D.: The cost of monotonicity in distributed graph searching. In: Tovar, E., Tsigas, P., Fouchal, H. (eds.) OPODIS 2007. LNCS, vol. 4878, pp. 415–428. Springer, Heidelberg (2007)
16. Kirousis, L.M., Papadimitriou, C.H.: Interval graphs and seatching. Discrete Mathematics 55(2), 181–184 (1985)
17. Kirousis, L.M., Papadimitriou, C.H.: Searching and pebbling. Theor. Comput. Sci. 47(3), 205–218 (1986)
18. LaPaugh, A.S.: Recontamination does not help to search a graph. J. ACM 40(2), 224–245 (1993)
19. Megiddo, N., Louis Hakimi, S., Garey, M.R., Johnson, D.S., Papadimitriou, C.H.: The complexity of searching a graph. J. ACM 35(1), 18–44 (1988)
20. Nisse, N., Soguet, D.: Graph searching with advice. Theor. Comput. Sci. 410(14), 1307–1318 (2009)
21. Parson, T.D.: Pursuit-evasion in a graph. Theory and Applications of Graphs, 426–441 (1976)
22. Peng, S.L., Ho, C.W., Hsu, T.S., Ko, M.T., Tang, C.Y.: Edge and node searching problems on trees. Theor. Comput. Sci. 240(2), 429–446 (2000)

23. Peng, S.L., Tang, C.Y., Ko, M.T., Ho, C.W., Hsu, T.: Graph searching on some subclasses of chordal graphs. Algorithmica 27(3), 395–426 (2000)
24. Petrov, N.N.: A problem of pursuit in the absence of information on the pursued. Differentsialnye Uravneniya 18, 1345–1352, 1468 (1982)
25. Skodinis, K.: Construction of linear tree-layouts which are optimal with respect to vertex separation in linear time. J. Algorithms 47(1), 40–59 (2003)

A Metastability-Free Multi-synchronous Communication Scheme for SoCs

Thomas Polzer, Thomas Handl*, and Andreas Steininger

Vienna University of Technology
Institute of Computer Engineering – Embedded Computing Systems Group
Treitlstrasse 3, A-1040 Vienna, Austria

Abstract. We propose a communication scheme for GALS systems with independent but approximately synchronized clock sources, which guarantees high-speed metastability-free communication between any two peers via bounded-size FIFO buffers. The proposed approach can be used atop of any multi-synchronous clocking system that guarantees a synchronization precision in the order of several clock cycles, like our fault-tolerant DARTS clocks. We determine detailed formulas for the required communication buffer size, and prove that this choice indeed guarantees metastability-free communication between correct peers, at maximum clock speed. We also describe a fast and efficient implementation of our scheme, and calculate the required buffer size for a sample test scenario. Experimental results confirm that the size lower bounds provided by our formulas are tight in this setting.

1 Introduction

Over the last decades, VLSI technology has been dominated by the trends towards shrinking feature sizes, increasing complexity and higher clock rates. The VLSI design style, however, was shaped by the synchronous abstraction and the assumption of relatively low component failure rates that do not match well the above VLSI technology trends: First of all, clock frequencies became so high (and chips so complex) that phase-synchronous clock distribution over the entire chip is a substantial challenge [1]. Chip designers are hence confronted with the erosion of the convenient globally synchronous clock abstraction, which makes GALS (globally asynchronous locally synchronous [2]) systems an attractive alternative. In GALS, the system is partitioned into modules that are compact enough to be designed safely using the synchronous paradigm. Each module is equipped with its own clock source, however, and communication across different clock domains is performed in an asynchronous way.

The second problem with contemporary VLSI technology are increasing error rates [3] due to smaller critical charges, lower voltage swings and high clock and signal frequencies. Hardening techniques at the technology and circuit level [4,5], and redundancy concepts at the architectural level [6], as known from dependable computing, are hence expected to become widespread in commercial

* This research is supported by the Austrian bm:vit FIT-IT project *DARTS*.

R. Guerraoui and F. Petit (Eds.): SSS 2009, LNCS 5873, pp. 578–592, 2009.

circuits as well. Interestingly, however, even such designs often rely on a single clock source, usually a quartz oscillator, that ultimately constitutes a (silently accepted) single point of failure: Typically, brute-force approaches for providing a robust clock, such as using very strong drivers, are employed here. More sophisticated alternatives like [7,8] provide very limited fault-tolerance only.

Again, GALS seems to come for a rescue. However, while multiple independent clock sources indeed eliminate the single point of failure, this comes at a high price: The global notion of time that was naturally provided by the synchronous clock does not exist anymore. The modules are running asynchronously to each other, which not only complicates the application design, but also prohibits TMR or voter-based fault-tolerant architectures. Moreover, asynchrony introduces the potential of metastability [9]: Synchronizers must be employed to mitigate these effects at the clock domain boundaries between modules. In order to cope with (slowly) drifting clocks, adaptive synchronizers have been proposed [10,11]. Although the meantime between metastable upsets can be made arbitrarily large, they cannot be eliminated completely. Moreover, synchronizers tend to degrade performance, since their designs need to be conservative [12].

Therefore, an inter-module communication scheme for GALS that rules out metastability by construction would be an appealing alternative to synchronizer-based asynchronous communication. In this paper, we describe such a communication scheme for GALS systems built atop a multi-synchronous clocking scheme. A multi-synchronous clocking scheme employs independent clock sources that, however, guarantee some known bound on the worst-case synchronization precision, typically in the order of a few clock cycles. One example is our fault-tolerant DARTS clocking scheme for SoC [13]. Although the synchronization precision of multi-synchronous clocking is much worse than that of a conventional synchronous clock, it turns out that its "loose" global synchrony is – in contrast to GALS – sufficient for implementing metastability-free communication at full clock speed, i.e., without reducing the data rate. Implementing this scheme only requires bounded-size FIFO buffers between communicating modules. To the best of our knowledge, there is no related work that targets similar goals.

2 System Architecture

We assume a system consisting of different functional units (FUs) that are internally complex synchronous designs with well defined interfaces to the outside. A typical example is a system-on-chip (SoC) built from IP modules. In the following we will hence treat the FUs as black boxes and concentrate on the inter-FU communication. Although we do not assume the individual FUs and channels to be fault-tolerant, we can actually restrict our attention to the communication between non-faulty FUs, along non-faulty communication channels: If required by the application, fault-tolerance is rather achieved at the architectural level by appropriate replication. Since the behavior of faulty FUs and channels can be disregarded here, we can safely disregard failures in the sequel.

2.1 Communication Issues

A fundamental requirement for every communication primitive is that a data item must not be changed by a write operation while being read. It is well known that, in this case, the receiver may remain undecided about the interpretation of the input for an arbitrary time and exhibit arbitrary behavior, such as self-oscillation or undecided output. This undesired effect is known as metastability [9], and causes the need to appropriately align the activities of source and sink.

In principle, the globally synchronous abstraction provides a very efficient solution here: A global clock source is used to clock all individual FUs and co-ordinate their activities. As outlined in the previous section, however, the globally synchronous abstraction is increasingly difficult to maintain, and enormous efforts are hence being made to establish a sufficiently tight co-ordination between sender and receiver at high clock frequencies.

Unfortunately, GALS does not solve this problem: Due to the lack of a common time reference, the communication between FUs needs to be explicitly coordinated by means of handshakes, which severely degrades communication performance. Moreover, a handshake can provide a coordination on a transaction level, but does not solve the synchronization issue at the signal level: The transfer of data across clock domains inevitably introduces the potential for metastability, even during fault-free operation. As already mentioned, synchronizers can only reduce (but not eliminate) this risk and introduce performance penalties [12].

2.2 Multi-synchronous Clocking

In between the globally synchronous and the GALS clocking schemes there is a "loosely synchronized" scheme termed multi-synchronous clocking [14,15]. With this approach, all FUs receive a clock of the same frequency on the long run, but with a significant short-term phase jitter that may amount to several clock periods. The worst-case phase deviation between any two FUs' clocks that will ever be encountered is termed the precision (measured in clock ticks), and is usually limited by design. A trivial example of a multi-synchronous solution is a globally synchronous system with significant skew in the clock distribution tree.

Interestingly, there are ways to implement a multi-synchronous clocking scheme also in a fully distributed and fault-tolerant manner: In our DARTS project, we adapted a simple Byzantine fault-tolerant distributed tick generation algorithm introduced in [16] for direct implementation in asynchronous digital logic [17]. Rather than using quartz oscillators, DARTS hence employs a special distributed fault-tolerant ring oscillator.

In [13], it was shown that DARTS clocks guarantee some bounded worst-case precision (π), provided that (1) some relatively uncritical layout timing constraints are met, and (2) that at most f out of the $n \geq 3f+2$ clock instances suffer from arbitrary (Byzantine) failures. Formulas for both the minimum (T^-) and maximum (T^+) clock cycle time have also been determined, as they are needed for determining the required communication buffer size in Sect. 4.2.

3 The Communication Layer

3.1 Fundamentals

The communication scheme traditionally used on top of the globally synchronous paradigm relies on a precision that is considerably better than one single clock cycle: The sender writes data at the active clock transition k, and the receiver reads these data at the next active clock transition $k+1$. Assuming perfect synchrony, this leaves one clock period for transmission and stabilization of the data. In case of non-perfect synchronization between sender and receiver, however, this interval may shrink, as transition k is determined by the sender's local perception of time, but $k+1$ by the receiver's. Evidently, this simple scheme will no longer work reliably in a multi-synchronous environment, where the synchronization precision may be as large as several clock periods.

In order to reason precisely about such communication schemes for multi-synchronous GALS systems, we employ the notation of precedence described by Lamport in [18]. Informally, the precedence relation $A \rightarrow B$ means that action A must have been finished before action B starts. Given a set P of FUs, termed nodes in the sequel, and denoting the ticks of our multi-synchronous clocking system by C_i^k, where i is the node and k the tick count, we can define the precision π of our system by requiring that

$$\forall i, j \in P, \forall k > 0 : C_i^k \rightarrow C_j^{k+\pi} \tag{1}$$

A simple approach would be to divide the native clock ("microticks") such that the resulting clock ("macroticks") has a precision better than one. The drawback of this approach is the limited throughput. To circumvent it, we suggest implementing metastability-free communication [18] using a pipelined communication scheme directly based on the microticks.

3.2 Pipelined Communication

Let us recall the requirement for metastability-free communication from Sect. 2.1: For the transfer of any given data item, we need to pair write and read transitions such that writing has finished safely before reading starts. In the above synchronous approach, clock transitions of the same direction (rising or falling) are considered indistinguishable. Hence, this pairing is applied strictly via subsequent *alternating* edges. Consequently the phase relation between any two FUs is of central importance and must be maintained within tight bounds.

However, if we could distinguish edges on an *individual* basis (e.g. by their index), then we could establish relations between arbitrary clock transitions, such as $W_i^{13} \rightarrow R_j^{22}$. Clearly this requires a globally consistent numbering of clock ticks, which is, however, nothing else than the global time base established by our multi-synchronous clock, provided that a consistent edge numbering is ensured by the synchronous start of all FU's local clocks at start-up.

Based on this idea, we can pipeline transmission activities at the microtick level, thereby avoiding the throughput penalty of macrotick-based communication. We simply exploit the precedence given in (1)

$$\forall i, j \in P, \forall k > 0 : W_i^k = C_i^k \rightarrow C_j^{k+\alpha} = R_j^k$$

with α being a sufficiently large time margin that separates writes and reads.

Note that writes and reads can be performed at every microtick here, which maximizes the throughput. As the synchronization precision, however, can be in the order of several microticks, one needs a FIFO buffer in between communicating nodes to avoid data loss. Clearly, minimizing the required buffer size is important, both with respect to costs and communication delay. In the following we will therefore formally derive the respective bound.

4 Formal Model and Proof

4.1 System Model

To be able to prove the correctness of our approach, we first create an algorithmic model of our system. In this model, the nodes are coupled by a single-writer single-reader buffer memory of unbounded size (see Fig. 1). Our proof will reveal that finite buffer size will be sufficient. The behavior of the system is modeled by a sender algorithm (Algorithm 1) and a receiver algorithm (Algorithm 2).

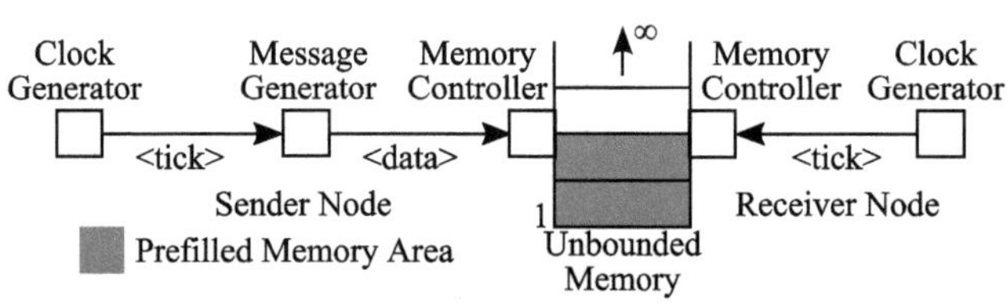

Fig. 1. System model used for the proof

Informal description of the algorithms: In our description, we use the term action for an operation with duration ≥ 0. For action A, $t_s(A)$ and $t_e(A)$, respectively, denote A's start and end time. An action with zero duration is called an event. The following actions and messages can be handled and/or produced by the sender node i:

Algorithm 1. Sender algorithm for node i

on C_i^k **do**
  Send $\langle$tick, $k\rangle$ to generate D_i // Simulate Clk Delay
on D_i^l: l-th receive of any $\langle$tick, $k\rangle$ from node i **do**
  Send $\langle$data, $l\rangle$ to generate W_i // Simulate Message Delay
on W_i^m: m-th receive of any $\langle$data, $l\rangle$ from node i **do**
  $mem(m + \alpha)$:= data // Memory Write Action

Algorithm 2. Receiver algorithm for node j

on C_j^k **do**
  Send $\langle$tick, $k\rangle$ to generate R_j // Simulate Clk Delay
on R_j^l: l-th receive of any $\langle$tick, $k\rangle$ from node j **do**
  $data := mem(k)$ // Memory Read Event

- C_i^k - This is the k-th clock tick of the sender node i. It is an event.
- $\langle$tick, $k\rangle$ - At every event C_i^k the clock generator of node i sends a message to its message generator to initiate the delivery of the data message. Its message delay $\Delta_{\text{send}}(i,k)$ is in the interval $0 < \Delta_{\text{send}}^- \leq \Delta_{\text{send}}(i,k) \leq \Delta_{\text{send}}^+$.
- D_i^l - This is the receive action for the l-th $\langle$tick, $k\rangle$ message at its message generator. It is an event.
- $\langle$data, $l\rangle$ - At every event D_i^l node i's message generator sends a message to its memory controller to initiate the memory write operation. Its message delay $\Delta_{\text{msg}}(i,l)$ is in the interval $0 < \Delta_{\text{msg}}^- \leq \Delta_{\text{msg}}(i,l) \leq \Delta_{\text{msg}}^+$.
- W_i^m - This action models the buffer memory write operation and is triggered by the reception of the m-th $\langle$data, $l\rangle$ message. It has a non zero duration $\Delta_{\text{mem}}(i,m)$ within the interval $0 < \Delta_{\text{mem}}^- \leq \Delta_{\text{mem}}(i,m) \leq \Delta_{\text{mem}}^+$.

The receiver node can produce/handle the following actions and messages:

- C_j^k - This is the k-th clock tick of the receiver node. It is an event.
- $\langle$tick, $k\rangle$ - At every event C_j^k the clock generator of node j sends its memory controller a message to initiate the memory read. Its message delay $\Delta_{\text{recv}}(j,k)$ is in the interval $0 < \Delta_{\text{recv}}^- \leq \Delta_{\text{recv}}(j,k) \leq \Delta_{\text{recv}}^+$.
- R_j^l - This is the actual read action. It is triggered by the reception of the l-th $\langle$tick, $k\rangle$ message and has a specified length of $\Delta_{\text{rd}}(j,l)$ within the interval $0 < \Delta_{\text{rd}}^- \leq \Delta_{\text{rd}}(j,l) \leq \Delta_{\text{rd}}^+$.

It is important to note that R_j^k reads memory location k, while W_i^k writes memory location $k+\alpha$. As a consequence of the shifted write index, the memory must be pre-filled with α elements (all zero), simulating that the writes $W_i^{-\alpha+1}, \ldots, W_i^0$ to the memory locations $1, \cdots, \alpha$ have already been finished before the first clock tick $k = 0$ (initial state). A sample execution of tick k for both algorithms can be found in Fig. 2.

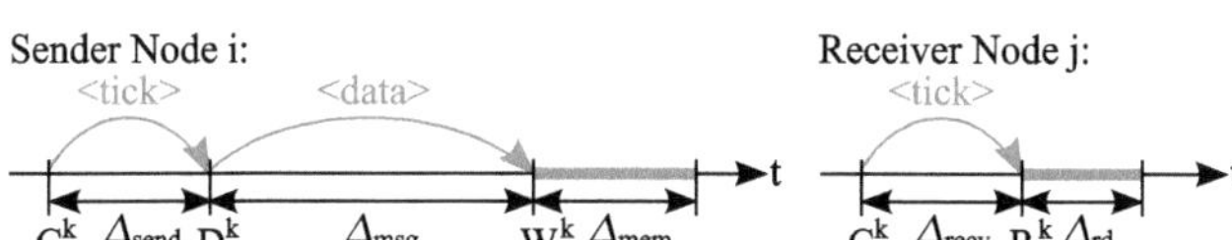

Fig. 2. Execution of tick k

4.2 Prerequisites

We require the clocking scheme to guarantee the following properties:

Assumption 1 (Precision). $\exists \pi : \forall i, j \in P, \forall k \geq 0 : C_i^k \to C_j^{k+\pi}$

Assumption 2 (Accuracy). $\forall i \in P, k > 0 : \exists T^- = \min_{i,k}(C_i^{k+1} - C_i^k) > 0$

Assumption 3 (Startup). *Before the first clock tick (initial state, $k = 0$), all memories are prefilled with α elements (all zero) and the precision π is zero ($\pi_0 = 0$). This is easy to guarantee in systems with a common reset.*

Assumption 4 (Message Order). *All message channels provide FIFO ordering. Furthermore, the actual delays must be such that every read and write operation is finished before the next one starts. This is always guaranteed if*

$$T^- + \Delta_{\text{send}}(i, k+1) + \Delta_{\text{msg}}(i, k+1) - \Delta_{\text{send}}(i, k) - \Delta_{\text{msg}}(i, k) > \Delta_{\text{mem}}(i, k)$$
and $$T^- + \Delta_{\text{recv}}(j, k+1) - \Delta_{\text{recv}}(j, k) > \Delta_{\text{rd}}(j, k)$$

For a more in-depth discussion of the delays in real systems see Sect. 5.1.

4.3 Problem Definition and Relation between Events

Properties of correct operation:

(WR) The write of memory location k must be finished before the read of this location starts ($W_i^{k-\alpha} \to R_j^k$).

(OV) In case of a bounded-size buffer, the read of an element must be finished before it is overwritten ($R_j^k \to W_i^{k+\pi+\beta}$, the size of β will be fixed later).

We will now prove essential relations between the events in our system model.

Lemma 1. *Algorithm 1, line 3: $\forall k \geq 1$, it holds that $k = l$ and $D_i^k \to D_i^{k+1}$.*

Proof. We prove this Lemma by induction.

- Induction start ($k = 1$): C_i^1 triggers the first send of a message $\langle \text{tick}, 1 \rangle$. By the FIFO property of the links it is also the first message to be delivered and therefore triggering event D_i^1. Since it is the first event the precedence relation is obviously true.
- Induction hypothesis: Assume the lemma holds for k.
- Induction step ($k \to k+1$): We know that the first k $\langle \text{tick}, l \rangle$ messages trigger the events $D_i^l | l \leq k$. By FIFO order, message $\langle \text{tick}, k+1 \rangle$ (generated by event C_i^{k+1}) will be the next one delivered, thereby triggering the event D_i^{k+1}. Since D_i^l is a zero-length event, this implies the precedence relation.

□

Lemma 2. *Algorithm 1, line 5: $\forall l \geq 1$. it holds that $l = m$ and $W_i^l \to W_i^{l+1}$.*

Proof. The proof is similar to above.

- Induction start ($l = 1$): D_i^1 triggers the first send of a message $\langle \text{data}, 1\rangle$. By the FIFO property of the links it is also the first message to be delivered and therefore triggering event W_i^1. Since it is the first event the precedence relation is valid.
- Induction hypothesis: Assume the lemma holds for l.
- Induction step ($l \to l{+}1$): We know that the first l $\langle \text{data}, m\rangle$ messages trigger the events $W_i^m | m \leq l$. By FIFO order message $\langle \text{data}, l+1\rangle$ (generated by event D_i^{l+1}) will be the next one delivered, thereby triggering the event W_i^{l+1}. By Assumption 4 we know that $t_\text{s}(W_i^{l+1}) > t_\text{s}(W_i^l) + \Delta_\text{mem}(i, l)$ and therefore W_i^l is finished before W_i^{l+1} is started. Therefore $W_i^l \to W_i^{l+1}$ holds. □

We now define a new relation $\rightsquigarrow$. It is used to model the triggering of events. $A \rightsquigarrow B$ means that event B was triggered by event A. Note that $A \rightsquigarrow B$ implies the precedence relation (A → B). Using this notation, the trigger dependencies implied by Lemma 1 and 2 read: $C_i^k \rightsquigarrow D_i^k \rightsquigarrow W_i^k$.

Lemma 3. *Algorithm 2, line 3: $\forall k \geq 1$, it holds that $k = l$ and $R_j^k \to R_j^{k+1}$.*

The proof is equivalent to the one of Lemma 2. In conjunction with Lemma 3, this implies $C_j^k \rightsquigarrow R_j^k$.

4.4 Write-Read Order Proof

For the proof of (WR) we fix an arbitrary sender-receiver pair. The sender node has the index i, the receiver node the index j. We will now derive the latest possible end of a write operation to a certain data item. We start with the first α items.

Lemma 4. $\forall -\alpha + 1 \leq k \leq 0 : t_\text{e}(W_i^k) = 0$

Proof. Follows directly from Assumption 3. □

Lemma 5 gives the latest possible end time for all other write operations.

Lemma 5. $\forall k > 0 : t_\text{e}(W_i^k) \leq t(C_i^k) + \Delta_\text{send}^+ + \Delta_\text{msg}^+ + \Delta_\text{mem}^+$

Proof. We already know that $C_i^k \rightsquigarrow D_i^k \rightsquigarrow W_i^k$. Since D_i^k is triggered by the k-th $\langle \text{tick}, k\rangle$ message, we get: $t(D_i^k) = t(C_i^k) + \Delta_\text{send}(i, k)$. Since W_i^k is triggered by the k-th $\langle \text{data}, l\rangle$ message, we get:

$$\begin{aligned} t_\text{s}(W_i^k) &= t(D_i^k) + \Delta_\text{msg}(i, k) = t(C_i^k) + \Delta_\text{send}(i, k) + \Delta_\text{msg}(i, k) \\ &\leq t(C_i^k) + \Delta_\text{send}^+ + \Delta_\text{msg}^+. \end{aligned}$$

We know that the event takes $\Delta_\text{mem}(i, k)$ time to finish, so its end time is:

$$t_\text{e}(W_i^k) = t_\text{s}(W_i^k) + \Delta_\text{mem}(i, k) \leq t(C_i^k) + \Delta_\text{send}^+ + \Delta_\text{msg}^+ + \Delta_\text{mem}^+.$$ □

We determine the earliest possible time a read operation can start.

Lemma 6. $\forall k > 0 : t_s(R_j^k) \geq t(C_j^k) + \Delta_{\text{recv}}^-$

Proof. We already know that $C_j^k \rightsquigarrow R_j^k$. Since R_j^k is triggered by $\langle \text{tick}, k\rangle$, we link: $t_s(R_j^k) = t(C_j^k) + \Delta_{\text{recv}}(j,k) \geq t(C_j^k) + \Delta_{\text{recv}}^-$. □

For proving (WR), we need to relate the latest possible end of a write with the earliest possible start of a read of the same item, namely, $t_s(R_j^k) - t_e(W_i^{k-\alpha}) \geq 0$. In particular, we will show that this condition is true if:

$$\alpha \geq \pi + \left\lceil \frac{\Delta_{\text{send}}^+ + \Delta_{\text{msg}}^+ + \Delta_{\text{mem}}^+ - \Delta_{\text{recv}}^-}{T^-} \right\rceil$$

Lemma 7. $\forall k > 0 : t_s(R_j^k) - t_e(W_i^{k-\alpha}) \geq 0$

Proof. We use a case differentiation to prove this Lemma:

- $1 \leq k \leq \alpha$: $t_s(R_j^k) - \underbrace{t_e(W_i^{k-\alpha})}_{=0 \text{ by Lemma 4}} = t_s(R_j^k) \geq 0$.
- $k > \alpha$:

$$\begin{aligned}
&t_s(R_j^k) - t_e(W_i^{k-\alpha}) \geq t(C_j^k) + \Delta_{\text{recv}}^- - t(C_i^{k-\alpha}) - \Delta_{\text{send}}^+ - \Delta_{\text{msg}}^+ - \Delta_{\text{mem}}^+ \\
&= \underbrace{t(C_j^k) - t(C_i^{k-\pi})}_{\geq 0 \text{ by Assumption 1}} + \underbrace{t(C_i^{k-\pi}) - t(C_i^{k-\alpha})}_{\geq(\alpha-\pi)T^- \text{ by Assumption 2}} + \Delta_{\text{recv}}^- - \Delta_{\text{send}}^+ - \Delta_{\text{msg}}^+ - \Delta_{\text{mem}}^+ \\
&\geq \left(\pi + \left\lceil \frac{\Delta_{\text{send}}^+ + \Delta_{\text{msg}}^+ + \Delta_{\text{mem}}^+ - \Delta_{\text{recv}}^-}{T^-} \right\rceil - \pi\right) T^- + \Delta_{\text{recv}}^- - \Delta_{\text{send}}^+ - \Delta_{\text{msg}}^+ - \Delta_{\text{mem}}^+ \\
&\geq T^- \frac{\Delta_{\text{send}}^+ + \Delta_{\text{msg}}^+ + \Delta_{\text{mem}}^+ - \Delta_{\text{recv}}^-}{T^-} + + \Delta_{\text{recv}}^- - \Delta_{\text{send}}^+ - \Delta_{\text{msg}}^+ - \Delta_{\text{mem}}^+ = 0.
\end{aligned}$$ □

This proof shows that if the buffer is prefilled with at least

$$\alpha = \pi + \left\lceil \frac{\Delta_{\text{send}}^+ + \Delta_{\text{msg}}^+ + \Delta_{\text{mem}}^+ - \Delta_{\text{recv}}^-}{T^-} \right\rceil$$

elements, no element is read before it is written.

4.5 Bounded Buffer Size

Now we replace the unbounded memory with a FIFO buffer of bounded size. We will now determine a lower bound for the buffer size such that (OV) holds.

As in the previous section, we will show the start and end time, respectively, for the read and write operations. To determine the required buffer size, we need the earliest possible start time of all write operations (excluding the first α writes, since they are prefilled).

Lemma 8. $\forall k > 0 : t_s(W_i^k) \geq t(C_i^k) + \Delta_{\text{send}}^- + \Delta_{\text{msg}}^-$

Proof. We already know that $C_i^k \rightsquigarrow D_i^k \rightsquigarrow W_i^k$. Since D_i^k is triggered by the k-th $\langle\text{tick}, k\rangle$ message, we get: $t(D_i^k) = t(C_i^k) + \Delta_{\text{send}}(i,k)$. Since W_i^k is triggered by the k-th $\langle\text{data}, l\rangle$ message, we get:

$$\begin{aligned} t_{\text{s}}(W_i^k) &= t(D_i^k) + \Delta_{\text{msg}}(i,k) = t(C_i^k) + \Delta_{\text{send}}(i,k) + \Delta_{\text{msg}}(i,k) \\ &\geq t(C_i^k) + \Delta_{\text{send}}^- + \Delta_{\text{msg}}^-. \end{aligned} \qquad \square$$

In addition to the start of the write operations, we need the latest possible end time of the read operations.

Lemma 9. $\forall k > 0 : t_{\text{e}}(R_j^k) \leq t(C_j^k) + \Delta_{\text{recv}}^+ + \Delta_{\text{rd}}^+$

Proof. We already know that $C_j^k \rightsquigarrow R_j^k$. Since R_j^k is triggered by the k-th $\langle\text{tick}, k\rangle$ message, we get: $t_{\text{s}}(R_j^k) = t(C_j^k) + \Delta_{\text{recv}}(j,k) \leq t(C_j^k) + \Delta_{\text{recv}}^+$. Knowing that a read operation finishes within $\Delta_{\text{rd}}(j,k)$, we get:

$$t_{\text{e}}(R_j^k) = t_{\text{s}}(R_j^k) + \Delta_{\text{rd}}(j,k) \leq t_{\text{s}}(R_j^k) + \Delta_{\text{rd}}^+ \leq t(C_j^k) + \Delta_{\text{recv}}^+ + \Delta_{\text{rd}}^+. \qquad \square$$

After calculating the start and end time of the operations, we will now show the maximum possible number of unread messages in the buffer.

Lemma 10. *There are always less or equal than $\pi+\alpha+\beta$ unread elements in the buffer (i.e., $\forall k \geq 0 : t_{\text{s}}(W_i^{k+\pi+\beta}) - t_{\text{e}}(R_j^k) \geq 0$) with $\beta = \left\lceil \frac{\Delta_{\text{recv}}^+ + \Delta_{\text{rd}}^+ - \Delta_{\text{send}}^- - \Delta_{\text{msg}}^-}{T^-} \right\rceil$.*

Proof. We have to distinguish two cases:

- $k = 0$: At the beginning there are the α prefilled elements in the buffer. Therefore the buffer size is surely sufficient.
- $k > 0$:

$$\begin{aligned} t_{\text{s}}(W_i^{k+\pi+\beta}) - t_{\text{e}}(R_j^k) &\geq t(C_i^{k+\pi+\beta}) + \Delta_{\text{send}}^- + \Delta_{\text{msg}}^- - t(C_j^k) - \Delta_{\text{recv}}^+ - \Delta_{\text{rd}}^+ \\ &= \underbrace{t(C_i^{k+\pi+\beta}) - t(C_j^{k+\beta})}_{\geq 0 \text{ by Assumption 1}} + \underbrace{t(C_j^{k+\beta}) - t(C_j^k)}_{\geq \beta T^- \text{ by Assumption 2}} + \Delta_{\text{send}}^- + \Delta_{\text{msg}}^- - \Delta_{\text{recv}}^+ - \Delta_{\text{rd}}^+ \\ &\geq \left\lceil \frac{\Delta_{\text{recv}}^+ + \Delta_{\text{rd}}^+ - \Delta_{\text{send}}^- - \Delta_{\text{msg}}^-}{T^-} \right\rceil T^- + \Delta_{\text{send}}^- + \Delta_{\text{msg}}^- - \Delta_{\text{recv}}^+ - \Delta_{\text{rd}}^+ \\ &\geq \Delta_{\text{recv}}^+ + \Delta_{\text{rd}}^+ - \Delta_{\text{send}}^- - \Delta_{\text{msg}}^- + \Delta_{\text{send}}^- + \Delta_{\text{msg}}^- - \Delta_{\text{recv}}^+ - \Delta_{\text{rd}}^+ = 0. \end{aligned} \qquad \square$$

Theorem 1. *For $\alpha = \pi + \left\lceil \frac{\Delta_{\text{send}}^+ + \Delta_{\text{msg}}^+ + \Delta_{\text{mem}}^+ - \Delta_{\text{recv}}^-}{T^-} \right\rceil$, a sufficient FIFO buffer size is given by*

$$2\pi + \left\lceil \frac{\Delta_{\text{send}}^+ + \Delta_{\text{msg}}^+ + \Delta_{\text{mem}}^+ - \Delta_{\text{recv}}^-}{T^-} \right\rceil + \left\lceil \frac{\Delta_{\text{recv}}^+ + \Delta_{\text{rd}}^+ - \Delta_{\text{send}}^- - \Delta_{\text{msg}}^-}{T^-} \right\rceil .$$

5 VLSI Implementation

The layout of a single FU, consisting of application logic, communication subsystem, and (DARTS) clocking subsystem, is shown in Fig. 3. As usual with GALS systems, we implemented communication subsystem and application logic according to the classic synchronous paradigm, using standard development tools.

The **transmitter** operates as a synchronous peripheral slave device of a controller implemented in the FU's application logic. Data to be transmitted is passed via an 8-bit register interface. In case no data is available from the controller, the transmitter is responsible for inserting idle patterns. In any case, the data is serialized and line coding is applied. To guarantee small skew between clock and data line, a matched (parallel) routing of the PCB traces for data and clock is employed. (Similar constraints are found in all modern high speed source synchronous systems like DDR memory). To relax the timing margins as far as possible, we introduce a 180° phase shift between data and clock.

The **memory element** is integrated into the receiver node. Its read port is controlled by the receiver clock, whereas the write port is under the control of the sender node. Recall that this buffer memory effectively compensates the (bounded) clock skew between sender and receiver clock, and thus ensures metastability-free data communication. As shown in Sect. 4, this can indeed be accomplished with a sufficiently large buffer size. The memory element itself is implemented as a ring buffer with individual address pointers for input and output. Since the only potential for metastability, namely a simultaneous access to the same address [18] is ruled out by construction, it can be written to and read from independently.

The **receiver** operates as a synchronous peripheral slave device for a controller unit implemented in the receiving FU. It takes the data out of the buffer using its own (i.e. its controller's) local clock. After de-serializing and decoding the data, it supplies them to its controller via a memory-mapped 8-bit interface.

5.1 Mapping the Model to the Implementation

The correctness of the algorithms presented and proved correct in Sect. 3 and 4 depends on Assumptions 1–4, which must be guaranteed by the underlying system. In our case, bounded precision and accuracy are inherently guaranteed by our DARTS clocking scheme, and the synchronous start is ensured by a system-wide reset (including DARTS). Finally, Assumption 4 is a timing condition known from classic synchronous systems. It bounds the uncertainty of

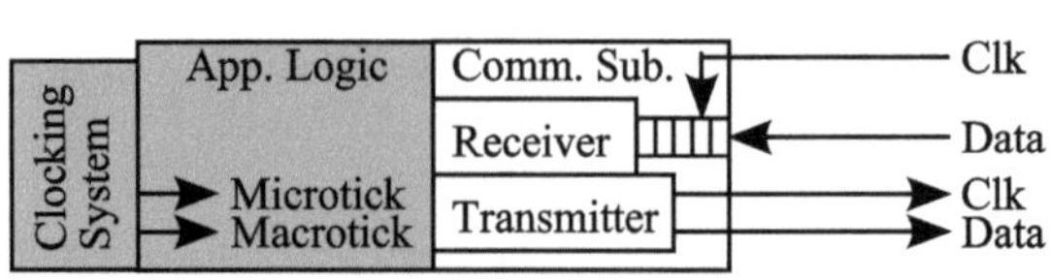

Fig. 3. Layout of a functional unit

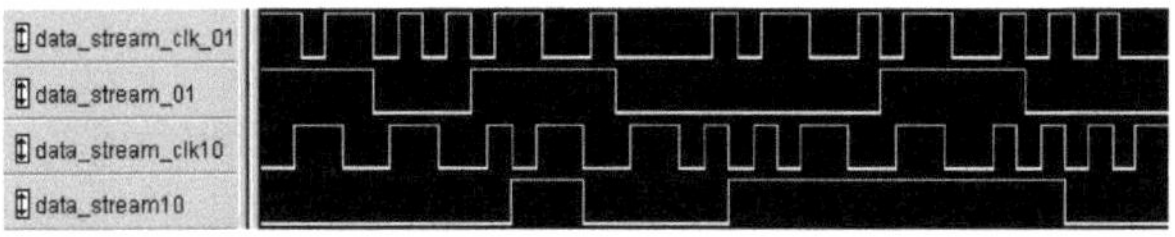

Fig. 4. Example communication within the test system

the involved delays and relates it to the clock period. Since delay uncertainties are caused by manufacturing variabilities and varying operation conditions only, guaranteeing Assumption 4 is easily accomplished by means of standard timing analysis tools.

The actions/events and messages introduced in the algorithmic model in Sect. 4 are mapped to the implementation as follows: The messages $\langle \text{tick}, k \rangle$ are just clock ticks. The delays $\Delta_{\text{send}}(i,k)$ and $\Delta_{\text{recv}}(j,k)$ are the times needed for the ticks to reach the sender output element and the read port of the memory element, respectively. The message $\langle \text{data}\ , l \rangle$ is implemented as the data and clock transition running on the serial communication link between the sender and receiver. The corresponding delay $\Delta_{\text{msg}}(i,k)$ is the sum of the involved output-, line- and input-delays and the memory setup time. Obviously the simple signal lines that convey all these messages respect FIFO order. The duration of the write operation $\Delta_{\text{mem}}(i,k)$ is the time needed for the new data to reach the output element of the memory (including all combinational logic on its path) after the clock edge and the setup time needed for the output element. $\Delta_{\text{rd}}(j,k)$ is mapped to the hold time of the memory output element.

5.2 Performance and Efficiency

A typical operation example of our communication subsystem is shown in the logic analyzer trace in Fig. 4. It was generated by means of our test system (see Sect. 6.1) using the random clock emulation mode with a precision of 4. The clock traces reveal that our approach also works under very unfavorable clocking conditions: The highly variable phase relation between the clocks would definitely upset any traditional (phase-)synchronous system, and would also violate the feasible operating conditions of synchronizer-based solutions like [10,11].

Our implementation achieves a (gross) data rate of 1 Mbps/MHz, since one data bit is transferred with every active clock edge. This leads to a data rate of 24 Mbps for our test system clock of 24 MHz, which uses a single data rail. Multiplying this throughput by using parallel data lines is straightforward. For a system with a clock frequency of 100 MHz, for example, using 16 parallel data lines for one clock line would result in a data rate of 1.6 Gbps.

6 Experiments

We now verify the claim that the buffer size derived in Sect. 4 (a) is sufficient for fault-free and metastability-free operation with clocks showing a precision of several clock cycles, and (b) gives a reasonably tight lower bound.

6.1 Test System

To evaluate our communication scheme under controllable and possibly very unfavorable conditions, we have implemented a test system. It consists of 3 Xilinx Virtex-4 FPGAs and a host PC. One of the FPGAs acts as a global test controller. The other two FPGAs host target FUs that exchange messages. They are randomly generated at the host PC and downloaded to both target FPGAs, such that the receiver of a message can check its correctness. If an error is detected, communication stops until the test controller has re-initialized the test system.

6.2 Clock Emulation

To systematically investigate worst case scenarios and reproduce interesting effects, we need full control over the speed and the relative position of the target FUs' clocks. To this end, we decided to use a clock emulation instead of the real DARTS clocking scheme, which would be much harder to control. This emulation is performed by the controller FPGA. The respective clock patterns are downloaded from the host PC where they have been a priori calculated. In essence, they are a sequence of integer multiples of a base clock period that determines the resolution of the clocking system.

In our experiments, we have used the following two types of clock emulation:

Worst case precision clock emulation. In this mode, the two clock signals are deliberately kept as far apart as the precision allows. This way we can check whether the system can indeed operate under unfavorable conditions. At the same time, chances are high that the communication will fail if the buffer size is too small, which gives an indication of whether the size calculated in Sect. 4 is a tight lower bound. To actually generate such worst case clock scenarios, we artificially stop one clock while the other one runs at its full frequency. As soon as the precision limit is reached, the stopped clock is speeded up to its full frequency again.

Random clock emulation. This mode is used to assess the performance of the system under continuously changing relative clock speeds. An example was already shown in Fig. 4. Clock frequencies are varied over time here, by utilizing a set of "clock primitives" (each one with a different frequency) that can be used by the host PC when constructing an emulation schedule: Clock primitives are randomly assembled into two different sequences that represent the clock traces of the two target FUs. Of course, care is taken to keep the emulated clocks within the precision limits.

6.3 Test Conditions

For the experiments reported here, we used a clocking system with a precision of 4. The emulation base clock (emulation resolution) was set to 48 MHz. This leads to a mean clock frequency of 24 MHz for the random emulation mode, and a clock frequency of 24 MHz for the worst-case emulation mode. The test system was implemented in a way that minimizes the required buffer size according to Theorem 1: The last term is zero, while the middle term evaluates to 1. This leads to a required buffer size of $2\pi + 1 = 9$.

6.4 Performed Tests and Test Results

Recall that the purpose of our experiments is to verify whether the calculated buffer size is (a) sufficient and (b) minimal. Since it is of course not possible to exhaustively emulate all possible clock relations, we can not *prove* the absence of any buffer overruns for a buffer size 9. We can, however, check the failure-free operation under adverse conditions during some period in order to increase the confidence in our modeling. Furthermore, by reducing the buffer size below the calculated limit, we can easily test the hypothesis (b).

The actual test runs were executed 5000 times for each buffer size and each clock emulation type. For each run, we calculated new clock traces for the emulation. If no failure has been encountered after 2 seconds of observation time, the run was considered fault-free. The resulting histogram, showing the error percentage, has been calculated after all the test runs have been completed.

Figure 5 presents the collected test results. First of all, the random emulation mode did not produce any error in case of a buffer size of eight, whereas the worst case emulation mode did. This indicates that the typical failure probability is actually very low, and becomes visible within limited observation time only if worst case conditions are artificially established. For smaller buffer sizes, the expected failures could be observed frequently. Therefore, our results give a good confirmation of our hypotheses (a) and (b) and, hence, of our analytical results.

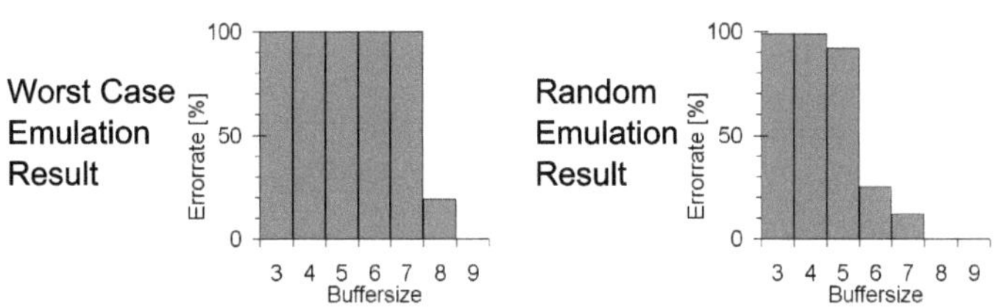

Fig. 5. Results of the experiments

7 Conclusion and Future Work

Multi-synchronous clocking is an attractive alternative to globally synchronous clocking in modern high-speed VLSI circuits, such as complex SoCs, which also allows to avoid the single point of failure usually represented by a central clock source. In this paper, we have shown how to employ the loose synchrony provided by multi-synchronous GALS system for implementing a high-speed pipelined communication scheme that is metastability-free by construction. It employs a bounded-size FIFO buffer for compensating the skew between the sender and receiver clock. We derived a reasonably tight lower bound for the required buffer size, and provided a formal proof of correctness and freedom of metastability. Furthermore, we have described an efficient implementation of our communication scheme, and experimentally demonstrated its feasibility using a custom test system. Part of our future work will be devoted to extensions of our approach, in particular, flow control and timing error detection.

Acknowledgments. Our thanks go to Matthias Fuegger for guiding us through the formal proofs and to Ulrich Schmid whose ideas initiated this work.

References

1. Metra, C., Francescantonio, S.D., Mak, T., Ricco, B.: Implications of clock distribution faults and issues with screening them during manufacturing testing. IEEE Transactions on Computers 53(5), 531–546 (2004)
2. Chapiro, D.M.: Globally-Asynchronous Locally-Syn-chronous Systems. PhD thesis, Stanford Univ. (October 1984)
3. Constantinescu, C.: Trends and challenges in VLSI circuit reliability. IEEE Micro. 23(4), 14–19 (2003)
4. Borkar, S.: Designing reliable systems from unreliable components: the challenges of transistor variability and degradation. IEEE Micro. 25(6) (November 2005)
5. Mavis, D., Eaton, P.: SEU and SET modeling and mitigation in deep submicron technologies. In: Proceedings 45th Annual IEEE International Reliability physics symposium, April 2007, pp. 293–305 (2007)
6. Nicolaidis, M.: Design for soft error mitigation. IEEE Transactions on Device and Materials Reliability 5(3), 405–418 (2005)
7. Fairbanks, S.: Method and apparatus for a distributed clock generator (2004)
8. Maza, M., Aranda, M.: Interconnected rings and oscillators as gigahertz clock distribution nets. In: Proceedings of the 13th ACM symposium on VLSI (2003)
9. Kleeman, L., Cantoni, A.: Metastable behavior in digital systems. IEEE Design & Test of Computers, 4–19 (December 1987)
10. Ginosar, R., Kol, R.: Adaptive synchronization. In: Computer Design: VLSI in Computers and Processors, ICCD 1998 (1998)
11. Panades, I.M., Greiner, A.: Bi-synchronous FIFO for Synchronous Circuit Communication Well Suited for Network-on-Chip in GALS Architectures. In: Proc. 1st Int. Symp. on Networks-on-Chip (NOCS 2007). IEEE CS Press, Los Alamitos (2007)
12. Dobkin, R., Ginosar, R., Sotiriou, C.: Data synchronization issues in gals socs. In: Asynchronous Circuits and Systems, ASYNC 2004 (2004)
13. Fuegger, M., Schmid, U., Fuchs, G., Kempf, G.: Fault-Tolerant Distributed Clock Generation in VLSI Systems-on-Chip. In: Proc. of the 6th European Dependable Computing Conference (EDCC-6). IEEE Comp. Soc. Press, Los Alamitos (2006)
14. Teehan, P., Greenstreet, M., Lemieux, G.: A survey and taxonomy of gals design styles. IEEE Design & Test of Computers (2007)
15. Semiat, Y., Ginosar, R.: Timing measurements of synchronization circuits. In: 9th Int. Symp. on Asynchronous Circuits and Systems, 2003. Proceedings (2003)
16. Widder, J., Schmid, U.: Achieving synchrony without clocks. Research Report 49/2005, Technische Universität Wien, Institut für Technische Informatik (2005)
17. Ferringer, M., Fuchs, G., Steininger, A., Kempf, G.: VLSI Implementation of a Fault-Tolerant Distributed Clock Generation. In: IEEE International Symposium on Defect and Fault-Tolerance in VLSI Systems (DFT 2006), October 2006, pp. 563–571 (2006)
18. Lamport, L.: Arbitration-free synchronization. Distrib. Comput. 16(2-3) (2003)

From Local Impact Functions to Global Adaptation of Service Compositions*

Liliana Rosa[1], Luís Rodrigues[1], Antónia Lopes[2], Matti Hiltunen[3], and Richard Schlichting[3]

[1] INESC-ID/IST
[2] Faculty of Sciences, University of Lisbon
[3] AT&T Labs Research

Abstract. The problem of self-optimization and adaptation in the context of customizable systems is becoming increasingly important with the emergence of complex software systems and unpredictable execution environments. Here, a general framework for automatically deciding on when and how to adapt a system whenever it deviates from the desired behavior is presented. In this framework, the adaptation targets of the system are described in terms of a high-level policy that establishes goals for a set of performance indicators. The decision process is based on information provided independently for each service that describes the available adaptations, their impact on performance indicators, and any limitations or requirements. The technique consists of both offline and online phases. Offline, rules are generated specifying service adaptations that may help to achieve the specified goals when a given change in the execution context occurs. Online, the corresponding rule is evaluated when a change occurs to choose which adaptations to perform. Experimental results using a prototype framework in the context of a web-based application demonstrate the effectiveness of this approach.

1 Introduction

Today's complex software systems and services (e.g., Apache, Tomcat, MySQL, virtual machines) offer different facilities for customizing their behavior, including loadable modules and numerous configuration options. Such facilities can be used to adapt the behavior of these services even during execution in response to changes in the operational envelope. These changes might be the result of, for instance, changes in system workload or in the available resources. While dynamic resource allocation (e.g., [1]) can be used to respond to such changes, adaptations that affect the service behavior itself can also be a powerful tool.

This paper addresses the problem of how to select appropriate service adaptations when the system behavior deviates from that which is considered optimal, for example, to provide a certain quality of service. This problem is extremely challenging since the best adaptation may depend not only on the particular

* This work was funded by REDICO project (PTDC/EIA/71752/2006).

R. Guerraoui and F. Petit (Eds.): SSS 2009, LNCS 5873, pp. 593–608, 2009.

configuration of the system—that is, the set of services and how these services are configured—but also on information that can be extremely dynamic and unpredictable, such as the pattern of service invocations. In this paper, we consider software systems built from one or more adaptable services. We assume that the behavior of such service compositions can be described using a set of *key performance indicators* (KPIs) that need to be maintained or optimized, and that the system behavior can be controlled by applying one or more adaptations.

There are several approaches to deciding on how to adapt a service composition. One approach is to consider the composition as a black box and use control theory and/or learning techniques [2,3,4] to derive adaptation policies. Unfortunately, this approach is expensive and the resulting policy is only valid for the specific configuration and workloads used during the learning process. Thus, if the system configuration changes, the entire process has to be repeated. The same applies for changes in the workload, where a small change can have a large impact on the set of adaptations that need to be selected. Another approach relies on the system architect or system administrator specifying a low-level adaptation policy for the system's service composition manually based on her own knowledge on the system operation [5]. Typically, these policies consist of declarative Event-Condition-Action (ECA) rules specifying how the system must adapt in the presence of specific events and conditions. Unfortunately, as the complexity of the system composition increases, this task becomes harder and more error-prone. Indeed, it often becomes impractical or even impossible for the system architect to manage all the possible interactions and side effects among the adaptations available for all services. The Cholla system [6] also addresses a similar problem, proposing a solution based on fuzzy control rules. While rules can often be developed independently, additional coordination rules specific to the chosen set of rules are often required. Also, this work does not provide an explicit mapping from KPI-based goals to adaptation rules. Note that our work is orthogonal to research on coordinating distributed adaptations [7,8]. In fact, such techniques could be combined with our approach in case distributed coordination is required.

While a complex system of this type is hard to understand, the developer of each individual component or module usually has a clear understanding of the ways the component can be adapted and the impact of each adaptation on the performance of the component in isolation. For instance, the designer of a graphical component G may implement two operational modes: one that produces high quality images and one that produces low quality images. The designer, knowing the implementation details, is fully aware of the tradeoffs involved, specifically that the low quality mode produces an image with lower image resolution, but consumes less memory and less processor time than the high quality counterpart. The challenge, of course, is to mesh this information with that from other components to devise the best solution.

The goal of this work, then, is to make services adaptive by leveraging information from service developers about the characteristics of each individual component considered independently of where it will be used. To realize this goal, we propose a technique that uses this information to select the best adaptations for a service when its execution deviates from the desired behavior. The selection process is driven by a high-level policy that specifies the desired behavior—and, hence, the goals the adaptations should strive to achieve—and relies on information provided for each component describing possible adaptations, their impacts on KPIs, and any limitations or requirements. The proposed technique consists of both offline and online phases; in the offline phase, a set of service adaptations that can help achieve the specified goals is created, while in the online phase, adaptations are selected from this set in response to a change in the execution context using the current system status and workload as input. For example, in the above example, if the graphical service G is heavily utilized (high workload), the change from high quality to low quality mode may yield significant memory, processor, and/or bandwidth savings, while if G is in fact lightly utilized, the same adaptations may have negligible impact. Thus, the adaptations selected by our technique take into account not only the impact of each adaptation, but also the contribution of each service to the performance of the entire composition.

The rest of the paper is organized as follows. Section 2 describes the way in which the impact of possible adaptations on system performance is specified, and also how high level goals can be captured in a policy. Section 3 then explains how ECA rules are derived offline from the policy, while Section 4 describes how these rules are evaluated online. The framework is illustrated and evaluated in Section 5 using a web based application built from the composition of several services that handle the process of replying to a HTTP request. Experimental results show that selected adaptations are effective for different compositions of the same services and different workloads. Section 6 concludes the paper.

2 Adaptable Services and Adaptation Goals

The proposed approach is based on adaptation goals defined in terms of a set of KPIs and requires information regarding adaptations, their impacts, and constraints for each service component. As mentioned above, KPIs are metrics that capture system performance, like CPU or memory use, among others [2].

The two key assumptions behind the approach are: (i) the value of each KPI for a service composition C is $\sum_{s \in C} s.KPI$, where $s.KPI$ is the "contribution" of service s to that performance indicator, and (ii) it is possible to express the (localized) impact of each adaptation of a service s in each of these KPI_s. For instance, the CPU used by a service composition is an example of a KPI that can be defined as the sum of the CPU used by each service in the composition. An adaptation of a service s that, if applied, changes the CPU used by s would have to give a function that estimates the new value of $s.cpu\_u$.

A KPI definition includes a name, the type of the expected value, and the acceptable *error_margin* in any evaluation of the KPI, as illustrated below.

```
KPI cpu_u: double Error 0.1
```

This means that two values of the KPI within *error_margin* of each other are considered indistinguishable from the point of view of goal evaluation.

2.1 Specification of Service Adaptations

Our approach relies on local information regarding each adaptation to assess how these adaptations can be used to change system behavior. These adaptations involve either changing service parameters or exchanging service implementations. The impacts of each adaptation on the system behavior is specified against a set of KPIs and a service model.

Service models describe the service components available for use in compositions and, for each component, the configurable parameters and available implementations. We consider service models as defined in our previous work [9], i.e., defined in terms of a type hierarchy reflecting the *is a* relationship, taking into account the functionality provided by the services. Service types can be concrete, designating a specific service for which an implementation is available, or abstract, representing simply the characteristics of a group of other service types. Below is the model for a concrete service that provides static webpages with a configurable parameter *ImgQlt* that controls image quality (resolution):

```
Service StaticContent
  Parameters
    ImgQlt:{low, regular}
```

The service model is needed to support the specification of adaptations, which must include: a) the concerned service or service component, b) the adaptation action(s) to be performed, c) constraints such as the required service state or other adaptations that have to be performed simultaneously, and d) the impact of the adaptation on each KPI. If a KPI is omitted from the impacts, it means that the KPI is not affected. The following example shows the specification of an adaptation of the *StaticContent* service:

```
Adaptation ToLowStatic
 Service:
  StaticContent
 Actions:
  setParameter(ImgQlt, low)
 Requires:
  ImgQlt == regular
 Impacts:
  StaticContent.cpu_u /= 1.21   //decreases
  StaticContent.resolution = 1   //changes to low
```

This adaptation changes the image quality from regular to low, with the impact being to decrease the CPU used by the service and the image resolution. The effect of the adaptation on the KPIs is described by *impact functions* under the label *Impacts*, which provides an estimate for the new value of s.KPI if the adaptation is performed given its current value. Impacts can also be expressed in terms of current values of the configurable parameters, the current version of a service, or the presence or absence of a given service component. Even when not explicitly stated, any adaptation is only applicable if the target service or service component is present in the current service composition. We assume that meta-information about the deployed and executing service compositions, as well as the value of their parameters, is available at runtime. The problem of deriving the impact functions for each adaptation is outside the scope of this paper, but existing approaches can be applied [2].

Additional adaptation constraints can be specified by listing which adaptations of different services cannot be applied at the same time. By default, adaptations of the same service that have impact on the same KPI are assumed to conflict, but it is possible to specify a single adaptation that considers several actions provided the joint impact of these actions over the KPIs can be defined. These conflicts are simply described as pairs of adaptations:

```
Conflict conflict_name Adaptations (serviceA.adapt1,serviceB.adapt2)
```

The complete specification therefore consists of the service model, the adaptations, and the conflicts.

2.2 Policies

Adaptation goals are specified in terms of a policy that describes the desired values for a set of KPIs. A policy describes: a) the KPIs that are relevant to the policy, b) the goals to be met by the system, and c) the values of configuration parameters related to the runtime operation of the adaptation engine. Besides identifying the relevant KPIs, the policy can further use them to specify *composite KPIs*, denoted by CKPIs. CKPIs are identified by a *ckpi_name* and their specification consists of a function of several KPIs, and an *error_margin*:

```
CKPI ckpi_name = f(kpi1, kpi2, ...) Error error_margin
```

This function also makes it possible to derive the impact of each adaptation in the CKPI from the impacts of the adaptations in *kpi1*, *kpi2*, etc. As an example, the definition of the CKPI *gdev* below measures the weighted deviation from target CPU and memory utilization values:

```
CKPI gdev = 0.5*|cpu_u-0.6| + 0.5*|mem_u-0.4| Error 0.1
```

Henceforth, we use KPI to refer to either a basic KPI or a CKPI.

A policy can have one or more goals that are ranked to prioritize goals in situations where it is not possible to fulfill all goals. The rank is implicit in the order goals are listed in the policy, where the first goal has the highest rank. Additionally, there are two types of goals: *exact* and *approximation* goals. Exact goals separate the values of a performance indicator in two disjoint sets: *acceptable* and *not acceptable*. We consider the following types of exact goals:

```
Goal goal_name: kpi_name Above threshold_down MinimumGain gvalue
Goal goal_name: kpi_name Below threshold_up MinimumGain gvalue
Goal goal_name: kpi_name Between thr_down thr_up MinimumGain gvalue
```

An *Above* goal states that the value of the KPI should be kept above the stated threshold, a *Below* goal that the value should be kept below the threshold, and a *Between* goal that the value should be kept within lower and upper thresholds. In all three, the *MinimumGain* specifies the minimum change necessary to perform the adaptation; that is, if the estimated change in the KPI value is below *gvalue*, the adaptation is not worth performing. The *gvalue* should be greater than the *error_margin* specified for the target KPI.

In contrast, instead of simply classifying the values of a KPI as good or bad, approximation goals specify a total order between these values, that is, for any two values, it specifies which one is better. We consider the following types of approximation goals:

```
Goal goal_name: kpi_name Close target MinimumGain gvalue Every interval
Goal goal_name: Minimize kpi_name MinimumGain gvalue Every interval
Goal goal_name: Maximize kpi_name MinimumGain gvalue Every interval
```

A *Close* goal states that the KPI value should be kept as close as possible to the *target* value, a *Minimize* goal states that the KPI value should be as small as possible, and a *Maximize* goal states that it should be as large as possible. As with exact goals, it is also possible to specify the expected minimum gain required in order to perform an adaptation. Furthermore, associated with each approximation goal, is a time *interval* that specifies how often the system should try to find an adaptation aiming for a better value for the KPI. Note that while adaptation towards an exact goal is only triggered when the current KPI value is unacceptable, an approximation goal opens the possibility of continuously attempting to improve the system behavior aiming for a better value.

Finally, a policy may also define the values of configuration parameters that control the runtime operation. For example, *mon_interval*, which controls how often the KPIs' current values are read, can be configured.

3 Rule Generation

Adaptation rules are generated offline from the policy using the specifications of the available adaptations. Each rule consists of an event and one or more alternative sets of adaptations A_i that may help achieve the specified goals when a change in the execution context occurs. These rules are evaluated at runtime to determine which set of adaptations should be executed given the current system state. The rules have the following format:

```
When event
 Select {A1, A2, ...}
```

The *When* clause defines the *event* that triggers the rule. This may be caused by a change signaled by a *sporadic event*—when some KPI exceeds a threshold, for example—or by the passage of time signaled by a *periodic event*. The *Select* clause lists all relevant sets of adaptations for dealing with that particular event. For instance, if a goal states that some KPI must be maintained above a given threshold, only those adaptations that affect this KPI and increase it are relevant. The sets A_i represent the viable combinations of the relevant adaptations, reflecting the fact that the combination of adaptations is subject to constraints imposed by conflicts or application conditions. Naturally, given that rules are generated offline, it is only possible to take into account the aspects that do not require runtime state information.

Extracting the rule sets offline in this way has two main advantages. First, it often simplifies the online phase and improves its performance as a result. Second, by capturing the online behavior in a human-readable form, the system operators can better understand the behavior of the system. This is especially valuable in cases where the observed behavior is counter-intuitive to the (expected) impact of the high-level policy.

3.1 Event Extraction

Event extraction is the first task of rule generation. This step relies on the assumption that the component that monitors the system performance, the *context monitor*, is able to generate different types of events divided into sporadic and periodic events. The *kpiAbove(kpi,x)* and *kpiBelow(kpi,x)* events signal when the value of *kpi* is detected to be above or below the value x, and needs to be decreased or increased, respectively. Similarly, *kpiIncrease(kpi,θ,condition)* and *kpiDecrease(kpi,θ,condition)* are periodic events generated every period θ, if the *condition* over the current value of *kpi* holds, and signals that the value of *kpi* needs to be increased or decreased, respectively.

As noted above, the high-level policy has two distinct types of goals. When an exact goal is violated, system adaptation should be triggered. For approximation goals, adaptations are triggered periodically, thus they require the use of periodic events. Table 1 summarizes the types of events generated for each type of goal and how these events are triggered.

Table 1. Events generated for each type of goal

Type	Goal	Event 1	Event 2	Trigger
Exact	Above	kpiBelow(kpi, x)	-	threshold exceeded
Exact	Below	kpiAbove(kpi, y)	-	threshold exceeded
Exact	Between	kpiBelow(kpi, x)	kpiAbove(kpi, y)	threshold exceeded
Approx	Close	kpiIncrease(kpi, θ, cond)	kpiDecrease(kpi, θ, cond)	periodic
Approx	Maximize	kpiIncrease(kpi, θ, cond)	-	periodic
Approx	Minimize	kpiDecrease(kpi, θ, cond)	-	periodic

The specific events that are extracted from a high-level policy depend on the different values used in the goals and KPI declarations. Here, we explain how the values in the event attributes are defined for each type of goal. Figure 1 provides examples of events for some goal types. For an *Above* goal, an event of type *kpiBelow* needs to be triggered when the value of the KPI falls below the specified threshold by a margin greater than the KPI *error_margin*. Similarly, for a *Below* goal, an event of type *kpiAbove* needs to be triggered when the value of the KPI exceeds the specified threshold. Since *Between* goals are a

```
Goal cpu_reserve: cpu_u Below 0.6 MinimumGain 0.2
Event kpiAbove(cpu_u,0.7)     // 0.6+0.1

Goal target_cpu: cpu_u Between 0.4 0.6 MinimumGain 0.2
Event kpiBelow (cpu_u,0.3)    // 0.4-0.1
Event kpiAbove (cpu_u,0.7)    // 0.6+0.1

Goal minimize_deviation: Minimize gdev MinimumGain 0.2 Every 10
Event kpiDecrease (gdev,10, true)

Goal target_cpu: cpu_u Close 0.5 MinimumGain 0.2 Every 20
Event kpiDecrease (cpu_u,20, ">0.6")    // 0.5+0.1
Event kpiIncrease (cpu_u,20, "<0.4")    // 0.5-0.1
```

Fig. 1. Example events extracted from goals

combination of the *Above* and *Below* goals, both previous events are needed. For the *Minimize/Maximize* goals, a periodic event of type *kpiDecrease*/*kpiIncrease*, respectively, needs to be triggered with the period specified in the goal. Finally, for the *Close* goals, two distinct events are extracted, one for when the KPI needs to be decreased and the other for when the KPI needs to be increased, as illustrated in Figure 1. For each extracted event or periodic event, a rule is created with the *When* clause stating the event as the trigger for the rule evaluation.

3.2 Selecting Service Adaptations

The second task of offline rule generation is to identify the sets of adaptations that need to be included in each rule. The purpose of a given rule is either to increase or decrease the value of a given KPI. Thus, the impact functions declared in the adaptation descriptions need to be analyzed to check if the adaptation increases or decreases the value of the relevant KPI. Consider, for instance, a rule of the form **When** *kpiBelow(cpu_u,0.3)* **Select** ... where the aim is to increase the value of the *cpu_u*, and we have an adaptation X that applies to service S with the impact function *S.cpu_u *= 1.8*. To assess if adaptation X should be used in the rule, one simply checks whether the function $f(kpi) - kpi$ has a positive derivative. In this example, since the derivative of $1.8 \cdot x - x$ is 0.8, the adaptation X helps to increase the CPU utilization. Hence, this adaptation will be used in the construction of the sets of adaptations to be evaluated when the event *kpiBelow(cpu_u,0.3)* is triggered.

Once all adaptations that contribute to achieve the goal associated with the trigger event are known, rule generation proceeds with the calculation of the set of viable combinations, i.e., the sets of adaptations that can be executed at the same time. When there are adaptations that apply to the same service or conflicts between adaptations in the main set, it is necessary to break the main set into several sets, where all adaptations in the same set are compatible, and have all their requirements satisfied. To help the system operator understand the behavior of the system, an intentional representation of the set of viable combinations is used. As illustrated in the example below (in human readable form), all adaptations that contribute to achieve the goal associated with the trigger event are listed, together with the pairs of conflicting adaptations and pairs of adaptations that need to be executed together.

```
When event
  Adaptations: S1.A, S1.B, S2.X, S2.Y, S3.Z
   Conflicts: (S1.A, S2.X)  Dependencies: (S2.Y, S3.Z)
```

4 Rule Evaluation

The rules that were generated offline are evaluated at runtime. The evaluation of a rule **When** e **Select** $\{A_1, ..., A_n\}$ occurs whenever event e is triggered, and consists of selecting a combination of adaptations from the subsets of A_i, for $i = 1, ..., n$. The selected set includes the adaptations to be applied to the system and, hence, the aim of the selection process is to find the combination that best satisfies the goals defined in the adaptation policy.

The process of rule generation ensures that each A_i includes only adaptations that can be executed at the same time. However, these sets may include adaptations that cannot be applied in the current configuration of the system. This happens if the target service is not part of the current composition or if the constraints expressed in the *Requires* section of the adaptation do not hold. Hence, the evaluation of the rule starts by removing non-applicable adaptations from every A_i. Then, rule evaluation proceeds by searching for combinations that best match the goals expressed in the adaptation policy, taking into account the current system state.

As mentioned above, the search space $\mathcal{S}$ is the set of all subsets of all A_i. Intuitively, the search involves analyzing the estimated effects of the different combinations on the KPIs addressed by the goals of the adaptation policy and deducing which ones best fit these goals. More precisely, recall that adaptation policies define a set of ranked goals $\{G_1, ..., G_n\}$, where G_1 is the goal with the highest rank. The comparison between different combinations of adaptations relies on their evaluation against these goals, starting from G_1. The evaluation of a combination against a goal G_i depends on the type of goal (exact or approximation), with the impact functions of the involved adaptations being used to estimate the effect on the KPI_i associated with the goal.

Let KPI_i^C be the estimated impact of a combination of adaptations C on KPI_i. (Note that if C is the empty set, then KPI_i^C is just the current value of KPI_i.) C *best matches* $\{G_1, ..., G_i\}$ only if the following conditions hold:

1. if $i > 1$, C best matches $\{G_1, ..., G_{i-1}\}$
2. if G_i is an exact goal:
   - if G_i is currently satisfied: KPI_i^C also satisfies G_i;
   - if G_i is currently violated: there is a gain w.r.t. the current value of KPI_i and it exceeds the specified minimum gain;
3. if G_i is an approximation goal:
   - $|KPI_i^C - KPI_i^{C^*}| < error\_margin^{kpi}$ and, if C is not the empty set, the gain w.r.t. the current value of KPI_i exceeds the specified minimum gain;

   where C^* is, among the combinations in $\mathcal{S}$ that best match $\{G_1, ..., G_{i-1}\}$, the one that puts the KPI_i closer to the target specified in G_i.

For instance, consider the exact goal *cpu_reserve* and assume that the current *cpu_u* value is 0.75 (the goal is currently violated). A combination with a single adaptation whose estimated effect brings *cpu_u* to 0.9 is excluded because it violates the goal. A combination with a single adaptation whose estimated effect brings *cpu_u* to 0.65 is also excluded because it does not meet the specified minimum gain. Two combinations with a single adaptation whose estimated effects bring *cpu_u* to 0.50 and 0.55, respectively, are both candidates for being selected. Thus, the next ranked goal would be used to tie-break among them.

5 Evaluation

To evaluate the proposed approach, we conducted a study to analyze how successfully the rules generated offline drive the runtime adaptation, given changes that carry the system outside the desirable or acceptable behavior defined in the goals. To do so, we implemented a prototype of the framework in Java^{TM}, and developed an experiment that illustrates the use of the proposed approach for the autonomic management of web-based applications.

5.1 Services, Adaptations and Policy

The case study consists of a web site that offers both secure and non-secure content; part of this content is static, and another part is dynamically generated. The content is produced by several services that are adaptable, which allows the quality of any provided content to be controlled.

Three services provide content: *StaticContent*, *DynContent*, and *SecureContent*. The first, *StaticContent*, provides the static content web pages that are not secure. The service can operate on *regular* or *low* mode; in *low* mode it offers lower image quality as well as de-animated GIFs. Thus, it is possible to have two adaptations of the *StaticContent* service: from regular to low quality and vice-versa. The first adaptation reduces resource consumption, while the second increases the quality of service. The second service, *DynContent*, generates user-tailored non-secure webpages. The service also features regular and low versions similar to *StaticContent*, which are implemented by adding, removing, or changing HTML tags using the approach described in [10]. Furthermore, two implementations of the *DynContent* service can be used: a *heavyweight* implementation that determines new recommendations and advertisements for a user on the fly, and a *lightweight* implementation that uses cached recommendations and advertisements [11]. Finally, the third service, *SecureContent*, handles webpages that deal with account login or sensitive data, such as order payment information; it also generates regular and low versions in terms of image quality and animated GIFs. The service specification is presented below. Space limitations prevent us from describing the entire set of services adaptations (which is presented in [12]), that includes the adaptation *ToLowStatic* introduced in Section 2.

```
Abstract Service DynContent
  Parameters
    ImgGIFFilter:{on, off}

Service LWDynContent
  subtype DynContent

Service HWDynContent
  subtype DynContent
```

```
Service StaticContent
  Parameters
    ImgQlt:{low, regular}

Service SecureContent
  Parameters
    Mode:{low, regular}
```

In our case study we used three KPIs. The monitored system resource is the consumed CPU (*cpu_u*); recent research has shown this to be the main bottleneck for this type of application [13]. The quality of service provided to the user is captured by two synthetic metrics, the *resolution* of the images returned to the user (*resolution*), and the *accuracy* of the recommendations included in the web pages (*harvest*). We have also considered a CKPI *qos*, defined as the composition of both the resolution and the harvest of the pages returned to the user as follows:

```
KPI cpu_u: double Error 0.1
KPI resolution: integer Error 0
KPI harvest: integer  Error 0
CKPI qos = (2*resolution + harvest) Error 0
```

Using these KPIs, we defined the simple policy presented below that aims to provide users the best quality of service possible without exceeding a pre-defined threshold of CPU utilization. This policy is broadly similar to policies that have been used in related work, including policies to achieve optimal resource use for webservers [2,14], intermediary adaptation systems [10,15,16], and web server and user experience improvement [13]. The policy describes two goals. The first limits the value *cpu_u* to a pre-defined threshold of 0.6. This limitation is imposed to maintain an available CPU margin to deal with workload peaks. The focus of the second goal is to maximize the quality of the content provided to the user, ensuring that when resources are available, the best image quality, animated GIFs, and up-to-date recommendations are returned. The policy additionally specifies that the monitoring interval is 1 second.

```
Goal limit_cpu: cpu_u Below 0.6 MinimumGain 0.15
Goal max_qos: Maximize qos MinimumGain 1 Every 60
Configuration mon_interval 1
```

From this policy, event extraction and rule generation was performed offline. The extracted events are presented in Table 2. The rules, in their human readable form, are as follows:

```
When kpiAbove(cpu_u,0.7)
  Select {ToLowStatic, ActivateImgGIFFilter,ToLW+FilterOn,ToLW+FilterOff,
      ToLW+MaintainOn,ToLW+MaintainOff, ToLowModeSecure}

When kpiIncrease(qos,60,true)
  Select {ToRegularStatic, DeActivateImgGIFFilter,ToHW+FilterOn,ToHW+
      FilterOff,ToHW+MaintainOn,ToHW+MaintainOff, ToRegularModeSecure}
```

5.2 Experimental Setup

The prototype implementation consists of the overall framework, several static webpages (*StaticContent*), and the web site's dynamic generation components (*DynamicContent* and *SecureContent*). Each component is an adaptable *CGI* that offers two distinct behaviors that trade off the quality of service provided to the user with the resources used, primarily CPU usage. Apache web server [17] running on Linux is used to execute requests. To monitor the execution context, i.e., CPU usage, a simple monitoring tool was implemented in Python and integrated with the framework prototype. The monitoring tool can be configured in terms of the interval between reads and the stabilization time after adapting.

To analyze how the policy drives changes in the quality of service when the resource consumption varies, we generated several workloads to force different adaptations. In periods when the load is high, then, the system will adapt one

Table 2. Events generated for the case study

Type	Goal	Event 1	Trigger
Exact	*limit_cpu*	kpiAbove(*cpu_u*, $0.6 + 0.1$)	*cpu_u*> 0.7
Approx	*max_qos*	kpiIncrease(*qos*, 60, true)	periodic

or more components to provide a lower quality of service, to keep CPU usage below the given threshold. After adapting, the KPIs readings are ignored until the end of a stabilization period.

The experimental testbed consists in three machines. One machine runs the Apache Web Server as well as the services, while the other two machines run a workload generator. The three machines are connected by a 100 Mbps Ethernet. The server machine is a 8 x 3.22 GHz processor with 8 GB RAM running Linux (kernel v2.6.24-21). We used Apache HTTP Server v2.2.8 configured with 150 *MaxClients* and a *KeepAliveTimeout* of 15 seconds, with CGI and SSL modules enabled. The client machines run Pylot [18], an open source tool for testing performance and scalability of web services based on an XML file that describes the workload. We modified the original Pylot tool to run several workloads in sequence, each for a period of time, thus, varying the workload.

The services in our case study are implemented as follows. First, the *StaticContent* service is implemented using several HMTL pages containing text and images with different sizes (from 5 to 500 KB), each one with a low and a regular version. Second, the *DynContent* service is implemented as a CGI that generates the HTML pages on the fly according to parameters passed in the HTTP request. The generated pages include images and text, again with two different implementations of the service. Finally, the *SecureContent* service consists of dynamically generated pages requested over HTTPS, with text and media.

In terms of adaptations, the change between different versions in the *StaticContent* service is achieved using file system links. The HTTP request will request a HTML file. If the low version is in use, the link will point to the low version. When the adaptation sets *ImgQlt* to regular, the link is redirected to the regular version. The same approach is used when the other remaining parameters are set, and, also, to exchange implementations of *DynContent* service.

The three different workloads used are determined by the type and frequency of requests, for each of the three services described above. The *light* workload allows all services to be offered with maximum *qos*. The *medium* workload requires the *qos* to be lowered in order to respect the *cpu_u* threshold. Finally, the *heavy* workload requires the system to operate with an even lower *qos*.

As defined in the policy, the consumed CPU is monitored every second. Due to the variability of the workload, a change is only signaled if it is observed for at least 10 out of 15 consecutive samples.

5.3 Results

Services were initially deployed with a configuration that yields the best quality of service: static web pages and secure content are served with regular quality, while dynamic content is deployed using the heavyweight version and with the content filter off. Then, we subject the system to a varying workload.

The workload consists of a collection of urls that are requested by each client. The order of this list is randomized for each client to ensure that the sequences will differ. Each client waits for a response before sending another request; this interval is 10 milliseconds. Our experiment used 100 clients that run concurrently. The client rampup takes 25 seconds, therefore, 4 clients are launched every second. The clients start sending requests as soon as they start. The workload is changed between three different levels: light (LW), medium (MW), and heavy workload (HW) characterized as follows:

LW: 60% of requests for static content, 30% for dynamic content, and 10% for secure content. This workload is not enough to violate any of the KPI constraints. The experiment starts and finishes with this workload.

MW: 35% of requests for static content, 55% for dynamic content, and 10% for secure content. This workload violates the CPU threshold defined by the first goal, thus, triggering an adaptation to decrease CPU use.

HW: 20% of requests for static content, 30% for dynamic content, and 50% for secure content. With this workload it is impossible to satisfy the CPU threshold without a substantial decrease in CPU use, forcing an adaptation with greater impact.

Figures 2 and 3 depict the described scenario under varying workloads. Each dotted vertical line marks a change in the workload. We begin with LW, changing to MW around time 134, then to HW at around time 405, and finally switch back to LW around time 740. The impact of the workload change on the CPU usage may be delayed, depending of the request distribution. Between each workload change, there's the current service composition and configuration. The solid vertical lines mark when adaptations take place. After each adaptation, the monitoring device ignores the readings during a stabilization period to allow ongoing requests to be processed until they are completed by the original components.

Figure 2 depicts the evolution of the KPI values during system execution. After changing the workload from LW to MW, the system detects that the

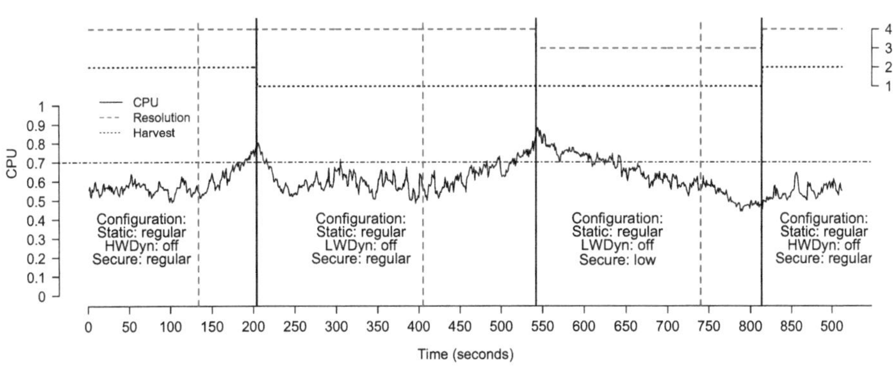

Fig. 2. Evolution of the KPIs of the system in the described scenario

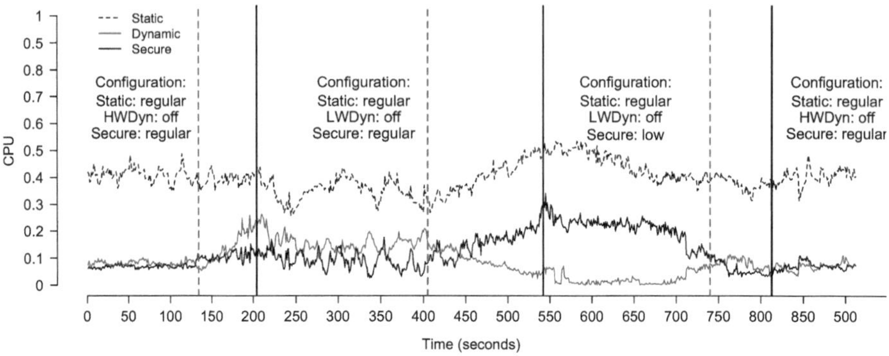

Fig. 3. CPU consumed by each service

CPU use is above the CPU limit plus the error margin (0.7), thus, it selects an adaptation that decreases the harvest KPI. Later, the workload is switched to HW, forcing an adaptation that lowers the resolution KPI to decrease the CPU use; note that this adaptation requires longer to take effect. Finally, the workload is changed back to LW and another adaptation takes place, increasing both the resolution and harvest KPIs. This increases the quality of service to a maximum, as in the beginning.

Figure 3 shows the contribution of each service to the global CPU utilization for the same scenario, allowing us to assess the impact of each adaptation. As a result of the first workload change, the system adapts around time 204 by changing the dynamic content implementation. This adaptation is selected because it lowers the CPU use to below the limit and also offers the highest *qos* CKPI value. This follows since it only decreases harvest, which has a lower weight in the *qos* CKPI. When the second workload change takes place, the system adapts around time 542 by changing the secure content from regular mode to low. This adaptation is selected because the CPU usage by secure content is clearly higher than the others, giving this adaptation a greater impact that the total of the others with a higher *qos* value. Finally, when the workload goes back to LW, the system adapts to its initial configuration with highest *qos*; this occurs at around 813 seconds and is triggered by a periodic event. These results demonstrate that the system adapts as expected given the characteristics of the workload and the performance of the deployed components, always offering the highest possible *qos*.

6 Conclusions and Future Work

This paper proposes a novel approach to managing adaptive behavior in customizable software systems. This approach uses information provided by each service designer about the impact of possible adaptations on the system KPIs to perform the automatic offline generation of a set of rules corresponding to a policy that describes the intended system behavior for those KPIs. These rules are then evaluated online to implement the adaptive behavior. Experimental results show that this approach is feasible and has a number of advantages. For example, each service configuration can be measured independently a single time to quantify the impact of adaptation, and still work for different configurations or workloads. The approach is also able to balance the trade-offs due to different goals when choosing an adaptation. Finally, as shown by experimental results, the approach considers not only how far the current state is from the optimal state—and, as a result, how large the impact has to be—but also uses the load of each service to realistically estimate the impact of an adaptation.

As future work, we plan to broaden application of the approach. Currently, for instance, we do not explicitly consider dependencies among services, so that when such dependencies exist, each adaptation must be applied separately. We plan to extend our model to consider such constraints.

References

1. Jung, G., Joshi, K., Hiltunen, M., Schlichting, R., Pu, C.: Generating adaptation policies for multi-tier applications in consolidated server environments. In: ICAC 2008, June 2008, pp. 23–32 (2008)
2. Diao, Y., Hellerstein, J.L., Parekh, S., Bigus, J.P.: Managing web server performance with autotune agents. IBM Syst. J. 42(1), 136–149 (2003)
3. Astrom, K.: Adaptive feedback control. Proceedings of the IEEE 75(2), 185–217 (1987)
4. Zhang, R., Lu, C., Abdelzaher, T.F., Stankovic, J.A.: Controlware: A middleware architecture for feedback control of software performance. In: ICDCS 2002, Washington, DC, USA, p. 301. IEEE Computer Society, Los Alamitos (2002)
5. Bahati, R.M., Bauer, M.A., Vieira, E.M.: Policy-driven autonomic management of multi-component systems. In: CASCON 2007, pp. 137–151. ACM, New York (2007)
6. Bridges, P., Hiltunen, M., Schlichting, R.: Cholla: A framework for composing and coordinating system software adaptations. IEEE Transactions on Computers (to appear, 2009)
7. van Renesse, R., Birman, K., Hayden, M., Vaysburd, A., Karr, D.: Building adaptive systems using ensemble. Softw. Pract. Exper. 28(9), 963–979 (1998)
8. Chen, W.K., Hiltunen, M., Schlichting, R.: Constructing adaptive software in distributed systems. In: ICDCS 2001, April 2001, pp. 635–643 (2001)
9. Rosa, L., Lopes, A., Rodrigues, L.: Modelling adaptive services for distributed systems. In: SAC 2008, pp. 2174–2180. ACM, New York (2008)
10. Mazzoni, F.: Efficient provisioning and adaptation of Web-based services. PhD in computer science, Università di Modena e Reggio Emilia (2006)
11. Sivasubramanian, S., Pierre, G., van Steen, M., Alonso, G.: Analysis of caching and replication strategies for web applications. IEEE Internet Computing 11(1), 60–66 (2007)
12. Rosa, L., Rodrigues, L., Lopes, A., Hiltunen, M., Schlichting, R.: From local impact functions to global adaptation of service compositions. Technical report (2009)
13. Souders, S.: High-performance web sites. Commun. ACM 51(12), 36–41 (2008)

14. Abdelzaher, T., Bhatti, N.: Web content adaptation to improve server overload behavior. In: WWW8 / Computer Networks, pp. 1563–1577 (1999)
15. Iaccarino, G., Malandrino, D., Scarano, V.: Personalizable edge services for web accessibility. In: W4A 2006, pp. 23–32. ACM, New York (2006)
16. Grieco, R., Malandrino, D., Mazzoni, F., Riboni, D.: Context-aware provision of advanced internet services. In: PerCom Workshops 2006, March 2006, p. 603 (2006)
17. Apache, `http://httpd.apache.org`
18. Pylot, `http://www.pylot.org`

A Wireless Security Framework without Shared Secrets

Lifeng Sang and Anish Arora

Department of Computer Science and Engineering
The Ohio State University, Columbus, Ohio, 43210
{sangl,anish}@cse.ohio-state.edu

Abstract. This paper develops a framework for wireless security that provides confidentiality, identity authentication, message authentication, integrity, sender non-repudiation, receiver non-repudiation and anonymity. Our framework is based on two physical primitives: collaborative jamming and spatial signature enforcement. Notably, it eschews the use of shared secrets, while providing a cryptosystem that is no less secure than conventional cryptosystems.

1 Introduction

Wireless security design has typically been based on cryptosystems and protocols used in wired networks. As such, the use of shared secrets as a cryptographic basis is the norm today in wireless security[3]. Nevertheless, wireless networks differ from their wired counterparts in a number of ways: they rely on a broadcast medium, often have higher densities of deployment, and —especially in the context of sensor and mobile networks— have severe resource limitations. As a result, they face a substantially more severe problem of secret management [7].

Towards reducing security management overhead, there has been academic interest in recent years in shared-secret-free security in wireless communications. Building on Wyner's seminal result [12] on the possibility of secure communication when the eavesdropper's channel is degraded with respect to the legitimate receiver's channel, diverse analyses have been performed for the capacity of confidential unicast: some model exploit feedback on receiver/channel state [5][11], some exploit the ability of the receiver to selectively jam the transmitter at secretly chosen times, some exploit multipath [10], and others exploit power level selection. Although the focus thus far largely been on theory, we recently took a first step in the development of codes for confidential communications at the physical layer [1], using the physical primitive of collaborative jamming.

In addition to this primitive for message confidentiality, recent work has also considered message authentication without the use of shared secrets [8][2][6]. In [8], we proposed the concept of the "spatial signature" of a node, which is a physical characterization of the signal that the node induces at each of its neighbors. We also designed a lightweight and robust primitive that validates the spatial signature of messages at run-time, and illustrated the use of the primitive for achieving message authentication without shared secrets.

R. Guerraoui and F. Petit (Eds.): SSS 2009, LNCS 5873, pp. 609–623, 2009.

Given these physical primitives for shared-secret free secure communications, we focus on the following question in this paper: *"Do physical primitives suffice to develop shared-secret free protocols for conventional security properties?"* We show for the first time that a wide variety of security services are possible without any shared secrets and with only a small basis of physical primitives. Specifically, we design a wireless security framework that encompasses confidentiality, authentication, integrity, non-repudiation and anonymity, not only for single-hop and end-to-end communications, but unicast and broadcast contexts as well.

The implications of reducing or eliminating shared-secrets for achieving secure communications are manifold: (i) the key management overhead is greatly reduced (if not eliminated) when there is no shared secret at all; (ii) shared-secret-free physical layer security can be seen as a way of increasing the security level of wireless networks wherein, say for reasons of resource limitation, a highly secure protocol cannot be implemented at higher layers; (iii) it can be used as a building block in efficiently bootstrapping the security parameters and configuration data required by higher layer protocols and applications; bootstrapping is widely regarded as being a hard and important problem for deeply embedded and potentially large scale wireless networks; (iv) finally, it is conceivable that in some application scenarios that it is possible to completely eschew the use of shared-secret based cryptosystems.

The rest of this paper is organized as follows. We review physical primitives for cooperative jamming and spatial signature enforcement in Section 2. In Section 3, we develop a rich suite of security protocols based on these physical primitives. We make concluding remarks as well as discuss future work in Section 4.

Table 1. Notation

j, k, l, e	nodes in the system
$\mathcal{S}$	domain of private messages
$\mathcal{X}$	domain of messages sent by j
$\mathcal{Y}$	domain of messages received by k
$\mathcal{Z}$	domain of messages overheard by e
Γ	domain of random time sequences
$j \langle k$	j shouts out a message, received by k
$j \langle\sim_\gamma k$	j shouts out a message, selectively jammed by k with random jamming sequence γ
N_j	the neighboring nodes of j
T_j	the trusted base of j
$j \lhd k$	j shouts out a message designated to k, authenticated by T_j via physical primitive
f, ϕ	coding functions s.t. $\phi(y, \gamma) \equiv s$ where s is a private message that j wishes to deliver, $f(s)$ sent by j is selectively jammed by k with jamming sequence γ, and y is the message k receives

2 Two Physical Primitives

In this section, we briefly review two physical primitives with which we will build security protocols. Table 1 contains the notations that we will use in the rest of the paper to abbreviate these primitives and other protocol concepts.

2.1 Cooperative Jamming

In [1], we proposed a cooperative jamming primitive that enables design of perfectly secure message communication. By perfectly secure, we mean that an eavesdropper cannot decode the message any better than it would by random guessing, even if it completely knew the coding and decoding schemes used for communication. We also introduced the following secure coding problem.

Given an arbitrary message s, $s \in \mathcal{S}$, which node j wishes to send privately to node k, and an arbitrary time sequence γ, $\gamma \in \Gamma$, which node k applies to cooperatively jam while j is sending. Design coding functions f and ϕ for $j \langle\sim_\gamma k$: x such that

1. $x = f(s)$, where $x \in \mathcal{X}$
2. $\phi(y, \gamma) = s$, where $y \in \mathcal{Y}$
3. $Pr(s) = Pr(s|z)$, where $z \in \mathcal{Z}$

Note that the third requirement directly implies:

Lemma 1. *Any solution to the secure coding problem ensures perfect secrecy of message communication from j to k.*

Our solution to the secure coding problem is called "dialog codes". These codes are derived from the following basic strategy: Each source bit is augmented with a redundant bit; the receiver randomly jams either bit in a pair. Since the eavesdropper does not know which bit is jammed or what the output would be, he cannot recover the jammed bit or decode the message correctly.

Let us illustrate the basic idea behind the jamming primitive in terms of the well-known "flipping model" in which a source bit gets flipped upon jamming. A simple mechanism then would be as follows. Let each bit in s be represented by two bits,

$$x_{2i-1}\ x_{2i} = \begin{cases} 0\,0 & if\ s_i = 0 \\ 1\,1 & if\ s_i = 1 \end{cases} \tag{1}$$

Hence the signal transmitted from j is a stream of pairs, with values 00 or 11. k's cooperative jamming strategy is to jam either position of each pair, and to recover the input simply by looking at the remaining bit within each pair. Since the bit corruption resulting from jamming is deterministic (i.e., value flipping) as a result of the definition of the channel model, what the eavesdropper sees would always be either 01 or 10, which is equally likely the result of jamming either 11 or 00. So the probability for the eavesdropper to make a correct guess for each pair is $\frac{1}{2}$. Therefore, the eavesdropper's chance of correctly guessing s is $\frac{1}{2^m}$, where m is the number of bits in s, and that gives us perfect secrecy.

By way of an example, this time letting $s = 1101$, s would be encoded as 11 11 00 11 by j. If k were to corrupt the first bit in each pair, then the eavesdropper would receive the corrupted value 01 01 10 01 and ?1 ?1 ?0 ?1 would be received at k. k can certainly recover s simply by looking at the second bit within each pair, however, the eavesdropper has no way of knowing that whether "01" is produced by "0" or "1".

In [1], we provided an extended class of dialog codes for diverse channel models and receiver models. We also implemented a prototype and validated the algorithms on both *CC2420 (IEEE 802.15.4)* and *CC1000* platforms.

2.2 Spatial Signature Enforcement

In [8], we proposed the concept of a node's "spatial signature", which is a physical characterization of the signal that the node induces at each of its neighbors. We showed experimentally that a spatial signature of nodes based on physical features such as Received Signal Strength Indicator (RSSI) is unique, with high probability, in multiple radio platforms and in diverse network topologies that range from rather sparse to very dense. We also designed a lightweight and robust primitive that validates and enforces the use of spatial signature in authenticating messages at run-time.

The basic idea of this primitive lies in the following proposition: if nodes are in a K-dimension space, $K+1$ neighbors in general (i.e., non-degenerate) position suffice for defining a unique spatial signature for nodes. The geometric argument underlying this proposition is straightforward, and is in essence that of ranging-based device positioning.

We illustrate the idea with an example in $2-D$ space. If a node i has only one neighbor j, then an adversary A located anywhere on the circle of radius $dist_{ij}$ centered at j can convince j that A is i. If i has two neighbors, j and k, as shown in Figure 1(a), A can convince both j and k that it is i by being located at point A. But in Figure 1(b), where i has three non-collinear neighbors j, k, and l, there exists no location at which A could be confused with i. By the same token, i cannot hide its identity from its signature basis (i.e., all of j, k, and l) when it sends a message. Thus, three (which is $K+1$ in this example) neighbors in a general position suffice for defining a unique spatial signature.

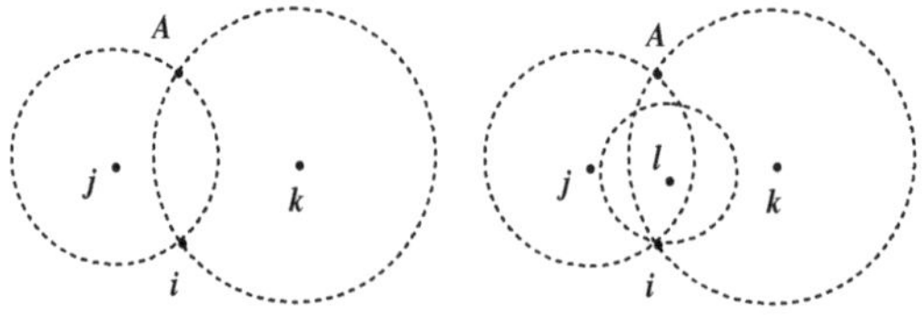

(a) Adversary at A cannot be distinguished from i by j and k

(b) Adversary cannot imitate i without being detected by j, or k, or l

Fig. 1. Example of minimum density required for *uniqueness*

Based on the spatial signature primitive, we presented a simple cooperative protocol for message authentication that exploits the broadcast nature of wireless communications: any receiver in the signature basis of a node complains if a sender claims the identity of the node but the signature does not match locally. In other words, a message is authenticated if no node in the signature basis of the node complains. This idea has been validated in some other works too [2][6]. We use $j \lhd k$ to denote the use of spatial signatures to enforce reception of a message sent by j to k. The cooperative protocol has the following properties:

Lemma 2. *Liveness: if $j \lhd k$: x, x is delivered at k.*

Lemma 3. *Safety: if x is delivered at k as a result of k's role in protocol $j \lhd k$: x, x must have been sent by j.*

3 Security Protocol Suite Based on Physical Primitives

We now build upon the primitives described above to describe and validate a diverse set of security protocols, including protocols for confidentiality, identity authentication, message authentication, integrity, sender non-repudiation, receiver non-repudiation and anonymity. We consider communications in a wireless network of the following sorts:

- one-hop unicast and broadcast
- end-to-end unicast and broadcast

3.1 System Model

The system consists of a wireless network of static, and potentially resource-constrained, nodes. Let j and k be two legitimate nodes in the system; legitimate nodes, unlike adversarial nodes, are trusted to execute their protocols correctly. And let T_j and T_k be the respective "trusted bases" of j and k; the trusted base of a legitimate node consists of at least c legitimate nodes in its one-hop neighborhood, for some strictly positive constant number c (c is typically two or three). It follows that the system has nontrivial density in the neighborhood of each node.

We assume the following system properties:

- When some node impersonates j in a communication with k, any trusted base node of j complaining of a signature failure communicates the complaint to j.
- j can discover the trusted base of k, if k is in its one-hop neighborhood.

3.2 Threat Model

The adversary in this wireless setting has, in the spirit of Dolev-Yao, the capability to: (1) eavesdrop on messages in its reception range; (2) block messages sent within its interference neighborhood; (3) replay older messages, possibly modifying the payload; and (4) inject arbitrary messages to nodes. The adversary may physically operate via devices other than the legitimate nodes or it may operate via nodes that it compromises. If a node is compromised, its state becomes known to the adversary. Compromised nodes may collude with other compromised nodes within their communication range to launch attacks.

Note that we are not in the position of dealing with communication disruption that results in more message loss, e.g., malicious jamming. (This problem is common to all wireless applications, and may be compensated by retransmission or routing around jammed regions.) Instead, we are interested in whether the proposed protocols are secure in the sense that the system satisfies its security properties despite the adversary, and the adversary is not able to convince the system to launch malicious or denial-of-service actions.

3.3 Confidentiality

One-hop Unicast. There are numerous contexts of message communciation where one or both the sender and the receiver demand privacy: a sender communicating an "alarm" communication and a receiver receiving a "query response" may each require privacy regardless of whether the other party requires privacy or not. Now, confidentiality in this one-hop setting is readily achievable via the cooperative jamming primitive, assuming the receiver faithfully performs its cooperative role. If the receiver does not cooperate, the sender's message would be sent in the clear.

A step towards ensuring that the receiver cooperates is to coordinate with it before a transmission. Our protocol for one hop secure unicast, denoted by $UniSec(j \rightarrow k)$, is formally stated below.

UniSec($j \rightarrow k$): s

$j \; \lhd \; k$:	hello
$k \; \lhd \; j$:	hello_ack
$j \; \langle\sim_\gamma \; k$:	$f(s)$

In this protocol, j initiates by sending k an authenticated "hello" message. After receiving "hello", k knows that j intends to send a private message. If k does not want to proceed, it can simply ignore the "hello" message; otherwise, it acknowledges with an authenticated "hello_ack" message, confirming to j that k is in sync to jam j's transmission. Note that the message authentication itself is achieved by using the spatial signature enforcement primitive for authenticating the principals.

After j receives the "hello_ack" from k, it encodes s with the coding function f, and sends $f(s)$ in the clear immediately. In sync, k jams with a random sequence γ that is (ideally) known only to itself, it can then decode the remaining information it receives to recover s via ϕ and γ, as described in the secure coding approach above. The proof sketch for this protocol can be found in [9].

Two-way (Two-Hop) Unicast. We develop next an extension of the previous protocol for the special case where cooperative jamming is used by two senders, as opposed to a sender-receiver pair. The extension allows two nodes to exchange information concurrently, without either communication being revealed to other nodes.

Two-Way UniSec

```
Message exchange step:
    l ⟨| j,k: ready to help

    j ⟨ l: s_j
    ||
    k ⟨ l: s_k

    l ⟨ j,k: s_j ⊞ s_k
```

In Figure 3, l servers as an intermediate router for the exchange between j and k. We directly apply the cooperative jamming primitive in a symmetric form as follows: j and k transmit roughly at the same time. l shouts back the raw signal which is a combination of j's signal and k's signal. If the wireless channel follows the "addition" model, both j and k can decode the message because they know what they have sent. The router l simulates a full-duplex transceiver at both j and k; that is, if j and k were full-duplex transceivers as opposed to half-duplex, they could perform the exchange themselves and l would not be necessary. In theory, j and k can simply subtract the signal they have sent from the signal they hear from the router, and decode the message if the channel is additive [4]. In practice, the development of coding scheme is however more complicated, and beyond the scope of this paper. Note that this extension may by attacked by allowing l to send a bogus signal instead of what it heard. This attack is dealt with by adding a checksum/hash value at the end of the message. Since l has no way of knowing the value of s_j and s_k, it is hard for l to make up a legitimate message that passes the checksum validation.

End-to-end Unicast. A key requirement of confidentiality for an end-to-end unicast is that nodes in the middle of the network that forward a message should not themselves be aware of the content of the message.

In traditional shared-key security, this is easily achieved if the message is encrypted with an end-to-end shared secret (notwithstanding the difficulty of initializing the end-to-end secret). Unfortunately, with the physical primitives described above, it is difficult not to reveal the message to nodes in the middle. Any node that helps to hide the communication via cooperative jamming is able to decode the message if it knows the jamming time sequence. Even if nodes on the path between two parties of interest can be trusted, this approach still violates the requirement for end-to-end confidentiality.

A standard idea is to split the message s into multiple pieces, and to send all pieces separately along node disjoint paths. As long as intermediate nodes from all the paths do not collude, s is safe.

Our protocol for end-to-end secure unicast is formally stated below.

e2eUniSec($j \rightarrow k$): s

$s = (s_1, s_2, \cdots, s_n)$	
$\forall i, 1 \leq i \leq n$,	
{	
$UniSec(j \rightarrow l_i^1)$:	$f(s_i)$
$UniSec(l_i^1 \rightarrow l_i^2)$:	$f(s_i)$
...	
$UniSec(l_i^{m_i-1} \rightarrow l_i^{m_i})$:	$f(s_i)$
$UniSec(l_i^{m_i} \rightarrow k)$:	$f(s_i)$
}	

A message s is first divided into n pieces assuming that there are at least n node disjoint paths between j and k, as shown in Figure 2. Let l_i^t ($t = 1, 2, \cdots, m_t$) be the nodes on path i between j and k. j first securely transmits s_i to l_i^1 via the $UniSec(j \rightarrow l_i^1)$ protocol. l_i^1 then forwards s_i to its next forwarder along the path to k securely. In the end, $l_i^{m_i}$ forwards s_i to k. The same procedure is followed on all n paths in parallel (for pedagogical reasons, we omit discussion of the scheduling necessary to deal with potential self-interference in this process). As long as the adversary does not compromise n or more nodes, with at least one each from a distinct path, the message s is safe.

One-hop Broadcast. Recall that in the cooperative jamming primitive, only those nodes that know the jamming sequence can decode the message from the residual information. In essence, the jamming primitive is designed for unicast communication, as only the node that helps to jam knows the sequence that it has applied. In order to send a packet to all the neighboring nodes securely, a straightforward approach is to send the packet to each neighboring node in sequence, but the communication overhead would be high. We may optimize this approach by letting all potential receivers share a jamming sequence, which

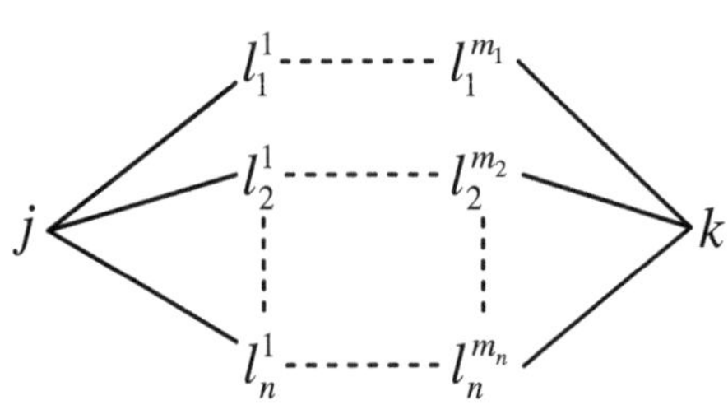

Fig. 2. End-to-end unicast confidentiality via multiple paths

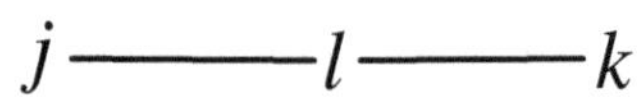

Fig. 3. End-to-end unicast confidentiality for line topology

introduces a one-time cost in the initialization. All subsequent jamming sequence can be derived from the knowledge of the previous jamming sequence and the received message.

Our one-hop secure broadcast protocol is formally stated below.

A node j initializes the jamming sequence with nodes in its neighborhood, informing every node in N_j to use $\gamma_{j,0}$ as the initial jamming sequence. When a broadcast is initiated from j, it chooses one node k in N_j to help hide the first message s_1. Since k jams with $\gamma_{j,0}$, which is known to all other nodes in N_j, every node in N_j can decode $f(s_1)$ to obtain s_1, while nodes not in N_j can not discover s_1 without the knowledge of $\gamma_{j,0}$. In all following messages, the new jamming sequence is generated by a one way function on the previous jamming sequence. For initialization, the system can either perform this step for all the senders at the very beginning or lazily in the sense that this step can be performed only upon request. We relegate the proof to [9]. Frequent update of the jamming sequence increases the level of difficulty for the adversary to break the secure broadcast.

BrdSec($j \langle N_j$): s

Initialize the jamming sequence (one–time cost):

$\forall k \in N_j$, $\{UniSec(j \rightarrow k): (\gamma_{j,0}, brd)\}$

First broadcast:

$j \langle\!\sim_{\gamma_{j,1}} k$: $f(s_1)$

Second broadcast:

$j \langle\!\sim_{\gamma_{j,2}} k$: $f(s_2)$

...

m^{th} broadcast:

$j \langle\!\sim_{\gamma_{j,m}} k$: $f(s_m)$

...

where $\gamma_{j,1} = \gamma_{j,0}$, $\gamma_{j,2} = H^1(\gamma_{j,1})$, and $\gamma_{j,m} = H^{m-1}(\gamma_{j,m-1})$

Secure Flood. Flooding is a common service in many applications. We realize secure flooding by extending the *UniSec* and *BrdSec* protocols, for two cases.

Case 0: the network has no structure. If the underlying network does not provide any structure, we can simply adopt a typical flood service such as a naive flood, gossip, etc. The main difference is that the old broadcast is replaced by our *BrdSec* protocol. A duplicate suppressing mechanism may be used to reduce overhead.

Case 1: the network is partitioned into groups, each having a leader node. This approach exploits a tree structuring of the system, to reduce communication overhead. specifically, we use a tree that spans all the group leaders, and subtrees by which each group leader spans its group. The secure flood involves using a secure one-hop broadcast within each group and a secure one-hop unicast on the leader tree. This protocol is stated below.

Secure flood(j)

$UniSec(j \rightarrow L_j)$:	s
$UniSec(L_j \rightarrow NL_{L_j})$:	s
$BrdSec(L_i \ \langle\ N_{L_i})$:	s

First, the source node j sends a packet securely to its group leader L_j, then L_j forwards the packet securely to its neighboring leaders NL_{L_j} and so forth. After that, each leader L_i securely broadcasts the message to all nodes in its respective group. As in other flood protocols, a duplicate suppressing mechanism may be used to minimize unnecessary retransmissions.

3.4 Authentication

One-hop Unicast and Broadcast. For authentication in a one-hop setting, there is not much difference between the case of unicast and that of broadcast when using the spatial signature primitive, because a node is authenticated by another node as long as it is authenticated by all of its trusted neighbors. Identity authentication and message authentication are also quite similar in this setting.

One-hop authentication is achieved by the physical primitive alone. If s is indeed sent by j, no one in the neighborhood of j would complain by the definition of spatial signature enforcement, thus s can be authenticated.

One hop message authentication

$j \ \langle\!\langle\ k:\ s$

In identity authentication, node j claims that it is j, and this is validated by its trusted neighbors. If it is the very node that he claims, no one in N_j would complain, and its identity is authenticated.

Identity authentication

$j \ \langle\!\langle\ k:\ (j, s)$

End-to-end Unicast and Broadcast. For authentication in an end-to-end setting, similarly, there is not much difference for unicast and broadcast. To solve the end-to-end authentication problem, we assume, as is common in many network applications, that trust is transitive in the sense that if a trusts b and b trusts c, then a trusts c. The basic idea is that if in a hop-by-hop fashion each receiver trusts the preceding sender that forwards the message, then the intended destination can authenticate the message.

Letting l be a node between j and k, the protocol for end-to-end message authentication is formally stated below.

End-to-end authentication

$$j \llparenthesis l:\ (j, s)$$
$$l \llparenthesis k:\ (l, (j, s))$$

j informs l that it intends to send a message s along with its identity j. l authenticates this message and j's identity as well, and then forwards this message with its own identity (l) to k. If k authenticates l, by the transitivity property, k can authenticate that s is from j. Note that the same protocol applies to cases where there are multiple intermediate nodes along the path from j to k.

Authentication via Certificates. This protocol allows two nodes to mutually authenticate each other, even if they are new to each other in the system. The protocol uses a version of certificate exchange, so that the two can learn each other's signature base. Specifically, their one-hop neighbors serve as the certification authority (CA). As long as they have common neighbors in their trusted bases, they can enforce trust in each other through their common neighbors.

Our certificate-based authentication protocol is formally stated as follows.

Authentication via certificates

$$j \llparenthesis k:\ T_j$$
$$k \llparenthesis j:\ T_k \cap T_j$$

In this protocol, j shouts out its trusted base, T_j, which is verified by the nodes in T_j. k now knows T_j. k replies with the common nodes in both its and j's trusted bases, which in turn is verified by T_k. Although j and k do not know each other a priori, as long as $T_k \cap T_j$ is not null, they can derive trust in each other according to the transitivity of trust. A proof sketch is provided in [9].

3.5 Integrity and Non-repudiation

For our purpose, there is not much difference between integrity, sender non-repudiation and authentication, especially in the one-hop case. For end-to-end integrity and sender non-repudiation, the receiver may send back a traversal that checks whether the message has in fact been sent by the sender, by checking the sender's immediate neighbors' reception history.

Our protocol for message integrity and sender non-repudiation is stated below.

One hop sender non-repudiation

$$j \llparenthesis k:\ (j, s)$$

k itself can verify (j, s), and j can not lie that it has sent s because nodes in N_j have seen an authenticated message (j, s), by the definition of the $\llparenthesis$ operator.

End-to-end sender non-repudiation

$$
\begin{array}{l}
j \;\langle\!\langle\; l:\ (j,s)\\
l \;\langle\!\langle\; k:\ (l,(j,s))\\
k \;\langle\!\langle\; l:\ \texttt{verify}\ (j,s)
\end{array}
$$

In the end-to-end case, k checks back with j's immediate neighbor l to verify that j has sent s. This provides sender non-repudiation. In both the one-hop and the end-to-end case, we may attach a fingerprint, computed by a well-known hash function, to the message, to enhance the its integrity.

For receiver non-repudiation, we need to ensure that the receiver indeed obtains the message. We achieve this by requiring an acknowledgement, which allows the reception to be verified.

The protocol is formally stated below.

One hop receiver non-repudiation

$$
\begin{array}{l}
j \;\langle\; k:\ s\\
k \;\langle\!\langle\; j:\ ACK(s)
\end{array}
$$

Note that here we only need receiver non-repudiation, therefore, we do not need to authenticate the message sent by j. To check that the receiver k has in fact received the message, j establishes that it has one or more ACKs for the query in its history. Note that $ACK(s)$ are authenticated by T_k so k can not lie about receiving s. If k chooses to not respond to s, in other words, k does not reply with an ACK message after he receives s, then k violates the protocol, and be regarded as suspect.

End-to-end receiver non-repudiation

$$
\begin{array}{l}
j \;\langle\; l:\ s\\
l \;\langle\; k:\ s\\
k \;\langle\!\langle\; l:\ ACK(s)\\
j \;\langle\!\langle\; l:\ \texttt{verify}\ ACK(s)
\end{array}
$$

For the end-to-end case, the source can query the receiver's immediate neighbors to see whether they have seen the ACK. This makes sure that k cannot lie that it has received s. The protocol fails iff all the nodes in $T_k \cap T_j$ are compromised, but in this event no other protocol can do better. If there are multiple intermediate nodes on the path between j and k, the protocol remains essentially the same, except that we need to add one or more intermediate forwarders for the message s and to verify that one or more ACKs were sent.

3.6 Anonymity

In addition to confidentiality and authenticity, anonymity—the requirement of preventing the sender's identity from being revealed—is an important one. A potential problem in realizing anonymity using physical primitives is that two or more receivers have a good chance of identifying the sender, if the sender sends a message in the clear—the receivers can learn the spatial signature of the sender and collude in the identification. The induced signature at its neighbors is likely to match with the one learned before, especially if the sender uses the same transmission power for each communication.

One simple idea then is to let a node vary its transmission power, to intentionally change its induced signature, and make neighbor collusion somewhat harder. Another idea is to let a trusted node to first help to hide the communication and to then forward the message. Because the message is jammed by the trusted node, others can not learn the spatial signature of the sender. The trusted node that helps jam may be able to learn the signature of the message, but can not figure out the identity of the sender by itself.

The basic procedure is as follows: First, a node that is willing to help shouts out and it is verified by its trusted base including the potential sender. Then, the sender desiring anonymity sends its message, in the presence of cooperative jamming by the helper. Finally, the helper forwards the message in the clear. Since wireless networks, especially sensor networks, enjoy node density, such a helper is expected to be easy to find.

The protocol is formally stated below.

Unicast for Anonymity

One hop anonymity for unicast

$l \lhd j$: ready to help
$j \langle\!\sim_\gamma l$: $f(s)$
$l \langle k$: s

where l is a neighbor of both j and k

End-to-end anonymity for unicast

$l \lhd j$: ready to help
$j \langle\!\sim_\gamma l$: $f(s)$
$l \langle h$: s
$h \langle k$: s

where h is a common neighbor of j, l and k

Broadcast for Anonymity

One hop anonymity for broadcast

$k \lhd j$: ready to help
$j \langle\!\sim_\gamma k$: $f(s)$
$k \langle N_j$: s

End-to-end anonymity for broadcast

$l \langle\!\vert\ j$:	ready to help
$j \langle\!\sim_\gamma l$:	$f(s)$
$l \langle N_l$:	s
$N_l \langle N_{N_l}$:	s

It is worth noting that a sender can simply shout out a message without its identity attached, so as to achieve anonymity. This is because it could lie that the message is owned by someone other than itself. However, one potential problem is that if the channel is not busy shortly before this transmission, colluding neighbors may be still able to identify that this message belongs to the sender. That is why a volunteer is exploited to help hide the identity of the sender.[1] We provide a proof in [9].

4 Discussion and Conclusion

In this paper, we developed a wireless security framework based on two physical primitives: cooperative jamming and spatial signature enforcement. The former is essentially for confidential wireless communication, while the latter essentially for message authenticity. The derived protocols include a variety of common security services, including confidentiality, identity authentication, message authentication, integrity, sender non-repudiation, receiver non-repudiation and anonymity, for a variety of wireless network communication contexts. This work, together with the previous work on physical primitives, illustrates a new approach in the field of wireless security: that communications without shared secrets while providing the same level of security is feasible and, in fact, relatively simple.

We should emphasize that have not attempted to address the energy efficiency problem in this paper, even though it is conceivable that the physical primitive based framework may be realized with low power consumption. Rather, we have attempted to reduce the key management task that involves significant overhead and manual effort, especially in large scale networks. By the same token, we have not attempted to handle the problem of bootstrapping trust either. Our physical spatial primitive assumes an initial period of trust, which motivates further study to effectively handle bootstrapping.

Since the proposed protocols rely heavily on the correctness and efficiency of the two primitives, future work includes further justification of these existing primitives and development of new alternatives to enrich the primitive set. Another direction is to provide an automatic "InstallShield" for easy deployment of the whole protocol suite. Last but not least, investigating the feasibility of

[1] In order to cover N_j, the helper may increase its transmission power to forward the message. An alternative would be to perform 2-hop anonymity forwarding with a cost of increased communication overhead.

combining this framework with the existing cryptography based security infrastructure to provide better domain-specific security services is worthy of further study.

References

1. Arora, A., Sang, L.: Dialog codes for secure wireless communications. In: ACM/IEEE IPSN, pp. 13–24 (2009)
2. Danev, B., Capkun, S.: Transient-based identification of wireless sensor nodes. In: ACM/IEEE IPSN (2009)
3. Fischer, R.J., Green, G.: Introduction to security. Butterworth-Heinemann (2003)
4. Katti, S., Gollakota, S., Katabi, D.: Embracing wireless interference: Analog network coding. In: ACM SIGCOMM (2007)
5. Lai, L., Gamal, H.E., Poor, H.V.: The wiretap channel with feedback: Encryption over the channel. IEEE Transactions on Information Theory 54(11), 5059–5067 (2008)
6. Patwari, N., Kasera, S.: Robust location distinction using temporal link signatures. In: Mobicom (2007)
7. Perrig, A., Tygar, J.D.: Secure broadcast communication in wired and wireless networks. Kluwer Academic Publishers, Dordrecht (2003)
8. Sang, L., Arora, A.: Spatial signatures for lightweight security in wireless sensor networks. In: IEEE Infocom Miniconference (2008)
9. Sang, L., Arora, A.: A wireless security framework without shared secrets. Technical Report (2009), `http://www.cse.ohio-state.edu/~sang/paper/sang-suite-tech.pdf`
10. Sayeed, A., Perrig, A.: Secure wireless communications: Secret keys through multipath. In: ICASSP (2008)
11. Tekin, E., Yener, A.: The general gaussian multiple access and two-way wire-tap channels: Achievable rates and cooperative jamming. IEEE Transactions on Information Theory - Special Issue on Information Theoretic Security 54(6), 2735–2751 (2008)
12. Wyner, A.D.: The wire-tap channel. Bell Syst. Tech. J. 54(8), 1355–1387 (1975)

Read-Write-Codes: An Erasure Resilient Encoding System for Flexible Reading and Writing in Storage Networks

Mario Mense[1] and Christian Schindelhauer[2]

[1] Heinz Nixdorf Institute,
University of Paderborn, Germany
vodisek@upb.de

[2] Computer Networks and Telematics,
University of Freiburg, Germany
schindel@informatik.uni-freiburg.de

Abstract. We introduce the Read-Write-Coding-System (RWC) – a very flexible class of linear block codes that generate efficient and flexible erasure codes for storage networks. In particular, given a message x of k symbols and a codeword y of n symbols, an RW code defines additional parameters $k \leq r, w \leq n$ that offer enhanced possibilities to adjust the fault-tolerance capability of the code. More precisely, an RWC provides linear (n, k, d)-codes that have (a) minimum distance $d = n - r + 1$ for any two codewords, and (b) for each codeword there exists a codeword for each other message with distance of at most w. Furthermore, depending on the values r, w and the code alphabet, different block codes such as parity codes (e.g. RAID 4/5) or Reed-Solomon (RS) codes (if $r = k$ and thus, $w = n$) can be generated. In storage networks in which I/O accesses are very costly and redundancy is crucial, this flexibility has considerable advantages as r and w can optimally be adapted to read or write intensive applications; only w symbols must be updated if the message x changes completely, what is different from other codes which always need to rewrite y completely as x changes. In this paper, we first state a tight lower bound and basic conditions for all RW codes. Furthermore, we introduce special RW codes in which all mentioned parameters are adjustable even online, that is, those RW codes are adaptive to changing demands. At last, we point out some useful properties regarding safety and security of the stored data.

1 Introduction

An erasure (resilient) code maps a word x of k symbols drawn from an alphabet Σ into a codeword y of $n > k$ symbols from the same alphabet, and in the optimal case, any k symbols from the n codeword symbols are sufficient to recover x. This property has made erasure codes become very prominent in many application areas [1,7,16]. In storage networks such as RAID-*arrays* [13,14] and modern

R. Guerraoui and F. Petit (Eds.): SSS 2009, LNCS 5873, pp. 624–639, 2009.

storage area networks (SAN) [10] access to hard disks is comparably slow, and thus, data is scattered into fixed sized blocks which are evenly distributed among the storage devices to exploit access parallelism. If then some disks fail for reading (erasures), in the optimal case, any k symbols from y are sufficient to recover x, i.e. such codes can tolerate up to $n-k$ erasures which may be caused by failed, respectively temporarily not accessible disks. Since the number n of blocks (symbols) in a codeword y is fixed (called *data stripe*) and all blocks in a stripe are hosted by n different disk, *linear block codes* are mainly applied [13,5,14,8]. More importantly, linear block codes are *optimal codes*, i.e. they only require any k blocks from y to recover x what is important in a scenario that suffers from expensive I/O operations.

However, most codes applied in RAID-like storage networks almost aim at providing a (near-)optimal recovery behavior but what implies a serious drawback as any code that is able to reconstruct x from up to $n-k$ erasures suffers from a bad update behavior. In particular, if one information symbol changes from x_i to x_i', any codesymbol y_i must also be modified. If then any of the disk keeping y_i is not accessible, there is no chance to store the modified codeword appropriately (except merely the plain information word if a systematic code is applied such as given, for example, with the RAID 4/5 encoding).

In order to face this negative update behavior that is inherent to usual linear blocks codes and which turns to be pretty costly when such codes are applied in RAID-like storage environments, we introduce the *Read-Write-Coding-System (RWC)* – a very flexible framework for generating different linear block codes, called *Read-Write (RW) codes* in the following, which feature enhanced update properties for given codewords by simultaneously offering different degrees of fault-tolerance. In contrast to common linear block codes, an RWC defines further parameters $k \leq r, w \leq n$ which offer enhanced possibilities to adjust the redundancy, and thus, the fault-tolerance capability of an RW code. In the language of coding theory, for any fixed r, an RWC provides linear (n, r, d)-codes over some finite field $\mathbb{F}_q$ that have (a) minimum (Hamming) distance $d = n-r+1$ (thus, are MDS codes if $r = k$), and (b) for each codeword there exists a codeword for each other message with distance of at most w, i.e. the two code words differ in at most w symbols. More specific, an RWC generates appropriate sub-codes of Reed-Solomon (RS) codes (see e.g. [9] for details on RS codes) of dimension r and length n in which any two codewords have distance at least w. Depending on the values r, w and the field $\mathbb{F}_q$ chosen, different block codes can be generated, e.g. parity codes (if $q = 2$).

The ensured degree of redundancy mixed up with the improved update behavior offered by an Read-Write code provides significant benefits for the observed storage systems which, driven by the application's read and write behavior, on one hand, suffer from very costly I/O operations, and on the other hand, have to ensure some defined level of fault-tolerance at any time. Clearly, a Read-Write code provides best improvements for write-intensive applications because, given an n-sized codeword y and parameters r, w, it can decode the information from **any** r symbols of y whereas only **any** w symbols of y must be updated whenever the information word x changes completely (recall that we can choose $w < n$). Again, this is different to other linear codes, like e.g. Reed-Solomon codes, which always must rewrite the codeword y completely as x changes. This novel redundancy property comes with cost of additional necessary disk space for compensating the absence of writable disks, i.e. the data rate of RW-codes decreases with increasing w.

For most applications it is necessary to read the data and then to update the information such that the condition $w \geq r$ seems natural. Our encoding systems allows the update without prior reading, i.e. the difference vector δ of the old and new message is needed. E.g. if an empty file is overwritten with the first data entries then only w disks need to be written. In such cases RW-codes with $w < r$ become interesting.

An example. Consider a RAID 4-parity code with $n = 4$ hard disks storing a data file bit by bit, $\Sigma = \{0, 1\}$. We encode $k = 3$ bits x_1, x_2, x_3 to symbols $y_1 = x_1, y_2 = x_2, y_3 = x_3$ and $y_4 = x_1 + x_2 + x_3$, where addition denotes the XOR-operation and the code symbols y_i, $1 \leq i \leq 4$, are stored separately on distinct disks. The XOR-operation enables to recover the original three bits from any combination of $r = 3$ hard disks, e.g. giving y_2, y_3, y_4 we have $x_1 = y_2 + y_3 + y_4$, $x_2 = y_2$, and $x_3 = y_3$. Thus, if any one disk is temporarily not available, reading data is still possible. However then, writing data is not possible since a complete change of the original information involves the change of the entire code; we call this *code consistency* (this also holds for any other erasure code applied in storage environments). The second example shows an RW-code. Again, consider $n = 4$ hard disks with code bits y_1, y_2, y_3, y_4. Now, we encode $k = 2$ information bits x_1, x_2 such that any $r = 3$ code bits y_i, y_j, y_k can be used to recover the original message, and furthermore, only any of such $w = 3$ code bits $y_{i'}, y_{j'}, y_{k'}$ need to be changed to encode a completely new information. For instance, start with the codeword $(0, 1, 1, ?)$. According to Table 1, the information is $(1, 1)$ and therefore the complete code is $(0, 1, 1, 0)$. Now, we want to encode $(0, 1)$ without changing the second entry. For this, we choose line 0 for information $(0, 1)$ and get code $(0, 1, 0, 1)$.

Moreover, RW codes can exploit system information about existing erasures, which are caused by failed or blocked disks and that have rather long-term character in a SAN, for encoding and decoding. For instance, consider a codeword y with symbols stored on n disks from which $b \leq n - w$ disks are unreachable (e.g. failed or blocked). Then, using an RW code, y can still be updated to the codeword y' in a code consistent manner. Furthermore, if then some of the formerly blocked disks become available again while some other $b' \leq n - r$ disks turn to be unreachable, we can still recover the new information word x' by simply selecting any r of the remaining $n - b'$ accessible disks. Therefore, as long as sufficient disks are accessible, an RW code provides code consistent operations by circumventing blocked disks.

At last, some RW codes offer the possibility to change any of the parameters k, r, w and n during runtime, that is, a (k, r, w, n)-RW code can be changed to

Table 1. A $(2,3,3,4)_2$-Read-Write-Code for contents x_1, x_2 and code y_1, y_2, y_3, y_4. Every information vector has two possible code words. Even if only three of the four code words are available for reading and writing, the system can perform read and write operations (see Figure 1 for the encoding). Variable v is an internal variable of our RW-code introduced in Chapter 5.

Contents		Code				Line
x_1	x_2	y_1	y_2	y_3	y_4	v
0	0	0	0	0	0	0
0	0	1	1	1	1	1
0	1	0	1	0	1	0
0	1	1	0	1	0	1
1	0	0	0	1	1	0
1	0	1	1	0	0	1
1	1	0	1	1	0	0
1	1	1	0	0	1	1

(nearly) any choice of (k', r', w', n') giving such codes the ability to adapt to changing system conditions.

2 Related Work

The most popular codes used are parity-based schemes, like RAID [13] or EVEN-ODD [4] that have low storage consumption which is given by a factor $(k+1)/k$ and $(k+2)/k$, respectively, and that base on simple but efficient XOR-operations. Unfortunately, parity codes are able to tolerate only one or two erasures at a time, what is often not sufficient, even in large SANs. Therefore, since in large SANs an increased fault-tolerance is often the major focus, a code should be used that provides a high minimum distance between any two codewords. Codes providing this feature are called *MDS codes* (Maximum Distance Separable), which ensure distance $d(Y) = n - k + 1$ for any two codewords [8,9]. Nevertheless, many variants of MDS codes, like *MDS array codes* [3] or *X-codes* [2] also suffer from high rates. Alternatively, *Hamming codes* have good rate but distance of at most 3, and *Reed-Muller codes* have high distance but bad rate (c.f. [9]). Therefore, *Reed-Solomon (RS) codes* have become very popular in distributed storage systems [15,11] and disk arrays [6,14] since they combine a good rate of $(n-k)/k$ with distance $d(Y) = n - k + 1$. Unfortunately, as RS codes are MDS codes, they also suffer from an undesired update overhead because if x is modified, all blocks of y must be rewritten, what is dismal in a SAN suffering from expensive I/O accesses.

Thus, due to their beneficial properties, applying RW-codes in a SAN seems quite self-evident. From now on, we call a $(k, r, w, n)_b$-Read-Write code a coding system with a k-symbol message and an n-symbol code with symbols drawn from a b-symbol alphabet, and a parameter r for recovering the message and w

for modification with $k \le r, w \le n$. In the next section, we state the operations of the RWC formally. After that, we prove general bounds for the parameters of RW codes and present a general scheme to generate $(k, r, w, n)_b$-RW codes as long as $k + n \le r + w$ holds for an appropriate choice of b. Then, we introduce adaptive RW codes called *Chameleon codes*, where any of the given parameters can be subject to changes. At last, notice that the following description is given in more operation-based terms rather than conceptual since RW codes base on the same well-studied algebraic principles as RS codes.

3 The Operational Model

Read-Write codes encode information words into codewords. The information is given by a k-tuple over some finite alphabet Σ, and since Read-Write codes are linear block codes, the codeword is an n-tuple over the same alphabet Σ, $k < n$. Now, for what follows, let $b = |\Sigma|$ and $\mathbf{P}(M)$ denotes the power set of some set M. Moreover, let $\mathbf{P}_\ell(M) := \{S \in \mathbf{P}(M) \mid |S| = \ell\}$.

Then, the following operations are provided by a $(k, r, w, n)_b$ Read-Write-Coding-System (RWC):

1. **Initial state** $x_0 \in \Sigma^k$, $y_0 \in \Sigma^n$
   This is the initial state of the system with information x_0 and codeword y_0. This state is crucial because all further operations ensuring the beneficial features of an RW code depend on this initial state.
2. **Read function** $f : \mathbf{P}_r([n]) \times \Sigma^r \to \Sigma^k$
   This function reconstructs the information by reading r symbols of the codeword whose positions are known. The first parameter shows the positions (indices) of the symbols in the code, and the second parameter gives the corresponding code symbols. The outcome is the decoded information.

3a. **Write function** g :
   $\mathbf{P}_r([n]) \times \Sigma^r \times \Sigma^k \times \mathbf{P}_w([n]) \to \Sigma^w$
   This function adapts the codeword to a changed information by changing w symbols of the codeword at w given positions. The first two parameters describe the reading of the original information. Then, we have the new information as a parameter, and the last parameter indicates which code symbols to change in the codeword. The outcome are the values of the new w code symbols.

3b. **Differential write function** $\delta : \mathbf{P}_w([n]) \times \Sigma^k \to \Sigma^w$
   This is a restricted alternative to the write function whose parameters are the positions S of symbols available for writing as well as the difference of the original information x and the new information x' but without reading the w code entries. The outcome is the difference of the available old and the new codeword symbols. Thus, for two functions $\Delta_1 : \Sigma^k \times \Sigma^k \to \Sigma^k$ and $\Delta_2 : \Sigma^w \times \Sigma^w \to \Sigma^w$ and w given positions $\nu_1, \ldots, \nu_w \in [n]$ from y, we can describe the write function g above by the differential write function as

$$(y'_{\nu_1}, \ldots, y'_{\nu_w}) = \Delta_2((y_{\nu_1}, \ldots, y_{\nu_w}), \delta(S, \Delta_1(x, x'))).$$

while the original write function needs to read at positions $\rho_1, \ldots, \rho_w \in [n]$ and produces the same result by the following.

$$(y'_{\nu_1}, \ldots, y'_{\nu_w}) = g(\{\rho_1, \ldots, \rho_r\}, (y_{\rho_1}, \ldots, y_{\rho_r}), x', \{\nu_1, \ldots, \nu_w\})$$

All RW codes presented here have such differential write functions where Δ_1, Δ_2 denote the bit-wise XOR-operations. The goal is that e.g. a controller in a storage device i can, by itself, update its kept block y_i by simply adding (XOR) the received difference γ of y_i and y'_i, i.e. $y'_i = y_i + \gamma$, if, for example, the device is blocked between reading the old and writing the modified block.

For a tuple $y = (y_1, \ldots, y_n)$ and a subset $S \in \mathbf{P}_\ell([n])$, let $\text{CHOOSE}(S, y)$ be the tuple $(y_{i_1}, y_{i_2}, \ldots, y_{i_\ell})$ where $i_1, \ldots, i_\ell$ are the ordered elements of S. Furthermore, for an ℓ-tuple d, let $\text{SUBST}(S, y, d)$ be the tuple where according to S each indexed element $y_{i_1}, y_{i_2}, \ldots, y_{i_\ell}$ of y is replaced by the element taken from d such that $\text{CHOOSE}(S, \text{SUBST}(S, y, d)) = d$ and all other elements in y remain unchanged in the outcome.

Now, for $S' \in \mathbf{P}_r([n])$, define the read operation

$$\mathbf{Read}(S', y) := f(S', \text{CHOOSE}(S', y))$$

and for $S \in \mathbf{P}_w([n])$ and $x' \in \Sigma^k$, the write operation

$$\mathbf{Write}(S, S', y, x') := \text{SUBST}(S, y, g(S', \mathbf{Read}(S', y), x', S)).$$

Since any Read-Write code needs to start at some initial state, we define the set of possible codewords Y as the *transitive closure* of the function $y \mapsto \mathbf{Write}(S, S', y, x')$ starting with $y = y_0$ and allowing all values S, S', x. Then, an RW code is correct if the following statements are satisfied.

1. *Correctness of the initial state:*

$$\forall S \in \mathbf{P}_r([n]) \ : \ \mathbf{Read}(S, y_0) = x_0 \ .$$

2. *Consistency of read operation:*

$$\forall S, S' \in \mathbf{P}_r([n]) \ \forall y \in Y \ : \ \mathbf{Read}(S, y) = \mathbf{Read}(S', y) \ .$$

3. *Correctness of write operation:*

$$\forall S \in \mathbf{P}_w([n]), \forall S' \in \mathbf{P}_r([n]), \forall y \in Y, \forall x \in \Sigma^k : \mathbf{Read}(S', \mathbf{Write}(S, S', y, x)) = x \ .$$

4 Lower Bounds

The example of a $(2, 3, 3, 4)_2$-RW code in the previous section stores two symbols of information in a four symbol code (c.f. Table 1). Unfortunately, this storage overhead of a factor two is unavoidable, as the following theorem shows (moreover, this implies that e.g. no $(3, 3, 3, 4)_b$-RWC exists).

Theorem 1. *For $r+w<k+n$ or $r,w<k$ and any base b, there does not exist any $(k,r,w,n)_b$-RWC.*

Proof: Consider a write operation and a subsequent read operation where the index set W of the write operation ($|W|=w$) and the index set R of the read operation ($|R|=r$) have an intersection: $W \cap R = S$ with $|S| = r+w-n$. Then, there are b^k possible change vectors with symbols in S that need to be encoded by the write operation since this is the only base of information for the subsequent read operation. This holds because all further $R \setminus S$ code symbols remain unchanged. Now, assume that $|S| < k$. Then, at most b^{k-1} possible changes can be encoded, and therefore, the read operation will produce faulty outputs for some write operations. Thus, $r+w-n \geq k$ and the claim follows.

If $r < k$, only b^r different messages can be distinguished while b^k different messages exist. Then, from the pigeonhole principle, it follows that such a code does not exist. For the case $w < k$, this is analogous. □

Thus, in the best case $(k,r,w,n)_b$-RW codes have parameters $r+w=k+n$. We call such RWC codes *perfect*. Unfortunately, such perfect codes do not always exist as the following lemma shows.

Lemma 1. *There is no $(1,2,2,3)_2$-RWC.*

Proof: Consider a read operation on the code bits y_1, y_2 and a write operation on y_2, y_3. Then, y_2 is the only intersecting bit which must be inverted in case of an information bit flip. The same holds for bit y_3 when considering a read operation on y_1, y_3 and a write operation on y_2, y_3. Thus, together, both y_2 and y_3 have to be inverted if the information bit x_1 flips. Now, consider a sequence of three write operations on bits $(1,2), (2,3), (1,3)$ each inverting the information bit x_1. After these operations, all code bits have been inverted twice bringing it back to the original state. In contrast, the information bit has been inverted thrice and is thus inverted. Therefore, all read operations lead to wrong results. □

However, if we allow a larger symbol alphabet, we can find an RW code.

Lemma 2. *There exists a $(1,2,2,3)_3$-RWC.*

Proof: See Table 2 for an example. The correctness is straight-forward. □

Clearly, concerning operational complexity, $b=2$ (i.e. $\mathbb{F}_2$) is the best choice for codes applied in SANs because XOR-based I/O operations can often efficiently be realized in hardware. However, as common RAID 4/5 schemes as well as parity-based Reed-Solomon codes correspond to an $(n,n,n+1,n+1)_2$-RW code, $n \geq 1$, the following lemma shows that there is no parity-based placement scheme offering better update properties.

Lemma 3. *For $n \geq 1$, there is no $(n,n,n,n+1)_2$-RW code.*

Proof: The proof follows directly from Theorem 1. □

5 Encoding and Decoding

We show that perfect RW codes always exist if the symbol alphabet is large enough, and as being closely related to Reed-Solomon codes, RW codes can also be constructed by matrix operations over finite fields. More formally, for given information tuples $x = (x_1, \dots, x_k) \in \Sigma^k$ whose underlying alphabet Σ is a sufficiently large finite field $\mathbb{F}_q$ (and thus, x is a k-dimensional vector in the vector space $\mathbb{F}_q^k$) and additional parameters $k \le r, w \le n$, we examine special subcodes of larger Reed-Solomon codes that have dimension r and length n and in which for each codeword $y = (y_1, \dots, y_n) \in \Sigma^n$ there exists a codeword for each other message with distance of at most w.

For what follows, we consider the information vector $x = (x_1, \dots, x_k) \in \mathbb{F}_q^k$, the corresponding codeword $y = (y_1, \dots y_n) \in \mathbb{F}_q^n$, and for any modification in x, let $\delta = \Delta x$ be the information change vector. Moreover, let $v = (v_1, \dots, v_\ell)$ denote the vector of internal slack variables with $\ell = n - w = r - k$ and which carry no particular information. Then, the aforementioned operations are realized by the following linear mapping using an appropriate $n \times r$ generator matrix M with $M_{i,j} \in \mathbb{F}_q$; the sub-matrix $(M_{i,j})_{i \in [n], j \in \{k+1,\dots,r\}}$ is called the *variable matrix*. In particular, an RW code relies on the following *matrix approach*:

$$\begin{pmatrix} M_{1,1} & M_{1,2} & \cdots & M_{1,r} \\ M_{2,1} & M_{2,2} & \cdots & M_{2,r} \\ \vdots & \vdots & & \vdots \\ M_{n,1} & M_{n,2} & \cdots & M_{n,r} \end{pmatrix} \begin{pmatrix} x_1 \\ \vdots \\ x_k \\ v_1 \\ \vdots \\ v_l \end{pmatrix} = \begin{pmatrix} y_1 \\ y_2 \\ \vdots \\ y_n \end{pmatrix}$$

Operations

- **Initialization:** We start with an arbitrary given information vector $x_0 = (x_1, \dots, x_k)$, for which the variables $(v_1, \dots, v_\ell)$ can be set to arbitrary values (if one wants to benefit from the security features of this coding system (see section 6), these slack variables must be chosen uniformly at random). Then, compute the codeword $y_0 = (y_1, \dots, y_n)$ using the matrix approach above.
- **Read:** Given r code entries from y, compute x We rearrange the rows of M and the rows of y such that the first r entries of y are available for reading. Let y' and M' denote these rearranged vector and matrix. The first r rows of M' describe the $r \times r$ matrix M'' that we assume to be invertible. Then, the information vector x (and the variable vector v) is obtained by: $(x \mid v)^T = (M'')^{-1} y$.
- **Differential write:** Given the information change vector δ and w code entries from y, compute the difference vector γ for the w code entries. Recall that y is updated by γ without first reading the information of y at the w code positions.

  The new information vector x' is given by $x'_i = x_i + \delta$. This notation allows to change the vector x' without reading its entries. Clearly, only the choices $w < r$ make sense. Now, due to the matrix approach, given the new k-dimensional information vector x', the task is to find another $(r-k)$-dimensional vector ρ with $v' = v + \rho$ such that the new codeword $y' = M\,(x' \mid v')^T = M\,(x+\delta \mid v+\rho)^T$ is a vector of weight at most w. Since we only consider at most w positions of y', we may, without loss of generality, assume that the last $n-w$ positions are zero, so that $M\,(x' \mid v')^T = (y'_w \mid 0)^T$, with y'_w of length w, and the vector $0 = (0,\ldots,0)^T$ is of length $n-w$. Clearly, we must rearrange the rows of the matrix M due to the vector $(y'_w \mid 0)^T$. After that, we partition M according to the lengths of the sub-vectors involved, and obtain

$$\left(M^{\leftarrow\uparrow}\right)x' + \left(M^{\uparrow\rightarrow}\right)v' = y'_w$$
$$\left(M^{\leftarrow\downarrow}\right)x' + \left(M^{\downarrow\rightarrow}\right)v' = 0\;.$$

An important precondition of the write operation is the invertibility of the submatrix $M^{\downarrow\rightarrow}$. The code symbol vector is then updated by the w-dimensional vector $\gamma = ((M^{\leftarrow\uparrow}) - (M^{\uparrow\rightarrow})(M^{\downarrow\rightarrow})^{-1}(M^{\leftarrow\downarrow}))\,\delta$, such that the new w codeword y' is derived from the former code symbols at the w given positions by simple addition, that is, $y' = y + \gamma$.

Table 2. A $(1,2,2,3)_3$-Read-Write code for an information word x and codeword y consisting of symbols y_1, y_2, y_3. For every information, there are three possible codewords, and if only any two of them three are available for reading and writing, the system can perform read and write operations (see Figure 2 in the next section for the encoding.

Contents	Code			Line
x	y_1	y_2	y_3	v
0	0	0	0	0
0	1	1	1	1
0	2	2	2	2
1	0	1	2	0
1	1	2	0	1
1	2	0	1	2
2	0	2	1	0
2	1	0	2	1
2	2	1	0	2

In fact, the $(2,3,3,4)_2$-RWC in Table 1 can be generated by this matrix based approach whose encoding is given in Figure 1 (compare also the $(1,2,2,3)_3$-RWC in Table 2 and Fig. 2).

Definition 1. *An $n \times k$-matrix A over any base b with $n \geq k$ is* row-wise invertible *if each $k \times k$ matrix constructed by combining k distinct rows of A has full rank (and therefore is invertible).*

$$\begin{pmatrix} 0&0&1 \\ 0&1&1 \\ 1&0&1 \\ 1&1&1 \end{pmatrix} \begin{pmatrix} x_1 \\ x_2 \\ v_1 \end{pmatrix} = \begin{pmatrix} y_1 \\ y_2 \\ y_3 \\ y_4 \end{pmatrix}$$

Readable code symbols	x_1	x_2
y_1, y_2, y_3	$y_1 + y_3$	$y_1 + y_2$
y_1, y_2, y_4	$y_2 + y_4$	$y_1 + y_2$
y_1, y_3, y_4	$y_1 + y_3$	$y_3 + y_4$
y_2, y_3, y_4	$y_2 + y_4$	$y_3 + y_4$

Write code	$(x_1', x_2') = (x_1 + \delta_1, x_2 + \delta_2)$			
	$y_1' = y_1+$	$y_2' = y_2+$	$y_3' = y_3+$	$y_4' = y_4+$
$1, 2, 3$	$\delta_1 + \delta_2$	δ_1	δ_2	0
$1, 2, 4$	δ_1	$\delta_1 + \delta_2$	0	δ_2
$1, 3, 4$	δ_2	0	$\delta_1 + \delta_2$	δ_1
$2, 3, 4$	0	δ_2	δ_1	$\delta_1 + \delta_2$

Fig. 1. A $(2, 3, 3, 4)_2$-Read-Write-Code over the alphabet $\mathbb{F}_2 = \{0, 1\}$ modulo 2

$$\begin{pmatrix} 0&1 \\ 1&1 \\ 2&1 \end{pmatrix} \begin{pmatrix} x \\ v \end{pmatrix} = \begin{pmatrix} y_1 \\ y_2 \\ y_3 \end{pmatrix}$$

Readable code symbols	x
y_1, y_2	$2y_1 + y_2$
y_1, y_3	$y_1 + 2y_3$
y_2, y_3	$2y_2 + y_3$

Writable symbols	$x' = x + \delta$		
	$y_1' =$	$y_2' =$	$y_3' =$
y_1, y_2	$\delta + y_1$	$2\delta + y_2$	y_3
y_1, y_3	$2\delta + y_1$	y_2	$\delta + y_3$
y_2, y_3	y_1	$\delta + y_2$	$2\delta + y_3$

Fig. 2. A $(1, 2, 2, 3)_3$-Read-Write-Code over the field $\mathbb{F}_3 = \{0, 1, 2\}$ modulo 3

Theorem 2. *The matrix based RWC is correct and well-defined if the $n \times r$ generator matrix M as well as the $n \times (r - k)$ variable sub-matrix M' is row-wise invertible.*

Proof: Follows from the definition of row-wise invertibility and the description of the operations. To prove the correctness of the coding system we show that after each operation the matrix based mapping is valid. This is straight-forward for the initialization and read operations. It remains to prove the correctness of the write operation.

Again, consider the additive vector $(\rho_1, \ldots, \rho_\ell)$ denoting the change of the variable vector v and the vector $(\gamma_1, \ldots, \gamma_w)$. With this and the information change vector δ, we obtain $x' = x + \delta$, $v' = v + \rho$ and $y' = y + \gamma$.The correctness of the write operation then follows by combining:

$$M\begin{pmatrix} x' \\ v' \end{pmatrix} = M\begin{pmatrix} x+\delta \\ v+\rho \end{pmatrix} = M\begin{pmatrix} x \\ v \end{pmatrix} + M\begin{pmatrix} \delta \\ \rho \end{pmatrix} = \begin{pmatrix} y_1 \\ \vdots \\ y_w \\ y_{w+1} \\ \vdots \\ y_n \end{pmatrix} + \begin{pmatrix} \gamma_1 \\ \vdots \\ \gamma_w \\ 0 \\ \vdots \\ 0 \end{pmatrix}$$

This equation is equivalent to the following.

$$\begin{aligned} (M^{\leftarrow\uparrow})\delta + (M^{\uparrow\rightarrow})\rho &= \gamma \\ (M^{\downarrow\rightarrow})\rho + (M^{\leftarrow\downarrow})\delta &= \mathbf{0}\ . \end{aligned}$$

Since δ is given, the variable vector ρ can be computed as

$$\rho = \left(M^{\downarrow\rightarrow}\right)^{-1}\left(-M^{\leftarrow\downarrow}\right)\delta\ ,$$

and γ by the last upper equation. If ρ is known, then the product $M \cdot (\delta \mid \rho)^T$ (reduced to the first w rows) gives the difference vector γ which provides the new code entries of y' by $y' = y + \gamma$. □

Theorem 3. *For any $k \leq r, w \leq n$ with $r+w = k+n$ there exists an $(k,r,w,n)_b$-RWC for an appropriate base b. Furthermore, this coding system can be computed in polynomial time.*

Proof: Follows from the following lemma and the fact that we use standard Gaussian elimination for recovery. □

Lemma 4. *For each $n \geq k$ and basis $b \geq 2^{\lceil \log_2 n+1 \rceil}$, there is a row-wise-invertible $n \times k$-matrix over the finite field $\mathbb{F}_b$. Furthermore, each submatrix is also row-wise invertible.*

Proof:
Define an $n \times k$ Vandermonde like matrix V for non-zero distinct elements $(c_1, \ldots, c_n) \in \mathbb{F}_{[2^{\lceil \log_2 n+1 \rceil}]}$.

$$V = \begin{pmatrix} c_1^1 & c_1^2 & \ldots & c_1^k \\ c_2^1 & c_2^2 & \ldots & c_2^k \\ c_3^1 & c_3^2 & \ldots & c_3^k \\ \vdots & & \ddots & \vdots \\ c_n^1 & c_n^2 & \ldots & c_n^k \end{pmatrix}$$

Then, erase any $n-k$ rows resulting in an $k \times k$ matrix V'. This submatrix is also a Vandermonde-matrix. Since all Vandermonde-matrices are invertible, the lemma follows. □

6 Security and Redundancy

Depending on the usage of additional slack variables, in this section, we show that Read-Write codes furthermore offer useful properties concerning data availability and security. Consider, for instance, the very extreme scenario of a combination of hard disks of n portable (laptop) computers in an office. If then a $(k, r, w, n)_b$-RWC is used for encoding for at most n laptops, it is sufficient if at least $\max\{r, w\}$ computers are accessible at the office at any time for data access and changes. If merely r computers are connected, at least the read operations can be performed. Now, what happens if computer hard disks are broken or information on some hard disks has changed ? Then, the inherent redundancy of the $(k, r, w, k)_b$-RWC allows to point out the number of wrong data and repair it (to some extent).

A different problem occurs if computers are stolen by some adversary to achieve knowledge about company data. The good news is that, for every matrix based RWC, it holds that one can give away any $n-w$ hard disks without revealing any information to the adversary. If the slack variables are chosen uniformly at random from Σ, the attacker will receive hard disks with perfect random sequences, absolutely useless without the other hard disks. As a surplus, this redundantizes the need for complex encryption algorithms.

Theorem 4. *Every $(k, r, w, n)_b$-RWC system can detect and repair ℓ faulty code symbols if $\frac{n!(r+\ell)!}{(n-\ell)!r!} < \frac{1}{2}$. Additionally, it can reconstruct $n-r$ missing code symbols.*

Proof: If $n - r$ code symbols are missing, then by the definition of a RWC system the complete information can be recovered from any r code symbols. Furthermore, if then ℓ out of these r code symbols are faulty, we simply test any combination of the $\binom{n}{r}$ combinations of r code symbols and take a majority vote over the information vector. In this vote, at least $\binom{n-\ell}{r}$ produce the correct result. This results in a majority if $\binom{n-\ell}{r} > \frac{1}{2}\binom{n}{r}$ which, by transformation, is equivalent to $\frac{n!(r+\ell)!}{(n-\ell)!r!} < \frac{1}{2}$. □

If the coded symbols are stored on distinct storage devices, with an (k, r, w, n)-RWC the loss of at most $n - \max\{r, w\}$ device can be tolerated. For instance, if these storage devices were stolen, then the following theorem shows that the thief cannot reveal any information whatsoever from the encoded information: the attacker sees only a completely random sequence vector.

Theorem 5. *Every matrix based $(k, r, w, n)_b$-RWC with $k + n = r + w$ can be used such that every choice of $n-w$ coded symbols does not reveal any information about the original information vector.*

Proof: Choose random vectors $v_1, \ldots, v_\ell$ for the initialization. Then, there is an isomorphism between these slack variables and the stolen coded symbols leading b^ℓ possibilities for the stolen coded symbol to be changed. If more symbols are added, this starts to reveal some information. □

7 Adaptive Read-Write Codes

In a SAN, adding and removing hard disks are the most delicate maneuvers, and provided that the size of the underlying symbol alphabet is chosen appropriately, we show in the following that perfect RW codes exist which allow to seamlessly continue all operations without forcing the system to be in some intermediate and, more importantly, invalid state. For instance, assume 10 disk in a SAN using an $(8, 9, 9, 10)$-RW code. Then, for better space utilization, the system administrator wants to switch to a $(4, 7, 7, 10)$-RW code. In a usual encoding, all disks have to be available for such a switch. In this section, we show that there exist some special RW codes, called *Chameleon codes*, that allow to switch while only 9 disks are accessible for read and write. If the 10th disk returns after computing the re-encoding of all data on the 9 disks, it can immediately participate in the new $(4, 7, 7, 10)$-RW code. Moreover, if the 10th disk is permanently lost, it can be reconstructed from the new $(4, 7, 7, 10)$-RW code. In particular, a *Chameleon code* is a set of RW-codes $(k, r, w, n)_b$ with fixed alphabet, and, unlike the initial codes, has a switch function. If the code is switched, all parameters k, r, w, n can be subject to change. Regarding the codeword y, not all of the code symbols have to be read or changed.

Theorem 6. *For a sufficiently large constant M, there is an (M, b)-Chameleon-RWC with $b \geq 2^{\lceil \log_2 M+1 \rceil}$. In this system, it is possible to switch at any time from a $(k, r, w, n)_b$-RWC to any $(k', r', w', n')_b$-RWC provided that $n, n' \leq M$ and $k' + n' = r' + w'$ only by reading any set of r encoded symbols and changing any set of w' encoded symbols.*

Proof: First, we select a base $b \geq 2^{\lceil \log_2 M+1 \rceil}$ and take the Vandermonde Matrix based approach as shown in Section 5. We change the main equation to the following.

$$\begin{pmatrix} c_1^1 & c_1^2 & \cdots & c_1^M \\ c_2^1 & c_2^2 & \cdots & c_2^M \\ \vdots & \vdots & & \vdots \\ c_M^1 & c_M^2 & \cdots & c_M^M \end{pmatrix} \begin{pmatrix} x_1 \\ \vdots \\ x_k \\ v_1 \\ \vdots \\ v_{r-k} \\ 0 \\ \vdots \\ 0 \end{pmatrix} = \begin{pmatrix} y_1 \\ \vdots \\ y_n \\ z_1 \\ \vdots \\ z_{M-n} \end{pmatrix}$$

Again, $x_1, \ldots, x_k$ are the content symbols, $v_1, \cdots, v_{r-k}$ are the slack variables and $y_1, \ldots y_n$ are the code symbols. The variables $z_1, \ldots, z_{M-n}$ can be ignored for the beginning; they are neither contents, slack nor code symbols and can be generated from the content and slack symbols at any time. The initial vector as well as the read and write function are chosen as in the matrix based approach. Then, the switch operation, that is, switching from a (k, r, w, n)-RWC to a (k', r', w', n')-RWC, works as follows.

First, we read r code symbols at given positions and decode the vectors x and v according to the matrix based approach. Then, we adapt the size of the former code to the new code size. If $n' > n$, we compute the corresponding variables z_i from x and v. If $n' < n$, we rename $n - n'$ code variables to z-variables, and thus, reduce the code size. If $r' > r$, the content/slack-variable vector $(x \mid v)^T$ is extended by $(r' - r)$ 0-entries. We assume that new contents are written during the switch-operation (especially, if $k \neq k'$). For this, let $v'_1, \ldots, v'_{r'-k'}$ be the new set of slack variables. Furthermore, we suppose at most w' code symbols (positions) available for writing.

We start by erasing the rows $n' + 1, \ldots, M$ in y and in the Vandermonde matrix since they are of no interest for this operation. Then, like in Section 5, we rearrange the residual matrix and the residual code vector such that the first w positions are the writable variables. We additionally rearrange the columns of the Vandermonde matrix and the contents/slack vector such that the new slack variables are on the rightmost columns, respectively lowermost lines. This results in the generator matrix M' (c.f. Section 5), and the original vector x is rearranged up to the lowest $r' - k'$ entries (possibly containing a mixture of old contents, old slack variables, and 0-entries). Let x' be the vector of the new contents (adequately rearranged), and let v' be the new slack vector with $r' - k'$ entries. If $r' \geq r$, x has k' entries, and otherwise, x (x') has $r - r'$ additional entries resulting from former slack or content variables that must to be set to 0.

We first consider the case $r' \geq r$. The number of entries in x is k'. Then, we can perform an RWC write operation changing w' code symbols. Let $\ell' = r' - k' = n' - w'$ and partition M' like in Section 5. That is, let $M^{\leftarrow\uparrow}$ be a $w' \times k'$-sub-matrix of M', $M^{\uparrow\rightarrow}$ a $w' \times k'$-sub-matrix, $M^{\leftarrow\downarrow}$ an $\ell' \times n'$-sub-matrix and $M^{\downarrow\rightarrow}$ an invertible $\ell' \times \ell'$-sub-matrix of M'. Again, according to the matrix based approach, the new (rearranged) code vector y' is obtained by

$$y' = y + \left[(M^{\leftarrow\uparrow}) - (M^{\uparrow\rightarrow})(M^{\downarrow\rightarrow})^{-1}(M^{\leftarrow\downarrow})\right] \cdot (x' - x) \tag{1}$$

using the old (rearranged) writable symbol vector y. The proof of correctness is analogous to Section 5.

Now, consider the case $r' < r$. Then, the number of entries in x and x' is $\tilde{k} = k' + r - r'$. Again, let x' be the new (adequately rearranged) vector containing the $\tilde{k}$ new symbols, and v' is the new slack variable vector with $r' - k'$ entries. Note that $x' - x$ can be computed at this stage. We now perform a slightly adapted matrix based RWC write operation that changes w' code symbols. Clearly, compared to the previous case, that matrix consists of additional $r - r'$ columns but what does not cause any problem since we only have to adapt the sub-matrices. Furthermore, let $\ell' = r' - k' = n' - w'$ and $\tilde{w} = w + r - r'$. Then, let $M^{\leftarrow\uparrow}$ be a $\tilde{w} \times \tilde{k}$-sub-matrix of M', $M^{\uparrow\rightarrow}$ a $\tilde{w} \times \ell'$-sub-matrix, $M^{\leftarrow\downarrow}$ an $\ell' \times \tilde{k}$-sub-matrix and $M^{\downarrow\rightarrow}$ an invertible $\ell' \times \ell'$-sub-matrix of M'. As usual, y denotes the old and y' the new writeable symbols. Then, applying the defined matrices, the new vector y' is obtained as given with Equation 1, and again, the proof is analogous to the proof given in Section 5. □

8 Conclusions

The Read-Write codes, presented here, provide linear block codes that, in contrast to commonly applied strategies, such as parity schemes or RS codes, feature advanced possibilities to update any codeword, and to adjust the redundancy and thus, the fault-tolerance capability of the code. In general, RW codes seem to be well-designed to any setting in which I/O operations are very costly, that feature high frequencies of write operations, and that are of dynamic behavior, like modern storage area networks. Further results and applications of RW codes can be found in [12].

References

1. Adler, M., Bartal, Y., Byers, J.W., Luby, M., Raz, D.: A modular analysis of network transmission protocols. In: Israel Symposium on Theory of Computing Systems, pp. 54–62 (1997)
2. Aguilera, M.K., Janakiraman, R., Xu, L.: Reliable and secure distributed storage using erasure codes
3. Blaum, M., Brady, J., Bruck, F., van Tilborg, H.: Array codes. In: Pless, V.S., Huffman, W.C. (eds.) Handbook of Coding Theory, ch. 22, vol. 2 (1999)
4. Blaum, M., Brady, J., Bruck, J., Menon, J.: Evenodd: an optimal scheme for tolerating double disk failures in raid architectures. In: ISCA 1994: Proceedings of the 21st annual international symposium on Computer architecture, pp. 245–254. IEEE Computer Society Press, Los Alamitos (1994)
5. Blaum, M., Brady, J., Bruck, J., Menon, J., Vardy, A.: The EVENODD code and its generalization: An efficient scheme for tolerating multiple disk failures in RAID architectures. In: Jin, H., Cortes, T., Buyya, R. (eds.) High Performance Mass Storage and Parallel I/O: Technologies and Applications, ch. 14, pp. 187–208. IEEE Computer Society Press and Wiley, New York (2001)
6. Burkhard, W.A., Menon, J.: Disk array storage system reliability. In: Symposium on Fault-Tolerant Computing, pp. 432–441 (1993)
7. Byers, J., Luby, M., Mitzenmacher, M.: A digital fountain approach to asynchronous reliable multicast. IEEE Journal on Selected Areas in Communications 20(8) (October 2002)
8. Mac Williams, F.J., Sloane, N.J.A.: The Theory of Error Correcting Codes. North-Holland Mathematical Library, Amsterdam (1977)
9. Huffmann, C., Pless, V.: Fundamentals of Error-Correcting Codes. Cambridge University Press, Cambridge (2003)
10. Tate, A.J., Kanth, R.: Introduction to Storage Area Networks. Technical report, IBM (May 2005)
11. Kubiatowicz, J., Bindel, D., Chen, Y., Eaton, P., Geels, D., Gummadi, R., Rhea, S., Weatherspoon, H., Weimer, W., Wells, C., Zhao, B.: Oceanstore: An architecture for global-scale persistent storage. In: Proceedings of ACM ASPLOS. ACM, New York (2000)
12. Mense, M.: On Fault-Tolerant Data Placement in Storage Networks. PhD thesis, University of Paderborn (January 2009)
13. Patterson, D.A., Gibson, G., Katz, R.H.: A Case for Redundant Arrays of Inexpensive Disks (RAID). In: Proceedings of the 1988 ACM Conference on Management of Data (SIGMOD), June 1988, pp. 109–116 (1988)

14. Plank, J.S.: A tutorial on Reed-Solomon coding for fault-tolerance in RAID-like systems. Software, Practice and Experience 27(9), 995–1012 (1997)
15. Rhea, S., Wells, C., Eaton, P., Geels, D., Zhao, B., Weatherspoon, H., Kubiatowicz, J.: Maintenance-free global data storage (2001)
16. Rizzo, L.: Effective erasure codes for reliable computer communication protocols. ACM Computer Communication Review 27(2), 24–36 (1997)

Distributed Sleep Scheduling in Wireless Sensor Networks via Fractional Domatic Partitioning

André Schumacher and Harri Haanpää

Helsinki University of Technology, Department of Information and Computer Science,
P.O. Box 5400, FI-02015 TKK, Finland
Andre.Schumacher@tkk.fi, Harri.Haanpaa@tkk.fi

Abstract. We consider setting up *sleep scheduling* in sensor networks. We formulate the problem as an instance of the *fractional domatic partition problem* and obtain a distributed approximation algorithm by applying linear programming approximation techniques. Our algorithm is an application of the Garg-Könemann (GK) scheme that requires solving an instance of the minimum weight dominating set (MWDS) problem as a subroutine. Our two main contributions are a distributed implementation of the GK scheme for the sleep-scheduling problem and a novel asynchronous distributed algorithm for approximating MWDS based on a primal-dual analysis of Chvátal's set-cover algorithm. We evaluate our algorithm with ns2 simulations.

1 Introduction

In *sleep scheduling*, sensor-network nodes switch between active and inactive states to save energy, thus extending network lifetime. A variety of protocols have been proposed for having a sensor network self-organize by choosing subsets of nodes to be active and serve as a *backbone* for routing or providing coverage; see e.g. [1,2,3,4]. Many protocols are heuristic and do not provide performance guarantees.

The sleep-scheduling problem can be modeled using a pairwise redundancy relationship between sensor nodes. In the resulting *redundancy graph* adjacent nodes represent sensors that can measure the same data. When backbone connectivity is not a concern, e.g., because data generation and collection phases are separated, the network can be considered operational as long as at any time each inactive node has an active neighbor in the redundancy graph. Although our coverage model is very simple, we consider it useful when node density is rather large, so that nodes nearby typically measure similar data. In graph-theoretic terms, the problem reduces to finding dominating sets in the redundancy graph and computing an assignment of dominating sets to time slots that achieves maximum length while satisfying node-battery constraints. This notion of sleep scheduling assumes a global clock to determine at any time the set of active nodes. It is usually sufficient, however, that nodes are loosely synchronized.

Floréen et al. [5] and Suomela [6] use the same redundancy model. Cărbunar et al. [7] consider a geometric setting where nodes have a fixed sensing radius.

R. Guerraoui and F. Petit (Eds.): SSS 2009, LNCS 5873, pp. 640–654, 2009.

They construct a graph of nodes which each individually could become inactive without sacrificing coverage. By introducing edges between nodes that share an edge in the *Voronoi diagram* and searching for large independent sets in this graph, battery capacity of some nodes can be preserved while retaining network-wide coverage.

Assuming uniform battery capacities and a node can only participate in one dominating set during the operation of the network, the sleep-scheduling problem is also known as the *domatic partition problem*. In the version we consider, dominating sets can be active for an arbitrarily long period while satisfying battery constraints. Removing integrality constraints enables us to apply approximation techniques for Linear Programming (LP) and allows for a longer lifetime in some networks, such as the five-cycle with unit capacities.

In Section 2, we formulate the sleep-scheduling problem as an LP packing problem and apply the Garg-Könemann [8] (GK) technique to obtain a distributed approximation algorithm for general redundancy graphs. General redundancy graphs are interesting for sensor networks, as other models, such as *unit-disk graphs*, do not capture non-uniform sensing capabilities or obstacles in the terrain. We also present a novel asynchronous distributed algorithm for approximating the *minimum weight dominating set* (MWDS) problem, which we will then use within the GK scheme. We develop our algorithm in Section 3 and first describe a centralized implementation. In Section 4 we present an efficient distributed implementation which does not require network-wide clock-synchronization. Further, in Section 5 we provide `ns2` [9] simulation data, which indicate a low number of messages required in practice. Section 6 presents our conclusions.

2 Domatic Partition

The domatic partition problem is a well-known problem in graph theory. The maximum number of disjoint dominating sets of a graph is called the *domatic number*. Feige et al. [10] show that the domatic number can be approximated in polynomial time within a factor of $O(\log n)$, where n is the number of nodes, but that it is hard to approximate it within a $(1-\epsilon)\ln n$ factor for any $\epsilon > 0$. Moscibroda and Wattenhofer [11] extend the results of Feige et al. and obtain a distributed, randomized algorithm for the same problem.

In this section, we give a formal description of the sleep-scheduling problem that allows arbitrary activation periods and formulate it as an LP. We then describe the application of the Garg-Könemann algorithm and a distributed implementation that is suitable for wireless sensor networks. For simplicity, we assume that all nodes have unit battery capacity. We note, however, that the extension to arbitrary capacities is possible.

2.1 Problem Formulation

We assume a given connected *transmission graph* $G(V, E)$ that models the sensor network with unique node identifiers. The edges in E represent the links between the radio nodes, which we assume to be undirected. Denote by $N(v)$ the neighbors of v in G and define $N^+(v)$ to be the *extended neighborhood* $N(v) \cup \{v\}$ of v. Define $\delta = \min_{v \in V} N(v)$ and $\delta^+ = \min_{v \in V} N^+(v)$ to be the minimum degree and minimum extended degree, respectively. Similarly, define Δ and Δ^+ to be size of the largest neighborhoods. By $N_k^+(v)$ we denote the k-hop extended neighborhood of v, i.e., all nodes at a hop-distance of at most k from v and define $N_0^+(v) = \{v\}$, so that $N_1^+(v) = N^+(v)$.

For simplicity of exposition, we consider the redundancy graph and G to be identical, so that the problem involves finding dominating sets in G. This assumption could be removed, when nodes know their neighbors in the redundancy graph and can communicate with them over only a few hops in G. However, note that we do not require any specific structural properties on either graph.

We introduce variables x_D that correspond to the total activation time of dominating set D. The domatic partition problem can be formulated as the following LP with a possibly exponential number of variables.

FRAC_DOMPART_PRIMAL

$$\max \sum_D x_D$$

$$\text{s.t.} \quad \sum_{D: v \in D} x_D \leq 1 \quad \forall v \in V \tag{1}$$

$$x_D \geq 0 \quad \forall D$$

The objective $\sum_D x_D$ is the length of the sleep schedule and (1) is the capacity constraint for node v. From (1) and since there is a node that can be dominated by at most δ^+ different dominating sets it follows that δ^+ is an upper bound on the total lifetime of any feasible solution. For the domatic number problem x_D must be integral. As we assume that nodes can participate in several dominating sets, we do not require integrality of x_D. This problem has only been rarely addressed in the literature. It was shown in [6] that the hardness of approximation result of [10] for the domatic number problem also holds in this case. Floréen et al. [5] propose a local algorithm that achieves a constant approximation factor in so-called *marked* graphs, which are bounded-degree graphs that contain specially distributed marked nodes for breaking symmetry. Since we consider general graphs we can only aim at a logarithmic approximation factor.

We propose a distributed version of the Garg-Könemann scheme for approximating LP packing problems, which requires a solution to the following dual problem. The dual is formulated by introducing dual variables y_v for the capacity constraints of node v.

FRAC_DOMPART_DUAL

$$\min \sum_v y_v$$

$$\text{s.t.} \quad \sum_{v \in D} y_v \geq 1 \quad \forall D \tag{2}$$

$$y_v \geq 0 \quad \forall v \in V$$

Validating constraint (2) for given y_v corresponds to solving an instance of the minimum weight dominating set (MWDS) problem with y_v as constant node weights. Our algorithm for approximating MWDS does not require network-wide synchronization or geometric restrictions on the dependency graph. Suomela [6] applies the GK scheme in a centralized setting to so-called *local graphs*, where $V \subseteq \mathbb{R}^d$, all edges have length at most 1 and node density is bounded by a constant. It was shown in [6] that the MWDS problem in these graphs can be solved efficiently. Berman et al. [12] propose to use the greedy set-cover approximation algorithm by Chvátal [13] within the GK scheme. Although their approach is similar to ours, their algorithm is centralized. See also [4] for a survey of algorithms for variations of lifetime maximization problems within the context of *sensor network coverage*, which can be also seen as heuristics for problems similar to domatic partition.

2.2 Garg-Könemann Scheme

For simplicity of exposition, we first describe the GK scheme as applied to problem FRAC_DOMPART_PRIMAL in a centralized setting and then elaborate on a distributed version suitable for implementation in sensor networks. The GK scheme takes as input an LP packing problem and a small positive constant ϵ. After termination the primal objective value is guaranteed to be at least $(1-\epsilon)^2$ times the optimum (for details see [8]). The algorithm proceeds in iterations, as described in Algorithm 1.

```
initially :
    β ← (1 + ε)((1 + ε)L)^(-1/ε)
    for all D: x_D(0) ← 0
    for all v ∈ V: y_v(0) ← β

in iteration k ≥ 1
  use oracle to find MWDS D* using y_v(k − 1) as node weights
  if (Σ_v y_v(k − 1) ≥ 1)
    for all D: x_D(k) ← x_D(k−1) / log_{1+ε}((1+ε)/β)
    return
  else
    x_{D*}(k) ← x_{D*}(k − 1) + 1
    for all v ∈ V
      if v ∈ D* then y_v(k) ← (1 + ε)y_v(k − 1)
      else y_v(k) ← y_v(k − 1)
```

Algorithm 1. GK scheme for fractional domatic partition

Denote by $y_v(k-1)$ the value of the dual variable y_v at the beginning and by $y_v(k)$ its value at the end of iteration k and define $x_D(k)$ similarly. In iteration k one selects the MWDS D^* depending on the current node weights and increases its activation time by one. If the total weight of all nodes in the networks is at least one, the primal variables are scaled down by a value depending on the size of the instance, and the algorithm terminates. Otherwise, the dual variables for the nodes in D^* are multiplied by $(1 + \epsilon)$. For the value L in the scaling factor it is sufficient to choose $L = |V|$, the maximum size of any dominating set. Note that the dominating sets found in different iterations do not need to be disjoint.

Instead of solving the MWDS subproblem in each iteration exactly, we use an approximation oracle with approximation factor $\phi > 1$. The resulting sleep schedule is guaranteed to have a length of at least $(1 - \epsilon)^2/\phi$ times the optimal length, where ϵ can be chosen arbitrarily small. For details on the application of the GK scheme in combination with an approximation oracle see the paper by Tsaggouris and Zaroliagis [14].

In Section 3 we propose a distributed MWDS algorithm with an approximation factor of $\phi = O(\ln \Delta^+)$, so that the combined algorithm is asymptotically optimal for the sleep-scheduling problem. By choosing a different MWDS approximation algorithm it is likely that better approximation guarantees can be achieved for certain graph classes.

2.3 Distributed GK Implementation

We now describe a distributed implementation of Algorithm 1 and how we combine it with the MWDS subroutine of Section 4. We assume the existence of a single initiator node which knows the number of nodes $|V|$.

First we construct a spanning tree of the transmission graph in style of the *Shout* protocol [15]. The spanning tree is used to send and receive control messages within the network. While constructing the spanning tree, the node weights are initialized to β, as in Algorithm 1.

In the first iteration, the initiator node broadcasts an initiate message in the network. This is a signal for the nodes to solve the subproblem within the inner loop of the GK algorithm, in our case the MWDS problem. The nodes then solve the subproblem, and a convergecast follows, whereby the initiator obtains the sum of the weights $y_v(0)$ that is needed for testing the termination condition.

Until the termination condition is met, in subsequent iterations the nodes update their weight y_v according to the solution of the subproblem in the previous iteration. In our case, the nodes found to be in the dominating set in the previous iteration set $y_v \leftarrow (1 + \epsilon)y_v$ before solving the MWDS problem in the current iteration. When the termination condition is satisfied, the initiator broadcasts a final message to inform the other nodes of the termination.

In our implementation, nodes need to remember the iterations in which they were in the dominating set. The sleep schedule results from this information. As an implementation note, during the broadcast and convergecast in each iteration, we let the nodes collect some data they need for the MWDS computation. Namely, at the start of the MWDS algorithm the nodes have to know not only their own weight but also the weights of their neighbors, as well as the number of neighbors each neighbor has. Instead of having separate phases for collecting this data, this is convenient to embed in the GK scheme.

3 Minimum Weight Dominating Set Approximation

This section describes an approximation algorithm for MWDS inspired by parallel algorithms based on linear programming duality proposed by Rajagopalan and Vazirani [16] for weighted set-cover. Although we use it within the GK scheme, we consider the more general MWDS setting. Dominating sets can be used among other purposes for network coverage, routing, and sleep scheduling. For an overview of the relevant literature see [17].

3.1 Problem Formulation

We first formulate an LP for the problem. Introduce variable z_v for each v corresponding to v being selected for the dominating set, whereby we initially do not require integrality of z_v. Denote the weight of node v by w_v.

FRAC_DOMSET_PRIMAL

$$\begin{aligned} \min \quad & \sum_{v \in V} w_v \, z_v \\ \text{s.t.} \quad & \sum_{u \in N^+(v)} z_u \geq 1 \quad \forall v \in V \\ & z_v \geq 0 \quad \forall v \in V \end{aligned}$$

Algorithm 2 is Chvátal's algorithm applied to MWDS that obtains an integral solution to the previous LP. It repeatedly adds to the dominating set the node with the lowest ratio of weight to *span*, the number of uncovered nodes that the node would cover, until all nodes are covered. The algorithm gives a dominating set with weight at most $\phi = H_{\Delta^+}$ times the optimum, where $H_i = \sum_{j=1}^{i} j^{-1}$ is the i-th *harmonic number*. This follows from the results in [13], as Δ^+ is the size of the largest set in the corresponding set-cover instance.

---

initially :
  $C \leftarrow \emptyset$
  for all $v \in V$: $z_v \leftarrow 0$

while $C \neq V$
  $v' \leftarrow \arg\min_v \frac{w_v}{|N^+(v) \setminus C|}$
  $z_{v'} \leftarrow 1$
  $C \leftarrow C \cup N^+(v')$

Algorithm 2. Greedy algorithm MWDS based on [13]

When one assumes unit node weights, one can easily obtain approximation algorithms that achieve a constant approximation factor in unit-disk graphs [18], and even polynomial-time approximation schemes (PTAS) are possible [19]. In general graphs, however, the inapproximability results for the set-cover problem [20] imply that Chvátal's algorithm is essentially the best-possible polynomial time approximation algorithm under standard complexity assumptions.

Distributed algorithms based on Chvátal's algorithm have been proposed for both unit and arbitrary weights. Most of them, however, assume a synchronous message passing model. Jia et al. [21] remark that the straightforward distributed implementation of the greedy algorithm in the synchronous model has linear time complexity. They propose randomized algorithms with polylogarithmic time complexity and approximation guarantees similar to Chvátal's algorithm, but their implementation requires careful clock synchronization in the network. Alternatively, synchronization techniques proposed by Awerbuch [22] can be applied, which further complicate the algorithm and require message overhead. Our algorithm is deterministic, requires no synchronization, is simple to implement, and shares the approximation guarantee of Chvátal's algorithm.

Wang et al. [23] propose a distributed asynchronous algorithm for connected MWDS based on a hybrid approach between the independent set approach [18] and Chvátal's algorithm applied locally in each neighborhood. However, for general graphs the approximation guarantee in [23] can be worse than for Chvátal's algorithm and may further depend on the weights of adjacent nodes.

3.2 Centralized Implementation

We first describe our algorithm for approximating MWDS in a centralized setting. Introduce dual variables α_v for the coverage constraint of node v in problem FRAC_DOMSET_PRIMAL. We formulate the dual as follows.

FRAC_DOMSET_DUAL

$$\begin{aligned} \max \quad & \sum_{v\in V} \alpha_v \\ \text{s.t.} \quad & \sum_{u\in N^+(v)} \alpha_u \le w_v \quad \forall v \in V \\ & \alpha_v \ge 0 \quad \forall v \in V \end{aligned}$$

Algorithm 2 can be translated into an algorithm that maintains a pair of primal and dual solutions. The primal solution is initially infeasible and becomes feasible at termination. The dual solution is initially feasible but may become infeasible. However, as one is able to bound the maximum dual constraint infeasibility, a dual feasible solution is obtained by the technique of dual fitting [24].

The algorithm is best explained in its continuous version. Denote by $z(t)$ and $\alpha(t)$ the value of a pair of primal and dual solutions at time t respectively (not necessarily feasible). At start, $z(0) = \alpha(0) = 0$. Start increasing all $\alpha_v(t)$ at unit rate until the first dual constraint holds with equality, say the constraint for z_v. This happens at time $t_1 = w_v/|N^+(v)|$, so the node first chosen has the least ratio of weight to span. Fix $z_v(t) = 1$ for $t \ge t_1$ and for all $v' \in N^+(v)$ let $\alpha_{v'}(t) = 0$ for $t > t_1$. Keep raising the other dual variables and proceed as before, breaking ties arbitrarily. As $\alpha_{v'}(t) = 0$ for all t after v' was covered, they no longer contribute to the dual constraints. The order in which these get tight is exactly the same in which Algorithm 2 adds nodes to the dominating set, and each node is chosen at a time that equals its weight divided by the number of its uncovered neighbors. Assume that k nodes got tight at time points $t_1, \ldots, t_k$.

One can show the following pair of primal and dual solutions is feasible and at most a factor of H_{Δ^+} apart, therefore establishing the approximation guarantee based on weak duality.

$$z_v = z_v(t_k)\ \forall v \in V, \quad \alpha_v = \frac{1}{H_{\Delta^+}} \max_{t_1,\ldots,t_k} \alpha_v(t_i)\ \forall v \in V$$

4 Distributed MWDS Approximation

In this section we obtain a distributed approximation algorithm for the MWDS problem from the centralized dual-increase algorithm described above. Although the order in which nodes enter the dominating set can be different, the resulting dominating set is guaranteed to be the same. We assume that each node is aware of the weight and degree of all its neighbors and also knows its neighbors in a spanning tree rooted at the initiator by executing the steps of Section 2.3.

The previously described algorithm is only feasible in a strictly synchronized setting, since nodes need to increase their α_v variables uniformly. We now describe a voting scheme that does not require synchronization. After termination each node knows all dominators in its one-hop neighborhood. We first explain the basic ideas of the algorithm in 4.1 and then describe it in more detail in 4.2.

4.1 Algorithm Outline

Throughout the algorithm, each node is in one of three *cover states*: *uncovered*, *covered*, or *dominator*. Denote by U the set of uncovered nodes, where initially $U = V$. Each node v maintains its own *price*

$$p_v := \begin{cases} \frac{w_v}{|N^+(v) \cap U|} & \text{if } N^+(v) \cap U \neq \emptyset, \\ \infty & \text{otherwise.} \end{cases}$$

In the continuous time version, node v would become a dominator at time p_v if the set of its uncovered neighbors stayed unchanged until then. To estimate p_v node v must know the state of its neighbors.

The straightforward method of repeatedly having each node compute its price and letting the node with the minimum p_v in the network become a dominator would be inefficient. Instead, it suffices to consider two-hop local neighborhoods only. The crucial observation is that as the algorithm proceeds, p_v can only increase, as the number of uncovered neighbors can only decrease. Thus, if node v has the minimum p_v in $N_2^+(v)$, it is guaranteed to become a dominator at time p_v, since $N^+(v) \cap U$ stays unchanged until then. Then the idea of the distributed algorithm is clear: whenever node v has the minimum p_v in $N_2^+(v)$, add it to the set of dominators and let its neighbors know they are dominated.

During the algorithm each node v monitors whether it has the minimum p_v in $N_2^+(v)$. If so, v declares itself a dominator and informs its neighbors, who then mark themselves as covered. A node becoming covered may affect the prices of its neighbors, as the prices depend on the number of uncovered neighbors. The algorithm terminates when all nodes are covered.

Each uncovered node v monitors the weights of the nodes in $N^+(v)$ and votes for the neighbor with the lowest price. If some node receives votes from all of its uncovered neighbors, and there is at least one of those, it has the lowest price in $N_2^+(v)$ and may therefore declare itself dominator.

To reduce the number of messages, when u votes for v, it also informs v of a limit; the vote is valid as long as the price of v does not exceed the limit. When u votes, it votes for the neighbor with the lowest price and sets the limit to that of the neighbor with the second-lowest price. If v raises its price above the limit, it will notify u so that u can decide again which node to vote for.

As a technical point, nodes only inform the nodes that are currently voting for them about price updates. If a node receives a vote with a limit that is lower than the current price of the recipient (e.g., if the voter has old information about the price of the recipient), then the recipient will reply by informing the voter of its current price.

4.2 Voting Scheme

We now describe the distributed implementation given in Algorithm 3. Each node v keeps a tuple $\mathrm{NL}_u = (\mathrm{id}, \mathrm{weight}, \mathrm{degree}, \mathrm{span}, \mathrm{limit}, \mathrm{notify})$ for each $u \in N^+(v)$, which together form the *neighbor list* NL, where id $= u$, *degree* is the degree of u, *span* is the number of uncovered nodes in $N^+(u)$, *limit* is the highest price limit received in any vote from u for v, and *notify* is a boolean variable which indicates whether u needs to be notified of a change in the price of v. The list is kept in increasing order of price, where ties are broken using node identifiers. Additionally, v maintains a set $U(v) \subseteq N^+(v)$ of uncovered neighbors, a set $D(v) \subseteq N^+(v)$ of neighbors that have become dominators, and a set $S(v) \subseteq N^+(v)$ of *supporters* of v, i.e., neighbors that are voting for v.

Initially, $\mathrm{NL}_u = (u, w_u, \delta_u, \delta_u + 1, 0, \mathrm{false})$ for all $u \in N^+(v)$, where δ_u is the degree of u, and v calculates its price $p_v = \frac{w_v}{\delta_v+1}$. Node v also initializes $D(v)$, $S(v)$ and $U(v)$ accordingly. After receiving an initialization message, node v votes for the node at the head of the list NL. We denote the kth entry of the list by $\mathrm{NL}(k)$, where $1 \leq k \leq |N^+(v)|$. So v sends the message VOTE(limit) to the node with id NL(1)[id], say u, where limit $= p_{\mathrm{NL}(2)[\mathrm{id}]}$. Note that $|N^+(v)| > 1$ because G is connected. When u receives the vote, it first checks whether the vote is valid, i.e., it checks whether limit $\geq p_u = \frac{w_u}{\delta_u+1}$. If it is valid, u records v entering its set of supporters $S(u)$ and stores the limit value in its local neighbor list. If v and u are the same node, node v performs exactly the same changes in its own neighbor list without transmitting the message.

Whenever v receives a valid vote or if one of its neighbor was covered, it checks whether there is at least one uncovered node in $N^+(v)$ which also votes for v. If so, i.e., if $S(v) = U(v)$ and $|S(v)| > 0$, then v declares itself dominator and informs all its neighbors with a DOMINATOR($N(v)$) message. It includes the ids of its one-hop neighbors to let each recipient $u \in N(v)$ update its own price based on the number of nodes in $N^+(v) \cap N^+(u)$ that were covered by v.

```
initially :
  D(v) ← ∅; U(v) ← N⁺(v); S(v) ← ∅; NL ← ∅
  for all u ∈ N⁺(v)
     NL ← NL ∪ (id: u, weight: w_u, degree: δ_u, span: δ_u + 1, limit: 0, notify: false)
  schedule price_update_timer() after T_1 seconds
  cast_vote() after T_2 seconds

if v receives VOTE(limit) from u
  if (NL_v[weight]/NL_v[span] < limit) // vote is valid
     S(v) ← S(v) ∪ {u}
     if (NL_u[limit] < limit) NL_u[limit] ← limit
     if (check_all_covered_and_voted()) declare_myself_dominator()
  else send PRICE(NL_v[span], v ∈ U(v) ? UNCOVERED : COVERED) to u

if v receives PRICE(new_span, new_state) from u // (either overheard or unicast)
  old_first ← NL(1)
  if (u ∈ U(v) and new_state == COVERED) // u informs of becoming dominated
     U(v) ← U(v) \ {u}
     NL_v[span] ← NL_v[span] − 1
     for all w ∈ S(v) do
        if (NL_w[limit] < NL_v[weight]/NL_v[span])
           NL_w[notify] ← true
           S(v) ← S(v) \ {w}
  NL_u[span] ← new_span
  if (v ∉ D(v) and check_all_covered_and_voted()) declare_myself_dominator()
  else check_and_terminate()
  if (v ∈ U(v))
     if ( old_first != NL(1)[id] or (old_first == u and message was unicast))
        cast_vote()
     if ( old_first == NL(1)[id] and old_first == v)
        NL_v[limit] ← NL(2)[weight]/NL(2)[span]
        if (check_all_covered_and_voted()) declare_myself_dominator()

if v receives DOMINATOR(N(u)) from u
  D(v) ← D(v) ∪ {u}
  NL_u[span] ← 0
  if (|U(v) \ N⁺(u)| < NL_v[span])
     NL_v[span] ← |U(v) \ N⁺(u)|
     for w ∈ S(v) with NL_w[limit] < NL_v[weight]/NL_v[span]
        NL_w[notify] ← true
        S(v) ← S(v) \ {w}
  if (v ∈ U(v))
     for all w ∈ N(v) \ (N⁺(u) ∪ D(v))
        send PRICE(NL_v[span], COVERED) to w
        NL_w[notify] ← false
  U(v) ← U(v) \ N⁺(u)
  if (v ∉ D(v) and check_all_covered_and_voted()) declare_myself_dominator()
  else check_and_terminate()
```

Algorithm 3. Distributed MWDS as executed by node v

```
void function cast_vote() at v
   limit ← NL(2)[weight]/NL(2)[span]
   if (NL(1)[id] ≠ v)
      send VOTE(limit) to NL(1)[id]
   else
      NL_v[limit] ← limit
      S(v) ← S(v) ∪ {v}
      if (check_all_covered_and_voted() and v ∉ D(v))
         declare_myself_dominator()

void function declare_myself_dominator() at v
   D(v) ← D(v) ∪ {v}
   U(v) ← ∅
   for all u ∈ N(v)
      send DOMINATOR(N(v)) to u
   NL_v[span] ← 0
   stop price_update_timer()
   check_and_terminate()

bool function check_all_covered_and_voted() at v
   if (S(v) = U(v) and |S(v)| > 0) return true
   else return false

void price_update_timer() at v
   for all u ∈ U(v) with NL_u[notify] == true
      NL_u[notify] ← false
      if (NL_u[limit] < NL_v[weight]/NL_v[span])
         send PRICE(NL_v[span], v ∈ U(v) ? UNCOVERED : COVERED) to u
   if (v ∉ D(v)) schedule price_update_timer() after T_1 seconds

void check_and_terminate() at v // test for local termination, perform convergecast
   if (U(v) = ∅ and all child nodes in spanning tree have reported weight of their subtree
   for current GK iteration)
         send terminate message to parent, include sum of weights of local tree branch
```

Algorithm 3. (*Continued*)

If v receives from u an invalid VOTE(limit) (with limit $< p_v$), then v replies with PRICE(span, state), informing of its current span and cover state instead of recording the limit for u. The set $S(v)$ remains unchanged in this case. When receiving the reply, u updates the span and state for v in its local memory. This update may initiate a price update to be transmitted by u if v indicated it is covered but $v \in U(u)$ prior to receiving the price update from v.

When the price of a node v changes because the number of uncovered nodes in $N(v)$ decreases, v goes through its set of supporters and sets the notify flag for those nodes $u \neq v$ that are required to leave $S(v)$ because v's price just exceeded the limit $NL_u[\text{limit}] < p_v$. To these neighbors v later sends a price update PRICE(span, state).

Upon receiving a price update, each uncovered node v checks whether the lowest-price entry NL(1) has changed. Let u be the neighbor with the former lowest entry and let $u \neq v$. If it has changed, i.e., if $u \neq \mathrm{NL}(1)[\mathrm{id}]$, then v sends a vote to the new best entry as described above. If it stayed the same and if the price update message originated from u, then v sends a new vote to u with a –now larger– limit value than previously and thus reenters $S(u)$. If $u = v$, then v records the new limit value for NL_v.

If a node v receives a DOMINATOR($N(u)$) from node u and if v was previously uncovered, it sends a message PRICE(span, state), where state = covered, to all neighbors in $N(v) \setminus N(u)$ that are not marked as dominators in $D(v)$, independently of their limit value.

Communication Complexity. Assuming fixed-length fields for node identifiers, weights, and number of neighbors, the communication complexity of the distributed algorithm is $O(|V|\Delta^2)$. The price of a node can change at most Δ^+ times. Each price change can trigger at most Δ price updates, each of which may require sending one vote. So the total number of vote and price update messages is $O(|V|\Delta^2)$, each of constant size. At most $|V|$ nodes may become dominators. Each dominator sends at most Δ dominator messages to inform its neighbors, and each dominator message contains information on at most Δ neighbors.

4.3 Practical Considerations

One advantage of wireless networks is their broadcast nature. As a further improvement, we let nodes overhear price updates sent between neighbors. Furthermore, the length of network-interface queues is typically limited. To prevent packet drops due to buffer overflows, instead of sending price updates immediately the neighbors are marked for notification, and marked nodes are notified periodically. We study the effect of the price update interval by experiments.

5 Experimental Evaluation

We evaluate our algorithm in two parts. After generating a number of test instances, we first use Matlab to compare the actual performance of the algorithm with the theoretical guarantee and to compute the number of GK iterations required. After that, we simulate our distributed algorithm with `ns2` to verify the correctness of our algorithm and to determine the number of messages required.

5.1 Performance Evaluation of the Centralized GK Scheme

We generated a set of 20 disk graphs by scattering 150 nodes onto square areas of various sizes uniformly at random. Connectivity was determined by the `ns2` default transmission range. We varied the average node density by changing the size of the area and discarded disconnected graphs.

Figure 1(a) shows the performance for different ϵ compared to the approximation bound using the upper bound on network lifetime δ^+. One observes that

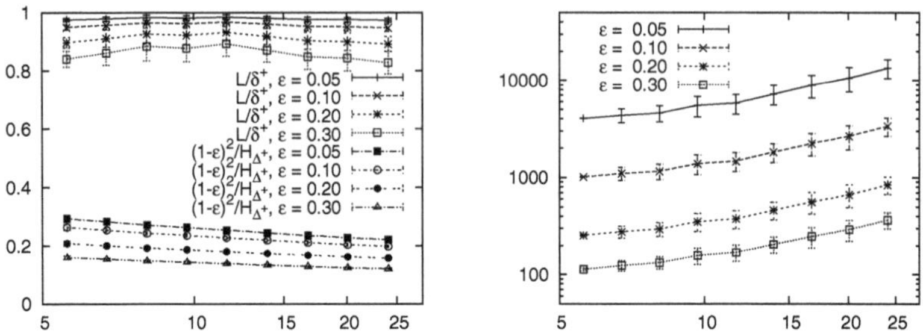

(a) Lifetime/δ^+ for different ϵ (b) Number of iterations for different ϵ

Fig. 1. The x-axis shows the expected node degree on a logarithmic scale disregarding terrain boundary effects; a) also shows the bound for the approximation factor

the total lifetime is close to its upper bound and the algorithm performs better than what one might expect from the approximation guarantee. Figure 1(b) shows the required number of iterations for the same set of instances. In all plots errorbars show the standard deviation over a set of 20 instances.

5.2 Network Simulations

We implemented the combined distributed algorithm of Sections 2.3 and 4 as a routing agent in `ns2` and consider the number of control messages and simulated termination time for the same network instances used in the Matlab experiments. Additionally, we evaluate the effect on the simulated running time achieved by choosing different values for the length of the price update interval (PUI).

Figure 2(a) shows the number of messages per node per iteration required for a fixed value of PUI and $\epsilon = 0.2$. The total number of messages per node

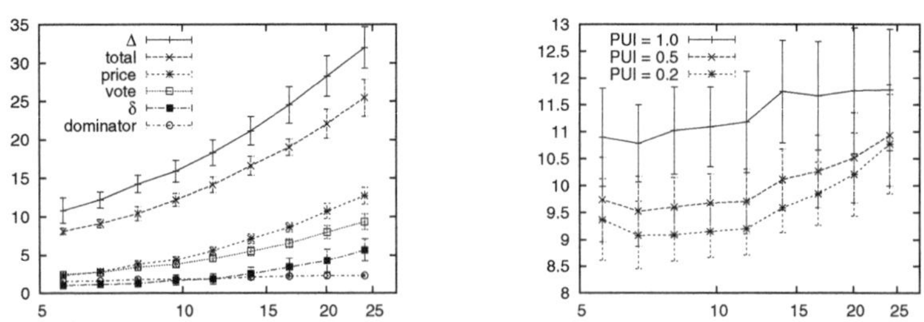

(a) Messages per node per iteration according to type for PUI=1.0 (b) Seconds per iteration for different PUI length

Fig. 2. Number of messages and second per iteration versus expected node degree; data on x-axis is shown on a logarithmic scale disregarding terrain boundary effects. Message Counts also include retransmissions due to collisions.

generally lies between the maximum and the average degree in the graph. Figure 2(a) also shows the number of messages split according to type. The price update messages have the largest contribution to the number of messages, followed by votes and dominator messages. Figure 2(b) shows the average duration of a single iteration of the algorithm for different lengths of PUI. One observes that the actual value of PUI generally has a minor effect on the average duration of a single iteration of the GK scheme, particularly when the network is dense.

6 Conclusions

We present a distributed approximation algorithm for the sleep-scheduling problem based on the Garg-Könemann scheme and linear programming duality. A key component of the algorithm is our efficient distributed implementation of Chvátal's greedy set-covering algorithm. The set-covering problem is a central combinatorial problem and we believe our implementation to be useful also in other problem settings; moreover, the LP duality technique used to obtain locality may be useful also for other problems. Our algorithm is based on a mathematical framework that provides a guarantee on the solution quality. Moreover, our simulation results suggest that the algorithm also performs well in practice.

Acknowledgements. The authors thank Pekka Orponen for fruitful discussions on the topic. A. Schumacher has been supported by the Helsinki Graduate School of Computer Science and Engineering and by the Nokia Foundation.

References

1. Chen, B., Jamieson, K., Balakrishnan, H., Morris, R.: Span: an energy-efficient coordination algorithm for topology maintenance in ad hoc wireless networks. Wirel. Netw. 8(5), 481–494 (2002)
2. Basagni, S., Mastrogiovanni, M., Petrioli, C.: A performance comparison of protocols for clustering and backbone formation in large scale ad hoc networks. In: Proc. IEEE Int. Conf. on Mobile Ad-hoc and Sensor Systems, pp. 70–79 (2004)
3. Wang, L., Xiao, Y.: A survey of energy-efficient scheduling mechanisms in sensor networks. Mobile Networks and Applications 11(5), 723–740 (2006)
4. Dietrich, I., Dressler, F.: On the lifetime of wireless sensor networks. ACM Trans. Sen. Netw. 5(1), 1–39 (2009)
5. Floréen, P., Kaski, P., Musto, T., Suomela, J.: Local approximation algorithms for scheduling problems in sensor networks. In: Kutyłowski, M., Cichoń, J., Kubiak, P. (eds.) ALGOSENSORS 2007. LNCS, vol. 4837, pp. 99–113. Springer, Heidelberg (2008)
6. Suomela, J.: Locality helps sleep scheduling. In: Working Notes of the Workshop on World-Sensor-Web: Mobile Device-Centric Sensory Networks and Applications (2006), `http://www.sensorplanet.org/wsw2006/8_Suomela_WSW2006_final.pdf`
7. Cărbunar, B., Grama, A., Vitek, J., Cărbunar, O.: Redundancy and coverage detection in sensor networks. ACM Trans. Sen. Netw. 2(1), 94–128 (2006)
8. Garg, N., Könemann, J.: Faster and simpler algorithms for multicommodity flow and other fractional packing problems. SIAM J. Comput. 37(2), 630–652 (2007)

9. McCanne, S., Floyd, S., Fall, K., Varadhan, K.: The network simulator `ns2`, The VINT project (1995), `http://www.isi.edu/nsnam/ns/`
10. Feige, U., Halldórsson, M.M., Kortsarz, G.: Approximating the domatic number. In: Proceedings of the thirty-second annual ACM symposium on Theory of computing (STOC 2000), pp. 134–143. ACM, New York (2000)
11. Moscibroda, T., Wattenhofer, R.: Maximizing the lifetime of dominating sets. In: Proceedings of The 19th IEEE International Parallel and Distributed Processing Symposium (2005)
12. Berman, P., Calinescu, G., Shah, C., Zelikovsky, A.: Power efficient monitoring management in sensor networks. In: Wireless Communications and Networking Conference, WCNC 2004, pp. 2329–2334. IEEE, Los Alamitos (2004)
13. Chvátal, V.: A Greedy Heuristic for the Set-Covering Problem. Mathematics of Operations Research 4(3), 233–235 (1979)
14. Tsaggouris, G., Zaroliagis, C.: QoS-aware multicommodity flows and transportation planning. In: Jacob, R., Müller-Hannemann, M. (eds.) ATMOS 2006 - 6th Workshop on Algorithmic Methods and Models for Optimization of Railways, Internationales Begegnungs- und Forschungszentrum fuer Informatik (IBFI), Schloss Dagstuhl, Germany (2006)
15. Santoro, N.: Design and Analysis of Distributed Algorithms. Wiley Series on Parallel and Distributed Computing. Wiley-Interscience, Hoboken (2006)
16. Rajagopalan, S., Vazirani, V.V.: Primal-dual RNC approximation algorithms for set cover and covering integer programs. SIAM J. Comput. 28(2), 525–540 (1999)
17. Blum, J., Ding, M., Thaeler, A., Cheng, X.: Connected Dominating Set in Sensor Networks and MANETs, pp. 329–369. Kluwer Academic Publishers, Dordrecht (2005)
18. Marathe, M.V., Breu, H., Hunt III, H.B., Ravi, S.S., Rosenkrantz, D.J.: Simple heuristics for unit disk graphs. Networks 25, 59–68 (1995)
19. Nieberg, T., Hurink, J., Kern, W.: Approximation schemes for wireless networks. ACM Trans. Algorithms 4(4), 1–17 (2008)
20. Feige, U.: A threshold of ln n for approximating set cover. J. ACM 45(4), 634–652 (1998)
21. Jia, L., Rajaraman, R., Suel, T.: An efficient distributed algorithm for constructing small dominating sets. Distrib. Comput. 15(4), 193–205 (2002)
22. Awerbuch, B.: Complexity of network synchronization. J. ACM 32(4), 804–823 (1985)
23. Wang, Y., Wang, W., Li, X.Y.: Distributed low-cost backbone formation for wireless ad hoc networks. In: Proceedings of the 6th ACM international symposium on Mobile ad hoc networking and computing (MobiHoc 2005), pp. 2–13. ACM, New York (2005)
24. Jain, K., Mahdian, M., Markakis, E., Saberi, A., Vazirani, V.V.: Greedy facility location algorithms analyzed using dual fitting with factor-revealing LP. J. ACM 50(6), 795–824 (2003)

Network-Friendly Gossiping

Sabina Serbu[1], Étienne Rivière[2,*], and Pascal Felber[1]

[1] University of Neuchâtel, Switzerland
first.last@unine.ch
[2] NTNU Trondheim, Norway
etriviere@gmail.com

Abstract. The emergence of large-scale distributed applications based on many-to-many communication models, e.g., broadcast and decentralized group communication, has an important impact on the underlying layers, notably the Internet routing infrastructure. To make an effective use of network resources, protocols should both limit the stress (amount of messages) on each infrastructure entity like routers and links, and balance as much as possible the load in the network. Most protocols use application-level metrics such as delays to improve efficiency of content dissemination or routing, but the extend to which such application-centric optimizations help reduce and balance the load imposed to the infrastructure is unclear. In this paper, we elaborate on the design of such *network-friendly* protocols and associated metrics. More specifically, we investigate random-based gossip dissemination. We propose and evaluate different ways of making this representative protocol network-friendly while keeping its desirable properties (robustness and low delays). Simulations of the proposed methods using synthetic and real network topologies convey and compare their abilities to reduce and balance the load while keeping good performance.

1 Introduction

We have observed a major paradigm shift in distributed computing over the last decade, with the emergence of many large-scale and widely distributed applications based on the peer-to-peer (P2P) paradigm, such as BitTorrent or Skype. These applications rely on overlay networks that connect participating nodes via application-level communication links. While these links may be built while considering application-level quality of service metrics, usually their construction does not consider their impact on the underlying support infrastructure itself as a primary goal. Given the prevalence of P2P traffic in today's Internet, it is important to understand the impact of protocols that are not aware of the underlying network, and develop solutions to minimize their traffic. This impact can be measured in two main ways: what is the stress imposed on each component of the infrastructure (routers, links), and how is this load balanced over all such components?

* This work was carried out during the tenure of an ERCIM "Alain Bensoussan" Fellowship Programme.

R. Guerraoui and F. Petit (Eds.): SSS 2009, LNCS 5873, pp. 655–669, 2009.

Some P2P protocols try to build efficient peering relations using application-level measurements, such as the round-trip time (RTT) obtained by ICMP measurements, e.g., as performed during the construction of routing tables in the Pastry distributed hashtable [22]. These techniques are used mostly to enhance the performance as experienced by the user, by reducing communication delays, but it remains unclear whether this approach is really effective at reducing the burden on the network. That is, preferring low-delays routes does not necessarily lead to using shortest paths and it tends to saturate low-delay links and associated routers. Therefore, the length of the communication paths, i.e., the number of traversed routers, is a better indicator of the stress on the infrastructure (a long path obviously loads the network more than a short one). This information is not, however, readily available to the application.

In this paper, we study the problem of network-friendly P2P communication. We focus on gossip-based dissemination protocols, because they are very simple yet extremely robust, they are highly dynamic by nature and rely on random interactions with a set of neighbor peers that changes over time, and they are perfectly adapted to large-scale decentralized systems. Most importantly, classical gossip-based protocols are not particularly friendly with the infrastructure (notably because they select random peers to communicate with) and thus they represent good candidates to illustrate our approach.

In order to make gossip-based dissemination more usable, we propose network-friendly gossip protocols that can use various metrics for selecting, in a semi-random manner, application-level communication links between peers. The objective is to reduce the impact of the dissemination on the infrastructure while keeping good performance. These protocols are based on network-aware peer sampling services and use a combination of push- and pull-based gossiping. We specifically consider metrics based on delay and path length on different topology models, both synthetic and real-world. We study the efficiency of the protocols in terms of performance of dissemination and load distribution. As such types of protocols are lightweight in terms of bandwidth consumption (their primary usage is the robust dissemination of small messages or meta-information with sizes in the order of kilobytes), we do not consider the cap bandwidth of links nor the usage of available bandwidth as being potential sources of bottlenecks in the system.

Related work. A first approach to network awareness consists in introducing a bias in the selection of peers in a peer-to-peer system by leveraging ISPs' knowledge of their infrastructure [3]. The ISP proposes an oracle node which, given a list of IPs, returns this list sorted in decreasing order of network friendliness (as determined by the ISP). While this solution is appealing because it allows more knowledge and control by the infrastructure, in particular regarding the peering relations of the ASes, it is unclear whether ISPs are willing to deploy such services in the near future.

There exist other application-level solutions like ours. Synthetic coordinates have been proposed to model the delay and the load associated with traffic in a content delivery network [4]. Although this approach allows the network to balance the load on the peers and on the routers, it is only helpful for long-lasting communication patterns with non-fluctuating bandwidth and its applicability to gossip-based dissemination is unclear. The contribution of this paper focuses on protocols where no stable communication patterns between peers can be leveraged, yet the load has to be reduced and balanced on the infrastructure. Here, bandwidth is not the primary concern, but the presence of a multitude of lightweight operations that, summed up, can represent a considerable load for the network. Knowledge about the network layer structure can also be used to perform various application-level optimization [23] (e.g., balancing the routing load by mapping the routes in the overlay onto those in the infrastructure, or recovering faster from failures). Such knowledge is, nonetheless, not readily available to the application nor easily exploitable in a decentralized manner.

Roadmap. We first present the basic gossip-based dissemination and membership management protocols in Section 2, as the context for the presentation of our solution. We then elaborate in Section 3 on the tools required for network friendliness. In Section 4 we present variants of gossip-based dissemination, from complete unawareness of the underlying infrastructure to network-friendly solutions. We evaluate the resulting protocols in Section 5, in terms of performance and impact on the network using various topologies. Finally, we conclude in Section 6.

2 Gossip-Based Protocols

Gossip-based protocols, also known as *epidemic* protocols, are a class of fully decentralized protocols that are particularly adapted for implementing self-organizing behaviors in dynamic networks. They were first introduced in the context of database synchronization [9] and they have since received considerable attention, mostly due to their ability to support large scale information systems with a simple, yet efficient and robust approach. They rely on periodic, pairwise exchanges of small-size state information between peers. Their scalability stems from the balance of communication amongst peers, and from the fact that each node only needs to know a small part of the network, which is usually called its *view*. Periodically, each peer chooses one other peer in its view to perform an information exchange. The nature of this information, as well as the result of the exchange (i.e., what information is exchanged and what is eventually kept on each side), defines a gossip-based protocol. The following algorithm presents the abstract operation of the protocol at each peer:

Each node runs both an *active* and a *passive* thread. The active thread on a node n_a periodically selects from the local view a partner n_b to gossip with by using the `selectPartner()` operation. The data sent by n_a to n_b is determined by the means of the `selectToSend()` operation. The passive thread on node n_b receives this information, merging it into its own state (by using the `selectToKeep()` operation), and optionally sends back some data to n_a, which may in turn update its state. Note that while `selectToSend()` and `selectToKeep()` operations are most often the same for both the passive and

```
// Active thread: periodically
   send gossip request (n_a)
n_b ← selectPartner()
buf_send ← selectToSend()
send buf_send to n_b
receive buf_recv from n_b
view ← selectToKeep()
```

```
// Passive thread: reply to
   incoming gossip request (n_b)
receive buf_recv from n_a
buf_send ← selectToSend()
send buf_send to n_a
view ← selectToKeep()
```

active threads, this is not mandatory: for instance, the selection of elements to be sent back can be based on different policies for the active or the passive threads. The size of the state is usually of bounded size, and it often consists of the view itself. These protocols can be used for a variety of tasks [18] (e.g., computing aggregates of distributed values [17, 21], failure detection [24] or group management [14]). We present here their use for application domains relevant for this paper: membership management, clustering and dissemination.

Creating random overlays. We first discuss *peer sampling* [15] protocols. Their objective is to create, for each peer, a view composed of peer samples drawn *randomly* from all peers in the network. The resulting graph, when considering bounded view sizes, is close to an Erdös-Rényi random graph [10].

Cyclon [25] is an example of a peer sampling protocol. It operates on a view of c peers. Each node n_a periodically exchanges a subset of its view, plus its own identity, with the peer n_b from its view that was contacted the least recently (`selectPartner()`). The result of the exchange is that links from n_a to this subset are *shuffled* with the links received from n_b, in such a way that peers keep the same in-degree.

A simple addition [19] to a peer sampling protocol such as Cyclon allows us to estimate the size of the system at each peer, an information that can be fundamental to many distributed algorithms. Random identifiers are assigned to nodes and then hashed into a key space; next, collecting the closest hashes around n_a's identifier and considering their density, one can obtain a sound estimation of the network's size with a very limited overhead.

Emerging structure. The second and more general kind of view management protocols construct overlays whose structure emerges in a totally decentralized fashion (e.g., distributed hashtables [20] or semantic overlays [26]). T-Man [13] and Vicinity [26] are two generic protocols for expressing emerging structures. Both operate on the same principle. Each node constructs a view, usually of fixed size t, that satisfies some constraints expressed as functions over the neighbors characteristics. The goal is to make views evolve towards a set of peers whose "sum of desirability" is the highest possible, as defined by a *proximity function.* `selectPartner()` selects a partner node n_p in the view (e.g., the least recently contacted peer) and `selectToSend()` picks a subset of the view (e.g., by choosing nodes with the lowest proximity scores w.r.t. n_p). `selectToKeep()` simply merges the received elements with the local view, sorts the nodes according to the proximity function, then keeps the first t elements.

Gossip-based dissemination. The most common use of gossip is arguably for information spreading [16,6,11]. The information spreads much like an epidemy in a human population. We distinguish two types of pairwise contaminations between an "infected" and a "non-infected" node: by *push* and by *pull*. In a *push* model, a node that receives a message for the first time sends it during the next round to f other peers. The message is tagged by a *hops-to-live (htl)* value, which is decreased at each peer encountered; the message is no further propagated if *htl* reaches 0. A *pull* operation is a periodic request sent by an active thread on node n_a and handled by a passive thread on node n_b. Node n_a sends its set of message identifiers (`selectToSend()`) to node n_b, which sends back the messages that n_a is missing. Note that pull requests can be piggybacked on top of existing gossip-based messages such as the ones used for membership management. A push-only dissemination protocol reaches all nodes in the network w.h.p. in $O(\log N)$ rounds if $f = O(\log N)$. The nodes that have not been infected by a push operation can later obtain the message by pull requests. As such, a dissemination protocol combining synchronous push and pull operations exhibits a two-phase scenario. First, the number of infected nodes follows an exponential growth; then, as the probability to infect *virgin* nodes by a push operation decreases, the number of virgin nodes decreases in a quadratic manner. The dissemination in the first phase is mostly due to pushes, while the second phase relies essentially on pulls [6].

3 Network Friendliness

We define *network friendliness* as the ability of a protocol to limit and balance the load it imposes on the elements of the network upon which it operates. In this section, we elaborate on the facilities, available to the protocol designer, that we will use for making gossip-based dissemination network friendly.

We consider a network composed of multiple entities (autonomous systems or ASes, each composed of multiple routers), in which a communication between two nodes follows a path of routers: $n_a \rightarrow r_a \rightarrow ...r_i... \rightarrow r_b \rightarrow n_b$, where $r_a, r_i, ..., r_b$ belong to the set of all routers R. A message of size m between n_a and n_b loads each router on the path by m. Network friendliness aims at (1) reducing the overall load on all routers, i.e., $\sum_{r \in R} load(r)$ and (2) balancing the load on each router, reducing the differences between $load(r)$ for all $r \in R$. Intuitively, one can approach both objectives by preferring short routes and using routers that lie in the vicinity of n_a and n_b (e.g., in the same AS). It is clear that randomly selecting communication partners will lead to configurations that are far from network-friendly, with actual message paths that unnecessarily traverses routers over several continents. We now present the two main metrics that are available to an application for choosing nearby communication partners: using the *delay* as an estimation of the route size, or discovering the actual *route size* by lightweight probing of the IP network. We will use both these metrics in our network-friendly solution presented in Section 4.

$t \leftarrow T$ (expected median length)
$r_{\max} \leftarrow 2t$, $w_{\text{found}} \leftarrow \bot$
while $(r_{max} - r_{min}) > 1$ **do**
  send a packet with TTL t
  if *no reply within timeout* **then**
    if $w_{found} = \bot$ **then**
      $r_{\max} \leftarrow \min(r_{\max} + T, 255)$
    $r_{\min} \leftarrow t + 1$
  else
    $r_{\max} \leftarrow t$, $w_{\text{found}} \leftarrow \top$
  $t \leftarrow \lfloor \frac{r_{\min} + r_{\max}}{2} \rfloor$
return t

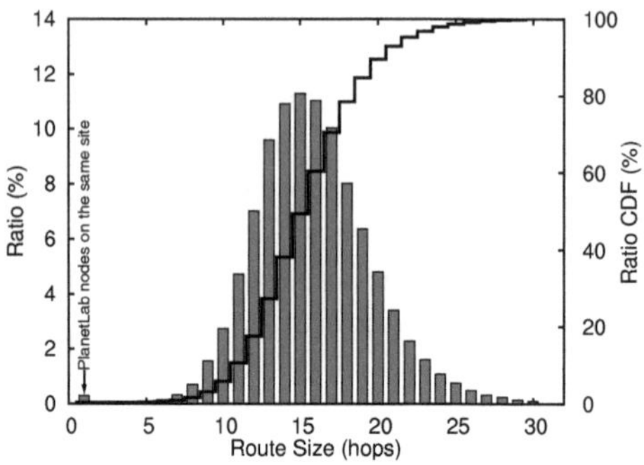

Algorithm 1. Lightweight probing of path length using the TTL field in IP messages (left). Route sizes distribution for 610 PlanetLab [1] nodes (right).

Application level round-trip times (RTT). The first metric, which is also the most commonly used (e.g., when constructing routing tables in Pastry [22]), is the time required for a message to go from a node n_a to another node n_b, estimated as half the round trip time of a small packet exchanged between n_a and n_b (RTT). The RTT can be measured either at the application level, which can benefit from pre-established connections, or by using the ICMP layer (`ping`). Note that this metric is usually leveraged for enhancing the application performance, not for improving network friendliness. While the relation between low delays and low path length may seem intuitive, it is interesting to investigate whether using the RTT estimation for path lengths achieves *the best possible* network friendliness.

Routes lengths. The knowledge of route lengths is usually a metric that is available to the infrastructure manager only, i.e., the Internet service provider (ISP). In the general case, when collaboration between the application and the ISP [3] is not available, it is necessary to *probe* the network for retrieving this information. The *traditional* way of discovering a route (and hence determine its length) is to use the `traceroute` tool. This poses two problems: (1) this tool requires administrator rights, which is not desirable for an application and (2) its load is quite high as it obtains additional information (e.g., the name and addresses of all routers in the path) that are not needed in our context.

We use instead a lightweight mechanism to obtain route length at the application level, using regular ICMP packets. Every packet sent from a node n_a to another node n_b contains a TTL field. On each router $r_a, r_i, ..., r_b$, IP specifies [7] that the TTL is decreased by the number of seconds the message has passed onto the router, or by one if this time is less than a second. Obviously, the latter case largely dominates in today's Internet, that is, it is safe to consider that on each router the TTL is reduced by 1. Messages that reach TTL 0 are dropped. It follows that a probe message sent with TTL x will only reach its destination if $|r_a, r_i, ..., r_b| \leq x$. The lowest necessary TTL t for successfully *probing* n_b from n_a thus indicates the path length from n_a to n_b. Algorithm 1 presents a simple

Local computations:

$dir \leftarrow u(c_b - c_a)$; // Direction (unit vector)

$m_v \leftarrow ||c_a, c_b||$; // Vivaldi estimation

$diff \leftarrow m_v - m_r$; // Estimation vs. measure

$\delta \leftarrow \max(\delta_{\min}, \delta - \delta_{\text{decr}})$; // Adaptive delta

Apply force:

$c_a[i] \leftarrow c_a[i] + dir[i] * diff * \delta$; // Local coord.

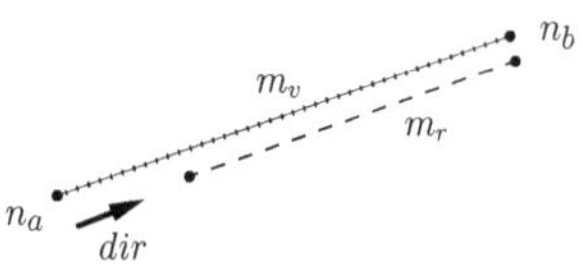

Algorithm 2. Vivaldi network coordinates update

method to determine t. This algorithm uses a divide-and-conquer approach to determine the lowest TTL for a message to reach its destination. The expected median value of the TTL is T which, properly set, allows for faster probing but this is not a requisite. The expected number of sent probes is $O(\log_2 T)$. We tested this algorithm by discovering the path lengths between all nodes-pair in a set of 610 worldwide nodes on PlanetLab [1]. The method successfully detected all route lengths, in most cases within 5 message exchanges (T was set to 15).

The use of the TTL field in TCP packets for discovering infrastructure characteristics without relying on tools such as `traceroute` has been successfully used in a different way by the *Recursive Packet Train* (RPT) method [12], whose goal is to discover bottlenecks (i.e., links that are limiting the overall bandwidth offered by the route) in the path between any two Internet end hosts.

Network coordinates. An overlay substrate for gossip-based dissemination is likely (and willingly) dynamic. It is contrary to the objective of network friendliness, and particularly to the reduction of the load, to have each single peer probe any possible neighbor node it encounters. It is not necessary either to use *perfect* measurements (especially if the act of performing them produces as much load as they were meant to avoid). An appealing technique for reducing measurements is to use *network coordinates* [8]. The idea is to embed all nodes in a metric space of moderate dimensionality,[1] such that the distance between the points representing two nodes in this space provides a good estimate of the metric (delay or route length). Each node "bootstraps" its coordinates by evaluating the metric with a set of landmark nodes. The evolution of coordinates is similar to that of a spring-mass relaxation system: the goal is to reduce, gradually, the differences between the predicted and experienced metrics. Algorithm 2 details the coordinate update of a node n_a, after probing the peer n_b chosen by `selectPartner()` for the exchange (in case of delays, this probing is done using application messages, while for path length an explicit probing is needed). Node n_a knows its coordinate, c_a, and the coordinate of n_b, c_b. The actual measure is m_r while the estimate m_v is given by $||c_a, c_b||$ (distance between n_a's and n_b's coordinates). The difference between m_r and m_v is compensated by slightly moving n_a's coordinate, covering part of the difference between the estimate and

[1] We use 5 dimensions, as it represents a good tradeoff between the accuracy of the estimations, and associated computational costs and convergence times [8].

the measurement. Note that the whole distance between c_a and c_b is not compensated, in order to avoid oscillations of coordinates. The portion of the difference is given by δ, which is moderate for the first adjustments (we use $\delta = 0.1$) and decreases down to its minimum value as the node converges towards its "ideal coordinate" for each exchange (we use $\delta_{\text{decr}} = 0.005$ and $\delta_{\text{min}} = 0.05$). The initial setup is done by probing 20 landmarks.

4 Network-Friendly Gossip-Based Dissemination

This section describes the design of network-friendly gossip-based dissemination protocols, based on the building blocks that have been presented in the previous sections. We first discuss the *limited push* approach, intended to reduce the load of useless duplicate messages, then describe the creation of the support overlay, and finally elaborate on the various dissemination scenarios.

Limited push. Gossip-based push propagation reaches all N nodes in the network w.h.p. in $O(\log N)$ rounds if the fanout $f = O(\log N)$. During dissemination the number of messages sent by push grows exponentially, and so does the number of *duplicates* (messages received more than once), because the probability of reaching an already infected node increases. Figure 1 presents the behavior (simulated, and averaged over 1,000 runs on a 100,000 nodes network) of a push-only dissemination, in terms of coverage and redundancy. We observe that close to 100% coverage is achieved with $f = 4$ and $htl = 8$ but much higher values of f and htl are required to ensure that all peers get all messages. Yet, the number of duplicates is extremely high even with $f = 4$ and $htl = 8$, which is contrary to our objective of network friendliness.

We thus propose to combine push and pull in the following way. An initial, limited push *seeds* the network, leveraging the initial exponential growth phase, but stops before yielding many duplicates. Periodic, lightweight pull messages are then used to disseminate the message to all peers. The values of f and htl have to be set properly to reach a certain proportion (e.g., 10%) of the network. Obviously, these values depend on the size of the network, an information that is not known to the peers directly, but that can be calculated by a simple mechanism [19] on top of membership management messages. As the desired coverage

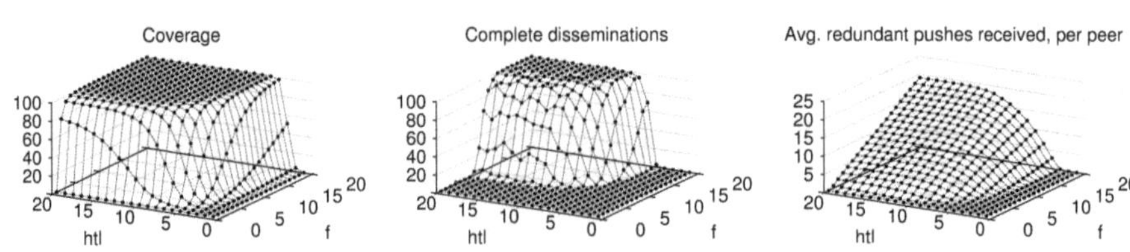

Fig. 1. Push-only dissemination: coverage (ratio of peers notified), complete (ratio of dissemination that notify *all* peers) and redundancy ratio for various f and *htl*

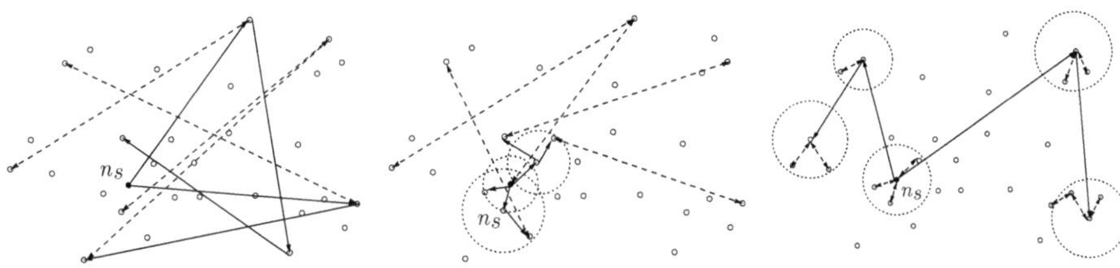

(a) push rand., pull rand (b) push close, pull rand (c) push rand., pull close

Fig. 2. Peer selection strategies. Dotted circles represent close views. Solid lines correspond to pushes and dashed lines to pulls.

is small enough for not having duplicates, the number of nodes touched by a push can be estimated as $\sum_{h=0}^{htl} f^{htl}$. Since f is fixed, a node n_i issuing a new message uses the *htl* value that best approximates the desired coverage (almost 10% in our experiments). Alternatively, different push messages can be initiated by n_i, with different *htl* values for getting closer to the target coverage.

Construction of the support overlay. Gossip-based dissemination relies on some randomness in the peer samples available at each node. We call the set of peers constructed by regular sampling "random peers", gathered in the "random view". These views are constructed using Cyclon [25]. Moreover, we use the T-Man protocol [13] along with Vivaldi coordinates [8] to construct a set of *close* peers, called the "close view" at each node. Both Cyclon and T-Man use views of size 20, and 8 peers are exchanged at each cycle. The proximity function between a node n_a and a potential neighbor n_i is the distance between their coordinates (based on delay or route length). Obviously, the overlay composed of only close peers is not likely to be connected (e.g., all peers from the same institution will form a separate overlay), thus both views are necessary to ensure dissemination termination and we need to use appropriate peer selection strategies, as discussed next.

Peer selection strategies. Classical gossip-based dissemination [16, 6, 11] uses random partner selection for both push and pull. Instead, we choose to use two `selectPartner()` operations, depending on whether the transmission of information is by push (i.e., finding a partner to send data to) or by pull (i.e., finding a partner to ask data from). Each selection can be made in any of the two views (of random or close neighbors), yielding thus four possible strategies. An important point is that a push message is of a greater size than a pull request: the former contains the epidemic message, while the latter only contains a digest of the epidemic messages the requesting node already holds (e.g., a Bloom filter).

The *push-close/pull-close* strategy can be dismissed right away: the clustering made by the selection of close peers will most likely produce non-connected overlays which, lacking random links, cannot preserve robustness nor ensure termination. The *push-random/pull-random (RR)* strategy, depicted in Figure 2(a), refers to "classical" gossip without close view. It imposes the highest load on the network, as arbitrarily long routes are used. Nonetheless, its performance is expected to be good as the network is uniformly seeded by the limited push, and the probability to touch an infected node by pull requests does not depend on the position of the requester in the network. The two network-friendly strategies are *push-close/pull-random (CR)* and *push-random/pull-close (RC)*, shown respectively in Figure 2(b) and Figure 2(c). CR seeds by limited push the vicinity of the initiator n_s. This increases the risks of duplicates in n_s's vicinity but presents the advantage of using short paths for the push phase. Intuitively, the better strategy is RC: n_s pays the price of seeding remote nodes through long routes, and these nodes are then in charge of propagating the message by pull requests to their vicinity, using smaller routes. However, if no node has been touched by push in a cluster of nearby nodes (possibly not connected with the rest of the networks by their close views), RC may produce large delays for message delivery, or even lead to some messages not being delivered at all. To avoid this scenario, we force RC to sometimes select a random partner for a pull request (with 5% probability).

5 Evaluation

We evaluate metrics and strategies for network-friendly gossiping by the mean of simulations of both the application layer *and* the network layer. Our discrete time simulator considers the network as a set of routers and links between them. Each application node is attached to a router, and messages follow the shortest path in the network in terms of the sums of delays for all traversed links. We chose to use simulation rather than a deployment for being able to compare inter-router delays and routes lengths w.r.t. the ones estimated by Vivaldi at the application layer. Each application node runs the Vivaldi coordinates system, a Cyclon peer sampling service, our route length measurement algorithm, a T-Man protocol for clustering nodes in local views according to the chosen metric, and the dissemination protocol. To allow for a fair modeling of Vivaldi and the associated estimation error, delays on each link are subject to a ±10% variance.

Topologies. We use both *synthetic* topologies representing classical network models found in the literature, as well as a *real* topology model collected from a university network. All topologies are composed of 651 routers to match the size of the real one. Their characteristics are presented in Figure 3: (i) distribution of route sizes (bottom); (ii) dispersion of routes lengths for each route size (scatter plot on top), as well as the evolution of the distribution of delays for each route length for the real topology.

Synthetic topologies are helpful for understanding the behavior of network friendly gossiping in various well-studied graphs models. We use 4 different synthetic topologies that are representative of global characteristics of real networks, and that are the most commonly used for modeling these networks characteristics. Unless explicitly noted, all links between routers have a delay of 50 ms ±10%.

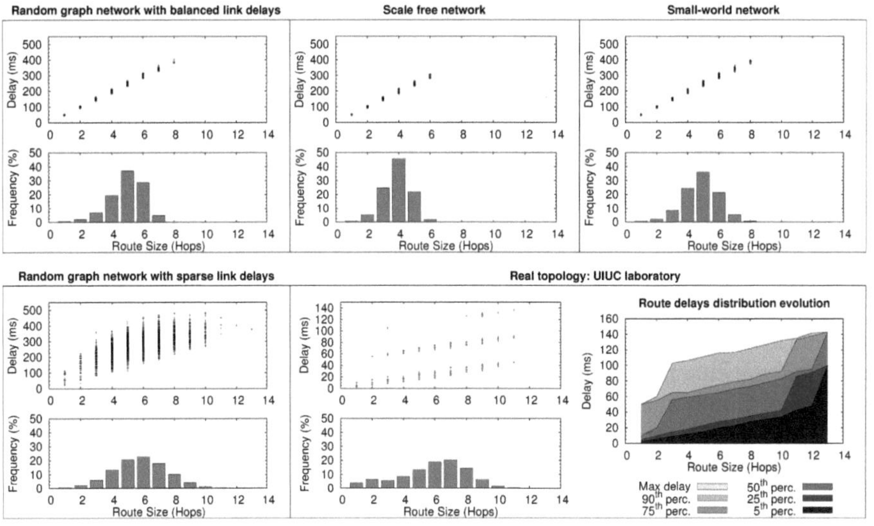

Fig. 3. Characterization of the five topologies

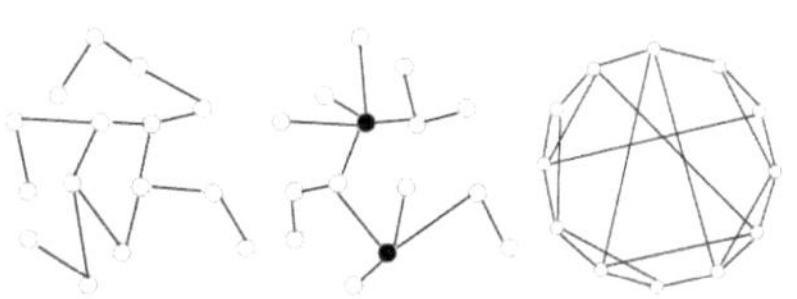

Fig. 4. Synthetic topologies

Figure 4 illustrates the characteristics of synthetic topologies. (1) The "random/balanced" topology links routers in an Erdös-Rényi random graph [10], each router being linked to two other routers drawn at random. This topology has a low clustering, low diameter and a balanced distribution of in-degrees. (2) The "scale-free" topology is representative of networks where central elements are acting as *hubs* in the network, e.g., the main routers in each linked institution on a campus. It uses a *preferential attachment* incremental construction (Albert & Barabási [5]): each link constructed from a router r has a probability to target a router r_d that is proportional to r_d's current in-degree. This topology presents a high clustering and a low diameter, and a sparse distribution of in-degrees. (3) The "small-world" topology is built according to the shuffling model of Watts & Strogatz [27]: starting with a ring composed of all routers (each router being linked to its two neighbors in the ring), randomly chosen links are shuffled and directed to random routers, creating shortcuts. This topology presents a high clustering, low diameter and balanced in-degrees. (4) The "random/sparse" topology is similar to the random/balanced one, but links are assigned highly varying delays: 50 ms -75%/+150%. As can be observed in Figure 3, this topology presents a high dispersion of delays for a given route length. The random/balanced and random/sparse topologies can be considered as the two extreme cases for this study. In the former, using delays as a metric for deciding on low-length routes is likely to succeed most often, while for the latter

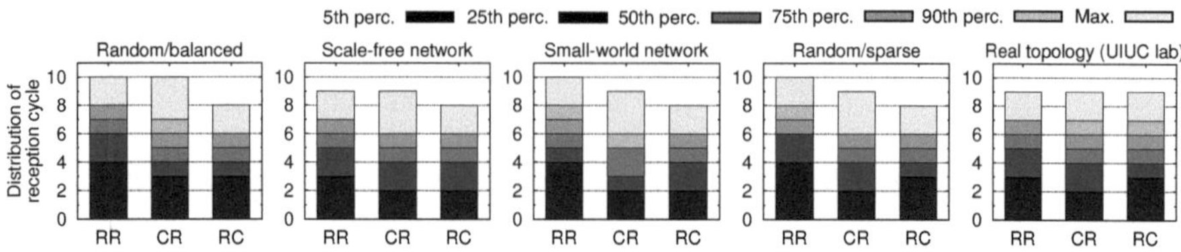

Fig. 5. Distribution of the number of cycles required for receiving the *first* message

it is not. (5) Finally, our last topology, "UIUC laboratory", is part of a set of real Internet topologies [2] that were produced by collecting BGP routing maps and benchmarking inter-router delays. This topology corresponds to a large local area network on a university campus, composed of 448 pure routers, 203 routers and attachment points, connected by 8,486 links.

Experimental setup. Each experiment involves 10,000 nodes randomly distributed over routers. We measure the time used for propagation in *cycles*, that is, the cycle period of all gossip-based protocols. As we assume that Vivaldi coordinates are bootstrapped (e.g., provided by an external service), we let the system run for 200 cycles to let them stabilize using a set of 20 landmarks nodes, before the actual gossip-based dissemination (push and pull) takes place. 500 messages from random initial peers are then published, each of size 10kB, and the simulation stops when all peers have received all messages. We monitor the loads on routers only during the dissemination phase. The parameters for the push dissemination are $f_{push} = 3$ (fanout) and $htl = 6$, which seeds 10% of the nodes. The dissemination is done synchronously with the cycles (a node that receives a message m forwards it to f_{push} other random peers during the next cycle, when it also sends 1 pull request).

Time efficiency of the dissemination. We first evaluate the impact of network-friendly gossiping strategies on the actual performance of the dissemination, i.e., if the number of cycles required to notify a given percentage of the network varies. Figure 5 shows the distribution of the number of cycles required, by the means of percentiles. The 50th percentiles (mid-shaded grey) is the median value. The dissemination takes up to 9 or 10 cycles, and half of the nodes receive the message within 4 or 5 cycles. We observe that using network-friendly gossiping has a small positive impact on the dissemination delays, which is slightly more important when using RC. This conveys the fact that our protocols can reduce the load without affecting dissemination efficiency.

Impact on the load at each router. We evaluate the impact of our strategies on the load imposed on each router in the network, both in terms of number of messages and bandwidth. The first criterion is important as a longer path stresses more routers for every connection established and message sent along that path, while the second criterion represents the actual routing load at each router and is a fundamental concern to ensure true network friendliness.

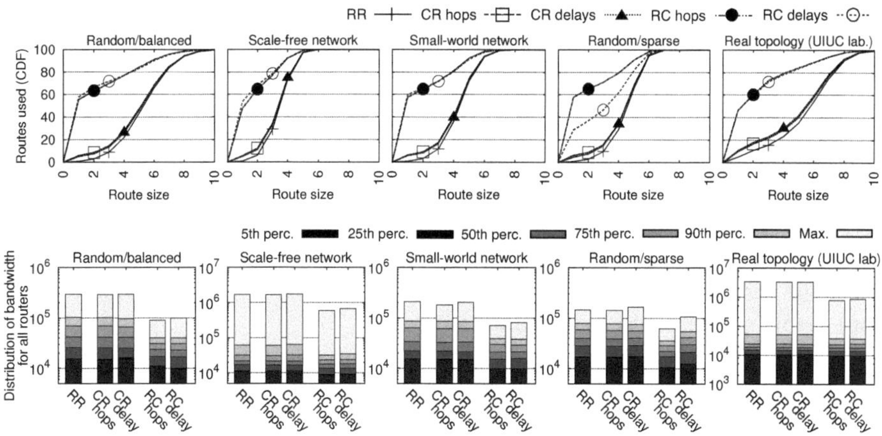

Fig. 6. Distribution of load on all routers: (a) route lengths and (b) bandwidth

Figure 6(a) presents the distribution of the route lengths, for all routes used during one simulation, regardless of the size of the message. We observe that, as expected, the CR strategy produces nearly as much load as RR in terms of number of messages on the routers, as the pull requests largely dominate. Using the number of hops as a metric instead of the delays yields better results in all cases, but this is more noticeable in the random/sparse scenario due to the mismatch between both metrics.

Figure 6(b) presents the distribution of bandwidth on all routers, for all messages sent during one simulation. 500 messages of size 10kB are sent, with pull requests and empty replies of 50 bytes. Note the logarithmic scale for the ordinates. We observe on all topologies that the RC strategy greatly reduces the amount of data imposed on each router. Moreover, it appears clearly that the CR strategy is not very efficient with respect to bandwidth because messages are much bigger than pull requests. We also observe that RC is able to reduce not only the load on all routers, but also the difference between the median and the maximal load in all cases. Finally, in the random/sparse topology with the RC strategy, the load is much lower when using the number of hops as a metric rather than the delay, highlighting the benefits of the former metric for infrastructures where there is no clear matching between path lengths and delays. Note that this matching can be tested online by the protocol itself, by comparing measures of path lengths and delays between random pairs of nodes, and switching to actual route length measurements when necessary.

Experimental results summary. The experiments conducted and presented in this section bring three main observations. First, using infrastructure-awareness for gossip-based dissemination protocols does not impact the performance (delays and coverage) of the diffusion, and that regardless of the metric used for implementing the network awareness. Second, the best policy for ensuring the completion of the dissemination in a short time with no or very few duplicates reception and an overall short dissemination delay, is Random/Close (RC). The principle of RC is to seed the network by an initial set of random limited push operations, followed by pull operations that use *close* links for the majority of the exchanges. Finally, the best results achieved for reducing the load on the infrastructure are obtained with the same RC policy. Noteworthy, the load reduction that can be achieved by using application-level delays/RTT as a metric for constructing infrastructure-aware links is limited, and is depending on the correlation between path lengths and delays. This correlation is not necessarily present in real networks or common synthetic network topologies. Therefore, the use of the measured route length as a metric for constructing close-links yields more stable and effective load reduction.

6 Conclusion

We presented network-friendly algorithms for disseminating messages by gossip on multi-hops networks such as the Internet. By clustering peers that are at short distances, an important part of the burden usually imposed on the infrastructure can be avoided, and the remaining load is better balanced amongst routers. It also appears that using application-level delays as a primary metric for choosing good (network-friendly) neighbors does not work well on all types of topologies. Route lengths, which can be determined by a lightweight probing method, can provide a better metric. As for the gossiping strategies, the best results are achieved by combining a limited push-based *seeding* of the network using random links, followed by periodic pull-based dissemination using short routes. Network friendliness has no impact on the efficiency of the gossip dissemination itself, which makes our solution particularly appropriate for real networks.

References

1. `http://www.planet-lab.org/`
2. `http://www.crhc.uiuc.edu/~jasonliu/projects/topo/`
3. Aggarwal, V., Akonjang, O., Feldmann, A.: Improving user and ISP experience through ISP-aided P2P locality. In: Global Internet Symp. (2008)
4. Ball, N., Pietzuch, P.: Distributed content delivery using load-aware network coordinates. In: ROADS 2008 (2008)
5. Barabasi, A.-L., Albert, R.: Emergence of scaling in random networks. Science 286 (1999)
6. Birman, K.P., Hayden, M., Ozkasap, O., Xiao, Z., Budiu, M., Minsky, Y.: Bimodal multicast. TOCS 17(2), 41–88 (1999)
7. Braden, R.: Requirements for internet hosts: Communication layers. Internet Engineering Task Force RFC 1122 (October 1989)
8. Dabek, F., Cox, R., Kaashoek, F., Morris, R.: Vivaldi: a decentralized network coordinate system. In: SIGCOMM 2004 (2004)
9. Demers, A., Greene, D., Hauser, C., Irish, W., Larson, J., Shenker, S., Sturgis, H., Swinehart, D., Terry, D.: Epidemic algorithms for replicated database maintenance. In: PODC 1987 (1987)

10. Erdös, P., Rényi, A.: On the evolution of random graphs. Publications of the Mathematical Institute of the Hungarian Academy of Sciences 5, 17–61 (1960)
11. Eugster, P.T., Guerraoui, R., Handurukande, S.B., Kermarrec, A.-M., Kouznetsov, P.: Lightweight probabilistic broadcast. TOCS 21(4) (2003)
12. Hu, N., Li, L.E., Mao, Z.M., Steenkiste, P., Wang, J.: Locating internet bottlenecks: algorithms, measurements, and implications. In: SIGCOMM 2004: Proceedings of the 2004 conference on Applications, technologies, architectures, and protocols for computer communications, pp. 41–54. ACM, New York (2004)
13. Jelasity, M., Babaoglu, O.: T-man: Gossip-based overlay topology management. In: Brueckner, S.A., Di Marzo Serugendo, G., Hales, D., Zambonelli, F. (eds.) ESOA 2005. LNCS (LNAI), vol. 3910, pp. 1–15. Springer, Heidelberg (2006)
14. Jelasity, M., Kermarrec, A.-M.: Ordered slicing of very large-scale overlay networks. In: P2P 2006 (2006)
15. Jelasity, M., Voulgaris, S., Guerraoui, R., Kermarrec, A.-M., van Steen, M.: Gossip-based peer sampling. TOCS 25(3), 8 (2007)
16. Karp, R.M., Schindelhauer, C., Shenker, S., Vocking, B.: Randomized rumor spreading. In: IEEE Symposium on Foundations of Computer Science (2000)
17. Kashyap, S., Deb, S., Naidu, K.V.M., Rastogi, R., Srinivasan, A.: Efficient gossip-based aggregate computation. In: PODS 2006 (2006)
18. Kermarrec, A.-M., van Steen, M. (eds.): ACM SIGOPS OSR, s.i. on Gossip-based computer networking, vol. 41(5). ACM, New York (2007)
19. Kostoulas, D., Psaltoulis, D., Gupta, I., Birman, K.P., Demers, A.J.: Active and passive techniques for group size estimation in large-scale and dynamic distributed systems. Journal of Systems and Software 80(10), 1639–1658 (2007)
20. Montresor, A., Jelasity, M., Babaoglu, O.: Chord on demand. In: P2P 2005 (2005)
21. Mosk-Aoyama, D., Shah, D.: Computing separable functions via gossip. In: PODC 2006 (2006)
22. Rowstron, A., Druschel, P.: Pastry: scalable, decentralized object location and routing for large-scale peer-to-peer systems. In: Guerraoui, R. (ed.) Middleware 2001. LNCS, vol. 2218, p. 329. Springer, Heidelberg (2001)
23. Hilt, V., Hofmann, M., Seetharaman, S., Ammar, M.: Preemptive strategies to improve routing performance of native and overlay layers. In: INFOCOM 2007 (2007)
24. van Renesse, R., Minsky, Y., Hayden, M.: A gossip-style failure detection service. Technical Report TR98-1687. Cornell university (1998)
25. Voulgaris, S., Gavidia, D., van Steen, M.: Cyclon: Inexpensive membership management for unstructured P2P overlays. Journal of Network and Systems Management 13(2), 197–217 (2005)
26. Voulgaris, S., van Steen, M.: Epidemic-style management of semantic overlays for content-based searching. In: Cunha, J.C., Medeiros, P.D. (eds.) Euro-Par 2005. LNCS, vol. 3648, pp. 1143–1152. Springer, Heidelberg (2005)
27. Watts, D.J., Strogatz, S.H.: Collective dynamics of 'small-world' networks. Nature 393(6684), 440–442 (1998)

Black Hole Search with Tokens in Interconnected Networks

Wei Shi

University of Ontario Institute of Technology, Canada
wei.shi@uoit.ca

Abstract. We study the Black Hole search problem using mobile agents in three interconnected network topologies: hypercube, torus and complete network. We do so without relying on local storage. Instead we use a less-demanding and less-expensive *token* mechanism. We demonstrate that the Black Hole can be located with a minimum of two (2) *co-located* agents performing $\Theta(n)$ moves with $O(1)$ tokens, in each of these three topologies. Then we study the Black Hole search problem with *scattered* agents. We show that the optimal number of moves can be achieved with the optimal number of mobile agents using $O(1)$ tokens.

Keywords: Black Hole, Mobile Agent, Token, Ring, Scattered, Un-oriented.

1 Introduction

Computational and algorithmic research has just recently started to consider security issues, mainly in regards to the presence of a *harmful host* (i.e., a network node damaging incoming agents) or of a *harmful agent* (e.g., a mobile virus infecting the network nodes), see [1,2]. With respect to the computational issues related to the presence of a harmful host, the focus has been on a *black hole* (*BH*), a node that disposes of any incoming agent without leaving any observable trace of this destruction [3,4,5,6,7,8]. In this paper, we continue the investigation of the *black hole search* (*Bhs*) problem. Our research concern is to determine under what conditions and at what cost, within finite time, at least one of a team of mobile agents can survive and know all the links leading to a *BH*.

Most of the existing investigations on *Bhs* have assumed the presence of a powerful inter-agent communication mechanism, *whiteboards*, at all nodes. In the *whiteboard model*, each node has a local storage area where information can be written and read by the agents (e.g. see [9]). In this research, we investigate the *Bhs* in a *token model*. Communication between mobile agents is considerably more restricted (and complex) in a *token model* than in a *whiteboard* one: information-rich messages written to and read from a whiteboard must instead be represented using a limited number of tokens. The question then is whether this additional constraint complicates significantly token-based solutions to the *Bhs*. In this paper, we show that is not the case for the following three interconnection networks: hypercube, torus and complete network. We also answer the following

R. Guerraoui and F. Petit (Eds.): SSS 2009, LNCS 5873, pp. 670–682, 2009.

question: under what conditions and at what cost is the *Bhs* problem solvable. Notice that the use of tokens introduces another complexity measure: the number of tokens. Indeed, if the number of tokens is unlimited, each information-rich message of a whiteboard environment can be mapped to a specific configuration of tokens and thus it is possible to simulate a whiteboard environment. The question then is how few agents are truly required by a solution to *Bhs*.

The problem of locating the *BH* using tokens has been examined in the ring topology in both cases of *co-located* agents (i.e., all the agents start from the same node in the network) [4, 10] and of *scattered* agents (i.e., the agents start from different unknown nodes in the network) [7, 8]. In [4] it is demonstrated that in order to locate the *BH* without *whiteboards*, $O(\Delta^2 M^2 n^7)$ moves suffice with $\Delta+1$ mobile agents and one token per agent.[1] Also, a recent solution proposed in [11] solves the *Bhs* problem in an arbitrary network with a team of two asynchronous agents with a map, using $\Theta(n \log n)$ moves, where n is the number of nodes. All existing solutions except for [7, 8], solve the *Bhs* problem using *co-located* agents. Here we propose to solve the *Bhs* problem for some specific network topologies, hoping to achieve better complexity than for the *Bhs* problem on an arbitrary network. We first consider the *Bhs* problem in hypercube, torus and complete network using *co-located* agents. We then study the *Bhs* problem in torus and complete network with a group of *scattered* agents. The *scattered* initial locations of the team of agents significantly complicate the solution of the problem. Yet, we show that for *Bhs* in these network topologies, the *token model* is computationally and complexity-wise as powerful as the whiteboard model, regardless of the initial position of the agents and of the orientation of the topology. Also, with specific knowledge of the network, the number of moves executed by a team of two asynchronous agents can be reduced to $\Theta(n)$. The results hold even without using a map for a team of two agents in a complete network. In the *scattered* agents case, we show that the *Bhs* problem can be solved in a complete network with $O(n^2)$ moves, where n is both the number of *scattered* agents and the number of nodes in the network. We then show that, with 3 *scattered* agents and 7 tokens per agent, a black hole can be located with $\Theta(n)$ moves in a torus. We also observe that, when the number of *scattered* agents in a torus increases, the problem becomes significantly more complicated. A simple algorithm we develop solves *Bhs* with k ($k > 3$) *scattered* agents, with $O(k^2 n^2)$ moves using only 1 token per agent.

2 Model, Assumptions and Terminology

Let $\mathcal{G} = (V, E)$ denote a simple connected undirected graph, where V is the set of vertices or nodes and E is the set of edges or links in $\mathcal{G}$. At each node $x \in V$, the incident edges are labeled by an injective mapping λ_x. Hence, each edge (x, y) has two labels, $\lambda_x(x, y)$ at x, and $\lambda_y(x, y)$ at y. $\lambda_x(x, y)$ and $\lambda_y(x, y)$ will be called the port numbers. We say a graph is *oriented*, if there is a globally

[1] Here, M is the number of edges in the graph, n is the number of nodes in the graph, and Δ is the maximum degree of the graph.

consistency of such labeling (or sense of direction) of all the edges (links), *unoriented* otherwise [7,8].

Operating on $\mathcal{G}$ is a set of k agents $a_1, a_2, ..., a_k$. The agents have limited computing capabilities and bounded storage. They all obey an identical set of behavioral rules (referred to as the "protocol"), and can move from node to neighboring node. We make no assumptions on the amount of time required by an agent's actions (e.g., computation, movement, etc.) except that it is finite. Thus, the agents are *asynchronous* [5]. Also, these agents are *anonymous* (i.e., do not have distinct identifiers) and *autonomous* (i.e., each has its own computing and bounded memory capabilities). If *co-located*, agents start at the same node, called *homebase* ($\mathcal{H}$ for brevity). *Scattered* agents start at different $\mathcal{H}$s.

We postulate that, while executing a *Bhs*, the agents can interact with their environment and with each other only through the means of *tokens*. A token is an atomic object that the agents can see, carry, place in the middle or on a port of a node, or remove. Several tokens can be placed at the same location. The agents can detect such multiplicity, but the tokens themselves are undistinguishable from each other. Initially, there are no tokens in the network, and each agent starts with $O(1)$ number of tokens.

The basic computational behavior of an agent (executed either when an agent arrives at a node, or upon wake-up) consists of three actions called *steps*. First an agent need to *examine* its current node and evaluate (as a non-negative integer) the multiplicity of tokens at the middle of the node and/or on its ports. (An agent therefore may have to evaluate several multiplicities for its current node.) Second, an agent may *modify* tokens (by placing/removing some of the tokens at the current node). Third, an agent may either become *Passive*(i.e., temporarily stop participating to the *Bhs*) or *leave* the node through a port. Finally, an agent may become *DONE*, namely terminate the whole algorithm. A step is performed as a single atomic (i.e., none interruptable) operation. We assume that there is a fair scheduling of the steps of the operation at the nodes, so that, at any node at any time, at most one computational step will take place, and every intended step is performed within finite time. This computation is *asynchronous* in the sense that the time an agent sleeps or travels is finite but unpredictable. It is known that in an *asynchronous* system, it is *undecidable* to determine if there is a *BH* or not [6]. The consequences of this fact are numerous and render the asynchronous case considerably difficult. Hence, in this research, we assume that there is one and exactly one *BH* in the network. All the agents are aware of the presence of the *BH*, but, at the beginning of the search, the location of the *BH* is unknown. The goal of this search is to identify all the links leading to the *BH*. At the end of the search, there must be at least one agent that has survived (i.e., not entered the *BH*) and knows the location of the *BH*.

We will consider three complexity measures for the *Bhs* problem. The first one is *size*: the number of agents needed to locate the *BH*. The other two complexity measures of interest are the *token size* (i.e., the number of tokens each agent needs to start with) and the *cost* (i.e., the total number of moves executed by the agents in the worst case over all possible timings). We study the following three topologies in such model and under such assumptions: hypercube, torus and complete network.

3 Basic Tool and Technique

3.1 *CWWT*

Cautious Walk with Token (henceforth *CWWT* for brevity) is an adaptation of the *cautious walk* technique used in systems with whiteboards [5]. It is a basic step in all our algorithms and is explained below.

At any time during the execution of this algorithm, a port will be classified either as *With Tokens* (i.e., one or more tokens have been placed on this port) or *Without Tokens* (i.e., no tokens on this port). The details of how to establish that a port is with or without tokens will differ across the algorithms that we introduce throughout this paper. During a *CWWT*, having a certain number of tokens on a port indicates that the link of this port is currently being *explored* by an agent. The exact number and location of tokens required to determine that a port is being explored may vary between the algorithms that use *CWWT*. Clearly, a port under exploration may be *dangerous* (i.e., possibly leading to the *BH*). To prevent unnecessary loss of agents, we require that no two agents enter the *BH* through the same link. In order to achieve this, we establish two basic rules for the agents that use *CWWT*. The first rule is:

When an agent a arrives at a node u with a port p under exploration, that agent is not allowed to move through port p. In fact, agent a can only leave through port p once p becomes *safe*.

In order to explain how a port becomes *safe*, consider an agent a that leaves token(s) on a port p of node u in order to explore the node v through the link of p. Our second rule captures how p becomes *safe*:

Upon reaching node v through port q, if v is not a *BH*, then a immediately returns to u and removes tokens on p. Thus, p necessarily becomes *Without-Tokens* and both its link and itself are thereafter considered *safe*. Port q is also considered *safe* once visited by a.

3.2 *Bypass* Technique

The *Bypass* technique is used in the algorithms to solve *Bhs* in both hypercube and torus with *co-located* agents. For those topologies, in contrast to a ring, each node has more than two links and ports adjacent to it. This significantly complicates the communication between agents using tokens, but also offers multiple paths between any of the two nodes in the graph. In fact, we get the following observation:

Observation 1. *Both hypercube and torus topologies contain one or more ring subgraphs, as shown in Figure 1.*

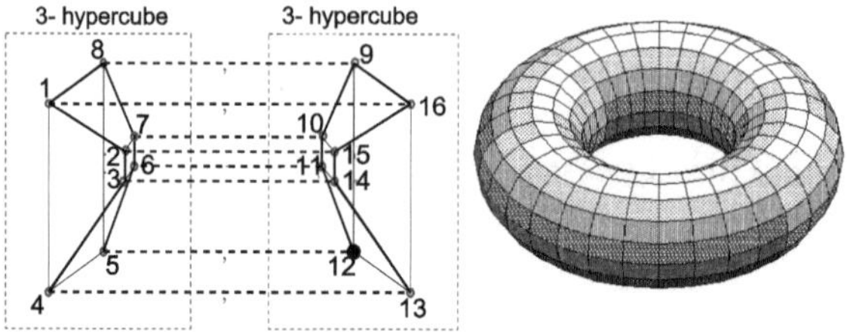

Fig. 1. Hypercube and Torus

According to our assumption that "there is one and only one *BH* in the network", we remark:

Observation 2. *It is impossible that the* BH *is in both* ring *a and* ring *b*.

We then call the ring without the *BH* a *safe ring*; a *dangerous ring* otherwise.

The basic idea of the *Bypass* technique is to use the links and nodes on a *safe ring* to create a bridge over an unknown node (possibly *BH*) on the *dangerous ring* that is under exploration by an agent. This bridge will allow a second agent to continue exploring the rest of the *dangerous ring*. This technique ensures a) that two agents do not explore the same node at the same time; and b) that all the nodes in the network get traversed using a linear number of moves, so that the total number of moves for locating the *BH* stays linear. Details follow:

Once in the "*Bypass*" procedure, an agent acts differently whether advancing in a *safe ring* or in a *dangerous ring*. Let A_d denote the agent that is exploring a node I in the *dangerous ring*, and A_s denote the agent that is going to *bypass* node I through path J, K, L, M, N (see Figure 2). When A_s arrives at node J , it moves the token(s) from port J_d to J_s if J_s is *without token*. Otherwise, A_s picks up the token(s) from port J_d, then A_s walks through J_s to node K. A_s then walks to node M through node L. If port M_s is *with token*, then A_s moves the tokens from port M_{s1} to port M_{s2}, then walks to the next node on the *safe*

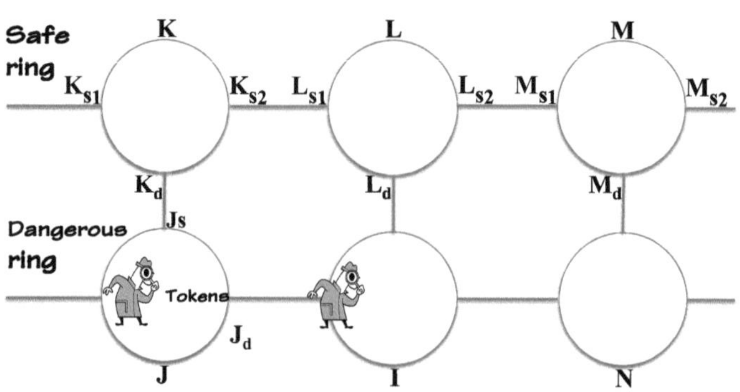

Fig. 2. Two agents executing "*Bypass* on a *dangerous ring and a* safe ring

ring. Otherwise, A_s leaves a token at port M_d, then it becomes ready to go back to the *dangerous* ring. From this point on, A_s becomes an agent exploring the *dangerous ring* M_d' in the next stage. If the old A_d does not die in node I, then it becomes an agent trying to *bypass* node N that is under exploration by the other agent. Namely, in the new stage, agent A_d will become a new A_s'. These two agents keep changing roles to *bypass* a node in the *dangerous ring* that is under exploration, until one dies in the *BH*.

4 *Bhs* with *Co-located* Agents

4.1 *Bhs* in Hypercube — Algorithm *Two Rings*

The following well-known property of a hypercube is the key to our solution to the *Bhs* problem in this topology:

Property 1. $\mathcal{Q}_d$ consists of two $d-1$-hypercubes connected by 2^{d-1} links labeled as d.

Given this property, we find a way for two mobile agents (given 2 is the minimum team size for the *Bhs* problem) to traverse the hypercube with tokens. The basic idea can be carried out using the following three steps[2]:

- let one agent stay in the common $\mathcal{H}$, and the other agent move to the other ring through the connecting link using *CWWT*.
- have both agents explore a Hamiltonian Cycle (i.e., a ring) of each $(d-1)$-hypercube according to a specific permutation (see below) with *CWWT*. After an agent has finished exploring its ring, we call this ring a *safe* ring, and call the other ring, which has not finished being exploring, a *dangerous* ring.
- let the agent that finished exploring the *safe* ring go to the other ring through a connecting link. This agent will help the other agent exploring the *dangerous ring*. It keeps walking on the *dangerous ring* until it sees the marker of the other agent. The two agents then repeat multiple stages of the *bypass* technique until one agent dies in the *BH* and the surviving agent finishes exploring all but one nodes in the entire hypercube. The only node the surviving agent has not visited is the *BH*.

The detail we need to address is how do we make the agents only walk on an appropriate Hamiltonian cycle and 2^{d-1} links labeled as d, in a labeled $\mathcal{Q}_d$. The following technique makes it possible:

We define a permutation that can construct a unique Hamiltonian cycle when a starting node is given. Let $\mathcal{P}_d$ be a permutation of length n: $\{p_1, p_2, ..., p_{n/2}, p_1, p_2, ..., p_{n/2}\}$. The sequence is constructed as follows:

[2] Due to the page limit, most Lemmas and Theorems and their proofs are omitted. Details can be found in: http://www.scs.carleton.ca/~swei4/FinalThesis(VF2007May23).pdf

- when $d = 2$, $n = 2^2 = 4$, $\mathcal{P}_2$: $\{1, 2, 1, 2\}$;
- when $d = 3$, $n = 2^3 = 8$, $\mathcal{P}_3$: $\{1, 2, 3, 2, 1, 2, 3, 2\}$;
- when $d = 4$, $n = 2^4 = 16$, $\mathcal{P}_4$:
  $\{1, 2, 3, 2, 4, 2, 3, 2, 1, 2, 3, 2, 4, 2, 3, 2\}$;
- when $d = 5$, $n = 2^5 = 32$, $\mathcal{P}_5$:
  $\{1, 2, 3, 2, 4, 2, 3, 2, 5, 2, 3, 2, 4, 2, 3,$
  $2, 1, 2, 3, 2, 4, 2, 3, 2, 5, 2, 3, 2, 4, 2, 3, 2\}$;

  If we let $\mathcal{P}\prime_d$ denote the sequence from the second digit to the $2^{d-1}{}^{th}$ digit of $\mathcal{P}_d$, then:
- when $d = i - 1$, $n = 2^{i-1}$, $\mathcal{P}_{i-1}$: $\{1, \mathcal{P}\prime_{i-2}, i - 1, \mathcal{P}\prime_{i-2}, 1, \mathcal{P}\prime_{i-2}, i - 1, \mathcal{P}\prime_{i-2}\}$
- when $d = i$, $n = 2^i$, $\mathcal{P}_i$: $\{1, \mathcal{P}\prime_{i-1}, i, \mathcal{P}\prime_{i-1}, 1, \mathcal{P}\prime_{i-1}, i, \mathcal{P}\prime_{i-1}\}$

While d increases, each permutation $\mathcal{P}_d$ can be constructed by executing the following two steps on permutation $\mathcal{P}_{d-1}$:

a) replace the second occurrence of '1' found in the sequence by '*d*';
b) duplicate this modified sequence and append it to its own end (effectively creating a sequence that consists of the modified sequence followed by itself).

Given all the agents know the size of the hypercube $n = 2^d$, they can all come up with such a permutation individually. All their permutations will be the same, because they construct it according the same rules. Each element in the permutation represents a label of a link. Every such number indicates which link an agent is going to explore next.

Theorem 1. *Permutation $\mathcal{P}_d$ computed by an agent constructs a Hamiltonian cycle of $\mathcal{Q}_d$.*

4.2 *Bhs* in Torus — Algorithm *Cross Rings*

Informally, a torus is a mesh with "wrap-around" links that transform it into a *regular* graph: every node has exactly four neighbors. We develop an algorithm *Cross Rings*, to locate the *BH* in a torus with *co-located* agents when the torus is *oriented*, that is, when the ports of each node in the torus are consistently labeled as: *East*, *West*, *North*, and *South*.

Let $\mathcal{R}-NS$ denote a ring with only links labeled *South* and *North* in a labeled torus and, let $\mathcal{R} - EW$ denote a ring with only links labeled *East* and *West* in a labeled torus. Starting from a node, there are two obvious paths that allow an agent to traverse the torus and go back to the starting node. See Figure 3:

It is clear that a *north-south* ring $\mathcal{A}$ and an *east-west* ring $\mathcal{B}$ share exactly one node, say v. If node v is not the *BH*, we know the *BH* cannot be on both $\mathcal{A}$ and $\mathcal{B}$. We then get the following observation:

Observation 3. *Let* 2 *agents start from v. If we let one agent traverse the* north-south *ring $\mathcal{A}$, and another agent traverse the* east-west *ring $\mathcal{B}$, then there is at least one agent that survives its traversal.*

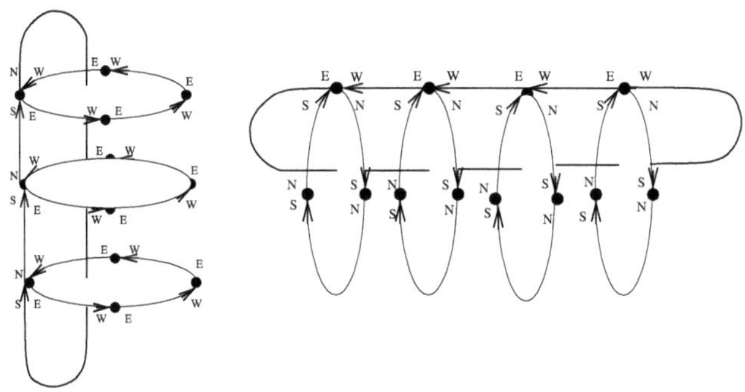

Fig. 3. Two paths that allow an agent to traverse all the nodes in a labeled $3*4$ torus: 1. an *east-west* ring, plus every *north-south* ring that starts with a node in this *east-west* ring, and 2. a *north-south* ring, plus every *east-west* ring that starts with a node in this *north-south* ring

If only one agent finishes traversing a ring (i.e., the other agent died in the *BH*), then we call this ring a *Base* ring. If both agents finish traversing their rings, then we call the ring that is traversed the earliest, a *Base* ring, which is also a *safe* ring. Hereafter, we assume that the *Base* ring is a *north-south* ring. (The algorithm would be essentially the same if the *Base* ring were an *east-west* ring). Now, we let the surviving agent(s) (either one or two) explore all the *east-west* rings, each of which starts from a node on the *Base* ring. In order to prevent the two agents from both dying in the *BH*, we let both agents explore a *dangerous* node using *CWWT* with 1 token on a port.

Before one agent starts exploring an *east-west* ring, it puts 1 token in the middle of the *homebase* u. This agent then explores the first *east-west* ring. When this agent finishes exploring an *east-west* ring, it will move the single token it left in u to the next node to the North of u on the *Base* ring. We call the *east-west* ring marked by this token, a *RUE* (*R*ing *U*nder *E*xploration). An agent continues exploring *east-west* rings one by one, until it sees a token in the next node. It then puts a second token in the next node to the *north*, comes back to pick up the token it left in the previous node, goes to the next node to the *north* again and starts exploring a new *east-west* ring. Given there is only one *BH*, and there is no common node(s) shared by any two *east-west* rings, we obtain Lemma 1. Given one agent a_1 will finish exploring all but one *east-west* ring. The other agent a_2 is either exploring the *RUE* or died in the *BH* in the last *RUE*. Then a_1 will go and help a_2 to explore the last *east-west* ring. Because we assumed that one of the *north-south* rings is the *Base* ring, we say that an agent finishes a *stage* as soon as it finishes exploring an *east-west* ring. An agent a_1 will not visit a *RUE* (by a_2) until this is the only *east-west* ring left. Also, a_1 follows the path that a_2 took on this last *east-west* ring, until it sees the *CWWT* token of a_2. Now a_1 and a_2 will execute the procedure "*Bypass* on Torus", sketched out earlier. Eventually the algorithm terminates when there is only one node that is not explored in the last *RUE*. The only node left unexplored is the *BH*.

Lemma 1. *Eventually all but one* east-west *rings are explored.*

4.3 *Bhs* in a Complete Network — Algorithm *Take Turn*

In this subsection, we present the solution to the *Bhs* problem in a complete network without using *sense of direction*, that is, no ports of any node is labeled. However, it is important to note that, even without a common labeling, the *co-located* agents share a common reference (e.g., indexing) mechanism for the $n-1$ links of their $\mathcal{H}$ and thus can share a common order of traversal of these links.

For simplicity, we will say that the links are traversed 'clockwise' when going from the lowest to the highest index, 'counterclockwise' otherwise (This is merely a convention and the actual order of traversal could be defined differently, as long as it is shared by the *co-located* agents.). A team of two *co-located* agents is used to solve the problem. We can imagine the complete network as a star-shape network with a node (which we will take to be the $\mathcal{H}$ of this pair of *co-located* agents) in the middle.

The idea is very simple: once an agent a_1 wakes up, it puts one token on a port of its node, which it views as its $\mathcal{H}$. a_1 then explores the node reachable from this port. When a_1 comes back to its $\mathcal{H}$ after exploring a node, if the token of a_1 is still at the port where it was left, then a_1 will move this token to the next port clockwise, and repeat this exploration step. Once the second agent a_2 wakes up, it moves the token of a_1 to the next clockwise, and explores the node accessible through this port. When an agent comes back from the exploration of a node, if it sees the token it left is missing, then this agent continues clockwise until it finds the port with one token. It moves this token to the next port clockwise and starts exploring another node through this port. During this process, an agent keeps counting the number of ports it visited (i.e., ports it used to access nodes to explore) or passed (i.e., ports that are between the port this agent just visited and the port that currently has a token). As soon as one agent notices that this total (of ports being counted) reaches $n-1$, it terminates the algorithm immediately. It is important to know that we use a variable *bhlocation* to record the location of the *BH*. Each time an agent a_i moves the token used by partner a_j to the next port, a_i resets the variable *bhlocation* to 0, then keeps increasing it by one each time it explores a new node. Also, variable *nCount* is incremented as ports are used. a_i terminates the algorithm as soon as it realizes *nCount* reaches $n-1$, at which point *bhlocation* indicates the location of the *BH*: the $bhlocation^{th}$ port counter clockwise leads to the *BH*.

Theorem 2. *Using two (2)* co-located *agents and one (1) token in total, the* BH *can be successfully located in a complete network of n nodes, with* $\Theta(n)$ *moves in total.*

5 *Bhs* with *Scattered* Agents

5.1 In a Complete Network

The algorithm for locating the *BH* with *scattered* agents follows: upon one agent waking up, it leaves a token in the middle of its $\mathcal{H}$ and waits. This agent starts executing algorithm *Take Turn* as soon as its token is moved to a port of its $\mathcal{H}$. If an agent wakes up in a node that has a token in the middle, then this agent starts executing algorithm *Take Turn* immediately. Once an agent wakes up in a node that has a token on a port of its $\mathcal{H}$, it becomes *Passive* immediately. Eventually, a maximum of $n/2$ pairs of agents will execute algorithm *Take Turn* and finally locate the *BH*. Given algorithm *Take Turn* requires n moves, $n/2 * n = n^2$ moves in total suffice with n *scattered* agents. 1 token per agent for n agents suffice to correctly locate the *BH*. Hence we get the following theorem:

Theorem 3. *Using* n scattered *agents, one (1) token per agent and* $O(n^2)$ *moves, the* BH *can be successfully located in an un-oriented complete network* $\mathcal{K}_n$.

5.2 In a Torus with Minimum Number of Agents

Again in this section, we assume the torus under investigation is *oriented*. We also assume no agent wakes up in the *BH*. It is possible that 4 agents could die immediately after the first move: one enters the *BH* through the *North* port, one through the *South* port, one through the *East* port, and one through the *West* port. In order to minimize team size, we program each mobile agent to enter each node through only the *South* or *West* ports[3], and thus a maximum of two agents die after the first move. Hence, we conclude:

Lemma 2. *At least* 3 *scattered agents are needed to locate the* BH *in an* oriented *torus* .

The basic idea for solving the *BH*s problem with *scattered* agents is to let two of the three agents form a pair that execute algorithm *Cross Rings* starting from the node (their $\mathcal{H}$) where they formed this pair. In the following paragraphs we will explain how the agents form a pair and how a pair of agents finds a *Base* ring. Then, the rest of the algorithm is almost the same as algorithm *Cross Rings*. In algorithm *Cross Rings*, there are only two agents working on the *Bhs*. But in the *scattered* agents case, we need to find out a way to eliminate the third *scattered* agents. Consequently, we work out a way for the third agent to become *DONE*, in order to simplify the communication between the working pair: as soon as an agent goes into a node with 2 tokens on any of a port (the indication of a single agent), it will pick up all the tokens and then continue.

[3] In order for an agent to traverse an oriented torus, each agent must visit at least two ports of each node.

Procedure "Initialization" and "Single Agent Explores a *north-south* Ring: upon waking up, an agent becomes a single agent and it immediately executes procedure "Single Agent Explores a *north-south* Ring" to the *north*. In procedure "Single Agent Explores a *north-south* Ring", an agent a_1 explores the *north-south* ring starting from node u ($\mathcal{H}$), with $CWWT$ (two tokens on the port). a_1 keeps counting the number of nodes in this *north-south* ring.

Case 1: When a_1 goes into a node with one token in the middle of a node, a_1 becomes $DONE$ immediately.
Case 2: When a_1 goes into a node with two tokens on the *east* port, it executes "Paired agent finds a *Base* ring" to the *north*.
Case 3: a_1 goes into a node with two tokens on the *north* port, it leaves one extra token in the middle of the node. It then executes "Paired agent finds a *Base* ring" to the *east*.
Case 4: When a_1 comes back to the node where it left its $CWWT$ tokens, if two tokens are in the middle and at least one token on the *east* port of the node, it then executes "Paired agent finds a *Base* ring" to the *north*.
Case 5: When a_1 goes into a node, if any of the following three situations happens, a_1 will become *Passive* immediately. All three situations indicate that a pair was formed. The situations are: either there is at least one token in the middle of the node (there may be also token(s) on a port of that node), or there is a token on the *north* port, or there is a token on the *east* port.
Case 6: When a_1 finished exploring the *north-south* ring, it then executes procedure "Single Agent Explores an *east-west* Ring".
Case 7: When a_1 comes back to the node where it left its $CWWT$ tokens, if all the $CWWT$ tokens are no longer there, it becomes $DONE$.
Case 8: When a_1 finishes exploring one *east-west* ring, it immediately explores the next *east-west* ring that starts from the next node to the *north* on the *north-south* ring. a_1 then executes procedure "Single Agent Explores an *east-west* Ring" again.

Procedure "Paired Agent Finds a *Base* Ring": As a single agent, as soon as a_1 sees two tokens on a port of a node (the $CWWT$) *of another single agent* a_2, it modifies the token configuration in this node and becomes a paired agent immediately. After a_1 becomes a paired agent, it executes procedure "Paired Agent Finds a *Base* Ring". Once an agent a_2 becomes a paired agent (after seeing the modified token configuration a_1 left to it) it also executes procedure "Paired Agent Finds a *Base* Ring". We call this node with the modified token configuration the *homebase* ($\mathcal{H}$ for brevity as used earlier) of these two paired agents. It is worth repeating that if a_1 executes "Paired Agent Finds a *Base* Ring" to the *north*, then a_2 will execute "Paired Agent Finds a *Base* Ring" to the *east*, or vice versa.

Upon starting "Paired Agent Finds a *Base* Ring" to the *north*. A paired agent a_1 keeps walking to the *north* with $CWWT$, until it goes back to the $\mathcal{H}$ of this pair. It is possible to have the following token configurations in this node:

1. there is 1 token on the *north* port and two tokens in the middle of their $\mathcal{H}$ (and maybe another token on the *east* port if the other paired agent a_2 is exploring the node to the *east* after being a paired agent). In this case, the *north-south* ring becomes the *Base* ring. a_1 informs a_2 of this result by picking up the token on the *north* port.

2. there are 2 or 3 tokens in the middle of the node. In this case, 2 tokens in the middle of the $\mathcal{H}$ shows that the second agent a_2 finished exploring the *east-west* ring before a_1 finished exploring the *north-south* ring. So, the *east-west* ring becomes the *Base* ring.

In either case, a_1 then keeps walking to the *east* until it sees 1 token in the middle of a node. It then executes algorithm *Cross Rings* to the *east* port. If there are 3 tokens in the middle (a_2 is exploring the first *east-west* ring as a paired agent), a_1 executes algorithm *Cross Rings* to the *east* port immediately. When agent a_2 walks back to the $\mathcal{H}$ of this paired agent after exploring an *east-west* ring, there are either

a) 2 tokens in the middle of the $\mathcal{H}$ (a_1 informed a_2 that the *north-south* ring is the *Base* ring). So a_2 keeps walking to the *north* until it arrives in the node with a token in the middle. It then executes algorithm *Cross Rings* to the *north.*

b) or 3 tokens in the middle of the $\mathcal{H}$ or 1 token on the *north* port and 2 tokens in the middle of their $\mathcal{H}$ (this means that not only a_1 informed a_2 that the *north-south* ring becomes the *Base* ring, but also that a_1 is exploring the *east-west* ring that a_2 just finished). Then a_2 will execute algorithm *Cross Rings* to the *north.*

c) or, in the third case, a_2 decides that the *east-west* ring is the *Base* ring and picks up the token on the *north* port of the pair's $\mathcal{H}$. a_2 then executes algorithm *Cross Rings* to the *east.*

During the execution of procedure "Paired Agent Finds a *Base* Ring", there are two other possible scenarios: 1) as soon as a_1 or a_2 goes into a node with 2 tokens on any of a port, it will pick up all the tokens then continue. 2) as soon as a_1 or a_2 notices its $CWWT$ token is moved, it will continue using the *Bypass* technique as a paired agent.

5.3 In a Torus with *k Scattered* Agents

We also study the *Bhs* problem in a labeled torus with k ($k > 3$) *scattered* mobile agents. Here, k is not known to any of the agents. From the result shown in Theorem 4 we conclude that: not only an increase of team size does not help to reduce the total number of moves, but also drastically complicates the communication mechanism and increases the total number of moves performed during the *Bhs.*

Theorem 4. *Using* k ($k > 3$) scattered *agents and one token per agent, the* BH *can be successfully located using* $O(k^2n^2)$ *moves in a labeled torus with* n *nodes.*

6 Conclusion

In this paper, we developed a set of token-based algorithms for locating a *BH* in three interconnected network topologies. We sketched out solutions with both *co-located* agents and *scattered* agents. This set of algorithms suggests that the token model is computationally and complexity-wise as powerful as the whiteboard model, regardless of the topology of the network, and with the knowledge of a specific network topology, the cost of *Bhs* is improved from $\Theta(n \log n)$ to $\Theta(n)$. Moreover, in section 5, we show that *Bhs* with a team of *scattered* agents is rather complex but solvable in some dense graphs. We are now exploring a solution for *Bhs* on Hypercube with optimal complexity using *scattered* agents.

References

1. Greenberg, M., Byington, J., Harper, D.G.: Mobile agents and security. IEEE Commun. Mag. 36(7), 76–85 (1998)
2. Oppliger, R.: Security issues related to mobile code and agent-based systems. Computer Communications 22(12), 1165–1170 (1999)
3. Dobrev, S., Flocchini, P., Kralovic, R., Prencipe, G., Ruzicka, P., Santoro, N.: Optimal search for a black hole in common interconnection networks. Networks 47, 61–71 (2006)
4. Dobrev, S., Flocchini, P., Prencipe, G., Santoro, N.: Exploring a dangerous unknown graph using tokens. In: Navarro, G., Bertossi, L., Kohayakwa, Y. (eds.) TCS 2006. IFIP, vol. 209, pp. 169–180. Springer, Heidelberg (2006)
5. Dobrev, S., Flocchini, P., Prencipe, G., Santoro, N.: Mobile search for a black hole in an anonymous ring. Algorithmica 48(1), 67–90 (2007)
6. Dobrev, S., Flocchini, P., Prencipe, G., Santoro, N.: Searching for a black hole in arbitrary networks: Optimal mobile agent protocols. Distributed Computing 19(1), 1–9 (2006)
7. Dobrev, S., Santoro, N., Shi, W.: Scattered Mobile Agents Searching for a Black Hole in an Unoriented Ring Using Tokens. International Journal of Foundations of Computer Science(IJFCS) 19(6), 1355–1372 (2008)
8. Dobrev, S., Santoro, N., Shi, W.: Scattered black hole search in an oriented ring using tokens. In: Proc. of 9th Workshop on Advances in Parallel and Distributed Computational Models (APDCM 2007), IEEE International, vol. (26-30), pp. 1–8 (2007)
9. Fraigniaud, P., Ilcinkas, D.: Digraph exploration with little memory. In: Diekert, V., Habib, M. (eds.) STACS 2004. LNCS, vol. 2996, pp. 246–257. Springer, Heidelberg (2004)
10. Dobrev, S., Kralovic, R., Santoro, N., Shi, W.: Black hole search in asynchronous rings using tokens. In: Calamoneri, T., Finocchi, I., Italiano, G.F. (eds.) CIAC 2006. LNCS, vol. 3998, pp. 139–150. Springer, Heidelberg (2006)
11. Flocchini, P., Ilcinkas, D., Santoro, N.: Ping Pong in Dangerous Graphs: Optimal Black Hole Search with Pure Tokens. In: Taubenfeld, G. (ed.) DISC 2008. LNCS, vol. 5218, pp. 227–241. Springer, Heidelberg (2008)

Oracle-Based Flocking of Mobile Robots in Crash-Recovery Model

Samia Souissi, Taisuke Izumi, and Koichi Wada

Graduate School of Engineering,
Nagoya Institute of Technology, Gokiso-cho,
Showa-ku, Nagoya, Aichi, 466-8555, Japan
Phone: +81-52-735-5438, Fax: +81-52-735-5408
{souissi.samia,t-izumi,wada}@nitech.ac.jp

Abstract. This paper considers a system of autonomous mobile robots that can move freely in a two-dimensional plane, and where a number of them can fail by crashing. The crash of a robot can be either permanent or temporary, that is, after its crash the robot either executes no action or it recovers from its failure. These robots repeatedly go through a succession of activation cycles during which they observe the environment, compute a destination and move. In particular, we assume weak robots, in the sense that robots cannot communicate explicitly between each other. Also, they cannot remember their past computations (i.e., oblivious). Finally, robots do not agree on a common coordinate system.

In this paper, we address a fault-tolerant flocking problem under the crash-recovery model. That is, starting from any initial configuration, a group of non-faulty robots are required to form a desired pattern, and move together while following a robot leader on a given trajectory, and keeping such a pattern in movement. Specifically, we propose a fault-tolerant flocking algorithm in the semi-synchronous model that allows correct robots to dynamically form a regular polygon in finite time, and maintain it in movement infinitely often. Our algorithm relies on the existence of two devices, namely an eventually perfect failure detector oracle to ensure failure detection, and an eventual leader oracle to handle leader election. The algorithm tolerates permanent crash failures, and also crash recovery failures of robots due to its oblivious feature. The proposed algorithm ensures the necessary restrictions on the movement of robots in order to avoid collisions between them. In addition, it is self-stabilizing.

1 Introduction

During the past decade, increasingly more research has been focussing on the coordination and self-organization of mobile robot systems involving multiple simple robots working together, rather than a single highly-complex one. This view is motivated by a variety of reasons, including reduced manufacturing costs, increased fault resilience, improved overall maneuverability, or simply better polyvalence of the system. The challenge is however to ensure enough coordination so that the multiple robots appear as a single coherent system rather

R. Guerraoui and F. Petit (Eds.): SSS 2009, LNCS 5873, pp. 683–697, 2009.

than as a set of independent entities. Consider for instance, a group of robots working together in unknown environment to carry out missions such as search and rescue, cooperative localization, or scouting. To maximize the capability of performing tasks collaboratively as a team, robots need to achieve and maintain a coherent group movement. This problem is referred as *flocking*. That is, robots need to move together while keeping some shape in movement like a flock of birds or soldiers. Flocking is not an end in itself, but rather can be used as a component of a larger multi-robot system, for instance simplifying the transport of objects by a large number of robots, or organizing the nodes of a distributed sensing system.

Model and problem. We consider a system in which the robots are represented as points moving in a plane. Each robot executes its own instance of the same algorithm which consists of repeatedly (1) observing the environment, (2) computing a destination, and (3) moving toward it. Robots are semi-synchronous in the sense that if robots are activated simultaneously, they see the same thing. Otherwise, the robots can see the environment only when the other robots has already finished their moves. In addition, we assume that robots do not share a common coordinate system, except the unit distance. Besides, they are identical (i.e., the algorithm cannot distinguish them), and they are oblivious, meaning that they do not retain any information between activations. This last assumption is useful both for memory management and because an algorithm designed for such robots is inherently self-stabilizing.[1]

In this paper, we focus on an agreement problem, called flocking in a system where robots can fail by crashing. The crash of robots can be either permanent, that is after the crash, the robot executes no action, or it can be temporary, and after which the robot recovers again from its failure. In short, the problem of fault-tolerant flocking requires that non crashed robots, located at random locations, move in such a way that they eventually form a pattern in finite number of steps, and then they keep such a pattern while moving. In the literature, the flocking problem was mainly addressed based on a leader-followers approach [1,2], where the leader is predefined or fixed, and robots followers will adjust their moves by following the movement of a robot leader.

Gervasi and Prencipe [1] have provided a flocking algorithm for asynchronous robots based on a leader-followers model, but introduce additional assumptions on the speed of the robots. In particular, they proposed a flocking algorithm for formations that are symmetric with respect to the leader's movement, without agreement on a common coordinate system (except for the unit distance). However, their algorithm requires that the leader is distinguished from the robots followers.

Canepa and Potop-Butucaru [2] build upon the work of Gervasi and Prencipe [1], and they proposed a flocking algorithm, also in an asynchronous system with oblivious robots. First, the robots elect a leader using a probabilistic algorithm. After that, the robots position themselves according to a specific formation.

[1] Self-stabilization is the property of a system which, starting in an arbitrary state, always converges toward a desired behavior [8].

Finally, the formation moves ahead. Their algorithm only lets the formation move straight forward. Although the leader is determined dynamically, once elected it can no longer change. In the absence of faulty robots, this is a reasonable limitation in their model. Note that, the above two algorithms do not work properly in the presence of failures of robots, and that their adaptation is not straightforward. The first result on fault-tolerant flocking was by Souissi et al. [3], and then the result by Yang et al. [4] follows it. In these two works, the fault-tolerant flocking problem was only studied in the permanent crash failure model. In particular, fault-tolerant flocking algorithms in both the asynchronous and semi-synchronous models were proposed when robots' activations follow a k-bounded scheduler. The algorithm developed in the asynchronous model [3] allows robots to realize the flocking by maintaining an approximation of a regular polygon while moving. However, the algorithm does not allow the rotation of the formation. In the later algorithm [4], which is developed in the semi-synchronous model, the rotation of the formation is allowed. Although, the above two works investigated the problem of flocking only in the permanent crash model, achieving the flocking was quite difficult. In fact, the authors made a lot of additional assumptions and restrictions on the movement of robots, which were mainly necessary to the detection of faulty robots, and the election of a leader of flocking. So, we can easily imagine that handling crash and recovery becomes quite complicated, and needs a large number of tedious assumptions. To avoid such a complication, we suppose the help of a failure-detection oracle, which encapsulates the necessary assumptions to identify faulty robots. In particular, our algorithm uses an eventually perfect failure detector oracle as a building block, together with an eventual leader election oracle to handle leader election. This algorithm appropriately handle the complication caused by the crash and recovery. We believe that this algorithm is a good example to show the benefit of modular based approach for mobile robot algorithms. The weak assumptions made on the capabilities of robots (such as, oblivious, no common coordinate system) made the problem of flocking difficult to solve. For instance, correct robots need to find a way to determine their targets on the formation since they do not agree on a common coordinate system. Besides, robots need to avoid collisions between each other, and with crashed robots, especially when the failure detector and leader election oracles output erroneous information on the status of robots.

Contribution. This paper proposes a fault-tolerant flocking problem rigorously where, a group of correct robots dynamically form a regular polygon in a finite number of steps, and maintain it infinitely often in movement by following the movement of a robot leader in a given trajectory. In particular, our algorithm allows correct robots to solve the flocking problem in the semi-synchronous model, by tolerating permanent and crash-finite-recovery failures of robots. Although our algorithm relies on the existence of a failure detector and a leader election oracles, we exhibit solvability of weak robots for the flocking problem. Finally, considering oblivious robots makes the proposed algorithm very robust in that it can tolerate additions, removals and relocations of any of the robots, and it is intrinsically self-stabilizing.

Structure. The remainder of this paper is structured as follows. In Section 2, we introduce the system model and the terminology used in the paper. In Section 3, we describe our flocking algorithm in the crash-recovery model, and in Section 4, we prove its correctness. Finally, in Section 4.3, we conclude the paper.

2 Preliminaries

2.1 System Model

Robot model. In this paper, we consider the system model of Suzuki and Yamashita [7], which is defined as follows. The system consists of a set of autonomous mobile robots $\mathcal{R} = \{r_1, \cdots, r_n\}$ roaming on the two-dimensional plane devoid of any landmark. Each robot is modelled and viewed as a point in the plane, and equipped with sensors to observe the positions of the other robots. In particular, each robot proceeds by repeatedly observing the environment, performing computations based on the observed positions of robots, and moving toward the computed destination. This behavior constitutes its cycle of *sensing*, *computing*, and *moving*. The sequence *look-compute-move* is called the *cycle* of a robot.

The robots are *anonymous*, in the sense that they cannot be distinguished by their appearance, and they do not have any kind of identifiers that can be used during their computation. In addition, there is no direct means of communication among them. Hence, the only way for robots to acquire information is by observing each other's positions. In this paper, we assume that the robots are *oblivious* or *memory-less*, which implies that they are unable to remember their past actions and observations, and thus, their computations cannot be based on previous observations.

In this model, time is represented as an infinite sequence of discrete time instants $t_0, t_1, t_2, \ldots$, during which each robot can be either *active* or *inactive*. When a robot becomes active, it performs a look-compute-move cycle. In particular, the robots execute their activities of observation, computation and movement instantaneously, and thus a robot observes the other robots only when a cycle begins.

The cycle of a robot is finite, and the activation of robots is determined by an activation schedule, which is unpredictable and unknown to the robots. At each time instant, a subset of the robots becomes active, with the guarantees that: (1) Every robot becomes active at infinitely-many times (fairness), (2) At least one robot is active during each time instant, and (3) The time between two consecutive activations is finite.

In this model, each robot uses its own local x-y coordinate system which includes an origin, a unit distance, and the directions of the two x and y axes, together with their orientations. However, the robots share neither knowledge of the coordinate systems of the other robots, nor of a global coordinate system, except the unit distance.

Failure model. In this paper, we address *permanent crash and crash-recovery failures* of robots. Before we define the failure model in more details, we classify robots as follows: A robot is called *stable* if eventually it becomes *up (correct)*, or eventually it becomes *down* (i.e., the robot executes no actions forever). A robot is called *unstable* if it alternates between the two states *up* and *down* infinitely often. A robot is called *good*, if it is *stable* and it is *eventually up*. On the other hand, a robot is called *bad*, if it is *stable* and *eventually down* or it is *unstable*.

In this model, we assume that robots are equipped with an eventually perfect failure detection device to ensure failure detection. Intuitively, an eventually perfect failure detector is responsible for monitoring the operational state of all robots in the system. The failure detector may make mistakes in the beginning, however, it eventually gives a correct view of the system. If robot r_i believes robot r_j to be down, we say that r_i *suspects* r_j. Otherwise, if r_i believes r_j to be up, we say that r_i *trusts* r_j. So, the output of the eventually perfect failure detector is the list of trusted robots, that is robots that are detected to be correct. An eventually perfect failure detector or $\diamondsuit P$ for the crash-recovery model as defined by [9] has the following properties:

Definition 1 (Eventual Perfect Failure Detector for crash-recovery).

- *Completeness: (1) every bad and stable robot is eventually permanently suspected by all good robots. (2) every bad and unstable robot is either eventually permanently suspected by all good robots, or suspected and trusted infinitely often by all good robots.*
- *Accuracy: every good robot is permanently trusted by all good robots.*

Note that, if there are no unstable robots in the system, then eventually all good robots agree on which robots are currently up. Since unstable robots may cause infinite number of mistakes by the eventual perfect failure detector oracle, we assume a crash-finite-recovery model, in which there exists no unstable robots, and eventually every robot stays up or down. In other words, the crash-finite-recovery model includes *permanent* and *temporary* crash failures of robots. A crash is *permanent* if the robot is stable and eventually down. However, the robot stays physically in the system, and it is seen by the other correct robots. Alternatively, a crash is *temporary* if a robot crashed, and then it recovers within reasonable amount of time, and becomes *eventually up*. The above definition of crash-finite-recovery model implies that there is a time GST_0, called Global Stabilization Time, which is unknown to robots, after which all robots detect and agree on the same set of correct robots.

2.2 Problem Definition

The problem addressed in this paper is the fault-tolerant flocking by a group of oblivious mobile robots. Before we define the problem more rigorously, we first provide the following definitions:

Definition 2 (Formation problem). *Let* $\mathcal{R} = \{r_1, ..., r_n\}$ *be a set of robots, and* $F = Formation(P_1, ..., P_n)$ *a given formation with* $n \geq 3$*, we say that robots* *in $\mathcal{R}$ solve the formation problem, if starting from any arbitrary configuration at time t_0, there exists $t \geq t_0$ such that, each robot $r_i \in \mathcal{R}$ occupies a point $P_i \in F$.*

In this paper, we assume that the formation F is a regular polygon. We denote by d the length of the polygon edge (known to the robots), and by $\alpha = (n-2)180°/n$ the angle of the polygon, where n is the number of robots that form F. Note that, to form a polygon, n should be greater than or equal to three robots.

Definition 3 (Fault-tolerant formation problem). *The fault-tolerant formation for a set of robots $\mathcal{R} = \{r_1, ..., r_n\}$ is defined as the formation problem for the set of correct robots $\mathcal{R}' \subseteq \mathcal{R}$. That is, among all robots in the system, the remaining correct robots $\mathcal{R}'$ are required to form the formation F, where $|\mathcal{R}'| \geq 3$.*

Using the above definition, we define the fault-tolerant flocking problem as follows:

Definition 4 (Fault-tolerant flocking problem). *Given a trajectory $\mathcal{T}$, and a group of robots $\mathcal{R} = \{r_1, ..., r_n\}$, we say that the robots solve the* **fault-tolerant flocking problem** *if (1) there exists infinitely many time instants $t_0, t_1, ...$, such that at any time t_i, robots in $\mathcal{R}$ solve the fault-tolerant formation problem, and a correct robot $r* \in \mathcal{R}$ is on the trajectory $\mathcal{T}$. (2) Given p_j and p_k the positions of robot $r*$ on the trajectory $\mathcal{T}$ at time t_j and t_k, with $t_j \neq t_k$, then $p_j \neq p_k$.*

We assume that the trajectory $\mathcal{T}$ is given as a sequence of discrete points online. That is, the robots do not know the points of the trajectory a priori.

Following the definition of fault-tolerant flocking, the robot that is moving on the trajectory is called a robot *leader*, and the other remaining robots are called *followers*. The leader computes its trajectory T in real time, and it is not known to the other robots in the system. Therefore, we need some leader election mechanism to elect the robot leader that will lead the formation. In this paper, we assume that the leader election is given by an eventual leader oracle, called Ω, which is defined as follows:

Definition 5 (Eventual leader Ω). *Given a set of correct robots S, there is a time $GST \geq GST_0$, which is unknown to robots, such that after GST, every invocation of the eventual leader oracle by a correct robot returns r as leader, with $r \in S$.*

Note that, before the time GST, that is between GST_0 and GST, there can be no leader, or there exist many leaders in the system. However, after GST only one single leader exists in the system , and all robots agree on the same robot leader.

2.3 Notations

Smallest enclosing circle. The *smallest enclosing circle* of a set of points P is denoted by $\mathcal{SEC}$, and its center is called o. It can be defined by either two opposite points that form the diameter of $\mathcal{SEC}$, or by at least three points. The smallest enclosing circle is unique, and can be computed in $O(n)$ time [5]. We shall denote by $p \in boundary(\mathcal{SEC})$, the point p that belongs to the circumference of $\mathcal{SEC}$. Also, we denote by $q \in inside(\mathcal{SEC})$, the point q that is located on the interior of $\mathcal{SEC}$, and does not belong to its boundary.

Voronoi diagram. The *Voronoi diagram* Voronoi(P) of a set of points $P = \{p_1, \ldots, p_n\}$ is a subdivision of the plane into n cells, one for each point in P. The cells have the property that a point q belongs to the Voronoi cell of point p_i, denoted $\text{Vcell}_{p_i}(P)$, if and only if, for any other point $p_j \in P$, $\text{dist}(q, p_i) < \text{dist}(q, p_j)$, where $\text{dist}(p, q)$ is the Euclidean distance between p and q. In particular, the strict inequality means that points located on the boundary of the Voronoi diagram do not belong to any Voronoi cell. Significantly more details about Voronoi diagrams are surveyed by Aurenhammer [6].

Before we proceed, we give the following notations that will be used throughout this paper. Let A and B be two points, with $\overline{AB}$, we will indicate the segment starting at A and terminating at B, and $dist(A, B)$ is the length of such a segment. We also denote by $[AB)$, the ray starting at A and passing through B. Given a region $\mathcal{X}$, we denote by $|\mathcal{X}|$, the number of robots in that region at time t. Finally, let S be a set of robots, then $|S|$ indicates the number of robots in S.

3 Fault-Tolerant Flocking in the Crash-Recovery Model

In this section, we present a fault-tolerant flocking algorithm for mobile robots in the semi-synchronous model with crash and recovery. The algorithm allows a group of oblivious correct robots to dynamically generate a regular polygon, and move together by following the movement of a robot leader on some trajectory. The algorithm solves the flocking problem in the crash-finite-recovery model, and relies on the existence of an eventually perfect failure detector, and an eventual leader election oracles.

Algorithm 1. Fault-tolerant Flocking (code executed by robot r_i)

When r_i **is activated**
r_i takes a snapshot of the positions of robots;
$\mathcal{R}$:= the set of positions of all robots in the system including faulty ones;
$S_{correct}$:= Output of $\diamond P$ Failure Detector Oracle on $\mathcal{R}$;
L := Output of Eventual Leader Oracle on the set $S_{correct}$;
if ($|S_{correct}| \geq 3$) **then** {*at least three correct robots*}
  if ($r_i = L$) **then** {*leader*}
    Flocking_Leader($\mathcal{R}$, $\mathsf{S_{correct}}$, L);
  else {*follower*}
    Flocking_Follower($\mathcal{R}$, $\mathsf{S_{correct}}$, L);
  end if
else
  Do_Nothing();
end if

Algorithm 2. Flocking Leader: Code executed by a robot leader L

```
procedure Flocking_Leader($\mathcal{R}$, $S_{correct}$, $L$)
  $d$ := the desired distance of the polygon edge;
  $\mathcal{T}$ := the trajectory of the leader;
  $n := |S_{correct}|$;
  $\alpha := (n-2)180°/n$;
  Compute Voronoi($\mathcal{R}$);
  Compute $\mathcal{SEC}(S_{correct})$;
  $o$ := Origin of $\mathcal{SEC}(S_{correct})$;
  if ($L = o$) then                                   {the leader is at the origin of $\mathcal{SEC}$}
    Move within $\text{Vcell}_{r_i}(\mathcal{R})$ to different nearest point from trajectory $\mathcal{T}$;
  end if
  if ($L \notin \mathcal{T}$) then                          {the leader is not on trajectory}
    if ($\mathcal{T} \cap \mathcal{SEC} = \emptyset$) then
      Move within $\text{Vcell}_{r_i}(\mathcal{R})$ to nearest point from trajectory $\mathcal{T}$;
    else                                                      {$\mathcal{T} \cap \mathcal{SEC} \neq \emptyset$}
      if ($L \in boundary(\mathcal{SEC}) \wedge n = 3$) then
        Move within $\text{Vcell}_{r_i}(\mathcal{R})$ toward $p \in \mathcal{T}$ by Restriction 1 and Restriction 2;
      else
        Move within $\text{Vcell}_{r_i}(\mathcal{R})$ toward $p \in \mathcal{T}$;
      end if
    end if
  else                                                        {the leader is on trajectory}
    if ($n = 3 \wedge L \in inside(\mathcal{SEC})$) then
      if ($\mathcal{T} \cap \mathcal{SEC} \not\subseteq \{r_j, r_k\}$, with $\{r_j, r_k\} \subset S_{correct}$) then
        Move within $\text{Vcell}_{r_i}(\mathcal{R})$ to $p \in (\mathcal{T} \cap \mathcal{SEC})$;
      else
        Move within $\text{Vcell}_{r_i}(\mathcal{R})$ to $p \in boundary(\mathcal{SEC})$;
      end if
    else
      if ($\forall r_j \in S_{correct}$, $F = Formation(P_1, ..., P_n)$ is formed) then
        if (no faulty robot on $\mathcal{T}$ prevents leader from moving) then
          Move within $\text{Vcell}_{r_i}(\mathcal{R})$ to a desired point on trajectory $\mathcal{T}$;
        else
          Move within $\text{Vcell}_{r_i}(\mathcal{R})$ to some point $p \notin \mathcal{T}$;
        end if
      else                                                    {formation is not formed}
        $\Delta$ := Ray starting at leader's position $L$, and passing through $o$;
        $\alpha_L$ := angle equal to $\alpha$ and having as bisector $\Delta$;
        Compute $F = Formation(P_1, ..., P_n)$ with $P_1 = L$, and $\alpha = \alpha_L$;
        if (Some targets on $F$ are occupied by faulty robots) then
          Move within $\text{Vcell}_{r_i}(\mathcal{R})$ to some different point on $\mathcal{T}$;
        else if ($\forall r_j \in S_{correct} - \{L\}, r_j \in boundary(\mathcal{SEC})$) then
          Compute the rays $\Delta_1$ and $\Delta_2$ starting at $L$, and at angle $\alpha/2$ from $\Delta$;
          $p_1 := \Delta_1 \cap \mathcal{SEC}$;
          $p_2 := \Delta_2 \cap \mathcal{SEC}$;
          if ($\forall r_j \in S_{correct} - \{L\}$, $r_j$ is unable to move on $\mathcal{SEC}$ to $p_1$ or $p_2$) then
            Move within $\text{Vcell}_{r_i}(\mathcal{R})$ to some point that breaks $\mathcal{SEC}$;
          end if
        else
          Do_Nothing();
        end if
      end if
    end if
  end if
end
```

Algorithm 3. Flocking Follower: Code executed by a robot follower r_i

```
procedure Flocking_Follower($\mathcal{R}$, $S_{correct}$, $L$)
  $d$ := the desired distance of the polygon edge;
  $n := |S_{correct}|$;
  $\alpha := (n-2)180°/n$;
  if ($F = Formation(P_1, ..., P_n)$ is formed) then          {regular polygon is formed}
    Do_Nothing();
  else
    Compute $\mathcal{SEC}(S_{correct})$;
    $o$:= origin of $\mathcal{SEC}(S_{correct})$;
    $\Delta$:= Ray starting from leader's position $L$ and passing through $o$;
    $\alpha_L$ := angle equal to $\alpha$, with $\Delta$ its bisector and formed by two correct robots;
    Compute the two rays $\Delta_1$ and $\Delta_2$ starting at $L$, and at angle $\alpha/2$ from $\Delta$;
    Compute Voronoi($\mathcal{R}$);
    if ($\alpha_L$ is formed) then          {angle with leader is formed}
      Compute targets of $F = Formation(P_1, ..., P_n)$ with $P_1 = L$, and $\alpha = \alpha_L$;
      if ($r_i \in \Delta_1 \wedge r_i$ is nearest to $L$ in $\Delta_1$) $\vee$($r_i \in \Delta_2 \wedge r_i$ is nearest to $L$ in $\Delta_2$)
      then
        Move linearly on $\Delta_1$ or $\Delta_2$ within Vcell$_{r_i}(\mathcal{R})$ toward target;
      else if ($\exists P_i \in$ Vcell$_{r_i}(\mathcal{R})$) $\wedge(P_i \notin \Delta_1 \wedge P_i \notin \Delta_2)$ then
        Move to nearest target $P_i$ in Vcell$_{r_i}(\mathcal{R})$;
      else
        Move to last point on Vcell$_{r_i}(\mathcal{R})$ toward a nearest target $P_i$;
      end if
    else          {$\alpha_L$ is not yet formed; keep $\mathcal{SEC}$ invariant}
      if ($r_i \notin$ boundary of $\mathcal{SEC}$) then
        if ($n = 3$) then
          Move within Vcell$_{r_i}(\mathcal{R})$ to the boundary of $\mathcal{SEC}$;
        else          {$n > 3$}
          $Zone_1$ := Vcell$_{r_i}(\mathcal{R}) \cap \mathcal{SEC} \cap \Delta_1$;
          $Zone_2$ := Vcell$_{r_i}(\mathcal{R}) \cap \mathcal{SEC} \cap \Delta_2$;
          if ($Zone_1 \neq \emptyset$) $\vee$ ($Zone_2 \neq \emptyset$) then
            Move linearly to last point in $\overline{r_i p}$, such that $dist(L,p) = d$ within the
            non empty zone $Zone_1$ or $Zone_2$ ;
          end if
        end if
      else          {$r_i \in$ boundary of $\mathcal{SEC}$}
        $P_c(t)$:= the set of robots on the boundary of $\mathcal{SEC}$ at time $t$;
        if ($|P_c(t)| = 2$) then          {only two robots are on $\mathcal{SEC}$}
          Do_Nothing();
        else
          $p_1 := \mathcal{SEC} \cap \Delta_1$;
          $p_2 := \mathcal{SEC} \cap \Delta_2$;
          $P_c(t)$:= the set of robots on the boundary of $\mathcal{SEC}$ at time $t$;
          $prev_{r_i}(t)$ := direct clockwise neighbor of $r_i$ on $P_c(t)$;
          $next_{r_i}(t)$ := direct counter-clockwise neighbor of $r_i$ on $P_c(t)$;
          $\alpha_{prev_{r_i}}(t)$:= the angular distance from $r_i$ to $prev_{r_i}(t)$;
          $\alpha_{next_{r_i}}(t)$:= the angular distance from $r_i$ to $next_{r_i}(t)$;
          $\alpha_m(t+1)$:= the angular movement of $r_i$ at time $t+1$;
          Move within Vcell$_{r_i}(\mathcal{R})$ on boundary of $\mathcal{SEC}$ to nearest point $p_1$ or $p_2$,
          with $\frac{\alpha_{prev_{r_i}}(t)-\pi}{2} \leq \alpha_m(t+1) \leq \frac{\pi-\alpha_{next_{r_i}}(t)}{2}$;
        end if
      end if
    end if
  end if
end
```

The flocking algorithm is depicted on Algorithm 1, and it must guarantee that (1) there is no collision between robots, especially when there is instability in the system, that is when the failure detection device makes mistakes about the status of robots, and also before the leader election oracle gives the same output for all correct robots (2) The robot leader moves on the trajectory (3) eventually correct robots form dynamically the regular polygon with the leader in finite time. The overall idea of the algorithm is as follow. Recall that robots are anonymous, and they do not share a common coordinate system, so correct robots need some way to find their targets on the polygon. The polygon construction starts from the position of the leader, which is given by the eventual leader oracle. After that, two correct robots must form the first angle of the polygon having as a vertex the position of the leader. In order to restrict the number of angles that can be formed at the position of the leader with two correct robots to a unique angle (called, α_L), α_L must have as bisector the ray starting as the position of the leader, and passing through the center of the smallest enclosing circle (referred as $\mathcal{SEC}$) of the positions of correct robots. Therefore, as long as α_L is not formed, correct robots need to keep $\mathcal{SEC}$ invariant. When the angle α_L is formed, correct robots are allowed to break $\mathcal{SEC}$, and move to the remaining targets of the polygon within their Voronoi cells.

Before we describe the algorithm in more details, we first give the following restrictions that are imposed on the movements of robots that are located on the boundary of $\mathcal{SEC}$ before the construction of the angle α_L in order to preserve the invariance of $\mathcal{SEC}$ until α_L is formed:

Restriction 1. *If α_L is not formed, then correct robots located on the circumference of the smallest enclosing circle do not move unless there are at least three such robots with distinct positions. That is, when only two robots are located on the boundary of $\mathcal{SEC}$, they are not allowed to move.*

Restriction 2. *Let $P_c(t)$ be the set of correct robots on the boundary of $\mathcal{SEC}$ at time t, and r_i one such robot. Let $prev_{r_i}(t)$ (resp., $next_{r_i}(t)$) denote the direct clockwise (resp., counter-clockwise) neighbor of r_i on $P_c(t)$. Let also $\alpha_{prev_{r_i}}(t)$ and $\alpha_{next_{r_i}}(t)$ be the angular distance from r_i to $prev_{r_i}(t)$ and $next_{r_i}(t)$, respectively. Then, the angular movement of r_i at time $t+1$, denoted by $\alpha_m(t+1)$ is restricted as follows:*

$$\frac{\alpha_{prev_{r_i}}(t) - \pi}{2} \leq \alpha_m(t+1) \leq \frac{\pi - \alpha_{next_{r_i}}(t)}{2}$$

The above restriction ensures that the movement of correct robots located on the smallest enclosing circle $\mathcal{SEC}$ does not leave an empty angle greater than π, or else $\mathcal{SEC}$ would no longer be the smallest circle enclosing all correct robots.

We now describe the algorithm in more details as follows. First, when robot r_i becomes active, it executes the following steps:

- Robot r_i calls the eventually perfect failure detection module to get the set of correct robots, $S_{correct}$.

- Robot r_i calls the eventual leader election module, and gets the position of the leader, L.
- Depending on the status of robot r_i, r_i executes the procedure described in Algorithm 2; Flocking_Leader($\mathcal{R}$, $\mathsf{S}_{\mathsf{correct}}$, L) if it is a leader. Otherwise, it executes the procedure described in Algorithm 3, Flocking_Follower($\mathcal{R}$, $\mathsf{S}_{\mathsf{correct}}$, L).
- If robot r_i is a *leader*, then first it has to move to a point that is located on its trajectory $\mathcal{T}$. We distinguish the following cases depending on the leader' position:

1. If the leader r_i is located at the origin of the smallest enclosing circle, then it needs to move toward a different point on its trajectory, and within its Voronoi cell, otherwise robots cannot compute the ray Δ, which represents the bisector of the angle α_L (Algorithm 2, line 10).
2. If the leader is not located on its trajectory $\mathcal{T}$, then it has to move within its Voronoi cell to some point on $\mathcal{T}$ (Algorithm 2, line 14).
3. If the leader is located on $\mathcal{T}$, but inside $\mathcal{SEC}$, and the number of correct robots is equal to three (including the leader), then the leader needs to move to the boundary of $\mathcal{SEC}$ (Algorithm 2, lines 24 – 27) in order for the two other correct robots forming $\mathcal{SEC}$ to be able to move on the boundary of $\mathcal{SEC}$, without breaking it, and form the angle α_L. After being on the boundary of $\mathcal{SEC}$, the leader needs to move on the boundary of $\mathcal{SEC}$ toward a point on $\mathcal{T}$ by following Restriction 1 and Restriction 2 (Algorithm 2, line 17). The whole idea behind this special case of three correct robots in the system is to have eventually the robot leader located on the boundary of $\mathcal{SEC}$, and on its trajectory $\mathcal{T}$. After that, the two other robots followers can construct the angle α_L of the formation.

Note that, we assume that the portion of the plane delimiting the trajectory of a robot leader is larger enough than the portion of the plane enclosing the smallest circle of the positions of correct robots $\mathcal{SEC}$. It follows that, when the leader is located on $\mathcal{T}$, there exists at least one point that intersects $\mathcal{T}$ with $\mathcal{SEC}$.

After being on the trajectory, the leader r_i checks if the formation F is already formed. Then, two cases follow: if the formation F is formed by correct robots, then the leader r_i computes the Voronoi diagram of all robots in the system, including faulty ones, and moves within its Voronoi cell to a desired point on its trajectory $\mathcal{T}$ (Algorithm 2, line 32). In the situations where, some faulty robots are located on its trajectory, and block robot r_i from moving, robot r_i can deviate from its trajectory until it passes the positions of faulty robots, and then goes back again to its trajectory (Algorithm 2, line 34).

In the case, where the formation F is not yet constructed, the following cases arise. If some targets of the formation F are occupied by some faulty robots, then the leader moves within its Voronoi cell to some different point on its trajectory in order to free the targets of the formation from faulty robots (Algorithm 2, line 41). Finally, in the case where all correct robots are located on the boundary of $\mathcal{SEC}$, and all of them are unable to move on its boundary because they are blocked by faulty robots, then the leader needs to move to some different point in its trajectory $\mathcal{T}$ within its Voronoi cell in such a way it breaks the current $\mathcal{SEC}$.

- If robot r_i is a *follower* then it has to find its target on the formation F if it is not formed yet. Todo so, robot r_i needs to compute an angle, called α_L, which is equal to α, and having as vertex the leader's position L, and with the bisector the ray passing through the origin of $\mathcal{SEC}$(computed on correct robots). The algorithm for a robot follower distinguishes the following two cases:

  1. The angle α_L is already constructed by the leader and two correct robots located respectively on the two rays Δ_1 and Δ_2 (delimiting α_L), robots followers need to move toward the remaining targets of the formation within their Voronoi cells, by excluding the two targets on Δ_1 and Δ_2.[2] In the case when many correct robots form the angle α_L, each of the two nearest robots from the leader that are located respectively, on Δ_1 and Δ_2 will move to the target that belongs to the same ray it is located (i.e., Δ_1 or Δ_2) within its Voronoi cell (Algorithm 3, line 17).
  2. The angle α_L is not yet formed. In this case, robots followers need to keep the smallest enclosing circle of correct robots invariant until that angle is constructed. So, if the number of correct robots is equal to three (including the leader), and robot r_i is located inside $\mathcal{SEC}$, then it has to move to the boundary of $\mathcal{SEC}$ (Algorithm 3, line 26) within its Voronoi cell. Such a movement will result on three robots that are located on the boundary of $\mathcal{SEC}$, which will allow two of them to move on the boundary of $\mathcal{SEC}$ to construct the angle α_L. Then, if a robot follower r_i is located on the boundary of $\mathcal{SEC}$, in addition to the restriction of moving within its Voronoi cell, Restriction 1 and Restriction 2 are imposed on its movement in order to preserve the invariance of $\mathcal{SEC}$ until α_L is formed.

In this paper, we studied the fault-tolerant flocking, when the formation is a regular polygon, however even if the problem is defined for the partial polygon, we can solve the problem similarly.

4 Correctness of the Algorithm

In this section, we prove the correctness of our algorithm by first showing that no two robots ever move to the same location (Theorem 3). Second, we prove that the smallest enclosing circle remains invariant until the first angle of the polygon is formed by correct robots (Theorem 4). Then, we show that all correct robots form the regular polygon in finite time after the global stabilization time

[2] We mean by the angle α_L is constructed, the fact that two correct robots are located respectively in Δ_1 and Δ_2, and they are located at angle $\alpha/2$ from the ray passing through the position of the leader and the center of $\mathcal{SEC}$. This does not mean that the two robots are in their final targets of the formation.

GST (Theorem 5). Finally, we prove that the flocking algorithm tolerates crash-finite-recovery failures of robots due to its oblivious feature (Theorem 6). The proofs of some lemmas are omitted due to lack of space.

4.1 Collision Avoidance

Lemma 1. *By Algorithm 1, at any time t (before or after GST), there is no collision between any two robots in the system.*

Theorem 3. *Algorithm 1 is collision free.*

4.2 Polygon Formation

In this section, we first prove that Algorithm 1 allows correct robots to form the regular polygon deterministically after the global stabilization time GST. In the following, we consider the system after time GST has been reached. Thus, all robots agree on the same set of correct robots, and also on the eventual leader. We first prove show that the leader can be located on its trajectory within finite time, and then we prove that the smallest circle enclosing all correct robots $\mathcal{SEC}$ remains invariant from the time when the leader is located on its trajectory until the angle α_L having as vertex the position of the leader is constructed with two correct robots.

Lemma 2. *After the time GST, the robot leader can be located in finite time on some point on its trajectory $\mathcal{T}$.*

Theorem 4. *After GST, the smallest circle enclosing all correct robots remains invariant until the angle α_L is formed.*

Lemma 3. *The angle α_L is constructed in finite time by two correct robots and the position of the leader as the angle vertex after the time GST.*

Proof (Lemma 3). We consider the system after the time GST has been reached, and thus by the definition of the eventually perfect failure detector, and the leader election oracle, all robots agree on the same set of correct robots, and there exists exactly one single leader in the system. First, by Lemma 2, the leader can be located on its trajectory $\mathcal{T}$ in finite time. Second, observe that there exists exactly one ray Δ that starts at the position of the leader, and that passes through the center of $\mathcal{SEC}$ because the leader is unique. Also, the center of $\mathcal{SEC}$ is unique since $\mathcal{SEC}$ is invariant before the construction of α_L by Theorem 4. So, there exists exactly one angle α_L having as angle vertex the position of the leader, and that has Δ as its bisector.

Let Δ_1 and Δ_2 be respectively, the two rays starting at the position of leader r_i, and located at angle $\alpha/2$ from Δ. The angle α_L is constructed by the position of r_i as the angle vertex, and the two correct robots that will be located respectively, on Δ_1 and Δ_2. Let p_1 and p_2 be the intersection respectively, of Δ_1 and Δ_2 with $\mathcal{SEC}$. We first prove the case for three robots, and we distinguish the following cases:

- The leader r_i, and the two correct robots followers r_j and r_k are located on the circumference of $\mathcal{SEC}$. We also, assume that r_j and r_k are not blocked by faulty robots to move on $\mathcal{SEC}$, then we will easily show that in finite number of steps, r_j and r_k will reach p_1 and p_2. By the algorithm, the leader r_i is on its trajectory, then it does not move. Robots r_j and r_k are able to move on $\mathcal{SEC}$ by following Restriction 2, besides their activation cycle is finite, and at each cycle they can progress by non-zero distance toward p_1 or p_2, and thus α_L can be constructed in finite time.
- The leader r_i is located inside $\mathcal{SEC}$, and the two other correct robots r_j and r_k form $\mathcal{SEC}$ (i.e., they are located on the circumference of $\mathcal{SEC}$). This case is the most interesting one because the leader has to move to the boundary of $\mathcal{SEC}$ (otherwise, r_j and r_k cannot form α_L because they are not allowed to move by Restriction 1), and also to a point on its trajectory $\mathcal{T}$. By Lemma 2, the leader r_i can be located in finite time in some point on its trajectory $\mathcal{T}$, and also without modifying $\mathcal{SEC}$. It results that, this situation is reduced to the above case.
- The leader r_i, and one correct robot r_j (without loss of generality) are located on the circumference of $\mathcal{SEC}$, and robot r_k is located inside $\mathcal{SEC}$. This case is trivial, since robot r_k has to move to the boundary of $\mathcal{SEC}$ by the algorithm, and then this situation is also reduced to the same case discussed above.
- All correct robots are located on the boundary of $\mathcal{SEC}$, and they are unable to move because they are blocked by faulty robots. This case is handled as a special case by the algorithm, where the leader has to move in order to modify the current $\mathcal{SEC}$, and make free correct robots. So, this case can be also reduced to the general case in finite time after the movement of the leader to a different point on the trajectory.

As a conclusion, in every possible case where the number of correct robots is equal to three, α_L is constructed in finite time. When $n > 3$, the rest follows by induction. □

Theorem 5. *All correct robots reach their targets on the polygon in finite time after the time GST.*

4.3 Fault-Tolerant Flocking

Theorem 6. *Algorithm 1 is a fault-tolerant flocking algorithm that tolerates permanent crash failures, and also finite-crash-recovery failures of robots.*

Proof (Theorem 6). Let us consider the system after the global stabilization time GST. By the algorithm, stable correct robots are determined in finite time by the eventually perfect failure detector oracle. Also, unstable robots that crash for some arbitrary periods, and then they recover and become correct will be included in the list of correct robots by the eventually perfect failure detector oracle. Since, Algorithm 1 is oblivious and does not depend on past computations and observations, handling the recovery of some robot can be seen as a new activation for that robot. Thus, the recovery of robots is implicitly encapsulated by the oblivious feature of the algorithm.

By Theorem 3, there is no collisions between any two robots in the system, and by Theorem 5, the polygon formation is constructed dynamically in finite time by correct robots. By the algorithm, after the construction of the polygon, the robot leader changes its position on the trajectory, and robots followers adjust their movements. Consequently, Algorithm 1 is a dynamic flocking algorithm that tolerates permanent and crash finite recovery failures of robots. □

Acknowledgments

This work is supported in part by the JSPS (Japan Society for the Promotion of Science) postdoctoral fellowship for foreign researchers (ID No.P 08046), KAKENHI no. 21500013 and The Telecommunication Advancement Foundation.

References

1. Gervasi, V., Prencipe, G.: Coordination without communication: the Case of the Flocking Problem. Discrete Applied Mathematics 143(1-3), 203–223 (2004)
2. Canepa, D., Potop-Butucaru, M.G.: Stabilizing flocking via leader election in robot networks. In: Masuzawa, T., Tixeuil, S. (eds.) SSS 2007. LNCS, vol. 4838, pp. 52–66. Springer, Heidelberg (2007)
3. Souissi, S., Yang, Y., Défago, X.: Fault-tolerant Flocking in a k-bounded Asynchronous System. In: Baker, T.P., Bui, A., Tixeuil, S. (eds.) OPODIS 2008. LNCS, vol. 5401, pp. 145–163. Springer, Heidelberg (2008)
4. Yang, Y., Souissi, S., Défago, X., Takizawa, M.: Fault-tolerant Flocking of Mobile Robots with whole Formation Rotation. In: Proc. 23rd IEEE International Conference on Advanced Information Networking and Applications (AINA 2009), pp. 830–837 (2009)
5. Welzl, E.: Smallest enclosing disks (balls and ellipsoids). New Results and New Trends in Computer Science 555, 359–370 (1991)
6. Aurenhammer, F.: Voronoi Diagrams—A survey of a fundamental geometric data structure 23(3), 345–405 (1991)
7. Suzuki, I., Yamashita, M.: Distributed Anonymous Mobile Robots: Formation of Geometric Patterns. SIAM Journal of Computing 28(4), 1347–1363 (1999)
8. Dolev, S.: Self-Stabilization. MIT Press, Cambridge (2000)
9. Freiling, C.F., Majuntke, M., Mittal, N.: On Detecting Termination in the Crash-Recovery Model. In: Kermarrec, A.-M., Bougé, L., Priol, T. (eds.) Euro-Par 2007. LNCS, vol. 4641, pp. 629–638. Springer, Heidelberg (2007)

Speculation for Parallelizing Runtime Checks

Martin Süßkraut, Stefan Weigert, Ute Schiffel, Thomas Knauth, Martin Nowack, Diogo Becker de Brum, and Christof Fetzer

TU Dresden
Computer Science Department
{suesskraut,stefan,schiffel,thomas,martin,diogo, christof}@se.inf.tu-dresden.de

Abstract. We present and evaluate a framework, *ParExC*, to reduce the runtime penalties of compiler generated runtime checks. An obvious approach is to use idle cores of modern multi-core CPUs to parallelize the runtime checks. This could be accomplished by (a) parallelizing the application and in this way, implicitly parallelizing the checks, or (b) by parallelizing the checks only. Parallelizing an application is rarely easy and frameworks that simplify the parallelization, e.g., like software transactional memory (STM), can introduce considerable overhead. ParExC is based on alternative (b). We compare it with an approach using a transactional memory-based alternative. Our experience shows that ParExC is not only more efficient than the STM-based solution but the manual effort for an application developer to integrate ParExC is lower. ParExC has – in contrast to similar frameworks – two noteworthy features that permit a more efficient parallelization of checks: (1) speculative variables, and (2) the ability to add checks by static instrumentation.

1 Introduction

Despite several decades of intensive research, software bugs and execution failures are still major threats to software dependability. Compilers can not only help to detect software bugs by performing type checks during compilation but also by adding runtime checks to a program to enable self-repairing and self-healing. Unsafe languages like C/C++ are particularly prone to software bugs – some of which enable, for example, buffer overflow attacks. Buffer overflows are especially a problem in distributed systems as they might enable remote attackers to gain access via the network. Buffer overflow attacks can be detected via precise out-of-bounds checking which can introduce an up to 12x slowdown – even for state of the art bounds checkers [1]. A lower-cost alternative is, for example, data-flow integrity checking [2] which does not prevent buffer overflows but instead detects invalid data flows and effectively prevents attacks that exploit buffer overflows. Nevertheless, data-flow integrity checking has still a slowdown of 2.5x or higher.

In future, hardware failures are expected to become more likely [3]. To ensure the correctness of critical programs, one might need to detect the incorrect execution of programs. One can use replicated execution to detect simple transient hardware failures. However, if one needs to detect hardware design failures

R. Guerraoui and F. Petit (Eds.): SSS 2009, LNCS 5873, pp. 698–710, 2009.

and compiler failures, one needs to use other alternatives. Arithmetic encoding with an AN-code [4] is one such alternative. Our own measurements show a 45x slowdown when encoding almost all operations of a program with an AN-code.

Given the potentially very large slowdowns introduced by runtime checks, our goal is to make runtime checking more palatable by reducing its impact on the runtime of applications. Given the prevalence of multi-core CPUs and the difficulty of many applications to harness the full power of multi-core CPUs, it makes sense to use additional cores to try to mask the overhead of the runtime checks. This could be accomplished by (a) parallelizing the application and in this way, implicitly parallelizing the checks, or (b) by parallelizing the checks only.

The problem with alternative (a) is that parallelizing existing applications and even writing new parallel applications is very difficult and introduces new sources of software bugs resulting in, e.g., data races and deadlocks. To simplify the parallelization of applications, one could use software transactional memory (STM). STM alleviates several drawbacks of lock-based and also lock-free mechanisms.

Alternative (b), i.e., the parallelization of runtime checks has recently been investigated by *Speck* [5]. While Speck scales very well with the number of cores, the performance measurements of [5] do not seem to result in any performance gain when compared to sequential checking. The parallel taint analysis of Speck has a slowdown of 18.4x on an 8-core CPU [5] . This is in the same order of magnitude than checking without parallelization on one core [6]. Newer sequential taint checking approaches using static instrumentation perform even better: slowdowns are between 1.58x and 2.06x [7].

Given the current state of the art, it is not clear if one should choose alternative (a) or (b) or maybe, even just use sequential checks using static instrumentation? The main question is on how much we can reduce the overheads of the competing alternatives. We have been working on reducing the overheads of STM and with TinySTM [8] we have a very efficient – and according to our own measurements – the most efficient STM. In our analysis of alternative (b), we have identified two sources for the high overheads of existing parallelized checking frameworks:

(1) If runtime checks need to exchange state between epochs, state accesses are serialized. Parallel Dynamic Information Flow Tracking (DIFT) [9] uses a non-trivial hardware extension to stream meta data to another core and Speck [5] streams taint data to a single core. This limits scalability and performance.
(2) Runtime checks are added by dynamic binary instrumentation (DBI). DBI introduces a high overhead that must be compensated by additional cores. Our goal is to be faster than the sequential execution of statically instrumented code and DBI does not seem to be competitive in that regard. Furthermore, some checkers cannot be implemented by DBI. For instance, bounds for objects on the stack are not available in binaries without debug information. Therefore, it is not possible to build a precise out-of-bounds checker with DBI for stack objects.

Based on the above two observations, we developed a new framework, *ParExC*, for writing parallelized runtime checkers. It parallelizes the runtime checks only, i.e., it does not require the application itself to be parallelized. To demonstrate the effectiveness and versatility of our approach, we implemented checkers for two very different threats: buffer overflow attacks and hardware errors. Furthermore, we compare ParExC with an STM-implementation using two parallelized STM-benchmarks, i.e., benchmarks for which STM implementations have been optimized. We describe how to add checks to parallelized applications using software transactional memory in Sec. 3.

Our approach for parallelizing runtime checks is introduced in Sec. 2. A *checker* instruments applications with runtime checks. When a check fails at runtime, the application is aborted. The basic approach is very similar to Speck [5]. We execute the original application as *predictor* without any runtime checks on one core. The predictor's execution is partitioned into *epochs*. Each epoch is replayed with runtime checks enabled by an *executor*. Because of the runtime checks, the executor is typically an order of magnitude slower than the predictor for the same epoch. We achieve a speedup by running the executors in parallel to each other and to the predictor.

We make three novel contributions in this paper:

(A) Speculative Variables. To scale, executors run out-of-order and share the runtime state of the checkers. Nevertheless, accesses to the shared state have to happen in-order to preserve semantic correctness of the runtime checks. We solve this problem with *speculative variables* (see Sec. 4). Executors access the shared state speculatively and later verify the validity of those accesses. With that, we overcome the limiting single core used in Speck [5] and the meta data stream of DIFT [9].

(B) Static Instrumentation. We have implemented three checkers using static instrumentation: a precise out-of-bounds checker (OOB), a data-flow integrity checker (DFI) [2], and an AN-code checker (AN) [10]. The OOB and AN checker cannot be implemented using DBI, as they rely on information only available at compile time. Furthermore, static instrumentation enables – in contrast to DBI – more optimizations such as inlining. We discuss the implementation of these checkers in Sec. 5.

(C) Comparison to STM. ParExC parallelizes an application by speculating on the correct execution of epochs. On the other hand, STM parallelizes by speculating on the absence of memory-contention between concurrent data accesses. In Sec. 6, we demonstrate that checking an application with ParExC can scale better than checking an application which was already parallelized using an STM.

2 ParExC

ParExC reduces the performance impact of expensive runtime checks by parallelizing these checks (Fig. 1). At compile time, runtime checking code is added

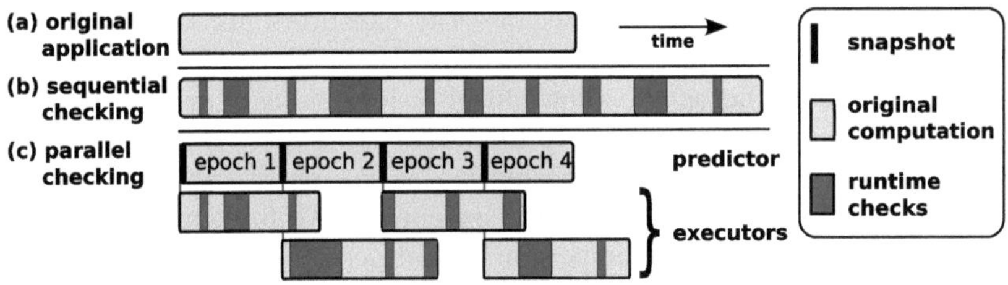

Fig. 1. (a) Original application execution without checks. (b) Sequential execution with checks. (c) Parallelized execution with checks. Unchecked predictor for fast state prediction. Parallelized executors including slow checks.

to the original application. Our approach supports the addition of one or more runtime checkers to the same application, e.g., a bounds checker and a data-flow integrity checker can be used together. These checkers are executed in parallel and each checker itself is also parallelized. We focus on using just one kind of checker to simplify the presentation. The overall approach is very similar to [5] with two important exceptions: (1) to reduce the overall overhead, we use static instrumentation instead of DBI, and (2) we introduce speculative variables (Sec. 4) to decouple the execution of the individual epochs of a checker.

An execution with runtime checks (Fig. 1 (b)) introduces, in general, a substantial overhead compared to the original application (Fig. 1 (a)). To parallelize the runtime checks (Fig. 1 (c)), we execute the original application without checks by a *predictor* process. The predictor's execution is partitioned into *epochs*. The objective of the predictor is to predict the state of the application at the start of each epoch. An *executor* process re-executes the epoch with runtime checks activated. Executors run on additional cores in parallel to each other and to the predictor.

At compile time, ParExC generates the checker code base by duplicating the original (predictor) code base. ParExC instruments both code bases to enable switching from the predictor code base to the checker code base at epoch boundaries. After these preparations, checkers can analyze and instrument the checker code base. The instrumentation process is the same as for checking without parallelization. For instrumentation, ParExC uses the LLVM compiler framework [11] which provides very nice support for static instrumentations using the LLVM intermediate code. However, our approach does not depend on LLVM specifics, i.e., LLVM could be replaced by another compiler framework.

At runtime, we provide a copy-on-write snapshot mechanism (similar to the UNIX system call `fork`) to copy the application state from the predictor to the new executor at the beginning of a new epoch. The executor replays the same computation for an epoch e as the predictor performed for e but with additionally added runtime checks. Therefore, any input received by the predictor is deterministically replayed in the executors. All externally visible side-effects (issued via system calls) of the predictor are held back by ParExC until they are verified by the executors. An executor explicitly approves an epoch e to make

e's side-effects externally visible. Because the executors are running in parallel, the verification order of system calls might be different from the order they were issued in the predictor. We allow out-of-order issuing of system calls by the executors but ensure their in-order retirement.

The deterministic replay and speculative execution of external side-effects at runtime is mostly transparent to the executors. We implemented these two features as kernel-module for Linux similar to Speck [5]. To be able to log any non-determinism we require that accessing any non-determinism has to happen via system calls, e.g., instead of reading the time stamp counter (`rdtsc`) the application has to call `gettimeofday`.

To allow the deterministic replay, an application-developer has to mark potential places in the code where ParExC should take a snapshot, i.e., start a new epoch. Ideally, these snapshot-places are executed periodically with constant frequency at runtime. Therefore, using ParExC is not completely transparent to the application developer, but the manual instrumentation overhead for using ParExC in an application is small.

3 Runtime Checking in STM-Based Applications

Software transaction memory (STM) provides transactions at the programming language level. An STM detects read/write and write/write conflicts of transactions and aborts or delays a conflicting transaction. On abort, all state changes are rolled back and the transaction is then retried. STMs require all shared data accesses within a transaction to be instrumented. This instrumentation incurs synchronization and book-keeping overhead. However, this book-keeping overhead can often be amortized by achieving better scalability through speculation.

In our experiments, we used a C++ version of TinySTM [8]. Instead of instrumenting the code by hand, we used Tanger [12] which is an extension for LLVM [11] that automatically transactifies applications. The programmer only has to mark the start and the end of the transactions. The instrumentation delegates all shared data accesses in these regions to an STM.

To parallelize the application with runtime checks, we perform two steps. First, we apply the same compiler transformations as the ParExC checkers. Second, we apply the Tanger transformations on the code resulting from the first step. Due to this ordering, Tanger automatically puts the book-keeping state of the runtime checks under the control of TinySTM.

Note, an application-developer who wants to use an STM to parallelize the runtime-checks themselves would have to identify (1) where to spawn threads and (2) critical sections and encapsulate these in transactions. If the application is not yet parallelized, the developer would have the additional burden of parallelizing the application itself. We therefore believe that an STM is more difficult to use for the application-developer than the ParExC approach. Furthermore, while an application must itself be parallelizable to parallelize its runtime-checks using STM, this restriction is not the case for ParExC.

4 Speculative Variables

In ParExC, runtime checks need to update and read checker specific book-keeping state. For instance, the out-of-bounds checker (OOB) adds for each executed `malloc` the address and size of the newly allocated object to its book-keeping state. OOB verifies that each memory access reads from or writes to a currently allocated memory area. Fig. 2 shows that in the predictor, a `malloc` and a memory `write` are in a causal order. However, the `malloc` and the `write` may happen in a different order in the executors as can be seen in Fig. 2: the `write` access in the second executor happens before the `malloc` in the first executor. Therefore, the OOB checker cannot immediately verify that the `write` accesses an allocated region in the memory. (Note that the predictor allocates the memory for the executor but the predictor does not update any book-keeping information).

We propose to use speculation to decouple the accesses to shared state. Book-keeping state is stored in *speculative variables*. At runtime, each executor has a private view of the speculative variables. After finishing the checking of an epoch, an executor merges its private view into a shared view. Merges happen exclusively and in the order of the epochs, e.g., executor E_i has to wait for executor E_{i-1} to finish before E_i can merge its private view into the shared view.

Interface. Speculative variables have a generic interface so that different checkers can use the same speculative variable implementation. The semantic of the values stored in speculative variables depends on the checker. For example, the OOB checker maintains for each memory object a speculative variable storing the bounds of the memory object. Speculative variables are addressed by ids. The OOB checker uses the memory address of an object as id.

A speculative variable provides two operations: *read* and *write*. `read (id, ob)` returns the value of the speculative variable addressed by `id`. The read operation only operates on the private view. Therefore, if there is not yet a speculative variable for `id`, the value `ob` is returned. Additionally, a new speculative variable is created in the private view and its current value is set to `ob`. We call `ob` an *obligation*. A check must always provide an obligation to a read operation. The obligation is calculated by assuming the current check succeeds. Hence, the obligation is a speculative value. For instance, an OOB check speculates that the checked memory access is valid. Therefore, the obligation is the memory area size at least required for the checked memory access. We explain in Section 5 how to calculate the obligations for our other checkers. The obligation is also stored within the speculative variable for later validation.

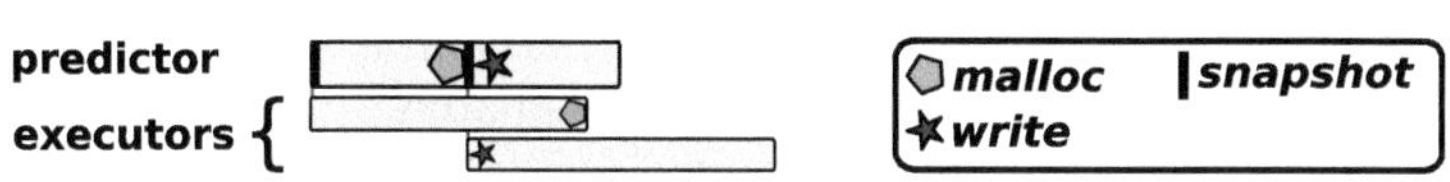

Fig. 2. The temporal order of `malloc` and the write access are different between predictor and executors. Checks use speculative variables to defer the check of the write.

The write operation `write(id, val)` stores `val` in the speculative variable addressed by `id`. A write does neither create an obligation nor does it change or delete an existing obligation with the same `id`. The latter property is important: Consider that the `write` in Fig. 2 would be followed by a `realloc` in the same epoch. Although, we know which size the buffer has after the `realloc`, we still do not know which size it had before the `realloc`. But we need this knowledge to check the validity of the preceding `write`. Thus, the obligation has to remain until it is verified using the shared view.

After the epoch e_i is completely replayed, all its obligations need to be validated. Therefore, executor E_i, checking epoch e_i, waits for E_{i-1} to finish checking e_{i-1}. After E_{i-1} finishes its checking, it updates the shared view. E_i validates all obligations of its private view against the view shared by all executors. The shared view does neither contain speculative values nor obligations. The exact semantics of the validation is provided by the checker via a callback function. The OOB checker validates that bounds stored in the obligation of a speculative variable are *within* the bounds stored in the shared view. A failed validation is treated as a failed check, i.e., the application is aborted. After the validation, E_i updates the shared view with the current values of all speculative variables.

Deadlock avoidance. Because of the use of speculative variables, we need to post-pone the commit of external actions until all obligations are validated. If a checked application in the same epoch sends out a request to a server and then waits for a reply, it could block forever. The reason is that the request is held back until all obligations are validated at the end of the epoch. Hence, it is never made visible to the server and the reply will never be sent. Therefore, we implemented a second validation scheme to overcome this problem. After executor E_{i-1} successfully finishes checking epoch e_{i-1}, E_{i-1} validates the obligations of the private view of E_i. As soon as all obligations are validated and no new obligations were created during the validation, E_i can commit all outstanding external actions and also all new external actions immediately.

5 Experience

We used the ParExC framework to create three parallelized checkers. The parallelization itself is in most parts transparent to our checkers. The major exception is the usage of speculative variables for holding the checkers book-keeping state. Furthermore, system calls which are additionally introduced in the executors have to be excluded from replay. Therefore, ParExC provides a library of commonly used functions such as allocating memory or performing IO which has to be used by the checkers for performing, e.g., logging. This library is not subject to any replay and speculation restriction. It marks the system calls such that the ParExC kernel module executes these immediately.

Data Flow Integrity. The motivation of the *data-flow integrity checker* (DFI) [2] is to protect against memory access errors. DFI checks that a read value was written from an allowed store instruction, i.e., variables are only allowed to be written at certain positions in an application. Our DFI checker conservatively extracts for each memory location m a set of stores that are permitted to write to m. All loads and stores are instrumented. At runtime, each used memory location has a speculative variable that contains a unique writer ID. Each executed store updates the corresponding writer ID. For each load, we check that the writer ID of the last writer of the read location is within the set of allowed stores. If we do not find a writer ID for the loaded memory location, the store was executed in a previous epoch. In that case, our obligation contains the set of allowed stores for this location. On obligation checking, we verify that the writer ID in the global view is indeed an element of the set of allowed stores.

AN-Encoding. Our *AN-encoding checker* (AN) detects hardware errors, which if undetected, could lead to arbitrary failures [10]. The whole encoded state is stored in speculative variables. When a variable is loaded for the first time in an epoch e_i, the executor E_i does not know its encoded value. E_i speculates by encoding the value which it got from the predictor's snapshot for this variable. The obtained value is the obligation. The global view after executing E_{i-1} contains the complete encoded state of the application at the end of e_{i-1}. The application is aborted by E_i if the value of an obligation is not equal to the encoded state in the global view at the end of e_{i-1}.

Out-Of-Bounds. Our *out-of-bounds checker* (OOB) detects buffer overflow bugs. The checker instruments all memory allocation code for the heap and the stack. In this way, it can keep track of all currently allocated buffers. Loads, stores and address computations are also instrumented. Address computation is statically identifiable in LLVM since a special instruction is used. By instrumenting these address computations, the checker can at runtime identify the buffer accessed by a load or a store. For each load and store, the used offset is checked against the allocated size of the identified buffer. If the offset is larger than the allocated size, the program is aborted. The OOB checker makes use of the fact that allocations on the stack are identifiable in the LLVM intermediate code. The size of individual allocations on the stack are not necessarily known at runtime. Thus, DBI-based checkers cannot implement precise out-of-bounds checking for buffers allocated on the stack.

We already introduced in Sec. 4 how OOB makes use of speculative variables when allocation of a buffer `buf` and access to `buf` happen in different epochs.

Transactification. To transactify the out-of-bounds checking with Tanger/TinySTM, it is sufficient to perform every access to the book-keeping state inside a transaction. The out-of-bounds checker is the only checker that has been enriched with STM-support for the following reasons: (1) The AN-checker does not yet support all features (in particular, floating point numbers) to run the STM benchmark suite STAMP [13]. Also, the micro-benchmarks we use for the AN-checker are not yet parallelized. (2) The data-flow integrity checker cannot easily be extended to support parallel accesses to its state because the assumption that for each load the last writer-id is actually the last writer-id cannot hold if more than one thread writes to the same location in memory but from different locations in the code.

6 Evaluation

Our evaluation focuses on the scalability of our checkers and the comparison between Tanger/TinySTM and ParExC. For out-of-bounds checking (OOB) and data-flow integrity checking (DFI), we used two STAMP [13] benchmarks. We performed all measurements using Fedora 8 on a 2xIntel Xeon E5430 with 2.66 GHz (8 cores) and 16 GB RAM. Every measured value is the median of 3 runs. For the comparison between ParExC and Tanger/TinySTM, every measured value represents the median over 5 runs. Like [5], we used the *real* time, reported by the `time` command to measure the runtime.

6.1 Speedup

We compared the performance of sequential and parallel checking using the checkers introduced in Sec. 5. The focus of our experiments is on scalability. We limited the number of parallel executors to simulate CPUs with fewer cores. If the maximum number of parallel executors is reached, the predictor blocks before spawning a new executor until at least one of the currently checking executors finishes. In our experiments, we measured either throughput or runtime.

Fig. 3 shows the runtime for parallel and sequential DFI checking of the Vacation and Labyrinth STAMP benchmarks. To adapt both benchmarks to ParExC we manually added 3 and 1 calls to our checkpointing function, respectively. For Vacation, we plot transactions per second and for Labyrinth the total runtime. Vacation performs 363,000 transactions per second without runtime checks. Thus, according to the measurements in Fig. 3, DFI has a slowdown of 7.26x in the sequential execution without ParExC and 1.91x with ParExC. Labyrinth runs for 56.21s without runtime checks on a 512x512 maze. The DFI slowdown without ParExC is 7.14x and 1.37x with ParExC.

For the AN checker, we used three micro-benchmarks: `md5` calculates the md5 hash of 500,000 bytes at 69.0Mbyte/s. `primes` calculates all primes up to 700,000 at 5.0 million primes/s. `PID` is a proportional, integral, derivative controller. It

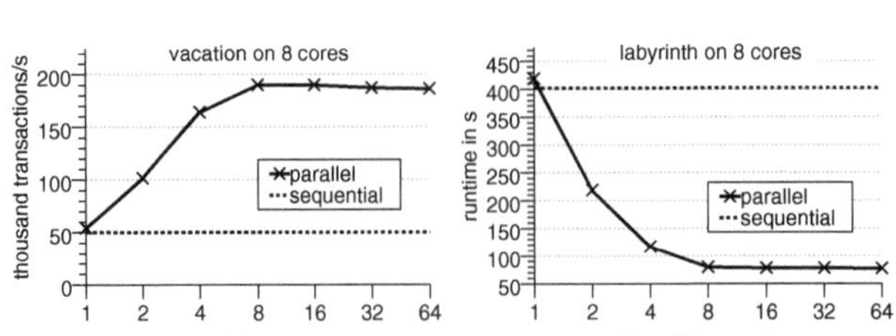

Fig. 3. Runtime of sequential vs parallel DFI checker for two STAMP benchmarks

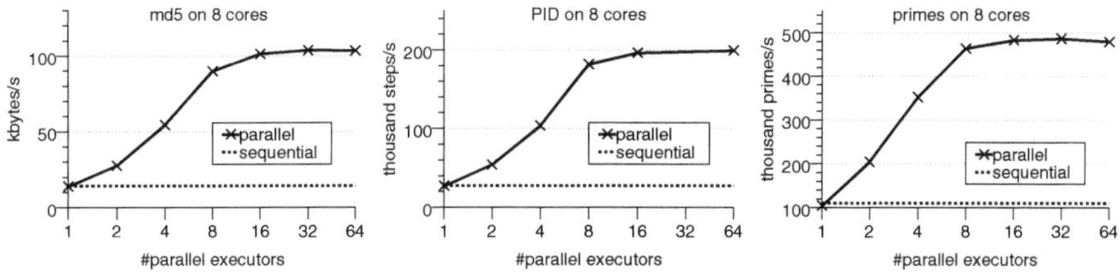

Fig. 4. Runtime of sequential vs parallel AN checker for 3 micro-benchmarks

performs 500,000 steps at 27 million steps/s. All previous numbers were measured without checking. Fig. 4 compares the runtime of sequential and parallel versions of the AN checker. The throughput scales well with the number of parallel executors. 16 parallel executors are faster than 8 on an 8 core machine because some executors need to wait for their predecessor executors to finish. During this wait time, the CPU idles when running only 8 parallel executors.

6.2 Comparison between ParExC and Tanger/TinySTM

The STAMP benchmarks are explicitly written for benchmarking STM libraries. Therefore, all shared memory accesses have been marked explicitly by experts. However, as we focus on as few manual changes as possible, Tanger ignores these markings (except the transaction boundaries) and puts all potentially shared memory accesses under the control of TinySTM. We expect different results if TinySTM would be used directly without Tanger. But this would additionally involve the manual transactification of the OOB checker, what we want to avoid. As the STM-version of Labyrinth contains some very sophisticated optimizations for the shared memory accesses, which cannot be automatically generated by Tanger, we decided to use Genome instead.

We also measured the percentage of application runtime executed sequentially, in particular the startup and the cleanup phase of both benchmarks without any instrumentation. These parts have not been parallelized by the benchmark-developers. In Vacation, only 0.16% of the execution runs sequentially. In contrast, Genome's startup phase takes very long, i.e., 14.3%. While ParExC can parallelize the checks of this phase, Tanger cannot be used for this purpose.

For both benchmarks, the measurements depicted in Fig. 5 show that the sequential overhead is higher with the Tanger instrumentation than with the ParExC instrumentation. In contrast to applications instrumented with ParExC, those instrumented with Tanger need to acquire and check locks for every memory access within transactions *and* in the OOB runtime library.

Furthermore, we can see in Fig. 5 that both benchmarks scale better when instrumented with ParExC than when instrumented with Tanger. Vacation instrumented by Tanger actually scales worse if more threads are used than cores are available. One reason could be increased contention, which would lead to higher abort rates. Another reason could be the lack of transaction scheduling

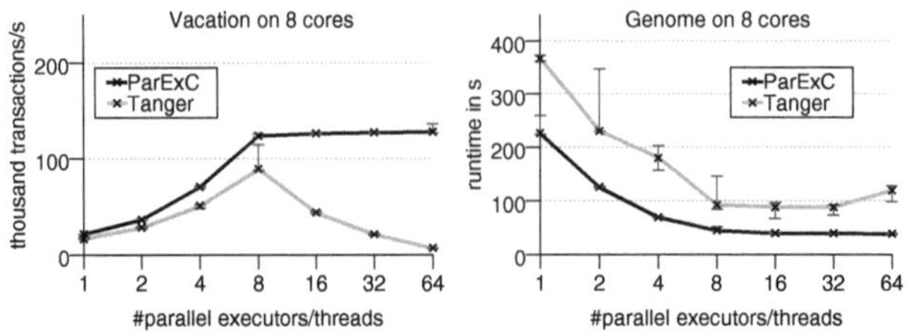

Fig. 5. Runtime of the OOB checker with ParExC and Tanger/TinySTM. The error bars show the minimum and the maximum of our measurements, respectively.

by TinySTM. Both issues do not arise using the ParExC approach. First, there is no contention between executors. Second, executors are scheduled by the OS transparently. However, more measurements are necessary to clarify this issue.

Since only the checks are parallelized, the application parallelized using the ParExC framework cannot be faster than the original application. Therefore, if the workload is easily parallelizable, and enough cores are available, the Tanger approach will eventually result in better scaling applications. On the other hand, the ParExC approach also works with applications or parts of applications that are difficult to parallelize, as long as heavy runtime checks have to be applied.

7 Related Work

Parallel checking has been introduced using dynamic binary instrumentation (DBI) [5,9,14]. The general approach is similar to ParExC: the original application (our predictor) runs on one core and is partitioned into epochs. Each epoch is deterministically replayed with runtime checks on another core. Replayed epochs run in parallel to each other. This basic approach was already presented by [15]. However, there it was used for parallelizing the application itself with modest performance gains and not for runtime checks. SuperPIN [14] does not hold back externally visible side effects. Therefore, it can only detect errors but not prevent their propagation into other components of the system. Parallel DIFT [9] uses a non-trivial hardware extension to stream data from the core running the original application to the cores used for checking. This hardware extension enables very low overheads for taint analysis checking. [9] reports slowdowns between 1.2 and 3.1. In contrast to Parallel DIFT, Speck [5] is as ParExC a software only approach. As already discussed, Speck scales well, but incurs a high overhead due to DBI and serializing checking on a single core. FastTrack [16] uses the same approach as Speck for parallelizing an out-of-bounder checker. Like ParExC, it uses static instrumentation. However, FastTrack tracks the array-bounds in the predictor. Fig. 1 shows that the predictor's runtime limits the overall speedup for all related work including ParExC. We avoid the slowdown of the predictor by using speculative variables. In contrast to Speck and ParExC, FastTrack has to wait for all outstanding executors to finish before each system call. Hence, FastTracks scalability is reduced in applications with many system calls.

ParExC uses speculation in two ways: (1) it speculates on the failure free execution of the predictor, and (2) uses speculative variables to decouple executors. Thread-level speculation tries to exploit parallelism in sequentially programmed applications. Therefore, applications are divided into parts, similar to our epochs. This requires either code analysis or hints by the programmer [17]. The obtained epochs are characterized by no or minimal data dependencies and are executed in parallel [18,19]. Our speculative variables are similar to value speculation used in thread-level speculation [18,19,20]. Transactional memory (TM) [13,8] provides atomicity for critical regions. Optimistic TM implementations speculate on low contention between concurrently executed critical regions. If a conflict between two concurrently performed critical regions is detected, at least one of the critical regions is rolled back and its changes are undone. ParExC speculates on a failure free execution. Thus, we abort the application as soon as we detect a failed speculation.

8 Conclusion

In our experience, the ParExC framework is relatively easy to use by programmers of checkers because it is mainly transparent - except for the use of speculative variables. The overhead of the ParExC instrumentation is low when compared to dynamic binary instrumentation or transactional memory. Moreover, ParExC has demonstrated that it can scale well with the number of cores for various checkers. From our evaluation, we conclude that for applications instrumented with heavy-weight runtime checks, it seems to be more promising to parallelize the runtime checks than the application itself. When the number of cores is getting larger than the slowdown introduced by the runtime checks, we expect that STM will eventually do better for parallelized applications that scale well with the number of cores.

References

1. Ruwase, O., Lam, M.S.: A practical dynamic buffer overflow detector. In: NDSS. The Internet Society (2004)
2. Castro, M., Costa, M., Harris, T.: Securing software by enforcing data-flow integrity. In: OSDI 2006: Proceedings of the 7th symposium on Operating systems design and implementation, Berkeley, CA, USA. USENIX Association (2006)
3. Borkar, S.: Designing reliable systems from unreliable components: The challenges of transistor variability and degradation. IEEE Micro. (2005)
4. Oh, N., Mitra, S., McCluskey, E.J.: ED4I: Error detection by diverse data and duplicated instructions. IEEE Trans. Comput. 51 (2002)
5. Nightingale, E.B., Peek, D., Chen, P.M., Flinn, J.: Parallelizing security checks on commodity hardware. SIGARCH Comput. Archit. News 36(1), 308–318 (2008)
6. Newsome, J., Song, D.: Dynamic taint analysis for automatic detection, analysis, and signature generation of exploits on commodity software. In: Proceedings of the Network and Distributed System Security Symposium (2005)

7. Xu, W., Bhatkar, S., Sekar, R.: Taint-enhanced policy enforcement: a practical approach to defeat a wide range of attacks. In: Proceedings of the 15th USENIX Security Symposium, Berkeley, CA, USA. USENIX Association (2006)
8. Felber, P., Fetzer, C., Riegel, T.: Dynamic performance tuning of word-based software transactional memory. In: Proceedings of the 13th ACM SIGPLAN Symposium on Principles and Practice of Parallel Programming, PPoPP (2008)
9. Ruwase, O., Gibbons, P.B., Mowry, T.C., Ramachandran, V., Chen, S., Kozuch, M., Ryan, M.: Parallelizing dynamic information flow tracking. In: Proceedings of the 20th annual symposium on Parallelism in Algorithms and Architectures (SPAA), USA. ACM Press, New York (2008)
10. Schiffel, U., Süßkraut, M., Fetzer, C.: An-encoding compiler: Building safety-critical systems with commodity hardware. In: The 28th International Conference on Computer Safety, Reliability and Security, SafeComp 2009 (2009)
11. Lattner, C., Adve, V.: LLVM: A Compilation Framework for Lifelong Program Analysis & Transformation. In: Proceedings of the 2004 International Symposium on Code Generation and Optimization (CGO 2004), California (2004)
12. Felber, P., Fetzer, C., Müller, U., Riegel, T., Süßkraut, M., Sturzrehm, H.: Transactifying applications using an open compiler framework. In: TRANSACT (2007)
13. Cao Minh, C., Chung, J., Kozyrakis, C., Olukotun, K.: Stamp: Stanford transactional applications for multi-processing. In: IISWC 2008: Proceedings of The IEEE International Symposium on Workload Characterization (September 2008)
14. Wallace, S., Hazelwood, K.: Superpin: Parallelizing dynamic instrumentation for real-time performance. In: 5th Annual International Symposium on Code Generation and Optimization, San Jose, CA, March 2007, pp. 209–217 (2007)
15. Zilles, C., Sohi, G.: Master/slave speculative parallelization. In: MICRO 35: Proceedings of the 35th annual ACM/IEEE international symposium on Microarchitecture, pp. 85–96. IEEE Computer Society Press, Los Alamitos (2002)
16. Kelsey, K., Bai, T., Ding, C., Zhang, C.: Fast track: A software system for speculative program optimization. In: CGO 2009: Proceedings of the 2009 International Symposium on Code Generation and Optimization, Washington, DC, USA, pp. 157–168. IEEE Computer Society Press, Los Alamitos (2009)
17. Olukotun, K., Hammond, L., Willey, M.: Improving the performance of speculatively parallel applications on the hydra cmp. In: ICS 1999: Proceedings of the 13th international conference on Supercomputing, USA. ACM Press, New York (1999)
18. Steffan, J.G., Colohan, C.B., Zhai, A., Mowry, T.C.: A scalable approach to thread-level speculation. SIGARCH Comput. Archit. News 28(2), 1–12 (2000)
19. Steffan, J.G., Colohan, C.B., Zhai, A., Mowry, T.C.: Improving value communication for thread-level speculation. In: HPCA 2002: Proceedings of the 8th International Symposium on High-Performance Computer Architecture, Washington, DC, USA, p. 65. IEEE Computer Society Press, Los Alamitos (2002)
20. Pickett, C.J.F., Verbrugge, C.: Return value prediction in a Java virtual machine. In: Proceedings of the Second Value-Prediction and Value-Based Optimization Workshop (VPW2), October 2004, pp. 40–47 (2004)

Optimistic Fair Exchange Using Trusted Devices

Mohammad Torabi Dashti

ETH Zürich, Switzerland

Abstract. Efficiency of optimistic fair exchange using trusted devices is studied. Pfitzmann, Schunter and Waidner (PODC 1998) have shown that four messages in the main sub-protocol is optimal when exchanging idempotent items using non-trusted devices. It is straightforward that when using trusted devices for exchanging non-idempotent items this number can be reduced to three. This however comes at the cost of providing trusted devices with an unlimited amount of storage. We prove that exchanging non-idempotent items using trusted devices with a limited storage capacity requires exactly four messages in the main sub-protocol.

1 Introduction

Fair exchange protocols (hereafter called FE) aim at exchanging items in a *fair* manner. Informally, fair means that all involved parties receive a desired item in exchange for their own, or none of them does so. Deterministic fair exchange protocols cannot be constructed with no presumed trust in the system [4]. Therefore, many FE protocols rely on impartial processes which are trusted by all the protocol participants, hence called trusted third parties (TTPs). In the *optimistic* family of FE protocols, normally the participants execute an optimistic (or, main) sub-protocol which does not involve the TTP at all. However, if a failure maliciously or accidentally occurs, the participants are provided with fallback scenarios, which enable them to recover to a fair state with the TTP's help. When failures are infrequent, optimistic protocols are preferred over those which involve the TTP in each exchange.

In this paper, we study optimistic FE between *trusted computing devices* (TDs). TDs, by construction, follow their certified software, and are guaranteed to observe the terms of use and distribution of digital contents. These devices are nowadays becoming prevalent, particularly in entertainment and multimedia industries. A very common application of TDs pertains to protecting digital contents from unauthorized access (e.g. rendering a media file) and illicit distribution.

Using TDs in optimistic FE protocols is hardly new. TDs have previously been used in order to enrich services provided by FE protocols, e.g. for exchanging time-sensitive data [23], for exchanging electronic vouchers [18], and for robust efficient multi-party computation, which is a general form of fair exchange [7]. Moreover, in [5] a class of FE protocols using TDs is developed which also tolerate accidental failures of devices. Note that TDs are not necessarily operated by

R. Guerraoui and F. Petit (Eds.): SSS 2009, LNCS 5873, pp. 711–725, 2009.

honest owners, and usually have to communicate over insecure media. Therefore, using TDs does not entirely obliterate the need for security protocols to ensure fairness in exchange. One would however expect that using TDs results in simpler, more efficient, or value-added FE protocols. Our main contribution here is a negative result concerning two-party FE between TDs: Using TDs does not increase the *efficiency* of optimistic fair exchange protocols in *common practical scenarios*. In the following, we describe what is meant by efficiency and common practical scenarios.

The premise of optimistic FE is that failures are infrequent, and consequently fallback sub-protocols are executed rarely. Therefore, a meaningful measure of efficiency in these protocols is the number of messages exchanged in the main sub-protocol. This number will serve as our measure of efficiency for FE protocols as well. As a convention we refer to n-message FE protocols, where n refers to the number of messages exchanged in their optimistic sub-protocol.

Most existing protocols for fair exchange assume that the items subject to exchange are *idempotent*, meaning that receiving (or possessing) an item once is not different from receiving it multiple times [1,15]. For instance, once Alice gets access to Bob's signature on a contract, receiving it again does not add anything to Alice's knowledge. The idempotency assumption reflects mass reproducibility of digital contents. Certain digital items are however not idempotent. Electronic vouchers [10,9] are prominent examples of non-idempotent items. Depending on the implementation, right tokens in various digital rights management schemes are as well digital non-idempotent items, e.g. see [12,20]. As mentioned above, a common approach to secure use and dissemination of non-idempotent items is to limit their distribution to TDs. We focus on practical scenarios in which fair exchange between TDs needs to ensure that non-idempotent items are not cloned arbitrarily.

Contributions. We confine to two-party exchange protocols. Pfitzmann et al. [16] have shown that four messages in the optimistic sub-protocol are sufficient and necessary for secure fair exchange of idempotent items between non-trusted devices. We show that when exchanging non-idempotent items between TDs, the number of messages in the optimistic sub-protocol can be reduced to three. This would however come at a cost which is often intolerable in practice: The TDs need to keep record of *all* their previous exchanges. If TDs are provided with limited non-volatile storage capacity (hence not being able to store fingerprints of all their previous exchanges), four messages in the main sub-protocol are proved to be necessary. In order to prove our minimality results, we give a knowledge-based model of optimistic FE protocols between TDs. Our formalization mainly follows [2]. Logics of knowledge have proved to be a useful tool in deriving communication lower bounds in various distributed systems, cf. [6].

Related work. In this paper, we investigate to which extent using trusted computing devices can increase the efficiency of optimistic FE protocols. The only papers on the optimal efficiency of FE protocols, to our knowledge, are [16] for two-party protocols, and [13] for protocols with more than two participants. The bounds derived in these work are relevant for non-trusted participants, and their focus is on exchanging idempotent digital signatures over contracts.

Road map. Section 2 gives an informal introduction to optimistic FE protocols, idempotent and non-idempotent items, TTP logic, etc. In section 3 we develop a knowledge-based model for optimistic FE protocols using TDs. The main result of this section is to formally determine the *resolve pattern* of three-message optimistic FE protocols, by proving that a TD p can successfully complete an exchange only if p *knows* that his opponent q can also successfully complete the exchange. Intuitively, a resolve pattern describes alternatives available to protocol participants in case they are waiting for a message from their opponent and the message does not arrive in time, or received messages at that point do not conform with the protocol. Section 4 concerns FE of non-idempotent items between TDs with limited storage capacity. We give a four message protocol which satisfies the desired security requirements. To prove that four messages in the optimistic sub-protocol are necessary, we build upon the result of section 3 and give a generic replay attack on all the three-message protocols between TDs with limited storage which aim at exchanging non-idempotent items. We also show that the mentioned replay attack can be countered if TDs possess an unlimited storage capacity, by presenting a 3-message protocol for this case. Section 5 concludes the paper. Proofs omitted in the text due to space constraints can be found in [19].

2 An Informal Introduction to Optimistic FE

Non-idempotent items. We consider *electronic vouchers* as a generic model for non-idempotent items. An electronic voucher, according to RFC 3506, is "a digital representation of the right to claim goods or services" [9]. A voucher v is a tuple $v = (\langle I, P \rangle, H)$, where I is the voucher's issuer, who guarantees the contents of the voucher, H is the voucher's owner, and P is I's promise to the owner of the voucher (i.e. H). Voucher forgery and alteration are assumed infeasible: No one, except I, can create $\langle I, P \rangle$, and once it is created, no one can alter P. This can be realized, e.g., using secure digital signature schemes. Duplicating vouchers is nonetheless possible, and has to be prevented.

Two voucher duplication scenarios are conceivable: (1) local duplication, where H, the owner of $\langle I, P \rangle$, duplicates the voucher for its own (excessive) use, and (2) remote duplication, where H', a device different from H, gets a copy of $\langle I, P \rangle$ and stores it for its own use, without H destroying its copy of the voucher. Using TDs to store and spend vouchers can prevent local duplications. Security protocols designed for distribution, exchange and use of vouchers are in charge of preventing remote duplications, by ensuring that H destroys $(\langle I, P \rangle, H)$ before H' stores the voucher.

Trusted computing devices. Trusted devices are tamper-proof hardware that, though possibly operated by malicious owners, follow only their embedded sealed software. Trusted devices typically contain a secure scratch memory and (a limited amount of) non-volatile storage capacity. Device X maintains a multiset of vouchers V_X. Before adding the voucher $v = (\langle I, P \rangle, Y)$ to V_X, the device transforms v to $(\langle I, P \rangle, X)$.

The owner of a TD can deliberately turn the device off, or permanently destroy it. We assume that TDs are stateful: If a TD is abruptly turned off, it would resume its previous state when turned on later. This can be realized using various logging systems. For TDs, thus, we assume the crash-recovery failure model with no amnesia, e.g. see [11]. For the moment, we ignore the possibility that the owner delays, blocks or tampers with the messages destined to the device, or transmitted by the device. These issues are discussed within the system and communication model below.

The TTP is a trusted device, which is immune to failures, and has access to an unlimited secure persistent database. It is assumed that the identity of the TTP is a common knowledge in the system.

A computing device which is not trusted, called *non-trusted*, can be faulty. In this case, it would follow the Byzantine failure model.

System and communication model. We assume a fully connected asynchronous message passing network which connects all TDs; computations are asynchronous, and communication delays, although being finite, are not bounded. The communication channels between any two device X and Y are assumed to be *reliable*, meaning:

- (resilience) No messages are lost in transition.
- (authenticity) A message delivered at Y, has been previously sent by X.
- (confidentiality) Messages sent from X to Y are readable only to Y.

We remark that over reliable channels messages *can* be delayed, reordered or replayed. These operations are usually attributed to an omnipresent *adversary* in the system.

Authenticity and confidentiality can be guaranteed using standard secure encryption and digital signature schemes, assuming a deployed secure public key infrastructure. Below, we discuss the prerequisites and implications of the resilience condition.

Assuming resilient channels, as observed in [1], is unavoidable, in order to guarantee termination of FE protocols (cf. Gray's generals paradox). In practice, if two principals fail to properly establish a channel over computer networks, they can ultimately resort to other communication means, such as various postal services. These services, although being much slower, are very reliable and well protected by law.

The resilience assumption may however seem to be unrealistic when TDs are operated by malicious owners, who may block messages destined to the devices. Below, we argue that such communication failures are subsumed in our device failure model and communication model. Assume that X is a TD which expects to receive a message. Device X either (1) has alternative actions to take if the message does not arrive in time, or (2) no such option is available. The effect of blocking the message in case (1) is the same as delaying the message in the communication network, which is allowed in our model. As a convention, when a message is delayed long enough so that the intended recipient device takes an alternative action, we say that the message has been *intercepted*. In case (2), however, the device would not take any steps unless it receives that very message. Preventing the message to ever arrive, thus, corresponds to turning the device off; this is indeed allowed in our device failure model (see above).

Optimistic fair exchange. Below, we briefly introduce optimistic FE. For an extensive exposition of FE in general see [1]. In the following, we opt for a high level description that underlines the exchange patterns, and for the moment we do not focus on exchanges between TDs. Exact message contents are abstracted away, and all messages are assumed to contain enough information for protocol participants to distinguish different protocol instantiations, and different roles in protocols. Detailed specification of these issues is orthogonal to our current purpose.

Optimistic protocols typically consist of three sub-protocols: *main* or *optimistic* sub-protocol, *abort* sub-protocol and *recovery* sub-protocol. Figure 1 depicts a generic main sub-protocol between A and B. The regions in which the other two sub-protocols are alternative possibilities are numbered (1–4) in the figure. In the main sub-protocol, that does not involve the TTP, the agents first *commit* to release their items and then they actually release them. The items subject to exchange, and commitments are respectively denoted by i_A, i_B and $c_A(i_A), c_B(i_B)$. In figure 1 we have $m_1 = c_A(i_A)$, $m_2 = c_B(i_B)$, $m_3 = i_A$ and $m_4 = i_B$. If no failures occur, the participants exchange their items successfully using the main sub-protocol.

If an expected message does not arrive in time, or the arrived message does not conform to the protocol, then the participant expecting that massage can resort to the TTP using abort or recovery sub-protocols. Here we introduce the notion of *resolve patterns*. This notion helps us in reasoning about optimistic FE protocols. Consider again the generic four message protocol shown in figure 1. A resolve pattern characterizes the alternative sub-protocols which are available to participants when they are waiting for a message from their opponent in the main sub-protocol; namely, the alternative sub-protocols envisaged for points 1, 2, 3 and 4 in figure 1.

Four different symbols can be assigned to a point in the resolve pattern: *abort* (a), *recovery* (r), *quit* (q), and *none* ($-$). Intuitively, a (r) means that the device can initiate an abort (resolve) sub-protocol, and q means that in case the expected message does not arrive in time, the participant can safely quit the exchange. Naturally, if no message has been exchanged, the participant quits the protocol, e.g. B is figure 1 quits the exchange, if it does not receive the first message in time. A 'none' option ($-$) indicates that the participant has no alternatives but following the optimistic protocol. It will be proved later (in theorem 3) that 'none' options undermine termination of optimistic FE protocol. This is intuitively because TDs may crash and never send the message their opponent is waiting for. When communicating with the TTP (using resolve sub-protocols), however, TDs know that

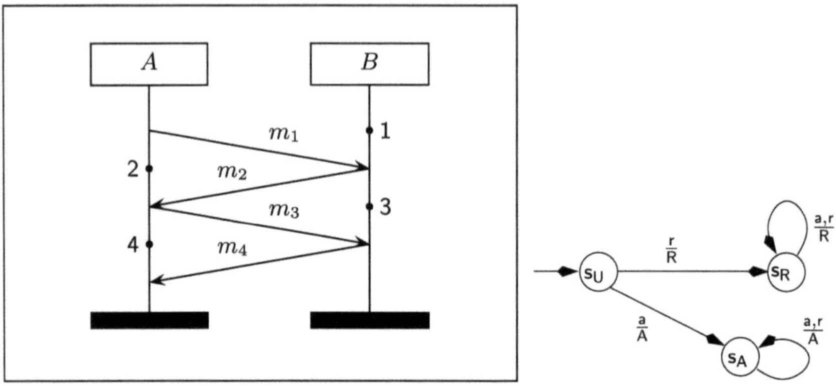

Fig. 1. Generic four message protocol (left); Abstract Mealy machine of TTP (right)

the message they send to and expect to receive from the TTP will be delivered in a finite time. This is due to resilience of the channels, and the fact that the TTP is immune to failures (see TTP assumptions, above). We use tuples for representing resolve patterns. For instance, a resolve pattern for the protocol of figure 1 can be $\pi = (\mathsf{q}, \mathsf{a}, \mathsf{r}, \mathsf{r})$; then we write $\pi_1 = \mathsf{q}$, $\pi_2 = \mathsf{a}$, etc.

The resolve sub-protocols (abort/recovery) involve the TTP. Without loss of generality we assume that the participant sends its message history (all messages sent and received up to now by the participant in the current execution of the protocol) to the TTP, and based on these the TTP either returns an *abort token* A, or a *recovery token* R. Token A often has no intrinsic value; it merely indicates that the TTP will never send an R token in the context of the current exchange. Token R should however help a participant to recover to a fair state. Although it is impossible for B alone to derive i_A from $c_A(i_A)$ (and vice versa), it is often assumed that the TTP can generate i_A from $c_A(i_A)$, and i_B from $c_B(i_B)$, and that R contains i_A and i_B. In case the TTP cannot do so, usually an affidavit from the TTP is deemed adequate, cf. *weak fairness* [15].

The TTP logic matching the resolve pattern $(\mathsf{q}, \mathsf{a}, \mathsf{r}, \mathsf{r})$ for the protocol of figure 1 is also shown in figure 1. For each exchanged item, the finite state (Mealy) machine of the TTP is initially in the *undisputed* state $\mathsf{s_U}$. If the TTP receives a valid abort request (from A) while being at state $\mathsf{s_U}$, then it sends back an abort token, and moves to *aborted* state $\mathsf{s_A}$. Similarly, if the TTP is in state $\mathsf{s_U}$, and receives a valid resolve request (from either A or B), then it sends back R, containing i_A and i_B, and moves to *recovered* state $\mathsf{s_R}$. When the TTP is in either of $\mathsf{s_A}$ or $\mathsf{s_R}$ states, no matter it receives an abort or a recovery request on this exchange, it consistently replies with A or R, respectively.

Security requirements. A process is *correct* if it does not deviate from the terms of the protocol; otherwise it is *faulty*. In particular, a TD is correct if it does not crash. Due to our assumptions, TTP is always correct. A fair exchange protocol is *secure* iff it satisfies the following conditions in presence of any number of faulty processes [1]:[1]

- Timeliness: Any correct process can terminate the protocol in a finite amount of time, with no help from its opponent.
- Fairness: When the exchange terminates, if A owns i_B (or R) and B does not own i_A, then we say the protocol is *unfair* for B. A protocol is *fair* iff it is not unfair for any correct process.
- Functionality: If A and B are correct, and communication delays are negligible, then the A gets i_B and B gets i_A, with no contact to the TTP.

Furthermore, any secure protocol for exchanging non-idempotent items (between TDs) has to guarantee the following requirement [9]:

- No-duplication: The total number of instances of any non-idempotent item v is never increased in the system (i.e. in the V_X sets collectively maintained by TDs).

The scenario in which issuer I injects new vouchers to the system is here considered to occur out-of-band. We remark that assigning unique (serial) numbers to non-idempotent items does not in general address the problem of ensuring no-duplication.

We recall the following theorem from [16].

Theorem 1. *Four messages in the main sub-protocol is sufficient and necessary for secure fair exchange of idempotent items, using non-trusted computing devices.*

Remark 1. The four-message FE protocol that is given in [16] as a witness has the resolve pattern $\pi^{in} = (\mathsf{q}, \mathsf{a}, \mathsf{r}, \mathsf{r})$. It can easily be verified that π^{in} is the *only* resolve pattern suitable for secure fair exchange of idempotent items using non-trusted devices.

3 A Formal Model for Optimistic FE Using TDs

We introduce a minimal formal system for reasoning about FE protocols. The formalization mostly follows the knowledge-based approach of [2], see also [6].

A formal model for protocols. For finite set Σ we write Σ^* for the set of all finite sequences of elements of Σ, containing the empty sequence ϵ. Concatenation of sequences x and y is denoted xy. For two sequences $x, y \in \Sigma^*$, we write $x \leq y$ iff x is a prefix of y, i.e. $\exists z \in \Sigma^*.\ xz = y$; we write $y - x$ for z. We write $x < y$ if $x \leq y$ and $x \neq y$. The *prefix closure* of set $Y \subseteq \Sigma^*$ is defined as $\underline{Y} = \{x \in \Sigma^* \mid \exists y \in Y.\ x \leq y\}$. Set Y is *prefix closed* iff $\underline{Y} = Y$.

[1] Fairness is a safety trace property, timeliness is a liveness trace property, while functionality is not a trace property: It concerns existence of particular traces in the system.

We define the set of actions as $Act = S \cup \bar{S} \cup I$, where S, $\bar{S}$ and I are pairwise disjoint, and respectively contain the set of send, receive and internal actions. We assume there is a bijective function $\bar{\cdot} : S \to \bar{S}$ such that $\forall s \in S.\ \bar{a} \in \bar{S}$. Intuitively, $a \in S$ denotes the event of sending a message, and $\bar{a} \in \bar{S}$ stands for the corresponding receive event.

A *process* is a prefix closed subset of Act^*. A *protocol* $\mathcal{P}$ is a finite number of processes. We assume the set of actions appearing in different processes are disjoint. This makes it possible to associate a unique process to each action. Let $x \in Act^*$, and write x_p for the sequence of actions that results from x after erasing all the actions *not* performed by process p. We say x is a *computation* of protocol $\mathcal{P}$ iff (1) for all $p \in \mathcal{P}$, x_p belongs to process p, and (2) any $\bar{a} \in \bar{S}$ which appear in x is preceded by a in x. It follows that computations of protocols are prefix closed. That is, any protocol can be seen as a process in itself. We write $a \in x$, with $a \in Act, x \in Act^*$, if a appears in x.

Let us fix a finite nonempty set of propositions Φ, and an *interpretation* function $\mathcal{I} : Act^* \to \Phi \to \{\mathsf{tt}, \mathsf{ff}\}$ which assigns truth values to the elements of Φ, given a computation. We augment the set of propositions with the standard negation and disjunction operators, and also a knowledge-based operator $\mathcal{E}$, in order to define the syntax of our knowledge-based logic *EL*: (1) Every element of Φ is an *EL* formula; (2) If e is an *EL* formula and p a process, then $\mathcal{E}_p(e)$ is an *EL* formula; (3) If e and e' are *EL* formulas, then so are $\neg e$ and $e \vee e'$. Read $\mathcal{E}_p(e)$ as "p knows e".

In the following we introduce the notion of *isomorphism*: Two computation x and y are isomorphic w.r.t. process p iff $x_p = y_p$. Clearly the isomorphism relation is an equivalence relation on the set of all computations. Isomorphism is the core of *EL*'s semantics: Processes have only local views, and cannot therefore distinguish computations which are isomorphic in their view [2]. Models of *EL* formulas are computations. For computation x and *EL* formula e, the relation $x \models e$ is inductively defined as:

- $x \models e$ with $e \in \Phi$ iff $\mathcal{I}(x)e = \mathsf{tt}$.
- $x \models \mathcal{E}_p(e)$ iff $y \models e$ for all computations y that are isomorphic to x w.r.t. p.
- $x \models \neg e$ iff $\neg(x \models e)$.
- $x \models e \vee e'$ iff $x \models e$ or $x \models e'$.

A formal model for fair exchange protocols using TDs. Below, TDs are referred to as processes. We assume that any process p which finishes the optimistic subprotocol successfully executes an internal action $\top(p)$ and terminates: (Recall that the set of computations of p is prefix closed.)

$$\forall x \in p.\ \top(p) \in x \implies \neg \exists y \in p.\ x < y$$

Since communications with the TTP are over reliable channels, and the TTP is indeed always correct, we choose to model these communications as internal actions for processes. We write $\mathsf{R}(p)$ and $\mathsf{A}(p)$, with $p \in \mathcal{P}$, for receiving the recovery and abort tokens by p. Notation $\mathsf{Q}(p)$ denotes p quiting the exchange. Immediately after executing any of these actions, the process terminates:

$$\forall x \in p.\ \mathsf{A}(p) \in x \vee \mathsf{R}(p) \in x \vee \mathsf{Q}(p) \in x \implies \neg\exists y \in p.\ x < y$$

This condition in particular implies that only one of $\mathsf{A}(p)$, $\mathsf{R}(p)$ or $\mathsf{Q}(p)$ can appear in any execution x.

When a process p crashes it simply executes $\bot(p)$ and terminates:

$$\forall x \in p.\ \bot(p) \in x \implies \neg\exists y \in p.\ x < y$$

Since any process p (except TTP) may crash at any moment (before terminating) we assume:

$$\forall x \in p.\ \top(p) \notin x \wedge \bot(p) \notin x \wedge \mathsf{A}(p) \notin x \wedge \mathsf{R}(p) \notin x \wedge \mathsf{Q}(p) \notin x \implies x\bot(p) \in p$$

The consistent behavior of the TTP is captured via considering only *TTP-consistent* computations, as defined below. Computation x of an FE protocol is TTP-consistent iff

– If $\mathsf{R}(p)$ appears in x for process p, then $\mathsf{A}(q)$ does not appear in x for any $q \in \mathcal{P}$.

We also need to assert that if a correct process has the choice to, e.g., contact the TTP in computations x, then the computations x also allows (or, covers) this possibility. That is, we confine only to *maximal* computations. For a computation of protocol $\mathcal{P}$ like x, we say x is maximal iff

– For any $p \in \mathcal{P}$, for all $y \in p$ such that $x_p < y$ and $\bot(p) \notin y - x_p$, we have $x(y - x_p)$ is not a computation in $\mathcal{P}$.

This constraint, intuitively, implies that computation x is considered maximal only if no process p can progress further in computation x except by crashing. Note that since processes are prefix closed, if p can progress further than x_p, then there exists a $y \in p$ such that $y - x_p$ contains only one action.

TTP-consistence and maximality can be seen as *fairness constraints* on protocol computations, cf. [8]. From this point on, by a computation we mean a TTP-consistent and maximal computation, unless otherwise stated.

Fair exchange security requirements. A protocol $\mathcal{P}$ is a secure fair exchange protocol iff it satisfies the following properties. Here, $x : \mathcal{P}$ stands for "computation x belongs to protocol $\mathcal{P}$".

– Functionality:

$$\exists x : Prot. \forall p \in \mathcal{P}.\ \top(p) \in x$$

– Timeliness:

$$\forall x : \mathcal{P}. \forall p \in \mathcal{P}.\ \mathsf{Q}(p) \in x \vee \mathsf{A}(p) \in x \vee \mathsf{R}(p) \in x \vee \top(p) \in x \vee \bot(p) \in x$$

– Fairness:

$$\forall x : \mathcal{P}. \forall p, q \in \mathcal{P}.\ (\mathsf{R}(p) \in x \vee \top(p) \in x) \implies (\mathsf{R}(q) \in x \vee \top(q) \in x \vee \bot(q) \in x)$$

The following theorem is the main technical result of our formalization that relates fairness to knowledge. For a computation x and $p \in \mathcal{P}$, we write $\mathcal{I}(x)\mathbb{G}(p) = $ tt iff $\top(p) \in x \vee \mathsf{R}(p) \in x$.

Theorem 2. *For any computation x in a protocol between p and q that satisfies fairness, $x \models \mathbb{G}(p)$ only if $x \models \mathcal{E}_p(\mathbb{G}(q) \vee \bot(q))$.*

Proof. Let $x \models \mathbb{G}(p)$, and assume y is any computation in the protocol such that $x_p = y_p$. We need to show that $y \models \mathbb{G}(q) \vee \bot(q)$. From $x_p = y_p$ we conclude $y \models \mathbb{G}(p)$. As the protocol satisfies fairness we get $y \models \mathbb{G}(q) \vee \bot(q)$. □

Intuitively, the theorem states that p can add an item i_q to V_p iff p *knows* that a correct q would add i_q to V_q.

3.1 Three-Message Protocols for FE Using TDs

In this section we determine the resolve pattern of any three-message FE protocol that satisfies functionality, timeliness and fairness. Figure 2 shows a generic three message protocol. Our focus in this section is on *optimistic non-redundant* protocols, as defined below. A protocol is optimistic iff it satisfies functionality and $\pi_1 \notin \{\mathsf{r}, \mathsf{a}\}$. The intuition behind this definition is that by functionality the protocol has at least one successful computation without contacting the TTP, and the condition $\pi_1 \notin \{\mathsf{r}, \mathsf{a}\}$ implies that in case the receiver of the first message, say Bob, in the protocol does not receive this message he can either wait, or quite the exchange, but may not contact the TTP. In other words, if no messages are exchanged in Bob's view, then he does not contact the TTP.

An optimistic protocol with ℓ messages is non-redundant iff the protocol has no computation of length less that $2\ell + 2$ which contains both $\top(p)$ and $\top(q)$. Here, 2ℓ counts all the m_i and $\bar{m}_i$ for $1 \leq i \leq \ell$, and then two actions $\top(p)$ and $\top(q)$ are added to the result. Intuitively, this implies that all the messages of the protocol are required to be exchanged in order to successfully complete the protocol, with no TTP interventions.

Below, in order to capture the intuitive meaning of resolve patterns we require that given resolve pattern $\pi = (\pi_1, \pi_2, \pi_3)$ and any computation x in which only, say p, contacts the TTP at a point corresponding to π_i, the TTP answer with R if $\pi_i = \mathsf{r}$ and the TTP will answers with A if $\pi_i = \mathsf{a}$. This is in accordance with the description of TTP logic in section 2. The proof of the following theorem relies on theorem 2, and can be found in [19].

Theorem 3. *The resolve pattern of any three-message optimistic FE protocol between p and q that satisfies fairness, timeliness and functionality, is necessarily* $\pi = (\mathsf{q}, \mathsf{a}, \mathsf{r})$.

The resolve pattern determined in theorem 3 is a necessary, but not generally sufficient, condition for satisfying fairness, timeliness and functionality. If processes are not trusted, there is no 3-message protocol for secure FE, see theorem 1.

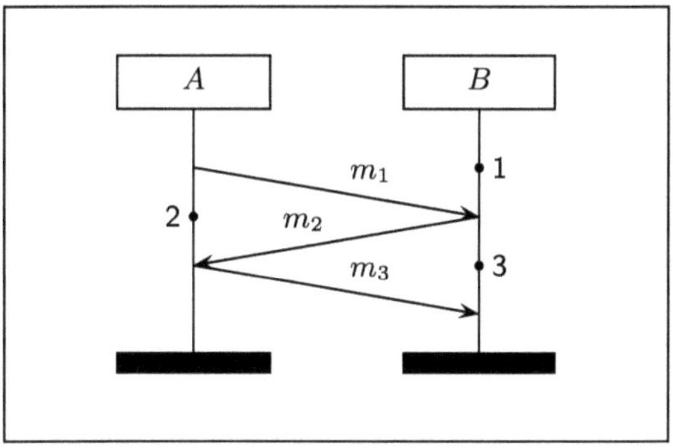

Fig. 2. Generic three message protocol

4 Optimistic FE of Non-idempotent Items between TDs

Below, we focus on exchanging non-idempotent items between TDs. In section 4.1 we give a four-message FE protocol for exchanging non-idempotent items between TDs with limited storage capacity. It is worth mentioning that the resolve pattern of the protocol of section 4.1 is different from π^{in} (see remark 1); using π^{in} would require TDs with unlimited storage capacity. In section 4.2 we show that four messages in the optimistic sub-protocol are necessary by giving a generic replay attack on any three-message FE protocol between TDs with limited storage capacity. Protocols with one or two messages in the optimistic sub-protocol are not discussed, due to their trivial inadequacy. In section 4.3 we give a three-message FE protocol for exchanging non-idempotent items between TDs with unlimited storage capacity.

4.1 A Four-Message FE Protocol between TDs with Limited Storage

It can be easily verified that the resolve pattern π^{in} is not suitable for exchanging non-idempotent items. Namely, there exists a generic replay attack on protocols with resolve pattern π^{in} which can be countered only if the TDs have access to an unlimited amount of secure storage. The attack is due to the no-duplication requirement. The proof of the following proposition is given in [19].

Proposition 1. *The resolve pattern* $\pi^{in} = (\mathsf{q}, \mathsf{a}, \mathsf{r}, \mathsf{r})$ *is not secure for fair exchange of non-idempotent items, using TDs with limited storage capacity.*

Next, we present a protocol with resolve pattern $(\mathsf{q}, \mathsf{q}, \mathsf{a}, \mathsf{r})$ for exchanging non-idempotent items using trusted devices with limited storage capacity. This protocol is inspired by a protocol of Terada et al. [18].

In order to give a detailed description of the protocol, we relax the integrity, authenticity and confidentiality assumptions on communication channels (cf. section 2) for proving theorem 4, and also theorem 6. Below, $[M]_X$ denotes message M signed by participant X; and M can be extracted from $[M]_X$. We write $h(M)$ for the hash value of M, where h is a one-way secure hash function. A secure PKI infrastructure is also assumed to be in place. The cryptographic apparatus are assumed to be *ideal*, as in Dolev and Yao [3].

Theorem 4. *Resolve pattern* $\pi = (\mathsf{q}, \mathsf{q}, \mathsf{a}, \mathsf{r})$ *can be used for secure fair exchange of non-idempotent items, using TDs with limited storage capacity.*

Proof. Consider an instantiation of the 4-message protocol and the TTP logic of figure 1, with resolve pattern π. Initially $v \in V_A$, $v' \in V_B$, and A and B want to exchange v for v'. We assume that

1. A temporarily removes v from V_A when starting the exchange. If A receives token A, it puts v back into V_A. Upon a successful exchange with B, or receiving token R, A adds v' to V_A and destroys v. A similar assumption is made for B.
2. A and B are programmed such that once they start the resolve sub-protocols, they will ignore all the messages from the main sub-protocol.

These assumptions are tenable, since A and B are trusted devices. The specifications for initiator A and responder B are given in table 1. We assume that confidentiality of the vouchers v and v' is not a concern (otherwise, communications between A, B and the TTP have to be encrypted in the following). The message contents for the protocol (referred to in table 1) are described below. We recall that messages are communicated over resilient channels, and A and B are TDs.

- $m_1 := [v, v', B, n]_A$, where n is a fresh nonce generated by A.
- $m_2 := [h(v, v', A, B, n), h(n')]_B$, where n' is a fresh nonce generated by B.

Table 1. Specification of processes in theorem 4

Specification of initiator A	**Specification of responder** B
$V_A := V_A \setminus \{v\}$	recv m_1 from A
send m_1 to B	IF recv times out THEN quit
recv m_2 from B	$V_B := V_B \setminus \{v'\}$
IF recv times out THEN quit	send m_2 to A
send m_3 to B	recv m_3 from A
recv m_4 from B	IF recv times out THEN
IF recv times out THEN	send abort request a to TTP
send recovery request r to TTP	IF recv abort token A from TTP THEN
IF recv abort token A from TTP THEN	$V_B := V_B \cup \{v'\}$
$V_A := V_A \cup \{v\}$	ELSE IF recv recovery token R
ELSE IF recv recovery token R	from TTP THEN
from TTP THEN	$V_B := V_B \cup \{v\}$
$V_A := V_A \cup \{v'\}$	ELSE
ELSE	send m_4 to A
$V_A := V_A \cup \{v'\}$	$V_B := V_B \cup \{v\}$

- $m_3 := [h(n')]_A$
- $m_4 := n'$

We assume upon receiving a message, the TDs check the integrity of the message, and its conformance to the protocol. A bogus message is destroyed, and considered as not having been received. For contacting the TTP, the following messages are used:

- $\mathsf{a} := [f_1, A, B, v, v', n, h(n')]_B$
- $\mathsf{r} := [f_2, A, B, v, v', n, h(n')]_A$
- $\mathsf{A} := [ack(f_1), A, B, v, v', n, h(n')]_{TTP}$
- $\mathsf{R} := [ack(f_2), A, B, v, v', n, h(n')]_{TTP}$

Here f_1, f_2 and $ack(f_1)$ and $ack(f_2)$ are unique flags respectively denoting an abort request, a resolve request, an abort token, and a recovery token. Notice that in this protocol, the TTP can readily extract v and v' from m_1 and m_2. In fact, to recover to a fair state, the participants do not require the contents of their opponent's item, but rather the permission to add the item to their local voucher set. A complete security analysis of the protocol is omitted due to space constraints. We however note that assumption (1) in the beginning of this proof, and fairness imply that during exchanges no items are duplicated. A subtlety here is to ensure that replay attacks are not possible. Note that abort option for B (that is $\pi_3 = \mathsf{a}$) thwarts the replay attack described in proposition 1. □

4.2 Four Messages Are Necessary for FE between TDs with Limited Storage

Theorem 3 maps out the resolve pattern of any three-message FE protocol that satisfies fairness, timeliness and functionality; namely, $\pi = (\mathsf{q}, \mathsf{a}, \mathsf{r})$. Below, we use this result to show that any three-message protocol that is used for exchanging non-idempotent items between TDs with limited storage capacity is susceptible to a generic replay attack.

Theorem 5. *There is no three-message protocol for secure exchange of non-idempotent items between TDs with limited storage capacity.*

Proof. Assume there exists a three-message FE protocol for secure exchange of non-idempotent items. The resolve pattern of the protocol needs to be $(\mathsf{q}, \mathsf{a}, \mathsf{r})$, due to theorem 3. Now, assume the protocol is repeatedly executed between processes p and q. Let computation x be one of these computations which has completed successfully without resorting to the TTP. Such a computation exists due to the functionality property. Let

$$x = m_1\bar{m}_1 m_2\bar{m}_2 m_3\bar{m}_3 \top(p)\top(q)$$

Since the processes have limited storage capacity, there exists a point in time θ, when all the information about computation x is erased from the storage of p and q. Note that at time θ, the adversary can replay m_1. Now the computation $y = m_1\bar{m}_1 m_2 \mathsf{R}(q)$ is a valid computation: It is maximal, and indeed

TTP-consistent. Note that p has no actions to perform in this computation, and is in fact not even "aware" that the exchange is happening. Clearly y violates the no-duplication property of non-idempotent items. It is worth mentioning that fairness is not violated in computation y. □

Remark that simply assigning sequence numbers to different transactions between TDs A and B *does* prevent the replay attack described in theorem 5. However, such sequence numbers must be of an unbounded length, in order to prevent repetition. That is, TDs require an unbounded storage capacity to store the sequence numbers in general.

4.3 Three-Message FE Protocols between TDs with Unlimited Storage

For exchanging non-idempotent items between TDs with unlimited storage capacity one can use a three-message FE protocol with resolve pattern $(\mathsf{q},\mathsf{a},\mathsf{r})$. The main idea of the protocol is that TDs can use their unlimited storage to counter the replay attack described in theorem 5. The proof of the following theorem is similar to theorem 4, and can be found in [19].

Theorem 6. *Resolve pattern* $\pi = (\mathsf{q},\mathsf{a},\mathsf{r})$ *can be used for secure fair exchange of non-idempotent items, using TDs with unlimited storage capacity.*

Remark 2. Micali has proposed [14] a three-message protocol for fair exchange of idempotent items between non-trusted devices, which has the resolve pattern $(\mathsf{q},-,\mathsf{r})$. That is, A cannot run the abort sub-protocol (A's access to abort jeopardizes fairness if A is non-trusted). As A is not provided with any means to contact the TTP in Micali's protocol, in case A does not receive m_2, timeliness is violated (as observed in [1]), since A can terminate the protocol only when B takes actions. The resolve pattern $(\mathsf{q},\mathsf{a},\mathsf{r})$ of theorem 6 has also been used in [17] and [22] for secure fair exchange of the so-called *revocable* digital contents; intuitively the TTP's testimony is necessary for the validity of (some of) the exchanged items in these protocols.

5 Concluding Remarks

We analyze the efficiency of optimistic protocols for fair exchange of non-idempotent items using trusted devices. Four messages in the main sub-protocol is proved to be necessary, given that the trusted devices have access to a limited amount of storage. With an unlimited non-volatile storage, this number can however be reduced to three.

It must be interesting to explore the efficiency of FE protocols which guarantee *atomicity* for non-idempotent items, that is no-duplication and also no-destruction. Atomicity is a typical requirement for financial transactions [21].

References

1. Asokan, N.: Fairness in electronic commerce. PhD thesis, Uni. Waterloo (1998)
2. Chandy, K., Misra, J.: How processes learn. Distrib. Comput. 1(1), 40–52 (1986)

3. Dolev, D., Yao, A.C.: On the security of public key protocols. IEEE Trans. on Information Theory IT-29(2), 198–208 (1983)
4. Even, S., Yacobi, Y.: Relations among public key signature systems. Technical Report 175, Computer Science Dept., Technion, Haifa, Isreal (March 1980)
5. Ezhilchelvan, P.D., Shrivastava, S.K.: A family of trusted third party based fair-exchange protocols. IEEE Trans. Dependable Secur. Comput. 2(4), 273–286 (2005)
6. Fagin, R., Halpern, J., Moses, Y., Vardi, M.: Reasoning About Knowledge. MIT, Cambridge (2003)
7. Fort, M., Freiling, F., Draque Penso, L., Benenson, Z., Kesdogan, D.: TrustedPals: Secure multiparty computation implemented with smart cards. In: Gollmann, D., Meier, J., Sabelfeld, A. (eds.) ESORICS 2006. LNCS, vol. 4189, pp. 34–48. Springer, Heidelberg (2006)
8. Francez, N.: Fairness. Springer, Heidelberg (1986)
9. Fujimura, K., Eastlake, D.: Requirements and Design for Voucher Trading System (VTS). RFC 3506 (March 2003)
10. Fujimura, K., Kuno, H., Terada, M., Matsuyama, K., Mizuno, Y., Sekine, J.: Digital-ticket-controlled digital ticket circulation. In: USENIX Security 1999, pp. 229–240 (1999)
11. Guerraoui, R., Rodrigues, L.: Introduction to Reliable Distributed Programming. Springer, Heidelberg (2006)
12. Kuntze, N., Schmidt, A.: Trusted ticket systems and applications. In: IFIP SEC 2007. IFIP, vol. 232, pp. 49–60. Springer, Heidelberg (2007)
13. Mauw, S., Radomirovic, S., Torabi Dashti, M.: Minimal message complexity of asynchronous multi-party contract signing. In: CSF 2009, pp. 13–25. IEEE CS, Los Alamitos (2009)
14. Micali, S.: Simple and fast optimistic protocols for fair electronic exchange. In: PODC 2003, pp. 12–19. ACM Press, New York (2003)
15. Pagnia, H., Vogt, H., Gärtner, F.C.: Fair exchange. Computer Journal 46(1), 55–67 (2003)
16. Pfitzmann, B., Schunter, M., Waidner, M.: Optimal efficiency of optimistic contract signing. In: PODC 1998, pp. 113–122. ACM Press, New York (1998)
17. Schunter, M.: Optimistic fair exchange. PhD thesis, Universität des Saarlandes (2000)
18. Terada, M., Mori, K., Ishii, K., Hongo, S., Usaka, T., Koshizuka, N., Sakamura, K.: A framework for distributed inter-smartcard communication. IPSJ Digital Courier 2, 120–132 (2006)
19. Torabi Dashti, M.: Optimistic fair exchange using trusted devices. Technical Report TR 635, Dept. of Computer Science, ETH Zürich (2009)
20. Torabi Dashti, M., Nair, S.K., Jonker, H.: Nuovo DRM Paradiso: Designing a secure, verified, fair exchange DRM scheme. Fundam. Inform. 89(4), 393–417 (2008)
21. Tygar, J.: Atomicity in electronic commerce. In: PODC 1996, pp. 8–26. ACM Press, New York (1996)
22. Vogt, H.: Asynchronous optimistic fair exchange based on revocable items. In: Wright, R.N. (ed.) FC 2003. LNCS, vol. 2742, pp. 208–222. Springer, Heidelberg (2003)
23. Vogt, H., Pagnia, H., Gärtner, F.C.: Using smart cards for fair exchange. In: Fiege, L., Mühl, G., Wilhelm, U.G. (eds.) WELCOM 2001. LNCS, vol. 2232, pp. 101–113. Springer, Heidelberg (2001)

Application Data Consistency Checking for Anomaly Based Intrusion Detection

Olivier Sarrouy, Eric Totel, and Bernard Jouga

Supelec, Avenue de la Boulaie, CS 47601, F-35576 Cesson-Sévigné CEDEX, France
firstname.lastname@supelec.fr

Abstract. Host-based intrusion detection systems may be coarsely divided into two categories. Misuse-based intrusion detection systems, which rely on a database of malicious behavior; and anomaly-based intrusion detection systems which rely on the comparison of the observed behavior of the monitored application with a previously built model of its normal behavior called the reference profile. In this last approach, the reference profile is often built on the basis of the sequence of system calls the application emits during its normal executions. Unfortunately, this approach allows attackers to remain undetected by mimicing the attempted behavior of the application. Furthermore, such intrusion detection systems cannot by nature detect anything but violations of the integrity of the control flow of an application. Although, there exist quite critical attacks which do not disturb the control flow of an application and thus remain undetected. We thus propose a different approach relying on the idea that attacks often break simple constraints on the data manipulated by the program. In this perspective, we first propose to define which data are sensitive to intrusions. Then we intend to extract the constraints applying on these data items, afterwards controlling them to detect intrusions. We finally introduce an implementation of such an approach, and some encouraging results.

1 Introduction

Two approaches co-exist in the domain of intrusion detection: the misuse-based approach and the anomaly-based approach. The misuse-based approach consists in looking for known attack signatures in the data collected by the intrusion detection system. However, this method cannot detect unknown attacks. The anomaly-based approach requires to build the normal application behavior. At runtime, the observed application behavior is compared with the normal behavior, and if a deviation arises, we consider an intrusion has occurred.

In the domain of intrusion detection at application level, the anomaly detection approach is largely preferred. Either the normal behavioral model is derived from the specification [1], or it is learned dynamically. This last approach is the basis of most work. In this domain, literature focuses mostly on the system calls, on the basis of the work of Forrest et al. [2]. The goal of these methods is to detect if the control flow of an application is corrupted or not. However, such an

R. Guerraoui and F. Petit (Eds.): SSS 2009, LNCS 5873, pp. 726–740, 2009.

approach is nowadays considered as insufficient because it is possible to perform mimicry attacks to evade from intrusion detection systems. These attacks can take two different aspects: the attack can execute additional code and generate an additional sequence of system calls that appears licit from the point of view of the intrusion detection system, or the attack can focus on modifying the program internal state by executing application legal code (e.g., data attacks with no impact on the application executed control flow). These kinds of attacks aim thus at corrupting either the control flow integrity or the application data integrity.

To enhance the detection of the first category of attacks, a lot of recent work have focused on adding processes internal information in the application behavioral model. Such information may consist in the content of the process call stack or the value of the program counter at the time of the system calls. However if such approaches may be efficient to detect hidden control flow modification, they remain blind to non-control data attacks, i.e., attacks that impact the value of program variables without modifying its control flow, as it is explained in the article of Chen et al. [3].

In this paper, we focus on a method that would enhance the detection of this last category of attacks. This approach consists in building a data oriented application model. The core problem of such an approach is to have access to the internal state of the application. This is performed by emulating a processor on which the monitored application is executed. Then we try to discover relations between the variables of the executed program, which would permit to detect inconsistencies between them at runtime.

This paper is organized as follows: we first discuss the existing work on this topic, then we show how we build the application data model. At last, the paper exhibits how we can implement such an approach to detect intrusions at the application level, and the results we obtain.

2 Related Work

Most recent application level anomaly-based intrusion detection systems rely on an approach introduced by Forrest et al. [2]. This approach consists in monitoring the sequence of system calls emitted by the applications hosted on the system [4]. The idea behind this approach is that these sequences of system calls constitute a good model of how applications interact with the remains of the system and thus constitute a good model of the behavior of the applications. Such intrusion detection systems are efficient against classical attacks, which obviously modify the expected sequence of system calls emitted by an application. For instance, a classical attack which exploits a buffer overflow to spawn a shell will likely call the `socket()`, `bind()`, `listen()`, `accept()`, `read()`, `fork()` system calls, which is quite unlikely what a classical web browser would do.

However, it is possible to easily evade system call monitoring based intrusion detection systems for two main reasons. First of all, the model used to define the normal behavior of the monitored applications is quite coarse, in that sense that it observes the application from an external point of view and with a relatively high granularity. Given this limitation, an attacker may adapt his attack in such a way that it does not modify the behavior of the exploited application in the eyes of the intrusion detection system. In other words, an attacker may indeed take control of the application control flow, but yet make this control flow appear normal to the intrusion detection system. As they mimic the expected behavior of the monitored application, these attacks are often called *mimicry attacks*. In [5], Wagner et al. thus describe various possibilities to adapt classical attacks which modify the control flow of the application and make them unseen to most intrusion detection systems. To contend with this kind of attacks, a lot of recent work in intrusion detection has focused on extending the part of an application one could actually monitor. In this perspective, many process internal information have been added to the original behavioral model based on system call sequences. As they go and look inside the application, such approaches are called *gray-box approaches* in opposition with *black-box approaches* which limit their observation to the interactions of the application with the rest of the system through the system calls they emit. A few examples of gray-box attempts can be found in [6] or [7]. Thus, in [6], Sekar et al. propose to extract the value of the program counter at the time of a system call. With the same goal, in [7], Gao et al. suggest to examine the content of the stack at the time of each function call. By enhancing the accuracy and the granularity of the control flow model, gray-box approaches indeed make mimicry attacks quite difficult to succeed. However, these approaches carry their limitations in their nature itself. Indeed, as they focus on the monitoring of the control flow, these works are unable to detect anything but control flow integrity violation. This objective is quite pertinent as most of the attacks indeed modify the control flow of the application. Nevertheless, as shown in [8] and [3], another kind of attacks exists, which does not disturb the control flow of the application but nonetheless leads to the same threat than classical attacks.

This second class of attacks focuses on the pure data manipulated by the program, i.e. on the data which do not influence the application control flow, and are thus called *pure data attacks* or *non-control data attacks*. In [8], Wagner et al. show that these attacks constitute an important threat for the confidentiality and the integrity of the data, all the more so it cannot be detected by none of the actual intrusion detection system. Furthermore, in [3], Chen et al. prove that there exists a realistic danger concerning these kind of attacks by analyzing several memory corruption vulnerabilities in different real-world applications and showing how a lot of them can be exploited without modifying the control flow of the program but still gaining the same privileges on the host than classical attacks. As such attacks cannot be detected by the monitoring of the application control flow, they bring us to the study of the data manipulated by the application.

Several approaches have been investigated to detect pure data attacks. Castro et al. [9] propose to build the normal data-flow graph from a program static analysis, and verifies at run-time the data-flow integrity, detecting thus incorrect affectations. Some articles propose (such as [10,11]) a taint-check based approach, in order to know which variables of a program are dependent on the user inputs, and must then be considered as potentially incorrect. Larson and Austin [12] propose to detect out of bounds errors in programs by using tainted data analysis (i.e., data that depend on a user entry, and can be incorrect) and predicates on most used string related functions. In this approach, the predicates are defined statically. In the method we propose in this paper, we try to discover dynamically from the program execution which invariants must be verified, in order to detect incorrect behaviors. This approach relies on the definition of the set of variables that are sensible for intrusion detection, and thus on the notion of tainted data.

3 Pure Data Attacks

As explained in the previous section, if actual intrusion detection systems manage to detect quite accurately what we call classical attacks, *i.e.*, attacks which violate the application control flow integrity, they remain helpless in detecting what we call pure data attacks, *i.e.*, attacks which do not violate the application control flow integrity. In order to understand how these attacks may be characterized and thus how they may be detected, we first introduce in this section an example of such a pure data attack, and then study it in the perspective of the properties it breaks concerning the data it modifies.

3.1 An Example of a Pure Data Attack

A typical example of a pure data attack may be found in the exploitation of the WU-FTPD *Site Exec Command Format String* Vulnerability [13] described in [3]. This vulnerability, among other things, allows an attacker to overwrite a `C` structure, denoted `pw`. The severity of this vulnerability resides in the fact that this `pw` structure owns an important role in the security logic of the application as it contains the uid of the authenticated user. It thus basically allows an attacker to authenticate beside the WU-FTPD server as an unprivileged user and afterwards overwrite the `pw` structure to gain administrative privileges. More precisely, the successive steps of the attack, illustrated on Figure 1, may be described as follows. First, the attacker authenticates himself beside the WU-FTPD server as an unprivileged user. His password is then checked and the `pw->pw_uid` is set to the value of its *uid*. At this time, the attacker can exploit the *Site Exec Command Format String* vulnerability to overwrite the `pw->pw_uid` field and set its value to `0`. A soon as the attacker performs a `GET` or a `PUT` command, the server call `seteuid(0)` to gain the privileges necessary for a call to `setsockopt()`. After the call to `setsockopt()` has returned, the server call `seteuid(pw->pw_uid)` to drop its privileges. As, the `pw->pw_uid` has been overwritten to `0`, the privileges of the attacker are set to those of the root user, allowing him to overwrite the `/etc/shadow` file and thus to gain permanent administrative privileges on the host.

As explained above, this attack is interesting as it clearly does not disturb the control flow of the application, and thus would not be detected by any of the

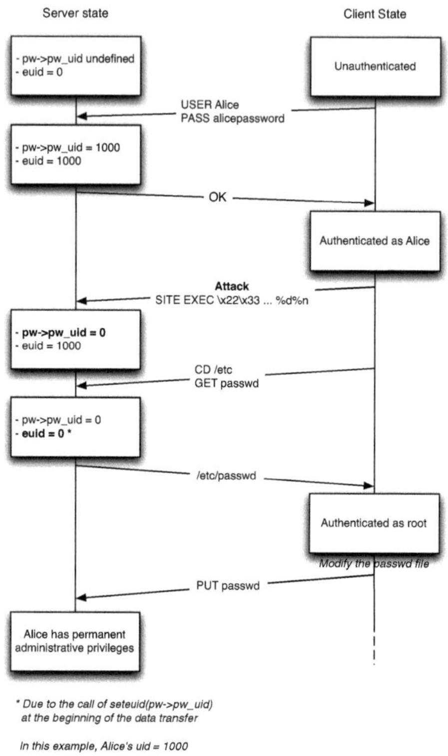

Fig. 1. WU-FTPD pure-data attack

classical system call based approaches or more accurate gray-box based intrusion detection systems, although it appears quite critical as it allows an attacker to gain administrative privileges on the host. An other interesting point in the study of this attack is that it appears to be characteristic of the properties pure data attacks break when they are performed. We discuss this idea in more details in the next subsection.

3.2 Attack Characterization

The pure data attack described in the previous subsection appears to be interesting in how characteristic it is in the disturbance of the expected properties of the application data. Indeed, this attack breaks a very simple property verified during a normal use of the application, which is that the `pw->pw_uid` variable should remain constant during a given session. In this perspective, denoting $\texttt{pw->pw\_uid}_1$, $\texttt{pw->pw\_uid}_2$, ..., $\texttt{pw->pw\_uid}_n$ different values of `pw->pw_uid` during the execution of a given session, this attack may be characterized by the fact that whenever $\texttt{pw->pw\_uid}_1$, $\texttt{pw->pw\_uid}_2$, ..., $\texttt{pw->pw\_uid}_n$ are extracted, it breaks the simple following constraint :

$$\texttt{pw->pw\_uid}_1 = \texttt{pw->pw\_uid}_2 = ... = \texttt{pw->pw\_uid}_\texttt{n}$$

More generally, it appears that most pure data attacks - and even more classical attacks - can be characterized by the fact that they break one of the constraints which qualify the normal use of the application. In other words, we can say that these attacks break the properties verified by the application data when this application remains in a " normal " state, *i.e.*, when it runs without being attacked. In this perspective, we first introduce in the next section a formal model of an application state to work with. Then, we propose a definition of an attack in the eyes of this model. Finally, we suggest a detection model based on that previously established definition of an attack.

4 Data-Based Intrusion Detection Model

As explained above, pure data attacks can be characterized by the fact that they break some properties verified by the application data when this application remains in a " normal " state. Thus, we believe that extracting and afterwards controlling these properties would allow us to detect intrusions more accurately. In this section, we first introduce a formal definition of a process state and propose an abstraction of this definition focused on the properties verified by the application data. Then, we intend to define the notion of an attack in the eyes of this abstraction, still focusing on the properties verified by the application data. Finally, we propose a detection model based on that previously introduced considerations.

4.1 State of a Process

For each discrete time i, the *snapshot state* s_i of a process may be defined by :

$$s_i = \langle pc_i, v_{1_i}, ..., v_{n_i} \rangle$$

where pc_i is the location in the process of the executed instruction at time i, i.e. the value of the program counter, and v_{1_i}, ..., v_{n_i} the values of the various data manipulated by the program at time i (registers, environment variables, global and local variables, etc ...).

This definition of the state of a process may be insufficient in the perspective of intrusion detection. Indeed, controlling the consistency of snapshot state s_i at a given time i sometimes requires the knowledge of all the previous snapshot states $s_0, ..., s_{i-1}$. We thus define the *global state* S_i of a process - in its temporal meaning - at time i by :

$$S_i = \langle s_0, ..., s_i \rangle = \langle pc_0, ..., pc_i, v_{1_0}, ..., v_{n_0}, ..., v_{1_i}, ..., v_{n_i} \rangle$$

The set of all potential global states of a process, denoted $\mathcal{S}$, is a set whose elements depend on the definition sets of its variables which are platform dependent (for example, on a 32 bit platform, an unsigned integer is constrained to the interval [-2147483648, 2147483647]). However during the " normal " executions of a given program, all global states cannot be reached. For instance, a given integer variable may be constrained by the program to remain in the interval [0, 4]. In the same way, access rights on a given file are likely to be the same at the time the program checks it and at the time the program reads or writes it. Though, we may define the set of allowed global state of a process, denoted $\mathcal{A}$ as the set of licitly reachable global states of a process. However, the notion of licitly reachable global state is quite difficult to define. Indeed, if an attack against a given application is possible, it is precisely because it is possible for an attacker to lead this application in a problematic state, which is therefore reachable. We finally may define the set of allowed global states $\mathcal{A}$ as the set of all states which can be reached in a " normal " use context, *i.e.*, in a context where no attack against the application is performed. We suppose in addition that these states would be those described by a complete specification of the application if such a specification could exist.

In practice, it appears that $\mathcal{A}$ constitutes a quite small subset of $\mathcal{S}$ that we would like to define in order to discern the " allowed " states and the " unallowed " states. As it seems impossible and probably not much relevant to explicitly define $\mathcal{A}$, we propose to abstract the state definition to implicitly define it by expressing the various constraints on the values that application data can effectively take when this application is in an allowed global state. In other words, we define a number of relationships which constitutes a constraint system $\mathcal{C}$. Given a global state $S_i = \langle s_0, ..., s_i \rangle = \langle pc_0, ..., pc_i, v_{1_0}, ..., v_{n_0}, ..., v_{1_i}, ..., v_{n_i} \rangle$ we consider that :

$$S_i \in \mathcal{A} \iff \langle pc_0, ..., pc_i, v_{1_0}, ..., v_{n_0}, ..., v_{1_i}, ..., v_{n_i} \rangle \text{ verifies } \mathcal{C}$$

In this subsection, we have thus given a definition of a process state and have proposed an abstraction of this definition which brings us to consider the state of an application through the properties or the constraints verified by its data. In the next subsection we propose an attack model based on this proposition.

4.2 Attack Model

In the perspective of the state model proposed above, we may assume that the application is in an unallowed global state, *i.e.*, a state $S \in \mathcal{S} \backslash \mathcal{A}$ when one of the constraints of $\mathcal{C}$ is broken. Thus, we propose, on the basis of our data constraint based state model, a definition of an attack. In this model, we can indeed affirm that an attack can be characterized as a sequence of " user actions " leading the application from a state $S_i \in \mathcal{A}$ into a state $S_f \in \mathcal{S} \backslash \mathcal{A}$, therefore breaking the constraints on the application data which characterize the set $\mathcal{A}$. In the pure data attack example given in section 3, the attack is thus characterized by the fact it breaks the simple $\texttt{pw->pw\_uid}_1 = \texttt{pw->pw\_uid}_2 = ... = \texttt{pw->pw\_uid}_\texttt{n}$ constraint.

Given this definition of an attack, focused on the constraints verified by the application data when this application is in an allowed global state, we can now propose a model to detect these attacks. In the next section, we introduce such a detection model, based on the previously stated attack definition, and therefore focused on the data and the constraints they verify.

4.3 Detection Model

In this perspective of the attack model proposed in the previous subsection, we now define a detection model focused on the constraints verified by the application data. Our detection model relies on the assumption that it is possible to extract in whatever manner the set of constraints $\mathcal{C}$ which characterize the set of allowed global states $\mathcal{A}$. Supposing this assumption verified, we thus propose to monitor the application by controlling the enforcement of this set of constraints $\mathcal{C}$ and to raise an alert as soon as one of these constraints seems broken. The major interest of such an approach is the accuracy of the detection, as it potentially enables the detection of both control flow integrity attacks and pure data attacks, what classical intrusion detection systems would not allow. However, this detection model relies on the quite complex extraction of the set of constraints $\mathcal{C}$ on the application data. Nevertheless, our goal in this paper is not to fully qualify the consistency of a given state, but only to qualify this consistency with regards to security concerns. In this approach, it clearly appears that not all the data manipulated by the application would be of interest for us, and therefore allows us to restrict our study to a smallest security critical data set. In the next section, we thus try to define which data can be critical in a security focused perspective and then examine a way to practically extract this data out of the whole application data set.

5 Intrusion Sensitive Data Set

As explained in the previous section, not all data items are interesting for our model. In this section we first try to define which data can be considered as critical in a security perspective and then introduce a formal characterization of these data in order to clearly define which data must be studied out of the whole application data set.

The set of interesting data we try to extract, henceforward called *intrusion sensitive data set* and noted *ISDS*, is defined by the two main properties it verifies. First, in an immunological approach, we may consider that this intrusion sensitive data set constitutes a subset of the data which may influence, directly or indirectly, the system calls or their arguments. Indeed, if a data item has no influence on the system calls or their arguments, it cannot have any influence on any critical behavior (reading a file, writing on a socket, modifying the uid of a process, etc ...). Thus, we may consider that the data which do not influence the system calls or their arguments is of little interest for an attacker and thus is of little interest in an intrusion detection perspective. Secondly, we may consider that the intrusion sensitive data set constitutes a subset of the data being influenced, directly or indirectly, by user inputs. Indeed, one must remind that an attack always occurs through a pernicious user input (configuration file, data read on a socket, etc ...). In this perspective, the data we are interesting in must be influenced, directly or indirectly by user inputs. These data are said to be *tainted* as the threat they sustain propagates through them.

The notion of influence between two or more data can be formally defined by the notion of causal dependency largely tackled in [14], [15] and [16]. Denoting *(o,t)* the content of the data object o (a byte or a variable depending on the level of granularity) at time t, we may then denote *(o',t')* $\rightarrow$ *(o,t)*, with $t' \leq t$ the causal dependency of *(o,t)* in relation to *(o',t')*. The relation $\rightarrow$ being transitive, we may then define the causality cone of a point *(o,t)* as :

$$cause(o,t) = \{(o',t')/(o',t') \rightarrow (o,t)\}$$

In the same way, we may define the dependency cone *dep(o,t)* as the set of points which causally depends on *(o,t)* :

$$dep(o,t) = \{(o',t')/(o,t) \rightarrow (o',t')\}$$

More informally, the causality cone of a given point *(o,t)* represents the set of point *(o',t')* influencing, directly or indirectly, the set *(o,t)*. In the same way, the dependency cone of a given point *(o,t)* represents the set of points *(o',t')* influenced, directly or indirectly, by *(o,t)*. The notions of causality cone and dependency cone are the expression of the notions of information flow and/or control flow.

The notions of causality cone and dependency cone being introduced, we may now give a more formal definition of the intrusion sensitive data set. As explained above, the first property characterizing the intrusion sensitive data set is that it constitutes a subset of the data influencing, directly or indirectly, the system calls emitted by the application and their argument. Thus, we may denote (with *sc* the set of system calls):

$$ISDS \subseteq cause(sc)$$

Furthermore, the second property characterizing the intrusion sensitive data set is that it constitutes a subset of the tainted data, *i.e.*, of the data being

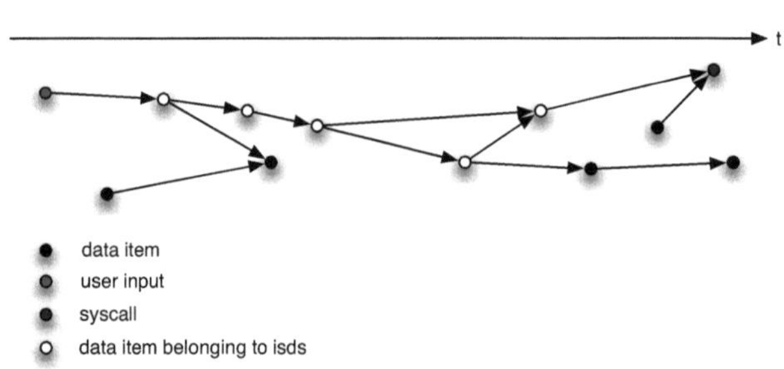

Fig. 2. Intrusion Sensitive Data Set

influenced, directly or indirectly by user inputs. Thus, we may denote (with ui the set of user inputs):

$$ISDS \subseteq dep(ui)$$

Finally, we may define the set of intrusion sensitive data set as the intersection of both the causality cone of system calls or their arguments and the dependency cone of user inputs (c.f. Figure 2):

$$ISDS = cause(sc) \cap dep(ui)$$

In this section, we have explained how to reduce the application of our detection model to a small subset of all the data manipulated by the application. The set of data to which we restrict our detection model has been defined, in a security perspective, as the intersection of the causality cone of the system calls and their arguments and of the dependency cone of the user inputs. In the next section, we present the kind of constraints we aim at extracting. Then we introduce an implementation of our detection model, describing how to technically extract the intrusion sensitive data set execution traces and how to extract the set of constraints $\mathcal{C}$ out of this execution traces.

6 Constraints Determination

As explained in section 4.2, we state that an attack breaks the constraints applying on the sensitive data manipulated by the application. The simple example we have given shows that an equality relationship between many instances of the same variable at different times must be fulfilled. In a more general approach, we have formulated the hypothesis that attacks aim at modifying one or more variables, and that this modification leads to the violation of invariant constraints on the variables.

Our main problem is thus to automatically extract these constraints, which constitute the basis of our behavioral model. To do so, we have used an automated tool called *Daikon*, and developed by Michael Ernst [17], [18]. Daikon is a likely invariant discovery tool which analyzes the execution traces of a given application and try to extract invariant properties out of it. In this goal it implements an algorithm based on a property grammar which contains the set of all invariants looked for in the execution traces. These invariants are thus exhaustively verified on the execution trace data. These invariants can be very complex: constant data item (e.g., x = a), data item taking only a few distinct different values (e.g., x ∈ {a, b, c}), definition set (e.g., x ∈ [a..b]), non-nullity, linear relationship (e.g., x = ay + bz + c), order relationship (e.g., x ≥ y), single invariants on x + y, x - y, etc.

As explained above, these invariants are extracted out of the execution traces of the monitored application. In the next section, we introduce our implementation of an intrusion detection prototype, and explain how to generate the execution traces needed to extract the invariant properties out of the intrusion sensitive data set.

7 Implementation

The implementation of an intrusion detection system based on the ideas introduced in the previous sections raises several issues. Firstly, we must wonder how to generate the execution traces necessary to the analysis of the various data manipulated by the application during the learning phase of the intrusion detection system deployment. Secondly, we must determine how to analyze this execution traces to extract the constraints characterizing the integrity of the application state.

7.1 Processor Emulation

In order to generate the execution traces used during the learning phase of our approach, we need a runtime access to the data manipulated by the monitored application. Several solutions exist which may coarsely be divided into two categories. A first approach consists in using the debugging facilities provided by the operating system, such as the `ptrace` system call. A second approach consists in emulating a processor controlled by the intrusion detection system and to execute the monitored application in this context. We have decided to follow this second approach, using the Valgrind dedicated dynamic binary instrumentation framework [19,20].

Valgrind is a dynamic binary instrumentation framework which aims at easing dynamic binary instrumentation. In this goal, it offers a dedicated programming interface and exposes an emulated processor to the studied binary (c.f. Figure 3). More concretely, Valgrind proposes the writing of plugins to which it delegates the control of the application. Thus, when a monitored application is executed, Valgrind first extracts its current basic block, *i.e.*, the current sequence of code until the next jump. It then translates this basic block into an intermediate representation (IR), build over a set of C structures representing the various instructions and their operands. Once this operation achieved, Valgrind transmits the translated basic block to the plugin. The plugin can then analyze the

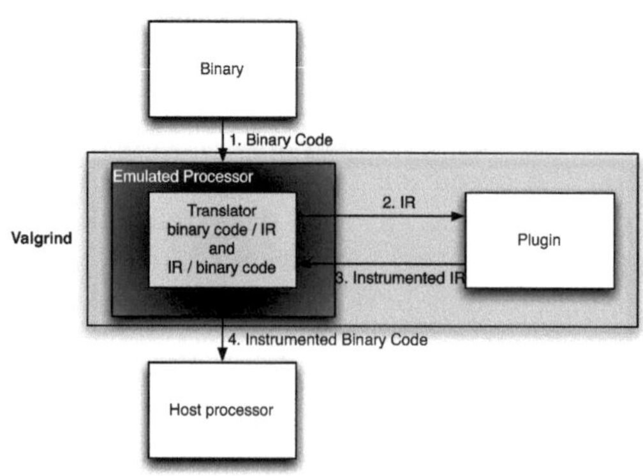

Fig. 3. Valgrind architecture

instructions contained in the block and modify it by adding or removing instructions and by inserting internal C function calls. Once this operation finished, the plugin transmits the modified block back to Valgrind which translates it back into binary code and executes it on the host processor. The instructions or the function calls inserted by the plugin are then executed dynamically. A cache system is furthermore implemented in order to instrument each block only one time. One of the main advantages of Valgrind is that it aims at making all of this processing as transparent as possible.

Thus, our intrusion detection system prototype, called *Fatgrind*, has been designed as a plugin to Valgrind. Through the dynamic binary instrument abilities Valgrind provides, this prototype is able to dynamically determine the intrusion sensitive data set and to generate the associated execution traces.

7.2 Execution Traces Generation

As said above Fatgrind, our intrusion detection system prototype, has been designed as a plugin to Valgrind. This plugin mainly aims at dynamically extracting the intrusion sensitive data set *ISDS*, and at dynamically generating the execution traces containing the values of the various intrusion sensitive data items. In order to achieve these goals, Fatgrind builds a shadow of the memory of the monitored process [21]. This shadow memory keeps a trace of which data items are tainted and which are not. Furthermore, it keeps a copy of the value of the data which are tainted. Each time a byte of the monitored process memory is written, Fatgrind draws the causality cone of this byte. Once the causality cone has been determined, Fatgrind inspects whether this byte is tainted or not. In the case the byte is indeed tainted, it is shadowed for further use. Finally, each time a system call is emitted, Fatgrind draws the causality cone of the system call and of its arguments. Each tainted byte belonging to this causality cone is then considered as belonging to the intrusion sensitive data set and is dumped into a file.

7.3 Likely Invariants Extraction

Once enough executions of a given application have been done, the execution traces generated are considered complete enough and are analyzed by *Daikon* to automatically extract the likely invariants it contains. Of course, the quality of the extracted invariants depends on the exhaustivity of the normal application behavior learning.

8 Results

To evaluate our model, we have studied the following snippet of code, equivalent to the one studied in section 3:

```
1. int main(int argc, char ** argv)
2. {
3.       char buffer[256];
4.       uid_t uid;
5.
6.       uid = 1000;
7.       seteuid(uid);
8.
9.       while(gets[buffer])
10.      {
11.            seteuid(0);
12.            printf(buffer);
13.            seteuid(uid);
14.      }
15.
16. }
```

This example is representative of the wu-ftpd vulnerability (*i.e.*, of a format string attack at line 12, which allows the modification of the `uid` variable), although generating very few traces and thus very few invariant properties, allowing us to easily check their consistency. Indeed, we have focused here on the validation of our approach, that is on the validation of the extracted invariants. We have thus tried to control one by one the invariants inferred by Daikon out of the execution traces generated by Fatgrind. Among the various properties extracted by Daikon, we obtain in particular the equality of the `uid` variable at the beginning of the loop and at the end of the loop. Moreover, given the obtained results, it appears that most of the attacks described in [3] would be detected by our approach. Indeed, the attack against the NULL HTTPD server described in this article modifies a configuration variable allowing to define the root of the cgi scripts. This variable remains constant during a normal use of the server, thus we could extract an invariant property out of it. In the same way, the TOCTTOU (Time Of Check To Time Of Use) attack against the GTTPD server, rely on an abnormal modification of a variable between the time it is checked and the time it is used. As this variable remains constant between these two instants during a normal use of the server, we should be able to extract an invariant property out of it. The attack against the SSH server could however be more difficult to detect. Indeed, this attack exploits a memory corruption vulnerability allowing one to modify an authentication control data, but this data is whatever modified during a normal use of the application. It is thus not obvious that we could extract an invariant property which would be broken by the attack.

The obtained results therefore show the viability of the approach on the previous examples, which although small are quite representative of the attacks we aim at detecting. This report thus encourages us to pursue the prospective work we have engaged. Nevertheless, a lot of enhancements could be brought to our approach. We are going to discuss them in the next section.

9 Conclusion and Future Work

The work presented in this paper proposes a way to enhance application level intrusion detection by introducing a data-oriented detection model. This approach relies on the automatic generation of a behavioral model based on the relationship between application data aiming at detecting state inconsistency at runtime. In order to pursue such an approach, it is necessary to determine which data are sensitive to intrusions and how these data items are related to each other. These two goals are fulfilled through the use of a dynamic binary instrumentation framework, namely Valgrind, and of an automatic invariant discovery tool, namely Daikon.

As shown by the results, the proposed approach indeed enables the detection of pure data attacks. However, regarding the conclusion of this prospective work, it appears that several enhancements could be brought. Indeed, the binary level does not allow us to access a high semantical level, as, for instance, we do not get any information about the type of the manipulated data. We therefore plan to apply this approach to programming language using a native intermediate representation (Java, .Net, PHP, etc.). Through the direct modification of the virtual machine or interpreter, we thus expect to access richest information than those available at the binary level.

Acknowledgement

This work has been funded by the french DGA (General Delegation for Armament) and the french CNRS (National Center for Scientific Research) in the context of the DALI (Design and Assessment of application Level Intrusion detection system) project.

References

1. Uppuluri, P., Sekar, R.: Experiences with specification-based intrusion detection. In: Lee, W., Mé, L., Wespi, A. (eds.) RAID 2001. LNCS, vol. 2212, pp. 172–189. Springer, Heidelberg (2001)
2. Forrest, S., Hofmeyr, S.A., Somayaji, A., Longstaff, T.A.: A Sense of Self for Unix Processes. In: Proceedings of the 1996 IEEE Symposium on Research in Security and Privacy, pp. 120–128. IEEE Computer Society Press, Los Alamitos (1996)
3. Chen, S., Xu, J., Sezer, E., Gauriar, P., Iyer, R.: Non-control-data attacks are realistic threats. In: Usenix Security Symposium, pp. 177–192 (2005)
4. Hofmeyr, S.A., Forrest, S., Somayaji, A.: Intrusion detection using sequences of system calls. Journal of Computer Security 6(3), 151–180 (1998)
5. Wagner, D., Soto, P.: Mimicry attacks on host-based intrusion detection systems. In: CCS 2002: Proceedings of the 9th ACM conference on Computer and communications security, pp. 255–264. ACM, New York (2002)
6. Sekar, R., Bendre, M., Dhurjati, D., Bollineni, P.: A fast automaton-based method for detecting anomalous program behaviors. In: Proceedings of the 2001 IEEE Symposium on Security and Privacy, Oakland, CA, May 2001, pp. 144–155 (2001)

7. Gao, D., Reiter, M.K., Song, D.: Gray-box extraction of execution graphs for anomaly detection. In: Proceedings of the 11th ACM conference on Computer and communications security, pp. 318–329 (2004)
8. Parampalli, C., Sekar, R., Johnson, R.: A practical mimicry attack against powerful system-call monitors. Technical Report SECLAB07-01, Secure Systems Laboratory, Stony Brook University (2007)
9. Castro, M., Costa, M., Harris, T.: Securing software by enforcing data-flow integrity. In: Proceedings of the 7th USENIX Symposium on Operating Systems Design and Implementation, vol. 7, p. 11 (2006)
10. Cavallaro, L., Sekar, R.: Anomalous taint detection. Technical report, Secure Systems Laboratory, Stony Brook University (2008)
11. Newsome, J., Song, D.: Dynamic taint analysis for automatic detection, analysis, and signature generation of exploits on commodity software. In: Proceedings of the 12th Annual Network and Distributed System Security Symposium (NDSS 2005), San Diego, CA (February 2005)
12. Larson, E., Austin, T.: High coverage detection of input-related security faults. In: Proceedings of the 2003 Usenix Conference, Usenix 2003 (2003)
13. Cert advisory ca-2001-33 multiple vulnerabilities in wu-ftpd (2001), `http://www.cert.org/advisories/CA-2001-33.html`
14. Denning, D.E.: A lattice model of secure information flow. Commun. ACM 19(5), 236–243 (1976)
15. Sabelfeld, A., Myers, A.: Language-based information-flow security (2003)
16. d'Ausbourg, B.: Implementing secure dependencies over a network by designing a distributed security subsystem. In: Gollmann, D. (ed.) ESORICS 1994. LNCS, vol. 875, pp. 249–266. Springer, Heidelberg (1994)
17. Ernst, M.D., Perkins, J.H., Guo, P.J., McCamant, S., Pacheco, C., Tschantz, M.S., Xiao, C.: The daikon system for dynamic detection of likely invariants. Science of Computer Programming 69, 35–45 (2007)
18. Ernst, M.D., Cockrell, J., Griswold, W.G., Notkin, D.: Dynamically discovering likely program invariants to support program evolution. IEEE Transactions on Software Engineering (2001)
19. Valgrind, `http://www.valgrind.org`
20. Nethercote, N., Seward, J.: Valgrind: A framework for heavyweight dynamic binary instrumentation. In: Proceedings of ACM SIGPLAN 2007 Conference on Programming Language Design and Implementation (2007)
21. Nethercote, N., Seward, J.: How to shadow every byte of memory used by a program. In: Proceedings of the Third International ACM SIGPLAN/SIGOPS Conference on Virtual Execution Environments (2007)

Self Adaptive High Interaction Honeypots Driven by Game Theory

Gérard Wagener[1,2], Radu State[1], Alexandre Dulaunoy[2], and Thomas Engel[1]

[1] University of Luxembourg
{radu.state,thomas.engel}@uni.lu
[2] SES S.A.
{gerard.wagener,alexandre.dulaunoy}@ses.com

Abstract. High-interaction honeypots are relevant to provide rich and useful information obtained from attackers. Honeypots come in different flavors with respect to their interaction potential. A honeypot can be very restrictive, but then only a few interactions can be observed. If a honeypot is very tolerant though, attackers can quickly achieve their goal. Having the best trade-off between attacker freedom and honeypot restrictions is challenging. In this paper, we address the issue of self adaptive honeypots, that can change their behavior and lure attackers into revealing as much information as possible about themselves. The key idea is to leverage game-theoretic concepts for the configuration and reciprocal actions of high-interaction honeypots.

1 Introduction

Simulating failures in order to lure attackers was reported for the first time in the classical paper "An Evening with Berferd" [1], where manual interactions from a human system administrator lured an attacker into revealing many of his tactics and tools. During the operation of an high-interaction honeypot we observed that attackers follow a dedicated goal. We manually interfered with the tools installed and operated by attackers and noticed that some attackers connected back to the honeypot and tried to solve the problems. Some attackers even tried to harden the system aiming to lock out other attackers. Thus, we assume that attackers are rational and follow a specific goal during attacks. We address in this paper a first step towards an automated failure injecting honeypot aiming to disclose as much information as possible about an attacker. According to Lance Spitzner, a honeypot is a resource dedicated to be attacked [2]. Honeypots are frequently used to monitor or lure attackers and serve as baits for attackers. Once honeypots are compromised, attackers can be traced and attacking techniques can be learnt. On the one hand, if a honeypot has too limited capabilities some attack goals can not be reached and not much can be learnt. On the other hand, if a honeypot exposes to many and easily accessible features to an attacker, the attack goal can be easily reached and only a part of the attack can be observed. The goal of an attacker is also often unknown. The challenge addressed in this work is to elaborate an adaptive high-interaction

R. Guerraoui and F. Petit (Eds.): SSS 2009, LNCS 5873, pp. 741–755, 2009.

honeypot that tries to optimize the retrieval of knowledge from an attacker. The level of interaction is a consequence of the capabilities of a honeypot. The more features are implemented in a honeypot, the more interactions are possible between attackers and the honeypot. One way to obtain more interactions, is to partially allow attackers to execute some programs, leading them to explore alternative execution paths and reveal more information about themselves (attack tools) and to disclose other repositories, used for malicious purposes. Similarly, an adaptive honeypot can abnormally terminate the execution of programs by an attacker and lead the attacker to perform other activities, that can provide insightful information to the security community. We address in this paper, the design, implementation and validation of adaptive high-interaction honeypots. The major research challenges that we had to address were:

- to design an adaptive behavior for a honeypot that should be optimal and remain stealthy.
- to implement an effective Linux kernel monitoring solution capable to trace attacker activities on a system.

The remaining paper is organized as follows: Section 2 explains our high-interaction honeypot model. Section 3 formally describes the game between attackers and the honeypot and shows that our honeypot model can be fed with data delivered from a deployed high-interaction honeypot. Our experiments are shown in section 4 and the state of the art activities are summarized in section 5. Finally, the article is concluded in section 6 and future work activities are announced.

2 Modeling a High-Interaction Honeypot

We consider high-interaction honeypots operating a Linux operating system exposing a SSH server to attackers. The rationale behind this choice is that attackers often use specialized tricks or side effects to detect or evade from low-interaction honeypots and that SSH is a popular attack vector for attackers [3], [4]. We model high-interaction honeypots with a hierarchical probabilistic automaton. This model, as detailed in the following, is needed to frame the honeypot capabilities in the context of game theory.

2.1 Honeypot Hierarchical Probabilistic Automaton

Probabilistic automata are often used in the field of pattern recognition [5]. An attacker can connect to a high-interaction honeypot and can execute programs. Downloads can be performed with tools like `wget, curl, ftp`, archives can be extracted with programs like `tar` and `gzip` and so on. We define the states of the automaton as the programs that can be executed on the honeypot. Moreover, we add a state labeled *unknown* in order to describe the fact that new and unseen tools could be installed and used later on. Each program has some program arguments that are passed as array to the `main` function. If no command line arguments are explicitly passed to the program, the first command line argument

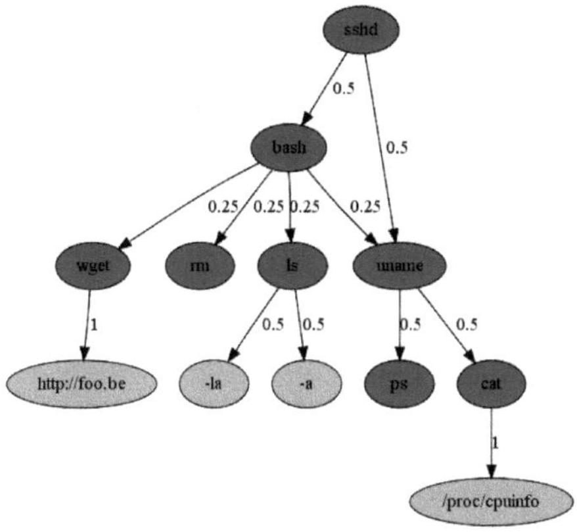

Fig. 1. Honeypot hierarchical probabilistic automaton example

corresponds to the program name [6]. Moreover, a program can have the same command line argument than another one but with a different semantic. Thus, we introduce a hierarchy between programs and command line arguments. Each program is formalized as automaton where each state represents a command line argument. The states in an automaton representing a program are called macro states and each macro state contains micro states (i.e. the command line arguments). Some transitions between programs or command line arguments are more likely than others. The program `wget` is often executed previously to the program `tar`. Therefore, each transition can be modeled using a transition probability. The same notation as proposed by Thollard et al. [5] is used. The set Q_A contains the programs installed on the honeypot including an *unknown* state and the set of states for a given program is denoted Q'_A. Attackers penetrate the honeypot through the SSH server. Thus, the initial probability for the state */usr/sbin/sshd* is 1 and 0 for all the other states. Moreover the alphabet consists of the commands executed by the attacker. An example of such a hierarchical probabilistic automaton is shown in figure 1[1]. An attacker connects to the honeypot via SSH and stays in the `sshd` state. Next he or she can execute the program `bash` or `uname` with the equal probability of 0.5. After the execution of the program `bash`, the programs `wget`, `rm` and `uname` have the same likelihood to be executed, namely 0.25. The program `ls` is executed with the command line arguments `-la`, `-l` with an equal probability of 0.5.

2.2 Process Vectors

The transitions between programs are described by the conditional probabilities, capturing the likelihood of one program being executed after a previous one. We use sequences of program executions from a deployed high-interaction honeypot

[1] For the purpose of understanding a simplified automaton is presented.

to determine these probabilities. Such a sequence of programs is considered as process vector which is observed from one attack and where each element is a program that is executed during an attack. An attacker who executes the programs `/bin/bash`, `/usr/bin/wget` and `/usr/bin/tar`, generates the process vector $< /\ bin/bash\ ,\ /usr/bin/wget\ ,\ /usr/bin/tar >$.

2.3 Attacker Process Trees

In order to obtain the process vectors, we have to dig into the kernel data structure (on the honeypot) holding process tree information. After having compromised the honeypot, an attacker usually executes programs. Such an execution triggers a `clone` or `do_exec_ve` system call which should be monitored. Multiple attackers can be connected to the honeypot at the same time and the operating system itself is using `do_exec_ve` and `clone` system calls. The system calls that are related to a given attack can be identified as follows: In a Linux operating system each process has a process identifier (PID) and a parent process identifier (PPID) [7]. An attack usually starts with a privilege separated process of the SSH server [8], denoted p_0. The process p_0 then forks, resulting in a `clone` system call or directly executes a program via the `do_exec_ve` system call. We consider that the process p_0 executes a program and creates another copy of the process, denoted p_1. The parent process of p_1 is thus p_0 and the result of the execution of a sequence of programs is a process tree of an attack which is a subtree of the Unix process tree on the honeypot. We define a process tree as a tree structure where each node can contain a process id, a timestamp, a program name or a command line argument resulting from a `do_exec_ve` or clone system call. An edge links two process identifiers with each other, which represents the parent child relationship. Furthermore, in a process tree, each parent of a leaf represents a program name and each leaf represents command line argument (at least the program name [6]).

One process tree is shown in figure 2. The privileged separated process of the SSH server has the process identifier 4121 and is the root of the tree. Two `clone` system calls are done; one results in a process with the process identifier 4127 and another one in the process identifier 4129. The process with the identifier 4127 is

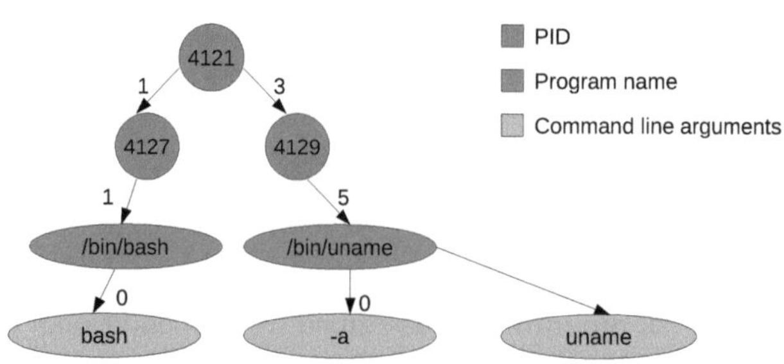

Fig. 2. Process tree example

created after one second and the process with the identifier 4129 is created after 3 seconds. Then the process with the identifier 4127 executes a program called `/bin/bash` after one second and the process with the identifier `4129` starts the `/bin/uname` program after 5 seconds. The program `/bin/uname` is started with the argument `-a` and the command line arguments `bash` and `uname` represent the respective program names.

2.4 Inducing a Honeypot Hierarchical Probabilistic Automaton

We model the honeypot capabilities as a hierarchical probabilistic automaton where each state represents a program. Each state is furthermore an automaton on its own, where combinations of command line arguments build the states of the sub-automaton. From a deployed high-interaction honeypot we have extracted the process trees related to an attack. A process tree can be composed of PID nodes, nodes containing the programs that were executed and nodes modeling command line arguments. Due to the fact that the process identifiers change from one attack to another, we are interested to transform these process trees in process vectors describing the sequences of programs that were executed during an attack. The order of program execution is important. A good example is when a tool was downloaded that is then extracted and executed. To recover the order we use the timestamps in the process trees. The time difference of each leaf with the root enables us to determine the position of a program in the process vector. In the example shown in figure 2 the process vector $\overrightarrow{v}$ is $< /bin/bash, /bin/uname >$ because the program `/bin/bash` was executed before the program `/bin/uname`. Each attacker generates a process tree that is converted to a process vector. All these vectors are now inserted in a two dimensional matrix transition matrix. The observed programs are used as labels for the columns and rows respectively. Each cell contains the frequency of how often a couple of programs was observed. The transition probability P_A is computed from the transition matrix. Each cell is divided by the sum of the row. The automaton containing the macro states is created from the transition matrix. In figure 1, each state is represented by a circle and the edges are labeled with the transition probability. For instance, a transition from the macro state `sshd` can be done to the macro state `bash` with a probability of 0.5. Another transition can then be done to the macro state `ls`. The program `ls` can operated in different modes by accepting different command line arguments. In this example the states denoted by "l" and "-la" are micro states and belong to the automaton `ls`. First, the hierarchical probabilistic automaton may be incomplete because it is constructed from honeypot observations. Therefore, we integrate a state in the automaton which is called "unknown". Second, rare transitions may be unobserved. To counteract this phenomenon we smooth the probabilities that we derived from honeypot observations, where the smoothing factor is denoted ϵ. In this case each probability > 0 is multiplied by $(1 - \epsilon)$ and from a given state, transitions are created to all other remaining states. If we assume that our automaton has N states and the number of transitions for a given state is n, then

$N - n$ transitions are created having the probability $\frac{\epsilon}{N-n}$. The automaton has now N^2 transitions and is able to capture all possible transitions. In practice, the automaton could be periodically induced in order to adjust the transition probabilities.

3 The Honeypot Game

Intuitively, the fact that attackers connecting to the honeypot can be seen as game between the honeypot and the attackers. We assume that attackers try to achieve their goal as fast as possible. They want to minimize the number of interactions with the honeypot. The honeypot aims to maximize the number of interactions or to learn as much as possible from attackers or to distract them as long as possible from real assets. In this article we define two possible actions for the honeypot and three different strategies for an attacker. We determine Nash Equilibriums [9], providing the optimal strategies for both the attacker and the honeypot.

3.1 Modeling Attacker and Honeypot Actions

Our current adaptive honeypot can accept or block the execution of a program which is implemented by allowing or blocking the `do_exec_ve` system call in a Linux kernel [7].

Block a `do_exec_ve` system call. The honeypot can crash a tool of an attacker which can be derived from blocking the `do_exec_ve` system call. In that case an error code is immediately returned instead of executing the regular code of the `do_exec_ve` system call. Let $Pr(Block)$ be the probability that the adaptive honeypot blocks the system call `do_exec_ve`. This decision is taken at each `do_exec_ve` system call[2].

Allow a `do_exec_ve` system call. The honeypot behaves like a normal high-interaction honeypot. The probability to allow a system call is $1-Pr(Block)$.

Attackers often find out that the honeypot is not immediately ready for their malicious activities. Thus, they download their tools, install them and execute them. They download tar balls containing a pre-compiled version of their program or the source code is downloaded and compiled on the honeypot. In both cases attackers often configure their programs on the honeypot. All these actions results in interactions with the honeypot. In our hierarchical probabilistic automaton, the interactions with the honeypot result in transitions from one state to another one. We assume that attackers are rational and that they select the next transition on the most probable path in the automaton. In the game between attackers and the honeypot we define three actions for attacker when their transitions are blocked.

[2] Practically, an explicit error code of the system call could be returned.

Retry of a command. Attackers can retry a command from a failure. First a failure might be due to a syntax error. The second reason might be a time-out that emerged during the program execution. For instance, an attacker may to download a file and a network timeout may emerge. In this case another repository might be disclosed. Third, the execution of a program might produce an undesired effect. A wrong command line argument might have been used. The program is executed again with a different command line argument. Let $Pr(Retry)$ denote the probability that attackers execute the same command again.

Select an alternative solution. A downloaded program may fail during execution. Some attackers try to debug the problem on the honeypot. They can check the configuration file of the program or run an inspection tool like `strace` on the program. They might try to download another program or to download the source code of the program that will be compiled on the honeypot. No matter which option they select, their behavior can be classified in a category describing the actions of choosing an alternative solution for obtaining their goal. Let $Pr(Alternative)$ denote the probability that attacker select an alternative command to achieve their initial goal.

Quit. Some attackers check the capabilities of the honeypot and if they suspect a trap or a worthless system, then they will leave. Let $Pr(Quit)$ describe the probability that attacker quit.

The relation 1 holds for the attacker strategies.

$$Pr(Quit) + Pr(Retry) + Pr(Alternative) = 1 \tag{1}$$

An example of attacker and honeypot strategies is shown in figure 3. We observe that an attacker tries to invoke the command `nmap` (a popular network scanner). The honeypot might allow the execution (with the probability $1 - Pr(Block)$) and in this case the attacker continues and executes the program `wget` (with a probability of 0.95). If the tool `nmap` is not allowed by the honeypot, the attacker can decide to either quit (with a probability of $Pr(Quit)$) or to retry the execution of `nmap` or to execute another command (for instance `uname` - with a probability of 0.6). The execution of `nmap` was blocked and its probability was equally distributed among the transitions to the states `wget` and `uname`. The probabilities used by attackers to choose the next command to be executed can be estimated from an operational high-interaction honeypot. The probabilities used by the honeypot to block the execution of a command is a configuration setting and reflects the strategy played by the honeypot. Similarly, the probabilities used by the attacker to either quit the session, or retry a command (and consequently to choose another command) give the strategy played by the attacker.

The main question is related to what are the optimal settings for both the honeypot ($Pr(Block)$) as well as for the attacker ($Pr(Quit)$, $Pr(Retry)$, $Pr(Alternative)$).

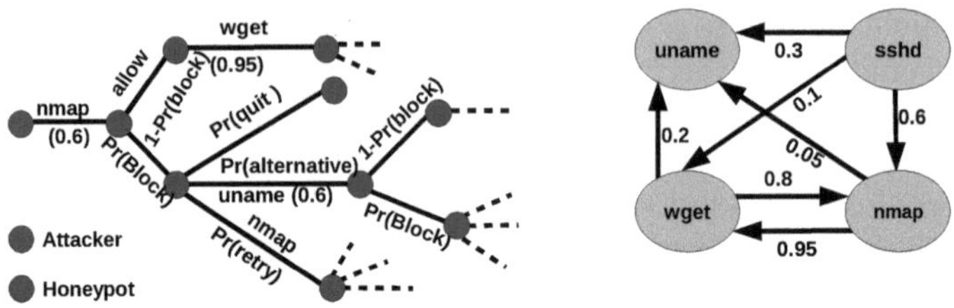

Fig. 3. Honeypot game example

3.2 Modeling Attacker and Honeypot Games

We reuse the definitions and notations proposed by Amy Greenwald [9] in order to formally describe our games between attackers and the honeypot. The game between the attacker and the honeypot has two players. Thus, $N = \{honeypot, attacker\}$. The honeypot can block `do_exec_ve` system calls with different probabilities. The set A_h corresponds to the set of blocking probabilities the honeypot can choose. An attacker can choose to retry a command, to search for an alternative command or to leave. We define an attacker strategy with a 3-tuple $(Pr(Retry), Pr(Alternative), Pr(Quit))$ and the set A_a contains all these strategies. One purpose of game theory is to compute the optimal strategy profiles for the players which results in the computation of Nash Equilibrium. A Nash Equilibrium in the context of honeypot game means that neither the honeypot nor the attacker can increase their expected payoffs assuming that neither player does not change his strategy during the game.

Computing Payoffs. Respective to attacker and honeypot strategies we propose two honeypot games. The games are different with respect to the payoff computation. We propose the following payoff computations[3]:

Number of transitions. We assume that attackers are rational and that they want to achieve their goal as fast as possible. Thus, an attacker tries to minimize the number of transitions in the hierarchical probabilistic automaton. The honeypot tries to learn as much as possible from the attacker. Potential useful information for a honeypot is to collect tools owned by attackers or to discover the sources where they are downloaded from. Hence, the honeypot tries to maximize the number of transitions performed by an attacker. The payoff for the honeypot R_h^t returns the number of transitions performed by an attacker. The more transitions an attacker does, the better it is for the honeypot. Attackers try to minimize their transitions and their payoff function returns -1 multiplied by the number of transitions. The less transitions attackers do, the less they are punished in terms of payoff. This game seems at first glance unfair regarding attackers. If we assume that attackers want

[3] Which can be setup on two different honeypots.

to be undiscovered while they are doing their attack, they have already lost because they connected to a monitored honeypot instead to real assets. The only chance they have is to divulge less information as possible and thus try to minimize the number of transitions.

Path probability payoff. The payoff computations purely based on the state transitions ignores the fact whether attackers reached their goal or not. Moreover, the payoff should take into account how likely a path is regarding observations from a deployed honeypot. We are looking for a payoff computation that rewards the honeypot for blocking and that penalizes the attacker when being blocked.

The payoff for the honeypot is shown in definition 2 and the payoff for the attacker is presented in definition 3. The probability $Pr(path)$ denotes the probability of the path the attacker has chosen and $Pr^*(path)$ denotes the probability of the most probable path from the source to the selected destination by the attacker.

$$R_a^p = \frac{Pr(path)}{Pr^*(path)} \tag{2}$$

$$R_h^p = 1 - \frac{Pr(path)}{Pr^*(path)} \tag{3}$$

The more the path probability gets close to the most probable path probability, the payoff for the attacker converges to 1. In this case, the payoff of the honeypot gets close to 0 which is the minimum payoff for the honeypot. If the path of the attacker is diverted due to blocked programs, the path probability chosen by the attacker diverges from the most probable path probability and gets lower than the most probable path probability. Hence, the payoff gets minimized for the attacker and maximized for the honeypot.

3.3 Computing Payoffs with Simulations

In order to compute the payoff values for all possible combination of strategies, we use a Monte Carlo simulation. We have built a simulator that uses bootstrap data obtained from an operational honeypot deployed over a period of 3 months. Due to computation and deployment constraints we are forced to do simulations since, doing real world experiments for all possible behaviors would require 2684 different honeypots setups.

Honeypot Simulator. Attackers and the honeypot select their strategies according to a given discrete probability. These probabilities are fixed and an attack is simulated. The simulation provides the number of transitions an attacker did, the optimal path probability, the path probability for the attacker, the fact that the attacker left and the fact that the maximum number of transitions was reached. The variable *src* specifies the initial state and the variable *dst* stands for the destination state in the hierarchical probabilistic automaton. Hence, the final state probability, required by the automaton, is 1 for the state *dst* and 0 for all the other states. During a simulation, the transitions performed by an attacker are recorded. The states, that an attacker passed through are kept in a list. When the simulation starts, the attacker enters the initial state. We assume that an attacker chooses the next transitions on the most probable path. If the attacker is not blocked, the attacker follows the same path. An attacker has a fixed goal. If this goal is reached then the simulation ends. ($src = dst$). Moreover the number of transitions during a simulation is recorded and if this number exceeds a defined threshold the simulation ends because we want to avoid endless transitions. The attacker can retry a command or compute the next state and the step is recorded. The honeypot decides to block or allow this step according to the probability $Pr(Block)$. The attacker now decides whether to quit or continue the game according the probability $Pr(Quit)$. If the attacker quits, the simulation ends. If the attacker decides to choose an alternative command, the hierarchical probabilistic automaton is modified due to implementation issues. The probability for the blocked transition is set to 0 and the probability for this transition is equally distributed for all outgoing transitions. An attacker always computes the most probable path and the same path could not be selected due to the 0 probability transition. Of course this effect is undone for the next simulation round. If the attacker decides to retry a command the state *alternative* is set to false, the loop ends and the next round starts.

4 Experimental Evaluation

We set up a high-interaction honeypot capable to record `do_exec_ve` and `clone` system calls. We directly patched the Linux kernel in order to avoid a detection by address arithmetic which is an attack described by McCarty [10]. We transmit the collected data in kernel space directly to the hardware level in order to avoid that collected information passes through the hands of the attacker. The honeypot is operated with the Qemu a x86 emulator [11]. The kernel inside the Qemu was modified such that process ids are logged. On the host machine this data is put in a database. The honeypot has also an additional network interface where system logs are transmitted to a syslog-ng server like it is the case for current production systems. The default running service is a SSH server which serves as entry point for attackers. We could configure the SSH server that the PAM module `pam_permit` should be used. In this case no password is asked, which may be very suspicious for attackers. Thus, we preferred to modify the `pam_unix` module, which is responsible for password authentication in a Linux operating system. With our patch, the system asks for a password but then neglects all non-privileged user passwords. This implementation choice is also resistant against password changes performed by attacker, because the password is not checked anymore. In theory an attacker could also change the PAM modules but we did not observe this phenomenon during the operation of our honeypot. Moreover, we observed that some attackers installed their own shell in order to be sure that they do not use a shell with additional monitoring features. Furthermore some attackers replaced the SSH server on the honeypot. An alternative solution is to perform a MITM attack in order to filter the command executed by attackers. However, from an engineering perspective this solution requires additional efforts to become stealthy. From this honeypot we recovered the process trees related to attackers which are sub trees of the Unix process tree on the honeypot. Then we transformed these process trees in process vectors. Each vector corresponds to an attack. From the observed process vectors we created a hierarchical probabilistic automaton to drive the simulation. Our data sets and developed software are publicly available[4].

4.1 Data Sets

The honeypot was operated on one public IPv4 address and consisted of a Ubuntu Linux 7.10 operating system. The Linux operating system was executed in a virtual machine operated by Qemu, version 0.9.1. We patched the `pam_unix` module, version 0.99.7.1 in order to facilitate access to the attackers and to mitigate the effects of an attacker that changed the password of a compromised account. We extended the Linux kernel, version 2.6.28-rc6 with the `do_exec_ve` and `clone` monitoring features.

The honeypot was operated from 2009-01-21 until 2009-03-09. In this period we observed 637 successful ssh logins and 12140 ssh failures. Despite the patched `pam_unix` module, a high number of ssh failures was discovered. Our `pam_unix` module patch lets the `pam_unix` module ignore passwords for non privileged user accounts on the honeypot. For 61% of the failed ssh attempts the root account was targeted which was explicitly blocked by our `pam_unix` module patch. Besides the 13 system accounts, we created 12 additional user accounts. Thus, we have 25 non privileged user accounts. Attackers tested 1763 non existing accounts with different passwords which is another explanation for the high number of SSH failures. For the successful logins we observed 183 different IP addresses. Some attackers modified the kernel but the virtual machine was configured in such a way that a reboot was translated into a power off. The kernel changes are noticed because the file system of the honeypot was periodically mounted (loop back) and checksums were computed to detect changes. If the kernel was changed we replaced the modified kernel with the original.

Process Trees. We recovered 637 process trees. The root of each process tree was the privileged separated process by sshd. The smallest trees have only one node and the tree with the maximum nodes has 1954 nodes. The small trees can be explained due to the fact that a brute force attacks against the SSH server was performed by some attackers with automated tools. The automated tool managed to break into the honeypot and immediately left. The maximum length of a process tree is due to bots that were installed on our honeypot. The bot master had long sessions with the bot in order to operate it. Due to data processing capabilities we stopped to reassemble the tree if the length is longer than 100 nodes. The average number of nodes per process tree is 105 with a standard deviation of 231.

[4] `http://quuxlabs.com/~gerard/jogy-experiment`

Process Vectors. Each process tree was converted in a process vector aiming to extract the program sequences done by an attacker. The longest process vector is composed of 85 programs and the smallest one contains only 1 program. The average process vector length is 6.16 with a standard deviation of 2.81.

4.2 Simulation Results

The hierarchical probabilistic automaton was set up using the process trees. We obtained 91 different programs (states). Each program is on its own an automaton based on the command line arguments. To simplify the automaton, we removed the first command line argument which corresponds to the program name in a Linux operating system. On average, programs have 9.72 command line arguments. The program with the most observed command line arguments has 181 arguments and some programs have one program argument. The standard deviation of the program arguments per program is 23.5. A large number of command line arguments can be explained by substitutions done by the program `bash` [12]. For instance the argument `*` is substituted by the program `bash` with a file list in the current directory. Moreover the hierarchical probabilistic automaton contains 581 different transitions. To model unknown or unseen transitions we smoothed the transition probabilities. Due to the fact that in our simulator the attacker selects the path with the highest probability, the smoothing factor is selected in such a way that the path probabilities are not affected. We evaluated the smoothing factor from $4.48 \cdot 10^{-15}$ to $4.48 \cdot 10^{-3}$ which are multiples of 10 of the lowest path probability. For each smoothing factor, we computed the average number of transitions from the initial states (always /usr/sbin/sshd) until the final states (last programs executed by attackers). In the range of $4.48 \cdot 10^{-15}$ to $4.48 \cdot 10^{-6}$ the average number of transitions remains constant and for values larger that $4.48 \cdot 10^{-6}$ the average number of transitions linearly decreases due to the fact that an attacker can select artificial shortcuts. We used a smoothing factor of $4.48 \cdot 10^{-08}$, which does not change the number of average transitions and is large enough to avoid rounding errors. The number of transitions increased to 8281 which is the square of the number of states which can be explained that we have a fully interconnected automaton.

The hierarchical probabilistic automaton was used to simulate attacks in order to compute the average payoff. We simulated the honeypot strategies ($Pr(Block)$) and attacker strategies ($Pr(Quit)$, $Pr(Retry)$, $Pr(Alternative)$) in a range of 0 and 1 in a step of 0.10 respecting the relation 1. In a first step we evaluate the impact of blocking system calls of an attacker. We noticed that the average of transitions performed by an attacker increases with the blocking probability.

In a second step, we computed Nash Equilibriums using the game theory simulator Gambit [13]. Only mixed equilibriums have been found. If we consider the first game (upper half of the table 1) then one mixed Nash Equilibrium exists: for instance, the honeypot can decide to use either a blocking probability of 0.10 or of 0.90. It should use 0.10 in 54% of the cases and 0.9 in 46% of the cases. The attacker should use $Pr(Quit)$ equal to 0.3 or 0.4 with associated

Table 1. Gambit simulation results

R_h^p		R_a^p			
q	$Pr(Block)$	q	$Pr(Quit)$	$Pr(Retry)$	$Pr(Alternative)$
0.54	0.1	0.73	0.3	0.4	0.3
0.46	0.9	0.27	0.4	0.2	0.4
R_h^t		R_a^t			
0.3	0.4	0.14	0.6	0.2	0.2
0.51	0.7	0.26	0.8	0	0.2
0.19	1	0.6	0.8	0.1	0.1

probabilities 0.73 and 0.27 respectively. Similarly, value choices according to the table can be set for $Pr(Retry)$ and $Pr(Alternative)$. The second game, (lower half of the table 1), has also a mixed equilibrium: the honeypot should use three different blocking probabilities (0.4, 0.7, 1) with corresponding probabilities 0.3, 0.51 and respectively 0.19. This is interesting, since blocking all transitions ($Pr(Block) = 1$) should be done in 19% of the cases. The attacker can also set his optimal strategies with respect to this table.

5 Related Work

The article of McCarty [10] describes an arm race between honeypots and attackers: attackers improve their techniques as soon as new monitoring techniques are deployed, which furthermore leads to defenders improving their previous approach. Some researchers modified shells aiming to observe the commands that an attacker used [2]. The major assumption of such a strategy is that the attacker does not change the shell on the honeypot. Other papers considered kernel patching [10] to mitigate this attack. Recently, virtualization based solutions [14] allowed to monitor from an external point of view high-interaction honeypots. Our operational deployment results are in line with the observations made by Eric Alata et al. [4] and Daniel Ramsbrock et al [3]. However, we preferred to patch the Linux authentication module PAM in order to avoid the case where attackers can lock out other attackers by changing the password of a compromised account. Next, we preferred to extract the process trees related to a SSH server instead of patching SSH as it is proposed by Eric Alata et al, because we have observed several times that attackers changed the SSH server. Although our implementation is based on a modified kernel running in Qemu, the conceptual approach using game theory with high-interaction honeypots can also be used in the context of virtualization based solutions. Garg et al. [15] also used game theory, where they established a different game: an attacker is rewarded if he or she probes a real machine and punished when he or she probes a honeypots. Bistarelli et al. [16] propose high level attack trees and associated attacks with countermeasures, where each action is linked to a cost or payoff. Game theory was also used in the general context of dependability and network security [17] for predicting future attacks.

Our honeypot model is based on a hierarchical probabilistic automaton bootstrapped with operational data from a high-interaction honeypot. Attacker actions are frequently grouped in high-level attack categories which describe the automaton [3]. Our approach is different from the work described by Kong-wei Lye et. al [18], because we recover the states and the transitions probabilities from a deployed honeypot compared to a manual definition. In order to compute the payoffs for the formal game, we used a simulation strategy that is similar to the approach used by Shishir et al. [19].

6 Conclusions and Future Work

This paper proposes a new paradigm for adaptive high-interaction honeypots that rely on game theoretical concepts as main driving force. We modeled the interaction between the honeypot and an attacker as a game, where appropriate payoff functions model the behavior goals observed in the real world. We derive the best strategies from the well known Nash Equilibrium and use operational honeypots in order to parametrize the game model. We make the strong assumption that hackers are always rational - this might be not the case with all attackers. The obtained results permit practical solutions for designing adaptive high-interaction honeypots. The adaptability is given by blocking one system call according to the optimal blocking probabilities. We leveraged data obtained from a deployed high-interaction honeypot in order to parametrize our model. We plan to investigate other game theoretical models, where repetitive and iterative learning from the past is possible. From an implementation point of view, we are not focusing on indirect attacks: for instance, we do not fully model attacks, where a script is added and gets executed later by the system itself. Moreover, our automaton may be biased by the specifics of the deployed honeypot and attackers that are aware of the game could poison the transition probabilities. This motivates further research on simplifying and comparing hierarchical probabilistic automata from different honeypots. We also planned to compare adaptive and non adaptive honeypots.

References

[1] Cheswick, B.: An evening with Berferd in which a cracker is lured, endured, and studied. In: Proc. Winter USENIX Conference, pp. 163–174 (1992)

[2] Spitzner, L.: Honeypots: Tracking Hackers. Addison-Wesley Longman Publishing Co., Inc., Boston (2002)

[3] Ramsbrock, D., Berthier, R., Cukier, M.: Profiling attacker behavior following SSH compromises. In: DSN 2007: Proceedings of the 37th Annual IEEE/IFIP International Conference on Dependable Systems and Networks, Washington, DC, USA, pp. 119–124. IEEE Computer Society, Los Alamitos (2007)

[4] Alata, E., Nicomette, V., Kaaniche, M., Dacier, M., Herrb, M.: Lessons learned from the deployment of a high-interaction honeypot. In: Sixth European Dependable Computing Conference, EDCC 2006, pp. 39–46 (2006)

[5] Vidal, E., Thollard, F., de la Higuera, C., Casacuberta, F., Carrasco, R.: Probabilistic finite-state machines-part I. IEEE Trans. Pattern Anal. Mach. Intell. 27(7), 1013–1025 (2005)
[6] Mitchell, M., Samuel, A.: Advanced Linux Programming. New Riders Publishing, Thousand Oaks (2001)
[7] Love, R.: Linux Kernel Development, 2nd edn. Novell Press (2005)
[8] Provos, N., Friedl, M., Honeyman, P.: Preventing privilege escalation. In: SSYM 2003: Proceedings of the 12th conference on USENIX Security Symposium, Berkeley, CA, USA, p. 16. USENIX Association (2003)
[9] Greenwald, A.: Matrix games and nash equilibrium, Lecture (2007)
[10] McCarty, B.: The honeynet arms race. IEEE Security and Privacy 1(6), 79–82 (2003)
[11] Bellard, F.: Qemu, a fast and portable dynamic translator. In: ATEC 2005: Proceedings of the annual conference on USENIX Annual Technical Conference, Berkeley, CA, USA, pp. 41–46. USENIX Association (2005)
[12] Newham, C., Vossen, J., Albing, C., Vossen, J.: Bash Cookbook: Solutions and Examples for Bash Users. O'Reilly Media, Inc., Sebastopol (2007)
[13] Turocy, T.: Gambit (2007), http://gambit.sourceforge.net/
[14] Dinaburg, A., Royal, P., Sharif, M., Lee, W.: Ether: malware analysis via hardware virtualization extensions. In: CCS 2008: Proceedings of the 15th ACM conference on Computer and communications security, pp. 51–62. ACM, New York (2008)
[15] Garg, N., Grosu, D.: Deception in honeynets: A game-theoretic analysis. In: Information Assurance and Security Workshop, 2007. IAW 2007. IEEE SMC, pp. 107–113 (2007)
[16] Bistarelli, S., Dall'Aglio, M., Peretti, P.: Strategic games on defense trees. In: Dimitrakos, T., Martinelli, F., Ryan, P.Y.A., Schneider, S. (eds.) FAST 2006. LNCS, vol. 4691, pp. 1–15. Springer, Heidelberg (2007)
[17] Sallhammar, K., Helvik, B.E., Knapskog, S.J.: A framework for predicting security and dependability measures in real-time. International Journal of Computer Science and Network Security 7(3) (2007)
[18] Lye, K.W., Wing, J.M.: Game strategies in network security. International Journal of Information Security 4(1), 71–86 (2005)
[19] Nagaraja, S., Anderson, R.: The topology of covert conflict. Technical report, University of Cambridge (2005)

Cooperative Autonomic Management in Dynamic Distributed Systems

Jing Xu[1], Ming Zhao[2], and José A.B. Fortes[1]

[1] ACIS Lab, Electrical and Computer Engineering, University of Florida
[2] Computing and Information Sciences, Florida International University
{jxu,fortes}@acis.ufl.edu
mzhao@fiu.edu

Abstract. The centralized management of large distributed systems is often impractical, particularly when the both the topology and status of the system change dynamically. This paper proposes an approach to application-centric self-management in large distributed systems consisting of a collection of autonomic components that join and leave the system dynamically. Cooperative autonomic components self-organize into a dynamically created overlay network. Through local information sharing with neighbors, each component gains access to global information as needed for optimizing performance of applications. The approach has been validated and evaluated by developing a decentralized autonomic system consisting of multiple autonomic application managers previously developed for the In-VIGO grid-computing system. Using analytical results from complex random network and measurements done in a prototype system, we demonstrate the robustness, self-organization and adaptability of our approach, both theoretically and experimentally.

1 Introduction

Scalability, cost and administrative overheads make it desirable for large dynamic distributed computing systems to be self-manageable. This is a particularly challenging goal in dynamic environments, such as grids, where large numbers of resources are discovered or aggregated on-demand and are subject to hard-to-predict loads, failures or off-times. With the increasing complexity of system management, the need for self-managing systems, as proposed in [24], has never been more important than today. Extensive research [11][12][22] has focused on providing autonomic capabilities to individual system components, such as databases, application servers and middleware components. In general, these autonomic components use an application-level manager that is capable of monitoring and/or predicting performance and allocating resources as needed to deliver reliable applications with the expected Quality of Service (QoS). One can envision the use of these or similar components and their autonomic capabilities as the basic building blocks of large distributed systems.

Three questions that arise in this context are addressed in this paper. First, what interactions should take place among individual components, in order to achieve system-level self-management needed to support application-level autonomics? Implicit in this question is the need for information sharing among different components. Second,

R. Guerraoui and F. Petit (Eds.): SSS 2009, LNCS 5873, pp. 756–770, 2009.

what type of network should be used to support the interactions? Implicit in this question is the need for the network to be highly scalable and robust to failures. Third, how should autonomic managers be designed to interact with other components, and enhance their autonomic ability? Implicit in this question is the need for cooperation among managers to efficiently collect and share information.

This paper proposes an approach for distributed-system self-management arising from interactions among the autonomic components deployed in the system. The key features of the proposed design are the effective use of components' limited monitoring and communicating capability, and their adaptation to the surrounding environment on the basis of information provided through a management overlay. The proposed system has the following properties:

- Self-adaptation: The system can dynamically respond to a changing environment to provide individual application managers with information and resources needed for achieving the desired QoS.
- Self-organization: The decentralized coordination enables the system to adapt to changes without external control. The global optimization is achieved through local decisions and interactions among neighbors.
- Robustness: There are no central resources that could become single points of failure or performance bottlenecks. Reconfiguration mechanisms effectively deal with dynamic resource availability.

An application of proposed approach in the context of the In-VIGO grid-computing system [1], is presented in this paper. In-VIGO provides a distributed environment where multiple application instances can coexist in virtual or physical resources. A virtual application manager (VAM) is a middleware component used to process user requests and manage application execution. Previous work considered the integration of autonomic capabilities into VAM to achieve self-optimizing and self-healing computation [22]. In this paper, a decentralized autonomic virtual application management system (DAVAM) is designed and implemented to further improve the scalability, efficiency and robustness. The DAVAM system is deployed on a large testbed that consists of tens of dynamic VAMs managing continuous jobs on hundreds of virtual machines with time-varying loads. Compared with our previously proposed centralized approach, the DAVAM system produces much lower job execution time and higher throughput in highly dynamic environments.

The rest of the paper is organized as follows. Section 2 describes the architecture of the decentralized autonomic system. Section 3 presents an analytical analysis of the system. The case study on DAVAM is presented in Section 4 and its experimental evaluation is discussed in Section 5. Section 6 reviews related work and Section 7 concludes the paper.

2 Autonomic System Model

We consider a highly dynamic distributed computing system consisting of a large collection of autonomic components [10]. Multiple components share distributed resources, as exemplified by grid-computing systems.

2.1 Autonomic Manager (AM) Model

The distributed system contains multiple autonomic components, each consisting of one or more managed components (e.g. jobs and resources) and an autonomic manager (AM). The behaviors of the components are independently managed by their AMs. To make optimal decisions towards desired states, AMs require global knowledge of the changing environment. However, in large distributed systems it is not scalable to collect and provide global knowledge through a central location.

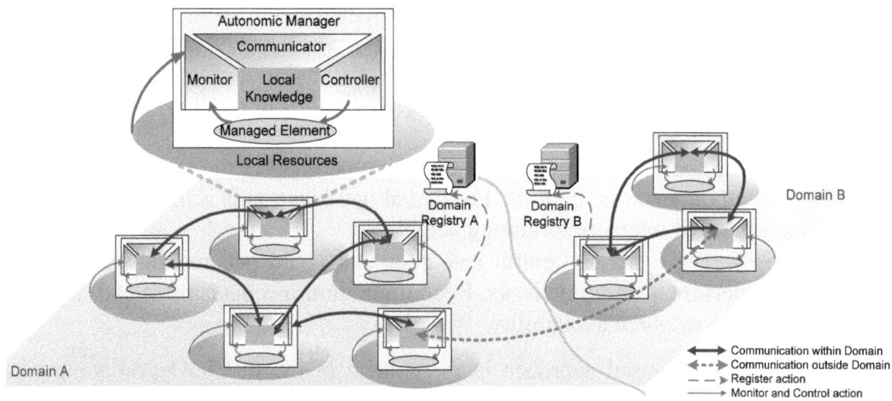

Fig. 1. A distributed autonomic system consisting of autonomic managers (AMs) across two domains, each with a registry indexing resources in the domain. Each AM contacts its domain registry to choose both the resources to be monitored (called local resources) and other AMs (called neighbors) to exchange local information.

To solve this problem, individual AMs are extended to monitor a small piece of their environment (hereon called *local* resources). Each AM has only a local view of the whole environment. However, interactions among the managers provide them with a global view of the system. The AM model (Fig. 1.) consists of the following components:

- **Monitor:** it collects, aggregates and filters the status information from its managed elements and its local resources.
- **Controller:** it manages the elements' behaviors based on analysis and prediction using the local knowledge.
- **Communicator:** it supports information exchanges with other autonomic managers.
- **Local Knowledge Base:** it stores the information obtained locally and through information exchanges between neighbors.

2.2 Decentralized Autonomic System

Because the computing resources are organized into domains which may correspond to administrative domains, a distributed domain registry infrastructure is designed to provide scalable and reliable resource location and AM discovery services. Each registry maintains an index of resources and the list of existing AMs in its domain.

When an autonomic component joins the domain, its AM registers its unique id in the registry, and chooses some existing AMs to cooperate with and selects some resources in the domain as its local resources. To improve reliability, nearby domain registries periodically exchange information so that each registry's local resource and AM lists are replicated in some other registries.

Local resource claiming: Each AM randomly selects a number of resources in the domain which have not yet selected by other AMs registry and claims them by marking the corresponding entries with its id. Once a resource is claimed by an AM, its status is monitored by the AM and stored in its local knowledge base during the claiming period. An AM disclaims its resources by unmarking them in the registry before its departure from the system.

Neighborhood building: When an AM joins a domain it selects *m* existing AMs in the same domain as its potential neighbors. AMs in the same neighborhood cooperate with each other by exchanging information. The neighbor selection can take place randomly, or preferentially which means that some AMs are more attractive and have a better chance to get neighbors. When departing from its domain, an AM unregisters itself by deleting its id from the domain registry and sends a message to its neighbors. In case an AM needs other domain's information, it can ask its domain registry for AMs in other domains to build a "cross-domain" neighborhood.

Information sharing and filtering: During its lifecycle, each AM becomes a dynamic information source by monitoring its local resources. This local information can be propagated through multi-AM cooperation. Every AM that receives a message from a neighbor must store it and later forward it to its other neighbors. Two approaches are used toghether to reduce the number of messages transmitted among the AMs. One is to define an obsolescence relation [14] between messages: a message m_1 is recognized as obsolete if m_2 contains more recent information that subsumes m_1. The other way is to evaluate how useful each message is, and drop the low-value messages.

2.3 Dynamic AM Network

The AM neighborhoods define a dynamic overlay network that changes as the AMs join and leave the system, in a manner similar to a peer-to-peer network [18][17]. The AMs must adapt their behaviors and interactions to the changing state. For example, an AM leaving or crashing may cause serious effects - claimed local resources may be no longer monitored by anyone, and some AMs may become isolated from others. To prevent and repair the damages, the following mechanisms are proposed.

Dynamic resource claiming: By periodically checking the domain registry, AMs can obtain the domain information such as the number of resources and AMs currently in the system, and then adjust the number of resources it should monitor to balance the monitoring load over the network. However, the information provided by domain registries might be incorrect because of AMs' unpredictable failures. To solve this problem, once an AM detects its neighbor's failure, it informs the domain registry and reclaims the resources that became unmonitored because of the failure.

Dynamic neighborhood building: If an AM decides to leave, it informs its neighbors by sending them a farewell message. In the case of AM or network failure, each AM measures the interval between two successive messages sent from the same neighbor and sets a timeout to detect the failure. When an AM is informed of a neighbor's departure or detects a neighbor's failure, it chooses its new neighbor with probability p (set to 0.5 as explained in Section 3.3). This mechanism allows AMs to maintain network connectivity.

3 Analytical Evaluation

3.1 Network Model

We use the conceptual framework and notations from complex network theory [2][6] to model the AM network and analyze its topology features. The decentralized autonomic system is modeled as a network in which each AM is represented by a node, and two nodes are linked if they are neighbors. The following notations are used to describe the network.

$n(t)$: the total number of nodes at time t.

$r(t)$: the total number of resources at time t.

m : the number of neighbors a node connects to when joining the network.

$k_i(t)$:the degree (the number of neighbors) of the ith node at time t.

$o_i(t)$: the local load (the number of claimed resources) of the ith node at time t.

The first two parameters describe the entire network and can be obtained directly from the domain registry, while the rest of the parameters describe the behavior of individual nodes.

3.2 Node Joining and Neighbor Selection

Consider the case where the network starts with one node, and at each step, a new node joins and connects to m existing nodes. At time t the network has a total of $n(t)$ nodes ($n(t) >> m$, for a large system). It is well known that the resulting network has the following properties [6].

$$\text{Total number of links: } e(t) = mn(t) - (m^2 + m)/2 \approx mn(t) \tag{1}$$

$$\text{Average degree: } \bar{k}(t) = 2e(t)/n(t) \approx 2m \tag{2}$$

$$\text{Diameter: } d(t) = \ln n(t)/\ln \bar{k}(t) \approx \ln n(t)/\ln 2m \tag{3}$$

Eq. (3) shows that the network diameter (shortest-path length between any two nodes) is small even for a large network. This "small world effect" [20] ensures that local information of one node can be propagated to any other node very quickly even in large networks. Different neighbor selection policies result in different network degree distributions. The random selection results in exponential distribution. In contrast, the preferential linking (the likelihood of connecting to a node is proportional to the node's degree) leads to a power-law distribution [2]. The major differences between these networks are their robustness against random network errors as discussed next.

3.3 Neighborhood Rebuilding

The effect of random damage on networks was simulated in [2] and the results show that scale-free networks display a high degree of tolerance against random failures. For exponential networks, Eq. (4) indicates that average degree decreases linearly with growing f (the fraction of removed nodes), which in turn increases network diameter (see Eq. (3)).

$$\bar{k}' = \bar{k}(1-f) \tag{4}$$

A dynamic neighborhood rebuilding mechanism is proposed to avoid this impact. When a node leaves the network, a fraction p of its neighbors establish new relationships with other nodes. Eq. (5) indicates that by choosing p equal to 0.5 the average degree can remain approximately constant, so does the network diameter.

$$\bar{k}' = 2e'/n' \approx 2\left(\bar{k}n/2 - (1-p)\bar{k}fn\right) / n(1-f) \overset{p=0.5}{\Rightarrow} \bar{k} \tag{5}$$

3.4 Local Load Adjustment

We use $\tilde{o}(t) = r(t)/n(t)$ to express the average ratio of the number of resources $r(t)$ to the network size $n(t)$ at time t. To balance the load on all the nodes, when a node joins the network, $o_i(t)$ is initialized as follows:

$$o_i(t) = \begin{cases} \lceil \tilde{o}(t) \rceil & \text{if} \quad \tilde{o}(t) < o^{\max} \\ o^{\max} & \text{otherwise} \end{cases} \tag{6}$$

The maximum number of resources each node can monitor is bounded to avoid overloading. Because the value of $\tilde{o}(t)$ may change as the network size and resource availability vary, each node periodically compares its current load with $\tilde{o}(t)$ and adjusts it accordingly.

3.5 Communication Cost

Each node in the network sends messages to its neighbors at constant time interval ΔT. With information filtering, the message size s_i can be bound to a fixed value S. The global communication cost of the network is

$$C = \sum k_i(t) \cdot s_i \le 2e(t) \cdot S = 2m \cdot n(t) \cdot S \tag{7}$$

which grows linearly with the network size. But from the perspective of a single node, the average communication cost stays almost constant.

$$\bar{c} = C / n(t) \approx 2m \cdot S \tag{8}$$

4 Case Study: DAVAM System

In order to validate the proposed model, we used In-VIGO [1] grid middleware to implement a decentralized Autonomic Virtual Application Management (DAVAM) system.

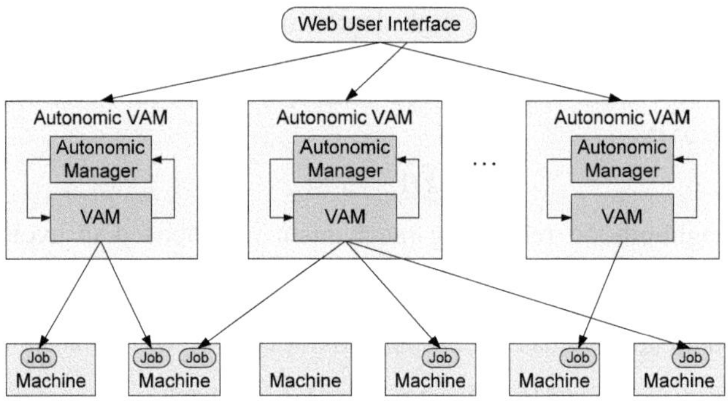

Fig. 2. The high-level view of autonomic VAM in In-VIGO. This figure shows multiple VAMs that submit jobs on multiple machines.

4.1 Background

In-VIGO is a grid-computing infrastructure that uses virtualization technologies to provide secure application execution environments. Fig. 2 provides a high-level view of the role of the autonomic Virtual Application Manager (AVAM) in In-VIGO (detailed in [22]). Typically, a user initiates an application session to run instances of a computational tool on grid resources[1].

Each session is managed by a middleware component, called the Virtual Application Manager. Autonomic features including self-optimization and self-healing are integrated into the AVAM. It relies on monitoring of job and resource conditions, predicting violations of user- and/or system-expected execution times, and restarting jobs in resources capable of delivering acceptable times. To achieve desired performance, each AVAM requires global knowledge of the time-varying resource information. However, the centralized approach in [22] using a global controller to collect and maintain the whole system status does not scale well in large-scale distributed systems.

4.2 Cooperative AVAM

Fig. 3. shows the major functions implemented in an AVAM. The local knowledge base stores information such as dynamic local resources' status, application run-time performance, the list of the neighbors and local resources claimed by the AVAM.

[1] A "tool" or "application" can consist of more than a single application, e.g., it could entail the execution of a workflow of application.

4.2.1 Controller

The controller is responsible for controlling the application execution to achieve reliable and optimized performance. The functions in the controller are listed below:

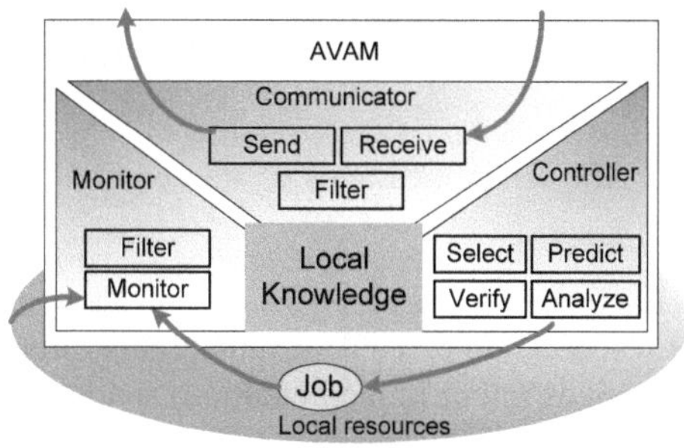

Fig. 3. The functions and information flow of a cooperative AVAM

Predict function: A memory-based learning algorithm [22][9] is used to predict resource usage for a given job, such as CPU cycles and memory usage. The basic idea is that the resources consumed by a job often depend on the input parameters supplied to the tool. Therefore, the "similarity" of two jobs is defined by the distance metric of two sets of inputs and resource usage is predicted based on the tool execution history.

Select function: The controller scans the list of resources in the local knowledge base and ranks them based on the job's resource requirements and the resources' capacity. To optimize the job's performance, the controller selects the resource with the highest score. However, resource contention may happen if multiple AVAMs try to submit jobs to the same "best" resource simultaneously. A ε-random rule is used to deal with this problem. A randomly generated small number ε in the range [-0.1, 0.1] is added to each resource's score, and then *Select* function ranks the resource list with these "modified" scores. By setting a small number ε, the ε-random rule is able to mitigate resource contention to a certain extent.

Verify function: After a resource is selected, this function checks the current status of the resource and verifies whether its score is still valid. If not, the controller selects the next candidate resource in the ranked list and repeats this verification process.

Analyze function: After a job is submitted to the chosen resource, the monitor keeps collecting the job's running status (e.g., current CPU time, elapsed time, and CPU utilization consumed by the job), which is used to estimate the job's progress (see [22]). If it is predicted that the job cannot finish before the deadline, the controller will try to find a better resource that can satisfy the job requirements and reschedules the job to that resource. In the case when all the resources in one domain are heavily loaded, the controller selects its "cross-domain" neighbors and communicates with them to quickly get the resource information in other domains and determine on which resource it can submit the job.

4.2.2 Monitor and Communicator

The monitor periodically collects local resources' status information and checks every submitted job periodically. If the job finishes successfully, the monitor collects some statistic data about this execution and reports it to the local knowledge base for historical records. The communicator is responsible for sending and receiving messages to and from neighbors. There are four types of messages exchanged between neighbors.

Joining/leaving: An AVAM sends messages to its neighbors to notify its arrival or departure.

Local resource table: Each AVAM has its own current view of the resources' status and stores it in a local resource table. To disseminate this information, every AVAM periodically (every 10 seconds in our implementation) sends its local resource table to the neighbors.

Rewiring: Before leaving, an AVAM selects a fraction p (set to 0.5 in our case) of its neighbors and sends them rewiring messages. The receivers then choose some other AVAMs as their new neighbors.

4.2.3 Information filtering

The resources information collected by an AVAM must be filtered before being added to the local resource table to reduce message size. Each record has an *age* attribute to indicate the time elapsed since the last update. If two records contain the same resource's status, the older one gets filtered out.

Information filtering also happens by purging the lower-values records from the table. Concentrating on CPU-intensive applications, AVAMs are interested in resources with high CPU processing power. Thus, the value of the ith resource is defined as follows. If CPU utilization stays below 100%, the CPU capacity is calculated by the CPU speed and utilization; otherwise, it is computed using the CPU load (the queue length of the runnable processes). A weight of 0.01 is used to make these two measurements comparable.

$$Value_i = \begin{cases} CPU\_Speed_i \times (1 - CPU\_Utilization_i) & \text{if CPU\_Utilization}_i < 100\% \\ CPU\_Speed_i / CPU\_Load_i \times 0.01 & \text{otherwise} \end{cases} \quad (9)$$

Due to the dynamic nature of grid resources, the older a resource record becomes, the less accurate it is. Therefore, the record's value is reduced by a factor corresponding to its age, represented as α ($\alpha = 1 - age / max$), where the max is set to 60 seconds in our implementation. With this information filtering, a local resource table's size is reduced by only retaining the resources with high CPU processing capability.

5 Experimental Evaluation

This section evaluates the proposed DAVAM system with respect to scalability, efficiency and robustness.

5.1 Setup

The experiments were conducted on a subset of the In-VIGO system. The computer resources consist of 200 VMware-server virtual machines (each has 128 MB memory and runs Red Hat 7.3) hosted on a cluster of ten dual 2.4GHz hyper-threaded Xeon nodes. In the experiments, a considerable amount of background load was also introduced into the resources by launching CPU-intensive jobs. Dynamic loading environments were created by randomly choosing and loading different subsets of the resources (100 randomly chosen resources, unless otherwise noted) every 50 seconds. The domain registries are implemented with MySQL. TunProb (Numerical Calculation of the Transmission Probability for One-Dimensional Electron Tunneling), a tool available on the In-VIGO portal, is used as a benchmark representative of CPU-intensive workloads. In the experiments each AVAM was used to manage the execution of one or more instances of TunProb.

The DAVAM system initialization process starts with one AVAM. Then at each increment of time (one second) one new AVAM is started until the expected system size is reached. Each AVAM establishes connections with *m* (0~6) existing AVAMs in its domain. Each AVAM monitors up to five virtual machines as its local resources, and updates their status in its local resource table every ten seconds. AVAM neighbors exchange their local resource tables every ten seconds and the table can only keep up to ten records.

5.2 Experimental Evaluation of Efficiency

The efficiency of the DAVAM system is reflected by each AVAM being able to quickly obtain the current status of the entire system and find good resources for its jobs. The first experiment investigates how the performance changes with different numbers of neighbors each AVAM contacts when joining the system. Fifty AVAMs were initially started in the domain, and ten seconds later another five AVAMs joined and each selected *m* (0~6) neighbors. After ten seconds of their arrivals, the five AVAMs began to submit jobs continuously until they left the domain 140 seconds later.

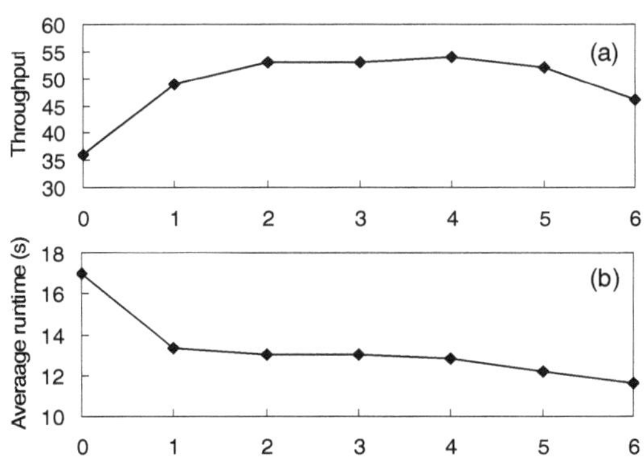

Fig. 4. The comparison of the total number of jobs finished by 5 AVAMs (a) and the TunProb jobs' average execution time (b) with different values of m during 150 seconds

Fig. 4. compares the average job runtime and the throughput (the total number of jobs completed by the five AVAMs) with different values of *m*. As expected, the worst performance occurs when each AVAM does not have any neighbors. As the value of *m* increases, the performance improves because AVAMs can learn more resources' information through interaction with their neighbors and select resources more wisely. Figure 4 also indicates that, when *m* exceeds five, the throughput drops because the benefit from contacting more neighbors is outweighed by communication overhead.

5.3 Experimental Evaluation of Scalability

In the second experiment, we studied the system scalability by comparing the performance of DAVAM with *centralized* and *round-robin* approaches. Forty AVAMs join the domain and each one submits jobs continuously for 150 seconds. In the DAVAM approach, each AVAM selects two neighbors. The neighbor selections, with and without preference, lead to two types of networks, *power-law* and *exponential networks* [2], respectively. The *centralized* approach uses a central monitor to collect and store resources' status in a central database. Each AVAM chooses the best resource currently available in the database to submit its jobs. The *round-robin* approach does not need any resource status information and chooses resources in a round-robin manner. The experiments were conducted in three loading environments – low, medium and high, in which 30%, 50% and 70% of randomly chosen resources were loaded with CPU-intensive processes, respectively.

Fig. 5. shows the average job runtime and the overall throughput of the different approaches. Both *exponential* and *power-law* AVAM networks deliver similar best performance because the small world property makes sure that each AVAM in the network can obtain the latest system-wide resource status very quickly. Furthermore, the ε-random resource selection rule avoids resource contention among multiple AVAMs. In contrast, the *centralized* approach suffers from database-access contention between the AVAMs and the central monitor. The *round-robin* approach gives the worst performance because it does not consider any dynamic information for resource selection.

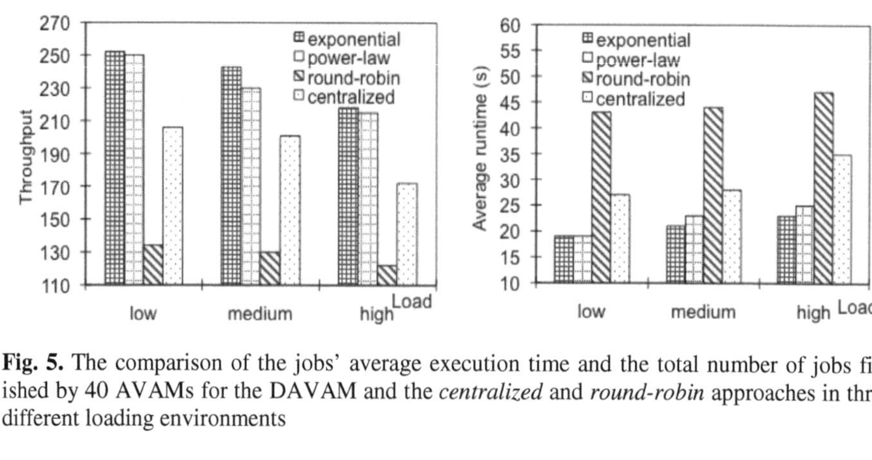

Fig. 5. The comparison of the jobs' average execution time and the total number of jobs finished by 40 AVAMs for the DAVAM and the *centralized* and *round-robin* approaches in three different loading environments

5.4 Experimental Evaluation of Robustness

The third experiment studies the robustness of the DAVAM approach, where the system-level information is constructed by the distributed cooperative AVAMs, in contrast with the centralized approach, where a central database is used to store the global knowledge. In the experiment, 50 AVAMs were started at the same time. After 200 seconds, half of them left and the others continued to work and submit jobs for another 200 seconds. In DAVAM the remaining AVAMs react to system changes by contacting new neighbors and reclaiming resources from the domain registry. The neighborhood rebuilding mechanism maintains the DAVAM network connectivity, and the resource reclaiming ensures that most of the resources are monitored by at least one AVAM. Fig. 6. compares the average job runtime and the throughput by the 25 AVAMs before and after the other AVAMs' leaving. For both exponential and power-law networks, the performance of the remaining AVAMs is almost unaffected even if a high number of AVAMs left the system.

For the *centralized* approach, on the contrary, if the central database fails, none of the AVAMs can retrieve any new information from the database, so they have to continue using the resources chosen before the database failure. Figure 6 shows that, without the dynamic resource information provided by the database, the performance drops dramatically. Similar effects can be observed if the central monitor fails.

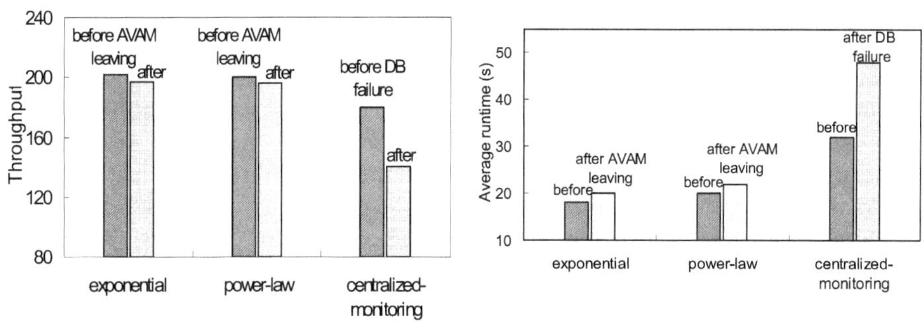

Fig. 6. TunProb jobs' average execution time and the total number of jobs finished by 25 AVAMs before and after AVAM leaving, for DAVAM exponential and power-law networks, and before and after failure of a central database when it is used for centralized monitoring

5.5 Discussion

It may possible to design a hierarchical system to circumvent scalability issues caused by a purely centralized approach and also achieve the similar performance with the p2p approach. However, in a dynamic environment where nodes can join and leave at any time, it is very difficult to construct and maintain a balanced, optimal hierarchical structure. Moreover, the supernodes (root notes) at the top level in the hierarchical system can potentially cause single-point system failures and/or lead to isolated nodes in the system. Although replication can compensate for potential unstable behavior of a supernode, it will add resource costs and communication overhead to keep replicas consistent.

6 Related Work

Agent-based [8][16] modeling is a very natural and flexible way to model distributed interconnected systems. In [2] several distributed and self-organizing algorithms are proposed for placement of services on servers. For each service a service manager is instantiated to create multiple “ants” (agents) and send them out to the server network. The ant travels from one server to another, choosing the servers along the path based on locally available information. The ant then finally makes a decision, based on the knowledge it has accumulated on its travel. Service manager and the spawned ants work with local information, which ensures scalability. Similarly, Messor proposed to use “ants” wandering over the network to explore load conditions. The goal is to achieve load balancing by ants moving jobs from the most overloaded node to underloaded ones.

In our system, each autonomic component can be identified as an agent, and the autonomic system as a multi-agent system. Each autonomic component is both cooperative (sharing its local knowledge with neighbors) and selfish (trying to find and allocate the best resources for its own jobs). The authors in [8] claim that no obvious gain can be achieved from communication between agents. The reason is that if all the agents have a "better" picture of the whole system, they all tend to use the best resources and thus cause competition. In contrast, the resource verification and ε-random selection mechanisms applied to our system can prevent this problem and their effectiveness is proved by the experiments.

The peer-to-peer model offers an alternative to the traditional client-server model for many large-scale applications in distributed setting. Epidemic (or gossip) algorithms [7][4] have proved to be effective solutions for disseminating information in large-scale systems. The basic idea is that each process periodically chooses a random subset of processes in the system and sends them the new information it has received.

Traditional epidemic algorithms rely on each process having knowledge of the global membership which is not realistic for large groups of processes. Our system uses a very simple membership protocol to establish and rebuild neighbor connectivity with support from the decentralized domain registry service.

7 Conclusions

This paper presents an autonomic computing system in which multiple autonomic components collaborate to optimize the behavior of the system. A general autonomic manager model is designed to control the managed elements’ internal state and manage its interactions with the surrounding environment. The autonomic manager is lightweight, making it suitable for many distributed systems. Each has a local view of the system state and communicates periodically its partial knowledge to its neighbors, thus contributing to building a common, shared global view of the system state. A decentralized registry provides scalable and reliable neighbor and resource discovery service for the system. The overlay network structured by the neighbor relationships is demonstrated to be highly reliable and efficient. The results show that the decentralized and cooperative nature of the system yields a number of desirable properties, including efficiency, robustness, and scalability under a highly dynamic environment.

In Introduction we raised the question of what component interactions are needed for system-level self-management to support autonomic applications. Our results show that simple exchanges of local information suffice to enable application managers to find resources that best suit performance requirements of an application. Another question asked which network should be used to support the communication needed to establish connectivity and share information. We found that both exponential and power-law networks yield small diameters to support low-latency communication needed for timely sharing of information among system components. The question of how to design autonomic managers capable of cooperatively interacting with each other has been answered by describing a set of functions implemented by the typical components of an autonomic manager: monitor, communicator, controller and a local knowledge base. The interaction between managers consists of simple information exchanges and each manager has a small cache to store partial "global" information to enhance its autonomic ability. The resulting design is rather lightweight and applicable beyond the concrete In-VIGO scenario used in this paper to validate the proposed approach.

There are additional questions that require further research. Among them, to what degree does our design mitigate the occurrence of races or oscillations among requests or job allocations? Our approach reduces their likelihood because communication latencies are small, age attributes are used to avoid using very dated information and an ε-random resource selection rule is used to mitigate the probability of resource contention. A complete answer would require a characterization of the conditions that lead to oscillations and races in distributed systems without (and with) our techniques. This is outside the scope of this paper and left as a challenge for future work.

Acknowledgments. The US National Science Foundation partially supports this work under grant numbers IIP 0925103, CNS 0855123, CNS 0821622, IIP 0823896, IIP 0758596. We also acknowledge the support of the Bell-South Foundation and Shared University Research grants from IBM.

References

1. Adabala, S., et al.: From Virtualized Resources to Virtual Computing Grids: The In-VIGO System. In: Future Generation Computing Systems (2005)
2. Albert, R., Barabási, A.: Statistical mechanics of complex networks. Rev. of Mod. Phys. 74 (2002)
3. Andrzejak, A., et al.: Algorithms for Self-Organization and Adaptive Service Placement in Dynamic Distributed Systems. HPL Tech. Rep. 9/02
4. Barabasi, A., Albert, R., Jeong, H.: Mean-field theory for scale-free random networks. Physica A (1999)
5. Birman, K.P., Hayden, M., Ozkasap, O., Xiao, Z., Budiu, M., Minsky, Y.: Bimodal Multicast. ACM TOCS 17 (1999)
6. Cohen, R., Erez, K., ben-Avraham, D., Havlin, S.: Resilience of the Internet to random breakdowns. Phys. Rev. Let. (2000)
7. Dorogovtsev, S.N., Mendes, J.F.F.: Evolution of networks. Adv. Phys. 51 (2002)
8. Eugster, P.T., Guerraoui, R., Kermarrec, A.M., Massoulie, L.: Epidemic Information Dissemination in Distributed Systems. IEEE Computer 37 (2004)

9. Jennings, N.R.: Building complex, distributed system: the case for an agent-based approach. Communications of the ACM 44(4), 35–41 (2001)
10. Kapadia, N., Fortes, J.A.B., Brodley, C.E.: Predictive Application-Performance Modeling in a Computational Grid Environment. In: Proceedings of the 8th IEEE international Symposium on High Performance Distributed Computing (August 1999)
11. Kephart, J.O., Chess, D.M.: The vision of autonomic computing. Computer (2003)
12. Liu, H., Parashar, M., Hariri, S.: A Component-based Programming Framework for Autonomic Applications. In: Proceedings of the First international Conference on Autonomic Computing (June 2004)
13. Melcher, B., Mitchell, B.: Towards an autonomic framework: Self-configuring network services and developing autonomic applications. Intel Technology Journal 8(4) (2004)
14. Pereira, J., Rodrigues, L., Oliveira, R.: Semantically Reliable Multicast: Definition Implementation and Performance Evaluation. IEEE Trans. Computers 52 (2003)
15. Qiao, Y., Bustamante, F.: 'Elders know best -handling churn in less structured p2p systems. In: 5th IEEE Intl. Conf. on Peer-to-Peer Computing (2005)
16. Schaerf, A., Shoham, Y., Tennenholtz, M.: Adaptive load balancing: A study in multiagent learning. J. A.I. Res. (1995)
17. Schoder, D., Fischbach, K.: Core Concepts in Peer-to-Peer (P2P) Networking. In: P2P Computing: The Evolution of a Disruptive Technology. Idea Group Inc., Hershey
18. Steinmetz, R., Wehrle, K. (eds.): Peer-to-Peer Systems and Applications. LNCS, vol. 3485. Springer, Heidelberg (2005)
19. Thrun, S.B.: The Role of Exploration in Learning and Control. In: Handbook of Intelligent Control: Neural Fuzzy and Adaptive Approaches. Van Nostrand Reinhold (1992)
20. Watts, D., Strogatz, S.: Collective dynamics of 'small-world' networks. Nature 393 (1998)
21. White, S.R., Hanson, J.E., Whalley, I., Chess, D.M., Kephart, J.O.: An architectural approach to autonomic computing. In: Proceedings of the First international Conference on Autonomic Computing (2004)
22. Xu, J., Adabala, S., Fortes, J.: Towards Autonomic Virtual Application Manager in In-VIGO system. In: Proceedings of the Second international Conference on Autonomic Computing (June 2005)
23. Xu, J., Zhao, M., Fortes, J.: Cooperative Autonomic Management in Dynamic Distributed Systems. Technical Report (April 2006)
24. IBM's Perspective on Autonomic Computing, `http://www.research.ibm.com/autonomic/`

Brief Announcement: Consistent Fixed Points and Negative Gain

Hrishikesh B. Acharya[1], Ehab S. Elmallah[2], and Mohamed G. Gouda[1,3]

[1] The University of Texas at Austin, U.S.A.
{acharya,gouda}@cs.utexas.edu
[2] The University of Alberta, Canada
ehab@cs.ualberta.ca
[3] The National Science Foundation, U.S.A.

Abstract. We discuss the stabilization properties of networks that are composed of "displacement elements". Each displacement element is defined by an integer K, called the displacement of the element, an input variable x, and an output variable y, where the values of x and y are non-negative integers. An execution step of this element assigns to y the maximum of 0 and $K + x$. The objective of our discussion is to demonstrate that two principles play an important role in ensuring that a network N is stabilizing, i.e. starting from any global state, network N is guaranteed to reach a global fixed point. The first principle, named consistent fixed points, states that if a variable is written by two subnetworks of N, then the values of this variable, when these two subnetworks reach fixed points, are equal. The second principle, named negative gain, states that the sum of displacements along every directed loop in network N is negative.

1 Introduction

A network of communicating elements is stabilizing iff, starting from any global state, the network is guaranteed to reach a fixed point [1]. The theory of network stabilization, though highly studied, has not yet identified the general principles which can explain the stabilization of rich classes of networks. We identify two such general principles, and illustrate their utility by showing how these principles can be used to design interesting classes of stabilizing networks. In our study, we focus on a simple model, called displacement networks.

A displacement network consists of one or more displacement elements. Each element is defined by an integer K, called the displacement of the element, an input variable x, and an output variable y, where the values of x and y are non-negative integers. The execution step of this element assigns to y the maximum of 0 and $K + x$ (provided that this assignment changes the value of y). Later, we generalize the model to allow elements with multiple inputs.

We propose two general principles to adopt while designing a stabilizing displacement network N: consistent fixed points and negative gain. The principle of consistent fixed points states that, if a variable is written by two or more subnetworks of N, then the values of this variable written by these subnetworks, when

R. Guerraoui and F. Petit (Eds.): SSS 2009, LNCS 5873, pp. 771–772, 2009.

these subnetworks reach fixed points, are equal. The principle of negative gain states that the sum of the displacements along every directed loop in network N is negative.

These two principles have counterparts in control theory. Specifically, the principle of consistent fixed points is analogous to the requirement that a control system be free from self-oscillations; the principle of negative gain is analogous to the requirement that the feedback loop of a control system be negative.

2 Results

1. An acyclic network N is stabilizing iff every two chains, that terminate at the same variable in N, are consistent.
2. Given a particular assignment of input values, a stabilizing acyclic network has exactly one fixed point.
3. A loop network is stabilizing iff one of the following two conditions holds:
   - the total gain of the loop is negative.
   - the total gain of the loop is zero and the loop has no more than two elements.
4. A stabilizing loop network has exactly one fixed point.
5. A composite network (composed of stabilizing acyclic and loop networks) is stabilizing iff it is consistent.
6. If the gain of each directed loop in an m-bow network N is negative, then N is stabilizing.
7. A composition of a stabilizing loop or m-bow network with a stabilizing acyclic network, is stabilizing if every variable shared by both components is an input variable of the acyclic network.

3 Concluding Remarks

Our two principles, of consistent fixed points and negative gain, are seen to be sufficient (and sometimes also necessary) to establish stabilization of many classes of networks. It would be interesting to study whether these principles remain sufficient to ensure self-stabilization if we allow a richer network model, in which an element can perform any linear operation on its inputs and output the result.

Reference

1. Dijkstra, E.W.: Self-stabilizing systems in spite of distributed control. Commun. ACM 17(11), 643–644 (1974)

Brief Announcement: Induced Churn to Face Adversarial Behavior in Peer-to-Peer Systems

Emmanuelle Anceaume[1], Francisco Brasileiro[4], Romaric Ludinard[2,⋆], Bruno Sericola[2], and Frederic Tronel[3]

[1] CNRS / IRISA, Rennes, France
[2] INRIA Rennes Bretagne-Atlantique, Rennes, France
[3] Supelec, France
[4] Universidade Federal de Campina Grande, LSD Laboratory, Brazil

Awerbuch and Scheideler [2] have shown that peer-to-peer overlays networks can only survive Byzantine attacks if malicious nodes are not able to predict what will be the topology of the network for a given sequence of join and leave operations. A prerequisite for this condition to hold is to guarantee that nodes identifiers randomness is continuously preserved. However targeted join/leave attacks may quickly endanger the relevance of such an assumption. Inducing churn has been shown to be the other fundamental ingredient to preserve randomness. Several strategies based on these principles have been proposed. Most of them are based on locally induced churn. However either they have been proven incorrect or they involve a too high level of complexity to be practically acceptable [2]. The other ones, based on globally induced churn, enforce limited lifetime for each node in the system. However, these solutions keep the system in an unnecessary hyper-activity, and thus need to impose strict restrictions on nodes joining rate which clearly limit their applicability to open systems.

In this paper we propose to leverage the power of clustering to design a provably correct and practically usable solution that preserves randomness under an ϵ-bounded adversary. Our solution relies on the clusterized version of peer-to-peer overlays combined with a mechanism that allows the enforcement of limited nodes lifetime. Clusterized versions of structured-based overlays [1,3] are such that clusters of nodes substitute nodes at the vertices of the graph. Nodes are grouped together according to some distance function. Our solution is based on the partitioning of the cluster population into two sets, called resp. core and spare sets. Core members are responsible for implementing the overlay. By using classical quorum-based active replication mechanisms among core members, the impact of a minority of malicious nodes is easily masked. The spare set is used to reduce the management overhead caused by the natural churn that is present in typical overlay networks. Nodes in the spare set that leave the system cause next to no overhead, and so do most of the nodes joining the system as they are inserted in the spare set of their corresponding clusters. On the other hand, whenever a core member leaves the system, new core and spare sets are possibly generated.

We propose two strategies to handle these leaves. These strategies mainly differ in the amount of randomisation they impose to introduce the unpredictability

⋆ Supported by the Direction Générale des Entreprises - P2Pim@ges project.

R. Guerraoui and F. Petit (Eds.): SSS 2009, LNCS 5873, pp. 773–774, 2009.

required to deal with attacks. In the first one, a core member that leaves is replaced by a randomly chosen spare member, while in the second one, the departure of a core member leads to the renewal of the whole core set by randomly selecting new core members within both core and spare sets. Then we model each strategy as a game.

The long term behavior of both games is evaluated by using a homogeneous Markov chain $X = \{X_n, n \geq 0\}$ that represents the evolution of the number of malicious nodes in both core and spare sets of a cluster. Both games are played against an adversary whose strength represents the amount of induced churn at a cluster level. In its stronger version, the adversary is free to keep the nodes it manipulates forever in the cluster, while in its weakest form, manipulated nodes are forced to move (they can rejoin later if they wish). The adversary wins the game when process X reaches a set of polluted states from which it can never exit. A state is polluted if the fraction of malicious nodes in the core set exceeds ϵ (i.e., a collusion is mounted). A state that is not polluted is *safe*.

The first step of our work shows that the amount of randomization implemented at cluster level does not prevent a strong adversary from winning in both games in a bounded number of steps, however randomization together with cluster size influence the speed at which this pollution is reached. In particular, the second game alternates, for a random number of steps, between safe and polluted states.

The second step evaluates the benefit of constraining the adversary by limiting the sojourn time of its manipulated nodes in both sets, so that randomness among manipulated and honest nodes is continuously preserved. We first show that none of the games exhibit an absorbing class of states (i.e., both games never ends). Next we prove that process X reaches a stationary distribution which is surprisingly the same for both games. Specifically

Theorem 1. *For both games 1 and 2, the stationary distribution is the same. For all $x = 0, \ldots, c$ and $y = 0, \ldots, s$, where c (resp. s) represents the upper bound of the core (resp. spare) sets, we have*

$$\lim_{n \longrightarrow \infty} \mathbb{P}\{X_n = (x, y)\} = \alpha(x, y),$$

where

$$\alpha(x, y) = \binom{c}{x} \mu^x (1-\mu)^{c-x} \binom{s}{y} \mu^y (1-\mu)^{s-y}. \quad (1)$$

References

1. Anceaume, E., Brasileiro, F., Ludinard, R., Ravoaja, A.: Peercube: an hypercube-based P2P overlay robust against collusion and churn. In: Procs. of the IEEE Int'l Conference on Self-Adaptive and Self-Organizing Systems (2008)
2. Awerbuch, B., Scheideler, C.: Towards scalable and robust overlay networks. In: Proceedings of the Int'l Workshop on Peer-to-Peer Systems (2007)
3. Fiat, A., Saia, J., Young, M.: Making chord robust to byzantine attacks. In: Brodal, G.S., Leonardi, S. (eds.) ESA 2005. LNCS, vol. 3669, pp. 803–814. Springer, Heidelberg (2005)

Safer Than Safe: On the Initial State of Self-stabilizing Systems*
(Brief Announcement)

Sylvie Delaët[1], Shlomi Dolev[2,**], and Olivier Peres[2,***]

[1] Univ Paris Sud, LRI, CNRS, Orsay F-91405
sylvie.delaet@lri.fr
[2] Department of Computer Science, Ben-Gurion University of the Negev, Beer-Sheva, Israel 84105
dolev@cs.bgu.ac.il,olivier@bgu.ac.il

Introduction. A self-stabilizing algorithm [2] is a distributed algorithm with an additional property: it guarantees to eventually execute its task, by reaching a *legitimate configuration*, regardless of the state in which the processes and communication links are started.

Some algorithms are supposed to remain *safe* at all times while they carry out their task. Safety, however, is impossible when very high levels of failures overwhelm the system, e.g., when more than a third of the processes are Byzantine, or in the extreme case, when all the processes disappear.

To combine the safety of non-stabilizing algorithms and the eventual safety of self-stabilizing algorithms, we argue that each self-stabilizing algorithm should have *initial configurations*. If the system is started in an initial configuration, there is no need to overcome any problem stemming from the starting configuration. Thus, **safety** is guaranteed throughout the execution. Since the system is self-stabilizing, it guarantees convergence from any configuration to a legitimate configuration, thereby also providing **eventual safety**.

An initial configuration is intended as a good starting point for a self-stabilizing algorithm. Such a configuration must be safe, introducing the notion of *initial safety*. Roughly speaking, an initial configuration is an "empty" configuration, in which the algorithm has not yet obtained any information. It is therefore not a legitimate configuration. For example, in the initial configuration for an algorithm that maintains routing tables, all tables should be empty. For a spanning tree algorithm, each process should have no parent and no child.

Contributions. To illustrate the notion of initial configuration, we apply it to the Update protocol, a self-stabilizing routing table algorithm. We prove that if the system is started in a configuration, where all the routing tables are empty, then it never acquires any wrong information, such as a routing table entry for a nonexisting process or a distance shorter than the actual distance.

* A detailed version appears in a technical report [1].

** Partially supported by the ICT Programme of the European Union under contract number ICT-2008-215270, US Air Force, and Rita Altura chair in computer science.

*** Partially supported by the ICT Programme of the European Union under contract number ICT-2008-215270.

R. Guerraoui and F. Petit (Eds.): SSS 2009, LNCS 5873, pp. 775–776, 2009.

We generalize the notion of initial configurations by characterizing all the configurations of a system with regards to initial configurations using a framework that classifies configurations into categories. In addition to the *legitimate* and *initial* configurations, we identify configurations that are *reachable* from an initial configuration. All the other configurations are *corrupted*. We apply this framework to information gathering algorithms, like census and routing table algorithms. The framework can be extended to *composed* algorithms, i.e. self-stabilizing algorithms obtained by merging several algorithms.

We then introduce a special tool for composed algorithms: self-stabilizing stabilization detectors. We provide, as an example, an algorithm that detects whether the Update protocol is in a legitimate configuration. If the system is started in a non-initial configuration, it converges toward a legitimate configuration where the Update protocol has converged and the detector outputs *true*. The detector can wrongly output *true* before the Update protocol has converged. However, if the system is started in an initial configuration, the stabilization detector only outputs true when the Update protocol has converged. This indication assists in scheduling higher layers only when lower layers are stabilized, and thus allows smoother restarts following a distributed invocation of a reset.

To illustrate the combination of safety and eventual safety, we provide a self-stabilizing n-modular redundancy (NMR) implementation. NMR is a fundamental tool for fault masking. Consider a state machine with transition function T and a function *out* that maps states to outputs. NMR replicates this state machine n times and allows tolerating faults in any minority of the machines. Our self-stabilizing NMR is thus **safe**, like a regular NMR system, if started in an initial configuration. Moreover, being self-stabilizing, after any sequence of transient failures, it converges toward a legitimate configuration. Therefore, while the behavior of the regular NMR system is unpredictable following an overwhelming number of transient faults, the self-stabilizing NMR system eventually places all the processes in the same state, and then, correctly executes the transition function. Thus, the self-stabilizing NMR system is also **eventually safe**.

Conclusion. Our main contribution is the definition of *initial configurations*, i.e. preferred starting configurations, from which a self-stabilizing algorithm can safely converge toward a legitimate configuration. Being self-stabilizing, the algorithm converges if initialized in any other configuration too. We believe that specifying initial configurations with self-stabilizing algorithms should be the standard. It provides the user who wants to run the algorithm with instructions on how to start the system in order to obtain the best possible conditions, combining safety, in normal conditions, and eventual safety, in the presence of a very high number of failures. We thus argue that self-stabilizing systems should no longer be regarded as only eventually safe, but as **safe and eventually safe**.

References

1. Delaët, S., Dolev, S., Peres, O.: Safe and eventually safe: Comparing stabilizing and non-stabilizing algorithms on a common ground. Technical Report 0905, Ben-Gurion University of the Negev (August 2009)
2. Dolev, S.: Self-Stabilization. MIT Press, Cambridge (2000)

Brief Announcement: Unique Permutation Hashing*

Shlomi Dolev, Limor Lahiani, and Yinnon Haviv

Department of Computer Science, Ben-Gurion University of the Negev, Beer-Sheva, 84105, Israel NSF grant and the Israeli ministry of defense
{dolev,lahiani,haviv}@cs.bgu.ac.il

Introduction. We propose a new *open addressing* hash function, the *unique-permutation hash function*, and a performance analysis of its hash computation. A hash function h is *simple uniform* if items are equally likely to be hashed to any table location (in the first trial). A hash function h is *random* or *strong uniform* if the probability of any permutation to be a probe sequence, when using h, is $\frac{1}{N!}$, where N is the size of the table. We show that the unique-permutation hash function is *strong uniform* and therefore has the lowest expected cost; each probe sequence is equally likely to be chosen, when the keys are uniformly chosen. Thus, the unique-permutation hash ensures that each empty table location has the same probability to be assigned with a uniformly chosen key.

For constant load factors $\alpha < 1$, where α is the ratio between the number of inserted items and the table size, the expected time for computing the unique-permutation hash function is $O(1)$ and the expected number of table locations that are checked before an empty location is found, during insertion (or search), is also $O(1)$.

Hashing. Given a hash table of size N, a hash function h maps a key to a table location in $1, 2, \ldots, N$. The *probe sequence* of a key, defined by the hashing method and h is, in fact, a permutation of $1, 2, \ldots, N$. For a given key x, assume that the probe sequence is $i_1, i_2, \ldots, i_N$. In such case, when inserting an item with key x to the hash table, the first location which is checked is i_1. If location i_1 is filled, location i_2 is then checked and so on until finding an empty location into which the item is inserted. Similarly, the same probe sequence also defines the sequence of table locations that are checked when searching for x. In such case, table locations are checked until x is found or until an empty location is found, indicating the search has failed (x is not on the table).

Unique permutation. Given a hash table of size N, with locations denoted by $1, 2, \ldots, N$. Let $\Pi(N) = \{\pi_1, \pi_2, \ldots, \pi_{N!}\}$ be the set of all permutations of $1, 2, \ldots, N$, lexicographically ordered. The *unique-permutation hash function* maps a key to a unique probe sequence in $\Pi(N)$. That is, if for an item x, $h(x) = \pi \in \Pi(N)$ and $\pi = i_1, i_2, \ldots, i_N$, then π is the probe sequence used for insert-

* Partially supported by EU ICT-2008-215270 FRONTS, Rita Altura Trust Chair in Computer Sciences, and the Lynne and William Frankel Center for Computer Sciences. See [1] for a detailed version.

R. Guerraoui and F. Petit (Eds.): SSS 2009, LNCS 5873, pp. 777–778, 2009.

ing x, as well as for searching for x. As there are $N!$ permutations of the N table locations, the items can be divided into $N!$ classes $[\pi]$, where $[\pi] = \{x : h(x) = \pi\}$.

We show that our unique-permutation hash function is a *random hash function*, (also defined *strong uniform hash function*), which ensures that each empty entry has the same probability to be filled with a uniformly chosen key. Obviously, the *random* property neither holds for linear probing, nor for double hashing, since when probing a filled location, according to these methods, some locations have a higher probability to be tried next, as we demonstrate in [1]. We distinguish *local steps*, which refers to the hash function computation from a hash *table entry access*. In case keys are given as integers and obviously, when keys are explicitly given as permutations, we present a simple algorithm that (locally) calculates the next probe number in the probe sequence upon a request. The expected number of local steps done by this algorithm, during insertion, is a function of the load factor (i.e. $\frac{1}{(1-\alpha)^3}$). For a bounded load factor, both the expected number of local steps and number of table entry accesses are constants.

Given two integers N and k, we use an algorithm which generates the kth permutation in $\Pi(N)$ (when lexicographically ordered). We compute each number in the permutation only upon a request. For the sake of presentation completeness, we present a simple algorithm which finds the first j numbers in the kth permutation in $O(j^2)$ operations. Roughly speaking, this algorithm is based on modular operations, starting with computing the key mod N, next the key mod $N-1$, and so on until the key mod 2, using the resulting indexes as an indexes in the non yet explored locations. In fact we prove in [1], that it takes $O(1)$ expected number of operations for inserting an item, when α is bounded, say $\alpha < \frac{2}{3}$.

Number of keys. We also address the cases in which the number of items inserted is greater than or smaller than $N!$. In case the number of items is $c \cdot N!$, where c is a positive integer, our function satisfies the random property. Note that when c is a non integer number greater than 1, there are some permutations that are chosen with probability $\frac{\lfloor c \rfloor}{N!}$, while other permutations are chosen with probability $\frac{\lfloor c \rfloor + 1}{N!}$. The ratio between these probabilities is negligible for a large enough c. In case the number of items is less than $N!$, we can *start probing the first table locations in a uniform fashion*, using our hash function (mapping the key to an index of a permutation in shorter permutations domain $N!/k!$, largest domain that is equal to or smaller than the domain of the keys) and continuing in any deterministic fashion (say in a linear probing fashion) that probes the rest of the table locations.

Applications. In addition to the obvious possible usage of the unique-permutation hash function being an optimal hash function, the unique-permutation hash function has an application for parallel, distributed and multi-core systems that avoid contention as much as possible. See [1] for some relevant references to such applications.

Reference

1. Dolev, S., Lahiani, L., Haviv, Y.: Unique Permutation Hashing. Department of Computer Science Ben-Gurion University, Technical Report, TR-#3-09 (2009)

Randomization Adaptive Self-stabilization*

(Brief Announcement)

Shlomi Dolev and Nir Tzachar

Department of Computer Science, Ben-Gurion University of the Negev, Beer-Sheva, 84105, Israel NSF grant and the Israeli ministry of defense
{dolev,tzachar}@cs.bgu.ac.il

Introduction. Self-stabilizing algorithms are designed to start from an arbitrary state and eventually exhibit a desired behavior. Self-stabilizing algorithms that use randomization are able to achieve tasks that cannot be achieved by deterministic means. In addition, in some cases, randomization enables faster convergence of self-stabilizing algorithms. Often, randomized self-stabilizing algorithms are designed to use an infinite amount of random bits to operate correctly. However, the creation of (real) random bits is considered expensive; thus, a *randomization adaptive* self-stabilizing algorithm which uses random bits during convergence but does not use random bits following the convergence is desirable. Such a notion of adaptiveness has been studied in the past, where the resource demands of a self-stabilizing algorithm are reduced upon convergence, be it memory requirements, or communication requirements.

We suggest a new scheme for converting randomized self-stabilizing algorithms to randomization adaptive self-stabilizing algorithms. Our scheme can be employed when every execution of the algorithm, starting in a safe configuration, is legal, regardless of the random input – as opposed to legal with some probability. Our scheme can also be applied in case there is at least one random sequence that implies liveness from every safe configuration. Generally speaking, the scheme is based on collecting the entire history of the system at each node, and examining this history to check if the algorithm has converged. If so, no randomization is used. We demonstrate the scheme on a leader election algorithm derived from the token circulation algorithm of Ted Herman, 1990. We also obtain token circulation with deterministic behavior following convergence.

When Byzantine nodes are introduced, we suggest a scheme based on *unreliable stabilization detectors*. The unreliable stabilization detector gives an unreliable indication whether the algorithm is in a safe configuration. Roughly, when the algorithm has converged, the detector *eventually* notifies all nodes of this fact; before the algorithm converges the detector notifies at least one node that randomization is still needed. The other part of the conversion scheme is a *randomization surrogate*, where each node that gets an indication on non-convergence from the unreliable stabilization detector supplies random bits to all

* Partially supported by EU ICT-2008-215270 FRONTS, Rita Altura Trust Chair in Computer Sciences, and the Lynne and William Frankel Center for Computer Sciences. See [1] for a detailed version.

R. Guerraoui and F. Petit (Eds.): SSS 2009, LNCS 5873, pp. 779–780, 2009.

the nodes including itself; each node xors the random bits received from all nodes in the system and uses the result as its source for random bits. Roughly speaking, in the presence of Byzantine nodes, such randomization assistance must be done atomically, avoiding the Byzantine nodes' choice which can potentially nullify the random bits selected.

We demonstrate our second scheme over the non-randomization adaptive self-stabilizing clock synchronization algorithm presented by Ben-Or, Dolev and Hoch in 2008. The application of our scheme results in the first constant time Byzantine self-stabilizing clock synchronization algorithm that uses an expected bounded number of random bits.

Self-stabilizing stabilization detector. The detector is based on collecting a historical view, similar to the monitoring suggested by Afek and Dolev in 1997. The history collection algorithm maintains, at each node, an array of the last d system configurations – the $history_p$ array. At each pulse, each node p first shifts p's $history_p$ array to the right, discarding the last entry $history_p[d-1]$, and places the current partial configuration $\{s_p\}$ (the state of p) in $history_p[0]$. p then proceeds to send $history_p$ to all of p's neighbors. Finally, p merges the histories p receives from p's neighbors with p's history array (the identifiers of the nodes are used to facilitate a simple merge).

Eventually, each node has the correct state of the system d rounds in the past, where d is the diameter of the communication graph. At each round i, each node p examines the history of round $i-d$ to check if the system was in a safe configuration. If the system was in a safe configuration in round $i-d$, p uses no random bits. Otherwise, p uses random bits.

Randomization adaptiveness in the presence of Byzantine faults. Assume that the communication graph is complete, thus, preventing interference of the Byzantine nodes with communications between non-Byzantine nodes.

In each round each node p directly collects information about the current configuration from the rest of the nodes. In case p detects that the system is not stabilized, p proceeds to send a different random number to each node (including itself). Otherwise, p sends a fixed default number to all nodes. All the (random/default) numbers received by a node are xored to replace the original result of the random function. Thus, if at least one non Byzantine node identifies the current configuration as unstable, then all non-Byzantine nodes use random numbers. Moreover, when all non Byzantine nodes identify a stable configuration, none of them invoke the random function.

Reference

1. Dolev, S., Tzachar, N.: Randomization Adaptive Self-Stabilization. CoRR, abs/0810.4440 (2008)

Brief Announcement: On the Time Complexity of Distributed Topological Self-stabilization*

Dominik Gall, Riko Jacob, Andrea Richa,
Christian Scheideler, Stefan Schmid, and Hanjo Täubig

1 Introduction

This brief announcement proposes a new model to measure the distributed time complexity of topological self-stabilization. In the field of topological self-stabilization, nodes—e.g., machines in a p2p network—seek to establish a certain network structure in a robust manner (see, e.g., [2] for a distributed algorithm for skip graphs). While several complexity models have been proposed and analyzed over the last years, these models are often inappropriate to adequately model parallel efficiency: either they are overly pessimistic in the sense that they can force the algorithm to work serially, or they are too optimistic in the sense that contention issues are neglected. We hope that our approach will inspire researchers in the community to analyze other problems from this perspective. For a complete technical report about our model, related literature and algorithms, the reader is referred to [1].

2 Case Study: Graph Linearization

Our model is best understood with an example. We hence examine a concrete problem, namely *graph linearization*: Given a connected overlay network with unique node identifiers, we want to construct a chain network which is sorted w.r.t. these IDs. For simplicity, we consider undirected graphs only.

We study two distributed algorithms $\mathrm{LIN}_{\mathrm{all}}$ and $\mathrm{LIN}_{\mathrm{max}}$ that work on *node triples*: A so-called *linearization step* involves three nodes u, v, and v' with the property that u is connected to v and v' and either $u < v < v'$ or $v' < v < u$. In both cases, u may command the nodes to move the edge $\{u, v'\}$ to $\{v, v'\}$. If $u < v < v'$, this is called a *right* linearization and otherwise a *left* linearization (see Figure 1). Since only three nodes are involved in such a linearization, this is an efficient operation.

Algorithm $\mathrm{LIN}_{\mathrm{all}}$ is very simple: Each node constantly tries to linearize its neighbors according to the *linearize left* and *linearize right* rules. In doing so, *all* possible triples on both sides are proposed to a hypothetical scheduler. $\mathrm{LIN}_{\mathrm{max}}$ is similar to $\mathrm{LIN}_{\mathrm{all}}$: but instead of proposing all possible triples on each side, $\mathrm{LIN}_{\mathrm{max}}$ only proposes the triple which is the furthest (w.r.t. IDs) on the corresponding side.

* Research supported by the DFG project SCHE 1592/1-1, and NSF Award number CCF-0830704.

R. Guerraoui and F. Petit (Eds.): SSS 2009, LNCS 5873, pp. 781–782, 2009.

3 Parallel Time Complexity

We define the *distributed runtime* of a self-stabilizing algorithm as the total number of *rounds* required in the worst-case to establish a desirable topology (e.g., a linearized one) from an *arbitrary* initial network.

A round should capture what can be done in a distributed setting per unit time. In our approach, in each round, the scheduling layer may select any set of *independent operations* to be executed by the nodes, in the sense that each node v can only be part of *one* operation (i.e., one linearization triple): if multiple neighbors of v (or v itself) want to change—i.e., add or remove—edges incident to v, at most one edge change is scheduled. Thus, no node is overloaded.

Fig. 1. Left and right linearization step

We studied the runtime of LIN_{all} and LIN_{max} for different scheduling regimes: (1) *Worst-case scheduler* $\mathcal{S}_{\text{wc}}$: This scheduler must select a *maximal* independent set of possible linearization steps in each round, but it may do so to enforce a runtime (or work) that is as large as possible. (2) *Randomized scheduler* $\mathcal{S}_{\text{rand}}$: This scheduler considers the set of operations in a random order and selects, in one round, every operation that is independent of the previously selected operations in that order. (3) *Greedy scheduler* $\mathcal{S}_{\text{greedy}}$: This scheduler orders the nodes according to their degrees, from maximum to minimum. (4) *Best-case scheduler* $\mathcal{S}_{\text{opt}}$: The round triples are selected in order to minimize the runtime (or work) of the algorithm.

The analysis of the different schedulers provides interesting insights into an algorithm's performance. In particular, the randomized scheduler can be regarded as a distributed mechanism where node coordinate their operations by local control. We have derived the following bounds [1].

Theorem 1. *Under a worst-case scheduler $\mathcal{S}_{wc}$, LIN_{max} terminates after $O(n^2)$ work (single linearization steps), where n is the total number of nodes in the system. This is tight in the sense that there are situations where LIN_{max} requires $\Omega(n^2)$ rounds under $\mathcal{S}_{wc}$. LIN_{all} runs at most $O(n^2 \log n)$ rounds under $\mathcal{S}_{wc}$ and at most $O(n \log n)$ rounds under $\mathcal{S}_{greedy}$. On the other hand, there are situations where both LIN_{all} and LIN_{max} require at least $\Omega(n)$ rounds, even under an optimal scheduler $\mathcal{S}_{opt}$.*

References

1. Gall, D., Jacob, R., Richa, A., Scheideler, C., Schmid, S., Täubig, H.: Modeling scalability in distributed self-stabilization: The case of graph linearization. Technical Report TUM-I0835, Technische Universität München, Computer Science Dept. (November 2008)
2. Jacob, R., Richa, A., Scheideler, C., Schmid, S., Täubig, H.: A distributed polylogarithmic time algorithm for self-stabilizing skip graphs. In: Proc. PODC (2009)

Brief Announcement: An OS Architecture for Device Self-protection*

Ruan He[1], Marc Lacoste[1], and Jean Leneutre[2]

[1] Orange Labs, France
[2] Telecom ParisTech, France

What is VSK? By introducing context-awareness in the system layer, pervasive computing is a turning point in OS design. Device mobility and dynamicity of situations raise strong challenges for run-time adaptability of embedded software, while at the same time inducing new, serious threats to device security. Paradoxically, due to the multiplicity of protection requirements specific to each environment illustrated by the heterogeneity of network security policies, the solution may come from applying context-awareness to security itself. The idea is to tune security mechanisms to match the protection needs of the current device environment, such as the estimated level of risk. A manual adaptation is ruled out by the administration overhead and error potential of human intervention. To automate reconfiguration, security needs to be autonomic [2]. But how?

In the case of access control, the OS should satisfy two main requirements: (1) full run-time customization with limited performance overhead[1]; and (2) flexible policy-neutral access control[2].We present a new OS authorization architecture called *Virtual Security Kernel (VSK)* which meets these requirements, making it applicable to make pervasive devices self-protected.

VSK completely separates a minimal kernel from execution resources. The kernel performs efficient run-time reconfiguration of resources. It also manages authorization through a policy-neutral reference monitor, protection being non invasive thanks to an optimized access control strategy. The architecture is completely component-based, which allows flexibility both at resource level for customization, and in the kernel to support multiple authorization policies and enable their run-time reconfiguration. The result is a highly adaptable OS architecture where security mechanisms may be self-managed.

Solution Overview. Our architecture for self-protection of devices can be divided into 3 layers (see Figure 1): (1) the *execution space* provides a run-time environment for components, either application- or system-level; (2) the *VSK* controls the execution space, both to enable application-specific customization and to guarantee security of resources; and (3) the *autonomic layer* performs automatic adaptation of authorization policies enforced in the VSK.

* This work has been partially funded by the ANR SelfXL project.

[1] The OS should be flexible enough to tune running services, while meeting embedded device resource limitations.

[2] Devices will roam betwen multiple networks, each with its own authorization requirements which cannot be embraced by a single policy. The OS should thus support several classes of authorization policies with run-time reconfiguration capabilities between them to select the most adequate policy when changing network.

R. Guerraoui and F. Petit (Eds.): SSS 2009, LNCS 5873, pp. 783–784, 2009.

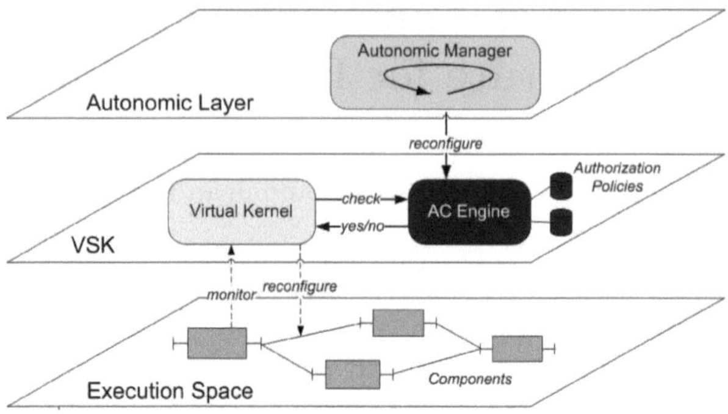

Fig. 1. A 3-Level OS Architecture

The VSK consists of a *Virtual Kernel (VK)* and of an *Access Control Engine* (ACE). The VK provides run-time management capabilities over components and their bindings to reconfigure the execution space. Access control to components is optimized by enforcing ACE decisions at binding creation time only, a binding being considered secure for subsequent access requests until the next change of authorization policy. Apart from these operations, the VK remains hidden in the background to minimize interactions between kernel and execution space for performance optimization. The ACE is a flexible decision engine allowing run-time selection of different authorization policies. The ACE design is compliant with the attribute-based vision of access control, by managing separately security attributes and permissions, both of which may be dynamically updated [3]. The VSK is supervised by an *Autonomic Manager* which triggers reconfiguration of security policies depending on context information received from the environment. This layer implements two autonomic loops, respectively for self-protection of the device and the network.

Current and Future Work. A first prototype of VSK architecture was implemented on a Nokia N800 Internet tablet using the Think [1] component-based OS framework. The prototype was tested on self-protection scenarios for home networking, and evaluated in terms of performance, flexibility, and security. Preliminary performance assessments are promising, showing that the VSK design yields significant improvements, notably compared to micro-kernels. Future work will focus on: hardware mechanisms to guarantee VSK integrity; and a policy management framework in the autonomic layer to control the VSK.

References

1. Anne, M., et al.: Think: View-Based Support of Non-Functional Properties in Embedded Systems. In: International Conference on Embedded Software and Systems (2009)
2. Chess, D., Palmer, C., White, S.: Security in an Autonomic Computing Environment. IBM Systems Journal 42(1), 107–118 (2003)
3. Lacoste, M., Jarboui, T., He, R.: A Component-Based Policy-Neutral Architecture for Kernel-Level Access Control. Annals of Telecom 64(1-2), 121–146 (2009)

Brief Announcement: Towards Secure Cloud Computing

Christian Henrich[1], Matthias Huber[2], Carmen Kempka[1], Jörn Müller-Quade[1], and Mario Strefler[1]

[1] IKS/EISS
[2] IPD
Fakultät für Informatik
Universität Karlsruhe (TH)

Abstract. Security of cloud computing in the strict cryptographic sense is impossible to achieve practically. We propose a pragmatic security approach providing application-specific security under practical constraints.

Keywords: Software as a Service, Cloud Computing Security.

Introduction and Motivation. Cloud computing enables flexible and resource-efficient services [1], but privacy concerns prevent its application in sensitive scenarios. Most service providers offer protection against external threats arising from insecure communication. But a provider that has full control over the data makes an insider attack an intolerable risk.

Solutions provided by theoretical cryptography have impractically high costs. On the other hand the security properties of practical approaches are not well understood. In this brief announcement we propose a pragmatic security approach to provide application-specific security under practical constraints (better-than-nothing security).

A Pragmatic Approach. Privacy issues that arise from cloud computing [2] are twofold: The intellectual properties of both the client and the service provider have to be protected.

The confidentiality of the client's private data can be achieved by encrypted cloud storage. However, this prevents providers from executing services on this data. Application-specific encryption (e. g. searchable encryption [3], order preserving encryption [4] or homomorphic encryption) enables the provider to offer specific functionalities such as database services. However, the server may still gain additional information by observing access patterns and through other side channels. By adding fake data and queries the amount of information leaking can be reduced. Another approach is to reduce the amount of information the server can extract by using coarse indices (similar to range queries [5]) and post-processing the results on the client.

To prevent malicious behavior of the service provider, software certification may be used. Additionally, techniques like digital rights management (DRM) [6]

R. Guerraoui and F. Petit (Eds.): SSS 2009, LNCS 5873, pp. 785–786, 2009.

can ensure that only trusted software can access the sensitive data. Depending on the application context it may even be sufficient to obtain forensic evidence for illegal behavior.

Some of these approaches require postprocessing or even execution of complete services on the client. For the provider this raises the problem of protecting his intellectual property. DRM techniques or code obfuscation [7] may be used to protect code from being copied or reverse-engineered by the client. To protect the client from malicious code, certification can be used.

Conclusion and Open Problems. Theoretical cryptography became very successful by abstraction. However, application-specific security can be by far more efficient. We propose a pragmatic approach to the security of cloud computing. This will lead to the development of usable techniques providing a sufficient level of security depending on the application.

Pragmatic security cannot provide ideal protection in general. An open problem is to formally define and quantify the level of security reached by pragmatic approaches. Further research has to be done to find combinations of existing and new pragmatic approaches. This will allow for individual trade-offs between the workloads and security concerns of both service provider and client.

References

1. Vouk, M.A.: Cloud computing - issues, research and implementations. In: ITI 2008. 30th int. conf. on information technology interfaces, pp. 31–40. IEEE, Los Alamitos (2008)
2. Pearson, S.: Taking Account of Privacy when Designing Cloud Computing Services. HP Laboratories (2009)
3. Curtmola, R., Garay, J., Kamara, S., Ostrovsky, R.: Searchable symmetric encryption: improved definitions and efficient constructions. In: Proceedings of the 13th ACM conference on Computer and communications security, pp. 78–88. ACM, New York (2006)
4. Agrawal, R., Kiernan, J., Srikant, R., Xu, Y.: Order preserving encryption for numeric data. In: SIGMOD 2004: Proceedings of the 2004 ACM SIGMOD international conference on Management of data, pp. 563–574. ACM, New York (2004)
5. Hore, B., Mehrotra, S., Tsudik, G.: A privacy-preserving index for range queries. In: VLDB 2004, Proceedings, pp. 720–731. ACM, New York (2004)
6. Safavi-Naini, R., Yung, M.: Digital Rights Management: Technologies, Issues, Challenges and Systems. LNCS. Springer, Heidelberg (2006)
7. Hofheinz, D., Malone-Lee, J., Stam, M.: Obfuscation for cryptographic purposes. In: Vadhan, S.P. (ed.) TCC 2007. LNCS, vol. 4392, pp. 214–232. Springer, Heidelberg (2007)

Brief Announcement: Robust Self-stabilizing Construction of Bounded Size Weight-Based Clusters

Colette Johnen[1] and Fouzi Mekhaldi[2]

[1] LaBRI, Univ. Bordeaux, CNRS, F-33405 Talence Cedex, France
[2] LRI, Univ. Paris-Sud XI, CNRS, F-91405 Orsay Cedex, France

Introduction. The clustering problem consists of partitioning network nodes into groups called clusters. Each cluster has a single clusterhead that acts as local coordinator of cluster.

A technique for designing solutions that tolerate transient faults is self-stabilization. Self-stabilizing protocols are attractive because they need not be initialized: they converge from any configuration to a legitimate one. Also, they are adaptive to topological changes. If the current configuration is inconsistent with the network topology, the self-stabilizing protocol eventually converges to a legitimate configuration. Nevertheless, self-stabilizing protocols do not guarantee any property during the convergence period. In addition, the convergence time may be proportional to the size of the network; particularly, in weight-based clustering protocols. In order to overcome these drawbacks, we are interested to the robust stabilization. Robust stabilization guarantees that from an illegitimate configuration, the system reaches quickly a safe configuration, in which the safety property is satisfied. The safety property has to be defined such that the system performs correctly its task in a safe configuration. During the convergence to a legitimate configuration, the safety property stays always verified.

Related works. In [1], a robust self-stabilizing protocol building a minimum connected dominating set is proposed. In a safe configuration, the built set is a dominating set. A robust self-stabilizing weight-based clustering protocol for ad hoc networks is proposed in [2]. In [2], a configuration is safe if and only if the network is partitioned into clusters.

To our knowledge, the only protocols building bounded size clusters are [3,4,5]. In [5], the size of obtained clusters is bounded by a lower and an upper bound. This solution cannot be applied to one-hop clusters, because the degree of nodes may be less than the lower bound. However, [3,5] are not self-stabilizing, and [4] is self-stabilizing but it is not robust.

Contributions. We propose the first robust self-stabilizing protocol that constructs 1-hop clusters whose size is bounded, and the clusterhead selection is weight-based. The detailed version can be found on [6].

Our protocol is weight based: the clusterhead selection criteria is based on the weight of nodes. Each node has an input variable, its weight, named w, representing its capacity to be clusterhead. The higher the weight of a node, the more suitable this node is for the role of clusterhead. The weight value can increase or decrease reflecting the changes in the node's status.

R. Guerraoui and F. Petit (Eds.): SSS 2009, LNCS 5873, pp. 787–788, 2009.

The proposed clustering protocol provides bounded size clusters; at most $SizeBound$ ordinary nodes can be in a cluster. This limitation on the number of nodes that a clusterhead handles, ensures the load balancing over the network: no clusterhead is overloaded at any time.

As clusters are bounded, several clusterheads may be neighbors. To limit the number of clusterheads locally, a node v may become clusterhead only if it does not have a suitable clusterhead in the neighborhood. Furthermore, v stays clusterhead only if it cannot join a neighbor cluster : neighbor clusters are full (they contain $SizeBound$ members), or v is the leader having the highest weight.

The obtained clusters have to satisfy the *well-balanced clustering* properties:

- *Affiliation* condition: each ordinary node affiliates with a neighboring clusterhead, such that the weight of its clusterhead is greater than its weight.
- *Size* condition: each cluster contains at most $SizeBound$ ordinary nodes.
- *Clusterhead neighboring* condition: if a clusterhead v has a neighboring clusterhead u such that $w_u > w_v$, then the size of u's cluster is $SizeBound$.

Convergence and time complexity. Our protocol is silent; no node executes an action once a legitimate configuration is reached. Starting from an arbitrary configuration, the protocol reaches a safe configuration in 4 rounds.

Once a safe configuration is reached, each node belongs to a cluster having an effectual leader, and each cluster contains at most $SizeBound$ members, but clusters may not satisfy the well-balanced clustering properties. During the construction of the final clusters, that satisfy the well-balanced clustering properties, the safety property is preserved under any computation, and also under the following input changes: (1) change on node's weight, (2) crash of an ordinary node, (3) failure of a link between: (a) a clusterhead and a nearly ordinary node, (b) two clusterheads, (c) two nearly ordinary nodes, or (d) two ordinary nodes, (4) joining of a sub-network that verifies the safety property.

The time of convergence to a legitimate configuration is at most $\frac{7*N}{2}+5$, where N is the number of nodes in the network.

References

1. Kamei, S., Kakugawa, H.: A self-stabilizing approximation for the minimum connected dominating set with safe convergence. In: Baker, T.P., Bui, A., Tixeuil, S. (eds.) OPODIS 2008. LNCS, vol. 5401, pp. 496–511. Springer, Heidelberg (2008)
2. Johnen, C., Nguyen, L.H.: Robust self-stabilizing weight-based clustering algorithm. Theoretical Computer Science 410(6-7), 581–594 (2009)
3. Chatterjee, M., Das, S.K., Turgut, D.: WCA: A weighted clustering algorithm for mobile ad hoc networks. Journal of Cluster Computing 5(2), 193–204 (2002)
4. Johnen, C., Nguyen, L.H.: Self-stabilizing construction of bounded size clusters. In: ISPA 2008, pp. 43–50 (2008)
5. Tomoyuki, O., Shinji, I., Yoshiaki, K., Kenji, I., Kaori, M.: An adaptive maintenance of hierarchical structure in ad hoc networks and its evaluation. In: ICDCS 2002, pp. 7–13 (2002)
6. Johnen, C., Mekhaldi, F.: Robust self-stabilizing construction of bounded size weight-based clusters. Technical Report N° 1518, LRI (2009), `http://www.lri.fr/~bibli/Rapports-internes/2009/RR1518.pdf`

Brief Announcement: A Stabilizing Algorithm for Finding Two Disjoint Paths in Arbitrary Networks

Mehmet Hakan Karaata[1] and Rachid Hadid[2]

[1] Department of Computer Eng., Kuwait University
P.O. Box 5969, Safat 13060 Kuwait
karaata@eng.kuniv.edu.kw

[2] Clinical Research Laboratory, Saad Specialist Hospital
Saudi Arabia P.O. Box 3053, Al-Khobar 31952
rhadid@saad.com.sa

The problem of finding disjoint paths in a network is a fundamental problem with numerous applications. Two paths in a network are said to be (node) disjoint if they do not share any nodes except for the endpoints. The two node disjoint paths problem is to find two node-disjoint paths in $G = (V, E)$ from source $s \in V$ to the target $t \in V$. The two-node-disjoint paths problem is a fundamental problem with several applications in diverse areas including VLSI layout, reliable network routing, secure message transmission, and network survivability. The two node disjoint path problem is fundamental, extensively studied in graph theory.

In this paper, we present the basis of the first stabilizing distributed algorithm to find two possible node-disjoint paths between two distinct nodes s and t in anonymous arbitrary networks. Since the proposed solution is self-stabilizing, it does not require initialization and withstands transient faults. The proposed algorithm constructs the two node-disjoint paths in two concurrent phases, namely the *shortest path construction* and the *node-disjoint paths construction phase.* The disjoint paths construction phase is based on the shortest path construction phase, i.e., the progress of this phase is ensured only after the shortest path construction phase terminates successfully. Upon termination of the shortest path (path $\mathcal{P}_0$), two disjoint paths (denoted by $\mathcal{P}_1$ and $\mathcal{P}_2$) are constructed from the source node s to the target node t using the shortest path as follows.

Let $d_s(x)$ denote the distance of node x on path $\mathcal{P}_0$ from source s. After the construction of $\mathcal{P}_0$, the source process finds two paths P_2 and P_1 disjoint from each other and P_0 from s to two distinct nodes x_2 and x_1, respectively, on $\mathcal{P}_0$ such that x_2 and x_1 are the farthest and the second farthest nodes on $\mathcal{P}_0$ (see Figure 1). The two sub-paths P_1 and P_2 are constructed in a way to include the minimum number of nodes of $\mathcal{P}_0$. Observe that after the construction of P_1 and P_2, if $x_1 = x_2 = t$, then two node-disjoint paths (P_1 and P_2) between s and t are found. Otherwise, if $x_1 \neq t$, then, we find nodes x'_1 and x_3 on $\mathcal{P}_0$ such that $d_s(s) < d_s(x'_1) < d_s(x_2)$, $d_s(x_2) < d_s(x_3)$, x'_1 and x_3 are connected by a path P_3 disjoint from P_1 and P_2, and x_3 and x'_1 are selected to maximize first $d_s(x_3)$ and then $d_s(x'_1)$. Subsequently, we combine P_1 and P_3 and the segment of $\mathcal{P}_0$ from x_1 to x'_1 to extend $\mathcal{P}_1$. Observe

R. Guerraoui and F. Petit (Eds.): SSS 2009, LNCS 5873, pp. 789–790, 2009.

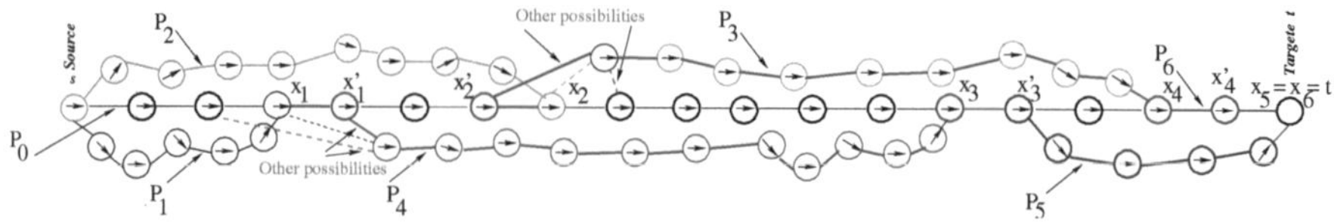

Fig. 1. Example showing the construction of the two disjoint paths

that, now $\mathcal{P}_1$ is a path from s to x_3 disjoint from $\mathcal{P}_2$. Similarly, if $x_2 \neq t$, then we find nodes x_2' and x_4 on $\mathcal{P}_0$ such that $d_s(x_1) < d_s(x_2') < d_s(x_3)$, $d_s(x_3) < d_s(x_4)$, x_2' and x_4 are connected by a path P_4 disjoint from (extended) P_1 and P_2, and x_4 and x_2' are selected to maximize first $d_s(x_4)$ and then $d_s(x_2')$. Subsequently, we combine P_2 and P_4 and the segment of $\mathcal{P}_0$ from x_2 to x_2' to extend $\mathcal{P}_2$. Observe that, now $\mathcal{P}_2$ is a path from s to x_4 disjoint from $\mathcal{P}_1$. The process of alternately extending paths $\mathcal{P}_1$ and $\mathcal{P}_2$ continues in this manner until they both reach target process t. Thus, after each step, alternately the length of the two disjoint paths ($\mathcal{P}_1$ or $\mathcal{P}_2$) increases. In Figure 1, after the construction of the two sub-paths P_3 and P_4, since we did not reach the target process t, the construction of the two disjoint paths ($\mathcal{P}_1$ and $\mathcal{P}_2$) is not terminated. Thus, additional steps are needed to finish the construction. In the following step, we find the farthest node on $\mathcal{P}_0$ reachable from x_4 via a path disjoint from P_4 to be target node t. Hence, the construction of the first disjoint path ($\mathcal{P}_1$) terminates. Subsequently, iterating the same process, a new sub-path (P_5) is constructed from node x_3' such that P_5 is disjoint from P_3 and P_4. Then, P_5 is used to extend $\mathcal{P}_1$ in the earlier manner. Observe that the farthest process on $\mathcal{P}_0$ from x_3' is the target process t. So, the construction of second disjoint path ($\mathcal{P}_2$) terminates.

The following lemma establishes the basis of the proposed algorithm.

Lemma 1. *Let $\mathcal{P}$ be an arbitrary path between two arbitrary but distinct nodes s and t in $G = (V, E)$. Let $x_0, x_1, x_2, ..., x_n$, for $n > 0$ be a sequence of vertices on $\mathcal{P}$ such that $d_s(x_i) < d_s(x_{i+1})$, $0 < i < n$, $x_0 = s$ and $x_n = t$, where $d_s(x_i)$ denotes the distance of process x_i from process s on path $\mathcal{P}$, and if two node disjoint paths exist between s and t, then the following two conditions hold.*

1. There exists a path P_1 from s to x_1 node-disjoint from path $\mathcal{P}$ or there exists two paths P_1 and P_2 node-disjoint from $\mathcal{P}$ and each other to x_1 and x_2 on $\mathcal{P}$, respectively, such that $d_s(x_2)$ and $d_s(x_1)$ are the largest and the second largest values among all possible nodes x_1, x_2,..., and x_n on $\mathcal{P}$.

2. For each $k, 1 < k \leq n$, if x_k is not the target process t, there exists a path P_{k+1} from x_k to x_{k+1} disjoint from paths P_1 through P_k and x_{k+1} is the node on $\mathcal{P}$ that makes $d_s(x_{k+1})$ largest.

The above lemma implicitly presents additional algorithmic details to further describe the presented approach. However, the details that make the algorithm stabilizing is out of the scope of this version of the paper due to space restrictions. It is anticipated that the entirely new proposed approach will initiate further research in this area with numerous useful applications.

Relocation Analysis of Stabilizing MAC* Algorithms for Large-Scale Mobile Ad Hoc Networks (Brief Announcement)

Pierre Leone[1], Marina Papatriantafilou[2], and Elad M. Schiller[2]

[1] University of Geneva, Switzerland
[2] Chalmers University of Technology, Sweden
pierre.leone@cui.unige.ch, {ptrianta,elad}@chalmers.se

The designers of media access control (MAC) protocols often do not consider the relocation of mobile nodes. Alternatively, when they do assume that the nodes are not stationary, designers tend to assume that some nodes temporarily do not change their location and coordinate the communications among mobile nodes. An understanding is needed of the relationship between the performances of MAC algorithms and the different settings by which the location of the mobile nodes is modeled. We study this relationship with an emphasis on stabilization concepts, which are imperative in mobile ad hoc networks (MANETs). We show that efficient MAC algorithms must balance a trade-off between two strategies; one that is oblivious to the history of local broadcasts and one that is not.

Modeling the location of mobile nodes. Let us look into scenarios in which each mobile node randomly moves in the Euclidian plane $[0,1]^2$ and in which two mobile nodes can directly communicate if their distance is less than a threshold $\chi \in [0,1]$. This scenario can be modeled by a sequence of evolving communication graphs, $\mathfrak{G} = (G_0, G_1, \ldots)$, such that at time instant t, the communication graph, $G_t = (V, E_t)$, includes the set of mobile nodes, V, and the set of edges, E_t, which represents pairs of processors that can directly communicate at time t. Let us consider two consecutive communication graphs, $G_t, G_{t+1} \in \mathfrak{G}$. In this short run, it can be expected that many of the mobile nodes have *similar neighborhoods* in G_t and G_{t+1}, say, when the threshold $\chi \to 1$.[1]. In the long run, this similarity may disappear because there are *(independent) random relocations* of the mobile nodes due to their random motion, e.g., G_t and G_{t+x} are independent when $x \to \infty$. These properties of neighborhood similarity and (independent) random relocation motivate the studied system settings in the context of MAC algorithms. To model the evolution of the communication graphs, we assume that between every two consecutive communication graphs, $G_t, G_{t+1} \in \mathfrak{G}$, a fraction of the mobile nodes, α, relocates from their neighborhood, where $\alpha \in [0,1]$ is the relocation rate. The relocating nodes and their new neighborhoods are chosen randomly. This leads to a mixed property of *short-term* (independent) random relocation and *long-term* neighborhood similarity. The mix is defined by the relocation rate, α, that can be viewed as the ratio of non-stationary nodes over (temporarily) stationary ones.

* An extended version of this work appears in ALGOSENSORS'09 and http://tinyurl.com/LPS08. The 1st author is partially supported by the ICT Programme ICT-2008-215270 (FRONT'S).

[1] Neighborhood similarity refers to situations in which a number of the neighbors remain neighbors after a broadcasting round.

R. Guerraoui and F. Petit (Eds.): SSS 2009, LNCS 5873, pp. 791–792, 2009.

Our contribution. We start by considering arbitrary values of the relocation rate and then focus on bounded values. We show that when the relocation rate is arbitrary, the best that you can hope for is a randomized oblivious strategy that ignores the history of broadcasts. This claim considers the extreme scenario in which the communication graph is always connected, but can drastically change between any two algorithm steps. We focus on demonstrating a throughput-related trade-off between oblivious and non-oblivious strategies of algorithms for MAC protocols. We view the relocation rate as the ratio of non-stationary mobile nodes over (temporarily) stationary ones. We identify a critical threshold, α_c, of the relocation rate and we show that above this critical threshold, it is best to employ an oblivious strategy (Fig. 1). The non-oblivious algorithm is a fault-tolerant MAC algorithm for which we analytically estimate the throughput in settings that model the location of mobile nodes, and wireless communications in which broadcasts can collide. The algorithm is TDMA based and has natural self-stabilizing version. The analysis considers saturation situations in which the number of transmitters is equal to the number of slots in the TDMA frames. We verify that the algorithm converges to a guaranteed throughput, within $\widetilde{\mathcal{O}}(\log n)$ broadcasting rounds, where n is the number of nodes.

Conclusions. This work is an analytical study of the relationship between a fundamental protocol for MANETs and the settings that model the location of mobile nodes. The study focuses on a novel throughput-related trade-off between oblivious and non-oblivious strategies of MAC algorithms. The trade-off depends on the relocation rate of mobile nodes. The non-oblivious algorithm can balance such trade-offs and can be extended to consider stronger requirements of fault-tolerance as well as other trade-offs. The studied algorithm is the first of its kind, because it is a "stateful" and fault-tolerant one. Thus, our methods can simplify the design of "stateful" self-stabilizing algorithms for MANETs, because we explain how to consider practical details, such as broadcast collisions and the location of mobile nodes. Moreover, we expect that the methodology used in this paper can study more trade-offs in this context. Expressive models facilitate the demonstration of lower bounds, impossibility results and other limitations, such as trade-offs. It is difficult to discover negative results by employing approaches that perform numerical or empirical studies. In addition, Kinetic models can be restrictive and difficult to analyze; it is hard to consider arbitrary behavior of mobile nodes and transient faults when algebraic equations are used. Interestingly, the simpler analytical model is more expressive than the existing approaches; in the context of MANETs, it is the first to facilitate the analysis of "stateful" algorithms as well as negative results.

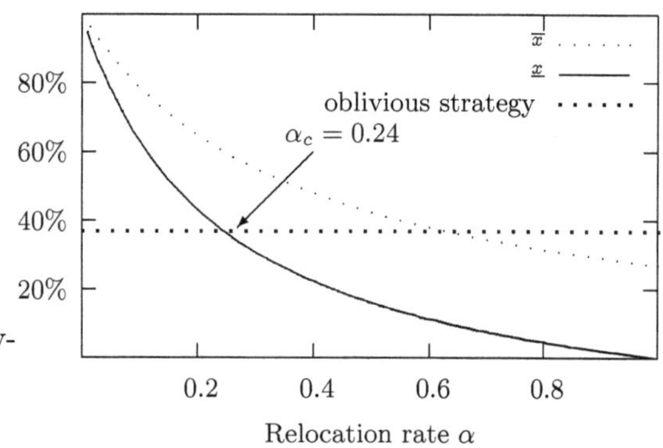

Fig. 1. Throughput of oblivious and non-oblivious strategies; $[\underline{x}, \overline{x}]$ bounds the latter

Brief Announcement: A Simple and Quiescent Omega Algorithm in the Crash-Recovery Model*

Cristian Martín[1] and Mikel Larrea[2]

[1] Ikerlan Research Centre, 20500 Arrasate-Mondragón, Spain
cmartin@ikerlan.es
[2] The University of the Basque Country, 20018 San Sebastián, Spain
mikel.larrea@ehu.es

Abstract. We present a simple algorithm that implements the Omega failure detector in the crash-recovery model. The algorithm is quiescent, i.e., eventually all the processes but the leader stop sending messages. It assumes that processes have access to a nondecreasing local clock.

1 Introduction and System Model

Omega has been shown to be the weakest failure detector for solving consensus [2]. Informally, Omega provides an eventual leader election functionality, i.e., eventually all processes agree on a common process. Several consensus algorithms based on such a weak leader election mechanism have been proposed [3].

This brief announcement presents a new algorithm implementing Omega in the crash-recovery model. Contrary to the algorithms proposed in [5], this algorithm does not rely on the use of stable storage, but on a nondecreasing local clock that each process has access to. Besides this, the algorithm is quiescent, i.e., eventually all the processes but the elected leader stop sending messages.

We consider a system S composed of a finite and totally ordered set Π of synchronous processes that communicate only by sending and receiving messages. Processes can only fail by crashing, and crashed processes can recover. In every execution of the system, Π is composed of the following three disjoint subsets: *eventually up* (processes that eventually remain up forever), *eventually down* (processes that eventually remain crashed forever), and *unstable* (processes that crash and recover an infinite number of times). By definition, eventually up processes are correct, while the rest are incorrect. We assume that the number of correct processes in any execution is at least one.

Concerning communication reliability and synchrony, we assume that for every correct process p, there is an eventually timely link [1] from p to every correct and every unstable process. The rest of links of S, i.e., the links from/to eventually down processes and the links from unstable processes, can be lossy.

Each process has a nondecreasing local clock that can measure intervals of time with a bounded drift. The clocks of the processes are not synchronized.

* Research supported by the Spanish and Madrid Research Councils, grants TIN2007-67353-C02-02, TIN2006-15617-C03-01 and S-0505/TIC/0285.

R. Guerraoui and F. Petit (Eds.): SSS 2009, LNCS 5873, pp. 793–794, 2009.

Finally, the Omega failure detector, adapted to system S, satisfies the following property [4]: *there is a time after which (1) every correct process always trusts the same correct process l, and (2) every unstable process, upon recovery, always trusts first $\perp$ (i.e., it does not trust any process), and —if it remains up for sufficiently long— then l until it crashes.*

2 The Algorithm

Figure 1 presents a quiescent algorithm implementing Omega in system S. With this algorithm, the elected leader l will be the "oldest" correct process, i.e., the process that first recovers definitely. The waiting instruction at the beginning of Task 1 guarantees that, eventually and permanently, unstable processes always change their leader from $\perp$ to l before the end of the waiting.

```
Initialization:
   leader_p ← ⊥
   Timeout_p ← clock()
   ts_p ← clock()
   ts_min ← ts_p
   start tasks 1, 2 and 3

Task 1:
   wait (Timeout_p) time units
   if leader_p = ⊥ then
      leader_p ← p
   else
      reset timer_p to Timeout_p
   repeat forever every η time units
      if leader_p = p then
         send (LEADER, p, ts_p) to all except p

Task 2:
   upon reception of (LEADER, q, ts_q) do
      if (ts_q < ts_min)
         or [(ts_q = ts_min) and (leader_p = ⊥)
                             and (q < p)]
         or [(ts_q = ts_min) and (leader_p ≠ ⊥)
                             and (q ≤ leader_p)] then
         leader_p ← q
         ts_min ← ts_q
         reset timer_p to Timeout_p

Task 3:
   upon expiration of timer_p do
      Timeout_p ← Timeout_p + 1
      leader_p ← p
      ts_min ← ts_p
```

Fig. 1. Quiescent Omega algorithm. Code for process p

References

1. Aguilera, M., Delporte-Gallet, C., Fauconnier, H., Toueg, S.: On implementing Ω with weak reliability and synchrony assumptions. In: Proceedings of the 22nd ACM Symposium on Principles of Distributed Computing (PODC 2003), Boston, Massachusetts, July 2003, pp. 306–314 (2003)
2. Chandra, T., Hadzilacos, V., Toueg, S.: The weakest failure detector for solving consensus. Journal of the ACM 43(4), 685–722 (1996)
3. Lamport, L.: The part-time parliament. ACM Transactions on Computer Systems 16(2), 133–169 (1998)
4. Martín, C., Larrea, M.: Eventual leader election in the crash-recovery failure model. In: Proceedings of the 14th Pacific Rim International Symposium on Dependable Computing (PRDC 2008), Taipei, Taiwan, December 2008, pp. 208–215 (2008)
5. Martín, C., Larrea, M., Jiménez, E.: Implementing the Omega failure detector in the crash-recovery failure model. Journal of Computer and System Sciences 75(3), 178–189 (2009)

Brief Announcement: How to Overcome the Limits of Bounds*

Olivier Peres**

Department of Computer Science, Ben-Gurion University of the Negev
Beer-Sheva, Israel 84105
olivier@bgu.ac.il

Abstract. A distributed system consists of processes linked to one another by communication links. A classical problem is how to realistically model these links so that it is possible to write correct algorithms. This paper presents a new solution that results in more natural executions and removes the need for artificial workarounds.

1 Introduction

Distributed systems are an abstraction over computer networks, where machines communicate with one another via specialized hardware, like wires and wireless links, themselves linked by routers and other networking equipment. Various models, and algorithms using them, have been described in the literature [4].

It is common to assume bounded FIFO channels, based on the observation that a real wire does not reorder messages and has a finite capacity. Bounded FIFO channels do have their shortcomings, though. This is illustrated by the method that Afek and Bremler had to design in order to work around these shortcomings for their *power supply* spanning tree algorithm [1]. They assume that it is possible to detect the message loss that occurs when one tries to send a message into a full channel and set up buffer variables in which lost messages are stored, to be sent again later. This hypothesis is stronger than it appears, since it requires observing a link into which no message can be sent.

Contemporary systems are commuted networks. The "channel" between two processes is a set of links, routers and other processes. Since several routes exist between any two processes, such a channel is not FIFO and has no fixed bound. Hence the idea of moving the constraints from the channels to the scheduler.

This new approach is called *IO-fairness*, because the scheduler is forbidden to make unrealistic decisions (*fairness*) related to the messages. More precisely, it cannot store an infinite amount of messages in the channels. The channels are unbounded, they are not FIFO, and no attempt is made at making them FIFO.

This is not equivalent to a bound on the channels in the traditional sense, because no individual channel has a fixed bound. Therefore, sending a message cannot fail and processes cannot measure the bounds on their channels, a trick commonly used to turn a non-FIFO channel into a FIFO one.

* A more detailed version appears as a technical report [3].

** Partially funded by the ICT program of the European Union under contract number ICT-2008-215270.

R. Guerraoui and F. Petit (Eds.): SSS 2009, LNCS 5873, pp. 795–796, 2009.

variable : state $\in$ {0,1,2}
true $\longrightarrow$ send +; send −; send −
reception of − $\longrightarrow$ state $\leftarrow \max(0, \text{state} - 1)$
reception of + $\longrightarrow$ if state $\neq 0$ then state $\leftarrow \min(2, \text{state} + 1)$

Fig. 1. +/− Algorithm

2 An Application of IO-Fairness

One would expect the +/− algorithm, provided in Figure 1, to work in any realistic system. Each of the two processes in the system has a state in $\{0, 1, 2\}$, initialized arbitrarily. Each process periodically sends to the other the sequence of messages +, −, −. + increments the state of the receiver and − decrements it, however the state cannot be greater than 2 or change if it is 0. In other words, the system should *converge* towards a *legitimate configuration* where all the states are 0, which the system cannot leave. This algorithm is thus *self-stabilizing* [2].

Suppose that the initial state of both processes is 2. If the scheduler is not IO-fair, it can prevent convergence by first almost filling the channel with messages, leaving space for only one or two of them. Then, it lets the +, −, − sequence be sent, so that one or two of the − are lost. With bounded FIFO channels, one would have to work around this problem by detecting the message losses and compensating for them.

An IO-fair scheduler, on the other hand, forbids this pathological behavior, even though the channels are not FIFO and unbounded. Indeed, not converging would mean storing an infinite amount of − messages in the channels. Any scheduler allowing this would, by definition, not be IO-fair.

3 Conclusion

This paper presents IO-fairness, a new point of view on communication channels that moves the constraints from the channels to the scheduler, more accurately modeling the reality of a commuted network by preventing the system from exhibiting a pathological behavior. IO-fairness allows to use directly unbounded non-FIFO channels, without any trick to make them FIFO and without having to detect message losses and account for them.

References

1. Afek, Y., Bremler, A.: Self-stabilizing unidirectional network algorithms by power-supply. In: Proceedings of the Eighth Annual ACM-SIAM Symposium on Discrete Algorithms (SODA 1997), pp. 111–120 (1997)
2. Dolev, S.: Self-Stabilization. MIT Press, Cambridge (2000)
3. Peres, O.: How to overcome the limits of bounds. Technical Report 0908, Ben-Gurion University of the Negev (August 2009)
4. Tel, G.: Introduction to distributed algorithms. Cambridge University Press, Cambridge (1994)

Brief Announcement: The Design and Evaluation of a Distributed Reliable File System

Dalibor Peric, Thomas Bocek, Fabio Hecht, David Hausheer, and Burkhard Stiller*

University of Zurich, CSG@IFI, Binzmuehlestrasse 14, CH-8050 Zurich, Switzerland
{peric,bocek,hecht,hausheer,stiller}@ifi.uzh.ch

Network file systems provide access to data in a networked environment. If such systems operate in a client-server (C/S) mode, *e.g.*, NFS (Network File System) or SMB (Server Message Block), issues concerning the scalability, the presence of a single point of failure, and fault tolerance emerge. Scalability issues, such as coping with an increasing number of clients, need to be addressed, since bandwidth on the server side may be limited and expensive. Peer-to-peer (P2P) systems are, in contrast to C/S systems, fault-tolerant, robust, and scalable. Distributed file systems based on P2P networks can help to avoid such problems. Besides, P2P systems are self-organizing, requiring less management, thus reducing maintenance costs.

A categorization of existing P2P file systems is provided in [1]. This survey outlines P2P file systems with distinct features and it focuses on particular problem areas. A disadvantage is that some of them do not support the write operation for all peers. Another shortcoming is that some store data at locations related to the content. Other systems offer access to stored data using specialized, less-transparent interfaces.

Allowing all peers write access may cause data consistency issues, if the operation is executed concurrently on the same data and security issues arise, if peers cannot be trusted. According to [2], in corporate distributed file systems "file sharing is rarely concurrent and sharing is usually read-only. Only 5% of files opened by multiple clients are concurrent and 90% of sharing is read-only." Thus, a weaker consistency model can be applied. The use case considered in this extended abstract is a small to medium-sized office LAN, in which trust among participants is assumed. Each workstation runs an instance of DRFS, dedicating disk space and bandwidth.

Distributed Reliable File System (DRFS) Design and Evaluation

This extended abstract presents DRFS (Distributed Reliable File System), a P2P file system, which uses content-independent identifiers for data storage, while maintaining high performance and low overhead. A dynamic replication mechanism ensures data availability, under high churn. Files in DRFS are accessed transparently through the Filesystem in Userspace (FUSE) interface. DRFS offers a tree-based view of the file system structure, together with read-write

* This work has been performed partially in the framework of EU IST Project EC-GIN (FP6-2006-IST-045256) and EU IST NoE EMANICS (FP6-2004-IST-026854).

R. Guerraoui and F. Petit (Eds.): SSS 2009, LNCS 5873, pp. 797–798, 2009.

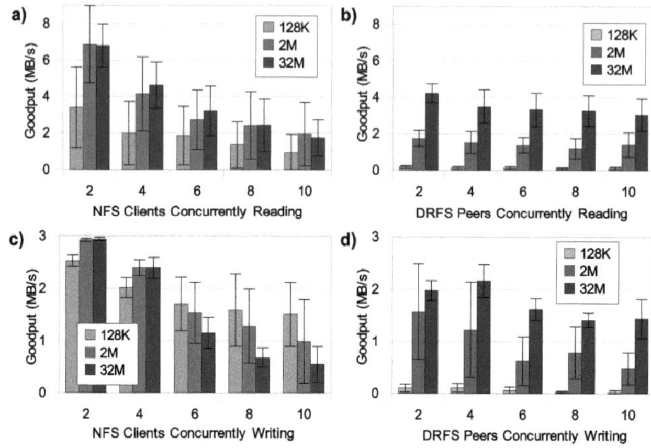

Fig. 1. NFS and DRFS read and write performance with concurrent access

support for all participants. Data is stored under random keys, independently of the data content. Thus, in case of updates, it does not have to be moved to other nodes. Modifying data stored according to its content can be an expensive operation: if a file saved under the hash of its data is modified, the hash value will change and thus its new location, which brings communication overhead. To address those issues, DRFS introduces random chunk addressing. The key idea of DRFS is to split each file in chunks and abstract chunk addresses from its content. DRFS combines active and passive replication, to prevent data loss due to peer failures. DRFS has been designed and implemented as a prototype. The source code of the DRFS implementation is available for download [3].

The current implementation has been evaluated with respect to performance, reliability, and overhead, and is compared to NFS as shown in Figure 1. Those experimental results indicate that the DRFS implementation is scalable, and the performance of read and write operations is not influenced by the size of the system. DRFS shows better performance than NFS for many peers and with large file sizes. DRFS has the advantage of avoiding a single point of failure. However, the experiments showed also that failure of peers storing the root directory resulted in complete loss of data. Thus, this information needs to be replicated more to prevent complete data loss. Further future work will comprise the implementation of an optimistic consistency mechanism and possibility of introduction of user access rights.

References

1. Hasan, R., Anwar, Z., et al.: A Survey of Peer-to-Peer Storage Techniques for Distributed File Systems. In: ITCC 2005, Washington, DC, USA (April 2005)
2. Leung, A.W., Pasupathy, S., et al.: Measurement and Analysis of Large-Scale Network File System Workloads. In: USENIX 2008, Boston, MA, USA (June 2008)
3. DRFS download, `http://www.csg.uzh.ch/publications/software/TomP2P#DRFS`

Author Index

MIX
Papier aus verantwortungsvollen Quellen
Paper from responsible sources
FSC® C105338

If you have any concerns about our products,
you can contact us on
ProductSafety@springernature.com

In case Publisher is established outside the EU,
the EU authorized representative is:
Springer Nature Customer Service Center GmbH
Europaplatz 3, 69115 Heidelberg, Germany

Printed by Libri Plureos GmbH
in Hamburg, Germany